ENCYCLOPEDIA OF KITCHEN HISTORY

Mary Ellen Snodgrass

Fitzroy Dearborn

An Imprint of the Taylor & Francis Group
New York • London

Published in 2004 by
Fitzroy Dearborn
An Imprint of the Taylor and Francis Group
270 Madison Avenue
New York, NY 10016
www.routledge-ny.com

Published in Great Britain by
Fitzroy Dearborn
An Imprint of the Taylor and Francis Group
2 Park Square
Milton Park, Abingdon
Oxon OX14 4RN
www.routledge.co.uk

10   9   8   7   6   5   4   3   2   1

ISBN 1-57958-380-6

Printed on acid-free, 250-year-life paper
Manufactured in the United States of America

Library of Congress Cataloging-in-Publication Data

Snodgrass, Mary Ellen.
  Encyclopedia of kitchen history / Mary Ellen Snodgrass.
      p. cm.
  ISBN 1-57958-380-6 (alk. paper)
  1. Kitchens--History--Encyclopedias.   2. Cookery--History--Encyclopedias.   I. Title.
  TX653.S57 2004
  643'.3'09--dc22
                                                    2004018161

Dedication

In loving memory of my aunt, Nan Whitlock,
whose Old South kitchen on Stonewall Avenue in Richmond
was her true source of strength

Preface

To study kitchen history is to examine, appreciate, and even celebrate the culture of domestic life. In all its diverse forms and functions, the kitchen is a space common to all people. It reflects the practical challenges posed by daily necessity, but also the human ingenuity and invention that creates and shares domestic culture. The search for clues to the domestic past leads over surprising terrain. How the story of the kitchen begins is found in the remains of prehistoric settlements around the globe. Piecing together the findings from Catal Höyük, Pompeii, Fontevrault, and Monticello demands the combined studies of archeologists and anthropologists who excavate firepits and middens to find the gnawed bones and shards of dinners that nourished humanity's ancestors. Historians record how the cultural practices around the kitchen developed in unique ways, each instrument, method, and invention a response to the environment in which everyday people lived. They catalog domestic inventions that contribute to practices as diverse as fire science, home building, ovens, woodworking, pottery, horn-working, weaving, masonry, and metal-craft. They note how travel and trade brought these inventions and kitchen cultures from one area of the world to another—further influencing the growth and development of culinary practices. They observe how, by the nineteenth-century, profitable kitchen industries emerged to supply the domestic sphere with new conveniences that altered daily life. Such transformations and economic incentives eventually led to innovations in such things as plastics, synthetic coatings for cookware, electronics, and modern canning. We see how improvements to packaging and processing changed the experience of food shopping as well. Where consumers once measured handfuls of goods and weighed them on a balance-beam scale at the open-air market, they now find clean, pure foodstuffs measured out in even quantities in the jars and cans on the shelf of the corporate superstore. These facts form the bare skeleton of kitchen history.

In fleshing out the evolution of the kitchen, the historian is also acknowledging the ideas and experiments of everyday cooks, the people who tried new combinations of pasta and tomatoes, tasted *couscous* and olives for the first time, applied new water purification technologies, and amended and added to the stock of folksay and food lore passed on by their ancestors. From these risk-takers came the rules for roasting and basting lamb, for trussing a goose and cooking savory mixes in a pastry crust, and for creating sustaining oat cereals and banana purées for toddlers. The cook's hands were the first to master the ulu and *bain-marie*, stoke the first coal stove, and plug in the mixer, toaster, and microwave oven.

Why do we want to record this history? History allows current generations to appreciate the hardships of skinning rabbits in a tepee and packing chopped meats into animal intestines for trail food, the significance of organizing St. Lucia Day breakfasts and *kaffeeklatches,* and the importance of bartering for hen eggs and breadfruit in the world's first markets. From these common practices that often go unacknowledged come the customs that give meaning to today's major rituals—the communion of the first American Thanksgiving, the welcome of guests to a seder, the preparation of rice cakes for the new year, and the sharing of baklava after Ramadan. What we discover is that the first kitchens were not merely places to eat. They were sources of warmth and family togetherness, the beginnings of division of labor, the place for child care and hemp spinning, scrubbing tile and ironing ribbons, gardening and treating colds and dropsy, and the vast schedule of minuscule chores that constitute homemaking. Pots and turnspits at the kitchen cookfire have long shared place with dyepots of madder, dried peppermint, lavender-scented hand lotions, cherry bark curatives, Paris green rat poison, and rose petal love potions. The same cauldrons that heated water for laundry and children's baths also reduced pulp to apple butter and scalded pigs for salting and milk for cheddar cheese. The hearth on which young girls learned bayberry candle dipping also heated pork fat and oak-ash lye for soap and dried willow withes for basketry and basil for potpourri.

From home fires, the products of kitchen work spread to the streets with sticky rice and noodle soup vending, to buffets at inns and restaurants, on horseback with dinner safely packed in parfleches and thermos bottles, and over the seas in galleys supplying the comforts of cooked rice cereal and hot ginger tea to the sailor and submariner. Kitchen history includes Conestoga wagons on the Oregon Trail, the chuckwagons of Charles Goodnight's drovers, the Orient Express, and the *Hindenburg* and the *Titanic*, where galley cookery reduced space regimens to the barest limits, influencing designers of rowhouses, Levittown, camping trailers, and the first streamlined counters of the Frankfurt Kitchen. Into the skies, the same philosophy of cookery served the airplane passenger and NASA's voyagers to the moon and beyond.

The nuances of the world's cookery participate in so much human activity—the soldier's slap-dash pan-fry on the march, the Zoroastrian rituals that dedicate *homa* to god, Asian celebrations of birthings and weddings, and the presentation of savory roast pigs and whole sea bass to Turkish potentates and Georgian slavemasters. Objects of the kitchen include face jugs, calabashes, bamboo mats, chopsticks, hot pots, kabobs, carvery, and aprons. The activities of the kitchen lead us to the histories of hand-washing, etiquette, and the styles and methods of daily work, histories that describe the digging of hops beds with a dibble, pruning grape vines and fertilizing herb beds, and loading head and shoulders and arms with fresh manioc, yams, and banana leaves. Kitchen history is also the history of endless human labor, in which the harvest prefaces salting and drying candlefish, threshing rice and barley for beer, caching maize and fermenting *koumiss*, molding blancmange and bottling cherry juice, and preparing Yuletide banquets and tribal feasts.

This labor is also a shared labor from which we have much to learn. Without prejudice to male or female, slave or free, the global understanding of kitchen history supplies more than enough faith in humankind's ability to warm, clothe, and feed itself. Along the way, the student of domestic history acquires an earful of new words and phrases—osmazome and Maillard reaction, frankenfood and shea nut butter and slow food, MREs and graywater. The huge vocabulary of the kitchen records in words how domestic work has changed with the invention of yogurt, poi, kimch'i, woks, *chinampas*, tumplines, hornos, Japan ware, forcing bags, *obentos*, floorcloths, and *nouvelle cuisine*. The mixing of languages, like the blending of flavors in the olla, attests to the kitchen as the starting place of multicultural harmony, the sharing of techniques and dishes that invites each member of humankind to the world's table.

How to Use this Book

The organization of *Encyclopedia of Kitchen History* presents for student, teacher, historian, researcher, librarian, chef, and domestic worker an A-to-Z overview of over 300 topics ranging from inventors like Nils Dalén and such cookbook authors as Isabella Beeton to baby food, cannibalism, vermin, Bakelite, ramadas, and prison kitchens. Each entry presents in chronological order the advances in technique and imagination up to current times in many fields such as baking and fire safety. Following generous *See also*s, each entry concludes with a list of sources from books, CDs, journals, newspapers, and online databases and electronic media. At the back of the book there is an appendix of Common Sources, the works that I have found most helpful and have added to my personal shelf of domestic histories, including the *Larousse Gastronomique*, *The African Kitchen*, *The Rituals of Dinner*, *Culinaria*, *The Oxford Companion to Food*, and *A Mediterranean Feast*. Illustrations are numerous and were chosen from a variety of sources with the intention not to decorate kitchen history, but to document and explain it, and to communicate the richness of domestic culture. A thorough index directs the reader to the people, writings, recipes, inventions, processes, and foodstuffs that have formed the homemaker's history from the discovery of fire to the missions in space.

Mary Ellen Snodgrass
Hickory, North Carolina

Acknowledgments

I would like to thank Bob Arendt, editor of *Aramco World,* the reference staff at the Academy of Sciences in San Francisco, California; Peter Dargin, folklorist, Dubbo, New South Wales, Australia; Thor Dunnmire, staff technician at *Aquarius,* Key Largo, Florida; Dr. Bob Hart, historian, Hickory, North Carolina; Bill Jenkins, reference librarian, Harold Washington Library Center, Chicago, Illinois; Joan Lail, writer, Hickory, North Carolina; Dr. Steven Miller, Director of *Aquarius*; Don Murphy, camping enthusiast, Charlotte, North Carolina; Diana Norman, researcher and novelist, Stevenage, England; Curtis Robinson, barbecue cook, Hickory, North Carolina; Wanda Rozzelle, reference librarian, Catawba County Library, Newton, North Carolina; Mark Schumacher, reference librarian, UNC, Greensboro, North Carolina; Dr. Marsha J. Stone, chemical engineer, Reading, Pennsylvania; Patti Tyndall, educator, UNC-W, Wilmington, North Carolina.

Special thanks to Wanda Rozzelle, who remained an e-mail away throughout my research, and to an old friend and colleague, Jeff Willhelm, photographer for the *Charlotte Observer,* for his advice and help. Much of the photography was the work of Hugh Snodgrass and of Dr. Bob Hart, preserver of frontier Americana at Hart Square in Catawba County, North Carolina.

List of Entries

A

ACTON, ELIZA (ELIZABETH)

England's nineteenth-century culinary pacesetter Elizabeth Acton, author of *Modern Cookery for Private Families* (1845), introduced exact measurement of ingredients, specific cooking temperatures and times, and pioneered the modern cookbook. A native of Sussex, she was born on April 17, 1799 at Battle. Her father, John Acton, an Ipswich brewer, moved his family back to Suffolk, but Elizabeth, who suffered from physical weakness in childhood, was sent to France for recuperation. While living abroad, she became accustomed to French cuisine, which may have initiated her interest in cooking.

Content at her London home as a sedate but independent spinster, Acton developed her writing style by composing articles for journals and periodicals and publishing *Poems* (1826). When a publisher spurned Acton's work and urged her to turn her talents to cookbooks, she settled in Tonbridge, Kent, and compiled her famous compendium of recipes, intended primarily for young English housewives.

Acton's contributions to food history include the formulation of precise directions, application of the nutritional theories of chemist Justus von Liebig, promotion of nutritious low-budget meals, and faithful recreation of English cuisine, including the nation's first recipe for brussels sprouts, which she may have eaten on the Continent. She anthologized recipes conceived in her own kitchen as well as those prepared by her friends, including Lady Judith Montefiore, author of *The Jewish Manual* (1846), the first Jewish

MODERN COOKERY,

FOR PRIVATE FAMILIES,

REDUCED TO A SYSTEM OF EASY PRACTICE.

IN A SERIES OF

CAREFULLY TESTED RECEIPTS,

IN WHICH THE PRINCIPLES OF

BARON LIEBIG AND OTHER EMINENT WRITERS

HAVE BEEN AS MUCH AS POSSIBLE APPLIED AND EXPLAINED.

BY ELIZA ACTON.

"It is the want of a scientific basis which has given rise to so many absurd and hurtful methods of preparing food."—Dr. GREGORY.

NEW EDITION.

LONDON:
LONGMANS, GREEN, READER, AND DYER.
1877.

Title page, *Modern Cookery* (1877).

cookbook published in English. Acton also cleared up confusion about types of pasta and their cooking times and explained the use of the conjuror, or necromancer, a fuel-efficient meat cooker heated with burning paper that John Rich invented in 1735.

Acton alleviated the grimness of contemporary cookbooks with sparkling humor and gave her dishes pleasant names, such as Publisher's Pudding. For maximum clarity to the beginning cook, her instructions for stewing sole in cream moved step by step through simmering, draining, seasoning, and stewing. For shaping an apple dumpling, she suggested wrapping it in textured cloth to pattern the surface. Her text focused on food preparation and omitted the recipes for face creams and essays on etiquette that some of her contemporaries added to their homemaking compendia. She also initiated the inclusion of recipes that suited both Catholic and Jewish kitchen protocols.

Acton joined other voices of the era in protesting impure and adulterated foodstuffs. In 1857 she produced *The English Bread Book,* which railed against low-quality commercial baked goods. She died at her Hampstead home after a lingering malady in February 1859. Her writings remained available through numerous reprints and influenced the domestic content of Isabella Beeton's classic, *The Book of Household Management* (1859). The popularity in the United States of *Modern Cookery for Private Families* derived from *Modern Cookery in All Its Branches* (1848), a version of Acton's cookbook issued by Sarah Josepha Hale, editor of the women's magazine *Godey's Ladies Book.*

See also **Victorian Kitchens; Leibig, Justus von**

Further Reading

Shattock, Joanne. *The Oxford Guide to British Women Writers.* Oxford: Oxford University Press, 1993.
Zlotnick, Susan. "Domesticating Imperialism: Curry and Cookbooks in Victorian England." *Frontiers,* 1996, 51–58.

AIR CONDITIONING

Air conditioning enables the control of indoor air quality, humidity, and temperature, all factors that affect cookery. In ancient times, various applications of evaporation produced tentative improvement in the home environment. In India, people used evaporative cooling, suspending water-soaked grass mats in windows to cool the incoming air. One innovator, the Syrian Elagabalus, who was Rome's emperor until his murder by the palace guard in 222 CE, tapped nature's own atmospheric coolant. To ease the discomfort of a summer heat wave, he dispatched slaves with donkey carts to retrieve snow from the Appenines. When they returned, he ordered them to heap it about his villa garden to cool sweltering dinner guests.

During the Italian Renaissance, Leonardo da Vinci sketched plans for a water bellows, a drum air-cooling device he devised for the bedroom of Beatrice, Duchess of Milan. The huge cooling system required the labor of a servant, whose measured step activated the treadmill that rotated the drum. In the 1800s, textile mill owners cooled and humidified factory environments by spraying the air with fine jets of water, a concept that had flourished in Arabian dining salons in the Middle Ages. In the United States in the 1830s, John Gorrie tinkered with a mechanized cooling system in Florida, where control of kitchen environments eventually boosted tourism and dining out during sticky summer months. In 1880 engineers at New York City's Madison Square Theater improved comfort by circulating outside air through a cheesecloth filter over four tons of ice.

Twenty years later, mechanical engineer Willis Haviland Carrier, an employee of the Buffalo Forge Company in New York, developed the first air conditioning system at Brooklyn's Sackett-Wilhelms Lithographing and Publishing Company. His apparatus, patented in 1902, achieved humidity control by directing cold water through heat-transfer coils. A fan propelled air over the chilled coils. Centrifugal force directed cool air streams overhead rather than to the floor.

Four years later, the mill owner Stuart W. Cramer and I. H. Hardeman of Charlotte, North Carolina, assisted Carrier in cooling the Chronicle Cotton Mills in nearby Belmont. Cramer coined the term *air conditioning* in an address to the National Cotton Manufacturers Association. In 1907, Carrier's employers established the Carrier Air Conditioning Company of America. In 1915, he took control of the company and named it the Carrier Corporation, which air-cooled Graumann's Metropolitan Theater in Los Angeles in 1922 and later installed a cooling device in J. L. Hudson's department store in Detroit.

Before its application to homes, the ideal of a comfortable working environment spread to cigar factories, bakeries, breweries, and theaters. For hotels, department stores, and theaters, Carrier created a centrifugal chiller, which suited these larger, more open spaces; for residences, he created the Weathermaker, a model developed in 1928. Within two years, air conditioning cooled the U.S. Capitol, Library of Congress, Supreme Court, the White House, the Kremlin in Russia, and some 10,000 homes. The advent of air-conditioned homes put an end to the tradition of separate summer kitchens and the misery of canning in a hot, steamy atmosphere.

Advertising helped sell mechanized cooling to the dubious homeowner. In a huge cone called the Igloo of Tomorrow, Carrier displayed his air conditioners in a chill atmosphere to four million attendees at the 1939 New York World's Fair. His installers worked out the logistics of cooling chicken coops, greenhouses, museums, and hotel and hospital kitchens.

Carrier introduced a central home system in 1952; two years later, Fedders brought out a three-quarter horsepower room unit. Critics of Carrier's invention dubbed it the "Great Isolator." Some homeowners, immured indoors in summertime, looked with nostalgia to the porch-centered summers of earlier decades when attic fans, curtains, awnings, and shade trees were the best investments for a comfortable home atmosphere. Contributing to their discontent was the high cost of electricity and the clatter of whirring condensers and fans, particularly in apartment complexes and closely spaced condomium units. For all its faults, however, air conditioning made possible comfortable hospitals, offices, and vehicles as well as climate-controlled microchip labs. In home kitchens, the control of heat and humidity during the hot months lightened the seasonal tasks of jelly-making and canning of fresh fruits and vegetables.

Further Reading

"The Coolest American of the Century," *U. S. News and World Report*, December 27, 1999, 61.

AKABORI, MINEKICHI

As Japan threw off feudalism in the late 1800s, Minekichi Akabori updated women's education at the same time that he introduced the nation to modern cuisine. A native of Shizuoka, he was born in 1816 and developed a reputation as restaurant chef in Tokyo. An egalitarian educator, he supported compulsory schooling. Akabori's enthusiasm for domestic improvement influenced the careers of other members of his family, including a son, Kumauemon, called Minekichi the Second, a foods instructor at the Women's University of Japan; a daughter, Kiku, a lecturer in cookery and co-author of her father's second book; Kiku's son Kichimatsu, a chef in the Japanese imperial kitchen; Kumauemon's son, Matsutarô, called Minekichi the Third, a proponent of Fanny Farmer's *The Boston Cooking School Cookbook* (1896) and an advocate of Western-style menus; Michi, wife of Minekichi the Third, a member of a cooking faculty; and a great granddaughter, Fusae, called Masako, a domestic science writer for magazines, radio, and television, and author of 14 books on Japanese and multicultural cuisine. Together, the Akabori clan produced 61 cookbooks.

To introduce housewives to quality home cookery, in 1882 Akabori founded Tokyo's Akabori Kappô Kyôjô (Akabori Cooking Class), for which Kumauemon developed a curriculum strongly influenced by French haute cuisine and by Isabella Beeton's classic advice in *The Book of Household Management* (1859). Within six years, Akibori offered a course in Western cooking techniques. As of 1910, the faculty augmented regular, weekend, and ten-day courses with correspondence courses. They issued monthly installments of a text, *Akabori Ryôri Kôgiroku* (Akabori Cooking Manual), featuring lectures on side dishes, seasonal meals, Chinese and Western-style cooking, sweets, etiquette, the invalid diet, and nutritional chemistry.

Akabori's emphasis on variety derived from his ability to improvise new dishes and to introduce middle-class cooks to such foreign ingredients as Western seasonings, beef, and pork. He promoted typical Western meats for use in dumplings, rolls, stews, croquettes, and cutlets, the recipes for which he compiled in a menu calendar published in a 1915 issue of *Fujin Zasshi* (Lady's Magazine). By preparing meat Japanese style with standard home implements, he removed some of the stigma of foreign food culture and increased the amount of fat and protein in the spare national diet. Family recipes in *Katei Nichiuô Ryôri, Ge* (Dishes for Daily Use at Home, Part II), published in 1911 by Minekichi the Third, introduced cabbage, onions, and potatoes, among the most economical elements of Western cooking.

Akabori supported notions of cleanliness, nutrition, and economy. In *Katei Jûnikagetsu Ryôribô* (Home Cooking for Twelve Months, 1905), he advocated that cooks have clean hands, hair neatly tied out of the way, and white caps and aprons, the traditional Western kitchen uniform. He extended personal sanitation to include cleanliness of cutlery, pans, and plates. For the sake of economy, he explained how to dampen firewood to slow a cooking fire.

Akabori's influence extended far beyond his life span. The prestigious family culinary academy took a new name, the Akabori School of Cookery, and, within 80 years, graduated more than 800,000 food preparers. During the rise in urbanization and living standards following World War II, a cook's claim to a diploma became a status symbol. In 1972 the directorship passed on through the Akabori family line to Chiemi, daughter-in-law of Masako. Akabori's vision reached into the next generation of family kitchen specialists with the culinary career of Hiromi, Chiemi's daughter.

Distillery.

ALCOHOL

Strong drink has been equated with worship and hospitality in many cultures, making the lifted glass a symbol of spirituality, conviviality, respect for the host, and demand for a refill. The history of such alcoholic beverages as the Aztec tequila, Hindu *pauch* (punch), Mexican mescal, Chaco *algaroba* (beer), and Japanese *sake* (rice wine) is so ancient as to be virtually untraceable.

India

In India the distillation of *sura*, a liquor made from barley or wild paddy, dates to the early settlers of the Indus Valley, but, like the practice of meat eating, produced conflicting opinion among religious groups. The sutras, a series of ethical guidebooks, encouraged the serving of wines made from honey, jaggery, or mahua flowers as a sign of hospitality; however, Indian scripture lists drunkenness from *sura* among the five mortal sins, with intemperance second only to violating a guru's bed. The Buddhist *jataka* tales, moral fables outlining right behavior, also described controlled consumption of liquor among men, women, and ascetics. Buddhist monks prescribed wine for sickness, but Jainists would not allow monks to reside in a dwelling where wine jars had merely been stored. In 947 CE a Muslim visitor, Al-Masudi of Baghdad, author of a thirty-volume world history, summarized a sensible philosophy with his statement that Hindus abstain and condemn drinkers and strong drink "not because their religion forbids it, but in the dread of its clouding their reason and depriving them of its powers."

Caucasus

Among shepherds in the Caucasus, the traditional fermentation of camels' milk into *kéfir* (milk wine) has a long history, one early reference appearing in *The Travels of Marco Polo* (ca. 1299). Whether whole or skimmed, the drink consisted of an inoculation of milk with grains of bacteria-rich starter to produce a pleasant, soothing beverage similar to yogurt. The process consisted of blending cultured milk with fresh milk, stoppering it in bottles, and storing it in a hot cupboard.

Over three days, the fermentation process increased the strength of the intoxicant. The strongest was a sour, frothy, but highly digestible liquid strained from sediment. Variations included drinks cultured from cow, goat, sheep, coconut, rice, or soy- milk or from powdered *kéfir* grains. Turkish cooks valued their own specialty drink called *koumiss,* a fermented mare's milk. Devout Muslims considered these intoxicating dairy drinks a gift from Allah.

Because *kéfir* is a self-carbonated drink containing beneficial yeasts, Russian peasants recommended it for feeding invalids and pets and for creaming the face. In 1908 Élie Metchnikoff, the Nobel prize-winning Russian zoologist and microbiologist, discovered the drink's ability to stimulate salivation and peristalsis, the muscular motion that propels food through the digestive tract. Folk healers have championed *kéfir's* microflora as an aid in recovery from abdominal surgery and a treatment for difficult cases of flatulence, irritated mucosa, troubled sleep, overeating, learning and behavioral disabilities, and depression.

Kvass, another traditional Russian drink, is a healthful low-alcohol beverage mentioned in Elena Molokhovets's *A Gift to Young Housewives* (1861), a classic Russian cookbook. It is a home-brew concocted from yeasty grain, beets, fruits and berries, or rye bread mixed with sugar and raisins. An additive to soups, *kvass* reached its height of popularity in the czarist period, when itinerant vendors sold it at farmers' markets and on the street. As political factions distanced landed aristocrats from peasants, drinking the beverage of the common people took on patriotic significance.

China

In China the first experiments with fermenting *chiew* or *jiew* (grain alcohol) occurred in 2000 BCE Whether made from millet, rice, wheat, or sorghum, alcohol became a standard offering at feasts, on holidays, and for temple and ancestor worship. By 800 BCE, distillers were extracting whiskey from rice beer cooked down in porcelain vats. The first Chinese home brew was the work of Du Kang, who lived during the Zhou dynasty around 770 BCE. For sharing his restorative, energizing drink with the emperor, he earned the title of "immortal of wine." Du Kang's name became so well known that in China—like Dionysus in ancient Greece, Bacchus in Rome, and John Barleycorn in England—it served as a synonym for drink.

Chinese historians summarize the choice of alcoholic beverages as *li, lào, láo,* and *chang.* Brewers fermented *li, láo,* and *chang* from millet and made *lào* from milk. The earliest date for these drinks was 1500 BCE, during the Shang dynasty. Archeologists have located ceramic and bronze drinking cups and a brewery from the era. To vary the alcohol content of their vintages, wine makers used different kinds of yeast. In *Records of the Investigation of Things* (290 CE), the encyclopedist Chang Hua preserved an even older tradition from central Asian nomads, noting that they made a strong wine drink capable of intoxicating the drinker for days.

Because of the emperor Wang Man's wish to control the brewing and distilling industries around 20 CE, the Chinese concealed their methods as a national secret. In the fifth and sixth centuries, the imperial monopoly and secrecy met their stiffest challenges. First came the bootlegging of the 400s, when government agents threatened death to lawbreakers. In the next century, distillers circumvented the law by producing brandy, which they called "burned wine," the same concept characterized in the Dutch *brandewijn*, source of the English term *brandywine.*

Around 534 Jia Sixie composed *Ch'i Min Yao Shu* (Important Skills for the Well-being of the People), an agricultural handbook that named forty alcoholic beverages and described methods of fermenting wine from broom corn, millet, rice, and eight types of yeast. Domestic wine makers stored vessels in the dark under controlled hermetic conditions. In the 600s, alcohol was so precious a commodity that a Turfan tribe from Sinkiang province paid tribute in frozen wine. From communication with Mongols and Turks, the Chinese learned about *alaji,* or *koumiss,* a Mongol beverage churned and fermented from mare's milk. It was not until 1117 that Zhu Gong compiled *Beishan Jiujing,* which revealed Chinese distillation techniques, including the fermentation of cereal mash, which distillers had mastered in the 600s.

Arab World

After Mohammed's followers gave up gambling, pork, and alcohol following his death in 632, the spread of Islam reduced the number of places in the Arab world where alcohol was available. In Muslim Spain, laws forbade the serving of alcoholic drinks except as an ingredient in cooking or an accompaniment to food. Barkeepers began serving drinks in mugs capped with a lid, or *tapa.* From the practice of placing small morsels of food on the lid came the Spanish tradition of *tapas,* small dishes of bar food that made drinking legitimate. As described by the Spanish food critic Alicia Rio, these tasty bites encouraged diners to admire the cook's art and to engage in genial conversation. Today, the small savory servings come in three types: *cosas de picar* (finger food) such as olives, *pinchos* served on toothpicks, and *cazuelas* (small servings), dishes topped with sauce.

Europe

The scientific study of distillation in the Middle Ages raised the public's interest in the properties of *aqua vitae* (water of life), which the Florentine physician Taddeo Alderotti categorized in *De Virtutibus Aquae Vitae* (On the Qualities of Alcohol) (ca. 1275). Less documentation survives from a parallel tradition of the Gaelic *uisge beatha* (water of life), forerunner of the Irish whiskey that crofters home-distilled from malt. Used as a casual beverage and restorative, Irish whiskey was the basis for Irish coffee, a popular nightcap topped with whipped cream.

In the 1200s, the Franciscan friar William of Rubruck (Willem van Ruysbroeck) accepted a diplomatic mission from Louis IX to China. Accompanied by Bartholomew of Cremona and several other monks, he met with Sartach, a Mongol chief on the Volga, to acquire full diplomatic status in Tartary. On this journey, he learned the method of fermentation for *koumiss,* which Mongols distilled in a two-stage pan. The creation of such alcoholic wonders earned the praise of the thirteenth century Majorcan scientist and philosopher Raymond Lull, who pronounced the process a natural stage in human maturity.

In Britain, cider, popular in the 1200s, offered an alternative to the standard ale, mead, and metheglin. In about this same period, Albertus Magnus, a Dominican monk from Swabia, published in *Secretis Mulierum* (Women's Secrets) recipes for distilled *aqua ardens* (fire water), a pure pharmaceutical alcohol. At least a century later, Bonne of Bourbon heated an alembic (a distillation device) before the Savoy court to refine rosewater, a common ingredient in desserts, medicines, and kitchen-made cosmetics and lotions. In supplying the burgeoning distilling market with glass, the glass blowers of Murano greatly boosted their industry. In 1309 alchemist Arnaud de Villeneuve, author of *Tractatus de Aquis Medicinalbus* (Treatise on Medicinal Waters), declared distilled alcohol a panacea—a cure for humoral imbalance, heart failure, and aging, as well as gallstones, dropsy, colic, fever, and paralysis.

Into the Renaissance, the use of alcohol in cookery and medicines increased the complexity of kitchen work at the same time that recreational imbibing transformed etiquette and public behavior. Tudor England perpetuated the table ritual of the toast. As explained in Alexandre Dumas *père's* five-volume *Le Grand Dictionnaire de Cuisine* (The Great Dictionary of Cooking) (1873), the kitchen staff sent to the table a decanter or pitcher of ale or beer along with a toasted crust of bread. Sunk to the vessel's bottom, the bread remained there until the last draft, which brought a blessing of health to the drinker. When Anne Boleyn, second wife of Henry VIII and mother of Elizabeth I, allowed fanatic admirers to sip her bathwater, she was curious about one abstainer. He replied that he was holding out for the toast.

Throughout the seventeenth century, still rooms required equipment for producing flavorings, scent, essences, cordials, liqueurs, and spirits. In addition to a copper boiler with spout, distilling called for an iron firebox below, wet cloths for cooling condensate, and quantities of water. A worm tub mounted on a wood frame held enough water to cool the liquids that ran from a large still into the condenser tube. To cool a dry chamber, a nearby cauldron or tank held enough water to prevent an explosion.

The distillation of fruit juice such as citron water began, like cider making, with mashing pulp in a wood press and straining the pomace through several horsehair cloths or mats. The juice ran down a lead spout to tubs and casks. Distillers drew samples from stone jars with a tin pump. Smaller implements included a scoop called a pewter crane, fire tongs and rake, foreceps, bungs, and a hypocras bag for infusing spice. For sealing leaks, the brewer kept on hand a paste of bean meal or wheat and rye meal. A taster's pewter pipette, called a *valencia,* assisted in regular checks on clarity, flavor, and strength. If the resulting product was clouded, the brewer made a filter by sprinkling powdered alabaster in a flannel sleeve suspended in a willow hoop, then poured the liquid through until it ran clear.

In Spain, Basque all-male cooking clubs survive as a relic of earlier drinking cliques. In the 1850s, the first *txokos,* a Basque culinary gathering for middle-class men, got its start in San Sebastian, Spain, during a boycott of cider shops. Stockpiling beverages for sharing in a shop or home, they formed a buying and cooking group that allowed them autonomy and freedom from restrictions. During Franco's rule, they came under suspicion of harboring nationalist rather than cultural intent. By 1999, the groups, numbering more than 1,000, offered professional cooking in modern kitchens, where members took turns preparing meals and shared the cost of supplies.

Australia

In colonial Australia, European settlers' reputation for strong drink paralleled the low reputation of the island nation's cuisine. In 1853, a street preacher named Nathaniel Pidgeon reported that in a single week in

April, Sydney harbor had received 312,000 bottles of brandy, 90,000 barrels of beer, 70,000 bottles of beer, 48,000 gallons of rum, 34,000 gallons of brandy, and 31,000 gallons of gin. From the unseemly behavior of the hopeless convicts who inhabited the first English penal colonies, the grog tenters in the Ballarat gold fields, and the sailors who overran its harbors, Australia deserved bad press for seedy alehouses, where food was a mere sideline. To rescue urban areas from blight, planners of Sydney and other towns stressed the establishment of food markets, where shoppers gathered for produce rather than rum. By the mid-nineteenth century, both Sydney and Melbourne had turned the tide by supporting proper restaurants, boardinghouses, inns, and hotels. Wine distributors advertised the qualities of table vintages that complemented good food, a new concept to the hard-drinking Aussies.

The Americas

Cooks have long known of alcohol's uses as a food flavoring and preservative. In Curaçao homemakers mixed the eponymous liqueur, distilled from dried peel of the bitter orange, in flambéed omelettes to add a piquant flavor and aroma. Colonial American cooks made two products in one by brandying fruit in applejack, commonly known as "apple squeezin's." The fruit was useful for winter pies and meat stuffing; the liquid was a brandy suitable for entertaining and flambéing specialty dishes.

According to folklore, a New England tavern keeper turned out the first sophisticated American drink, the cocktail. During the American Revolution, Elizabeth "Betsy" Flanagan hosted local militia in Yorktown and listened to their complaints about English loyalists who prospered at the expense of the colonies. She served her guests a blend of fruit juice and rum and, in jest, adorned each glass with a feather from a Tory rooster. A Frenchman got into the spirit of the occasion with a cry of "Vive le coq's tail!"

Cognac, gin, and whiskey shared the New World spirits market with cheap rum from the Caribbean. Rum makers competed with the island traders by producing enough "kill devil" to supply each drinker with fifteen quarts per person. Farther south, in colonial Williamsburg, families turned to rum, fruit liqueurs, and brandy as tonics and cures. For daily health maintenance, they drank alcoholic beverages to ward off fever and flux. At Mount Vernon, George Washington favored imported claret and wrote of looking forward to sharing a cask with its donor, the Marquis de Chastellux. At Monticello, Thomas Jefferson preferred foreign wines, which he considered a cooking and table necessity. Social taboos against drunkenness kept excessive tipplers in line.

In place of water, the colonists relied on such alcoholic beverages as beer, ale, cider, mead, wine, bumbo punch, and syllabub, in the belief that the sources of amoebic dysentery, cholera, and typhoid could not survive in "hard drinks." To assure military readiness, army suppliers distributed brandy and rum along with provisions until 1832, when President Andrew Jackson ended the ration and replaced it with coffee and sugar. Lydia Maria Child's *The American Frugal Housewife* (1836) advocated New England rum as a quality hair cleanser and restorative. In her opinion, the alcohol rid the scalp of disease and promoted growth better than Macassar oil, the era's established hair dressing.

For variety, American distillers replicated alcoholic drinks from many parts of Europe and welcomed immigrants who brought new technologies. For instructions on making authentic Irish whiskey, they turned to a classic recipe in the Scottish food writer Margaret "Meg" Dod's *The Cook and Housewife's Manual* (1826). At Mrs. Goodfellow's Cooking School in Philadelphia, the first culinary academy in America, an unnamed pupil compiled *Cookery As It Should Be: A New Manual of Dining Room and Kitchen* (1853), which described brandied cherries and cherry bounce liqueur, an imitation of the Dalmatian drink Maraschino di Zara, for use as a condiment and flavoring.

Traveling in the Bahamas in 1860, Gaspare Campari discovered the appetite-enhancing properties of cascarilla bark, obtained from a tree that was native to Crooked Island at the southeastern end of the chain. After stripping the bark and soaking it for weeks, he created an aperitif that he aged in oak casks and served at Biffi, his Milan café. Sippers surmised that the secret recipe for the bittersweet Campari contained Chinese rhubarb, quinine bark, and seville orange zest, along with cochineal to color it bright red. It became a standard additive to colorful punches and other libations.

During the American Civil War, medical officers of the U.S. Army regularly examined and tasted servings of camp cookery to monitor the quality of the enlisted men's diet. The surgeon issued discretionary amounts of "old tanglefoot" (spirits) only after heavy exertion as an antidote to exposure and fatigue. On 1 March 1863, from the Medical Director's Office at headquarters for the Army of the Potomac near Falmouth, Virginia, surgeon Jonathan Letterman advocated a gill (about 4 oz or 118 ml) of alcohol diluted in three-quarters of a canteen of water at the end of each march. Control of alcohol assured the army that heavy drinkers did not sap the regiment's strength and render their bodies useless for fighting or vulnerable to slow-healing injuries and wounds.

ALCOHOL

In the southern Appalachians, moonshining was a way of life. Home brew, also known as corn squeezin's, apple brandy, and white lightning, was the base of such kitchen cures as cough syrup, compounded from alcohol and rock candy. During the Great Depression, poor farmers of Scotch-Irish heritage could not get a fair price for their corn. To survive, they turned grain into corn liquor and sold it illegally as non-tax-paid contraband. According to Eliot Wigginton's *The Foxfire Book* (1968), a compendium of folk traditions, moonshine was so remunerative that distillers warred openly against federal tax-collection agents, called "revenuers," and willingly risked fines and imprisonment for ready cash.

When Prohibition ended in the United States on December 5, 1933, alcohol returned openly to home bars and kitchens, where homemakers had previously concealed the stores saved for use in fruit cakes and sauces. The cocktail party, with its shakers of martinis, became an emblem of sophistication. Crucial to the flow of conversation were circulating trays of canapés and buffets of hot snacks that slowed the flow of alcohol to the bloodstream and kept friendly gatherings from degenerating into drunkenness.

Away from the Puritanic constraints of home, Americans found a host of traditions concerning strong drink. When U.S. mariners brought alcohol to the South Seas, they discovered a world unacquainted with intoxicating liquors. The popular drink of the islands was *kava*, a traditional euphoric beverage that women made from chewing the fibers of *Piper methysticum*, a shrub native to Australia. They spit the juice into warm water and brewed a mild ritual liquid that was imbibed in honor of the ancestors. In the estimation of Thor Heyerdahl, author of *Fatu-Hiva: Back to Nature* (1974), the *kava* ritual parallels the *kasava*-drinking culture of Mexico and Peru, where the brew is called *aqha, chicha,* or *kawau*. Heyerdahl cited the similarities between the rituals as proof of his theory that South Americans had traveled west by raft and shared elements of their culture with South Seas islanders. When Europeans arrived with more potent alcoholic drinks, the *kava* culture disappeared and islanders began distilling their own fermented grog from oranges.

In the West Indies rum remains a stable commodity offered under 1,500 labels and valued since the 1700s as a medicine and anesthetic. Although their products were harsh and volatile during the colonial period, distillers smoothed out the rough edges with charcoal filters invented in 1862 by Don Facundo Bacardi y Maso. Around 1898, U.S. doughboys in the Spanish-American War married rum to Coca-Cola at a Havana bar. Their toast to a free Cuba resulted in the drink known as the *Cuba libre.*

The lightest rum, called "white" or "clear," is the basis for the daiquiri, devised by engineer Jennings Cox and named for a copper-mining town in Cuba's Sierra Maestra. Darker categories of rum begin with *oro* (golden), aged for two years in oak barrels and used to make mai tais and mojitos, and end at "dark" or "black" rum, which is aged for four years and valued for making hurricanes or serving on the rocks. Viscous, strong-flavored fruit rums, made with island fruits, are the key ingredient in punch, piña coladas, and old-fashioneds. Rum also has wide culinary uses, adding an edge to savory dishes, complementing allspice and ginger and sparkling in pork glazes, sweet fruit salads, and soups made from coconut milk, sweet potatoes, honey, brown sugar, guava, pineapple, mango, or bananas. Bajans, Guyanans, and Jamaicans apply island rums to much of their entertaining and cooking, such as rum swizzle and soaked black cake.

The twenty-first century has produced some new approaches to alcoholic drinks. In 2000 Mike's Hard Lemonade Company of San Francisco marketed seven million cases of a so-called soft-hard beverage. Like the English Hooper's Hooch, Anheuser-Busch's "Doc" Otis, Rick's Spiked Lemonade, Two Dogs, and other "alcopops," the fizzy lemonade with a punch blurred the edge between alcoholic and nonalcoholic beverages. Like wine coolers, these drinks contained five percent alcohol, a fact that prompted criticism from the Marin Institute for the Prevention of Alcohol and Other Drug Problems, which claimed that such products introduced the young to hard drink.

Local Traditions

Where, when, and how to serve alcohol defines local traditions. In Russia, Georgians begin the meal with a toast and down entire glasses of alcohol or pass the *kantsi* (animal horn) from diner to diner; Lithuanians also toast the cook and host at lunch and supper. Swedish hosts precede the *skål* (toast) with a formal welcome. Danes prefer a shot of caraway-spiced Aalborg aquavit, which they chase with beer. Bulgarians typically end their evening meal with coffee or alcoholic drinks, as do Estonians, who favor vodka, and the French and Italians, who are famous for their dessert wines and brandies. German hosts offer both beer and wine. In Lebanon, non-Muslims indulge in *arak,* a strong traditional liquor. Turkish home brewers ferment grapes to make *raki,* which is also a favorite beverage in Albania. Chileans age grapes into *pisco* (grape brandy), their national beverage; Slovenians also make traditional table wines and fruit brandies. In Latvia, home brewed *balzams* blends herbs with alcohol for a healthful beverage or coffee additive. Zambians also make a home brew.

Around the globe, prevailing religious law influences attitudes toward alcohol. To the Afghan, consumption of alcoholic drinks violates Islam, but tobacco, hashish, and opium are common recreational pleasures. Likewise, Algerians, Guineans, Eritreans, Egyptians, Syrians, Tanzanians, Palestinians, and Guinea-Bissauans abstain from alcohol according to the dictates of the Koran. Moroccans tend to observe Islamic prohibitions by abstaining; those males who indulge are shunned. The Sudanese abide by Islamic injunction but brew a domestic drink called *marisa* (sorghum beer); Tunisians also waver on strict prohibition of alcohol. Tajiks openly violate Islamic injunctions by toasting guests with vodka on special occasions. Iranians, Pakistani, and Jordanians outlaw alcohol in any form.

See also **Banquets; Graham, Sylvester; Grog; Hale, Sarah Josepha; Mead; Monastery Kitchens; Soft Drinks; Wine**

Further Reading

Fredriksson, Lars, "The Liquor from Luzhou and the Secret of the Earth Cellar," *Oriental Studies*, No. 49–50, 1984.
Lovegren, Sylvia. *Fashionable Food: Seven Decades of Food Fads*. New York: Macmillan, 1995.
Skabelund, Grant P., man. ed. *Culturgrams: The Nations Around Us*. Vols. I & II. Salt Lake City, Utah: Brigham Young University, 1997.

ALUMINUM

Ductile and stain resistant, the metallic element aluminum contributes a silvery sheen to cookware and reduces weight in a variety of appliance frames, utensils, and cooking implements. The extraction of aluminum from bauxite ore in 1824 was the innovation of Hans Oersted, also claimed three years later by the German chemist Frederick Wohler. In 1850 a Frenchman named Henri Sainte-Claire refined the extraction process from aluminum chloride, but so little aluminum was produced that it was considered rare into the 1860s. Charles Martin Hall initiated the aluminum implement industry in Oberlin, Ohio, in 1886 when he passed an electric current through ore to separate pure metal. Within two years, items crafted from pliant aluminum sheets entered the iron- and tin-dominated kitchenware market.

A bit of domestic history in a 1917 issue of *House Furnishing Review* identified Griswold Manufacturing Company, working with Pittsburgh Aluminum Company, as the first to produce cast aluminum domestic goods in 1890, the first year that aluminum cookware

was made. A contrasting statement in the April 30, 1892 issue of *The Metal Worker* claimed that Auburn Hollow Ware of Auburn, New York, cast the first piece, a tea kettle. By the early twentieth century, lightweight aluminum storage containers were common. English biscuit-makers marketed their products in aluminum boxes, which homemakers recycled as canisters. In France aluminum foil was pressed out on rollers. The Aluminum Cooking Utensil Company, later a part of Alcoa, began marketing Wear-Ever in 1903, when its familiar logo appeared on inexpensive domestic goods. In 1911 the American West Bend Company began distributing its aluminum cookware through Sears, Roebuck & Company.

Although early models of aluminum blinds, lamps, tables, cruet stands, trays, candlesticks, and kitchenware were flimsy and poorly constructed, homeowners prized the bluish metal for its strength and smooth, unpitted surface. Shoppers elevated it to a preferred material for bridal and housewarming gifts. Another plus for aluminum, its resistance to harsh solutions, made it impervious to wine, brandy, pure alcohol, hot tea and coffee, beer, and acetic, citric, lactic, and tartaric acid. Manufacturers of aluminite, a metal sulfate invented in Germany in 1807, shaped it into sauce and sauté pans, gratin dishes, vegetable steamers, plates, soufflé dishes, ramekins, and shells. A popular French pot, the aluminum casserole used for the dish known as *pommes de terre Anna* (Anna potatoes), kept thin slices of potato from disintegrating while they cooked in butter.

When the poet Filippo Tommaso Marinetti, author of the 1909 manifesto of futurism, issued his *Manifesto of Futurist Cooking* (1930) in *Le Figaro,* he turned Italian cooking upside down. His dicta demanded newness and proposed annihilating the past by cloaking homely tiled kitchens and iron stoves in aluminum, a shiny evocation of technological advancement. His lack of cooking experience was obvious because he did not take into account that, although a quilted aluminum hot pad was serviceable, the thin aluminum vessels of the day had notoriously short life spans.

The emergence of cast aluminum enabled manufacturers to surpass in quality the early utensils cut from single sheets and shaped in one piece. Cleanup of cast items was easier than for ironware, which required much scouring followed by oiling to prevent rust in any implement that came in contact with salt. In 1915 domestic specialist Helen Atwater commented in *Selection of Household Equipment* that aluminum containers heated quickly and saved on fuel. Because discoloration caused by alkali was difficult to remove, she recommended the use of aluminum in double boilers, pot and pan lids, and teakettles. After World War I, coffeepots and filters made from anodized aluminum sheets duplicated the sheen of silver or pewter. By the 1920s the cookware starter sets produced by Club Aluminum of Chicago became a popular wedding gift. Still featured in women's magazines in the post-World War II era, Club Aluminum thrived in an era when homemakers favored matched items that also coordinated with linoleum, tile, paint, and cabinetry.

The 1923 Sears, Roebuck catalog featured a set of functional, inexpensive aluminum cookware. For a mere 90¢, the homeowner could buy three top-grade saucepans in three-pint, two-quart, and three-quart sizes. A trio of two-, four-, and six-quart kettles cost $1.95. The ad also listed a teakettle, dish pan, and convex-lipped kettle with lid at comparable prices. Subsequent applications of aluminum to kitchen equipment included firm nonslip handles on Wear-Ever pans and one-step juicers, such as the Handy Andy, a top-cranked device patented in 1935.

Using aluminum, American kitchenware manufacturers were able to produce medium-priced goods that sported a Continental panache—for example, aluminum egg crates for the eggs-by-mail business and sleek aluminum thermos bottles that paired with compartmentalized lunch boxes. In the January 1925 issue of *Good Housekeeping,* Wagner Manufacturing of Sidney, Ohio, marketed cast aluminum housewares, including serviceable kettles, double boilers, and roasters heavily clad in metal to resist denting, warping, breaking, and burning. In the April 1925 issue, Foulds' Macaroni Products featured a large-lidded cooker with a perforated liner for draining pasta and steamed vegetables.

Five years later, ads featured Wagner's upscale French drip coffeemaker in cast aluminum. Unlike the standard enamelware pot, this 1930 innovation displayed a curved shape topped with a simple lid and included an internal grounds basket. With its svelte silhouette ending in a scalloped bottom edge, the vessel also served as a cold-liquid pitcher; by filling the basket with ice, the housewife could serve ice water, lemonade, or tea.

In the December 1930 issue of *Good Housekeeping*, Walter H. Eddy, the author of a question-and-answer column, fielded queries about aluminum. To an Indiana reader who feared that aluminum cooking utensils caused cancer, he dispelled rumors about the effects of the metal on the body. As proof, he cited data from Allerton S. Cushman's article "The Truth about Aluminum" and Harvey W. Wiley's corroboration. Both specialists declared aluminum to be safe. Another health concern—a possible link between aluminum cookware and Alzheimer's disease—surfaced several decades later, but no convincing evidence was found to support this claim.

Illustrated with silvery line drawings of foil-wrapped mints and ice cream bars and aluminum-capped bottles, along with aluminum-lined tank cars carrying oils and dairy products, advertisements from the Aluminum Company of America featured full-page tributes to the versatility and flexibility of the metal. Text promised that aluminum foil protected flavor and purity by reflecting heat and light, retarding moisture, halting corrosion, and maintaining internal temperatures to guarantee long shelf life. An ad in the April 1947 issue of *Woman's Home Companion* touted the Maytag washer's aluminum agitator and seamless cast-aluminum tub for snag-free clothes washing. Another lauded Presto glass canning jars with aluminum screw bands, which carried the Good Housekeeping seal of approval. Text for a full-color column from the West Bend Aluminum Company in West Bend, Wisconsin, recommended the aluminum Serving Oven, a domed bread-and-roll basket with strainer to drain away the collected moisture that caused sogginess.

In the late 1940s Wear-Ever and Ekco courted housewives with the latest in pressure cookers. A sleek fuel- and time-saving pot with a technologically advanced cover, it offered safety as well as beauty. To relieve the cook's jitters over the possibility of an explosion, the Wear-Ever company offered closure with one hand and a lid lock that secured the lid handle to the main handle below. A simple temperature control fit over the release valve, which featured seven openings to channel steam. A full-color ad for a simpler Ekco model in the February 1947 *Woman's Home Companion* promised lima beans in one minute, rice in five, and fried chicken in fourteen.

To sort out developments in domestic goods, Elizabeth Beveridge, home equipment editor of *Woman's Home Companion,* advised brides on the best and latest developments in cookware. She and staff member Arlean Pattison characterized aluminum as the most widely used cookware material for its light weight and modest price and its no-polish finish. She recommended sheet aluminum for baking pans and stovetop pots and cast aluminum, which heated evenly and retained heat, for Dutch ovens, waterless cookware, and skillets.

Despite media claims, housewives encountered the same liabilities with thin aluminum ware as they had with tinware, which required constant repair and resoldering. Beveridge warned that pots made from the thinnest grade of aluminum tipped over easily and were prone to denting from daily use. In the 1940s an American firm marketed Mendets, a solderless disk or plug of aluminum for sealing holes in metal pots and pans. Using a wrench and a nut, the homemaker attached the plug to the backside of the vessel. At 10 cents per kit, Mendets were cheap and simple to apply, but patched cookware looked unsightly and was difficult to clean.

In 1949 Northland Aluminum Products of Minneapolis started a kitchen sensation by replicating in aluminum the German *bundt* pan, an earthenware or ceramic cake pan imprinted with harvest sheaves. The aluminum version, a tube pan divided into eight segments marked by scallops and spires, turned out a cake with a convoluted crust suited to streusel rather than icing. The molded cake was a popular midcentury bazaar, county fair, and church supper item.

The 1950s found new home uses for aluminum. Designer Eero Saarinen created dining chairs similar to the lightweight aluminum chairs and tables installed on the *Hindenburg* and the garden furnishings that George Steedman had made in the 1930s. The emergence of aluminum as a container for convenience foods came in 1954 with the introduction of TV dinners. The lightweight, reusable stamped trays served for both cooking and eating. The advent of aluminum foil altered the practice of food storage; foil sheets made easily shapeable containers for leftovers and foods bound for the freezer. Foil was cheap enough to be disposable, yet malleable enough to be straightened, washed, and reused.

The master chef James Beard, a compiler of *The Cook's Catalogue* (1975), exulted over a casserole both useful and beautiful, which he discovered at the Nambé factory outside Santa Fe, New Mexico. Its eight-metal, aluminum-based alloy created at the Los Alamos National Labs in the 1940s contained no silver or lead. It was so smooth and glossy that it won awards from the Museum of Modern Art. The company continues to market nontoxic metal kitchen and table goods that mimic the sheen of sterling silver and the durability of iron. The pieces—each cast in sand as a single unit—resist chipping, cracking, peeling, and tarnishing and maintain food temperatures for hours.

As the twentieth century drew to a close, aluminum continued to serve kitchen needs with unique packaging, tools, vessels, and novelties. Containers made from aluminum included oven roasters, garlic presses, cream whippers, tomato tongs and slicers, Kaiser roll stamps, and stovetop coffee pots. A heavy, steel-banded aluminum roaster from Commercial Aluminum provided ample space for a whole turkey or venison roast. The Perfex aluminum pepper or salt mill contained a pull-out chute for refilling and a steel grinding mechanism that adjusted from coarse to fine. Alessi introduced a sleek, fashionable tripod lemon reamer by the French designer Philippe Starcke.

See also **Canning**

AMANITE KITCHENS

The Amana colonies brought to the United States a flair for wholesome cookery and domestic economy. Founded in 1714 by pietist separatists from the Lutheran church, the religious society began in Darmstadt, Germany from the work of mystics Johann Friedrich Rock and Eberhard Ludwig Gruber. In 1842, to escape persecution, they immigrated to the United States. On 5,000 acres in Buffalo, New York, they formed the Ebenezer Society and supported their *Gemeinde* (commune) on profits from a nursery, greenhouse, and vegetable farm.

In 1864, a splinter group resettled on 26,000 acres outside Cedar Rapids, Iowa, and established a complex of seven communities—Amana, East Amana, Homestead, High Amana, Middle Amana, South Amana, and West Amana. Home-centered in their philosophy and focus, community planners worked at placing barns, wells, apiaries, kitchen gardens, grape arbors, and orchards to best advantage. The farm and trade center profited from wool weaving, a winery, a cooperage that manufactured barrels, and an abattoir that slaughtered and processed meat.

Brewers in the Amana colonies made batches of beer at four locations—Amana, Homestead, Middle Amana, and South and West Amana. Each commune obeyed local laws and paid federal taxes on its yield. In a brick brewhouse and cellar, the village brewmaster made a supply for adult residents, producing at Amana, the largest brewery, an average of 16,606 gallons per year from 1872 to 1883. Residents preferred homebrew for wedding receptions, where the groom and his friends supplied the gathering and washed the empty bottles for reuse. After 1884, the commune abandoned brewing, perhaps because of costs.

Community tradespeople milled lumber and shaped hardware for the first housing, which segregated male and female. Food service for groups of thirty to forty-five residents began in fifty-five communal kitchens. Members shared meals in dining halls seating up to 40 and managed by a *Küchebaas* (kitchen overseer), *Vizebaas* (assistant supervisor), and *Rüstchwestern* (vegetable cook), all appointees of the *Bruderrat* (council of elders). Providing supplies were breweries, garden plots, and gristmills. Agents for the commune peddled extra goods door to door. The next generation of workers entered apprenticeships after completing eight years of school. By 1881, the Amanite community had doubled in size.

Amanite carpenters built communal kitchens on a variety of floor plans, generally a roomy two-story frame, brick, or stone edifice with a one-story addition. They placed kitchen and dining area on ground level and reserved the upstairs as the living quarters of the supervisor and her family. A coal- or wood-fired oven stood at the center of food preparation for production of round four-pound loaves. With plain or yeast-raised dough, the staff baked twenty or more pies every few weeks from apples, rhubarb, plums, peaches, cherries, and grapes and cooled them on porch benches. Twice a week they made braided loaves, coffee cake, and sweet rolls with dough raised overnight. Flanking the oven was an ample brick hearth stove and six-foot sink and washstand, originally supplied with water from the pump of the courtyard well and hand-carried indoors. With improved technology, Amanites added an indoor hand pump, replaced eventually by a cold-water tap.

In honor of each *Küchebaas,* the kitchen house bore the woman's surname. As of 1932, sixteen had been so honored: the Christen *Küche,* Frey *Küche,* Goerler *Küche,* Graf *Küche,* Heinze *Küche,* Hertel *Küche,* Leichsenring *Küche,* Moershel *Küche,* Neubauer *Küche,* Osterle *Küche,* Rettig *Küche,* Winzenried *Küche,* Zimmerman *Küche,* two Noé *Küches* (run by Mrs. Charles Noé and Mrs. John Noé), and the Hotel. Upon a manager's retirement, she surrendered her place to the member of the staff best suited to the commune's routines and demands.

Commune members respected and honored supervisors for their control of foods and sanitation. They managed supplies and requisitions from the butcher, miller, baker, and keepers of icehouse and orchard. It was important to smooth operation that they remain on good terms with the dairy staff, who delivered goods on schedule by horse and wagon. To keep milk fresh, kitchen workers placed cans in a trough cooled with spring water and covered with old rugs.

Baking was a six-day-a-week job, requiring 100 pounds of flour a day. In addition to making the traditional four-pound loaves of white bread, the kitchen staff used locally milled flour to raise dough for pies and shape coffee cakes twice a week. Central to the Christmas holiday were the sweet aroma and the array of tins and crocks of cooled cookies; the baking of Christmas cookies began early in December. Ingredients included the colonies' own flour and yeast and local honey. The traditional holiday meal remained constant: rice soup, creamed chicken and noodles, mashed potatoes, cole slaw, stewed peaches and prunes, and *Stollen* (sweet yeast bread) filled with nuts, citron, and raisins. For New Year's Day, a special iced pretzel made of coffee cake was a colony treat also sold to the community. Bakers topped their pretzels with coconut or chopped nuts.

Managers kept detailed records of the surplus eggs and garden produce that they delivered to the general store for sale to the outside world. In exchange, they stated the amount of food they used, listing kitchen, number served, and individual commodity, such as coffee, sugar, and tea. Because of the *Küchebaas's* importance to the commune's survival, well-trained kitchen staff worked hard at brick and iron stoves preparing appetizing beef stew in fifteen-gallon kettles and ladling up generous platefuls. Each neophyte got lessons in cooking fried potatoes, soup, roast meat, and creamed vegetables and in shaping traditional Amanite sweet roll and coffee cake from yeast dough.

Kitchens serving a total of 1,500 residents had to be models of efficiency. Tall wall shelves, pie safes, and cupboards and corner or hallway iceboxes stored the necessary supplies. On the walls hung basins, tubs, and baskets, and additional vessels were handy under the sink. To redeem the area from institutional grimness, cooks covered windows with white calico curtains and brought in potted violets and geraniums.

For unautomated tasks, workers used a variety of hand utensils—cherry stoners, apple peelers, cheese and pudding molds, and noodle boards for shaping *Spätzle,* a Swabian dumpling. Vessels included varied sizes of sieves, ladles and spoons, and pots and pans made by the order's tinsmiths in Amana, Homestead, and East and West Amana. For the children, the tin worker created cookie cutters in a variety of shapes. For specific needs, the supervisor requested a pail or boiler of the appropriate size and shape. From the cooper came buckets, barrels, and tuns as well as immense winery barrels.

According to the memoir of Henrietta Ruff of South Amana, food preparation included care and cleaning of work stations and equipment. Commune philosophy of appreciating every task meant that workers mastered how to care for, use, and store each item, down to the lowly broom. New girls learned to light and clean the stove, polish kettles, scrub the sink and floor, and neaten cupboards. For soap making, they preserved wood ash from the hearth and oven in a collection box. A solution of ashes and lard from the butcher's animal scraps went into an open kettle for three days of cooking into a smooth, creamy *Schmierseif* (soft soap) and cooling into fifteen-inch bars for personal use. Crews delivered casks of soap for housework, laundry, and dish washing. In winter, the staff completed their chores by kerosene lamplight.

Menu planning followed the rhythms of commune life, with special breakfasts and suppers on Saturdays and a standard Sunday lunch of rice soup, boiled beef, creamed spinach, fried potatoes, coffee cake, and hot tea or coffee. When egg and milk production lessened in winter, cooks used more dried and canned supplies and vegetables from the root cellar, where salsify and horseradish lay buried in barrels of sand. Custards, cakes, and cheeses were more plentiful in spring, as were garden salads and fresh fruits and vegetables.

At sunrise, girls dressed in long calico dresses and walked to work in the kitchens, which was their assignment until marriage. Males and females ate at separate trestle tables in a large refectory. A separate table accommodated hired laborers and offered meals to guests at the cost of 15 cents to 20 cents. The High Amana General Store coordinated a voucher system to account for meals taken by outsiders, usually customers who came to buy paint, tires, and farm supplies. To acknowledge visiting relatives, the staff served special pies or *Eispudding* (ice pudding). They also delivered meals to mothers nursing infants and to those too sick to come to table. Following a German blessing, the supervisor and those waiting on tables passed bowls and platters and provided refills. Amanites ate in silence, offered a post-meal prayer, and thanked the *Küchebaas* on their way out.

After breakfast, a bell rang to summon Amanites to their jobs, which included peeling potatoes, canning fruit, making cheese, and churning butter as well as tending poultry, weaving baskets, and turning brooms. Additional crews raised poultry, tended the dairy, and preserved and pickled. The kitchen followed a rigid seven-day schedule, with specific tasks allotted to each day of the week. Young cooks took turns at cookery, beginning with lighting the stove and brewing coffee. Assigned chores included mixing cakes, shaping cheeses, gathering mushrooms, and collecting eggs. After a week's rotation, the cook got an extra hour's sleep and reduced workload. The third week of the system required setting tables and washing dishes. Whatever the chore, women aided each other and sang as they worked in a spirit of camaraderie and commitment.

The first Amanite kitchen gardeners started their beds with seeds and cuttings from Germany. Among their prized crops were the tall Amana string bean, Ebenezer onion, yellow leaf lettuce, multicolored radish, citrus melon, celeriac, European black salsify, and ground cherry. They saved seed, which they sorted, weighed, and labeled for storage. At the two- to three-acre gardens attached to each kitchen, work crews composed of three or more women and retired male farmers hoed herb beds, watered seedlings, aired cold frames, and weeded berry patches daily.

Crops went into the ground according to the phases of the moon—plants growing above ground were planted when the moon was on the increase and root crops begun in the waning moon. Insect control consisted of dusting with ashes, hand-plucking grubs, interplanting marigolds among the vegetables, and killing cabbage worms with saltwater. Weed pulling filled the period in the dark of the moon. The garden crew hired extra workers during plowing and harvesting or recruited children to help. Under the direction of the *Gartebaas* (garden supervisor), each crew produced enough herbs and vegetables to feed forty residents.

Amanite communes made bee keeping a spring ritual. On the first sunny day of the growing season, workers hauled bee boxes from the cellar to awaken hibernating insects to the fragrant orchard, garden, and grape arbor. Each village's beekeeper tended the hives through the summer, collected honey, and divided it into equal shares, one per residence. The season concluded with the dragging of boxes back downstairs for the cold months.

The utopian dream of self-sufficiency collapsed in the 1920s and 1930s, in part because Amanites began questioning six decades of rigidly silent meals. At the beginning of the twentieth century, they experimented with the distribution of foodstuffs to individual housewives, who carried them home in baskets to serve family-style meals. Although the order abandoned the institutional atmosphere of communal dining halls, the *Küchebaas* and unmarried Amanites continued to dine in the old style.

On August 12, 1923, the commune suffered fires in two mills. The lure of new ways of thinking and working began weakening consensus, and the Great Depression brought an end to unity. On June 1, 1932, during an era known as the Great Change, members disbanded the commune and created the Amana Society, Inc., to manage business and farming operations. They formed the Amana Church Society to reorganize the faith. Home units replaced dormitory-style living; communal dining ended completely, giving place to the nonsectarian ideal of one family at one table.

See also **Baking; Cheese; Corn**

Further Reading

"History of Amana Colonies," http://www.amanacolonies.com/ history.htm.
Hoppe, Emilie. *Seasons of Plenty: Amana Communal Cooking.* Ames: Iowa State University Press, 1998.
Searle, Bonita Cox, "A Brief History of the Amana Society," http://www.ipfw.edu/ipfwhist/home/searle.htm.

AMISH KITCHENS

The Amish, who were philosophically conservative and strict, lived by a gender-specific code that separated cooking chores for male and female. Women traditionally concentrated on cooking, baking, and seasonal preserving of foods, including oven-dried corn for meal. According to John A. Hostetler's *Amish Society* (1993), women traditionally shelved 800 quarts of home-canned fruit and vegetables per family each year.

Lancaster County, Pennsylvania. This Church Amish Housewife is engaged in the rapidly disappearing practice of baking bread. Note the devotional head-covering, which is worn in accordance with I Corinthians 11:1-16.
[© *Courtesy of National Archives and Records Administration.*]

Cooks rose early to provide hearty meals, such as a breakfast of eggs, fried scrapple and potatoes, corn-meal mush, and hot wheat hearts or whole-wheat cereal plus jelly and apple butter with bread and butter. Dinners featured Amish "kitchen specialties"—home-cured ham with chow-chow and pickled beets, stinky cheese, floury rivel soup, and shoo-fly or green tomato pie and apple dumplings for dessert. In recognition of her importance to the family, the mother occupied a place at the table beside her husband, the head of the household, who signaled the beginning and end of a silent grace.

Of the typical six or seven rooms in an Amish home, four were allotted to food preparation. In addition to a large kitchen, the homemaker pursued duties in a room-sized pantry, closed porch, summer kitchen, and indoor washhouse. As described in Stephen Scot and Kenneth Pellman's *Living Without Electricity* (1999),

Amish kitchens perpetuated pre-Edison technology with domestic and farm devices powered by wind, horse, and muscle. For refrigeration, housewives depended on the icebox. In Iowa, Wisconsin, and On-tario, ice harvesters labored in the coldest weather to cut block ice and store it in icehouses. The success of the operation launched a community business in home ice delivery. Eventually, kerosene-powered refrigera-tors replaced some iceboxes. Beef, chicken, and sau-sage were preserved by canning. For the storage of large haunches of meat, householders rented space in frozen-food lockers.

Greens were valued for their medicinal properties. A cook from Leola, Pennsylvania, collected tender spring dandelions, which she fried in butter until crisp and topped with eggs, a dish she called "bacon dan-delion." Another Amish herb collector, Ben E. Byler from Selinsgrove, Pennsylvania, boiled dandelion flowers with citrus fruit to make a general-purpose home remedy.

In her lyrical *Amish Women: Lives and Stories* (1994), Louise Stoltzfus reflected on the domestic skills of her grandmother Fannie Ebersol, a German-speaker from Lancaster, Pennsylvania, who kept an orderly house and neatly weeded garden until her death at the age of 100. The women in her family upheld frontier traditions in food preservation and all-day quilting. They established such kitchen customs as growing celery to stuff for wedding dinners and gathering seasonally for the communal making of cream-filled doughnuts.

The traditional wedding meal required that the cooks—including the parents of the bride and groom—arrive at the bride's kitchen early in the morning the day before the ceremony. After the men beheaded and plucked fowl, the women dressed and stuffed the birds and cracked nuts and peeled fruit for an array of pies. Their male helpers assisted by keeping kettles of hot water boiling, carrying parings to the mulch heap, and erecting pine trestle tables about the house to serve as many as 100 guests. The meal consisted of a generous serving of roast fowl with dressing, mashed potatoes and gravy, ham, cole slaw, and cookies, candy, and cake, along with cider and tea, and concluded with mints and digestive aids.

During the 1930s, the Amish abandoned outdoor bake ovens and began to cook on wood, kerosene, and propane stoves. In summer, they resorted to Coleman camp stoves to keep kitchens from overheating and to serve as auxiliary stoves. Their low-tech bake ovens were the brick or stone types once favored on the American frontier. For washing clothes and stirring up batches of apple butter, they depended on the kettle stove, a small but powerful workhorse designed to heat large amounts of liquid with a limited expenditure of fuel.

Amish technology expanded in the 1970s, when Elmo and Mark Stoll invented the first American airtight stove, a model intended to burn all night. Similar to the Scandinavian Jo-Tul wood-burning stove, the Amish Pioneer Maid stove kept the stainless steel firebox lit from twelve to fourteen hours by nurturing a slow, steady burn within a lining of fire brick. It featured wooden control knobs, a polished surface, and a hopper that held up to six weeks' worth of ash. In 1979, the design went into manufacture in Aylmer, Ontario.

See also **Pennsylvania Dutch Kitchens**

Further Reading

Hostetler, John A. *Amish Society.* Baltimore: John Hopkins University Press, 1993.

Igou, Brad. *The Amish in Their Own Words.* Scottsdale, Penn.: Herald Press, 1999.

Scott, Stephen, and Kenneth Pellman. *Living Without Electricity.* Intercourse, Penn.: Good Books, 1999.

Stoltzfus, Louise. *Amish Women: Lives and Stories.* Intercourse, Penn.: Good Books, 1994.

AMPHORA

In ancient Phoenicia, Greece, and Rome, the amphora was a double-handled oval-shaped clay jar holding around six gallons and seven pints of wet or dry commodities. Its name derived from the Greek *amphiphoreus* (carried on both sides), a reference to the two handles located at either side of the vessel's shapely neck. As pictured in William Clarke's *Pompeii: Its Past and Present State* (1847), amphorae came in a variety of styles, some smooth-sided and

Amphora urn.
[© *TH Foto / Alamy*]

some coiled. Designed for packing in a cargo vessel, the amphora served for storage and lengthy or cumbrous transport of oil, olives, capers, dried fish, honey, fruit, fruit syrup, wine, and grain. Users lined with pitch or hot resin those jars that held wine or the pungent sauce called garum. Thick olive oil seeped into crevices in the clay and served as its own waterproof sealant. Larger, more stylized amphorae served as wedding and funeral urns and grave markers.

The typical amphora was was a long, narrow-necked, two-handled vessel ranging from one to five feet in height. It ended in a spike or button, which the user could grasp to steady the jar for two-handed pouring or carrying. An iron amphora stand held the vessel upright in kitchen or storage room. The trade from Rome to southern Spain was so active that a Roman city dump on the Tiber shore accumulated a pile of jar shards 140 feet high and 3,000 feet around. The original containers may have numbered 40 million and carried 440 trillion gallons of oil. Their weight and sturdiness altered over time from heavy and fragile to lighter and stronger. Late models could carry three times their weight.

The origins of amphorae were sometimes recognizable from official stamps on the handle or from graffiti, symbols such as a rose for the island of Rhodes, magistrate or inspector's name, or painted inscriptions listing the *modius* (capacity), measured in units equal to two gallons. Some wine amphorae inscriptions labeled the vintage and the consulate under which wine-growers harvested the grape. The presence of pottery vessels and shards in excavated buildings and at shipwreck sites has made it possible for archaeologists to study the economy and diet of the ancient world, as well as the spread of pottery styles from one region to another.

Mention of amphorae in Greek sources specified the importance and daily uses of storage jars for home use and transportation. Homer's *Odyssey* (ca. 850 BCE) describes how Telemachus, embarking on his search for his long-lost father Odysseus, packed twelve jars of wine from the household store. Two centuries later, Thucydides mentioned that householders stored water in amphorae as a safety measure in case of fire; in the fifth century BCE, the historian Herodotus characterized Egyptian amphorae as water containers. Xenophon's *Anabasis* (ca. 400 BCE) cited amphorae as storage containers for barley and slices of dolphin meat and fat. Strabo's *Geography* (ca. 20 BCE) recounted how the Cimbrians slit the throats of their captives over amphorae to retain the blood.

The wide dispersal of amphorae attests to Rome's inability to feed its populace on locally grown foods. Without shipping and overland trade, particularly in wheat from Egypt, Sicily, and North Africa, Romans would have starved. Outgoing trade in food and wine

kept the economy healthy. In the first century BCE, when Julius Caesar campaigned in Gaul, Roman exporters moved goods with the troops, who absorbed some of the risk and cost of overland distribution. Simultaneously, importers brought some 40 million amphorae into the area. Counts of amphorae attest to fluctuations in trade of foodstuffs and wines, including the emergence of competitive vintners in Spain and Provence.

Although barrels and kegs would have been lighter and more efficient users of space, clay was more readily available than wood and nearly indestructible for the shaping of amphorae and *dolia*, the storage vats found in Roman warehouses. Amphora packers preferred cork stoppers for wine and terra cotta for garum and olive oil. These plugs, cemented with lime, kept contents pure over long periods. In *De Agri Cultura* (On Agriculture, ca. 150 BCE), the orator Marcus Porcius Cato declared that properly stored wine must (the fruit pulp and skins from crushed grapes) would stay fresh for a year. Other prized foods, notably English oysters, *boleti* (mushrooms), and truffles, remained fresh for long-distance shipping.

Aboard ship, packers stacked amphorae vertically between small branches or straw bundles in a ship's hold, with the pointed ends of the upper layer fitting between the shoulders of the preceding layer. Harbor draymen unloaded them individually, and delivery teams loaded them onto carts for delivery to homes or religious houses, where cellarers nestled them in sand in a cool room. One molded terra cotta bas-relief from Pompeii depicts two male slaves bearing a jar tied with a thong and slung over a pole.

Further Reading

"Amphorae and the Roman Wine Trade," *Athena Review*, Vol. 1, No. 4, 15.

Betz, Virginia, "Bread, Wine, and Villas: Agriculture in Roman Gaul," *Athena Review*, Vol. 1, No. 4, 51–55.

Casson, Lionel. *The Ancient Mariners*. Princeton, N.J.: Princeton University Press, 1991.

Koehler, Carolyn, and Philippa M. W. Matheson, "The Amphoras Project," http://archaeology.about.com/science/archaeology.

Tyers, Paul. *Roman Pottery in Britain*. London: Routledge, 1999.

APHRODISIACS

Belief in aphrodisiac substances intended to promote sexual potency or arouse amatory interest permeates much of world history and literature. Aphrodisiacs have come in many forms, from drinks and foods to lotions and ointments, and have served a variety of purposes—increasing virility, enhancing seductive powers, bolstering sexual allure, prolonging coitus, reawakening waning sexual potency, or rekindling interest in a former love. Although science has confirmed the effects on libido and sexual performance of only a select few hormones, drugs, and herbs, the search for and distribution of "love potions" continues, often at great price and much danger to the user.

Folklore links the cooking and eating of certain ordinary foods—for example, oysters and asparagus—to a surge in passion. Select herbs and plants, including true-love, hops, jasmine, lettuce, lily, orchids, rhubarb, strawberries, and staves-acre, all allegedly cured frigidity. Australian natives ascribed aphrodisiac properties to lizard meat and accordingly limited lizard in the diet of young men lest they ruin their health with too much sexual indulgence. Ginseng root, powdered rhinoceros horn, and scrapings from deer antlers are among substances traditionally believed to awaken erotic powers in males. Another plant, datura, a dangerous hallucinogen, appeared on aphrodisiac lists throughout Europe, Asia, and the Americas.

In the ancient world, the baking of cakes shaped like phalluses or labia was a common impetus to love. Mountebanks peddled mandrake root (*Mandragora autumnalis*), damiana (*Turnera diffusa*), and absinthe, a drink flavored with wormwood (*Artemis absinthium*), as well as arsenic and marijuana (*Cannabis sativa*), which could be administered through food, drink, or inhaled smoke. Late in the third century BCE, the Greek Dioscorides, author of lusty epigrams, promoted the blending of goat milk and orchid tubers into a paste as an aid to lechery. Celtic lore concerning Tristan and Isolde attributed the failure of their love match to a powerful elixir that doomed their hearts' cravings. In Mesoamerica, cooks venerated mushrooms as tonics, panaceas, and aphrodisiacs.

During the late Middle Ages, the kitchens of midwives and folk healers were often the source of love-enhancing concoctions blended from plants, minerals, and common foods, especially bay leaves, peppers, almonds, aloe, hibiscus, jasmine, marigolds, rose petals, vanilla, and raw honey or mead, the "grandfather of aphrodisiacs," mentioned in the Kama Sutra and the Bible. Much of the effectiveness of aphrodisiacs was ascribed to fragrance, as was the case with anise, basil, caraway, chamomile, coriander, fennel, lavender, licorice, rose, rosemary, sage, and summer savory. As a deterrent to seduction, charm makers made drinks and dishes with calamint, poppy, and lettuce, all thought to protect a virgin from violation. The kitchen staff of the Mexican emperor Montezuma II whipped frothy cups of bitter *chocólatl* or *cacahuatl*, rich in phenyl ethylamine, to stimulate the desires and sexual performance of his women.

During the Renaissance, cooks believed that foods that caused intestinal bloating and flatulence, such as beans, oats, or cabbage, improved potency by performing a parallel swelling of tissue in the genitals. French recipe books recommended bean or truffle soup as an antidote to waning sexual urges. In Italy, food writer Bartolomeo Scappi, compiler of *Opera dell'Arte dell Cucinare* (Compendium on the Art of Cookery, 1570) and chef to Pope Pius V, earned renown for his recipe for a pie containing bull testicles, which were believed to confer the animal's potency when ingested. In the 1700s, the Marquis de Sade procured candies laced with so-called Spanish fly, which caused the deaths of some of his courtesans.

While discrediting most of these sexual myths, science acknowledges the anatomical affect of cantharides, substances derived from crushed portions of *Lytta vesicatoria,* the blister beetle (also called Spanish fly), which stimulate the pelvic area by irritating the genitourinary tract. A second substance, yohimbine, a deadly alkaloid extracted from the yohimbé tree (*Corynanthe yohimbe*) native to Cameroon, Gabon, and Zaire, is used to promote blood flow to the genitals to encourage stallions or bulls to mate with mares and cows in estrus. Another acknowledged libido enhancer is derived from bois bandé, a tree found on the Caribbean isle of Grenada, where the local people brew a romance-boosting infusion by blending the bark with rum. Into the twenty-first century, herbs reputed to have aphrodisiac properties continued to be marketed in nutritional specialty stores and on the Internet.

See also **Chocolate; Mead**

Further Reading

Nordenburg, Tamar, "The Facts about Aphrodisiacs," *FDA Consumer Magazine*, January–February 1996.

Severson, Kim, "The Foods of Love," *San Francisco Chronicle*, February 9, 2000.

Stewart, Ian, "Love Could Kill Off Popular Aphrodisiac," *South China Morning Post*, January 31, 2001.

Walsh, Robb, "A Rosy Repast," *Natural History*, May 1, 1999, 96.

APICIUS, CAELIUS

The Roman food expert Caelius Apicius is credited with writing *De Re Coquinaria* (On Cooking, late 300s AD), the world's oldest cookbook. Although he provided a wealth of detail on food selection, preservation, and cookery, he left only bits of information about his life. According to conflicting accounts, he earned his nickname because he was as bald as an *apica* (ewe's stomach) or because he was as sweet as the food of the bee, *apis*.

Further confusing the identity of this legendary food lover, at least four Apicuses are known from Roman history of this period. The first was the profligate Apicius who lived under Sulla in the last half century of the Republic, during the rise of Julius Caesar. The second, the wealthy Marcus Gavius (or Gabius) Apicius of Minturnae, Campania, taught elegant cookery under the first two emperors, Augustus and Tiberius, in the early first century CE. He left a legacy of original stews, which the encyclopedist Pliny the Elder praised in his encyclopedia, *Natural History* (ca. 77 CE). Pliny also recorded Apicius's cruel force-feeding of pigs with dried figs, doping them on *mulsum* (honeyed wine), and slaughtering them to extract their tasty livers.

A third candidate, mentioned by Athenaeus of Naucratis in his *Deipnosophistai* (The Learned Banqueters, ca. 200 CE), lived during the reign of Trajan in the early second century CE. The fourth and final Apicius lived nearer the end of Rome's empire, when cultural decline triggered a yearning for the golden era of the Augustan Pax Romana.

Apicius's text, alternately titled *De Opsoniis et Condimentis sive de Re Culinaria Libri Decem* (Ten Books on Catering and Seasoning), first came to print in Milan in 1498. It appears to be incomplete, for it lacks dessert and pastry recipes, both Roman favorites. The vague generalities of Apicius's style dismayed readers until the 1984 publication of a new translation by the Latin master John Edwards.

Extant chapters display a limited command of grammar and rhetoric, but the cook's *joie de vivre* is evident in chapters on spicing wine, chopping meat, raising a kitchen garden, and slow-cooking duck, venison, mutton, squid, and eels. The glory of Apicius's recipes was the range of spices he obtained from Greek and Roman traders. Overall, 90 percent of his dishes called for seasoning. With spices such as cinnamon, cloves, and nutmeg and foodstuffs from the Near East, North Africa, and the Black Sea, he cultivated a sophisticated and demanding palate that rejected the dull and soggy fare of the average Roman diet.

Apicius's original compilation survived because of the efforts of a little-known food writer, Vinidarius, who used a transcription in late Latin as the basis for his own extracts in the early 400s CE. In eleven chapters—ten Apician originals plus Vinidarius's addition—the collection characterizes the great Roman chef's flair for flavor, for example, his pairing of contrasting sauces, sweet against sour. For sourness, he used vinegar; for sweetening, he chose wine must, honey, or raisin wine. As thickeners, he preferred dumplings and soft bread. He displayed a weakness for such standard condiments as *liquamen* (fish sauce) and chose as preservatives honey, wine must, vinegar, myrtle berries, and salt. He simmered meat with chives, leeks, onions, and squills and sauced dishes with a veritable cornucopia of tastes and textures— myrtle berry wine, roasted and chopped almonds, chestnuts, damsons, dates, hazelnuts, pine nuts, pistachios, quince-apples, and raisins.

The inventiveness of Apicius's culinary writings attests to real kitchen experience. He enlivened salads with cheese and capers, gave new life to traditional Roman *puls* (pottages of fava beans), stuffed pig paunch with brains and seasonings, and honored the philosopher Lucretius with Patellam Lucretianam (Lucretian Dish), a salt fish stewed with onions and vinegar. For storing grapes, Apicius devised a system of boiling down rainwater and pouring it over fresh grape clusters in a vessel sealed with pitch and gypsum and shielded from light. He suggested using the liquid as a sweetened beverage for invalids. He even worked out a means of shipping fresh oysters to the Emperor Trajan on campaign in Parthia.

The two oldest copies of Apicius's writing are housed at the New York Academy of Medicine and the Vatican Library. In 1705, the London physician Martin Lister issued an annotated edition that carried the imprimatur of physicist Isaac Newton and architect and city planner Sir Christopher Wren. In 1829, the waggish Dick Humelbergius Secundus published *Apician Morsels; Or, Tales of the Table, Kitchen, and Larder: Containing, a New and Improved Code of Eatics; Select Epicurean Precepts; Nutritive Maxims, Reflections, Anecdotes, & c.* Humelbergius appended to the Roman gourmet's book his own extravagant instructions for breakfasting and dining out, including commentary on table manners and anecdotes about cooking.

See also **Cookbook; Herbs; Roman Cookery; Spices; Wine**

Further Reading

Edwards, John. *The Roman Cookery of Apicius*. Point Roberts, Wash.: Hartley & Marks, 1984.

APPERT, NICOLAS

The chef, distiller, and chemist Nicolas-François Appert earned a place in the annals of domestic and military science for his invention of *appertizing*, a method of creating a heat-generated hermetic seal that allowed food to be preserved in bottles as easily and safely as had been done centuries earlier with wine. Among his other innovations were the bouillon cube, a gelatin-extraction method, and a sterilizer. Born on November 17, 1749 in Chalons-sur-Marne, France, he mastered Champagne wines while working for his father as a bottle corker. Appert apprenticed in cooking at the Palais Royal Hotel in Châlons and worked in brasseries and in the private kitchen of the duke and duchess of Deux-Ponts. An accomplished candy maker, at age thirty-one he earned the unofficial title of "confectioner of Lombard Street."

In 1795, during a period of intense rivalry between the French and British to keep their armies and navies adequately fed, Appert devoted himself to kitchen experimentation to solve a key problem—how to save seasonal crops for later table use. When the curtailment of overseas food supplies jeopardized the forces of General Napoleon Bonaparte, the Directoire issued a general appeal for comestibles. Appert began testing new procedures at Brest in 1804 and opened a bottling works at Massy outside Paris, employing fifty workers.

At age fifty-seven Appert achieved the breakthrough that led to the safe and secure packaging of food in wide-mouth glass bottles. The concept preceded by several years the work of an English inventor, Peter Durand, who created a technology for preserving food in tin cans. Appert's method required a kettle, boiling water, glass champagne bottles, corks, wax, and wire. He assured an air-tight closure by sealing the bottles with wax and wire before immersing them in water and boiling them to kill the microbes responsible for food spoilage. An article in the February 1809 issue of *Courier de l'Europe* declared that Appert had "discovered the art of fixing the seasons. With him spring, summer and autumn exist in bottles like delicate plants that are protected by the gardener under a dome of glass against the intemperance of the seasons."

The experiment impressed the Belgian horticulturist André Parmentier and the French physicist Joseph-Louis Gay-Lussac, although the latter questioned Appert's belief that heat destroyed or neutralized natural fermentation. In 1807, the English emulated the Appert canning method after the London Society of Arts remunerated Thomas Saddington for canning fruit for use by the British navy. Napoleon, by then emperor of France, issued Appert the 12,000-franc prize offered by the Directoire to the first person who developed a method of food preservation to aid in the shipboard transport of naval provisions. The honor included the requirement that Appert publish a description of thermal-activated vacuum bottling. This work, published in 1810, was entitled *Le livre de tous les ménages ou L'Art de conserver, pendant plusieurs années, toutes les substances animales et végétales* (The Book of all Housework, or The Art of Preserving All Kinds of Animal and Vegetable Substances for Several Years). His text explained the results of bottling on milk,

partridge, *pot-au-feu* (stew), bouillion, consommé, fresh eggs, fruit, herbs, peas, sorrel, spinach, and tomatoes.

Immediately, Appert abandoned candy making and invested the prize money in pure laboratory research at the firm of Chevalier-Appert in Ivry-sur-Seine. The application of his findings benefited military men at a time when the navy boosted its ranks from 25,000 in 1793 to more than 145,000 and required shipmasters to provision their galleys for six-month cruises. Two years after his breakthrough, following the French invasion of Russia with more than a million soldiers, Appert became a national hero. He earned a gold medal from the *Société d'Encouragement pour l'Industrie Nationale* (Society for the Encouragement of National Industry) for his contribution to the nation's food supply. In 1814 he began manufacturing bouillon cubes, another timesaving kitchen aid, and experimented with replacing the glass canning jar with the tin can.

Three years after Appert's factory burned during the invasion of 1814, he restarted his operation in Paris, which remained active until 1933. Appert himself died penniless on June 1, 1840, leaving his investigative work to a successor, Raymond Chevallier-Appert, who controlled the high temperature of the autoclave by inventing a pressure gauge. William Underwood further developed the Appert model at his Boston canning business, producing Underwood's Deviled Ham, a popular home convenience food. In Appert's memory, the U.S. Institute of Food Technologists named its highest honor the Nicholas Appert Award.

APRONS

The apron, a garment of variable size, usually tied around the waist, has a long history as both a protective and decorative accessory. The simplest were little more than loincloths worn for modesty's sake; among the most elaborate were the jeweled ritual aprons worn by priests in ancient Assyria as a sign of their rank and power. In its most widespread form, however, the apron was—and still is—used as a covering worn for kitchen tasks and other, often domestic, work.

Aprons for serf and master date to medieval customs from Western Europe. On seaside piers and in market stalls, tradespeople and fishmongers protected their clothes with oilskin or wool aprons as they dispensed food or sorted, gutted, and scaled their slimy prey. For the garbage picker scooping through debris in search of usable items, the apron provided protection from the muck.

In the thirteenth century well-dressed female diners covered their laps with a surface wrap of fabric. It spread outward into a communal banquet cloth, which

Woman with apron preparing meal.

could shield the laps of several banqueters at once. Workers had their own versions, particularly the familiar leather apron of the smithy or tanner and the cook's white apron with matching cap; other adaptations of the apron suited the work of nurses, servants, gardeners, and florists. Colors and styles established the types of work performed by each: white for professional cooks and stonemasons, green for butlers and furniture movers, blue for weavers, blue stripes for butchers, black for cobblers, and a checkered pattern for barbers. To at-home models, kitchen staff and housewives added oval bags or pockets suspended from a tie at the waist as receptacles for keys and aids to domestic work. Some of the more protective models even included long skirts and sleeves. To keep hemlines out of the way, kitchen workers tucked them into the underside to form panniers at the back and sides. Over top, the bib or a full-sleeved smock kept the front clean.

From the fourteenth to the sixteenth centuries, aprons were standard garb for peasant and middle-class women. The Swiss wore a white version with black embroidery that spread widely over the skirt. In the Elizabethan era, the apron developed into a long skirt covering for ordinary dress. Around the time of the rise of Puritanism in England, the apron became a fashionable accessory protecting embroidered panels. Made of gauze and silk and edged in lace, cutwork, and fine stitchery, the fancier model allowed the underskirt to show through. For plainer attire, white holland or linen aprons sufficed. The apron grew long and narrow during the Puritan regime from 1649 to 1660. With the return of the monarchy to power and the restoration of Charles II, aprons were once more relegated to serving staff and commoners.

In the colonial Americas, women carrying ale and baskets of bread to field workers wrapped a loose length of cloth about the waist to protect their skirts. For housework, colonists stitched together homespun pockets, some with expansion pleats, which tied about the waist on a tape or string. A valuable and handy carry-all, it held the oddments of the day—seeds and herbs saved from last year's garden, bodkins and cake testers, string, baby "clouts," yarn, or a letter from relatives in the old country. The loss of a pocket containing keys to the food chest or cellar would have caused a massive search, perhaps by rushlight in woodpile, pig sty, dairy, or henyard until the missing pocket was found.

The late seventeenth century reduced aprons to small lap coverings made of fashionable fabrics and embroidered or edged with frills and lace. These garments altered in the first quarter of the 1700s into silk and satin drapings. In midcentury, the serviceable apron changed into a pair of pouches tied about the waist for carrying practical household items. The muslin apron embroidered white on white remained a standard of polite, ladylike dress. At the beginning of the 1800s, the long, bib-front apron gained popularity.

For housework and kitchen duties, Victorian women protected their garments with wraparound pinafores or bibbed pinners that reached from neck to feet and buttoned in back for full coverage. For messy work such as dusting ceilings and overhead light fixtures, fastidious workers sometimes tied on two aprons, one to the front and another to protect skirts to the rear. The punctilious nanny wore a nursery apron and sometimes carried a nanny whistle in the pocket. One toot warned children to come at once for tea or to stop scruffy behaviors before facing stiffer penalties.

In Germany, the Professional Teacher's Institute in Frankfurt established a curriculum of classroom study and practicum. When the curriculum called for work in the laboratory kitchens, students dressed in uniforms and starched white aprons. The costume symbolized the school's attitude toward the "new woman," who approached domestic work scientifically in a sleek metal-and-glass environment powered by gas and electricity. These cook trainees were the first generation of food specialists who did not have to dread the drudgery and heavy clean-up of the nineteenth-century kitchen worker.

In the United States, the starched white apron became the uniform of an emerging home economics profession, symbolized by the American domestic authority Fannie Farmer, the lecturer, demonstrator, and published food writer in 1891 at the Boston Cooking School. Emma M. Hooper sang the praises of the kitchen apron in an 1894 issue of *Ladies Home Journal,* proclaiming the humble but useful garment "indispensable."

From the American frontier days to the Depression era, aprons indicated the woman at work, whether plucking fowl in the Appalachian hills, fanning a campfire along the Oregon Trail, or crimping fruit pies for the master in the plantation bakehouse. For illiterate slaves who made their own aprons, embroidery and patchwork were outlets for dreams and family history, for which they had no written words. Letitia M. Burwell, the author of *A Girl's Life in Virginia Before the War* (1895), recalled that the apron was a wardrobe essential for domestic slaves, who "were always dressed in the cleanest, whitest, long-sleeved aprons, with white or red turbans on their heads."

Housekeepers preferred the freedom of cobbler aprons, a shortened version of the Victorian pinafore that ended below the waist and featured a row of deep pockets along the bottom edge to hold scissors, dust cloths, potholders, and other domestic needs. With the advent of printed chicken feed sacks, farm women recycled the brightly printed material for aprons, kitchen towels, and curtains. The canning apron was a high-bibbed variant of the cobbler and extended below the hipline to protect the cook from hot splashes, melted paraffin, and indelible berry and beet juice stains. A waterproof black dairy apron of oiled duck with leg straps, which sold in the 1923 Sears, Roebuck catalog for $1.95, offered protection for such heavy, messy dairy jobs as straining milk and scalding pans and skimmers.

With the advent of the twentieth century, the apron proved its adaptability. During World War I women designed the Hooverette, a wrap-around body covering whose name honored Herbert Hoover, at the time national Food Administrator. On the man-less home front of World War II, the mythic Rosie the Riveter donned the industrial apron of the shop floor, as well as the factory worker's coveralls, welding mask, and work gloves. The U.S. National Livestock and Meat Board issued a pamphlet of recipes for liver, tongue, kidney, and tripe and encouraged the war era cook to think of the kitchen and victory garden as combat zones and of the apron as a uniform—"she may wear it proudly; for there is no more important responsibility than hers." During sparse times in Great Britain, Ann Hathaway's *The Homecraft Book* (1944) advised Irish housewives to get the most out of old mackintoshes by cutting them into waterproof aprons to keep their skirt fronts dry while cycling.

After the armistice, the apron changed shape as women returned to the kitchen and their former roles as wives and helpmeets. No longer needed on the assembly lines, women factory workers retreated to home sewing machines and produced a demure front-flap apron sashed at the back and suspended on a tight band over the lap to emphasize a waspish waistline. Patterns sold in *Woman's Home Companion* offered a full range of styles, from the scalloped dirndl to the button-down-the-side apron dress. Ties grew from a simple cloth tube to a wide band at the waist flaring into a frilled sash that was starched and tied in back in a perky bow.

At the height of the vogue for coordinated kitchen goods, domestic shops touted matching sets of apron, hot pads, oven mittens, tea towels, and dishwashing cloths. Variations of the tie-back apron include whimsical models made of tea towels and homey handmade aprons stitched from sewing scraps and embellished with patch pockets, colored bias binding, felt shapes, and cutwork. Before guests arrived, some housewives preferred to change from practical aprons to airy, ornate hostess aprons stitched from dotted swiss, chiffon, or silk voile. When the backyard barbecue became the rage, durable unisex aprons of canvas, denim, and sailcloth offered a convenient protective covering. This garment, usually consisting of a small bib and broad wrap-around bottom, was sometimes inscribed with comments about the cook's skills.

After eight years' study, in 1957, the creation of a plastic cocklebur by Swiss engineer George de Maestral led to the introduction of Velcro, a nylon fastener suited to myriad uses. In the kitchen, the placement of Velcro on aprons ended fumbling with buttoned straps and ties and enabled the user to alter at will the size and fit. An additional advantage was Velcro's ability to survive machine washing and drying.

Entering the twenty-first century, aprons—like caps, T-shirts, jackets, and myriad other garments—

became instruments of marketing. Workers in retail stores, cafes, retirement homes, school cafeterias, day-care centers, garages, and other business establishments sported colorful aprons or smocks featuring company names and logos.

Further Reading

Bentley, Amy. *Eating for Victory: Food Rationing and the Politics of Domesticity*. Urbana: University of Illinois Press, 1998.
Bradfield, Nancy. *Historical Costumes of England*. New York: Barnes & Noble, 1971.
Hooper, Emma M., "The Indispensible Apron," *Ladies' Home Journal*, April 1894, 27.

ARCHESTRATUS

An Athenian-born Epicurean and food writer during the Hellenistic Age, Archestratus—alternately called Archestratus of Gela (Sicily)—lived in Syracusa in the mid-fourth century BCE. More culinary guide than chef, Archestratus composed *Hedypathia* (Luxury, ca. 350 BCE), a fifteen-volume verse text composed in a playful parody of the hexameter-based style of the classical epics. Now lost except for sixty-two fragments, the work, sometimes called Europe's oldest cookbook, expressed the fundamentals of classical Mediterranean cuisine.

The intense pleasure Archestratus took from food is apparent in his writings: "Eat what I recommend. All other delicacies are a sign of abject poverty—I mean boiled chickpeas, beans, apples, and dried figs. The flat cake made in Athens deserves praise, though. If you can't get hold of that, demand some Attic honey, as that will set your cake off really well. This is the life of a freeman! Otherwise one might as well...be buried measureless fathoms underground!" He wrote chiefly about sensual banquet fare—fish- and meat-heavy menus devoid of vegetables. His commentary lauded the white bread of Lesbos and Bybline wines from Phoenicia and mentioned dishes made from lentils, herbs, yogurt, hare, goose, conger and moray eels, boar-fish, and a favorite, lightly-seasoned and oiled fresh fish for roasting or grilling.

A stickler for details, Archestratus was given the nickname the "Hesiod of the Gourmets." He influenced Athenaeus of Naucratis, author of *Deipnosophistai* (The Learned Banquet, ca. 200 CE), who preserved much of the master's tastes. According to Athenaeus, Archestratus "diligently traveled all lands and seas in his desire . . . of testing carefully the delights of the belly." He loved such appetizers as olives, barley breads, small birds, and pickled sow's womb and spoke knowledgeably of the different textures of flesh from different parts of the fish—fin, belly, head, and tail. He divided fish into two categories: the tough varieties, which required marinating to tenderize, and the fine-quality species that needed only attentive grilling. Among the flavorings he mentioned were honey and silphium, a pungent form of fennel used as a condiment. One delectable seafood dish he cooked in a sheaf of grape leaves. A translation of his book, titled *The Life of Luxury,* was published in 1994 by John Wilkins and chef Shaun Donovan Hill, a member of the Académie Culinaire de France; the English food writer Andrew Dalby discussed Archestratus's cooking style and ingredients in *Siren Feasts: A History of Food and Gastronomy in Greece* (1996).

For his compilation of cookery and recipes, Archistratus traveled to Greece, southern Italy, and Sicily, the coast of Asia Minor, and the Black Sea and kept notes on ethnic food preferences, kitchen arrangement, and eating styles. He knew the best places to secure quality foodstuffs, especially scarce items. In the style of food writers Matro of Pitane and Philoxenus of Leucas, he delighted in dishes well cooked for the elegant table. Of the *amia,* a fish similar to bonito, he says in Book VII: "You could not possibly spoil it even if you wanted to. . . . Wrap it in fig leaves with a little marjoram. No cheese, no nonsense! Just place it gently in fig leaves and tie them up with a string, then put it under hot ashes." He warns the cook to watch the bundle carefully to keep it from burning. He concludes with a casual, almost offhand remark about quality food: "Let it come from Byzantium if you want the best."

Among the fads Archestratus disdained was the use of overpowering sauces with herb pickles, which obscured the natural flavors of Mediterranean seafood but served well as a disguise for an inferior catch. Against more casual timing of service, he insisted that skewers of meat should come immediately to table while guests were still drinking: "[Meat] should be hot, simply sprinkled with salt, and taken from the spit while it is still a little undercooked. Do not let it distress you to see the divine ichor dripping from the meat, but eat it greedily. All other methods are mere sidelines to my mind, thick sauces poured over, cheese melted over, too much oil over—as if they were preparing a tasty dish of dogfish."

During a period of culinary exchange between Roman cooks and Greek colonials in southern Italy and Sicily, the Roman poet Quintus Ennius reprised Archestratus's text in *Hedyphagetica* (ca. 200 BCE).

Further Reading

Lesky, Albin. *A History of Greek Literature*. London: Gerald Duckworth & Co., 1996.

AUTOMAT

Horn & Hardart's Automat (H&H) was the most high-tech eating establishment of its time. The idea came from two Philadelphia restaurateurs, Joseph V. Horn and Frank Hardart. The latter, an immigrant to the United States, imported the concept from a German original. The two went into partnership in 1888. In New York City, Horn & Hardart's Automat, like the Statue of Liberty and Empire State Building, was a must-see for visitors. Local residents became satisfied regulars.

A primly elegant glass-and-chrome hall lined with high-backed booths and frequently wiped tables, the first Automat sold fast food with less fuss than a cafeteria but less warmth than a café. In an era preoccupied with cleanliness, the shiny tables and stand-up counters reassured customers of a pristine dining experience. At the first location near Independence Hall in Philadelphia in 1902, patrons retrieved individual cold dishes from the lighted cubicles and drew milk and coffee from self-serve urns topped with a dolphin head, a Roman symbol of luck copied from a fountain in Pompeii. Those needing change received nickels from clerks in glassed-in change booths. The retrieval of a self-selected meal was a simple matter of dropping nickels into a slot, turning the knob, and retrieving the ham sandwich, baked beans, fish cakes, cucumber salad, dollop of slaw, or wedge of apple pie on the other side of the glass. Hot dishes could be obtained at steam tables.

The owners kept staff on a tight rein. Cooks worked directly from ingredients ordered from the commissary. Provisioning and cooking were centralized, and the 400 original recipes were standardized down to exact portion size and placement on the dish. Plated foods entered small automated cells at the right temperature and remained at optimum flavor as customers passed by. Workers drip-brewed fresh coffee every twenty minutes; the food was only hours from the kitchen, never held over from the previous day. Leftovers were dispatched each evening to outlets in working-class neighborhoods for sale as day-old goods.

In its heyday in the 1950s, the user-friendly Horn & Hardart chain served 800,000 meals daily and 90 million 5-cent cups of coffee per year at forty-five locations in Philadelphia and New York. Its appeal sprang from the wide selection of dishes, the reliable quality of the food, and the absence of such restaurant add-ons as cover charges and tips. The motto said it all: "Less Work for Mother." (Crowley, 2001, 24)

Daily traffic at the Automat was a human mosaic. The social and economic range of its patrons included executives in gray flannel suits, female shoppers come to the city for the day, out-of-towners weary of hotel room service, teenagers on dates, children on roller skates, and the down-and-out. Two regulars each day were the owners themselves, who sat at a special table to monitor the quality of items such as the popular macaroni and cheese and coconut custard pie and to spot-check coffee from different stores within the metropolitan area. From their confabs came additional recipes for plain, appetizing dishes, which the company field-tested for six months at its Philadelphia and New Jersey sites before offering them to customers.

Within a decade of the opening of the first location, New Yorkers had their own Automat in Manhattan, a sleek establishment fitted out with marquetry, marble, and long expanses of mirror. H&H introduced the city to drip coffee, just as it had in Philadelphia. It was for this savory beverage that Irving Berlin composed "Let's Have Another Cup of Coffee," the H&H theme song. The Automat concept survived for seventy years before finally yielding to Ray Kroc's McDonald's chain and the ubiquitous White Castles. H&H sold out to Burger King in 1968; the last Automat—located two blocks from New York's Grand Central Station at 42nd Street and Third Avenue—closed in April 1991.

The original H&H Automat inspired similar serve-yourself convenience foods—frozen food vending machines at U.S. Navy installations, glass cases of baked goods at supermarket delis, personalized meal selection on NASA spaceflights, and waiterless dining on trains, beginning with toasters and hot soup dispensers on the Southern Pacific Sunset and the Nebraska Zephyr. When short-haul lines began to thrive in the northeastern corridor in 1997, the Southern Pacific and Burlington railroad emulated the quickie automat meals on low-cost, self-serve Amtrak Automat Cars. Neat and functional vending machines plopped out chocolate bars, Fritos, juices, Cokes, coffee, and White Castle hamburgers and burritos that the diner heated in a microwave oven while the train sped from Chicago to Grand Rapids. In 1998, architect James Biber designed the Globe restaurant on Manhattan's Park Avenue South with the decor of an updated Automat, right down to the shine on terrazzo floors. The trim but uncluttered H&H look survives in a replica of the original Philadelphia counter in the Smithsonian's National Museum of American History.

Further Reading

Crowley, Carolyn Hughes, "Meet Me at the Automat," *Smithsonian*, August 2001, 22–24.

Gray, Christopher, "New York's First Automat," *New York Times*, June 30, 1991, R6.

Maxwell, William, "In Little Boxes, the Automat Lives On," *New York Times*, April 5, 1998.

B

BABICHE

For general household chores, such as binding dried birds or suspending herbs from the top of a longhouse, hogan, or tepee, Native Americans have traditionally made *babiche,* the Algonquian-Canadian French term for a lacing or cord cut from semi-softened rawhide, leather, bark, pelts, or sinew. These thongs might be used to tie back skin tepee walls to allow cooking fumes to escape or to lace and hang a cradleboard, a flat board to which the mother strapped an infant to keep it safe while she attended to household chores.

The Blackfoot and Cree thinly sliced buffalo skin into cording; the Micmac of Nova Scotia and Pacific Coast Indians from Alaska to California wove babiche into creels and fishnets. Kitchen workers used babiche for lanyards to suspend cutting tools at the waist or to tie them securely in pouches to protect sharp points. Another necessity was the stringing of a bow drill to use in fire making. From Indian cooks American colonists learned to truss game birds and poultry with babiche and to suspend them from a tripod of bent limbs. Another technique involved binding oyster-stuffed cod to a green wood rack for roasting over a slow fire. A pottery urn nestled in the ash caught the juices for basting or adding to vegetables.

The Cherokee strung leather britches beans on babiche over a slow fire to preserve the pods from mildew and weevils. To prepare the beans for eating, they presoaked and parboiled them, then cooked them with slabs of fat, meat chunks, salt, and seasonings. This method of preserving beans passed to settlers, who also called them shucky beans. They emulated the

Babiche with fur strip.
[Original illustration by Dan Timmons.]

cutting of babiche and threading of beans; the strings of beans were then tied to cabin beams. Leather britches beans passed to the White House kitchen when Andrew Jackson, the seventh U.S. president, was inaugurated.

See also **Bow Drill**

Further Reading

Pennington, Campbell W. *The Tepehuan of Chihuahua: Their Material Culture.* Salt Lake City: University of Utah Press, 1969.

BABY FOOD

Appropriate food for weanlings has been the concern of parents throughout human history. The different child-feeding practices of cultures around the world have long been a topic of fascination for travelers, explorers, and, later, anthropologists. According to the French *coureurs de bois* (woodsmen) traveling the Great Lakes region in the eighteenth century, the Chippewa fed their infants fish heads seasoned with maple sugar. On his Arctic expeditions in search of a northwest passage, the nineteenth-century explorer Sir William Edward Parry observed the child-rearing practices of the Eskimo people. Newborns were breastfed, but when it came time to introduce solid foods, the women masticated bites of food from their own meal and then pressed their lips to the child's mouth, passing the chewed food directly without the use of fingers or utensils. To heat water for their infants, the women held it in their own mouths till it reached body temperature before passing it to the babies. The men also participated, as Parry noted: "Some fathers are very fond of taking their children on their knees and thus feeding them." (Parry 1842, II, 214)

In the world's temperate zones, the first solid food introduced to most babies is rice or oat cereal. Early records of infant feeding in Ireland reported that the offspring of the poor ate "stirabout," a pabulum consisting of oatmeal thinned with buttermilk or water. Chiefs' sons thrived on barley, milk, and butter, but only royal princes ate wheat bread, milk, and honey. Two utensils essential to family welfare were the spouted infant or invalid cup, a covered tin cup for feeding hot milk or pabulum to babies, and the caudle cup, a two-handled feeding dish that held egg mixtures, gruel, or broth for administration to the sick or elderly.

Like a minor rite of passage, the transition from soft to hard food took on ceremonial significance in some cultures. The ritual baking of the first teething biscuit appeared in *Notes on the Folk-Lore of the North-East of Scotland* (1881), compiled by the folklorist Reverend Walter Gregor, one of the founders of the Folklore Society. The mother made an oatmeal bannock dough with butter or cream and placed a ring inside the finished biscuit. After the child broke the biscuit in play, each family member and the child got a small bite, as though partaking of the same nourishment meant that the child had attained full membership in the family.

In industrial countries, the convenience of canned foods has relieved mothers of the task of daily preparation of digestible foods for the young. Ever since the French inventor Nicolas Appert perfected the process of canning in 1807, manufacturers have applied techniques of heating and condensing to infant formulas and solid foods. The pharmacist Henri Nestlé, a German-born researcher who sought an economical alternative to breastfeeding to combat infant malnutrition, began experimenting with combinations of sugar, wheat flour, and cow's milk in the 1860s. He named his product Farine Lactée (milk cereal); it was manufactured in Vevey, Switzerland, and was sold across Europe. An industrialist, Jules Monnerat, subsequent owner of the Nestlé Company, introduced a condensed milk in 1874.

From the mid-1800s into the twentieth century, researchers and inventors continued to seek new methods for producing commercial baby food. In 1866, the American entrepreneurs Charles and George Page founded the Anglo-Swiss Condensed Milk Company, which sold cheese and infant formula. In 1907, Nestlé made foods in Australia and warehoused them in Singapore, Hong Kong, and Bombay to supply Asian markets. Heinz baby food products got their start in Canada two years later. The company began producing foods for all stages of childhood, including fortified cereal, fruit, vegetables, desserts, meat, and processed meals. In 1923, food handlers added kosher preparation to their purity standards and produced Hebrew Strained Foods and Hebrew Junior Foods. In this same period, Nestlé began marketing Milo, a powdered infant formula.

The success of prepared baby foods required an efficient system of distribution and a concerted advertising effort to educate and entice parents. The 1923 Sears, Roebuck catalog offered, along with wide-mouth nursing bottles and four styles of nipples, a selection of foods that included Horlick's Malted Milk, Nestlé's, Dextra Maltose, Imperial Granum, Robinson Barley, and Sugar Milk. In 1928, Gerber began preparing baby food at a family cannery in Fremont, Michigan. Before labeling its jars with an appropriate logo, the company held a contest to choose a picture of the quintessential Gerber baby. The winner, a charcoal sketch of Ann Turner Cook, was drawn by Boston artist Dorothy Hope Smith, who had also drawn the baby used by Procter & Gamble in its ads for Ivory hand, dish, and laundry soap. In the 1930s, the Gerber Company offered two Gerber dolls, a boy and girl, as premiums to customers.

To encourage the acceptance of packaged products, advertisers filled women's magazines of the 1930s with messages intended to convince mothers to give up making their own infant foods. Monthly, *Good Housekeeping* ran pictures of the smiling Gerber baby accompanied by copy emphasizing the wholesomeness of Gerber's strained vegetable products. The ads noted that canned foods preserved vitamins and minerals that would be lost if the same vegetables were simmered in water on the kitchen stove. Because packers picked fresh produce and washed, cleaned, and cooked it in steam pressure cookers, preparation excluded oxygen while sterilizing foods at 240 degrees Fahrenheit. In *Good Housekeeping*, Sunshine bakeries, a division of the Loose-Wiles Biscuit Company, lauded its arrowroot biscuits, promoted as the child's first adventure in solid food. Easily digested and containing no eggs, the thin wafers required only saliva and gum action to melt in a baby's mouth.

One series of products promoted confidence that children would grow up strong, healthy, and straight on commercial baby food. In an era of scoliosis and devastating childhood diseases, food supplements such as Ovaltine, which Swiss physician George Wander marketed in Europe in 1910 as Ovomaltine, and Coco-malt, made by R. B. Davis Company of Hoboken, New Jersey, promised parents that children would put on weight, which, the ad implied, protected young bodies from illness and bone deformity. Sold in grocery stores and pharmacies and served cold or hot, these milk additives allegedly aided digestion and bolstered the nutritional value of milk by providing extra vitamin D for strong bones and teeth. Junket was introduced in 1925 with ads in *Good Housekeeping* for tablets and powder that would turn milk into puddings and desserts and thereby increase children's milk consumption. In 1935, the makers of Ovaltine appealed directly to children with a radio program, the Ovaltine Club, broadcast Sundays at 5:30 p.m. from Radio Luxembourg. Advertisers enticed young listeners with membership in a secret society, complete with badges, club regulations, and secret codes. Within four years, the club grew to five million members. A rival product, Postum, invented in 1893 by cereal maker C. W. Post, claimed to benefit child health with a grain beverage more wholesome than caffeinated drinks and flavorful enough to induce milk-haters to drink up.

The choices available to mothers continued to expand into the mid-twentieth century. Beech-Nut entered the growing baby food market in 1931. The company followed the example of Clapp's baby foods to become one of the first infant-food marketers to seal its products in glass jars rather than metal cans. The jars enabled parents to clearly view the wholesome food inside and offered the additional attraction of allowing them to heat the food in the container. Gerber enlarged its offerings to mothers with boxed oatmeal, barley, and other cereals that could be poured directly into a baby's dish and moistened with heated milk or formula for spoon feeding. As busy mothers demanded more convenience, the company advertised warm-and-serve meals in the form of glass jars of strained fruit, vegetables, and soups. Unused portions could easily be capped and stored in the refrigerator. By 1948, the beginning of the post-war baby boom, Gerber was selling two million jars per week. In 1979, the company began marketing puréed bananas from Productos Gerber de Centroamerica in Costa Rica.

In many third world countries, soft foods for infants lacked the scientific basis in nutrition claimed by mass-produced baby foods. In Uganda, for example, when a second pregnancy began, mothers of infants traditionally ended breastfeeding and introduced youngsters to *matoke,* a macerated banana pulp served in a communal family bowl. Fed solely on carbohydrate-rich bananas, children could develop kwashiorkor, a form of protein-deficiency malnutrition responsible for the death of millions of children in central Africa. In the 1970s, health agents instructed the women on the danger of diets low in protein. In home cooking demonstrations, they taught classes on how to add peanuts, beans, fish, or fried termites to banana purée to assure children sufficient nutrients for proper growth.

In the closing decades of the twentieth century, the emergence of new health concerns prompted some changes in commercial baby foods. In 1981 Beech-Nut pioneered salt-free baby foods. As families began to demand all-natural foods, Beech-Nut eliminated the use of modified starches as food thickeners and rid all infant products of refined sugar, artificial coloring, flavors, and preservatives. The firm currently markets 100 food items for infants. Purity controls subject them to more than 480 quality tests and hold them to standards ten times stricter than those mandated at the federal level. Gerber, too, responded to health fads and trends. Late in the twentieth century, the company announced that it would use no genetically engineered foods in its baby products. In this same era, the increasing interest in organic foods encouraged the growth of Earth's Best Baby Foods, a U.S. company whose products were also popular among health-conscious French parents.

In 1997, the American Council on Science and Health (ACSH) reported that parents had developed unfounded fears that manufactured infant food was inferior to and less safe than homemade. In defense of commercial baby foods, the council pointed out that, in an era when most mothers were busier than ever before, kitchen-prepared foods required time, effort, and an understanding of infant needs and digestion. It also noted the dangers of microbes and pesticides in the food supply and pointed out that government regulations allow higher levels of these substances for adults than for infants. The ACSH targeted peaches and pears as foods with the highest levels of pesticide residues; next in order of impurities were applesauce, plums, sweet potatoes, green beans, and squash.

For those parents who choose to make their own baby food, in 1995 Elisabeth Schafer, a professor of nutrition at Iowa State University Extension, offered guidelines for making soft foods that infants can swallow by four to six months of age. She instructed homemakers to thoroughly wash hands, utensils, and equipment before beginning. She also advised separating infants' portions of fresh foods intended for the family meal before adding any seasonings. She warned parents to observe expiration dates on products and to warm formula on the stove rather than in a microwave, which heats unevenly and thus increases the risk of scalding an infant's tongue and throat. Any food not refrigerated, frozen, or eaten in two hours should be discarded to prevent contamination. Schafer's timetable for introducing foods called for cereals mixed with breast milk or formula from birth to six months of age, introduction of vegetables at seven months and fruit at eight months, meat and egg yolks at ten months, and cheese and yogurt by ten to twelve months. Beets and spinach, she suggested, are best left until after the first year.

See also **Borden, Gail; Graham, Sylvester; Home Economics; Liebig, Justus von**

Further Reading

Embree, John F. *Suye Mura: A Japanese Village.* Chicago: University of Chicago Press, 1939.
La Fay, Howard, and George F. Mobley, "Uganda: Africa's Uneasy Heartland," *National Geographic*, November 1971, 708–735.

BAIN-MARIE

From the alchemist's laboratory and dyer's vats to present-day banquet halls and restaurant kitchens, the concept of the *bain-marie*, or water bath, is essential to baking, stove-top cooking, and canning. The mythic inventor was the alchemist Miriam the Prophetess (or Mary the Jewess), sister of Moses, near the beginning of the first century BCE, who is mentioned in Exodus and the Talmud. A more likely figure, the alchemist Maria or Marianne of Alexandria, a shadowy scientist from the third century CE, may have created a two-stage water bath, a forerunner of the autoclave. Called the *kerotakis,* or double boiler, it was essential equipment for her work with condensers, sublimation, and distillation during her study of sulfides. According to Isabella Beeton's *The Book of Household Management* (1861), Roman food maven Caelius Apicius, the author of *De Re Coquinaria* (On Cooking, late 300s CE), the world's oldest cookbook, used the *bain-marie* as a means of keeping food warm and moist when the dinner hour was uncertain. In the late thirteenth century, the French physician Arnaud de Villeneuve corroborated the claim that Miriam the Prophetess invented a hot bath or alembic called the *balneum Mariae* (Mary's bath).

Italians offer another etymology, claiming that the *bagno maria* was created by the Spanish alchemist Maria de' Cleofa and introduced to the French court chef by Catherine de Médicis. Alexis Soyer, the author of *The Modern Housewife* (1850), proposed that the English version, called a Beauméré pan, derived from the alchemical boiling of sea water and from the resulting term *bain marie,* or seawater bath.

Whatever its provenance, the water-filled container applies moist, gentle heat to paraffin wax, canning jars, egg cream, butter sauce, organ meats, fish loaf, or meat loaf in an upper container, which sits above a pot of boiling water but touches only the steam during the cooking. The method prevents curdling or the breaking up of soufflés, custards, and mousses.

The kitchen version of the *bain-marie* was a large, high-sided rectangular, oval, or round basin made of aluminum, copper, or iron. The cook partially filled it with hot water and placed small pots of food or baby bottles in the water to keep them hot. Another application was in the slow or indirect cooking of milk or chocolate, which scorch easily when they come in contact with open flame or a stovetop. In a treatise known as *Mackenzie's Five Thousand Receipts in All the Usefull and Domestic Arts: Constituting a Complete Practical Library* (1829), the author, an unidentified American physician from Philadelphia, explained the problem of milk cookery in more detail: "Milk only burns on the edges of its surface, or where it comes in contact with the sides of the vessel in which it is heated, which is obviated by placing kettles one within the other."

The water bath method of cookery crops up throughout culinary history. The traditional Russian method of churning butter called for a simmer or scald of raw milk in a double boiler to increase yield, hasten curd formation, enhance flavor, and lengthen shelf life. Early in the 1800s, the meticulous chef Marie-Antoine Carême, founder of inspired French cuisine, explained béchamel sauce as a velouté thickened with cream and egg yolks, then buttered, sieved through white cloth, and warmed in a *bain-marie*. In Helsinki, Finland, in 1889, the chemist Rudolf Rempel devised a method of boiling milk in a *bain-marie* to pasteurize it for infant feedings, a means of reducing the nation's high infant mortality. The German merchant Johann Weck, founder of J. Weck & Company, marketed the sterilization equipment for home use. In 1900, a Philadelphia manufacturer offered an urn-shaped variant. Set on high legs to accommodate spitted meat at the bottom of the chamber, it steam-heated as much as one hundred gallons of bouillon.

Although microwave ovens have replaced the *bain-marie* in some kitchen procedures, the device continues to be used for banquet and steam table service worldwide. At Brisas del Mar Restaurant on the island of Aruba, the kitchen turns out a sophisticated *quesilo* (caramel dessert) made in a *bain-marie*. A countertop electronic appliance applies the *bain-marie* concept to home production of yogurt.

See also **Double Boiler; Dyes and Colorants**

BAKELITE

In 1909, the formulation of a synthetic polymer resin called Bakelite—the first true plastic—greatly enhanced domestic work by offering manufacturers of kitchen utensils a strong, lightweight, nontoxic, and inexpensive material to replace wood, ceramic, horn, ivory, ebonite, and metal. Bakelite's name honors the chemist Leo Hendrik Baekeland, who also invented Velox, a silver chloride photographic paper. Born in Ghent, Belgium, on November 14, 1863, he was apprenticed in shoe repair, his father's trade, at age thirteen, but attended night school. After graduating first in his class, he studied chemistry on scholarship at the University of Ghent.

Baekeland taught at Bruges, but abandoned the teaching profession to follow a more lucrative career in industrial chemistry. He married Celine Swarts, daughter of his mentor, the organic chemist Theodore Swarts, and in 1889 emigrated to the United States to work in dry-plate photography. He succeeded in enriching himself by selling the patent for Velox photographic paper to George Eastman of Eastman Kodak.

Wealth enabled Baekeland to indulge himself in research in the laboratory he assembled in his barn in Yonkers, New York. In 1904, while seeking a substitute for shellac and hard rubber, he accidentally synthesized the Bakelite resin, the prototypical thermoset plastic, from a powdered mix of phenols and formaldehyde, a process originally pioneered by the German organic chemist Adolf Bayer (or Baeyer). When heated, the insoluble mass hardened in patterned molds or under a press, could be cured in ovens, and accepted color in a broad range of transparent or translucent shades. Baekeland patented his discovery, created a cook pot he called a Bakelizer for controlling temperature and pressure, and in 1910 launched the Bakelite Corporation.

Bakelite became a familiar trademark in England and the United States. As a replacement for the flammable substance known as celluloid, Bakelite plastic did not conduct electricity and resisted heat, flame, and chemical solvents. When mixed with ground corusco nuts, wood flour, or asbestos, it could withstand high levels of force. In industrial applications it was a breakthrough in the manufacture of electrical insulators, chemical equipment, electrical components, adhesives, paint, and baked enamel. The influx of plastics into the market began in 1914 and expanded with the manufacture of telephone receivers, radios, lamps, bearings and bushings, batteries, electric plugs and insulators, plastic buttons, thermos bottles, toys, pens and pencils, candlesticks, umbrella handles, and tobacco pipes.

Bakelite inundated the kitchen with products the inventor termed "fancy goods." (Meikle 1995, 46) The new plastic was used to form creamers and syrup dispensers, food scales, toasters, juicers, salt- and pepper shakers, napkin holders, trays, coffee grinders, and the casings of kitchen clocks. The use of Bakelite handles and knobs on cookware, tableware, and stoves reduced the danger of burned fingers. Bakelite earned Baekeland the Willard Gibbs Medal and, in 1924, the presidency of the American Chemical Society.

After the inventor's initial patent expired in 1927, the Catalin Corporation began manufacturing and marketing plastic goods. To the already available jet, amber, carnelian, and emerald, the firm added fifteen new colors and a marbleized effect, such as that used in the popular Fada radio. The public bought Catalin's domestic products at B. Altman, Bonwit Teller, and Saks Fifth Avenue as well as Sears, Roebuck and Woolworth's. Catalin plastics earned the respect of *Vogue* editor Diana Vreeland and fashion designer Elsa Schiaparelli.

Ads in women's magazines lauded Bakelite for its cool surface. In *Woman's Home Companion,* a happy picture of children pouring hot drinks from a Thermos School Kit, a product of the American Thermos Bottle Company in New York City, Toronto, and London, accompanied the advertiser's assurance that the cool plastic cup would not burn lips. The Blue Boy model contained three nested plastic cups to simplify the pouring of drinks for children. The December 1930 issue of *Good Housekeeping* featured Bakelite bedside water carafes and Remington kitchen knives with one-piece Bakelite handles, which replaced the earlier riveted wood or bone handles. The ad copy, reflecting the era's germ mania, noted that seamless plastic offered no places for grime or microbes to hide.

The popularity of Bakelite for domestic manufacture waned in the 1940s. During World War II, Bakelite and Catalin dropped domestic manufacture to concentrate on pilot goggles, field telephones, electric insulators, and other durable, lightweight products for wartime use. After new technology produced lucite, fiberglass, vinyl, and acrylic, early Bakelite items became prized collectibles.

Further Reading

Meikle, Jeffrey L. *American Plastic: A Cultural History.* New Brunswick, N.J.: Rutgers University Press, 1995.

BAKING

Whether it involves a simple cake baked in the oven, a pudding boiled in a cloth bag, or a delicate, airy soufflé, baking is the most complex and sophisticated of culinary arts. It is also an ancient art. In Neolithic Syria, the cultivation of natural cereal plants in 12,000

Bakers at work from *The Shepherd's Great Calendar*, 15th century.

BCE preceded a shift from a hunting-and-gathering culture to a settled lifestyle, a requisite for a cook depending on an oven. Einkorn, the earliest wheat species, dates to 5000 BCE, when grain was added to wild seeds, roots, and berries as an additional forage food. Syrian grain growers also cultivated polygonum and antragalus wheat, which they gathered and stored in silos. To ready grain for cooking, women crushed the seed heads between polished stones, a kitchen technology that developed before oven baking.

Evolution of the Art

Within the millennium, the consumption of bakeable grains extended beyond the Mediterranean to the Fertile Crescent, Europe, the Americas, China, and the Indian subcontinent. Around 4000 BCE, Mesoamericans applied beater and foraging basket to the gathering of seed heads. Five centuries later, Chinese farmers improved their yield by means of the swidden system, which allotted plots for working and wild acreage to lie fallow in a rotating system of grain cultivation. Farming as a way of life supplanted earlier subsistence practices as far north as Scandinavia and produced communities in the Indus Valley in 3200 BCE. Faulty application of irrigation caused the Indus Valley culture to fail in 1750 BCE after farmers introduced too many salts and ruined their fields, thus depriving families of grain for bread making.

North Africans and farmers on the Mediterranean rim produced both wheat and barley, thus doubling their choice of grain staples. In this same period, the Sumerians along the Tigris and Euphrates Rivers to the east and Egyptians along the Nile to the south were the first peoples to enhance productivity by irrigating fields. To work the grain into usable form, early wheat harvesters ground it by hand, using a metate, a flat-bottomed stone thinned at the center into a depression by the friction of a mano, or hand-held rubbing stone. To the crude flour that filtered from these grinding surfaces, they added liquid and shaped bread loaves or patties.

In ancient Egypt baking and brewing were the provinces of one social group, which controlled the yeast supply. By 2000 BCE, professional bakers supplied Egyptian tables with yeast-leavened bread. As early as 1425 BCE, harvest scenes from the Tomb of Menena in Egypt show ritual sowing, cultivation, and transportation of grain heads in a huge basket balanced on the shoulders of two workers. Farm workers equipped with wood rakes are depicted in such tasks as threshing, treading from the husk, and winnowing emmer wheat. The dough was placed in a triangular or lozenge-shaped mold to produce fragrant bread. For the poor living in mud huts, an onion or garlic stem and a mug of beer completed the bread-based meal. Work scenes from the tomb of Ramses III, built around 1125 BCE, show the progression of dough from troughs, where it was kneaded by the feet of laborers, to shaping tables and, finally, beehive ovens. Nearby, workers stoke fires under vats of hot oil, where cooks fry dough into spiral pastries.

From *magis* (barley bread), the early Greeks developed the word *mageiros,* which first meant "baker" but broadened to name any kind of cook. Greek cooks excelled at hearth bread, the forerunner of *focaccia* and pizza, and invented a more sophisticated *filo* or *phyllo* (leaf) dough, the basis for light, flaky dinner rusks and desserts. A time-consuming task, the making of phyllo involved building up fragile strata by over-layering dough with cuts of butter. The result was a fine, brittle crust that readily absorbed the chopped nuts, spices, and honey used in baklava, *bourekakia* (cheese rolls), and *tyropitakia* (cheese pastry). During the Middle Ages, Crusaders from western Europe admired Greek baking artistry and spread word of their phyllo pastries in letters from the front. Today, even with the advent of the food processor, this prized baking staple is more often purchased from the grocery store freezer than made at home the traditional laborious way.

To the west in ancient Italy, bread was a luxury item because it required finely ground flour. From the third Punic War, which ended in 146 BCE, the Roman *pistor* (baker), a food professional introduced from Greece, flourished alongside a guild of freedmen bakers and freelance *fornarii* (oven tenders). To improve the nation's diet, around the beginning of the second century CE, the emperor Trajan established Rome's first baking school. It produced professional bakers who used special ovens and tools to relieve urban cooks of the onus of regular dough-making and loaf-baking. The flour they chose varied in quality and type, ranging from simple rye or wheat to an exotic blend of grain and pounded gladiolus bulbs. The cheapest loaves were made from *puls,* an inexpensive cereal grain found in plebeian homes. For *satura* (fruit cake), cooks added honeyed wine, pomegranate seeds, nuts, and dried fruits to barley mash. These and other recipes the professional bakers kept as family trade secrets, which they passed along with the trade to sons and sons-in-law.

Bakers sold several grades of goods: *panis subcineritius,* or ashcake, *artopticius,* or pan rolls baked in a covered kettle similar to a Dutch oven, and *siligineus,* top quality white bread made of a Campanian wheat flour so fine that women used it to powder their faces. With advancements in trade goods, implements, and ovens, professional bread makers developed sourdough bread, honey-and-oil loaves, gritty Silician bread, suet or cheese loaves, poppy seed bread, spit-baked rolls, pancakes, pepper rolls, milk and wine wafers, and cheese and aniseed squares. Bakers shaped bread dough in molds to produce a round perforated loaf suitable for pulling apart with the hands. Four eight-inch rounds of white bread scored into eight triangular sections survived at Pompeii following the eruption of Vesuvius in 79 CE. Stamped in the top was a list of ingredients—"Siligo. Cranii. e. Cicer"—indicating that bakers added chickpeas to white flour. To produce the best crust, they placed containers of water in the oven to enhance moisture.

In the New World, the technology of baking was determined by the foodstuffs at hand. In upper Michigan and Wisconsin, the Menominee dug a deep trench for baking corn; Virginian tribes baked tuckahoe, or arum, a starchy root that mixed well with corn meal. To the southwestern Great Basin and into Central America from about 1000 CE, the Chiricahua, Lipan, and Mescalero Apache lined pits with stone to slow-bake agave, a sturdy desert plant from which they obtained mescal for drying and storage. In the same area, Navaho bakers used the ubiquitous prickly pear, the pulpy fruit of the common opuntia cactus, to dry and pulverize for flour and for thickening a custard similar to tapioca.

Emergence of a Profession

The burgeoning towns of medieval Europe increased the demand for commercially baked bread. In the 1100s, bakers evolved the recipe for Scottish shortbread, a biscuit baked in a round called "petty cotes tallis" (little sheep pen tallies), a reference to the sheepcotes where sheepherders notched their headcounts on sticks or to the bell-hooped underskirts of fashionable ladies at the Scottish court. John of Garland, a Latin teacher at the universities of Paris and Toulouse, captured the bustle of pastry sellers in the English marketplace in his *Dictionary* (1220): "Streetcriers…call out through the night, selling waffles and wafers and meat pies in baskets covered with a white towel; and the baskets are often hung at the windows of clerks who are damned by dice." He described the shop windows of his day piled with cake, pie, and hearth cake alongside cheeses and sulfur candles. The types of bread available included *tourte, bis,* and *trete,* three types of dark, coarse-grained loaves, as well as *manchet* and *paindemaigne,* the lighter top grades. In great detail, Garland described Paris bakeries where pastry chefs made up dough by weight and measure. They cleaned the ovens with a scouring cloth before sliding in fruit bread wreathes and loaves of chaff, bran, rye, barley, and oatmeal bread. In the main kitchen, the baker often attached to the ceiling a "bread car," a crate hoisted on ropes to a cool, dry space safe from rodents. When weighing bread dough for customers, dishonest bakers often concealed a slit in the table, through which an accomplice pinched off small amounts from each loaf. To deter such fraud, authorities confiscated underweight loaves to give to the poor; they also confiscated and disposed of unclean or adulterated bread.

By 1250, Jewish bakers were making made *pretsls,* the forerunner of pretzels (or bretzels) and bagels. Legend connects the creation of these shaped breads with an Alpine monk in 610 CE who twisted leftover dough into a *pretiola* (small reward) for children. A specialty of the Ashkenazi Jews of central Europe, these chewy breads were daily food as well as common refreshments at festive occasions. In 1483, a German baker peddled pretzels from a wheeled oven. When Turkish forces tunneled under Vienna in 1510, they awakened local pretzel bakers, who became heroes by alerting the military to defend the city. The king conferred on the bakers a crest featuring a pretzel and charging lion. The classic pretzel remained an honored refreshment at Swiss weddings as symbols of the lover's knot.

In 1280, baking had become so essential to city growth that Florence alone claimed 146 bakeries. In England, women created kitchen businesses from pastries, which they baked in characteristics shapes with such distinctive names as checky pig (a pastry treat made like a pig's body with pastry strips forming ears and tail), Cornish pasty (a hand-sized meal made from dough sealed to hold in fillings and gravy), and Lancashire foot (a foot-shaped turnover filled with cooked fruit and secured in a flap of pastry).

Throughout Europe, the work of the estate pastry chef turned the kitchen into an assembly line much like those in the kitchens of ancient Rome. The ordinary cook ground, minced, steamed, or cooked foods to be used as fillings for dough. The pastry specialist received from *sous chefs* the makings of pies, pasties or turnovers, and tarts for wrapping in dough and baking. Maintaining heat required a team of bakery workers, who saw to the cleaning, stoking, and supplying of bake ovens and the removal of ashes. Finished goods cooled on worktables, awaiting the attentions of the master chef, who would ready them for the table. The cost of the operation dipped in 1300 with the invention of the windmill, but government intervention persisted with such intrusions as a London law requiring the baker to "have a basket with his bread in the King's market" rather than to sell from his own oven or house. (Counihan & Van Esterik 1997, 355)

In the mid-1300s, Asian baking took on political significance when Chinese women used traditional moon cakes to launch a revolt against militaristic Mongol overlords, who ruled the nation like a colony. Within the bean-filled pastry shells, the bakers concealed anti-Mongol sentiments written on paper slips. Distributed every year for the Moon Festival, the cakes containing these revolutionary urgings reached friends, kin, and neighbors, gradually fomenting a grassroots uprising.

From the sixteenth century, the English developed the trifle, a sweet comprising sponge cake, wine or sherry, and a layer of jam, custard, and whipped cream garnished with cooked or glacéed fruit and almonds. Begun as a boiled renneted cream, the treat appeared in T. Dawson's *The Good Hyswife's Jewell* (1596). Within a century, the dish had metamorphosed into a featured banquet item admired by the Tudor and Stuart courts. By the 1700s, it had evolved into layered dessert based on macaroons, ratafia cake, or Naples biscuit topped with boiled custard and syllabub. Parallel to the evolution of trifle was the invention of the banbury cake, an Oxfordshire yeast cake dotted with currants.

Baking became big business for professionals. Kneading at ten-foot wood troughs preceded shaping of the dough in round rye baskets and sprinkling with flour and meal to prevent the dough from sticking. For reasons of piety, bakers topped buns with a cross, impressed them with the profile of Christ, or initialed them with the letters IHS, the English equivalent of the abbreviation of the Greek *iesous* (Jesus). Although bakers may not have known the meaning, they recognized the letters from pulpit drapes and altar cloths and interpreted them as conferring good on those who ate their buns. North and west of England, Scottish and Irish bakers relied less on wheat and more on oat breads, a commodity still much in use. The concept of the half-circle patty spread to the West Indies, where Jamaican cooks emulated English methods so well that visitors felt at home in island bakeries.

Frontier Traditions

In the North American colonies before 1650, the cook baked several types of loaves at one time in a dooryard oven or at the hearth in a biscuit pan or in a Dutch oven. Upgrades to settlers' cabins included ovens built into the back wall of the fireplace. Tin reflectors augmented oven heat. The homemaker was adept at building a fire out of steady, clean-burning birch or maple limbs. When the coals burned down to red, the baker spread them across the oven floor for a half hour, then gauged the temperature by holding a hand or arm in the center of the oven space. Before scraping out the coals or sweeping them out with a baker's mop or birch broom, she could vent the oven by leaving the door open to feed oxygen to a slow fire.

For the weekly baking, thrifty cooks layered baking dishes on the soapstone floor and placed hams and slower-cooking items in Dutch ovens at the oven back. Near the end of loading the chamber, they lifted pie plates into place with a wire-ended pie peel or pie lifter, a long handle that slid the dish into position, and concluded by placing quick breads on oak leaves or cabbage leaves near the door. As kitchen businesses took shape, professional *baxsters,* the era's term for "baker," produced native specialties, including a corn meal pudding called "hasty pudding" as well as batter biscuits. After removing goods from the oven, bakers cooled them for an hour and removed them to racks on the baker's barrow or wagon for the apprentice baker to deliver.

Some bakers kept an hourglass nearby for timing, then shut the door and moved on to other chores. Keeping an eye on baking required concentration, especially during trips to the lean-to for fuel or to the barn for eggs. Retrieval of loaves from the oven required the use of a bread peel, a long wooden paddle sprinkled with coarse corn meal, a method still in use at pizzerias. Like the distaff, the peel became a symbol of a married woman's chores. The gift of a peel at a wedding symbolized good fortune and a stable household.

In colonial Quebec, bread was sacred to the household. It was blessed, sliced, and shared according to the age and status of each person at the table. From loaves that failed, women compounded a tea to aid a parturient mother or fashioned a poultice for bee stings or insect bites. Farmers distributed less-than-perfect loaves to pigs and chickens or fed them to ruminants as a cure for the scours (diarrhea), a potential killer of calves. Dry bread became the base for bread pudding. Homemakers saved burned crusts to grind with toasted barley into a quasi-coffee, served French style with hot milk. Another beverage common to the Gaspé peninsula and valued as a source of energy was a wine made from oranges, raisins, yeast, burned bread crumbs, and sugar. After fermenting in a pot for up to four weeks, it tasted like porter.

As towns and villages took shape, some cooks completed their baking in communal ovens. Families gathered to make Christmas cookies, marzipan, and chocolate drops. Along with fruit pies, the traditional mince pie was a holiday treat that required chopping meat. If domestic livestock dwindled, bakers substituted bear meat, which was still plentiful along the frontier.

To sweeten the mix for a pie, the home baker added maple or sugar syrup, raisins and dried apples, nut meats, and spices. Latticing crusts and sealing juices inside crimped edges of pies and tarts required the use of a wood, tin, brass, or bone jagger—also called a coggling wheel, dough spur, pie crimper, jagging iron, runner, or rimmer, which might have points cut into the opposite end for pricking crust to let steam escape. Extra pies could remain layered in an outdoor shed during winter until needed.

For home bakers in the United States, a bright idea and time-saver in biscuit making was the earthenware or metal biscuit tank, a mounted bowl for mixing beaten biscuits that the historian Thomas Masters described in *A Short Treatise Concerning Some Patent Inventions and Apparatus for the Production of Ice, and Artificial Cold, Soda Water, Lemonade, Nectar, and All Aerated Beverages* (1850). The framework was a hollow basin with plugged spout. By pouring hot or cold water into the base, the biscuit maker could control the temperature of the dough. In the 1860s, glass, enamel ware, and tin items began replacing crockery for baking.

On the Australian goldfields, gold-panners were desperate for groceries, which arrived by itinerant provisioners and sold for exorbitant rates. At the top of the prospector's shopping list was flour, the staple of most meals. When other foods ran low, flour, salt, baking powder, and water were shaped into dampers, johnny cakes, puftaloons, doughboys, pikelets, and scones, all variations on the same recipe. Lacking the appropriate baking pans or an oven, they mixed ingredients on the clean side of a bark sheet (or a tent corner, saddle cloth, or shirt), shaped cakes with their hands, and buried them in ashes to cook.

Advent of Mechanization

The work of milling and baking eased in 1760 with the invention of the steam engine to turn grinders of various sizes. For a smooth product, North American and European bakers worked up dough at a wooden table or molding board with a rolling pin, wood mallet, dough scraper, or cook's ax. The pin evolved from a handle-less wood column to a lathe-turned roller that tapered at the ends to accommodate the fingers. The first pins with handles had only a single handle. One model set double pins in a frame to control thickness, much like the cranking of clothes through a wringer. Rolling pin materials shifted from maple, cherry, and lignum vitae to marble and, a late twentieth-century innovation, a hollow stainless steel version that held ice water to maintain gluten in the dough.

Shaping dough for flat pastries involved pressing with a cracker stamp, pounder, or tamp that pierced the surface with needles to produce cracknels. To achieve a uniform scone shape, the baker applied a biscuit cutter, dipping it in flour between cuts to keep the edges dry. Cookie rollers applied grooved surfaces to a single dough slab, which the baker then cut apart into individual cookies. Another separator, the Naples biscuit pan, separated dough into vertical fingers to make individual cakes or crackers. For a decorative cake, wooden hoops called *garths* were used for shaping.

The nineteenth century was an era of growth in the baking industry. A clever invention introduced in 1802, the dough brake was a bladed device that fit into a metal basin. The user turned a crank to knead moist materials without soiling the hands. Other mechanical dough kneaders and mixers eased the backbreaking job of manipulating dough to develop gluten. A large-lidded dough trough was doubly serviceable as a covered receptacle for raising dough and as a table for rolling out, shaping, and slicing into loaves with a wooden blade. By 1834, the Swiss invention of the roller mill produced a consistently fine flour that made it easier for bakers to turn out quality baked goods.

In 1830, Naples got its first pizzeria, opened under the aegis of Umberto and Margherita, members of the royal family. The pizza business required its own tools and techniques, including the peel, a paddle for sliding crusts and loaves into the oven. Slicing dough for individual loaves or pizza crusts required a break, a flat wooden utensil dipped in flour to keep it from sticking to the dough. In France, the renowned chef Marie-Antoine Carême, the author of *Le Patissier Pittoresque*

BAKING

(The Picturesque Confectioner, 1854), and other great *pâtissiers* created the *richelieu* (sweet pastry), *savarin* (ring cake), and *napolitain* (large buffet cake), the crowning achievements of the culinary age.

Baking powder became a reality in 1857, after a Harvard professor, Eben Horsford, the Rumford Chairman in applied science, studied the nutritional value of baked goods. He concluded that adding calcium and phosphates in baking powder would alleviate some of the nutrient loss that occurred in the milling of flour. As a result of his investigation, he founded the Rumford Company. In 1859 the Rumford Chemical Works began manufacturing a calcium phosphate baking powder, the first of its kind.

Twentieth-Century Innovations

Electricity revolutionized baking by taking the drudgery out of kneading. In 1908 Herbert Johnson, an engineer, created a twenty-gallon dough mixer for Kitchen-Aid. After World War I, the company concentrated on redesigning the commercial mixer for the home. In 1925, assembly lines began turning out a unique mixer that rotated the bowl in one direction and the beater mechanism the opposite way. The product suited the home kitchen so well that, in the 1930s, the company hired the home products designer Egmont Arens to smooth out the rough edges. The sleek Art Deco shape became the standard by which buyers judged competing brands of mixers for decades to come.

In 1921, Betty Crocker, America's most famous symbol of domestic womanhood, came into being at the Washburn Crosby Company. In answering customer's questions about baking, the Home Service Department concluded its letters with the fictitious signature compounded of a cheery first name and the last name of a former company officer. Because homemakers accepted Betty as the essence of wholesome home cooking, in the 1940s, the company, which had been acquired by General Mills, attached its imaginary master cook to waffle irons, fry-cookers, coffeemakers, cake mixes, and a best-selling publication, *Betty Crocker's Picture Cook Book* (1950).

The 1923 Sears, Roebuck catalog recognized the home cook's desire to turn out fancy baked goods for special occasions. In addition to crêpe nut cups and birthday candles and holders, ad copy offered wedding cake decorations along with candy sprinkles, rosettes, and flowers. According to Dorothy Hartley's *The Countryman's England* (1935), English cooks managed well without such niceties. They continued to raise crust for pork pies around wood pie molds, a top-knobbed cylinder suited to stretching and turning as the pastry casing took shape. She exclaimed, "Those

were *good* pies! Any pig might have been proud to be in pies like that!" (Hartley 1980, 54)

Baking powder, nearly eighty years after its creation, came into its own in the 1930s, when women's magazines featured whole-page ads promoting the sensational results of various brands. In *Good Housekeeping,* Calumet presented a brief tutorial on double-action leavening, which creates its first gas production in cold liquids and a second bubbling with application of heat. Sprinkling the ad copy with words such as "astonishing" and "marvelous," the company promised excellent results even when the batter was stored in the refrigerator for several days. For free recipes, readers could write the company in Chicago, addressing their requests to Marion Jane Parker, a name rather than a department, thus suggesting a knowledgeable female baker at the helm to guide women as they improved their baking.

In 1950, Pillsbury introduced its national biennial bake-off. The annual event promoted the company's brand-name flour, cake mixes, boxed brownie mix, dinner rolls, refrigerated biscuits, pizza and pie crusts, canned vegetables, and mashed potato flakes. By the early 1990s, prizes had grown to $40,000 and a kitchen makeover for the top winner and a variety of cash prizes, ranges, food processors, and mixers for runners-up. Judges screened recipes; home economists selected the best entries for testing in Pillsbury food laboratories. Finalists prepared their dishes in mini-kitchens at a test site in Phoenix, Arizona.

The State of the Art

Baked goods continue to epitomize the culinary labors of many nations. In Greece, Bulgaria, and Turkey, baklava is a national treat; in Austria, the oven delicacy is *sachertorte* (sugar cake), a chocolate cake spread with chocolate icing and apricot jam. Estonians have a reputation for meat- and fish-heavy meals, but their pastries are ample and inexpensive. Croatian *strukli* (cheese strudel) is an inland delicacy; Slovak cooks specialize in *torta* (cake) and *kolác* (seeded rolls). Farther to the north, the Dutch pride themselves on beautiful pastries and *stroopwafels* (syrup waffles). Bakers in Iceland make a unique *hverabraud* (hot spring bread), a gummy treat produced at underground sites stoked by geothermal heat.

Bakers worldwide can choose from teflon pans, spouted or tubed pans, and enamel, tin, aluminum, or earthenware cake molds in a variety of shapes. A piece of cookware that gained popularity in the United States during the 1950s is the cast aluminum bundt cake pan, which originated in Europe in the previous century. The convolutions of its turk's head design allows drizzled icing or streusel to nestle in the cake's crevices. For pizza cooks, the pizza stone absorbs, holds, and radiates dry heat to maintain even cooking after the opening of the oven door. Available in clay or terra cotta, baking stones for domestic use ensure a crispy crust by ridding dough of excess moisture.

A new generation of gadgets, including crimpers, pastry blenders and brushes, jaggers and cutters, and pie weights, offer the cook of the twenty-first century a measure of control over some of baking's uncertainties. Among the advances in gadgetry are the following:

- A nonstick, silicone-surfaced kneading mat, which lessens the problems of rolling and shaping sticky dough
- A flour wand, a coiled globe that holds dusting flour for sprinkling dough boards and crusts and opens with a squeeze of the handle
- A mechanical baking thermometer that gauges temperature in water for yeast and in baked breads and roast meats
- Cake strips that require soaking before encircling custard and cheesecake batter to keep them flat and distribute heat uniformly
- Bun pans that shape dough into hot dog and hamburger buns
- A *pain de mie* or Pullman pan for baking thin-crusted, square-cornered sandwich bread
- A nonstick steel baguette pan that dimples the crust through tiny holes in the sleeve
- The one-hand plastic cake decorator that extrudes whipped cream, buttercream icing, or meringue through a choice of six different-shaped tips
- A cookie press that provides one-press production of cookies through twenty different metal discs and four decorating tips to shape and adorn desserts for everyday and holiday use
- Stacked steel racks that allow the cook to bake several layers at a time
- For maximum flakiness of pie crusts, hollow rolling pins that hold ice or ice water
- A stainless steel beaded pie chain that lies on a baking pie shell to inhibit bubbles and prevent lifting of the crust
- An aluminum foil or a metal pie crust shield for the outer edge to prevent overbaking
- A push-button, battery-powered vacuum bakery keeper that removes air and locks out moisture to keep baked goods fresh
- A line of flexible silicone bake ware that produces baked goods heated evenly throughout

See also **Biscuit; Bread; Cooking Stone; Ovens; Tinware; Yeast**

Further Reading

Boily, Lise, and Jean-François Blanchette. *The Bread Ovens of Quebec.* Quebec: National Museums of Canada, 1979.
Earle, Alice Morse. *Colonial Days in Old New York.* New York: Scribner's, 1896.
Jacob, H. E. *Six Thousand Years of Bread: Its Holy and Unholy History.* Garden City, N.Y.: Lyons Press, 1997.
Mandelbaum, David G. *The Plains Cree: An Ethnographic, Historical and Comparative Study.* Regina, Sask.: Canadian Plain Research Center, 1979.

BALDWIN, BESSIE

An English woman transported to Australia as a criminal, Bessie Florence Baldwin was a touchstone of authentic regional dishes and cookery. She got her culinary start in London, but practiced her art far from home. Born on a farm in Kent in 1818, she came to London at age nineteen and studied baking and pastry making with Thomas Edenwell near the House of Commons. Two years later, she demanded a raise from one cent per week to fivepence. The ensuing uproar earned her a seven-year prison term for assaulting her employer with a pie dish.

Along with 182 other female prisoners, Baldwin boarded the *Gilbert Henderson* on December 14, 1839 for transportation to the Colony of Van Dieman's Land, now called Tasmania, an island south of the province of Victoria. On January 11, 1840 she earned a permanent stay in the brig for bashing Sir John Hamett, the libidinous ship's surgeon, with a candlestick for improprieties. He chose not to press charges and withdrew to his quarters for the remainder of the voyage.

At the Hobarton penal colony, Baldwin passed to the Female Factory, where convicts wore yellow garb during their incarceration. She took part in a scandalous display of bare backsides toward the viceroy, Sir John Franklin, and his wife and attendants. The ruckus could have earned her solitary confinement at Port Arthur Prison and starvation rations of twelve ounces of flour a day, a mug of water, and eight drams of salt plus five of soap. Nonetheless, in 1842, the governor assigned Baldwin as cook's assistant and pastry cook to the Government House kitchen, where she performed admirably. By the end of his service to the colony, Sir John determined that she was rehabilitated and pardoned her. She departed for Tasmania at age thirty-one and left no more of her colorful history.

Baldwin's legacy arises from a lengthy compendium of colonial recipes, recorded by the Franklins' governess. Baldwin's simple but nourishing food covers the spectrum of English cookery—mulligatawny, lemon sauce, savory tomatoes, fish hash, kidney on toast, date pudding, Cornish pasty, and ginger sponge. Added to the list were her inventions, including Australian sauce and steamed kangaroo. As with jugged hare, the recipe for the latter calls for layering meat, bacon, and veal balls in a jar and steaming it for up to four hours. Baldwin lived well in the governor's employ—leaving behind the standard convict diet of gruel, bacon, potatoes, bread, and tea—and apparently caused him no difficulty.

Further Reading

The Convict Recipe Book (pamphlet). Rosny Park, Australia: Southern Holdings, 1996.

BAMBOO

An outsized grass with a remarkably versatile woody stem, bamboo is widely distributed over the world's tropics and subtropics into temperate zones across Asia, Oceania, and the marshlands of the southern United States. Some 1,200 species have been identified. No other plant grows so rapidly to a usable size or produces so light an inner fiber, strengthening and stabilizing the stalk. The prolific bamboo plant provides edible seeds and shoots to serve with *wakame* (seaweed) or to garnish broth, leaves for weaving into table and sleeping mats and sunshades, hollow stalks for shaping into stirring utensils for making soybean curd or weaving into sieves for drying shiitake mushrooms, and pith that Indian cooks use to form a *kudu,* which they place over cooked food to protect it from insects. Bamboo also makes fodder for cattle, pulp for paper, and tough, lightweight timbers as tall as 120 feet for building platforms, coffins, homes, dining pavilions, bridges, boats, masts, and rafts.

In 211 BCE Chinese workers used pu bamboo and drill bits to bore 500 feet into the ground to free natural gas from pockets lodged west of Chungking. By the tenth century CE, they had made a portable fuel cell by putting petroleum fuel into bamboo shafts. They subsequently used split bamboo to scrub iron woks. The dietary importance of the plant was recognized by 618 CE, when the pharmacologist Meng Shen listed bamboo among health-restoring plants. Bamboo shoots were limited to Chinese markets before canning made them more widely available. For the tenderest varieties, farmers harvested them in winter before fiber formed. In addition to being a favorite ingredient in Asian cookery, bamboo—in the form of poles balanced *tan tsu* style (shoulder-to-shoulder between two carriers)—was used to transport cooking implements and stoves.

Kazuyoshi Kudo's *Japanese Bamboo Baskets* (1980) documents bamboo's profound influence on home life in the island nation. As early as 794 CE, the Japanese were using bamboo in the serving of *neri-seihin* (fish paste), which composes 20 percent of the nation's sea catch. The glutinous blend of high-protein fish flesh, concocted from several species plus egg white, starch binders, and flavorings, produced a favorite food that was difficult to manage in the kitchen and at the table. To simplify handling, the cook molded the paste onto bamboo skewers like a kebab for grilling.

Bamboo continues to have wide domestic uses. In Japan's steep mountains, farmers carry bamboo baskets with tump lines or back or shoulder straps while planting and weeding, winnowing, and sieving. They gather garden produce into bamboo baskets and woven trays that can be held under running water and hung up to drain, making a separate colander unnecessary. For carrying crops and fish to market, a shoulder yoke balances two baskets at each end for even distribution of weight. Bamboo baskets are also handy for hauling food on carts and bicycles.

The clever householder can hollow, cut, and splice bamboo into wattle for walls, fencing, rakes, canes, umbrellas, tables and chairs, fans, lanterns, brooms and brushes, garden stakes and arbors, fences, sun shades, and fishing poles. In food preparation, cooks rely on bamboo buckets, vessels, canisters, tea whisks, and other household utensils. Bamboo baskets are used for air-drying rice and vegetables and for storage of fish and mushrooms. Lidded baskets can be turned into crab pots, eel traps, and cages for storing live catch under water or creels for transporting fresh fish to the kitchen counter. Bamboo skewers, a standard item in Asian kitchens, are useful for retrieving such items as teabags or *bouquet garni* from boiling liquids and for propping sprigs of kitchen herbs on window sills. The skewers require soaking before use on the grill to lengthen their life span over flame.

Throughout Asia, bamboo is the traditional raw material for making some of the world's most flexible, lightweight, and inexpensive household goods. In Hunan, archeologists discovered a Chinese woman buried with pottery, bamboo food containers, and 300 bamboo slips on which were listed culinary recipes and methods of frying, roasting, steaming, pickling, salting, and drying meats, game, and poultry, including dogs and pheasants. In New Guinea, the kitchen knife handle is bamboo. The traditional bamboo steamer has made the transition from Asian cooking to the Western kitchen and is now available in specialty catalogs and kitchenware shops. It consists of tiered baskets and a lid for layering fish, poultry, rice, and vegetables for a one-pot cooking procedure that preserves texture, moisture, and nutrients.

In the 1960s, the Samo of Papua, New Guinea, lacked cash for trade with the industrialized outside world. In their jungle environment, they made the most of sago palm and bamboo. Sago provided starch and fiber for roofing their traditional longhouses. From the latter material, they steamed wild shoots as *pit*, a favorite dish, and carved smoking tubes, knives, building material, hand tools, and water tubes. Farther north on Tonaki Jima, Okinawa, tillers of terraced fields traversed the long walk to work with bamboo carry poles across their shoulders. Slung to each end, mats strung on cords bore the implements and seedlings used in the cultivation of rice.

In the twenty-first century, bamboo is a source of weaving material for Montagnard basketmakers and the preferred cooking vessel in Papua New Guinea, where cooks work over an open hearth. Papuans and the Aeta, Negrito nomads of Mount Pinatubo in the Philippines, steam greens over a hot flame by securing them in bamboo tubes with banana leaves for lids. In like manner, Sikkimese cooks have for centuries used the end nodule of bamboo as the tube bottom and stuffed the other end with bamboo leaves to form a cooking chamber for fish, which they bake over a charcoal brazier. They also sip homemade millet beer through bamboo straws. Off the southeastern coast of Africa, the brewers of the Seychelles ferment *calou* (coconut palm toddy) and sell it in bamboo vessels.

In China, bamboo still serves numerous domestic purposes. In Xishuangbana, wooden pavilions on sturdy bamboo stilts form a living area with open bamboo porch for cooking. Women drop peelings and scraps to chickens and pigs that live below the veranda. For threshing outside Fanch'eng, a bamboo basket attached to a scythe gathers barley as it falls. In homes, food shops, and restaurants, bamboo mats and chopsticks are the most common table accoutrements. The food historian F. T. Cheng, author of *Musings of a Chinese Gourmet* (1962), explained the importance of bamboo pouches to the cooking of shark's fin to protect the strands of cartilage within. In Canton, cooks encase the fin in a net to preserve its integrity. However, this method sacrifices the pure fish taste for looks by imparting a bamboo flavor to an Asian delicacy. An alternative is a net woven of silver filament.

In India, winnowing from a curved bamboo tray uses natural air currents to separate grain from chaff. For Bangladeshi householders, bamboo is the building material for the cookhouse, a stand-alone structure from the home equipped with a mud *chula* (oven). On small stools on the earthen floor, members of the extended family gather to share rice and curry cooked by the daughter-in-law. The separation of cookhouse from dwelling helps keep the family cool during the hot season. Bangladeshi farmers operate bamboo foot pumps to irrigate kitchen gardens. To the southeast in Indonesia, the building of a new bamboo house calls for the recycling of the old house as a kitchen, which forty to fifty community laborers maneuver into position

much like the North American Amish at a barn raising. The move requires some helpers on the inside and more on the outside awaiting the count of three to walk the structure into place.

The bamboo worker requires a hatchet, punch, pliers, scissors, and ruler to fashion practical objects. In the United States bamboo adds an exotic air to Asian-style table settings, mats, and teapot and implement handles and supports cucumber vines and tomato stalks in patio gardens. On his television cooking show *The Galloping Gourmet,* Graham Kerr introduced viewers to the carved bamboo spurtle, originally a Scottish paddle/spatula used for stirring and turning pancakes.

See also **Chopsticks**

Further Reading

Cort, Louise Allison, and Nakamura Kenji. *A Basketmaker in Rural Japan.* New York: Weatherill, 1994.
"First Glimpse of a Stone Age Tribe," *National Geographic*, December 1971, 880–884.
Griffin, P. Bion, and Agnes Estioko-Griffin, "Ethnoarchaeology in the Philippines," *Archaeology*, November-December 1978, 34–43.
Kudo, Kazuyoshi. *Japanese Bamboo Baskets.* Tokyo: Kodansha International, 1980.
Rajah, Carol Selva. *Makan-Lah!: The True Taste of Malaysia.* Sydney, Australia: HarperCollins, 1996.
Shaw, R. Daniel. *From Longhouse to Village: Samo Social Change.* New York: Harcourt Brace College Publishers, 1996.

BANANAS

The banana, a relative latecomer to the diet of the Northern Hemisphere, today rivals the apple and grape in popularity. Native to the East Indies or Malaysia, the plant flourishes in the tropics of Africa, Oceania, the Caribbean, Central and South America, and the West Indies. Shipped from Costa Rica, Guatemala, Honduras, Nicaragua, Panama, Colombia, Jamaica, Guadeloupe, Martinique, Ethiopia, Cameroon, Guinea, Nigeria, Taiwan, and Mexico, it is a common fruit in home orchards in these countries and is enjoyed virtually free of preparation. In addition to this easily digested sugar- and carbohydrate-rich foodstuff, the banana tree also produces fiber for paper-making, leaves suitable for wrappings, and manila hemp for the twine industry.

The use of bananas for food is widely documented in Arab, Greek, and Latin literature, including commentary on Alexander the Great and his campaign in India. Pliny the Elder's encyclopedia, compiled around 77 CE, describes the banana as the food of India's gurus, who took shelter under the tree's shady fronds

With the help of a donkey, an agricultural worker transports bananas on a farm in the southern region of Bahia, Brazil. [© *Courtesy of Agricultural Research Service, USDA. Photo by Scott Bauer.*]

and consumed the fruit. The Hindu devotees of Vishnu, Lakshmi, and Ganesha prepared ceremonial dishes of bananas and their leaves and honored the plant as the earthly incarnation of Kali, goddess of agriculture.

After the Portuguese introduced the banana to the Canary Islands from Africa in 1482, it gained greater recognition. In the Americas in 1516, Father Tomas de Berlanga, bishop of Panama and emissary to Peru during the explorations of Francisco Pizarro, planted banana trees on the island of Hispaniola as a potential food source for slaves. From there, Bishop Vasco de Quiroga of Michoácan, a church reformer and ecclesiastical judge, carried the plant to Mexico as part of his program to save the peasants from colonial predations. In the mid-eighteenth century, the Swedish naturalist Carl Linnaeus gave the plant the Latin name *Musa paradisiaca* (heavenly muse), a romantic image drawn from a legend identifying the banana as the forbidden fruit of Eden.

The banana tree spread quickly to stands planted about the Caribbean, where vendors distributed the fleshy fruit door to door. Children ate freshly picked and peeled ripe bananas without further pulverizing or straining. Cooks added the pulp to drinks, pies, puddings, and baked goods. They especially prized the plantain, a less-sweet cooking variety suited to frying, roasting, and boiling Cuban style. The banana was also milled into flour or pounded into meal, preserved in jams, and fermented into wine or beer, a use also common in Tanganyika.

In the 1670s, the English traveler William Dampier learned to vary the cookery of bananas while managing a Jamaican plantation. He wrote: "The Darien Indians preserve them a long time by drying them over the fire, mashing them first and molding them into lumps. The Moskito Indians will take a ripe banana and roast it; then take a pint and one-half of water in a calabash; and squeeze the banana in pieces with their hands, mixing this with water; then they drink it off." (*The Wise Encyclopedia of Cookery*, 45)

He also listed as home uses slicing, grating, sun-drying, and cooking banana pulp as pie filling and described the substitution of mashed bananas for batter in a bag pudding, which he called a "buff-jacket." (Ibid., 44)

In industrialized nations, the unusual shape and size of the banana was its major selling point. The fruit appeared in still-life paintings and the lithographs of Currier and Ives and Louis Prang and was a hit at the 1876 Centennial Exposition in Philadelphia, where exhibitors wrapped each banana in tinfoil to heighten its exotic appearance. Young ladies made waxed copies for arranging in decorative displays.

To shoppers in the United States, the banana was virtually unknown until its introduction to produce markets in the 1880s. It was a luxury item until engineers mapped out regular transportation in specially built slatted rail cars. *First Principles of Household Management and Cookery* (1882), by Maria Parloa, the founder of the Boston Cooking School, confirmed the health-giving quality of the fruit, but ranked it below the apple for ease of use in the kitchen. A popular home economics textbook, Mary Johnson Lincoln's *Mrs. Lincoln's Boston Cook Book* (1888), declared otherwise, however, singling out the banana as a time- and work-saver that should appear on the table daily.

Although bananas were purchased primarily by the middle class, an article in *Scientific American* dated September 23, 1905, hailed the fruit's arrival in the American diet and characterized it as "the poor man's fruit." In the early decades of the century the growing demand for sweet foods and new serving ideas increased the popularity of bananas and other exotic foods such as pineapples, grapefruits, marshmallows, and flavored gelatin. The *Boston Cooking School Magazine* proposed that the home cook mold a salad of banana balls and gelatin in a banana skin. The United Fruit Company made the banana a standard year-round produce and fruit market item nationwide and the most common fruit for casual eating and for cooking, either fresh or powdered. The *Journal of the American Medical Association* debunked rumors that the banana was hard to digest.

In 1929, the Fruit Dispatch Company assigned consultants to survey American consumers and produce dealers. Advertisers touted the banana as a source of nutrition for children and a revitalizing food for the sick and elderly. Ads in *Good Housekeeping* proclaimed the banana as a sanitary food wrapped in its own microbe-proof cover. The text stressed words such as *tender* and *mellow* and offered free recipes from the Banana Growers Association. In the October 1930 issue, Dorothy B. Marsh, staff member of the Good Housekeeping Institute, composed a three-page article with photos of methods for preparing fruits for the table. For the cook contemplating bananas, she noted, "Always available, always in season, and economical in price—in them we have one of nature's most wholesome fruits." She demonstrated how to bake bananas in the skin to serve with rice or potatoes and how to fry battered halves or sauté slices dipped in milk, flour, pepper, and paprika for the main course. A smiling Chiquita Banana danced nimbly across posters, subtly selling the fruit as a fount of energy and contentment. Bananas began appearing in kitchen fruit bowls, wholesome desserts, and school lunch boxes; Boy Scout manuals pictured children happily roasting bananas on sticks over an open fire.

The banana was absent from U.S. kitchens during World War II, when shipping took second place to combat. The American Friends of France established a fund for freedom fighters by compiling a recipe book, *Spécialités de la Maison* (Specialties of House). First Lady Eleanor Roosevelt contributed her recipe for a delicacy made scarce by war—Prewar Bananas Flambés Kirsch. Families welcomed the banana once more in 1946, when shipping resumed from South American and Caribbean ports.

In the 1970s journalists writing for *National Geographic* described the banana-centered diet of Uganda. West of Mbala in eastern Uganda, the Gweretene cultivated kitchen beds of maize, peanuts, cassava, and millet alongside banana groves. Cooks gathered bunches of fruit for mashing and steaming into *matoke,* which they served in communal family bowls. They crushed and fermented bananas into beer, sliced them raw for desserts and snacks, and folded the ample leaves into plates, table mats, dish covers, even clothing. To prevent the deadly form of malnutrition known as kwashiorkor, along with the carbohydrate-rich banana, children's diets included sources of protein such as peanuts, beans, fish, or fried termites.

In the 1980s, the Seaside Banana Gardens of La Conchita, California, began producing a number of banana species, including a Polynesian variety suited to cooking. Established by Doug Richardson and Paul Turner, the commercial venture was the only banana plantation to succeed in the United States. The use of bananas in cookery flourished from a campaign to make recipes available in cookbooks, newspaper cooking sections, and the electronic media. By the twenty-first century, the banana was equally likely to be served by a flight attendant over Minneapolis or a street vendor in Mali.

Further Reading

Jenkins, Virginia Scott. *Bananas: An American History.* Washington, D.C.: Smithsonian Institution, 2000.

BANQUETS

Banquets—lavish celebratory meals—have marked special occasions from early times. The first banquets may have been clan ceremonies or festivals honoring a birth or death or launching a hunt, as described in Greek commentary on Ethiopian banquets prepared for the gods, pictured on paintings at the Trois Frères in Ariège, France, and characterized in the writings of the American anthropologist Hortense Powdermaker after her sojourn in Melanesian New Ireland in the 1930s. The dissection of slaughtered animals into prime portions for the gods and servings for priests and worshippers set a precedent of dividing meat equitably. Another aspect of banqueting was the proper entertainment of important guests, the purpose of the banquet by which King Alcinous welcomes Odysseus in Book VII of Homer's *Odyssey* (ca. 850 BCE). In Robert Fables's translation, the elder Echeneus prompts the king, "Come, raise him up and seat the stranger now, in a silver-studded chair, and tell the heralds to mix more wine for all so we can pour out cups to Zeus who loves the lightning, champion of suppliants—suppliants' rights are sacred. And let the housekeeper give our guest his supper, unstinting with her stores." (Homer 1996, 184–185)

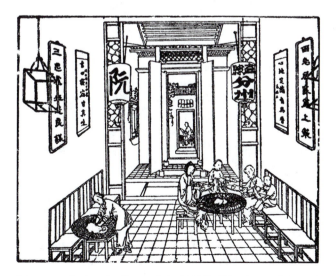

A banquet during the Feast of the Middle Kingdom celebrated by the Chinese.

No Expense Spared

At his death around 718 BCE, palace staff in Gordion, Anatolia, honored the Phrygian monarch Midas with a banquet. In addition to the display of the king's remains on an open log catafalque, servants assembled sacrificial food and beverage for the gods and a sizeable spread for the mourners. Microscopic samples taken from cauldrons, bowls, and bronze *situlas* (buckets), when subjected to infrared and mass spectroscopy and liquid and gas chromatography, provided details of the menu. Sommeliers blended grape wine with honey mead and barley beer permeated with the calcium oxalate of beerstone, a settling agent. The main course was roast goat sliced from the bone, accompanied by lentil stew, spiced with bitter vetch and fenugreek. Ornate walnut-topped serving stands inlaid with boxwood and juniper and *omphalos* bowls accompanied Midas to his tumulus.

For in-house banqueting, Greek hosts spared no expense to set a fine table and organize their domestic staff to serve abundant food and drink. Of the custom of parting gifts, the Roman architectural chronicler Vitruvius wrote around 20 BCE about *xenia* (friendly gifts): "When the Greeks became more luxurious, they began to provide…stores of provisions for their guests from abroad, and on the first day they would invite them to dinner, sending them on the next [day] chickens, eggs, vegetables, fruits and other country produce. That is why artists called pictures representing things sent to guests 'xenia.'" (Hollander 1999) The packaging of small kitchen delicacies expressed a deepened friendship that extended from the host's residence to the guest's home; the packages might include servings of dishes that the guest had remarked on during the meal.

Herodotus described lavish Thracian feasting in his *Histories* (ca. 440 BCE): "When a rich Thracian is buried, the custom is to lay out the body for three days, during which, after a preliminary period of mourning, a feast is held of all sorts of animals slaughtered for the purpose." (Herodotus 1961, 313) A generation later, the historian Xenophon contributed to the history of Thracian feasting in *Anabasis* (ca. 400 BCE), in which he described the use of couches for dining and the drinking and singing that preceded dancing to flute music, brandishing of swords, and the acting out of combat technique.

In Asia, banquets featured flavorful, aromatic condiments and spices. At the royal court of China around 200 BCE, the palace employed 4,000 servants, of whom more than 2,000 prepared and served food and beverage. As described by Su Jan Lee in *The Fine Art of Chinese Cooking* (1962), "The Chinese kitchen was more than a kitchen—it was a laboratory, a factory, a marvel of efficiency" (p. 62). Yet, for large numbers of guests, the cook created such dishes as Peking duck and shark's fin with only three necessities—a sharp knife, chopsticks, and wok—and followed the kitchen dictum of a maximum of selection and preparation and a minimum of cooking.

The Chinese emperor required 162 dietitians for menu planning and 256 chefs, half for family meals and the other half for company. Kitchen crew included 62 cooks and a cadre of specialists—28 for drying, 62 for game, 342 for fish, 24 for shellfish and turtles, and 335 for cereals, vegetables, and fruit. The staff of condiment specialists included 62 whose job was to procure and serve salt and 62 who were devoted to sauce making and pickling. In addition to 110 sommeliers, there were 340 cup fillers. The Chinese taboo against gluttony or immoderate consumption assured that frequent feasting did not overtax digestion, cause obesity, or threaten longevity. One labor-intensive method of removing fat from a duck carcass required the continuous pouring of boiling water through the gullet of the bird suspended over an open fire. The process eroded most of the heavy fat and continued until the meat was cooked through.

In Canton, the formal multicourse banquet shrank to an informal ritual or celebratory meal called the *sihk puhn* (eat pot). Compressing nine courses into one, the cook offered a wooden basin of meat, poultry, bean curd, fish balls, turnips, and shellfish fried in peanut oil and flavored with a sweetened onion and soy bean sauce. Diners received individual rice bowls and chopsticks. While squatting at table, they fished in the commensal bowl for morsels of food, ate without regard to pacing or socializing, and departed when they were filled. This unstructured meal required neither elegant accoutrements nor serving staff and called for no forced conviviality.

As described by the historians Herodotus, Athanaeus, and Plutarch, at banquets honoring wealthy Egyptians, women took charge of the kitchen and organized staffing and table service. Stewards welcomed guests to the antechamber with basins and towels for rinsing hands and feet. When the meal was ready, staff decked diners with flower wreaths and led them to cushions on the floor. After serving drinks and joining in prayers, waiters began distributing baskets of food. Harpists and other musicians entertained while mimes and tumblers performed. For the *silicernium* (funeral feast), planners concluded with a touch of the macabre—presentation of a coffin with mock corpse, a reminder that the living should enjoy their pleasures while they could. More uplifting, the *cena novendialis* (ninth-day feast) ended the mourning period with nonstop cooking and eating.

Assyrian kitchens served huge banquets, such as those of Ashurbanipal in Nineveh. According to French Egyptologist Gaston Maspéro's *Lectures Historiques* (1892), Assyrian kitchen staff opened the palace doors for a week to all visitors, adult and child, male or female. Workers hung multihued drapes around courtyards to transform them into dining halls. The king ordered his cooks and stewards to package dishes and beverages for presentation to soldiers on duty.

Greek and Roman Extravagances

Hebrew and Persian banqueting prefaced the extravagance of the Greeks and Romans. Like the Hebrews, who perfumed their table wines and wreathed guests with flowers, the Greeks accorded luxuries to visitors to make them feel festive. Euripides's *Ion* (ca. 417 BCE) describes the preparations for a public feast:

> The boy knew just what to do.
> He set up a framework of poles,
> A hundred feet by a hundred feet—
> Or so they say who measured it—
> Across the whole town square,
> Big enough to shelter everyone in Delphi
> At noon.

Skilled at table service, the boy carried in tables and cups and sent out a crier to invite all within his hearing to wear a garland, laugh, eat and drink well, and share the *euergetes'* (benefactors') kitchen bounty with everyone.

The culinary staff of Alexander the Great, a master entertainer, set the example of hospitality by roasting whole animals stuffed with delicacies. In huge tents decked in purple and gold, carvers served portions on flat-bread. Like the banquet meals of the Persians, who launched a massive slaughter of horses, camels, oxen, asses, deer, ostriches, geese, and cocks, Roman menus exhibited the largesse of the host, who sought to impress guests with exotic meats cooked in home kitchens or purchased from caterers and skillfully arranged and garnished on platters. The satirist Petronius's fictional *Satyricon* (first century CE) described a grotesque list of dishes that marked the end of a bloated meal: "To wind up, we had some soft cheese steeped in fresh wine, a snail apiece, some tripe hash, livers in pastry boats and eggs topped with more pastry and turnips and mustard and beans boiled in the pod—but enough's enough. Oh yes, and they passed around a dish of olives pickled in caraway, and some of the guests had the nerve to walk off with three fistfuls. But we sent the ham back untasted." (Hollander, 1999)

Among the more unusual banquet dishes that have survived in food histories are puppies, elephant trunks, guinea pigs, peacocks, and dormice. As described by the Greco-Syrian philosopher Poseidonius the Athlete around 90 BCE, diners squabbled over the slaughtered animal's legs, a gift presented to the bravest guest. Each bit directly into huge joints of meat and cut into tough pieces with the small knife that each carried in a small scabbard attached to his sword. The whole company shared diluted wine in ox horn cups ringed with gold or silver or in the skull of enemies defeated in combat. A more sentimental vessel was the skull of a deceased parent. The Gauls, whom Julius Caesar epitomized in his *Gallic Commentaries* (52 BC), preferred tableside cooking to the impressive platter presentations of the Romans. From braziers and cauldrons placed nearby, guests seated on straw bundles observed spit roasting and grilling.

Romanized Gauls, depicted in E. de la Bédolière's *Moeurs et Vie Privée des Français* (Customs and Private Lives of the French, ca. 1865), rejected the Roman custom of reclining on couches. Instead, they sat on wood stools or benches draped with carpet. Staff poured *mulsum* (diluted wine) into their cups and carved joints ferried from the kitchen still sputtering from the heat. Cooks prepared tarts, honeyed pastry, soft cheese, medlars, chestnuts, figs, and grilled snails as desserts. Servers ended the meal by distributing hot wine and wood-and-silver toothpicks topped with feathers.

Feasts of the Middle Ages

No era of banqueting has received the intense interest bestowed on the Middle Ages. According to the description of the Lyons-born correspondent Caius Sollius Sidonius Apollinaris written around 450 CE, Frankish hosts set lavish silver tables topped with utensils in precious metals and rose-petal-strewn tablecloths. German hosts distributed *widerkomms,* large glasses that kitchen staff filled with spirits for pre-meal toasting. A central trough in the early Saxon hall held an elongated fire around which serving staff positioned trestle tables. The English great hall also boasted a central hearth paved with brick or stone, a source of warmth and cheer for banqueting and welcoming important guests. The first technological advance to benefit feasting was the twelfth-century placement of fireplaces on the room's outer walls. Ovens in the side of the fireplace allowed for controlled baking. Supplanting boiled vegetables and meats that cooks once spit-roasted over blazing fires were more complex dishes, savory stews, and sauces stirred over a slower, more controlled heat.

In the fourteenth century, according to Sir Walter Scott's *The Fair Maid of Perth* (1828), Scottish highlanders observing a chief's funeral ended their mourning with an outdoor banquet. At the *al fresco* kitchen, a cadre of cooks stoked coal and wood fires and lined pits with heated stones for stewing beef, mutton, and venison. On wood spits, they roasted whole goats and sheep, while fish broiled over embers and sundry joints boiled in cauldrons made of animal hides. Guests ate in arbor rooms, on sod tables, and in hastily nailed-together plank sheds. In 1618, the English poet John Taylor accompanied the Earl of Mar on a shooting trip to the Highlands and found the same bankside cookery in temporary *lonchards* (lodges), where cooks baked, roasted, and stewed four kinds of meat, eight varieties of poultry, and fresh salmon to serve with ale, sack, claret, and *aquavitae* to 1,400 guests. At all levels of society, Britons cooked commensal meals and shared entertainments on Plough Monday, Mayday, Midsummer's Eve, and harvest home. The church supervised the more dignified celebration of St. Valentine's Day, Christmas, and Lent. Home-cooked viands and drinks accompanied maypole dances, mumming, and the playing of pipe and tabor.

One of the most elaborate meals recorded in church history took place at the installation of Pope Clement VI at Avignon, France, on May 7, 1342. Against the backdrop of Provence's wretched poverty, ecclesiastical festivities pressed fourteen butchers to work preparing 219 calves and cows, 914 goats, 1,023 lambs, and 10,000 chickens. With less hospitality toward guests, in Poland, Queen Jadwiga, who came on the throne in 1384, demanded that the royal kitchen prepare celebratory meals, but instructed them to cook her own food separately. Her reason was less antisocial behavior than disdain for her husband Ladislaus, a Lithuanian who demanded less sophisticated dishes from the kitchen staff.

Medieval banquets were feasts for the senses that commenced with a bustle and flourish. Lighting was provided by flaming torches that servants held aloft. Meals began with the sounding of a trumpet. Servants conducted guests to Roman-style couches. In token of trust in the good will of the host and his staff, all shared a communal wine or loving cup, which pages refilled throughout the meal. Before foods came from kitchen to table, tasters determined if they were toxic and touched them with a talisman to protect royal diners from poison.

For feasting, only the lord and the most honored guests sat in chairs, which were often fitted with false seats that could be lifted to reveal a hidden storage compartment for silver, prize dishes, or costly linens. The privilege of individual seating resulted in the term *chairman* as a token of high rank. The surveyor of ceremonies entered a festal hall singing a welcome that has since become a familiar Yuletide carol:

Here we go a-wassailing among the leaves so green,
Here we go a-wandering so fair to be seen.
Love and joy come to you
And to our wassail too;
And God send us a happy New Year!
(Pelner-Cosman 1981)

After presenting an ornate container of salt to honorees at the high table, he established that the elite ate above the salt, while those of lower social standing took their places below it. Such positioning of people by status was essential to a society ordered under the rigid classifications of feudalism.

After a church dignitary delivered a blessing, the surveyor summoned the pantler with a wave of the key to begin the presentation of bread. The noblest, holiest, or most socially prominent "upper crust" guest received the top crust, on which the baker sprinkled spices. A cup-bearer accepted wine poured by the butler or bottler for an assay, a test to determine the purity of the vintage, either by tasting it or dropping into it a bezoar (a calcified stone formed in a ruminant's stomach). The bezoar supposedly changed hue if the drink was poisonous.

At table, ewers or laverers presented *acquamaniles* (also spelled *aquamaniles*), animal-shaped hand basins from which they poured fragrant herbed or spiced water for hand washing. One gold-alloyed specimen crafted in Nuremberg, Germany, around 1400 and now housed in the Metropolitan Museum of Art in New York City, takes the form of a prancing lion. The servant filled it through a hole in the top of the head and tilted it by a dragon-shaped handle over guests' hands so that water poured from a spigot in the chest. Before presenting these amenities, servants tasted the water and kissed the towel to prove them poison-free. Throughout the meal, waiters provided finger bowls and refreshed them with clean water. Lesser attendees performed their ablutions in a lavabo inset in the wall of the Great Hall's vestibule.

The order of the multicourse medieval banquet began with fish and smaller dishes, followed by *relevés,* which replaced anything removed from the table, and continued with the spectacular *pièce de resistance* or entrée and subsequent meat courses. In the anonymous etiquette manual *The Boke of Curtasye* (ca. 1440), serving staff were advised to place pieces of bread unobtrusively around hot soup pots, much like hot pads, to prevent them from burning their hands on the long walk from hearth to table. The peacock, a favorite culinary showpiece, was skinned and the head and tail preserved for redressing the roasted carcass. By positioning a cotton ball dipped in spirits or a chunk of camphor in the beak, the server could light the bird's mouth just before entering the room and present a flame-breathing firebird. Around the focal dishes were small garnishes and *hors d'oeuvres,* a decorative presentation enhancing the main course. Dessert, derived from the French verb *desservir* (to clear the table), was a light, palate-clearing dish accompanied by small bonbons, fennel stalks for cleansing the breath, and rosewater for rinsing greasy fingers.

Master Chiquart Amiczo's *Du Fait de Cuisine* (On Cooking, 1420) offers readers a sampling of the huge menus common to the era's banquet tables, including his recipe for boar's head. He advocated food coloring and cited saunders (sandalwood) and galingale as the best for red tints. For feeding "kings, queens, dukes, duchesses, counts, countesses, princes, princesses, marquis, marquises, barons, baronesses and lords of lower estate, and nobles also a great number" whom Duke Amadeus of Savoy invited, Chiquart called for an ample supply of foodstuffs. He listed the following:

- 200 kids and lambs, 100 cattle, 30 sheep, 120 pigs, 100 piglets, and 60 fatted pigs for soups and for larding plus venison, hares, conies, partridges, pheasants, pigeons, cranes, herons, and wild birds
- 6,000 eggs
- 320 pounds of white ginger, ginger, cinnamon, "grains of paradise," and pepper as well as six pounds each of nutmeg, clove, mace, and galingale and 25 pounds of saffron
- 30 loaves of sugar plus almonds, rice, raisins, figs, prunes, dates, pine nuts, turnsole, alkanet, gold leaf, and camphor
- Two casks of vinegar, two of wine, one each of verjuice and oil
- 120 quintals of cheese

He also called for leather bags, cauldrons and hanging pans, fry pans, 62 casks, 12 mortars, 160 bowls, six graters, two two-handed knives, 26 ordinary knives, 125 spoons, 100 baskets, 12 grills, six hooks, 120 iron spits, 20 shovels, 20 rotisseries, and fine cloth for straining. For the kitchen staff, he projected at least three or four months of training and preparation. Heating required 1,000 carts of firewood and a store of coal. For serving, he estimated 4,000 vessels of wood, pewter, gold, and silver; for drapery and light, the tables required 60 ells of linen, 60 torches, 20 pounds of wax candles, and 60 pounds of tallow candles.

New Heights of Luxury

In this same era, the fabled banquets of the Ottoman Empire carried court cuisine to new heights of luxury. For the sultan, the imperial cook catered meals for meetings of the *divan* (cabinet), which seated as many as 5,000 people or accommodated twice that many for the reception of a foreign embassy. Supervision of a phalanx of cooks called for codification of kitchen protocol. Under strict rule, trainees learned the basics of classic Islamic cookery.

In Italy, no one rivaled the dukes d'Este in hospitality. Court cooks created golden strands of pasta to honor the arrival in 1502 of a blonde beauty, Lucrezia Borgia, the intended of Alfonso, the future Duke d'Este. For a January 1529 dinner at which Don Ercole d'Este honored his father, Duke Alfonso, the family invited an emissary from Venice, the Milanese archbishop, and 100 others to dine on 120 menu items. To accompany special music and a comedy by the poet Ariosto, the cook baked tall pies and gilded them with an egg yolk wash, which turned to a golden glow in the oven. In 1549, Christoforo (also Cristoforo or Christofaro) di Messisbugo (or Messisburgo), *scalco* (steward) of Hippolyte d'Este, cardinal of Ferrara, wrote *Banquetti Compositioni di Vivande, et Apparecchio Generale* (Foods and General Necessities for Banquets), a description of a Lenten banquet serving 54. The menu called for 140 dishes filling fifteen platters and fifty-four separate plates. He served seafood, gelid dishes, sausage, mortadella, ravioli, lasagna, and tarts. At the conclusion of the meal, his cleaning staff washed more than 2,500 dishes.

Venetian lawmakers attempted to curb excessive dinners, especially wedding celebrations. Statutes discouraged these *al fresco* extravaganzas, which extended to numerous banquets served to hundreds of guests in public for maximum display of wealth and prestige. To circumvent the law, in the 1500s, the wealthy developed a villa culture, which perpetuated fine cookery and festal dining in bucolic vacation homes outside of Venice. The shift created a competition between city and country dwellers for the best cooks and stewards. Hosts who entertained at multiple locations transported their staff to the setting that demanded the most service. The concept of dining as a display of personal property spread to lower social levels, creating a demand for new technologies in glass, napery, cutlery, salt cellars, candelabra, braziers, and pottery as well as local and imported antiques.

In Central America, huge banquets were a delight to Montezuma II, the Aztec monarch who ruled 5,000 Mexicans until his murder by the Spanish *conquistadores* of Hernán Cortés in 1520. He invited hordes of guests, but chose to eat his meal behind a screen for maximum privacy. From the royal kitchen, his staff carried pottery crocks of flaming oil and placed them under food containers to keep them hot until he asked for them.

Joy in feasting continued into the late sixteenth and seventeenth centuries, according to Carlo Nascia, the chef to Ranuccio II, Duke of Parma, Piacenza, and Castro. Nascia recorded a dozen recipes for turkey, called the "Indian rooster," in *Il Quatro Banchetti Destinati per le Quatro Stagioni dell'Anno* (Four Banquets Destined for the Four Seasons of the Year, 1652). One recipe adorned the bird with morello cherries; others employed galantine, candied fruit, verjuice, cream and sugar, herbed kidney sauce, and Borgia sauce, named after the famous line of Spanish popes. Likewise opulent in their menus and table presentations, Bartolomeo Scappi, chef to Pope Pius V and author of *Opera dell'Arte dell Cucinare* (Compendium on the Art of Cookery, 1570) and Bartolomeo Stefani, author of *L'Arte di Ben Cucinare* (The Art of Cooking Well, 1662), advanced the late Renaissance tradition of cooking with panache. Of such galas, Mikolaj Rej, the father of Polish literature, complained that cooks were more interested in show than in tasty food. Royalty promoted their ostentation as a means of currying political favor. By the late seventeenth century, heavy drinking, quarreling, and bloodshed caused many Polish feasts to end with broken glass and serious injuries.

For these extravaganzas, organization was the key to success. Kitchen staff dispatched chargers or platters of foods that complemented each other. The twelve-course medieval meal contained foods subtly contrasting in taste, aroma, texture, and nutrition, as displayed by this menu:

> First course: a medley of apple, pear, plum, and quince spiced with basil, rosemary and rue and ladled into a pastry tart
>
> Second course: St. John's Urchin, a carob-flavored pastry holding minced meat and molded like a hedgehog
>
> Third course: an almond "eyroun" or omelet flavored with nuts, currants, honey, and saffron
>
> Fourth course: salmon roasted in onion and wine marinade
>
> Fifth course: Fruits Royal Rice, a dish of artichokes stuffed with blueberry rice
>
> Sixth course: Aigredouncy (sweet with sour), roulade of sliced honeyed chicken, mustard, pine nuts, and rosemary
>
> Seventh course: an astrological herb cake intended to balance the body's humors
>
> Eighth course: an astrological cheese
>
> Ninth course: roast pheasant or chicken wings
>
> Tenth course: elderberry divination pastries in assorted shapes
>
> Eleventh course: platters of almond spice cake in circlets topped with roundels or verses for the guests to sing, giving rise to the term *roundelay* for recitations
>
> Twelfth course: the parade of subtleties, the carving and service of dessert sculpture

The seventh course represented a perpetuation of the dietetic theory of the Greek medical experts Hippocrates and Galen. According to their concepts of digestion, food triggered excesses in the body that required careful selection and balance of contrasts.

Paired diners shared servings from dishes made of precious metals. Meat frequently came to table on metal spits. Only the head table enjoyed the services of a carver. From the *écuyers tranchants* (carving squires), diners might receive gobbets or pre-cut meat on bread trenchers or *manchets*, thick slabs of coarse, four-day-old bread accompanied by bowls of sauce for dipping. They typically pulled at the pieces with their teeth and dripped sops, or juices, onto the trencher below, which established the part of the table and servings they claimed as their own.

Finger food was the order of the day. Servings arrived in segments that could be skewered with the point of the knife, eaten with a spoon, or held in the fingers. A favorite baked item was the tart or pasty, which contained rich, juicy fillings held in place by a sealed crust. The hall butler's staff poured beverages into tankards or bowls for sharing, concluding with hippocras, a spiced wine reserved as an end-of-meal digestive. The formal dinner ended with grace and another round of drinks. Afterward, when servants put all away, brushed up crumbs, and returned the area to normal, kitchen staff passed the used bread trenchers to free-roaming dogs or tossed them from the back door to the poor.

Renaissance Refinements

Renaissance banqueting retained the opulence of the Middle Ages, but added refinements of Italian cookery. For example, the anonymous Italian *Epulario* (The Italian Banquet, 1516) reprised recipes from Platina but transformed a simple poultry tart into the great pie celebrated in "Sing a Song of Sixpence." When the server slit the crust, the pie disgorged live birds "to delight and pleasure shew to the company." (Aresty 1964, 33) In France in the early 1500s, Francis I revived festive meals and heavy drinking. Hosts displayed finely chased and crested plate of precious metals, surrounded with Nevers porcelain, Faïence, and hand-blown Venetian glass. The use of forks and spoons ended earlier gaucheries and ushered in an era of more polished manners. Kitchens refined the earlier dependence on haunches of meat with prepared dishes, soup, hash, salad, and fricassée. In 1631, the Italian cookbook author Antonio Frugoli, compiler of food history in *Practica e Scalcaria* (Practical Matters and Carving), summarized the complex job of providing tables with fish, meats, vegetables, and beverages and appended a history of cookery and table service from ancient times.

At the court of Louis XIV, meals were served under a splendid canopy. At Versailles on May 6, 1664, a banquet on the theme of *Les Plaisirs de l'Isle Enchantée* (Pleasures of the Enchanted Isle) honored the royal couple and the queen mother. It featured a theme of the four seasons for which ballet dancers performed steps suited to the signs of the zodiac. Twelve waiters per season processed a quarter mile from the main kitchen and the special *l'office de la bouche* (office of the mouth), a temporary dessert station, to the king's crescent-shaped table. Borne aloft, their salvers displayed the candied and preserved fruit and blossoms appropriate to fall, winter, spring, and summer.

For this lengthy introit of *la viande du Roi* (the King's food) past courtiers, plating staff topped trays with domes. The purpose was simply to keep food hot and unpolluted as well as to guard against assassination attempts by poison. Those volunteers chosen to taste the food gained immense prestige, as did those individuals whose meal was tested. As Margaret Visser states in *The Rituals of Dinner: The Origins, Evolution, Eccentricities, and Meaning of Table Manners* (1991): "It was flattering to be considered so great as to be a likely candidate for assassination, and flattering to watch such elaborate care being taken to prevent any harm to one's person—while other people looked on, waited, and were not given the same regard." (p. 140)

Small porcelain dishes and bowls simplified the serving of desserts, which consisted of marzipan, sugared nuts, preserved fruit, and blancmange. The king's demand for the best of preparation and service caused the suicide of his cook, Jean François Vatel, who died rather than suffer the embarrassment of running out of meat for the royal entourage. An amateur cook, Prince Louis II de Bourbon Condé, nicknamed "Le Grand Condé," honored the king with a feast begun with a grand procession. After the waiters lost hold of a giant turbot and dropped it on the floor, Louis called for the cook to send in the second fish and the parade continued. Such lavish cooking, table decoration, and presentation of dishes reached its highest point in the eighteenth century with the court of Louis XVI and Marie Antoinette, whose self-indulgence precipitated the French Revolution.

Catering to Modern Tastes

In defiance of the table fantasies designed by architectural confectioner Marie-Antoine Carême, the first of the grand French chefs, Jean-Anthelme Brillat-Savarin preferred a less fussy table. His eight-volume classic, *Physiologie du Goût, ou Méditation de Gastronomie Transcendante, Ouvrage Théorique, Historique et à l'Ordre du Jour* (The Physiology of Taste, or A Meditation on the Best of Dining, a Theoretical and Historic Work on the Order of the Day, 1825), characterized a meticulous but restrained banquetry. He indicated that the best menu should present food in order from heaviest to lightest and wines from lightest to the most fragrant. He advised cooks to served the hottest coffee and only the liqueurs that the host himself preferred.

In nineteenth-century Russia, the opulence of Europe's banquet tables spilled over into west country estates, where hosts prided themselves on a lavish welcome. In the opinion of Madame Germaine de Staël, a salon wit, the Russians were more hospitable than the French. For guests arriving from twenty to thirty miles away, from 11:00 a.m. to 3:00 p.m., servants began distributing *zakuski* (*hors d'oeuvres*), such as meat pasties, caviar, smoked fish, pickled mushrooms, and vodka. Outside Moscow, staff at Mikhalka, the Orlov family estate, astounded diners with exotic foods. One featured dessert, an Astrakhan melon, traveled 1,000 miles by carriage. For the four-hour meal, cooks prepared fifty to sixty dishes. A winter feast featured such out-of-season fare as asparagus and oversized grapes.

The tradition of the banquet continued into the twentieth century, although the host might as easily have been an industrialist as an aristocrat. Around the world, monarchs, presidents, and even dictators of Socialist countries continue to mount extravagant entertainments. In October 1971, the Shah of Iran attempted to reclaim some of the glory of ancient Persia by setting his staff to work on *Jash'n* (Celebration), a lavish international dinner. The occasion was the 2,500th anniversary of the founding of the Persian Empire by Cyrus the Great, who ruled a wide swath from the Danube to the Nile and from the Aegean Sea to India. For catering, he called on the French, who made bimonthly flights and sent truck convoys from France to provision the affair. For livery, he dressed fifty staff members in designer uniforms from the house of Lanvin at a cost of $50,000. The dinner for fifty heads of state required the services of Maxim's, a world-class Parisian restaurant established in 1893. The famous restaurant dispatched 165 chefs, sommeliers, and waiters. Provisions, shipped over the previous month, consisted of 25,000 bottles of wine, nearly four tons of meat, four tons of cheese and butter, and 1,000 pints of cream. The menu included quail eggs stuffed with caviar, moussed crayfish tails, and roasted rack of lamb. The signature dish, roast peacock, required preparation of *foie gras* for stuffing. The five-and-a-half-hour meal ended with cake, champagne, sherbet, figs with raspberries, and coffee.

See also **Carême, Marie-Antoine; Medieval Kitchens; Renaissance Kitchens; Servants**

Further Reading

Girouard, Mark. *Life in the English Country House: A Social and Architectural History.* New Haven, Conn.: Yale University Press, 1978.
Kasper, Lynne Rossetto. *The Splendid Table.* New York: William Morrow & Co., 1992.
Waterson, Merlin. *The Servants' Hall.* New York: Pantheon Books, 1980.

BARBECUE

Barbecue is at once a name for a cooking method, the outdoor pit or grill used in the process, and the food produced by this method. Although ancient, it flourishes today in many corners of the globe. Around 375 CE, at the height of Aryan India, Chandragupta II, known as Vikramaditya (or Vikrama Ditta; Son of Power), a legendary Gupta king, was a patron of the arts and adherent to traditional culture. He accommodated Hindu vegetarianism to barbecuing by inventing a way to spit-roast spicy vegetable kebabs. In China *kao* cookery calls for a traditional charcoal-fired grill or hibachi for spit-cooking meats on skewers, a cooking style developed in the fourteenth century from the Mongol nomads descended from Kublai Khan. At informal gatherings, diners traditionally threaded morsels onto bamboo sticks and turned them over embers at the table for immediate eating. Variations allowed for deep frying or broiling, depending on the texture of the food, which might include delicate shrimp and chicken livers.

Barbacoa in the Americas

Barbecue as a cooking method is indigenous to the Americas. From the Taino culinary style of the *barbacoa* (roasting scaffold) came the concept of roasting or smoking whole oxen or sheep over a timber framework. A seventeenth-century engraving by Théodore de Bry pictures Native Americans smoking or roasting fresh-caught fish over one of these scaffolds, which they elevated enough from the flame to spare the wood from charring. The Caribe, who moved north into the Caribbean isles from the Orinoco Basin of Venezuela, cultivated a similar method, marinating flank meat or fish strips in salt water and then roasting them in a pit oven over a low fire. In a separate strand of culinary history, slaves carried the African version of barbecuing to Grenada, Jamaica, and enclaves around the Gulf of Mexico, where cooks often dressed meat with a sauce made from the fiery hot scotch bonnet pepper, an equal in heat to the habañero pepper. Similarly, the Caribou Eskimo, Chipewyan, and Naskapi broiled caribou head over a low fire.

A form of barbecue still common in Jamaica, jerk, or jerked meat, the island's national dish, results from a labor-intensive process of marinating, basting, and tenderizing meats with an acidic sauce blended from brown sugar, chilies, onion, tomato, and vinegar and cooking over aged wood. Mountaineers altered the term *charqui* to jerky because they could yank a piece of jerked meat from a saddlebag and eat without stopping to cook. The Jamaican barbecue cooking on Mount Diablo, Jamaica, continued to draw tourists

Woman selling char grilled Guinea
Pig in Peru.
(© *Shoosh/Up the Res/Alalmy*)

since the early days of colonization. Outside small grocery stores, the traditional grilling of yams, corn, plantains, breadfruit, saltfish, and barbecue plus akee (or ackee), a succulent island fruit, requires little more than a steel drum on legs with a hinged lid.

Among Hispanic settlers of southern Texas, a cultural specialty, the *barbacoa de cabeza* (barbecued beef head), began with an in-ground roasting and supplied meat plus brains, eyes, lips, and tongue for family reunions, weddings, and funerals. Of the traditional Western barbecue, food historian Foster Rhea Dulles wrote in *A History of Recreation: America Learns to Play* (1965): "Dinner was a gargantuan feast; a barbecued beef or hog, roasted in a deep hole lined with hot stones; quantities of buffalo steaks, venison, baked 'posum or wild turkey; and always hominy, corn dodgers, and wheatcakes fried in bear's oil."

The Inca of Ecuador, Chile, and Peru applied the fire pit cooking method to the drying of llama meat. In Argentina, Chile, Paraguay, and Uruguay, the cooking of sausage, sweetbreads, baby goat, suckling pig, beef brisket, and ribs takes place at the *asado* (spit-roasting) and *parilla* (grill). In Ecuador, barbecue sparks a rice dish called *arroz con menestra*; in Brazil, a mixed-meat barbecue called *churrasco* dates to the 1530s, when importers brought the first cattle from Cape Verde to São Paulo. They built brick pits for the first home barbecues. As characterized in John Mier's *Travels in Chile and La Plata* (1826), while on the move, the *vaquero* (cowboy) carried a saddle pack meal of *carne seca* or *charqui* (jerky), a strip of beef or llama meat that could be eaten with one hand. Argentinian barbecues developed into an all-day cookout broken into courses that focused on particular specialties, such as chicken, lamb, and *chinchulin* (cow's udder).

The U.S. Tradition

In the southern United States, according to D. Allen Willey, an essayist writing for the December 1896 issue of *Home-Maker's Magazine*, barbecue was to the Georgians "what the clambake is to Rhode Island, what a roast-beef dinner is to our English cousins, what canvas-back duck is to the Marylander, and what a pork-and-bean supper is to the Bostonian." (Walsh 1925, 95) He extolled the role of barbecue at socials, political rallies, and entertainments for strangers.

In the Carolinas, barbecuing remained a regional kitchen art that began with roasting shoulders or whole carcasses over oak or hickory coals. Unlike Texas-style barbecuing, the Carolina method called for succulent minced meat. Armed with cleavers and boning knives, cooks lopped away fat, chopped the softened meat into

fine cubes, and moistened it with an apple-cider vinegar sauce mixed with salt and pepper. A barbecue meal typically balanced spicy meat with hush puppies or corn cakes, dried beans, pickles, and cole slaw, all washed down with iced tea or beer.

Throughout the Jim Crow South, the reputation of black barbecue cooks enticed whites who otherwise shunned black restaurants. To avoid socializing with African-American diners, white customers ordered take-out, preferably from a drive-up window. Eventually, whites and blacks managed to eat together at community and church pits made famous by black cooks. The barbecue or pig-pickin' became a staple of candidates ranging from hopefuls for the office of sheriff to presidential candidates Andrew Jackson, John Tyler, Jimmy Carter, Lyndon Baines Johnson, Bill Clinton, and George W. Bush.

During the Republican presidential campaign of Rutherford B. Hayes in 1876 in Brooklyn, New York, Northern barbecue cooks led two oxen to Myrtle Park on October 18. They abandoned the traditional pit for a coke fire and iron pans paralleling the spit. The cooking area was roofed with metal to force drippings into the pans. The meat was ready on October 20. Within twenty minutes, some 50,000 diners descended on the scene and consumed chopped meat sandwiches while political speakers addressed the crowd.

Upon Lyndon Johnson's accession to the presidency after John F. Kennedy's assassination, the emphasis on Texas fare so unnerved the Kennedys' French chef René Verdon, he resigned rather than learn the "curiosities" of down-home Tex-Mex cooking. (Cannon & Brooks 1968, 515) The White House kitchen staff continued to barbecue for Lady Bird and Lyndon, who imported Fort Worth caterer Walter Jitton to throw a barbecue bash complete with cole slaw, potato salad, and apple turnovers in honor of first daughter Lynda Bird Johnson. To the consternation of Washington socialites, the Johnsons kept barbecue on the menu at White House dinners, both indoor and out.

The craze for barbecued meat moved to the suburban back yard after 1952, when George and Stephen Weber recycled two marine buoys as a grill, the original Weber charcoal-fired kettle cooker. The extension of kitchen work and dining to the patio accommodated the informality of American casual elegance. Outside the overheated kitchen, the barbecuer, often male, could put on an apron, don padded mitt, brandish oversized tools, and make a show of saucing and slicing. One indoor version placed the elevated barbecue spit on the den fireplace, above which an oversized hood carried cooking smells and grease away from table and floor.

The macho flair of campfire cookery inspired James A. Beard and Helen Evans Brown's *The Complete*

Book of Outdoor Cookery (1955). The book offered a plan for a homemade grill constructed of pipe, cinder blocks, and wire mesh. Whether at costly rotisserie or simple hibachi, the authors declared, "It is primarily a man's job and a woman, if she's smart, will keep it that way." (Lovegren 1995, 168) The text added that men enjoy charcoal grilling because it provides an opportunity for them to prove their culinary skills. The authors relegated women to a peripheral role as meal planners, marketers, prep cooks, and hostesses.

One enterprising Southern barbecue cook, Curtis Robinson, made a successful kitchen business of barbecue. To end a twenty-five-year career with the U.S. Postal Service, he chose to cook in his personalized mobile restaurant and pit cooker. Born in Hartford, Connecticut, he began cooking on weekends for neighbors and special customers. For research, he went to Lexington, North Carolina's barbecue capital. From local preferences, he learned to please the tastes of piedmont North Carolina and Virginia with a special sauce made of red pepper, black pepper, cayenne pepper, lemon juice, vinegar, mustard, and ketchup. At his numerous stops, he set up a van with a walk-up window to sell pork ribs, bulk barbecue, or barbecue sandwiches with sides of cole slaw, pinto beans, and soft drinks. In addition to selling barbecue and gourmet sauce to motorists and shoppers along highway 127 North in Hickory, North Carolina, he traveled to the campus of Appalachian State University in Boone, North Carolina, and catered private parties in Blowing Rock and Winston-Salem.

Farther west in the Southern states, barbecue cooks thicken sauce with tomatoes or ketchup. Across the Mississippi River into Arkansas, Louisiana, and Oklahoma, cooks balance barbecued pork with beef; Tennesseeans add ribs to the mix; Texans prefer beef only. Cooking in the Mississippi area calls for a burlap wrap and underground smoking or cooking in a pit over mesquite, hickory, or oak coals. Cooks baste with a sauce of vinegar, ketchup, butter, Worcestershire sauce, lemon juice, sugar, salt, and pepper. Across the Rio Grande, the barbecuers of Tlaxcala, Mexico, line their pits with fresh *pencas,* the leaves of the maguey, which impart a distinctive flavor.

Global Grilling

In Africa, barbecuing sets the tone for artful food preparation. On the Ivory Coast, cooks barbecue ears of corn alongside brochettes of meat. Called *braais* in Namibia, barbecuing is a standard cooking method, beginning with the purchase of sheep and goats for home slaughter of fresh meat. In Niger, cooks specialize in *kilshi*, a spicy jerked beef. South African cooks prepare *braaivleis* (barbecue) as a weekend treat cooked over a *jikka* (barrel grill) and slow-roast chewy *biltong* (jerky) for snack food and pizza topping. At the *slaghuis* (butcher shop) in Northern Transvaal, the *biltong* maker insists on selecting tender meat from Bonsmara cattle, fattened in the bushveld. Before marinating and drying slices, he hangs the meat for up to two days in the warm exhaust of his shop's refrigerators.

Josie Stow and Jan Baldwin's *The African Kitchen* (2000) describes the sounds, fragrance, and rhythms of a safari barbecue in the wilds of South Africa. Before cooks can sizzle meat, they collect camel thorn and limbs of the lead wood tree (*Combretum imberbe*) to produce dense fuel for long-lived embers lasting through the night. The hottest coals cook thin-sliced *braai* and heat *roosterkoek* (grilled bread) on a grate scraped clean with a wire brush.

In China, where farmyards have housed domesticated pigs from early times, pork is a major meat choice across the land. Barbecued pork, called *char siu* (held on a fork over flame), predates the oven. A version created in 1700 is *jan yau tai pong* (red cooked pork shoulder), a Shanghai specialty requiring searing and slow cooking. Cooks serve this barbecue for home celebrations, observances of birthdays, weddings, a son's first month of life, and funerals.

In Afghanistan and into the Himalayas, the traditional village barbecue celebrates weddings. A festive, uninhibited gathering with drinking and dance, the *barra kebab* (young goat roast) begins with the construction of a clay barbecue dais. The cook builds a charcoal fire on the platform and suspends sides of goat meat over the flame to roast. Diners slice away the pieces nearest the heat for eating as the cooking process continues.

In the 1970s, the American fad of home barbecuing spread from the United States to Europe, creating new markets for compressed hardwood briquettes, charcoal, liquid smoke, Japanese hibachis, grill lighters, and barbecuing tools. Gas grills became the rage at the end of the 1980s and have since outsold charcoal-burning models nearly two to one. Although more expensive than charcoal burners, gas grills acquired panache, especially among males. The best models grilled and slow-cooked faster than a charcoal user could bring conventional briquettes to the ember stage. One manufacturer offered a convection system that circulated hot air around meat. Competitors added porcelain-coated cast-iron or stainless steel grates for corrosion resistance, hood thermometers, smoke drawers, removable drip pans, trays for wood chips, and wheels for easy movement of the grill from storage to deck or poolside.

In the United States, home barbecuing in the twenty-first century kept pace with multicultural trends in cookery. According to Steve Raichlen, the author of *How to Grill: The Complete Illustrated Book of Barbecue Techniques, A Barbecue Bible!* (2001), backyard cuisine expressed the shared food preparation styles of many nations: "The Indonesian satay guy, the Indian tandoori master, the Argentinian *asador*, the Mexican *carnita* lady all have a lingua franca with the Texas brisket guy." (Luscombe 2001, 43)

Further Reading

Dulles, Foster Rhea. *A History of Recreation: America Learns to Play.* New York: Appleton-Century-Crofts, 1965.

Neustadt, Kathy. *Clambake: A History and Celebration of an American Tradition.* Amherst: University of Massachusetts Press, 1992.

BASKETRY

The craft of basket weaving evolved from the necessity for food gathering, preparation, transportation, and storage. The shape and design of the oldest examples suggests that early practitioners may have imitated birds' nests. Basketry developed into woman's work by its connection with home, childcare, and, especially, food storage and cooking.

From 10,000 to 8000 BCE, coil-and-plait-style basketry worked by Nile Delta artisans served to line subterranean granaries. Around 7500 BCE, basket makers plied their craft at Danger Cave, Utah; five hundred years later, natives living in Huachocana Cave, Argentina, made coiled baskets, evidenced by extant coiling tools. Around 5270 BCE, basket weavers left matrix impressions in the mud of Jarmo, Iran. In 5000 BCE, southwestern American aborigines molded cook pots in baskets wattle-and-daub style before developing pottery as a craft on its own. The waterproof pot quickly reduced the need for baskets, particularly in the preparation, transportation, and storage of watery foods or grains small enough to slip through all but the tightest grid.

A group known as the Basketmakers flourished in the Rio Grande Valley from 100 to 500 CE. Among their works were yucca-leaf vessels woven tightly enough to hold water. By 600 CE they had expanded the foodstuffs preserved in their kitchen storage pits to include beans and dried turkey meat. Within a century, a shift in housing construction earned them the name the Pueblos.

For harvest collectors, cook pots, serving trays, and storage vessels, early Native Americans wove or netted lightweight baskets from pine needles, spruce root, cane, raffia, grass, reeds, straw, or twigs. Baskets containing foodstuffs such as seeds, nuts, and dried fruits were suspended above the floor to keep the contents safe from gnawing rodents and weevils. Along South America's west coast, the Inca, who inhabited Ecuador, Peru, and Chile, wove vines and withies into kitchen tools. With a winnowing basket, they could separate the chaff from threshed stalks of quinoa, or pigweed, a cereal grain that they simmered into porridge or soup, baked, or used in brewing.

In ancient Greece, basket makers wove travel containers and knotted twig nets for seining. Greek grain winnowers used a woven scoop called a *liknon*, modeled on the cradle of the infant Dionysus, god of wine. A Roman parallel survives in the cornucopia, symbol of harvest plenty and thanksgiving.

In northern Europe, artisans chose bulrushes and willow withies as materials for the slat (or slath) basket and rush mat. In Scotland, a framed wicker scull, a flat-bottomed receptacle with one raised side, carried coiled fishing line. Throughout the islands, fishermen depended on woven eel pots and herring swills for transporting their catch from dock to cook pot. On the Orkney and Shetland islands, weavers used heather stalks and roots to make the fish *caizie* (creel).

The medieval British homesteader braided straw into rope on a throw cock or spindle for coiling into bottle covers, lidded baskets, bread trays, and other domestic items. The Skye hen or ose basket, called a Scotch basket in Sweden, carried broody hens from one croft to another. Because marketers had to provide their own containers, the oval shopping basket was useful for holding odd-shaped staples. A dual-lobed egg basket, also called a shoe basket or granny's fanny, kept eggs from rolling together and cracking. A malt skip aided the brewer in shoveling barley. The huckmuck or barrel strainer fitted over a tap on the vessel's interior to separate liquid from dregs. A deep fruit picker, with a more ample body than the garden basket, accompanied the gatherer up a ladder for selecting ripe pears, apples, or grape clusters. In the kitchen, the bottle basket kept glass containers from clinking together, while a willow tray, dish frame, and plate holders were useful for carrying meals to sick family members.

American colonists brought their own weaving traditions and adapted the more delicate Indian berry basket to farm chores by pounding thin wood strips for weaving. The Dutch, who had to smuggle the *Salix americana* willow into the United States, made a basket of green twigs, kept it moist on the Atlantic crossing, then dismantled it upon arrival and planted the ends as cuttings. The Pennsylvania Dutch added dough baskets and skeps, coiled straw beehives that adorned gardens and encouraged bees to make their hives close to human habitations for easy recovery of honey and wax, both domestic essentials. Other immigrant peoples copied Indian splinting and wove new designs—a nonslip hexagonal pattern for ox muzzles, clam and cheese baskets, eel traps and fish creels, charcoal and winnowing sieves, egg baskets, cheese drainers, and vinegar funnels.

Around 1700, slaves brought from West Africa a tradition of tightly woven, coiled storage baskets. On the coast of South Carolina and Georgia, they made the most of bulrushes, longleaf pine needles, palmetto leaves, and soft, pliant sweetgrass, a swampland treasure that produced a waterproof basket that could be washed, dried, and reused. Still produced by the descendents of slaves, these baskets represent one of the nation's oldest African-American crafts. The tradition involves the entire family—men and boys gather the materials, while girls and women create the initial round disk and stitch the tight, multi-hued weave.

One noted East Coast basketry style employed men, particularly the sailors staffing the first Nantucket lightship, the *Nantucket South Shoal*, built in 1853. Three years later, Yankee seamen who were familiar with basketry in ports in China, India, and the Philippines brought basket molds on board and wove farm and home baskets to occupy them during an eight-month assignment on the floating lighthouse. In port from 1854 to 1905, they created Nantucket Lightship baskets, a style modeled on Indian examples. Beginning with a wood base ribbed to hold withies of rattan, oak, or hickory, they pounded ribbing into grooves to make them sturdy. By weaving over molds, they developed nested baskets, lunch baskets, and a distinctive lidded oval carryall enhanced with cherry and walnut staves, bone knobs, pairs of carved drop handles, and ivory, ebony, and bone scrimshaw insets.

In the Appalachian hills, farmers carried a cropping or field basket for harvesting cabbage heads and ears of corn. The storekeeper used bartering or measurement baskets to mete out pecks and bushels of goods to home shoppers. To size a new basket, the maker poured in a known quantity of loose corn, oats, or barley and marked on the edge the height of a pint, quart, or gallon or of various degrees of dry measure. The standard for a bushel was an English model, the Winchester Bushel, a 2150.42 cubic inch cylinder that was eight inches high and 18.5 inches in diameter. The next size up was the firlot, a Scottish dry measure that held 50 percent more.

Late in the twentieth century, South African basketry recovered traditional methods. The native basket makers of Hlabisa outside Durban in Zululand relearned their failing art after 1972, when the Reverend Kjel Lofroth, a Swedish missionary, set up the Vukani Association in Eshowe's former post office. Out of respect for Zulu traditions, he fostered indigenous

domestic arts, such as setting tables with stick mats. Local artisans once again gathered and hand-rolled grasses, palm fronds, and rushes and made natural dyes. They were best known for the saucer-shaped *imbenge* used as a girdle for a clay beer jug, the crater-sided *unyazi* for storing millet or pulse, and the *iqoma*, an ample container for carrying foodstuffs on the head. They also made the bulbous *isichumo*, a close-stitched, watertight carafe and lid for transporting and serving beer. The secret of its impermeability was a fiber that swelled when wet. An addition to the Zulu basket trade was the *ivovo*, a narrow, woven sieve for straining sprouted millet from the neck of a *ukhamba*, a broad-bellied clay beer vat.

In the same era, English weavers sometimes began with a stout oak rectangle or square pierced with holes to hold rush withies for interlacing. In Ireland, the farm wicker worker often shaped a nesting basket for hens, eel traps, a *sciathóg* for holding potatoes during planting, and a trug, the squat harvest basket that held freshly dug potatoes and carrots. Other European styles reflected idiosyncratic basketry shapes and techniques, such as the woven fish traps of the Khanty, seminomadic reindeer herders of the west Siberian tundra. Weavers in the Balkans equipped mushroom baskets with a shoulder strap to leave the gatherer's hands free for a smaller basket in which to put herbs and greenery gathered along the way.

Despite industrialization and the development of materials such as aluminum, stainless steel, and plastic, the traditional kitchen uses of baskets have persisted. Fine antique baskets have brought high prices, although many stay in use despite their increasing value as collectibles.

See also **Sieves and Strainers**

Further Reading

Brown, Carol, "Zulu Basketry," *Lantern*, August 1994, 23–26.
Goodrich, Frances Louisa. *Mountain Homespun*. Knoxville: University of Tennessee Press, 1989.
Kudo, Kazuyoshi. *Japanese Bamboo Baskets*. Tokyo: Kodansha Internaitonal, 1980.

BEARD, JAMES

American food and cooking expert James Andrews Beard promoted excellence and variety in dining experiences. A native of Portland, Oregon, he was born on May 5, 1903 to Mary Elizabeth Jones Beard and Jonathan A. Beard, a shipyard appraiser. His mother taught him cookery of all types, including informal dishes suitable for picnics, backyard feasts, and barbecues. In the introduction to *The Cook's Catalogue* (1975), Beard quipped, "I grew up in the Iron Age of

American cookery. We had a cast-iron wood stove.... For stove top cooking we used iron skillets, iron Dutch ovens, and iron stew pots." He declared iron the king in his mother's kitchen in Gearhart, seventy miles northwest of Portland, but conferred some culinary credit on "earthenware, tin, some copper, and the ghastly enameled pots known as graniteware."

After expulsion from Reed College on the grounds that he was a homosexual, Beard studied at the University of Washington. He took up a career in singing and drama, taking roles on radio and on the stage in *Othello* and *Cyrano de Bergerac* in the 1920s until nodes on his vocal cords impaired his voice. In 1933, he gave private cooking lessons and worked briefly as a teacher of English, French, and history at a private school in New Jersey. On an intuition that American cuisine was ripe for a renaissance of its various immigrant traditions, he embarked on a culinary career, establishing an eclectic Manhattan catering business, Hors d'Oeuvre, Inc., which served French, Italian, and Russian menus at Upper East Side tables.

Like other men of his generation, Beard was drafted during World War II. After a stint as a decoder for the army air corps, he returned home to work at a dairy and truck farm in Reading, Pennsylvania. He followed a trend in world cookery while directing military officers' clubs in Cristobal, Marseilles, Naples, Puerto Rico, and Rio de Janeiro. A natural organizer, he adeptly managed kitchen workers and serving staff and published his first food book, *Fowl and Game Cookery* (1944), which launched his reputation for gourmet cuisine.

In the infancy of television, Beard became one of a coterie of pioneer TV cooks. In 1948, he demonstrated kitchen techniques on the Borden Company's *Elsie Presents*. He developed a varied career as a public speaker, restaurant consultant, hobby and food festival demonstrator, benefit organizer, and author of a second book, *The Fireside Cook Book: A Complete Guide to Fine Cooking for Beginner and Expert* (1949), which contained 1,217 recipes and 400 color photos. Chapters covered the usual menu items plus outdoor cookery, frozen foods, pick-up meals, menus for warm and cold weather, and wines and liquors. He stripped food preparation of European pretensions and did away with multicourse feasts served on exquisite china. Primarily American in focus, his presentations returned to the basics but avoided the humdrum by appealing to the senses.

At age fifty-two, Beard opened a cooking school and experimental kitchen, originally at New York's Lexington Hotel and later at the corporate headquarters of *McCall's* magazine with a branch in Seaside, Oregon. He gained further recognition by promoting Green Giant vegetables, Planter's peanuts, and Spice Islands seasonings. At age fifty-six, he chose New York City's Greenwich Village as his base and set about boosting America's confidence in its own kitchens. At a half-moon-shaped workstation, he taught amateur cooks how to create party platters, buffets, crêpes, soufflés, omelets, breads, and sauces. A key to preparation, he taught, was constant tasting to determine how combinations and heat altered flavor and texture.

To maintain a fresh perspective, Beard traveled Europe, studied regional cuisine, critiqued restaurants, and traded in-crowd gossip with West Coast food historian Helen Evans Brown. His correspondence with the latter was the source of his memoir *James Beard: Love and Kisses and a Halo of Truffles: Letters To Helen Evans Brown* (1994). He was one of the first food critics to denounce lowered standards in venues that catered to tourists. His touchstone was L'Auberge de Père Bise, a two-star Michelin restaurant south of Geneva, Switzerland, on Lake Annecy, which he declared the hallmark of discriminating cookery. In the 1950s, America's golden age of cooking, he wrote columns for *Woman's Day, Harper's Bazaar,* and *Vogue* and published works on Parisian foods, fish, barbecue and rotisserie cooking (including the popular 1975 book *Barbecuing with Beard*), entertaining, patio cooking, and budget recipes. Of his eight books from that decade, *The James Beard Cookbook* (1958) became a national classic in hardbound and paperback. Reprising his life's work, *American Cooking* (1972) summarized his regard for the nation's cuisine and earned him an honorary degree from Reed College.

Sparkling and witty until his death at age eighty-two, Beard left unfinished his last memoir, *Memories and Menus*. To fans, he epitomized hospitality and fun. His preference for bold color, prize wines, and new developments in food processors, microwaves, and kitchen gadgetry continued unabated. A link between the prominent chefs of his homeland and those of Europe, he valued regional traditions and fresh produce from local markets. He admired a melange of American dishes featuring corn and beans, nuts, and strawberries and revived such working-class treasures as fried tomatoes, Indian pudding, and scrapple. Against the tide of Julia Child chic, he spoke the language of common eating pleasures. Friends transformed his home into the James Beard Foundation and established annual James Beard awards for cookbooks and chefs as a tribute to the "Father of American Gastronomy."

Further Reading

Beard, James. *Beard on Bread.* New York: Alfred A. Knopf, 1973.

_____. *Delights and Prejudices*. New York: Atheneum, 1964.

Jacobs, Jay, "James Beard, an American Icon," *Gourmet*, February 1984, 26–39.

BEECHER, CATHARINE ESTHER

An educator, social reformer, and home economist Catharine Esther Beecher, sister of abolitionist and writer Harriet Beecher Stowe and author of *A Treatise on Domestic Economy for the Use of Young Ladies at Home and at School* (1841), spoke eloquently and forcefully on behalf of the overtaxed housewife. The eldest of eight children, Beecher was born in East Hampton, New York, on September 6, 1800, to mill worker Roxanna Foote and the Reverend Lyman Beecher, New York's foremost Congregationalist preacher. Imbued with a blend of her father's Calvinist idealism and her mother's pragmatic home skills, Catharine spent her girlhood in Connecticut and enrolled at Miss Pierce's School for young ladies in Litchfield, where she learned artistic refinement and literature as well as mathematics and science.

At age twenty-three, Beecher opened the Hartford Female Seminary on funds from her father and $5,000 in contributions from like-minded local women. Still educating herself in the classics and science, she added courses in philosophy, history, modern foreign languages, mathematics, home economics, the arts, and chemistry to elevate her school to the level of comparable institutions for men. Ignoring detractors who scorned equal opportunities for female students, she offered physical education and equipped her school with laboratory equipment and a slide projector to demonstrate astronomy. Her faculty enlarged to eight teachers and drew girls from other states to a teaching regimen recognized as one of the country's most enlightened.

Unwilling to bide her time until marriage, as her family advised, Beecher developed leadership potential and, at age thirty-one, shifted her coursework to concentrate on teacher training. Leaving the school in the control of eighteen-year-old Harriet, Catharine took a principal's post at Cincinnati's Lane Theological Seminary and, in 1833, opened the Western Female Institute, where she focused on moral improvement to combat the barbarism of the unsettled West. Public outrage at her notions of social and racial betterment forced her to return to New England, from whence she launched an egalitarian vision of education through a speaking tour of the Atlantic seaboard.

Beecher's books on home economics greatly increased her fame and influence on young women and educators. As an authority on domestic conditions, she lectured and wrote on the future of systematic home

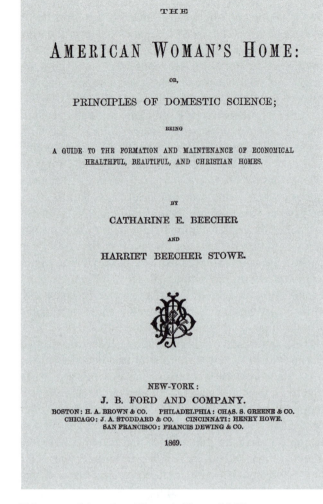

Title page of *American Woman's Home* (1869).

cleaning, kitchen maintenance, child care, gardening, diet and health, hygiene, hobbies, etiquette, and nursing—all elements of the woman's domestic role. Among her hopes for the future were hot-and-cold water systems and efficient kitchen appliances. In her view, there was a strong irony in the behavior of people who attended little to their own personal hygiene while devoting hours to the washing and grooming of their horses.

Beecher affirmed the role of the housewife in the trans-Mississippi cities she visited by riverboat, carriage, and stage. In her estimation, housewifery was an "honorable and serious profession, one which requires training and specialized knowledge, one which embraces high responsibilities." (Cheney 2000, 16) In *Letters to Persons Engaged in Domestic Service* (1842), she established a familiar credo: "A place for everything and everything in its place." (Hoy 1995, 21)

Beecher continued her work for women by founding the American Woman's Educational Association in 1852. She also promoted the cause in her writings, including *The Duty of American Women to Their Country* (1845), *The Evils Suffered by American Women and American Children* (1846), *Letters to the People on Health and Happiness* (1854), *Physiology and Calisthenics for Schools and Families* (1856), and *Common Sense Applied to Religion* (1857). With Harriet's aid, but mostly on her own initiative, she augmented her *Treatise on Domestic Economy* into a pro-female classic, *The American Woman's Home, or Principles of Domestic Science* (1869). The text championed the physical reorganization of the home, placing the kitchen alongside the dining room and thus restoring the cook to her place at the family table.

The most famous of the Beecher sisters' collaborations was *The American Woman's Home.* The elevated moral tone if its subtitle—"Being a Guide to the Formation and Maintenance of Economical, Healthful, Beautiful, and Christian Homes"—clearly derived from Victorian standards. Harriet summarized the need for home science with a restatement of Benjamin Franklin's aphorism, "Silk and satins put out a kitchen fire." To her way of thinking, it was not luxury and pretense that jeopardized contentment, but the lack of training in domestic skills.

As a model of the efficient kitchen, Catharine chose the ship's galley, which contained every vessel and utensil needed for cooking for 200 crew members and was arranged to maximize effort and reduce steps. Following chapters on the Christian family, the coauthors presented drawings of a two-stage kitchen and stove room lined with shelves and fitted with a pot box, drain and sink, and locked closet. The plan included a laundry, an ice closet, linen closet, ironing table, and bins for storing vegetables and fruits.

The authors expressed the importance of protecting the family from poisonous air with drawings of the respiratory system. They warned of using gas burners in unventilated parlors and explained the physics of a flue, chimney, stove, and furnace. Their use of geometry to explain the superiority of a corrugated firebox argues for the acceptance of educated women as domestic experts.

The chapter on healthy foods, which follows entries on healthful living and exercise, dismisses the "Grahamite" or vegetarian philosophy, which elevated vegetable foods over animal. (Beecher and Stowe 1994, 122) Ranking foods in order of their nutritional importance, they placed bread and butter first and second, followed by meat, vegetables, and tea and other beverages. As was common among Calvinists, they dismissed alcoholic drinks, opiates, and tobacco as destructive.

In Chapter 30, the authors considered the cleaning and upkeep of specific rooms. They advocated teaching young girls to maintain a "neat and cheerful kitchen." (Ibid., 371) Their requirements were practical—a room above ground and well lighted, with a large sink, an underground drain, and attractive plantings cultivated around doors and windows. They preferred whitewashed walls, a painted or oilcloth-covered floor, and a sink scalded daily with hot lye.

Rules for dishwashing included the use of a linen swab, towels and dishcloths, hard soap on a fork, and a slop pail. Their advocacy of recycling dictated the first stage in the dishwashing process, scraping of plates into a pail, placing grease in a catch basin, and saving used tea leaves for sweeping. The second stage suggested washing "the nicest articles" first, then rinsing, and draining. The third stage demanded the addition of hot water for washing greasier dishes and sudsing the ends of knives and forks. The last stage involved a clean supply of suds for washing milk pans, tins, and buckets before scouring roaster, griddle, posts, and kettles. The meticulous housekeeper would empty and scald the slop pail, dry teapots and tins to prevent rust, order the fireplace, and sweep and dust before retiring from the kitchen.

Catharine Beecher's *The New Housekeeper's Manual* (1873), a guide to household economy, health, beauty, and the home, included "The Handy Cook-Book." Published late in her career, it contained a sentimental drawing opposite the title page that reflected her home-centered philosophy: A mother, bending over a child reading a book, sits at the center of a family of six. In addition to three children, she is flanked by an elderly man and a contemporary, presumably her husband. A lamp suspended from the wall casts a radiance on the woman's neatly dressed hair. The picture captures Beecher's contention that a strong mother is the fount of the home and source of character and strength in the community. At Catharine Beecher's death on May 12, 1878, she was one of the nation's most respected experts on education, teacher training, and domestic science.

Further Reading

Beecher, Catharine E. *The New Housekeeper's Manual.* New York: J. B. Pond & Co., 1873.

BEER

Beer is a low-alcohol drink produced in different forms by peoples around the world. All beers have in common the use of starchy materials, such as cereal grains, and yeast for fermentation. In Europe and North America, the most common varieties are made from malted barley, with hops added for flavoring.

Home-brewed beer has traditionally served as a beverage and an additive to bread and porridge as well as a ritual item, used, for example, by ceremonial dancers of the Bobo in Burkina Faso and among Surma mourners at funerals in Ethiopia. The burial site of an Ethiopian woman dating to around 2800 BCE suggests that she may have been respected for her role as cook and brewer. From 3000 to 1500 BCE, the Valdivians of Las Vegas, Ecuador, managed a thriving civilization in which beer occupied a central position in home cookery. At a ritual plaza at Real Alto, ceremonial beer consumption was a focus of communal activity.

Early Brewing Methods

In the eastern Mediterranean, Mesopotamian brewers earned a high status that carried prestige as well as a top salary. Their equipment included mills, crucibles, filters and sieves, and drip bottles. Before 2000 BCE, Sumerian brewing of barley and emmer wheat resulted in nineteen recipes for beer. As outlined in the "Hymn to Ninkasi" (ca. 1900 BCE), the job was a labor-intensive process that involved watering, soaking, and spreading mash on reed mats and filtering it into vats. The addition of malt, cereal grain, herbs, and honey varied the standard liquid. Brewed primarily by women, who received brewing equipment as bridal gifts, Mesopotamian date beer became an in-house kitchen business. These home pubs caused concern to Hammurabi, the supreme lawmaker who set legal price limits for drinks in 1750 BCE. Any homemaker found cheating customers received a dunk in the river for breaking the law. For serving criminals, the barmaid earned a death sentence.

The alliance between the bake oven and the brewery was crucial. As described in Astri Riddervold and Andreas Ropeid's *Food Conservation* (1988), the beer-making process began with kneading, molding, and lightly baking beer bread. Loaves made from barley or spelt corn cooled on mats before the brewer broke them up to soak in a clay vat or wood canoe-trough filled with water. The pulp, mashed and stirred with pestles or by treading underfoot, went from tank to basket or trough before workers sieved the liquid into fermenting tubs.

Egyptian brewmasters, who monopolized yeast for baking and brewing, systematized the process of preparing grain for *hekit* (beer). With a gang of slaves, the brewer oversaw the cracking of grain in a mortar, rolling of cracked grain into flour with a grinding stone, and kneading of dough for oven baking. In the next stage, the fresh loaves went to the treaders, who dampened it and stamped it into pulp. Strainers passed the mash through sieves. From clay vats, workers poured pure liquid beer through midriff spouts to rid it of barm (yeast formed by fermentation) and dregs. At the brewery built for Nefertiti in El-Marna about 1350 BCE, workers made beer and baked holy bread for rituals. Glyphs depicting this work show a male slave tramping mash in a shoulder-high vat.

Celtic brewing was the work of brewsters, female workers who chewed grain and spit it into fermentation vats. After warming the slurry, they mounded the vats with soil and left the mix to make alcohol by the action of salivary enzymes, which transformed starch into sugar. Before the beer jar could be reused, it had to be cleansed of its "beer strong" by several weeks of steeping. Even with this precaution, the container was suitable only for cold liquids. Around 360, the Roman emperor Julian, a snob who belittled Celtic drink as uncouth, penned snide doggerel about Celtic beer and resulting flatulence.

When the Greco-Syrian travel writer Poseidonius the Athlete visited Celtic Gaul late in the first century BCE, he described table service and etiquette among a people who took dining and drinking seriously. In a strongly masculine warrior society, male drinkers sometimes fought to the death over the choicest portions of meat. The wealthy drank imported French or Italian wine, while the poorest people drank *corma,* a honeyed wheat beer.

The remains of drinking paraphernalia and massive beer storehouses offer proof of the centrality of beer drinking in ancient times. Finds in the eastern Mediterranean indicate that the beer tankard came with its own sieve to separate husks from liquid. Archeologists discovered the oldest surviving beer cache in the Roman province of Bezirk near Vienna, Austria. The Latin name for the drink was *cerevesia* after the grain goddess Ceres. The beer found in Bezirk had remained undisturbed in a round jug beneath the cellar steps of a house built in 300 CE. When diggers removed the jug, the remaining dark brown mass proved to be a recognizable form of beer that Czechs still call by its Latin name. In Joya de Cerén, El Salvador, destroyed by a volcanic eruption in 595 CE, the remains of a large vat of beer marked a building that appears to have been a men's club.

Those skilled in beer making stood to advance in society. Around 800, Charlemagne, king of the Franks, took a personal interest in the royal brewery. He invited all brewmasters to come to his court, where he personally instructed them on methods of producing a quality brew. Just as he handpicked his counselors and military commanders, he sorted through the brewers to find the best superintendents for the royal staff. In the time of King Gorm the Old Jutland, who came to the throne in 899, Danish brewers earned honor for their profession, as did Scandinavia's monastery brewmasters. The monks at Burton-on-Trent, England, discovered that the secret ingredient to a sparkling beverage was the local water, celebrated in song and verse for its clarity.

Bavaria was especially rich in cloistered breweries, which supported the monks while providing them and their guests and pilgrims with drink. In 859, a Bavarian brewer added hops to the mash, a development recorded in the writings of the German herbalist Hildegard of Bingen in the eleventh century and adopted by abbey beverage makers. The monastery of Weltenburg, possibly the world's oldest monastery brewery, established production in the 1000s, about the same time that St. Gallus founded St. Gallen, site of a large brewery. Another local beer producer, the Weihenstephan abbey, owned a recipe for ale that dated to the 900s.

Drink of the Common Folk

Anglo-Saxon peasants considered beer a dietary staple. The *Kalevala* (ca. 1200), Finland's epic, warns of overindulgence: "Beer isn't such a blessing to men as it's supposed to be; the more you swallow, the less you stay the master of your mind." (Terry 1990, 12) Because of beer's link to the barbarian tribes of Gallia and Germania, Roman insurgents distanced themselves from the proletarian drink and stocked their pantries with wine.

Among the learned, medieval beer earned less medical respect than wine, primarily because the most prestigious physicians of the era were Arabian, Spanish, or Italian—all wine-making and wine-drinking ethnic groups. Members of the servant class, who received no wine allotment, contented themselves with ales and beer, which they made from barley, oats, wheat, or a blend of grains. The castle alewife superintended brewing from grain harvested on local fiefs. In Finland, brewers strained mash in a long *kuurna* (tub) carved canoe-style with a hatchet and adze from a tree trunk. For a sieve, the brewer layered wood shavings on the bottom and covered them with rye or oat straw. To heat the mix to enhance fermentation of microorganisms in the wood, the technician dropped in heated stones. For additives and flavorings, Scandinavian brewers preferred yarrow, marsh tea, meadowsweet, cowslip, wormwood, or sweet gale. On the Continent, the favorites were juniper bark and berries.

Beer, purer than most of the available drinking water, prompted many a caution on moderation. A medieval alert about malting warned, "The drying mault steam is soporific, it is almost impossible not to become drowsy [so the worker should keep singing, to prove she is awake and not falling asleep and letting it burn.]" (Hartley 1979, 192) In the early thirteenth-century text *Le Régime du Corps* (Regular Care of the Body), Aldobrandino of Sienna warned that beer harmed brain function and digestion, rotted the teeth and soured the breath, caused gas, and led to inebriation. On its positive side, he noted that the drink, taken with meals, aided the urinary tract and lightened the complexion.

As of the 1300s, beer and ale were the regular choice of English, Dutch, and German drinkers. In the Dutch province of Utrecht, Amersfoort alone boasted 350 breweries. In a gesture of friendship, Henry V, on his betrothal to Catherine of Valois in 1420, sent her father, Charles VI of France, a beer mug, a symbol of everyday pleasure from one male to another. Andrewe Boorde, author of *A Dyetary of Helth* (ca. 1530), cleared the reputation of malt ale, but he declared beer a drink suitable only for the Dutch and predicted that it would be the downfall of the English tippler, who would grow fat and big-bellied. In the Elizabethan era, ale brewers produced a varied number of strengths, ranging from small ale to double, along with a potent multiple-strength ale nicknamed "Mad Dog," "Huffcap," "Father Whoreson," and "Dragons' Milk." (Singman)

In 1525, home brewing of household beer, also called March beer, from hops, added to the number of table beverages. Flavorings extended to hops and fruits, a source of yeast, and included herbal blends, common to Westphalian brands. Although Alexander Nowell, Dean of St. Paul's in London, invented bottled beer in 1568, home concoctions remained the norm. In his *Description of Elizabethan England* (1577), the clergyman William Harrison described how his wife ground eight bushels of malt in a quern or hand mill, then stirred in a half bushel each of oats and wheat meal before dispersing it in 240 gallons of boiling water. Heating over a flame required testing the liquor and adding hops for a two-hour simmer until the appropriate color of ale appeared and the drink lost all tartness. He commented that "beer that is used at noblemen's tables in their fixed and standing houses is commonly a year old, or peradventure of two year's tunning or more…but, for the [ordinary] household, it is usually not under a month's age."

Harrison made definitive statements about the purity of beer and about tippling. Of the brewer's choice of water for the process, Harrison preferred "the fattest standing water" as opposed to the "fenny and marsh." He offered a tip to the drinker who suspected the alewife of adulterating his drink with salt and resin. To remove the latter, a red-hot knife blade pushed to the bottom of the stein caused the resin to cling to the tip for easy removal. Salt, he noted, only increased thirst, forcing the drinker to drink himself into a stupor "and so doth he carry off a dry drunken noll to bed with him, except his luck be the better."

Drinkers passed a communal tankard or loving cup marked with wooden pins to indicate one draught. An invitation to "have a peg" invited a newcomer to an equal share, but Archbishop Anselm decreed that "priests shall not drink to pins." (Pinto 1949, 13) A whistle ("weesil" or "wizzel") carved into the handle allowed the last drinker to summon the bartender for a refill—hence the phrases "wet your whistle" and "whistle for it." At the inner base of the drinking bowl, a boss or medallion—called a founce, frounce, or print—carried stars or animal shapes, family crests, or profiles of the Virgin Mary, depending on the company sharing a drink.

In the seventeenth century, the tedious task of stirring barley brew with rowers and of removing it to mash vats with scavels and jets preceded the steeping of malt in boiling water. Additives and treatments required a list of special equipment—a copper coil, cooler, chunk, yealding vat, and tubes called cowls. Along with yeast tuns and casks and a leaded trough, the brewer needed a pulley to load the finished brew onto carts for transportation to a storage room. On a smaller scale, one recipe from Hannah Wooley's *The Queen-like Closet; or Rich Cabinet* (1670) suggested that the home cook stir up a draft of small beer, a cold summer drink for children, from beer and sack, a manchet (small loaf), currants, sugar, and nutmeg.

In the 1770s, Captain James Cook, the English explorer who mapped the New Zealand coastline, brewed that island nation's first beer. Adapted from an English recipe, the formula may have included spruce bark, tea leaves, molasses, and malt essence. Cooks' purpose was medicinal: He used beer along with sauerkraut and island fruit to prevent scurvy in his sailors, who suffered loose teeth, aching joints, and eventual death if they did not ingest ascorbic acid in some form. His contribution to the history of beer survives in New Zealand's Captain Cook brand.

In the British Isles, the coopered oak keg bound in willow or cane, the standard vessel for beer and ale, was known as a costrel, beaver barrel, or beaver keg. From these large vats, Irish hosts served ale to peasant guests in *lámhógs* and *methers* made from willow, ash, beech, and elm; Welsh barkeeps preferred goblets of yew wood. An 1818 painting by the Scottish portraitist Sir David Wilkie entitled "The Penny Wedding" shows Scots serving brew from an oak-jack (barrel) to a staved bicker (pitcher) to be poured into individual *cuachs* or *quaichs* or small *coggies* or *luggies,* straight-sided tankards similar to beakers. Scots woodworkers carved their drinking vessels with a pocketknife and banded them in willow from the bottom to an inch from the top. An unusual example, the *quaich* of Bonnie Prince Charlie, featured a glass spy panel at bottom and a sage warning against assassins: "For its bottom

is of glass that he who quaffed might keep his eye the while upon the dirk hand of his [enemy]." (Pinto 1949, 26) In *Furth in Field* (1900), a volume of essays on the life, language and literature of old Scotland, Hugh Haliburton (pseudonym of James Logie Robertson) wrote that barley first earned fame for its use in beer making: "From the Lothians in the south, to the scarcely inferior barley-soils of Moray in the north, the great mass of the harvest is destined for distillation and brewing, and only an insignificant proportion will find its way to the mill." (McNeill 1929, 14) The lightest, least worthy leavings went to the cereal mill for the making of porridge and oatcakes.

Brewing in the American Colonies

In 1620, the pilgrims aboard the *Mayflower* chose a Massachusetts landing site because they were running low on beer aboard ship. In colonial America, beer and other alcoholic beverages were preferred to water from wells or springs, which was often a source of disease. The first breweries at the Massachusetts Bay and Rhode Island colonies began business in 1637 and 1638; in Virginia, George Fletcher set up as brewer in 1652, but with limited success.

A number of North American garden plants and natural substances served the brewer, including pumpkins, persimmons, and maple sugar as well as spruce tips, hemlock branches, sassafras, and birch sap. Suppliers of alehouses malted beer by drying sprouted barley to add sweetness to the mash, which steeped slowly at a low simmer to keep it from souring. At the brewing stage, the mash plus hops and herbs boiled before the addition of yeast, obtained either from bread or an existing beer batch. Within a day, the mix began to bubble. Drinkers usually diluted the native brew with water to produce a watery, low-alcohol small beer that required little fermentation.

Breweries thrived in Pennsylvania, where German farmers raised ample barley and hops and bouncing bet, or soapwort *(Saponaria ocymoides)*, a common lavender-flowered herb that produced foamy heads. Householders supplied horn and glass cups, also stone jugs, Flanders jugs, or "tipt" (spouted) jugs; the privileged could offer German gresware (ceramic) tipped in silver, such as that owned by Massachusetts governor John Winthrop. (Earle 1975, 99) Another type of vessel, the Fulham jug, bore the initials G.R. for Georgius Rex, the first English Hanoverian monarch. Beginning brewers consulted an English source, William Cobbett's *Cottage Economy* (1821), which listed home beer-making equipment, including copper kettle, mash tub, underbuck, tun, and coolers. The text explained how to store beer casks in an earth-bermed cellar, preferably dry and undisturbed, during the fermentation period.

Twentieth-Century Traditions

Brewing has influenced numerous recipes. Beer cookery characterized Belgian cuisine until World War II, when old methods faded from use. In the 1950s, the master chef Raoul Morleghem revived the tradition of beer-based cooking. As a result of his promotion of traditional home cooking, Belgian restaurants returned to such national dishes as Lapin du Brasseur (Brewer's Rabbit) and Ballekes à la Bière (Rissoles in Beer Sauce). Regional cookery reflects the emphasis on beer in sweet-and-sour sauce and *carbonnades,* rich cottage stews flavored with beer and onions.

In the 1970s, the Sherpa of Nepal considered beer a necessity for hospitality. Among guests, they distributed flasks of *chhang,* a thick drink brewed from barley or millet. To enhance the taste, they smeared the rims of the flasks with rancid butter. Each guest had to drink three glasses of *chhang* to satisfy local beer-drinking etiquette. In the same period in the United States, beer drinkers could buy their own complete microbrewery system, a home kit consisting of barrel with spigot, starter for West Coast pale ale and Oktoberfest Vienna lager, plus recipes for thirty variations producing twenty twelve-ounce servings.

At the end of the twentieth century, beer remained a traditional kitchen specialty in Sweden. In Skåne, householders brewed a domestic supply of small beer, as they had since the 1700s, for serving in jug, pitcher, or tankard at every meal. Generally available especially in farm kitchens during haying and reaping were refreshments of beer and rye bread, whether eaten separately or combined into *drickasupa* (hot small beer soup) or *drickablandning* (cold small beer mix). Another combination, small beer and milk, complemented meals heavy with fried potatoes or other salty foods. The drink was a standard tonic for women who gave birth at home. Nils-Arvid Bringéus's article "A Swedish Beer Milk Shake" cited one diner's memory of a meal that featured "a big dish or bowl with small beer and milk" from which the assembled company "each took a sup with their horn spoons now and then." (Lysaght 1994, 141)

See also **Monastery Kitchens; Yeast**

Further Reading

Beckwith, Carol, and Angela Fisher. *African Ceremonies.* 2 vols. New York: Harry N. Abrams, Inc., 1999.

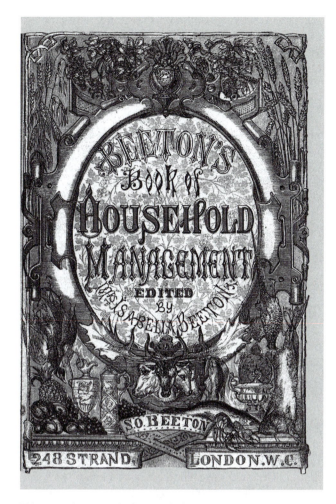

Title page from *Book of Household Management* (1861).

BEETON, ISABELLA

No name from Victorian English cookery is as well known as that of Isabella Beeton, a food writer, editor, and doyenne of the kitchen. Born Isabella Mary Mayson on March 14, 1836, in Cheapside, London, to Benjamin and Elizabeth Mayson, she was the eldest of three children. Her father died when she was young, and her mother married the racecourse entrepreneur and publisher Henry Dorling of Epsom, Surrey, when Isabella was four. The family grew to twenty-one children, a brood that gave Isabella considerable experience in childcare and domestic duties. After years of piano lessons in London, she studied music, modern foreign languages, and pastry making at Heidelberg and learned confectionery at Barnards School in Epsom.

At age twenty, Isabella married Samuel Orchard Beeton. They settled in Epsom and had four children. Samuel Beeton published middle-brow magazines and popular books, including *Uncle Tom's Cabin.* In 1860 he issued his wife's classic *Book of Household Management,* which took Isabella three years to compile.

For the illustrations and text, she studied culinary history and, with the aid of her kitchen staff, personally tested recipes from numerous English, French, and German sources as well as the works of Homer and Pliny the Elder, the first century CE Roman encyclopedist.

Her search for suitable middle-class cuisine began in 1857; her sources included friends, relatives, and two cookbooks of the day—Eliza Acton's *Modern Cookery for Private Families* (1845) and Alexis Soyer's *The Modern Housewife* (1849). In all, she gathered recipes for 100 soups, 200 sauces, 128 fish dishes, and such end-of-meal delights as "Dutch flummery," a jellied custard made with Madeira. The only original recipe in the collection was her "Soup for Benevolent Purposes," the result of a soup kitchen she opened in the hard winter of 1858. She issued the work serially in two dozen installments beginning September 1859.

Beeton's domestic writing was both creative and energetic. In addition to dispensing advice on the outfitting of kitchens, she advised young brides on etiquette, efficient household management, and the hiring and supervising of servants. Supremely practical, she told women how much a meal should cost and how to train a kitchen maid. Her goal of dispensing wholesome as well as elegant food information endeared her to generations of women in Britain, Canada, Australia, and the United States. The book was an unprecedented success, selling 60,000 copies in the first year. Beeton also wrote columns on food, child care, and household hints for her husband's *Englishwoman's Domestic Magazine.* She was a media success, entertaining readers with epigrams and to-the-point style. Among Beeton's succinct dicta were commands to clear the work area at each stage of cooking and to put implements back where they belonged.

In 1861, she began editing *Queen* magazine and planned *Young Englishwoman.* That same year, she issued a second edition of her book, in which she commented specifically on a significant kitchen-to-table matter—the shift from *service à la francaise* to *service à la russe*: "Dinners *à la russe* are scarcely suitable for small establishments; a large number of servants being required to carve, and to help the guests; besides there being a necessity for more plates, dishes, knives, forks, and spoons, than are usually to be found in any other than a very large establishment. Where, however, a *service à la Russe* is practicable, there is, perhaps, no mode of serving a dinner so enjoyable as this." (Molokhovets 1992, 29) The text illustrated the boiler, brass spigot, hot plate, oven, and toaster attachment of the Leamington Kitchener open range, exhibited at the 1851 Great Exhibition and the 1853 Dublin Exhibition and marketed by Messrs. Richard & John Slack of London.

On February 6, 1865, while reading copy for the *Dictionary of Cookery,* an abridgment of her earlier works, Beeton died at age twenty-eight of exhaustion and puerperal fever. She was buried in a family plot in London's Norbury Cemetery. In honor of his beloved wife, her husband appended a eulogy to the dictionary.

Sam Beeton's collapsing finances forced him to sign over Isabella's first book to Ward, Lock and Tyler, which kept it in print with minor revision for 125 years. The company augmented the 1912 edition with details of electric, gas, and oil cookery and appropriate kitchen accessories.

More than other Victorian food writers such as Acton and Agnes B. Marshall, Beeton was read like scripture and her advice followed, in part because of her unerring taste and sensible tone. Her work influenced Sarah Tyson Rorer, the founder of the Philadelphia Cooking School, and Minekichi Akabori, the modernizer of Japanese cuisine. Prolific food writer Bridget Jones—editor of *Mrs. Beeton's Healthy Eating* (1984), *Mrs. Beeton's Book of Baking* (1991), *Mrs. Beeton's Traditional Cake Decorating* (1991), *Mrs. Beeton's Christmas Menus* (1996), and *Mrs. Beeton's Best of British Home Cooking* (1998)—declared Beeton the forerunner of modern home economics. In 1998, Southover Press brought out a facsimile edition of *Book of Household Management,* illustrated in color.

See also **Victorian Kitchens; Women's Magazines**

Further Reading

White, Cynthia L. *Women's Magazines 1693–1968.* London: Michael Joseph, 1970.
Wilson, Bee, "Good Egg," *New Statesman,* September 18, 2000.

BELLARMINE

Identified by its distinctive shape and predominantly brown color, the Bellarmine, or *Bartmannkrug,* was a popular form of working-class crockery from the sixteenth through the eighteenth centuries and the major contribution of the Low Countries and Rhineland to *steinzeug* (stoneware). Perhaps in mockery of Catholic prohibition of drinking, Bellarmine ware takes its name from the late sixteenth-century Roman Catholic cardinal and theologian Roberto Bellarmino, who was canonized in 1627. Among Protestant Low Country tipplers, however, who knew nothing of Italian prelates, people assumed that the imposing face on the jug was that of Charlemagne.

Produced from the 1500s into the eighteenth century, the bulbous jugs originated in the Rhineland about 1520; early examples were small, handled jugs with a man's facial features—hairline, eyes, nose, mouth, and beard—etched in relief below the lip of the vessel. Colors ranged from browns and grays to a mottled tiger glaze, the result of iron rust. Some bellarmines bear blue and purple markings over a gray core and display decorations incised in relief. Around 1550, the distinctively plump Bellarmine pot entered production in Cologne and Raeren. Wood carvers stamped jugs with additional decorative shapes including vines, foliage, acorns, acanthus leaves, sashes, coin-shaped buttons, and a corded ring separating neck from body.

Standing six to seven inches tall, the droller versions sported belts around the girth inscribed with mottoes or aphorisms. Around 1550, innovators added a hinged pewter lid. When Frechen's pot yards supplanted the Rhineland's centers in the late 1500s, potters began touching up the surface with cobalt blue and adorning the pear-shaped Bellarmine ware with metal medallions and small plaques that advertised the producer or seller. These markings evolved into armorial symbolism of towns and regions and badges and monograms identifying ruling families, classical figures, nobles, and religious leaders.

Produced east of the Rhine River, Westerwald stoneware so dominated the Bellarmine trade that Westerwald ware became a generic name for all such vessels. Made in Höhr, Grenzau, and Grenzhausen in the late 1500s, pots and jugs derived from kiln yards that thrived on abundant supplies of gray clay and wood for the requisite white-hot firing. As an aid to merchants and homemakers, Bellarmine potters marked their wares with units of liquid measure, designated by such terms as anker, cask, coomb, firkin, flagon, hogshead, jack, jackpot, kan, kilderkin, nipperkin, pail, pottle, runlet, and strike. To the characteristic clayware painted Prussian blue and manganese purple were added portraits, geometric motifs with religious and civic themes, reeded necks, incised stems, and scrollery. The brisk trade in clayware earned Westerwald the name *Kannenbäcker-land* (country of the pot bakers). Local goods, exported throughout Europe, India, Africa, North and South America, and Australia, were the most common in the American colonies, where local potters emulated the Rhenish original.

England entered the Bellarmine market in the 1670s with the establishment of John Dwight's pottery at Fulham in London. The trade, influenced by immigrant German potters, spread to Staffordshire and Liverpool but never approached the commercial success enjoyed by the Rhenish clayworks. Under the conditions imposed by mass production, stylized English jugs lost their distinctive faces in the 1600s, when the neck reliefs stretched to an oval shape and the medallions took on light generic patterns rather than detailed crests. Larger and fuller, the jugs took on a spherical shape with a thinner, slightly longer neck and acquired classical handles, tavern medallions, and facemasks. English examples featured wire markings on the base caused by friction from the pottery wheel. Enhanced English versions added silver mounts, portrait busts of William III and Mary II, and three distinctive royal markings—WR (Wilhelmus Rex) for William III, AR (Anne Regina) for Queen Anne, and GR (Georgius Rex) for the three Georges—which boosted the rulers' popularity among drinkers in the laboring class. By the 1700s, domestic stoneware and black glass bottles compromised the world trade in Bellarmine ware.

Further Reading

Thwaite, Anthony, "The Chronology of the Bellarmine Jug," *Connoisseur*, April 1973.

BENTZ, MELITTA

The coffee filter was the idea of Melitta Bentz, a housewife and inventor born in Dresden, Germany, in 1873. At age thirty-five, she developed a method of removing grounds and bitterness from drip coffee without marring the taste. After experimenting with linen towels, in 1908 she shaped a blotting-paper filter from sheets from her son's notebook. She pierced a brass container with holes, lined it with a filter, and placed the ground coffee in the filter. To market her idea, she engaged a tinsmith to manufacture aluminum pots used solely for making filtered coffee.

To increase the absorbency of the filter, Bentz replaced the paper insert with a more porous fiber. After her sons began a filter delivery route to neighborhood customers, her idea caught on. On December 15, 1908, she and her husband Hugo established a business to market her filtration system. A year later, the Melitta Coffee Company had sold 1,250 coffeemakers at the Leipzig trade show. Three years later, the family-owned firm began marketing the paper filters as a stand-alone product in 150 countries. In 1925, the company adopted its familiar red and green logo.

By 1930, the Melitta paper filtration disc gave way to the conical filter, which further reduced the amount of grounds that ended up in the brewed coffee. A decade later, the company introduced the porcelain filter cone, thus eliminating the metallic flavor caused by the original brass basket. The company also patented the *filturtuten* (filter bag) in 1937 and vacuum packing in 1962. Another improvement, a plastic filter cone, proved more durable than the porcelain version and less expensive. A subsequent shift to a dioxin-free oxygenated paper whitener, introduced in 1992, and natural brown filter paper in 1998 eased some users' fears of the toxic bleaches applied in papermaking. A filter paper with microfine openings admitted more taste and aroma. In honor of its founder, the Melitta Company established the Melitta Bentz Woman of Innovation and Invention Award, which carries a $5,000 purse plus a $1,000 donation to charity and a replica of the inventor's original brass coffee pot.

Further Reading

Vare, Ethlie Ann, and Greg Ptacek. *Mothers of Invention*. New York: Quill, 1987.

BIRDSEYE, CLARENCE

The father of the frozen food industry, inventor-naturalist Clarence Birdseye was an ordinary man with more than the usual amount of intellectual curiosity. Born on December 9,1886, in Brooklyn, New York, to Ada Underwood and attorney Clarence Frank Birdseye, he was proud of the family name, which legend linked with the rescue of an English queen from a hawk by an archer firing a single arrow through the bird's eye. From the renaming came a family motto, "Stay right on the target." (Rothe 1946, 44)

Birdseye showed an interest in taxidermy at age five and advertised his service in a sports magazine. After a cooking course in high school in Montclair, New Jersey, he earned money by supplying rats for breeding experiments at Columbia University and frogs to feed snakes at the Bronx Zoo. The rats were rare black specimens he trapped in a butcher shop bone room. This unusual work paid tuition for two years of study in biology at Amherst University. Some three decades later, in recognition of his achievements, his alma mater awarded him an honorary master's degree.

From jobs as office boy for an insurance agent and snow checker for the New York City street department, Birdseye advanced to a position as a field naturalist in the Arctic for the U.S. Department of Agriculture biological survey. He trapped wolves in Michigan and studied Rocky Mountain spotted fever in Montana; the latter endeavor led to the compilation of *Some Common Mammals of Western Montana in Relation to Agriculture and Spotted Fever* (1912). While in the Arctic, he observed how the Inuit quickly froze their fresh-caught fish, rabbits, ducks, and caribou to preserve them for later use. At -50 degrees Fahrenheit, the process allowed only small ice crystals to form in the cells, thus preserving the meat's texture, natural juices, vitamin content, flavor, and color.

During thousands of miles traveled on a four-year fur-trading expedition in Labrador, Birdseye acclimated to dog sleds and small boats. While living in Canada with his wife and firstborn, he became fascinated with the notion of frozen foods. Upon his return to the United States, he experimented with freezing fresh produce in barrels of water. At age thirty-one, he began work on the commercial application of frozen foods for the domestic market. This work halted during his service in World War I, followed by two years as assistant purchaser for Stone and Webster and the U.S. Housing Corporation and as aide to the president of the U.S. Fisheries Association.

While managing Granite Spring Bottling, Birdseye labored for seven years at a New Jersey icehouse to develop a method for packaging foods and rapidly reducing the temperature to freezing. His equipment was crude—a brine bucket, ice cakes, and an electric fan. In 1924, at his laboratory in Gloucester, Massachusetts, he borrowed on his life insurance to launch Birdseye General Foods with his first quick-frozen products, haddock fillets and rabbits packed in discarded candy boxes. He asked local sea captains to save their excess catch for test freezing, thawing, and sampling. In collaboration with Charles Seabrook, he developed the technology for deep-freezing bricks of cooked fish, meat, and vegetables. He cranked out portions on a quick-freezing machine between two refrigerated presser plates and placed them in waxed cardboard cartons for easy removal. To assure freshness, he adapted the factory freezing mechanism into a portable assembly line that he could set up at the source of supply.

Birdseye patented the food freezing process in 1926. *Fortune* declared that freezing was "one of the most exciting and revolutionary ideas in the history of food." (Rothe 1946, 44) Despite this endorsement, Birdseye still had to contend with the public's qualms about the purity and wholesomeness of frozen foods. After making $1 million chilling fish fillets from the Fulton Fish Market for the General Seafoods Company, in 1929, he sold the concept for some $20 million to the Postum Company, although he remained employed as a consultant. On Birdseye's orders, the owners kept the name *Birds Eye* as a product trademark, but they renamed the firm General Foods. To avoid the negative image of freezing, the company referred to its product as "frosted." (Landau 1986, 69)

Birdseye successfully test marketed twenty-six foods in Springfield, Massachusetts, in 1930, making available to the American homemaker frozen fish, meat, cherries, peas, and spinach. His success encouraged farmers to select varieties of produce that would withstand freezing without destabilization due to internal crystallization. Because few kitchens had freezers, shoppers had to cook and serve frozen foods the day of their purchase or rent space in neighborhood freezer lockers, which catered to consumers who bought food in bulk.

Birdseye continued working as president of Birds Eye Frosted Foods and the Birdseye Electric Company. In 1934, he helped the American Radiator Corporation manufacture low-cost freezer cases for lease to grocery stores. Within five years, he added frozen chicken, turkey, and beef products to shopper's choices. He developed a method for quick-freezing loose vegetables, a cost-saving move that enabled cooks to pour out the amount needed rather than thaw a whole package. In 1944, he leased insulated refrigerator rail cars to carry his goods to market. During the rationing of commodities during World War II, frozen foods became more popular, garnering a large percentage of the consumer's dollar.

With the end of rationing in 1945, *Consumer Reports* predicted a bright future for the food-freezing process, although it warned of inconsistencies in quality. The following year, the magazine predicted home delivery of complete frozen meals, apartment house storage lockers, electronic defrosting ovens, and frozen meals cooked and eaten from disposable dishes. This vision of the future was prophetic. By 1946, frozen foods were available in England; in 1950 "frostmobiles" were delivering frozen goods to U.S. housewives. (Landau 1986, 69) The development of the microwave oven and microwaveable disposable plastic trays and bowls further enhanced the sale of frozen foods in the 1990s.

Until Birdseye's death from heart attack on October 7, 1956, in New York City, he kept busy writing *Growing Woodland Plants* (1951), playing Chinese checkers, and reading Western fiction. Altogether, he patented some 300 ideas, including anhydrous freezing of quick-cook products and a recoilless shoulder-fire harpoon for whalers. He also traveled to Peru to study the recycling of sugar cane fiber into pulp for paper.

Within a half-century of Birdseye's innovation in food storage, processors were selling $17 billion worth of frozen foods a year. By 1961, his company was marketing sixty products in the United States and United Kingdom. In 1980, the average American was consuming 220 pounds of vegetables per year—double the amount in 1920—thanks in part to the increased availability of frozen goods to smaller towns. The Birds Eye Company continued to lead innovation in frozen foods, developing a foil overwrapping to retain moisture, boil-in-the-bag portions, and frozen pasta.

BISCUIT

Once a staple food of army camps and naval vessels, biscuit is a class of flat, hard, unleavened bread that satisfies hunger and settles queasy stomachs. One of the major kitchen inventions of goods baked from wheat, biscuit derived from the Roman *lagani* (pasta). Shore bakers formed biscuit of wheat flour and little water and cooked it twice, slowly, into a hard, durable crust that held its shape during buffeting at sea. Iberian sailors called them *mazamorra* (or *massamorda*); for their density and unappetizing texture, the blunt English dubbed them *hardtack*. Among other innovations in culinary history, biscuit ranks with couscous and macaroni in its impact on working-class cuisine.

In the 800s CE, references to *panis biscoctus* (twice-cooked bread) suggest that biscuit got its formal start during the early Middle Ages. According to Petrus Tudebodus (or Peter Tudebode) of Poitiers, author of *Historia de Hierosolymitano Itinere* (History of the Route to Jerusalem, 1095–1099), crusaders transported containers of biscuit to Jerusalem by camel and donkey after the siege of Ascalon in August 1153. Late in the era, crusaders' biscuit acquired the Latin name *panis Africanus* (African bread) and *panis Alexandrinus* (Alexandrian bread). By the 1200s references to biscuit recur on naval provisioning records in Genoa and Marseilles, two of Europe's busiest ports.

Jean Froissart's *Chroniques de France, d' Angleterre, d' Ecosse, et d' Espagne* (Chronicles of France, England, Scotland, and Spain, ca. 1405), a history primarily covering the Hundred Years' War and the Crusades, mentions English soldiers' envy of Scots regulars. Rather than gnaw the stale, hard biscuit of the English, Scots infantrymen packed oatmeal and cooked hot oat cakes over their campfires. Froissart concludes, "Hence it is not surprising that they can travel faster than other armies." (*Froissart* 1978, 47)

In the 1700s, Portsmouth, England, became the source of biscuit for government victuallers. In the royal dockyards, an assembly line of bakery personnel produced hardtack at the rate of seventy four-ounce biscuits per minute. The fluctuating demand of the military during war and peace caused local staff to maintain a basic crew to be supplemented by contractors when need arose. Thomas Grant reduced labor costs and improved quality in 1833 by inventing a steam mechanism to crank out biscuit. Several years later, Carr, a Quaker bakery in Carlisle, applied the same factory system to the production of quality biscuit, thus decreasing the dominance of two rival products—the buttery Bath Oliver biscuit, named for its inventor, William Oliver of Bath, England, in 1750, and the semisweet Abernethy biscuit, invented early in the 1800s by John Abernethy, the Scottish chief of surgery at St. Bartholomew's Hospital.

In North America, the biscuit was a part of colonial culinary history. When the *Mayflower* sailed for New England, according to William Wood's *New-Englands Prospect* (1634), the hold contained 15,000 brown biscuits and 5,000 white to accompany bacon and smoked herring. In the colonies, biscuit production provided opportunity for a professional bakery in a harbor town. According to an ad in the September 10, 1722, issue of the *New England Courant,* a Boston baker offered his services to "any Persons wanting good brown Bisket fit either for the Fishery or for Shipping Off, may be supplyed by *Lately Gee* at the Sign of the Bakers Arms in Hannover Street." (Dow 1988, 122) His offerings, per bushel or per hundred-count, depended on the market price for wheat. The next week, competitors offered to match Gee's prices and countered, "They being willing to avoid the Curse of the Common Sailors, those employ'd in the Fishery, etc., generally make their Bread better, and sell it for a better Price." (Ibid.)

In 1841, George Palmer and Thomas Huntley opened a biscuit factory in Reading, England, where "biscuit boys" delivered fresh goods to travelers on the Bath-London highway. Demand grew for the Huntley-Palmer biscuit, which the company stored in tins and delivered fresh to outlying grocers. The availability of a regular supply of biscuit reduced the need for kitchen staff and eased the homemaker's daily job of toasting bread for breakfast.

At sea, galley cooks stored biscuit below decks in the bread room in canvas bags or tin chests, which were better than wood crates at keeping out weevils and maggots. The purser's assistant, or "bread-room jack," issued biscuit from the ship's stores as if it were coin of the realm. If biscuit became infested with vermin, the warder might bait the barrel top with fish or meat. When maggots crawled upward, the warder captured and discarded them. For the more elegant taste of passengers aboard the luxury liner *Titanic,* the chef imported cabin biscuits from Spillers & Bakers.

During the American Civil War, in addition to other supplies, ration clerks allotted each soldier eight to ten saltless hardtack biscuits, which the men dubbed worm castles, sheetiron crackers, purser's nuts, and tooth dullers. (Mitchell 2000, 18) In honor of hardtack, they altered the lyrics of "Hard Times Come Again No More" to "Hard Bread Come Again No More." (Glass & Singer 1964, 143-144) When they had no alternative, messmates dropped weevilly biscuit into hot coffee and skimmed off vermin that floated to the surface while grumbling that the hardtack stores were probably army surplus from the Mexican War fought two decades earlier. The wise seaman chewed up rations wiggling with maggots after dark "when the eye saw not, and the tender heart was spared." (Riddervold & Ropeid 1988, 150) Sailors in Hawaii crumbled biscuit into milk and sweetened it with brown sugar to create a humble but not very nutritious *panada*. Others, disillusioned by poor rations at sea, turned to contempt for authority and mutinous mutterings.

To vary this dismal diet, military cooks dreamed up recipes such as skillygalee, military biscuit soaked in water or broth and fried like croutons in pork grease, as well as "hell fired stew" or "hish and hash" of cracker, meat, potatoes, tomatoes, salt, pepper, and garlic. (Mitchell 2000, 20) For a mess kitchen dessert, they pounded crackers into powder, blended it with water, sugar, and raisins, and boiled the mass into a pudding. It is not surprising that the men looked forward to mail call, when packages from home brought spice cookies, ginger snaps, dried fruit, and the occasional home-cured ham.

Additions to the biscuit line eventually raised hardtack to culinary respectability. In 1875, the Peek Frean Biscuits & Cakes Company of England made a biscuit recipe to commemorate the marriage of the Grand Duchess Maria of Austria to the Duke of Edinburgh. The Maria, a crisp round, carried the duchess's name stamped on top. It attained popularity in Spain in the late 1930s as an item for dunking in coffee, milk, and tea. Another historic biscuit, the Anzac, a variant of Scottish oat cake dispensed by Red Cross workers during World War I, honored the Australia and New Zealand army corps, who distinguished themselves after landing at Gallipoli on April 25, 1915.

See also **Borden, Gail, Jr.; Frontier Kitchens; Galley; Military Kitchens**

Further Reading

Glass, Paul, and Louis C. Singer. *Singing Soldiers: A History of the Civil War in Song.* New York: Da Capo Press, 1964.
Kemp, Peter, ed. *The Oxford Companion to Ships and the Sea.* Oxford: Oxford University Press, 1988.

BORDEN, GAIL, JR.

Although inept as a businessman, Gail Borden, Jr., was a man with great ideas. He was responsible for the development of America's first staple convenience foods: meat biscuit and canned condensed milk. Born in Norwich, New York, on November 9, 1801, he was poorly educated. He served as a captain of the militia and worked as a surveyor after his family moved to the Indiana Territory. After teaching school, he moved to Stephen Austin's Texas colony and served as superintendent of official surveys and cartographer of topographical maps. In San Felipe in 1835, Borden and his brother Thomas established the first permanent Texas newspaper, the *Telegraph and Texas Land Register*, which they moved to Houston. He assisted in drafting the Texas constitution and aided Sam Houston as collector of port of Galveston and agent for Galveston City Company.

Borden knew nothing of formal science, but was able to apply pragmatic solutions to everyday problems. After the death of his wife and son from yellow fever in 1844, he dreamed up a refrigeration system to cool those stricken with the disease, who tended to sicken and die only in summer. He also invented a multipurpose horse-drawn "terraqueous" machine intended to operate on land and water. A wagon fitted with square sail and pulleys attached to paddle wheels, it capsized on its trial run from Galveston to the Gulf of Mexico.

A venture into the food industry brought Borden notice as the inventor of meat biscuit, a powdered convenience food that blended flour with dehydrated meat reduced in weight from 120 pounds to ten pounds. He obtained the recipe from Mrs. Joseph Osterman, whose husband financed Borden's store and dehydrating ovens. A second backer, Washington Green Lee Foley, provided $1,000 as start-up money.

By reconstituting Borden's powder with water, Westerners, campers, explorers, and sailors could quickly cook a wholesome meal in a skillet or Dutch oven. At the height of gold fever, Borden offered his meat product to friends setting out for the California mining fields. Arctic explorers and Alaskan adventurers ate meat biscuit without complaint—despite its gluey consistency and unpleasant taste—primarily because it saved work and fuss, the main drawbacks to standard homemade biscuits. At the First Lone Star State Fair, held in May 1852, the new product won first prize.

Although it had wide popular appeal, meat biscuit lacked official backing. Military authorities found the substance unpalatable and sickening. By 1842, Borden's meat biscuit foundered in the wake of shrewd competitors, but received the support of a backer, Ashbel Smith, a Yale-educated U.S. commissioner to the 1851 London Industrial Exposition, who touted the product in England. Another promoter, the Texas soldier of fortune Arthur Goodall Wavell, recommended reconstituted biscuit to the Royal British Admiralty. As a result of successful promotion, in 1851 meat biscuit won Borden a gold medal from the London Society of Arts.

Humanistic concerns prompted Borden's greatest culinary contribution. Having witnessed the death aboard ship of starving children, he resolved to find a way to make a safe source of milk available on long voyages. After pondering Brother Alonzo Hollister's airtight chamber for condensing fruit juice into sugar at a Shaker enclave in New Lebanon, New York, Borden studied the application of canning technology to milk.

Borden devised a copper vacuum pan gently warmed by a heating coil as a means of evaporating the water from milk solids. To assure cleanliness, he enforced strict sanitation measures in dairies. He was able to can pure, wholesome milk without discoloring, scorching, or souring it. Patented on August 19, 1856, his method of producing vacuum-packed concentrated milk boosted the fortunes of the dairy industry. The Committee of the Academy of Medicine lauded Borden in 1858 for finding an economical way to produce milk that could be stored safely without refrigeration.

In 1861, Borden went into business in Wassaic, New York, and sold his thick milk concentrate door to door. The philanthropist-investor Jeremiah Millbank underwrote production at Borden's New York Condensed Milk Company. The lengthened shelf life made milk available to pioneers, campers, ships' crews, and soldiers in the field. At the beginning of the Civil War, Borden sold his canned milk to the Union army, which ordered more cases than he could produce. After the war, condensation of milk made him rich.

Still tinkering, Borden pursued ill-conceived schemes for making condensed apple cider, pumpkins, potatoes, and melons. His success at condensing blackberry juice for the U.S. Army earned him a commendation from General William Tecumseh Sherman, who thanked the inventor for aiding Union soldiers stricken with dysentery. Borden also patented methods of making concentrated beef, tea, coffee, and cocoa. He used his experience to found schools and train dairy workers in sanitation. At his death in 1874, the inscription on his tombstone read: "I tried and failed, I tried again and again and succeeded."

In the 1920s, Borden's company promoted infant welfare by teaching immigrant mothers that the best way to provide their infants with pure milk was to open a sterilized can of milk rather than buying powdered milk in bulk from a milk station. The Borden name survives in a diversified corporation that produces chemicals, adhesives, processed food, housewares, and dairy products marked with the smiling visage of Elsie, the Borden cow.

Further Reading

Crowley, Carolyn Hughes, "The Man Who Invented Elsie, the Borden Cow," *Smithsonian*, September 1999, p.32.

BOW DRILL

The rotary fire drill, alternately known as a bow drill, hand drill, pump drill, or thong drill, was the first technically assisted method of fire making. Early examples have been found around the world—among primitive domestic goods dating to 5500 BCE at Aomori in northern Japan; in a Bronze Age ship sunk off Ulun Burun, Turkey, after 1300 BCE; among Harappan artifacts in ancient India; in King Tut's tomb; among the Inuit of Newfoundland and Labrador; and at archeological digs at Neolithic sites around the Great Lakes and in Cyprus, India, Indonesia, Australia, Scandinavia, and northern Asia. A primitive two-handed or hand-and-mouth device, it operated by means of a back-and-forth sawing or spinning motion. After looping a thong or cord around a vertical shaft of wood or bone, the operator rotated the cord in the manner of a drive belt for three to seven minutes, winding and unwinding it while pressing the pointed end of the shaft into an oiled or waxed socket in a fire board below, made from soft wood, bone, stone, or coconut shell. A forerunner of the bow drill, the thong drill lacked the attachment of the loose cord end to end.

Early Native Americans of the plains or Great Basin fashioned bow drills from a strip of wood or from cottonwood or yucca root pulled into an arc by a babiche, or thong, tied to each end. After setting up the simple mechanism, the user could saw the bow horizontally until friction produced sparks. A skilled bow-driller supplied flammable material—bark, buffalo chips, feathers, moss, shredded wood pulp—with the free hand and blew on the sparks until a flame appeared.

In the best-selling trail guide, *The Prairie Traveler: A Hand-Book for Overland Expeditions* (1859), containing advice, maps, and intineraries over the principal westward routes between the Mississippi River and the Pacific Ocean, army captain Randolph Barnes Marcy, a veteran of the Mexican War and inspector general of the Department of Utah, described the native method of fire-by-friction with a bow drill made from two dried stalks of Mexican soap plant, which Indians held in hands and feet. He wrote, "This is an operation that is difficult, and requires practice; but if a drill-stick is used with a cord placed around the centre of the upright stick, it can be turned much more rapidly than with the hands, and the fire produced more readily." (Marcy 1978, n. p.)

A similar fire-making staff was the pump drill, a wheel placed over a stick and tied to the end with babiche. It served at sea in ship's galleys, such as the seventh-century Byzantine ship downed on a reef just off the island of Yassi Ada between Turkey and Cos.

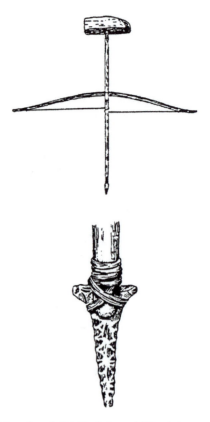

Bowdrill (above) and detail of stone drill point [*Original illustration by Dan Timmons.*]

A variant on the broomstick, or vertical, churn was the pump churn, which the dairy worker activated with a bow drill. Shaped like a vertical churn, it contained a series of paddles attached to a spindle. The user rotated the mechanism at top with each pull on the drill. The advantage of the pump churn was an end to the tiring up-and-down motion of the dasher, which the pump churn replaced with a less-tiring back-and-forth-sawing motion. It also allowed a seated user to read or nurse an infant while operating the bow drill with a free hand.

Further Reading

Field, David, "Bury the Dead in a Sacred Landscape," *British Archaeology,* April 1999.

Rudgley, Richard. *The Lost Civilizations of the Stone Age.* New York: The Free Press, 1999.

BRASS

Brass, a bright gold alloy of tin and copper or zinc and copper, was a traditional material for making and lining kitchen utensils. In medieval England, housewives depended on the three-legged brass pot for mundane cookery. Although iron was available, they valued brass because it did not rust and rapidly conducted heat. To maintain the kitchen fire during the night, a bell-shaped *couvre-feu* (fire cover), also called a curfew or nightcap, kept embers glowing and ready for the cook to start a flame the next day with a puff of the bellows. It also protected the kitchen floor from flame caused by downdrafts. The device hung within arm's reach of the hearth from attached loop or handle. When upended, it could hold hot ash for heating a cup or dish or for warming a dining or sleeping chamber.

In the fifteenth century, the Ashante of southern Ghana began importing brass across the Sahara or through port cities from Holland and Portugal to make two types of vessels. For the first, *forowa* (canisters), they shaped hammered metal sheets of fabricated basins and bowls from Europe into lidded storage jars for shea butter. Artistic detailing with incised geometrics, lotus blossoms, rosettes, waves, idealized quadrupeds, and figure eights centered on Akan and Islamic concepts of symmetry and nature. The second category of vessels, called *kuduo* (altar vessels), made from cast brass, served ceremonial and ritual purposes. To shape *kuduo*, the caster modeled forms in wax and coated them with clay. By melting the wax, pouring it out, and refilling the hollows with molten brass, they achieved artistic results in Islamic and North African styles.

Until people recognized the health risks of brass cookware in the 1850s, the malleable metal provided malleable material for pastry jaggers, graters, ladles, cream pans, skillets, and deep mixing bowls for whisking eggs and beating meringue. Fanciful nutcrackers, whether levered or screwed, often held the nut between the jaws of a wooden alligator, monkey, or dog lined in brass for extra grip. Brass could also underlay other metals; latten, a beaten brass sheet plated with tin, was the source of inexpensive church altar plates and vessels.

Among immigrants to the New World, the fifteen-gallon brass kettle was a treasured item, one of the few kitchen furnishings ferried from the motherland in weeks-long voyages. In the American colonies, brass kettles worth three English pounds sterling were the most expensive and valuable household vessels. When Native Americans acquired their first brass cook pots, they requested that the lustrous vessels be buried with them at death.

In the Victorian era, when middle-class merchants and importers thrived on the riches of the colonies, home fireplaces grew more ornate, although they performed fewer utilitarian functions. Brass andirons and grate fronts complemented tile with metallic inlays and matched sets of brass fireplace tools and warming pans, all requiring cadres of servants to keep them gleaming. Servants jumped at the ring of the brass wire-and-pulley house bell, a summons issued to the service passage. Bells rang in varying tones intended

to single out butler, maid, or kitchen staff. The advent of electricity for home lighting replaced the familiar bell pull with a brass push-button face plate and brass ringer.

In the twentieth century, brass returned to favor as the metal of choice for indoor plumbing. An advertisement in the February 1925 issue of *Good Housekeeping* extolled household conduits made by Anaconda Brass Pipe of Waterbury, Connecticut. The copy declared that Anaconda products lasted a lifetime without expensive repairs. An illustration of a toddler happily eating in a highchair implied that children deserved the pure water that flowed through brass. At the start of the twenty-first century, brass fittings are still components of kitchen plumbing.

See also **Bentz, Melitta**

BRAZIERS

A broad, flat-bottomed pan or metal receptacle for holding hot coals, the brazier was originally a portable slow cooker elevated on three or four legs. Called a *brasière* or *sauteuse* (heater) in French, it was the forerunner of the barbecue grill and the candle- or sterno-powdered *réchaud* (table heater), or chafing dish. The high-sided charcoal brazier remains a standard item among nomad households of the Mediterranean and among the Rom, or gypsies, worldwide. In Mexico, cooks prefer the mobile tin *elanafre* brazier, which holds wood or charcoal for heating small batches of food on a patio or balcony. Small, stationary pot braziers installed in a kitchen nook serve the cooking needs of villagers in Thailand.

Potters were shaping braziers in the western Mediterranean as early as 2000 BCE. In Italy, cooks heated clay braziers with charcoal. Arab cooks traditionally set up a portable brazier outdoors away from their dwellings. From the fifth century BCE, Greek housekeepers in townhouses preferred the brazier to the hearth for heat and cooking. Roman cooks might place a brazier outdoors in a courtyard during hot weather. A tableside brazier allowed the skilled cook to gain favor through an impressive presentation. One Roman model illustrated in chef Alexis Soyer's translation of Adolphe Duhart-Fauvet's *The Pantropheon: History of Food in All Ages* (1853) had a square base built like a crenellated fortress. Water poured into the hollow walls of the receptacle absorbed heat from charcoal burning at the center. The book cites the Roman philosopher Seneca as a proponent of the tableside bronze chafing dish, a dainty device that ended the uncivilized practice of eating cold food. Julius Caesar, who epitomized regional cookery in his *Gallic Commentaries*

(52 BCE), noted that the Gauls were especially fond of tableside food preparation in braziers.

Braziers were also used for cooking in the New World. In the first millennium CE, the Aztec of Tlajinga at Teotihuacán, Mexico, lived in interlinked apartments featuring cobbled patios and private storage and living quarters. Unlike other Indian groups, they cooked at ceramic braziers similar to single-burner stoves. Archaeological evidence suggests that one clan or perhaps one family specialized in brazier production.

One ornate bronze brazier made in the ninth century returned to Sweden aboard a trading vessel that traversed the Volga River from Baghdad to Scandinavia. Its body, a two-stage cube, was pierced with ornate slotting and topped with a dome. It stood on four legs. A handle jutting out from one side enabled the user to carry the brazier from fireplace to table.

An inventory of the belongings of Sicilian cooks in the Middle Ages attests to their poverty. From records of the taxes levied on street foods, historians have concluded that the laboring class, whose homes had no kitchens, relied largely on food vendors, who cooked outdoors on portable braziers. In large medieval fireplaces, a brazier attached to the andiron cap allowed for dishes to be cooked or heated away from open flame. Some of the braziers contained central dividers. Thus, cooks could warm four dishes at a time, two to an andiron.

Domestic inventories from Italy listed spits on tripods, fry pans, and pots more often than *foculàri* (braziers), the latter being a more sophisticated method of home cookery found in prestigious kitchens. In the high Renaissance, Christoforo (also Cristoforo or Christofaro) di Messisbugo (or Messisburgo), steward of Hippolyte d'Este, cardinal of Ferrara, compiled *Il Libro de Arte Coquinaria* (The Book of Culinary Art, 1548), a cookbook illustrated with valuable glimpses into court cookery. In illustrating the court kitchen of the d'Estes at Ferrara, he represented the kitchen staff in figures sized according to their importance. Thus, at the feet of an elaborate brazier, a tiny servant works the bellows to keep the fire hot. To the sides, two spit boys turn broaches, one skewering a fish and a snake and the other holding the carcass of a small animal. The largest figures in the picture are the cooks, who baste poultry with long-handled ladles. As the lower classes began emulating the refined cookery of the d'Este family and other aristocrats, their festal banqueting created a demand for braziers and other ornate dining implements.

Despite advances in fireplace, chimney, and range construction, the brazier remained a useful cooking device. Tending a brazier was not pleasant work, however. In 1833, Marie-Antoine Carême, a master chef who cooked for Napoleon, Talleyrand, Metternich, and Tsar Alexander I, complained of the discomfort cooks suffered in the damp, poorly lit subterranean kitchens of the era, not the least of which was having to breathe "the poisonous gas from the charcoal braziers…every moment of the day."

A more recent version of the brazier is a showy tabletop egg boiler, some models of which are crafted from silver and decorated with curving braces and ornate lid finial. The fondue pot, used variously for cheese and chocolate, is yet another variation on the brazier.

See also **Charcoal**

Further Reading

Gabriel, Judith, "Among the Norse Tribes," *Aramco World*, November-December 1999, 36–42.

Hess, Karen, intro. *Martha Washington's Booke of Cookery*. New York: Columbia University Press, 1981.

Yzábal, María Dolores, and Shelton Wiseman. *The Mexican Gourmet*. McMahons Point, Australia: Thunder Bay, 1995.

BREAD

Bread has been an integral part of human history from the family ritual of breaking bread together to the tumultuous revolution ringing with the cry for loaves. Worldwide, the bread created by different peoples has reflected their views, aspirations, and creativity. Arab dietitians prescribed white bread as a restorative of health. A Catalan children's rhyme declared that the hungry child, denied a portion of bread, will steal it. Ribald Italian folklore referred to *sciarbuzzia* (fake pudenda), unleavened breads shaped into female genitalia; a similar Greek baking tradition was reported by Heracleides of Syracuse in *On Institutions* (ca. 75 BCE). Humble English bakers, recognizing IHS, an abbreviation of the Greek *iesous*, inscribed on church pulpit, communion vessels, and altar cloth, scratched the Greek letters on buns and made up such folk interpretations of the initials as "in his steps."

In the Russian fairy tale "The Frog Princess," the Slavic ritual of bread making is central to the search for wives worthy of the king's sons. A wily frog princess bests the human brides with trickery. When she magically turns into the beautiful Elena, she marries Prince Ivan and fills his days with merry feasting. Russian traditionalists perpetuate the token loaf—a test of housewifery—that a prospective bride must bake for her husband.

Today, men and women in many nations engage in time-honored baking traditions, shaping the round loaf with rough side down, rolling oval loaves with extended fingers, scissoring oblongs of dough into ear-of-wheat

Taos (vicinity), Taos County, New Mexico. Spanish-American woman removing baked bread from outdoor earthen horns (oven) by means of a long wooden paddle.
[© *Courtesy of Agricultural Research Service, USDA. Photo by Russell Lee.*]

A loaf of bread found at Pompeii. Note the baker's stamp.

Distributing the blessed bread during mass.

shapes, cupping the oiled palm to form Parkerhouse rolls, braiding festive loaves of challah, or pushing their fingertips into a stretched lump of dough before pinching the two long sides together to form a baguette. In their classic work on homemaking, Ellen Henrietta Richards and Sophronia Maria Elliott, the authors of *The Chemistry of Cooking and Cleaning* (1912), declared that "the most important of all the articles of diet which can be classed under the head of starchy foods is bread." (p. 33)

Staff of Life

Baking followed fire and clay ovens in the history of technological development. Bakers built the first crude ovens in the Ukraine around 25,000 BCE; the first grain growers cultivated seed-bearing plants starting around 10,000 BCE. In the Bronze Age, bread baking required a cast-iron or clay *sac,* or sheet, that went into the heat with an iron cloche perched like a bell jar over the loaves. Bakers heaped embers on the domed lid much as Dalmatian bakers baked potato, millet, and black breads in the nineteenth century. The system resembled colonial open-hearth Dutch ovens, which cooks mounded with fresh coals to bake fireplace breads.

The evolution of sophisticated bread-making skills began with the simple cooking of grain heads into cereals. In 1500 BCE, Egyptian agronomists hybridized a variety of wheat that required no toasting. Unlike millet, barley, and oats, it was the first grain to accept leavening and rise into moist, fluffy loaves.

In ancient Greece, bread makers wielded pestles in baked clay mortars or hollow tree trunks to dislodge kernels from chaff. From the stripped and winnowed grain they made the common *maza* (barley flour) or the more luxurious *artos* (white wheat flour), food of royal, priestly, and privileged classes. Bread became the single most important menu item for serving with *opson* (side dishes) of honey, cheese, olives, and oil; it also served as the basis for gruel or broth. For banquets, hosts displayed untouched white loaves as symbols of their wealth and status.

According to Roman myth, Vesta, goddess of the hearth, conspired with her associate Ceres, the grain goddess, to build an advanced and powerful culture nourished on bread. The introduction of baked goods to the early Roman diet relieved the tedium of *puls* (porridge). Cooks flavored various types and shapes of bread with honey and cheese. They raked out coals from a hot stone or brick oven, then put uncooked loaves on the oven floor and shut a heavy iron door to hold in the heat. As the growth of cities promoted specialization of labor, the home baker could choose to make her own bread in kitchen or community oven or, if finances allowed, could buy pastry, cake, or rolls from a professional bakery.

After the Anglo-Saxons supplanted the Roman conquerors of the British Isles, cooks relied on bread as part of the dietary triangle, the other points of which were roasted meats and dairy items and mead, the beverage that accompanied meals. The term *hlaf* (loaf) took such significance in Old English that it appeared in the translation of the Lord's Prayer for "daily bread." It also recurred in common speech to delineate the wife as *hlaf-dige* (loaf-distributor) and the servant as *hlaf-oetan* (loaf-eater).

The Loaf as Status Symbol

In medieval times, a variety of grains served as the basis of flour; the type of loaf a person ate depended on his or her social class. Fine-textured wheat flour became loaves for the feudal lord's table. Irish cottagers presented guests rounds of soda bread scored with an X for breaking into four portions. Scot bakers made barley and mixed-grain bannocks and oatcakes on a girdle.

According to the Castilian abbey of Santa María de Benevivere in Palencia, Spain, prestigious lay diners ate *candidus* (white) wheat loaves, called *paindemayne* (hand bread), the food of royalty. The masses subsisted on *grossus* (inferior) peasant loaves, scorned as the bread of dogs. Bakers made the humblest loaves from barley, rye, poppyseed, millet, spelt, sorghum, or, in the absence of grain, fava beans. In the worst of famines, people made flour from acorns, ferns, the sawdust of palm trees, fig roots, chestnuts, straw, almond husks, hornbeam, and sloes. The coarsest concoctions abraded the gut, aggravating epidemics of cholera and fever among the poor. On Sundays after mass, the laity blessed pieces of *panis benedictus* (holy bread) and distributed it to the poor, who valued it as a miracle cure for disease and a charm to cure dog and rat bites.

Among Polish cooks, bread baking, which they learned from the Goths, took on both mundane and religious significance. Cracow bakers invented the humble bagel around 1610. Home bakers made loaves for pagan and Christian ritual, marking the latter with the sign of the cross. If they dropped a loaf, they retrieved it, apologized, and kissed it. For weddings, they baked loaves as gifts, to be offered on the couple's doorstep with a bag of salt, symbols of the kitchen.

Balkan bread took on a sacred quality from the time the seed entered the furrow until the loaf was sliced. An engraving by S. Kamtz dated 1862 depicts devout Serbian Catholics gathered by a table centered with a wide, thin loaf topped with symbols of the Trinity. With heads bowed above long tapers, they stand quietly to bless the Yuletide meal. A Hungarian tradition explained that the baker topped the *császárzemle* (emperor's roll) with a cross to commemorate a Christian victory over Turkish invaders. The baker earned the right to the symbol in honor of bakers who heard insurgents tunneling toward the center of town and sounded the alarm that saved the people from slaughter. A similar legend accounts for a baking style of the Austro-German *kipfel.*

In northern Europe, bread came to the lord's table in its finest form. The pantler carried the freshest *manchet* (lord's loaf), a wheaten *pain de main* (hand bread) baked of the highest grade of flour. The high-status diner received the best portion, or "upper crust." (Scully 1995, 172) A groom served slices of bread to guests from a linen sling or a furled or pleated napkin. Individuals shared pitchers, platters, napkins, and loaves. From sharing came the term *companion,* referring to those who broke bread together.

Grist for Regulation

As specialized skills evolved into trades, bakers advanced from amateurs to professionals under the control of the royal pantler. In France, bakers were divided into three classes, each with its own status and salary. The lowest, the *fournier,* was a poor bread baker; second in prestige was the *pâtisserier,* a dough maker. After four years of apprenticeship, a lowly baker became a second-level tradesman, who could buy certification from the king. The third and most revered was the *boulanger,* who owned the shop in which bread was sold. In some instances, both gristmill and bakery belonged to the lord of the manor.

During the decline of meat consumption following the Black Death of 1348, bread assumed a mythic aura. The word *breads* became a synonym for groceries. In Italy, a worthy neighbor was *buono come il pane* (good as bread); a desperate matron with hungry children was said to yield her honor for bread when she turned to prostitution. Contract law specified tithe and rent in individual *de pane* (bread share) units and called farmsteads *terre da pane* (bread lands) and their produce a *recoltu panis* (bread harvest). Italians ate up to twenty-eight ounces of bread per day; Sicilians, who never approached their neighbors in wealth and variety of foodstuffs, ate more than thirty-six ounces. If bread hardened before it could be used, cooks shredded it into crumb dishes—the Spanish *migas,* Egyptian *fatta,* Bedouin *fattita,* and French *quenelles.*

French bakers formed a confraternity, a religious brotherhood known as the *talemeliers* (also *tameliers* or *talemetiers,* mixers of bread), protected by Saint Honoré. The confraternity set standards for loaf quality, size, and price. Estienne Boileau's *Registres de Métiers* (also *Livre des Mestiers,* or Registers of Trade, ca. 1260) collected these specifications, including a punishment for selling undersized loaves, which the offender had to donate to the poor. Because of the importance of baking to peasant contentment, in 1372, King Charles V set the price of loaves on a sliding scale affixed to the price of grain.

During a scarcity of grain during the reign of Charles VI, some bakers abandoned the confraternity and destroyed their ovens. The king intervened in 1415 and ordered them to rebuild the ovens and go back to baking. He forbade bakers' monopolies and the ownership of weapons, allowed no free days except specified holidays, and set the guild uniform—shirt, pants, and cap, but no hose—so citizens could easily recognize bakers. To protect buyers from being cheated, the king required bakeries to sell all goods within three days and destroy any stale leftovers. Longer apprenticeships and additional burdens on bakers increased stress and encouraged more men than women to enter the profession illegally. The French Revolution failed to dismantle the old bureaucracy, which hampered bakers until their total liberation in 1863.

In Ferrara, Italy, while the poor continued to bake crusts from whatever grain was available, the d'Este family put on a show of wealth and privilege with baked peacock, gilded pies, and intricate breads. The most famous loaf, called *coppia* (couple), a sculpted star-shaped bread, required costly white flour and shortening or olive oil for the shaping. For bakers who saw Christian symbolism in the *coppia,* it became a crucifix suitable for holy feasts; under an earthier interpretation—as a representation of human copulation—the twisted loaf honored state and family occasions, such as family alliances, weddings, and christenings.

To assure fair practice and steady output in late medieval England, where bakers tended to ignore statutes that dated back to King John, professional breadmakers formed guilds and codified detailed regulations to govern the making and sale of bread. In 1266, the English Assizes of Bread superintended bakeries and standardized weights and pricing. In 1419, pillorying was the punishment for bakers who used molding boards, perforated tabletops through which they could press the dough sent by householders for baking, enabling them to filch a portion of the mass. The introduction of sifted flour in 1650 lightened bread made of bran and ended the licensed baker's sideline of pig raising to use up wheat chaff. That bread was important to social and political stability was confirmed in 1482 in a decree of the dukes of Saxony that listed the foods owed to artisans each day and ended with a promise of bread twice a day.

Complaints continued into the late eighteenth century. In 1771, Tobias Smollett, the Scottish-born novelist and travelogue writer, complained of adulterated baked goods in England's capital: "The bread I eat in London is a deleterious paste, mixed up with chalk, alum and bone-ashes...the good people are not ignorant of this adulteration; but they sacrifice their taste, and their health and the lives of their tender infants…and the miller or the baker is obliged to poison them and their families." (Farmer 1985) In contrast to conditions in London, bakers emigrating from the British Isles to the New World gained respect for their honesty.

Rye Bread and Beaten Biscuits

In New England, until colonists perfected the planting of English wheat in American soil, bakers contented themselves with rye. They concocted a "rye-an'-injun" bread blended from rye and corn meal, the latter a gift from forest Indians. In Philadelphia, it was the mayor's job to supervise and inspect bakeries to assure homemakers that they were getting a fair deal. By law, the standard commercial loaf of rye, white, or coarse bread weighed a standard eight pounds. Bake staff cut chunks from a dough box and weighed them individually before leaving them to rise in oiled dough trays or bowls. The local baker initialed loaves as proof of professional pride.

Biscuit-making instructions from the colonies varied with regional style. In Maryland, the beaten biscuit required beating with an ax to soften the dough. For some bakers the biscuit break—a wood mangle that the baker hand-cranked to work the dough across a corrugated oak or poplar cylinder—lessened the work. The funeral biscuit bore a stamped design such as those mentioned in *The Secret Diary of William Byrd of Westover, 1709–1712.* Cooks lent their stamps to those memorializing a deceased family member.

By 1748, Benjamin Betterton was merchandising a line of decorated burial "biscakes," which he advertised in the *Pennsylvania Journal.* (Weaver 1989, 108) Among Lutherans of Montgomery County, Pennsylvania, a girl carrying a plate of cakes and a boy holding a tray with a whiskey or wine cup offered refreshments to each mourner in procession to the cemetery. Symbolic shapes on these biscuits included thistles, roses in bud for those who died young, roosters to represent resurrection, wheat sheaves representing the harvested soul, and plumes, the headgear of the horses that pulled the hearse. The wine-and-biscuit custom ended when temperance drives sought to stamp out the consumption of alcohol.

Biscuits were star attractions in prestigious homes in the eighteenth and nineteenth centuries until the railroads began distributing white flour and baking powder to most communities. In the American South, cooks stirred up buttermilk biscuits, thrice-raised angel biscuits, sweet potato biscuits, and catheads, craggy drop biscuits covered in natural ridges. Lacking shortening, cooks in Maryland and Virginia invented a new type of bread called *beaten biscuits.* To whip up a

batter of flour, butter, warm milk, and salt required eight hundred strokes with a steady hand, which aerated the mix. Some church-reared homemakers set the rhythm of their labor to the seven verses of the hymn "Abide with Me." The recipe survives from the presidency of Zachary Taylor, when his daughter, Betty Taylor Bliss, superintended the White House kitchen.

Health Food

In 1839, the writer Sarah Josepha Hale, editor of *Godey's Ladies Book,* published *The Good Housekeeper,* a systematic study of foods for the purpose of improving health. Hale considered bread the most important element of the diet. Because the baker was the only person to certify the quality of the ingredients, she advocated baking at home from good flour ground at the rate of no more than one or two bushels at a time. To assure purity, she suggested that the purchaser test a pinch of flour between two fingers moistened with sweet oil to see if the miller had adulterated his supply with whiting, the common named for ground calcium carbonate, or chalk. For all its thorough coverage, her text failed to deal with the problem of baker's carts hauling unwrapped loaves in the open air exposed to dust, insects, and humidity.

Hale was not the only writer to link bread with health. The distinguished Massachusetts author Mary Tyler Peabody Mann, author of *Christianity in the Kitchen: A Physiological Cook Book* (1857), made a direct connection between cooking and spiritual and physical wholeness. In her preface, she denounced wheat bread raised with saleratus (a leavening agent) and soda and warned homemakers about baker's flour adulterated with magnesia and carbonate of ammonia. She decreed that the woman of the house should make the bread herself: "Bread should be home-made. In this country, it is the general custom to make bread in families, but as our domestics are not scientific, it is absolutely necessary that it should not be left to them." (Mann 1857, 15)

What kind of bread to eat and how to make it became the subject of debate. Sylvester Graham, the father of graham flour, extolled the virtues of home-made whole-grain bread and recommended chewy bread as an answer to the health problems and moral decline of his day. Catharine E. Beecher and Harriet Beecher Stowe, the authors of *The American Woman's Home, or Principles of Domestic Science* (1869), also had much to say about bread, "the very foundation of a good table." (Beecher and Stowe 1994, 170) They contrasted "civilized" bread with the leaden flour and watery lumps baked by the savage. Mourning the passage of light, airy rolls and loaves, they bemoaned "the green, clammy, acrid substance, called biscuit, which many of our worthy republicans are obliged to eat in these days." (Ibid., 171) They advised the baker to buy quality yeast and a variety of flours, including rye and corn meal. With an ominous allusion to digestive problems, they remarked on "the unknown horrors of dyspepsia from bad bread...a topic over which we will draw a veil." (Ibid., 176)

From Home to Factory—and Back

To meet family needs, homemakers demanded equipment that would simplify bread making. The 1908 Sears, Roebuck catalog offered a cylindrical hand-crank bread mixer and kneader for $1.79. A sturdy tin-plated machine capable of handling ingredients for eight loaves, the machine required three minutes of cranking the gear-driven assembly to turn the entire covered apparatus around stationary paddles. In praise of the machine, the text claimed, "The White House Bread Kneader is simple, nothing to get out of order, and with ordinary care ought to last a lifetime. It is as easy to clean as a tin pail, can be clamped to any table and is the most convenient device of its kind ever invented." (Schroeder 1971, 464) For $4.82, the buyer could get the mixer plus thirty-seven additional pastry-making items, including patty pans, tube cake pan, pie plates, bread box, rotary flour sifter, and spice cabinet. On the same page were bulk bags of flour available in 25-, 50-, and 100-pound sizes for less than 3 cents per pound.

For bread baked in a brick oven, the cook used an iron bread rasp, a sander that removed dark, ashy crust and burned spots from the surface. Before the advent of window screens, bakers placed cool loaves in a ventilated tin or wood breadbox to protect them from insects and keep them from drying out. Sears, Roebuck marketed breadboxes with hinged lids and roll-tops.

The first electric dough-kneading machine, a model that held twenty gallons of dough, came from the workshop of Herbert Johnson for Hobart in 1911. It was never modified for home use, however, as the outbreak of World War I turned the company's machinery to military use. KitchenAid began marketing its dough mixer in 1912. A cheaper but less efficient hand-cranked tin bread maker or mixer introduced in the 1920s allowed the baker to rotate internal paddles on a central rod to create a uniform gluten dough.

In urbanized areas of the United States, homemakers stopped making bread when cheap, pre-sliced, pre-wrapped loaves became available at local markets. No longer a luxury for the wealthy, white bread found a loyal market in working-class households, where the busy housewife had less time than her predecessors

for raising and kneading dough for homemade loaves. On May 21, 1920, the Taggart Baking Company of Indianapolis launched Wonder Bread, a 1.5-pound loaf of white bread. Company vice president Elmer Cline merchandised the commercial loaf with a balloon logo he conceived at the International Balloon Race, held at the Indianapolis Speedway. Five years later, when Continental Baking of St. Louis bought the bakery, Wonder Bread, a mid-twentieth century kitchen phenomenon, became a national trademark. In 1939, at the New York World's Fair, the company constructed a modern bakery in a futuristic pavilion marked with the familiar crayon-colored bubbles that characterized the brand. Wonder Bread popped out of automated pans at the rate of 10,000 loaves per hour.

In 1941, the makers of Wonder Bread joined a national campaign to enrich white bread by restoring vitamins and minerals removed in the refinement of white flour. Additives supplied nutrients needed to prevent deficiency diseases such as beriberi and pellagra. The federal government also forced bread manufacturers to remove nitrogen trichloride bleach and petroleum derivatives that kept crumbs soft. When Hopalong Cassidy and Howdy Doody appeared on television's first color offerings, Wonder Bread sponsored the kid-pleasing programs. After ITT bought the company in 1968, Wonder Bread wrappers carried baking dates and nutritional information.

A competitor, Pepperidge Farm, turned Margaret "Maggie" Rudkin into a baking millionaire. In hopes of curing her son's asthma, in 1937 Rudkin began making home-baked bread free of chemical additives. She used stone-ground unbleached flour and added molasses, honey, butter, and whole milk. The boy's health improved, and Rudkin opened a mail-order business set up in her garage. Soon she was making 4,000 loaves a week. Publicity in the *New York Journal and American* necessitated a move to a permanent mill in Norwalk, New York, followed by a second mill in Pennsylvania in 1949. The addition of another mill in Illinois in 1953 enabled her to add cookies, frozen pastries, croutons, stuffing mix, and brown-and-serve rolls to her line of baked goods.

In Florida, where the novelist Marjorie Kinnan Rawlings, author of *Cross Creek* (1942), learned swampland cookery, the word *bread* did not stand for the white pre-sliced loaves bought by city dwellers. To lowlanders, *bread* signified a hierarchy of foods beginning with cornbread and working down to pone made in a skillet and hoecake cooked in a Dutch oven over a campfire. To the far end of respectability came hush-puppies, the fried cornmush croquettes that accompanied fresh-caught fish. "I assure you," she wrote, "that under the open sky [hushpuppies] are so succulent that you do not care whether you have the rest of your dinner or not." (Rawlings 1942, 210)

Tools of the Trade

Globally, bakers have created a large market for kitchen vessels and implements. The wire whisk is the tool of choice for blending shortening into flour. The metal dough scraper, topped with wood or plastic handle, ends in a rectangular blade for slicing dough into exact portions and is useful for lifting chopped vegetables into a wok, dicing butter, and scraping clean a work surface. A bread board, paste board, or ventilated wire bread rack aids in cooling and slicing loaves, either directly on the surface or atop a bread cloth.

In 1975, the master chef James A. Beard, a contributor to *The Cook's Catalogue*, listed the types and styles of loaf pans he preferred. In addition to tinned steel, Pyrex, and stoneware, he advocated the tin-coated steel Pullman loaf pan, which produced a nearly crustless *pain de mie* (soft-crumb bread) for sandwiches and canapés. The sliding cover kept out air to lighten the surface and caused the dough to swell up the straight sides and into the corners and top of the box. A silicone glaze on the preoxidized surface simplified removal of near-perfect loaves, ideal for slicing.

In the 1990s the bread machine applied the technology of the crockpot and the automatic coffeemaker to the bread making process. West Bend pioneered the all-in-one electric breadmaker in 1993, a breakthrough in the multiple stages of mixing, kneading, proofing, and baking. Early in the twenty-first century, features in the Salton Breadman Plus—a nonstick loaf pan, eighty-one settings, a fruit-and-nut add-in, instant recall and delay bake timer, and power failure backup—assured home bakers perfectly timed loaves. At the January 2001 International Housewares Show in Chicago, West Bend displayed a model that made bread for four in forty-five minutes.

Persisting Traditions

Bread remains central to the diet of people around the globe. Shoppers in Bucharest queue at neighborhood bakeries for the same bread that country women baked daily in their home ovens. Bakers in Yugoslavia, Albania, and Bulgaria recoil from delicate French flour and insist that hearty bread must be brown and robust to accompany substantial meals and tankards of beer.

The Malaysian *roti* maker twirls dough in the air, then folds it much like a handkerchief and places it on the grill. Niue islanders select local fruit for traditional coconut bread; Estonians, Latvians, Lithuanians, and Finns use plentiful rye in their dark breads. Swedish cooks base breakfast on *knäckebröd* (crisp bread) and serve open-faced lunch sandwiches called *smörgåsar*. Danes characterize a ready hospitality with pumpernickel, *rugbrød* (rye bread), and open-faced sandwiches built on *smørrebrød* (buttered bread), the basis for *koldt bord*, a spread of cheese, salami, salad, and smoked fish. In Norway the crisp, crackerlike *flatbrød* is baked on a *takke* (flat griddle). A sweet loaf Norwegians call *verterkake* derives from *verterol* (brewer's wort), which moistens the mix.

Ethiopians bake injera, a raised flat bread made from fermented *teff* (millet dough), cooked on a clay board over a log fire, and served on a round basket-shaped table. Diners wrap it around a fiery hot *doro wat* (chicken stew). The Gurage of southwest Ethiopia rely on the false banana plant (*Ensete edulis*); they strip the plant of its inner tissue, ferment the pulp in deep pits, then bake it into *wusa* (bread). In South Africa, breakfast begins with tea or coffee and dry rusk, a seed-studded biscuit introduced by the Boers as safari food. For snacks, South Africans stir up dough for *shraak*, a crisp unleavened pocket bread that accompanies pickles and cheese. A more substantial loaf, elephant foot bread, is a yeast bread made from mashed potatoes and flour and worked up to cover the entire bottom of an oven. Incised with mock elephant toes, the oversized loaves serve a crowd.

In French Polynesia, round metal containers resembling newspaper boxes receive fresh-baked commercial loaves that are delivered each morning without wrappings. Colonialism has influenced the Togolese dependence on English loaf bread and the French *baguette*. The Kyrgyz vary their breads by choosing from flat rounds of *tahngdyr nahn* or long, dark loaves of *byolko*; Mauritians also choose between French bread and *roti* (flat bread) and serve bread with *varaynya* (preserves) as a dessert. The Hunza of northern Pakistan liven mundane dough into *kimochdun*, a holiday bread made with milk and almonds and cooked in a hot skillet.

Flat bread prevails in numerous lands. The primitive desert version, baked in hot sand and embers in Algeria, Tunisia, and the Sinai, requires no utensils. In India, tandoori-baked *chapatti* is the standard; Moroccans call their variety *k'sra*; Bedouins, *fatir*; and Turks, *lahmajun*. To create a chewy, flat center and softer outer edge, Turkish bakers stamp dough with a *durtlik* (bread stamp) attached to a wood handle. Jordanians base their meals on pita bread, a chewy flat bread that the nomads of Petra cook on hot metal disks over campfires; Israeli and Palestinian menus feature *falafel*, pita bread with a filling of fried chickpeas. The Mexican version of flat bread is the tortilla; the Puerto Rican equivalent is *pan sobao*.

Choices and service of breads may reflect the lifestyle of a region and the state of its economy. In Belgium, a leisurely breakfast of breads, jam, and a hot beverage is the norm; in Ecuador, cooks bake hot bread for afternoon snacks. Where baking is a longstanding profession, families stock their larders with a wide variety of breads. In the United Arab Emirates, cooks can choose from twenty-three bread types, the most popular being a thin loaf called *raqaq*. Choices in France, Italy, and the Czech Republic are similarly broad. Poverty often reduces families to bread alone. In 1975, when famine stalked villagers of India and Bangladesh, mothers traded goods for wheat and cooked only one meal a day. Some days the single meal consisted of *chapaties* and salt. In Sardinia, the shift from home-baked bread to bakery loaves accompanied the shift in the island economy from peasant farms to industry. In the 1960s, as homemakers gave up drying figs, salting olives, and preserving tomatoes, they also ceased making bread. The purchase of bakery goods became a mark of women's liberation from the oven.

See also **Graham, Sylvester; Kosher Kitchens; Medieval Kitchens; Yeast**

Further Reading

Alford, Jeffrey, and Naomi Duguid, "On the Flatbread Trail," *Amsco World*, September–October 1995, 16–25.
Hale, Sarah Josepha. *Early American Cookery: "The Good Housekeeper, 1841,"* Mineola, N.Y.: Dover Publications, 1966.
Jacob, H. E. *Six Thousand Years of Bread: Its Holy and Unholy History*. Garden City, N.Y.: Lyons Press, 1997.
Mann, Mrs. Horace. *Christianity in the Kitchen: A Physiological Cook Book*. Boston: Ticknor and Fields, 1857.
Reinhart, Peter. *Bread Upon the Waters*. New York: Perseus, 2000.
Richards, Ellen H., and S. Maria Elliott. *The Chemistry of Cooking and Cleaning*. Boston: Whitcomb & Barrows, 1912.
Sheraton, Mimi. *The Bialy Eaters: The Story of a Bread and a Lost World*. New York: Broadway Press, 2000.

BRERETON, MAUD ADELINE

In the days preceding the enactment of women's suffrage, Maud Adeline Cloudesley Brereton, the publicist for the British Commercial Gas Association (BCGA) and author of *The Mother's Companion* (1909), championed a domestic revolution to liberate women through improved, affordable home technology. From her conviction that education and health benefited the nation, she wrote and lectured in America and Europe, stressing the multiple roles of women as wives, mothers, and family and home managers. Her

activism earned her an award from France in 1907 for service to international public health.

Hired by the BCGA in 1912, Brereton promoted gas as kitchen fuel. At her urging, the industry targeted its advertising toward a female audience. With the average homemaker in mind, the BCGA marketed its product as a "silent servant" and "working man's friend." (Clendenning 1998, 5) The association pointed out that not only was gas an efficient, labor-saving fuel, it also had health benefits, eliminating from the home air pollutants that caused respiratory irritation and asthma.

In 1913, Brereton, representing the BCGA, stood on a platform with engineers and businessmen. She denounced the low standards of domestic sanitation due to the absence of hot water; she spoke of the "repetitive and soul-killing drudgery" that debilitated housewives. (Clendenning 1998, 14) With twenty years of experience in public health, she had the data to back up her claim that benefits to women through improved home heating would uplift the nation as a whole. At Brereton's urging, the association erected model homes, hosted cooking contests, offered free lectures, and demonstrated the advantages of gas over coal and even electricity, which Thomas Edison had touted since 1882.

To counter the image of electricity as the latest in technology, promoters of gas had to revamp their position in the marketplace. Brereton organized conferences, edited two trade magazines, and issued a monograph on the value of gas technology to the home. Her media blitz reached architects, housing magnates, and health officials. Her writing and speaking skills earned her the vice presidency of the Society of Women Journalists and a job as consultant for the British Ministry of Food during World War I.

Central to Brereton's demands for reform was a shift in society's definition of *home* and *wife*. She deplored the enslavement of women to the kitchen and protested limitations on their imagination, creativity, and work. She proposed that gas companies establish reading rooms stocked with source material on domestic science and that they hire technical experts and female demonstrators who could advise women on the use of gas for cooking. She urged industry managers to involve themselves in issues of health and women's liberation.

Brereton championed free lunch programs for hungry children and home economics classes for girls and women to teach hygienic food handling and preparation. Doctors supporting her agenda advocated study of such home health hazards as arsenic-laced wallpaper, toxic paint, damp areas that sheltered vermin, inadequate plumbing, and poor ventilation. Home designers targeted the numerous health risks of the standard four-story Victorian home: coal cook stoves in basement sculleries, open water cisterns, and multiple flights of poorly lit stairs. Using her own home as a model of a healthful environment, Brereton urged architects to rethink the plan of the typical house to minimize stress on housewives and servants.

See also **Gas; Victorian Kitchens**

Further Reading

Clendinning, Anne, "Gas and Water Feminism: Maud Adeline Brereton and Edwardian Domestic Technology," *Canadian Journal of History*, April 1, 1998, 2–24.

BROOMS, BRUSHES, AND MOPS

The kitchen business in brooms, brushes, and mops derived from a domestic need for tools to clean food preparation areas and cooking utensils. Bird wings, burs, and brushes with wood, bone, or ivory handles or grips served utilitarian purposes in prehistory. The *Codex Mendoza* (1540), a key native manuscript describing Aztec culture, recorded injunctions to young girls to "Seize the broom, be diligent with the sweeping." Native Americans of the Southwest used the sturdy, fibrous yucca plant to make brooms and brushes for sweeping out pueblos and scouring *comals,* the hot baking stones on which they shaped tortillas. Archeologists have found these household items preserved intact in the dry desert climate. To the southeast, in the Caribbean, St. Lucia islanders wrapped coconut fronds around a stick to make yard brooms, which they used to sweep up debris around open hearths.

Special Purpose Brushes

Over time and around the world, specialized brushes and brooms have been created to serve many purposes in the kitchen.

Baby bottle brush is a narrow, soft-bristled, flexible column with flanged brush ends for scrubbing baby bottles and removing residue from decanters

Blacking brush is a stiff-bristled tool for removing rust from grills and cast iron ranges and reblacking them with black lead

Broom cake tester is a circle of 4.5-inch corn husk bristles attached to a dowel and thong for hanging; bakers can snap off a clean straw for testing cakes for doneness

Garbage disposer brush is a columnar brush of polypropylene bristles used to dislodge residue in the disposer tank

Glass and tumbler brush is a long-handled scrubber bearing a column of bristles for reaching into the bottom of drinking glasses, bottles, coffeepots, wine decanters, and vases

Glazing brush is a long-napped brush with stiff bristles for spreading gelatin and glazes over baked goods, broiled fish, and roasted birds and meat

Hearth besom is the homemade Irish hearth broom composed of a bundle of twigs bound to a stick to return spreading ash to the hearthstone

Pastry brush is a simple tip of natural hog bristle shaped like a flat or round paint brush banded with stainless steel; also, a round fluff of goose feathers secured on a wire handle used for buttering, basting turkeys, or glazing pastry

Pot brush is a long-handled tool with tampico (a stiff fiber similar to jute) bristles for use in institutional kitchens for heavy scrubbing; a shorter version made from palm fiber, the material used in doormats and boot brushes, is meant for cleaning griddles

Potato brush is a West German specialty that blends nylon, natural fiber, and brass wire bristles on a rounded head set at an angle from the handle for removing soil from tubers and chemical residues from fruits

Scouring brush is a coarse-fibered brush attached to a durable wood handle for scrubbing potatoes and winter squash

Sink brush is a sturdy fiber or steel mesh brush that fans into a semicircle for removing crusts from pots, griddles, waffle irons, and sinks.

Spout brush is a tiny brush composed of a wire handle wrapped in a spiral around a thin sheaf of stiff bristles for debriding spouts of iceboxes, lemonade coolers, percolators, urns and samovars, and teapots; one version is adapted for cleaning the narrow spaces between the buttons of telephones and kitchen appliances

Twin bar brush is a ruff of nylon bristles on dual hardwood posts attached to a metal base and mounted on suction cups to enable the user to scour the interior and exterior of a glass or mug in one motion

Vegetable brush is an all-purpose kitchen tool composed of bristles set in a circle of twisted wire and attached to a short wood handle for silking corn, removing pin feathers from hens, and other jobs requiring moderate friction

Visp is a Swedish coarse-fiber brush head bound with wire and attached to a wood handle for scouring pots

Homely Implements

Essential to the home brewer's task was the traditional besom, a bunch of broomstraw bound to a stick at top and bunched together with a cord below. Like a baker's whisk, the homely broom swished through fermenting liquids. According to the domestic expert Dorothy Hartley's *The Land of England* (1979), the brewer hung the besom to air-dry by a leather cord or laid it across wall pegs. Because it had no other uses that might have rid it of residue, it held yeast spores that were returned to the mix when it was used again and sped the brewing process. As a symbol of the brewing trade, every alehouse, the most common gathering place in Tudor England, displayed an ale-stake or broom.

European housekeepers favored a variety of brushes and brooms. Cooks in the time of Elizabeth I used brushes made of fine hair to color and adorn marchpane (marzipan). According to John Partridge's *The Treasurie of Commodious Conceits and Hidden Secrets* (1584), the job of gilding confections and tarts with edible gold leaf called for the use of "Conies tailes" (rabbit's tails), natural brushes that aided the decorator in applying designs or words to paper for transferring to the surface of the cake or tart. (Denny, n.d., 29)

In 1770, the English inventor William Addis, incarcerated for debt, improvised a toothbrush in his jail cell by boring holes in a bone and inserting bristle, which he glued into place. The brush evolved into a family of domestic implements suited to such meticulous chores as cleaning small crevices and spreading egg-wash glazes on pies and loaves. The common birch besom, made of springy twigs with a stick handle, required an ash-strip binding, which the broom maker pulled free from an ash log soaked in a running stream. The besom had many uses at the hearth and about the kitchen, dooryard, and garden.

A baby-bottle brush from the 1870s had a crank attached to the wooden handle for easy rotation in tight confines. Brewers used bottle washers and bristle brushes to scour bottles and casks. To reach the bottom, the cleaner applied a chain brush, a long-handled implement that bore a flexible tail of chain links, metal beads, or wire and rounds of bristles. Bakers needed the flat yeast-tub brush, made of a wood grip fitted with tampico fiber and marketed in England by W. Jaburg & D. J. Barry.

In addition to a stiff broom, brushes, abrasive powder, and sand, the cleaner of floors relied on a homemade device composed of old rags sliced into strips and spiked onto a mop nail that was driven into a handle. The mop bucket sometimes contained a tin attachment pierced with holes to support the soap and allow dissolved portions to drain back into the mop water. A three-stage mopping required soaping, rinsing, and carrying the mop outdoors to spin dry between the palms before the final going over, which sometimes included the spreading of a few drops of paraffin for a shiny finish. To protect the knees, kitchen help wore kneeling pads made of shredded toweling and buckled to the leg or placed their knees on scrubbing mats woven of rushes or coconut fiber. For added convenience in mopping floors, in 1893 Thomas W. Stewart patented a long-handled mop with a T-head. To stabilize the fibers, he created a spring-loaded, pivoting clamp-and-rod device similar to the mop handles still in use in the twenty-first century.

American Innovations

On the American frontier, householders centered cooking, childcare, crafts, and home schooling around the fireplace, a source of light, heat, and—unavoidably—grit. To keep the hearth brushed clean where manufactured brooms were unavailable, thrifty folk made their own. A sturdy sweeping or scrubbing broom consisted of a limb or pole surrounded with stiff brush. To create a tight, nonslip binding, the maker soaked rawhide and stretched it over the brush ends. When the broom dried, the bristles remained straight and stiff enough to dislodge spills from the hearth.

American-made brooms required broom corn imported from Italy or wild panicles that Native Americans cleaned of seeds and shaped around a stick for sale to white housewives. In the Appalachian hills, home besom or broom makers collected twigs to dry for soaking, then bound or wired them to a stout ash, oak, or hickory stick. With more effort, they fashioned a fast-selling hickory broom from a single piece. To make bristles, carvers sliced thin slivers and bound them back with wire to produce a tough scrubber suited to puncheon floors. A sturdy institutional broom expedited the oiling of a floor by removing residue that clung to sawdust. This method suited slaughterhouses, cannery kitchens, industrial plants, courthouses, and schools, where heavy traffic prohibited regular soap-and-water mopping.

The founder of the American broom trade, Benjamin Franklin, salvaged seed from a French broom and planted it in his kitchen garden plot. In 1785, Thomas Jefferson, the keeper of an enlightening garden and farm daybook, did likewise at Monticello, his estate in rural Virginia, thus creating a useful job for idle slaves and children and a new product for local markets. After introducing his brooms in Pittsfield, New London, Albany, and Boston, he started an industry that, by 1810, was turning out 70,000 brooms a year. The broom became a standard part of the fireplace set, a wrought iron stand holding poker, tongs, shovel, and iron-banded hearth brush.

As described by Samuel M. Sener, a state folklorist writing in the New Year 1892 edition of *Christian Culture,* an early winter tradition was the gathering of neighbors to slaughter pigs. The thrifty Pennsylvania housewife saved the bristle derived from this process to clean, dry, comb, and sell to brush makers, who exported their goods to Europe. In the late nineteenth century, quality bristle brought 75 cents per pound for the long and 40 cents for short. The money came in handy for buying Christmas gifts.

Handcrafting of brooms became a task of the elderly and handicapped and a money-making project for institutions that housed orphans and the blind or deaf. In the mid-nineteenth century, machinists facilitated the task of broom making with winders, presses, and trimmers. Broom sellers covered routes door-to-door and added to their stock the brush mat, scrub brush, hearth broom, and cob broom, a long-handled round brush used to remove spider webs from upper shelves, window frames, rafters, light fixtures, and cornices. They also sold child-sized brooms as educational toys for prospective homemakers.

The sister inventors Emma and Mary Dietz contributed to housekeeping efficiency with their dust pan and crumb receiver, which they exhibited at Philadelphia's 1876 Centennial Exposition. In the same year, the inventor Susan Hibbard simplified a humble but necessary cleaning chore with a low-cost implement: a feather duster made of turkey feathers. Pitted against her husband, George Hibbard, for rights to the patent, she proved her ownership of the idea of turning feathers into a dusting aid.

Keeping the housekeeper clean while engaging in this dirty work was the purpose of other devices. Jonathan Periam's handbook *The Home & Farm Manual: A Pictorial Encyclopedia of Farm, Garden, Household, Architectural, Legal, Medical and Social Information* (1884) explained how to sweep in short strokes and how to employ salt, fresh grass, moist corn meal, or tea leaves as a strewing medium to prevent clouds of dust. He added that toughening brooms weekly with boiling suds and hanging them up to dry kept plenty of sweep in the bristles. In August 1897, a black inventor, Lloyd P. Ray, patented a dustpan. He made his wood-handled device out of sheet metal, which he fashioned into a collection bin. Subsequent models came in varied styles and materials, including decorative covered pans in japanned metal or tole painted in flowered designs.

The 1908 Sears, Roebuck & Company catalog pictured an array of brushes to lighten unpleasant household chores. For stoves, the curved tampico brush with hardwood back provided five rows of bristles and a separate heel brush for 13 cents. For windows, a 34 cent-brush head with two-inch bristles fit standard handles; a 28 cent-counter brush with extended end handle fit into odd corners to dust and clean. The 63 cent-floor scrubber with bristles radiating in all directions suited hardwood and painted floors but was too abrasive for carpets. For the thrifty homemaker, the catalog touted an assortment of five floor, dusting, scrubbing, and stove brushes for $1.63 to "end your brush troubles." (Schroeder 1971, 467)

Fifteen years later, the Sears catalog was featuring an even larger variety of brushes, brooms, and mops for the well-equipped home. An appealing combination deal offered a triangular dry dust mop for reaching into corners, a matching oil mop, spare handles, and can of mop oil for $1.30. Only minimal ad copy accompanied products that needed no introduction—the flat broom at $1.25, floor brush for $1.20, self-wringing mop for 85 cents (58 cents more than in 1908), extra mop head (19 cents), palmyra fiber scrubber (15 cents), and hand duster (50 cents). Two years later, a discreet ad in the January issue of *Good Housekeeping* lauded the Brown Daisy polishing mop, a wax-treated dry swab that ended dependence on messy buckets and wringers.

In 1929, a decade after mechanical refrigerators gained popularity, keeping them free of spills and odors became a preoccupation of homemakers. *Collier's* magazine warned that "slime accumulates in [the drainpipes] constantly and should be removed with a long-handled circular brush." (Lovegren 1995, 10) The same era saw the invention of the coffeepot brush, a miniature bristled coil on a slender wire, used to remove residue that, if left in the pot, ruined the flavor of the coffee.

Factory broom makers improved on the round-head broom by flattening straws and stitching them into place before inserting the sharpened handle and lopping off uneven ends. Sewing originally required looping hanks of straw with a half-hitch of cord. Later technology allowed waxing the broom head to keep straws in place and securing bristles with the aid of a heavy-duty industrial sewing machine. In 1983 Henry Hadley of the University of Illinois ended dependence on hand-harvested Mexican broomcorn by hybridizing the world's first machine-harvestable variety, which produces numerous shades of green, yellow, and red.

Persisting Need

In industrialized countries, brooms have largely been replaced by vacuum cleaners, power washers, and leaf blowers, although they still command a sizeable market of specialty items such as the cobweb broom, a quaint hearth tool still in use in high-ceilinged rooms. Other specialized adaptations of broom and brush include the tiny coffee spout brush, a double-handled sling for scrubbing the backs of faucets and taps, a coiled brush for removing mold from the tracks of sliding windows and doors, and the flexible, hair-catcher brush, a long wire snake with short, stiff bristles for removing plugs from drains. A formidable implement, the polypropylene disposer brush removes malodorous residue from garbage disposers. Despite the availability of synthetic bristles and machine-made brooms and brushes for specific jobs, old-style Appalachian, Pennsylvania Dutch, and Shaker broom makers have continued to present their craft at demonstrations of hand-made wares. Late in the twentieth century, Arcola, Illinois, became the broom corn capital, raising broom corn and selling seeds worldwide.

Brooms, brushes, and mops remained kitchen necessities throughout the twentieth century and into the new millenium. Third-world marketing entered a new phase with the production of attractive, bamboo-handled brooms made in Thailand from sorghum grass. Continuing the trend toward specialization, a telescoping duster fitted with a lamb's wool head allowed housekeepers to reach recessed and track lighting. For many busy housekeepers, the so-called electric broom, basically a low-power upright vacuum cleaner, replaced its homely predecessors.

See also **Shaker Kitchens**

C

CABINETS AND CUPBOARDS

Cabinets and cupboards are extensions of early forms of food storage—caches and canisters—both designed to assure a supply of foods such as game, nuts, and plants abundant during only part of the year. The Havasupai, who resided near the Grand Canyon, sun-dried local desert fruit and berries. They puréed squawbush and desert thorn berries, dried the purée, and stored it in buckskin sacks. To protect precious supplies from rodents and human raiders, they created a storage system under canyon ledges away from the village. Out of sight at a level above possible flooding, they constructed storage cists, stone chambers cemented with clay. When they had filled the cache with one season's harvest, they sealed the outer surface with mud.

Open Cabinet left.

Rustic Furnishings

The wood cupboard first came into use for the storage and display of dinnerware and utensils. The original European kitchen cabinet, the ambry (or aumbry) cupboard, which the French called an *armoire,* is a relic of the Medieval Merchant's House in Southampton, England. It represented an improvement over a simpler method of storage: a recess in a wall used to hold clothing and dishes or a niche in abbey kitchens and churches where vestments and ceremonial silver were stored. The high Middle Ages produced the ambry cabinet as a free-standing food and dry goods "livery and dole" furnishing four feet high and three feet wide. (Banham 1997, 193) The cabinetmaker provided a single shelf, called a *borde,* and pierced the front of the cupboard with ventilation holes in an ornate pattern.

Used by a wholesaler or retailer as a wine cabinet, the ambry cupboard suited the needs of a neighborhood inn or small-scale private kitchen. The center door, attached by a butterfly hinge, featured a woven screen that let wine breathe. For commercial kitchens, it held jacks (pitchers) of various vintages, from which customers poured smaller portions into take-home containers. For security, the cabinetmaker attached a long, decorative hinged tang forked at the end. The catch plate and barrel bolt accommodated an iron lock. In modern reproductions, the ambry cabinet holds vials of chrism, the sacramental oil used in anointing ritual.

The ambry evolved into a larger, more solid structure, the pierced livery cupboard, which held plated servings for absent diners as well as salt, verjuice, bread, cheese, pickles, pasties, game, and meat along with napkin wrappers for the making of quick meals or snacks to be eaten out of hand. The Scottish version, called an *aumry,* served as a cupboard. The almerie was a plain dish press, in contrast to the dressing burd, a workstation for dismembering and fileting meat. In Poland, where Queen Jadwiga came to the throne in 1384, a smaller chest resembling a jewelry box held her dried fruit, almonds, and spices, which she locked to ensure access by none other than her own personal kitchen staff.

The typical Irish household sported a bolting hutch or meal ark, a cabinet built by an arkwright to hold flour, oatmeal, and bran, the staple foods at every meal. Richard Ainsworth's *The Old Homesteads of Accrington & District* (1928) characterized a family heirloom of the Ainsworth's of Clayton-le-Moor as a "meal ark." In Wales, the Welsh dresser offered drawers; the Merioneth variant had doored compartments for storage. These evolved into a farmhouse showcase for crockery, Delft china, noggins (small cups or mugs) and piggins (drinking pails), pewter, and ornate trumpery and treen souvenirs carved as gifts. The Yorkshire and East Anglia variety had a plate rack (or Delft rack) faced with guard rails. Dressers from Brittany, Northumberland, and the Midlands enhanced shelving with bobbined galleries. The largest dressers held fish, poultry, and whole meat and game carcasses for garnishing, saucing, and carving and could support a corpse for prefuneral viewing. When these rather crude cabinets began to be used in dining rooms, they took on such refinements as inset clocks and cabriole legs, becoming more showpieces than functional kitchen furniture.

In a similar manner, the French developed *armoires, dressoirs,* or *buffets* into richly decorated dressers or cabinets with massive carved panels, columns, and feet. As Alienor de Poitiers explained in the 1330s, observers could estimate the owner's status by the number of tiers a cabinet featured, from a single tier for a knight to five for a queen. To enhance the display of plate and create a contrast to the dark wood, owners decked the wall unit with a tester, or canopy, to impress upon guests their social prominence.

The English ambry combined with the cupboard in the early 1500s to complement room paneling. Placed at a bedside, it held night refreshments and a beverage set for an aristocrat or an honored guest. The two-tiered cupboard, a standard furnishing of the Elizabethan or Jacobean dining room, displayed pitcher and cups, sugar chest, cruets for vinegar and oil, and condiment pots. With the emergence of silver as a status item, Baroque sideboards held unusual pieces, including a fountain for rinsing glassware, a wine cooler, and tools for crushing salt along with an ivory knife for dispensing it. Before dinner, the staff placed on top a wash basin and flagon of water and gold and silver salvers for serving loose items such as table implements.

Refinements and Decoration

As the European cabinet evolved into the credenza, an art object rather than a utilitarian chest, it acquired veneers, painting, inlays of tortoiseshell, metal, and ebony, marble plaques, marquetry, mirrors, leather covering, brass medallions, and moldings and carvings. The French created the latticed *panetiére* (sideboard) solely as a decorative dresser for bread. More ornate, the Spanish *vargueno* (cabinet) of this period consisted of a moveable furnishing displayed on a stand, an offshoot of church furnishings.

Cabinets never divorced themselves completely from their original task of supplying the table with needed items. In the early 1700s, Lady Grisell (or Grizel) Baillie, mistress of Mellerstain, one of Scotland's great Georgian houses, made her personal list of necessities for the sideboard in her domestic account book, *The Household Book of Lady Grisell Baillie*

(1733). The list read, "Bread, Water, Peper, Vinegar, ail, wines, Mustard, Shalot, Smal Beer, sugerr, Oyle, Sallad." (Banham 1997, 194).

An essential to European and American kitchens, the cupboard, patterned after dressers, offered two areas of storage. On the open shelving at top, dishes and serving pieces stood ready for use. Attractive glass, pewter, and china received maximum display space to brighten simple homesteads and reflect glints from firelight and candles. Below, closed shelving secured linens, place mats, and such humble items as tea cozies, canisters, cutlery, and everyday flatware. In some homes, a notched cabinet adjacent to the cupboard held spoons vertically in neat rows. Tin sconces attached to the wood held candles and lamps at eye level, enabling the housekeeper to search for needed items.

Other parts of Europe established unique cabinetry traditions. Elena Burman Molokhovets's classic Russian cookbook *A Gift to Young Housewives* (1861) urged the beginner to opt for built-in cupboards with insulated doors. She pictured them placed on the outside wall of the house, one for warm storage and another ventilated to the outdoors. In Transylvania, a small decorated *szuszék* (chest) was used to store salt. Throughout the Continent and the United Kingdom, the stodgy, middle-class Biedermeier cabinetry and the dark, often massive Victorian buffet, with its ornate carvings, columns, doors, turrets, and mirrors, formed the nerve center of table service. Status-conscious hosts kept glassware, china, linens, silverware, and faience and majolica on display for use by guests and during holiday meals.

Among the colonists of North America, cabinets tended to be built into walls as a means of making full use of floor space. Because they framed their homes with vertical timbers eight inches wide, there was ample space for recessed shelving in between the uprights. Clean lines and functional, unfussy construction appealed especially to the Shakers, who arrived in New York aboard the *Mariah* in 1774 and established a permanent complex at Niskayuna (now Watervliet) south of Albany, New York. The nook-style storage shelves in the New England saltbox home paralleled a matching alcove bench by the fireplace, which made good use of chimney heat.

Edward Brown set up as a joiner and carpenter in Ipswich, Massachusetts, in 1637. Until his death twenty-two years later, he provided settlers with cabinets and sideboards as well as chairs and spinning wheels. The April 8, 1736 issue of the *Boston News-Letter* bore an advertisement from cabinet-maker John Davis of Summer Street, who offered to sell English glue for furniture-making and repair of wooden joints,

which would have easily loosened on exposure to wide fluctuations in temperature near open fireplaces.

Finished pieces occupied central positions in the household. In *Good Wives: Image and Reality in the Lives of Women in Northern New England, 1650–1750* (1991), the historian Laurel Thatcher Ulrich summarized the kitchen furnishing in the home of Beatrice and Francis Plummer of Newbury, Massachusetts, in 1672: a "cupboard, a 'great chest,' a table, and a backless bench called a 'form,' plus a second bed." (Ulrich 1991, 18) Like fireside spiders and cook pots, cabinets stood on long, sturdy legs, sometimes ending in a wooden globe for maximum contact with flooring. The purpose was two-fold—to support heavy hardwood construction and to lift unwieldy furnishings from the floor for ease of mopping and vermin control.

For the manor house or inn, the wood dresser was a laborsaving workspace. Built like a cupboard, it contained upper shelves to hold linens, utensils, plates, and serving items. The shelf at waist level was a meat-dressing board, a place for boning roasts, trussing fowl, and readying large cuts of meat for serving. To keep tools such as mallets, whetstones, cleavers, and boning knives at hand, the user often nailed leather loops to the edge of the shelf. Drawers and bins below offered additional storage space.

A valuable adjunct to the appearance and durability of cabinets were the lift and the waterboard. To protect the feet and fascia of the cabinet from mop water and accidental flooding, homemakers elevated the pieces on slate, tile, or pottery blocks. Ornate lifts bore crests and impressive bosses. Also providing decoration along with functionality was the breakwater, a board that attached to the skirting board and thus covered the space under the cabinet. It kept out dust balls, mice, and vermin while concealing nicks, splits, or damage to the finish of the piece. Some of these floor-level additions were drilled with holes to ventilate the under-cabinet area.

A low cupboard from the 1780s, the Dutch *kas* secured foodstuffs behind two hinged doors. Ball feet held the framework high enough off the floor to allow for cleaning underneath. A tall eighteenth-century Canadian version doubled the low Dutch piece by mounting chest on chest for storing foods and table linen. Decorative New England chests and cabinets sported painted scenes and folk art symbols on front, top, and sides. The Welsh cupboard added a decorative molding to open shelving to set off the family's collection of dishes and treen. The New Mexican *trastero* (cupboard) often sported grooves, insets, and wrought iron hinges and latches. More sedate, the punched-tin cupboard held jars of food behind ventilated doors that encouraged the circulation of air.

So-called safes enclosed foods behind doors that could be padlocked. The meat safe, a four-legged cabinet screened with wire gauze to keep out vermin, provided ventilated sides and pierced shelving for storing game; a similar cabinet, the pierced tin pie safe, decorated kitchens with patterned holes rayed like suns and stars or imitating common quilt motifs. The butter-and-cheese safe, a hexagonal version for the dairy, described in the *American Agriculturist* in December 1875, stored stoneware crocks of milk and cream away from dust and insects. Workers could reach the contents by rotating shelves fitted to a central post. The origin of the term *safe* as applied to kitchen storage is unclear. The U.S. writer James Agee once speculated that "farm families, whose most urgent treasures are the food they eat, use for its storage-box the name used among middle-class people for the guardian of money, ledgers, and 'valuable papers.'" (Agee 1960, 162)

A May 1876 issue of *American Agriculturist* presented L. D. Snook's ideal farmhouse kitchen, a utilitarian arrangement that suited the housewife who lacked servants. He placed the wood or iron sink and pump at a window. Below the sill, a slatted dish drainer received wet dishes, which dried quickly in the sunlight. The elongated counter separated upper and lower cabinets. An obvious workstation opposite the stove side of the room, the window unit prefigured paired counters and modern wall-hung cabinetry.

The American cabinet took on a unique form and style late in the 1800s. From a family of six furniture makers, designer Gustav Stickley of Osceola, Wisconsin, worked in his uncle's factory in Brandt, Pennsylvania, and learned to value natural color, grain, and texture. When he established his own firm in Binghamton, New York, in 1884 with brothers Charles and Albert, he lacked the machinery for crafting elegant English reproductions. Instead, his shop turned out hand-made designs in simple, unadorned shapes based on cabinetry he studied at the Shaker settlement in New Lebanon, Pennsylvania.

After moving to Grand Rapids in the 1890s, Stickley began manufacturing colonial and European reproductions that he copied from the Art Nouveau innovations of France and Germany. He used quartersawn oak treated with ammonia to enhance wood grain and added doors with decorative glass panes. His pieces were the forerunners of the American Arts and Crafts Movement. In 1901, he issued *The Craftsman*, a magazine on fine cabinetry that inspired designer Frank Lloyd Wright. From an atelier in Manhattan, until his death in 1942, Stickley displayed his homey artistry, which included the gracious cupboards, corner china closets, and sideboards that homemakers purchased as investment furniture and treasured as family heirlooms.

Emphasis on Function

As women were liberated from the home-and-husband mindset, their needs changed. A camouflaged kitchen cabinet designed with the lone working women or student in mind came from an unnamed home economics teacher who lived in a boardinghouse. She devised an attractive piece of mahogany furniture, perfect for a parlor or bedroom, that accommodated the utensils needed for preparing simple meals. The 1900 Sears, Roebuck catalog featured four sideboards that had evolved from a utilitarian storage unit to carved and mirrored furnishings fitted with swell-front drawers, some lined with felt to accommodate silverware. The 1908 catalog offered the Wilson Kitchen Cabinet, a multi-drawer hutch and workstation that featured fine craftsmanship in walnut. The well-executed design organized baking tools, food scale, grinder, and serving pieces in a single kitchen furnishing that ranged in price from $13.25 to $19.85, as compared to less elaborate models selling for as low as $5.45.

The 1923 Sears, Roebuck catalog reserved a full-page ad for its kitchen cabinet. A four-door, six-drawer oak or enamel work station, it featured a white enamel top, swinging sugar and flour bins with see-through windows, secure latches, and a bracket for supporting a food chopper. The copywriter stressed a mouse-proof bread box drawer with perforated lid, cutlery drawer, meal bin, and a sliding drop curtain. A handsome furnishing for the kitchen, the cabinet sold for $43.85 in golden oak and $48.85 in white enamel, a popular surface as cooks began to concern themselves with bacteria.

An innovation of the late nineteenth century, the Hoosier cabinet, made by the Hoosier Manufacturing Company in Newcastle, Indiana, was an attractive all-in-one work organizer and forerunner of the built-in cabinets of the 1940s. A tall oak structure, it contained a flour bin with built-in sifter, sugar bin, clock, and canisters to hold tea, coffee, and up to six spices. The baker, either standing or seated on a tall stool, had access to a work surface on which to roll out dough and could easily reach into drawers for cutters, crimpers, and cornmeal. The Hoosier Manufacturing Company advertised the cabinet as a step-saver that systematized staples and equipment within hand's reach of where they were needed. This line of thinking accompanied a revolution in housekeeping characterized by the emerging concept of kitchen design, the development of time and motion study, and the evolving discipline of home economics. One model, the Napanee Dutch Kitchenet, earned the admiration of efficiency expert Harrington Emerson, author of *Twelve Principles of Efficiency* (1911), who counted the steps of the 1920s housewife. He determined that all-in-one cabinetry could reduce the traffic incurred in a day's kitchen work by more than 75 percent, from 2,113 to 520 steps.

Home economists, working for manufacturers of domestic items, glorified the kitchen cabinet as the heart of food work. Lois M. Wyse, director of the Hoosier Test Kitchens, published "How to Equip the Modern Kitchen" (1924), a picture essay that touted the cabinet as scientifically planned and organized to replace the butler's pantry. Without the fuss of remodeling, the home planner could add a baker's work station or a one- or two-door equipment cabinet to end problems of clutter and wasted space. In 1925, the British domestic magazine *Ideal Home* joined the campaign to promote kitchen shortcuts, advertising the Easiwork Kitchen Cabinet, one of numerous streamlined products that offered the homemaker assistance in managing the "servantless" home.

Technology boosted women's morale and nurtured an image of domestic management rather than home drudgery. The monthly forum in the July 1930 issue of *Good Housekeeping* reported on the replacement of earlier porous porcelain-enamel finishes with a stainless porcelain veneer that was both attractive and easy to clean. Increasing its appeal was the chromium-plated trim that was safe from tarnish and discoloration from acid foods. The following month's issue featured Mutschler Porce-Namel, a cabinet and cupboard company in Nappanee, Indiana, that made refectory tables, work stations, and cabinet suites with leaves that slid out of sight when not in use. The 1938 Cussins and Fearn Company catalog praised the White House kitchen cabinet, a multi-drawered work station that offered combinations of shelves, door racks, dish space, porcelain-topped counter, roll-top canister concealment, and flour bin with sifter for all-in-one baking convenience. Brand names were important to pricing: White House cabinets cost as much as $20 more than others equipped with similar features.

These early-twentieth-century developments in cabinetry paralleled the trend toward scientific organization of the kitchen. In January 1925, Katharine A. Fisher, director of the Good Housekeeping Institute, presented methods of grouping tasks according to purpose and materials. The focus of the orderly kitchen was the cabinet work space, which held canisters, spice jars, implements, bowls, even cutlery strapped to the outside of the frame. Augmenting the dresser-style cabinet was the teacart, a small kitchen table on wheels that organized serving dishes or smaller projects and could be rolled up to the sink, stove, or worktable. Fisher's motto summed up the philosophy of the well-organized kitchen: "Everything in daily use in sight." (Fisher 1925, 71)

Five years later, Fisher's regular column published a floor plan and photos of the "pre-planned kitchen," a two-room module bisected by a swinging pantry door. In the kitchen, cabinets above and below the L-shaped work area provided for baking and food preparation within easy reach of the refrigerator, sink, and drain board. Other cabinets above and below additional food preparation space flanked the range and warming closet. In the adjacent laundry room, the matching cabinetry above and below the laundry preparation station enabled the homemaker to attend to starching, sprinkling, and ironing without moving too far from the kitchen. To simplify daily cleaning, Fisher recommended washable wainscoting and tile and linoleum or floor cloths finished with paint or varnish. She also suggested wall and overhead lighting fixtures to keep the cook's shadow from blocking the light falling on work surfaces.

For the post-World War II generation of cooks, Elizabeth Beveridge, home equipment editor for *Woman's Home Companion*, presented design tips to help the bride make the most of built-in cabinetry and coordinated appliances. For the cupboard, she suggested a pass-through dish organizer; clean dishes removed from the drain board went into one side of the cabinet and could be removed on the other side for use at the eat-in kitchen counter. She recommended that homemakers opt for a five-foot-long counter linking refrigerator and stove—long enough to accommodate utensils, mixer, and serving pieces and within reach of the wall-mounted cabinet holding other implements and supplies.

See also **Chests; Smoked Food**

Further Reading

Agee, James. *Let Us Now Praise Famous Men*. New York: Ballantine Books, 1960.
Beveridge, Elizabeth, "The Kitchen Does the Work," *Woman's Home Companion*, July 1947,72–73.
————, "She Models Her Kitchen," *Woman's Home Companion*, March 1947, 102–104.
Fisher, Katharine A., "Making the Kitchen This Year's Model," *Good Housekeeping*, October 1930, 88–89, 254.
————, "Planning for Saving Work," *Good Housekeeping*, January 1925, 70–71, 96.
"The Forum for July," *Good Housekeeping*, July 1930, 131.

CACHES

The use of caches, subterranean cavities in which food is stored, may have preceded habitation in permanent dwellings. The practice of caching appears to have set the Cro-Magnon apart from their predecessors, the Neanderthals. The successful protection of foodstuffs and consequent improvement of the food supply was

Sideview of an underground cache of food and supplies.

a decisive factor in enabling the Cro-Magnon to survive the cold Northern European winters. Nomadic hunter-gathering clans dug deep holes in the frozen earth to hold meat during heavy snows and periods when game was scarce. The creation of this system of meat preservation may have enabled them to outlast the Neanderthals, who died out entirely.

As agrarianism replaced the wandering lifestyle, caches became a part of early grain-growing, bread-baking societies. The Celts of Danbury Hill Fort in Britain buried their wheat and barley in unlined granaries near their circular houses between 1000 and 500 BCE. The technology was surprisingly effective. The harvester sealed the stash with an airtight, watertight layer of clay. When the outer layer of grain germinated, it used up the oxygen, enabling the rest of the grain to survive in a state of suspended animation for up to two years. After that, the stored grain succumbed to fungi.

The early Native American equivalent of the pantry or root cellar, the cache, dug as much as eight feet deep, concealed food supplies as well as tools, harness, and clothing. The Omaha of the Great Plains used an adze or dibble to hollow out a pit for storage of meat or corn. To protect the food from contamination, they lined the sides of the hole with grass, moss, or willow withies and topped it with ash, bark, bear grass, litter, or sod. The Hidatsa dug bell-shaped granaries about eight feet deep, six feet wide at the bottom, and half that wide at the top; an attached rope ladder provided access. They lined the walls with ears of corn and placed squash and shelled corn at the center. The Mohawk added a bark-lined cellar to their longhouses for caching staples for the winter.

Styles of caching differed according to locale and type of foodstuff. The Carrier of north-central British Columbia preserved smoked fish, their staple meat, in caches; Inuit *giviak,* a form of treepies (sausage) made by stuffing baby birds into sealskin, ripened for several months in a subterranean cache. The Kutchin of Alaska and the Yukon preferred platform caches, which raised stores above the ground to protect them from foraging animals; likewise, the Ingalik of the Lower Yukon River stored food in logs elevated on posts, while the Sekani of British Columbia used trees as storage sheds. As described by French *coureurs de bois* (woodsmen), the Ojibwa dug mortar holes in the ground, lined them with skins, pounded meat with a stone pestle, and packed the blended pemmican in hide containers. Used as trail food, it could remain unspoiled up to three years in the ground.

In the maple groves of Mille Lacs, Minnesota, Ojibwa sugar-makers buried cedar-bark bags of rice, cranberries, potatoes, and apples. These supplies fed workers during the long cold nights when they camped on snowy hills to drain sap and boil it into syrup and crystalline sugar. The Métis of the Great Lakes cached pemmican along the waterways they frequented, thus freeing space in their canoes for trade goods.

In the 1850s, the Red River Métis, who traded at the Hudson Bay Company headquarters, cached pemmican as trail food for long canoe and ox-cart journeys to St. Paul, Minnesota, and across the Dakota border along the Red River Valley to Fort Edmonton in Canada. While dominating the pemmican market, they specialized in dried meat, a flavorful, low-bulk provision that obviated the need for a cook fire. The company provisioned northern outposts and the *voyageurs* of the boat brigades with pemmican, which they stored on rock beds, layered like fire logs, to reserve for hard times.

The caching of perishables in ice wells began in Russia and Slovakia in the fifteenth century. These chambers, lined with straw, kept cherries for up to eighteen months. In her classic Russian cookbook, *A Gift to Young Housewives* (1861), Elena Burman Molokhovets provided instructions for storing a variety of foodstuffs. She told cooks to wrap lemons in paper, pack them among green birch branches in a chest, and store them on ice. She also explained how to preserve meats such as marinated eel, salted ham, corned beef, sturgeon, and poultry in barrels buried in ice. Other foods, including raspberry juice, *shipovki* (sparkling beverages), jars of plums, and cherry brandy, could be preserved in caches of dry sand. Slovakian cooks packed fresh or smoked haunches of meat in wooden troughs and buried them in soil or ash to preserve them over the winter freeze.

A similar caching system in Ireland preserved surplus butter. Housekeepers stored it in wooden tubs and buried the tubs in caches dug in the bog. The antiseptic loam kept the butter from turning rancid. Turf cutters often discovered forgotten caches in which the yellow rounds were still sweet smelling and pliant.

On the tundra, Eskimo cooks used caches to protect fresh fish, blubber, or meat from spoiling. They topped the hidden store with turf and stone to conceal the odor from predatory animals and marked it with a stick set at an oblique angle in case snow covered the spot. An unwritten law forbade one group from opening another's cache. In *Life with the Esquimaux* (1862), written by Captain Charles Francis Hall during an expedition to Greenland and Baffin Island, the author commented, "I noticed an instance of honesty and good faith which deserves mention. . . . The Innuits with me noticed all this, and saw the meat thus deposited, yet *not one would touch a morsel of it*. They knew it belonged to others, and therefore it was sacred in their eyes, unless in cases of actual extremity." (Hall 1972, 401)

On an expedition to Greenland and the Baffin Bay islands from 1907 to 1909, Frederick Cook, one-time associate of explorer Robert Peary, joined forces with two Eskimo companions, Ahwelah and Etukishook. After building a moss-and-stone hut for winter quarters, the trio skewered a bull walrus with a lance. It provided 300 pounds of meat—enough to keep them comfortably fed through the dark months—and 100 pounds of tallow. Caching was crucial to survival as temperatures could drop as low as -50 degrees Fahrenheit. Upon returning to the spot, Cook lamented, "We found to our dismay numerous bear and fox tracks. Bears had opened the cache and removed our hard-earned game while the foxes and ravens had cleared up the very fragments and destroyed even the skins. . . . The bear out-generalled us in nearly every manoeuvre." (Mowat 1989, 429)

Residents of the polar regions perpetuate Cook's method of storing meat during the coldest months. On Victoria Island in Nunavut, Canada, for example, hunters dig caches to store sections of caribou that are too valuable to waste but too heavy to carry home.

See also **Canisters; Ice; Pemmican**

Further Reading

Reed, Evelyn. *Woman's Evolution from Matriarchal Clan to Patriarchal Family.* New York: Pathfinder Press, 1975.

CAMP COOKERY

Hiking, backpacking, and camping present unique challenges to cooks. Preparing wholesome, palatable meals in a tent or camper-trailer requires the right provisions and the right equipment. For early campers—explorers, trappers, and pioneers—utensils were

Field Kitchen. Engraving from *Il Cuoco Segreto Di Papa Pio V* (The Private Chef of Pope Pius V) by Bartolomeo Scappi, Venice, 1570.

often improvised and meals were unpredictable. With the rise of recreational camping, however, an industry emerged that was dedicated to making trail meals easier to prepare, more varied, and better tasting.

Settlers' and Explorers' Meals

During the European settlement of South Africa after 1700, ox-drawn wagons transported salt, sugar, canned milk, coffee, and tea; the wagoneers foraged and hunted for the rest of their provisions along the way. When conditions permitted, cooks set up three-legged *potjiekos* (hunters' pots) to stew venison with vegetables and local greens. As they shot additional guinea fowl, wart hog, bush pig, and rabbit, the cook added new meat to the mix and used marrow as a thickener. When the wagon halted each evening, the pot was returned to the fire for additions of meat and replacement of old bones with new.

Among European settlers of Australia, bush cooks were sometimes jokingly referred to as "bait layers," named after the poisoners of the rabbits that overran the wild. Food preparers carried authority and demanded the respect of workers at trail camps and shearing sheds. For removing pans and lids from the fire or embers, they bent a series of custom-made hooks out of wire and used them to retrieve dampers (bread) from the ash. By way of parrying complaints about the quality or quantity of servings, the cook threatened to "take me'ooks and orf," a sure sign of annoyance.

One essential of the cookfire, the tinderbox, accompanied most outbackers, particularly settlers of the American frontier. Those who carried a powder horn and flintlock could bypass flint and steel by flashing powder in the pan to ignite a rush or paper spill, wood shavings, or twist of tow. A rustic alternative to the clay tankard was the stoppered leather bottle, a stitched hide-covered glass bottle, a forerunner of the thermos. Slung over the shoulder by a thong, the leather bottle resembled the canteen, a military container that Roman legionaries had carried on overland marches.

A clever device, the iron Conjuror camp kettle, sold in London and described in *An Encyclopaedia of Domestic Economy* (1848), applied controlled heating in little space for quick cooking of meat. To maximize the burning of a sheet of brown paper, users placed raw meat in a shallow tin dish, covered it with the lid, and placed it in the cylinder top. Through a side door, they set fire to the paper and closed the door on the combustion. The text noted that the kettle was useful to "fishing or shooting parties, and other occasions where a dinner might be required at a distance from home." (Franklin 1997, 549)

In the 1880s, field naturalist Mary T.S. Schaffer camped out while scouring the Canadian Rockies in search of wild animals and plants. In *Old Indian Trails: Incidents of Camp and Trail Life, Covering Two Years' Exploration through the Rocky Mountains of Canada* (1911), she described the careful selection of flour, baking powder, cocoa, coffee and tea, sugar, dried fruit and potatoes, beans, and rice. She learned the hard way that dried cabbage gave off a repulsive odor and that "granulose," a much ballyhooed lightweight sugar substitute, did not deliver enough sweetening to supplant sugar. (Riddervold & Ropeid 1988, 159) She was also disillusioned with dried eggs and milk, finding them far removed from the real thing. From an experienced camper she encountered, Schaffer learned of pinole, a ground dried corn product that became her most valued stock. However, when she finally cooked it with sugar and cream, "it had a taste which hung on for hours, its consistency was that of a mouthful of sand, and its grittiness was all over you, inside and out . . . on the fourth day a mere smell of it caused a howl to go up." (Ibid., 160) Even her horses rejected it.

Not all women adapted readily to overland travel and rustic campfire cookery, which required that they sling pots from hooks attached to a rod over the flame. The difficulties of green wood and wet buffalo chips,

unpredictable weather, burned food, and smoke in the eyes diminished the usual joy in domestic chores. Helen M. Carpenter, a pioneer bride still on her honeymoon, was disenchanted with the inconvenience of having no stable kitchen. She complained, "By the time one has squatted around the fire and cooked bread and bacon, and made several dozen trips to and from the wagon—washed the dishes . . . and gotten things ready for an early breakfast, some of the others already have their night caps on." (Schlissel 1982, 78) Woman's work, she found, was a progression of washing clothes, baking bread, gathering wood, hauling water, making fires, and daily packing and unpacking. Lodisa Frizzell wrote that such campfire drudgery "goes agin the grane." (Ibid., 80)

Pioneer camping often required extremes of innovation. The Irish-born anthropologist and journalist Daisy O'Dwyer Bates, a bush country healer in the Murray River Basin and author of *The Passing of the Aborigines: A Lifetime Spent among the Natives of Australia* (1938), described the challenges of cooking oatmeal gruel in a two-gallon billy can over an open flame. At one point, when the wind shifted, she suffered singed hair and a scorched face. After four hours of stirring, she was finally able to remove the can from the heat and feed strengthening porridge to a patient recovering from measles.

When Frederick Cook, one-time associate of the explorer Robert Peary, set out on a foray during his expedition to Greenland and the Baffin Bay islands (1907-09), he and Eskimo companions Ahwelah and Etukishook limited their equipment to fifty-two pounds each. For cooking and light, they carried one blow fire lamp and two pounds of wood alcohol. With the temperature at −48 degrees Fahrenheit, he struggled to economize on fuel to melt ice chopped with an ax and to heat their morning tea, the day's only luxury. When the lamp flame wavered, Cook carelessly gripped the fuel line cleaning needle and burned his fingers, leaving skin frozen to the metal.

Camping for Fun

By the turn of the twentieth century, the descendants of the pioneers could buy equipment specifically designed to make camping convenient and enjoyable. The need for lighting in dark and forested settings brought multiple responses from makers of camping lanterns. In 1901, Arthur Kitson, a British inventor, created a vaporized kerosene oil burner, a boon to lighthouse operators. Burning mineral oil in an incandescent mantle, it produced more light with less effort than previous wick lights. Manufacturers adapted it for pressure lamps and camp stoves.

In 1908, the Sears, Roebuck catalog listed a complete "Kamp Cook's Kit" for $5.48. The twenty-pound parcel included two boilers and a fire jack, plus fry pan, coffeepot, cutlery, and tableware for six. For an additional $1.55, the camper could purchase a separate thirty-one-piece cutlery and tableware set that included butcher knife, fish scaler, and a can opener that fit into a two-part cooking pan suited to baking and roasting. For more complex baking, the Rival camp stove, at $3.08, offered two steel chambers and a stovepipe that nested inside for easy portability.

Some kitchen implements, convenience foods, and vessels have traditionally suited the demands of outdoor cooking. Folding pocket knives or barlow knives have chopped kindling, scaled fish, gutted small animals, punched holes in cans of condensed milk, and stirred tin cans of soup. For the fussier camp cook, the lidded fireless, or fuelless, cooker made it possible to cook in a cylindrical well in a tin or zinc box. Heat derived from a pre-heated soapstone disk that fit into the bottom of the well; food cooked in a cooking cylinder that slid into the well. The camper could load the box, put out the campfire, and move on while the next meal simmered.

The outdoorsman Horace Kephart issued *Camp Cookery* (1933), a food directive for the serious camper. He explained how to pack lightly, cook staples such as bacon and eggs, and create varied meals using limited supplies. His specialty was instruction on cleaning, butchering, and cooking game and scaling and preparing fish; among the recipes were such delicacies as roasted beaver tail, barbecued squirrel, and broiled bittern.

In the late twentieth century, "roughing it" became less rough than ever before. Improvements in readily available packaged foods made them suitable for camp fare; also a boon to the camp cook were freeze-dried items, a by-product of aerospace research. The invention of the Sierra Cup offered the hiker a ten-ounce stainless steel drinking vessel stabilized with a wire handle mounted under a rolled lip. Light and handy, the cup could be attached to the belt. Although later plastic models were cheaper and tougher, the steel cup also served as a vessel for heating food or sterilizing water and a receptacle for kindling a small fire.

In 1990, Robert C. Birkby updated *The Boy Scout Handbook* for the Boy Scouts of America with information on camp stoves. He suggested stoves that burn kerosene, gas, butane, or propane, all of which can be stored in bottles or cartridges. Noting the potential hazards of camp cooking, he warned of the danger of cooking inside a cabin or tent and of igniting fuel containers with flame from a camp stove. For cooking with charcoal, he suggested making a stove from a coffee can pierced with holes.

In Australia, camping attracted devout trekkers, curious tourists, and adventurous retirees. In 2000, the Range Rover Club of Victoria posted suggestions for camping safety, which recommended, among other tips, screw-top plastic jars to secure margarine, tissue wrapping for unripe tomatoes, long-life packets of fruit juice and milk, and newspaper for storing lettuce, cabbage, celery, and carrots. For dish washing, the club suggested pouring detergent into a plastic screw-top container to churn the best lather from bore water. An essential in mosquito country, the mozzie coil burned slowly and emitted a noxious fume to drive away swarms. A sponge dipped in oil of lavender discouraged flies.

A necessity of campfire cookery, the jaffle iron, a long-handled hinged sandwich toaster of aluminum or cast iron, brought fond memories to Aussies who once cooked their home lunches over a gas jet. A handy device to protect meals in rainy weather, the iron had a long but humble history of making sandwiches filled with tomato and bacon, sardine and egg, and ham and pineapple. Quick and simple to use, the versatile iron functioned like a mini-grill, requiring only a thick slathering of butter or margarine on the outside of the bread to keep it from sticking.

Australian contributions to camp oven cooking focused on the cast-iron model for baking bread, cooking stew or casseroles, and roasting meats. New ovens required seasoning with olive or vegetable oil and baking for an hour before they were ready for coals. Cleaning with hot water and a natural fiber brush restored them better than washing in detergent, which precipitated rust. Utensils that accompanied the camp oven included a long lid hook, long-handled tongs, pot scraper, oven mitt or heavy pot holder, and whisk broom for removing ash. The experienced camp cook knew to take into account high temperatures, sunlight, and wind, which raised cooking temperatures, and humidity, shade, and high altitude, which lowered them.

Camping held its appeal into the twenty-first century, especially among those urbanites who considered sleeping outdoors and cooking over an open fire a suitable way to introduce young children to survival skills. According to research conducted for the Coleman Company, adults cited the campfire as the best part of cooking outdoors. Nine percent of campers said eating outdoors was the most enjoyable aspect of the experience, but 42 percent said gathering around the fire with family and friends was the best part of "roughing it."

Camper-Trailers: The Comforts of Home

The first camping trailers, called house cars, carried stoves, equipment, and staples for cooking dried foods and canned goods as well as fresh-caught fish and game. They were followed by a second generation of camping vehicles—tent trailers, converted double-decker buses, stylish Pierce-Arrow campers, and home-built wooden campers mounted on car bodies. One variant, the Motor Chapel of St. Peter, funded by the Catholic Women's Auxiliary, carried missionaries across Texas in 1913. The vehicle contained an altar, a confessional, a lighted fold-out chapel, lockers, berths, and cooking space.

Several millionaires numbered themselves among the devotees of the gypsy lifestyle, including cereal magnate Charles William Post and department store owner Louis D. Shoenberg. Entrepreneur Thomas Coleman du Pont, founder of the E. I. du Pont de Nemours Company, designed a camping car for supervising highway construction. The body featured food lockers and a metal icebox. Henry B. Joy, president of the Packard Motor Car company, enjoyed his camper, made habitable with a grate, canvas water buckets, self-cooling water bags, food containers and airtight tin cans, a fireless cooker, and matched sets of dishes and utensils.

In 1916, Gustav de Bretteville, a realtor from San Francisco, traveled in the first collapsible steel camper, which attached to his Model T. Called the Automobile Telescope Touring Apartment, it contained a pantry, oil stove, folding table and chairs, drawers for utensils, and electric lights. Later models boasted iceboxes, sinks, and showers. In 1921, the Lamsteed Kampkar, made of metal panels, added aluminum pots and pans and flatware to the Kamp-Kook stove and refrigerator. Advertised in *Field and Stream,* the assembly could be tailored to fit trucks or autos for $535. For an extra $30, the buyer received a stove, cooking equipment, and tableware as well.

In England, caravaning got its start after Gordon Stables popularized a horse-drawn land yacht, called the *Wanderer,* now housed in the Bristol Museum. The first manufactured campers in England appeared after World War I. The Eccles Saloon Caravan, made in Birmingham, was a rudimentary arrangement of seat and locker on one wall and a two-burner camp stove and wash bowl attached to the opposite wall.

The safety and quality of life in motor camps declined during the Depression, then revived in the late 1930s, when Alexius R. Pribil and professional racer Ray Harroun engineered a bullet-shaped self-propelled camper. By the 1940s camping in trailers had become a family tradition. In the United States during the post-World War II economic boom, Larry Vita invented the Vita-Home Cruiser, which mimicked the suburban ranch home. With shingled sides, gabled roof, and casement windows, it looked like a cabin on wheels. In England, the Knight's caravan kitchen, built by Coventry Steel in Warwick, equaled the amenities of home, with full-sized appliances and a sink that folded out of the way when not in use.

Into the mid-twentieth century, motor coaches came to resemble vacation homes complete with water heaters, built-in coffee makers, screened porches, upper decks, and outdoor grills. The kitchens were sometimes called galleys because of their resemblance to ships' galleys. By 1964, the growing camper business had its own magazine, *Family Motor Coaching.*

Another upgrade in camping vehicles was the 1960 Sani-Cruiser, a Ford truck topped with an oak cabin featuring all-gas appliances, sink with hot and cold water taps, and full shower-bath. The 1961 Traveliner from the Pickwick Company offered gas oven and stove and convertible dinette-bed. The 1962 Ford Condor further developed the home on wheels with wood-paneled kitchen, Formica counters, metal wall tiling, wood cabinets, and butane gas range and oven.

The 1960s brought the Volkswagen Campmobile. Popular in Europe and the United States, it opened wide on the passenger side to reveal a compact kitchen and side-mounted table balanced on one leg. During the course of a decade, the company sold 50,000 units. To compete, General Motors put out a front-wheel-drive camper called L'Universelle. It featured Frigidaire appliances and a stylish exterior that bested the boxy VW. The idea foundered as market analysis showed a dearth of buyers. In 1965, Dodge produced the Camp Wagon, a pop-top camper roomy enough to stand in. A truck, wagon, and camper in one, it cost $3,000 and handled like a car. Volkswagen countered with the Campmobile, which sported a kitchen floored in linoleum.

The counterculture embraced the roving lifestyle, pursued in personalized hippie buses and camper vans. One American classic, the VW bus, was a New World success for a German vehicle augmented in 1947 by Dutch importer Ben Pon and manufactured two years later. In 1991, Volkswagen produced one of its most popular rear-engine camper vans, the box-shaped pop-top "Westy," outfitted by Westfalia. Behind the two front seats and opposite the sliding side door, the yard-long galley boasted a two-burner gas stove alongside a minuscule sink with cold water tap attached to a 14-gallon tank. As many as four campers could relax in air-conditioned comfort around two swing-out table-tops, from which they could also reach the gas or electric refrigerator, utensil drawer, and storage below; a slender broom closet and pantry space were located near the back. Books such as Janet Groene's *Cooking*

Aboard Your RV (1993) offered beginners tips on dish washing, substituting for missing ingredients, and getting through rainy-day meals in cramped space.

See also **Frontier Kitchens; Pemmican; Sanitation**

Further Reading

Parry, W. E. *Three Voyages for the Discovery of a Northwest Passage.* New York: Harper & Brothers, 1842.
Schlissel, Lillian. *Women's Diaries of the Westward Journey.* New York: Schocken Books, 1982.

CAN OPENERS

Since the advent of commercial canning in the mid-nineteenth century, kitchens have required heavy-duty openers suited to heavy metal containers. The original can opener was a hammer and chisel, followed by awkward, sharp-pointed metal flanges attached to a knobbed wooden handle. The types of patented opening devices varied from bladed steel gouges, forked sardine-can openers, iron rotary wheels, wall-mounted and table-mounted openers, gear-driven and blade-and-cogwheel models, and cranked cutters that removed both lid and lip of the metal cylinder, leaving a dangerously sharp edge. In the same family or sometimes combined with the can opener were the bottle opener, a metal loop that fit over one side of a crimped metal lid for prying upward, and the beer opener, a triangular punch that waggish imbibers dubbed a "church key."

To end disasters from forcing lids open, Robert Yeates came up with a claw-ended opener in 1855, a hand-operated tool that haggled its way around the metal top. In 1858, the inventor Ezra Warner devised a puncturing tool. By pressing the point into the can top and allying a guard to stop the blade from protruding into the food, he created a workable tool that moved smoothly around the upper rim, leaving a safer edge. Around 1865, tinned meat merchants popularized the bull's head opener by offering the tool free with a purchase of canned beef.

Competition quickly made new models obsolete. One version, sold in Helsinki in the 1870s, maneuvered around the outside of the rim, prevented the can lid from falling into the food, and left a smooth edge. Safe and sanitary, it also kept its gears free from contact with the can's contents. A Finnish inventor, F. Wattne, patented a simpler tin opener in 1900 but met competition from master builder E.A. Gutzén, who proposed an alternate design two years later.

The can opener with cutting wheel became available in the 1880s. In 1907, Taylor Manufacturing Company of Hartford, Connecticut, was marketing the Yankee opener, patented in 1902, a combination tool that lifted vacuum caps or stabbed and removed lids from cans. The 1908 Sears, Roebuck catalog offered a steel-bladed piercing can opener for seven cents to open round or square cans of any size.

In the 1930s women's magazines featured the Speedo wall-mounted can opener. While the operator turned a handle, the blade gripped the can and opened it without spilling contents or hacking ragged edges around the rim. In the 1950s, the development of pop tops and removable tear tabs simplified the problem of opening containers, especially for children and adults unable to use conventional openers. In 1968, Sunbeam invented a dual-function model that opened cans and sharpened knives.

At the start of the twenty-first century, can openers were available in hand-held, wall-mounted, and under-cabinet-mounted models. Whether hand-cranked or electric-powered, the most efficient applied ergonomics to the problem of holding the can, piercing or removing the lid or uncrimping it from the cylinder, and maintaining sanitation by keeping the often dusty lid from falling back into the contents. The can colander, a pierced cap for an already open can, enabled cooks to drain liquids from canned meats, vegetables, or fruits.

CANDLES

Candles are simple light sources made by dipping, molding, or rolling wicked strings in a flammable substance such as tallow, beeswax, or pine tar to form multiple coats evenly about them. From the second century BCE, records detailing the sale of beeswax demonstrate the importance of this versatile commodity to the world economy. Demands on Rome by the Corsicans and on Pontus, Syria, and Africa by the Romans made wax collection a political issue in international trade. In Scandinavia, the Norse demanded a tribute of wax from the Slavs, which they collected in standardized *krugi* (balls). Throughout England, Scotland, Germany, the Faroe Islands, and Russia, candles were so vital that civic and ecclesiastical authorities accepted wax in lieu of currency for payment of fines, tithes, and rents.

The burning of wax lights led to a variety of candle and lamp shapes. In Egypt as early as 1550 BCE, candles took the shape of a twisted candy cane or a flat paddle banded with bark, which may have compacted the wax interior to keep it from crumbling. The letters of Pliny the Younger around 100 CE speak of wax-dipped pith from meadow rushes and of flaxen threads permeated with wax and tar. Under Alfred the Great in the late ninth century, the court at Wessex relied on grooved beeswax tapers to record the passage of time.

By 1100 European markets supported professional chandlery as well as kitchen-dipped varieties. English candle making began with twisting fiber wicks, supplied by a *caneurykestrete* (wick-maker), and dipping repeatedly to produce fine layering for a clean burn. (Hartley 1979, 293) When candle molds replaced the dipping method, the straining of fat also refined the quality of light. The place of use of each candle, whether in a passageway or over a table or chair, called for a different height and thickness, which became the business of the professional chandler (also called candler, chaundler, tallow chaundler, or waxechaundeler). (Ibid., 291) A constant household task was the trimming of wicks several times an hour to produce a stronger flame. Only in modern times did chandlers do away with that chore by employing a curling wick that trims itself.

A medieval improvement in lighting was the mirrored wall sconce, which augmented a single flame through reflection. The moveable candle arm allowed some choice in directing the light. For the kitchen, tallow tapers were sufficient. Less acrid, oily, and smoky were beeswax candles, which lighted dinner tables and gave off a sweeter fragrance. To lengthen the life of a candle, the householder refrained from blowing it out or pinching the brittle wick or beating it down into the soft wax. Instead, to preserve the tip, a snuffer was used. Saucers and bronze tip covers were employed to channel drips into a reserve for reuse.

Chandlery supported a steady trade among nations. As Christianity progressed from Western Europe overland into Russia and by the Black Sea from Turkey to the Caucasus, the wax trade thrived for the illumination of churches and monasteries. In the early nineteenth century, wax—along with slaves, gold, and ivory—was a key export of Senegal and Angola. Likewise, Timor, Indonesia, traded sandalwood and wax to the Chinese.

The making of candles was one of the demanding but necessary jobs in the North American colonies. Home chandlers set up kettles on trammels from a lug pole at the fireplace for boiling water to melt scalded and skimmed beef tallow, deer suet, moose fat, or bear grease. Because of the danger of tipping over a pot of wax or splashing boiling tallow on the hands or face, homemakers supervised children at the dipping process and stocked their kitchen first-aid kits with herbal remedies for burns.

If given a choice of the best material, colonial householders preferred wax from the stingless bee; also prized were spermaceti, derived from whale oil, and the waxy substance from the fruit of the bayberry, or candleberry (*Myrica pensylvanica*), a common Atlantic coast plant. When boiled in cauldrons, bayberries exuded a fat that layered evenly on the wick and burned with a pleasant fragrance.

In homes along the Atlantic seaboard, only the wealthy could afford to hire itinerant candle makers. Professional chandlers were available as early as 1748, when James Clemens advertised in the March 30 issue of the *Boston News-Letter,* boasting of his candles' sweet scent, longevity, and large flame. He declared that his goods offered three times the quality of home-dipped tallow candles. On July 24, 1750, a competitor, Edward Langdon, advertised in the *Boston Gazette* that his chandlery stocked bayberry candles, either dipped or molded, for retail sale by the box.

In 1836, Lydia Maria Child, a Massachusetts-born domestic writer, set down instructions for the new homemaker in *The American Frugal Housewife*. She reminded the bride to "look frequently to the pails, to see that nothing is thrown to the pigs which should have been in the grease-pot." (McCutcheon 1993, 96) She listed ingredients for a hard, clear taper as mutton tallow mixed with camphor, beeswax, and alum, all common kitchen commodities. In the West, pioneers molded candles from pan drippings or deer tallow melted at the hearth in one easy motion. They tied wicking to cylindrical molds, poured in the liquid fat, and cooled the columns outdoors.

Procter & Gamble, a partnership that joined a chandler with a soap maker, marketed tallow candles from the late 1830s and, in mid-century, added stearate candles made from stearic acid to produce a clear glow. The factory process ended the intense labor previously associated with home candle making and described in painstaking detail in the journals kept by many housewives of the day.

Catharine E. Beecher and Harriet Beecher Stowe, authors of *The American Woman's Home, or Principles of Domestic Science* (1869), regarded professionally made candles as an unnecessary expense. In their book, the Beecher sisters offered a recipe for candles, calling for a pound of white wax, one quarter ounce of camphor, two ounces of alum, and ten ounces of suet or mutton tallow. After soaking wicks in lime water and saltpeter, the candle maker attached them to molds, straightened them, and dried them until hard. Before the dipping began, the authors suggested that the wicks be twisted and dipped in lime water or vinegar. Finished candles, they advised, should be stored in a cool, dry place.

CANDY

Candy—any of a variety of sweet treats, or confections, made with sugar, honey, molasses, or other sweet substances and often called simply *sweets*—has long been associated with children and good times. The word is derived from the Arabic *qand* and Sanskrit *khand.* In ancient times sweets often appeared during festivals and were used to appease the gods. In the religion of ancient Egypt, the soul may have bought its way through the underworld with molded sweets. Similar connections between deities and confectionery can be found among the Aztecs, Hindus, ancient Hebrews, Cree of Canada, and Ainu of Japan.

A Roman treat made with honey and pine nuts was the forerunner of a sweet concoction called *halva* or Turkish honey. A recipe for *halva* from a Syrian cookbook compiled in Baghdad in 1226 called for heating equal parts of almonds or pistachios, sesame oil, sugar, and honey. Related to the Oriental *malebi,* the recipe is still in use in Egypt, the Balkans, India, and Greece. Hungarian, Yugoslavian, and Bulgarian cooks made their own boiled version from almonds and grape must.

During the Middle Ages, sugaring joined drying, salting, brining, and pickling as a method of preserving foods, in particular scented pastes, nuts, fruits, seeds, and fruit peels. Sugar, honey, or the sugary syrup from boiled sweet wine could be used to produce comfits of pine nuts, almonds, hazelnuts, and other nuts as well as spices such as coriander, cinnamon, and anise. Sometimes a drop of dye enhanced the eye appeal of foods that lost their natural color in the heating process. When the bright-hued coatings hardened, they turned conserves into candy. In England, the production of sticks of penide or pennet from barley and sugar as a treat or cold remedy suggests that the Arabic method of sugar boiling influenced northwestern European sweets.

Sweet Artistry

The addition of eggs to existing recipes for confections resulted in sweets that were more appealing than their predecessors and less gummy or brittle in texture. In 1441, an Italian court confectioner created the original *torrone,* a nougat candy made from egg white, honey, sugar, and nuts. For the marriage of Bianca Maria Visconti to Francesco Sforza, the innovative chef layered the ingredients into a *torre* (tower), a model of Cremona's landmark. The sweet, originally called *torrione,* evolved into *torrone,* a popular dessert that found favor in home kitchens and sweet shops all over Europe. In sixteenth-century Italy *torrone* developed into a complicated family of sweets, sugared fruit and berries, and sugar sculpture that required training and skill at elaborate layering. Still found in confectioners' shops in the twenty-first century, these sweets reach their height of beauty and appeal at Christmas and Easter, when traditional shapes in chocolate, nougat, and block sugar display seasonal colors adorned with ribbon, sequins, and metallic foil.

Platina, author of *De Honesta Voluptate et Valitudine* (On Right Pleasure and Health, 1475), contributed a recipe for marzipan (also called marchpane, massepain, and matzabaum), an exceptionally malleable candy dough made from almond paste, confectioner's sugar, and rosewater, which may have originated in Baghdad. He warned that cooking the delicate treat in an oven or at the hearth required careful monitoring, but the effort was, in his opinion, well worth the trouble: "I have eaten nothing more pleasant with my friend Patricius of Siena where they make it as a specialty." (Platina 1999, 167)

Leonardo da Vinci, the Italian Renaissance painter, sculptor, and inventor, applied his talents to the sculpting of marzipan. Because of its plasticity, it could easily be shaped with a rolling pin, carved with sculptor's tools, and painted to represent flora and fauna. In his *Notes on Cuisine* (1470), written when he was eighteen, Leonardo told of carving figures from sugared almond paste to present to Prince Ludovico Sforza of Milan. He reported that the greedy prince did not appreciate his artistry: "I have observed with pain that my signor Ludovico and his court gobble up all the sculptures I give them, right to the last morsel, and now I am determined to find other means that do not taste as good, so that my works may survive." (Eigeland 1996, 34) When Leonardo turned to military engineering, he sculpted marzipan models for Lorenzo de Médicis of Florence but again lost his creations to candy thieves, who happily devoured his ramparts and parapets.

In the Tudor era, marzipan required extensive painting and trimming with edible gold leaf, which was costly and difficult to apply. The astrologer John Partridge's *The Treasurie of Commodious Conceits and Hidden Secrets* (1584) described the process of grinding blanched almonds, cooking them in sweet water, and shaping them into circles using a template of "green hazell wand, of the thickness of halfe an ynche." (Denny, n. d., 29) After filling the confection with comfits and glazing it with sugar and rosewater, the candy-maker began the tedious process of gilding:

Take and cut your leafe of golde, as it lieth upon the booke, into square peeces like Dice and with a Conies [rabbit's] tailes end moysted a little, take the golde up by the one corner, lay it on the place beeing first made moyste, and with another tayle of a Conie drie presse the golde downe close. And if ye will have the forme of an Harte, or the name of *iesus,* or any other thing whatsoever: cut the same through a peece of paper and lay the paper upon your Marchpane. (Ibid.)

The process required a steady hand and eye and skills that took years to develop. The food writer Sir Hugh Platte's still-room book, *Delightes for Ladies to Adorne Their Persons, Closets, and Distillatories: With Beauties, Banquets, Perfumes and Waters* (1602), presented instructions for modeling marzipan into birds and beasts, crests, knots, and initials for use in enhancing banquet tables.

Convent Confectioners

In Palermo, Sicilian nuns claimed candy making as a rare outlet for feminine creativity. Cistercian women at Santa Trinità del Cancelliere, founded in 1190, accepted into their number a few patrician ladies who made *fedde* (slices), a clamshell-shaped pastry made in hinged molds and filled with egg custard and apricot jam. At the Monastery of the Martorana, a cloister that once stood adjacent to the Arab-Norman church of Santa Maria dell' Ammiraglio, the sisters created an almond paste that they hand-shaped and painted to resemble fruits and vegetables. Teamwork was necessary to produce the quantity of sweets required for All Soul's Day, when they were handed out as a traditional gift to children. The Santa Trinità del Cancelliere supported itself with sale of *fedde* until the 1500s, when the diocese of Mazara del Vallo banned the convent confectionery. The nuns' fund raising revived in the eighteenth century, when they held pastry parties for holidays, but these, too, were halted on orders from the Marchese of Villabianca. Until its closure, the convent of San Carlo at Erica also produced marzipan, which is now the province of candy molders at commercial Sicilian pastry shops. Simultaneously, the cloistered and missionary Spanish sisters in Mexico continued making chocolate confections to raise money for their order. Export of their delicacies brought the rare cacao-based treats to Europe, where traders sold them along with candied fruit and sugared confections.

For royalty and aristocrats, the arrangement of candy into a grand decorative display occupied confectioners of the seventeenth through the nineteenth centuries, including the Benedictine sisters of Moret-sur-Loing, makers of *sucre d'orge,* a barley sugar candy. The fashion reached a height with Marie-Antoine Carême's *Le Pâtissier Royal Parisien* (The Royal Parisian Pastry Chef, 1815), in which he described how to arrange molded sugar baskets and a three-tiered set piece with each level individually decorated. Skilled at concocting sugared pastes for shaping into animals, flowers, human figures, and buildings, Carême often turned sweets into a table centerpiece called a *pièce montée* (mounted presentation). For a base, the confectioner set up a tiered plinth, a wooden stand on which to squeeze out *pâte d'office* (sugared paste) from a forcing bag in fantastic shapes that could be hand-painted or silvered or gilded with foil wrap. For beginners, he suggested less daunting bases, such as waffles, nougats, puff pastry, nut toffee, and *duchesse* or Genoese cakes.

Elevation to a Profession

The establishment of candy making as a profession occurred in the seventeenth century. Edinburgh, Scotland, got is first confectioner in 1665, when an Italian set up shop. Street vendors called Sweetie Wives strolled streets and markets selling hawick balls, soor plooms (sour plums), and Berwick cockles. In England, Hannah Wooley's *The Queen-like Closet; or Rich Cabinet* (1670) offered a Renaissance recipe for candying fresh garden blossoms, a wedding specialty. The task began with the application to the petals of a coating of sugar and rosewater, followed by a sprinkling of sugar; the flower was then left to dry by the fire or in the sun. Delicate sugar violets and pansies accompanied plates and platters to the table and adorned cake tops, petits fours, and plates of candies handed round as party favors.

Confectionery vocabulary took shape in France in 1691, when François Massialot, author of *Le Cuisinier Royal et Bourgeois* (The Royal and Middle-Class Cook), standardized terms for candy coatings by describing stages from smooth and pearled to blown, feathered, cracked, and caramelized. Lady Grisell (or Grizell) Baillie, refined mistress of Mellerstain, Scotland, and author of *The Household Book of Lady Grisell Baillie* (1733), applied the term *tablet* to candy. She listed in her domestic account book the kitchen chore of making tablets for the bairns (children), which consisted of pouring a sweet mix into a tray for slicing into rectangles.

A romantic addition to candy lore was the praline, a crispy nut-and-sugar treat invented in France. It became the signature love token of Count Cesar du Plessis-Praslin, ambassador to Turin and commander of the French army in Lombardy during the Thirty Years War. He courted famous women with almond candies that his cook devised in 1649. The sugared gifts became the count's calling card. One of his sweethearts, who had emigrated to New Orleans, longed for the almond treats. Her cook substituted local pecans and applied the count's name to the confection. The name evolved from *Praslin* to *praline,* and the candy developed into a southeast Louisiana specialty.

The food writer William Gunter's *The Confectioner's Oracle* (1830) cataloged the great variety of candies available in the early decades of the nineteenth century. In addition to standard fudge, peanut brittle, popcorn balls, pralines, spruce gum, and taffy were milk chocolates, chewy fruit jujubes and gumdrops, and lozenges, which clerks in general stores sold by the piece from glass cases or canisters. Late in the century, Mrs. Robert Shields devised a method of slicing lozenges, a step-saver for candy manufacturers. In 1892, the women's magazine magnate Ebenezer Butterick published *The Correct Art of Candy Making.* The booklet, which went through several editions, explained home candy making and advised the homemaker on appropriate types of storage containers.

In 1858, a challenge from Lady Canning, vicereine of India and wife of Charles John Lord Canning, who, as governor general, had suppressed the Sepoy Mutiny, resulted in a confection replete with meaning for the British Raj. She urged renowned Bengali *moira* (confectioner) Bhim Chandra Nag to concoct a candy for her birthday. A large, syrupy glob of chickpeas flavored with cardamom and fried to a dark brown, it came to be known as the "Lady Canning" or by the pidgin variants "Lady Kenny," "Ladikanee," or "Ledikeni." In this same period, Elena Burman Molokhovets, author of the classic Russian cookbook *A Gift to Young Housewives* (1861), depended on cones of cane sugar for confections. To make lozenges and gum candy, which required that powders be suspended in candy solutions, she used tragacanth, or gum dragon, a natural gum derived from shrubs of the genus *Astragalus.*

In the southern Appalachians of the United States, hill people produced a traditional molasses candy. To make a sweet dough for pulling and cutting, the cook boiled a one-to-one ratio of salted water to molasses. After the mass reached the hard ball stage, it had to cool before it was ready for hand working. Pulling taffy was a favorite activity for rural children and an occasion for a party.

Asian Sweets in Hawaii

Hawaiian cooks used a cutting board to finish a sweet cookie bar called *mochi,* made from sugar, eggs, butter, coconut milk, cornstarch, and vanilla. They folded the sticky substance into a sweet rice flour called *mochiko* and pounded it in a wooden tub with a mallet. Similar to Turkish delight and the Filipino treat called *bibingka* (coconut pudding), it is a hybridized confection born of the island chain's blended ethnic cookery. *Mochi* answered the Japanese Hawaiian's craving for *koshian* (bean paste), the Filipino's delight in *ube* (purple yam paste) or black beans, and the chocolate cravings of *haoles,* or Caucasians. A specialty for family occasions, *mochi* usually required baking but was also available as a deep-fried fritter or as a coating for ice cream.

Additional kitchen treats from Hawaii centered on rice and crystallized sugar. Filipino cooks rolled cascaron balls from sticky rice flour, coconut, and brown sugar, then deep-fried them before cooling the mix on a skewer. They also deep-fried *bitsu-bitsu* patties, shaped from grated sweet potato, flour, and sugar. Chinese shops displayed crystallized fruit to celebrate New Year. A cookie-shaped wheat pastry, the Japanese *manju* required stuffing with bean paste. Japanese confectioners also shaped sweet rice flour into a boiled or steamed dumpling called *chichidango* or just *dango.*

Factory-Made Treats

Candy took two routes in the twentieth century. Amateur aficionados continued devising and improving home recipes for fudge and fondant. At the same time, more factory-made goods came on the market to be sold in stores, movie theaters, street stalls, and vending machines. In 1920, factories began making one of the most popular brands, Baby Ruth candy bars, which were named for the daughter of President Warren G. Harding and not, as some have assumed, for the period's legendary baseball player. In March 1925, an advertisement in *Good Housekeeping* magazine suggested a tip for elegant entertaining: the nut-encrusted Oh Henry! Bar could be sliced at the dinner table and presented to guests.

In candy kitchens, professional confectioners used wheels equipped with steel knives to cut hard-boiled candy into uniform bites and rotating, beveled candy cutters for slicing horehound. The gooseberry cutter, similar to an apothecary's pilling machine, was a hand-operated device that rolled perfect balls of marzipan. Levered confectioner's presses produced uniform lozenges, "kisses," wafers, ovules, suckers, drops, and other shapes. For specialty shops, Thomas Mills & Brothers of Philadelphia marketed a candy-curling device with hand crank for turning candy strands into opera curls.

Allegations that candy was not a healthy food for children prompted the Mars Company of Chicago, maker of Cream Caramels and Milky Way, to buy advertising space in the November 1930 issue of *Good Housekeeping.* Mars claimed that because candy lacked water, it was a quickly absorbed source of energy. Touting its products as an antidote to fatigue, Mars noted that candy had been a boon to the Olympic swimmer Gertrude Ederle and the polar explorer Admiral Richard E. Byrd, who carried 1,000 pounds of candy in his camping gear when he explored Antarctica. A citation from a medical journal, *Canada*

Lancet, declared that the absence of sugar from the diet was more injurious to teeth than was excessive sugar residue in the mouth.

Special Tools of the Confectioner

In addition to a variety of ordinary kitchen utensils—sieve and sugar sifter, ladle, enamel double boiler or kettle, skimmer, muslin bag, basin, cooling slab, and spatulas—candy making also requires some special tools and supplies, including the following:

Candy cups—fluted, plain, foiled, or decorated cups made to contain individual treats for gift-giving and easy transportation without spilling

Candy modelers—a collection of cutters, gouges, rosewood shapers, tools for crimping edges and creating bands, and pointers or dotting implements for incising tiny markings

Candy thermometer—an accurate gauge for candy- and jelly-making that registers the change in sugar as it heats to form frosting, taffy, nougat, jam, and marmalade

Comfit, or crystallizing, pan—a rectangular tin or enameled pan equipped with a mesh tray for preserving seeds in sugar syrup

Cutting board—a wooden or marble surface used for kneading sugary masses and shaping or cutting them into bite-sized pieces

Hoarhound cutter—a rolling cutter on a wire handle used to slice stick candy in a pan or on a marble cooling slab

Molds—containers for shaping *pâtes officinales* (pastilles), aromatic jellied or gum candies or lozenges dried in a slow oven and coated in crystallized sugar.

Oil of sweet and bitter almonds (*huile d'amondes douce et amères*)—a flavoring pressed from nuts tied in linen bags

Fond Memories

Perhaps because of its happy associations with holidays and celebrations, candy has long had a place in literature, especially in memoirs. Adults remember the candies of their childhood, immigrants recall the sweets of their homeland, and travelers record in their journals the delights of newly discovered treats. In Fulco di Verdura's memoir *Estati Felici: Un' Infanzia in Sicilia* (Happy Summers: A Childhood in Sicily, 1977), he wrote of the street vendors who sold homemade nougat, crystallized almonds, and hard candies. One of these merchants, di Verdura recalled, held a sucker on a string in one hand and a stopwatch in the

other. Each youthful customer was given one minute to lick the candy. When the minute was up, the next impatient child got his or her turn.

In *La Sicilia* (Sicily, 1897), Gastone Vuillier marveled at the verisimilitude of marzipan miniatures made by the Sicilian nuns:

Figs just opened from which a crystalline drop is oozing, little strawberries, pears, bananas, walnuts with the shell broken so that the inside is visible, roast chestnuts sprinkled with a faint trace of ashes, nor do they forget the legumes. There are entire collections of peas, of fava beans, of artichokes, of asparagus; I saw even some snails! And all this in almond paste." (Simeti 1989, 245)

In his 1945 chronicle of Bosnian history *Na Drini Cuprija* (The Bridge over the Drina, 1945) Nobel prize-winner Ivo Andric described the making of *halva* in an outdoor market: "On the square which linked the bridge with the market palce, *halva* was cooked in cauldrons and served piping hot to the people." (Chamberlain 1989, 427) Andric noted that the practice spread to surrounding villages, where candy enthusiasts wished good health to the Turkish Vizier. Children returned so many times for refills that the cooks waved them off with their stirring spoons.

See also **Carême, Marie-Antoine; Chocolate**

Further Reading

Coe, Sophie D., and Michael D. Coe. *The True History of Chocolate*. London: Thames & Hudson Ltd., 1996.
Eigeland, Tor, "Arabs, Almonds, Sugar and Toledo," *Aramco World*, May–June 1996, 32–39.
Namboodiri, Udayan, "Syrupy Salvo," *India Today*, September 7, 1998.

CANISTERS

To ensure the safety and purity of granular items, most cooks rely on canisters, a set of wood boxes, metal cylinders, or glass or earthenware jars with tight-fitting lids that keep out air, moisture, mold spores, rodents, and insects. As described in Elaine Morgan's *The Descent of Woman* (1972), in anticipation of times of scarcity, female hominids developed the practice of storing extra rations in a lair. To keep berries, roots, fungi, grubs, and nuts safely collected in one spot, preferably near the family fire, they used ostrich shells, coconut halves, and gourds as containers. With the development of pottery, they molded clay into storage vessels. From these rudimentary beginnings in the Kalahari, early Africans evolved the concepts of home, hearth, pottery, and pantry.

The Harappa of the Indus Valley, who flourished in 2500 BCE, constructed granaries of mud. These consisted of chambers divided into four bins and set on stone lifts to allow for ventilation. At Lothal, the storage chamber perched atop a square brick platform.

Study of the palace of Knossos, built on Crete around 2000 BCE, suggests that food preservation was the building's purpose. The complex appears to have stored agricultural produce in a centralized location as a form of palace economy. As a citizen refuge in hard times, the palace depended on fair-minded provisioners to distribute reserves to laborers. In exchange for food, they committed themselves to labor at public works. Thus, skilled woodworkers and masons bound themselves to the palace staff, which sustained their families during the course of massive building projects. To accumulate enough staples to pay work gangs, the palace staff acquired stone vessels, lead-lined stone chests, and clay *pithoi* (storage jars). Placed in narrow magazines, these containers stored such foodstuffs as barley, wheat, lentils, vetch, and grapes. A similar storage system at Pylos positioned stone *pithoi* to hold oil and wine in the royal warehouse.

Excavations at Ceren, El Salvador, a Mayan village buried by a volcano about 600 CE, disclosed details of early food storage practices. Payson D. Sheets of the University of Colorado, who directed the project, found vessels and pots in high niches, suspended on ropes, and stacked on rafters and columns.

Pre-industrial cultures carried storage many steps forward with leaf wrapping, basketry, caching, and the use of the leather parfleche, a folding pouch or portfolio. The Cupeño of San Diego, California, and the Cahuilla of California's Bernardino Mountains advanced the use of woven grass canisters covered with layers of pine pitch. The nearby Chumash made a similarly tight storage container by spreading their water baskets with asphaltum. The Karuk of Siskyou County, California, carved their canisters from wood. The Havasupai, who resided near the Grand Canyon, recycled the shells of baked squash for caching seeds.

To the north, the Quileute of Washington's Olympic Peninsula twined kelp, reeds, grass, spruce root, cedar, and willow bark into canisters; the Kalispel of the lake district and the Shuswap of British Columbia wove skins into food storage bags. In the Queen Charlotte Sound of British Columbia, the Bella Coola wove canisters and burden baskets from cedar bark. The Kwakiutl of Queen Charlotte Strait used a variety of wooden boxes, baskets, chests, and kelp tubes as canisters. Along Canada's west coast, the Nisqually stored meat and carried food on journeys in flexible elk hide parfleches. The Dogrib of central Canada erected a tripod of saplings and suspended food bundles out of the reach of marauding animals. Among the Lenni

Lenape of the Delaware River, gourds were the preferred canisters.

In the Fertile Crescent, Mesopotamian housewives were sensitive to the issue of home hygiene, particularly contamination from rats and flying and crawling insects. They used animal skins, baskets, woven hampers, lidded bins, and wood chests to store staples and placed vegetables in crates. To store liquids, they waterproofed the vessels and labeled the capacity of wine jars. Greek and Roman households improved on these devices with advanced models of *pithoi,* pottery flagons, glass bottles, and amphorae (clay jars with a distinctive oval shape).

In Japan, the itinerant straw weaver kept villagers supplied with storage baskets and lidded containers for grain, sardines, shiitake mushrooms, and dry and cooked rice. Hand-made lidded bentwood containers, which resembled the Shaker nested oval box, came in a variety of heights and widths and doubled as vessels for holding cooked rice to keep it warm until served. Made from the wood of the silk tree, the boxes absorbed moisture and prevented food from becoming soggy, making them ideal for use as lunchboxes for fieldwork or travel.

At the splendid Hamilton Palace in Lanarkshire, Scotland, Duchess Anne Hamilton established a heated room as a larder in 1690, described in Rosalind K. Marshall's *The Days of Duchess Anne: Life in the Household of the Duchess of Hamilton 1656–1716* (1973). Hamilton's storage of food by type and length of shelf life required boxes, dishes, chests, and canisters. In additon to barley, meal, and herring barrels, she kept cheese, sugar loaves, and dishes of dried fruit on shelves above casks of bread and candles. Other goods in pewter trenchers, stone jugs, and glass bottles shared space with silver table vessels. A half-century later, Anne Gibbons Gardiner, author of *Mrs. Gardiner's Family Receipts from 1763*, enlightened the homemaker on the storage of powdered mushrooms in a tightly sealed pantry canister.

The tidiness of the pantry was also of concern to the American homemaker-kitchen adviser Sarah Josepha Hale, author of *The Good Housekeeper* (1839). Hale recommended closed earthen pots for storage of bread crusts and pork fat. She kept lard and suet in tin canisters, yeast in wood or clay crocks, vinegar in glass bottles, and jelly and preserves in glass, china, or stoneware. Also valuable were paper bags for herbs and dried fruit and pig intestines for sausage and bladders for lard.

In more recent times, housewives have valued mouse-proof tin and wood containers, which they labeled with the names of the contents—tea, coffee, brown and white sugars, corn meal, cake, bread, and wheat, self-rising, or all-purpose flour. Forerunners of these canister sets include cracker boxes, powder horns, and tobacco humidors. Housekeepers in hot, moist climates inserted bay leaves or sage in muslin bags taped to the inside of the lid to ward off weevils.

The Civil War placed privations on Southern kitchens that left fears and insecurities after the surrender. In Sarah A. Elliot's *Mrs. Elliot's Housewife* (1870), the author instructed readers to keep their canisters polished and well filled, the sign of an ample supply of staples. In 1887, the food authority Maria Parloa, author of *Kitchen Companion*, disdained wood buckets and promoted tin cans for meal and sugar and stone jars for salt. She suggested recycling cracker boxes from the grocery store in lieu of purchased canisters.

Adaptations to simple cylinders include the flour bin sifter, a japanned canister modified in the 1890s to hold flour in its upper compartment. By operating the sifter mechanism, the user could measure directly into a container or drawer below. Another model placed the sifting tray at the top of a tin-lined copper canister. By the end of the 1800s, the possum-belly table and Hoosier cabinet combined the canister with a work station, thus placing flour, meal, rice, salt, sugar, potatoes, and onions at the site of kitchen food preparation. In 1905, another adaptation of the canister, a glass container mounted to the wall, dispensed supplies into cups and pans through a bottom opening controlled with a twist knob.

The 1908 Sears, Roebuck catalog indicated the importance of fresh coffee to the home with its 32-cent japanned tin canister and steel coffee mill. Handy and discreet, the cylindrical canister, marked "Coffee" in elaborate scrollery, held a pound of beans in an airtight, moisture-free enclosure until the user was ready to measure a serving into the hand-cranked mill. Multiple settings regulated ground coffee falling into the cup below at coarse, medium, or fine grade. For another 15 cents, the catalog shopper could choose a more practical glass-fronted wood model that displayed the quantity of beans left in the hopper. Two additional wall-mounted canisters, one for salt at eight cents and a multidrawer cabinet for eight spices at 48 cents, spared the counter an excess of storage items while glamorizing humble elements of home cookery with their polished wood cabinetry.

In 1925, the Thomas Goodwin Green Company—maker of yelloware teapots and domestic items in Church Gresley, Derbyshire, England, since the 1860s—softened the hard edge of working-class kitchens with white Cornish ware banded in blue. Available in thirty-two styles, including the neatly labeled staple and spice canister sets and vinegar cruets as well as matching mugs, rolling pin, egg cups, and electric clock, the kitchen ware pieces also came in red, yellow, and a gold tone that complemented pine cupboards.

Still made at the Cloverleaf factory in Swindon, Cornish ware rose to prominence as a late-twentieth-century collector's item, with its own aficionados, a collector's club, and a guide book, Paul Atterbury's *Cornish Ware: Kitchen And Domestic Pottery* (1996). At the top of the list of collectibles were unbroken sets of canisters and spice jars in pristine condition.

The post-World War II kitchen sported canisters in plastic, the wonder material of the age. Primarily polystyrene, injection-molded sets dominated kitchenware because of their bright colors, light weight, and low cost. DaPel Plastics of Worcester, Massachusetts, brought out a whimsical line of spice holders with shaker tops. Lined up in a double row within a plastic frame topped with a chef's head, the ten canisters fit into the bend of the chef's arms as though he were presenting them to the cook as a gift. Catalin Styrene of New York City added see-through windows to display the amount left in each bin. The ad copy proclaimed, "No bushel hides their light! Not only are they welcome, out-in-the-open show pieces but they also offer exceptional utility values and appreciated handling features." (Wahlberg 1999, 98)

With the rise of the fashion for coordination, manufacturers designed matching sets that included, in addition to a canister set, a bread box, towel dispenser, butter keeper, cake box, pitcher and cups, cookie jar, wastebasket, utility tray, picnic set, and garbage can. Earl Silas Tupper exploited the market with lustrous, color-coordinated, tight-sealing sets sold under the name Tupperware. His employee, Brownie Wise, helped to propel the line to international success through home demonstration parties. Her favorite sales pitch was to toss a sealed canister filled with water to prove it leak proof and thus vermin- and moisture-free.

With the arrival of the twenty-first century, canister sets remained on the bride's must-have list. Tightly lidded containers came in a variety of shapes, sizes, and materials, including ceramic, tin, stainless steel, and glass-lined wood. Glass apothecary jars provided the advantage of expanding upward from a small base, thus using up less precious counter space. Increasing the safety of food from moisture and vermin were silicone rubber gaskets, which sealed in freshness better than cork, which tended to crumble. One variety of clear polycarbonate bins featured chrome-plated clasps and airtight silicone seals. Other models bore measurement marks, and one line incorporated measuring compartments that made a separate measuring cup unnecessary. One manufacturer developed a pleated polymer canister that expanded to suit the amount of food to be stored inside.

See also **Basketry; Caches; Coconut; Gourd; Plastics; Pottery**

Further Reading

Clarke, Judith, "Blue and White Cornish Ware," *Collectibles*, December 1998.

Papanek, John L., ed.-in-chief. *Hunters of the Northern Forest*. Alexandria, Vir.: Time-Life Books, 1995.

Scott, Susan, "Hot Collectibles: Cornish Ware," *Canadian House and Home*, October 1997, 44, 46.

CANNIBALISM

Cannibalism, also known as anthropophagy—the practice of eating human flesh—has extended to peoples worldwide and is well documented by archaeological evidence. There is also considerable anecdotal evidence of cannibalism, in the form of eyewitness accounts by explorers, missionaries, and travelers. Whether to protect the privacy of their cultures or to deflect the criticism of Western moralists, participants in flesh-eating rituals have often denied their actions and disavowed their beliefs.

Archaeological Evidence

Skeletal remains from the Neolithic Period, around 50,000 BCE, in Switzerland attest to the consumption of brain matter and bone marrow, primarily those of women and children. Paleolithic eaters of human flesh appear to have begun the practice as part of defense of their hunting and gathering territories; interlopers were captured, killed, and turned into food. In the Middle Paleolithic Period, nearer 30,000 BCE, brain and bone marrow tissue appear as elements of sacrifice for religious or magical purpose connected with membership in secret societies, initiation of youths into adulthood, funeral rites, or propitiation of fertility gods. In the prehistoric Valdivian cultures of the northern Andes, ritual cannibalism occurred at the cult center of Chavín de Huántar as an adjunct to religious worship. Others known to have practiced cannibalism include Navaho shamans, Haitian voodoo priests, and warriors in Basutoland. Australian aborigines traditionally practiced ritual consumption of dead relatives as a gesture of respect.

The term *cannibalism* dates to the late fifteenth-century confrontation of Spanish explorers with the Carib, a West Indian nation of the Lesser Antilles, Orinoco, and Guiana, whom the Spanish called Caríbales or Caníbales. Christopher Columbus's dispatches from Cuba in December 1492 described the Carib as a belligerent, cannibalistic nation. After settling in Guiana, they targeted the Arawak of Puerto Rico, whom they slaughtered and devoured. In retaliation, the Arawak instituted flesh-eating against the Carib. According to anthropologist J. A. MacCulloch, writing for the *Encyclopedia of Religion and Ethics* (1951), by the 1590s, the word *cannibal* was in general use among people who considered the eating of human flesh the ultimate taboo. In modern times, the few surviving Carib charged that the Spaniards had invented incidents of cannibalism to cover up their own blood crimes during systematic slaughter of indigenous tribes.

Rationale

As is evident from the above accounts, groups may indulge in cannibalism for a variety of reasons—tribal and religious ritual, family custom, famine, or inaccessibility of other food sources as a result of shipwreck or blizzard. The practice has alternately been extolled and cursed, celebrated and punished, depending on the circumstances and locale. The following examples are representative:

- The female Gimi of Papua swallowed flesh of the dead to consume and retain the spirit of the deceased.
- The Cree of the Hudson and James bays and Alberta ate human flesh when game was scarce.
- Some African groups devoured choice parts of human victims as a sacrament or a trophy. In central Nigeria, the victors ate only the heads of the dead. Thus, cephalophagy became a ritual means of acquiring the enemy's power.
- The Witoto (Huitoto) of southeastern Colombia and northern Peru ate mature prisoners of war as a religious act.
- Warriors in Basutoland used roasted herbed flesh as a charm against evil.
- The Amahuaca of Peru consoled grieving families with a beverage made from the ground bones and teeth of the dead. A similar custom in Venezuela preserved body fluid as a drink to strengthen medicine men.
- During the Middle Ages, starving villagers turned to hanged criminals for food or robbed graves of corpses that had not yet decomposed.
- Chao-hui, the Chinese general who conquered East Turkistan in 1757, placed his soldiers under such privation that they were forced to eat human flesh in place of military rations.
- California-bound pioneers of the infamous Donner party ate the corpses of the dead when the train was stranded during a disastrous crossing of Utah's Sierras in the winter of 1846–47.
- During twenty-four days at sea, survivors of the *Mignonette*, which strayed off course in the South Atlantic in 1884, murdered and consumed raw an ailing cabin boy.

- In the winter of 1932–33, the failure of Josef Stalin's collectivized farms in Russia forced some seven million people into starvation. Reports of cannibalism were common among entire villages that perished under the close watch of Communist Party guards.
- In 1975 Cambodian troops selected heart, lungs, liver, and biceps and lower leg meat from enemies for eating.

Into recent times, anthropological documentation, oral tradition, and eyewitness accounts confirm incidents of cannibalism in Fiji, New Guinea, Australia, New Zealand, Polynesia, Sumatra, west and central Africa, and North and South America. The custom of sarcocannibalism—the eating of human corpses as a duty to the dead—has persisted into twenty-first century. In Indonesia, survivors allow the remains of the dead to decay, then drizzle their rice with the liquid as a means of preserving the dead in the bodies of the living. Writing about such funerary practices in the early decades of the twentieth century, the anthropologist Bronislaw Malinowski noted that participants were typically reluctant to perform the holy act and immediately disgorged the unpalatable meal.

Further Reading

Berndt, R. M. *Excess and Restraint, Social Control Among a New Guinea Mountain People.* Chicago: University of Chicago Press, 1962.

Diamond, Jared M., "Archaeology: Talk of Cannibalism," *Nature*, September 7, 2000, 25–26.

Malinowski, Bronislaw. *Magic, Science and Religion.* New York: Oxford University Press, 1987.

Marlar, Richard A., "Biochemical Evidence of Cannibalism at a Prehistoric Puebloan Site in Southwestern Colorado," *Nature*, September 7, 2000, 74–78.

Rawson, Claude, "Unspeakable Rites: Cultural Reticence and the Cannibal Question," *Social Research,* Spring, 1999, 167.

Sanday, Peggy Reeves. *Divine Hunger: Cannibalism as a Cultural System.* New York: Cambridge University Press, 1986.

Tannahill, Reay. *Flesh and Blood: A History of the Cannibal Complex.* New York: Dorset, 1974.

White, Tim D., "Once Were Cannibals," *Scientific American*, August 2001, 58–65.

CANNING

Canning revolutionized kitchen work and menu preparation by simplifying the heavy job of preserving foods, previously accomplished by salting, drying, smoking, or pickling—all chores that date to the earliest eras of domesticity. A forerunner of the tin can was a variety of sealable glass and crockery vessels that contained preserved foods such as sauerkraut, pickled eggs, gherkins, or brandied fruit. An ingenious *in vitro* preservation method influenced Thomas Saddington, who earned the London Society of Arts award in 1807 for preserving fruit for home and galley.

Appert's Contribution

The real breakthrough in 1809 followed the work of the French inventor Nicolas Appert, whose extensive experiments in food preservation produced the first sterilized food in its own glass container, which he prepared for the French military. The simplicity of Appert's approach made it suitable even for the average housewife. As explained in the *Journal de Paris,* "henceforth, everybody will be able to preserve the treasures nature bestows on us in one season and enjoy them in the sterile season when she refuses them." (Schärer & Fenton 1998, 204) About the time that an English patent extended canning to glass, pottery, and tin containers, Appert published a handbook on canning for the home cook. Because of the tedious nature of the sterilization method, however, few homemakers bought his brochure. In 1812, the journalist and food writer Grimod de la Reynière surmised that canning required such skill, patience, and experience that few home cooks felt equal to the task. Perhaps because of time and labor constraints on housewives and doubts about the sturdiness and transportability of glass containers, Appert's concept of home sterilization in jars failed to take hold in France until Louis Pasteur popularized it in 1861 by explaining how boiling killed the microbes that caused food to spoil.

For the food industry, canning was an economic boon—a method of extending the value of farm produce. In 1810, the English engineer Peter Durand received a royal patent from King George III for the invention of the cylindrical sealed can. His method required cutting cans from tin-plated sheet metal with foot-powered shears, then forming the body around a cylindrical mold and soldering the seams. Two years later, an English foundryman, Bryan Donkin (or Dorkin), and John Hall of the Dartford Iron Works used Appert's method to preserve meat, vegetables, and soup in tins and established the first commercial cannery. They claimed to have paid £1,000 for the use of Appert's patent. They offered boiled beef and mutton, boiled veal, corned round of beef, mess beef, mess beef and vegetables, mutton with vegetables, roasted veal, seasoned beef and mutton, soup and bouilli (boiled meat), veal and vegetables, and vegetable soup. The first commercial canners filled tin cans through a large hole, topped them with lids, and concluded by soldering the opening. The technology replaced the laborious, expensive job of manufacturing iron cans, which workers produced at the rate of sixty a day.

A 4-H Club member storing the food canned from the vegetables grown in her garden, Rockbridge County, Va. *[© Library of Congress, Prints and Photographs Division (LC-USZ62-99891)]*

Stocking the Navy's Pantry

Canned foods immediately began making culinary history. In 1814, English provisioners began stocking the pantry at the navy's Bermuda hospital with canned goods. In that same period, when Britain's Pacific penal colonies were relieving English jails of an overflow of criminals, transporting and growing enough food was so great a problem that both prisoners and jailers risked malnutrition and starvation. The first shipment of canned food left the British Isles for Australia in 1814. The next year, Arctic expeditioners Otto von Kotzebue and Sir William Edward Parry, on voyages to locate a Northwest Passage, improved their chances of survival by stocking ship and camp larders with tinned food and matches. Likewise, in 1818, the explorer John Ross packed tinned food during his trek to Baffin Bay; simultaneously, Lord William Pitt

Amherst carried canned food on a state embassy to China. In 1820, the arctic expeditioner Sir John Richardson, surgeon and naturalist in Sir John Franklin's exploration of the Canadian Arctic coast, advanced the primitive style of making pemmican by drying it in a malting kiln and preserving it in tins.

The advent of canned foods was a special boon to the navy. Captain Basil Hall of the *Lyra*, escort to Lord Amherst, wrote that he looked forward to provisioning in cans. It had distinct advantages over the practice of bringing aboard livestock, which drank up the vessel's water supply and could tumble overboard, lose flesh from the roll of the ship, or die from falls or disease. Moreover, cans stacked easily and were immediately ready to serve, hot or cold. Hall summarized, "[Canned food] is not exposed to the vicissitudes of markets, nor is it scourged up to a monstrous price as at St. Helena, because there is no alternative. Besides these advantages it enables one to indulge in a number of luxuries which no care or expense could procure." (Riddervold & Ropeid 1988, 156) Naval surgeons attested to the value of canned goods in improving the health and morale of officers and crew. In 1825, the *Regulations and Instructions for the Medical Officers of His Majesty's Fleet* established the daily allotment of canned meat at two to six ounces per man in sick bay. Within six years, the shift in galley cookery affected all sailors.

In the quarter century before the invention of the can opener, the navy issued each mess a lever knife for opening tins along with instructions for testing the quality of the contents, which sometimes spoiled from rough handling during transport. The worst such instance occurred in 1845 on Sir John Franklin's doomed arctic expedition aboard the *Erebus* and *Terror,* when many of his men, marooned by thick ice, died of starvation and scurvy. Authorities blamed the spoiled canned meat that an innovative processer, Stephen Goldner, had put up in large tins rather than single-serving cans and had underheated them. The failure temporarily altered military opinions of canning at England's Victualling Yards and prompted a parliamentary investigation of food contractors. Sailors groused at the shift from time-honored salt beef and pork and dubbed tinned Irish beef "clews and lashings," a reference to the cords that slung their hammocks from the bulkheads. (Ibid. 156)

Growing Consumer Acceptance

In the United States, canned foods slowly worked their way from institutional use to home kitchens and westward to the Indian reservations, where the availability of tinned food rapidly separated Native Americans from their traditional diet. By 1819, a factory in New York City was turning out tins of fish. Because of the difficulty of opening cans with hammer and chisel and the waste incurred when the top was hit too hard, home cooks bought few tinned products. In the 1820s, while pilchard and sardine canning began in Nantes, France, and salmon tinning in Aberdeen, Scotland, and Cork, Ireland, William Underwood of Boston widened the application of the Appert sterilization model, canning meat products in bottles and extending the technology to berries, jam and jelly, ketchup, milk, and pickles. In a move to counter prejudice against American canned foods and assure acceptance of his goods in English colonies, he affixed an English label to his wares.

In 1825, Thomas Kensett and his father-in-law, inventor Ezra Draggett, patented hermetic (airtight) canning in glass and marketed lobster, oysters, and salmon from their New York factory. Extensive breakage forced them to abandon glass in favor of tin. Within

a decade, provisioners could also purchase friction matches sealed in a can. These handy, waterproof containers of supplies found their way to wagon trains and homes on the North American frontier. Canning cost and efficiency improved in the mid-1800s. The first collapsible metal tube came on the market in 1842, introducing flexible packaging for such necessities as stove blacking and toothpaste. Henry Evans's invention of a die-cutting operation in 1846 sped up can production tenfold, from six to sixty an hour. The U.S. inventor Allen Taylor refined machine stamping of tin cans the following year.

Because hopes remained high for the canned food industry, the Great Exhibition of 1851, held at London's Crystal Palace, exhibited canned meat from Australia as an example of the unity of the British colonies in the task of feeding the world. The search for new ways to cap containers passed through several stages; among the substances considered were leather, waxed paper, skin, cork stoppers, and wax. Over two decades, from 1850 to 1870, various soldering processes enhanced the tightness of the seal to prevent botulism and decay in tinned foods. In 1856, the U.S. entrepreneur Gail Borden marketed condensed milk in a familiar red-and-white tin can manufactured in Walcottsville, Connecticut. Along with Van Camp's pork and beans, canned milk was a staple of miners in the American West. To supply cook shacks on the gold fields of California and Alaska, shippers sent canned goods around Cape Horn by clipper.

Cheap canned meats from the United States flooded the markets in the 1860s. During the Civil War, canners added calcium chloride to canning water to raise the temperature. Canned cherries, tomatoes, corn, and peas from Northern canning factories helped the Union army and navy keep fit and well nourished while Southern soldiers, still dependent on agrarian methods of food preservation, often went hungry. One of the rebel army's prize captures was a Union mess pantry, which yielded some of the first canned foods the Confederate men had ever encountered. Survivors from both sides returning from combat spread the word to wives at home that tinned food was safe and storable. When peace returned to the nation, H. J. Heinz added pickles, horseradish, sauerkraut, and macaroni dishes to the homemaker's choices. To assist homemakers in recycling cans, the *American Agriculturist* published line drawings of cans reshaped into feed and grain cups, paint buckets, rat traps, scoops, saucepans, long-handled fruit pickers, graters, muffin rings, and mica-sided lanterns.

The canning jars used in home kitchens mimicked the stoneware crock favored by home canners but with a narrower neck to limit air-borne contamination. The factory-made canning jar, which came on the market in the 1850s, grew more popular in the late 1860s. Competing with patented goods were Peoria tomato jars from Illinois and yellow ware fruit jars made by John Bell in Waynesboro, Pennsylvania, and by H. H. Melick in Roseville, Ohio. In the 1870s, a home recipe explained how to reseal tin cans for reuse. The process called for heating block tin in a pot with gum shellac, brick dust, beeswax, and rosin. Lids stayed firmly on can necks dipped into the sealant. When it came time to open the can, the cork chipped away sealant with a sharp blade.

Improved Caps, Better Cans

Several advances in technology simplified the capping process. John B. Bartlett's unique jars, invented around 1865, featured small glass feet to elevate the jar above boiling water and a complicated metal crossbar system that secured elastic bands over the cap. The Mudge cannery, promoted by Sarah Tyson Rorer, America's first dietitian, was a patented cylindrical processor that held jars sealed with wire bail handles.

Simultaneous with the wire-bound cap, the familiar zinc cap and rubber ring came into use. These suited the high-shouldered Mason jar, the invention of the New Yorker John Landis Mason in November 1858. Formed of greenish-blue glass in a mold, the jars offered visual proof that the contents had retained their original color and shape. By matching neck threads to the screw cap, the canner could form a seal as hot liquids cooled. As noted in C. D. Tuska's *Patent Notes for Engineers* (1947), Mason was a prime example of the unwary inventor who fails to file a patent until too late. In Mason's case, a lawsuit carried to the U.S. Supreme Court found in favor of the thief. In 1869, Lewis Boyd's patented glass-lined zinc cap further eroded the value of the original Mason patent.

For commercial canneries, a removable tear-strip and keywind simplified the use of cans in 1866; side-seaming of cans became commercially feasible in 1877. Another technological advance, the combination of Allen Taylor's drop press and A. K. Shriver's pressure-cooking "retort," enabled canners to surround containers with steam that equalized pressure in the contents to speed cooking. By 1880, canners in Baltimore were turning out 45 million pound-sized cans of food annually. Franco-American boosted selection in the 1880s with production of canned entrées.

Home canners continued putting up their own fruits, vegetables, and meats in glass jars submerged in a boiling water bath. Essential implements to the task included a broad-mouthed canning funnel or fruit jar filler, a knife for dislodging air pockets, a metal jar lifter or jar tong for removing jars from the water bath,

and hot pads on which the jars cooled. Optional were the fruit jar wrench, which tightened or loosened threaded zinc caps or screw-on jar lids, and a jar wrench or jar opener, which lifted flat canning lids to release the vacuum seal.

In 1890, Amanda Theodosia Jones, the inventor of an exhaust system, opened an all-woman canning factory that revolutionized the industry. At the end of the century, when canned foods became a kitchen standard, Campbell Soup Company's John Dorrance expanded canned foods to include condensed soups. Women's magazines featured recipes designed around canned ingredients. Full-page advertisements pictured smiling, contented women in their own kitchens opening packaged crackers and cookies and canned ham and corned beef.

The history of the canning industry in Australia paralleled that of Europe and the United States and freed the island nation from dependence on British food processors. In 1846, Sizar Elliot opened the island nation's first cannery in Sydney. Queensland canners dominated the export market in 1869. Victoria and Ardmona entered the business in the early 1900s by tinning fruit. At Bathurst in 1926 Edgell & Sons canned the first tinned asparagus; in 1935, at Richmond, Victoria, Heinz & Company marketed tinned baked beans in tomato sauce. During World War II, Australian canners added cauliflower, brussels sprouts, and whole tomatoes to their line of goods. In 1957, island manufacturers reduced costs by plating their own tin for cans.

Globally, canning innovations continued in the twentieth century with J. F. Pont's Amsterdam firm, which capped wide-mouth glass milk bottles, and the Ball canning jar company, which began producing glass canning jars in 1886. Ball's market dominance lasted into the 1940s with tall wide-mouthed freezer jars, which sealed food odors and flavors inside to protect the environment of home freezers and commercial lockers. The introduction of canning to the Hawaiian Islands early in the twentieth century provided American and European markets with the exotic taste of pineapple year-round. In 1906, the collaboration of the American Can Company with Oahu Rail and Land Company railroad and the development of a peeling and coring device by Honolulu Iron Works expedited the processing of canned pineapple rings, a popular item in home recipes and on buffets. The publication of recipes calling for canned pineapple quickly established it as a novel and affordable taste sensation. James Dole of the Dole Pineapple Company earned enough profit to buy the island of Lanai and plant 20,000 acres.

An important innovation, the sanitary lid, introduced in 1900, folded over rather than being soldered to seal a can. The technology worked well for ripe olives, which had never been preserved in sealed containers. Ball brought out the Sure Seal jar in 1908, when the company added the Lightning Closure, a wire bail that held the glass lid against a rubber sealing ring. Zinc compounds strengthened can liners and extended shelf life in the 1920s. By 1922, the introduction of the crimped lid sped up the canning process and reduced costs, making canned foods more affordable.

Advantages: Cleanliness, Convenience

Aiding the progress of canned fruits and vegetables from emergency supplies to pantry staples were product endorsements from such famous domestic experts as Fannie Farmer, Mary Johnson Bailey Lincoln, and Sarah Tyson Rorer. In 1898, Anna Barrows, founder and editor of *New England Kitchen Magazine,* declared that canned foods could not compare with garden-fresh produce. By 1914, however, she had changed her mind, claiming that she actually preferred canned goods to fresh-picked goods. She based her endorsement on improved sanitation in canning factories, where food passed rapidly through the process without being contaminated by human hands or exposed to the air to wilt or spoil. She stated, "The advantages offered by all these processes in preserving food in perfect cleanliness cannot be overlooked by the housekeeper who struggles to keep her kitchen and its contents free from dirt, germs, and consequent disease." (Shapiro 1986, 203)

Improved technology aided both commercial and domestic canning. In 1926, canning entered a new phase with the research of Norwegian chemist Erik Rotheim, developer of the aerosol can. Lyle Goodhue and William Sullivan applied the technology to home spray cans. Marketers embraced the technology first for distributing wax, paint, and home pesticides and later for spraying cooking oil on frying pans. The lifting of jars in home canners entered a new era with the marketing of the Iron Horse Cold Pack, invented by Oscar Herman Benson in his own kitchen and made by the Rochester Can Company in 1930. The cylindrical tin kettle held a wire frame to accommodate eight one-quart jars, which the canner lifted in one motion by grasping handles that extended above the boiling water.

In the November 1930 issue of *Good Housekeeping,* the magazine's institute reported on new U.S. labeling requirements for canned goods. Two months earlier, President Herbert Hoover had signed into law the McNary-Mapes Act, which strengthened the Pure Food Law of 1906. The new act required canneries to label all low-grade products except milk and meat, which were regulated under another statute. By distinguishing the bottom grade of a substandard season from high quality produce from better harvests, the Department of Agriculture began the move toward complete standardization of canned food.

After World War II, the Hak family of Giessen, Holland, advanced from marketing potatoes to selling groceries and canned foods. Their line started with applesauce, which they canned in a home kettle. They were more successful with beets, broad beans, butter beans, and carrots. In the 1960s, the firm shifted to glass jars, which allowed consumers a full view of what they were buying. Consumer preference for glass jars over tin cans soon established the Hak label with its slogan "Natur-Garten" as a sign of quality. Through successful advertising, the company expanded to worldwide sale of more than forty products.

Pop Tops and Squeeze Tubes

The first canned drinks appeared in the 1930s in three-ply, bottle-shaped cans with a cork at the conical top. The first easy-open aluminum cans, developed in 1963 for Alcoa by Ernie Fraze of the Dayton Reliable Tool Company, simplified the task for children, the handicapped, and elderly consumers. An extrusion method developed in 1964 ended the three-ply can and reduced the amount of metal necessary for canning, thus lessening shipping weight and cost. The next year, chromium and chromium oxide replaced earlier metal bases for cans. Solid-sided and flexible metal containers, such as squeeze tubes for cheese spreads and cake icing, rapidly changed from metal to plastic by the 1960s. The development in 1989 of the ring top further simplified opening. By 2001, the manufacturing process could turn out more than 2,500 cans per minute. Innovation continued at a slower pace from the late 1900s into the twenty-first century. Early in 2001, StarKist, a division of H.J. Heinz in Pittsburgh, Pennsylvania, introduced dry-pack tuna in a lightweight plastic packet that did not require a can opener and did not need to be drained.

See also **Appert, Nicolas; Baby Food; Jones, Amanda Theodosia**

Further Reading

Grierson, Bill, "Food Safety Through the Ages," *Priorities*, Vol. 9, No. 3, 1997, 14–17.

CARÊME, MARIE-ANTOINE

Called Antonïn the Prodigy, the Parisian chef and master confectioner Marie-Antoine Carême, one of the founders of French cuisine, turned food preparation into an art. Legend connects his surname to an ancestor whom Pope Leo X dubbed Jean de Carême (John of Lent) after he devised a flavorful Lenten soup. Born in a shed on June 8, 1784, the sixteenth child of a poor laboring-class family, Carême was abandoned at the city gate in 1795. His father, a stonemason, felt that the boy had a better chance of survival on his own. He immediately found work in a tavern kitchen. Advanced to the pastry shop of the master confectioner Bailly, the top Paris *pâtisserie,* he learned candy making as well as reading and art. By age fifteen, he was apprenticed in a restaurant kitchen.

In his spare moments, Carême read cookbooks and studied classical architecture at the Bibliothèque Royale and applied neoclassical structural design to his famous *pièces montées* (mounted presentations). Using spun sugar, dough, and wax, he constructed elegant temples, ruins, crenellated castles, and belvederes and set them on elaborate china pediments to grace Napoleon's table. For the natural glue needed for *pastillage* (sugar paste decorations), he chose tragacanth, or gum dragon, a natural gum that exudes from a shrub of the genus *Astragalus.* Of his creative sweets he wrote, "The fine arts are five in number, to wit: painting, sculpture, poetry, music, architecture— whose main branch is confectionery." (Montagné 1977, 186)

Driven by art rather than greed, Carême devised aspics, galantines, borders of greenery, and fruit baskets and invented *mille-feuille,* a flaky pastry; *sultanes,* a large pastry set on sugar lattice and topped with sugar plums; and *croquembouche,* a crunchy casing for sweets. From orange rinds, he made decorated baskets with handles for holding orange gelatin. From Monsieur Eugène, chef to Prince Schwartzenberg, the Austrian ambassador, he learned to make *kugelhopf* (or *kougloff*), a lofty risen pastry that Queen Marie Antoinette admired. He defended *roux,* the butter-flour mixture used as a base and thickener for gravies and sauces.

While working for Charles-Maurice de Talleyrand, the French foreign minister, Carême abetted his master's manipulation of meals and buffets into undercover political coups by serving as master cook and spy. Among the dinners he engineered were the celebration of Napoleon's brother's marriage, Napoleon's wedding to Marie-Louise of Austria in 1810, and the birth of their child the following year. Carême rose quickly into the service of the Baron James and Baroness Betty de Rothschild, in whose kitchen at Boulogne he cre-

ated Lady Morgan's English fish soup. He moved on to cook for Tsar Alexander I of Russia at the Paris peace talks of 1814–1815. The next year, Carême catered a feast for the Allies in Champagne.

On a visit to Russia in 1819, Carême admired hothouse pineapples and concocted strawberries Romanov from strawberries grown under glass. He rejected offers to work at the Russian palace, where his cuisine would have come under constant scrutiny. Rejuvenated by travel, he returned home to western Europe with a myriad of fresh ideas. Among them was a recipe for Paskha, a traditional Russian Easter dessert. By molding a cream-cheese mix in heart-shaped pans, he invented Coeur à la crème, which was served with cream and wild strawberries. As illustrated in his book *Le Patissier Pittoresque* (The Picturesque Confectioner, 1854), he created a Russian *dacha* (summer house) in *pastillage.*

Carême's whimsy evoked praise from great and powerful people. For composer Antonio Rossini, he invented Tournedos Rossini. For George IV, who was then prince regent, he superintended the royal kitchens at Carlton House in London and Brighton's Royal Pavilion. Pressed to stay on, he abandoned the foggy, depressing English landscape to return to France. Content in his homeland, he created such table sensations as Charlotte à la Parisienne—later renamed Charlotte Russe—a creamy dessert molded on top of sponge cake fingers; a cream-based béchamel, named for Louis de Béchameil; and Bavaroise, a beverage prepared from tea, syrup, and milk and named for the Bavarian princes who took refreshment at the Café Procope.

As though born to privilege, Carême presided over the kitchen at the Court of Vienna, the British Embassy in Paris, the Congress of Aix-la-Chapelle, St. Petersburg Palace, the Tuileries, Hôtel de Ville, Elysée-Napoléon, and private mansions and châteaux. Armed with the best of ingredients, utensils, and staff, he placed dishes on decorated *socles* (bases) and perfected for them his signature complex sauces—salmis, Robert, Sauce Supremé, Sauce Hollandais, and bourguignonne, the sauce that popularized the snail.

To would-be chefs, Carême was honest about the painstaking work of making fragile food presentations. After creating vol-au-vent, an entrée made from flaky pastry casing filled with brown and white sauce, he pronounced it "pretty and good without a doubt," but noted that "to cook it perfectly demands the utmost care." (Montagné 1977, 970)

The key to Carême's popularity was his discipline of under-chefs and his coordination of dishes into compatible textures, flavors, and aromas. Although he witnessed *service à la russe* at the table of Tsar Alexander I in 1818, he preferred the grandly dramatic *service à la francaise*, which survived in Europe only a few more years. By imposing order on chaotic banquet tables, he elevated the role of the chef as chief engineer of gustatory pleasure.

In 1815, Carême published *Le Pâtissier Royal Parisien* (The Royal Parisian Pastry Chef), a riposte to the uneducated and tasteless food writers of his day. He followed with *Maître d'Hôtel* (1822) and, in 1833, three parts of his five-volume *Le Cuisinier Parisien, ou l'Art de la Cuisine au Dix-neuvième Siècle* (The Parisian Cook, or The Art of Nineteenth-Century Cuisine), a salute to grand cuisine that also revealed his reservations about dark kitchens and smelly charcoal braziers, the hazards of the trade. He dedicated the work to Laguipière, his tutor, who died in 1812 while serving cavalryman Joachim Murat, marshal of France, during Napoleon's disastrous retreat from Moscow. Carême tinged praise for a fine teacher with regret that the great man had left nothing of his cooking expertise in print.

Perhaps in reaction to Laguipière's failure to document his accomplishments, Carême exceeded the usual quantity and range of publications from a master chef. His compilation of recipes and menus for daily use and special occasions accompanied a history of French cuisine, drawings of his centerpieces, and instruction for the beginning cook on food shopping, kitchen organization, decoration, and garnish. In this same period, he redesigned the cook's uniform, selecting white as a model of sanitation and choosing the double-breasted jacket as a dignified style for the professional man. To distinguish the ranks of kitchen pecking order, in 1821, while he was working for Lord Stewart, Carême designated short caps for apprentices and, for chefs, the tall pleated toque that remains the symbol of culinary mastery.

For his creativity and attention to detail, Carême earned the title "Le Cuisinier des Rois et le Roi de Cuisiniers" (the Cook of Kings and the King of Cooks). (Montagné 1977, 185) Near the end of his career, he declined numerous offers to head staffs for royalty and nobility. Wearied by a life of hard work, he retired to Paris to dictate commentary and anecdotes to his daughter. He died a poor man at age fifty-seven on January 12, 1833. Buried at Montmartre Cemetery, Carême lies beside his wife under an obelisk reading, "Un de Profundis" (One of the Profound). It fell to a pupil, Pluméry, to complete his masterwork according to the chef's outline. The influence of Carême shone through the writings of Urbain Dubois and Émile Bernard, co-authors of *La Cuisine Classique* (Classic Cookery, 1856), which dominated the profession until the rise of chef Georges-Auguste Escoffier.

See also **Candy**

Further Reading

Mennell, Stephen. *All Manners of Food: Eating and Taste in England and France from the Middle Ages to the Present.* New York: Basil Blackwell, 1985.

CARVER, GEORGE WASHINGTON

A major contributor to agricultural science, George Washington Carver developed by-products of the peanut, soybean, and sweet potato. The sickly son of slaves, he was born in July 1861 outside Diamond Grove, Missouri. In 1871 he entered a one-room school at Neosho, Missouri, and, at age twenty-four, completed high school in Minneapolis, Kansas. After first attending Simpson College in Indianola, Iowa, Carver moved on to the State Agricultural College in Ames, Iowa, and worked in botany and mycology at the Ames Experiment Station while completing a master's degree.

In 1896, Booker T. Washington invited Carver to join the department of agriculture at Tuskegee Institute in Alabama. The focus of his work was the remediation of farmland depleted by erosion, lack of moisture, and overcropping with cotton. Beginning by nourishing the soil with nitrogen-generating crops such as cowpeas and soybeans, he went on to specialize in the cultivation of peanuts, soybeans, and sweet potatoes. He took his courses on the road to teach established farmers new and better methods and to encourage homemakers to use peanut oil and homemade peanut butter to enrich their menus. His school on wheels succeeded and influenced the U.S. Department of Agriculture to set up a similar program in other states and territories.

To boost the marketability of local crops, Carver studied hybrids and fertilizers. His experiments in the creation of agricultural by-products rejuvenated the rural Southern economy. He bolstered family nutrition with recipes for homemade peanut butter and peanut-based meal, and he urged home cooks to add peanuts and peanut sprouts and oil to meatless casseroles, bisques, wafers, fudge, brownies, cake, candy, salads, sauces, pickles, mayonnaise, shortening, milk, and coffee. He created peanut-based livestock feed and taught women to make their own sweeping compounds, washing powder, home cosmetics, and remedies from peanuts, including lotions, shaving cream, soap, anti-dandruff shampoo, antiseptics, rubbing compounds, cough syrup, castor oil substitute, iron tonic, goiter treatment, and laxatives. From peanuts he extracted wood stain, leather dye, and paint and made charcoal and fuel bricks for wood stoves, insecticide, wood filler, plastics, lubricants and axle grease, gas and diesel fuel, paper and ink, glue, metal polish, siding and insulation, even nitroglycerine and linoleum. From

Carver declined a $100,000 a year job with Henry Ford to continue teaching at Tuskegee for $1,500 annually. He advised U.S. presidents as well as Josef Stalin, the Prince of Wales, and Mohandas Gandhi. For his altruism and genius, Carver was elected to the British Royal Society of Arts and the Hall of Fame and earned the 1923 Spingarn Medal and the Roosevelt Medal and Thomas A. Edison Foundation Award in 1942. Before his death at his home on January 5, 1943, Tuskegee Institute set up the Carver Research Foundation, to which he contributed his savings and left his estate. The university's Carver Museum houses some of his laboratory equipment and samples of the products he was instrumental in developing. At the Moses Carver farm, the George Washington Carver National Monument honors his contributions to agronomy.

Further Reading

Mabunda, L. Mpho, ed. *The African American Almanac.* Detroit: Gale Research, 1997.

CAULDRONS

Cauldrons, the kings of the unlidded cooking pots, have served large-scale kitchen and laundry tasks since early times. In Hunan, an ancient grave reveals a *fu* (Chinese cauldron) along with a rod and *teng* (steamer). Similar vessels were used in the Middle East. According to chef and Assyriologist Jean Bottéro, the Mesopotamian cook of 1700 BCE appears to have invented a metal cauldron for browning and parboiling foods. Archeologists of the Hopewell culture in Loy, Illinois, reassembled a 1,900-year-old cauldron that retained charred traces of its contents. The leftovers, which included fish bones, suggested that the pot once held a long-simmering stew that was doled out in impromptu servings whenever families were hungry.

In the late Neolithic era, European metal smiths made bronze cauldrons mounted on four-spoked wheels, an improvement on wagons that bore leather bags, staved barrels, or vats. Traced to early rotund Hungarian burial vessels, these wheeled cauldrons developed into decorative chased metal containers, which, filled with mead, were placed in graves for use by the deceased in the afterlife. In 1895, a farmer in Skallerup, Denmark, found one such embossed kettle-wagon in a burial barrow. Similar drink pots on sledges, made in Hungary or Romania in the early Bronze Age, have also surfaced at Ystad, Sweden; Sesto Calende, Italy; and Milavec, Acholshausen, and Peccatel, Germany. They probably carried a standard honeyed wheat drink flavored with cranberries and bog myrtle.

George Washington Carver, full-length portrait, standing in field, probably at Tuskegee, holding a clump of soil.
[© *Library of Congress, Prints and Photographs Division* (*[LC-USZ62-114302]*)]

the sweet potato, he produced flour and meal, sweetener, molasses, vinegar, yeast, coffee, synthetic coconut and ginger, chocolate substitute, paste, tapioca, and starch. He published forty-three instructive pamphlets, beginning with "Feeding Acorns to Livestock" (1898).

Moving Cauldron. Engraving from *Il Cuoco Segreto Di Papa Pio V* (The Private Chef of Pope Pius V), by Bartolomeo Scappi, Venice, 1570.

Cauldron on open fire and pig to be scalded.

Multipurpose Vessels

In the Greco-Roman world, cooking in iron *ahena* (cauldrons) was the traditional method for boiling water and preparing pulses, the hot cereal eaten by soldiers and peasants alike. A single pot could weigh more than thirty pounds—or sixty pounds when filled with water or food. To ease the chore of moving the pots over a fire, cooks slung the heavy vessels from overhead chains.

In domestic settings, cauldrons had multiple uses—for bathing children, boiling or bleaching cloth, or cooking a pudding in an animal paunch, as with the Scottish haggis. Thrifty cooks could place various linen sacks and jugs in a single cauldron and heat them all on the same fire. In Ireland, the "pig's pot" was a cauldron large enough to hold kitchen scraps, which the cook boiled down for hours and then poured into the slop trough in the sty. Hearths were large enough to support the large fire under the pig's pot as well as ancillary fires for simultaneously heating kettles of food and beverage for the family. During the Middle Ages, Cairo's workers made public and private use of *qidras* (public cauldrons), which stokers heated each day to supply water to the Princess Baths. In the evening, when the cauldrons stood empty, cooks put them to work simmering fava beans to serve the next morning as breakfast *ful* (cereal).

According to Dorothy Hartley, author of *Food in England* (1954) and *Water in England* (1964), home cauldrons enabled thrifty householders of the twelfth century to simultaneously boil poultry, onions, and eggs in broth, bag a pudding of cereals, and suspend beef on birch twigs over the steam. For roasting beef in a clay jar, the cook crisscrossed branches in the bottom of the cauldron as a trivet; the jar, sealed with a waxed cloth or damp parchment, rested on the bottom of a cauldron in water to the level of the neck of the jar. The slow simmering of meat by this means extracted natural juices that had numerous uses—as infant or invalid food, for flavoring of root vegetables, or as a base for a steaming cup of beef tea on a winter's journey. A German drawing from the 1400s shows a peasant woman stirring ricotta cheese in an outdoor cauldron. Behind her, a long-handled draining spoon, pot strainer, and ladle lie ready for the next steps in the process.

Returning Crusaders brought from the Middle East various shapes and types of ewers and cauldrons in copper, bronze, and iron, which European artisans began to copy and produce. In Castelnaudray, France, during the siege of 1355, hungry townspeople rationed their food stocks in a centralized cauldron, from which custom came Languedoc's regional bean stew, cassoulet. Peasant cooks later simmered the dish in a clay pot or slow-cooked it over gorse-wood fires in farm kitchens of the nearby Black Mountains. Similarly, Paduans, who first planted corn in the early sixteenth century, turned the kernels into polenta, a filling mush stirred in a copper *paioli* (cauldron).

At hospices, taverns, and castles, cauldrons heated over an outdoor fire functioned as sinks for dishwashing and bathing and for scalding pigs. When householders moved several separate cauldrons indoors to the hearth of an enclosed fireplace, they prefigured the arrangement of the kitchen stove. Perched on three-legged pot stands over a log or peat fire, cauldrons stood secure on a spoked iron wheel that conducted heat directly to the outer edge of the vessel.

As soups acquired panache in the late Middle Ages, the *oulle,* a miniature of the grand cauldron, served the cook who wanted to refine mass cookery into a more delicate art. Transported north from Italy to Spain and France, the small bulge pot hung easily from a trammel hook or simmered on a trivet among embers. In the marketplace, measurement by *oulle* standardized the dispersal of loose items and some liquids. The pot became a kettle after it acquired a close-fitting top for

enhancing steam cookery and a hot pad for removing the lid or lifting the bail. Over time, the *oulle* found its way to the dining table for service of hot stews and broths directly into the bowl or porringer. Early in the 1400s, Henry IV mentioned the *oulle* in his call for warring religious factions to return to the communal pot, an emblem of shared meals and reconciliation.

Women valued the large communal cooking vats for preparation of large batches of goose and pork preserved in *confit d'oie* and *confit de porc.* In untinned copper pots, they made jam and preserves. Ironically, during the witch hunts of the fifteenth to the seventeenth centuries, church inquisitors connected the same ample cauldrons with witches' sabbaths and the preparation of illicit potions, such as abortifacients and love charms, or for cooking unwholesome concoctions alleged to contain human remains. Religious courts accused witches of using large vats for the boiling of animals and human infants.

In the 1600s, Breton sailors shared a day's catch in a communal stew of cream, onions, pepper, and potatoes called *la chaudrée,* named for *la chaudière,* the cauldron in which it was cooked. In English, the name of the fish stew was corrupted as *chowder.* In North America, the tradition of stewing fish in large pots thrived in New England, Nova Scotia, and Newfoundland and became the basis for a hearty cooking style that characterized American Atlantic coastal dining. An additional use of the cauldron, according to Anne Gibbons Gardiner's *Mrs. Gardiner's Family Receipts from 1763,* was the transportation of nourishing broth and soup during visits to slaves and the sick. The cauldron was also valuable for carrying food on wagon journeys.

On July 2, 1898, inventors of Brunswick stew on St. Simons Island off the coast of Georgia enshrined the cauldron that held the first batch. This Low Country ragout of pork, chicken, corn, tomatoes, and onions emerged as a local favorite in the Carolinas and Virginia. Conflicting oral traditions blur the truth as to who developed the recipe and what ingredients were obligatory. The filling dish, which once included squirrel and venison, is still a sea islands menu option, served with the traditional cornbread and iced tea.

Ethnic Traditions

A multitude of local dishes have relied on the cauldron to meld the different ingredients. Peasants of the Swiss Alps blended buttermilk and flour in a cauldron to make a traditional *fenz* (gruel) and layered the pot with stale bread and cheese sprinkled with milk for *chääs schoppe.* For *cocina criolla* (creole cookery), Puerto Rican cooks preferred the *caldero,* a round-bottomed iron pot, for such staples as fried *empanadillas* (turnovers), chicken with rice soup, and *bacalaitos* (cod fritters). Cooks on Margarita, an island off the coast of Venezuela, used a cauldron to boil *hallacas*, Christmas treats consisting of corn dough wrapped around meat filling and encased in banana leaves tied with string. In Grenada, the oil dong was a communal boil-down stew served with flour dumplings. The street cooks of Curaçao used wooden paddles to stir cauldrons of corn meal soup, a favorite lunchtime dish, and cactus soup, a thick green pulp pounded, then boiled and stirred with a pronged iron swizzle.

In Japan, cooks made huge batches of *shoyu*, a cereal condiment, in hermetically sealed cauldrons. The liquid flavoring began with roasted ground corn, simmered for three or four hours before the addition of soaked soya beans. The blend fermented several days before being pressed, strained, and preserved in kegs or bottles.

In Africa, the communal cauldron allowed women to share the heavy work. For a Zambian feast, cooks reduced white mealie-meal to *nshima* (cornmeal porridge) in thirty-gallon lots, taking turns at the wooden paddle as it thickened. A similar cast iron cook pot simmered *maltabella*, a hot sorghum cereal that South African cooks made at home and on safari over *jikkas* (barrel grills). They flavored the mass with vanilla, brown sugar, and *amarula*, a wild-fruit cream liqueur.

In the latter decades of the twentieth century, Egyptian cooks continued to prepare the traditional bean dish, *foul* (or *ful*) *madamis,* for the morning meal. Each night, they set fava beans boiling in tightly lidded copper cauldrons over the lowest possible charcoal fire. Overnight, at every kiosk, restaurant, and luxury hotel, the same scene occurred as cooks ladled cooked beans into vessels and plates for dressing with lemon, garlic, and olive oil or with pine nuts and butter. For weddings, neighborhood cooks converged at a single kitchen to fill a meter-wide propane-heated cauldron with eggplant, macaroni, meat, and rice to accompany honey-fried pastry and salad for a nuptial meal.

In Haiti in the early 1990s, a farmer too poor to hire laborers organized a *kombit* (community work day) and involved neighbors, relatives, and friends in readying corn fields for planting. The few women who remained at home in the kitchen teamed to fill a cauldron for a communal meal. Together, they hauled water, picked over beans, pounded garlic, washed and sifted meal, chopped cabbage, and stirred the ingredients over the traditional three-stone firepit. The hostess served the food in equal portions according to the Creole principle of "Bon mama kon partagé bien" (Good mother can divide well), a valuable bit of logic governing life

on a poor island where there was often mass hunger. (Schlabach 1991, 140)

Female farmers of Burkina Faso use cauldrons to produce shea butter, a substitute for cocoa butter that is the basis for many pharmaceutical creams, soaps, sunscreens, moisturizers, and foods. After gathering the nuts, the women grind and pound them into pulp, then cook them down in cauldrons over an open outdoor fire. Bankrolled by the United Nations Development Fund for Women and educated in collective bargaining, they have greatly increased the returns on their kitchen industry.

Further Reading

Adkins, Lesley, and Roy A. Adkins. *Handbook to Life in Ancient Greece*. New York: Facts on File, 1997.

McLaughlin, Jack. *Jefferson and Monticello: The Biography of a Builder*. New York: Henry Holt & Co., 1988.

Rausing, Gad, "The Wheeled Cauldrons and the Wine," *Antiquity*, December 199, 994–999.

Roden, Claudia, "Middle Eastern Cooking: The Legacy," *Aramco World*, March–April 1988, 4–5.

CEREALS

Judging from evidence provided by pollen studies, coprolites, stomach remains, and tomb and altar offerings, anthropologists have concluded that pulses (the edible seeds of leguminous plants) and cereals, both parched and raw, have contributed greatly to the human diet. Cereal grains dominated food cultivation of Ali Kosh, Iran, after 8000 BCE. Einkorn wheat (*Triticum monococcum*) has been identified at sites in Anatolia and Jarmo from around 6700 BCE. In Crete and Greece, emmer wheat was grown along with einkorn beginning around 6000 BCE, forming the basis for a diet heavy in baked barley and wheat loaves and boiled gruel; the latter was especially suited as a food for travelers and soldiers.

A subgroup of cereals, the pulse family of vetch, lentils, chickpeas, beans, soybeans, and field peas, has for centuries supplied humankind with vegetables that are easily grown and stored. In the Americas, farmers at Huaca Prieta in Peru grew green beans and lima beans for pottage as early as 5000 BCE. The chickpea was a common food in the eastern Mediterranean around 4000 BCE and spread to farms in Anatolia, Assyria, and Babylon. From 2800 BCE, the Chinese cultivated soybeans for their oil, a material for making a cheese curd and oily butter.

Early Uses

Among Germanic, Helvetian, and Scandinavian peoples, rye and oats were staples after 1000 BCE. Rye

Kellogg Company, 1934. Women inspecting filled boxes of cereal before boxes go to sealer.
[© *Courtesy of National Archives and Records Administration.*]

spread to farmland throughout the British Isles, Turkey, and central Europe and remained a mealtime standard into modern times. The Chinese wrote sophisticated commentary on millet in the *Fan Shêng-Chich Shu* (ca. 100 BCE).

In the Fertile Crescent, Mesopotamian and Kurdistani cooks were feeding their families club wheat in 3000 BCE. Despite Herodotus's statement to the contrary, the Egyptians also valued beans and peas, as evidenced by tomb offerings of a pulse paste made from farro, a common Mediterranean wheat variety. Cretan cereal cultivation paralleled that of the Fertile Crescent. North of Egypt, their clay *pithoi* (storage jars) held the island's stock of legumes, which appear to have thrived from the Neolithic era.

Among the Berbers, Algerians, Moroccans, and Tunisians, the making of couscous was a time-consuming process that required hand rubbing of large-grained durum semolina (*Triticum durum*) with finer grains soaked in salt water, causing the small shape to attach to the larger one. Moroccans completed this process on a *gas'a* (platter) of faience or wood before drying grains in a *miduna,* a lattice basket made

from palm fronds or esparto grass. Dried coucous rested in a *tabaq,* a finely woven basket, before the cook returned it to the *miduna* for additional rolling. For uniformity, cooks sieved the refined couscous before sun-drying the grains on a white cloth for up to five days. From there, the cook steamed or boiled the paired grains with broth in a *kiskis* or *couscousière,* a two-stage clay vessel bulbous at bottom and topped with a tightly fitting steamer basket.

Before the introduction of bread, early Romans cooked *far* (farro, or husked wheat) into cereal mush to eat with their vegetables and meat. Daily, cooks roasted farro before a fire and ground it into *puls* (porridge), a dietary staple. Householders sacrificed the grain to their deities and, for weddings, formed it into *panis farreus* (farro bread), a ceremonial loaf that honored newlyweds. Pulses dominated the diet of the poorest citizens, along with parched seeds and chickpeas sold by street vendors. Apicius, a connoisseur of Roman foods and author of *De Re Coquinaria* (On Cooking, late 300s CE), the world's oldest cookbook, preferred a Baian strain of beans to ordinary grain or peas.

Hearty Meals

In the Middle Ages, Scots made a porridge from recently threshed grain husks. After soaking them for a day, cooks skimmed away the chaff on top and boiled the brown flour at bottom into a thick sludge. From the same makings, English shepherds often brewed a cereal broth in a wooden vessel. By placing a handful of oatmeal in a small cask of water and slinging it from the shoulder when embarking on the day's rounds, the shepherd assured the mixture a continuous churning action. With the aid of fermentation by bacteria in the wood, the mix produced a hearty meal and sustaining drink. For liquid refreshment, the Scot carried a hoggin of *brose,* an oatmeal drink aerated and fermented during a long walk.

Scottish oats were an egalitarian nourishment. In the evening, according to Sir John Sinclair's *Statistical Account of Scotland* (1799), the laird and herder both dined on the same fare—*brochan,* a humble cereal made from oatmeal and herbs stirred into the water previously used to boil the mutton or venison. The Welsh *brewis* or *potes pigtegill* was a similar cereal broth made from oat bread and fat or drippings served hot with cheese and seasonings.

For home use, European cottagers served cereals in pot-bellied porringers made of clay, metal, or wood. Porringers or a matched set of bowls and spoons were considered a suitable gift for newlyweds. Communal diners typically shared a bowl and dipped independently into the same portion. From the French *écuelle* (porringer) arose the saying "manger à la même écuelle" (to dine from the same bowl).

Marco Polo discovered that cereals were as important to the diet in Asia as in Europe. On his journey east to Cathay, he observed the dominance of cereals in the kitchens of Tartars and Chinese. In *The Travels of Marco Polo* (1299), he noted that the sowing of millet, panic, and rice produced a hundred-fold yield; these grains, boiled with milk or meat, were the staples of the family diet. Wheat, a lower-yield crop, he described as being formed into noodles and pasty foods, a reference that some culinary historians have assumed to mean a form of macaroni.

Among Poles, the mastery of kasha, a buckwheat cereal grain dating to the group's beginnings, preceded other housewifely skills. Women learned to turn nourishing kasha into soup, baked dishes flavored with mushrooms and plums, and side dishes for meats. A forerunner of potatoes in the Polish diet, kasha was the cook's gift to the newborn and was once an offering to the goddess of childbirth. In the mid-1500s, the Dowager Queen Anne Jagiellon required her staff to cook the buckwheat kasha common to the laboring class in her private kitchen. As a gesture of good will,

she sent parcels of the cereal to the royal court in Warsaw.

Early in the 1600s, the beginning of Japan's Edo period, somen noodles and soba (buckwheat) noodles gained popularity in Tokyo and along the east coast. Because of a demand for soba as a breakfast and festival food and as street fare, farmers began sowing more grain. Colorful additions to the basic soba dough included green tea, shrimp, eggs, sesame seed, seaweed, mountain yams, and chrysanthemum petals. The noodles evolved into a kitchen staple for dipping in sauce, adding to soup, and frying in tempura.

In the British Isles, cereal cookery of the nineteenth century focused on pearl barley and cracked wheat, which cost the cook hours of steaming in a double boiler to make them palatable as porridge, gruel, or pudding. For ease of preparation, cooks gradually replaced barley with oats as the centerpiece of Irish and Scottish breakfasts. As described by the food historian Margaret "Meg" Dod, author of *The Cook and Housewife's Manual* (1826), the thrifty Scots cook "skinked" (aerated) gruel by lifting spoonfuls and dribbling them back into the pan, then sliced the hard rind of cereal left in the pot into slabs for frying in butter and serving with supper. (Beard *et al.* 1975, 166) The *Edinburgh Review,* founded in 1800, took as its motto: "Tenui musam meditamur avena" (We cultivate the muse on a little oatmeal). The main holdout against oats were the English, who denigrated the Irish and Scots and served oatmeal only in prisons or horse barns.

The Dutch favored porridge as a quick home grain dish. They cooked heavy, hearty masses of *bierenbroot* (beer porridge) and *melkentweebak* (rusk porridge and milk) to serve at breakfast or as a dinnertime appetizer, main dish, accompaniment, pudding, or dessert. More common among the poor, who could not afford commercially baked bread, porridge boiled with leftover buttermilk or skimmed milk was standard kitchen fare at student refectories, orphanages, hospices, and jails. Middle-class cooks made porridge from rice, wheat, or white bread and added cream, eggs, brown sugar, currants, or almonds, thus elevating the dish from its humble beginnings

New World Practices

In the New World, the wild mesquite bean, a relative of the pea, nourished the Cocopa, Mexica, Mojave, Papago, Pima, and Yuma of the Sonora desert. Pueblo housewives collected its sugary pods in fiber bags and then spread them out to dry on the flat roofs of their dwellings. When the supply of small animals and garden produce failed, families could rely on *mesquitamal,* a cooked cereal flavored with salt, berries, and seeds. They cooked the versatile bean into stews and ground it into flour used to make beer, bread, dumplings, mush, and pudding. The Quechua of Central America made a similar cereal, flour, and beer from quinoa, their mother grain; the Aztec preferred amaranth, which they grew on floating garden plots called *chinampas*.

Beginning about 4000 BCE, hot cereal was a favorite meal of the Incas, who inhabited South America's west coast. Cooks used quihuicha, a species of amaranth, to make a traditional meal. The tiny grains, cooked in water or broth, produced a crunchy texture and nutty taste; the dish was eaten with milk and honey or as a snack. The grain was also formed into confections and used as a coating for fried chicken and fish.

The Pueblo used a coil pot to cook *atole* or *atolli*, a favorite hot cereal broth. According to a description in Josiah A. Gregg's *Commerce of the Prairies* (1844–1845): "A sort of thin mush, called atole, made of Indian meal, is another article of diet, the preparation of which is from the aborigines; and such is its nationality, that in the North it is frequently called *el cafe de los Mexicanos* (the coffee of the Mexicans). How general so ever the use of coffee among Americans may appear, that of atole is still more so among the lower classes of Mexicans." (pp. 153–154) After the cook flavored the coarse grain porridge with honey or peppers, Aztec diners sipped the mixture from clay saucers as a nourishing liquid breakfast.

The French *coureurs de bois* (woodsmen) recorded the division of labor in the harvesting and cooking of wild oats among the Illiniwek. The men harvested the grains by shaking them into a passing canoe; women then cleaned them of chaff and spread them on wooden lattice over a fire for several days of drying. Nelson Algren summarized the rest of the process in his 1992 book *America Eats*: "They put the oats in skin bags, forced it into holes in the ground, treaded out the grain, winnowed it, reduced it to meal, boiled it in water, and seasoned it in bear grease." (p. 2).

In *Mourning Dove: A Salishan Autobiography* (1990), the author describes how native women threshed wheat by hand and winnowed it from dishpans. For cereal-making, she recounts, "the kernels were boiled until soft, with tallow flavoring and a little flour thickening. This dish was as common as beans are today." (*Mourning Dove*, 1990, 167)

English colonists cooked oatmeal for children and invalids, serving it to adults only when Scottish or Irish visitors sat at their tables. In *Good Wives: Image and Reality in the Lives of Women in Northern New England, 1650–1750* (1991), the author Laurel Thatcher Ulrich includes an inventory of the supplies of Beatrice and Francis Plummer of Newbury, Massachusetts, in 1672; the family's stores ran heavily to cereal grains—twenty-five bushels each of barley, oats, rye, and wheat. For everyday breakfasts Beatrice Plummer cooked oats into flummery, a porridge flavored with dried fruit and spice.

In the nineteenth century, because of the connection between oats and infant or invalid food, American shoppers bought their supplies from apothecaries. Because of demand from Scottish and Irish immigrants, dry goods dealers began dispensing rolled oats from barrels. It was not until 1856 that a Hanoverian grocer, Ferdinand Schumacher, began milling oats at the German Mills American Oatmeal Company outside Akron, New York for general distribution in grocery stores. Homemakers proved such faithful customers that Schumacher opened a second mill in 1883.

Staple of the Breakfast Table

During the American Civil War, Union soldiers were glad to get a hot breakfast, especially when they were on the march or cut off from supply trains. Cooks used foodstuffs on hand to make panada, a hot breakfast gruel affectionately known as "bully soup." (McCutcheon 1993, 234) The main ingredients were watery corn meal and crumbled hardtack, both of which were standard issue. The nourishing, belly-filling cereal required a brief cooking with wine and ginger before cooks' assistants ladled it into tin cups that the soldiers eagerly thrust over the camp cauldron.

Late in the nineteenth century, cereal began its transformation into standard breakfast food for American children of all classes. In 1870 the *Akron Beacon* carried the nation's first cereal advertisement, the beginning of a long tradition of wooing mothers to become devotees of hot cereal. An integral part of the advertising strategy was to emphasize the connection between a nourishing, filling morning meal and parental duty. As the dish lost its tie to the lower classes, the Lowell and Cabot families, pillars of Boston aristocracy, began eating oat porridge as part of a daily regimen. Oatmeal received favorable mention in two food influential reference books, *Miss Beecher's Housekeeping* (1873) and *Anna Maria's Housekeeping* (1884).

Meanwhile, the Quaker Oats Company got its start in Ravenna, Ohio, in 1881 with Henry Parsons Cromwell's Quaker Mill. Cromwell allied with Schumacher in 1888, and the two men formed a monopoly of oat cereal production, which lasted until Cromwell controlled the firm in 1906. Henry D. Seymour and William Heston, who registered the cheery-faced Quaker in 1877 as their official trade character, bought out Schumacher's shares in 1901. Schumacher's firm merged with Quaker Oats, headquartered in Cedar

Rapids, Iowa, and St. Joseph, Missouri. The company's cereal lines have provided American kitchens with oat, corn, barley, masa harina, and granola products for a century. The company's greatest contribution to kitchen efficiency was a quick-cooking Quaker Oats, introduced in 1922, which reduced preparation time from fifteen to five minutes.

In Europe, Dr. Maximilian Oskar Bircher-Benner, an advocate of muesli, a Swiss fruit, nut, and cereal dish, started a health-food fad for crunchy breakfast food. Born in Aarau, Switzerland, in 1867, he entered medical study in Vienna. After matriculation at Dresden, Berlin, and Zurich, he completed his degree in 1891. He first cured himself of weak appetite and jaundice by following the advice of Pythagoras, the Greek philosopher-mathematician who recommended that patients with poor digestion eat raw food. From experience with naturopathy, hydrotherapy, and dietetics in Zurich, where he practiced, Bircher-Benner developed a health regimen based on the observation of sensible health practices and a diet of raw vegetable foods.

In 1897, Bircher-Benner opened a small private clinic to treat his own patients. In 1902, he advanced to a large sanitarium, where he wrote texts on combating disease with diet and built the reputation of alternative medicine, then in its infancy. Emphasizing the benefits of harmony with nature, he promoted healthful grains, fruit, and vegetables over a meat-heavy diet and offered daily exercise in sunshine and fresh air. At his death in 1939, his *birchermuesli,* a blend of rolled oats, apples, and lemon juice, remained a focus of his natural diet. In the 1960s, muesli gained respect among vegans and health-food proponents for its high fiber and nutrients.

Wheat cereal has its own history. It was the dream child of food reformer Alexander Milton Ross of Toronto, who longed to find a suitable condensed wheat food. The dream became reality after Henry D. Perky, a devotee of wheat berries, got the idea for Shredded Wheat in 1890 after watching a dyspeptic diner blend wheat with cream. In his Denver kitchen, Perky processed wheat into biscuits and strips to make a product attractive to buyers seeking a food with a long shelf life. He first found buyers in vegetarian restaurants. One health-minded publication, *The Chicago Vegetarians,* suggested using his wheat pillows as croutons in soup. By 1892, his Cereal Machine Company was leasing cereal-making apparatus to bakers in Colorado Springs and Denver.

After meeting Perky and contracting to purchase a wheat processor, Dr. John Harvey Kellogg, spokesman for better technology and high standards of food processing, became an admirer of Shredded Wheat, which was distributed from a Niagara Falls factory. Although he chose not to buy Perky's patent on wheat cereal, it was Kellogg rather than Perky who became the father of breakfast cereals. To an audience consisting primarily of wealthy hypochondriacs and semi-invalids, Kellogg warned of "cholera morbus," the collywobbles, the results of a diet of health-endangering foods. (Carson 1957, n. p.) He denounced pork and promoted a water cure, vegetarianism, exercise, and sexual abstinence.

First "Health Food"

At the "San," affluent patients gathered at the dull, abstemious table of Kellogg's boardinghouse and hospital, which advocated a diet centered around grains, nuts, and a new invention, peanut butter. A lecture program for patients emphasized religion, moral reform, asceticism, and relaxation in a country club atmosphere. Observing the eating habits of patients, Kellogg realized that the flaccid, pasty appearance of hot cereal kept it from being enjoyed. He became determined to transform cereal mush into crisp, dry, digestible flakes. Working out of his own kitchen, he experimented with an extrusion process, which failed. Using paired rollers similar to those of a washing machine wringer, he successfully solved the problem of how to press wheat paste without destroying natural fiber.

Harvey Kellogg's brother, Will Keith Kellogg, kept at the rolling process until he accidentally let a batch of wheat mush sour. When the mush passed through the rollers, Keith cranked out the first batch of thin, crispy flakes, which he named Granose. After patenting their process, the two set up shop in a barn in 1895 and baked wheat flakes in an oven built by Swedish machinist Adolph Johnson. The assembly line reduced flakes to grains by sieving them as they dried to make them dissolve in milk. By 1905, the Sanitarium Health Food Company was operating night and day to produce more than 113,000 boxes of cereal a year. The following June, it began advertising directly to housewives in *Ladies' Home Journal.*

Other Battle Creek entrepreneurs began manufacturing such health foods as crackers, coffee substitutes, and cereals. In Detroit, the Beck Cereal Company made oat flakes, and the Lauhoff Brothers sold Crystal Malt Flakes. In Indianapolis, the Cerealine Manufacturing Company and the United States Frumentum Company entered the corn flake market. Charles W. Post, a former sanitarium patient, tried healing as a profession, then succeeded as the manufacturer of three products—Postum, an ersatz coffee; Elijah's Manna, renamed Post Toasties in 1908; and Grape

Nuts, a health food cereal that he advertised in 1919 with homey Norman Rockwell illustrations.

The market quickened with competition. One entry, Ralston Purina, advertised whole-wheat cereal as a good choice for toddlers, claiming that it promoted sturdy growth and deep sleep. To compete with its rivals, W. K. Kellogg Company emphasized the flavor and convenience of its products and the free tokens and toys in each box, an enticement to children to eat cereal for breakfast. Kellogg spread the message for Toasted Corn Flakes with a million-dollar ad campaign launched in 1931, when radio came into its own as an advertising medium.

Another rival cereal got its start in 1921 after a nutritionist accidentally dropped bran gruel onto a stovetop. He produced a crisp flake that was the prototype for Wheaties. In an ad campaign targeted at young breakfast eaters, the company sought to link its product to health and athleticism, calling it the "Breakfast of Champions." Although Wheaties never threatened the popularity of Corn Flakes, its manufacturer outlasted many other makers of breakfast cereals.

Enduring Popularity

By the mid-twentieth century, the popularity of cereal owed less to health wisdom and more to ubiquitous ad campaigns and marketing ploys. By the 1950s, cold cereal such as Weetbix, Rice Bubbles, Sultana Bran, Muesli, Vitabrits, and Weetflakes sold twice as well to Canadians and Australians as did Cheerios, Rice Krispies, and Wheat Chex in the United States, despite the introduction of sugary cereals such as Sugar Pops, Sugar Smacks, and Sugar Frosted Flakes. Part of the allure to Australian children was the discovery of a toy soldier, trading card, or pass for amusement park rides concealed in the box. In 1955, the first U.S. television generation got its introduction to cold cereal from Tony the Tiger, an animated character developed to instill brand loyalty in children rather than parents. Competitors followed the example with the Trix Rabbit and Post's Sugar Bear. Post, a marketing genius, increased cereal's appeal to children by offering a choice of ten small boxes in a packet called "Post Tens." Users could press open the perforated flap of the box, pour milk directly into the leak-proof waxed paper liner, and eat breakfast without dirtying a dish.

Advancements in cereal production, storage, and packaging have increased the popularity of this staple grain food found in most home kitchens. One manufacturer produced a variation on the standard breadbox: a chrome-plated electric crisper that revived wilted packaged cereals. In 2001, researcher Philip Ball applied the principles of physics to a persistent problem in cereal packaging—the "Brazil nut effect." Studies going back to the 1960s had demonstrated a sieving effect that allowed small particles to sink to the bottom of the package through gaps between larger grains. A manipulation of variables, such as the order in which packagers place grains in the container and the amount of agitation they receive, appeared to be the answer to producing optimum distribution in a box of muesli.

See also **Kellogg, John Harvey; Kellogg, Will Keith; Post, Charles William; Steaming; Tagines**

Further Reading

Beckwith, Carol, and Angela Fisher. *African Ceremonies.* 2 vols. New York: Harry N. Abrams, Inc., 1999.
Carson, Gerald. *Cornflake Crusade.* New York: Rinehart & Co., 1957.
Mourning Dove: A Salishan Autobiography. Lincoln: University of Nebraska Press, 1990.
"A Simple Change," *Good Housekeeping,* September 1930, 234.

CHAFING DISH

A Greek invention, the double-bottomed chafing dish contained coals in the lowest level. Used at tableside, it applied gentle heat to delicate ingredients, particularly eggs and fruit. In medieval Tunis and Muslim Spain, the dish took the place of the oven in the small home kitchen. Cooks relied on a cooking hearth, fueled by charcoal or manure, and heated foods and sauces in a *radaf,* a warming dish heated with embers. During epidemics or long home illnesses, the *radaf* burned fleabane to rid the home of vermin and charred angelica seed and root to disinfect and freshen the air.

The chafing dish first reached colonial America in 1720. Enamel, tin, and silver models provided a well or bottom container for charcoal or burning spirits, which heated the shallow lidded pan perched above on a stand or legs. A model heated over a spirit lamp—the design of the English cooking master Alexis Soyer—reached its height of popularity in the 1890s. Another variation was the hash lamp or hash dish, a footed chafing dish that perched over an alcohol lamp.

Contributing to the popularity of the chafing dish was the decline of in-house cooks and the demands on the homemaker who had little or no domestic help. Thomas Jefferson listed two brass chafing dishes on the inventory of Monticello's kitchen. For gentry such as Mary Randolph, author of *The Virginia Housewife: or Methodical Cook* (1824) and the posthumous text *Chafing Dish Possibilities* (1898), a long-legged portable chafing dish afforded more variety in cuisine than could be achieved by open-hearth cooking. The hotel kitchen of the Waldorf-Astoria popularized chafing dish dinners by serving them to actress Lillian Russell and financier J. P. Morgan. In 1898, one spokeswoman for the average housewife, Sarah Tyson Rorer, founder of the Philadelphia Cooking School, extolled the chafing dish as a godsend on laundry day.

At the Boston Cooking School the chafing dish served lecturers and demonstrators as the presenter's tool. Students sported lapel pins featuring the chafing dish, the institution's esthetically appealing emblem. At its competitor, Miss Farmer's School of Cookery, the chafing dish was a focus of classes for the home cook. Professional food writers compiled guidebooks introducing tidy, refined tabletop cookery, for example, Sarah Tyson Rorer's *How to Use a Chafing Dish* (1894), Fannie Farmer's *Chafing Dish Possibilities* (1898), and *Salads, Sandwiches and Chafing Dish Dainties* (1899) by Janet McKenzie Hill, editor of the *Boston Cooking School Magazine.* Such advocacy prompted an editor of *American Kitchen Magazine* to call the chafing dish "a missionary in disguise which would induce many young women to a more thorough study of combinations of food." (Shapiro 1986, 103)

The three-part dish gained popularity for cooking sauces and shellfish at table or for flambéing exotic desserts such as bananas Foster, Crêpes Suzette, and cherries Jubilee, an innovation claimed by Henri Charpentier, head cook for the Rockefellers. As stated in *American Kitchen Magazine,* proponents Kate Douglas Wiggin, a respected educator, and author Mary E. Wilkins Freeman delighted in the tabletop cookery of chopped and premeasured ingredients, which they stirred together with eggs, sauces, and other binders at the table. They extolled the ease of cooking and freedom from exertions over a hot stove. The stylish implement encouraged men to take up tabletop cooking, including Frank Schloesser, author of *The Cult of the Chafing Dish* (1905).

Chafing dish cookery enjoyed a resurgence in the home-centered 1930s and in the domesticated 1950s and 1960s, when cooks balanced glamour with intimacy for informal entertaining. To avoid hours in the kitchen, wives cooked jiffy Sunday night suppers in the waffle iron, toaster, percolator, and chafing dish. A necessary adjunct to chafing-dish cooking was the tea cart, which functioned as an extension of the kitchen counter for tableside preparation of such comfort foods as grilled cheese sandwiches, Welsh rarebit, and creamed beef on toast as well as the more elegant chicken à la king, lobster Newburg, beef stroganoff, crêpes Suzette, and sukiyaki. Touted as a conversation enhancer, the chafing dish received approval from an article in the February 1953 issue of *Better Homes and Gardens,* which cooed, "If you wish, you can cook before guests with all the fanfare of a magician." (Lovegren 1995, 206)

The chafing dish preceded the fondue pot, a tabletop heating vessel popular in the 1960s and 1970s and revived for relaxed dunk-and-dine cookery in the late 1990s. The smorgasbord buffet called for the warming dish to keep small nibbles impaled on toothpicks at a suitable temperature. In James Beard's *The Cook's Catalogue* (1975), the text praised a chafing dish with ornate scrollery, wooden handle, brass legs, and tin lining and heated by Sterno, a methanol and diethylene-glycol jell. Commentary described the low-heat cooker as a party or buffet centerpiece, a holding dish for hot appetizers, and a useful family server at Sunday suppers as well as a tasteful wedding or hostess gift. In 2000, the addition of a flame-retardant skirt around the dish protected cooks from flare-ups and reduced heat loss.

See also **Braziers**

Further Reading

Hess, Karen, intro. *Martha Washington's Booke of Cookery.* New York: Columbia University Press, 1981.
Lovegren, Sylvia. *Fashionable Food: Seven Decades of Food Fads.* New York: Macmillan, 1995.

CHANG CH'IEN

Chang Ch'ien (also spelled Zhang Qian), sometimes called "China's Marco Polo," was the first explorer to report on central Asia and eastern Europe to the Chinese court. He brought back new plants that enriched the Chinese culinary tradition. According to the *Shiji* (Chronicles, 91 BCE) of the court historian Sima Qian, in 138 BCE during the Han dynasty, Wu Ti, the notorious martial emperor, dispatched Chang Ch'ien, an officer of the palace bodyguard, some 2,000 miles west on a diplomatic mission. With a following of 100 retainers and his slave Kan-fu, he sought out the Yüeh-chih tribe, from whom he hoped to receive military concessions and acquire the Ferghana horse, a breed of cavalry mount from Turkistan noted for strength and stamina. The Hsiung-nu, or Huns, barbaric horse raiders to the west of China, captured Chang Ch'ien and held him under house arrest for a decade. After marrying and siring a son, he gained his freedom and, following a three-year journey, returned to Wu Ti, who refused to give up on the expedition to unknown parts of Asia.

Almost immediately, the emperor promoted Chang Ch'ien to the post of head imperial counselor, but he lost prestige during a disastrous war against the Hsiung-nu. He accepted a second mission, this time among the Indo-European-speaking Wu-sun of the

Tarim Basin in Russia. Accompanied by 300 horse soldiers, he set out with silk, precious metals, and other enticements. He delegated visits to Uzbekistan, Afghanistan, and Turkestan to an aide. On his own, he assembled a dossier on Parthia, Bactria, and India and returned to Wu Ti with news of a diplomatic link with Greece. Because of his persistence, China gained ambassadorial status with central Asia.

From this victorious foray into the West, Wu Ti acquired the horses he wanted. Among the amenities that Chang Ch'ien's explorations brought the average citizen were a host of new foods, including grapes and pomegranates, walnuts, sesame and caraway, cucumber, coriander, peas, and onions. As a result of his travels, the variety of plants grown in kitchen gardens increased and the Chinese entered a new culinary era of refined food flavors, aromas, and textures.

Further Reading

Hood, John, "Chang Ch'ien's Far-Ranging Diplomacy Laid the Groundwork for Han Conquest—and the Link Between East and West," *Military History*, April 1996.

CHARCOAL

Before the mining of coal, cooks depended on charcoal for fuel. It also served as a fertilizer, polishing abrasive, and medicine. A dig at a 4,000-year-old Russian *kurgan* (mound) produced remnants of a red wagon that held three clay braziers filled with charcoal, a burial offering that accompanied ceramic kitchen offerings of mutton and milk to a couple's grave. Around the Mediterranean, olive oil millers recycled olive pits into a low-smoke charcoal to supply kitchen braziers. Thrifty Sicilian bakers shoveled embers from their ovens into metal canisters to save for charcoal and recycled the ashy residue for polishing copper pots.

The making of charcoal in the British Isles involved stacking cords of wood cobhouse or log cabin style into a conical rick either on the ground or in a pit. After heaping the rick with dirt, sod, or clay, the charcoal maker dug a small side entrance and started a slow fire that smoldered as the wood carbonized. After seventy-two hours of careful tending and stoking, the heat sufficiently charred the wood. The burner cooled the briquettes and loaded them into sacks for delivery to homes or market stalls. Archaeological excavations at Hay Tor, a British settlement dating to 3000 BCE, produced barrowfuls of charcoal, the fuel for open-hearth cooking.

In medieval Tunisia and Muslim Spain, cooks who used communal ovens relied on simple heating measures at home. They burned charcoal and dried manure in chafing dishes and on low hearths. Street *tabbakhun* (cookshop owners) turned rotisseries within walls lined vertically with hardwood charcoal, the same method applied today via the vertical electric rotisserie.

After the denuding of England's vast oak forests for ship-building, the demand for charcoal increased. It was needed for heating homes and for filling charcoal irons used to smooth linens. A brazier atop andirons held charcoal for warming or cooking individual dishes. In 1595, the quality of sea coal, mined from pits in northern England, raised concerns in the Privy Council for the comfort of the urban poor, who could not afford to supplement expensive heating fuel with oak logs. Commentary on household health hazards condemned charcoal as a dangerous substance because of the fumes that it emitted.

In the New World, to make the most of burnables, colonial Americans made sturdy splint sieves to separate crumbled sticks from incombustible substances. The heavy pieces became charcoal fuel. Fine charcoal grit was used to polish tools and implements and to line the inside of knife boxes for whetting knives, awls, gimlets, skewers, bodkins, and choppers. Lydia Maria Child's *The American Frugal Housewife* (1836) suggested blending pulverized charcoal with honey for a handy abrasive toothpaste.

In the mid-nineteenth century, charcoal was available in Philadelphia at 35 cents per barrel. Street vendors cried, "Charcoal by the bushel, Charcoal by the peck, Charcoal by the frying pan, Or any way you lek!" (McCutcheon 1993, 136) For good reason, homemakers listened closely for the cry, horn, or bell that announced the hawker and his cart. He spared them the dusty, grimy job of lugging home a burlap sack of briquettes. In Russia, cooks carried on a centuries-old kitchen business making *sbitien,* a hot spiced honey drink, in copper samovars stoked with charcoal.

Compared with log fires, charcoal had the advantage of controlled heating, particularly in summer kitchens. Catharine E. Beecher and Harriet Beecher Stowe, authors of *The American Woman's Home, or Principles of Domestic Science* (1869), advocated the use of the portable iron or clay charcoal burner for hot weather tasks such as washing and ironing, stewing, or making preserves. The Beecher sisters were concerned with household health issues, including the importance of adequate ventilation. Writing of charcoal burners, they warned, "If used in the house, a strong draught must be made, to prevent the deleterious effects of the charcoal."

French cooks roasted spitted joints on a *coquille,* a boxed metal charcoal hearth with a scalloped front. The user fitted it with a grate to direct heat from the coals to a limited cooking space. Later *coquilles* of porcelain and tempered glass held foods that had already been cooked in a conventional oven. Culinary historian Marian F. McNeill's *The Scots Kitchen* (1929) compared the gentle heat of the French charcoal stove with the Scottish peat embers, which gently boiled broth, baked potatoes, and toasted oatcakes on the *greadeal* (griddle).

In the 1900s, during a period of great fascination with the Middle East, French homemakers often set aside a room or porch for a *salon turc* (Turkish room). Romanticized draperies, arabesques, and scrollery covered walls, floors, and ceilings. Reclining on pillowed divans, guests smoked water pipes, passed trays of Arabic sweetmeats, and sipped exotic coffees that the hostess heated over charcoal braziers. The containers doubled as room heaters in a land far chillier than most of the Middle East.

In Sicily charcoal delivery by mule was an essential for small fry shops. Douglas Sladen admired the tiled stoves in *Sicily, the New Winter Resort* (1910), a travelogue given to romanticizing burners "dotted like a cribbage board with little holes to contain charcoal embers." (Simeti 1989, 268) By the mid-twentieth century, the cheery cry of the charcoal seller—*Minni vaiu, minni staju ennu, min'ivi* (I'm going, I've gone, I went!)—was heard no more, as charcoal gave way to cleaner, less cumbersome, and more practical bottled gas.

In Japan, to make fuel from mountain hardwood, families built a kiln for slow burning, then winnowed out the ash with a scoop-shaped charcoal sieve woven from bamboo. The finished charcoal, baled in rice-straw matting, went into home storage or was traded to dyers and blacksmiths. Farm wives dried shiitake mushrooms on a tray atop a bamboo stand over a charcoal stove, the central furnishing in earth-floored kitchens or lean-tos attached to the end of the house. During the privations of the post-World War II era, people who had abandoned charcoal for oil returned to the primitive burners of their ancestors.

In China charcoal was still being used to heat homes and food in the late twentieth century. During the 1970s, journalists for *National Geographic* visiting Fanch'eng on the Han River found that poverty segregated some families into a rigid division of labor. In tile-roofed brick homes, grandparents who cared for small children while the parents worked the fields warmed *k'angs* (beds) with charcoal heaters encased in concrete. Small kitchen or living room stoves heated broth for dumplings and water for tea over a charcoal blaze.

In Africa, Indonesia, and Central America, as Peace Corps workers engineered various masonry stoves to suit village projects of the 1970s and 1980s, they had to adapt to areas where charcoal was the dominant fuel. To assist families in making the most of fuel, designers created one-pot cookers over sunken grates that brought the pot bottom as close as possible to the embers. To maximize heat conduction, they surrounded grates with metal collars to prevent wind from robbing the stove of heat. To improve oxygen intake, they opened the bottom of the stove to ventilate tightly packed briquettes.

One variant, the *feu malgache,* or malagasy stove of West Africa, required riveting or welding sheet steel or recycled material into single-pot braziers. The design, shaped like a spool, shielded charcoal from the wind while directing the fuel down the slanted walls to the grate in an automatic stoking process. Strong and sturdy, the stoves were affordable and took up little space in small dwellings. On the negative side, they lacked pot supports and thus posed a danger to cooks, especially children. They were also too unstable for foods that required vigorous stirring. Peace Corps volunteers experimented with burying the stove in sand to stabilize it and reduce heat loss. They also insulated the firebox with clay. The addition of a windshield reduced heat loss but encumbered the cook with a heated surface that could cause serious burns.

In Indonesia, similar charcoal stoves made from terra cotta and fitted with recessed metal grates could be fitted to most room shapes. Although less durable than metal and too heavy for easy portability, clay was superior in heat retention. It also saved on fuel, could be crafted from cheap local materials, and provided more safety to the cook from burns and tipping. An improved version, made at the Ceramics Institute of Bandung, Indonesia, had thicker walls and included clay grates and iron dampers for flame control.

Another shape, the Thai charcoal bucket stove, was a two-stage heater composed of a terra cotta vessel in a metal shell. By packing the air space between with ash and sealing with cement, the builder increased durability and heat retention. The bucket stove burned less fuel than stand-alone metal or terra cotta models and retained more heat. Although tough and shielded from the wind, it posed greater problems for its weight, cost, and inflexibility for use with varying sizes of cookpots.

Today, charcoal cooking produces a small controlled flame necessary for outdoor one-pot cooking. In rural St. Lucia, families rely on stewed goat, sheep, conch, pork, and vegetables for a single-dish meal. Chadians use a single kettle over a fire pit or cook on a *ganoon* (charcoal basket). In Kenya, workers in cook stalls skewer goat meat and roast it along with cassava and corn over *jikos* (charcoal burners). For Filipinos, a family celebration calls for a charcoal fire to roast *lechon* (stuffed pig). In Calcutta, the many charcoal grills in operation barbecuing kebabs during the winter months produce thick pollutants that block the sun. In Russia, an internal sleeve of charcoal fuels the samovar, from which tea drinkers fill their glasses with hot water to dilute a strong brew.

Charcoal cookery enabled Japanese cooks to develop *sukiyaki*, a favorite dish of fried vegetable, oyster, mussel, and beef slices that compares to the French fondue and the Mongolian hot pot. The hosts seats diners at a circular table centered with a charcoal brazier. Individuals watch as the sliced vegetables and meat sizzle and then serve themselves, selecting cooked morsels to dip into bowls of raw egg.

In developed countries, charcoal cooking is popular for relaxed outdoor meals. Catalogs offer many varieties of charcoal grills for patio, porch, campsite, boat, beach, camper, and balcony cooking.

See also **Chafing Dish; Mongolian Hot Pot**

Further Reading

Clark, Arthur, "The Orient of Pierre Loti," *Aramco World*, July–August 1992, 2–7.

Cort, Louise Allison, and Nakamura Kenji. *A Basketmaker in Rural Japan*. New York: Weatherill, 1994.

Limberis, Natalya Y., and Ivan I. Marchenko, "Caucasus Kurgan Cache," *Archaeology*, September/October 2000, 12–13.

Openshaw, Keith. *A Comparison of Metal and Clay Charcoal Cooking Stoves*. Morogoro, Tanzania: University of Dar es Salaam, n.d.

CHEESE

Perhaps because of its portability and long shelf life, cheese has been a popular food from antiquity to the present among all socioeconomic classes and for all occasions. Anthropologists surmise that as early as 6000 BCE, herders in Iraq's Fertile Crescent unintentionally created cheese from the milk of wild and domesticated goats, sheep, and cows. Egyptian tomb murals from 2000 BCE illustrate the skills required to make cheese and store it in skin bags. According to the chef and Assyriologist Jean Bottéro, who deciphered twenty-four clay tablets written in cuneiform script, Mesopotamian cooks knew enough about cream cheese to record the elements of lactic fermentation.

Food of the Ancients

The ancient Greeks injected cheese with powdered thyme to make *fromage persillé* and served it with vinegar and thyme. Both Homer and Aristotle mention the milking of sheep and goats and refer to cheese and cheese-makers; the early comedy writer Pherecrates remarks on the sizzle of melted cheese, a treat still made in Greece in the two-handled *saganaki* as an accompaniment to a glass of ouzo. Aristotle names the source of hot cheese as mare's and ass's milk.

Die Landleüt Heluetiæ habēd dreyerley gewerb/etlich den Acker-bauw/ vnd das ist der gröste teil: die anderen bauwend den weyn: die dritten / deren auch gar vil ist/ vmb alle gebirg erneerend sich allein des vychs/des sy so vil habend / das nit die weyber allein / sonder starcke menner vnd knecht die küy melckend/käß vñ ziger machend. Die werdend genennt Sennen / jre wonungen vnd werckstatt Señhütten/ɀc. Herum̄ der merteil käß vñ schmalɀ ɀåbereitet werdēd/dar-ɀů kein frauwen hand kumpt/ɀc.

Making Cheese. Engraving from the *Schweizer Chronik* by J. Stumpf (1548).

In ancient Rome large farms had a *caseale*, a separate house for aging and storing cheese rounds. Cheese nourished Roman athletes and legionaries and accompanied troops on expeditions to the outer reaches of the empire. When men mustered out of the service, they settled on distant *coloniae* (farmsteads), where they established Roman-style dairies. During their occupation of Britannia, the Romans observed that the Celts shaped perforated clay bowls to drain curds. Celtic artifacts at Mont Beuvray, France, included a huge draining rack erected to begin the cheese-aging process.

Roman dairying supplied goods into the late empire, when the exporting of cheese carried local types around the Mediterranean. Cheese-makers tended to soak cheese in brine or vinegar, then roll it in an herbal blend, which hardened and flavored the crust. The Roman encyclopedist Pliny the Elder, author of *Natural History* (77 BCE), mentions Gallic roquefort, the cave-cured, blue-veined specialty made from sheep milk and moldy bread crumbs. The gourmet Columella explained the curd-making process; the poet Varro summarized the digestability of regional cheeses. Athenaeus, writing around 200 CE, admired Sicily's "tender" cheese, a possible reference to ricotta, which was made by boiling whey with whole sheep's milk and straining the curds through a basket. As described in Platina's *De Honesta Voluptate et Valitudine* (On Right Pleasure and Health, 1475), the method remained unchanged from the Italian Renaissance and appeared in Elio Vittorini's *Le Città del Mondo* (The City of the World, 1955).

European Traditions

Early in the Middle Ages, local herders throughout Europe flourished. When Italians drained the Po valley in the late 1200s, they kept larger herds and inundated kitchen vessels with excess milk, which they made into cheese. Their process called for forming a curd with rennet in a cauldron, then using wood paddles to scoop the mass into cheesecloth to drain. Molded in wood frames, the parmigiano-reggiano rounds began drying and aging in dairy rooms. To the north, the Helvetians of the Swiss Alps developed a regional cheese making process and succeeded with emmental, their most formidable undertaking. French cheesemakers of Provence and the Atlantic coast flourished in the soft cheese trade. In contrast to the mighty eighty-pound wheels of Italian parmesan, Dutch cheese makers mastered gouda and edam, the familiar small, hard rounds brined and waxed to preserve them for distribution to a broad market.

In 1299 the Venetian explorer Marco Polo intrigued the reading public with *The Travels of Marco Polo*, an account of his long overland trek to the East. He reported that the Mongols made a skim-milk cheese from the whey left in the butter churn. After removing the butter, dairy workers placed the watery remains in the sun to curdle. They then boiled it into a mass and pressed it into solid shapes.

The forerunner of mozzarella, buffalo milk cheese first appeared in a recipe in 1520 compiled by a papal cook, Bartolomeo Scappi, author of *Opera dell' Arte dell Cucinare* (Compendium on the Art of Cookery, 1570). According to tradition, Longobards had brought the Italian buffalo to Italy in 586 CE. Alternate versions claim that the animal was native to Italy or that Normans or Arabs imported it. Whatever its origins, buffalo milk made a distinctive cheese. In the 1600s, Italian dairy workers evolved a more complex technology calling for a *bufalare,* a circular trough heated in the middle. From this, the *mastro casiero* (master cheesemaker) transformed milk into butter, ricotta, and provola.

North of Hadrian's Wall in Scotland, the Pict and Scots clans that the Romans had failed to subdue received little of the dairy technology that flourished along the Mediterranean shores. But as the Scottish monarchy gained stability under David I and Good Queen Maud in the eleventh and twelfth centuries, it required a royal cheese. Made from whole milk, it was a richer version of the skimmed-milk cheese eaten and marketed by farm families. Scottish cheese took on a military significance when Robert the Bruce distributed cheese rations to the troops at the battle of Bannockburn on June 23, 1314, where the Scots defeated English insurgents.

Mention of cheese in medieval township records establishes its importance to farm families and marketers. Before making cheese, the English dairy worker had to complete a messy chore—securing a stock of rennet, or runnet. A medieval recipe recommended collecting the milk bag from a slaughtered calf, leaving it under stinging nettles for half a day, then washing it in milk, beaten egg, cloves, and mace. The final preparation of rennet required soaking it in a pot of salt water with blackthorn, burnet, and marjoram. The collected stomach juice was lactic acid, called cheeselip (rennet). Other dairy traditions allowed for rennet collection from pig stomachs; the Spanish used *gallion,* lactic acid extracted from the skin of a cock's gizzard. (Hartley 1979, 106) Tavern cooks preferred firm, sturdy Anglo-Saxon cheese, which kept well for a long period. Makers of softer curd cheese tied the mass in a linen bag and steeped it in saltwater as a preservative and mold deterrent. In Moravia the fermentation of *Olmützer Quargel* (sour cheese) began with the souring of skim milk with a bread crust to hasten the process. After a turn in the press to remove whey, the cheese was kneaded and formed into pellets to be flattened and sun-dried into hard disks for grating.

The serving of cheese at the end of the meal accorded with the medieval medical advice of Salerno's doctors, who considered the weight of slow-digesting cheese appropriate for clearing the stomach. In the poem *Regimen Sanitatis Salernitanum* (Salernian Health Regimen, ca. 1100s), the personified cheese speaks for itself and boasts that it aids weak stomachs and rounds out a meal. According to Platina, a conservative bite of cheese sealed the stomach, reduced the unpleasant fullness caused by fatty dishes, and aided both brain and digestion.

Le Ménagier de Paris (The Goodman of Paris, ca. 1394), an unsigned text that may have been written by Guy de Montigny, servant of the Duke of Berry, advised housewives to purchase warm-colored, dry, solid pieces of cheese that were heavy, resistent to pressure, and scaly of skin. Henry de Bracton's *De Legibus et Consuetudinibus Angliae* (On English Law and Customs, ca. 1258) advised purchasers to demand a cheese naturally rich in color and not one merely soaked in broth to improve a wan hue. Further details on Italian cheese making standards were recorded in Pantaleone da Confienza's *Summa Lacticiniorum* (Treatise on Dairy Foods), published in Turin in 1477, the first dissertation on the subject.

In the Renaissance, European cheese making became an artisanal process. Specialists followed regional methods to produce distinctive texture, flavor, and aroma. English cheese makers used the name of their towns to identify their unique contributions, as exemplified by the Stilton, Cheddar, and Cheshire varieties. Of the ideal environment for producing flavorful cheese, Dorothy Hartley's *The Land of England* (1979) disdained Essex and praised Wensleydale, where "the alder growing by the stream—often breaking into bud while melted snow still netted the fields—gave the special flavour to Wensleydale cheese, which could only be made to perfection in the early spring." (p. 108) In England, one workaday recipe got to the core of cheese's popularity. For a quick Welsh rarebit, the cook poured cheese over buttered toast and clapped a hot fire shovel over it.

Irish cheese making required stimulating milk with rennet and slicing the *giuncán* (coagulated junket) with curd knives for scalding. After draining and ripening, the cheese maker ground the mass into granules for salting and serving. Such curd cheese was the rule until the introduction of hard molded cheese in the 1800s, when the Irish first mistook the solid rounds for tallow cakes.

Scandinavian and Dutch cheese also displayed regional uniqueness. Olaus Magnus, a Catholic priest who compiled the *Historia de Gentibus Septentrionalibus* (History of the Northern Peoples, 1555), summarized the skill of Swedish and Finnish cheese-makers. Finns on the Åland Islands enhanced goat cheese by smoking it with fumes from Labrador tea (*Ledum palustre*), an evergreen popular in Russia and Scandinavia as a lung and respiratory tonic and skin purifier. The smoke also lengthened the shelf life of the cheese. For Dutch cheese, cooks treated crumbled cottage cheese with salt, sage leaves or juice, and butter.

In west central Europe, cheese technology evolved into specific procedures for a variety of products easily identified by taste, texture, and aroma. Traditional French cheese making developed into an art, requiring the draining of rounds on a *clisse* (wicker mat) and careful *affinage* (ripening) in a climate-controlled cellar. The Gruyère maker recycled *aisy* (whey), a sour

liquid that was poured off scalded milk, stored in barrels, and shaped into *serai,* an inferior cheese. In 1761 Norman cheese maker Marie Harel of Camembert village created the soft camembert. Napoleon III chose the name, a moment in kitchen history honored with a statue and huge plaque. However, the cheese did not achieve its fame until 1880, when packers placed it in chipboard cheese boxes. Farther south, the Swiss specialized in gruyère and emmenthal, a labor-intensive scalded-curd variety. Italians developed parmesan, caciocavallo, and gorgonzola. An Italian, Egidio Galbani of Melzo, improvised the semi-soft *bel paese* in 1906, naming it from the title of a book by Abbot Antonio Stoppani.

Early in the twentieth century, an Irish teacher, Maude Parkinson, recorded the cheese-making style in Bucharest. She observed the Romanian herder's skill at fooling ewes with a trap door, where he caught them by the hind leg as they attempted to flee captivity. From their milk, averaging a half-glass per udder, cheese makers formed *kashkaval,* a Balkan yellow cheese similar to Italian *pecorino,* and packed it into an oblong bark container, which lent the mass a woodsy, resinous taste. Cooks in Greece, Cyprus, and the Middle East valued its texture, which stood up to grating, toasting, and frying. In Czechoslovakia in the 1970s, suspending cheese rounds in nets over wood fire added a smoky pungency that suited peasant fare.

American Variations

Cooks in the American colonies, who made cheese in the hot summer months instead of churning butter, preferred hard wheel varieties. The cheese-making process involved collecting both fresh and day-old milk from cows, goats, and sheep for heating, forming curds with cheeselip, and processing. After the final skimming and draining through muslin cheesecloth, the solids had to be washed and turned before being packed into brine, salted, flavored with herbs, and colored with vegetables dyes, such as spinach juice, powdered sage, carrot scrapings, or boiled pigweed.

Other North American cheese makers broke up the mass with a cheese knife, rectangular curd knife, steel curd whipper, spatula, or a curd breaker, a box grinder with rotating pegs that separated the curds. The worker then placed the mass in a perforated metal or wooden mold, colander, or muslin bag and drained it before spreading it into a hoop or spring-form, a round collar that fastened with a spring clip. In the final stage, the cheese maker reshaped the pieces over several hours or days in a hoop or cylinder under a weight or screw press to force whey from solids. Before the final stage, the cheese maker had soaked the solids in warm water, then scooped them into cheese drainers, slatted baskets or boxes drilled with holes, which encouraged thorough drying. The thrifty farm wife reserved drainings as moisture for pig feed.

After the washing, drying, and cutting of the cheese into chunks, the surface required a rub of salt, herbs, oil, or paraffin to prevent mold, soft spots, and off flavors. The worker packed the cheese into earthenware jars or cheese bags. Among the implements connected with serving cheese were a semicircular cheese trier for sampling the water content and consistency, a pointed cheese scoop for dipping solids from a vat, and a wire-bladed cheese cutter for making thin slices for sandwiches, platters of cold cuts, and garnishes.

In colonial Portsmouth, New Hampshire, in November 1675, Mary Hunt took to court a cheese thief named Samuel Clark. As evidence, she raided his home and retrieved a leftover chunk that contained the mark she used to identify her best work. She won the case, but lost in June on the appeal, in which Clark accused her of selling cheeses without her husband's knowledge, then claiming that they were stolen.

Cheese figured in several episodes in American history, beginning with a 1,450-pound cheese presented by the women of Cheshire, Massachusetts, to President Thomas Jefferson. A second gift the size of a carriage wheel from the same county, given to President Andrew Jackson in 1837, caused a near riot. At Jackson's invitation, some 10,000 citizens came to a reception on February 22, George Washington's birthday, to share the huge cheese. The mob succeeded in grinding smelly cheese into carpets, damask walls, furnishings, and silk draperies.

Benjamin Harrison exploited the public's image of him as a rustic by wooing potential supporters with food. His campaign staff erected log cabins and invited men to a hearth-side meal of cheese and cornbread served with hard cider. The feasting reached such proportions that cooks at an elaborate spread hosted in Wheeling, West Virginia, prepared a half ton of cheese, four tons of bread, 4,500 pies, three-quarter tons of beef, 360 hams, 25 sheep, and 20 calves. For the swearing-in in 1841, William Parker sent a modest gift, a 194-pound cheese, the product of 32 milk cows in Beavertown, Pennsylvania.

The Amana communes processed hard and soft cheese, cottage cheese, cheese spread, and butter with limited equipment. The *Süsskäse* (sweet cheese) required heating in five-gallon lots, adding rennet, stirring curds, and pouring off whey through a cheesecloth-lined chesset, or wooden press. After a day's pressing, the surface of the block or circle was salted. The finished cheese was wrapped in clean cloth for storage in a basement pantry covered by a screened wood door. Ripening took up to six weeks. For *Handkäse,* a strong-smelling semisoft cheese with a hard rind, the commune's dairy workers began with soured milk. They curdled eight to ten gallons in a batch, mixed curds with salt in a dishpan, then kneaded them like dough. The workers shaped peach-sized cheeses, which they pressed with board or butter paddle into round loaves. After a week's air-drying, they nestled the batch in a crock, covered it, and stored it in the basement. Cheese tending required that the ripening mass be scraped of mold and scrubbed with bristle brushes. After weeks of tending, cheeses were wrapped in cabbage leaves and returned to the crocks.

Schmierkäse (cheese spread), also called smear cheese or *Kochkäse* (cooked cheese), was an Amana specialty. Flavored with caraway, it preserved a Hessian tradition begun during the sect's era of religious persecution. Cheese makers separated curds with their hands and ripened the mass in stoneware bowls. After the curds aged, dairy workers stirred and cooked them in a buttered iron kettle. The addition of caraway and salt produced a tasty spread, which they poured into crockery bowls.

In the Modern Kitchen

In the 1930s, women's magazines featured Velveeta, Kraft's "cheese food" sold in a handy "golden brick" box suited for slicing into sandwich squares for meals and canapés. The ad copy explained that Velveeta was a scientific breakthrough from Rutgers University College of Pharmacy, formulated to be sliced, blended, melted, or toasted according to the homemaker's needs. Promoted as calcium- and phosphorus-rich and laden with milk sugars, the cheddar product melted sufficiently at room temperature to slice like butter. Like other products of its time, Velveeta came with a free recipe book, "Cheese and Ways to Serve It." By the late 1940s, ads in *Woman's Home Companion* pictured two more Kraft blocks—Philadelphia cream cheese and Old English cheese spread—along with Smo-kay, Limburger, Pineapple, Roka, and Relish cheese spread. Colorful photos illustrated ways to entertain using cheese products.

In the twenty-first century, fondue returned to popularity as a festive method of serving cheese. Melted in an open fondue pot, cheese laced with wine reached a suitable temperature for dipping tidbits held on the tines of long fondue forks. Hosts served cheese fondue with cubed breads, *crudités*, and meatballs.

Late in 2000 aficionados of raw-milk cheese— Spanish manchego, Sardinian and Tuscan pecorino, parmigiano-reggiano, gouda, cheddar, gruyère, and roquefort—anticipated the end of a revered food industry. Passage of a law specifying a sixty-day aging period to kill salmonella, listeria, and *E. coli* stymied sales of many cheeses, both domestic and imported. The American Cheese Society feared that the Food and Drug Administration would pass a regulation requiring that all commercial cheese be made from pathogen-free pasteurized milk. In a bid to forestall any legislation that would hamper artisanal cheese makers, a defiant Cheese of Choice Coalition published scientific data on the health benefits and superior flavor of products made from unpasteurized milk.

See also **Dairying; Molds; Presses**

Further Reading

Kummer, Corby, "Craftsman Cheese," *Atlantic Monthly*, December 2000, 109–112.

Lysaght, Patricia, ed. *Milk and Milk Products from Medieval to Modern Times.* Edinburgh: Canongate Press, 1994.

Pennington, Campbell W. *The Tepehuan of Chihuahua: Their Material Culture.* Salt Lake City: University of Utah Press, 1969.

Platina. *On Right Pleasure and Good Health.* Asheville, N. C.: Pegasus Press, 1999.

Smith, John H. *Cheesemaking in Scotland: A History.* Glasgow: Scottish Dairy Assoc., 1995.

CHESTS

The earliest food chests, shaped from hollow logs, served to protect valuable kitchen stores from theft. In ancient Egypt, Greece, and Rome, the wicker or box chest was the standard home storage unit for barley and husked wheat along with olives, garum (fish sauce), and amphorae holding oil, wine, and preserved fruit. The Egyptian chests were lashed with cording and secured with the owner's seal. Other types of chests held household goods such as table linens and towels as well as domestic heirlooms. Some Egyptian chests were woven wicker; others were ingenious coffers, tomb storage, and caskets that also served as kitchen seats and divans.

Roman travelers depended on the *arca* (chest) to keep pantry goods and belongings safe while in transit around the empire. On board ship, where meals were the traveler's responsibility, the chest kept foodstuffs safe from pilferers, dampness, and vermin. Officers' chests attached to poles for carrying over rough terrain. Slaves bore them to new billets, sometimes lagging miles behind the vanguard in the supply train, which caught up with their owners days or weeks later. Byzantine models moved beyond the demands of function and utility to a sumptuous display of crests, veneer, and ivory paneling.

In the late Middle Ages, chests served so many important functions that they were found not only in grand manors but also in lesser homes. Wooden chests of drawers, bible boxes, escritoires, and humble corner cupboards augmented kitchen storage space. Chests with padded tops provided additional seating or even beds. Some house-proud homemakers displayed a chest in every room as a sign of affluence.

In the 1700s housekeepers lined chests with paper to protect precious contents. Whether domed or raised on legs to protect goods from damp floors, the chest sat against a wall or other piece of furniture, sometimes supplying an additional table top for steadying a beverage tray. Finer models received a veneer of fine leather or hammered gold or sported brass studding. Owners lifted the chests by means of iron, leather, or rope handles attached at the sides.

When the fur trader Alexander Mackenzie toured the Pacific Coast in 1789 and 1793 he found native tribes living in plank houses. Along boards that stretched the length of their residences, he identified storage chests containing provisions, utensils, and other personal items. In spaces between the chests, cooks prepared food, such as the roasted fish they hung from beams.

In European homes, the kitchen chest secured foodstuffs from pilferage and kept out rodents. The mule chest, which developed into a double chest featuring multiple cubicles, added drawers at the bottom of a deep storage container. The wood strongbox, fitted with an ornate lock or hasp and padlock, served as the family treasury and store for armor and valuable weapons. For guarding table linens, householders preferred cedar or cypress chests, which they rubbed with potpourri and vermin repellents. The bride's chest in Asia and Europe held household and kitchen items—napkin rings, tablecloths and runners, candlesticks, spice boxes—and saved them for marriage.

See also **Cabinets and Cupboards**

CHICKEE

The Seminole and other native Americans of the subtropics traditionally performed domestic chores in an airy pavilion known as a chickee or chiki. During the first human settlement of South Florida, the Calusa founded communities on the Gulf Coast's barrier islands of Pine, Marco, Sanibel, and Captiva and moved inland to a trading center at Mayaimi on Lake Okeechobee. In 1513, when Ponce de Leon encountered the Calusa, he admired their skill at shaping cypress trunks into dugout canoes and building their open-sided chickees, stilt houses raised above tide, flood, and swamp. The constant breeze through living

A Chickee of the Seminole tribe.
[*Original illustration by Dan Timmons.*]

quarters kept them free of gnats and mosquitoes. Blowing underneath as well, circulating air refreshed and cooled the simple structures. The Calusa died out from European diseases and mistreatment by the Spanish, but the Miccosuckee (also Miccosukee or Mikasuki), a Creek tribe, have survived. Still comfortable in their chickee homes, they acclimated to mound communities on a reservation pierced by Interstate 75 adjacent to Everglades National Park.

The chickee, their contribution to American architecture, took its strength from native raw materials—sawgrass, pine, and palmetto fronds. Semi-permanent at best, the rectangular framework huts afforded space for sleep, work, childcare, cooking, and eating. Extensions of cabbage palm thatch created an overhang that shaded women while they pounded grain in mortars. Framed in cypress wood, the roof, thatched from palmetto fronds, topped a raised platform that allowed a kitchen worker to enjoy a breeze and an unhampered view in all directions and to avoid ground-level insects, reptiles, and dampness from bayous and swamps. Furnishings consisted of hammocks, matting, and baskets. The gable and rafters overhead offered an attic for storing extra baskets and dry staples. The under-floor level accommodated poultry and domestic animals as well as watchdogs.

In the late 1960s, the Miccosuckee occupied a compound of chickees in the Everglades alongside the Tamiami Trail. Thatched huts clustered around a single cookhouse, the communal site of daily food preparation over an open fire, symbolically shaped like a star. As in ancient times, women preparing meals entertained youngsters in their care with storytelling. In 1999, the Miccosuckee and Seminole came into conflict with the white world on the issue of their right to harvest plants and trees in the Picayune Strand State Forest. Under an 1842 gentleman's agreement with federal authorities as well as the more recent Freedom of Religion Act, they retained access to natural resources, which they had previously enjoyed in the Big Cypress National Preserve. Exempted from hunting and fishing ordinances, camping fees, stay limits, and state laws governing public lands and forests, the twenty-first-century Indians continued to build chickees as they had from prehistoric times.

See also **Ramada**

Further Reading

Capron, Louis, and Otis Imboden, "Florida's Emerging Seminoles," *National Geographic,* November 1969, 716–734.

CHILD, JULIA

Much of the credit for increased sophistication of the national palate and cuisine of the United States belongs to one woman, Julia Child. Perhaps the most recognizable name in American cookery, whether on the printed page or television screen, she has earned respect for her dedication to quality food preparation from impeccably fine ingredients. A native of Pasadena, she was born on August 15, 1912, to Julia Carolyn Weston and John McWilliams, an agronomist. After graduation from Smith College, she wrote ad copy for the W.&J. Sloane furniture dealership in New York City.

A turning point in her career, work for the Office of Strategic Services (OSS) during World War II, moved Child first to Washington, D.C., and subsequently to assignments around the world. A perquisite of her job was dining in cosmopolitan restaurants. In 1943, on a mission in China, she met her future husband, cartographer and epicure Paul Cushing Child, who also worked for the OSS. While he entered the foreign service in Paris in 1949, she learned French and studied cooking at the Cordon Bleu, the supreme cooking school founded in 1895. Classes and tutoring by Belgian restaurateur Max Bugnard were the beginning of her focus on food preparation.

Child joined Le Cercle des Gourmettes, an exclusive dining society, and, in her apartment, formed L'Ecole des Trois Gourmandes (School of the Three Gourmands) along with two colleagues, food specialists Simone Beck and Louisette Bertholle. At her country house in Cambridge, Massachusetts, in the 1950s, Child prefigured the masses of bright young women who broke free of pre-World War II domesticity. In her hands, cookery was not the thrice-daily drudgery of a harried housewife but rather the dramatic art of a self-assured modern woman.

An international culinary masterwork, Child's popular *Mastering the Art of French Cooking* (1961), written in collaboration with Beck and Bertholle, preceded a long list of friendly tutorials on the chef's art and articles in *House and Garden, House Beautiful*, and the *Boston Globe*. On February 11, 1963, she made her television debut on Boston's WGBH as the "French Chef," marking the beginning of a food revolution. The long-lived program became a public broadcasting staple and earned her the George Foster Peabody award and an Emmy in 1966.

Into the 1970s, Child flourished as a touchstone of self-confidence and kitchen technique, which she demonstrated tirelessly to beginners in a down-to-earth manner guaranteed to dispel fear of failure at *haute cuisine*. Quick-witted and cheerful, she commanded her television kitchen like the captain of a ship, introducing her audience to soufflés, sculpted chocolates, fish poaching, and puff pastry, among others. At her insistence, U.S. grocers began stocking fine cake and bread flour, leeks, and shallots, all standard items in European food emporia.

Child found myriad ways of influencing the American palate. In addition to a TV sequel, *Dinner at Julia's*, columns in *McCall's* magazine, and appearances on *Good Morning, America*, Child expanded her sphere of influence with *The French Chef Cookbook* (1968), *From Julia Child's Kitchen* (1975), *Julia Child & Company* (1978), and *The Way to Cook* (1989), a compendium of homey photos and columns she had produced for average cooks in *Parade* magazine. When Rosalyn Carter became First Lady, Child suggested refinements for the White House kitchen.

In 1981 Child joined chefs James Beard, Richard Graff, Jeremiah Tower, and Alice Waters and wine connoisseur Robert Mondavi in establishing the American Institute of Wine and Food, an organization devoted to promoting the best in table experience. She summarized the philosophy of the institute: "Small helpings, no snacking, no seconds, a little bit of everything and have a good time." (Shriver 2000, 11D) Child also helped establish a food library at the University of California at Santa Barbara and supported the publication of *American Wine and Food* and *The Journal of Gastronomy*. In 1989, at age seventy-seven, she lectured at the Eighth Annual Food and Wine Classic in Aspen, Colorado.

When the health concerns of the 1990s overturned the rich kitchen fare of the previous half century, Child adapted to *nouvelle cuisine* and the organic food touted by J. I. Rodale. She mediated between vegans and other food cultists and restaurateurs by choosing the middle ground. Instead of renouncing the indulgences of French cuisine, she counseled moderation and advised people to eat the rich foods they enjoyed but in smaller portions. Into her eighties on the TV series *Julia and Jacques: Cooking at Home, with Chef Jacques Pepin,* she continued to advise and cajole, to debunk food folderol, and to encourage people to enrich their lives by mastering the complexities of world cuisine.

In December 2000, shortly after the French government awarded Child the *Legion d'Honneur,* PBS excerpted her original half-hour kitchen tutorials for *Julia Child's Kitchen Wisdom.* Late in 2001, she helped inaugurate the American Center for Wine, Food and the Arts in Napa, California, where the kitchen is named for her. Julia Child's kitchen was donated to and reconstructed at the Smithsonian Institution; the exhibit opened on August 19, 2002.

See also **Beard, James**

Further Reading

American Decades on CD-ROM. Farmington Hills, Mich.: Gale Group, 1999.
"A Holiday Bird and a Free-Range Chat with Julia," *Life*, December 1989, 95–100.

CHILDREN IN KITCHEN HISTORY

From birth, infants in cultures around the globe have occupied cradles and cribs at the fireside, where they could easily be watched and tended as their mothers performed their multiple roles as housekeepers, weavers, seamstresses, kitchen gardeners, herbalists, and cooks. As early as 3000 BCE, potters of the Indus Valley shaped vessels specially designed for the feeding of infants. With the advance of metalwork, mothers sterilized water for infant use by plunging a hot poker into a flagon or by bottling condensate from the steam that collected on kettle lids. In Ladakh in northern India, coopers fashioned barrels from staves and applied similar technology to shaping playpen-like kitchen enclosures to keep toddlers safe from fire and sharp knives. In Saxon England, the cooking of porridge and scraping of bones for children to chew introduced them to hearty fare soon after weaning and assisted with teething.

Mothers' Little Distractions

The words of many soothing songs for children attest to the fact that child care has from early times hampered women's domestic work. The Swiss tune "Now Then, Sleep My Child" tells of a mother gathering nuts from the hazelnut grove while lulling her baby with song. A lullaby from France, "Go to Sleep, Colas," pictures the mother baking a cake while putting a daughter to work rocking her *p'tit frere* (little brother) to sleep. (Commins 1967, 98) In northeastern Algeria the Mzouda lullaby "Harara Yourara!" seeks to calm a fretful infant with lighthearted teasing:

I will mix your gruel,
And grind some flies into it,
And give it to you so that you'll be satisfied! (Ibid., 149)

The Castilian song "Hush-a-bye Baby al Ron, Ron" explains to the whimpering babe that the mother is too busy churning to offer her breast for feeding. Less comforting are the Wanyakyusa and Wabunga song "O Son, Son," an expression of regret by a Tanzanian mother whose son has broken his father's calabash, and the Ceylonese song "Sleep My Baby," a lament in which a woman drops a milk pot into the river on her way to feed the child.

In the seventeenth century, the cook's baby sometimes remained safe from the hazards of hearth and door yard in a go-cart, a wheeled frame similar to a modern walker. In the Victorian era, a baby-runner offered some safety for toddlers by encircling their waists with a wooden hoop that attached to an iron pole fitted vertically, floor to ceiling, in slots. The circumscribed radius allowed play and limited freedom but kept the crawling or toddling child safely out of reach of scalding liquids, embers, or hot pans. By age six, children had had enough experience with kitchen work to stay out of danger and be of use.

In colonial Quebec, *les enfants* assisted in such projects as the treading of clay with straw or grass for a new bake oven, gathering withies for the framework, cementing the door into the frame, or sealing hairline cracks in the side with clay. When the work was complete, children danced and joined in merrymaking and games and modeled miniature ovens in which they emulated adult baking chores. In snowy weather, they made an early version of snow cream from snow and maple syrup. Children in Quebec sang kitchen-centered songs: "La Berceuse Blanche" (The White Lullaby), "Le Vol des Pâtés Chauds" (Theft of the Hot Pies), "Les Blés d'Or" (Golden Wheat), and "Le Bon Pain d'Habitant" (Good Country Bread). One favorite, "Le Pain" (The Bread), concludes with a rousing cheer: Le pain, le pain/Est du genre humain/Le Mets le plus sain/Vive le pain! (The bread, the bread/Is for humankind/A source of health/Long live bread!) (Boily & Blanchette 1979, 101) On baking days, mothers sang the old rounds as they worked, and the children were pressed into service as fire stokers, errand-runners, or messengers.

Occupying Small Hands

Canadian bakers made a family production of the weekly batch of loaves, involving young children in the yeast-making, wood gathering, and laying of a fire on the hearth floor. If time was short, adults dispatched a child with the stock jug or empty leaven pot to borrow yeast for the next baking. When bread pans migrated to other parts of the farmstead, children searched for them in barn and shed, sometimes locating them in feed bags, where the user measured oats and corn for horses and fowl. The finder was rewarded with a children's loaf, a miniature that was baked nearest the oven door and was the first to emerge.

In many cultures, women occupied with spinning and weaving kept a watchful eye on their children while performing these tasks. Among the Samo of Papua, New Guinea, mothers working together in a longhouse shared responsibilities and halted their work to breastfeed any crying infant, regardless of its parentage.

The logical method for occupying small hands was to begin in toddlerhood the lessons in kitchen gardening, cooking, and preserving. Thus, mothers' chores became lessons for small girls, whose growth years left no illusions about what would be required of them as adults. In the colonial Americas, children usually stood at mealtime, at least until after the table blessing, and left seats for their elders, whom they attended by passing dishes and refilling mugs. According to table manners dictated by publisher John Newbery's *A Pretty Little Pocket Book, Intended for the Amusement of Little Master Tommy, and Pretty Miss Polly* (1760), adults indicated when children might take a seat on backless benches called *forms*. When among adults, young people knew not to ask questions or speak until bidden. Youngsters learned to dip into the salt cellar only with a clean knife tip and to break bread into bite-sized pieces before eating. Strict rules regarding staring at other diners and leaving the table before being excused show little variation from current etiquette. For lighter moments, a rural mother valued dried kernels as children's game pieces and counters for checkers, fox and geese, and other board games. Such amusements lightened long, rainy winter days at the kitchen work table while mother attended to her tasks.

In Bozena Nemcova's village novel *Babicka* (The Grandmother, 1855), the text focuses on homely scenes in Czech kitchens, where Catholic folklore ruled. When the granny of the title baked bread laced with plums and apples, she created a party atmosphere that relieved her grandchildren's tedium. Nonetheless, she always warned them to brush crumbs into the fire—any that spilled underfoot she condemned as torments to the souls in purgatory. Her kitchen lessons included the virtues of straight slicing. In her philosophy, "If you can't be straight with bread, you can't be straight with people either." (Nemcova 1997, 1) To the child Jenik's request for a piece of crust, she remonstrated, "Haven't you heard that as bread is sliced, the feet of our Lord are cut? Leave it as it is, and learn not to play with your food." (Ibid.)

Frontier memoirs and diaries tend to glorify the civilizing touches missing from pioneers' daily life. Children had to grow up fast and take on adult responsibilities at an early age, beginning around age three with the task of gathering chips and pine cones for the cook fire. Privations of diet pushed food to the forefront of children's thoughts. In Nannie Tiffany Alderson's memoir *A Bride Goes West* (1942), she recounts both the tedium of the daily workload and the rare moments of indulgence. She recalled, "I got so tired of doing the same things every day—cooking and washing and ironing and making clothes for the children." (Alderson 1969, 174) A Christmas Eve memory centered on "the cookie horses—our inevitable horses!—which the children cut out, baked, and branded in our brands with colored icing, then hung on the tree." (Ibid., 232)

Play: Preparation for Adulthood

Varied types of nineteenth-century children's cookware, now considered valuable collectibles, allowed youngsters to emulate adult cooks. One such item, a miniature mechanical sifter, mimicked the larger model used by cooks to distribute flour over a board or into a pot for thickening soup and stew. For cleanliness, author Emma M. Hooper, writing in an 1894 issue of *Ladies' Home Journal*, offered this comment on aprons for little girls:

Tiny girls wear full, gathered skirts sewed to a waist shaped like a skeleton yoke and edged with a frill of the pretty colored embroidery now in vogue. Another style has a low, round baby waist, with a full, gathered skirt; belt for insertion and frill of embroidery around the yoke. Girls of ten years have a fitted bodice belt buttoning in the back, to which the full skirt is gathered. Sometimes the front of the waist is most elaborately trimmed in the shape of a vest of lace or the goods edged with jabots of lace. However, as aprons on children are intended solely for use it seems to be poor taste to trim them in such a fanciful manner. (Hooper 1894, 27)

The care with which Edwardian mothers styled girl-sized versions of adult aprons suggests that parents wanted to introduce future homemakers to the joy of remaining feminine while performing kitchen labors. The practice continued at girls' boarding schools, where kitchen helpers tackled dirty kitchen tasks and added aprons to the student laundry load.

Among the toys for young girls in the 1900 Sears, Roebuck catalog were nickel-plated working model ranges with skillet, stewpot, lifter, and stovepipe for 25 cents, a cookware set for 50 cents, and a tin kitchen for 25 cents. True to the gender stereotyping of the era, specifically labeled for males were tool chests and a garden wheelbarrow.

Anna W. Keichline, Pennsylvania's first female architect, had mothers and children in mind in the 1920s when she patented a labor-saving kitchen. For ease of child care around knives or a hot stove, she created a half-hexagon portable partition that transformed any wall or corner into an instant play area. Within the windowed and doored divider, she provided toy storage and a playhouse atmosphere. Following Keichline's concept, numerous female inventors created folding playpens, cribs, cradles, strollers, swings, and feeding chairs that suited the transition from one chore to another in the mother's daily routine—from kitchen to pantry, laundry room, kitchen garden, or patio.

By 1930, kitchen electrification had advanced to the point that little girls had their own toy toasters. One nickel-plated model with flip-out sides, advertised in the June 1930 issue of *House Furnishing Review*, actually toasted half slices of bread. The 1930 Sears, Roebuck catalog featured a full-page layout of upscale children's kitchenware, including an electric range complete with pots and pans, a vacuum sweeper, platters and serving dishes, coffee pot, cut-glass water server and tray, work table, aluminum baking set, cabinets, brooms and dust mops, and laundry needs, including wash tub, scrubbing board, clothes basket, clothesline, pins, ironing board, and iron.

Post–World War II innovations put working Singer sewing machines and pressed-metal and cardboard kitchen set-ups into Santa's bag. Little girls delighted in stitching cloth scraps and keeping house with sleek kitchen cabinets stocked with painted-on boxes and cans displaying the familiar labels of Betty Crocker and Campbell's Soup. More expensive models provided the young baker with moveable stove controls, stovetops painted to look like glowing cal-rod units, and cardboard replicas of bottles and jars found in grocery stores.

Introduced in 1964, the Easy-Bake Oven offered little girls an opportunity to bake like their moms. The company celebrated its thirty-fifth birthday with a "Baker of the Year" contest in 1998–99 for children eight to eleven years old. Contestants had to create a new recipe using one or more Easy-Bake mixes. Five finalists competed at a bake-off in New York City for the title plus $5,000 and a two-year supply of cake mixes.

In the twenty-first century, children continued to emulate the kitchen tasks of adults, using increasingly sophisticated "toy" kitchen equipment. One baking set for children contained an eight-cup mixing bowl, seven-inch rolling pin, easy-grip cookie cutter frame pierced with four shapes, and a set of recipe cards. Another contained all the necessities for making and icing birthday cake.

Further Reading

Abercrombie, Thomas J., "Ladakh—the Last Shangri-La," *National Geographic*, March 1978, 332–359.

Alderson, Nannie, and Helena Huntington Smith. *A Bride Goes West.* Lincoln: University of Nebraska Press, 1969.

Boily, Lise, and Jean-François Blanchette. *The Bread Ovens of Quebec.* Quebec: National Museums of Canada, 1979.

Commins, Dorothy Berliner. *Lullabies of the World.* New York: Random House, 1967.

Partridge, James, "Review: The Grandmother," *Central Europe Review*, August 9, 1999.

Shaw, R. Daniel. *From Longhouse to Village: Samo Social Change.* New York: Harcourt Brace College Publishers, 1996.

CHINAMPA

A model of early wetlands reclamation, from the fourteenth to the sixteenth centuries, the Aztec and Mexican *chinampa*—Montezuma's floating garden—was an ingenious fresh-water herb or kitchen garden. It reclaimed some forty-six square miles of land to support a dense urban population with fresh food. The idea took shape during a difficult period of taxation by the Tepámec. To grow more food, farmers began making floating gardens. The network extended with pilings and vines into 520 square miles of swampy environs of Lake Texcoco near Tenochtitlan and the Xochimilco-Chalco Basin in the Valley of Mexico plateau.

Without plows or dray animals, farmers planted long rectangular seedbeds, measuring about 150 by 15 feet each, in sod laid out on rich muck and wattle woven of rush and cattail. They mulched their plots with decaying grass and weeds and staked them out in shallow canals with small trees so the roots could penetrate to a ready water supply. Wooden posts and willow trees planted at the corners stabilized each segment. The surface was so fibrous that it could be planted and cultivated with nothing more than a dibble or digging stick.

The space between plots was wide enough for gardeners to pass through towing nursery beds with ropes or paddling a hollow-log canoe, from which they could transplant seedlings, weed, fertilize with human waste, and harvest into kitchen baskets. Irrigation involved a network of sluices, gates, and dams. Crops included maize, beans, avocados, greens, tomatoes, peppers, amaranth, tobacco, cacao, and sage as well as agave for brewing pulque (liquor). The plots also supported flocks of turkeys, ducks, and geese for sale to royalty and the upper classes, the only Aztecs who could afford them. Causeways led to the gardeners' huts in mid-system settlements. When the produce was ready for harvest, the gardener could pole the entire plot to market through lagoons and waterways.

In 1519, Hernán Cortés arrived at Tenochtitlan, where he forbade the growing of amaranth, a subsistence grain long valued by the Aztec as sacred to the war god Huitzilopochtli. To halt the practice of stirring grain into the blood of human sacrifices, he ordered the chinampas burned. Despite this disruption of a centuries-old agricultural system, the same form of hydroponic gardening was still in use outside Mexico City in the twenty-first century, where gardenias, roses, and hibiscus were still marketed by Aztec-speaking growers.

A parallel to the *chinampa,* the narrow floating gardens of the Intha in Inle, Burma, supplied food to families living in stilt huts along the mucky shoreline. Lacking natural cropland, Intha farmers made matted strips of dried reed and grass that reached 200 feet in length. Bamboo poles anchored the garden plots to the bottom. By dredging fertile lake mire onto scows, they transported enough growing medium to ready their strips for planting. Bamboo arbors overhead supported the growth of gourds, which were eaten, shaped into containers, or sold.

Some of these gardeners were agile enough to keep their beds going while towing segments of their floating turf to customers in the village. Tilling these reach-in beds from narrow pirogues, year-round, they planted tomatoes, eggplant, cabbage, cauliflower, cucumber, peas, and beans. Where sunken plots were numerous, they formed permanent masses of rich mire requiring no irrigation to keep plants healthy and productive. The most profitable kitchen beds supplied households with food and leftover crops for sale at the Inbawhkon market and throughout the Shan State. A similar system of aquaculture in Srinagar, Kashmir, provided melons, greens, eggplant, and cauliflower from floating gardens to the boat merchants at the floating market on Dal Lake.

Further Reading

Allen, Patricia, and Van Dusen, D. *Global Perspectives on Agroecology and Sustainable Agricultural Systems*. Vol. 2. Santa Cruz: University of California, 1988.

Calnek, E. E., "Settlement Pattern and Chinampa Agriculture in Tenochtitlan," *American Antiquity*, 1972, vol. 37, 104–115.

Garrett, W. E., and David Jeffery, "Burma's Leg Rowers and Floating Farms," *National Geographic*, June 1974, 826–845.

Lockman, Michael, "Living the Permaculture Dream," *Communities*, July 1, 1998, 31.

CHOCOLATE

Although chocolate would seem to have been a global dietary constant, in the sixteenth century it was a gift of the New World to the Old. Cacao originated in South America on the banks of the Amazon and Orinoco rivers and flourished among the Olmec around 1000 BCE. It played a significant role as food and symbol in the creation lore of the *Popol Vuh,* the Quichéan scripture composed in the Mayan language of the Sierra Los Cuchematanesa Mountains in north-central Guatemala and written down by historian Diego Reynos, a proselytized Indian, between 1554 and 1558.

A high-fat drink popular in the Mexican empire of Montezuma II, ruler of Central and South America, the original *chocólatl* or *cacahuatl* was a foamy, bitter beverage thought to have aphrodisiac powers. From around 100 CE, the Maya and Aztec, who learned to revere chocolate from the Olmec, favored it for ceremonies, festivals, and dinner tables. Its popularity spawned an industry that equated cacao with legal tender throughout Mesoamerica. Counterfeiters increased their profit in fresh beans by adulterating them with sand to make them heavier.

Cooks winnowed, then slow-roasted cacao beans in urns. They ground the beans with mano and metate, a pair of hand grinding stones. They mixed the resulting powder with maize flour, sugar, cinnamon, and vanilla and shaped the mass into a paste for cakes. The chocolate-proud stored their cache of cacao patties in screwtop canisters like coins in a bank. A tomb at Río Azul, Guatemala, contained one of these painted and stuccoed pottery urns, a ritual cacao vessel marked with its own glyph around 500 CE. An early convenience food, the chocolate disks required only the addition of water to

a calabash and a deft shake to produce chocolate froth. For banquets and receptions, Aztec cooks mixed cacao, maize flour, and chili peppers with water to make *xocoatl,* a bitter drink that disgusted the Spanish *conquistadores.* A throne-room scene drawn around 750 CE depicts a female preparer pouring the sacred liquid from an elevated pot to another on the ground, presumably to aerate it and create foam.

From *Historia General de las Cosas de Nueva España* (A General History of New Spain, ca. 1590) by Franciscan missionary and Aztec archeologist Fray Bernardino de Sahagún came a list of cacao beverages made at that time—honeyed chocolate, flowered chocolate, green pods, red chocolate, black chocolate, and white chocolate. He particularized the making of a secular chocolate beverage, which the poet-king Nezahualcoyotl extolled in the 1430s as part of a royal dance and song fest. Cooks toasted and fried fermented beans on griddles before peeling the outer shell and removing the inner membrane. After grinding, the solids went into a gourd sieve to be submerged into boiling water for *cacahuatl* (cacao water). Blended with toasted corn and a local vine, the mixture was beaten with a wooden *molinillo* (paddle). The foam was served atop corn porridge, while the pot liquid was reserved as an end-of-meal beverage.

For a sacred ritual, the sponsor's wife roasted cacao beans, ground them on mano and metate, and added a foaming agent, which frothed as she whipped with a stick. Before pouring the mixture into a holy pot, she flavored it with corn gruel or *blaché* (mead). When kitchen workers blended a similar drink in Guatemala, they stressed the flavor of black pepper over cacao, which was too expensive to be served generously.

New Taste in Europe

When Spanish explorer Hérnan Cortés traveled Central America, his historian, Bernal Diáz, described an Aztec sauce blended in a *molcaxitl* (jar), agitated to a froth with a stick, and served in a *jícara* (open bowl). When Cortés arrived in the capital city of Tenochtitlán, Mexico, in 1520, he was so taken with the spirited drink that he transported it to Europe, where it was sweetened and called chocolate. Iberian importers drove up the price of chocolate by concealing their cacao source from northern Europeans. Spanish merchants found an aficionado in Cosimo de Médicis, whom the King of Spain's staff served with huge cups of chocolate at bullfights in the 1660s. By 1680, Joseph de Olmo was ordering kitchen workers to prepare chocolates and bake sweet biscuit to serve to foreign ministers, church officials, and special guests at an *auto-da-fé* (public execution) in Madrid. As suggested by the recipe for chocolate ice cream in French food writer Menon's *La Science du Maître-d'Hôtel Cuisinier* (The Science of Cuisine Management, 1750), chocolate maintained its appeal to European nobility and royalty, who hired master chefs to keep them current on the best of Continental cuisine.

In the 1670s, Arab explorer Elias ibn Hanna drank roasted chocolate in Guayaquil, Ecuador. The new experience left him searching for comparisons:

You would imagine it to be coffee in color, taste and smell, but it is very oily, so that it forms a paste. They add as much sugar as is required, and cinnamon and ambergris. Then they mix it to a paste and place it in molds until it sets. They melt the bars of chocolate and drink it like coffee. (Lunde n. d., 60-61)

His description of the Ecuadorian cooking method concluded with the endorsement of the Franks, who imported chocolate for sale. The flavoring rapidly moved north. By 1697, Judge Samuel Sewall reported dining on "Venison and Chocolatte" at the home of the lieutenant governor of the Massachusetts Bay colony.

European chocolate preparers created cocoa by blending eggs, sugar, and milk with chocolate powder. As a sideline, they marketed oil and cocoa butter, a kitchen staple used as a food binder, lubricant, and moisturizing for chapped hands and face. Connoisseurs demanded enameled tin, earthenware, or silver chocolate mills, a spouted urn with lid and a handle positioned halfway down the body of the container. Inside, a wooden dasher (also called a muddler or muller) attached to an upright post that protruded through the lid for stirring solids and raising a froth. Food writer Philippe Sylvestre Dufour composed *Traitez Nouveux et Curieux Du Café, du Thé et du Chocolate* (A New and Curious Treatise on Coffee, Tea, and Chocolate, 1685). Subtitled "As It Is Used by Most Parts of Europe, Asia, Africa, and America, with Their Virtues," it explained that cakes of chocolate must be grated or pounded, mixed with sugar, and carefully melted in boiling water before the blend is frothed in a mill and drunk with the scum still on the surface. In the chocolate houses of 1700, young servants carried completed cups of beverage from the chocolate-maker's service window to tables where gentlemen sat drinking, smoking, and discussing the news of the day.

Chocolate became a European craze, spreading to St. Petersburg, Russia, in 1857 after Swiss confectioner Moritz Conradi established a chocolate factory. Chocolate lovers established the dominance of Swiss manufacturers Lindt, Nestlé, and Suchard-Tobler and English firms Cadbury and Mars, all of whom maintained their prominence in the candy industry into the twenty-first century. In Poland, royalty demanded chocolate as a breakfast drink until, in the mid-1600s, Chancellor Jerzy Ossolinski complained that the nation spent too much on expensive imported delicacies.

In 1667, food historian Antonio Colmenero Ledesma compiled *Della Cioccolata: Discorso Diviso in Quattro Parti* (On Chocolate: A Discourse Divided into Four Parts), the first European book devoted to cacao and covering its history, uses, and recipes. It was translated into Spanish to enlighten Iberian cooks. The French learned from Denis Diderot's *Encyclopédie* (1751–72) exactly how chocolate was ground over a heated metate and cooked in a pot over a charcoal range before being laid out on a cutting board into chocolate cheeses. In the early 1800s, French culinary authority Jean-Anthelme Brillat-Savarin, author of *Physiologie du Goût, ou Méditation de Gastronomie Transcendante, Ouvrage Théorique, Historique et à l'Ordre du Jour* (The Physiology of Taste, or A Meditation on the Best of Dining, a Theoretical and Historic Work on the Order of the Day, 1825), instructed chocolate-makers on a secret he learned from Madame d'Arestrel, Mother Superior of the convent of the Visitation at Belley. She boiled a chocolate blend in a Faience pot and left it overnight to concentrate and gain body.

American Tastes

Colonial Americans also preferred chocolate in drink form. Potters designed chocolate pots and sets suited to the preparation and consumption of the drink. They modeled their vessels after the standard pear-shaped brass urn with gooseneck spout made in France and Switzerland. In an advertisement in the September 5, 1737 issue of the *Boston Gazette,* a seller of kitchen-size chocolate mills promised that this latest innovation was a valuable labor saver: "It will in less than six Hours bring one Hundred weight of Nuts to a consistance fit for the mold." (Dow 1988, 128) As an added inducement, the device was guaranteed to preserve the "Oyly Spirit of the Nut" and needed little or no fire for the process. (Ibid.)

By the 1800s, chocolate had advanced from a drink in a cup to a base for confections and icing. Tin and pewter chocolate molds shaped candy pieces with animal, religious, and seasonal motifs, including the Christian fish and Passover lamb. In 1828, Dutch chemist Coenraad Johannes van Houten patented a process that produced powdered, low-fat chocolate by forcing it through a hydraulic press. The "dutching" of chocolate improved its miscibility and darkened the color. (Coe & Coe 1996, 242) With this change in chocolate consistency, in 1847, Joseph Storrs Fry of Bristol, England, was able to manufacture bars of

Chocolat Déliceux à Manger (tasty eating chocolate), a true candy for the masses.

In 1832, Franz Sacher, Prince von Metternich's sixteen-year-old apprentice cook, invented *sachertorte*, a rich Austrian confection made from chocolate sponge cake double-iced in apricot glaze and bittersweet chocolate, traditionally stamped with an official seal, and served with unsweetened whipped cream. When a rivalry erupted between the toney Sacher Hotel, where Beethoven debuted his Ninth Symphony, and Demel's, Vienna's prize confectionary shop, Sacher's family brought to court a complaint that Demel's had usurped the right to call their version the original and genuine *sachertorte*. The Sachers had purchased the name from Franz Sacher's grandson Edouard. After a seven-year deliberation, the court awarded "custody" of the dessert to the hotel.

In Australia, chocolate delighted children and drew them in packs to the journeyman sweet and soft drink seller, who traveled the outback and in a van or jalopy. Cadbury wooed parents by promising that each bar contained a "glass and a half of milk." (Fahey 1992, 100) Children liked chocolate flakes, chocolate-covered caramel Fantales, orange-chocolate Jaffas, and chocolate nonpareils, tiny rolls sprinkled on breakfast toast. For birthday parties and scout camp, cooks made chocolate crackles from rice bubbles, cocoa, coconut or sultanas, and copha, a solid form of hydrogenated shortening made from coconut oil. The mix went into patty cases (muffin cups) and chilled in the refrigerator. For a hot chocolate drink, Aussie children lapped up cocoa, made with copha, dried milk powder, carob, and powdered sugar.

The American classic chocolate cake was a late arrival in baking history. Appearing in Chicago in the 1880s, it quickly gained a following for its succulent flavor and springy crumb. When President Chester Alan Arthur and first lady Ellen Arthur added chocolate cake to the White House menu, velvety, fragrant devil's food cake, laced with coffee and sour milk, became a faddish American dessert. Additional advice came from Maria Willett Howard's *Lowney's Cook Book Illustrated in Colors: A New Guide for the Housekeeper* (1907). Alongside ads for the Walter M. Lowney Company's chocolate factory were recipes for chocolate blancmange and chestnuts with chocolate cream. An illustration depicting a cacao tree provided a note of authenticity.

In 1930, the candy egg dipper, a wire frame, allowed home confectioners to spear six cream eggs on hooks and dip them simultaneously into chocolate. During the Great Depression, ads in *Good Housekeeping* extolled Baker's Cocoa as a sure means of fattening up underweight children, characterizing it as "a banquet of those valuable food materials which help every

child become strong and sturdy and alert." ("The Weekly Treat" 1930, 217) To add scientific validity, the copywriter cited a survey in which 77 percent of dietitians, nurses, and editors of women's magazines backed Baker's Cocoa as a boon to child growth.

Into the 1940s, the advertisers of chocolate took full advantage of the era's concern over vitamins and minerals in children's diets, warning mothers of the dangers of malnutrition, poor weight maintenance, low energy, and illness. Vita Sert, a between-meal chocolate bar, claimed to energize children with the addition of vitamins A, B1, B2, C, and D. Bosco milk amplifier provided iron; Ovaltine promised five vitamins, protein, iron, niacin, calcium, and phosphorus and claimed scientific standardization of nutrition for supplementing children's diet. Bosco, Chocomalt, and Ovaltine, the most popular chocolate beverage additivies, appealed to mothers whose children refused to drink milk.

When Captain Robert Scott set out for Antarctica in 1910, he set up camp at Cape Evans, including in his food stock a can of Fry's Cocoa, a comfort food that expeditioners valued as a source of quick energy and warmth. Ken Meyer, a navy photographer documenting the McMurdo research station in the mid-1950s, sought the hut that Scott had built and supplied. Without thought of history, Meyer removed the cocoa. In 2001, upon learning of preservation efforts to maintain the historical camp, Meyer returned the cocoa to the Antarctic Heritage Trust.

Into the twenty-first century, chocolate was a beverage choice in many households along with tea and coffee. In the Andean states of Uruguay, cooks served it hot and foamy. Samoan families drank cocoa for breakfast with bread or rice. Dutch children got *hagelslag* (chocolate sprinkles) on their breakfast toast. An aid to the maker of chocolate baked goods and candies was the Sinsation II, an electronic device that tempered chocolate for dipping and recipes requiring melted white, milk, or dark chocolates. The Swiss, who had to import cocoa and sugar, continued to lead the world in production of fine milk chocolate, which home cooks have traditionally used in a festive dessert fondue heated over a spirit lamp or candle.

On a December 2000 cooking program, the New England food maven Martha Stewart centered her holiday confections on chocolate. To demonstrate methods of preparing it, she showed how to sift cocoa and add it to batter and how to cut blocks of chocolate for candy. For slices, she hacked at the bar with a chef's knife. For uniform chunks, she used a chocolate fork, a straight, broad-tined implement with a sturdy handle. For a fine powder, she cut the bar with a serrated bread knife.

Holiday catalogs featured chocolate in a variety of forms and flavors. Shapes varied from orange sections, animals, and gold foil-encrusted coins to standard bars for cooking, snacking, and breaking apart on scored lines for sharing. The latter came in a variety of flavors—mocha, raspberry, hazelnut, and vanilla, as well as milk chocolate, white chocolate, bittersweet, semisweet, and unsweetened. Home candy makers could purchase varying grades of chocolate blended with wax in bars or as liquid extract, a fragrant dessert additive and coffee flavoring made from roasted cacao beans since 1890. A reprise of a food fad from the 1970s, chocolate fondue sets made a reappearance early in 2000, offering bowl, stand, candle or liquid fuel source, and individual long-handled forks for dippers to use while coating bread, cake, or fruit chunks in melted chocolate. Another favorite of candy makers, the nonstick double boiler for chocolate consisted of nested steel sauce pans, from which the chocolate melter could fill tin candy molds.

See also **Candy; Mano and Metate**

Further Reading

Coe, Sophie D., and Michael D. Coe. *The True History of Chocolate*. London: Thames & Hudson Ltd., 1996.
"The Weekly Treat," *Good Housekeeping*, October 1930, 217.
Yzábal, María Dolores, and Shelton Wiseman. *The Mexican Gourmet*. McMahons Point, Australia: Thunder Bay, 1995.

CHOPSTICKS

Chopsticks are a distinctive Asian serving and dining implement. After the spoon, they are the world's second most popular utensil. In a reference to the rapidity with which they can be manipulated, the Chinese have called them *kuai zi* (lively, or swift, fellows). (Montagné 1977, 242) Pidgin English applied the word *chop,* meaning quick, to the paired sticks, a commentary on the user's dexterity. Speed of eating was a necessity in a land where cooks minced foods into tiny pieces that cooled rapidly after cooking.

To eliminate the presence of knives—and thus reduce the potential for violence at the table—chopsticks replaced bladed implements in China around 3000 BCE. They rapidly influenced eating styles in Korea, Vietnam, and Japan, where diners referred to the sticks as *hashi* (a bridge) between bowl and mouth. Until around 900 CE, the Japanese used the double sticks as tweezers joined at one end. In feudal Japan, the elite carried eating implements in ebony or bone cases covered in sharkskin. Each soldier tucked a set of chopsticks and knife into his obi; the Mongolian male secured chopsticks in his sash. The only Southeast Asian nation to retain chopsticks as the primary

dining implement is Vietnam, which overthrew a millennium of Chinese rule in 939 CE.

The Chinese originals measured around ten inches in length; Japanese implement makers preferred a classically proportioned stick, with length equaling 1.2 times the dimension of the hand measured from the base of the palm to the tip of the middle finger. Traditionally, the Chinese emperor's personal set of chopsticks was made of gold. The food tester used ivory chopsticks, which turned dark after coming in contact with certain poisons. Ordinary meals among the proletariat called for bamboo implements, while lacquered wooden pairs were reserved for company and special occasions.

When Asians and Westerners first witnessed each other's dining style, the response was often mutually negative. As observed by Father João Rodrigues in the 1600s, the Japanese recoiled from the sight of Westerners wiping their hands on napkins. Japanese diners preferred a gentle, precise method of handling food. The French cultural scholar Roland Barthes described their meticulous approach to dining in *L'Empire des Signes* (Empire of Signs, 1970): "There is something maternal, the same precisely measured care taken in moving a child. . . The instrument never pierces, cuts, or slits, never wounds, but only selects, turns, shifts. For the chopsticks. . . in order to divide, must separate, part, peck, instead of cutting and piercing." (Visser 1991, 180)

As an indication of refinement among the elite, chopsticks are a social detail described by Tsao Hsueh-Chin in the classic Chinese novel *Dream of the Red Chamber* (or *The Dream of Red Mansions,* 1764). In preparation for a company meal, handmaids pass towels and waft a fly brush over the lacquered table. One guest, Liu Lao-lao, confronted with old-style gilded ivory chopsticks, finds the heavy implements too difficult to manipulate and compares them to iron tongs. Chasing costly pigeon eggs around her bowl, she succeeds in getting one to her mouth but then dropped it on the floor. The hostess orders her servants to bring silvered ebony chopsticks, but the hapless diner confesses that she prefers wood, "the best for practical purposes." (Tsao 1958, 193) Phoenix, another of the diners, explains the use of precious metal sticks for determining whether food is poisoned. Tsao's vignette of ladies at their meal illustrates the social importance of graceful manipulation of chopsticks.

In the 1860s, the *Englishwoman's Domestic Magazine* published "A Sketch of Tea Land," an article on Chinese customs and table manners. An eyewitness to the use of chopsticks stated, "At dinner we were surprised to see no knives or forks, for which instruments they make use of a couple of chopsticks for the purpose of throwing food into their mouths. . . . John Chinaman has the reputation of being the most patient of animals in the harness of business, and he equally maintains it in his steady pursuit of pleasure." (Major 1986)

When Chinese miners camped among Latinos and Anglos during the California gold rush of 1849, they set themselves apart from diners with forks and tin plates, instead squatting around small pots from which individual bites they took by means of chopsticks. Whites and Mexicans looked with disdain on this practice of dipping into a communal pot, an act that, while dainty in execution, seemed unsanitary.

The manufacture of millions of chopsticks, from humble disposable pairs to lacquered sets with gold inlay, had a decided impact on the Asian economy. During the 1970s, when hardship gripped South Korea, the government chose unusual measures for controlling waste. One method of saving national resources was to decrease the length of disposable wooden chopsticks. Instead of the traditional nine inches, homemakers began buying pairs that measured only seven inches.

When Hu Yao Bang, a Chinese Communist Party official, sought to halt the spread of communicable disease in China in 1984, he tried to end the traditional practice of sharing dishes. He promoted the use of the Western knife and fork and urged homemakers to serve individual portions on plates rather than in bowls. The Chinese ignored his advise and continued carrying communal pots to the table for diners to forage in with their chopsticks.

Wherever they live globally, the Chinese continue using chopsticks for kitchen work and meals. With two straight sticks, cooks are able to fluff rice, transfer steamed grains and *t'sai* (accompaniments) to individual bowls, and separate skin from meat in the preparation of Peking duck. Available in plastic, jade, teak, ivory, silver, ebony, palisander wood, and the more familiar bamboo, chopsticks come in round- and pointed-tip versions for mixing, stirring, and serving as well as eating.

Western customs have made inroads into Asian dining practices. Cambodians, Malaysians, Mongolians, Taiwanese, Thais, and Indonesians apply pragmatism—they use fingers, spoons, and chopsticks, according to family custom and the type of food served. French Polynesians, whose culture is markedly Eurasian, eat Chinese dishes with chopsticks and Tahitian specialties with fingers. Similarly, Korean hostesses let the cuisine determine the tableware—chopsticks for most foods and spoons for soup. Cooks worldwide have used the chopstick or a skewer as a "story stick," a visible measuring tool on which they mark the level of a sauce or jam or jelly to indicate how much to reduce a liquid.

In Hong Kong, where cosmopolitan dining is more common than in rural China, selecting servings from bowls with chopsticks is still standard procedure at home. Malaysian and Vietnamese diners use both chopsticks and forks and spoons for eating such foods as *laksa* (curried noodles) and *pho bo* (beef noodle soup). Malaysians eschew knives because they look too aggressive for table setting.

The Japanese also embrace Western-style flatware but eat traditional foods with *hashi* (chopsticks). Japanese *obentos* (lunchboxes), prepared at home for school meals and available to commuters and shoppers at train stations, often include *o-hashi* (chopsticks). Typically, Japanese diners go through some 25 billion pairs of disposable chopsticks annually. Diners still prefer bamboo to lacquered wood, which can be slippery and awkward and requires hand washing rather than placement in a dishwasher. One popular style, kuwa chopsticks, made from varnished mulberry twigs, dominated table trends in the 1990s. Japanese etiquette regarding use of chopsticks specifies that, when not in use, they must be placed with their tips on a *hashi odi* (holder). Diners learning to eat Asian style are taught to avoid sorting through or stabbing food, forcing bites into the mouth, licking the sticks, or anchoring the pair in the bowl or standing them upright. Passing food on chopsticks is considered disrespectful because the act mimics a funeral custom in which bones from a cremation are passed from one mourner to another.

Early in the twenty-first century, many manufacturers sought out supplies of wood from nonendangered sources, crafting chopsticks from coconut palm, cypress, Judas tree, mulberry, and sandalwood. In the United States an aluminum version of the standard Chinese restaurant take-out container came complete with its own set of aluminum chopsticks. Mass marketers such as Crate and Barrel sold all the necessary implements for Asian-style dining, including rice bowls, chopsticks, and chopstick rests.

See also **Bamboo; Mongolian Hot Pot; Obentos**

Further Reading

Rajah, Carol Selva. *Makan-Lah!: The True Taste of Malaysia.* Sydney, Australia: HarperCollins, 1996.

CHUCKWAGONS

The cowboy mess hall, the chuckwagon—named for a slang term for chow or grub—survives in frontier legend and lore across the American West from Canada

Two-bar chuck wagon camped at Dry Fork Elkhead Creek, Spring of 1907.
[© *Courtesy of National Archives and Records Administration. Photo by J.H. Sizer.*]

to Mexico and the west coast of South America. Invented in 1866 by Colonel Charles Goodnight, the chuckwagon was originally an army surplus supply vehicle. Goodnight, a breeder of cattalo (a cross between cattle and buffalo) and founder of the Panhandle Stockmen's Association, had been a Texas Ranger and an Indian fighter and served in the Civil War as a guide for the Confederate Frontier Regiment. As co-founder of a new trail from Weatherford in Palo County, Texas, through New Mexico to Colorado, he needed the supply wagon for long hauls.

Goodnight's initial trip with the frontier kitchen began on August 26, 1866. Traveling southwest from Fort Belknap toward the Pecos River over the "Goodnight Trail," he stopped to make a sale of steers at Fort Sumner, New Mexico. He took his $12,000 profit home by pack mule. His partner, the freighter Oliver Loving, the first drover to herd cattle to the Chicago stockyards, pushed the herd farther north and east

toward Pueblo, Colorado, over the "Loving Trail." He died in a Comanche attack during the third drive. Along with his partner John Chisum, Goodnight continued the cattle drives for three years. In 1875, he standardized a route from Alamogordo Creek, New Mexico, to Granada, Colorado. It became one of the most heavily traveled U.S. livestock trails.

Goodnight's chuckwagon was the prototype for other kitchen wagons pulled by teams of oxen or mules. A carpenter built the body out of seasoned *bois d'arc* (also known as Osage orange or orangewood), a lightweight, flexible timber of the mulberry family that Indians favored as bow wood. Goodnight added the chuck box, a partitioned pantry that contained packets of coffee, beans, salt pork, cornmeal, onions, potatoes, canned milk, sourdough, and "long sweetenin'" (molasses), as well as tin or iron plates, utensils, and cutlery. (McCutcheon 1993, 246) The hinged lid opened downward to place a single scantling, or leg, on the ground at center to support the flat surface during use as a worktable. As described in the Alberta cowboy C. J. Christianson's *My Life on the Range* (1968), in the early 1900s, refinements to Canadian versions called for high, narrow wheels for light running under the weight of the two tons of provisions required to feed sixteen to twenty cowboys for up to six weeks.

Drawn by ten oxen rather than the standard four, Goodnight's unique vehicle halted at a grocery store at the beginning of a drive to load up on staples and canned goods; shoppers avoided glass jars, which would not survive the jolts of the trail. The structure held tent, stove, rope and rawhide, horseshoes, tackle, kindling and firewood, and more kegs of water than earlier models because the bed sat atop an iron axle instead of the usual wooden shaft. The chuckwagon preceded the herd all the way, although the driver occasionally detoured from the cattle trail in search of grassier, less rutted passages.

Large items, primarily a month's supply of food, fit in the wagon body. In addition, a hammock, called a caboose, cooney, or possum belly, was slung under the wagon bed to hold kindling and buffalo chips, chunks of dried dung jokingly named "prairie coal." (Soule 1976, 127) Other essentials attached to the bed included coffee grinder, water buckets, and a barrel equipped with a faucet and roped to the side for quick access when drovers needed a drink. Near the driver was a tool box, called the "jewelry chest," which held pot hooks and rod, pick, hammer and shovel, ax and hatchet, farrier's shoeing equipment, branding irons, guns, bullets, musical instruments, hobbles for the horses, tar for waterproofing, saw blades, extra wheels, and rawhide strips for quick ties and repairs. A medicine chest held quinine, laxatives, and "red-eye" (whiskey), the only nostrums available on the frontier. (McCutcheon 1993, 249)

The cook, usually a retired cowpuncher too arthritic and trail-worn to ride horseback, tolerated irreverent nicknames such as cooky, dinero, hash slinger, grub wrangler, biscuit shooter, dough puncher, pot rustler, Sallie, and dough roller and weathered complaints about "coffee varnish." (Ibid., 242) From the Spanish name *cosinero* (cook) came the English slang "cousie." Cooks' pay varied. For good reason, if the cowboy made one dollar a day, the cook might get twice that amount. According to ledgers from 1899, one cowwagon cook, Richard Jackson, earned $15 per month.

The cook answered only to the trail boss and ruled the campsite, which could get violent when tired men's tiffs escalated into blows. His job involved positioning the wagon in a suitable spot for digging a fire pit and kindling a campfire without starting a prairie blaze. At day's end, he pointed the wagon tongue toward the North Star as a guide for the next day's travels. When there was a death, he often buried the body and officiated at the graveside service.

In the pre-dawn, the cook lighted the lantern and tied on a flour sack apron before beginning the day's cooking. After grinding coffee beans, he started water for coffee in a broad-based tin pot, mixed sourdough with flour for biscuits, and set them to bake over hot coals in a cast iron Dutch oven, the most valuable piece of equipment, which the cook wrapped in burlap and stored in the wagon boot between the back wheels. The cooking structure above the fire pit consisted of two upright bars to hold the cross piece, which supported pot hooks to steady coffee pot, kettle, and cook pot. In the long-handled fry pan, he set bacon and steak to sizzle. At the drop table, he set out dried fruit and syrup or sorghum molasses for sweetening flapjacks.

From the Mexican border to Saskatchewan, the wagoneer's menu varied little in foodstuffs or preparation. To *llaneros* (plainsmen), Mexican cooks served up *sancocho* (stew), ribs, beef chunks and sweetbreads spitted on an *asador* (metal rod), black beans, and *arepas* (corn cakes). In the American Southwest, cooks dished up bacon, jokingly referred to as "overland trout," "airtight" (canned) peaches or dried apples, fresh meat and *frijoles* (red or pinto beans), eggs with salt pork, soda or sourdough buttermilk biscuits, coffee, and sometimes tea. (Slatta 1994, 139) According to a 1938 article in *Canadian Cattleman*, northern cowboys preferred a breakfast of meat and potatoes and jam and bread washed down with hot java. After a range lunch of dried fruit, dried beef, biscuits, and coffee heated over a campfire, the cowboys returned for a dinner that resembled breakfast.

Range etiquette made the cook the arbiter of behavior. Cowboys washed at a communal basin and shared a towel and comb. The man who emptied the water keg was obliged to refill it. Diners came only when the cook called them and stood in line to wait their turn for a serving from the cook's spoon and meat-turning fork. Their expectations were simple—plenty of fresh beef and hot coffee. All else was table dressing. Seated in the mess tent on bedrolls or boxes or outdoors on a log or the ground, the men cleaned their tin plates, made no complaints, and dropped dirty utensils in the wreck (or wrecking) pan before saddling up for the day's work. Any man dawdling at the coffeepot refilled cups. The cook insisted on order and required riders to depart down wind of the wagon to protect stores from dust. Out of respect for the cook's job, cowboys collected firewood and buffalo chips. If they found the cookfire untended, they stirred the beans before going on about their business.

During the day, the cook washed dishes at the wreck pan, stowed bedrolls, and soaked beef and beans for dinner. For slaughtering beef on the trail, he used an ax to split the carcass and hung each portion from the upright wagon tongue for chilling and draining. The next day, he wrapped the beef in wet tarpaulins after removing ribs for a special treat. With the addition of chili, spice, vinegar, and tomatoes, beef that had spoiled became Texas chili. Wranglers valued trail food for nourishment and for relieving tedium. E. C. "Teddy Blue" Abbott exulted, "I'd never seen such wonderful grub as they had at the D.H.S. [ranch]. They had canned tomatoes all the time, canned peaches even." (Soule 1976, 257)

The cook cared for his team and followed the scout's direction to a water hole or grazing area. For fording, he might cut cottonwood logs and lash them to the wagon body to float it over deep water. At lunch, rowdies returned for "nooning," a combination of lunch and break. (Soule 1976, 128) The cook took his afternoon break and also repaired clothing and harness, cut hair, and applied first aid to animals and men, such as rubbing tomato juice on alkali burns and applying a poultice of chewing tobacco and whiskey to a rattlesnake or tarantula bite. When a cowboy got too sick to ride, the chuckwagon became a combination ambulance and recovery ward.

Cooking demanded scavenging. If a river offered good fishing, the cook might cut a willow pole and try his luck, shoot quail or wild turkey, or take a bucket or rawhide pouch and pick berries. Treats from the chuckwagon ranged from venison steak, roast beef, and stew to turkey eggs, wild honey, and pastries and desserts made from leftover dough and fruit or syrup. Andy Adams's *The Log of a Cowboy: A Narrative of the Old Trail Days* (1903) describes the free-form cookery of Colorado stew and dumplings, a one-dish meal made by the gradual addition of meat, potatoes, onions, and dough to the kettle.

At supper, the cook dispensed fresh beef or game and "sop" gravy, canned corn or beans, and rice. Southwestern specialties included roasted calf testicles, called range oysters, and "son-of-a-bitch stew," a one-dish meal of calf meat and organs simmered in a thick pot liquor of chili, onions, flour, and brains. (Slatta 1994, 142) In the ground near the campfire, the Mexican camp cook roasted the head of a yearling wrapped in sacking or hide. *Vaqueros* (cowboys) relished the unveiling and shared the flesh, brains, and tongue. In Chile, gauchos delighted in *carne con cuero* (meat with hide), a range-roasted calf carcass stuffed and then wrapped in hide for slow roasting.

Cowboys did not expect extravagant amenities, but they did look forward to dessert. The typical meal ended with a sweet, such as stewed prunes, cake, bread pudding, turnovers, an open-faced pie called a "boggy-top," or fried pastry. (Ibid.) A blend of canned tomatoes, sugar, and bread produced a thirst-quenching meal conclusion that countered a day's mouthful of alkali dust.

In the evening, the chuckwagon became a cantina, a warm, welcoming fireside where cowboys eased into a circle and rested on their saddles. Content with coffee and camaraderie, they swapped stories and legends, sang, and played poker. Journalist J. Frank Dobie preserved chuckwagon folklore in his columns and books. John Avery Lomax collected the music and lyrics for such tunes as "Sweet Betsy from Pike," "Home on the Range," and "Whoopee-ti-yi-yo, Git Along, Little Dogies" in *Cowboy Songs and Other Frontier Ballads* (1910) and *Songs of the Cattle Trail and Cow Camp* (1917).

The portable cookhouse, the Australian version of the chuckwagon, consisted of a shed on wheels. One model circa 1925 was made of corrugated tin and served the sheep station cook as sleeping quarters. A fold-down side became a food-preparation table. The corresponding upper piece leaned out on a stake to form a sunshade. A necessity of the national cuisine was the portable mincer, a hand-cranked mill that provided meat chunks for pies. One ingenious cook turned a giant ant's nest into an oven. The best of outback cooks knew the right wood to select for heating or baking in a camp oven and could estimate the force of the wind, which fanned the fire while peppering food with dust and insects.

The chuckwagon remains in use at the Four Sixes Ranch (6666) in the Texas panhandle. An original chuckwagon survives from the Old West at the John E. Conner Museum at Texas A&M University at Kingsville. In 1995, the Saints' Roost Museum in Clarendon, Texas, began hosting an annual Colonel Charles Goodnight Chuckwagon Cook-off. In Alberta, Canada, enthusiasts originated chuckwagon racing in 1923 at the Calgary Stampede. In subsequent years, wagon loading contests and obstacle courses expanded events. The Canadian Professional Chuckwagon Association, established in Alberta and Saskatchewan in the late 1940s, perpetuated the wagon-racing tradition, which standardized entrants at a minimum of 1,325 pounds with a team of four horses. Local rodeo promoters arranged events at Lloydminster, Pierceland, and Meadow Lake. Around 1978, racers formed the Northern Chuckwagon Association, which perpetuates the tradition of trail cookery.

Further Reading

Adams, Andy. *The Log of a Cowboy: A Narrative of the Old Trail Days*. Williamston, Mass.: Corner House, 1975.

Baillargeon, Morgan, and Leslie Tepper. *Legends of Our Times: Native Cowboy Life*. Vancouver: University of British Columbia Press, 1998.

Slatta, Richard W. *The Cowboy Encyclopedia*. Santa Barbara, Calif.: ABC-Clio, 1994.

Soule, Gardner. *The Long Trail: How Cowboys and Longhorns Opened the West*. New York: McGraw-Hill Book Co., 1976.

CHURNING

Churning is the process of agitation of fresh milk to produce butter. The concept may have originated in Arabia, where desert travelers transporting skins of milk at warm temperatures found that, after hours on a swaying camel, the milk had turned to butter. The rudiments of churning appear on a Sumerian frieze from the temple in al-Ubaid depicting the shaking of milk in a corked jug and the straining of whey from butter, a series of actions that has changed little for much of the world's dairiers. In India, a frieze at a Lakshmana temple in Khajuraho presents a method that replicates the technology of the bow drill or fire drill—the pull of a rope wound around a stirring stick in an earthen pot of cream.

After a journey to visit Sartach, a mongol chief living on the Volga River in the 1250s, Father William of Rubruck, a Franciscan priest, wrote a formal travelogue for Louis IX of France. One thing that fascinated the missionary was the Scythian production of koumiss, a mare's milk beverage that formed the basis for the Central Asian diet during the era of Kublai Khan and his horsemen. The drink remained popular in Kazakhstan, Mongolia, Tajikistan, and Uzbekistan. Dating to Turk nomads of the Central Asian steppes and farther back to China, it depended on a ready supply of mare's milk. The khan's household reserved 10,000 white stallions and mares to assure a sufficient supply of koumiss.

Rubruck explained how milkers on the steppes tethered mares by their foals during milking. The milkers, he explained, "would pour [milk] into a large skin or *bucellum* [bag], and set about churning it with a club which is made for this purpose, as thick at the lower end as a man's head and hollowed out. As they stir it rapidly, it begins to bubble like new wine and to turn sour or ferment, and they keep churning it until they extract the butter." (Lysaght 1994, 131) Only after the dairier had stirred the milk vigorously was it ready for drinking. He compared the heady drink to a cross between two beverages, a thin wine and almond milk. Along with dried meat, the beverage served the military as saddle food during long gallops.

In *Beverages, Past and Present: An Historical Sketch of Their Production, Together with a Study of the Customs Connected with Their Use* (1908) food researcher Edward R. Emerson described the Asian

Mrs. Dillard Eldridge churning. Four Mile, Bell County, Kentucky (1946).
[© *Courtesy of National Archives and Records Administration.*]

method for churning koumiss. Mixed with water in a skin bag in a ratio of six parts milk to one of water, koumiss fermented from a residue of natural rennin in the bag, which the churner never rinsed out. After the mix frothed at the surface, the koumiss-maker agitated the bag, then let it rest for several hours before churning. With a few turns of a spoon, the drink was ready for consumption.

In the seventeenth century, Czechoslovakian buttermakers followed a standard method. They typically washed the churned mass of butter in water, rinsing it four times. The process concluded with the squeezing of the mass by hand on a board with a *trdlo* (cylinder). By the 1800s hand pressure had been replaced with a mechanical wood beater. Carrot juice or saffron was added to provide color to the stark white mass. The shaper finished off the surface with wood molds, trowels, and butter knives. For maximum sanitation, cooks washed vessels, rinsed them in thyme water, and dried them in the sun.

In Finland, where butter was the nation's leading agricultural export, farm wives and manorial dairy keepers made butter according to longstanding tradition. They strained fresh milk into wood vessels and left the skimmed portion to sour, sometimes with the help of sour milk from a kitchen pitcher. When the cream rose by the third day, they agitated it into butter.

Another method, warm churning, called for the ladling of sour cream into skim milk before agitation.

In the 1700s, Finnish entrepreneur Jaako Fellman introduced the first barrel-shaped rotating churn from England. He had a woodworker in Oulu make copies and placed one in each parish. In the nineteenth century, cold churning replaced the older method with churning of cream alone. The cottage industry in butter making for export faded in 1860, when Swiss dairy masters instructed manorial dairies on mechanization and efficient production, including separation of cream with ice water. Home churning gradually ended as commercial dairies took over butter production.

In Scotland and most of Ireland, the most commonly used implements were the wooden dash churn, wooden or ceramic plunger churn, or cylindrical plump churn with broomstick handle and lug handles. In the region above Cavan, Ireland, however, dairiers preferred the glaik churn. Operated with a spring mechanism, the latter required steady see-sawing of a lever against the body. Another butter-making implement that the user agitated with shifts of body weight was the swing churn, which was popular around Lough Neagh. Suspended from the rafters, it took up no floor space and allowed the housewife to churn while supervising other cooking tasks and toddlers at play.

Another domestic use of churns involved the beating of egg yolks. In Elena Burman Molokhovets's classic Russian illustrated cookbook *A Gift to Young Housewives* (1861), she explains a complicated recipe for yeast babas, a typical Russian festival cake. By churning eggs dozens at a time, the cook could avoid the tedious, arm-tiring method of beating with slotted spoon or wire whisk.

Laura Ingalls Wilder, author of the "Little House on the Prairie" series, wrote of family life on the American frontier in the 1860s. In the first of her books, *Little House in the Big Woods* (1932), set on Lake Pepin, Wisconsin, she recounted her mother's trials with colorless winter butter. The process involved many steps. First, she shredded a carrot with a grater that Pa Ingalls had made by punching nail holes in a leaky tin pan. She added milk and heated the mixture on the stove. Ma Ingalls then strained it through a cloth bag into the churn. The yellowish liquid produced a pleasant-hued butter. "At first the splashes of cream showed thick and smooth around the little hole," Wilder wrote. "After a long time, they began to look grainy." Ma finally removed the gold lump, washed it in cold water, turned it with a paddle, and added salt. The task ended with the molding of the butter in a loose-bottomed mold carved with a strawberry. In return for their help, Laura and her sister Mary earned a drink of buttermilk from the watery liquid left in the churn.

After the Industrial Revolution, some 2,500 patented models of hand churns could be found in Europe and the United States. They ranged in height from fifteen to twenty-four inches. The agitator was originally a vertical plunger equipped with slotted paddles to increase the motion of milk. Some variants on this basic design applied ingenious principles of movement. The barrel churn, for example, rocked in a frame with a crank on the side, which could be turned by hand or attached to a pulley rotated by a horse. The crank churn was a tin or japanned cylinder activated by a crank rotated at the top, while the Dazey churn, a tabletop model patented in 1877, consisted of a columnar vessel topped with wooden lid and operated by means of a cast-iron gear-driven crank. Different-sized churns accommodated different-sized batches: the diamond balance churn, a box churn in a frame, patented in 1889, held sixty gallons of milk; for churning small batches there was the eggbeater churn, a glass vessel equipped with an eggbeater attached to the lid. Similar to the eggbeater churn was the syllabub churn; this small table model, also called a cream whip, applied an egg beater to a basin or bowl below for whipping a frothy meringue, pie topping, or cream desert. The end-over-end churn, a latch-lidded barrel set in a frame that allowed 360 degrees of rotation, turned cream into butter in only forty minutes. Swing churns such as the piggy churn, a tin ovule, were suspended from overhead beams. The user pushed the vessel back and forth with a handle attached to one end. The rocker, or tumbler, churn rocked like a cradle from the tread of the butter maker's foot. Within the oval vessel, cream sloshed from side to side. This method left the churner's hands free to perform other chores. The treadmill churn, a dog- or sheep-operated device rotated by a pulley, was invented in the United States in 1889. A version offered in 1895 by Montgomery Ward featured a treadmill and frame equipped to hold two dogs, whose trotting turned a wheel and belt connected by an iron coupler to a churn/cream separator.

Whether a small cylindrical table model, stand-alone churn, or dairy-size butter maker, all churns operated on the same principle of steady, continuous motion. Decanting over a strainer separated the mass from the buttermilk, a by-product that, in the early 1900s, Scots heated in a cauldron and dried in a bag by a smoky peat fire to make poor man's cheese, a peasant's curd blended with bacon fat.

To complete the butter making process, the housewife or dairy worker rinsed the gathered mass with plain or salted water. As the butter took shape in a wooden tub, a butter ladle or spade was the best tool for working it into a solid lump. A triangular wooden tray equipped with a drain hole and wooden paddles called "butter workers" aided the shaper in manipulating and compressing the mass. A later table model placed a roller in a slotted butter worker. By pushing the roller across the mass, the shaper quickly and thoroughly forced fluid from the compressed butter; the excess fluid flowed through a drain via a sloping tray.

Having removed any residual whey, the butter maker often blended in the juice of cooked carrots, changing the color of the off-white butter to a more appealing yellow hue. Further additives included salt and chopped herbs, such as dill or thyme. To test for firmness, the shaper could insert an iron or steel needle, borer, or skewer, called a butter trier, to assess consistency from top to bottom. A final evaluation of the product included tasting, smelling, or rubbing between the fingers. Butter remained fresh in a creamery, spring house, or dairy house when stored in wooden tubs and set on ice or in cold water.

Before meals, the homemaker used a butter fork, a broad-tined wooden implement, to remove the mass from the cylindrical tub. The finished mass passed to a butter trowel, or "butter hands," also known as butter rollers or Scotch hands, a pair of grooved or corrugated wooden paddles manipulated to shape the butter into pats and balls. Butter solidified quickly in ice water and retained decorative shapes if served in a bowl of ice water or on a bed of ice chips. For storage, some cooks pressed butter into a glass, tin, or wooden mold and applied a wooden stamp to the end to create a seasonal or patriotic or religious symbol, an initial, or a family crest. The dairy worker who had an abundance of butter often tamped the extra into a tub with a flat-topped masher or cut it into packages for sale or barter.

In the United States, the process of butter making varied from one region to another. In New England, the heavy salting of commercial butter required the purchaser to wash and squeeze the mass a second time before using it in pastry or cake recipes. In the Amana colonies, the kitchen's *Vizebaas* (assistant supervisor), scheduled churning weekly, biweekly, or as milk supplies demanded. For large batches, the butter maker used a square wood churn paddled with a hand crank. For smaller ones, the user might choose a glass churn. To the south, Appalachian dairy workers operated a lap churn for small scale butter production and completed the job with a lap trough, a vessel adapted from the Cherokee bread-maker's work bowl, and a hand clasher, an adze-shaped tool whose name became a slang term for gossip.

As described in Eliot Wigginton's *The Foxfire Book* (1968), churning became a survival skill for the mountaineers of the southern Appalachians. Butter makers filled a stoneware churn half full of whole milk or pure cream. After leaving the liquid to clabber overnight or for up to three days, they tilted the container to test

the liquid's cohesion. If the mass moved cleanly from the side, it was ready. If it needed more settling, it was deemed sour, or "blinky," milk, which did not produce good butter. Agitation with a dasher took thirty to forty minutes of steady, even, vertical strokes. Mountain folk used a five-line verse to keep the rhythm steady:

Come butter come
Come butter come
Peter standing at the gate
Waiting for a butter cake
Come butter come. (Wigginton 1972, 188)

Depending on temperature and milk quality, the mass yielded soft, fluffy butter. If the liquid was too cold to gel, the butter maker added hot water and continued agitation. After lifting the lumps of butter from the buttermilk, he or she drained the mass, pressed out liquid, chilled the mass, then salted and molded the butter for table use, trade, or sale.

See also **Bow Drill; Dairying**

Further Reading

Lysaght, Patricia, ed. Milk and Milk Products from Medieval to Modern Times. Edinburgh: Canongate Press, 1994.

CLARK, AVA MILAM

Unlike the more parochial accomplishments of other home economics pioneers, the work of Ava Bertha Milam Clark was global in its influence. She was born on November 27, 1884, in Macon, Missouri. In the family's farm kitchen, she learned how to stoke a wood stove, milk and churn, and butcher hogs. For reading material, she had *Ladies Home Journal* and the writings of Catharine Beecher, the nineteenth-century American proponent of sound home management.

After attending the Macon District Academy and the Centenary Academy at Palmyra, Illinois, Clark taught at the Blees Military Academy in Macon before completing her education at the University of Chicago, where her instructors included Elizabeth Sprague, the developer of the oven thermometer. In her mid-twenties, Clark met another woman who was to be an important influence in her life, Ellen Richards, who established the American Home Economics Association, launched home economics curricula for secondary schools and colleges, and served as the first editor of the *Journal of Home Economics*.

Replacing Margaret Comstock Snell, the first home economics professor in the far western United States, Clark advanced to full professor and head of the Department of Foods and Nutrition at Oregon Agricultural College. Among the subjects taken by her home economics students was an outdoor camp cookery course, which influenced the upgrading of an extension bulletin for Boy Scouts and 4-H members.

Like Beecher in the previous generation, Clark promoted modern housewifery. She presented cooking demonstrations at the Panama-Pacific Exposition. For the enlightenment of the older generation, she developed short courses for farm wives. In speeches to Salem farmers, she urged that the men give their wives vacations, spending money, and labor-saving kitchen devices. In 1917, Clark accepted President Herbert Hoover's offer of the home economics directorship in the state of Oregon and received a promotion to the post of dean of the School of Home Economics, which she held until she retired at age sixty-six.

In the decade following World War I, Clark introduced home economics education in Asia and the Middle East. One of the foremost consultants on the establishment of foods and nutrition programs, she advised home economics colleges in China, where the first college course opened at Yenching University in Peking in 1923, followed a decade later with similar coursework at Lingnan University in Canton. She lauded Chinese cooks for their superior soups and their restrained use of sugar, which, compared with contemporary American and Japanese cooking, was more conducive to dental health. Of culinary expertise in China, she wrote:

In the art of seasoning—only poorly imitated elsewhere in the world—and in the skill of preparing a variety of dishes with a minimum of utensils and delivering them to the table piping hot, [Chinese cooks] impressed me as being unsurpassed. They knew how to prepare a variety of vegetables by cooking them for only a short time at high temperatures so that they retained their color, minerals, and vitamins.

After consulting with pioneer home economics teachers at Ewha College in Korea, Clark advised Japanese domestic scientists at Kwassui College in Nagasaki. In 1968 she received a distinguished service award from Yonsei University of Seoul. For the Foreign Mission Conference in North America, she surveyed education in the Philippines; for the United Nations' Food and Agriculture Organization, she advised the governments of Syria, Iraq, Lebanon, and Egypt on home economics curricula and civilian food conservation. After her death in 1976, Milam Hall on the Oregon State University campus honored her name and career.

Further Reading

Clark, Ava Milam, and J. Kenneth Munford. *Adventures of a Home Economist.* Corvallis: Oregon State University Press, 1969.

Peiss, Kathy L., "American Women and the Making of Modern Consumer Culture," *Journal for Multi Media History,* Fall 1998.

Stage, Sarah, and Virginia B. Vincenti, eds. *Rethinking Home Economics: Women and the History of a Profession.* Ithaca, N.Y.: Cornell University Press, 1997.

CLEAVER

The cleaver is a substantial hacking and cutting tool found in kitchens throughout history. In restaurant kitchens it is the favorite all-purpose cutting blade for gutting and scaling fish, cutting up poultry, hacking through bones, mashing garlic, and mincing herbs. Skilled users adapt it easily to cutting, dicing, shredding, slicing, and chopping all viands, including frozen foods.

The French version, the *feuille,* is weighty and sharp enough to halve a beef carcass. An essential to Chinese cooking is the heavy-duty, rectangular-bladed cleaver that is typically three times as long as it is wide. Sharpened like an ax to avoid bruising meats and vegetables, it succeeds primarily by an authoritative application of its weight on a downward stroke rather than by a back-and-forth sawing action. Available in both a man's or lady's version, the implement dices meats and vegetables with the clean edge appropriate for stir-frying in a wok.

Whether made of a single piece of carbon steel or fitted with a wooden handle, the heavy-balanced blade defines the dramatic actions of Asian cooks as they rapidly chop fibrous foods. More than a knife, the wrought iron or steel cleaver directs arm power toward joints of meat, enabling the chef to separate large cuts into smaller pieces or to prepare roasts. A lighter version, the *usuba,* or oriental vegetable knife, is the implement of choice for precision slicing and julienning of vegetables and garnishes or for pounding and mashing with the side of the blade.

In *Chinese Gastronomy* (1972), the mother and daughter authors Hsiang Ju Lin and Tsuifeng Lin recounted a fabled exchange between Prince Huei and his cook on the skillful dismemberment of a bullock. The cook explained that he had used the same chopper for nineteen years and kept its edge fresh with a whetstone and constant cleaning after use. He expounded on the technique of inserting a thin blade into the joints of the carcass and keeping his eye and hand steady while exerting pressure. According to the legend, the prince was so impressed by the lesson that he adapted the cleaver for use as a weapon.

The anthropologist Sulamith Heins Potter, author of *Family Life in a Northern Thai Village* (1977), described how village women used cleavers to prepare a favorite meal of water buffalo meat. By hacking at the meat in multiple directions, they managed to reduce it to a shapeless mass. After seasoning it with seedpods and chili peppers, they served bowls of the cooked meat with broth and steamed rice.

Along with the wooden chopping block, the Chinese cleaver is a necessity for preparing emperor's fish, a dish that requires the cook to make angled slits in skin and flesh to hold sliced mushrooms and marinade. Control for julienne or matchstick cuts requires that the user move the blade up and down with the cutting hand while carefully curling the fingers of the hand keeping the food in place. The vegetable pieces are held against the flat of the blade; the chef gauges the thickness of the slices by pressing with his or her knuckles. A roll-cut technique for eggplant involves chopping three-quarter-inch *fu tau* (ax wedges) diagonally while rotating the vegetables a quarter turn at each cut.

American cooks, too, have found uses for cleavers. As described in Josiah T. Marshall's *The Farmer's and Emigrant's Hand-Book* (1845), the mincing cleaver enabled the cook to hash meat for sausage and ensure the blending of pepper and spices throughout. A steel blade attached to a turned handle balanced the half-moon-shaped cleaving blade on one side with a steak maul on the other. A later introduction, the vegetable cleaver featured a rectangular blade smaller than that of a meat cleaver. It was particularly useful for quartering solid masses, such as potatoes, water chestnuts, or eggplants.

Further Reading

Potter, Sulamith Heins. *Family Life in a Northern Thai Village.* Berkeley: University of California Press, 1977.

CLOCK

Although the mechanical timekeeping device known as the clock has been in existence only since the fourteenth century, humankind's need for a reliable means of timekeeping arose long before. This need inspired numerous methods of measurement, including sundials, water clocks, and measured candles. Around 1000 BCE, Egyptian timekeepers made shadow clocks by measuring the shadows cast by posts. Within three centuries, they had refined the system into the sundial, a smaller and more delicate mechanism that relied on the shadow cast by a central gnomon, or indicator, on a circular or arched scale. Near the end of the fourth century BCE, Berosos, a Mesopotamian inventor, created a shadow clock by placing a gnomon at a slant in the ground. In 300 BCE, the seasonally corrected timekeeper of the inventor Ctesibius of Alexandria applied gears to a clepsydra, or water clock. The indicator was a floating pointer that established the hour of the day by indicating a mark on a pillar.

The first reliable mechanical clockwork was a product of the 1300s, when villages measured time by the chiming of the church campanile, or bell tower. An alarm clock, invented in Germany in 1350, brought timepieces into monasteries and the homes of the wealthy. The astronomer Christian Huygens built the first home pendulum clock in 1656, thus enabling kitchen workers to time food preparation by a system accurate to within five minutes. The pocket watch, which Huygens perfected to within two minutes' accuracy in 1675, became the token of professionalism among bakers and grocery draymen.

Using the hourglass or egg glass, a glass timer shaped like a figure eight, cooks began timing phases of the cooking process, such as the span required for blanching vegetables or sterilizing glass jars for canning. When the user upended the device, mercury, pulverized shell, or grains of sand slipped through the narrow neck from the upper globe into the lower one. Hourglasses were treasured items, often fashioned with wood or metal frames and leather bindings. On September 17, 1716, according to an ad in the *Boston News-Letter,* hourglass-maker and repairer James Maxwell had enough business among Massachusetts colonists to set up shop in his home on Water Street.

Colonial homes boasted few farmhouse clocks or pocket watches. Women and kitchen slaves, who rose to prepare breakfast before sunrise, timed the cooking of lunch for field laborers by setting up a noon marker or sundial. When inviting dinner guests, they indicated the time for a holiday meal or reception as sunset, dusk-dark, or early candlelight—all practical terms that people knew and understood.

Home clocks came on the U.S. market in 1806 and were standard household items by 1830, when they replaced the hourglass. In humble open-hearth cooking areas, the kitchen clock probably sat on the mantel. For the cook, key-wound clockworks turned spit jacks in an even round to cook meats on all sides. Portable pantries contained clock frames to ally time keeping with sifters, spice containers, and canisters. Later, battery-operated and electric models hung on the wall.

In February 1908, *House Furnishing Review* advertised a unique English clock that timed tea making. The ad copy chortled: "Johnny Bull likes his cup of tea upon rising….The clock wakes him up, lights a lamp, boils a pint of water, pours the water into handy teapot, puts out the lamp, and rings a gong announcing that tea is ready." (Franklin 1997, 561) The clever timer foretold an era that put increasing numbers of mechanisms to work to rid daily life of guesswork.

A discreet ad in the September 1930 issue of *Good Housekeeping* extolled the Miller line of electric and lever kitchen clocks for modernizing the home. A porcelain console model, molded to give the illusion of standing on a wall shelf, came in bright green, yellow, or blue. The text declared it homey in appearance and easily wiped clean of cooking grime. As was typical of ads of the period, it offered a free booklet, "Striking the Final Note in Kitchen Color Harmony." The next month's issue featured the Century, a model in a stepped case and the same cheery colors. A better grade of clocks, marketed in furniture and jewelry stores, came with eight-day or electric movements.

In the December 1930 issue of *Good Housekeeping*, a photo of a woman stretching precariously from a chair to wind a kitchen clock illustrated the potential hazards of old-fashioned timepieces. To simplify matters, the Portia kitchen clock from New Haven-Westinghouse substituted simple electrical operation for hand-wound technology. A variety of models offered alarm clocks and chiming or chimeless movements. By the post-World War II era, General Electric was targeting cooks with its Chef clock, a combination timekeeper and timer that could be set for increments up to an hour. Available in wall-mounted or shelf models, it came in red, green, ivory, or white to coordinate with the kitchen decor.

The evolution of kitchen electronics rendered the kitchen clock obsolete when manufacturers began installing digital clocks in ovens, microwaves, kitchen televisions, and undercounter radios and CD players. The ubiquitous electronic clock came to symbolize the time stress of the 1990s, the ever-present sense of urgency that threatened to overwhelm the harried populations of modern industrial societies. For cooks at the dawn of the twenty-first century, a rotary timer measured up to ninety-nine minutes and fastened to appliances with a magnet or to the pocket with a clip. Bakers relied on digital wall clocks and appliance clocks as well as portable timers, count-down timers, and extra-loud timers designed for the benefit of double-tasking homemakers who vacuumed or gardened while cooking or baking.

COAL

In northern Europe, coal—a solid fuel composed of highly compressed decomposed vegetable matter—began to replace peat and wood for cooking in the late eleventh century CE. Because it was more compact than wood, it could be burned in a smaller space. As a fuel, however, coal did not function especially well in an open hearth: it lacked sufficient draft, and it produced an unpleasant sooty residue. As early as 1285, Londoners were suffering the effects of smog from the burning of soft coal for heating and cooking.

Old-fashioned coal stoves.
[*© Library of Congress, Prints and Photographs Division (LC-USZ62-23763)*]

Small-holders in northwestern England, Scotland, and Ireland denounced coal fires as evil, stinking, and bad for health.

When fireplaces were repositioned from the center of the room to a side wall, masonry chimney technology alleviated the problem of smoky interiors. To feed oxygen to the interior of the fire, Irish chimney builders excised a shore, a narrow ground channel that fed fresh air from the outside wall to the fire of turf, gorse, *cipíns* (sticks), faggots, or *bom*, a ground local anthracite formed with clay into balls. This method of nourishing coal fires was effective but wasteful of heat, and it gave place to the mechanical floor bellows, which cooks could activate at will.

In the kitchen, coal offered certain advantages over wood. It was easily loaded into a basket or scuttle, and cooking with coal reduced some of the guesswork of temperature control. But the rapidity with which coal burned required piles of chunks, sufficient kindling, and sturdy barrows for frequent refilling of the wood box to keep the meal cooking once it was begun. Coal also created heavy ash and clinkers, which fell from the fire basket, choking the draft and requiring adjustment of the grate bolt to correct uneven burning and to protect the grate from cracking or warping. These logistical considerations made coal unsuitable for heating ovens.

Coal posed further problems as a cooking fuel. Coal fires burned through the bottoms of cauldrons, and they made an ember pile that was too high to accommodate a spider or to roast meat on a horizontal spit. Thus, blacksmiths created a vertical spit, which required new brackets suspended from above and clockwork mechanisms to turn the broach. The kitchen boiler took the place of older vessels, the first step in the development of the three-stage kitchen range. But even with the advent of new stove technology, coal presented challenges, among them the necessity of hiring a servant to fill scuttles, stoke hoppers, scoop out ash, and dispose of it. These activities only added to the general chaos that attended the preparation of a major feast. Late at night or before daylight, another kitchen crew had to work at wiping down surfaces and cleaning flues of the oily soot and dust.

Coal came into general use as a fireplace fuel in New England in the seventeenth century. It was available in Boston as early as 1739, according to an advertisement in the June 4 issue of the *Boston Gazette*. Commander William Foster sold Sunderland Coal directly from his ship *Betty*, which was moored at Long Wharf. In the kitchen, the householder positioned pieces of coal in an iron grate or fire basket made of iron rods. In front, firedogs held spits for the roasting of meat. Useful implements include a scuttle or hod, a shovel-lipped bucket or cylindrical container with a bail and a side handle; holding on to both handles, the fire tender could direct loose coal chunks directly into a fire. A half lid kept coal dust from rising. The laundry copper, a built-in cauldron for heating wash water, sat above a flue heated with coal.

Coal smoke not only dirtied walls and ceilings, it also posed a health hazard to cooks. Denouncing the foul air of the early nineteenth-century kitchen, the French master chef Marie-Antoine Carême declared, "The coal is killing us!" (Montagné 1977, 527) When the smoke problem finally came under control late in the century, the fireplace began to take on more decorative trappings—cameos, plaques, mythological scenes carved in marble—than had the utilitarian models of past centuries.

The invention of the coal stove largely replaced the old-fashioned *paillasse* (charcoal burner) and increased fuel demand after 1819. New York stove maker Jordan Mott invented a stove that would burn anthracite, or "nut coal," formerly considered waste. From his marketing acumen came a generation of eye-catching coal stove advertisements accompanied by offers for extra utensils and pots. Although nut coal was lighter in weight per unit and easier to add to the firebox, it created clouds of greasy smoke and soot, a constant threat to health from flue fires and from particulates in the air.

By 1850, kitchen stoves were replacing fireplace cookery in North America. Because the stove was positioned away from the wall rather than flush against it, the source of heat was more centrally located, which resulted in a warmer room. The transition from fireplace

to stove also shifted the preponderance of the work to women, who could light, stoke, and clean a coal stove without help from men. In advice to the housewife in her book *Family Living on $500 a Year* (1888), Juliet Corson, superintendent of the New York Cooking School, explained:

The best result from coal as a fuel is obtained when the fire is of moderate size, replenished often enough to keep up a steady but not excessive heat. It is a mistake to choke the stove with coal. The heat of the fire can be maintained at an equal point if the fuel is supplied in small quantities often enough to give a clear, bright fire. (p. 268)

In view of coal's many disadvantages, Sarah Tyson Rorer, founder of the Philadelphia Cooking School, urged families to invest in gas as rapidly as possible. In 1900, she told an audience at one of her lecture-demonstrations, "I would feel my life work finished if I could emancipate women from coal cookery." (Weigley 1977, 72) Even after gas-fueled kitchen ranges had come into general use, some families continued to light a coal grate in the study, dining room, nursery, and bedroom.

During the Great Depression, coal companies placed ads in women's magazines emphasizing the cleanliness and efficiency of their fuel. In 1930, the Philadelphia and Reading Coal and Iron Company touted Pennsylvania's hard anthracite as the best fuel for heating and cooking. To encourage a switch to Reading fuel, the company offered free advice to consumers on what size equipment to buy and how to light and stoke it for the longest burn without soot or greasy film. A free booklet, disarmingly titled "Buried Sunshine," explained "the romance of hard coal" in story and pictures. ("A Cleaner, Warmer Summer" 1930, 296)

Further Reading

"A Cleaner, Warmer Summer in Your Home This Winter," *Good Housekeeping*, October 1930, 296.

Girouard, Mark. Life in the English Country House: A Social and Architectural History. New Haven, Conn.: Yale University Press, 1978.

Richards, Ellen H., and Alpheus G. Woodman. *Air, Water, and Food: From a Sanitary Standpoint*. New York: John Wiley & Sons, 1901.

Weigley, Emma Seifrit. *Sarah Tyson Rorer*. Philadelphia: The American Philosophical Society, 1977.

COCHRANE, JOSEPHINE

Although she was the granddaughter of John Fitch, a designer of hydraulic pumps and builder of steamboats, Josephine Garis Cochrane, creator of the first mechanical dishwasher, might seem to have been an unlikely inventor. Born in 1838 in Shelbyville, Illinois, she became the wife of William Cochrane, a wealthy merchant and politician, and lived in a large home well staffed with servants. Although widowed in her early forties, she remained socially active. In 1882, contemplating the delicate glassware and china her dinner guests had used that evening, she pictured the damage her fine pieces might incur at the hands of her kitchen staff and decided to wash them herself.

Four years later, tired of ruining her hands with hot soapy water, Cochrane measured the size and shape of her dishes and made a schematic drawing showing how jets of water could be aimed to strike the dish surfaces from several angles. The concept was more sophisticated than that of inventor L.A. Alexander, who, in 1865, had patented a hand-cranked geared device that spun a rack of dishes through water. Cochrane hired an engineer to build a mechanical dishwasher composed of dish compartments atop a wheel and brass boiler. In a woodshed, he assembled wire brackets and pulleys to be levered into the washtub. With a soap-and-water assembly at the base, the user hand-pumped a continuous spray for the wash cycle. The washing procedure ended with boiling rinse water poured on by hand. Dishes then air-dried in the rack.

After patenting the idea, Cochrane hired an Illinois firm to build her dishwasher. The first customers of the Garis-Cochrane Dish-Washing Machine Company were her friends. The company also placed ads, written by Cochrane herself, in periodicals aimed at hoteliers, stewards, restaurateurs, innkeepers, and managers of hospitals. Chicago's two largest hotels installed her washers at a cost of $150 each. At the 1893 Columbian Exposition in Chicago, she promoted the apparatus, winning first prize in international competition for a durable, adaptable mechanical construction. Her booth drew nine buyers from concessions needing a dishwasher.

Practical and ideological obstacles hampered widespread adoption of the device. Some potential customers did not have enough hot water to operate the whirling jets. The notion of relieving women's burden of household labors earned the scorn of some clergymen, who believed kitchen work the god-assigned task of females, as specified in the book of Genesis. Familiar with the fate of seamstresses after the invention of the sewing machine, professional kitchen workers objected to any machine that would replace them or deny them work. The most irate of these workers in Chicago and New York attempted to unionize to fight mechanization.

Nonetheless, Cochrane's corporation produced numerous upgrades, including the Garis-Cochrane Dishwashing Machine, patented in 1900, which featured an oscillating dish rack that could wash and dry 120 dishes in one minute. Her subsequent innovations added a revolving washer, centrifugal pump, and draining hose to the initial machinery. At her death from a stroke in 1913, she left a healthy business that her heirs sold a decade later to the Hobart Corporation, founders of the KitchenAid brand, which they introduced in 1949.

Further Reading

Longe, Jacqueline L., ed. *How Products Are Made*. Farmington Hills, Mich.: Gale, 2000.

COCONUT

The coconut is the fruit of the long-lived coconut palm, *Cocos nucifera*. In addition to providing valuable nutrients and rehydrating fluids, this graceful tree supplies the tropics with useful craft materials. According to an adage from Oceania, the planters of the coconut

A Manila dwarf coconut palm on the grounds of the Tropical Agriculture Research Station in Mayaguez, Puerto Rico.
[© *Courtesy of Agricultural Research Service, USDA. Photo by Scott Bauer.*]

tree guarantee their families food, drink, vessels, clothes, shelter, and a heritage for their offspring. Elaine Morgan's *The Descent of Woman* (1972) corroborated the belief that the coconut shell may have been among the earliest kitchen canisters. A staple in pre-Columbian South America, the fruit appears to have been transported around the Pacific from Indo-Malaya, where it originated. It passed from planters in the Indian Ocean to Egyptian gardeners around 500 CE. From there traders carried it over trade routes around the Mediterranean.

In *The Travels of Marco Polo* (1299), the celebrated Venetian traveler described the qualities of the "pharaoh's nut" to Europeans, who had little knowledge of it. Traders from the Indian Ocean to the Suez carried coconuts as curiosities and as natural refreshment for sailors between ports. In Indonesia, cooks drank the water from young fruit and spooned the flesh into cooling drinks. Older fruit produced milk and flesh for cooking, along with oil, a husk to fuel the cooking fire, and a hard shell for fashioning into kitchen implements and containers. A hand tool from the mid-1800s, the coconut grater, perhaps an English invention for use in the Caribbean, operated serrated blades with a hand crank to shred coconut meat still attached to the shell.

The American novelist Herman Melville, an authority on life in the southern Pacific islands, glorified the native cuisine in two semi-autobiographical works: *Typee: A Peep at Polynesian Life* (1846), an episodic summary of Nukuhivan life, and its sequel, *Omoo: Adventures in the South Seas* (1847). In the latter, he describes a lavish seaside feast that included steamed fish, calabashes of poi, and Indian turnips mashed and kneaded into cakes with coconut milk. The coconut also provided a beverage: "In the spaces between the three dishes, were piled young cocoa-nuts, stripped of their husks. Their eyes had been opened and enlarged; so that each was a ready-charged goblet." (Melville 1987, 260–261) In 1929, the anthropologist Bronislaw Malinowski, author of *The Sexual Life of Savages*, described how Trobriand Island women filled coconut-shell containers at the waterhole and stoppered them with twisted palm leaves.

The ringed trunk of the coconut palm creates a series of footholds that enable climbers to reach the top to harvest nuts growing under a topnot of feathery fronds. In southeast Asia and the South Pacific, the plant's gifts to the table and kitchen include a refreshing beverage of sterile water so pure that it was used as a substitute for plasma during World War II. The coconut palm supplies a milk substitute for cow's milk, a sweet meat called *copra,* a fermented toddy called *arrack,* palm cabbage, hearts of palm for salads, dessert and beverage flavoring, sugar, margarine, and vegetable oil, in addition to a number of nonedible products

such as skin emollients. From the fiber, called *coir,* comes material for thatching, rope, mats, baskets, fish nets, and many other domestic uses. The external surface is so tough that it works well as a grater for coconut meat.

Islanders in the South Seas consider the coconut shell a natural lunchbox. The pointed end of the tough, fibrous husk is a suitable shape for carving into cups, scoops, spoons, and scrapers; however, the rounded end containing the eyes must be discarded as too weak to hold liquids safely.

Although some historians assume that sea currents carried the coconut to the Society Islands, according to the native Hawaiian botanist Isabella Aiona Abbott, Polynesian immigrants brought the coconut palm. Polynesian adventurers who settled Kaho'Olawe, the smallest of Hawaii's eight major land masses, may have stocked their outrigger canoes with coconuts and hollow coconut shells filled with fresh water. The coconut's use in cuisine remained limited to stews and *haupia* (pudding) until newcomers from the Philippines and southeast Asia enlarged the number of recipes from their own traditions.

The coconut's unique natural package remained valuable into the 1940s. While sailing the *Kon-Tiki* raft from Peru to Polynesia in 1947, the Norwegian anthropologist Thor Heyerdahl depended on dried coconuts as the ideal food and liquid containers for the long sea voyage. His inquiry into Marquesan history proved that ancestors of the present-day population had carried the coconut on a long raft journey from South America. During his residence in the Marquesas Islands, he wrote *Fatu-Hiva: Back to Nature* (1974), in which he expressed admiration for the prolific banana but acknowledged that he preferred the coconut palm. As described in his account, the tall, swaying trees regularly dropped their fruits on fertile ground, which readily sprouted more palms. Cooks fried slices of breadfruit in oil from the coconut meat.

In the 1990s in Valley of Peace, Belize, Maud Adolphus, a local cook, demonstrated the baking of fresh coconut and coconut milk into *pan de coco* (coconut bread) for Mennonite recipe collectors from Reading, Pennsylvania. On her makeshift stove—a truck tire rim heated on open flame, topped with a barrel lid, and heaped with coals—the dough balls cooked into round loaves. Refugees at the Valley of Peace settlement declared that three small loaves of coconut bread nourished them for a many-day journey by bus and on foot when they fled north to Belize escaping civil unrest in El Salvador.

The coconut remains a culinary staple in many parts of the world. In the Seychelles, an island cluster off Africa's southeast coast, coconuts are the source of *calou,* a local beer, which distributors sell in bamboo containers. Malaysian cooks value the heavy cream that rises to the top of freshly pressed coconut milk as a thickener or topping. A second pressing produces a thinner liquid, used as the base for fish, rice, and vegetable dishes. In Hindu birthday and wedding rituals, celebrants break coconuts for good luck. A coconut palm planted at a child's birth records its age in the number of rings formed on the trunk.

Further Reading

Frawley-Holler, Janis, "The Coconut Palm," *Islands,* November 2000, 28.
Koene, Ada Henne, "Culinary Reconnaissance: Indonesia," *Aramco World,* January–February 1996, 18–27.
Rajah, Carol Selva. *Makan-Lah!: The True Taste of Malaysia.* Sydney, Australia: HarperCollins, 1996.

COFFEE

The enthusiasm for the beverage known as coffee dates to the discovery of the red berries of the evergreen shrub *Coffea* in Sudan and Abyssinia. According to legend, in the ninth century CE, the Ethiopian goat boy Kaldi observed the energizing effect of the berries on kids nibbling at the low-growing plants. He presented some of the berries to the local Christian abbot, who, fearing that coffee was a satanic plant, immediately jettisoned the lot into the fire. Thinking better of this hasty act, the abbot retrieved the toasted beans. He then mixed them with water and shared the drink with fellow monks. The fable conveniently manages to explain not only the discovery of the beans but also the origins of roasting and brewing.

Origins in the Middle East

Arabians and North Africans first ate coffee beans as a stimulant. They chopped them with fat and added them to their camel packs to provide energy for long journeys and military campaigns. Arab doctors advocated the consumption of coffee as a tonic or medicine. Muslims, forbidden by the Koran to drink alcohol, tentatively sampled the brew. Convinced of its value, they welcomed the new beverage, which brewers prepared in their tents and served in the open air. The magical drink, at first guarded as a secret, spread to the hosts of pilgrims and merchants who traversed the Middle East.

In the early 800s, after traders carried Ethiopian beans to Yemen, the Mufti of Aden became the first coffee drinker identified by name. An embroidered inscription claims that Chadely or Scyadly, a Sufi imam, drank coffee to keep him awake for late-night prayers and whirling, ecstatic dances. He passed along his discovery to other dervishes, who created a demand for coffee among Mohammed's most devout mullahs. Coffee makers were soon brewing the drink at mosques, before the Ka'aba at Mecca, at the tomb of the Prophet, and throughout the Muslim realm. The service of coffee and sweets to male guests extended the use of the Syrian *madafah* (guest hall), a room devoted to hospitality and business conferences.

By 1100, Arabian growers were cultivating plots of coffee plants, which workers soaked, depulped, and dried before seeding and husking. Coffee brewers evolved a system of roasting and boiling the residue into liquid to make *qahwa* or *gahwah*, Arabia's wine, served with peppercorns and salt. In the next century, the *qahveh khaneh* (coffee house) sprang up, providing refreshment, relaxation, music, and gambling. In the 1500s, Yemeni coffee growers grew rich from expanded trade.

Turks were the next to claim coffee, which they called *kahveh* or *kavé* and pulverized with a steel crank grinder. A shop owner specialized in thick, syrupy coffee in Constantinople in 1475; in 1554, two cafe owners founded the first coffeehouses, humorously called "schools of wisdom." The server offered small half-cups to friends, beginning with the eldest and most revered. Those receiving a full cup took the gesture as an insult. Traveling artist Jacques Le Hay's line drawing "Turkish Coffee" (1714) depicts the graceful Turkish hostess, armed with a towel, carrying a steaming *ibrik* pot in the left hand and tray of sweetmeats in the right. The ease with which her guest dips a cookie into a small handle-less cup imparts a serenity to social interaction, perhaps enhanced by coffee drinking.

Adoption by Europeans

In 1607, the Middle Eastern coffee craze migrated to Jamestown, Virginia, after Captain John Smith imported beans; eight years later, the drink advanced to the *botteghes* of Venice, a world port and natural disseminator of fad foods. With the rise in coffee consumption, the demand for sugar increased as an antidote to the bitter liquid. The first brew house opened in Oxford, England, in 1637 when a Turkish Jew named Jacob began pouring cups for customers. Coffee brewers served the drink with butter, spice, ale, and wine before settling on cream and sugar as the best additive. Temperance-minded crusaders connected beer with debauchery and coffee with sobriety and health.

Until a name for the drink crystallized in the public's mind, the English called coffee *chaoua,* then *cahoa,* which changed to *cahue* in 1615 and *coho* in

1638. It was not until 1650 that the term stabilized as *coffey* or *coffee*. Advertisements identified the popular beverages of the day by nationality—coffee was a Middle Eastern drink, chocolate was West Indian, and tea, Chinese. In 1669, Suleiman Aga, envoy to the court of Louis XIV, introduced the French to coffee. A French adventurer named Desclieux transported the coffee plant to Martinique, from whence it passed to French Guiana, Central America, and Brazil. Slaves were charged with the jobs of winnowing, cleaning, drying, and hulling the green beans.

In 1674, during the bawdy era that followed the end of Puritan rule and the restoration of Charles II to the throne of England, London women issued *The Women's Petition Against Coffee Representing to Publick Consideration the Grand Inconveniences Accruing to their Sex from the Excessive Use of the Drying, Enfeebling Liquor.* The anonymous authors signed the document "a well-wisher" and identified as spokespersons "several Thousands of Buxome Good-Women, Languishing in Extremity of Want." *(The Women's Petition,* 1674, n. p.) The ribald text charged that drinking this "boiled soot" cost men their "Old English Vigour." Too much coffee, they asserted, made men "as unfruitful as those Deserts whence that unhappy Berry is said to have been brought." They claimed that coffee led men "to trifle away their time, scald their Chops, and spend their Money, all for a little base, black, thick, nasty, bitter, stinking nauseous Puddlewater." (Ibid.)

Certain anonymous males riposted with *The Men's Answer to the Women's Petition Against Coffee* (1674), subtitled, "Vindicating Their Own Performances, and the Vertues of That Liquor, from the Undeserved Aspersions Lately Cast upon Them by Their Scandalous Pamphlet." It spelled out the value of coffee in promoting vigorous erections and full ejaculations. To justify their claims, the men cited earlier statements by William Harvey, the English physician who discovered the mysteries of the human circulatory system and advocated coffee drinking as a lubricant to the body's natural functions. In the 1670s, however, the racy debate over coffee's effects on sexual function gained little comment from the medical community.

Coffeehouse Culture

Despite prevalent misinformation that coffee caused mental illness and sterility, England opened its first faddish coffeehouse in 1652, when an Armenian (or Greek) named Pasqua Rosee set up a coffeehouse at St. Michael's Alley in Cornhill, London. Diarist Samuel Pepys noted that a London brew house, Miles's coffeehouse, offered the drink in 1660, the year in

which the royalists trounced the Puritans, ended the Commonwealth, and brought the exiled King Charles II to the throne. Pictorial business placards depicted a Sultan's profile or a Turkish coffee urn as an enticement to customers. Coffee bars, dubbed "penny universities," paired two essentials, conversation and a lively drink that boosted energy and overcame inhibition. Some establishments offered barbering, wig-fitting, games, music, and gambling as adjuncts to the relaxing, male-centered atmosphere. Patrons often received their mail at their favorite coffeehouses.

Political factions tended to gather at particular coffeehouses, a practice that was troubling to the crown. On December 29, 1675, Charles II proclaimed the "Suppression of Coffee-Houses," a stern admonition to rabble-rousers conducting their activities under the guise of polite socializing. He declared:

By occasion of the meetings of such persons therein, divers False, Malitious and Scandalous Reports are devised and spread abroad, to the Defamation of his Majesties Government, and to the Disturbance of the Peace and Quiet of this Realm; his Majesty hath thought it fit and necessary, That the said Coffee-Houses be (for the future) Put down and Suppressed. (Baxter 1998, 9)

To assure success, he dispatched justices of the peace to halt as well the consumption of "Chocolet, Sherbett or Tea, as [sellers] will answer the contrary at their utmost perils." (Ibid.)

New York City opened its first coffee establishments, the Tontine Coffee House and Merchants' Coffee House, both in what is now the financial district, in the 1670s. The drink caught on during the American Revolution in part because patriots boycotted tea to avoid heavy taxation by the English crown. The Tontine welcomed the entrepreneurs and financiers who founded the New York Stock Exchange. The custom of tipping came from coffee servers encouraging TIPS, an acronym for "To Insure Prompt Service," a monetary gift left by the cup or tossed into a tin on the counter as a bribe for front-row seating.

Vienna had its own coffeehouse in 1683, after defeated Ottoman forces fled the area, leaving behind sacks of coffee beans. The Viennese coffee bar became so popular a gathering place that artists and philosophers had their mail delivered to their tables. Venice became a coffee center in 1763, boasting more than 2,000 shops. The demand for coffee threatened to put sellers of lemonade and wine out of business.

Newly arrived in Paris in 1672, coffee was first served to the public in 1686 at Le Procope, owned by a Sicilian named Francesco Procopio de' Coltelli, who also sold fruit preserves and ices. At the St. Germaine Fair, Parisians patronized the first coffee kiosk in 1675; vendors wheeled the drink door-to-door in portable urns heated at the base with charcoal. Later, the plotters of the French Revolution gathered at the Café des Patriotes for coffee and sedition.

England's legendary insurance firm Lloyd's of London began in 1688 as Edward Lloyd's coffeehouse, an establishment where many maritime financiers and ship owners gathered to relax and discuss business. As early as 1696, English coffeehouses evolved into gentlemen's clubs, beginning with White's and followed by the Cocoa Tree, St. James, Boodles, Brook's, and the Reform Club, whose kitchen boasted the culinary talents of Alexis Benoît Soyer, chef extraordinaire. At first, amenities included beverages, gaming, free discussions, and the absence of women. In the Victorian era, members looked forward to gourmet fare presented by liveried servants and to an after-meal smoke, discussion, quiet reading, and perusal of the news. On the street, the wheeled coffee stalls offered cups and pitchers of cream at self-service urns.

The reputation of coffee went through many phases. One German prince dismissed the drink as a womanish beverage not suited to beer-quaffing males. After accession to the papal throne in 1592, Pope Clement VIII rejected a plea from Italian priests to ban coffee consumption as an adjunct to sin and sanctified the drink with a mock baptism. In 1656, the grand vizier of the Ottoman Empire closed coffeehouses, banned private, consumption, and punished scofflaws with a dunking in the Bosporus. In 1734, the composer Johann Sebastian Bach, sympathizing with neglected wives, wrote the "Coffee Cantata" in recognition of the dedication of men to the drink. His composition also acknowledged Frederick the Great's failed ban on coffee drinking for German women on the grounds that it impaired fertility.

In 1721, German drinkers acquired their first coffeehouse in Berlin but did not launch the popular afternoon tradition of the *kaffeeklatsch* until 1900. These informal gatherings for conversation, cards, and refreshments were a boost to women workers, whom patriarchal German males banned from coffeehouses, which they considered a threat to female morals.

After courtiers of August II of Poland established Warsaw's first café in 1724, coffee contributed to a crusade against drunkenness, which marred banquets and receptions. To promote the brewing of coffee rather than the fermentation of potatoes into vodka, Father Krusínski, a Jesuit priest, published a Latin treatise, *Pragmatographia de Legitimo Usu of Turkish Ambrosias* (Description of the Proper Use of Turkish Coffee, 1759). Polish housewives supported the campaign by roasting their own beans directly before brewing.

Worldwide Commodity

The enthusiasm for coffee spread via trade routes that linked countries and governments. Speculating and trading in coffee centered in Holland in 1690 after the Dutch began to cultivate coffee plantations in Java, a locale whose name became a synonym for the drink. Smugglers transported the jealously guarded plants from Mocha harbor in Arabia to Ceylon and the East Indies.

The Sun King, Louis XIV of France, developed the habit of drinking coffee with sugar after the Turkish envoy introduced the beverage at court. Louis received a coffee tree in 1713. Offshoots of the parent plant traveled from the Paris greenhouse of French botanist Bernard de Jussieu to Martinique in 1720. An alternate history claims that a French naval officer, Captain Gabriel de Clieu, brought the first commercial plant in the Americas to Martinique in 1723. Having survived sabotage by a Dutch passenger, a pirate attack, and a Caribbean hurricane, de Clieu placed his seedling under guard. Within four years, island coffee growers were cultivating millions of plants. However the first plant arrived in the New World, coffee planting spread to Jamaica, where growers developed the unique Blue Mountain strain. As the bean's popularity advanced to South America, Brazilian farmers acquired their first plants in 1727.

Coffee growing and production created a distinct chapter in Hawaiian history. The main island earned a reputation for high-quality kona, a full-bodied arabica coffee favored by gourmets and priced accordingly. Coffee cultivation was first attempted, unsuccessfully, in the early nineteenth century by Don Francisco de Paula Marin, a Spanish settler who established vineyards in Hawaii and brought the pineapple to the islands. After the deaths of King Kamehameha II and Queen Kamamalu in 1824 from measles during a state visit to Britain, Governor Boki of Oahu retrieved their remains aboard the H.M.S. *Blonde*. On the long journey to the Pacific, he halted at Rio de Janiero to buy coffee plants for cultivation in Hawaii. In 1825, Boki, aided by the agronomist John Wilkinson, sponsored a successful planting in Manoa Valley, Oahu, where the temperate climate and moist, fertile red soil nurtured the most flavorful beans.

From Oahu, the Reverend Samuel Ruggles brought *Coffea arabica* cuttings to Kealakekua-Kona, Hawaii. By 1898, coffee plants covered more than 6,000 acres of the Kona hills at a time when the vacuum pack revolutionized wrapping and shipping. Cultivation by native Hawaiians and Chinese labor prefigured the dominance of Asian farmers. Waves of Japanese and Filipinos continued the tradition, loading sacks of ripe beans on donkeys, called Kona nightingales.

The hybridization of the coffee plant in its many growing locations resulted in unique bean types becoming associated with specific countries. The table below lists the major types and their countries of origin.

Arabica	Cameroon, Colombia, Costa Rica, Ecuador, El Salvador, Ethiopia, Guatemala, Hawaii, Kenya, Mexico, Tanzania
Blue Mountain	Jamaica
Bourbon Santos	Brazil
Celebes	Indonesia
Chanchanati	Peru
Hawar	Ethiopia
Java	Indonesia
Kilimanjaro	Tanzania
Kona	Hawaii
Maracaibo	Venezuela
Mocha	Yemen
Mysore	India
Robusta	Cameroon, Java, southeast Asia, India, Madagascar, the East African coast
Santo Domingos	Dominican Republic
Sumatra	Indonesia

Innovations

In 1901, Sartori Kato began introducing the American public to powdered coffee at the Pan-American Exposition in Buffalo, New York. In 1903, Ludwig Roselius, a German importer of coffee beans, observed that seawater had accidentally decaffeinated beans in a ship's hold. He achieved his plan to make caffeine-free coffee with the invention of Sanka (the name was derived from the words *sans caffeine*). By 1905, Italian firms were selling their own versions of decaffeinated coffee.

In Guatemala in 1906, an Englishman named Washington observed the formation of coffee powder on the spout of a silver urn. After some experimentation, he began marketing instant coffee in 1909. Around this same time, the firm founded by Melitta Bentz, the German housewife who invented the coffee filter, began marketing drip coffeemakers. In the 1930s, the height of freshness was vacuum-sealed cans made of tinned steel; the special metal keys required to open them came with the cans.

Americans quickly made Maxwell House coffee a must-have commodity after its invention in 1880 by wholesale grocer Joel O. Cheek of Nashville, Tennessee. The emergence of restaurant chefs and professional cooks into the limelight increased the practice of endorsement of name brands in women's magazines. In the April 1925 issue of *Good Housekeeping*, an advertisement for Maxwell House Coffee from the Cheek-Neal Coffee Company quoted Antoine, the noted New Orleans chef, who testified that he had put an end to complaints about restaurant coffee by introducing diners to Maxwell House. The ad's whimsical scenario concluded with the rescue of the establishment's reputation through service of better-tasting coffee.

Distributors of G. Washington's instant coffee advertised in the October 1930 issue of *Good Housekeeping*, citing Samuel C. Prescott, an authority on coffee. The text stated that the product, made by the infusion method, was pure and unadulterated. A drawing pictured Prescott, a professor of industrial microbiology and director of biology and public health at the Massachusetts Institute of Technology, holding a test tube of coffee up to natural light for examination. The ads for Sanka Coffee in the same issue stressed the benefits of decaffeination: restful sleep untroubled by jangled nerves. The copy claimed that the manufacturing process removed 97 percent of the caffeine—without destroying flavor.

While aiding Brazil in marketing a surplus of beans, Nestlé, a Swiss firm, developed its instant coffee, Nescafé, which retained flavorful oils through a process of freeze-drying. In *Woman's Home Companion* and other domestic magazines, ads for hot and iced Nescafé pictured sophisticated drinkers enjoying drinks and camaraderie in relaxed settings. The name *Nescafé* became the generic European term for American coffee, which is thinner-bodied and less robust than European and Middle Eastern coffees.

Another Century of Sipping

At the turn of the twenty-first century, coffee remained a favorite mealtime beverage or after-dinner dessert-and-conversation drink for much of the world, including Cuba, Slovenia, Honduras, Finland, Saudi Arabia, Canada, France, Colombia, Costa Rica, and the United States. Finns led the world in coffee consumption, with an average of five cups per day. In Eastern Europe the cafés of Bucharest, Budapest, Cracow, and Prague survived the stultifying Communist regime to appeal to a burgeoning tourist trade. At the Berliner Kaffeehaus in Alexanderplatz, coffee drinkers still read the news in a daily tradition that dates to the bourgeoisie of pre-Marxist times. Turkish coffee is still premium stock worldwide for its strength and aroma.

As of 2000, London's International Coffee Organization computed the consumption of coffee in the United States at more than three billion pounds of beans per year. For the convenience of their patrons, hotels, motels, and cruise liners equipped guest rooms with small coffeemakers and the necessary supplies to brew the first cup of the day. In restaurants, offices, and home kitchens lightweight thermal carafes kept the beverage fresh and hot and dispensed a cup without dripping. In cars, on trains, and on foot commuters sipped from disposable cups or heat-retaining thermal mugs with tight-fitting tops that prevented spills.

Street vendors in Zanzibar serve small handleless cups of brew poured from a tall brass carafe capped with a conical top. Jordanians enjoy *qahwah saadah,* a bitter beverage sipped slowly from small cups. In Ethiopia, where coffee drinking began, hosts still pour after-dinner cups from ornate serving sets. Sudanese coffee makers prefer either Turkish brews or *jebbana,* spiced coffee. In other parts of Africa where coffee is scarce, drinkers substitute ground baobab seed. Malaysian brewers toss spiced masala coffee back and forth between two jugs held at arm's length until they produce a hand-made froth.

See also **Coffeemaker; Glass**

Further Reading

Baxter, Jacki. *The Coffee Book.* Royston, Hertfordshire: Eagle Editions, 1998.
"A German Coffee-Party in 1862," *English Woman's Journal,* December 1, 1862.
Khouri, Rami G., "Room for Tradition," *Aramco World,* May–June 1993, 10–17.
The Men's Answer to the Women's Petition Against Coffee. (reprint) London, 1674.
Römer, Joachim, and Michael Ditter, chief eds. *Culinaria: European Specialties.* Cologne, Ger.: Könemann, 1995.
Smith, Roff, "The Road to Zanzibar," *Islands,* July–August 2000, 82–97.
Williams, Jacqueline, "Food on the Oregon Trail," *Overland Journal,* Vol. 11, 1993.
The Women's Petition Against Coffee. (reprint) London, 1674.

COFFEEMAKER

The proper brewing of coffee has intrigued a host of inventors and tinkerers, prompting them to create innumerable devices for the introduction of water to ground coffee beans. In addition to coffeemakers per se, hundreds of methods and devices have been developed for the optimal roasting and grinding of the beans.

One of the earliest coffeemakers, the biggin drip coffee urn carried the name of its otherwise anonymous inventor. Devised around 1800, it was a table-model coffee server composed of a tin cylinder that slid over a rod and rested on a pot below. Boiling water poured onto the upper segment passed through the ground beans and dripped into the bottom container. A strainer on each piece removed any sources of bitterness. Somewhat awkward for its height, the biggin came in tin, granite ware, and flowered enamelware; silver models rested on ornate stands. In some models,

both segments sported handles. A table set paired the biggin with matching sugar bowl and creamer. The two-stage pot was a favorite of the French, German, and Dutch, who preferred a gentle brew. A still-popular version is the French biggin for making creole coffee.

In New England and along the Atlantic seaboard, coffee roasting took place in a large tin tumbler mounted over a range, a smaller cylindrical model, or a long-handled roaster with lid-mounted stirrer, suitable for camping and travel. A meticulous cook, Sarah Josepha Hale, editor of *Godey's Ladies Book* and author of *The Good Housekeeper* (1839), complained of the American style of coffee-making, which produced a beverage harmful to the dyspeptic and those inclined toward nervousness. For making a clear, rich drink, she urged "[breaking] into it an egg yolk, white, shell and all." (Hale 1966, 111) For settling the grounds, she advised the brewer to pour in a teacupful of cold water or adding a scraped cod skin.

In the mid-nineteenth century, cylindrical, round, and boxy coffee roasters came on the market in large numbers equipped with methods of agitating the beans to assure an even roast. In 1849, the inventor Thomas R. Wood of Cincinnati, Ohio, patented a hinged globe mounted on a three-legged frame with a bail for rotating beans as they heated on a hearth or stove. In 1854, William Law of London developed a similar commercial roaster that revolved horizontally to blend beans evenly over a firebox. A simpler iron roaster, advertised in the *American Home Cook Book* (1854) by "an American Lady," was shaped like a saucepan with a top-mounted stirring handle; it came with sensible advice to add a tablespoonful of water to each pound of beans to keep the mix from burning. More high-tech was a device produced by C. A. Mills of Hazel Green, Wisconsin, and patented in 1863. It consisted of a wire canister for holding beans in a cast-iron frame. The user capped the device with a tin cover and wound the clockwork key to set the beans on a steady rotation. The common wood, iron, or tin grinder came with either top- or side-mounted handles. The handles turned flywheels that powdered the beans, which fell from the hopper to the collection box below. By the early 1900s, most American families ground and roasted coffee beans for their breakfast beverage.

To end the need for a coffee roaster, some mid-nineteenth century packagers offered an innovation in labor-free freshness—pre-roasted or ground coffee sealed in waterproof, airtight packages and guaranteed to retain strength. During the Civil War, Union soldiers received their coffee allotment in paste form mixed with sugar and cream; Confederates roasted their green coffee beans in kettles and spiders. The Arbuckle Brothers of Pittsburgh patented a method of sealing in flavor by coating roasted beans with sugar and egg white. Because Arbuckle's coffee could be packaged and shipped, it was popular with campers and Westerners. Roasters began using hot air and natural gas in the process in 1885.

The popularity of the drink created a demand for ceramic beverage sets, resulting in unique coffee service in many lands. Coffee and coffee-making equipment evolved from awkward boiling-and-straining methods in enameled or tin boilers to ornate enamel urns and silver samovars. The first espresso maker was perfected in France in 1822, a year after Pierre-Joseph Pelletier isolated caffeine as a natural stimulant in the bean. In 1830, Robert Napier created the dual-chamber vacuum siphon, which evolved into a two-stage coffeepot accessed by a spigot on the side. In the 1830s, coffeehouses featured drip pots heated with alcohol burners. Italian-made home models by Pavoni and Snider applied steam pressure to drive hot water up a central tube and over ground coffee. As the brown liquid dripped through the mesh basket, it colored the liquid below and spread an appealing aroma. The brown spurt in the glass dome at the center of the lid attested to the readiness of the coffee brew.

During the twentieth century, coffee inspired additional innovations. The Kin-Hee pot, patented in 1900, was a topsy-turvy two-stage operation beginning with the removal of the top section to fill with coffee and boiling water. After attaching a straining cloth, the brewer plopped the coffeepot upside down over the top section, inverted, and poured. Manufactured by the James Heekin company in Cincinnati and by Eby, Blain in Toronto, the unusual pot debuted at the Chicago Pan-American Exposition along with the manufacturer's own brand of mocha-java.

For daily consumption, homeowners could operate the top-mounted crank on the box-shaped wood coffee mill that Sears, Roebuck offered for 52 cents in 1908. A cheaper model at 44 cents paled in comparison to the grand $4.68 coffee and spice mill with paired flywheels and attractive maroon and gold finish, suited to office or store use. Imported Turkish coffee mills met competition in the form of copies from Landers, Frary & Clark sold in the 1909 Albert Pick catalog, which offered an alternative to the discerning, penny-wise homemaker. Instead of gears and wheels, the sleek black japanned cylinder adorned with decorative banding bore a knobbed crank at top, the only evidence of its internal mechanism.

In 1910, Alfred Cohn created a seemingly effortless method of brewing the drink called the Cona vacuum pot, a two-chamber device that used the heating and cooling action of vapor to force hot water over ground coffee. Drinkers were so taken with the ritual of coffee and the sophisticated sets of table implements and cups designed for coffee serving that furniture designer began producing coffee tables around 1920. World War II was a high point in coffee consumption, when factory supervisors encouraged a coffee break to energize workers.

Innovations exploited the loyalty of coffee drinkers. In the 1920s, the Hobart coffee grinder simplified the task of cranking beans to powder; West Bend further demystified coffee making by marketing the filterless Flavo-Drip pot. A true deviation from the norm was the American Silen drip pot that perched on a stand-alone electric hot plate, thus freeing up space on the stove top. Both Alfonso Bialetti and Ernest Lily created automatic espresso makers in 1933; four years later, S. W. Farber produced a thermostatically controlled vacuum pot called the Coffee Robot, a boon to those who tended to wander away and forget they had left their brew on the stove. In 1941, Peter Schlumbohm designed a classic, handleless beaker vessel much admired for its sleek hourglass shape and bonded filters.

The year 1938 was an outstanding one for innovations in coffeemakers. KitchenAid introduced an electric coffee grinder that ended awkward hand-grinding in restaurants, coffee shops, and homes. Improvements to commercial and home coffeemakers continued in 1945 in Milan with Achilles Gaggia's double-valve pot that dispensed hot coffee with a foamy *crema* (cream top), produced under high pressure with a piston designed by Cremonesi. The piston coffee machine yielded so flavorful a beverage that it was soon found over much of Europe and the Americas. Within a few years, Gaggia began manufacturing the Gilda, a home-size espresso maker named for a 1946 *film noir* character played by Rita Hayworth. In the next decade, Milan's Faema Company competed with Gaggia by marketing an instantaneous system that heated water to 200 degrees Fahrenheit and pumped it through the coffee.

In post-World War II France, the café standard was the dramatic *cafetière,* a glass pot in which water was forced onto ground coffee with the downward stroke of a plunger. Bodum of Denmark pioneered the Presso Bistro, its own *cafetière,* in 1974. In the 1950s, electric coffee mills equipped with whirring blades refined grains to custom blend for percolator, drip pot, or filter pot. Canadian coffee machines dominated the market after 1991, when Caffè Carissimi Canada emulated equipment distributed by Franco Carissimi of Bergamo, Italy.

At the turn of the twenty-first century, the boom in popularity of chic coffee shops such as Starbucks was paralleled by a surge in new home brewing equipment that promised greater convenience and consistent quality. Home coffee roasters, grinders, brewers, and espresso makers proliferated, and manufacturers competed by offering innovative features such as cup warmers, thermal carafes, programmable timers, and dual brewing systems for making regular and decaffeinated coffee simultaneously.

See also **Bentz, Melitta**

Further Reading

Baxter, Jacki. *The Coffee Book*. Royston, Hertfordshire: Eagle Editions, 1998.

Hale, Sarah Josepha. *Early American Cookery: "The Good Housekeeper, 1841,"* Mineola, N. Y.: Dover Publications, 1966.

COLONIAL KITCHENS, AMERICAN

Like many who leave home to settle in unknown lands, the first colonists in the New World were intrepid souls endowed with a spirit of adventure. The most successful were those who readily shucked off European class distinctions, expected no luxuries, and acclimated to the use of hatchet and rifle. A willingness to partake of strange new foods was also crucial to survival.

The 101 newcomers arriving from Southampton, England, on the *Mayflower* had little room on board for household goods. The cookware and utensils that made the trip had to fit in small chests. Newly arrived cooks made do until they could duplicate items common in English homes with versions fashioned in New England workshops. Later voyages brought heirloom pieces—hutch tables, settles, rush-bottomed chairs, dining tables, sideboards, cupboards—to replace the plain, unfinished oak trestle tables, hewed from whole tree trunks, which colonists erected for meals and dismantled, washed, and set on end between meals. Subsequent arrivals also increased the population of coopers, carpenters, joiners, smiths, mechanics, and others whose specialized skills were much in need.

Colonial era fireplace.
[*© Library of Congress, Prints and Photographs Division (LC-USZ62-113458)*]

Adapt or Starve

The first meals in the new land consisted of strange new fish, game, and plants. In 1612, Captain John Smith of Jamestown, Virginia, wrote, "Wee had more sturgeon then could be devoured by dogge and man; of which the industrious, by drying and pownding, mingled with caviare, sorrel, and other wholsome hearbs, would make bread and good meate; others would gather as much tochwough roots in a day, as would make them bread a weeke, so that of those wilde fruites, fish and berries, these lived very well." (Grivetti 2001) He concluded on a poignant note that "such was the most strange condition of some 150, [if they had not been forced] to gather and prepare their victuall they would all have starved," a fate that did befall some of the newcomers. (Ibid.) Smith knew there were no alternatives to acclimatization. He ordered all to collect and eat unfamiliar plants.

In Massachusetts the Mayflower Pilgrims encountered a severe shortage of food during the first winter. Their ship-borne stores of fish, butter, cheese, biscuit, pork, and beef were inedible as a result of spoilage, and as recorded in Governor William Bradford's log, the failure of European wheat and seeds left them near starvation. From local Indians, the newcomers received five sides of venison and thirty- to forty-pound turkeys at the first Thanksgiving. They depended on native hunters to stock their larders with turkeys and fresh venison. In the absence of larger animals, families roasted squirrels, rabbits, and birds on a roasting jack or a piece of rawhide or cording. The carcass was wrapped in cord that gradually unwound, thus exposing all sides of the meat to the fire. The tedious job of tending the roast, which required frequent trips to the hearth to rewind the cord, was often relegated to a child.

In Quebec, colonists took immediate action to protect grain stores. The Compagnie des Cent-Associés (Company of One Hundred Associates) doled out wheat, an indispensable commodity for the French whose diet relied on bread as a staple. The settlers preferred high-gluten wheat, either the marquis or garnet variety, which made the chewiest bread. If necessary, they would accept easy-sprouting rye, tough barley, over-branned oats, heavy buckwheat, or, in a pinch, pea flour or vetch, which produced barely digestible loaves.

English-born bakers warmed milk to sour into bonny clabber and saved bits of dough from one batch for leavening the next. For sourdough pancakes, they preserved the starter in a spouted clay batter pot. In the absence of sourdough starter, they used a stock made from hops flowers and leaves soaked overnight in a jug. The liquid in which potatoes had been boiled could also leaven baking. Other recipes for yeast called for blends of hops, boiled potatoes, and flour left to ferment or for buckwheat cakes, the least dependable substitute. With a steady diet of batter cakes and twelve to fourteen pounds of bread each week, families placed a relentless demand on the grower, harvester, and baker. Thus, the building of granaries, mills, and ovens consumed the energies of families and communities.

Garret, Cellar, and Pantry

Essential to colonial cooking were the garret and cellar, where the cook stored apples, carrots, parsnips, turnips, beets, and potatoes in slotted bins that allowed air to circulate and prevented the development of mold. Hogsheads held salt pork and corned beef; tubs bore brined hams, salt mackerel, eels, and shad. Kegs and firkins stored butter, souse, lard, and pigs' feet. Householders built tumblers to contain spiced apples and pears, *rolliches* (pickled beef), and head cheese. They strung dried peppers, acorn squash rings, sausages, smoked beef, and sides of bacon from the rafters and above the mantel, and built tarred barrels to hold cider, vinegar, rum, madeira, and beer. With ample pompion (pumpkin), which kept well in cold weather, they invented a classic American dish, pumpkin pie, which became a tradition during the White House tenure of Abigail and John Adams.

Kitchen work in the thirteen American colonies required a long day, beginning before dawn with wood gathering, fire building, and water heating. Most of the toil fell to women. At daybreak, housewives, indentured servants, and slaves collected food and herbs from the kitchen garden, fruit and root crops from the root cellar, meats from the smokehouse, and beer from barrels. On baking day, an additional fire was readied in the bake house for loaves, pies, and cakes, which bakers transferred from wooden dough troughs and boards to tinware. Like orthodox Jews, the Puritans refrained from cooking on the Sabbath, preparing one-dish meals in advance for reheating at the fireside.

As Atlantic Coast settlers were able to replace their rough-bark, dirt-floored cabins with permanent dwellings, they constructed post-and-beam homes with many European features, including half-timber exteriors, jettied overhangs, low lime-washed ceilings, and wattle-and-daub paneling for maximum insulation and retention of fireplace heat. Elaborate plastered ceilings and lath-and-plaster walls painted in earth tones or sky blue added to the housekeeper's chores when soot and smoke took their toll.

Householders gradually acquired the kitchen accoutrements that lightened daily chores and made cooking less burdensome. An artist's rendering of King's

Reach, a farmstead in Calvert County, Maryland, shows a steeply gabled farmhouse with side chimney and picket fence and a small, sturdy barn accessible to the front yard. Glazed windows provided light to the kitchen area, and puncheon, or slab, floors ended the misery of packed dirt underfoot.

Simple, convenient shelving kept canisters in plain sight. Salt came in two grades, a white crystal for kitchen use and impure salt for the barn. The cornmeal container held a large rock, which kept grain from clumping and maintained a cool temperature. Hooks and pegs secured drawstring bags of foodstuffs as well as tin and wooden implements. Some versions of the kitchen worktable involved attaching a shelf to the wall with a leather hinge; the work surface could be folded away when not in use, thus reducing clutter. Until the Industrial Revolution around 1850, most implements and containers were homemade or heirlooms brought from the mother country.

To provide a full complement of foods for the household, a milk shed and pantry altered the open-hearth pattern of cooking. A milk room contained storage closets for presses, racks for drying implements and milk pans, and cupboards framed in muslin to screen drying cheese rounds from insects and dirt. The pantry extended the space available for cheese making and storage of herbs, vinegar and cider, wine and liquor, and sap and molasses. Also located in the pantry were dye tub, soft-soap barrel, meal and salting tubs, and a root cellar for storing root crops for winter. A stone or wood sink held cold water piped in from a spring or well. Water buckets, in constant use, were the first containers to wear out. The need for hot water kept homemakers constantly heating kettles over the fire. Lean-tos stored firewood close to the kitchen door and held strings of onions, dried apples, and leather breeches beans. An attic doubled as additional drying space near the flue for herbs and corn shucks, which thrifty housekeepers turned into scrubbers, mats, and mattress stuffing.

Acquiring New Tastes

In a new and challenging environment, colonial cooks were delighted with maple syrup, their only sweetener until the importation of bees in the 1630s. Colonial open-hearth cooking offered a broad menu from an ample supply of game—deer, elk, bear, rabbit, squirrel, boar, pigeons, turkeys, geese, quail, woodcocks, and teal. Turtles, eels, salmon, and clams added to the variety in the diet.

From the native peoples the settlers received Indian pudding, popcorn, hominy, and succotash; in exchange, they introduced the Indians to peaches, apples, apricots, grains, turnips and beets, lettuce, cabbage, purslane, asparagus, and cauliflower. African slaves also contributed new items to the Europeans' diet, including black-eyed peas, yams, and peanuts. The colonists readily took to some of the new foods—sweet potatoes, hickory nuts, wild rice, and cranberries, among them—but only slowly accustomed their tastes to such New World fare as potatoes, tomatoes, Jerusalem artichokes, local mussels and oysters, and avocados. Rice became a low country staple after 1720. The settlers traded these goods to Europe, where cooks gradually augmented the seventeenth-century menu with the exotic new foods.

Cultural exchange in the New World also brought English colonists Rhineland beer and wine and Dutch cabbage and cole slaw, sausage, lentils, soup, and rye bread. The colonies were a major market for Rhenish bellarmines, the common glazed storage jars for wine, beer, and cider. French Huguenots, who arrived after 1685, introduced chowder. After 1763, Minorcans in Florida added herbs, olive oil, vinegar, wine, goat, seafood, and Mediterranean bread making to the cultural and culinary mix.

Everyday Implements

Laurel Thatcher Ulrich's Pulitzer Prize-winning history *A Midwife's Tale: The Life of Martha Ballard, Based on Her Diary, 1785–1812* (1990) lists the possessions of newlywed colonists as "a few plates and bowls, some pewter spoons, knives and forks, a coffee pot, a couple of kettles, and a frying pan." (p. 143) Implements to ease the burden of heavy chores included a wooden shoulder yoke for carrying wooden buckets, wooden churns, and iron cranes that suspended heavy cauldrons over the fire.

In addition to the settlers' mundane ironware, wealthy homeowners possessed pewter, silver, and brass utensils, strainers and colanders, plates and chargers for keeping food warm, covered bowls, salt bowls and dippers, pepper boxes, and sugar casters. For daily use, there were candlesticks and snuffers, humidors, shallow porringers, lidded tankards, chocolate sets and tea services, caudle cups, communion services, and flatware.

By the mid-eighteenth century vessels and implements were available in the Boston area, as well as repair service and metal recycling. In an ad in the October 30, 1740 edition of the *Boston News-Letter* Thomas Russel, a brazier located near the drawbridge, offered the following:

Kettles, Skillets, Frying-Pans, Kettle-Pots, Sauce Pans, Tea Kettles, Warming Pans, Wash Basins, Skimmers, Ladles, Copper Pots, Copper Funnels, Brass

Scales, Gun Ladles, & c. makes all sorts of Lead Work for ships, Tobacco Cannisters, Ink Stands, & c. and buys old Brass, Copper, Pewter, Lead and Iron. (Dow 1988, 126)

In a June issue of the same newspaper, a competitor, Mary Jackson of Cornhill, Boston, advertised cookware wholesale and retail.

Cooks arranged kitchen implements on tables and hung on hooks about the room within range of the light cast by lanterns and sconces, the only source of light after sunset. Alongside long-handled dippers, skimmers, and ladles were funnels for transferring liquids from large earthen jars to smaller flagons, a balance-beam scale, and tinware shaped with separate pockets for shirred eggs and muffins. From the rafters hung braided strings of onions and a seed corn tree or wire corn dryers, on which ears of corn weathered in the dry heat emanating from the chimney. At the window or open door, the cook may have positioned a baking table for rolling out dough, shaping dumplings, and cutting biscuits and fancy cookies. Hanging alongside the cookware was the warming pan, a long-handled copper pan used for transporting hot coals from the fireside to chilly sleeping rooms, especially those of small children, pregnant women, and sickly elders. An alternative, the bed wagon, supplied a smaller warming pan with a wood-hooped frame to keep hot coals from charring delicate bed linens.

Colonial cooks favored cooking in a single cast iron stewpot or footed kettle and added the savory pot roast to American cuisine. Above the lid in the vapors, they steamed pudding in a cloth bag or muslin wrapper, as described in Susannah Carter's *The Frugal Housewife* (1772), and served it in a twiffler, the Scottish term for a pudding dish. Pivoting cranes mounted to lug poles supported some of the weight of heavy pots and reduced the danger of scalding or burns caused when skirts caught fire. Such accidents killed a quarter of female cooks in the American colonies and often killed or maimed children, who slept at the hearth while their mothers worked. Foods cooked on the corrugated surface of griddles varied a cuisine dominated by boiling and stewing. The pudding came to table first and stood at the center of other dishes as a "conceit" or table ornament. (Earle 1975, 104) Those who feared arriving late were glad to arrive "in pudding time." (Ibid.)

At the hearthside, the Southern cook made fried pies in a skillet from stewed dried fruit; she roasted root vegetables and fried meats in a spider. The meal was ready when beer appeared on the table in tankards, vegetables and main courses in covered bowls, and bread and bread knife on a wooden cutting board. Additional pottery pieces included plates and chargers, cups and mugs, jars, porringers, tureens and matching ladles, and monteith bowls, broad basins indented around the rim for rinsing wine glasses during the meal.

Two hours after the workday began, the kitchen staff served breakfast, a basic yeoman's portion of leftovers, toasted bread with cheese, and cider. Workers gathered once more at 2:00 p.m. for dinner, the heavy meal of the day, and ate a light supper when the workday ended. Among Puritans, dining did not necessitate sitting. Some groups clustered about the fireplace, sipping from gourds or a communal noggin, a one-piece pitcher carved from a vertical column of wood with a pouring lip on one side and a handle chiseled out on the other. Diners dipped into kettles with their hands or with bone, horn, or wooden scoops.

In more formal arrangements, children often stood behind adults at table and fetched fresh biscuits from the hearth and reheated beverages. For fireside hospitality, toddies made the rounds in lidded tankards. Cooks reheated the contents with a toddy stick warmed on the hearth. They stirred in sweetener with toddy spoons, a wooden implement resembling a speed boy or wheel driver for a spinning wheel.

Wooden trenchers five to fourteen inches in diameter served as plates and offered small wells at the side to hold salt and seasonings. Servers did not always offer separate plates but handed around a trencher to be shared by two or more diners. From a communal bowl, into which all could dip with gourd or ladle, the cook presented the main dish, usually a stew, porridge, and succotash, a vegetable medley that took its name from the Narragansett *misickquatash* or *sukquttahash*. Individual bowls were broad and shallow; cups with rounded handles ranged between soup bowls and mugs in size and shape. Until spoons and forks came into common use, the diner touched thumb to little finger and scooped with the three remaining fingers. One English custom that remained in use in the Americas was the eating of meat and vegetables from the "dinner side" of the plate, then turning it over to the unused "pie side" for dessert. In lieu of dessert, a syrup jug might hold molasses or honey for topping bread or pones. The jug's corrugated base kept it from tipping or sliding off an uneven tabletop.

Meals and mealtime customs varied among the diverse population. For the lone householder unaided by assistants, wash day and baking day often necessitated a light meal, sometimes served cold to leave the hearth free for heating water. For Catholics and among some New Englanders, Friday was a required fish day either out of religious observance of meatless days or in support of the fishing industry. For the elite, dining with pewter or silver service and china plates replicated home life in England. Among slaves and servants, eating before the fireplace from a common pot with wooden implements was the norm. For those who pressed westward over wilderness trails, only simple implements and cookware made the journey; often these were used under a wagon bed when inclement weather forced the cook to build a fire out of the wet.

Dessert, a daily expectation, varied from confections such as marzipan, candied ginger and citron, or rock candy to strawberry or blackberry preserves on a biscuit. In wealthy households, servants presented cake on porcelain epergnes or footed cake plates; beverages came to the table in tea and coffee services and chocolate pots. For more lavish holiday meals and communal feasts, diners enjoyed Sally Lunn bread, queen's cake, *buche de noël* (the traditional French Christmas cake shaped like a yule log), or king cake for Twelfth Night, and, after 1775, ice cream. Following dinner, guests cracked walnuts, hickory nuts, pecans, chestnuts, and beechnuts.

Living Heritage

Interest in colonial cookery has persisted into the twenty-first century among both social and culinary historians, as represented in collections of implements, compilations of brewing and baking lore, and cookbooks. For the nation's first centennial, New England women re-enacted scenes of colonial life at the 1876 American Centennial Exposition. The publication of collected recipes from the colonial era began in the nineteenth century with Lafcadio Hearn's *La Cuisine Creole* (1884) and Lucia Swett's *New England Breads, Luncheon and Tea Biscuits* (1891). In 1894, America's first dietitian, Sarah Tyson Rorer, researched colonial cookery and published *Colonial Recipes* (1894), a compendium that claimed authenticity for its pumpkin pie baked by Martha Washington. Visitors to historic recreations such as Williamsburg, Virginia, continue to enjoy dishes based on these 200-year-old recipes.

See also **Fireplace; Oilcloth**

Further Reading

Davidson, Marshall B. *The American Heritage History of Colonial Antiques.* New York: Simon & Schuster, 1967.
Gardiner, Anne Gibbons. *Mrs. Gardiner's Family Receipts from 1763.* Boston: Rowan Tree Press, 1989.
Ulrich, Laurel Thatcher. *A Midwife's Tale: The Life of Martha Ballard, Based on Her Diary, 1785–1812.* New York: Alfred A. Knopf, 1990.

COMMUNAL MEAL

A custom worldwide, the gathering of diners for a shared meal often marks an occasion of note—the welcoming of a guest, celebration of a holiday, or observance of a tradition or ritual, such as the Japanese tea ceremony. Such sharing of food may also indicate the absence of individual dishes, as was the case in war-ravaged central European lands early in the twenty-first century. Historically, communal meals around a fire were the standard in prehistoric times, when the only furnishings were logs or stones outlining the fire space. A common dish among the Tepehuan of Chihuahua, Mexico, and the Hupi and Pom of California, was *atole,* a mush made from stone-crushed corn, which was served in a communal pot. Diners dipped into the pot with their hands or ladled out servings with a mush spoon or paddle.

Medieval families began the tradition of sharing a one-dish meal from the oversized stew bowl in a time when homes lacked tableware for the serving of individual portions. Among the Dutch and German settlers of the Schoharie section of New York state, the sharing of a pewter dish of *sappaen* (mush) involved setting the gruel out to cool and harden, slicing it, and pouring on milk. Hosts offered pewter spoons to guests, who dug into the perimeter of the slices floating in their milky ponds.

Travelogues on Senegambian and Yoruban hospitality from the fifteenth century described the West African origin of shared food. Nineteenth-century French travelers René Caille and Theophilus Conneau admired similar dishes that sub-Saharan African cooks offered them. Central to the meal were platters and vessels of yams and sweet potatoes, leafy vegetables, peppers, peanuts, tomatoes, and melons, all eaten with hands rather than served on individual plates or bowls. Hospitality was essential to the local social order, which welcomed guests with finger food.

Church dinners, potlucks, basket suppers, and picnics expressed heritage and roots during African-American slavery. In the American South, blacks transported from West Africa took comfort in shared African-style meals. The rare holiday in the plantation slave quarters called for a communal eating ritual similar to those enjoyed by the ancestors at home.

The practice of communal cooking and eating was widespread among native Americans. On his expedition aboard the *Polaris* to Cumberland Inlet, Greenland, in 1871, Captain Charles Francis Hall observed a party of Inuit in their tent eating raw seal meat. His friend Koojesse concluded the meal by drinking from a communal dish of hot seal blood. From hand to hand, the dish passed among the dozen diners, who each carried a knife for slicing meat from the carcass.

Farther south, at a central food preparation hut, Creek and Seminole cooks soaked corn mush in ash water for *sofke* (corn soup), then simmered the mixture with pulverized nuts and marrow. Left bubbling on the fire night and day, the kettle was open to any diner who wanted to dip in a wooden, horn, or bone *sofkee* spoon for a snack or meal. Similarly, West Coast Indians softened and ground acorns for a communal staple served from a common stewpot.

Colonial American cooks often used communal plates, loving cups, and soup pots out of necessity. In the absence of enough utensils and vessels for each diner, they could offer wooden or horn spoons for dipping into a whole pumpkin cooked in the shell or a pot of "hotchpotch," a meat-and-vegetable stew. In 1777, General George Washington's cook staff invented the all-in-one convenience of the Philadelphia pepper pot—a soup of tripe and other scraps seasoned with peppercorns—during the Continental Army's disastrous winter at Valley Forge, Pennsylvania. Another common dish, milk and suppawn, named from the Indian term for porridge, appears to have been the origin of cornmeal mush, hasty pudding, or spoon bread, the Virginia term for an egg-and-cornmeal soufflé.

The rise of the Bolshevik government in Russia in 1917 precipitated an emphasis on the communal kitchen and dining room as an essential of universal equality. Marxist idealism, which came into its own amid widespread want, infused followers with a delight in communal cooking and state-run cafeterias at the same time that it shamed the private diner. In the repressive atmosphere that closed churches and communalized country estates, Soviet state dining rooms served the urban diner. Budding party leaders denounced restaurants as a waste of resources catering to the elite at the expense of the poor. To the Communist zealot, the best way to manage equipment, food, fuel, and labor was to cook large amounts at once to serve many people.

Alexandra Kollontai, a director of the women's section of the Russian Community Party, greeted attendees of the First All-Russian Congress of Women in Moscow in November 1918 with a prediction that communism would doom to extinction all housework. The source of liberation for the female was to be the widespread replacement of individual homes with communal laundries, kitchens, and dining rooms. Bolstering Kollontai's arguments was a pamphet, *Obshchestvennyi Stol* (The Public Table, 1919), signed with the initials F. Sh. The optimistic author gloried in the ideal group dining facility, "a cross between a temple uniting a community of worshippers and a cosy, family hearth." (Glants & Toomre 1997, 166) In reality, the state dining facilities and Proletkult clubs, with their inedible food and unbearable atmosphere, turned out to be a grim replacement for home cooking.

In rural Germany, communal meals served in traditional crockery bowls continued into the 1930s. The lower the social rank, the more people avoided elegant table manners and individual dishes. As real wages increased and people moved from laboring class to the bourgeoisie, they purchased more place settings and cooked less often in a communal pot. Rationalization of this shift in serving and eating hinged on hygiene and greater social mobility. Mechanical mass production of three-piece metal flatware ended dependence on wood spoons to be dipped into a central bowl.

In the twenty-first century, eating from a single, shared dish was still the norm in much of the world, for example, among Pakistani, Palestinian, Zambian, and Tanzanian families while dining informally at home. Traditionally, Bedouins of the Sahara have lived so closely in family units that they define "family" as people who share one bowl. In Catalonia, diners partook of the Yuletide *escudella* (stew bowl), a holiday treat made from root vegetables, grains and beans, or pasta according to individual family recipes. Andorran versions of this hearty, warming dish included sausages and meatballs.

The Kyrgyz placed a common plate at the center of their table and also passed individual plates for diners to serve themselves. Peasants preferred dining *pa kirghizi* (without flatware). In India and Nepal, hosts served food in a shared cup, which partakers held aloft in order to keep it from touching their lips. The Batswana fed themselves with their hands from common dishes but offered separate plates to guests and individual beverage containers to each diner. In the Middle East, the use of a small piece of flat bread to scoop up the popular dips *baba ghannouj* and *hummus* was a standard behavior for meals or snacks that extended a pleasant conviviality to friends and guests.

Similarly, African diners in Burkina Faso, Eritrea, Guinea, Ethiopia, Mauritania, Central African Republic, Chad, Niger, and Cameroon ate from a shared platter or bowls. Malians and Micronesians offered separate communal bowls for men and women, who seldom partook from the same vessel. Among the migratory Lapps of Norway, the communal pot served families living in tents during storms and heavy fog. For meals of dried reindeer meat, bread and butter, and coffee, they gathered around a large cauldron that cooks prepared family-style. In NaLao, Thailand, silk workers shared a lunchtime pot of sticky rice, which they shaped into balls with hands and then dipped into a sauce. The Hmong of Laos offered guests rice wine from a communal crock provided with four-foot-long straws for each sipper.

Social structure and cultural background continue to influence culinary and dining styles. Because of their Gallo-African heritage, the Senegalese may choose either to eat with their fingers on the floor or ground or to sit at tables French-style and eat from plates with flatware. Young girls study proper presentation of foods as their womanly duty and may learn both national African fare and French cuisine along with the dining manners of each tradition.

See also **Colonial Kitchens, American; Mongolian Hot Pot**

Further Reading

Garrett, W. E., "The Hmong of Laos: No Place to Run," *National Geographic*, 78–111.

Glants, Musya, and Joyce Toomre, eds. *Food in Russian History and Culture.* Bloomington: Indiana University Press, 1997.

Skabelund, Grant P., man. ed. *Culturgrams: The Nations Around Us.* Vols. I & II. Salt Lake City, Utah: Brigham Young University, 1997.

CONDIMENTS AND SEASONINGS

Strictly speaking, a condiment is any substance added to prepared food at the time of serving or eating to enhance its flavor. In this essay, however, the term encompasses the herbs and spices used to season food before and during cooking, along with sauces, such as ketchup, added at the table.

The earliest documented use of condiments dates back many thousands of years, and they continue to be widely enjoyed. The popularity of specific flavorings and condiments varies with cooking style, local geography, and trends and fashions. At the turn of the twenty-first century, research by Paul W. Sherman at Cornell University found that onions and black pepper—which, the data showed, were added to 60 percent of meat-based dishes—were the most widely used flavorings. The next most popular seasonings were garlic, chili peppers, and citrus juice. Horseradish, fennel, and savory were the least used.

Local Traditions

In the Western Hemisphere, the chili pepper has long been valued as both vegetable and seasoning. In Peru, where pepper plants may have grown in the first South American gardens, the practice of adding peppers to food began as early as 7000 BCE. Neolithic sites around the Mediterranean rim contain evidence of the use of such seasonings as poppy seeds and caraway. Cooks blended seasonings from ingredients such as asafoetida, anise, saffron, cassia, cardamom, myrrh, spikenard, ginger grass, capers, and mustard. They grew what they could in their own gardens and traded with others for specialty items.

Archaeological evidence indicates that ancient peoples loved garlic and onions. The royal gardens of Ur contained plots for onions and leeks around 2100 BCE. Clay tablets inscribed in the Akkadian language, translated by the chef and Assyriologist Jean Bottéro, testify

to the skill of Mesopotamian cooks in incorporating herbs and onions into recipes. For daily use, they fermented a common table condiment called *siqqu*, which consisted of fish, shellfish, and grasshoppers, a recipe remarkably similar to that of the Roman sauce known as *garum*. At Susa, cooks prepared more than fifty-five pounds of garlic daily.

The mention of onions and garlic permeates food writings from eastern Mediterranean lands. Turkish lore asserts that these were the first food plants to appear on earth. In the Fertile Crescent, peasants ate onions daily with bread. The Greeks, too, ate copious amounts of sauces, salad dressings, and condiments made with garlic and onions. The Roman satirist Juvenal ridiculed the Egyptian deification of leeks and onions, but all around him, commoners in Italy were stocking their pantries with the same seasonings and ate them daily. In Roman Spain, the soldier-agronomist Columella, author of *De Re Rustica* (On Agriculture, ca. 50 CE) described the drying and pickling of onions in salt and vinegar. Even the Emperor Nero declared that he toned his singing voice with leeks.

Roman cooks used condiments on a daily basis, favoring as food additives and recipe flavorings pine nuts and garum, a fish-based sauce similar to Worcester sauce, into which food was dipped. They also pickled turnips and other root vegetables in a blend of honey-mustard, oil, and vinegar, the forerunner of the Italian *mostarda di frutta* (fruit mustard), and whisked mustard seed into grape must to produce *mustum ardens* (burning must), a zesty seasoning for meats. Marcus Porcius Cato, author of *De Agricultura* (ca. 150 CE), described an appetizer that consisted of a mixture of olives served in a dressing of oil and vinegar, fennel, rue, mint, cumin, and coriander. Cooks in Italy's Abruzzi hills gathered and sun-dried *diavolino* peppers, the "little devils" that spiced the local lamb stew. In reference to Roman enthusiasm for condiments, the encyclopedist Pliny the Elder, author of *Natural History* (ca. 77 CE), complained that imported pepper was overrated and questioned the practice of selling ginger and pepper "by weight, as we do gold and silver." (Pliny 1962, 138) Three centuries later, Rome's chief food writer Caelius Apicius, author of *De Re Coquinaria* (On Cooking, late 300s CE), the world's oldest cookbook, explained the preparation of *columbades* with seawater to make an olive-rich sauce for boiled poultry.

When the Goth general Alaric overran Italy in 401, he forced the Roman soldier-master Flavius Stilicho to buy him off, in part with a ton and a half of pepper. Among Byzantines, the favored condiments consisted of *kabiari* (caviar), *rengai* (kippered herrings), and *oiotarichon* (egg pickle), a favorite salt roe. Among eastern Romans, the daring cook added rosemary to lamb, sprinkled nutmeg on pease pudding, and squill vinegar on salads, and introduced rose *zachar* (sugar) and saffron, an aromatic herb and food coloring, renowned for its great cost.

The Chinese, who developed soybean curd and *shih*, a fermented salt bean dish, valued them as relishes. The nomadic Hakka from northern China developed sugar-preserved vegetables that could be eaten on the move. A regional specialty, Chiu Chow cooking, derived from Shantou and Hakka cuisine, showcased seafood meals spiced with hot sauce and soups made from shark fins and birds' nests. This culinary style was also known for the use of pungent *lo soi* (old water), a sauce of the cooking juices collected from many meals. As it steeped, the mother, or dregs, gained flavor from each new use.

Additional Chinese sauces ranged from a salt-cured fish sauce to salted cabbage; preserves and marmalades; mustard pickles; peppered green leaves called *jun jiu choi* (pearl vegetable); and a pickle mix consisting of ginger, shallot, mustard greens, and garlic. When preparing seafood, cooks typically countered fishy flavors with soy sauce, wine, garlic, and scallions. To bland dishes, traditional Chiu Chow cooks added sweet soy, tangerine oil, and white rice vinegar.

In India, the dry roasting and grinding of spices preceded the blending of *garam masala* (hot mixture), a traditional seasoning used in, among other dishes, stewed lamb. The traditional kitchen blend was available from spice merchants, but many cooks made their own version, combining different proportions of ground peppercorns, cardamom, coriander, fennel, bay leaf, and caraway seeds. Garam masala was a rub for meats in addition to curry or to piccalilli, an East Indian vegetable and mustard spread.

The Arab delight in rotted barley dough dates to at least the tenth century, when a recipe for *budhaj* (or *fudanj*) appeared in the *Kitab al-Tabikh* (The Book of Dishes), a cookbook collection by Abu Muhammad al-Muzaffar ibn Nasr. By rolling raw dough in fig leaves and closing the loaves in containers for six weeks, the condiment maker prepared the mass for drying and mixing into such dishes as *bunn* and *kamakh*. One fermented condiment, *murri,* began with unleavened crumbs blended with the *budhaj* along with cinnamon, herbs, and saffron. A medieval phenomenon, these condiments vanished from culinary history in the 1300s. Among reasons cited for the shift in Arab cookery were the rise of Ottoman cusine, which disdained spices, and the influence of New World seasonings, which supplanted Old World tastes.

Sicilians made the chopping of onions and garlic a daily part of the kitchen routine. In 977 CE, when Baghdad merchant and cartographer Mohammed Ibn Hawqal visited Palermo, the island's thriving cultural center, he remarked on the pervasive onion taste and smell. In his *Book of the Routes and the Realms* (ca. 980), he claimed that eating too many onions had destroyed Sicilian rationality:

There is not one man among them, of whatsoever condition, who does not eat onions every day, and does not serve them morning and evening in his house. It is this that has clouded their imagination; offended their brains; perturbed their senses; altered their intelligence; drowsed their spirits; fogged their expressions, untempered their constitutions so completely that it rarely happens that they see things straight. (Simeti 1989, 99)

During the Italian Renaissance, Platina's *De Honesta Voluptate et Valitudine* (On Right Pleasure and Health, 1475), the first cookbook set in type, refuted Hawqal's diatribe with a description of tasty, sharp-flavored onions and a tribute to their curative value as anti-inflammatory and sleep-inducing agents. For removing the foul smell of garlic, he suggested eating it with toasted beets. Above all, he seemed partial to pepper sauce, for which he supplied a recipe.

Dissemination of Tastes

The medieval ferment that brought Jews and Moors to Spain and spread eastern Mediterranean cooking throughout the region produced a blend of condiments. From 1275, Jews escaping the Inquisition in Spain and parts of Italy found safe harbor from anti-Semitism in Ferrara and Modena. In the shadow of the wealth and power of the d'Este family, they flourished once more, contributing their recipes to sophisticated Christian tables. From the Jewish preference for *agresto*, a vinegar made from unripe grapes, Italians evolved *bagnabrusca* (literally, harsh bath), a sour marinade cooks used to baste poached meat and seafood. In English cookbooks dating to 1390, the time of Richard II, recipes for curry powder appear to have influenced the flavorings created by the royal cooking staff.

New World explorers brought new varieties of pepper plants to Iberia in 1514. Pepper cultivation reached India in 1611, perhaps an import of Portuguese sailors. Hot pepper sauce became a culinary specialty of cooks in Tunisia and the Mississippi Delta, especially New Orleans. In Tunis, ground chili peppers, pounded coriander and caraway, and chopped mint were the traditional bases for the hot *harissa* paste, an essential of north African dishes. Along the Gulf of Mexico, Mississippi hot pepper sauce became the condiment of choice to accompany oysters and other shellfish.

Mustard also had an impact on culinary history. Although Pope John XII, a fourteenth-century Frenchman, adored mustard on all foods and appointed his own private mustard maker to the papal kitchen staff, it was England that led the world in mustard production from the eighteenth century on. In 1720, a Mrs. Clements of Tewkesbury, England, successfully milled mustard seed into powder. In 1804, the miller Jeremiah Colman of Norwich concocted a blended mustard from white and black seed, turmeric, and flour. By 1814, he had begun to confine his business entirely to mustard. In Dijon, France, in 1853, Maurice Grey, advanced the technology of the mustard mill, adding steam power to pulverize and sift the oily seed. After partnering with Auguste Poupon in 1886, the two marketed Grey Poupon, a blend of black or brown seed, white wine and grape must, plus seasonings. Americans slowly acclimated to fiery mustard as a condiment after entrepreneur Francis French produced a milder recipe.

The introduction of Worcestershire sauce began in 1823 in an unlikely place—the pharmacy of John Lea and William Perrins in Birmingham, England. They manufactured medicinal goods, including Essence of Sarsaparilla and Taraxacum, a dandelion coffee recommended for liver ailments. Their shift to kitchen condiments began with a request by Marcus, Lord Sandys, former governor of Bengal recently retired to Ombersley Court. He asked the apothecary to compound an Indian sauce, which they did with spices and dried fruit. The result dismayed Lea and Perrins, but pleased Lord Sandys. After the remainder of the batch had fermented several months in the cellar, the sauce makers tasted it once again and found it savory and aromatic. Within three years, manufacture of the popular flavoring, which was being shipped throughout the British Isles as well as to Australia and North America, required a separate factory in Worcester.

The invention of mayonnaise is a detail of food history fraught with conflicting legends. As clarified in Alan Davidson's *The Oxford Companion to Food* (1999) and substantiated by the *Oxford English Dictionary*, the Duc de Richelieu admired a sauce that either he or his cook created in 1756 by emulsifying olive oil, vinegar, egg yolk, and seasonings. The duke coined a French adjective based on the name of Port Mahon, capital of Minorca. Thus, the term *mahonnaise* gave rise to the English "mayonnaise," first used in 1841.

In the North American colonies, farm families harvested wild garlic, shallots, or Catawissa onions to flavor plain venison roasts. For a sweet-and-sour sauce, they marinated cayenne pods and allspice in sherry and white vinegar as the base for pepper dram, or mandram, a blend of minced cucumbers or West Indian gherkins. The same sharp flavoring added life to bland bean and pea soups. By 1752, Boston homemakers could purchase prepared mustard from an expert, John Ingram of Lisbon, who declared that his condiment

"retains its Strength, Flavour and Colour Seven Years . . . and gives a most surprising grateful Taste to Beef, Pork, Lamb, Fish, Sallad, or other Sauces." (Dow 1988, 137) According to culinary expert Sarah Josepha Hale's edition of Eliza Acton's *Modern Cookery for Private Families* (1845), such quaint saucing had no place in the kitchens of gentry. Nonetheless, the deviled egg, a creaming of bland egg yolk with mustard, pickle, peppers, paprika, and vinegar, developed in the 1800s and earned a place in *Common Sense in the Household: A Manual of Practical Housewifery* (1871) by Marion Harland (pseudonym of Mary Hawes Terhune).

In the 1930s, condiments gained new attention in America and Europe. Advertisements in women's magazines lauded prepared mustards and sauces as a way of spicing up otherwise ordinary meals and pleasing bored husbands. To make a place for Colman's Mustard in American homes, advertisements in *Good Housekeeping* depicted it as racy, pungent, and tangy. The ad included an address where readers could write for free recipe cards for salad dressing, pickles, and spiced entrées.

Gebhardt's genuine Mexican chili powder, made in San Antonio, Texas, introduced an ethnic flavoring and bright red color to Anglo cooking. Most of the company's ads offered cookbooks that explained how to add excitement to bland foods with its Hispanic taste sensation. The food writer Alice Bradley, dean of the Boston School of Cookery, wrote *Ensaladas a la Mejicana* (Mexican Salads), which compiled color tutorials and details on how to use Mesoamerican seasoning to accent salad greens, add zest to meat loaf and hash, and brighten party tables. The text encouraged the reluctant cook to try such exotic dishes as chili con carne, Mexican beans, or tamales.

Seasonings Around the World

Traditionally, Chinese cooks have preferred a variety of sweet, sour, spicy, crispy, and salty pickles and appetizers as starters to serve with wine or tea—for example, lotus root chips, fried seaweed, boiled or fried peanuts, preserved lima beans, cauliflower pickles, sesame walnuts, jicama or cucumber pickles, honey pecans, pear or peach pickles, and various condiments based on bok choy, shallots, ginger, melon, plums, and mustard greens. One style of serving condiments they call *bot dai bot siu* (eight big, eight small), a reference to the number of relishes and tidbits a hostess offered at one sitting.

In Korea, the prize flavoring has long been *kimch'i*, a hot pickled cabbage that, for centuries, families chopped and fermented in clay jars buried in the ground. Many styles and variants of *kimch'i* are known, including one made from seaweed.

Indian, Sri Lankan, and Pakistani curries, which blend spices with other foods, have influenced the cooking style in many countries, particularly Guyana, Jamaica, and England. Pakistani cooks have traditionally made a chicken curry especially for wedding feasts. Yemeni cooks serve bread with *zhug*, a relish dip. In Turkey, cooks serve *cacik*, a relish blend containing chopped cucumber, garlic, dill, mint, and yogurt, as a *meze* (starter) or as an accompaniment for kebabs and meatballs.

Cooks in French Polynesia developed *poisson cru,* raw fish marinated in lime juice, into a Marquesan national dish. Micronesians prefer *wasabi*, a horseradish paste that originated in Japan. Samoans use coconut meat to make *pe'epe'e* (coconut cream), which they season with lemon juice or salt.

Farther north in Oceania, condiments tend toward vegetable and seafood blends. Lao cooks spice their rice with fermented fish or chili sauce; Singaporeans use fish heads, pineapple, and green onions. The Japanese use shredded, vinegar-soaked *kombu,* an algae, to flavor rice. For variety, they lace pickles and dress rice dishes with *miso* (soya bean paste). Other foods used to balance the blandness of rice include *daikon* (horseradish) and *ume-boshi* (salted plums). Vietnamese cooks have developed a reputation for *nuoc mam,* a salty fermented squid or shrimp dip, seasoning, or sauce with a strong fish smell; the Thai equivalent, called *nam pla,* is milder. Filipino cooks specialize in *lumpia* (egg roll) dressing blended from vinegar, garlic, and soy sauce and seasoned with sugar and hot sauce; they produce two versions of fish condiments, *patis,* a thin anchovy sauce used as a basis for *sinigang* (sour fish soup), and *bagoong,* a thicker sauce.

African condiments are among the world's most diverse. In West Africa fermented locust seed forms a popular, protein-rich flavoring for soup or stew. Senegalese cooks perk up *yassa,* a chicken-and-rice dish, by adding onion and spice sauce and serve *mbaxalusaloum,* a rice dish topped with ground peanuts, tomatoes, and meat. Ghanaians originated a traditional pepper mix to serve with meat or fish. In Burkina Faso, *tô* (millet porridge) requires the addition of peanut, sorrel, and okra sauces. Offshore, residents of the Comoros compound a hot pepper sauce called *putu* for serving on all foods; Ethiopians produce their own pepper condiment called *berbere,* sometimes served with raw meat.

Cooks in Poland make sweet-and-sour sauces to serve on game and carp, and, in England, piccalilli spices up a simple pub-counter plowman's lunch. Indulging in the traditional Icelandic *hákarl,* a shark delicacy ripened up to six months in sand and gravel,

requires some courage for outsiders unused to the smell. The Norwegian Yuletide treat of *lutefisk*, dried cod soaked into a pulp in lye, poses a similar challenge for the uninitiated.

King Ketchup

American families have relied on ketchup since its introduction. Andrew Smith's *Pure Ketchup: A History of America's National Condiment* (1996) traced the name to three sources: the Chinese *kë-tsiap* or *fan-kei chop,* the Indonesian *kecap,* and the Javanese or Malay *kitjap.* Whatever the derivation, food preparers derived the sauce around 1690 from a fermented salt pickle used to preserve fish. After British mariners tasted it, they ferried samples to England, where cooks imitated the condiment using either puréed anchovies, walnuts, or mushroom as a base. Cooks in the United States preferred a base of puréed tomatoes, from which they produced the food recognized by the *New York Tribune* in 1896 as the national condiment. Pennsylvania Dutch recipes for ketchup, published in *The Lancaster General Hospital Benefit Cook Book* (1912), preserved the spicy West Indian elements of clove, allspice, cayenne, and white pepper. By 1999, Americans were consuming 604 million pints annually.

See also **Garum; Herbs;** *Kimch'i;* **Pickles; Spices**

Further Reading

Bharadwaj, Monisha. *The Indian Pantry.* Weesp, Neth.: Kyle Cathie, 1996.
Kasper, Lynne Rossetto. *The Splendid Table.* New York: William Morrow & Co., 1992.
Smith, Andrew. *Pure Ketchup: A History of America's National Condiment.* Columbia: University of South Carolina Press, 1996.
Swahn, J. O. *The Lore of Spices: Their History, Nature and Uses Around the World.* Gothenburg, Sweden: AB Nordbok, 1991.
Zlotnick, Susan, "Domesticating Imperialism: Curry and Cookbooks in Victorian England," *Frontiers,* 1996, 51–58.

CONVENIENCE FOODS

Although generally regarded as a modern innovation, convenience foods—those requiring minimal or no preparation—derive from such time-honored methods of food preservation as drying. For centuries, Native American cooks made jerky and pemmican to preserve meat for times of scarce supply and to simplify the difficulties of cooking on long journeys. Desert peoples, too, traditionally dried fruits such as dates, grapes, and plums for easy storage and preservation of taste. The manufacture of dehydrated foods proved essential to the provisioning of the English navy.

Baby-cut carrots in the produce section of a supermarket in Virginia. [© Courtesy of Agricultural Research Service, USDA. Photo by Ken Hammond.]

Ship's galley cooks were familiar with biscuit, a powdered mix from which they concocted hardtack. Likewise, provisioners in Seattle, Portland, and San Francisco turned out evaporated potatoes, soup vegetables, and onions reduced by ninety percent and vats of egg yolk for sale in the mine fields of the Yukon. Annie Hall Strong, writing for the *Skagway News* in December 1897, declared commercially dehydrated goods "a grand success." (Murphy and Haigh 1997, 51)

In the early twentieth century, domestic scientists linked convenience with women's advancement and, ultimately, national prosperity. In support of nineteenth-century canning methods and other developments that made meal preparation easier and faster, Ellen Henrietta Richards and Sophronia Maria Elliott, coauthors of *The Chemistry of Cooking and Cleaning* (1912), wrote: "The family is the heart of the country's life, and every philanthropist or social scientist must begin at that point. Whatever, then, will enlighten the mind, and lighten the burden of care, of every housekeeper will be a boon." In the preface to the second edition, they assured readers that right conduct of homemaking saved time, money, and effort and predicted "the perpetuity, prosperity and power of the nation." (Richards & Elliott 1912, Preface to the Second Edition, n. p.)

A Brief History

The roll call of time-saving innovations includes developments in frozen, dehydrated, canned, prepared, or partly prepared foods that have reduced kitchen labor and made meals available in less time. The following list details some of the milestones in the history of convenience foods:

1741   Dr. William Brownrigg adds soda water to still room shelves.

1764   Baker's chocolate first reaches markets.

1777   Grey's Dijon Mustard introduces a prepared dressing.

1807   Dr. Philip Syng Physick of Philadelphia produces the first fruit-flavored soda water.

1820s   Saleratus replaces pearl ash for leavening baked goods, thus reducing the number of eggs called for in the recipe.

1829   Sylvester Graham concocts the graham cracker and touts it as a health food.

1835   Lea & Perrins introduce bottled Worcestershire sauce.

1842   Grocers offer the first packaged corn starch.

1847   Joseph Storrs Fry of Bristol, England, manufactures chocolate bars; around the same time, Burnett's vanilla essence becomes available to bakers.

1850   Burham and Morrill offer sweet corn in tins.

1856   Ferdinand Schumacher begins milling oats at the German Mills American Oatmeal Company for sale from barrels in dry goods stores. Gail Borden markets tins of condensed milk manufactured in Walcottsville, Connecticut.

1858   John Landis Mason introduces the mason jar for home canning.

1859   Rumford baking powder comes on the market; the product replaces calcium and phosphates lost in flour during milling.

1861   Van Camp markets canned beans in tomato sauce.

1867   Underwood introduces canned deviled ham.

1868   Charles and Maximilian Fleischmann begin selling packaged yeast.

1869 French chemist Hippolyte Mège Mouriès invents margarine as a substitute for butter.
The first Campbell's soup appears in markets.
Pennsylvania pickle maker Henry J. Heinz markets bottled grated horseradish, the company's first product.

1876 Heinz sells the first bottled ketchup.
Hires Root Beer and Premium Saltines are the first such foods to be available in sanitary individual servings rather than in open kegs and barrels.

1878 Chase & Sanborn packages ground-roast coffee in metal cans.

1880s Saccharin, synthetic vanilla, Wheatena, Thomas's English muffins, Oscar Mayer wieners, Tetley tea, Log Cabin syrup, Morton's salt, and sugar cubes become available, simplifying much kitchen work.

1886 Atlanta pharmacist John S. Pemberton concocts Coca-Cola, a global success.

1889 Aunt Jemima's pancake mix debuts on grocery shelves.

1890 Dr. John Harvey Kellogg invents peanut butter as a source of protein for vegetarians.

1892 Shredded wheat expands breakfast choices.

1893 Cream of Wheat and Cracker Jacks are invented.
Cereal-maker Charles W. Post creates Postum, a food supplement and coffee substitute.
Charles R. Knox, packager of gelatin sheets, begins manufacturing powdered gelatin, forerunner of Jell-O.

1896 Packaged fruitcake and Tootsie Rolls become available in the United States.

1899 Chemist David Wesson of Southern Oil Company produces Wesson Oil by deodorizing cottonseed oil through a high-temperature vacuum process.
Finnish inventor O. Siebold patents powdered meat.

1901 Japanese-American chemist Satori Kato introduces instant coffee powder at the Pan-American Exposition.

1902 Kellogg's corn flakes replace soggy cereals.

1904 Fair-goers at the Louisiana Purchase Exposition in St. Louis get their first view of Campbell's pork and beans, puffed rice, banana splits, and hamburgers.

1905 The Genesee Pure Food Company introduces Jell-O.

1907 Canners in San Pedro, California, pack the first canned tuna.

1909 Heinz pioneers baby food in jars in Canada.

1911 Procter & Gamble introduces Crisco, the first shelf-stable, hydrogenated vegetable shortening.

1912 Morton begins selling tumblers of table salt.

1916 Coca-Cola appears in stores in its familiar contoured bottle.

1920s Butter comes to markets machine-packaged by precise measure.

1920 The Taggart Baking Company of Indianapolis launches Wonder Bread.

1922 Clarence Birdseye establishes Birdseye Seafoods, the first successful seller of frozen fish fillets.
Quaker creates a faster-cooking oatmeal, reducing preparation time from 15 to five minutes.

1923 The H. J. Heinz Company begins canning and bottling kosher foods.

1926 Edgell & Sons produce the first tinned asparagus.
Potato chips in waxed-paper bags stock snack shelves.

1928 Otto Frederick Rohwedder pioneers commercially sliced packaged bread.
Peter Pan introduces homogenized peanut butter, which boosts the sale of sliced bread.

1929 Birds Eye markets the first frozen vegetables.

1930 Hostess invents Twinkies.

1931 Bisquick appears on store shelves.

1933 Borden introduces milk fortified with vitamin D.
Kraft develops Miracle Whip salad dressing.

1934 Mars Candy Company, owner of Petfoods Ltd., pioneers canned pet foods.

1937 Margaret Rudkin merchandizes whole wheat bread under the Pepperidge Farms label.
Kraft boxed macaroni-and-cheese offers a quick comfort food.

1939 Birds Eye markets frozen poultry and beef meals.

1945 Shoppers purchase the first frozen orange juice.

1946 R.T. French Company pioneers instant mashed potatoes the same year that R. H. Macy distributes the first frozen french fries.

1947 Grocery stores offer the first prepackaged produce the same year that Kraft begins marketing presliced cheese.
Reddi-Whip becomes America's first food sold in an aerosol can.

1950 General Foods introduces Minute Rice.
Charlie Lubin, a Chicago baker, launches Sara Lee cheesecake.

1953 Sara Lee Kitchens pioneers frozen baked goods.

1954 C. A. Swanson & Sons popularizes the TV dinner, a full meal heated in its own aluminum serving tray.

1957 Seabrook Farms invents boil-in-the-bag frozen entrees.
      General Foods introduces Tang, an instant orange juice substitute later used by NASA as a beverage for astronauts during space flights.
1963 Ermal Fraze patents the pop-top beverage can.
1965 General Foods debuts Shake'n Bake, a seasoned coating used in oven baking to simulate the crispy texture of deep-fried foods.
1970 The first Hamburger Helper and Orville Redenbacher's Gourmet Popping Corn appear in supermarkets.
1972 Snapple markets bottled fruit drinks as an alternative to soft drinks.
1973 General Foods introduces its line of instant International Coffees.
      Stove Top Stuffing debuts in stores.
1974 Miller Brewing Company bottles Miller Lite, a reduced-calorie beer.
1981 Nestlé launches the Stouffer's Lean Cuisine line of reduced-calorie frozen dinners.
1985 Rice cakes become a popular diet and snack food for bag lunches.
1986 The first microwave popcorn appears in stores.
1987 Campbell introduces low-salt canned soups.
1989 ConAgra markets Healthy Choice frozen meals.
1993 Progresso's Healthy Classics soups and RJR Nabisco's Snackwell cookies and crackers make their debut.
1998 Benecol, a margarine that lowers cholesterol levels, comes on the market, representing a new concept in foods—"nutriceuticals."

Meals in Minutes

In the second half of the twentieth century, when women entered the work force in unprecedented numbers, food manufacturers realized that they could boost sales by creating new convenience foods and marketing them as time-savers. Instant coffee, frozen vegetables, dehydrated potatoes and quick-cooking rice were just some of the innovative products that catered to the harried homemaker.

By the end of the century, makers of convenience foods recognized that diners were demanding more choices and shorter preparation times. In the 1990s alone, according to Paul Oliver, president of Pillsbury Bakeries and Foodservice, the amount of time homemakers spent preparing a typical meal had decreased from hours to minutes—often not more than fifteen minutes. To the roster of convenience foods were added such products as toaster pastries, soups ready to microwave in disposable cups, and school and office lunches complete in a single box. With developments in technology speeding the pace of life and families eating fewer formal meals, it appeared that the market for convenience foods—especially meals in individual servings catering to diners of varying ages and requiring minimal clean up—would continue to grow.

See also **Baby Food; Birdseye, Clarence; Canning; Kellogg, John Harvey; Kellogg, Will Keith; Knox, Rose; Military Kitchens; Patten, Marguerite; Post, Charles William**

Further Reading

Richards, Ellen H., and S. Maria Elliott. *The Chemistry of Cooking and Cleaning.* Boston: Whitcomb & Barrows, 1912.

COOKBOOK

Since the advent of written language, the cookbook—a compilation of recipes, often including menu plans, advice on service and presentation, nutrition information, and miscellaneous commentary on culinary matters—has served the needs of family cooks and professional chefs alike. As a record of the tastes, preferences, and standards of nutrition of families, ethnic groups, and historical eras, these texts offer a unique glimpse into human history.

Early Food Writing

Food writing in the ancient world consisted largely of practical applications of dietary knowledge. Babylonian recipes from around 1700 BCE describe meat and bean dishes seasoned with onion, leek, garlic, cumin, mint, coriander, and dorsal thorn, an unidentified flavoring. In the 1990s, when the chef and Assyriologist Jean Bottéro revealed the world's oldest cookbook, historians were astounded. The prevalent belief until then had been that the Mesopotamian diet consisted primarily of an unappetizing cereal pap. Composed at Ur in Akkadian, the twenty-four stone tablets recorded recipes for twenty-one spiced meats, four vegetable ragouts, bird dishes, garnishes, and pastries. Bottéro surmised that the brief culinary guides were intended to standardize and possibly ritualize kitchen procedures.

Early in the fifth century BCE, at the height of ancient Greek cookery, the physician Hippocrates of Cos classified many foods for their nutritional and healing properties. Foods that balanced the body's four humors—blood, black bile, yellow bile, and phlegm—and the four states—wet, dry, cold, hot—were regarded as sensual pleasures with physiological outcomes.

Hippocrates treated diet as a wellness regimen, suggesting the best way to cook different foods to make them more digestible.

Hippocrates's precepts from *Regimen II* (ca. 400 BCE) placed foods into eight categories—strong-tasting, moist, dry, salty, bitter, sweet, astringent, and oily. He wrote, "Take away the power from strong foods by boiling and cooling many times; remove moisture from moist things by grilling and roasting them; soak and moisten dry things, soak and boil salty things, bitter and sharp things mix with sweet, and astringent things mix with oily." (Albala, n. d., 2)

Similar concepts recurred in the writings of the military physician and pharmacologist Dioscorides of Anazarbos, author of *De Materia Medica* (On Healing Substances, ca. 50 CE). He instructed readers on the danger of poisonous mushrooms and the short shelf life of fish, melons, milk, and peaches. Likewise, Galen, a physician from Pergamum who tended the Roman emperor Marcus Aurelius and his successor Commodus, wrote about the therapeutic value of proper cooking in *De Alimentorium Facultatibus* (On the Means of Digestion, ca. 170 CE.)

In classical Greece, chefs were regarded as mere hirelings who competed for catering jobs among the rich. Although no whole cookbooks survive from Athens, greater classical Greece produced top chefs at Agrigento and Syracuse, two luxurious colonies in Sicily. They recorded regional cookery in two works of indeterminate date—*The Art of Cookery* (fifth century BCE) by Heracleides of Syracuse and the untitled food book of the Greek chef Mithaecus of Syracuse. More detailed is the Sicilian-Greek author Archestratus of Gela's amusing poem *Hedypatheia* (Luxurious Living, ca. 350 BCE), a segment of which Quintus Ennius translated into Latin verse.

The wit and themes of Archestratus's verse influenced an Egyptian-born Greek, Athenaeus of Naucratis, author of the 30-book symposium entitled *Deipnosophistai* (The Learned Banqueters, ca. 200 CE), a major source of information on Mediterranean dining practice. The text of the surviving fifteen books covers pantry essentials, cooks and servants, recipes for pastry and desserts, manners and conviviality, entertainment, dinnerware, and furnishings.

Surviving cookbooks attest to the Romans' wholehearted enthusiasm for good food. Even Marcus Porcius Cato, a consul and author of *De Re Agricultura* (On Agriculture, ca. 150 BCE), offered a recipe for a hearth-baked cheesecake. For the preservation of grapes, he instructed the bottler to seal them in an amphora with pitch and sink it into a pool. (Scully 1995, 80) The most punctilious of Roman authors, Caelius Apicius, heads the list of Mediterranean gourmands for the costly banquets that may have forced him into financial and emotional ruin. Surpassing his predecessors—the first century CE encyclopedist Pliny the Elder and the agronomist Columella, author of *De Re Rustica* (On Agriculture, ca. 50 CE)—Apicius left detailed lists of foods and suggestions of what paired well with what. His name is easily confused with that of Marcus Gavius Apicius, wealthy trader writing during Tiberius's reign (14–37 A. D.). The later Apicius, who thrived in the fourth century CE, published *De Re Coquinaria* (On Cooking) in the late 300s CE.

Texts on Medieval Fare

In the thirteenth century, cooking manuscripts began recording recipes and techniques. An anonymous Valencian author in the early 1200s recorded court cuisine for royalty in Muslim Spain. In a practical handbook of five hundred recipes, the compiler included an extravagant dish suited to a king's table: "One takes a fat young sheep. . .and puts a stuffed goose and in the goose's belly a stuffed hen, and in the hen's belly a stuffed young pigeon, and in the pigeon's belly a stuffed thrush and in the thrush's belly another stuffed or fried bird, all of this stuffed and sprinkled with sauce." The instructions concluded with burying the sheep in a calf, trussing the opening, and placing the carcass in a *tannur* (clay oven) until the skin crisped. (Eigeland 1989, 29)

A French-trained scholar, herbalist, and physician, Henrik Harpestraeng (also Harpstrang or Henricus Dacus), either collected or translated the first Danish cookbook. Proclaimed the oldest recipe compendium in Western Europe, the *Mittelniederdeutsches Kochbuch* (The Middle Lower-German Cookbook, ca. 1240) was a curious compilation of recipes in Icelandic, Danish, and Low German. The oldest copy, lettered by Knud Juul, survived from a monastery scriptorium at Sorø, Denmark, from around 1300. The text emphasizes various types of salt pickle as preservatives for fish, fowl, and meat. In the same period in Spain, the anonymous *Manuscrito Anónimo del Siglo XIII Sobre la Cocina Hispano-Magribi* (Anonymous Thirteenth-Century Manuscript on Spanish-Arabic Cookery) reflected shifts in typical Andalusian fare as two centuries of Arab infiltration beginning in the 1000s hybridized national dishes.

Italian cookbooks for nobility got their start in Florence with loose manuscripts and in England late in the Middle Ages with *Forme of Cury* [Cooking]: *A Rolle of Ancient English Cookery* (ca. 1390), a 200-page manuscript plus glossary and index written with health concerns in mind. It was composed by a consortium of professionals who probably cooked for King Richard II, a noted trencherman. Suited to the expansive fireplaces and staffs at Clarendon and Glastonbury, the compendium represents the grand cuisine of the fourteenth century or, as stated in the preface, "curyous metes for hyest astates" (curious foods for the highest estates). (Walker 1996, 45) The first entry is for frumenty, a grain drink mixed with almond milk for entertaining guests. The collection's listings of "brewet of almony," "oysters in gravey," "cawdels of muskels," "blank manng," "payn fondewe," and "lampreys in galyntyne," proves that the English were capable of sophisticated cookery.

From the same era, the European continent produced two compilers of cookery: Michel de Leone and Guillaume Tirel (or Tyrel), called Taillevent. Leone, a head clerk to the Archbishop of Würzburg, authored the first substantial German cookbook, *Das Buch von Guter Spise* (The Book of Good Food, ca. 1345), a forerunner of Renaissance compendia of kitchen advice. His fifty-seven entries detail the roasting of meat and preparation of flan, a term derived from the French *flaon* (custard). For a spectacular feast entrée, Leone explains how to roast and stuff a suckling pig. He gloried in pepper and salt, saffron, sage, parsley, ginger, anise, caraway, galingale, and garlic. His pasties were original and imaginative.

Taillevent, who was born in 1326 and worked his way up from *happelapin* (potboy) for Jeanne d'Evreux, cooked for Philippe VI de Valois and, from 1355 to 1368, headed the kitchen of Charles VI of France as royal chef. In his rise to fame, Taillevent earned the title of *premier écuyer de cuisine et maistre des garnisons de cuisine* (first squire of the kitchen and master of garnishes). In mid-climb to the top, under the influence of Charles V or Charles the Wise, he wrote *Le Viandier de Taillevent* (The Meat Cookery of Taillevent, ca. 1375), the first major French national cookbook. His text covers thickening soups with bread; preparation of substantial soups, meat, game birds, poultry, and fish; and seasoning with cinnamon, cloves, ginger, and nutmeg. In 1490, his cookbook became the first printed in French. It went through twenty-three reprints before 1615 and remained in circulation as a source of culinary and cultural history.

Early Cookbooks of India and China

A century before cookbook writing began in medieval Europe, King Someshwara III described the dishes cooked in the palace kitchens at his capital, Kalyana, India. After his crowning in 1126, he compiled the *Manasollasa* (Refresher of the Mind), a five-book compendium of royal delights. One chapter lists varied vegetarian and meat dishes and recipes for preparing them. With regal authority, he instructed his cook that

"even though food preparations served in earthen vessels taste well, kings must be served in vessels made of gold." (Achaya 1998, 89) A subsequent Indian poet-king, Basavaraja of Keladi, followed Someshwara's example by composing *Shivatattvaratnakara* (ca. 1714), an encyclopedia that described food preparation as essential to society and entertainment. Among Basavaraja's recipes fit for royalty, he lists bamboo rice, a delicacy that, because of the growth cycle, could be made available only twice in a century.

Parallel to the development of Western cuisine, China nurtured native food experts, including Huou, head cook for Kublai Khan in the mid-1200s. In 1368, Chia Ming published *Yin-Shih Hsu-Chih* (Essential Knowledge for Eating and Drinking), which supplanted the medicinal overtones of *Liang Fang* (Good Descriptions, ca. 1168). Its eight chapters contain a wealth of information on fifty types of beans, grains, and seeds, eighty-seven vegetables, thirty-four types of poultry, forty-two meats, and sixty-eight fish. He made a separate entry on sixty-three fruits and nuts and another division on thirty-three seasonings and sauces. He concluded with forty-three cookery methods involving water and heat. In addition to recipes, he explained the health benefits of foodstuffs and suggested methods of balancing the diet.

Renaissance Recipes in Print

The end of the Middle Ages and beginning of the Renaissance produced its own culinary experts—Chiquart Amiczo, master chef to Duke Amadeus of Savoy, and the humanist Bartolomeo de Sacchi, who went by the name Il Platina, a title derived from *piadina*, a flat bread indigenous to Emilia-Romagna, or from Piàdena, his home town. Chiquart's *Du Fait de Cuisine* (On Cooking, 1420) listed the enormous amounts of food he would need plus cookware and fuel for serving a sumptuous banquet. Platina's masterwork, *De Honesta Voluptate et Valitudine* (On Right Pleasure and Health, 1475), was the first cookbook set in moveable type. The text documents his philosophy of the good life, based in part on an ample table.

German cookbooks began to reflect the divergence of recipes for the elite and those of the *hausfrau*, or homemaker. In 1598 Anna Weckerin, a Swiss food writer, produced *Ein Köstlich New Kochbuch* (A Precious New Cookbook), the first such work compiled by a woman. One of her recipes prefigures the traditional *Rösti*, potato cakes patted out from shredded potatoes and minced onion.

In Tudor England, Sir Hugh Platte's still-room book, *Delightes for Ladies to Adorne Their Persons, Closets, and Distillatories: With Beauties, Banquets,*

Perfumes and Waters (1602), offers unusual suggestions for food preservation. For quinces, he advises an ale bath; for walnuts, he suggests covering them in the pulp left over from pressed crabapples. To rescue sailors from a diet of salted meat, his most exotic preservation method involved suspending beef in a barrel, drilling holes in the sides, and towing the barrel behind a ship. A more kitchen-specific work, *The Accomplisht Cook* (1660), by Robert May, a French-trained chef, catalogs more than 1,000, more than any other English compendium. Mary Tillinghast's *The True Way of Preserving & Candying* (1695) appears to derive from a confectionery training school, an emerging venue for kitchen careers for women.

That the French outpaced the English in culinary refinement was evident in Pierre Pidoux's *La Fleur de Toute Cuisine* (The Flower of All Cookery, 1543), the anonymous *Le Viandier de Taboureau* (The Cook of Taboureau, 1570), and Pierre François de La Varenne's *Le Cuisinier Français* (The French Cook, 1651), the first compendium to specify rules and principles of cooking and to promote natural flavors. Inspired by the heavy banqueting of Francis I in the early 1500s, the French had begun refining their unique style of saucing and stewing, with touches of cookery from Italian Renaissance sources imported by Catherine de Médicis.

Dining Advice for Princes and Peasants

The seventeenth century saw a burgeoning of texts by women. In Italy, Elisabetta Catanea Parasole produced *Prestiosa Gemma della Virtuose Donne* (Precious Jewels of Virtuous Ladies, 1600). In England, Queen Henrietta Maria, wife of Charles I, oversaw the compilation of *The Queens Closet Opened* (1655), a series of secrets for preserving, candying, and compounding of home cures. Among her recipes were instructions for collared beef, chicken salad, and a pumpkin-apple pie.

In the mid-seventeenth century an Englishwoman, Hannah Wooley (or Woolley), a governess to children of the nobility, published *The Cook's Guide* (1661), *The Queen-like Closet; or Rich Cabinet* (1670), and *The Gentlewoman's Companion: or, A Guide to the Female Sex* (1675), which listed recipes for candying flowers, advice on dairying and cleanliness in cupboard and larder, and remedies for common ailments. Her texts reflect the puritanic standards of the era, particularly admonitions to young women entering service of gentry.

The heightened sensibilities of Catherine and Marie de Médicis drew culinary artists and distinguished Italian *maîtres quex* (head cooks) to France. Period cookbooks, such as the encyclopedic *L'Ecole Parfaite des Officiers de Bouche* (Perfect Instruction for Table Staff, 1682), recorded energized kitchen techniques and the latest implements, table arrangement, and recipes. François Massialot, author of *Le Cuisinier Royal et Bourgeois* (The Royal and Middle-Class Cook, 1691), produced the first culinary dictionary and was the first to make a distinction between home cookery and princely cuisine.

The first break with past cuisine came from Vincent La Chapelle, chief cook to Lord Chesterfield. While serving in London in 1733, La Chapelle published a three-volume English work later expanded to the four-volume *Le Cuisinier Moderne* (The Modern Cook, 1735). Presaging the illustrated "coffee table" book, his anthology was the first of a series of expansive culinary treatises. The era's enthusiasm for food gave rise to new cooking pots of tin and iron, silver utensils, and varied menus highlighted with dishes named for kings, nobles, and distinguished individuals—such as béchamel, a creamy *velouté* sauce invented in a royal kitchen and named for the Marquis Louis de Béchamel.

Parallel to court cookbooks were the collected scrapbooks of home cooks, for example, the *Maddison Family Receipt Book, 1663–1688,* recorded in the handwritings of several contributors. For ordinary housewives, Mary Kettilby contributed a turkey-pickling recipe in *A Collection of Above Three Hundred Receipts in Cookery, Physick and Surgery* (1714), a folk approach to cookery that offered such casual directions as "boil a little longer" and "add [salt] when'tis cold." (Beard *et al.* 1975, 31) A competitor, Nathan Bailey, published *Dictionarium Domesticum: For the Use Both of City and Country* (1736), a catch-all text divided into six chapters: brewing, cooking, baking, and pickling; managing a kitchen, pantry, dairy, and henyard; herding; growing grapes for wine and cordial; raising bees; and making herbal remedies for the sick.

Eighteenth-century France profited from the cookbook of François Marin, compiler of *Les Dons de Comus: ou, L'Art de la Cuisine, Reduit en Pratique* (The Gifts of Comus: or, Kitchen Art, Reduced to the Practical, 1739), which included a comprehensive list of French sauces. His contemporary, known only as Menon, issued two important overviews of culinary fashion. For simple, practical menus, he wrote *La Nouvelle Cuisinière Bourgeoise* (The New Middle-Class Cook, 1746); its companion work, *La Science du Maître-d'Hôtel Cuisinier* (The Science of Cuisine Management, 1750), discussed the meal provider's job and appended many complex dishes for *les grandes tables* at any season of the year. Menon also wrote *Nouveau Traité de Cuisine* (New Treatise on Cookery, 1742), *La Science du Maître d'Hôtel* (The Science of the Master Chef, 1750), and *Les Soupers de la Court*

(Court Suppers, 1767). Among his specialties were waffles, ices and ice cream, pralines, macaroons, syrups, conserves, decorative sugar fantasies, mousses, and liqueurs set on tables adorned like gardens. Like La Chapelle, he abandoned slavish imitations of past dishes yet retained respect for antique and classic European cookery.

The first substantial Italian cooking encyclopedia was the work of the Neapolitan chef Francesco Leonardi, author of *L'Apicio Moderno* (The Modern Apicius, 1790). Working both in Italy and at the St. Petersburg court of Catherine the Great, he accumulated 3,000 recipes. His compendium surveys the food of six European countries but concentrates on Italian cookery, in particular, the Neapolitan preference for pasta in *sugo di pomodoro* (tomato sauce). Leonardi's culinary summary prefaced the writing of Ippolito Cavalcanti, Duke of Buonvicino, Italy's first official domestic food writer, who compiled *La Cucina Teorico-Pratica* (The Theoretical and Practical Kitchen, 1837).

In Barcelona, Juan Altamiras, author of *Nuevo Arte de Cocina Sacado de la Escuela de la Experiencia Económica* (New Cuisine Removed from the School of Everyday Experience, 1758), displayed the adventurous spirit of the kitchen innovator. He acknowledged the popularity of seafood dishes that included citrus fruits (which grew in abundance in Iberia), recommending, for example, that sea bream be simmered in a blend of fruit juice, pepper, garlic, and salt. His recipes reflect the lush visual banquets of Spanish art.

In the eighteenth century Polish cooks abandoned the nation's Latin standard, *Compendium Ferculorum* (Anthology of Dishes), written in 1682 by chef Stanislaw Czerniecki, in favor of a Gallic approach learned from a translated version of the French text *The Perfect Cook* (1786). Its sauces and pastries were a revelation to Polish cooks. The absence of cosmopolitan markets in Poland made it necessary for cooks to develop recipe substitutions—cherry juice or mead for wine, dried cherries for raisins, horseradish for pepper, mustard for ginger, mushrooms for olives and capers, and honey for sugar. Later editions revived old Polish cookery, as recorded by Lucyna Cwierciakiewiczowa, and energized a cultural spirit that allied Poland more with France than with Russia, its former culinary idol.

Czechoslovakian cooks found their champion in the nation's first cookbook author, Magdalena Dobromila Rettigova, a nineteenth-century Czech patriot and children's author, who published *Domaci Kucharka* (Domestic Cookbook, 1874). As described in its first cookbook, published in 1826, Hungary's cuisine drew on local Magyar, Turkish, Austrian, French, and Italian styles for sour soups and pot roast, meatballs, spitted fish, curd cheese, cheese spread, pancakes, and birch-sap cordial.

Evolution of Modern Cookbook Format

English food writers led the evolution of cookbooks to their current style and format. To provide home cooks with step-by-step guidance, Eliza Acton, England's popular middle-class cook and culinary advisor, issued *Modern Cookery for Private Families* (1845), the first text to quantify ingredients and list cooking times. The book achieved popularity in America through a version edited by Sarah Josepha Hale, editor of *Lady's Magazine*. The English author-editor Isabella Beeton published *The Book of Household Management* (1859), some 556,000 words devoted mainly to kitchen arts and management, lifted in part from Acton's book. Although she was criticized for plagiarism, Beeton's advice on cookery set a standard in England, the United States, Canada, and Australia. In addition to cooking advice, she offered home cleaning tips, such as sponging mirrors in gin and water, then dusting with powdered bluing and polishing with a silk handkerchief.

For the underclass, *A Plain Cookery for the Working Classes* (1852) provided valuable kitchen education from Queen Victoria's own chef and *maitre d'hôtel*, Charles Elmé Francatelli. Despite his large budget and phalanx of kitchen helpers, he displayed compassion for women who fed their families on limited expenditures and who cooked and baked at archaic hearths with primitive implements.

Eneas Sweetbread Dallas, the drama critic for the *London Times*, published a discriminating Victorian era cookbook, *Book of the Table* (1877) under the pseudonym of Auguste Kettner, chef to Napoleon III. Dallas held out little hope for the amateur cook and asserted that talent for cookery was a matter of soul. His overbearing rhetoric bolstered the image of the chef as an *artiste* who functioned above the plane of the ordinary kitchen worker.

Regional European cookery also found its way into print in nineteenth-century compendia. Karl Rumohr's *Geist der Kochkunst* (The Essence of Cookery, 1822), influenced by his cook Joseph König, looked back with affection on traditional peasant cuisine. The Scottish food expert Margaret "Meg" Dod produced *The Cook and Housewife's Manual* (1826), a major influence on F. Marian McNeill's *The Scots Kitchen* (1929), a repository of national dishes, beverages, measures, and festival foods.

In 1891, Tuscan cookery reached a wide audience with the publication of silk dealer Pellegrino Artusi's *La Scienza in Cucina e L'Arte di Mangiar Bene* (The

Science of Cookery and the Art of Eating Well), a readable collection spiced with anecdotes and advice on implements and method and concluding with an elegant menu for each month of the year. Subsequent editions reached best-seller status among middle-class cooks, who treated Artusi's compendium like a family heirloom and referred to as "L'Artusi," like the French "Larousse."

In 1895, the issuance of a French culinary newsletter, *La Cuisinière Cordon Bleu* (The Blue Cord Cook), expressed the high standards of the Institut de Saint-Louis, a private laboratory school founded in 1686 by the royal consort, Françoise d'Aubigne, Madame de Maintenon, to instruct 250 daughters of impoverished aristocrats and army officers. Those who did well in her classes earned the blue cord at graduation. The prestigious Le Cordon Bleu, an internationally renowned school of culinary arts, opened to the public in Paris in response to acclaim for the compendium.

American Cookery Classics

Valuable to New World settlers from Europe were the books they brought with them—Gervase Markham's *The English Hus-wife* (1615) was the most popular and influential household book of the period, featuring details of healing treatments, cookery, distilling, brewing, dairy work, dyeing, and fiber work. Published in the 1760s, Martha Bradley's *The British Housewife* was a revered work, as was Sarah Harrison's *The Housekeeper's Pocketbook and Compleat Family Cook* (1733). Another, Elizabeth Raffald's *The Experienced English Housekeeper* (1769), drew on her experience as a shopkeeper, confectioner, and manager of Arley Hall, Cheshire, England.

Typically pragmatic, North America's first published cookbook, Elizabeth (or Eliza) Smith's *The Compleat Housewife; or Accomplish'd Gentlewoman's Companion* (1727), attacked French pretensions—for example, such "preposterous recipes as stuffing a roast leg of mutton with pickled herring." (Aresty 1964, 112) In addition to six hundred recipes, Smith published menus for every month of the year.

A subsequent English volume popular in the United States, London-born Hannah Glasse's classic *The Art of Cookery Made Plain and Easy: Excelling Any Thing of the Kind Ever Yet Published* (1747), also rejected French exoticism and extravagance in favor of such wholesome folk fare as shoulder of mutton *en epigram*, "ragoo'd" hogs' feet and ears, and cod's head stew. She was the first food author to feature the clam, a common item at Wampanoag clambakes on the Atlantic shore. Perhaps because of Glasse's boastful subtitle and blatant pilferage of recipes from other sources,

Mary Cole, author of *The Lady's Complete Guide; or Cookery in All Its Branches* (1788), chided her for plagiarizing material and passing it off as original. Cole set an example by becoming the first food author to cite her sources.

The first American First Lady, herself a successful cook and recipe collector, added to colonial and federalist era cookery. Over five decades from 1749 to 1799, Martha Dandridge Washington, then a plantation homemaker and the wife of first husband Daniel Custis, worked at a kitchen project—compiling 104 recipes and commentary for her *Booke of Cookery: or, Accomplished Gentlewoman's Companion*. The compendium was a source of culinary secrets and heritage by which colonial housewives perfected cooking and invented and improvised kitchen shortcuts.

Bostonian Susannah Carter's *The Frugal Housewife: or, Complete Woman Cook* (1772) featured recipes for ample, filling cookery. One of Carter's menus begins with a first course consisting of "A dish of Fish, Vermicelli Soup, Chine of Pork, Veal Cutlets, Boiledt Turkey and Oyster Sauce, Beef Collops, Ox Palettes, Leg of Lamb and Spinach, Harrico." (Wolf & Byrd 1991, 119) Her derivative menus lack the fresh originality of those of food writer Amelia Simmons of Hartford, Connecticut, the author of *American Cookery* (1796), the first kitchen text written by an American-born food professional. One of Simmons' recipes, stuffed turkey, resembles the traditional turkey still being cooked and served in the twenty-first century.

The nineteenth century offered its own original kitchen advice, notably, Mary Randolph's *The Virginia Housewife: or Methodical Cook* (1824). Like Simmons, Randolph based her popular anthology of recipes on regional practice, local tastes, and produce common to America. Her dishes featured sweet potatoes, corn, field peas, squash, beans, pecans, and walnuts.

Additional works in the U.S. culinary canon include New England cook Lydia Maria Child's *The American Frugal Housewife* (1832) and Philadelphian Eliza Leslie's *Directions for Cookery* (1837). Leslie valued French method and American regional recipes. As the home economics movement took shape, books by Harriet Beecher Stowe, *Ladies Home Journal* editor Sarah Tyson Rorer, and Maria Parloa, the founder of the Boston Original Cooking School, enjoyed wide circulation.

Mary Tyler Peabody Mann, a member of a prominent Massachusetts family and the widow of educator Horace Mann, authored a cookbook with an unusual slant, *Christianity in the Kitchen: A Physiological Cook Book* (1857), in which she associated a healthful diet with religious virtue. Explaining why she favored simple dishes such as griddle cakes and vegetable stew over heavy suet puddings and rich turtle soup, she wrote: "If asked why I pronounce these and similar dishes *unchristian*, I answer that health is one of the indispensable conditions of the highest morality and beneficence." (Mann, 1857, p. 2)

Detailed texts became the norm late in the nineteenth century. Mary Johnson Bailey Lincoln's *The Boston Cookbook* (1883), was one of the first texts to begin a recipe with a list of ingredients. Because of limited literacy among indentured servants and slaves, the readers of these works were most likely the mistresses of the house rather than hireling cooks. Still, the informal methods of past cookbook writers did not instantly disappear. Thus, *The Economy Administration Cook Book* (1913) contained a brief recipe from a Maryland cook who followed a list of ingredients with instructions to "bake as quickly as possible." (Wilson & William Ferris 1989, 610) Obviously, the contributor assumed readers would have modicum of kitchen experience.

Cooking for Pleasure

Twentieth-century cookbooks generated a thirst for knowledge about the details of cooking, beginning with the phenomenally successful writings of Fannie Farmer, a columnist for *Woman's Home Companion,* and including *Echte Deutsche Kochkunst* (Genuine German Cooking, 1930) by the Milwaukee cooking teacher Lina Meier; Irma Rombauer's *Joy of Cooking* (1931); Lily Haxworth Wallace's *The Rumford Complete Cookbook* (1934); Ruth Berolzheimer's *The American Woman's Cook Book* (1938); General Mills' *Picture Cook Book* (1950); and the writings of the mid-twentieth century's popular experts James Beard, Julia Child, and Craig Claiborne, author of *The New York Times Cook Book* (1961). Elizabeth David's *A Book of Mediterranean Food* (1950) and the beautifully illustrated *Good Housekeeping's Picture Cookery* (1951), published by the National Magazine Company, introduced the same type of kitchen tutorial as featured in the appetizing color spreads in *Gourmet* magazine, which was first issued in 1950. Advancing from a format that consisted largely of text and the occasional line drawing to full-page color photos of hands at work in the kitchen, cookbooks entered a new era that boosted their appeal to beginners. The attractive images of beautifully presented foods elevated cookery from routine feeding of families to a form of artistry and a pursuit that brought pleasure to preparer as well as diners.

A trend toward historical recipe collections added immigrant memoirs and period collections to the body of cookery texts written strictly to instruct. One such work was *The Delectable Past* (1964) by the Iowa food historian Esther Bradford Aresty. Intrigued by exotic ingredients and unfamiliar cooking styles, Americans created a brisk market for ethnic cookbooks, including such popular volumes as Pu-Weï Chao's *How to Cook and Eat in Chinese* (1945), Maria Lo Pinto's *The Art of Italian Cooking* (1948), Ada Boni's *The Talisman Cook Book* (1950), Enriqueta David Perez's *Recipes of the Philippines* (1953), and Nancy Chih Ma's *Mrs. Ma's Chinese Cookbook* (1961). The masterpiece of the era, *Mastering the Art of French Cooking* (1961) by Simone Beck, Louisette Bertholle, and Julia Child elevated French kitchen art and taste above other national cuisines.

African-American cuisine found its way into print, both directly and secondhand through white cookbook writers such as First Lady Martha Washington and recipe collector Mary Randolph. Sue Bailey Thurman's classic *Historical Cookbook of the American Negro* (1958) and Jim Harwood and Ed Callahan's *Soul Food Cookbook* (1969) preceded a deluge of recipes from black cooks during the Civil Rights movement. The Creole and Cajun fare of the South influenced a wider audience with the publication of Chef Paul Prudhomme's *Louisiana Kitchen* (1984) and *Louisiana Tastes: Exciting Flavors from the State That Cooks* (1999).

A serious interest in Chinese cooking burgeoned in the West in the late twentieth century. One popular writer to make a reputation for himself, Kenneth Lo, originally named Lo Hsiao Chien in his native Fuzhou, China, worked as chef and restaurateur while producing more than thirty cookbooks, including *Chinese Food* (1972), *Cheap Chow* (1977), and *Encyclopedia of Chinese Cooking* (1990).

Two women, Mollie Katzen and Alice Waters, were at the forefront of the revolution in the American diet in the last decades of the twentieth century, when "natural" foods and sustainable agriculture became central concerns in cookery. Katzen appealed to the growing number of people turning to vegetarianism with her *Moosewood Cookbook* (1972), *The Enchanted Broccoli Forest* (1982), *Mollie Katzen's Vegetable Heaven* (1997), and *Mollie Katzen's Sunlight Café* (2002). Waters opened her own restaurant, Chez Panisse, in Berkeley, California, in 1971. To provide the fresh, seasonal produce that was the centerpiece of her recipes, she developed close working relationships with local farmers and other food suppliers. She wrote and coauthored a number of cookbooks, including *Chez Panisse Menu* (1994), *Chez Panisse Cafe Cookbook* (1999), *Chez Panisse Vegetables* (1996), and a cookbook/encyclopedia *Chez Panisse Fruit* (2002). Waters was one of the first in a growing list of U.S. chef-restaurateurs to become public figures by sharing their recipes, among them Lidia Bastianich (*La Cucina di*

Lidia, 1990), Mario Batali (*Simple Italian Food,* 1998), Rick Bayless (*Mexico One Plate at a Time,* 2000), Todd English (*The Figs Table,* 1998), Wolfgang Puck (*Live, Love, Eat!: The Best of Wolfgang Puck,* 2002), Julee Rosso (*The Silver Palate Cookbook,* 1982), and Charlie Trotter (*Charlie Trotter's Desserts,* 1998).

New Media in the Kitchen

Electronic cookbooks, which blossomed in the 1990s, offered search engines to locate specific ingredients and automatically adjusted dishes for half or double portions. Sophisticated programs printed shopping lists and narrated or demonstrated on-screen such intricacies as sewing up poultry or using a forcing bag to fill pastry shells. *The Digital Gourmet 2.6.2* from Books-On-Disk compiled one thousand recipes and allowed the cook to add to the collection. *Lilia's Kitchen, Volume 1: Exotic Vegetables from Electric Dreams* cooked on-screen in an animated format and provided an interactive instructional CD-ROM. The 350 recipes from Upstill Software's *Mangia* (2001) supplied rich detail of dishes originated in *Cook's* magazine, a no-nonsense professional publication known for its step-by-step instruction.

Two products combined recipe instructions with a tutorial. Coach Master International Corporation designed the *Kitchen Coach,* a remote-controlled television monitor with built-in compact-disc player that displayed professional cooking demos. Brother International's Kitchen Assistant, a handheld electronic recipe bank, allowed cooks to store and retrieve recipes and print out shopping lists.

Even more than these electronic devices, the Internet revolutionized the task of researching and comparing recipes. It also expedited the task of those preparing meals for people on restricted diets. Health-oriented recipes were available at www.foodfit.com. Food Network at www.foodtv.com boasted 15,000 recipes drawn from its television shows. Users could search by chef, cuisine, and ingredients, and a glossary provided definitions of technical terms. Cooking magazines launched Web sites such www.cooksillus-trated.com and www.epicurious.com in conjunction with their publications, and more than 700,000 international recipes were available from an ethnic cooking database at www.recipesource.com.

See also **Acton, Eliza; Akabori, Minekichi; Apicius, Caelius; Archestratus; Beeton, Isabella; Carême, Marie-Antoine; Escoffier, Georges-Auguste; Hale, Sarah Josepha; Knox, Rose; La Varenne, Pierre François de; Leslie, Eliza; Markham, Gervase; Marshall, Agnes; Pomiane, Édouard de; Raffald, Elizabeth; Renaissance Kitchens; Rorer, Sarah**

Tyson; Tselementes, Nikolas; Women's Magazines; Young, Hannah

Further Reading

Betty Crocker's Picture Cook Book. 2nd ed. New York: McGraw-Hill, 1956.
Bottéro, Jean, "The Cuisine of Ancient Mesopotamia," *Biblical Archaeology,* March 1985, 32–47.
Edwards, John. *The Roman Cookery of Apicius.* Point Roberts, Wash.: Hartley & Marks, 1984.
Hufton, Olwen. *The Prospect before Her: A History of Women in Western Europe, 1500–1800.* New York: Vintage Books, 1998.
Mann, Mrs. Horace. *Christianity in the Kitchen: A Physiological Cook Book.* Boston: Ticknor and Fields, 1857.
Ray, Elizabeth. *Alexis Soyer, Cook Extraordinary.* Lewes, Eng.: Southover Press, 1991.
Tselementes, Nicholas. *Greek Cookery.* New York: D. C. Divry, Inc., 1985.

COOKIE

Perhaps for its appeal to old and young, the bite-sized treat known as the cookie, derived from the Dutch *koekje* (cake), figures in much of kitchen history. The most famous specialty is gingerbread, invented on the Greek isle of Rhodes in 2800 BCE as *melitates* (honey cake) and popularized in the New World by the Ursulines of Quebec. The forerunner to the twenty-first century version of the delicately spiced cookie originated in England in the Middle Ages and took its name from the Old French *gingebras* for zingiber, a rhizome of the ginger family, Zingiberaceae.

Introduced into northwestern Europe in the late 1000s, perhaps by Crusaders returning from the Middle East, gingerbread became a favored holiday item. An early English recipe called for skimmed honey, saffron, pepper, grated bread, and powdered cinnamon. The recipe concluded: "When thou slycest hyt, caste Box leaves above, y-styked ther-on Cloves, and if thou wyll have yt Red, coloure yt with Saunderys y-now" ("When you slice it, sprinkle box leaves on top pierced with cloves. If you want it red, dye it with sufficient red sandalwood." (*The Wise Encyclopedia of Cookery* 1971, 542) Bakers cut the dough into seasonal shapes for saints' days and distributed it via strolling hawkers, who frequented carnivals and markets, such as St. Bartholomew's Fair in London and *Christkindlmarkt* (Christ Child Market) in Nuremberg, famed for its *Lebkuchen* (sugar cookie).

In the eighteenth century, the French pastry cook Avice invented a cookie called the *madeleine,* perhaps drawing on an earlier cake from Commercy. While cooking for the statesman Talleyrand, he molded bite-sized confections in an aspic mould. Encouraged by the renowned chef Marie-Antoine Carême, Avice

Baking cookies.
[© *Peter Usbeck / Alamy Images.*]

chose a feminine name for his cookie to please aristocratic diners at Versailles and in Paris.

In Russia cooks added potash or pearl ash to the batter as leavening, a practice also mentioned in the Dutch cookbook, *A Dialogue Between a Lady and a Pastrycook-Confiturier* (1752), and in American recipe compiler Amelia Simmons's *American Cookery* (1796), issued in Hartford, Connecticut. Artistic presentation of gingerbread involved pressing it into carved wood molds and decorating surfaces with gilt and colored icing, a stylistic detail mentioned in Elena Burman Molokhovets's classic Russian illustrated cookbook, *A Gift to Young Housewives* (1861). The most popular shape in Germany was the *Hexenhaeusle* (witches' house)—also called the *Lebkuchenhaeusel* (sugar cookie house) or *Knusperhaeuschen* (nibble house)—the dramatic woodland setting in the Grimm brothers' fairy tale of Hansel and Gretel.

At election day or training day exercises in New England, the militia paraded while onlookers enjoyed crisp gingerbread, stamped cakes, and beverages. The artist George Ropes painted one of these gatherings at Salem, Massachusetts, in 1808, depicting cooks' stalls open to display sweets and raised "election cakes" topped with a glaze of egg and molasses. (Weaver 1989, 104–105) Some colonial era cookie stamps bore royal crests; after the American Revolution, Indian figures, minutemen, George Washington, flags, and the American eagle were prominent. The horn book gingerbread, a reward for diligent students described in Andrew W. Tuer's *History of the Horn Book* (1897), carried numbers or letters in gold leaf.

A similar cookie-baking tradition derives from European settlers of Pennsylvania. As described by Samuel M. Sener, a state folklorist, in the New Year 1892 edition of *Christian Culture,* Pennsylvania cooks gathered their children by the wood stove to roll out sugar cookie dough on a cake board and stamp out cookies using tin cutters in animal shapes. A heart-shaped cutter produced a "sand tart," glazed with egg and sprinkled with hickory nuts. The name appears to derive from "sand heart" or "saint's heart." The dunking-size "apee" cookie took its name either from the English word *apiece* or the French *pain d'épice* (spice bread), another term for the Pennsylvania Dutch *lebkucha,* or gingerbread, which local immigrants pronounced "chinchbread." Another possible origin for the apee cookie was the name Ann Page, or A.P., cookie, a molasses-based dough spiked with nutmeg, cinnamon, mace, and caraway seed.

At Old Salem, the Bethabara Moravian community in North Carolina, members perpetuated traditions of hospitality and Christian good works by holding love feasts, holiday gatherings motivated by Christian unity and made fragrant by beeswax candles and their trademark spice cookie. Ingredients came from a steady trade with Charleston and Philadelphia, from which Moravian bakers bought almonds, mace, ginger, cinnamon, and nutmeg. In the twentieth century, one Carolina Moravian, Bertha Crouch Foltz, passed her cookie-baking methods on to her daughter, a seventh-generation Moravian. Rolled paper thin and cut into circles with scalloped edges, Foltz's dark brown, brittle confection, a Christmas tradition, adhered to the recipe of Old Salem's Winkler Bakery written down in 1821.

In the Amish community of Smicksburg, Pennsylvania, Mrs. Andy Miller created aggression cookies, a recipe that put restless hands to work. After her children dumped oatmeal, brown sugar, flour, butter, and baking powder in a bowl, they pounded, squeezed, punched, pinched, and slapped the dough before rolling it into small balls for baking. After ten minutes, they produced a sweet cookie—their reward for hitting dough rather than each other.

In the late nineteenth and early twentieth centuries, implement makers created jumble syringes, cookie presses that forced dough into bows, knots, and rings. The model that entrepreneur F. A. Walker offered in his 1870 catalog consisted of a tin cylinder with wood plunger. The operator gripped the dowels on each side and pressed the center post against his or her abdomen to force out a sweet stream of dough. Varied plates fitted into the end formed the dough into stars, half moons, diamonds, or other decorative motifs.

In 1903, the Kraft-Phenix Company went into business making Kraft cookie cutters, which later became popular collector's items. For specialty jobs, an Italian firm made Aspic tin symbols and number cutters, which included the four suits pictured on playing cards and ten integers for spelling out dates in cookie dough. At the turn of the twenty-first century, a baker making cookies for a special occasion could consult a Web site called cookiecutterfactory.com, which offered more than 600 hundred different shapes, including dinosaurs, musical symbols, tennis rackets, and cars.

See also **Molds**

Further Reading

Fries, Adelaide. *The Moravians in Georgia, 1735–1740.* Baltimore: Genealogical Publishing Co., 1967.
Shoemaker, Alfred. *Christmas in Pennsylvania.* Mechanicsburg, Penn.: Stackpole Books, 1999.

COOKING STONE

The use of a flat stone as a cooking surface, usually for baking a thin batter into a flat bread or toasting grains and seeds, is a tradition in many parts of the world. From early times, native peoples of the American Southwest, who had never been exposed to metal cookware, made pones, tortillas, and the paper-thin cornbread called piki on a duma, a greased, convex soapstone or steatite slab, which they heated at a fire pit.

At the Acoma Pueblo west of Albuquerque, New Mexico, cooks shaped their thin *mut-tze-nee* bread over hot stones. During long journeys, Choctaw cooks made flat corn cakes on portable dumas. In *The Raw and the Cooked: Introduction to a Science of Mythology* (1964), the anthropologist Claude Lévi-Strauss described how the Zuñi cooked maize cakes, a dietary staple, on dumas. The stone slabs had to be carefully rubbed with oil and resin to refine and lubricate the surface while they heated. Cooks so prized these stone griddles that they reduced their voices to a whisper while heating dumas to keep them from cracking. In contrast to the care lavished on cooking stones by the Zuñi, the Havasupai, who lived near the Grand Canyon, heated flat stones in the fire, pulled them aside for cooking piki, and then discarded them.

The hot-stone cooking method has been documented in other cultures and under other names. In Corsica, the *focolàre,* a baking stone heated over a hardwood fire, produced *mullade,* a large crêpe eaten with fresh goat cheese and fruit or jam. As described in Jean Froissart's *Chroniques de France, d'Angleterre, d'Ecosse, et d'Espagne* (Chronicles of France, England, Scotland, and Spain, ca. 1405), a detailed history of the Hundred Years' War, Scottish soldiers marching into Northumberland fortifed themselves with hot, fresh oat cakes cooked on baking stones, while English troops had to make do with rations of cold, stale military biscuit. Among the Andaman Islanders in the Indian Ocean, cooks used hot rocks to make chapati, the unleavened flat bread favored on the Indian subcontinent. Duma-style cooking also served explorers and trappers on the American frontier. Camp cooks made bannocks from a wild-rice dough cooked on preheated flat rocks balanced over an open fire. Duma-baked bannocks came into the twentieth century in such varied forms as raisin bannocks and cheese biscuits.

Further Reading

Pennington, C. W. *The Tepehuan of Chihuahua: Their Material Culture.* Salt Lake City: University of Utah Press, 1969.
Yzábalm M. D., and S. Wiseman. *The Mexican Gourmet.* McMahons Point, Australia: Thunder Bay, 1995.

COOKWARE

The broad array of metal cookware available at the turn of the twenty-first century—cast-iron, copper, aluminum, aluminum alloy, stainless steel—offered options to suit virtually every kitchen and cook. Some of these materials have been available for centuries, and others were introduced comparatively recently. The trusty iron kettle, sturdy cauldron, adaptable French *doufeu,* and Dutch oven were the mainstays of hearth, oven, and campfire for earlier generations. More durable than earthenware, iron pots can sit atop a stove or directly on embers to spread heat evenly and distribute it throughout the contents by forcing steam upward. The iron vessel requires an initial seasoning with oil or fat at high heat, a thorough rinse to remove old food flavors from the metal, and regular lubrication with salt-free oil after washing in detergent or soap to ward off rust.

The Chinese began making iron cookware in the fourth century BCE and developed the wok from earlier round pots. In Europe, the brazier with a small handle on each side evolved from the long-handled pots. The compact shape of the brazier, with its two small grips, proved advantageous: When ranges replaced brick wall ovens, it took up less space and made it easier for the cook to shift hot food from burner to burner or lift full vessels from the oven. Cast-iron

Assorted iron cooking ware.

skillets, which have served both civilian and military purposes, were a traditional favorite for blackening chicken and fish and baking biscuits and corn bread.

The development of coatings for iron improved the performance of cookware and lengthened its life. Because of its fragility, tin-clad iron became virtually extinct except as material for pastry molds. In 1925, Le Creuset in France simplified the use of cast iron by covering it with enamel, which eased problems with sticking and cleaning. Similar items such as the porcelainized cast iron made in Denmark by Copco and in England by H. E. Lauffer ended the problem of rust. Coated iron was capable of withstanding higher temperatures than traditional cast iron, but the coating reduced contact heat at the bottom of the pan during sautéing. In the late twentieth century, enthusiasm for retro design and the fad for collecting old kitchen equipment restored iron to kitchen use, especially in rustic mountain cabins and refurbished historic homes. For the everyday cook, the celebrated chef Paul Bocuse, invented a self-basting iron pot, which he marketed under his name.

Unlike mundane iron cookware, copper, which began supplanting ceramic and clay vessels during the Renaissance, brought warmth and panache to the kitchen. Copper easily took shape in many forms, including ladles, molds, teapots, kettles, trivets, and other utensils. In the Middle Ages, coppermongers set up shop in marketplaces and sold door to door, where they also offered their services for smoothing out dents, reattaching handles, and repairing loose rivets. Cooks welcomed copper cookware because it heated rapidly without creating hot spots and stored water in a pristine purity not possible with earthenware.

Copperware was substantial and serviceable, but its bright, shining surface discolored rapidly from oxidation, requiring either an internal tinning or constant scouring. Above the dresser at the Château de Champ de Bataille in France around 1660, kitchen workers hung a full range of copper bulge pots, strainers, warming pans, utensils, and basins turned bottom outward to display the diligence of the dishwasher. At Langton Hall south of Malton, Yorkshire, upended pots with handles extended lined the lower shelf of the kitchen dresser in close proximity to the work surface where foods were readied for cooking. The vessels' flat bottoms indicated use on a stove, another symbol of prestige and modernity as stove technology replaced openhearth cookery. Throughout Europe, proud owners listed their collection of copper pots in their wills as a legacy to the next generation of cooks. Artists such as the French still-life painter Jean-Siméon Chardin featured the glint of copper in their domestic scenes both as sources of light and evidence of kitchen hygiene.

Because of its softness, copper marred easily and reacted with acid to release toxicity into food. As a precaution against tarnished, stained cookware, a standard French copper casserole, dubbed a *fait-tout* (do-all) for its adaptability, combined a handsome copper shell with tin lining and brass handles for durability. Present-day manufacturers line their copperware pots and pans with aluminum or stainless steel to ally the strengths of the different metals.

Carbon or natural steel, which oxidizes and discolors from lengthy exposure to acid foods, was the next stage in cookware development. A competitor, stainless steel, developed in the late 1940s from chromium and nickel alloys, maintained attractiveness but heated unevenly and cost more than aluminum. Cleaner and more appealing than tin and iron, steel rapidly took over the kitchenware market, especially after clever marketing in the 1960s substituted the term *surgical steel,* with its hygienic connotations, for the less-scientific-sounding *stainless steel.* The addition of copper or aluminum to the bottoms of stainless steel pans improved heat distribution.

The addition of aluminum to the choice of metals for domestic use lightened the chore of lifting heavier metal cookware and reduced the cost of outfitting the kitchen. The use of chrome plating made aluminum stainless for use in egg trays, stew pots, fry pans, juicers, milk boxes, teapots, and coffeepots. Favorites included the Magnalite, Farberware, and Nambé versions, American products that alloyed aluminum with other metals to add beauty, durability, and grace. Attractive pieces like those made in Finland by Sarpaneva in the 1970s also provided burnished surfaces that went from oven to table.

Aluminum alloy cookware offers the advantage of conducting heat quickly and is more durable than pure aluminum, which dents easily and becomes dull with hard use. The main drawbacks of aluminum are the lightness of pot and pan lids, which fail to lock in vapor, and the discoloration of the metal caused by interaction with white wine and other ingredients. These faults earned aluminum cookware the disapproval of influential master chef James Beard. Sturdier sets, such as West Bend waterless cookware, gained popularity for their good looks, shiny exterior, and reputation for requiring only a few spoonfuls of water to steam most foods.

See also **Aluminum;** *Bain-Marie;* **Brass; Braziers; Double Boiler; Dutch Oven; Electric Cookery And Appliances; Enamelware; Frying; Griddle; Ironwork; Kettle; Metalwork; Mocucks; Ollas; Plunkett, Roy; Pyrex; Steel; Stone Boiling; Tagines; Teflon; Tinware; Woks**

COOPERATIVE KITCHENS

An alternative to a flawed servant system arose in the 1880s when American women proposed cooperative kitchens and group cookery. The idea had found two knowledgeable champions in 1869 with Catharine Beecher and Harriet Beecher Stowe, the authors of *The American Woman's Home, or Principles of Domestic Science* (1869), who suggested neighborhood laundries to relieve women of their most laborious chores. Both the reformer Jane Addams and the feminist Elizabeth Cady Stanton supported an idealized system of sharing work and delivering meals to others in the

cooperative that worked well in the beginning. Additional ammunition came from Edward Bok, editor of *Ladies' Home Journal* from 1889 to 1919. He wrote the column "Side Talk to Girls" under the feminine persona of Ruth Ashmore to support community co-ops and kitchenless homes. Holdouts like efficiency expert Christine McGaffey Frederick, product analyst for *Ladies' Home Journal* and author of *Household Engineering* (1920), rejected the use of outside agencies, claiming that professional laundries were rough on garments and might expose families to disease from mixing batches of laundry and by hiring disease-carrying launderers.

Christine Stansell's *American Moderns: Bohemian New York and the Creation of a New Century* (2000), explores some attempts at assisted housekeeping. The Cambridge Cooperative Housekeeping Society, founded by Melusina Fay Pierce in 1869, foundered before realizing its initial plan for a laundry, staples market, and cooperative kitchen. Another group, Chicago's Evanston Cooperative Housekeeping Association, worked out of a single building that turned out hotel-quality meals and laundry.

As reported in the American writer Dolores Hayden's *The Grand Domestic Revolution: Image and Reality in the Lives of Women in Northern New England* (1982), the servant situation worked no better for the group than it had for individuals. An inept manager and striking staff snarled work schedules. As a result, laundry piled up and soured, increasing the job of sanitizing and deodorizing it. Exacerbating the group's troubles were local wholesalers, who ceased supplying the co-op because of a merchant backlash.

Hayden also analyzed the utopian cooperatives proposed by the feminist urban planners Marie Stevens Howland and Alice Constance Austin. They assumed that by founding a functional commune they could free women of drudgery. Howland, in collaboration with the reformer Albert Kimsey Owen in 1885, planned a colony of cottages and residential inns kept up by a team of housekeepers at Topolobampo in Sinaloa, Mexico, but lacked the funds to actualize it. Pioneer colonists followed communitarian ideals, which Owen called integral co-operation. They established adobe houses and the beginnings of a railroad and self-sustaining model city that freed women of the preponderance of home drudgery. At the turn of the century, the colony dissolved from disorganization, disputes over private ownership, and difficulty securing water for their project.

In 1916, Alice Austin designed Llano del Rio, a socialist city of 10,000 residents of Los Angeles comprising laundryless and kitchenless homes connected by subterranean tunnels to central facilities for rapid delivery of finished laundry and meals. Her complex contained child care centers and underground utilities. As with Howland's feminist haven, Austin's plan lacked the financial backing to see it through and foundered from bad publicity and lack of water. In 1917, most of the remaining colonists tried a second time at Newllano, Louisiana, which survived until 1936.

See also **Amanite Kitchens; Amish Kitchens; Shaker Kitchens**

Further Reading

Degler, Carl. At Odds: *Women and the Family in America from the Revolution to the Present.* New York: Oxford University Press, 1980.

Hoy, Suellen. *Chasing Dirt: The American Pursuit of Cleanliness.* New York: Oxford University Press, 1995.

Peiss, Kathy L., "American Women and the Making of Modern Consumer Culture," *Journal for MultiMedia History,* Fall 1998.

Stansell, Christine. *American Moderns: Bohemian New York and the Creation of a New Century.* New York: Metropolitan Books, 2000.

CORDING

The use of cording and twine for domestic tasks dates to the earliest human settlements. In ancient Mesopotamia, cooks suspended pots from walls with rope handles, thus keeping stored foods free of low-crawling vermin. In Russia, hunters tied and suspended ducks from hooks or rafters while the meat aged. American Indians made tumplines to secure foodstuffs for the trek from forest or garden homeward.

As noted in Eliot D. Chapple and Carleton S. Coon's *Principles of Anthropology* (1942), the materials used depend on what was available locally:

Where skins are much used, as among the Eskimo, this cordage may consist mostly of thongs cut from hides, and animal sinews; people who use few skins and live in forests use vegetable fibers, such as rattan, hibiscus fiber, and spruce roots, which come in such long units that, like thongs and sinews, no secondary treatment is necessary to make them serviceable. (p. 112)

To create long, continuous cording, primitive peoples learned to twist and splice small lengths or to weave a plait, a development that preceded the basket industry. From cordage came fishing line, burden baskets, satchels, water bottles, parching trays, creels, and boxes.

At the Dolni Vestonice site in Czechoslovakia, impressions in clay from about 25,000 BCE revealed a twined netting. A similar textured pattern recurred at digs in the Spirit Cave in Thailand and Natsushima Shell Mound in Japan. In some prehistoric sites, fiber has survived. At the Lascaux caves in the Pyrénées on the French-Spanish border, bits of rope remain.

Needed for repairing woven vessels and making other necessities, cording was a familiar sight in native American hogans and tepees and among the Maya of Yucatán, who carried fresh produce in netted bags. The Aztec roasted squash blossoms stuffed with minced meat and spices and secured with cording. The Salish of Washington state tied layers of horn into place to shape it into table implements and cups. The Cree extracted oil from wild geese by trussing and suspending birds from the rafters of the cooking lodge. Householders among the forest Indians of the Great Lakes and the Cree of Alberta made kitchen cording from rolled and twisted bark of basswood, linden, willow bark, sinew, hide, or tulip poplar.

The Tepehuan of Chihuahua, Mexico, made cording from ixtle fiber, which they anchored to a post, scraped with a stone or iron scraper to remove leaves, then sorted fibers for washing and drying. The thinnest they rolled against the thigh; thicker lengths they attached to a post and twisted into an even length. With the finished cord, they netted gourd canteens and held broken ollas together until the glue could set. One special use of cordage was the construction of a fork of sapling branches for the gathering of cactus fruit. In early June, when the fruit was ripe, they anchored the two-tined implement to a pole with vine or ixtle cording and forced it into the top of the tall plant to dislodge fruits.

In Italy, Platina, the author of *De Honesta Voluptate et Valitudine* (On Right Pleasure and Health, 1475), stipulated that fish should be tied up in a wicker basket or onto a board before being suspending in a cooking pot. As described by the food historian Maria Dembinska, the author of *Food and Drink in Medieval Poland: Rediscovering a Cuisine of the Past* (1999), eastern Europeans also kept supplies of cording for cooking and drying. The Moravians strung circles of apples, pears, and apricots on cording and attached the ends to brackets above parlor stoves or in drying huts to preserve fruit for the winter.

In 1861 Elena Burman Molokhovets, a meticulous cook and housekeeper and author of the classic Russian cookbook *A Gift to Young Housewives,* gave explicit advice on cooking asparagus. For gathering the stalks into bundles, she specified Holland string, a cording taken from Holland cloth, a sturdy cotton or linen fabric. Her purpose was to avoid hemp cord, the everyday Russian string, which could impart an unwelcome flavor to the vegetables.

The French traditionally larded meats, game, and large fish with thin-sliced bacon or pork tied about the exterior with string or twine as a protection of delicate parts during braising. The French *carnier* (game bag) was a corded bag or net for holding fresh game or suspending it in the open air to drain before roasting.

In Scotland, the making of haggis, the national dish, began with the blending of spices and oats with sheep entrails. Cooks then stuffed the mix into a sheep's maw and tied the membrane securely before cooking.

In England and the United States at the beginning of the twentieth century, the strong holder or twine box allowed the housekeeper to reach for a free end of cording, pull out enough to truss a hen, and snip the required length with a scissors. Twine holders, which were round or spherical in shape, came in footed, columnar, beehive, and gimballed hanging styles in cast-iron, japanned tin, or brass. Through the use of decoration and fine materials, the humble object might be transformed into an ornate gift item. Worldwide, cord made from natural fibers retained its importance for kitchen chores into the early 1900s, when rubber bands and synthetic materials began to replace traditional string and twine.

See also **Babiche**

Further Reading

Barber, Elizabeth Wayland. *Women's Work: The First 20,000 Years*. New York: W. W. Norton & Co., 1994.
Clear, Caitriona. *Women of the House*. Dublin: Irish Academic Press, 2000.
Fitzhugh, William W., and Chisato O. Dubreuil, eds. *The Ainu: Spirit of a Northern People*. Washington, D.C.: Arctic Studies Center, National Museum of Natural History, The Smithsonian, 1999.
Mourning Dove: A Salishan Autobiography. Lincoln: University of Nebraska Press, 1990.

CORK

Because of its buoyancy, light weight, and resistance to moisture, cork—the bark of the evergreen oak *Quercus suber*—is a substance that lends itself naturally to use as a bottle stopper. The harvesting of cork is a painstaking process. A quarter century's growth is needed for the tree to produce a first layer of bark suitable for stripping. A second stripping about eight years later yields cork with a better consistency. It is the third stripping, however, that uncovers a layer with the even grain and supple consistency suitable for use as bottle stoppers and canister liners. Between the tree's upper limbs and roots, workers pry wedges of upper growth loose with a hatchet and air-dry it before boiling away sap and tannins. The process restores stability and elasticity within cells that are 50 percent air.

An article in the January 1854 issue of *Chamber's Journal* referred to the use of cork as a bottle stopper in Republican Rome. The Latin poet Horace told of popping the cork on a jar of vintage wine in 25 BCE. Traditionally, Mediterranean cooks and wine makers employed whittled oak pegs to seal wine bottles until the late 1600s, when they adopted the cork for bunghole stoppers in casks and shaped plugs for bottles. According to Prosper Montagné's *New Larousse Gastronomique* (1977), the replacement of the oil-soaked hemp stopper with cork may have coincided with Dom Pérignon's creation of champagne at the Benedictine abbey of Hautvillers in 1668. First cut for distribution in Ampurdan, Gerona, in the 1700s, cork enhanced red Spanish wines aged in the bottle.

Todd S. Goodholme's *Domestic Cyclopaedia of Practical Information* (1887) warned that corks could develop pores and allow evaporation. He advised particularly that home bottlers choose fine-grained, pliant material over hard, dry corks. The bottler left a space at the top of the bottle to allow the cork to rise under strong pressure, thus protecting the neck from splitting. A sealant of Spanish wax dissolved in hot water and softened with fat completed the seal. To recycle stoppers for *vin ordinaire* (table wine), users soaked them in boiling water, then air-dried them on a sieve to assure the removal of contaminants and mold. A final soak in brandy, alcohol, or marc (wine residue) assured cleanliness for home use, but not for capping drug containers. In 1999, the Neustadt Research Institute completed research into the recycling of cork that put an end to dunking in disinfectants and mold-killers to remove taint and off-flavors, substituting instead the use of a microwave oven. Nonetheless, by the millennium's end, wineries were turning in unprecedented numbers from natural stoppers to plastic.

Opening a corked bottle required a unique levering device to dislodge the plug. The *tire-bouchon* (corkscrew)—a domestic application of the bullet screw or gun worm, which extracted obstacles from rifle barrels—went through a series of reinventions before it became suited for food service. In July 1856, the New York designer George Blanchard adapted a tubular metal nutmeg grater into a corkscrew handle and attached the familiar wire helix corkscrew, an awkward device that slipped easily out of the user's grasp.

An invention of the mid-nineteenth century, the cast-iron cork press, a levered mechanism, shaped dampened cork into a variety of sizes. A cork puller or grapple, a four-pronged hand implement fashioned from twisted wire, secured a cork for removal or could be used to retrieve a cork that had sunk inward. Versions of the fifteenth-century French *tire-bouchon*, which lent its name to a ballet arabesque, applied the point of a steel spiral to a cork. Unscrewing the spiral caused the cork to pop out from the bottleneck. Another cork-working tool included the cork driver, a wooden bat or tamper that fit over a bottle top, and an ornate vertical bar press on a stand operated by a lever that recorked bottles by forcing a plug into the opening. In the late twentieth century, teflon coatings were applied to cork screws, making it easier to remove them from the extracted plugs.

During the Victorian era, cork aided the manufacture of kamptulican flooring, the forerunner of linoleum. A blend of gum, paint, and rubber solidifed with cork, kamptulican was a soft, vibration-absorbing surface inlaid in color. This material, which did not splinter or absorb dirt and revived with a damp mopping, made excellent washable kitchen flooring. Later, in the 1920s the Alaska Refrigerator Company of Muskegon, Michigan, produced a cork-insulated refrigerator. In its ads, the company promised that cork kept food fresh and unspoiled while lowering ice bills.

By the twenty-first century, cork had been adopted for many specialized uses in the kitchen, both practical and decorative. A renewable natural material that was nontoxic, nonallergenic, and biodegradable, cork became the major element in gaskets, expansion joints, coasters, hot pads, jar lids, wine racks, and candle holders. Devised in the late nineteenth-century but still in use was the fruit pricker, a piece of cork imbedded with needles. Cork also made a convenient surface for message boards and cushioned and sound-proofed ceilings and floors.

See also **Linoleum**

Further Reading

Clear, Caitriona. *Women of the House*. Dublin: Irish Academic Press, 2000.

CORN

First hybridized and grown in Mexico by Mayan farmers, the fresh yellow grain known as corn was originally called by the Taino or Arawak-Carib word *mahiz* (maize). A staple grain worshiped as a deity, it became the first human cereal, as documented by agricultural remains in Tehuacan Valley, Puebla, Mexico, from 7200 BCE. In his *Historia General de las Cosas de Nueva España* (A General History of New Spain, ca. 1590), the Franciscan missionary and archeologist Fray Bernardino de Sahagún characterized the reverence the Mexica, a Mesoamerican tribe, felt for dry grains: if kernels tumbled to the ground during cooking, the devout housewife snatched them up in fear that vindictive gods would let the family starve for committing sacrilege.

Maize was the prime staple of the Maya and farther south in coastal Ecuador, Peru, and Chile, where Inca cooks mixed a ritual pudding from llama blood and

A Guatemalan woman shells corn for tortillas.
[© *Courtesy of Agricultural Research Service, USDA. Photo by Ronald Riley.*]

cornmeal. Archaeological evidence dating to 4500 BCE indicates that corn cultivation extended as far north in the Americas as Bat Cave, New Mexico. About 2000 years ago, female gardeners of the eastern woodlands appear to have hybridized Mexican corn varieties into the Northern Flint species through selective breeding.

After 800 CE, the more prolific eastern corn varieties dominated native diets. The reduction of dried corn into flour made possible storage for hard times when game was scarce. Corn thus contributed to the health of the native peoples by providing steady nutrition year round. Improved diet, in turn, altered the basics of human life—population size, infant mortality rate, social structures, trade, land use, religion, tool making, basketry, culinary methods, even religion. By 1100 CE, corn had become the forest Indian's staff of life.

The earliest American strains were only inches long consisting of a cob and up to five kernels that ranged from white or yellow to ochre, orange, rust, and purple. Farmers valued dent corn, flint or decorative varieties, popcorn, soft flour corn, and sweet corn. The Aztec prized caterpillar-ridden corn ears and smut, a maize fungus that swelled and discolored grains. The Navaho sprinkled babies with corn pollen, a sacred dust. The Inca and Mexica fermented flour into a cidery alcoholic drink called *chicha*, which they manufactured in large vats for trade and sipped as a ritual drink from the skull of a slain enemy.

On the Atlantic seaboard, Indians were skilled at drying and grinding corn for meal to make bread. The Huron and Iroquois of Canada ate stone-boiled corn porridge as a daily staple, varying the dish with the addition of fish and game. The Iroquois also trench-roasted green corn in the husk. To simplify turning, they anchored a stick over the coals and leaned the ears against it. The value of corn to Indian civilization did not escape Christopher Columbus, who carried seeds back to Iberia, where they flourished in temperate areas and spread over most of the globe.

Colonists' Life Saver

After trial and error and with instruction from the Indians, in 1608, Captain John Smith, the founder of the Virginia colony, managed to break and plow forty acres and set it in corn. The natives who occupied the Massachusetts shore suffered an epidemic about the time that the Pilgrims arrived at Plymouth in 1620. Because elders buried victims with bags of corn and simple implements, New England's settlers discovered enough grain of "Guinny" or "Turkie" wheat to get them through a wretched first winter. (Earle 1975, 129) They experimented with planting corn grains but, in 1621, reaped a dismal harvest.

Governor William Bradford lauded Squanto, the Pemiquid translator and guide who, until his death from scarlet fever or smallpox in 1622, instructed the European newcomers in the sowing and tending of corn. Because it was easily stored, the corn the colonists raised was especially valuable during hard winters and in times of crop failure. Both native Americans and early European settlers relied on parching as a method of preserving corn. The Indians demonstrated how to dry, grind, and cook corn into hominy, *appone* or *oppone* (pone), *suppawn* or hasty pudding, and *sukquttahhash* (succotash). For its digestibility and wholesomeness to the English diet, Roger Williams praised corn samp, or nawsamp, a coarse porridge or mush the Indians flavored with maple syrup. The versatility of corn kernels beyond the table made it a valuable counter or game piece for children's games and an indication of an affirmative vote, a system used in the Massachusetts Bay Colony in 1623.

Corn on the cob was one native meal that found favor with Virginian Robert Beverley, the author of *History and Present State of Virginia* (1722), the first native colonial history. He reported that Indians "delight much to feed on Roasting-ears; that is, the *Indian* corn, gathered green and milky, before it is grown to its full bigness, and roasted before the Fire, in the Ear…And indeed this is a very sweet and pleasing food." (*The Williamsburg Cookbook* 1971, 97) In 1705, he also identified corn pone or ash pone by the local native name, *oppone,* and characterized it as a worthy snack and a handy, easily packed food for travel. In Louisiana, the humble grain did not meet the culinary standards of French colonists. They railed against the territorial governor, who tried to force them to eat corn, which they deemed unfit for the table.

An American Staple

Readying corn for grinding began with shelling, a tedious job that roughened the skin. One way to spare the sheller's hands was to rub two ears against each other or to scrape with a pegged hand sheller, which slid down the side of the ear, dislodging kernels as it went. A device called a husking pin duplicated the work of a hand sheller. Another method involved setting ears in a bucket and stripping kernels with an iron scraper. A streamlined shelling required pounding whole ears with a pestle into a shelling tub. The final stage of reducing kernels to meal or flour called for even greater exertion with a mortar and pestle, a hand technology that preceded the development of the grist mill. To remove meal from a grain bin or meal tub, the cook used a scoop or palette paddles, a pair of boards cut with thumb holes. Retrieval of the cornmeal was a simple matter of grasping the boards in each hand and forming a vee as a trough.

In the Dakotas, green corn time ushered in a period of hot fires and spirited gatherings. Cooks steam-baked ears in pit ovens lined with husks or boiled them in bark pots. William Cobbett's *A Treatise on Indian Corn* (1828) recommended that diners show no prissiness in picking over the ears, which he declared naturally clean in their husks. Eliza Leslie's *Directions for Cookery in Its Various Branches* (1837) advised a similar faith in nature, calling for cooking Indian corn in its inner leaves in boiling water for a half-hour.

As described by William W. Fowler in *Women on the American Frontier* (1976), corn-based meals were a model of kitchen pragmatism. For what it lacked in variety, the "hog and hominy" diet adapted well to different meals. Johnny cake or pone served as breakfast bread; supper consisted of mush with milk. Fowler noted, "When milk was scarce the hominy supplied its place, and mush was frequently eaten with sweetened water, molasses, bear's oil, or the gravy of fried meat." Historians have offered several explanations for the origin of the name "Johnny cake." The most feasible is that pone was a handy food for travelers, who took to calling it "journey-cake."

In the American south, African slaves made corn the centerpiece of their distinctive cuisine. Most slaves cultivated corn patches close to their quarters for their personal use. Along with collards, yams, okra, greens, and peas, roasting ears and cornbread were natural accompaniments to barbecued meat, fried fish, or chicken rolled in meal batter and fried in pork fat. Louisiana cooks added body and zest to corn dishes with okra, a natural thickener, and fiery red pepper.

In the Amana colonies, fall was the time for cutting broomcorn. Hand harvesting and husking corn ears was a job for Thanksgiving week. Using a leather husking glove, each worker applied the steel or iron hook in the palm to ears still attached to the stalk. After tossing the ears into a wagon, they stored the crop in corn cribs. When manufacturers added ornamental legs to stoves, cooks often placed pans on the floor beneath the firebox for parching corn, a slow process marked by frequent stirring.

International Appeal

In the Ukraine, as in much of the United States, boiled or roasted corn on the cob is a favorite of adults and children alike. Hungarian, Rumanian, and Slav cooks use cornmeal to make sponge cake, dumplings, pudding, and the Rumanian national dish, *mamaliga* (corn mush), which the nuns of the Rumanian Orthodox Sucevita Monastery serve in a communal dish in place of bread. At Polish weddings guests sing to the bride a traditional song telling of the importance of cornmeal to their husbands' comfort. In *From Carpathian to Pindus* (1906), Tereza Stratilesco wrote of the Aromanian Vlachs, a people who still speak a form of late provincial Latin and dine on the traditional *cucuosei* (corn mush).

In Italy, where ambassador Pietro Martire d'Angera reputedly introduced seed corn in 1494, the crop took hold on the Paduan plain. Modern Italian cooks made up batches of polenta, a thick salted cornmeal gruel cooked slowly in a copper *paioli* (cauldron) over low heat, as the base for other dishes or for topping with cheese or marinara sauce. As a thick paste, polenta accompanied sausage, quail, and herring dishes and could be formed into a roll, sliced with a string, and cut into strips for pastry.

In recent times, corn and corn products were the staple foods in many other locales worldwide, especially in Honduras, Belize, Cuba, Peru, Uruguay, El Salvador, Grenada, Guatemala, Iran, and Zimbabwe, and among the poor in the southern and southwestern United States. Iranian corn vendors soak ears in heavy brine before charcoal-roasting *balal*. The Tepehuan of Chihuahua, Mexico, and their neighbors, the Tarahumara, mixed toasted maize with water to make pinole, an everyday gruel. The labor involved rubbing two dry ears together, winnowing grain in a loosely woven basket, then heating it for thirty minutes in an olla or on a comal (cooking slab). Ground grain went into cloth bags or corncob-stoppered gourds for travel or into a pot for meals. Flavorings included native oregano, *yerba buena* (wild mint), thistle, garlic, and salt.

In the 1960s, the Hmong of Laos depended on rice as a staple but also valued corn for themselves and their livestock. The Hmong wasted no part of the plant. Daily domestic work began with milling in simple stone querns turned by hand. In addition to making cornbread, they distilled corn whiskey and fed stalks, cobs, and husks to their pigs.

African cooks have evolved their own style of corn cookery. The Ndebele of South Africa roast meat and cook corn porridge to serve to girls at their coming-of-age celebration. Swazis mix meat and vegetables with *liphalishi* (corn porridge). Namibians pound corn with *mahangu* (millet) into a fine flour for porridge; Tanzanians add millet, sorghum, and manioc to their *ugali* (corn porridge). In Botswana, *bogobe* (porridge), a cooked corn flavored with *mabele* (sorghum), is daily fare, either soft and soured at breakfast or simmered thick for noon and evening meals. Malawians and Zambians cook their corn flour into *nsima* (porridge), a standard dish. In the Cape Verde islands, the national dish of *cachupa* blends stewed corn and meat with manioc, a starchy tuber. Chadians make *boule*, their national dish of corn or millet; Lesothans and South Africans call yellow or white ground corn mealie meal, which they make into *papa* (mush). They shape corn gruel into balls or dumplings called, variously, *bogobe, mealiepap, krummelpap, sadza,* or *ugali.* The latter is a convenient accompaniment to *doro wat* (chicken stew) for dipping into the sauce.

African influence survives in Barbados, where cooks shape a dough of cornmeal and okra into *cou cou*. In the U.S. Virgin Islands, *fungi* is a blend of okra and cornmeal, a side dish cooks make to accompany *kallaloo*, a meat stew seasoned with the *kallaloo* green, which Africans imported to the Caribbean during slave days. Paraguayan cooks bake *sopa Paraguaya* (cornbread) with meat, onions, and cheese. Peruvians grill *choclo* (large-kerneled corn) over a brazier and top it with cheese.

See also **Mano and Metate; Mortar and Pestle; Querns**

Further Reading

Fowler, William W. *Women on the American Frontier.* Williamstown, Mass.: Corner House Publishers, 1976.

Fussell, Betty. *The Story of Corn.* New York: North Point Press, 1999.

Reid, Jefferson, and Stephanie Whittlesey. *Grasshopper Pueblo: A Story of Archaeology and Ancient Life.* Tucson: University of Arizona Press, 1999.

CORSON, JULIET

Juliet Corson, an editor for *Household Monthly* and home demonstration lecturer, promoted domestic science education for young girls and worked to improve the diet of the poor. Born on February 14, 1842, in Roxbury, Massachusetts, Corson grew up in New York City. At age eighteen, she worked for a teaching agency and on staff at the Working Women's Library at New York University.

In 1873 Corson set out to help working-class women learn to prepare low-cost, nourishing meals. To this end, she established the Free Training School for Women, a home-based school in sewing, bookkeeping, shorthand, proofreading, and cookery. She engaged a chef to hold live demonstrations, for which she provided underlying theory. In November 1876, she established home economics instruction at the New York Cooking School at St. Mark's Place, a pioneer in home economics education for women. Two years later, John Eaton, U.S. commissioner of education, hired her to write a history of European and American cooking schools and to lecture in Washington, D.C., at the Training School for Nurses.

An altruist who had experienced penury, Corson made her classes available to the poor without charge and published 50,000 copies of *Fifteen Cent Dinners for Workingmen's Families* (1877), which she used as a classroom text. She underwrote the publication and distributed it free with the aid of volunteers from the Woman's Education Association. The foods she recommended—broth, lentils, pasta, coarse-grained meats, and meat stocks—suited the needs of the disadvantaged, as did rice pudding, a wholesome dessert she advocated as a substitute for the empty calories of

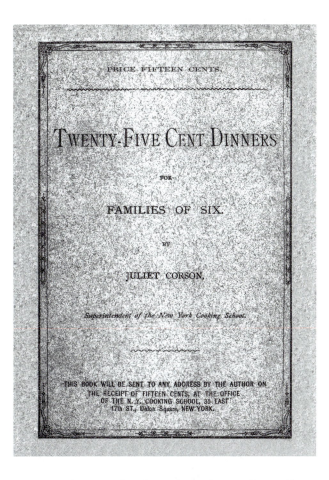

Title page of Twenty Five Cent Dinners for Families of Six (1878).

pie and cake. In the spirit of temperance, she promoted appealing and nutritious home-cooked meals as a means of discouraging male dalliance at saloons and grog shops.

In addition to many journal articles, Corson compiled *Cooking Manual* (1877); *Twenty-five Cent Dinners for Families of Six* (1878), a text reprised by the *Philadelphia Record* to aid the unemployed during the 1877 railroad strike; *Cooking School Text-Book* (1879); *Training Schools of Cookery* (1879); and "Hints on Domestic Economy" in the *Manual for Visitors Among the Poor* (1879), issued by a Philadelphia charity society. The latter influenced the food expert and dietitian Sarah Tyson Rorer at the beginning of her teaching career. Subsequently, Corson published *Juliet Corson's New Family Cook Book* (1885), *Miss Corson's Practical American Cookery* (1886), and *Family Living on $500 a Year* (1887), a compendium of articles she had written for *Harper's Bazaar*. She won an award for scientific meal planning and cooking at the Chicago World's Columbian Exposition, for which she compiled *The Home Queen World's Fair Souvenir Cookbook: Two Thousand Valuable Recipes on Cookery and Household Economy, Menus, Table Etiquette, Toilet, Etc.* (1893). She died on June 18, 1897, in New York City.

See also **Home Economics**

Further Reading

Bancroft, Hubert Howe. *The Book of the Fair.* Chicago: The Bancroft Company, 1893.

Corson, Juliet. *Cooking School Text Book and Housekeeper's Guide to Cookery and Kitchen Management.* New York: Orange Judd Co., 1879.

_____. *Family Living on $500 a Year.* New York: Harper & Brothers, 1888.

D

DAIRYING

An adjunct to livestock domestication, the consumption of milk and milk products as food dates back thousands of years. Historians know that Indian herders kept cows and buffaloes for their milk as early 3500 BCE. Activities related to dairying enliven frieze art from Ur (ca. 2900 BCE). Worldwide, communities varied in their acceptance of milk from different kinds of animals—asses, camels, cows, goats, reindeer, sheep, yaks, and possibly llamas. Goats have proved especially adaptable, enabling herders to settle such unpromising terrain as the mountains of Greece, the Mongolian plains, and the South African veldt, all of which offered suitable pasturage and a landscape the nimble animals could easily traverse.

Discovery of Dairy Goods

Nomadic families on the move milked, made yogurt, and turned their dairy goods into a variety of fresh dishes. Cuneiform inscriptions on Sumerian clay tablets describe a breakfast that typically began with milk and bread and concluded with dates. Early Kazakhistani and Irish cooks prized beestings (also beastings or biestings), the protein-rich colostrum or first milk produced in a ruminant's udder immediately after giving birth. Used in custard and rich pancakes, it bore a mystic aura for protecting the young in part because of a high antibody content that persisted for a few days after parturition.

Early milk producers in India, Scythia, Britain, and Germany serendipitously discovered a world of dairy goods—butter, sour cream, curds, yogurt, and soft and aged cheeses—from milk carried in skin vessels and inadvertently churned by the motion of pack animals. The Turks claimed to have brought yogurt from Asia to the Middle East. They still enjoy an iced yogurt drink called *Ayran*, a refreshing drink that Persians once called *musd*, Arabs recognize as *laban shrab*, and Indians know as *lassi*.

Over much of the world, animal-churned butter and cheese augmented an otherwise limited diet. In Anatolia, Hittites, who shared bread in religious ceremonies, found butter an economical alternative to oil, which was twice as expensive. On the Greek island of Santorini, remains of cheese survive from Late Bronze Age Therasia. A cheese pot from Palaikastro, Crete, contains a perforated base for draining whey. The Egyptians used small ceramic pots for cheese making and left offerings of cheese in tombs.

Classical writings abound with references to the importance of dairy foods in daily life. The Greek epicist Homer, writing about 850 BCE, mentions a pottage of barley, honey, and wine topped with grated goat cheese. The Greeks and Romans preferred olive oil to butter, which they valued at first only as a lamp oil, skin treatment, or medicine. Adults in ancient Italy drank beer, wine, or mead and reserved milk for children, the elderly, and invalids. Nonetheless, later Latin writings indicate a shift in attitude toward these foods, which came to be categorized as *oxygala* (salted curds), *melca* (milk soured in vinegar), and *schiston*, a curd manufactured in the first century CE. Plebe and

Wengern Alp cheese dairy herder milking cow, Bernese Oberland, Switzerland.
[© Library of Congress, Prints and Photographs Division (LC-DIG-ppmsc-06989)]

patrician alike added bread with cheese to the menu, including smoked and imported cheeses.

The desert nomads of Turkey and Arabia got their protein from yogurt, which they paired with dried figs and dates, onions and leeks, melons, and cucumbers. For ease of transportation, cooks jostled milk into yogurt in a skin *shakwa* (bag), then dried and salted the defatted, high-protein mass into small knobs of *jamid*, which could be reconstituted for later use. Ghee, a clarified butter boiled to remove milk solids, became a staple in Indian and Pakistani kitchens. In *Tuhfat al-Nuzzar fi Ghara'ib al-Amsar wa'Ajaib al'Asfar* (On Curiosities of Cities and Wonders of Travel, ca. 1354), describing his journey to Delhi, the famed Arab geographer Ibn Battuta mentions that he dined on honey cakes flavored with ghee.

Dairying took on an even greater significance to cooks in northwestern Europe than to those in the Mediterranean region. By the time of the Anglo-Saxon conquest of Celtic England in 449 CE, local food preparation centered on simple meals of spit-cooked meats, bread, milk, cheese, and butter.

Other peoples developed their own sources of milk. In western Asia, milk was a staple to the horse riders of the plains. In 1280, when Mongol invaders controlled China, they suppressed typical kitchen fare in favor of their own foodstuffs. In place of eastern China's rice-based diet, they introduced mare's milk as the standard and set milk above all other foods at their food festivals. In northeast Africa, the Somali relished camel milk, a sustaining drink that spoiled less quickly than other types of milk. Soured camel's milk was usable for weeks and sustained desert travelers who had nothing else to eat or drink.

On the European continent throughout the Middle Ages, milk was not a kitchen staple because of its short storage life and its reputation for endangering health. Milk was believed to cause headaches and tooth decay, and as a recipe ingredient, it turned foul in combination with fish. One major exception was the Low Country. Butter was a standard additive to oil in Dutch and

Flemish kitchens, and hard cow's and sheep's milk cheeses were common sights at Dutch markets. One Low-Country dish requiring milk was *furmenty* (wheat gruel), which appears in the first Dutch cookbook, *Notabel Boecxken van Cokeryen* (Notable Cookbook, 1510), an anonymous work compiled and printed in Brussels by Thomas van der Noot, and in Gheeraert Vorselman's *Eenen Nyeuwen Coock Boeck* (New Cookbook, 1560), printed at Antwerp.

Women's Work

When dairying gained popularity in Britain, it dominated much of the workday. The term *dairy* is derived from *dey* (milkmaid) and *erie* (the milk processing room). As described in Dorothy Hartley's cultural history *The Land of England* (1979), an efficient kitchen servant familiar with a "house cow" could slip a wood yoke about an animal, press the ground peg into the sod, milk the animal, and return to the hearth with a full pail in one quick operation. (Hartley 1979, 102) More exacting were the responsibilities of full-time cow tender, who was nearly always female.

Before working up butter, the dairymaid washed up to her elbows in cold salted water, with the rock salt scouring her hands to toughen them. The summer milk collection, salted at a ratio of one to sixteen, went into a barrel for knuckling and kneading into the mass to be sold in winter to shippers. For small quantities to be sold in summer, she pressed each batch with the farm's token, a carved symbol to identify the source. In East Anglia, the use of a ring gauge determined that each butter roll met standards for selling by the yard.

Dairy commerce enriched the farmstead, primarily owing to the long storage life and portability of cheese. In addition to churning and butter management, the dairymaid had to master different types of cheese making, attend to dairy vessels, and weigh and date each run of cheeses. She also had to be prepared for regular inspection by bailiff and provost to be certain that cheese production was in order and that farm staff had neither stolen nor whittled down the rounds. In addition to milking duties, the dairymaid had to remain on hand to winnow grain and to tend poultry.

For smallholders lacking servants, the moralist John Fitzherbert, author of *The Book of Husbandry* (1523), laid the task of kitchen and dairying to the goodwife, whose day spooled out into a predictable series of gender-specific domestic chores: "When thou art up and ready, then first sweep thy house, dress up thy dish-board, and set all things in good order within thy house; milk thy kine [cows], feed thy calves, sile [strain] up thy milk, take up thy children and array them, and provide for thy husband's breakfast, dinner,

supper, and for thy children and servants, and take thy part with them." (Fitzherbert, n. p.) The natural flow of daily labors continued with transporting corn and malt to the mill, baking, brewing, feeding swine, and then returning to the dairy house to make butter and cheese.

In *A Godly Form of Householde Government* (1598), the coauthors, the Puritan ministers John Dod and Robert Cleaver, ranked the servant hierarchy in Rutland, England, according to wages received: dairymaids got more than brewers, bakers, or drudges. A century and a half later, William Ellis, a diarist and domestic writer from Little Gaddesden, Hertsfordshire, commented in his eight-volume *The Modern Husbandman* (1750) that a good dairier was quite valuable, especially one who rose readily, worked diligently and skillfully, and maintained cleanliness. It is no wonder, then, that Hartley includes the plea of a "huswife" in need of dairy help: "Then neighbours, for God's sake! if any you see, Good servant for dairy house—waine [transport] her to me!" (Hartley 1979, 102)

If women bore sole responsibility for dairy work in England, they were excluded from it in Islamic countries. In *The Complete Book of Turkish Cooking* (1991), Ayla Esen Algar explained that in 1573 laws prohibited women from even entering the doors of special milk shops. Men tended to linger for conversation over the clotted cream of water buffalo milk, which cooks simmered on a tray, then chilled. To the thinking of the religious authorities, the lure of contented, idle men apparently drew the type of woman who was seeking romance.

In the English dairy house, tiling improved the sanitation and decor in the 1600s at the same time that it eased the dairymaid's hard job of scrubbing down walls and floor. The familiar blue-and-white delft tile adorned such model edifices as Queen Mary's dairy at Hampton Court in 1689, Howsam Hall in York, and Brocklesby Park, Lincolnshire, completed in 1779. The production of cream-toned dairy tile by Josiah Wedgwood in the 1780s gave local establishments a native distinction.

Throughout the Renaissance, Europeans relied on dairy foods, even during fast days. In 1611, the Archbishop of Hungary acquired a papal exemption permitting this practice, which was apparently already established, with or without Vatican consent. Traveler and historian Fynes Moryson's *Irish Wars* (1617) described with some disdain the native diet of the Irish, firm Catholics who dined primarily on oatcake, white meat, and "bonaclabbe" (bonny clabber), the local name for sour cream. (Davidson 1999, 405)

Advances in domestic technology during the Renaissance made few inroads on the long day and exhausting work of the dairymaid. In *The Gentle-woman's Companion: or, A Guide to the Female Sex* (1675), Hannah Wooley, a proponent of England's dairy industry, gave specific advice about milk collection. She advocated milking between 5:00 and 6:00 a.m. in spring and summer and again at 6:00 in the evening. She scolded the careless milkmaid for beginning late or leaving the udder partially stripped, both causes of an unprofitable dairy. Of dairy goods, Wooley believed that cream was the most nutritious and warned that an unclean dairy worker deserved to lose her reputation.

Before the discovery of bacteria, European dairies gave no thought to bacterial contamination. When Sicilian herders moved nannies through hamlets, customers would approach with empty containers and receive fresh supplies milked on the spot. Through the narrow streets of British towns, dairymaids bore open milk cans on their heads in range of night soil tossed from upper-story windows. As they approached likely customers, they called "Milkmaid below," a common seller's cry that elided to "Milko" and "Meow," an enticement to buy as well as a warning that dairy goods were at risk below open casements. (Pinto 1949, 39)

Dairies in the Americas

Unlike the rest of the world, the Americas had no butter or cheese until Christopher Columbus's second voyage in late September 1493, when his fleet of seventeen ships set out for the New World from Cadíz with dairy cows. The first settlers at Jamestown in 1607 and Plymouth in 1620 clearly recognized the need for dairying. In 1624, they transported a bull and three cows from England to Massachusetts, where dairying became a standard kitchen art. Five years later, newcomers aboard the *Talbot* added thirty heifers, twelve mares, and goats, which offered another source of milk, then selling in Maine for three pence to sixpence a pound.

American colonists respected the importance of cleanliness without understanding the concept of microbial contamination. For ease of sterilization, they chose glazed pottery for storing milk and employed tin milk pans, metal strainers, metal spoons, and fleeting dishes or skimmers. Butter molds, the dashers of churns, and the scored utility paddles known as "Scotch hands," traditionally carved of wood, required careful soaking to prevent mold and off-flavors. These precautions were a necessity to the dairy worker who sold tub butter at market, often after transporting goods a long distance by barrow or wagon.

Dairy animals increased in value as the colonies took hold. When bare subsistence gave way to a less

precarious lifestyle, dairy foods were popular to provide variety at table. For guests, a cook might melt cheese over plain vegetable casseroles and stir up a posset by curdling half-and-half with wine or ale. By 1700, the provision of dairy products for home use had evolved into a dependable butter and cheese business that provided families with cash for purchasing commercial foodstuffs.

Russian immigrants in America improved the butter-making process by demonstrating how fifteen minutes of simmering expedited the churning process, increased the yield, and improved flavor and storage life. From the *smetana* (whey), they blended beet stock to make borscht, the staple soup of the Russian table. Another favorite was the peasant specialty *varenets*, a fermented milk pudding.

In the American Southwest, Hispanic women made *asadero* (goat cheese) for home and trade, a kitchen business that employed the children of the family in tending and milking herds. When Anglos first settled parts of New Mexico, they engaged in labor-intensive dairy work calling for sterilizing pails and implements, sterilizing strainer cloths, and churning. To their surprise, there was no established market for their butter. The reason was a matter of kitchen tradition—local Hispanic cooks preferred lard for shortening and flavoring.

In 1825, Colin Mackenzie's popular kitchen guide *Mackenzie's Five Thousand Receipts in All the Usefull and Domestic Arts: Constituting a Complete Practical Library* advised homemakers on the choice of "milch cows." The text suggests that families consider Suffolk dun cows, small, polled animals that produced the best quantity and quality of milk. For larger stock, the monograph advocates short-horned Yorkshire or Holderness cows, claimed to be "great milkers." Of the last two, the author claims that the Yorkshire "make a picturesque figure in the grounds." (Powell 1974, 7) A less productive choice, the Alderney cow, gave a smaller quantity of rich milk, particularly in winter, and refused to fatten up for use as beef cattle. In his instructions to "the woman" who tended the stock, he advises that she establish a calm routine, forbid substitutes from handling her cows, and limit chitchat while working in the stall. As an aside, Mackenzie notes that cows withhold their milk if frightened by thunder, chased by a dog, or disturbed at milking time.

Of the rigors of dairying at her home in Cummington, Massachusetts, housewife Sarah Snell Bryant, mother of the poet William Cullen Bryant, spoke of the endless toil of weaning calves, scalding pails, washing muslin strainers, setting milk to sour, working up butter, selling veal, and hiring dairymaids to assist with the daily tasks. To guard against spoilage, dairy managers made butter only ten months of the year and reserved the hottest two months for making cheese, a task that Bryant preferred. For the greatest control over temperature, she withdrew to the north side of her home. Her favorite product was sage-flavored skimmilk cheese, which German immigrants called *shmierkase* (cottage cheese). Lovers of hard cheese disdained it as pig swill.

In 1857, the work of the French chemist and microbiologist Louis Pasteur culminated in the development of pasteurization, a process named in his honor. The process involved raising the temperature of milk to 158 degrees Fahrenheit, which killed bacteria and thus lengthened storage life and delayed souring. With the advent of pasteurization, homemakers were able to serve milk without fear of exposing their families to brucellosis, a disease of dairy cows, or to tuberculosis, a scourge of the era.

By 1860, American engineer L.O. Colvin had simplified dairy work by perfecting a bellows-driven vacuum milking process. His device relieved householders of enslavement to a twice-daily milking schedule. By applying four rubber cups to the cow's udder, the milker could extract milk and deliver it to an enclosed vessel via a sanitary hose line. A few years later, at the height of the American Civil War, Gail Borden, Jr., a floundering Texas entrepreneur, invented condensed canned milk, an easily storable form of milk that was welcomed by military provisioners.

In 1865, Martha Johnson Patterson, daughter of President Andrew Johnson, moved her family of five children from Greeneville, Tennessee, to the White House and superintended the kitchen for her father. To supply the first family's table with dairy goods, she started a dairy. Pasturing two jerseys on the grounds, she would "don a calico dress and spotless apron, then descend to skim the milk and attend the dairy before breakfast." (Cannon & Brooks 1968, 262)

Application of New Technologies

Four years after the end of the Civil War, inventor Anna Corey Baldwin, a farm wife in Newark, New Jersey, determined to make her dairy provide more income. She invented a cooling tube that forced raw milk against chilled baffles resembling the inner workings of an ice cream freezer. Her hygienic glove-milker increased the efficiency of automated milking by replacing rubber suction cups for each teat with an elastic sack that covered the entire udder and with feed lines attached to a suction pump. Another of her ideas was the straining of soured milk to recover curds to be made into chicken feed.

In 1876, Gustav de Laval, a Swedish engineer, and Oskar Lamm simplified the home job of skimming

cream from milk with their invention of the steam-powered centrifugal cream separator. The De Laval Company marketed the smallest of these machines, called Baby No. 1, which could process 150 pounds of milk per hour, for the home dairy. A testimonial lauded the device: "The use of the 'Baby' is a daily source of pleasure to my wife. No more carrying milk to and from the house and barn, tracking mud and filth into the house to the disgust and annoyance of the farmer's wife." (Jensen, 2000, 190) As advertised in an 1894 issue of *Farm and Dairy*, the hand-cranked model sold for $75, a high price for a home dairy but worth the investment if it simplified a daily money-making chore.

In the United States, women who ran home dairies began streamlining their work, keeping more cows, and selling the cream to butter factories for profit rather than churning butter for sale or trade at grocery stores. They separated the valuable cream at home and transported it in ten-gallon galvanized cans by wagon or truck to local creameries. Thus, they reduced the labor required to haul whole milk to market.

Dairy implement makers took note and met the demands for better equipment. The 1908 Sears, Roebuck catalog showed a cream separator that sold from $26.30 to $43.65, depending on capacity. A full-page schematic drawing illustrated the workings of the multiplex bowl, which saved the user three to ten times the butter fat that other machines lost. Fifteen years later, the mail-order giant was still supplying dairies with lidded steel milk containers, milk aerators, pint and quart bottles, sleek aluminum ladles, and a variety of churns. For $6.95, the dairy worker could buy a milk testing kit comprising a flagon of acid, test bottles, brush, measure, pipette, and directions for determining the quality of milk and cream.

Twentieth-Century Developments

Even after the turn of the twentieth century, dairying outside of the United States remained as wearying as it had been in the Middle Ages. On the Australian frontier, dairying was less a business than a farm necessity. Kathleen Peel, a housewife in Kyabram, Victoria, around 1912, began her day with barn chores. To expedite the job, she pushed her milk can on a two-wheeled cart. The long metal handles and suspended tray held baskets and equipment; her apron pocket carried the smaller implements needed for the job. In Munich, Germany, women continued to dominate the dairy labor force, a job that, according to one report from 1912, threatened the mental and physical health of milkmaids, who toiled from 5:00 a.m. to 9:00 p.m. in damp cellars.

In the United States commercial dairies gained the public trust with the passage of several state sanitary practice laws in 1921 and with the introduction of homogenized milk six years later. An ad in the January 1925 issue of *Good Housekeeping* urged homemakers to eschew fresh milk from the farm wife's pail: "Bottled milk is clean and protected…good evidence that your milkman is progressive and gives good service." ("A Bottle," 1925, 164) By 1939, families could purchase milk by the half-gallon in waxed cardboard cartons.

Americans and Europeans began to support a vast ice cream, gelato, and frozen yogurt industry. In part, the success of ice cream is credited to the unnamed girlfriend of Charles Menches. At the Louisiana Purchase Exposition in St. Louis in 1904, she had difficulty holding her beau's gifts of flowers and an ice cream sandwich. She removed a wafer from the sandwich and furled it into a cone to hold the ice cream. A New Jersey salesman, Abe Doumar, spread the idea to an ice cream vendor on the midway. The ice cream cone was not only a novel serving device, it also eliminated the labor involved in supplying and washing glass dishes. By 1948, American inventor Nancy Johnson had domesticated ice cream production with the invention of a home freezer. This same era saw the introduction of acidophilus milk, a flora-rich milk that allowed lactose intolerant individuals to enjoy dairy foods.

Universal Appeal

With the exception of China, where dairy products are not commonly available and therefore have little influence on cooking styles, dairy foods have become a part of the diet in virtually every corner of the world. Where camels or goats are plentiful in Saudi Arabia, Tajikistan, and Somalia, milk is a common beverage, and yogurt and ghee are widely used as food dressings. Filipinos have traditionally made their own fermented milk drink, called *halo-halo*, with sweetened beans and fruit to pour over crushed ice. Curds and whole milk remain a staple in Mongolia.

In Guinea-Bissau, where malnutrition has threatened the young, milk has become a common mealtime drink for those who raise cows. Dairy foods remain an important part of the diet in Chad, where cooks heat milk with sugar and cardamom or sour it for yogurt. Buttermilk has been the preferred meat tenderizer and marinade in South Africa; Ethiopian cooks use *niter kebbeh* (clarified butter) as an ingredient of a spicy stew called *doro wat*. For dessert, they top servings of yogurt with a sweet syrup of lemongrass and fresh berries.

Dairying has been problematic in some parts of Africa—in Niger, for example, where the health threat posed by the tsetse fly led to prohibition of cattle herding and pasturing. For dairy items, locals turned to powdered milk, cheese, and canned margarine. Only the Fulani successfully raised cattle and turned milk into yogurt for home use and sale. Cooks fermented *hura* from milk, millet, and hot pepper.

In Mauritania Nancy Abeiderrahmane, an engineer-dairywoman, established Laitière de Mauritanie, a commercial operation in camel milk, in the late 1980s. At her business outside Nouakchott, she convinced nomadic herders to abandon independent sales. Instead, they delivered fresh supplies of milk to her company for pasteurization, packaging, chilling, and delivery. In exchange, she offered fodder. Her business supplied small grocers and individual customers with clean, disease-free milk to replace the sterilized powdered milk once imported from Europe. She also developed "camelbert," a firm cheese made with camels' milk.

One of the most milk-centered diets in the world is that of the Maasai of Kenya, who feed their dairy herds on beer, milk, and herbs. Milk also plays an integral part in their rituals. The milking and slaughtering of goats accompanies the baby-naming ceremony, and unmarried girls offer drinks of milk to their sweethearts. At their rites of passage, boys are sprinkled with milk and honey beer by their mothers. Women provide delicacies and milk for a late-night ritual in which warriors earn blessings from the god Enkai, who watches over families and cattle.

See also **Borden, Gail Jr.; Cheese; Churning; Dalén, Nils Gustaf; Ice Cream; Kosher Kitchens; Margarine; Molds; Wood**

Further Reading

Beckwith, Carol, and Angela Fisher. *African Ceremonies*. 2 vols. New York: Harry N. Abrams, Inc., 1999.
"A Bottle of Milk Is a Bottle of Health," *Good Housekeeping*, January 1925, 164.
Ellis, William. *Country Housewife's Family Companion*. London: Prospect Books, 2000.
Hale, Sarah Josepha. *Early American Cookery: "The Good Housekeeper, 1841,"* Mineola, N. Y.: Dover Publications, 1966.
Jensen, Joan M., "Dairying and Changing Patterns of Family Labor in Rural New Mexico," *New Mexico Historical Review*, April 2000, 157–193.
Lysaght, Patricia, ed. *Milk and Milk Products from Medieval to Modern Times*. Edinburgh: Canongate Press, 1994.
Smith, Sylvia, and Richard Duebel, "Mauritania's Dromedary Dairy," *Aramco World*, November–December 1997, 32–35.

DALÉN, NILS GUSTAF

The Swedish engineer Nils Gustaf Dalén developed the Aga cooker and revolutionized the design of kitchen stoves. Born in Stenstorp on November 30, 1869, he grew up on a farm. After receiving a degree in mechanical engineering from Chalmers Technical Institute in Göteborg, he went on to post-graduate study at Zurich's Swiss Federal Institute of Technology.

Dalén worked briefly designing hot-air turbines for the De Laval Steam Turbine Company and formed a partnership to market a milking machine. After accepting a post as technical chief of Sweden's Carbide and Acetylene Company in 1901, he studied ways to automate the collecting, dispensing, and igniting of acetylene, a hydrocarbon that fed the flames of lighthouses, marine beacons, and harbor buoys. To tame explosive gas, he invented the sun valve and perfected a regulated container from a porous material that ended danger to gas users. In September 1912, when a valve failed at a quarry outside Stockholm during his research into control of acetylene, a sudden flare blinded Dalén. It was only weeks later that he learned he had been awarded the Nobel Prize in physics.

Substituting his phenomenal memory for data for his lost eyesight, Dalén spent the remaining quarter century conducting his own research. He studied his wife's difficulties in keeping her wood-burning kitchen stove lit and maintaining the right temperature for cooking. In 1929, he designed a stove that featured low combustion and heat storage in a cast-iron firebox insulated with a silicone dioxide called *kieselguhr.* His design resulted in a patent and a new appliance manufactured by the Aktiebolaget (Amalgamated) Gas Accumulator Company. Four years before his death on December 9, 1937, he won the Morehead Medal of the International Acetylene Association. His company patented 250 inventions, of which half were his own ideas.

Throughout Europe, the Aga stove—named for Aktiebolaget Gas Accumulator Company—became the most popular kitchen appliance of the era, particularly in regions not served by gas companies. A massive item, it typically included two ovens and an internal hot water boiler, a boon to cooks who constantly boiled water for laundry and cleaning as well as cooking. Additional features included a boiling plate, simmering plate, and simmering oven and a roasting oven with a door thermometer that regulated an air damper. Unlike the grimy black iron stove of the past, the creamy enamel surface of Aga wiped clean. Originally fired with wood, peat, or coal, it was subsequently converted to oil.

Hand-built in England and installed by technicians, the Aga country cooker is still a standard throughout the world for serious food preparation in hotels, restaurants, and institutional kitchens. In the mid-1980s, the expensive Aga stove became a status symbol featured in cookery classes and on the U.S. television series *Food and Drink.* Cookbooks accompanying the Aga explain how to use the compact cooking surfaces efficiently to save work and fuel while maintaining food quality and preserving nutrients.

Further Reading

Notable Twentieth-Century Scientists. Farmington Hills, Mich.: Gale Group, 1995.
Osband, Linda. *Victorian House Style.* London: David & Charles, 1991.

DAVID, ELIZABETH

England's most prominent twentieth-century food writer, Elizabeth Gwynne David is remembered for her vibrant memoirs of good food and good times. Born in Folkington, Sussex, in 1913 to a socially prominent family, she grew up amid cultural stimulus and dined from an eclectic menu. From boarding school, in 1929, she departed for Paris to study art. While living with a French family, she learned cookery in their kitchen.

David abandoned the debutante life and entered the theater. In 1937, while at Regent's Park Open Air Theatre, she began writing recipes in a copybook. At the end of World War II, after a turbulent period that took her around the Mediterranean, David took a job as librarian and code clerk for the Ministry of Information. She married an army officer, Tony David, and learned Anglo-Indian cuisine firsthand during a sojourn in Delhi. David returned to England in 1946. To recapture the experiences of her travels, she wrote *A Book of Mediterranean Food* (1950). A forerunner of the picture cookbook made popular in the 1950s and 1960s, it benefited from the decorative drawings of John Minton, who emphasized the exotica of the Riviera's foods and table setting. The book was an immediate sellout, appearing just as English cooks began to cast off the limitations of wartime food shortages and rationing. She followed with *French Country Cooking* (1951), also illustrated by Minton, and *Summer Cooking* (1955). She also compiled an enduring culinary history, *Italian Food* (1954).

Based in part on her travels to Malta, Cairo, and Provence, David's masterwork, *French Provincial Cooking* (1960), proved her capable of compiling an academic food history. She carefully explained the finer points of French cookery, for example, the difference beween a *dauphine,* a deep-fried potato ball, and a *dauphinois,* a potato casserole baked with a cheese topping. Her strength as a food writer was the ease with which she addressed her reader. For example, she describes a grand-sounding recipe for *La poule farci en daube a la berrichonne* (boned, stuffed chicken in jelly) as nothing more than "a method of turning an old boiling fowl into a civilized and savoury dish." (Beard 1975, 258)

For a time David sold imported goods at a kitchen shop near her home in London. She then entered a phase of column writing for *Spectator* and later anthologized short pieces in *An Omelette and a Glass of Wine* (1984). For her expertise, in 1976, she received the Order of the British Empire from Queen Elizabeth II. Her most scholarly effort, the classic *English Bread and Yeast Cookery* (1977), won her the Glenfiddich Writer of the Year award. After her death in 1992, editor Jill Norman completed her book *Harvest of the Cold Months* (1994).

David's opinions altered the focus of English culinary tastes by introducing the Mediterranean diet, rich in olives, olive oil, garlic, basil, tomatoes, and figs. She encouraged her contemporaries to abandon stiff presentation of ornate dishes and promoted earthenware goods that went from oven to table without doilies and fuss. At her prompting, cooks stocked their knife blocks with quality cutlery, stacked ramekins and casseroles on their shelves, provisioned their pantries with sun-dried mushrooms and tomatoes, and cultivated rocket (arugula) in their kitchen gardens.

Further Reading

Chaney, Lisa. *A Charming Monster, Elizabeth David: A Biography.* New York: Macmillan, 1998.

"Elizabeth David's Dream Kitchen," *London Independent*, November 11, 2000.

Oddie, Cornelia, "The Cook-Writer Extraordinary," *Contemporary Review*, July, 2000, 57–58.

DESIGN

Over the centuries, the location of the domestic cooking space—which eventually evolved into the kitchen—has been influenced by such variables as climate, building materials, household needs, and cultural customs. The first fire-keepers lived in caves or built huts, such as those found among the mammoth hunters of Moravia and Russia. When fireplaces dominated design, open-hearth kitchens tended to be round, as seen in the traditional *chum* (tepee), the temporary summer dwelling of the Khanty, seminomadic reindeer herders of the Russian tundra. Hunters living at Mezhirich in Russia around 18,000 BCE shaped mammoth bones into rounded piles covering a central fire. At Pushkari and in Siberia at Malta and Buret near Lake Baikal, skins stretched over a bone frame protected the family's heat and light source from inclement

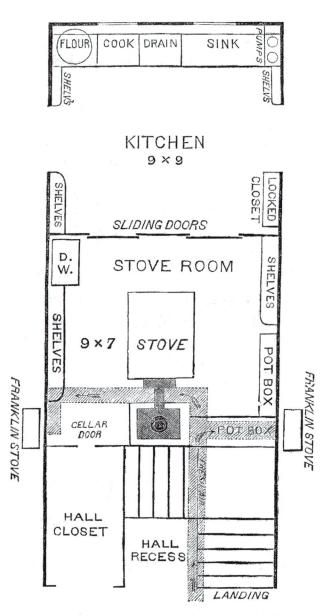

Kitchen design from *American Woman's Home* (1869) by Catharine Esther Beecher, 41.

weather. At Lazaret, a cave outside Nice, France, a circular fire pit of bone bits and stone chips is located at a side wall of the shelter.

Early Dwellings

A late thirteenth-century BCE dwelling discovered in the Madaba Plains in 1976 suggests that families in the Middle East favored a compact arrangement of domestic goods and equipment. At al-'Umayri (or'Umeiri), a highland site in Transjordan south of Amman, the two-story stone-and-mortar house topped with flat roof appears to have served as a space for the family's cooking, weaving, laundry, and livestock husbandry. The ground floor sheltered domesticated animals; a storage room held *pithoi* (storage jars) of dried grapes, chickpeas, broad beans, barley, and lentils. The second floor consisted of additional pantry space and a multipurpose room suited to sleeping, weaving, and cooking. Near the door, stone circles supported cook pots at a hearth. Remains of a millstone, bowls, jars, animal bones, and grinding implements attest to the level of culinary sophistication.

Rounded dwellings partially sunk into the ground near Aleppo, Syria, along the Euphrates River, took shape after 12,000 BCE, when the cultivation of cereal plants inspired hunter-gatherers to evolve a settled lifestyle. Home design advanced from a branch-and-daub matrix to *pisé,* a more malleable mud-and-straw construction. Standard floor plans called for placement of the cooking space near the door for maximum light and ventilation. Householders plastered floors and walls to keep out the rodents that ate and fouled their grain stocks.

By 9000 BCE, after stone masons had mastered the formation of right angles, round dwellings were superceded by the first rectangular homes. Builders of the prototypical rectangular house erected a community along the Jordan River in 7000 BCE. Two thousand years later, when the agrarian lifestyle supplanted hunting and gathering, the first permanent brick dwellings took shape from hand-molded mud clods sundried for durability. The technology remained crude until the Mesopotamians began firing their trademark brick in kilns in 3000 BCE.

Following Dame Kathleen Mary Kenyon's 1950s excavations at Jericho, which was first settled around 9000 BCE, she concluded that builders of larger homes grouped their rooms around courtyard kitchens, which sheltered the fire while leaving open space above for ventilation. A re-creation of Valdivian homes at the Real Alto site in Ecuador, dating from around 3000 BCE, reveals a circular or horseshoe-shaped domestic arrangement. For individual nuclear families, round houses shaped from wood and cane and covered in clay, mud, and grass provided cozy sleep areas and draft-free locales for open-hearth cooking. Simultaneously, British hut builders at Dartmoor settled within timber-framed dwellings, where the cooking place was situated on a beaten clay hearth surrounded by stones near the central support beam.

In early Egyptian villas a cooking shed was constructed apart from the house and near the steward's quarters to spare the wealthy homeowner from kitchen heat and odors. For similar reasons, Japanese householders paired their thatched hut with a separate kitchen fitted with a clay stove, and the Arabic cook set up a *tannur* (charcoal oven) outside the residence.

Deir el-Medina, an ancient Egyptian village situated on the west bank of the Nile opposite Luxor, the site of ancient Thebes, contains a rare glimpse of ordinary Egyptian home life from 1539 to 1075 BCE. The typical kitchen was an open-air room partially covered by a pillar and moveable thatched sunshade. The area served for food preparation, cooking, and laundry. Below stairs, a cellar held valuables, stores of food and drink, and a staircase connecting to the roof.

In cold, wet climates domestic design remained more rudimentary. The cooking area was usually sited at the heart of the dwelling, a pragmatic plan that spread warmth throughout the space. Around 1500 BCE, householders at Skara Brae on the Orkney Islands cooked over peat fires at a stone fire bed in the center of the house. At Jarlshof in the Shetland Islands, a shell-shaped house placed a central hearth below a smoke hole in the stone slab roof.

Domestic Arrangements in Disparate Climates

The Greeks and Romans were the first to modernize home styles with more family-friendly room arrangement. The fifth-century BCE townhouse reserved the ground floor for the kitchen; the Roman townhouse turned the ground floor into a garden, reception, and dining area and relegated the kitchen to a distant back corner. In the Roman country villa, the kitchen was a separate building.

Kitchen locations and layouts continued to be influenced by geography and local culture. In the Middle Ages, Mediterranean Jews adapted complex two-story floor plans in which the second floor, reserved for cooking, was entered by a separate door. To the south of the Mediterranean, Oman's architecture was adapted to suit the extreme temperatures common to the desert. In summer, affluent families occupied the front bedrooms of their mud homes, where palm frond walls admitted cooling breezes while filtering out street noise. The kitchen and well house stood apart near the center of the courtyard, where house staff could come and go without disturbing their masters. In winter, residents moved to the back of the court, where they sheltered within thicker-walled mud structures whose doors faced the kitchen for warmth.

After the Anglo-Saxons overran Roman Britain in 449 CE, they obliterated stone and plaster Mediterranean-style residences and raised their own wooden mead halls in place of existing country villas. At the center of the open common room blazed the bonfire, puffed into lively flame by the *boelig,* or bellows. Through ever-open doors, guests could draw near to warm themselves and seek shelter from harsh weather. Huge iron pots hung over the flame, suspended by a drop handle. Within each pot, thongs tied to a pair of horizontal bars welded level with the rim secured bags and jars of food cooked individually.

One sixth-century archeological site provides a glimpse of domestic life in the Americas. In August 595 CE, ash fall from a volcanic eruption of Laguna Caldera extinguished the pre-Hispanic village of Joya de Cerén, El Salvador, the so-called Pompeii of Central America, where natives lived in square huts, cooked in separate round kitchens, and worked at small roofed workshops. The disaster preserved a record of the last moments of home life, including the earliest kitchen garden, which produced manioc, agave, cacao, beans, chiles, squash, corn, avocado, and medicinal plants. Cooks hung *ristras* (plaits) of chiles from the beams and stored tools, colored paints, beans, and seeds in a shed. Diners enjoyed cool breezes while eating on benches or on the porch.

Multifamily dwellings established a high level of social cooperation in southwestern North America. The Anasazi, cliff dwellers who populated the American Southwest from 100 BCE to 1400 CE, were the builders of the apartment-like dwellings at Mesa Verde, Colorado, and Chaco Canyon, New Mexico. At Chaco Canyon they constructed walls from an earth-and-stone rubble faced with sandstone tablets. Each home unit contained large pantries to house the produce grown in kitchen gardens cultivated along irrigation ditches. Crops such as corn, beans, and squash were dried on the dwellings' flat roofs and stored in baskets and small-necked clay pots.

In a starkly contrasting environment to that of the Anasazi, the Eskimo created a variety of floor plans for their ice houses. The Inupiat of northern Alaska and the Seward Peninsula supplied their domed sod houses with a separate kitchen, which contained a meat cellar, storage niches, and a smoke hole as well as a formal entrance to the main quarters. The Inuvialuit of the Mackenzie Delta also supplied residences with kitchens but usually cooked outdoors over an open fire.

Among other indigenous American peoples, domestic arrangements varied immensely. In North America, the lodge was a sizeable structure built on a timber frame and support poles and covered in grass, reed thatch, or sod strips. The lodge ranged in shape from round to oblong to beehive-shaped. The largest could accommodate more than 100 residents. Cheyenne cooks transformed the lodge roof into a veranda for sun-drying corn and gourds and for preparing meat and fish for smoking and vegetables for winter preservation. The Mandan earth lodge, a round dwelling with a central cooking space, accommodated up to sixty people. At center, a fire burned constantly for cooking and heating. A rudimentary chimney at the smoke hole above directed fumes outside and admitted

natural light to illuminate such chores as skinning and cutting game and plucking birds.

The Japanese farmhouse with its earth-floored kitchen and attached storage lean-to accommodated the women of an extended family who worked in teams at a charcoal burner or wood stove at the center of the area. Overhead, out of reach of mice and crawling insects, beams held lidded fish baskets of dried sardines, noodle and dumpling scoops, and long-handled bean paste sieves that fit over a kettle. Bamboo shelving kept utensils within reach.

Hearth and Home in the Middle Ages

For the prosperous, the kitchen traditionally dominated the English home during the Middle Ages. Food cooked at an open hearth with a plaster-coated wood surround. Passageways often linked the cooking area to the buttery, pantry, and great hall, as was the case with the Bishop's Palace at Wells, Somerset. By the 1300s, stone kitchens had replaced the fire-prone wood structures. At manor houses such as Great Chalfield, Wiltshire, the layout accommodated a division of labors: kitchen, pantry, and buttery at the screen end of the great hall and cellar beneath the dais, the elevated seating place of dignitaries and royalty. Thus, presentation of dishes began at the entranceway and concluded with kneeling servants bearing uplifted trays to high-level attendants, who spread the meal before the host and hostess and their honored guests.

Separation of classes in Europe influenced home design and use. In Aix-en-Provence around 1375, the lower classes subsisted primarily on wine and bread. The reason emerges from a study of residence design: 58 percent of the residents had no kitchens.

During the Renaissance, kitchen design advanced in centrality to home life. Bartolomeo Scappi, head cook to Pope Pius V and author of the encyclopedic *Opera dell'Arte dell Cucinare* (Compendium on the Art of Cookery, 1570), wrote that the architect should place the kitchen in its own discreet space, "well arranged, with broad, high fireplaces." (Rowley 1999, 54) His list of necessities ranged from iron bars holding the chains that swung cauldrons over the fire to hooks and pegs holding implements along the mantelpiece. Above all, prefiguring the ideas of modern work zone design, he specified that the room should be arranged for the greatest possible productivity.

When the master of the house no longer ate in the kitchen, a sequestered location with covered stairs and passageways distanced kitchen labors from polite dining. In southern Germany, a style called the *stubenofenhaus* evolved, giving the kitchen its own space; it remained a standard house plan into the

1800s. The enclosed *stube* (living room) connected to an external *schwarz küche* (smoke, or black, kitchen) that housed the *ofen* (oven). In the separate chamber, a *herd* (cookstove) shared the oven *schlot* (chimney). The *stall* (stable) at the rear of the lot attached to a *keller* (basement), a storage chamber for root crops and dried and preserved foodstuffs.

Similarly differentiated to suit work and storage of utensils was the English croft. The crofter took his name from a small privately owned *croft,* or plot of land. A miniature version of an estate, it encompassed a country cottage, kitchen garden, livestock sheds and pens, and storage lean-tos. The well-to-do crofter might also own a separate kitchen, brewery, dairy, hen-yard, or mill. In this same period, Scottish builders knocked together the simple but-and-ben cottage, a two-roomed dwelling with but (kitchen) at one end and ben (living quarters) on the other. Cooks suspended vessels from chains on the three-legged iron arch over the hearth.

In the Elizabethan age, home building perpetuated separation of kitchen from living space but united both into a grandly symmetrical room arrangement. English gentry built fine homes of stone timbered with wood and laid out the rooms in an E or H shape. The sections differentiated work and lifestyle. One wing held bedrooms and private chambers. The middle consisted of a sumptuous hall, the principal gathering and entertaining room and dining area. The far wing housed servants' quarters, kitchen, and pantry.

To maximize light, builders equipped walls with bay windows, sunny niches with window seats on which to pare fruit, mend towels, and perform other meticulous domestic work for which the light from candles and lamps was inadequate. Choices of flooring ranged from inexpensive and durable flagstone or brick to costly oak planks and quarry tile. Hampton Court Palace went to the extreme with a host of specialty rooms, including a kitchen, small kitchen, cellar, larder, pantry, scullery, buttery, ewery, saucery, chaundry or candlery, spicery, poultery, and a victualing house for storing supplies.

Domestic arrangements were laden with class distinctions. Kitchen servants slept in the attic or garret and had to descend a private service stair to reach their posts. Andrea Palladio, the influential Italian architect of the high Renaissance, pronounced the working space of servants "less comely" than other regions of the home and thus initiated the banishment of the kitchen below stairs.

Around 1680, new residences separated living space from the kitchen, which occupied its own pavilion. Older homes underwent remodeling to accommodate shifts in attitude toward kitchen placement. By the 1720s, lesser kitchen staff, who were largely invisible to the gentry, ate in the servants' hall or kitchen. Only the clerk of the kitchen, head cook, butler, and groom of the chambers ate at a private staff table in the hall. In 1755, designers of Harleyford Manor, Buckinghamshire, placed the kitchen apart from the main residence and connected it by means of a tunnel, which shielded the kitchen staff totally from family and guests. In France, the evolution of formal and private apartments created a two-level arrangement: a downstairs cadre hired for cooking and garnishing foods for social gatherings and an upstairs serving staff devoted to the personal needs of the family.

European Influences Abroad

Colonists transported elements of English kitchen style around the globe to Canada, Virginia, Massachusetts, Hawaii, New Zealand, and Australia, yet, few colonial residences were grand enough to require staff regimentation. In many humble dwellings, the kitchen was a multipurpose space that blended cooking and preserving with weaving, entertaining, overnight guest accommodations, and child care. To economize on heat, New Englanders constructed hall and parlor to each side of the central chimney and oven. In Georgia, home builders placed kitchens in the basement or erected them outside to keep odors and heat out of the main quarters and lessen the chance of fire. In Tuvalu in the Ellice Islands and in other parts of the South Seas, island homes still feature a separate cookhouse called an *umu* where cooks work over open flame as they did in colonial times.

When families pressed west over known trails, they took up residence on virgin land. In Susan Louisa Moir Allison's *A Pioneer Gentlewoman in British Columbia* (1976), the Ceylon native reprises her trek across Canada's Brigade Trail to Hope, a town inland from Vancouver on the Fraser River. There she and her husband set up an Indian trading post and lived temporarily in a "cloth and paper lined shack." (Allison 1991, 12) Like other frontierswomen, she not only designed her own lean-to kitchen, she participated in its construction.

In Decatur House, the home of American naval hero Stephen Decatur at Lafayette Square a block from the White House, an unusual kitchen placement suited the lifestyle of succeeding generations of families who regularly entertained distinguished guests. The kitchen, designed by Benjamin Henry Latrobe, the father of American architecture, occupied the room adjacent to the front door. Placement of a family parlor and family dining room to the opposite side of the central hall assured hot meals delivered directly after preparation. Stairs led guests to the next floor to elegant sitting, music, and dining rooms. A parallel access for servants connected the kitchen to the upper festivities and enabled servants to move briskly from the cooking and plating area directly to dining areas. The focus on prompt service is apparent in the design of the structure, which is currently maintained as a museum by the National Trust for Historic Preservation.

Robert E. and Mary Anna Randolph Custis Lee resided at Arlington House, the genteel Southern home of the Custis family on a hill overlooking the fertile Potomac River bottoms below. Built in 1802 by George Washington Parke Custis, grandson of Martha Washington, the structure suited an agrarian family that owned a substantial slave kitchen staff. Like Decatur House, the Lee home featured a winter kitchen below stairs and near enough to the dining area to allow speedy delivery of hot dishes. In summer, the Lee family slaves cooked and served covered dishes from the summer kitchen, a separate cooking area behind the main residence that spared the family from intense heat and cooking odors during warm Virginia summers.

Preparing a King's Meals

An 1819 engraving of the cavernous royal kitchen at St. James's Palace by James Stephanoff shows the workplace of cook staff and butler dwarfed by the tall windows and skylight, which illuminate efforts to prepare the king's meals. Between the cook hacking meat at the range and a worker basting meat at the spit are two immense work tables. In the foreground, a serviceable baker's dresser offers adequate space for rolling out and raising dough, which lies neatly concealed under a white cloth. To the rear, an L from the front service extends more space for the task performed by two pastry cooks. A four-legged food preparation table at rear and a narrower table at the left wall offer the space staff would need for preparing numerous plates for presentation at a state dinner.

Residential design perpetuated much of medieval England's division of labor, for example, staffing the kitchen with a maximum number of cooks and undercooks and relegating to the housekeeper the preparation of tea and coffee and securing and serving of preserves, biscuits, and cake. Her quarters consisted of her room, which doubled as a linen press and china cupboard, plus a storeroom, still room for preparing tea and refreshments, and closet. Just off the dining room, the butler warmed dishes at the hot plate in the serving room. Coordinating the work of cook and housekeeper, he managed table linens and flatware, drinks, and pantry for storage, scullery, cellarage, filling oil lamps, and sharpening and cleaning knives.

Models of this arrangement survive at Ashburnham, Sussex, and Lanhydrock, Cornwall.

Influence of the Middle Class

As the availability of servants decreased in the United States, the size of houses diminished accordingly. With the middle-class homemaker doing all of the domestic work unaided, simplification of tasks and efficiency in performing them took precedence, presaging the emergence of the home economics movement, which applied scientific principles to domestic labor and equipment.

Arvada Nichols Metcalf, a reader of *Scribner's* and *Harper's* as well as of Harriet Beecher Stowe and Catharine Beecher's *The American Woman's Home* (1869), kept abreast of farm design and post-Civil War developments in home planning. She was among the first generation of U.S. householders to demand an above-ground kitchen with excellent lighting. Such an arrangement was detailed in *Miss Parloa's Kitchen Companion* (1887), an outgrowth of Maria Parloa's work at the Boston Cooking School. Innovations for maximum efficiency called for refrigerators or ice closets for storage of perishables, built-in pumps flanking the iron sink for well and rain water, and a food preparation center that organized dry staples, utensils, and cleaning supplies. In addition to sink and range, Parloa specified chairs, dresser, and a table with drawers, the latter a center of activity for rolling pie crusts, bathing infants, writing letters, making grocery lists, keeping household accounts, and cutting out garments.

The pantry, a rectangle of ninety-six square feet, was the command center for household equipment. It housed tables, cookware, pastry equipment, tinned foods, fresh fruit, and dried staples. Additional perishable goods, root vegetables, pickles, and meats belonged in the cellar, either an earth-floored storage chamber or finished basement. The homeowner often plumbed the china closet with a sink for the hand washing of breakables. A pie safe, a standard fixture after 1850, stored meat, cream, and perishables.

Streamlining

After the class leveling that followed World War I, residential design began to reflect a streamlining that required complex technology but fewer servants. As the home became more efficient in the 1920s, the so-called fitted kitchen, an idea recommended by time-and-motion experts Lillian Moller Gilbreath and Christine McGaffey Frederick, provided the homemaker with a workspace befitting a scientific approach to cooking. A bold move toward modernism came from

DESIGN

the Bauhaus, a revolutionary state-supported school of design, architecture, and applied arts founded in Berlin in 1919 by Walter Gropius. Balancing art with expert craftsmanship, the Bauhaus fostered high-quality machining for functional and aesthetically pleasing domestic design. In Weimar in 1923, Marcel Breuer created a galley-style kitchen called the Haus am Horn. Neatly arranged in limited space and touched with bright patches of color, it caught the public's attention and won media acclaim but failed as a commercial endeavor.

In Germany, the Viennese-born architect Grete Schütte-Lihotzky pioneered social architecture with her design for the Frankfurt Kitchen, one of the first low-cost, mass-produced kitchens. Her colleague, the architect Ernst May, designed built-ins that provided the first unitized work space paired with a continuous counter. By 1930, these units had been installed in 10,000 urban apartments. In 1938, the Bruynzeel Kitchen, a modular concept proposed by Dutch engineer Piet Zwart, extended streamlining with matched fittings and a single countertop sheltering cabinets, ovens, refrigerators, and bins.

A similar trend was represented in England by Middleton Park, Oxfordshire, an upscale residential project fitted with kitchens that sufficed without still room or steward's quarters. For convenience, designers moved the kitchen closer to the dining area; dumb waiters and service lifts lightened the tasks of hauling and serving. The gentrified owners adapted to life without a servant staff, pouring tea for themselves and guests and limiting the amount of in-house baking, distilling, brewing, and preserving by hiring caterers or local professionals when necessary.

Following the hardships of the Great Depression, American housewives, looking to better times, sought opportunities to brighten their surroundings while simplifying their work. With more money to spend than the previous generation of home buyers, they invested in new gas and electric ranges, updated lighting and plumbing, convenience foods, and the latest in time-saving gadgetry. An ad in a women's magazine of the period featured low-maintenance asbestos wall tile, a product of Johns-Manville of New York City, maker of fireproof shingles and asphalt siding. Other advertisements depicted smartly dressed women exclaiming over the affordability and ease of installation of scrubable kitchen wainscoting and paneling, available in colors to match paint, window treatments, and canisters.

Simultaneously, people in less developed countries—as well as rural residents in developed nations—continued to lived in squalid conditions no better than those in the Middle Ages. In rural Ireland, for example, stone barns provided family living quarters in spare and uncomfortable attic space under the thatch. The humans' lodgings were little better than those of their cattle. Some dirt-floored peat houses accommodated human inhabitants as well as livestock and poultry that wandered about at will. The traditional kitchen half-door was meant to keep out smelly, dung-footed ruminants and restrain crawling babies, while at the same time allowing sunlight and fresh air to penetrate the kitchen.

In the pre-World War II period changes in home design continued the trend toward bringing the kitchen and the meal-preparation process into the daily life of all family members. In 1934, the U.S. architect Frank Lloyd Wright designed the first floor plan to meld the kitchen with other rooms. An open plan reflecting the democratization of the American family, the design of the Malcolm Willey house in Minneapolis merged the cooking, dining, and home entertainment areas. These changes mitigated the housewife's sense of isolation and, at the same time, encouraged the husband and children to involve themselves more in kitchen activities.

In the 1950s, as home-ownership became a reality for the working class, the antiseptic white-and-stainless steel kitchen gave way to a more relaxed and welcoming space where guests felt free to join the cook. The space-saving built-in kitchens of Levittown, a huge development of prefabricated homes built outside New York City in 1947, are a case in point. Home decorators introduced bright enamel paint for kitchen cabinets and plastic utensils and accoutrements to match.

During the 1960s and 1970s, the kitchens of the prosperous offered the latest gadgetry, Formica and stainless steel surfaces, and color-coordinated appliances. Although apartment kitchens were often small, professional planning made them efficient. In the 1980s and 1990s, kitchen designers added multiple work stations, task lighting, rollout cabinet shelves, oversized cutting boards, secondary sinks for vegetable washing, easy-clean smooth top ranges, and a host of other conveniences. The U-shaped kitchen plan, a concept introduced in the 1920s by efficiency expert Lillian Gilbreth, increased efficiency by lessening steps from islands to appliances and sink. Skylights enhanced artificial illumination.

Wave of the Future

At the turn of the twenty-first century, architects, engineers, and designers continued to experiment with new appliances and innovative kitchen layouts. In addition to convenience and aesthetics, some experts sought to address issues such as conservation of resources. In

193

1993, under the leadership of professors Charles Lewis and Nancy Chwiecko, a group of graduate students in industrial and interior design at the Rochester Institute of Technology created futuristic kitchen devices intended to save energy, space, and labor and reduce waste. Engineers at Frigidaire's design center near Columbus, Ohio, applied the latest technology to tasks, creating a prototype countertop computer and automated cabinet dispensers that meted out herbs and spices and a gas-under-glass range in which foods cooked rapidly in induction heat. At the end of the meal, their ultrasonic dishwasher vibrated dishes clean with sound waves in three minutes.

The fitted kitchen reached its height with customized cook tops and modular ovens. Additions to the suite included a deep fryer, barbecue grill, and wok and electric burners set into the countertop for wipe-clean efficiency. The most elaborate designs provided customized pull-outs, drawers, and shelving. An innovative ventilation system replaced exhaust hoods with a telescoping arm that pivoted directly to the source of steam, smoke, and odor and retracted into a storage well when not in use.

Affluent cooks tired of the small but efficient galley kitchen sought a return to rustic roots with retro-style appliances, brick flooring, butcher block tables, and mock farmhouse touches, such as plank cabinet fronts, corner fireplaces, and wrought-iron cabinet hardware. No longer simply a functional space for preparing meals, the kitchen had become a reflection of the householder's personality and fluid, ever-changing self-image.

See also **Chickee; Colonial Kitchens, American; Feng Shui; Fireplace; Frederick, Christine McGaffey; Gilbreth, Lillian Moller; Ramada; Victorian Kitchens**

Further Reading

Cunliffe, Barry. *The Oxford Illustrated Prehistory of Europe.* Oxford: Oxford University Press, 1994.

Damluji, Salma Samar. *The Architecture of Oman.* Reading, Eng.: Garnet Publishing, 1998.

Girouard, Mark. *Life in the English Country House: A Social and Architectural History.* New Haven, Conn.: Yale University Press, 1978.

Hayden, Dolores. *The Grand Domestic Revolution: A History of Feminist Designs for American Homes, Neighborhoods, and Cities.* Cambridge, Mass.: MIT Press, 1985.

Waterson, Merlin. *The Servants' Hall.* New York: Pantheon Books, 1980.

Weisman, Leslie Kanes. *Discrimination by Design: A Feminist Critique of the Man-Made Environment.* Urbana: University of Illinois Press, 1994.

DETERGENT

A detergent is a substance with properties that enhance the cleansing action of soap. Detergents are capable of emulsifying oils and acting as surfactants, that is, breaking up the surface tension of water. In 1850, soap manufacturers compounded the first synthetic detergent, called turkey-red oil, a sulfated castor oil used in tanning and refining fabrics. Henkel, a German soap-making firm, made a perborate and silicate soap and, in 1907, offered the first household detergent, Nekal, which became popular during World War I when fats for home soap making were diverted for military use. Detergents were subsequently produced in flake, bead, and powder form. Additives such as abrasives and bleaches adapted some detergent formulations for specific uses, particularly washing dishes and clothes by machine, brightening dingy porcelain surfaces, removing hard water residue, and dissolving and lifting burned-on grease and crust from stovetops.

In the United States, Procter & Gamble introduced Dreft detergent in 1933. The product worked well on lingerie and knitted garments but earned mediocre marks for performance on heavily soiled articles. (Landau 1986, 47) Without comment on the product's fabric-sparing formulation, *Consumer Reports* omitted Dreft from a lab comparison of nineteen major laundry soaps conducted in 1936. All of the products tested contained alkali, a water softener that deactivated hard minerals to boost surfactant action. Even in their improved forms, however, these early detergents were too harsh for use on silk, synthetics, and wool. By 1940, the development of phosphate soap had solved the three most persistent home laundry problems— effectiveness without harm to fabrics, efficiency in hard water, and economy.

Detergents for home laundry use were in scarce supply during World War II, when rationing and import limitations reduced the availability of fat and oil. Responding to the needs of the war effort, chemists sped up studies of detergents that would perform in cold water. After the war, several new products were introduced, including Tide, Fab, and, in the United Kingdom, Surf. All three brands proved resilient in a volatile, ever-changing market. By 1953, consumers were buying more detergent than soap powder for home laundry. To capitalize on the growing appliance market, detergent manufacturers quickly turned out powders for use in the automatic dishwasher, liquids for washing machines, and milder formulas for dishwashing.

The romance with phosphate soaps ended in disillusion in the late 1950s when environmentalists cited suds from phosphate-containing housecleaning products as a major factor in water pollution. Ecologically-minded housewives were alarmed to learn that the detergents that made their laundry and dishes spotless were contributing to eutrophication, the premature aging of lakes from plant overgrowth, turbidity, sedimentation, reduced oxygen levels, and suppression of species diversity. Manufacturers moved quickly to reformulate the phosphate-heavy detergents, sales of which were banned in some areas.

In the 1960s and 1970s, the list of detergent choices grew with the invention of prewash treatments to rub or spray on stains and presoaks that broke down stains from blood or other natural substances with the enzymes amylase, lipase, and protease. The late 1970s added liquid hand soap, sheet fabric softener, and multifunctional detergents combined with softeners, stain removers, color protectors, and silicates to reduce foaming in front-loading washers. The last two decades of the century brought cold-water and biodegradable detergents, perfume-free products, liquid detergent for dishwashers, and concentrated laundry agents that weighed less than their predecessors and took up less cabinet space. By the early twenty-first century, detergents were compressed even further with formulations offering hard-milled tablets and pre-measured single-load packaging that ended problems with spillage and waste.

See also **Laundry**

Further Reading

Hunt, John A., "A Short History of Soap," *Pharmaceutical Journal*, December 1999, 995–999.
Richards, Ellen H., and S. Maria Elliott. *The Chemistry of Cooking and Cleaning*. Boston: Whitcomb & Barrows, 1912.

DIGBY, KENELM

A contributor to Renaissance cuisine, Sir Kenelm Digby (also Kenelme Digbie) combined the unusual careers of pirate, courtier, alchemist, and cook. He was born on July 11,1603, at Gayhurst, Buckinghamshire. His father, Sir Everard Digby, was hanged three years later for complicity in the Gunpowder Plot. At Oxford Digby studied mysticism under Richard Napier and alchemy and cooking with the mathematician Thomas Allen. In 1620, he left school, traveled in Europe, met the astronomer Galileo Galilei, and, in Spain, began a life-long collection of recipes.

At age twenty, Digby entered the service of Charles I at Madrid and earned a knighthood. He lived the life of a pirate, fleecing French ships at Iskenderun, Turkey, and ransoming English sailors from captivity. After his wife's untimely death, he turned again to science, performing chemical experiments at Gresham College and corresponding with René Descartes and Thomas Hobbes. Upon his release from imprisonment for Catholic leanings, he published his major titles in Paris: *Of the Nature of Bodies* (1644) and *Of the Nature of Mans Soule* (1644). His banishment at age sixty-one for court intrigue returned him to his former scientific studies, which he pursued until his death June 11, 1665. Among his projects was a study of the healthy diet.

The Closet of Sir Kenelm Digby Knight Opened (1669), an eccentric recipe collection, was compiled after Digby's demise by a still room steward named Hartman. Central to the text are still room and herbal lore and recipes for fermented honey beverages, possets, creams, and punch. Historians question the authenticity of much of the text, which may owe much to the steward's additions and corrections. Whatever their provenance, nearly a third of the 330 recipes describe the fermentation of mead, which Digby learned from Charles II's mead maker.

In addition to his record of contemporary methods of fermentation, Digby also recorded the queen's use of egg yolk to baste roasting meat. His collection included recipes for potages, calves' head hash, pear pudding, chocolate puffs, potato pie, a medieval fish stock, syllabub, quince jelly, cheesecake, a diet drink for the king, and the forerunner of white sauce. In honor of his expertise, another faithful royalist, Robert May, a professional chef to gentry from Elizabeth I through Charles II, dedicated to Digby *The Accomplisht Cook or The Art and Mystery of Cookery* (1660), one of the most admired food books of the seventeenth century.

Further Reading

Hall, Roland, "Unnoticed Words and Senses from Sir Kenelm Digby," *Notes and Queries*, March 1999, 21–22.

DISHWASHING

Because of the difficulty of removing congealed grease and baked-on crust from cooking and dining implements, dishwashing has traditionally been, as the essayist Christopher Morley described it, "an ignoble chore, a kind of hateful discipline." (Franklin 1997, 429) The job began in prehistory with sand-scouring of pottery and utensils at the nearest water source. In the Roman villa, slaves cleaned tabletops and scoured stone and tile floors with handfuls of sand. Another useful substance, cuttlefish bone, served as a cleaning abrasive, as did the horsetail (*Equisetum*), commonly called pewter wort, scouring rush, or shave grass, a plant with jointed stems suitable for scouring wooden utensils, dairy vessels, and pewter.

In the medieval castle, the lowest kitchen job fell to the pot boys, who faced a mountain of soiled cauldrons, spits, platters, and cups after each banquet. At the shallow work bench called the "slop stone" or at a stone slab sink, a sump dug near a tree and lined with stones, kitchen help cleaned fish and game, splintered bones, chopped vegetables, and scraped wet leavings into the pig pail and dry crumbs into the hen's tin. (Hartley 1964, 348) Other workers washed crockery in a separate tub, polished brass skillets with rhubarb juice or sorrel, and scoured pewter with *Hippuris vulgaris*, an aquatic plant with densely whorled shoots commonly called mare's tail. Delicate china and crystal were rinsed carefully in a vessel padded with soft cloth to prevent chips. According to the twelfth-century Arabic scholar and translator Gerard of Cremona, workers used soapwort (*Saponaria officinalis*), a perennial herb commonly known as bouncing bet, for cleansing and beautifying skin damaged by long stints at dishwashing.

Concern for personal safety turned dishwashing into a public ritual. At the dinner table, servants washed cups and flagons before the seated guests. The ceremony involved setting basins of water for all to see and extending the end of the drying towel to the highest dignitary. The purpose of this display was to demonstrate the purity of cups and to establish that no one had poisoned them on the long trek from the kitchen down torch-lit passageways to the great hall.

By the Renaissance, when cooking came into its own as a domestic art, dishwashing moved out of the main kitchen to a separate scullery or niche. In a trough or stone sink, the dishwasher poured well water from a bucket or basin or opened faucets to admit a steady flow of water from a cistern or town fountain for cleaning and rinsing. For air drying, stacked dishes remained on a table, shelf, wicker or wood drain board, or plate racks. The dreariness of the job in a stifling, windowless area remained the norm into the late 1800s.

A series of devices aided the housewife or scullery servant in cleaning and sanitizing dishes. Dishmops, powdered abrasive cleansers and polishes, plate scrapers, and wire and rubber scrubbers simplified the job; a soap saver—a wire mesh box on a handle—saved the soap bars from sinking to the bottom of the dishpan and dissolving into a gluey mess. Advice columns and household compendia suggested various cleaning aids, such as ketchup or a wedge of lemon topped with salt for shining dull copper. Hay and ash boiled in an iron vessel loosened rust, which the dishwasher could then remove by scouring the pot with soap and sand. Stove surfaces, the bane of kitchen cleaning, required sandpapering and oiling.

In *An Illustrated History of French Cuisine from Charlemagne to Charles de Gaulle* (1962), the historian Christian Guy described the poor *plongeur* (dishwasher), whose labors were long, low-paying, and malodorous. Shut into a small, windowless scullery closet, the worker worked in a veritable steam bath. One perquisite of the job was the layer of fat that collected on the surface of the washwater. It became the property of the dishwasher for collection in kegs and sale to soap manufacturers.

Household advice was a common subject of domestic manuals of the late nineteenth century. In 1884, the domestic adviser Jonathan Periam's *The Home & Farm Manual: A Pictorial Encyclopedia of Farm, Garden, Household, Architectural, Legal, Medical and Social Information* suggested that dishes soaked in hot soapy water required only a simple mopping with "an old linen towel, or candle wicking fastened to the end of a stick." (Periam 1984, 781) For washing good stemware, he advised rolling each glass thoroughly in hot water to equalize temperature throughout bowl and stem.

The mechanical dishwasher had a long and rocky history. In 1850 Joel Houghton invented a wooden hand-cranked water churn for soaking soiled dishes. L. A. Alexander devised the first mechanical dishwasher, patented in 1865, which he intended for institutional kitchens. Working by the principle of centrifugal force, his hand-rotated tub spewed water from the center outward to racks of dishes. Joseph Dauphin's Paris restaurant Marguery put the first dishwashing detergent to use in 1896 in a mechanized dishwasher, a frame with spray attachment operated by an overhead flywheel.

Inventor Josephine Cochrane of Shelbyville, Illinois, presented her dishwasher to the public at the 1893 Columbian Exposition in Chicago. It piqued the interest of restaurateurs and hoteliers but was too cumbersome for housewives. Later in the decade, her company devised a more petite cabinet dishwasher for the domestic market. Standing on four legs, it consisted of a lidded metal tub and racks for holding dishes. The user filled the interior with a hose, added soap, then cranked the paddlewheel to agitate the water. The device disappointed some because of its harsh treatment of delicate items, but Cochrane's company survived to become part of KitchenAid, a division of the Whirlpool Corporation.

Dishwashing was a source of numerous household goods sold in dry goods stores and through the mail. In 1900 the Sears, Roebuck catalog offered plain, four-legged kitchen sinks with drain and two taps for as little as $10.70. The lackluster advertising pictured only the encased sink set on a tiled floor against a tiled wall. Equally humdrum was a display of accessories—two gasoline-powered water heaters, soap cups, and folding towel racks. For the country kitchen, an enamel sink-and-bath tub combination turned the kitchen into a bathing area with the raising of the hinged sink casing.

Homemakers first began buying home dishwashers when the Walker Company demonstrated the hand-cranked washer at the 1910 New York State Fair. In England, a parallel product called the Polliwashup promised to save the homemaker time and effort. Within eight years, hand cranking gave place to an electric motor-driven model. The initial powerhouse in dishwashers was General Electric, which launched its first model in 1932, five years before the Hurley Machine Company marketed the Thor dishwasher in England. Prices fell after Hoover entered the competition and offered the homemaker additional choices in appliances. Electrolux produced a plastic sink-top dishwasher suited to apartment kitchens.

The market continued to accommodate both the modern electric kitchen and the traditional dishpan. The 1923 Sears, Roebuck catalog carried the humble equipment of earlier times—cast iron kitchen sink, stainless steel splashback, drain board, spigot and fittings, sink brackets, and cistern pump.

The task of dishwashing was eased with the introduction of synthetic sponges, soaps, and detergents. In 1913, New York attorney Milton B. Loeb established the Brillo Manufacturing Corporation, which produced steel wool pads permeated with soap to clean and shine aluminum. The February 1925 issue of *Good Housekeeping* presented the in-sink dishwasher, a heavy enameled tub plumbed directly into home water and sewer lines for automatic dishwashing. An advertisement in the July 1930 issue of *Good Housekeeping* extolled the virtues of Super Suds hollow dishwashing beads, a quicker dissolving cleanser than flaked, powdered, or chipped soap. A competitor, Chipso granules promised thorough dishwashing that required no hand-drying. Advertised in the same magazine was Mel'o, a water softener for dishwashing. With soft water, the dishwasher could remove grease and restore dishes and glassware to a pristine sparkle. In the same issue, an ad for the Walker Electric Dishwasher, manufactured in Syracuse, New York, showed a woman holding a dish up to natural light to inspect for cleanliness. Appealing to the germ-conscious homemakers of the day, an ominous statement warns, "Doctors have been the first to realize the dangers that lurk in the dishrag."("Yes" 1930) In yet another another ad from the same issue, delicate hands are pictured grasping S.O.S. scouring pads, a soap-permeated scrubber that promised to lift blackening from aluminum, smoke stains from enamel, and grease from skillets. Softer scrubbers came into vogue with the rise of kitchen plastics. Du

Pont engineers made the first manufactured sponge in the 1940s. The company sold its secret formula to General Mills in 1952, when cellulose sponges began supplanting sea sponge as a dishwashing essential.

At the end of World War II, American factories producing supplies for the war effort returned to manufacture of domestic goods. In 1947 Thor of Chicago and Toronto engineered an unusual appliance—the Automagic dishwasher-clothes washer, marketed for $269.95. By removing the dishwashing tub and replacing it with the clothes washing unit, the housewife could make double use of limited space, which was common to the small houses in developments such as Levittown and cramped city apartments. The Kaiser-Frazer motorless dishwasher, which debuted in the February 1947 *Woman's Home Companion*, used water pressure for power.

The last decades of the twentieth century brought numerous time- and work-savers to the market. A rinse additive for dishwasher detergents produced a sheeting action that rid clean dishes of film. Subsequent refinements in dishwasher design addressed the problems of noisy operation, vibration, and spotty dishes. New models featured such innovations as the soil sensor, an automatic mechanism that gauged the degree of soiling and set water temperature and length of cycle; insulated doors; sanitizing cycles; condensation dryers; waste grinders; and self-cleaning filters that increased the efficiency of the unit by determining needs as they varied from load to load. In the 1990s, appliance manufacturers introduced unobtrusive dishwashers built into drawers. Stacked one above the other, these "dishdrawers" shared plumbing but could wash independently or together.

See also **Brooms, Brushes, and Mops; Cochrane, Josephine**

Further Reading

"Innovative Dishwasher Product May Change Lives of 87 Million Americans," *PR Newswire*, August 22, 2000.

DOUBLE BOILER

Like the *bain-marie* and chafing dish, the double boiler is a cooking vessel that fosters gentle heat by positioning a pan of hot water under a container of a delicate food such as milk, cottage cheese curd, creamed corn or spinach, applesauce, custard, or chocolate. Also called a cereal cooker, milk boiler, fruit steamer, or farina boiler, the device had its beginning in Mediterranean history with the double-bottomed amphora, which Greek cooks used to temper the cooking of table delicacies. In the Middle Ages and into the late frontier

Double stock pot on kitchen counter.
[© *Foodcollection.com / Alamy.*]

period of the United States, jugged foods and boiled puddings simmered slowly in cauldrons of water that accommodated numerous containers of food requiring slow, steady heat. The modern version of the double boiler was developed by the physicist Sir Benjamin Thompson, the Count of Rumford, while serving in the Bavarian military. His smooth-fitting two-stage cooker replaced crude but effective combinations of vessels, such as a pail suspended on a stick across the mouth of a cauldron, an arrangement that the Anglo-Saxons had employed in their mead halls.

A forerunner of the patented double boiler, the double-potted custard kettle consisted of a tin pot nested inside an iron kettle, which could be filled with water for slow simmering. The kettle bail was dented inward at center to hold an S hook, which connected pot to pot. A variation on the double boiler, the glazing pot or kettle was a nested double cooker for stirring up glazes, sauces, and gravy. An opening in the lid admitted a slender glazing brush for daubing. The user then smeared thickened sauces on crusts of hams and pies. A competitor, the glass-enameled Savoy steamer-double boiler, advertised in the May 1925 issue of *Good Housekeeping*, was endorsed by Harvey W. Wiley, director of the Good Housekeeping Bureau of Foods,

Sanitation and Health. Wiley pronounced the Savoy model as the best equipment to soften starch and cellulose for nutritious cookery.

When Corning Glass Works developed a Pyrex double boiler in the 1930s, company officials allied contemporary wisdom with up-to-date design. Corning test kitchen manager Lucy Maltby examined a range of makes and designs on the market, including vessels of aluminum, enamelware, and glass. One of her goals was to minimize the potential for the device to tip over and scald the user.

After World War II, sophisticated hostesses were eager to provide tableside drama at their dinner parties. One popular dish, zabaglione, a wine, sugar, and egg yolk dessert heated over a chafing dish or double boiler, offered a perfect opportunity for such showmanship. *Esquire's Handbook for Hosts* (1949) warned that the delicacy of the eggs made the dish difficult to handle and slow to prepare. Delicacy, the book explained, was one of the reasons it was so expensive in restaurants. In magazines of the day celebrity cooks such as actress Joan Fontaine posed using the pot-in-pot method to impress guests with a smooth, lump-free zabaglione.

Late in the 1940s, Elizabeth Beveridge, the home equipment editor of *Woman's Home Companion*, recommended that the beginning cook assemble a set of cookware based on need. Among the most useful items, she named the double boiler, which she recommended for use in preparing hot cereals, custard, sauces, scrambled eggs, and any other foods that might easily overheat or stick to the pan if cooked over direct heat. She noted that cooks working in cramped quarters could break down the dual-stage vessel into two pots for a variety of uses.

When James Beard and his colleagues compiled *The Cook's Catalogue* (1975), he emphasized the value of the double boiler as a kitchen fundamental. He mentioned the white enamel model as excellent for heating baby food and making cocoa; even better, the Pyrex double boiler allowed the cook to observe the stages of boiling without disassembling it. He especially admired an aluminum-bottomed Farberware model, a stainless steel dual pot of excellent quality with a tight-fitting lid to control evaporation. He noted that the device offered an innovation—a steamer as an alternative use for the three-piece double boiler. "You wind up with a saucepan, or a double boiler, or a steamer, or all three at once," he explained. (Beard *et al.* 1975, 226) These variations allowed the cook to steam green beans, cook rice, and reheat creamed chicken, all on a single burner.

Further Reading

"'Cooking Up' a Double Boiler," *Corning Glassmaker*, April–May 1953.

Stage, Sarah, and Virginia B. Vincenti, eds. *Rethinking Home Economics: Women and the History of a Profession.* Ithaca: Cornell University Press, 1997.

DRYING FOODS

The development of food preservation methods improved human survival by enabling people to store food for a longer period than had been possible in the days of the earliest hunter-gatherers. The settled agrarian life produced supplies of crops that householders needed to guard from mold, decay, insects, and mice. One method of food preservation appeared around 2600 BCE, when Egyptians first dried vegetables in the sun. This primitive application of solar energy survives in southern Africa, where home gardeners cure squash on their straw roofs to harden and protect them. In ancient China, villagers dried foods any time their garden plots produced extra stock. Chinese cooks liked drying because it concentrated and enhanced flavors, particularly in mushrooms.

The Hopi of the Colorado Plateau sun- and fire-dried stores of yucca, berries and currants, corn, beans, squash, pumpkins, nuts, seeds, and prickly pear fruit as a hedge against drought and famine. Near the Grand Canyon, the Havasupai sun-dried the flesh of the prickly pear fruit and then pounded it into cakes for storage. Similarly, they pounded figs and yucca into paste to dry as fruit leather. To the west, the Cahuilla of California's Bernardino mountains dried meat strips in the sun.

The first specific information on dried foods comes from Herodotus, the Greek traveler and historian who wrote *The Persian Wars* (ca. 450 BCE). He described the Babylonian and Egyptian technique of gutting and slicing fish for sunning and airing. Of the Babylonian method, he explained in Book I, "These [fish] are caught and dried in the sun, after which they are brayed in a mortar and strained through a linen sieve. Some prefer to make cakes of this material, others bake it into a kind of bread." (Herodotus 1942, 108) Two other methods for preserving fish included dehydrating the flesh by filleting at a warm hearth or cooking it in a domed oven before a slower, more thorough air-drying. Babylonian cooks then stored the desiccated fish flesh by suspending it under the high eaves of their homes, away from rats. In Book II, Herodotus describes the

Two Dakota women hanging meat to dry on poles, tent in background.
[© *Library of Congress, Prints and Photographs Division (LC-USZ62-46993)*]

gathering of fish and lotuses along the Nile River for eating fresh or drying. The Egyptians extracted the center of the lotus blossom and dried it along with the root. The blossom flavored bread.

Dried food became the staple of travelers and nomads. When the Bulgar Slavs migrated south of the Danube in 681 CE, they gathered foodstuffs that could be prepared along the way. The easiest to obtain were wild apples, pears, and plums, which they dehydrated to make them lighter and easier to store. The food historian Maria Dembinska, author of *Food and Drink in Medieval Poland: Rediscovering a Cuisine of the Past* (1999) characterized the use of dried fish as a medieval survival method along the Baltic Sea. In the 1200s, King Jagiellon recorded how food preservers prized *streck-fuss* (dried fish), stocks of cod and herring which they desiccated until it was as compact as wood. They strung herring slabs on a stick, thirty pieces per length. In the 1500s, after Polish cooks developed more sophisticated food preservation methods, the poor continued drying fish and meat the traditional way. Provisioners for ship's galleys and military commissaries valued dried fish for long voyages and expeditions.

In Moravia, plum drying was a cyclical household job, beginning with boiling down fruit into a thick leather sweetened with fruit sugar. Housewives recycled heat by draping the fruit on hurdles in the oven after they removed bread. For apples, apricots, and pears, they strung slices on cording to place on the parlor stove. For residences with drying huts, processing began with the stoking of a central oven to dehydrate fruit draped over hurdles. These naturally sweet refreshments were favorite gifts to children on holidays and pocket snacks for field workers.

In 1703, writing of his journey to the western islands of Scotland, the traveler Martin Martin described the traditional Hebridean method of drying herring without salt. Homemakers suspended gutted fish in pairs on a heath rope strung across the house. Martin commented, "They eat well, and free from Putrefaction." (McNeil 1929, 112)

In the colonial Americas, families learned from local Indians how to dry and parch meat and grain to supply their tables in late winter and early spring. To make jerky, they layered thin slices of salted game, fish, and domestic meat over a slow fire or on a frame set up in the dooryard to make the most of wind and sun. They placed berries, beans, whole fruits, and fruit pulp in baskets to dehydrate in the sun. Overhead, they strung from kitchen or garden house rafters the braided onions and chili peppers, leather breeches beans, and herbs that sustained them once the root cellar was empty. Dehydrated goods also provided food for land journeys and long sea voyages.

Native Americans had a long tradition of drying *charqui* (jerky), the Quechuan name for dried meat. To ready venison or bison for packing on the trail, preparers boned and defatted haunches before slicing the meat into quarter-inch strips. To ward off worms, they dipped the meat in strong brine or rubbed it with salt. By rolling slices into a parfleche, or leather envelope, for a half day to cure it, they produced toughened meat that was resilient enough to sun-dry and pack in bundles. In the Caribbean, the Arawak perfected the island version of jerking. In Jamaica, where the meat-drying process was influenced by West African cookery, "jerked" foods became the national dish.

The Mandan of the American West worked out a method of air-drying buffalo meat, their staff of life. The nineteenth-century U.S. artist George Catlin, who documented Indian life in his paintings and drawings, wrote of the process, "Their mode of curing and preserving the buffalo meat is somewhat curious, and in fact it is almost incredible also; for it is all cured or dried in the sun, without the aid of salt or smoke!" (Catlin 1989, 127). Catlin remarked that Mandan cured meat could easily withstand the rigors of travel, being tough enough to "be carried to any part of the world without damage." (Ibid.)

In 1876 William W. Fowler, author of *Woman on the American Frontier*, described the value of jerky during perilous times. In colonial Lake Pleasant, New York, during the French and Indian War, scouting parties hid in rock crevices to observe movements of hostile tribes. While living on rainwater that collected in rock caches, "Their food was jerked beef and cold corn-bread, with which their knapsacks had been well stored. Fire they dared not kindle for the smoke would have brought a hundred savages on their trail." (Fowler 1976, 106)

When Captain James Cook, England's intrepid explorer of the Pacific rim in the late 1760s aboard the *Discovery*, he joined other adventurers searching for a northwest passage. Among the Nootka living on Vancouver Island in British Columbia, his men found native cooks working over an open fire in the large communal room of a log-and-plank house. Overhead, the smoke wafted through racks of drying fish, suspended row on row among massive cedar rafters. The smoke kept the fish flesh from moldering in the cool, dank climate by killing bacteria and mold.

In the pioneer bestseller *The Prairie Traveler: A Hand-Book for Overland Expeditions* (1859), the army captain Randolph Barnes describes the mountaineer's version of the jerking process. In the pure air of the nation's interior, hunters could cure fresh game without the use of salt by hanging it in the sun for slow drying. They packed the inch-thick jerk strips in sacks and transported it uncorrupted over long treks. For dehydrating meat while on the move, pioneers stretched lines along the sides of wagons and suspended meat strips to cure in the sun. Barnes advised travelers to apply this method when in contact with ample buffalo herds to supply jerked meat for emergencies and times when game was scarce.

During the Civil War, U.S. army cooks received regular issue of lightweight commercially processed desiccated potatoes and mixed vegetables. The foodstuffs underwent a factory process of cleaning, shredding, mixing, oven-drying, and pressing into hard wheels or sheets that softened when boiled in water or broth. Comprising potatoes, cabbage, turnips, carrots, parsnips, beets, tomatoes, onions, peas, beans, lentils, assorted greens, and celery, the sheets of compressed vegetables were easily stored. As described in the historian Henry Steele Commager's *The Blue and the Gray* (1950), cooks tore the flattened masses into pieces, plopped them into a kettle of water, and stirred with a broom handle. Upon crossing the Rappahannock River in mid-December 1862, Confederate Major G. Moxley Sorrel, General James Longstreet's chief staff officer, was amazed at the great slabs, which offered far more variety than the pathetic supplies that nourished rebel forces. In contrast to the major's enthusiasm, Union diners, less delighted with the tasteless mass, dubbed it "desecrated vegetables." (Mitchell 2000, 27)

Throughout the twentieth century, homemakers and commercial food processors retained drying as a preservation method because it assured a long shelf life for foods collected in the wild, such as cranberries, morels, and wild rice. The Swiss continued an ancient method of preserving beef for *Bindenfleisch* (bound meat), an air-cured table product. In the British Isles, diners favored the dried sea vegetables—tangle, Irish moss, sea-whistle, dulse, driftweed, purple laver, and sea cabbage—for thickening stew or eating like jerky. In Scotland, fishers sold "dulse and tangle," a sweet, nutty-tasting and nutritious food consisting of seaweed rinsed in fresh water and dried. ("The Coming World of Marine Cuisine" 1960, 21)

The tradition of rooftop drying continued in many parts of the world. Armenian cooks in eastern Turkey dried grapes for use in *bastegh* (fruit rolls). The process began with spreading a damp mass of fruit on white sheets, which were suspended on the clothesline. The fruit leather was then gently pried from the cloth and sprinkled with sugared water. From the same batch, the cook would dip strands strung with walnut halves into hot grape pudding for drying into sweet snack food.

Rationing and food shortages on the European continent forced homemakers to return to dehydrated supplies. In Norway during World War II, German occupation forces gathered and dried seaweed to grind into meal for bread. Bulgarians sun dried berries and fruits from their garden or from the wild and sprinkled them with a solution of ash and water to prevent mold in storage. The resulting *osay* (compote) was a favorite breakfast and holiday dish. In the September 1942 issue of *House Beautiful*, food commentator Clementine Paddleford's "What War Has Done to Life in the Kitchen" described how British cooks were coping with the shortage of fresh foods usually brought to the island nation by sea. Without these imported goods, cooks were being forced to rely on dried soup, egg yolk, fruit, milk, and entire dried dinners.

After the war, industrial drying ended the homemaker's laborious process of collecting, dicing, spreading, and turning foods. The Tupman Thurlow Company in New York City offered the home cook the convenience of dried onion bits in a glass jar. Processing reduced twelve fresh onions into a small bottle of flakes that occupied little space on the pantry shelf. Busy housewives, who had no time for mincing or dicing fresh onions, could quickly add onion flakes to soups, stews, salads, and roasted meats. In addition to saving the cook labor, the use of desiccated onions entailed no waste, no mess, no smelly hands, and no lingering cooking odors.

As pictured in Eliot Wigginton's *The Foxfire Book* (1968), mountaineers living in the isolated coves of the southern Appalachians depended on drying to preserve foods for winter. They strung green beans on cording for leather breeches beans, which had to be soaked before use. Rounds of pumpkin hung from the rafters, slices of sun-dried sweet potato lay in stacks for use in puddings, souffles, and pies. For drying corn kernels and okra, the gardener spread the vegetables across a tin sheet covered in butcher wrap and dried them in the sun. Sackfuls of field peas were bundled into a sheet and dehydrated in the same way. For apple or peach rings, the preparer peeled, cored, and sliced the fruit into rounds before stringing them on a broomstick to air- and sun-dry or braided them into wreaths to dry slowly at the hearth. To assure their survival without decay, mold, or insect infestation, some people further dehydrated the slices in a warm oven, then packed them in sacks for the winter. Berries also survived the winter if first dried, then layered in bags.

Into the twenty-first century, drying remained essential to the preparation of traditional foods, for example the Sicilian preparation of *'u 'strattu* (tomato extract), which involved hardening tomato purée into a claylike paste and storing it in a muslin-covered jar. Similarly, the nomadic Qermezi of southwest Iran preserved the first curds of the year by rolling them into small balls and placing them in reed mats elevated from the ground on tripods for sun- and wind-drying. Tanzanian women sun-dried *morogo*, a general term for edible leaves of buffalo-thorn, pumpkins, silver beet, or sweet potato, to preserve them for later use. In Sikkim, cooks air-dried pork strips in cool currents to dehydrate and texturize meat for stir frying. In El Coche and Cubagua off the coast of Venezuela, coastal cooks dehydrated fish roe on a griddle. Joined like hands of bananas, the strands of roe held their shape over the two-day drying period with the help of thin skewers extracted from the veins of coconut palms.

Dried food remains in production in Iranian, Iraqi, Syrian, and Turkish kitchens much as it was in the ninth century BCE. To ready wheat for winter storage, families make *byrghel*, also called *gurgur* and *hlula*. They retain up to a tenth of the wheat harvest to toast in sheet-metal kettles over a hot flame. After up to four hours of cooking, the softened grain, which children rifle for snacks, is ready for sun drying on rooftop matting or rugs. When the moisture content drops, the supply is ready for beating with wood hammers and mixing in a *gurno* (mortar). Another preservation method involves dehulling with stones. Similar sun-drying methods preserve raisins, salted meat, and tomato paste.

In the kitchens of industrialized nations, use of an electric dehydrator is the favorite method of making fruit leather and drying berries, beans, tomatoes, peppers, onions, garlic, and herbs. Unlike the stove-top drying boxes designed in the 1920s to fit over wood stoves and the expensive and complex electric cabinet dehydrators of the 1970s, late-twentieth-century models cost as little as $50. The fruits, mushrooms, and jerky dried in the electronic device offer the same advantages found in dried foods in ancient times: They require no added water, weigh less, and take up less storage space than their fresh counterparts.

Further Reading

Beck, Lois. *Nomad: A Year in the Life of a Qashqa'i Tribesman in Iran.* Berkeley: University of California Press, 1991.

Fowler, William W. *Woman on the American Frontier.* Williamstown, Mass.: Corner House Publishers, 1976.

Glants, Musya, and Joyce Toomre, eds. *Food in Russian History and Culture.* Bloomington: Indiana University Press, 1997.

Ross, John F., "People of the Reindeer," *Smithsonian*, December 2000, 54–65.

DUTCH OVEN

A familiar lidded pot, the Dutch oven—also called a bake kettle, bastable, bread oven, fire pan, bake oven, kail pot, tin kitchen, roasting kitchen, *doufeu* (gentle fire) or *four de campagne* (country oven)—originally replaced the roasting jack as the latest fireside cooking technology. Its forerunner, the pot oven or "oon pot," was an iron dome that sat directly on the hearthstone over baking bread, raised oatcakes, or pastry. (Schärer & Fenton 1998, 40) When using the Scottish kail pot, the baker intensified heat by heaping burning peat on top; the Irish cook renewed layers of embers on the bastable that roasted the Christmas goose. A Continental forerunner, the German *backhauben* (baking bonnet) was a flat open-hearth container into which the baker poured batter; it required covering with a lid, and heaping with glowing charcoal. Another version, called a "hang-over oven" in Isabella Beeton's classic *Book of Household Management* (1860), was a lidded pot hung from a fireplace trammel. Heat permeated from the hearth fire below and hot coals shoveled on the lid.

The Dutch oven combined the convenience of pot oven and hang-over oven. Standing on stout legs, the enclosed cooking chamber fit directly into hot coals or into an oven for slow cooking of pot roast, stewed meat or fruit, or baked beans. The *Mayflower* Pilgrims introduced the Dutch oven to the New World in 1620. They chose it over other cookware for its many uses during a long voyage where space was limited. According to folk tradition, Paul Revere, the esteemed silversmith and patriot of the late colonial era, adapted the Dutch oven by making the handle detachable. Because of its versatility—it adapted to stewing, baking bread, and heating water for dishwashing—it often accompanied overland travelers and was a necessity for pioneers and cowboys on the American frontier. A Western favorite called middling bread was a whole wheat bread baked for six hours in the Dutch oven; its thick, absorbent crust was especially suited to sopping up gravy, pan juices, or molasses. In the Australian outback, cooks fashioned baking powdered dampers (biscuits) for cooking directly in hot coals in Dutch ovens. Christian families often baked enough dampers to serve a congregation as communion bread.

As described in Alexandre Dumas's posthumous classic *Le Grand Dictionnaire de Cuisine* (The Great Dictionary of Cooking, 1873), the pot's flanged lid was flat or convex to accommodate hot coals on top, thus expanding the available cooking surfaces. The bail or falling handle allowed the cook to transport the pot and to suspend it from an overhead hook or rod, making it a valuable implement for open-hearth cooking and for use in lumber and mining camps, on military expeditions, and on chuckwagons.

The Dutch oven served great and humble as a casserole, pie pan, vessel for washing dishes, and receptacle for hot coals retrieved from a neighbor to relight a home hearth or start a campfire. In the Lincoln family home on Little Pigeon Creek in frontier Indiana, Nancy Hanks Lincoln slowly steamed jacket potatoes in a Dutch oven for a meager family supper. After placing the potatoes in salted water, she set the vessel in embers or on top of the stove. At the table, she served directly from the pot along with mugs of buttermilk.

In the 1930s, *Good Housekeeping* carried ads from Griswold Manufacturing of Erie, Pennsylvania, featuring the Tite-Top Dutch Oven, which enclosed steam without leakage. The company guaranteed that the lidded cook pot basted and enriched foods while they cooked without stirring or sticking. Sold in both cast iron and heavy cast aluminum, the pot became a family heirloom and collector's item after decades of use. The company enhanced sales by offering its "Booklet on Waterless Cooking," published under the cozy name of "Aunt Ellen," whose picture appeared on ad copy intended to appeal to female magazine readers.

Irish farm cooks had used pot ovens on open grates and hearth fires into the early 1900s. The Irish food writer Florence Irwin, author of *The Cookin' Woman: Irish Country Recipes* (1949), traveled around Northern Ireland in the early years of the twentieth century with a portable stove. Her intent was to introduce young farm women to domestic sciences and such Irish cooking traditions as soda bread, potato oaten cake, custard-baked fish, and curried rabbit and rice.

In 1968, Eliot Wigginton dispatched students from a Rabun Gap, Georgia, high school to learn the subsistence methods of householders in the Appalachians. The resulting text, *The Foxfire Book* (1968), the first of a successful series on lifestyles and survivalism, described in words and pictures the function of the Dutch oven for open-hearth or outdoor cooking. Student writers explained the purpose of the flanged lid and tongs, by which the cook maneuvered pot and lid during and after heating.

In the twenty-first century, the Dutch oven remained very much a part of cookery, particularly for camping.

The French cookware firm Le Creuset, known for its line of enameled cast-iron vessels, markets an oval *doufeu* with an indented top and paired handles, one on top and one on the bottom, at each side. The company recommends placing ice on the recessed lid to promote the development of pan juices.

See also **Chuckwagons; Hay-Box Cookers; Open-Hearth Cooking**

DYES AND COLORANTS

Before the creation of mineral and chemical dyes, cooks turned to nature for substances capable of enhancing the color of foods. Verifiable food additives date to 5000 BCE, when Egyptians applied natural colorants to pharmaceuticals and flavorings. By 1500 BCE color additives had evolved into food coloring. Chief among the brightly colored food dyes were yellow saffron, orange turmeric, and red paprika. The dyes appear to have been valuable to primitive people. A study of Pueblo gravesites from 1350 to 1500 CE at Hawikki near Zuñi, New Mexico, described paint pigments and grinding stones as worthy of accompanying female corpses as burial offerings.

In this same era, Mesoamerican harvesters in Tlaxcala and Oaxaca, Mexico, and others in Guatemala, Peru, the Caribbean, and the Canary Islands collected the fertilized female of the insect *Dactylopius coccus* from cacti. To extract the red colorant known as cochineal or carmine, harvesters dried the insects and crushed the bodies. Valued as food coloring in candy making—and also used to produce the fabric for the British army's red coats—these deep red dyes became

Dyeing cotton thread in Uruapan, Mexico.
[© *Brian Atkinson / Alamy.*]

a reliable trade item for export as far east as Turkey and China.

Writings about natural dyes from the Mediterranean rim indicate the high price these colorants brought on the market. In Italy Pliny the Elder, compiler of the Roman encyclopedia *Natural History* (ca. 77 CE), documented the dyeing technology of his time. Stew-cooks added *defrutum* (fruit paste), a deep-purple wine concentrate, to deepen the color of light dishes. The most treasured coloring of the era was royal purple, a product of the sea mollusks *Murex trunculus* and *Murex brandaris.*

In the Caribbean, a yellowish-red dye extracted from the seed of the annatto (*Bixa orellana*), served cooks as both flavoring and colorant. Columbus's sailors studied the Arawak and Taino's techniques for pit roasting, which produced foods of outstanding flavor, texture, aroma, and color. Cooks basted the crispy red skin of a skewered piglet with an annatto mixture. In Puerto Rico in the twenty-first century, cooks perpetuated the traditional use of red food colorants. Successive bastings of a roasting pig with annatto blended with the juice of the sour orange and oil or lard kept the crackly skin a bright red.

In the dye trade of the Middle Ages, dealers transported blue woad from Languedoc and cochineal red from Poland and Armenia across camel routes to the Arabian peninsula. Bright colors were a dinner-hour feature in Europe. In the typically dark great hall of the medieval castle, eye-appealing foods were a necessary complement to heavy furniture, smoky ceilings, and rich canopies and wall hangings. An opulent table established the host as powerful and generous and the hostess as sensitive to the tastes of guests.

Islamic cookery called for reds and yellows to enlivening table servings. Saffron—made from the dried stigmas of the purple crocus (*Crocus sativus*)—imparted both a yellow color and a distinctive flavor. This popular Arab specialty, discussed in al-Baghdadi's *Kitab al-Tibakhah* (A Baghdad Cookery Book, 1226), was costly because of the labor involved in harvesting it. A substance derived from the common broom plant, *Genista tinctoria*, produced a similar bright yellow color. To add a reddish color to dishes, Arab cooks used blood oranges, red currants, rose or mulberry conserves, dates, quince, prunes, wild cherries, or cinnabar (mercury sulfide), mined in Spain.

European cooks mixed their own food colorings, attaching a forked stick to a rock muller and grinding the pigments on a slab. John de Garland's *Dictionary* (1220) mentions the use of woad for blue and sandyx for vermillion and notes that the grinding of such substances caused cooks to have "fingernails colored in various colors, at times red, then black, sometimes

blue"—a characteristic that apparently handicapped them in matters of romance. (Rubin 1981, 55) In *Diversa Cibaria* (Diverse Provisions, early 1200s), an anonymous English cookbook, the author lists *sangdragon* (dragon's blood) as a red herbal colorant and advises that indigo can be made from pulverized cloves. Additional food dyes came from rose petals, strawberries, cherries, and hawthorn flowers.

During the Renaissance, vegetable dyes remained valuable trade items. In *Description of Elizabethan England* (1577), historian William Harrison declared madder second only to tin and wool in value. Cooks belonged to the same guilds as painters and apothecaries, all of whom ground their own spices and pigments with mortar and pestle. The cook who earned royal favor for skillful adornment was ranked as an artist, and his sauces, like the painter's pigments, were blended on the spot rather than being bought ready made.

Eastern Europe created its own traditions of culinary dyes. Before Easter, Polish women made bright gold *babas* (cakes), the traditional holiday dessert, which called for twenty-four beaten egg yolks, ten ounces of sifted wheat flour, and saffron dissolved in vodka. Elena Molokhovets, author of *Classic Russian Cooking* (1861), made her own cochineal powder and extract for coloring beverages and desserts. In the 1897 edition of her book, she chose for carmine hues a red gelatin manufactured in sheets at a St. Petersburg factory founded in 1887 by Swiss confectioner Moritz Conradi. By 1900, the city had three such food-dye factories and the Crimea, another.

In the heyday of artificial textile colorants, the makers of food dyes turned to minerals and metallic compounds. Toxic colorants, among them mercury and copper salts and arsenic poisons, enhanced the green of cucumber pickles and colored candies and marzipan in a variety of hues. Despite the fact that these metallic substances caused suffering and death, food distributors marketed around eighty such additives. Some were fiber dyes never intended for culinary use. In addition to brightening the natural color of foods, they masked low quality or spoilage. During the early decades of the twentieth century, dependence on toxic colorants in items such as ketchup, mustard, jelly, and wine continued unmonitored and unchallenged. The majority of the dyes were aniline- or petroleum-based derivatives called coal-tar dyes because they originated in bituminous coal. For reasons of cost and availability, the food dyes found in low-cost foodstuffs such as cookies and candy tended to come from chemical synthesis rather than plant and animal sources. With the passage of the first Pure Food and Drug laws in 1906, the U.S. government began to regulate food additives.

In the post-World War II era, shoppers demanded speed and efficiency in home products. One time-saving innovation was margarine that could be colored right in its own package, sparing the homemaker the task of mixing the pale vegetable shortening with yellow food dye. Delrich margarine from Chicago's Cudahy Packing Company came in a sealed plastic bag implanted with a coloring dot. By kneading the unopened bag, cooks could evenly distribute the dye throughout the mass. To create the standard rectangular block, the user returned the bag to the carton and chilled it in the refrigerator.

From the 1950s into the twenty-first century, inorganic and metallic dyes and bleaching agents earned scrutiny because of their importance to the appearance of processed foods (citrus fruit peels, potato skins, sausage casing, paprika and mustard, white bread and other baked items, candy and ice cream, butter and margarine, gelatin and drink mixes, and carbonated beverages) and in finished dishes in home and restaurant kitchens. Toxicity of dyes suggest a direct link to breast cancer and hyperactivity in children from red, yellow, orange, and violet colorings. Governments in Canada, Great Britain, and the United States have banned some of these substances from foods.

Further Reading

Bremness, Lesley. *The Complete Book of Herbs*. New York: Penguin Studios, 1994.

Wolinsky, Cary, "The Quest for Colors," *National Geographic*, July 1999, 72–93.

E

EGGS

Ever since the prehistoric hunting-and-gathering era, humans have valued fowl, amphibians, and their eggs as food. In some cultures, eggshells have also served as containers. Evidence of the early use of eggs comes from Patne, India, where artisans engraved ostrich eggs around 38,000 BCE. The Maya and the Caribe traditionally collected bird and turtle eggs from tree, ground, and seaside crannies and extracted fish roe from the catches in their seines. The Haida of the Queen Charlotte Islands, British Columbia, gathered eggs for storage in cedar-bark bags and relied on shore birds as a food source. The Eskimo enjoyed a dish called "duck not yet," made by boiling ducklings in the shell shortly before they hatched. The Philippine balut, sold by street vendors, parallels the Aleut dish with a duck egg boiled on the seventeenth day after fertilization until the liquid forms a sauce that marinates the unborn bird.

Early Culinary Use

Egg fanciers valued both shell and contents in Europe and Asia. In the Fertile Crescent, Mesopotamian housewives used ostrich eggs as serving vessels. In Egypt's Old Kingdom, tomb art at Saqqara shows servants at work cleaning female mullets and extruding batrakh, a roe that they dried in the sun. Egyptians also decorated friezes with pictures of ostrich or pelican eggs on trays. Around 1500 BCE, Greek tableware makers created egg dishes with slots of varying sizes to suit peacock, goose, and hen eggs. They also shaped

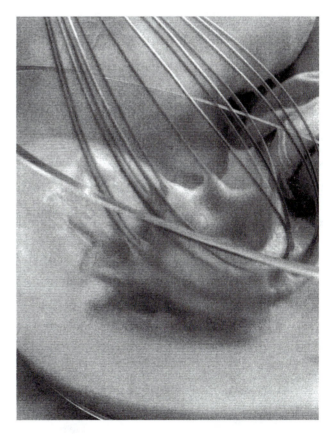

Beating eggs with whisk.

the first wooden dining spoon for serving and eating eggs. Roman cooks once outlined their menus methodically "ab ovo ad mala" (from eggs to apples), thus specifying eggs as an appetizer, the beginning of a good meal. The Chinese preserved eggs by encasing them in an airtight layer of clay and lime blended with wheat chaff and burying them for forty days.

In the Middle Ages, families relished eggs as a meat substitute on fast days and during Lent. They moistened stale bread to make pain perdu (lost bread), the original French toast. Gathering bird's eggs was a pleasant chore for British children. They provided the cottage kitchen with fresh eggs from ducks, bantams, and wild birds. To rifle a cliff side of gulls' eggs took ingenuity. The egg-fetcher worked from the cliff top down, placed the eggs in baskets, and lowered them to a waiting boat below. Welsh cottagers often made a goose hole under the stone kitchen step, where the bird became both egg-sitter and watchdog.

For open-hearth food preparation, cooks used the egg slicer or egg lifter, a simple turner with a flat shovel end pierced with small holes to allow fats to drain back into the pan. The egg fryer replaced the skillet by offering egg-shaped depressions in cast iron to separate each egg as it cooked. In ornate versions the depressions bore the shape of flowers, hearts, or stars. The cook could fry a dozen at a time, buttering or seasoning them to suit the tastes of individual diners.

The fifteenth century Italian cook and culinary writer Il Platina, author of *De Honesta Voluptate et Valitudine* (On Right Pleasure and Health; 1475), covered the topic of egg selection. In Book II, he observes: "Eggs, which produce life, are suitable for eating: geese, ducks, peacocks, ostriches, chickens; but those of chickens are better and more healthful, especially if they have been fertilized by the rooster." (Platina 1999, 41) Quoting the Roman encyclopedist Pliny and the philosopher Aulus Cornelius Celsus, author of *De Medicina* (On Medicine), both from the first century AD, Platina explains how whites and yolks heal and fortify. When desserts call for egg white, he advises the cook to reserve the separated yolks for warming the heart and nourishing the body.

Dishes Fit for a King

Because it demanded precise control, egg cookery became the province of the wealthy. A royal egg gourmand, Louis XIII, who came to the throne of France in 1611, was a failure as a soldier and monarch, but excelled at variety in egg cookery. In addition to poaching and hard-boiling, he experimented with a new dish containing chopped eggs with bacon. The indolent Louis XV, whose disastrous rule prefaced the French Revolution, became a hobby cook famous for an asparagus omelette, which he invented to please his mistress, Madame du Barry.

The production of a light, high-peaked meringue from beaten egg whites and finely ground sugar got its start in the 1500s in Europe. Chefs whipped egg whites and cream with birch whisks to make a topping known as snow, forerunner of the foamy confection dressing called meringue. A century later, meringue found its way into recipes under the name "sugar puff." (Davidson 1999, 497) A half century after the first experiments with meringue, courtier and alchemist Sir Kenelm Digby, author of *The Closet of Sir Kenelm Digby Knight Opened* (ca. 1667), passed on an eggnog recipe he obtained from a Jesuit to China in 1664. The restorative required the beating of sugar and egg yolks with a slow drizzle of hot tea, much as homemade mayonnaise is made by emulsifying eggs with oil. The transmission of the Chinese recipe coincided with the opening of the Asian tea market to the East India Company.

In the 1700s confectioners added cream of tartar to whipped egg white for stability and created a firmer type of meringue that could serve as a lightweight shell for fruit or custard. Mousse, another foamy confection, could be stabilized with egg white, whipped cream, or gelatin. In 1935, chef Herbert Sachse of the Esplanade Hotel, Perth, Australia, elevated the meringue by adding corn starch and filling the baked casing with fruit and fresh cream. The dessert, dubbed the Pavlova to honor the light dance confections of the Russian ballerina Anna Pavlova, became a national dish.

In *Pseudodoxia Epidemica* (1686) the seventeenth century English physician and writer Thomas Browne's connected the egg to witchcraft. He recommended that eggshells be broken to keep mischievous house sprites from inhabiting them. The precaution also prevented witches from writing or pricking their names in the shell to "veneficiously mischiefe ye persons." (Beard 1975, 431) He added that these customs prevailed in rural areas. In Scotland, the egg took on a more ambiguous use as a fortune-telling tool. The teller dropped the white into an ale cup, topped the vessel with the palm of the hand, and upended it. The future lay in the positioning of the viscous albumin in the container. The eggs then went into "dumb cakes," bannocks named for the silence of the subjects waiting for the telling of their fates.

The 1700s also saw the invention of a French masterwork, the soufflé (literally, "puffed up") which Russian and Ukrainian cooks emulated as drachena. Chef Antoine Beauvilliers, who established the first Parisian restaurant in 1783, drew customers with his puffy egg dishes. In *L'Art du Cuisinier* (The Art of the Chef; 1814), which he wrote near the end of his career, he gave precise instructions for the tricky job of adding beaten egg white to hot soufflé mix, the first printed recipe for the dish. His contemporary, Chef Louis Ude, compiler of *The French Cook* (1813), added more dessert soufflés to French cuisine. These dishes influenced the cookery of two culinary masters—Marie-Antoine Carême, who gave detailed accounts of egg-puffing techniques, and Georges-Auguste Escoffier, who featured soufflés in *Le Carnet d'Epicure* (A Gourmet's Notebook; 1911).

Housewives and Hens

Inspiring hens to lay more eggs was usually the job of the homemaker, who gathered, washed, candled, and sorted eggs for various uses, including sale or trade with neighbors. For the home hennery that produced too few eggs, A.W. Chase's handy *Dr. Chase's Recipes: Information for Everybody* (1866) advised readers to follow the advice of a housewife living in Maine on the Kennebec River. To perk up a dozen poor layers, she administered a teaspoon of powdered cayenne pepper daily. The regimen resulted in up to fourteen eggs each day.

Keeping eggs for winter could present a problem in homes where hens laid mainly in warm weather. In 1836, Lydia Maria Child published advice on egg preservation in *The American Frugal Housewife*. She suggested storing eggs in containers of lime water in a cool place, but she warned, "If there be too much lime, it will eat the shells from the eggs; and if there be a single egg cracked, it will spoil the whole." (McCutcheon 1993, 96) In her experience, the lime-water method retained egg freshness for up to three years. In 1869, *The Agricultural Almanac,* issued in Lancaster, Pennsylvania, by John Baer & Son, instructed housewives on pickling eggs in sugar, vinegar, salt, gingerroot, clove, peppercorn, and allspice for use as a plate garnish or a brightener for winter salads.

Elena Burman Molokhovets, compiler of the classic Russian cookbook *A Gift to Young Housewives* (1861), made ingenious use of sturgeon roe and poultry eggs. Roe, which she used liberally, flavored her sauces and sauerkraut and clarified bouillon. She set orange gelatin to firm in blown shells and removed the exterior to reveal perfect dessert ovules. She split hard-cooked egg, chopped and blended it with tasty ingredients, and stuffed the mix back into the shells for browning in the oven.

The delicacy and unique shape of the egg, whether fresh or hard-boiled, inspired a number of implements, one an ornate ovule that worked like a chafing dish for cooking eggs over a small flame at the table. The egg detector, patented around 1890, funneled the contents of a punctured eggshell directly into a cup below. The scissor-action topper, marketed by G. M. Thurnauer of New York City in 1904, slipped through the end of the shell without altering the insides or breaking the yolk. Various cast iron and japanned slicers lopped the boiled egg into quarters or horizontal slices by the action of a levered guillotine, press-action collar, or wire edges held in a swing-down frame.

"Candling" was a traditional method for assessing the freshness of eggs. The candler positioned a candle or kerosene-fed flame inside the lighted globe of an egg tester to illuminate the opaque shell. The purpose of such careful scrutiny was to determine the size of the air spot inside or the presence of an embryo in a fertilized egg. A large air pocket indicated an old egg. If blood spots or embryos were visible, the candler disposed of the eggs or fed them to the pigs. Further grading took place on a scale that determined the size and value of each egg.

Eggbeaters and Other Kitchen Aids

Worldwide, home production of eggs evolved from an activity that supplied family needs to a full-fledged kitchen business. The egg scale, a sheet-metal device patented in 1940 solely for the grading of eggs, held individual eggs on a small platform. A pointer indicated whether the egg was small, medium, large, or extra large. One model, the Jiffy-Way table model grading scale, made in Owatonna, Minnesota, provided a cupped lever to hold the egg while a pointer measured a range from 18 to 30 ounces.

The eggbeater was a boon to cooks seeking high, light peaks of egg white for folding into cream pies, crêpes, eggnog, and omelets. When it was patented in 1870, it largely replaced earlier whipping devices such as the fork, split cane, and the hickory rod whip. In *Common Sense in the Household: A Manual of Practical Housewifery* (1871), written by Marion Harland, pseudonym of author Mary Hawes Terhune, the text advised that with the aid of the egg beater, a meringue could be whipped up in as little as five minutes. According to the author, the recently introduced wire aerator whipped up "snow custard in less than half an hour with no tremulousness of nerve or tendon." (*The Williamsburg Cookbook* 1971, 136) Willie Johnson, an inventor from Cincinnati, updated eggbeater design in February 1884, when he made a drive wheel-and-pinion device to blend eggs, batter, and confections. Held in a frame, the socketed mechanism attached to two shafts that turned blades for stirring and mixing.

The task of separating yolk from white occupied other inventors. One egg separator contained a slotted upper cup that channeled the albumen into a small basin below. Around 1890 New Yorker Dollie Washburne marketed her original Dollie Egg Separator, which allowed the mass separation of eggs into a trough. The user rolled the eggs one-by-one down the length of the trough, where they broke against the end of the device. The white slithered through slits, while the yolks plopped into a basin.

A debate arose over the best way to purchase eggs. In a small ad in the January 1925 issue of *Good Housekeeping,* the Metal Egg Crate Company of Fredericksburg, Virginia, urged homemakers to save money and avoid disappointment in freshness and quality by buying direct from the producer by mail. The ad copy promised fresh eggs year round safely shipped in aluminum egg crates that limited breakage. In the next month's issue, Arthur E. Albrecht published an essay on grocery shopping that rebutted the mail-order distributor. He warned that shipping eggs by parcel post might not assure freshness: "If it is in the spring when production is heavy, the farmer's eggs, after reaching the city, may go into cold storage, to wait there several months before being placed on the market." (Albrecht 1925, 73)

Egg cookery spawned a large family of modern implements and containers, including vertical, horizontal, suspended, and long-handled poachers and wire egg stands for boiling eggs in a pot and the sablier [egg timer], an hour glass that timed the fall of sand from top half to bottom in one to three minutes. A unique egg manipulator, the Air-O-Mixer, patented around 1933, combined a cylindrical glass jar and metal lid with a metal shaft and conical mesh or perforated metal whipping blade. The device was useful for making homemade mayonnaise, an emulsion of egg and oil that had previously required tedious blending in minute amounts. Another device, a specialized pair of scissors, sliced through the end of a boiled egg and lifted the upper portion of shell out of the way. The lower shell perched in an eggcup, from which the contents of the egg could be scooped out with a spoon. The wire-bladed egg slicer produced uniform sections for use in decorating salads or garnishing platters.

Advances in technology yielded new methods for cooking eggs. The egg coddler was a two-stage tin box or basin that held boiling water below. The user lifted the egg frame, placed the egg in a wire circlet or wire basket, then plunged the frame into the water. An electric model, equipped with a timer, paralleled the original device. Large restaurant-sized cookers rotated eggs on a turntable. Some, like the ones favored by French hotels on the island of Guadeloupe, popped the frame up like an automatic toaster when the eggs were done.

Health Debate

Toward the end of the twentieth century, the healthfulness of eggs, previously an article of faith among nutritionists, became a subject of contention. Because eggs contain cholesterol—a fatty substance implicated in blockage of the arteries—people with coronary heart disease began excluding them from their diet. Egg producers altered the feed of their laying hens in an attempt to create eggs with less cholesterol; grocers offered "egg substitutes." With better understanding of the role of dietary fats in heart disease, however, the reputation of the egg was somewhat rehabilitated. Late in the 1990s, with the blessing of the American Heart Association, ad campaigns turned from warnings against egg consumption to cautious acceptance. Influencing the shift in thinking were reports such as the one in the April 1999 *Journal of the American Medical Association,* which declared that "up to one egg per day is unlikely to have substantial overall impact on the risk of [coronary heart disease] or stroke among healthy men and women." (Kummer 2000, 118) Around the same time, several outbreaks of salmonella were linked to eggs, triggering warnings that people should avoid eating raw or undercooked eggs and any dishes containing them.

Despite these periodic health debates, eggs remained a culinary essential into the twenty-first century. At Easter time in Christian nations, the decoration and eating of eggs symbolized rebirth and promise. Confections shaped like eggs perpetuated the age-old centrality of eggs in spring festivals. Nicaraguan cooks broke one egg per diner into every fresh pot of beans for *sopa de frijoles* (bean soup). Somali Muslims cooked clove-flavored egg crêpes on a griddle and served them with sweet tea to mark the completion of Ramadan, a month of ritual dawn-to-dusk fasting.

Egg producers, varying from the small farm to mass production agribusinesses, began competing in earnest for a share of the growing market in eggs from free-range chickens. Without the stress of living in close, factory-farm quarters or being subjected to heavy prophylactic doses of antibiotics, free-range hens produced the eggs that nutritionists exalted as the best choice for cooking. Three other additions to the egg trade were shelled eggs pasteurized and sold in liquid, frozen, or dried form in 1995; glass jars of yolks for infant meals; and rehydrated kosher whites, available in cans of fat-free, cholesterol-free, and pasteurized powder to be mixed with water for meringue and angel food cake.

New gadgets for egg cookery continued to simplify preparation. Using a stainless steel wire egg separator, cooks skip the old method of draining the yolk on a piece of shell. Instead, the cook breaks the egg directly into the device, which hold the yolk entire until the albumin separates into a container below. A two-handled version sits on a cup or bowl to free hands for breaking and separating shells. The Pedrini egg separator is a stainless steel cup with a wide rim. Albumin slips through two drain slots, keeping the yolk intact. Even faster were powdered products that simplify egg use and, for campers and backpackers in particular, carry no risk of breakage.

Additional egg gimmicks include a two-ended glass suited for serving juice on the large end and holding an egg on the other. An elegant Italian egg stand in stainless steel lowers four eggs at a time into boiling water and removes them in one motion when they are done. A French egg poacher contains four pierced egg cups arranged around a central stand for eggs Benedict or eggs Florentine. A popular kitchen catalog features porcelain egg coddlers with stainless steel lids. Polypropylene egg cups hold single servings for cooking eggs in the microwave. A plastic bowl with stainless steel inset at bottom supports the rapid strokes of a whisk for light, fluffy meringue.

Further Reading

Gentry, Patricia. *Kitchen Tools*. San Francisco: 101 Productions, 1985.
McGee, Harold. *The Curious Cook*. New York: HarperCollins, 1992.

ELECTRIC COOKERY AND APPLIANCES

Ever since the English physicist Michael Faraday produced the first electric motor in 1837, cooking and other domestic chores have become less labor intensive than in past generations. At his Menlo Park workshop, the U.S. inventor Thomas Edison directed electric current to the incandescent light, unveiled in 1879. It operated by means of a long-lived carbon filament, which glowed in a partial vacuum within a glass globe. Adaptation of the electric motor by the Italian inventor Galileo Ferrari and the Croatian physicist-engineer Nikola Tesla produced a small table-model fan in 1889, which Peter Behrens of Allgemeine Elektrizitats Gesellschaft streamlined in 1911. For Tesla's contribution to electronics, he earned the 1917 Edison Medal from the American Institute of Electrical Engineers.

Introduction of Kitchen Electronics

Public acceptance of kitchen electronics came much more slowly than did the installation of electric lighting. The European public got its first view of electric cookery at the 1883 Vienna Technical Exhibition, where technologists displayed an immersion heater. Within four years, an electric cook pot came on the Canadian market. The railroad entrepreneur and inventor George Westinghouse, who founded Westinghouse Electric and Manufacturing Company of Pittsburgh in 1886, bought Tesla's patents on alternating-current motors. At Chicago's 1893 Columbian Exposition, Westinghouse set out to persuade the American public to accept electrical gadgetry, made inexpensive after nickel-chromium alloys replaced platinum in electric coils. Application of electricity to broiling, boiling, deep-frying, toasting, coffee-making, and grilling presaged the changes to come—convenience, control of heat, and the end to hand-stoking fires.

Although the first all-electric kitchen in England had gone on display in 1891 at the Crystal Palace Electrical Exhibition, the engineer H. J. Dowsing of Dowsing Radiant Heat Company had already made limited inroads into the domestic scene with radiant space heaters. It was his restructuring of the naked heating element between metal plates in 1893 that removed fears of electrocution. A sketch of a model kitchen in a Scribner's handbook, *The Woman's Book: Dealing Practically with the Modern Conditions of Home Life, Self-Support, Education, Opportunities, and Every-Day Problems* (1894), pictured a cook at a counter covered with plug-in appliances. Because these devices were fragile and necessitated complex upkeep and cleaning, cooks used them mainly for heating water. However expensive and cumbersome, flameless cookery was well on its way to becoming an integral part of the kitchen of the future.

The closed wood- and coal-fired range marketed in the late 1700s dominated kitchens into the 1920s, especially in Germany and parts of the United States such as the Tennessee Valley, where a government project began supplying electric power in 1933. Cooks were initially suspicious of the cast-iron gas stove, which emerged from mid-nineteenth century technology; they took more readily to oil ranges. By 1900 they had accepted gas ranges—and were thus freed from wrestling with solid fuel and ash—but rejected the Edwardian electric model, which heated less rapidly than the gas stove. As of 1920, close to 50 percent of city homes were wired; within two decades, the number rose to 96 percent, but electrification affected only one-third of rural homes.

Smart manufacturers distanced themselves as much as possible from the era of flues, soot, and charred wood by offering electric ranges with slick, white enamel surfaces. After Albert Marsh invented Nichrome, a chromium-nickel alloy, in 1905, he provided the appliance industry with a suitable wire for heating elements. Within months, George Schneider of Detroit invented a boxed table-top electric toaster.

The first bread toasters to reach the mass market came from Pacific Electric Heating Company and General Electric, founded in 1878. In the wake of electric tea-kettles, waffle irons, and coffee percolators came table-top griddles, popcorn poppers, broilers, sewing machines, and vacuum cleaners. The electric table fan easily replaced the cumbrous kerosene model. Maud Lancaster calculated the price of progress in *Electric Cooking, Heating & Cleaning: A Manual of Electricity in the Service of the Home* (1914), in which she totted up how much electric power a dime would buy—enough to boil two quarts of water, perk four cups of coffee, run a small fan for two hours, operate a fry pan for twelve minutes or a griddle for eight minutes, cook a Welsh rarebit in a chafing dish, or sizzle a seven-minute steak.

The application of electricity to kitchen appliances soon extended to include coffee grinders, immersion heaters, portable space heaters, and the first thermo-statically controlled pop-up toaster, sold by the McGraw Electric Company. In 1917, when W. H. Hoover marketed the portable electric sweeper for under twenty dollars, the March issue of *House Furnishing Review* reminded retailers that summer would be a good sales opportunity for products that would free the housewife from hot-weather chores. The following year, Landers, Frary & Clark manufactured an electric waffle iron, which became a popular bridal shower and Christmas gift; General Electric (GE) produced an upscale set of appliances for use in the dining room—a chafing dish, hot plate, and percolator/urn. At the height of World War I, GE introduced the juicer and mixer on a single hinged stand.

Educating the Consumer

The fireless cooker began turning up in kitchens still dominated by the bulky gas or coal range. Thus, the two technologies existed side by side, and homemakers were able to assess their virtues and drawbacks. In this way, the issue of the fuel of the future gradually resolved itself. In a 1919 speech Raymond Marsh, secretary of the American Washing Machine Manufacturers' Association, attributed women's apparent eagerness to accept the new technology to the fact that factory work during World War I had rid them of their "unnatural fear" of machinery. But the public would never have been so accepting if marketers of the time had not acquired a firsthand knowledge of domestic needs and a sensitivity to the female shopper's opinions and attitudes. Fortunately for marketers, the burgeoning science of home economics had prepared large numbers of women for the work of demonstrating new

technology, answering questions about safety and economy, and training homemakers in its use.

For working-class Americans, the 1923 Sears, Roebuck catalog displayed the promise of the electric kitchen. Alongside electric washing machines and hot water heaters, pages of percolators, toasters, hot plates, and irons offered a new ease in housekeeping unknown in the time of wood, peat, and coal. One unusual item was a ten-pound electric table stove, which broiled, boiled, steamed, fried, and toasted, while simultaneously baking foods placed in a pullout drawer. Sold for $11.30, this handy item met the needs of travelers, college students, and apartment dwellers who did not have access to a full-size range. Another innovation, the electric doorbell, sold for 49 cents. At the touch of a button, it connected the homemaker in a back-of-the-house kitchen to visitors at the front door.

In 1924, Landers, Frary & Clark found a way to provide more usable electronic energy with less equipment and fewer cords and plugs. The company marketed a combination countertop appliance that used a single circuit for grilling, poaching eggs, cooking pancakes, and warming liquids. A multi-level device with a snap-on switch, it heated three areas and offered the flexibility of a removable rack and a poaching plate with indentations to hold four eggs. The appearance of an appliance engineered to solve a combination of kitchen problems prefigured the introduction of the electric range.

The William Campbell Company of Alliance, Ohio, began advertising its electric fireless cooker range in 1929. The Kitchen Queen, a sleek model with an oven and two burners, plugged into ordinary lighting outlets. It was ideal for the small home or efficiency apartment. To whet the interest of dubious cooks, the company offered the range at one-third off factory price on a thirty-day home trial. An even more intriguing ad from Monarch, made by the Malleable Iron Range Company of Beaver Dam, Wisconsin, boasted a time-clock and "positive, instant, clean, controlled heat at the touch of a switch!" (Celeher 1985, 52) The range was available on the installment plan in "pure white, Sunshine-Yellow, or Nile-Green," a deal that won over buyers who expected economy, convenience, and choice of colors. (Ibid.)

In 1934, the September issue of the *Edison Electric Institute Bulletin* reported on the electric company's advertising icon, Reddy Kilowatt, the electrical servant. A perky fellow with light bulb nose and red lightning streaks outlining his body, he gestured upward as though pointing toward an electrified future. Reddy's purpose was to humanize a public utility by simplifying the complicated process of generating and distributing electrical power. The public was not only ignorant about how electricity worked, it was fearful of what it did not understand. These attitudes were personified in characters such as the housewife in James Thurber's "The Car We Had to Push" (*My Life and Hard Times,* 1933), who was afraid the electrical outlets in her house would leak dangerous charges if she did not plug appliances into every socket. In a 1937 issue of *House Beautiful* an article entitled "Electrical Appliances at Your Service" featured a cartoon in which a mixer, iron, roaster, coffeepot, and toasters displayed accommodating smiles as they posed like willing household servants against a heart-shaped background.

The British public, too, required convincing of the benefits of kitchen electricity. During the 1920s and 1930s—a period when the United Kingdom saw an eleven-fold rise in the number of electrified homes—the British Electrical Development Association actively advertised the efficiency, ease of use, and cleanliness of electrical appliances. From 1924 to 1954, Dame Caroline Haslett, an English engineer and secretary of the Women's Engineering Society, headed the Electrical Association of Women, a public relations body that spread the word about new applications of electricity to domestic chores through demonstrations, brochures and pamphlets, schematic drawings, and home economics courses. In 1926 the consortium of women engineers issued a quarterly, *The Electrical Age for Women,* which featured articles on inventions and news from distant parts of the United Kingdom. As a result of this work displayed at the 1930 Bachelor Girls Exhibition, all-electric apartments and an all-electric residence set the standard in Bristol, England, in 1935.

Ads in women's magazines promoted electric appliances for the home with drawings and photos of slim, well-groomed "modern" women taking advantage of the new technology. In some of the illustrations, smooth hands with neatly manicured nails pressed the buttons or flicked the switches that promised to simplify the housewife's chores. One such ad featured the Hankscraft Bottle Warmer, which assured the correct temperature for baby feedings controlled by thermostat. Another ad showed the Armstrong Automatic Percolator, a dual-compartment coffeepot seated on a hot plate that brewed, then turned itself off before the water boiled and ruined the coffee. In yet another, a woman's hands lightly maneuvered the Ponsell Floor Machine, a polisher and refinisher that scrubbed and waxed wooden floors without buckets, rags, or hard labor. The dainty fingertips shown operating Edicraft's sandwich grill, toaster, and nine-cup siphonator coffeepot perpetuated the notion that cooking with small electrical appliances was virtually toil-free.

Also introduced around this time was the wall-mounted electric exhaust fan, which enabled the cook to rid the kitchen air of cooking odors and heat. In an ad in the July 1930 *Good Housekeeping,* a smiling woman with a perky bobbed hairdo reached up with one hand to turn on the Electrovent kitchen ventilator. The issue was timed to reach women at the height of the summer canning season, traditionally a miserable time in the kitchen. J. C. Akester's Vent-Axia Silent Six, introduced by De La Rue in 1935, represented the first of a series of upgrades that boasted variable speed and reversible blades and promised to filter grease from the air and remove condensation.

Trends: Proliferation and Specialization

In the United States the steady increase in ownership of electronic appliances was evident in the statistics compiled by the Rural Electrification Administration (REA) in the late 1930s and early 1940s. Data collected on REA farms (see table, below) showed a definite upward trend.

Percentage of homes equipped with appliances

appliance	1938	1939	1940	1941
coffeemaker	6.0	6.3	7.9	8.9
hot plate	12	19	15	15
iron	81	84	84	85
radio	86	82	88	90
refrigerator	26	32	33	42
toaster	24	31	29	32
vacuum cleaner	16	21	21	21
washing machine	47	59	55	55

(Stage and Vincenti 1997, 248)

World War II did not dampen manufacturers' enthusiasm for developing styling and features that would please women consumers. A Sunbeam ad in a 1940 issue of *Saturday Evening Post* pictured a toaster designed by George Scharfenberg in a streamlined, half-round shape, a classic that returned to popularity in retro kitchens at the end of the twentieth century. Following the hardships and deprivations of war, a proliferation of work-saving electric gadgetry revolutionized home, institutional, and restaurant kitchens. Articles rating and comparing the new appliances became popular features in women's magazines. In the December 1947 issue of *Woman's Home Companion,* the magazine's home equipment editor Elizabeth Beveridge summarized the best qualities of seven pop-up toasters and eight electric irons. She praised the warming feature in the Sunbeam toaster and Manning-Bowman's adjustable doneness control. In irons, she preferred the latest General Mills iron, which was tapered front and back, but made note of the cogwheel control and protecting plastic sheath on the Hoover model.

The majority of electrified homes contained water heaters, refrigerators, stoves, and washing machines, the "big four" of the modern kitchen. Manufactured in the United States by Emerson, Philco, Motorola, Capehart, Arvin, Jewel, Firestone, and Zenith, these electrical servants were capable of starting the coffee perking and turning on lights and fans. By 1955 portable televisions from General Electric had brought sound and picture to the kitchen counter. Philco marketed the Predicta TV in 1959, an adaptable model that attached to a swivel or sat on counter or table. For the affluent, the Rotissimat, invented in 1946, roasted poultry in the style of specialty restaurants; the next year, Nesco offered the automatic electric roaster. The Farberware Open Hearth broiler, marketed in 1962, made it possible for cooks to broil meat in an encased countertop appliance equipped with a heating element. Sunbeam began manufacturing a vertical rotisserie in 1963. Other models placed broilers and rotisseries in ovens above electric ranges for eye-level supervision.

Specialty items appealed to homemakers with a variety of needs. The all-purpose electric cooker from Raymen in New York City offered a hot plate pedestal for heating coffee, cooking meals, broiling, and toasting sandwiches. For coffee drinkers, the Silex two-stage coffee maker combined a timer and thermostatic control with a patented filtration system plus a pop-up handle for easy serving. For the cook who liked to entertain, electric warming trays in attractive frames replaced bulky sterno-heated chafing dishes for holiday brunches and receptions. The West Bend aluminum popcorn popper and the Fostoria glass-lidded model suited teen snack-makers entertaining friends.

In the 1970s, the Rival crockpot supplied the working wife with a versatile countertop cooker that slowly braised, roasted, and stewed overnight or while the homemaker was on the job. An improved model with removable ceramic liner simplified the job of soaking and cleaning by separating the crusty, greasy interior from an electric element that could not be submerged in water. The 1970s also witnessed refinements in roasting. In 1975, the roomy, porcelain-welled Hoover-Nesco roaster and chrome-lidded eighteen-quart roaster with adjustable racks and glass dishes earned the praise of the master chef James A. Beard, contributor to *The Cook's Catalogue*. A boom in home bread making followed Panasonic's introduction of the electric bread machine in 1987.

Late in the twentieth century, the slow cooker made a comeback in the United States as part of the "slow food" movement, a kitchen campaign against hastily gulped meals consumed on the run. Fueled by nostalgia for the homey comfort foods of their childhood—pot roast, meatloaf, mashed potatoes—baby boomers learned to tenderize stewing hens and inexpensive cuts of meat, simmer chili and bean dishes, and enjoy the convenience of ragouts and spaghetti sauce ready to serve after cooking overnight or during work hours. The downside of slow cookery was the possibility that foods might be kept at a temperature setting too low to kill microbes. Leaving an electric appliance unattended was also a concern.

In the 1980s, home computers entered the kitchen with multiple savings in time and information retrieval and storage. Electronic technology applied to building recipe databases for future use or for the selection of possible meals from a list of staples and supplies on hand. The advent of the Internet further increased the amount of available kitchen information with a proliferation of recipes and cooking methods from around the world plus mail-order venues for an endless supply of cookware and implements. At the January 2001 International Housewares Show in Chicago, an appliance whimsically called the Icebox offered no ice—rather, it combined television, home video, and DVD player with Internet connection in a state-of-the-art home media center.

Home communications, information, and entertainment systems ended the isolation of the kitchen and turned it into a pleasant, family-centered area. Homemakers stayed in touch with the rest of the house and outside world through wall-mounted, countertop, cordless, and cellular telephones and video security pictures of every room in the house. A wireless intercom allowed instant communication with family members in other rooms as well as surveillance of sounds in the nursery.

Stress on energy efficiency in the 1990s produced better application of energy through solid state controls for accurate temperature reading and refined design that increased efficiency. Manufacturers concerned themselves more intimately with homemakers' needs and ability to get the most out of fuel expenditures, for example, with convection ovens, braziers, exhaust hoods, and atmospheric steamers. Rebate programs enhanced energy management. Some systems developed cost-effective projects to reduce energy use, for example, by trading wasteful refrigerators for fuel-efficient models or converting dryers, water heaters, and grills from electricity to gas.

Robots Next?

In 1994, the unusual and the unique appeared on the electronic kitchen market. Welbilt premiered the Breakfast Express, a device that broke and fried two eggs, toasted two slices of bread, and brewed coffee automatically in ten minutes. Circle Manufacturing's Cooking Machine marketed a smokeless rotating spit to accommodate two large turkeys or six game hens alongside a heating element that directed fat into a pan rather than onto a hot coil. The Farberware Farber Peel robo-peeler rapidly stripped low and high density vegetables, including tomatoes. The smokeless One-Minute Grill Express used a steam jet to heat food as quickly as a microwave. In 1997, appliance makers injected flexibility into design to create do-all automatic breadmakers and an Capresso coffeemaker that automatically ground beans before brewing.

Late twentieth-century electronic wizardry relied on digital components that stored data and processed a range of commands. One example, the Sunbeam toaster, sensed voltage fluctuation and adjusted heating time. The chip in the Panasonic Electronic Rice Cooker selected an appropriate temperature for basmati, long-grain, brown, risotto, or Chinese sticky rice. The Sharp Multiple Choice microwave calculated reheat times and posted recipes and instructions at the touchpad. The Krups Espresso Novo came equipped with a programmable pump, automatic tamper, and steam froth-maker suited to latte, espresso, and cappuccino.

At the turn of the twenty-first century, manufacturers were continuing to introduce new levels of sophistication in electronic cookery. One new food processor included a sausage stuffer and pasta roller and cutters. A pressure cooker accommodated foods as large as a roast or whole chicken for programmable browning, steaming, cooking, and warming in a nonstick interior. Another new product was a vertical rotisserie that cooks meats on a rotating tower or basket or on eight kebab skewers, while a unit above cooks vegetables, rice, or casseroles in a nonstick aluminum casserole. Additional gadgetry—for example, the electric tortilla maker—allows cooks to prepare once-laborious ethnic dishes in record time.

See also **Garbage; Ice; Lamps and Lights; Microwaving; Mixers and Blenders; Refrigeration; Stoves**

Further Reading

Beveridge, Elizabeth, "New Toasters/New Irons," *Woman's Home Companion*, December 1947, 94–95.

Harwood, Catherine, "Housewives' Choice—Women as Consumers Between the Wars," *History Today*, March 1997, 10–15.

Stage, Sarah, and Virginia B. Vincenti, eds. *Rethinking Home Economics: Women and the History of a Profession*. Ithaca: Cornell University Press, 1997.

ENAMELWARE

A soft glass compounded from silica or flint, red lead, and soda ash or potash, enamel results from melting the components into a clear vitreous flux, also called frit or fondant. It gets its color from black oxide, carbonate of soda, stannic acid, arsenious acid, and other metallic pigments. Opaque enamel results from the addition of calx, a blend of lead and tin. Once the desired mixture has been achieved, the heated enamel is allowed to harden into cakes or slabs.

To ready enamel for application to an object, the enamel maker pulverizes cakes of enamel and rinses the resulting powder in distilled water. The metal surface to be enameled requires an acid bath, washing in water, and drying in sawdust. Wet enamel powder is applied to the metal and allowed to dry before the piece is fired in a furnace. Intense heat fuses the enamel into place. The hardest enamel, fused at very high temperatures, lasts longest and survives intense wear and tear, although it is easily scarred by scouring or stirring with metal spoons. Until relatively recent times, enameling was the province of skilled artisans who produced jewelry, liturgical objects, decorative serving pieces, and other ornaments. Later, the process adorned to a variety of utilitarian objects, especially cookware and kitchen implements.

The origin of enameling is unclear. It may derive from Mycenaean glass fragments applied to metalwork in Greece, Cyprus, and Crete as early as 1200 BCE. The next people to produce quality enamelware were the Kuban jewelers of the Caucasus around 800 BCE, followed by the Greeks, who applied white and blue enamel to gold filigree from the 700s to the 300s BCE, simultaneous with the development of Celtic, Scythian, and Sarmatian crafts, which were similar but inferior. Roman enamelers carried the technique to the outer limits of the Empire. Enameling flourished in Byzantium after 500 CE and reached its height around 1000 CE with the production of jewelry, scepters, cathedral ewers, sacramental plate, crosses, reliquaries, and chalices. Syrian workers appear to have duplicated these techniques on serving pieces. Although Chinese and Japanese enamelers perfected their version of the art by the 600s CE, the technique did not flourish in China until the mid-fourteenth century.

During the Renaissance, enamelware thrived in Sicily, Italy, France, Iberia, the Rhineland, the Low Country, and the British Isles. Fifteenth-century decorative, sacramental, and table serving pieces prefigured wider use of enameling on andirons and candlesticks in the 1600s in Europe and incense burners in China during the rule of emperor K'ang-hsi. Painting enamel on gold, an innovation of the goldsmith and watchmaker Jean Toutin of Châteaudun, France, around 1630, adorned boxes and cup. Toutin's sons, Henri and Jean II, carried the method across France to Sweden. In Japan around 1625, the enamel worker and metal engraver Donin Hirata I of Kyoto applied Korean techniques to enamel armor, doors, and sills. By the 1840s, Kaji Tsunekichi's Nagoya workshop was turning out artistic enameled vessels in conservative, pictorial, and exotic styles that influenced imitators.

Enamel cookware got its beginning in 1799 in the United States when a Dr. Hinkling surfaced iron and steel pans. In 1839, Clarke, a producer of domestic goods, produced a line of enameled cookware. Advertisements touted its low cost, beauty, light weight, and easy-to-clean surfaces that did not pit when they came in contact with acid, a common occurrence during canning. At first, most enameled pieces were one of three types. Agate ware had a blue-and-white speckled or mottled surface; common agate ware implements included watering cans and lidded slop buckets, in which homemakers carried water or other liquid waste from the kitchen to the yard or pig sty for emptying.

Glazed ware included the decked dinner carrier, an enameled tin dinner pail with multiple compartments and a wire bail. Gray-and-white granite ware was a typical choice for ornate nickel-plated soup tureens and lidded vegetable dishes

Demand for variety resulted in turquoise, gray, green, pink, and brown exteriors and white or ivory inner linings. One useful variation was the enameled wood teapot handle, which was attractive and nonconductive of heat. The success of the new technology lasted into the 1900s when aluminum cookware became available, providing more even conduction of heat and thus ending spontaneous boil-overs that required tedious clean-up.

In the twentieth century, industrial technology in Scandinavia brought the enameler's art within reach of ordinary people with the decoration of moderately priced tableware. Artisans in Western Europe and the United States manufactured boxes, basins, plaques, clock faces, and murals cut from factory-enameled steel sheets. These items could be used both indoors and out. The 1900 Sears, Roebuck catalog presented a two-page spread of such bath and kitchen items as steel muffin cups, lidded saucepans, bread pans, wash basins, and chamber pots at 20 cents each for the unlidded and 54 cents for the tall model with drop handle and domed cover. Enameling simplified the job of emptying toilet and sick room slops and cleaning and disinfecting the vessels for later use.

The February 1906 issue of *House Furnishing Review* touted enamelware as a promising development in domestic goods. The unnamed author castigated Americans for letting profit override taste and praised Austrians for developing enameled metal for vases, urns and pitchers, and mugs "that at first glance can scarcely be distinguished from pottery or fine china." (Franklin 1997, 539)

Residents of the British Virgin Islands valued the enamel "brekfuss pan," a sectioned container in which home cooks packed soup or stew, beans, salt meat, or fish. For the laborer or student away from home during the traditional breakfast, served from 10:00 A.M. until noon, the container evoked the ambience of a home-cooked meal that sustained the average islander until the evening meal.

In 1908, the Sears, Roebuck catalog featured improvements in enamel esthetics with True Blue brand enameled steel ware, including an ornate wall-mounted flower pot bracket with two shelves and a steel-mounted washbasin for back porch, barn, or in-house use. Ranging in price from a dime for a basting spoon to 76 cents for a lidded teakettle, enamelware items were available by the piece or by the set. For $4.58, consumers could purchase a fifteen-piece set suited to a particular size stove. Ad copy described the making of steel containers and implements coated four times with an enamel that was "chemically pure, free from all poisonous or harmful ingredients, and positively will not discolor from the acids of fruits and vegetables." (Schroeder 1971, 462) To enhance the aura of purity, the manufacturer lined the interiors of cooking and serving vessels in stark white enamel.

By 1923, Sears, Roebuck was offering a wide range of enamelware products, including foot baths, lidded chamber pots, soap dishes, and wash basins in white and speckled finish. For 65 cents, the homemaker could attach to the wall bracket an enamel soap basin within arm's reach of the dishpan. For rural families who bathed near the kitchen stove for warmth or on the back porch in warm weather, two-, three-, and four-piece sets offered pitcher and basin or basin and dipper for as low as $2.20.

Ads in *Good Housekeeping* in 1925 stressed the cleanliness and order of a kitchen dominated by enamelware, as with the enameled kitchen tables from Mutschler Brothers Company in Nappanee, Indiana, and the cookware produced by Sanitrox of Columbia Enameling & Stamping Company of Terre Haute, Indiana. The ad copy that accompanied pictures of women cooking with a full suite of enamel pans, dishes, and kettles emphasized the glossy white surfaces and the ease of keeping them clean. In 1926, Westinghouse introduced the first porcelain-enamel surfaced range. Initially available in black and white, it was later manufactured in a variety of colors.

In the 1930s, full-color ads featuring glossy enamelware appeared in most U.S. women's magazines. Vollrath of Sheboygan, Wisconsin, offered carafes, double boilers, percolators, colanders, and stock pots

216

in a range of colors, including terra cotta, red, blue, and cream edged in blue, green, or red. Ad copy promised a nonporous surface that required no scouring, to say nothing of a boost to kitchen chic. One specialty item, stackable lidded refrigerator containers, kept vegetables, sandwiches, ring molds, and milk fresh and ended the tainting of flavors and odors with those of other foods stored nearby.

In an era devoted to color coordination and matched sets, the Enameled Utensil Manufacturers Council showed off the gleam, smooth surface, and stain resistance of enameled steel goods in use in actual kitchens, as advertised in *Woman's Home Companion* and other women's magazines. Ads for Nesco pictured the perfectly groomed housewife glorying in the slick white surfaces of a percolator that required no scrubbing with harsh cleansers. As an inducement to consumers, National Enameling and Stamping Company of Milwaukee, Wisconsin, advertised that the wide bottoms and snug-fitting lids of Nesco products saved on fuel and time. A competitor, Memco of West Lafayette, Ohio, differentiated its products with a trademark ebony-black bottom and matching heavy lids.

Around the 1950s, enamelware—regarded as a remnant of homelier eras—declined in popularity and was largely supplanted by aluminum and Pyrex cookware. The older technology refused to die, however, and returned to favor as an element of the retro country chic that gripped Canada and the United States in the late 1990s.

Further Reading

"Enamelware Finds Its Niche with Today's "Country Chic," *Canadian House and Home*, October 1998, 36.
Sears, Roebuck and Co. *Consumers Guide*, Fall 1900. Northfield, Ill: DBI Books, Inc., 1970.

ERGONOMICS

Ergonomics, also known as human-factors engineering or, simply, human engineering, is the science of designing systems and tools that reduce or prevent work-related injuries. The term ergonomics comes from the Greek for "work law." By analyzing human factors such as capabilities, handicaps, and atmospheric limitations, designers of machinery, furniture, tools, and appliances are able to enhance users' safety, comfort, and productivity. Ergonomics has been widely applied in business and industry, improving assembly lines and executive offices. In the kitchen, ergonomic design might involve the addition of foam or other padding to handles and grips, substitution of lightweight metal parts for heavy ones, or cushioning

of floors to reduce stress on the cook's back, legs, and feet.

Ergonomics grew into a multidisciplinary science in the 1920s as a broad reaction to the contagion and filth of trench warfare in World War I and the worldwide 1918 influenza epidemic. In Germany, the Viennese domestic designer Grete Schütte-Lihotzky created the efficient, space-saving "Frankfurt Kitchen," an experimental kitchen plan intended to improve the working-class living environment. Ergonomics adapted machines and utensils to make kitchen workers more efficient and less likely to stress their joints, injure themselves in accidents, or develop musculoskeletal disorders from the repetitive motions of such tasks as ironing, kneading dough, churning, and washing dishes. Erna Meyer, a leader of the ergonomics movement and author of *Der Neue Haushalt* (The New Housekeeping: A Guide to Scientific Housekeeping; 1926), promoted the anthropometric table with the idea of matching the worker to the height of the work surface to save time and effort and prevent strain.

Late in the twentieth century, neomodern kitchen design sought to make the kitchen more attractive as well as more efficient. Basing their work on the Frankfurt Kitchen, designers and architects aimed to create a habitable workspace with bright lighting, functional cabinetry, and sturdy and reliable machinery. Redesigned items—rolling pins, step stools and kitchen ladders, telephone receivers shaped to the hand—prevented fatigue and waste of energy while improving kitchen workers' posture, balance, performance, and eye-hand coordination.

For those with special needs—for example, professional kitchen workers, and people with arthritis or carpal tunnel syndrome—ergonomic designers remodeled kitchen tools to simplify slicing vegetables, opening jars, gripping bones in fish, cutting up poultry and disjointing meat, and removing lids from food containers. In 1955, Rubbermaid earned a commendation from the Arthritis Foundation for marketing tightly sealed tubs with pop-off lids removed by means of large, easy-grip tabs. In 1992, Bulthaup, a kitchen manufacturer founded by Martin Bulthaup in 1949, introduced a modular designer kitchen that permitted flexibility in spatial organization. Five years later, the firm upgraded its unitized system to adapt appliances and work spaces to satisfy aesthetic as well as practical requirements of the user's anatomical positions. Another award-winner, the OXO Good Grips line of kitchen utensils, based since 1999 at World Kitchen, Inc., in Elmira, New York, became known for its handsome, durable tools. Good Grips kitchen tools, endorsed by the National Arthritis Foundation, were easily identified by their resilient, grippable rubber handles.

Other ergonomically designed implements helped to prevent cooking-related accidents. An oversized colander-scoop enabled the cook to remove pasta or rice from a large, steaming-hot pot without having to tip the pot to drain cooking liquids. An easy-grip meat tenderizer allowed the user to pound meat with a spiked mallet while grasping a soft handle suited to either right or left hand. A balanced pair of turkey lifters enabled the cook to force sharp prongs into the carcass and lift the bird from hot liquids without placing fingers near roasted skin and juices. The dual gripper and turner became a handy spatula for maximum control of foods cooking on a griddle or skillet. Clips attached stirring spoons and ladles to hot pots while keeping them elevated above the heat source. As ergonomically styled gadgets caught the public's attention, items continued to flood the market into the late 1990s and 2000s, including easy-grip peelers and zesters, a comfort-grip can opener, and a one-touch tool for removing twist-off bottle caps.

See also **Gilbreth, Lillian Moller; Lihotzky, Grete Schütte**

Further Reading

"Grips," *Design News*, March 1, 1999.
"New Ergonomically Designed Tools," *Successful Farming*, March 15, 1998.
Rozzi, Robert, "How to Find Truly Ergonomic Hand Tools," *Engineer's Digest*, November 1, 2000.

ESCOFFIER, GEORGES-AUGUSTE

One of the chefs who elevated French cookery to haute cuisine, Georges-Auguste Escoffier demystified professional kitchen skills and made them accessible to ordinary cooks. Born in Villeneuve-Loubet, France, on October 28, 1846, he grew up on the Côte d'Azur and entered culinary training in Nice at age twelve as apprentice saucier to his uncle. By age nineteen, he had moved to Paris to study at Le Petit Moulin Rouge, an apprenticeship that preceded taking charge of the Maire restaurant kitchen. During the Franco-Prussian War, he headed military food service for the Rhine army, the source of his interest in canning foods and imposing order on large cooking operations.

Returned to civilian cooking, in 1882, Escoffier worked on the Riviera as manager of the Swiss hotelier César Ritz's chain and became head chef at the Grand National Hotel at Lucerne. He was known for his watchword, *"Faites simple!"* (Do it simply). (Walker 1996, 25) To streamline food preparation, he stressed the basics. To simplify ordering in restaurants, he developed the à la carte menu. To tame the chaos of restaurant kitchens, he organized the *brigade de cuisine*

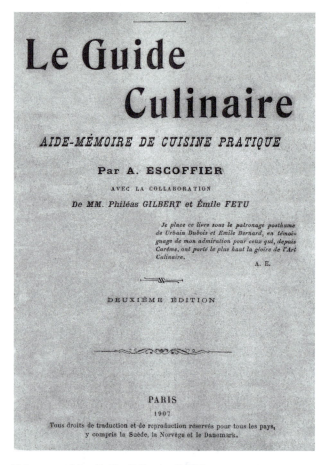

Title page of *Le Guide Culinaire* (1907).

(cooking team), an assembly-line system that prevails in restaurant and institutional kitchens, and supported the Russian method of table service.

Escoffier was a promoter of spit roasting over oven roasting as a means of preserving natural juices. He invented the fumet, a liquid flavoring whisked from natural pan juices and arrowroot, and the profiterole, a succulent ice-cream-filled puff pastry topped with chocolate sauce. He gave explicit instruction on how to whip a *bavaroise* (tea with sugared syrup) and serve it in special crystal beverage glasses. In 1890, he opened London's Savoy Hotel, where he prepared the coronation dinner for George V; eight years later he took up a similar post at the Carlton Hotel.

In addition to managing kitchens at the Grand Hotel in Monte Carlo and overseeing the kitchen of the Hamburg-America Line, Escoffier co-authored the classic *Le Guide Culinaire* (The Cookery Guide; 1903), which clarified changes to French cuisine. The work stresses what Escoffier considered the basics, beginning on page one with this advice: "In cooking, stock is everything, without it nothing can be done. If the stock is good, what remains of the work is easy. If it is bad, it is quite hopeless to expect anything even approaching satisfactory results." (Bensky 2000) The text demonstrates Escoffier's willingness to incorporate New World foods into his repertoire, for example with his recipe for pommes de terre Pont-Neuf, fried potatoes he described as crispy potato "batons," and his directions for steaming unhusked corn, peeling off the husk, and serving it on a napkin with butter. He followed with *Le Carnet d'Epicure* (A Gourmet's Notebook; 1911), *Le Livre des Menus* (Book of Menus; 1924), and *Ma Cuisine* (My Kitchen; 1934), a handbook for the home cook. Retired at age seventy-four with his wife, Delphine Daffis, he received the French Legion of Honor and advanced in honorary rank to an officer in 1928. He also earned respect among his peers for aiding poor, disabled, or substance-addicted chefs, for boosting military morale, and for publishing a book on poverty.

Escoffier died on February 12, 1935 in Monte Carlo. He contributed celebrated dishes to food history: sauce Robert, sauce diable, pear Hélène, dodine au Chambertin, strawberries Romanov, and chaud-froid Jeannette, a commemoration of an arctic shipwreck. In 1894, he named Melba toast and peach Melba (ice cream and peaches soaked in vanilla and topped with puréed raspberries) for the Australian opera singer Nellie Melba, who was a guest at the Savoy Hotel during his tenure. In his memoirs, he recalled a *petit souper* (little supper) she gave after a performance of Lohengrin. For the table, Escoffier sculpted a swan in ice; nestled between the wings was a silver bowl containing the ice cream creation he dedicated to the singer. For such panache, he was deemed "emperor of chefs" by the German emperor William II.

The Musée Escoffier, founded in his hometown by his pupil Joseph Donon, honored Escoffier's career with a display of menus and kitchen and restaurant memorabilia. In 1979, France issued a stamp picturing Escoffier. In 1996, to commemorate his 150th birthday, chefs served the same menu at 128 establishments in New Zealand, Japan, England, and the United States. French chefs held 82 honorary dinners.

Further Reading

Blake, Anthony, and Quentin Crewe. *The Great Chefs of France.* London: Marshall Editions, Ltd., 1978.
Quinzio, Jeri, "Visiting Escoffier," *Travel Lady,* April 5, 1999.

ETIQUETTE

Etiquette, a body of rules or principles outlining appropriate social behavior, permeates world cultures. In virtually every culture, a great number of these behavioral conventions involve the serving and eating of food—in other words, table manners.

Early Codes

The first recorded deportment guide, *The Instructions of Ptah Hotep,* appeared in Egypt around. 2500 BCE. Hebrew tutelage took the form of two essays in the *Derekh Eretz* (Correct Behavior, or Way of the Land) a code of conduct appended to the Babylonian Talmud to clarify all phases of human relations, including how to serve and consume food and beverages. At the core of the Derekh was respect of others' welfare and sensibilities. In the *Li Chi* (ca. 475 BCE), a manuscript explaining the social foundations of Chinese society, commentary on harmony explains the need to balance tones, flavors, diet, and colors.

When Poseidonius, the Syrian traveler and observer, visited the northwestern Gallic fringes of the Roman world in the first century BCE, he observed the table manners of the locals. He described diners seated according to their social status awaiting the cook's presentation of loaves and meat spitted or boiled over charcoal. Among some warrior groups, the serving of a choice cut of meat could set off a display of male rivalry. The Celt who claimed the best portion for himself risked a scrap with another male. The tableside set-to could result in a fight to the death.

The term etiquette may derive from the Old French *estiquer* (to affix), a reference to the daily rules of a royal court, which were affixed to the wall for all to read. Such rules explained the seating of honored guests on the host's right in southern Europe and on the left in Scandinavia.

The earliest medieval etiquette document, Count Anthimus's letter to the Frankish king Theodoric, written around 530 CE, instructed the king about the dangers of gluttony and intemperance. The underlying principle—to avoid extremes—derives from the familiar Roman dictum *nihil nimis* (nothing in excess). Anthimus insisted on self-control and inveighed against overindulgence at table. One polite custom he initiated, the use of no more than three fingers to pick up meat, put an end to unsightly grabbing.

The storyteller and moralist Petrus Alphonsi's *Disciplina Clericalis* (Training for a Gentleman; ca. 1100 CE), written in the form of a dialogue between father and son, explained the rudiments of offering guests water for washing hands. Rules for diners explained the necessity of eating only from one's own bowl, taking small bites, wiping the mouth before drinking, and emptying the mouth before speaking. Similar guidebooks reminded the polite guest never to dredge food in the salt cellar. Correct salting required lifting grains of salt by means of a clean knife blade or extracting a pinch at a time with clean fingers. An Italian guide, *The Treatise on Courtesy* (ca. 1200 CE) of Tommasino di Circlaria (or Thomasin von Zerklaere), rooted its advice in musings on gentility and correct behavior at table. The sensible precepts set forth in these and other early European books on manners has changed little up to the present time.

In Syria, the theologian Gregor Bar Hebraeus (also Gregor Bar'Ebraya or Gregor of Abulpharagus) summarized table wisdom and ethics in *Ethicon* (ca. 1265 CE). Mindful of the spiritual value of food, he urged diners to be clean, eat quietly and sparsely, and welcome outsiders to the family table. He recommended that meals be preceded by a religious blessing and instructed diners to maintain an upright posture while eating. He also urged that, out of respect for God's bounty, no crumbs should be left uneaten.

Gentility at Table

In the late Middle Ages, European behavior manuals introduced a new generation of advice to gentility and deportment. These guidebooks derived from the code of courtly manners intended to suit royalty and to quell altercations arising from the dispute over proximity to the king at table. Representative of these many volumes, which paralleled each other in tone and scope, were the German *Der Winsbeke* (ca. 1200s), the advice of a knight to his son; the Spanish *Castigas y Doctrinas que un Savio Dava a Sus Hijas* (Admonitions and Doctrines from a Wise Parent to His Daughters; 1400s), in which a father advised his offspring on restraint in drinking and eating and fairness in dealing with table servants; and the essayist Christine de Pisan's *Enseignements à Son Filz Jean de Castel* (Instruction to Her Son Jean de Castel; ca. 1430) and *Livre des Trois Vertus* (Book of the Three Virtues; 1405).

The English issued similar texts—*Boke of Curtasye* (1440), the *Book of Curtesye of Lytel John* (1477), and *Wynkyn de Worde's Boke of Kervinge* (Book on Carving; 1513), which assisted kitchen workers and table servants with the proper placement of meats and vegetables on platters, slicing of tarts and pies, and ladling of sauces.

The friar and rhetorician Bonvesin della Riva (or Bonvicino da Riva), author of *De Quinquaginta Curialitatibus ad Mensam* (Concerning Fifty Gentilities for the Table; ca. 1290), encouraged guests to speak graciously to others at table before sitting down to eat. He advocated courtly manners, proper attire, affability, good posture, and self-control. Among the most intolerable behaviors, he included overfilling the mouth, drunkenness, slurping, sneezing and coughing in the direction of other diners, and criticizing the food. He considered picking over dishes a disgrace and abhorred the practice of sopping bread in wine. As a gesture of

chivalry, he suggested that a man should cut up meat for any woman with whom he shared a platter. To ensure polite conversation, he forbade swearing and the raising of unpleasant, vulgar, or controversial topics.

Some of the guidelines for good manners sprang from sound principles of health and safety. For example, Petrus Alphonsi's admonition about chewing thoroughly before swallowing is sensible advice to prevent choking. For the conclusion of the meal, he admonished: "After eating, ask for hand-water, for this is required by medical teaching and it is the decent and easy thing to do." (Scully 1995, 176) An early fourteenth-century treatise on dining by Arnaud de Villaneuve, a physician and chemist from Montpellier, France, explained the role of sobriety and moderation in alleviating dullness and lassitude.

One author of a courtesy book, Francesc Eiximenis, a Franciscan friar from Catalonia, inveighed strongly against gobbling food and drinking too much. Chapters 29 through 37 of his text cover rules of conduct similar to those of Bonvesin. Concerning women, Eiximenis thought it best to sit beside rather than opposite a lady. He warned about spraying other diners with food, picking the teeth, and overdoing compliments to the host. He suggested that guests go to the toilet to rid the body of gas before sitting down at table. Serving with style and avoiding crude behavior during meals was, to Eiximenis, a form of patriotism—a way of elevating Catalonia among other European states.

In Germany, *Tischzuchten* (table etiquette guides), including Sebastian Brant's satiric *Das Narrenschiff* (Ship of Fools; 1454), established the importance of propriety at table, including thorough hand washing before meals.

Renaissance guides moved from simple admonitions against unseemly behavior in serving and dining toward matters of deference to lords and ladies. Unlike medieval etiquette specialists, Baldassare Castiglione, author of *Il Libro del Cortegiano* (The Book of the Courtier; 1528), emphasized grace and elegance over pragmatism. One mark of elegance was the male diner's spreading of his napkin over one shoulder as opposed to the female custom of covering the lap. Less pretentious and status conscious was the Dutch humanist scholar Erasmus, who published *De Civilitate Morum Puerilium* (On Civility in Boys; 1530), which took up such matters as the wiping of greasy fingers and blowing the nose at table.

To avoid excesses and indignities, the English consulted such texts as *Youth's Behavior, or Decency in Conversation Among Men* (1640), an anonymous work that remained a handy touchstone into the time of George Washington. The first printed guide, *The Fine Gentleman's Etiquette; or Lord Chesterfield's Advice* to His Son Verified (1776), established the pecking order between underlings and their superiors, who could retaliate against discourtesy with vengence or ostracism. In 1800, *Domestic Management* offered such instruction to the housewife as how to improve servants' manners. The footman, according to the text, should learn to open lobster claws in the kitchen rather than in the view of the dining room door. Gradually, the rules of proper behavior trickled down to the middle class via such books as *Etiquette, or a Guide to the Usages of Society* (1836), which offered warnings against vulgarity or improprieties that would offend their betters. Thus, newcomers to wealth learned how to conceal their social inexperience.

Manners for Colonists and Travelers

At Plymouth Colony standards of deportment were established from readings of the poet Richard Brathwait's *The English Gentleman and Description of a Good Wife* (1619). From the beginning, American society struggled with questions of identity, debating whether to create a uniquely American code of etiquette or merely to perpetuate the customs of the mother country. *Eleazar Moody's School of Good Manners* (1715) did little to differentiate New Englanders' manners from those of their cousins in Britain.

In 1883, People's Publishing Company compiled *Australian Etiquette or the Rules and Usages of the Best Society in the Australian Colonies,* a standard home guidebook concerning dinner parties, table conversation, and requirements of fine dining. The book served a self-conscious populace generally ridiculed by the supercilious English for its convict and laboring-class backgrounds. As Victorian manners reached the island nation, those who were moving up from billy tea to silverware and china had reason to study manners in private lest they humiliate themselves in public.

Travelers and explorers sometimes encountered customs that, although different from their own, prompted admiration. While living among the Mandan, the U.S. artist George Catlin, known for his depictions of Plains Indian life, remarked on a style of dining that allowed sitting cross-legged or reclining with the feet drawn close under the body. He noted that the Indian women gracefully served the diners and reseated themselves in a movement that allowed them modesty and poise at the same time that it left their hands free for lifting and maneuvering dishes.

More common for those traveling or living in unfamiliar climes were manners that struck the visitors as unsanitary—or worse. Sir William Edward Parry, Arctic expeditioner to the Canadian north from 1819–1822,

saw Eskimo etiquette from the point of view of a polite Englishman from the Regency period. He described how, when serving of food from the ootkooseek (cookpot) during a meal, the woman of the house lifted a lump of cooked meat with her fingers and handed it to the man of the house, who began the repast. After clenching the mass between his teeth, he sliced off a portion and passed both knife and remaining meat to the next diner. Another traveler, George French Angas, author of *A Ramble Through Malta and Sicily in the Autumn of 1841,* recoiled from the energetic eating style of villagers in Scaletta, Sicily. Upon arrival at a family cottage, he received a large dish of macaroni, which he thought was his personal serving: "To my surprise and astonishment, the whole family surrounded it instantly, and began to demolish it with wooden forks, cramming as much into their mouths as fast as possible, and then dexterously pushing in the depending filaments with their fingers. This is the true Sicilian mode of eating macaroni, though certainly not the most polite." (Simeti 1989, 169) When the hostess served him an individual trencher, he noted that she sprinkled salt on top of the portion with her fingers, another example of plebeian manners.

American Manners for Americans

The communal dining style common in farm families of North America dictated an etiquette suited to time and place. The absence of serving pieces required some restructuring of formal rules of table service. *Aunt Betsy's Rule, and How It Worked* (1863), issued by the Presbyterian Board of Publication and Sabbath-school, explained the use of personal knife and fork for removing meat, potatoes, vegetables, and pudding from a single shared dish. The text added, "In the same way, a piece of bread or butter was cut, and the tip of the knife dipped in the salt. The pitcher of water was passed round the table, and all drank from it." (Weaver 1989, 8)

The Shakers, who lived and worked in communes in New England, New York, Pennsylvania, Kentucky, and Ohio, observed a strict separation of the sexes in the commune refectory. Rules for decorum required that all wait until the elder began eating. Diners neatly cut their meat into square and equal parts and took some of all foods on their plates. They cleaned their plates and "shakered" them by laying knife, fork, and bones to one side before scraping up crumbs. The rules of the table mandated covering the nose and mouth with a handkerchief when sneezing or coughing, using a clean knife to cut butter, and swallowing chewed food and using a napkin before speaking or drinking.

In the 1880s, works such as *Social Etiquette of New York* demonstrated that the ongoing debate between traditional European manners and new American ways favored the Continent. In the late nineteenth century, however, Americans began to become comfortable with themselves and to formulate their own rules for formal table setting, serving, and eating. In this era of self-awareness, Emily Post became the American arbiter of good breeding. Her best-selling *Etiquette, the Blue Book of Social Usage* (1922) attempted to codify conduct for all social engagements. Her word remained law, even after the challenge of *Vogue's Book of Etiquette* (1948), Amy Vanderbilt's *Complete Book of Etiquette* (1952), and former First Lady Eleanor Roosevelt's *Book of Common Sense Etiquette* (1962).

The serving and eating of corn on the cob has been an enduring issue for American authorities on table manners. In *Hints on Etiquette* (1844) Charles Day decreed that rather than gnaw at the cob, the diner should scrape the kernels into his or her plate and eat them with a fork. Frederick Stokes's *Good Form: Dinners Ceremonious and Unceremonious* (1890) contrasted the crude gnawing from end to end with the more polite grasping with a folded napkin or doily. Food writer and *Ladies' Home Journal* editor Sarah Tyson Rorer, America's first dietitian, proposed a more demanding method of scoring each row of kernels and pressing out the contents with the teeth, leaving the hulls attached to the cob. The ever-practical Emily Post simply discounted corn on the cob as a suitable food for formal dining.

Cross-Cultural Quandaries

Meetings between cultures often produce table quandaries. On first contact with Southwestern cuisine, Susan Shelby Magoffin, the prim, well-bred daughter of Governor Isaac Shelby and author of *Down the Santa Fe Trail and Into Mexico* (1846), was dubious of a blue tortilla wrapped in a napkin. Knowing better than to insult her hosts, she ate the odd colored dish without protest but wrote of the experience, "Oh, how my heart sickened, to say nothing of my stomach." (Magoffin 1962, 94) It did not take long for her to discover that refinements such as eating utensils could easily be dispensed with: As Southwestern natives had done for centuries, she learned to fold a tortilla and use it as a food scoop.

Toward the end of the twentieth century, as the global economy pressed more Western business people into contact with the cultures of Japan, West Africa, India, and the Middle East, a demand arose for guides to unfamiliar dining experiences. American and English visitors pondered the proper way to remove their shoes before entering a Japanese or Turkish home and how to signal that chopsticks were unfamiliar and awkward. One of the most surprising taboos of the Sahara, India, Pakistan, and the Middle East, the prohibition against use of the left hand for eating, seemed strange to people accustomed to dining with both hands. Once foreigners learned that people in these societies traditionally used the right hand for dining and the left to perform toilet hygiene, the custom became understandable. To assist guests with these one-handed operations, Bangladeshi hostesses typically distributed basins for before- and after-dinner hand washing and remained on hand to serve plates rather than to join diners. In Botswana, before the table blessing, the business of the ritual hand washing fell to young girls, who filled a basin from an urn and extended a towel to diners.

In compliance with Islamic law, dutiful Muslims have traditionally welcomed any stranger seeking hospitality. Food writer Claudia Roden, author of *A New Book of Middle Eastern Food* (1985), explained the obligation of the Muslim cook to cater to diners' tastes. Guests customarily acknowledged the cook's effort and tasted what was offered to them, eating from the edge of a communal platter rather than serving themselves from the middle. Before ending a meal, the host circulated the communal *guerba* (beverage container) of milk or water—but not wine, which the Koran forbids. The polite diner refrained from breathing into the liquid. After the vessel made its round, participants relaxed with coffee and tobacco.

See also **Linens; Sanitation; Servants**

Further Reading

Andrews, Edward Deming. *The People Called Shakers: A Search for the Perfect Society*. New York: Oxford University Press, 1953.

Catlin, George. *North American Indians*. New York: Penguin, 1989.

"Knives, Forks, and Spoons," *Aramco World*, March 1960, 16–19.

EVELYN, JOHN

When physicians and nutritionists of the late seventeenth-century began recommending leafy greens for the health conscious, humanist John Evelyn's book *Acetaria: A Discourse of Sallets* (1699) spelled out the value of the kitchen garden to health and recorded the first salad recipes. Evelyn was born on October 31, 1620, in Wotton, Surrey, England, to a family made wealthy though the manufacture of gunpowder, a business begun in the time of Elizabeth I by his grandfather, George

Evelyn. He studied law but took no interest in the profession.

Evelyn was an avid reader with a special interest in the selection of foods and cooking for the everyday table. Over his lifetime, he published some thirty guides to cuisine, religion, forestry, coin collecting, fashion, and graphic arts. He became an amateur expert on air pollution and lambasted London officials for allowing the city's chimneys to foul its air. Among his interests was the planting of arbors, which he advanced with his own *Sylva, or a Discourse of Forest Trees* (1664) and a translation of De La Quintinyers's *The Compleat Gardner* (1693).

A major change in Evelyn's life occurred in 1699, when he inherited the family estate. As a neophyte country squire, he enjoyed horticulture, writing, and translation of medieval works on food and gardening. Among his recipes was one for seasoning a legume salad with wine vinegar; another provided instructions for pickling dill and "collyflowers" (cauliflower).

Unlike the cookbooks of the day, which were concerned only with food preparation, Evelyn's salad compendium summarized the knowledge of human digestion. He instructed the wise cook to sprinkle salad greens with water but not to drench them. He recommended draining wet greens in a colander or swinging them in a clean, dry napkin. Dressings, he remarked, should begin with a pale olive oil, such as the native oil he had enjoyed in Lucca, Italy. For tartness, he recommended infusing vinegar with blossoms and herbs and finishing off the salad blend with fine sea salt.

In a social climate that relegated the consumption of raw greens to livestock and savages, Evelyn's text prefigured later health regimens that replaced heavy meat-and-sauce menus with mixed greens seasoned to aid digestion. Of the thirty-five greens he chose for his kitchen bed, he selected from varieties of spinach, romaine, purslane, samphire (a member of the carrot family), lettuce, sorrel, cress, endive, chicory, celery, radish, mache, arugula, and nasturtiums. One of his favorites was fennel, which he peeled, dressed in the same manner as celery, and ate to induce a restful sleep. He recommended lettuce to reduce fever, soothe anger, quench thirst, stimulate appetite, provide nourishment, ease pain, and predispose the body to temperance, chastity, and sound sleep. For these health tips, he drew on an array of Hebrew, Greek, and Latin source material and on his own observations from his travels in Europe.

Evelyn promoted the establishment of kitchen gardens and classified seventy-three salad herbs, categorizing them as sallet, or salad, herbs, pot herbs for cooking, sweet herbs for flavoring, and simplex, a general category of medicinal compounds. Evelyn died on his estate February 3, 1706. The Evelyn Archive at the British Library contains his diary, manuscripts, and letters, purchased from the family in the late twentieth century.

See also **Herbs**

Further Reading

Capp, Bernard, "Particular Friends. The Correspondence of Samuel Pepys and John Evelyn," *English Historical Review*, April, 1999, 445.
Evelyn, John. *Sylva, or a Discourse of Forest Trees.* Woodbridge, Suffolk: Boydell and Brewer, 1995.

F

FARMER, FANNIE

A noted expert on dietetics and monthly columnist for *Woman's Home Companion,* Fannie Merritt Farmer taught her readers about kitchen equipment and the ongoing domestic processes of buying, preparing, and cooking food. Born in Boston on March 23, 1857, she grew up in Medford, Massachusetts. When her father's business faltered, the family was forced to move in with relatives in Boston. To earn extra money, Fannie, who had been prevented by illness from finishing high school, went to work. In Cambridge, she served in the kitchen of Mrs. Charles Shaw and cared for Shaw's daughter, whom she taught to cook.

Farmer mastered kitchen skills before entering the Boston Cooking School at age thirty-one with the encouragement of her parents and her former employer. After completing the course of instruction, she became assistant director of the school. Impeccably groomed and aproned for formal kitchen presentations, she set an impressive example that enlarged the enrollment. To challenge students, she revamped text materials and advanced the institution's reputation by adopting the principles of the emerging home economics profession.

Farmer expanded her knowledge of food chemistry through studies at Harvard University's medical school. She trained student nurses in invalid cookery and assisted in the research studies of the physician Elliott P. Joslin, the author of *A Diabetic Manual for the Mutual Use of Doctor and Patient* (1924). In 1891, she accepted directorship of the cooking school after the death of the co-director. Her approach countered

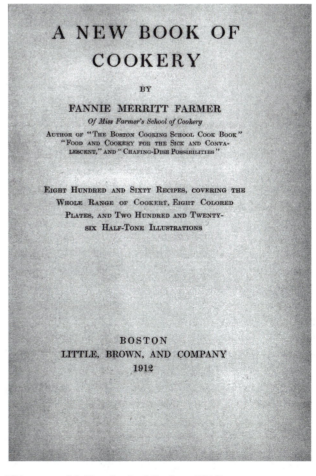

A NEW BOOK OF
COOKERY

BY

FANNIE MERRITT FARMER
Of Miss Farmer's School of Cookery

AUTHOR OF "THE BOSTON COOKING SCHOOL COOK BOOK"
"FOOD AND COOKERY FOR THE SICK AND CONVA-
LESCENT," AND "CHAFING-DISH POSSIBILITIES"

EIGHT HUNDRED AND SIXTY RECIPES, COVERING THE
WHOLE RANGE OF COOKERY, EIGHT COLORED
PLATES, AND TWO HUNDRED AND TWENTY-
SIX HALF-TONE ILLUSTRATIONS

BOSTON
LITTLE, BROWN, AND COMPANY
1912

Title page of *A New Book of Cookery* (1912).

the prevailing dreary domestic philosophy and practice with an infectious delight in food work. In *Woman's Home Companion*, she stated, "It is impossible to raise cookery above a mere drudgery if one does not put heart and soul into the work; then, and then only, it becomes the most enjoyable of household duties." (Shapiro 1986, 111) In an interview for *Good Housekeeping*, she stressed the zeal of the school's staff, who rated cooking as an art on a par with the fine arts.

To revamp the laboratory-minded approach of *Mrs. Lincoln's Boston Cook Book* (1884), the school's domestic science text, Farmer compiled her own. An American classic, *The Boston Cooking School Cookbook* (1896) outlined her straightforward tutorial stripped of condescending asides to housewives. She had to convince a reluctant publisher to accept her manuscript, agreeing to bear the financial loss if the book failed.

Moving systematically from a definition of nourishment through a discussion of meats, breads, vegetables, and beverages, Farmer's text concluded with sample menus and no-nonsense tips concerning measurement and kitchen streamlining. Among her classic recipes was the "one-two-three cupcake," named for the measurement of one cup butter, two cups sugar, three cups flour, and four eggs. In part because of its organization and concise data, the handbook was an overwhelming success that quickly sold out the initial printing of 3,000 copies. It went through three printings the first year and sold four million copies, becoming a touchstone of American culinary art. A year after publishing her cookbook, she witnessed unprecedented growth in the enrollment at the Boston Cooking School, which overflowed its quarters. Demand for Farmer's private lessons and requests for speaking engagements increased; attendees at her public demonstrations exceeded 3,000 annually.

Critics charged that Farmer had plagiarized recipes from Mary Lincoln's earlier compendium without crediting them to their originator, but such carping failed to quell public enthusiasm for Farmer's flair. Unlike more dogmatic nutritionists, she balanced the importance of food value with an insistence on flavor, appearance, and aroma. On the basis of her study of the agricultural chemist Wilbur Olin Atwater's chart of nutritive values, she listed the fat, protein, carbohydrate, and mineral content of her dishes. She commended soup for its physical stimulation, advocated mustard as a metabolic aid, and praised white fish for its digestibility. She retained her gift for whimsy, creating such holiday treats as Lovers' Sandwiches, Cupid's Deceits, and Heart's-Ache Pudding for Valentine's Day and green sherbet for St. Patrick's Day. From visits to metropolitan restaurants, she acquired novel ideas and occasionally daubed a calling card from her purse with an unfamiliar sauce, which she later attempted to analyze and re-create.

In the autumn of 1902, to escape boredom with a curriculum geared toward producing teachers, Farmer opened Miss Farmer's School of Cookery. In its ten laboratory kitchens, teaching aides helped pupils practice innovation rather than slavish emulation of past styles and philosophies. Rather than training graduate teachers, institutional cooks, and chefs, she sought to prepare young unmarried women, established housewives, waitresses, and nurses for pragmatic tasks such as food shopping, plain three-meals-a-day cookery, entertaining, and proper feeding of infants, the elderly, and invalids. More than 100 people filled her weekly demonstration-lectures on home cookery, at which she distributed printed copies of recipes and advised fledgling cooks on the most frequent causes for failure. Competition with the Boston Cooking School led to the sale of her school to Simmons College in 1903.

In part because of her advocacy of level measuring devices, Farmer's name became well-known to housewives, home economics experts, dietitians, and nurses. She stressed the importance of following tested recipes and promoted exact quantities meted out with graduated measuring cups and spoons, a culinary innovation of the era. Through lectures, articles, and a teaching tour to the U.S. West Coast, she became the nation's cooking teacher. She published six kitchen works, including *Chafing Dish Possibilities* (1898), a guide to home entertaining; *What to Have for Dinner; Containing Menus and the Recipes Necessary for Their Preparation* (1905); *Catering for Special Occasions, with Menus and Recipes* (1911); and *A New Book of Cookery* (1912), a compendium of 800 recipes intended to enlighten the middle-class homemaker.

Farmer took special pride in *Food and Cookery for the Sick and Convalescent* (1904), a major contribution to the field of dietetics. From personal experience with the dietary problems of invalids, Farmer urged hospital cooks and practical nurses to make no comment on meal preparation in front of the patient. She described appealing, stimulating food trays decked with digestible dishes served at appropriate temperatures.

Farmer's own health deteriorated from strokes, which deprived her of mobility but did not compromise her fame. For two years, she continued her lectures and demonstrations from a wheelchair. Her sister Cora assisted during a decade of column writing for *Woman's Home Companion*. After her death in Boston on January 15, 1915, Farmer's school remained in operation until 1944. Her writing influenced cooks worldwide, including one of Japan's most celebrated chefs and cookbook writers, Minekichi the Third.

Further Reading

Farmer, Fannie. *The Boston Cooking-School Cook Book*. Boston: Little, Brown, 1918.

FENG SHUI

The ancient Chinese concept of feng shui at one time governed the design of homes, gardens, tombs, stores, offices, temples, and palaces. Formalized around 2000 BCE from prevailing superstition, the ideal of feng shui nurtured positive energy and attitudes through appropriate configuration of windows, doors, and furnishings. The study of propitious positioning began with a floor plan indicating the shape of the house and the *ch'i* (energy) of the grounds. The term *feng shui* (wind-water) referred to the essential external elements. Many centuries later, in the 1980s and 1990s, the concept gained popularity in the West, spawning numerous books on the topic and a thriving business for consultants practiced in the art.

To create balance and harmony based on the Chinese principles, the residential designer adjusts home furnishings to surround inhabitants with an aura of peace and contentment. For the kitchen, proper alignment requires the following:

- Considering the relationship of the entrance to the placement of major appliances and furniture
- Providing the stove the largest view of the room
- Enabling the person preparing food to face the door of the room
- Ensuring that food preparers stand out of a direct line with the door

Additional adjustments seek to improve the enjoyment of a kitchen, considering such factors as the identity of the former owner, an intuitive appreciation of the room's energy, reduction of clutter, and improvement or redirection of energy. A stove with functioning burners and clean top, for example, is believed to warm and strengthen the family's prospects.

To create a scheme for the room, the designer sketches a *bagua* (map), an eight-sided diagram drawn from the *I Ching,* an ancient Chinese text. The map notes the positions of windows, the direction in which doors open, and the space between appliances. Superimposed over the geometric layout is a diagram of "power spots"—children, relationships, fame, wealth, family, knowledge, career, and helpful people.

According to the principles of feng shui, the best kitchen is one that absorbs natural sunlight and provides the cook a view of the outdoors. To radiate serenity, the placement of furnishings and incidentals is designed to energize and encourage rather than oppress or irritate. Feng shui advisers suggest ways to brighten with light or mirrors, to keep energy moving with sound or music, to enhance energy with color, to activate fortune with water, to enliven dead spots, and to stimulate the life force by means of living things such as plants and birds.

Further Reading

Carter, Karen Rauch. *Move Your Stuff, Change Your Life*. New York: Fireside Books, 2000.
Lagatree, Kirsten M. *Feng Shui*. New York: Villard Books, 1996.
SantroPietro, Nancy. *Feng Shui: Harmony by Design*. New York: Perigee Books, 1996.
Saunders, Steven, and Simon Brown. *Feng Shui Food*. Brunswick, Victoria, Australia: R & R Publishing, 2000.

FIREPLACE

The controlled use of fire—set and carefully tended in a dedicated enclosure, or fireplace—has enhanced human life for the past 200,000 years. The Romans made double use of their cook fires by establishing an *apotheca,* a wine making room next to the flue at roof level. By directing fireplace smoke upward, over a fifteen-year period, patient vintners reduced grape juice into the viscous Caecubum wine that the poet Horace lauded in his odes. After Anglo-Saxon conquerors replaced the Romans in Britain in 449 CE, they returned native cookery to open-hearth spit roasting and cauldron heating.

Open-Hearth Cooking

Throughout the British Isles and most of Europe, the working classes and poor made do with a variety of outdoor stone or earth fireplaces. One of the most rudimentary was the simple three-stone cooking fire that held a pot and heated fish, meat, and bread speared on toasting sticks and propped to receive the right amount of heat from the fire. Without added implements, the cook could suspend a bit of fat over a roasting fish for moistening dry flesh and pierce tidbits with a green stick to cook alongside the fire, with drippings falling into a seashell for basting or gravy.

Another form of outdoor cooking space was the earth oven, a stone hearth surrounded on three sides by an earth embankment that shielded wind from the flame. It provided a place to prop spits and skewers at top. Slovakian jam makers built an outdoor fireplace bricked on one side for cooking down jam in a copper kettle. The kelpie fireplace of Ireland had walls built up from stone slabs and an opening at one end for stoking and ash removal. Another variation was the trench firebox, an oven constructed by digging a long narrow ditch, lining it with stone, and heating with firewood for cooking dishes set over the narrow slit at top. Still another was the underground oven, a pit lined with stones. The cook stoked the flame through a separate underground flue. By wrapping meat in wet leaves and sealing the oven with stone and turf, the cook could produce succulent, tender servings moistened without hand basting.

Evolution of the Chimney

The "black kitchen" was a cook place at the center of a rustic house with a vented vault that dispersed smoke into an attic or outside through doors and windows. In the smoky environment of the black kitchens of southern Germany and Slovenia, cooks made meals and aged and preserved haunches of meat suspended from overhead beams. The sooty heat from the fire warmed the dwelling but posed a health hazard for residents, particularly the cook. Nonetheless, the black kitchen survives, for example at Casa de Carvalhinha in Trás-os-Montes, Portugal.

The wall chimney, an advancement of the Carolingian era, evolved slowly and randomly over a period of about 500 years, arriving in the British Isles in the 1300s and, two centuries later, in the Baltic provinces. A Swiss monastery contained the first chimney, built in 820 CE, with a flue system that carried smoke upward from several fires into three smokestacks. Originating in the late eleventh century, mural fireplaces built at or in a wall were luxuries found at Norman and Anglo-Norman palaces and Cistercian abbeys. Fireplaces with smoke pipes, like the stone model that survives at Peterburg Castle near Friesach, Slovenia, heated and cooked in banquet halls on upper stories, where building a centralized floor fire was impractical. The only way to accommodate fire safely was to attach a hearth to the outside wall—usually up the lateral peak—and to vent smoke upward through a hood or chimney. The appearance of a smokestack from the outside became a symbol of wealth and good living.

An unusual kitchen cook place, the herringbone masonry hearth of Canterbury Castle, completed around 1086, stood in one corner of a main room on the first floor. A circular fireplace nearly nine feet in diameter, it fed into a large wall flue and ended in a domed vault. At the corner buttress, the smoke filtered through loopholes. In the basement below, four large pantries provided stores. A niche hollowed out over the castle well—convenient and suited to fire fighting—allowed the cook to draw water without going outside.

The fireplace concept slowly made its way to the Mediterranean. The first fireplace in Piacenza, built in 1320, preceded similar improvements in Rome by a half century. The technology heated air currents as well and reflected radiant heat from the stone back wall, later augmented by a glazed tile or iron reredos. Smoke and gas rose through a roof-mounted louver covered with a sloping cap to keep out rain and snow. A cord allowed the person tending the fire to open and close the louver at will. Later in the 1300s, a revolving louver spun unaided according to the prevailing wind.

Tidy in shape and appearance, the cook's corner in Cotehele, the Edgecumbe family home built in Cornwall in 1485, made use of an enclosed space. To simplify cookery, the staff assembled dishes and implements on wooden shelves alongside, on the mantle, and suspended from wood laths mounted above the fireplace. A settle, or high-backed bench, walled off the area, retaining heat from the fireplace and stone floor.

Kitchen Fireplaces of the Fifteenth and Sixteenth Centuries

In the 1400s, fireplace technology influenced the design of the residential kitchen. In Scotland, homeowners differentiated between the sitting area "'fore'e fire" and the storage space "back o' the fire," the latter accommodating barrels, tubs, and drying peat stacks. (Schärer & Fenton 1998, 31) Above, nails and pegs on crossbeams held pots and pans, lids, the flat iron girdle, a tea caddy, trivets, and utensils. A curving wood toasting fender formed a small raised framework around the hearth. Bread fit on an oatcake toaster clipped to the front of a grate in reach of the cook. Around 1700, Dutch painter Gillis de Winter depicted the simple, floor-level fireplace in *Two Maids Preparing Food*, which shows three walls of a neat kitchen. On the far right wall, the hearthless fire heated a small cauldron suspended from above. The expansive hood overhead directed fumes and smoke upward to the ceiling and out the roof.

During the Renaissance, the raised hearth placed a centralized fire on a stone dais, which held cooking implements and vessels nestled in embers, over small side fires, or hanging from hooks above the flame. Stowage cubbies in the bottom of the hearth provided a space where green or wet wood could dry. One model, in the Nuremberg home occupied from 1509 to 1528 by the German engraver Albrecht Dürer, directed heat up a massive wood superstructure, a forerunner of the flue, which channeled smoke and fumes out an opening in the roof. Next to a cauldron swung over the flame, ladles and skimmers hung from pegs driven into the inner bottom rim of the framework. The elevated hearth was still a rarity. Farther north, Scandinavian homemakers kept a fire burning in a kitchen shed, while, around the Mediterranean, the portable brazier was still the heating and cooking source of choice.

Remodeling their old cottages, householders created gable hearths by inserting a flue between the timbers framing wattle-and-daub walls. The forerunner was the huge hooded fireplace or funnel flue, the development of which enabled home fires to be moved from the center of the floor to an outside wall. Sturdy *landiers* (andirons) held logs in place to keep them from spilling over the hearth and igniting floors. A cooking andiron held spits on hooks or supports; a basket spit attached to a wheel and pulley at the side for rotating meats within the framework. At the top of some andirons, a brazier allowed for cooking or heating individual dishes. Above, the *swey* (pot crane) held a heavy pot over flame.

Improvements to the medieval fireplace incorporated the flue into the wall itself, as seen on the fourth-floor living quarters of Carraig-an-Cabhlaigh (Rockfleet Castle), the seaside hideout of Grace O'Malley, unofficial queen of pirates in Connaught, Ireland. In Scandinavia and the Americas, builders fitted cottages with corner fireplaces. The flue was either a vertical tube connected to a chimney or a cylinder vented along the sides and capped with a cone. Amsterdam native Pieter Aertsen painted *A Wealthy Kitchen* (ca. 1550), a glimpse of men sitting beside a primitive brick fireplace to drink from steins while the cook skimmed the broth cooking in a cauldron suspended by chains in the hottest part of the fire. The technology varies little from the cookery of ancient Rome.

Andirons, also called brandirons or branddogs, were the standard fireplace equipment for burning wood for open-hearth cooking. In the Renaissance, the front was often ornamented with brass knobs and family escutcheons. Knobbed versions were called cobirons. The horizontal wood rest, called a billet bar, sometimes fit into a sleeve that enabled the cook to adjust the span. On a version called a spitdog, iron spits attached to the back of the andiron post on curved supports spaced at variable intervals for raising and lowering. For preserving coals overnight, the cook swept up ash, removed unburned segments of logs, then placed an ornate iron fire cover or nightcap over the remaining embers. The log holder gradually evolved from the combination of fire dogs and grate to the dog grate, an elevated iron basket, often trimmed with brass finials and slotted decorative plate.

Brick and stone-stacked chimneys enhanced homes at the same time that they directed smoke and sparks away from wood shingles. They also obviated the need for a smoke hole in the roof for venting of the open fire below. This advancement made it possible for people to build two-story houses. By the late 1500s, the fireplace units added a fire surround and such amenities as marble and slate interior lining, brass smoke canopy, tiled flooring and header, bricked chimney breast, and ceiling-high decorative embellishments as it shifted from utilitarian to room focus and center of warmth and hospitality. In the kitchen, the raised hearth became a design standard and simplified the job of cooking and removal of ashes, which fell through a slotted grating into a catch basin below.

In the peat cottage kitchens of Ireland, the chimney breast rested on the brace tree, a sturdy horizontal beam that supported wattle-and-daub or stone construction. For draft, the builder excised a shore, a narrow ground channel that let in air from the outside to feed a fire of turf or *bom*, ground-up anthracite blended with clay and formed into balls. Of necessity, the Irish householder sat close to the smoky flame on a three-legged stool, a useful article of kitchen furniture that balanced easily at an uneven hearthstone or on a blue-clay or flagstone floor. When chimneys were first built to vent the hearth in the 1700s, the stools, or creepies, began acquiring longer legs as they evolved into kitchen stools. For ease of carrying them to the barn for milking, the carpenter pierced the disk-shaped seat with a hole or slit wide enough to admit the hand.

Fire builders placed logs on low brick walls or in wrought-iron fire baskets or firedogs. The box seat, a variant of the box chest and settle, provided seating near the light for activities such as sewing and reading. For the cook attending a tricky, labor-intensive technique, such as basting or frying, these high-backed seats reduced chilly drafts from behind.

In sixteenth-century Europe, builders developed a penchant for adorning houses with strikingly handsome fireplaces. The affluent home boasted numerous chimneys. Period fireplaces typically took the walk-in or inglenook shape, named from the Scot-Gaelic *aingeal,* or corner, which provided heating and cooking facilities at its center and room for storage and intimate seating in the outer ends. For Sulgrave Manor, Oxfordshire, built in 1560 by Lawrence Washington, ancestor of George Washington, seventeenth-century additions provided a substantial hearth ten feet wide and four feet deep and set in place an oak beam five feet above the floor. It accommodated several small blazes rather than one huge, wasteful fire. The overall structure was large enough for the user to stand up and look skyward. At different points, the cook could roast in ashes, fry in a skillet, stew in a pot slung from a lug pole, or heat bread on the spiked toasting stand, a device that, according to Dorothy Hartley's *Food in*

England (1954) may have evolved from the stand on which archers impaled straw targets.

Along the chimney beam, the mantle held implements necessary to cooking of the Tudor period. A rounded niche at left served as a charcoal brazier that also heated flatirons. To the right and extending from the chimney wall into the understair, a firebrick-and-mortar bread oven with wrought-iron door and latch baked batch-cakes, a Renaissance term for loaves spaced close together to keep the sides from crusting. At center, an iron-lined hearth oven with hotplate flooring channeled air to the bake-fire through an adjustable vent in the door. An underfloor groove with iron trap door offered an alternate method of applying hot embers to the three-by-four foot chamber, where cooks made pastry, warmed platters, and kept foods until they were needed at table.

The Pleasures of Spit Roasting

The focal dish of the period was a whole meat haunch spit-roasted on wrought iron skewers, some of which were fitted with claws or prongs to grasp pieces of meat securely. Variants of the meat spit included the basket spit, a metal rod centered with a wire cage for holding small chunks, birds, or fish; the batter spit, a metal rod hoisted over a drip pan, from which the cook dipped juices and drizzled them over the meat to form a flavorful, textured crust; the bird spit, a thin rod for roasting small carcasses; and the fish spit, a metal rod that secured delicate fish in a metal cage. Holes pierced in the shaft of another form of spit enabled the cook to secure a cut of meat with cording.

A thrust pot, a cone-shaped vessel attached to a handle, accommodated the making of gravy or heating of a side dish, such as applesauce to accompany a pork roast. When all was done, the cook lifted the spit and cooked portions and carried the entire assembly to the table. While steadying the shaft with one hand, the server spit-carved in a circular pattern. In a servantless home, it is no surprise that the complexities of juggling baking and basting, gauging roasting times, carving meat, and stoking fires in addition to watching toddlers and caring for livestock contributed to the one-dish meal, a housewife's specialty born of necessity.

In the eighteenth century, a broad wooden beam in the Irish home served as a mantle and might hold a spit rack, toby jugs, candlesticks, tinderbox, and personal items. This construction augmented the medieval oak slab above a hearth, which gave families a place to store tinderbox, candlesticks, heirlooms, and memorabilia. A carving of intertwined Celtic knotwork or an overlay of decorative plaster was the only adornment to an otherwise utilitarian shelf. Manor houses

tended toward the wedge-shaped fireplace hood and classic pillars at each end. Placement of a flue and smoke vent to the rear drew fumes back, away from servants mulling wine and aristocrats drying wet boots or warming their hands.

Away from town centers, medieval fireplaces remained standard even into relatively recent times. In *Recollections of a Tour Made in Scotland* (1803), the English poet Dorothy Wordsworth wrote of a visit to a primitive highland cottage with a fire at the center of the floor and a hole in the roof to vent the smoke from smoldering peat. Overhead, hens roosted in rafters Wordsworth described as "crusted over and varnished by many winters, till, where the firelight fell upon them, they were as glossy as black rocks on a sunny day cased in ice." (McNeill 1929, 54) In a neighboring cottage, she saw a clever set of benches along the wall that housed peats to keep them dry.

In nineteenth-century Britain and northern Europe, householders imported fireplaces from Italy, Spain, Portugal, and France. For safety purposes, architects of the Gothic revival period created the stone or limestone fire surround, decorated with a central arch and spandrels, upright jambs, and elaborate friezes. Overhead, free-standing or wall-hung lamps of brass or iron burned oil or candles that dripped on incised stone pendants and furled crockets. The housekeeper expended much time and energy scraping spilled wax from these decorative elements.

Colonial Comforts

In the English colonies, early American kitchens were often called firehouses for the prominence of the hearth in cooking and heating as well as in brewing healing herbs and dyes for cloth and shaping bullets from melted lead. At colonial Salem, Massachusetts, newcomers burrowed fireplaces into the hillsides. In 1652, Edward Johnson, the town clerk of Woburn, summarized, "They make a smoky fire against the Earth at the highest side, and thus these poor servants of Christ provide shelter for themselves, their Wives and little ones." (Dow 1988, 17) The original bark-covered wigwams, which sufficed when settlers abandoned dugouts, offered a single room dominated at the far end by a stone and beam fireplace that encompassed the entire wall. Thomas Dudley reported in 1631 that the community limited the amount of wood in chimneys because "divers houses have been burned since our arrival and some English wigwams which have taken fire in the roofes with thatch or boughs." (Ibid., 19)

The first brickyard in the colonies, which opened in Salem in 1629, produced square-cut, stackable materials to even out a floor and brick a chimney. By sweeping sand between the pavers, the housekeeper created a durable floor that absorbed kitchen waste and slops, yet dried quickly. Inflammable catted chimneys framed in wood took shape in cobhouse fashion, with sticks placed two by two into a square; both inside and outside received a clay lining. Masons carried chimney bricking above the roofline by cementing bricks and stone with a mix of clay and lime. In 1716, Captain Arthur Savage of Boston was selling earthenware and glass as well as Holland tile for facing chimneys and hearths. By 1725, Richard Draper had set up at Cornhill, Boston, to sell Dutch tile, which he advertised in the *Boston News-Letter*. Thirteen years later, Captain Stephen Richard of Queen Street, Boston, was marketing "All sorts of Dutch Tyles, viz. Scripture (round and square), Landskips of divers sorts, sea monsters, horsemen, soldiers, diamonds, etc." as well as "Delph ware." (Dow 1988, 129)

The size of the fireplace was an indication of use and supply of wood. In the early colonial days of North America, massive space accommodated logs so unwieldy that they required a horse and logging chain to drag them into place. Inside, chimney shelves to right and left provided seating where, on the coldest nights, children enjoyed treats of roasted apples and popcorn. Of a particularly fetching Dutch model in colonial New York, a female visitor wrote in the late 1600s: "The chimney-places are very droll-like: they have no jambs nor lintell as we have, but a flat grate, and there projects over it a lum [mantel shelf] in the form of the cat-and-clay lum, and commonly a muslin or ruffled pawn [valance] around it." (Earle 1975, 55) By 1745, an ad in the February 7 issue of the *Boston News-Letter* offered upgraded technology in the "new-invented Pennsylvania Fire-Place." (Dow 1988, 141) Vendor C. Harrison of Cornhill promised to demonstrate the device's ability to warm rooms.

From the 1700s well into the mid-nineteenth century, English housekeepers purchased hearthstone and "Flanders brick" from pushcarts for scouring the hearth. After the removal of ash and scrubbing of the grate and andirons, the white or yellow stone mined in France and Surrey, England, whitened the fireplace base. A stout rubbing in a circular pattern revived the hearth color as well as the cleanliness of doorsteps, windowsills, and treadways. The finishing touch rid the kitchen hearth of grease and readied the flooring to receive tubs and coppers. Once revived with sweeping and scrubbing, the familiar stone hearth pattern attested to the pride, industry, and cleanliness of the householder.

An ambitious late colonial building project recorded in detail was the unsatisfactory flue system at Monticello near Charlottesville, Virginia. Owner Thomas Jefferson's design acumen conquered problems in gardening, cooking, supplying water and ice, and protecting wood structures from fire. He absorbed himself at length with the issue of flues because he wanted them concealed. He considered hollowing columns, piercing an obelisk with holes, or installing iron pipes to vent smoke away from the manse. When these ideas proved impractical, he chose to build flues into the terrace even with the balustrades. His structures rose symmetrically from Palladian Doric pedestals. Elegant, yet too low to vent smoke from the area, they threatened Jefferson's bedroom with fumes and odor from kitchen and smokehouse.

Varying Fortunes in Modern Times

In England, homebuilders and householders shared Jefferson's displeasure with poorly vented fireplaces. In the last half of the nineteenth century, the ubiquitous English chimney fell into disfavor for its unaesthetic appearance and constant belching of soot and fumes. The art critic John Ruskin declared chimneys appropriate to cottages but an eyesore on fine homes. In his opinion, they were not dignified. He belittled them as links to the laboring class—to common kitchen labor and the lowly task of spit turning. (McLaughlin 1988, 305)

Catharine E. Beecher and Harriet Beecher Stowe's classic of domestic science, *The American Woman's Home, or Principles of Domestic Science* (1869), devotes a chapter to fires and lights. Their practical text exhorts women to learn to figure cord measure, which is eight-by-four-by-four feet or 128 cubic feet. For safety, the authors suggest leaving no burning stick on the andirons at night and storing brushes and brooms at a safe distance from flames. As a precaution against house fires, they warn that kitchen hearths should hold two metal pails of water in a place where they are safe from freezing.

Throughout Europe and the Americas, the thoughtful home builder typically designed the parlor or keeping room fireplace with a hob, an inner wall or projected shelf of brick, stone, or iron, where containers of porridge and mugs of tea could be kept hot. When iron stoves replaced the fireplace, they retained the hob in a projecting surface called a side, or warming, shelf. The fireplace often sported a steel or iron fencing at the edge of the hearth to screen out sparks and popping embers and to keep women from brushing the edges of aprons and skirts in hot coals. The spot served as a prop for toasting forks, a place to heat ale or wine, and a drying rack for wet shoes and boots. A decorative steel, brass, or wrought iron footman emulated the humble trivet by supplying a place to heat water for tea or re-warm a tankard. The introduction of the iron stove and, later, gas and electric ranges gradually rendered the fireplace obsolete as cook space, although fireplaces used for home heating persisted, sometimes adapted with more efficient heat sources.

The development of central heating in the twentieth century prefaced a decline in fireplace building. Owners of older homes boarded up hearths and bored holes in floors for radiators, electric wall units, or forced-air ductwork. Builders reduced costs by constructing shallow, nonfunctional fireplaces or omitting them altogether. During the oil crisis of the 1970s, however, many U.S. homeowners rekindled their cold hearths and connected wood stoves to unused flues. Dual-heat systems increased the sale of chainsaws, stovepipe, coal scuttles and shovels, and Scandinavian fireplace inserts and cook stoves like the Jøtul, an iron firebox so airtight it could burn clay-surfaced magazine paper and household trash without emitting fly ash. These additions to the fireplace reacquainted the modern generation with the pleasures of slow-cooked stovetop stews, parched peanuts, and fragrant potpourri simmered in hydration containers, which rescued kitchens from the dry heat common in earlier, fireplace-dependent times.

For those with sleek, amenity-filled indoor kitchens, outdoor cooking became a form of recreation and relaxation, whether it involved rustic campfire cookery or a backyard cookout. For patio use, the Mexican *chiminea* supplied a quaint pot-bellied container with cylindrical chimney top for on-the-spot outdoor cookery. A more elaborate Italian import of reinforced quartz concrete boasted a steel-and-firebrick lined firebox, a stylish chimney, fuel and implement niches, and a surrounding food preparation and serving ledge.

See also **Rumford, Count von**

Further Reading

Agee, James. *Let Us Now Praise Famous Men.* New York: Ballantine Books, 1960.

Derven, Daphne, "Cooking with Fire," *Whole Earth,* Winter 1999, 50–52.

Fischman, Joshua, "A Fireplace in France," *Discover,* January 1996, 69.

Girouard, Mark. *Life in the English Country House: A Social and Architectural History.* New Haven, Conn.: Yale University Press, 1978.

Khouri, Rami G., "Room for Tradition," *Aramco World,* May–June 1993, 10–17.

FISH AND SHELLFISH

Fish and shellfish entered human cookery later than did the meat of mammals, but they were no less prized.

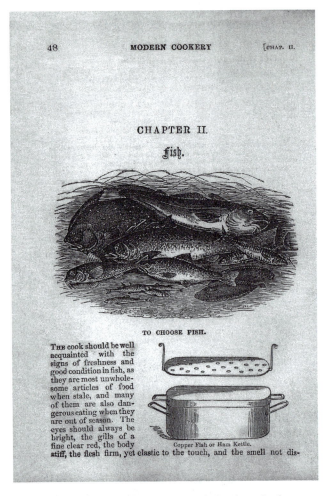

On choosing fish from Elizabeth Acton's *Modern Cookery* (1877).

Archaeological evidence indicates that as early as 10,000 BCE, seiners along the Mediterranean Sea were fashioning vines into nets for capturing finned fish and scooping up succulent shellfish from pools. In northern Africa, Egyptians enjoyed Nile perch, which they roasted whole on a spit. Greek settlements left remains of cooked tuna, shellfish, and snails. Savanna peoples of the Bolivian Amazon raised fields and heaped earth into mounds along causeways, forming fish weirs from which to harvest enough animal protein to supplement their diet.

Early Seafood Appreciation

Paleolithic peoples of Europe employed a variety of methods for catching fish, including spearing, clubbing, seining, and line fishing. Iron Age technology added sinkers and snelled hooks for catching bream, coalfish, cod, dogfish, eel, flounder, haddock, mackerel, perch, pike, pollack, tench, tuna, whiting, and wrasse. Evidence from Neolithic Danish shell mounds

Shellfish fisherman in Tenby, England, loading bag full of shellfish on the back of a truck. [© *Peter Evens / Alamy Images.*]

attests to the cooking of cockles, mussels, oysters, and periwinkles.

Along the Mediterranean, fish, whether grilled or cooked in a soup, were regularly referred to in early texts. The writings of Archestratus, who lived in Sicily around 350 BCE, described the best place to buy swordfish. In the third century BCE, one of the seven Greek masters of cookery, Aegis of Rhodes, specialized in cooking seafood and recording recipes. His contemporary, the Hellenistic geographer and historian Agatharkides, described the Boeotian obsession with Kopaïc eels. Separated from a mixed catch, the oversized eels came to the table garlanded, sprinkled with meal, and prayed over as sacrificial victims marked for the gods.

The Romans perpetuated the Mediterranean preference for lampreys and specialty fish. Cooks enhanced fish dishes with parsley, lovage, mint, cumin, pepper, bay leaf, celery seed, rue, and malabathrum, an unidentified aromatic leaf, as well as salt, honey, vinegar, oil, and *garum,* a fermented fish sauce. Around 50 BCE, the consul Gaius Hirtius, a renowned gourmet, constructed a black Carrara marble tank on his estate to hold some 6,000 eels as a commercial venture. From his stock, he supplied the kitchen of an honored friend, Julius Caesar. In the first century CE, the encyclopedist Pliny the Elder, the author of *Natural History* (ca. 70 CE), noted that swordfish were difficult to spear. He also described the *vivaria,* ponds in Baiae in which oysters were raised. A knowledgeable pisciculturist, Pliny judged the sturgeon of Rhodes the best, praised the turbot from Ravenna, eels from Sicily, and wolffish caught in the Tiber River. For oysters, he chose those from Brundisium, eastern Italy's major harbor.

The Roman snail specialist, Fulvius Lippinus, bred his stock in Tarquinius in the mid-first century BCE.

His food farm produced white Reatean, giant Illyrian, fertile African, and prime African sun snails. According to Pliny, Lippinus fattened his stock on spelt and grape must and grew shells so large that they yielded twenty pints each. On the extravagant menu for "Trimalchio's Feast," a section of Petronius's *Satyricon* (first century CE), the poet lists snails among the six dishes for the *mensae secundae* (second course).

A rich variety of fish were caught and raised in Canton, China. From 500 CE, the imperial staff included more than 300 experts devoted to the task of preparing fish for the royal table. Housewives and their servants traditionally shopped several times a day to get the freshest bass, grouper, wrasse, mullet, whitebait, pomfret, char, shark, or snapper, all of which they preferred to purchase alive. The Chinese shopper always inquired whether supplies were *hoi sin* (deepwater fresh) to be certain of quality fish. They watched as the seller clubbed the fish with a mallet, eviscerated and scaled it, and packed it in damp leaves.

The traditional Asian method for cooking a whole fish was steaming, particularly as the final course of a banquet. For shellfish, they searched out the best *bau yue* (abalone), a delicacy providing meat for the wok and shell for grinding into a healing powder to lower blood pressure and strengthen vision. Cooks boiled in salt water, dried, and stored in clay jars the meat of the premium *oma* abalone, gathered off northern Honshu or Hokkaido, Japan. The larger varieties, *yoshihama* and *amidori,* arrived in Chinese markets dried. Preparation began with soaking before cooking in clay pots.

On Kaho'Olawe, Hawaii's smallest island, a major *wahe pana* (religious shrine) Kohemalamalama'o Kanaloa honored the god Kanaloa from 400 CE. To the northwest at Honokoa Bay, a mythic builder named

Ai'ai erected *ko'a* (fishing shrines), an altar for the day's first catch and presentation of shells, coral, and shellfish to the god Lono, who promised peace and ample harvests. The growth of Hawaiian sea fishing depended in part on sailing, pond building, and navigation technologies. Chiefs constructed huge lava or coral walls along the shore to form seawater ponds averaging fifteen acres in size. Fish stockers attracted fry to the ponds with meals of breadfruit, mussel, seaweed, taro, and sweet potatoes borne on an influx of fresh seawater, which nourished shellfish, crustaceans, and sea turtles. To feed staff, retainers, and guests, royal stocks put 2.5 tons of fish on the king's table each day.

Continental Catch

The late Middle Ages saw the inclusion of snails in proper recipes and preparation instructions. A French delicacy for centuries, *escargot* first appeared in written instructions along with frogs in the anonymous *Le Ménagier de Paris* (The Goodman of Paris, ca. 1394), an unsigned text that may have been written by Guy de Montigny, servant of the Duke of Berry. The next major commentary appeared in Estienne Laigue's *A Noteworthy Treatise Concerning the Properties of Turtles, Snails, Frogs, and Artichokes* (1530), which suggested as substitutes for meat on Catholic meatless days.

Among the late medieval tuna-fishing communities of Sicily, an assembly line processed tuna for marketing to local kitchens and distributors. From fishhook to butcher, the fish passed to washer, salter, packer, and weigher before arriving at the transporter. The Italian cook and culinary writer Il Platina, author of *De Honesta Voluptate et Valitudine* (On Right Pleasure and Health, 1475), devoted the tenth and last book of his compendium to fish dishes. He observed that identification of species was difficult in a region where names given to fish varied from place to place. In general, he favored sea fish rather than those living in marshy waters. Beginning with tuna, the book's cooking instructions proceeded through recipes for mullet, eels, sea urchin, and cuttlefish. Platina's succinct prose grew more detailed in his description of turbot cookery, recommending that the fish be tied in a wicker basket or to a board before being dropped into the poaching liquid. Regarding caviar, he recommended draining in a cloth bag and storage in a perforated jar to assure complete evaporation of liquid. Platina also discussed snails, which he suggested storing in a jar of water overnight, then milk-feeding and cleaning to make them palatable. Frying was the preferred method of cooking snails, which cooks dressed with strong condiments.

Jewish and Greek workers in Sicily salted roe for *bottarga* and cut tuna steaks that were layered in casks for storage. Most of the island's rich catch left its harbors in the cargo holds of ships bound for distant ports. The same was true for Marseilles, where huge amounts of fresh fish were processed, while the workers ate mostly beef, mutton, and pork. The Mediterranean enriched the sea trade but sales left almost nothing for the fisherman's plate.

Along the Adriatic, however, from Dalmatia to Albania, fisherfolk maintained a direct relationship between the sea and the kitchen. Slavic cooks deep-fried fresh and saltwater fish and served shellfish at shore restaurants, where the menu offered a sizeable selection of anchovies, crayfish, dentex (sea bream), eel, hake, langouste (spiny lobster), mackerel, octopus, oysters, prawns, sardines, sea bass, sole, and squid. The link between maritime trade and fish-eating cultures produced traditional recipes and cooking methods, in particular, flavoring with rosemary, mint, and sage and serving fish whole with cooked chard.

Because of the scarcity of fresh fish in Poland, cooks regarded it as a luxury. During Lent, they relied on fish imported from the Baltic Sea. Carp raising began as a commercial venture in the 1200s, providing housewives a source of local fish. The food writer Lukasz Golebiowski reported that growers hand-fed the fish on malt and potter's clay baked with oil yeast, which so pleased the carp that they rose to the surface for a taste every time they heard the feeding bell ring. Before cooking carp, homemakers kept them in buckets of spring water, which they changed daily to retain freshness. To accompany the fish, cooks stirred up a gravy of carp blood, beer, honeyed gingerbread, and plum butter.

In France, the popularity of sturgeon with Louis XIV, the Sun King, prompted trade with Russia, where banquets showcasing sturgeon were the height of food service at the Hermitage in Moscow during the reign of Peter I. The czar's appetite for the luxury fish forced his mariners to ply the Caspian Sea and Volga Basin and beyond the rivers of Siberia to Asia's Pacific shore. Russian chefs demanded live fish, which they presented to diners and then killed on the spot.

The royal seafood tradition of England started in the time of Henry I, crowned in 1100, when cooks rolled crust over an annual Christmas lamprey pie. A separate tradition of Lenten fish pie required Yarmouth cooks to send the king two dozen pies containing 100 herrings. The customary gifts of fish in crust prevailed in 1530, when the prior of Llanthony, Gloucester, baked eels and carp into a pie for Henry VIII. The presentation of the royal eel pie continued in 1752, when bakers sent one to the Prince of Wales, and again during Queen Victoria's reign. In 2004, Elizabeth II turned down a nine-foot sturgeon caught off Wales.

New World Abundance

An abundance of fish varieties awaited European settlers in the New World. In Virginia, Captain John Smith wrote of the ample supply of seafood and freshwater fish in 1614: "Let not the meanness of the word *fish* distaste you, for it will afford as good gold as the mines of Guiana or Potosi, with less hazard and charge, and more certainty and facility." (Earle 1975, 115) From Squanto, the Pemaquid translator and guide from Pawtuxet, Massachusetts, who welcomed settlers to Plymouth in 1620, Pilgrim fishermen learned to tread and capture eels. Shipments of hooks, lines, nets, eel pots, rope, cable, and gaffs from England assured the continued dominance of seafood on the colonial table. From the Wampanoag and Algonquian, New Englanders learned to steam clams and mussels, developing the cooking tradition known as the clambake.

The French surveyor St. John de Crèvecoeur reported on the dependable food supplies of Nantucket in his *Letters from an American Farmer* (1782): "The shores of this island abound with the soft-shelled, the hard-shelled, and the great sea clams, a most nutritious shellfish. Their sands, their shallows are covered with them; they multiply so fast that they are a never failing resource. These and the great variety of fish they catch constitute the principal food of the inhabitants." (Crèvecoeur 1904)

The fur trader Alexander Mackenzie, author of *Voyages from Montreal on the River St. Laurence through the Continent of North America to the Frozen and Pacific Oceans in the Years 1789 and 1793* (1801), visited and wrote about Pacific Coast tribes. On one occasion he observed women preparing several hundred salmon at the door of the chief's residence. He described how they removed the fish heads for boiling, then sliced the meat from the backbone before gutting each fish. Making full use of the fish, they roasted the bones, collected the delicate roe, and dressed fillets for future use. By layering fish in troughs, they collected the oil, a valuable household stock.

To Newfoundlanders, fish was daily food. Families traditionally flensed and sliced whale meat on the shore, minced it for stew, and froze it in fifty-pound blocks for sale and local use. Home cooks smoked salmon over blackberry vines, dried kippers for breakfast food, and made a seafarers' stew called "fish and brewis," a blend of hardtack, cod, and fried salt pork cracklings. (Jennings 1974, 129) Young boys begged the offal from fish factories and plucked out cod tongues, which cooks sliced and fried as a delicacy.

For city dwellers such a supply of fresh fish and by-products was impossible. As second best, door-to-door fish delivery in the 1800s saved the shopper a separate trip to the fishmonger's stall or harbor. Pushing a barrow and blowing a horn, the fish seller advertised the qualities of his shad, mussels, and shrimp, calling out to the housewife, "Here comes the fishman! Bring out your dishpan, Porgies at five cents a pound." (McCutcheon 1993, 1360)

Families farther from shore had to rely on freshwater catch or chancier iced-downed loads of seafood transported on carts. Sophie Trupin, author of *Dakota Diaspora: Memoirs of a Jewish Homesteader* (1984), recalled that fresh fish were nonexistent on the prairie. She wrote of the surprise of an unexpected bucket of fish: "On the kitchen table sat a galvanized pail of fresh fish. True, it was only herring, the lowliest of fish, and it was not altogether fresh—they were frozen solid—but it was still a most welcome and unexpected treat. We had not seen or tasted fresh fish for as many years as we had lived in North Dakota." (Trupin 1984, 110) To Trupin, tinned salmon and sardines were pale copies of the fish that had been prepared in the Old Country each Friday for the Sabbath dinner. The only way to duplicate traditional Gefilte fish was with fresh stock.

In San Francisco, a cosmopolitan settlement that flourished under an influx of adventurers during the 1849 Gold Rush, fish dishes became the area's calling card. Chinese immigrants opened fishing camp kitchens to feed laborers. Along Fisherman's Wharf, cooks fired up iron cauldrons to steam daily catches of Dungeness crab, shrimp, oysters, and salmon. The Alioto brothers from Sicily opened a dockside stall in 1925. Their simple service of steamed crab and seafood cocktails evolved into one of the city's most famous restaurants.

Fish Eating Around the World

The Russian fishing industry specialized in salted fish, a commodity that traders carried around Scandinavia and Western Europe. In Elena Burman Molokhovets's classic Russian cookbook *A Gift to Young Housewives* (1861), the text specified marinated sprats from Tallinn, Estonia, a fish-curing center on the Baltic Sea. Into the twenty-first century, the area remained a respected source for cured Baltic herring and sprats, which cooks often used as a substitute in recipes calling for sardines.

The Dutch saying about herring, "Haring in' t land, docter aan de kant," was roughly the equivalent of "A herring a day keeps the doctor away." (Montagné 1977, 505) Whether salted or smoked, herring were the cook's choice for family meals and banqueting. On the coast, the Dutch once celebrated the year's maiden catch by sending the first barrel of herring to the queen.

In Japan, where no kitchen is more than sixty miles from the coast, fish and seafood have traditionally been daily staples. From both cold and warm marine currents, fishermen retrieved a variety of whale, carp, bonito, tuna, shark, bream, sole, and shellfish. Cooks had many ways of preparing the catch, from slivers of *sashimi* (raw fish) added to rice or steeped in vinegar, to whole grilled fish. Accompanying fish dishes were a variety of tangy condiments such as *shoyu* (soy sauce), mustard, sweet rice wine, grated horseradish, lemon, salt, or ginger.

Both fishing methods and fish cookery vary widely in different parts of the world. In the 1960s, Bahraini fishermen supplied restaurants and home kitchens with fish trapped on the shore. In the outgoing tide, they cast circular nets or positioned *hadra* (traps) woven of palm branches. In Malaysia, night fishing on deep-sea *kelong* (fishing platforms) was the source for *gerago* (krill), a microscopic prawn found in the Melaka Straits. Using lights, fishermen guided their catch into curved nets. In the kitchen, the prawns highlighted a sweet-and-sour sambal, a condiment made from chilies, coconut, bean paste, fish sauce, lime, and kaffir lime leaves.

Fugu, a potentially lethal pufferfish favored by connoisseurs in Japan, first appeared in culinary history in 720 CE. Certain tissues of the fish contain a deadly toxin that can be removed only through careful preparation by an experienced chef. In one historic catastrophe in the late 1500s, poisonous meat from fugu caused the death of Japanese soldiers awaiting an invasion of Korea. From that point on, fugu grew in mystique as a result of a nationwide ban on cooking and serving it that drove fugu cooks underground. In 1888, Prime Minister Hirobumi Ito reprieved the fish, initiating a new round of feasting. In the twentieth century, to prevent further disasters, fish cooks had to complete a three-year apprenticeship under a master chef and pass licensing tests before serving fugu. Although six Japanese diners died from eating the fish in 1997 and more in 1999 and 2004, it maintained its allure. Waggish food preparers arranged fugu sashimi to resemble a chrysanthemum, a flower commonly displayed at funerals.

Questions of Health

In the industrialized countries, high rates of heart disease became a focus of intensive medical research in the second half of the twentieth century. Scientists concluded that diet—and in particular, dietary fat—was largely to blame, and they proceeded to analyze and categorize the fat content of food. One result of this work was the finding that fish contained "heart-healthy" fats that could help to prevent heart attack and stroke. Physicians and nutritionists began to urge people to eat fish more often; newspapers and magazines abounded with fish recipes, sparking a resurgence in the popularity of seafood. But with concern over water pollution growing in the late decades of the century, reports of high levels of toxins in fish, especially methylmercury, a known neurotoxin, began to tarnish the reputation of fish as a health food.

Next, the public health community began to warn about the dangers of food-borne diseases. In February 2001, *Consumer Reports* found that 4.4 percent of foodborne illnesses in the United States were attributed to seafood. Tests of fish from several markets conducted in the magazine's laboratories discovered unacceptable levels of substances such as the bacterium *E. coli*, a major cause of food-borne disease. Some 25 percent of fresh fish tested was on the brink of spoilage. Although the experts did not advise people to stop eating fish altogether, they did warn that certain groups—e.g., small children and pregnant women—should limit their consumption of species known to harbor hazardous chemicals or bacteria. Instructions for safe handling advised keeping fish below 40 degrees Fahrenheit on the way home from the market and in the refrigerator, thawing frozen fish in the refrigerator, not on the kitchen counter, and separating raw fish from other foods during preparation.

Further Reading

Edwards, John. *The Roman Cookery of Apicius*. Point Roberts, Wash.: Hartley & Marks, 1984.

Foster, Nelson. *Kaho'olawe: Na Leo o Kanaloa*. Honolulu: Ai Pohaku Press, 1995.

Garrett, W. E., and David Jeffery, "Burma's Leg Rowers and Floating Farms," *National Geographic*, June 1974, 826–845.

Jennings, Gary, "Newfoundland Trusts in the Sea," *National Geographic*, January 1974, 112–141.

Neustadt, Kathy. *Clambake: A History and Celebration of an American Tradition*. Amherst: University of Massachusetts Press, 1992.

Rajah, Carol Selva. *Makan-Lah!: The True Taste of Malaysia*. Sydney, Australia: HarperCollins, 1996.

FISHER, M. F. K.

The creator of the food essay, Mary Frances Kennedy Fisher acquired an unusual blend of culinary credentials. Born in Albion, Michigan, on July 3, 1908, she grew up in Whittier, California, an Irish Episcopalian among Quakers. In a 1974 article for the *New York Times,* she described herself as the rebellious offshoot of a prim Irish grandmother: "The effects of her culinary discipline still affect my own manners at the stove and table or rather they still shape my revolt against my grandmother's gastronomical rules." (Fisher 1974)

From early childhood, Fisher loved good food and good company and knew in her youth that she wanted to be a writer. At age twenty-one, she settled in Dijon, France, to be near the university where her husband, Albert Young Fisher, was a Ph.D. candidate. While studying sculpture and drawing at the École des Beaux Arts, she steeped herself in the savor and aroma of Provence and spent long afternoons reading antique cookbooks at the local library. These influences inspired her to record the gustatory pleasures of the Mediterranean coast.

Her husband's career took her to Los Angeles in 1932, where she compiled an essay collection, *Serve It Forth* (1937), her first travelogue and kitchen history. A characteristic precision and fine turns of wit suffuse her essay "I Was Really Very Hungry," in which a servant remarks, "Any trout is glad, truly glad, to be prepared by Monsieur Paul. His little gills are pinched, with one flash of the knife he is empty, and then he curls in agony in the *bouillon* and all is over. And it is the curl you must judge, Madame. A false *truite au bleu* cannot curl." (Levy 1997, 135) Such piquant humor, blended with an understanding of foodstuffs and flavors, earned Fisher a more literary following than that of the standard cookbook writer.

After a second marriage in 1938, Fisher made her home in Vevey, Switzerland, and penned a novel, *Touch and Go* (1939). In 1942 her husband's suicide uprooted her once more. Resettled in Hollywood, she modeled, wrote for the movies, and, under the alternate name Mary Frances Parrish, completed *The Gastronomical Me* (1943), a deft blend of food lore and anecdote about appetite and love that exemplifies the controlled sybaritism that drew food-centered readers to adore her works. She followed with more books—*Here Let Us Feast* (1946), *An Alphabet for Gourmets* (1949), and *With Bold Knife and Fork* (1968)—and contributed to *The Cooking of Provincial France* (1969), a Time-Life volume in the *Foods of the World* series.

Among Fisher's accomplishments, the definitive translation into English of Jean Anthelme Brillat-Savarins' *Physiologie du Gout* (The Physiology of Taste, 1825), published in 1949, assured her a place in kitchen history. Her most successful food work, *The Art of Eating* (1954), won the James Beard Cookbook Award. The text showcased her most popular essays, including "How to Cook a Wolf" (1942), a commentary on eating well during the food rationing and privations of World War II.

Based in southern France, she continued to write about food, folk healing, and travel in *A Cordiall Water: A Garland of Odd and Old Recipes to Assuage the Ills of Man or Beast* (1961) and *Maps of Another Town: A Memoir of Provence* (1964). Before her death on June 22, 1992, she also completed an autobiography, *To Begin Again*. A resurgence of interest in her writing in the 1980s returned to print some of her titles and the hundreds of articles she wrote for *The New Yorker*. In her honor the Dames d'Escoffier International, an organization of women culinary professionals, bestows the M. F. K. Fisher Award to women in midcareer whose work has had a direct impact on the areas of food, beverage, and table arts.

Further Reading

Fisher, M. F. K., "Food: The Arts (Fine and Culinary) of 19th Century America," *New York Times*, September 15, 1974, 5.
_____. *M. F. K. Fisher: A Life in Letters*. Washington D. C.: Counterpoint, 1997.
_____, "Savoring Winter," *The Times Magazine*, October 27, 1985, 8.

FLATWARE

Following the introduction of the fork, knife, and spoon, known collectively as flatware, to table setting in the Middle Ages, use of these eating utensils became the norm for the Western world and beyond. Workers shaped most from base metal; only royalty could afford solid silver and gold table service. In 1750, the development of the Sheffield method of plating tea urns, serving pieces, candelabra, and knife handles created a new industry in Sheffield and Birmingham, England. In 1860, the old coating technology gave place to electroplating, a fusion process that bonded buffed silver to copper and nickel alloy and nickel to brass. Eventually, a less expensive domestic flatware, made from stainless steel, simplified the chores of removing stains and oxidation from tableware.

The stamping of flatware by a calendering method pioneered by Alfred Krupp preceded twentieth-century manufacture. The Krupp process involved passing a sheet of metal under a rotating drum fitted with sharp edges in the shape of the implements. Dye-cut as unadorned blanks from the metal sheets, the implements moved on to an annealing process to prevent staining, then tine-formation, bowl-shaping, trimming, and smoothing with emery wheels and belts. Finally, after the pieces received a finer detailing, hand polishing with rotating mops dipped in jeweler's rouge produced the satiny finish of expensive flatware.

Nineteenth-century serving styles and table setting required a host of specialized pieces, such as soup ladles, fish knives, sugar shells, and shellfish forks. A customary wedding gift to elite couples was a place setting of elegantly patterned and monogrammed flatware. The silver chest, lined in felt permeated with tarnish-preventing vapors, organized dinner knives and several types of forks and spoons between upright dividers. Separate leather straps in the lid held serving and carving pieces. Less expensive sets featured silver or silver-plated implement heads affixed to inexpensive handles of bone, coral, horn, or mother-of-pearl.

Throughout the 1930s, as flatware gained in popularity, especially as a gift for newlyweds, women's magazines carried lavish color spreads featuring silver flatware in tony settings. In an ad in the October 1930 issue of *Good Housekeeping,* one manufacturer emphasized that its quality sterling flatware was bolstered with extra metal at table-touch points for long-wearing beauty at an affordable price. Ads pointed out that in contrast to silver plating, in which workers merely dipped pieces in molten metal, sterling flatware advanced to heirloom status.

After World War II, the emphasis in flatware marketing shifted dramatically from snobbery to romance as a prelude to housekeeping. A 1947 ad for Community silverplate from Oneida featured a snuggly couple under a headline that read, "Let's make it for keeps." ("Let's" 1947, 49) The burgeoning domesticity of the postwar period stressed commitment to marriage and family, symbolized by flatware with deep-etched initials.

Modern flatware from such revered manufacturers as Gorham, International, Kirk-Stieff, Lunt, Reed and Barton, Towle, and Wallace remains a treasured adornment to formal table settings. For those who can pay for luxurious solid silver, the display of heirloom crests and patterns is a mark of taste and tradition. Social occasions such as weddings, holiday buffets, and club meetings provide opportunities for the glamourous host and hostess to set a fine spread, often marked by heavier pieces, particularly the canapé server, sugar tongs, and punch ladle. Families pass on valued silver service as legacies from the past to the tables of their children and grandchildren.

See also **Fork; Horn; Knives; Precious Metals; Spoons; Steel**

Further Reading

"Let's Make It for Keeps," *Woman's Home Companion,* March 1947, 49.

FORCING BAG

One of the tools of the master cook, the forcing bag, also called a piping, or pastry, bag, is a cone-shaped pouch that dispenses creamy semisolids capable of holding their shape as candies or icings. From the pointed end, the user extrudes icing, filling, meringue, or mashed potatoes for edging or latticing cakes, stuffing manicotti shells, and shaping chou pastry. Exchangeable fittings shape the oozing cream for edging platters with a decorative trim. One example of forcing bag artistry, *suspiros* (kisses), a bakery specialty on the island of Margarita, off the coast of Venezuela, requires piping a sweet mix into tall pyramids on wax paper for baking.

In the late Middle Ages, culinary artists used canvas or leather forcing bags to create masterful entrées for banquets. One culinary triumph consisted of whole, cooked fowl in the shape of a living bird, feathers and all. The dish required removal of the meat, which, after

OF EXTRA RECIPES—BREAKFAST DISHES, ETC.   317

stirring it occasionally; remove it from the stove and let the mixture cool a little, then add by degrees three whole raw eggs, working the paste quickly with a wooden spoon. When it is quite smooth add two large tablespoonfuls of grated Parmesan cheese, mix up well, put the paste into a forcing bag with a plain pipe and force it out on to a greased baking-tin in lengths of about three inches by one inch, as shown in

design; brush them over with whole beaten-up egg, and bake in a moderate oven for about twenty-three minutes; then remove and cut them longways, and fill them by means of a forcing bag and pipe with the Cheese custard (see recipe) or whipped cream; dish them up in a pile on a dish-paper or napkin. Serve hot or cold for luncheon or dinner savoury.

Timbal à la Jardinière

Timbale à la Jardinière

Line a fancy border mould, as shown in design, with aspic jelly about the eighth of an inch thick, then garnish it with little fresh sprigs of raw chervil and tarragon, and here and there place in the mould some quarters of hard-boiled eggs that are garnished with strips of French red chilli, and then set in the mould with a little aspic jelly, and fill up the inside of the mould between the egg with a cooked macedoine of vegetables; set this with cool aspic jelly and place on ice till quite firm, then dip the mould into hot water and turn out on a flat cold dish, and fill up the centre of the timbal with any nice cooked meat, such as

Woman using a forcing bag from A. B. Marshall's *Larger Cookery Book of Extra Recipes* (1891).

being chopped, cooked, and spiced, was returned into the hollow shell of the skin by means of a forcing bag. Medieval cooks also sliced beef and mutton for shaping into imitations of fowl, which they stuffed with herbed forcemeat, marrow, suet, and egg. They turned pig stomachs into *urchins* (hedgehogs) by filling them with forcemeat and prickling the exterior with pastry quills or slivered almonds. The technique of forcing of food into decorative outlines and shapes on platters and banquet centerpieces attained high artistry in the Arab cooking guide *Kitab al-Wusla ila l'habib* (Book of Friendly Bond, ca. 1250).

Complex cookery became the hallmark of French haute cuisine, which originated in the royal kitchens of Louis XIV for feasts held at the palace of Versailles. The first true Renaissance cook, La Varenne, author of *Le Cuisinier Français* (The French Cook; also *Le Vrai Cuisinier* [The True Cook], 1651), described the use of forcemeat for *Poulet en ragout dans une boteille* (ragout of chicken in a bottle), an elaborate dish made by forcing egg yolks, mushrooms, pigeons, sweetbreads, truffles and suitable seasonings into a bottle along with the boned meat. The sealed container, gently cooked in a bain-marie, went to table still seething, making for a dramatic presentation. Another grand display, a Spanish *pottewys*, began with forcemeat molded and spit-roasted in a flowerpot. Servers brought it to table with pastry blossoms and stalks concealing the spit hole. (Wilson 1991, 16)

The first recorded use of a forcing bag to create lettering was the work of the Viennese baker Franz Sacher, personal chef to Prince von Metternich. To please his master, in 1832 Sacher signed his desserts in discreet chocolate lettering. The concept spread from Austria to Hungary, where it became standard practice for chefs to inscribe their cakes with their name or the cake recipe in an icing made of egg white and powdered sugar. By the 1920s, self-trained cooks mastered the art of inscribing cakes for weddings, anniversaries, birthdays, bar mitzvahs, and holiday observances. The more inventive pastry chefs added lines of verse, scripture, family crests, personal messages, or dates of events.

As explained by Marie-Antoine Carême, France's master chef, in his five-volume *Le Cuisinier Parisien ou l'Art de la Cuisine au Dix-neuvième Siècle* (The Parisian Cook, or The Art of Nineteenth-Century Cuisine, 1833), the forcing bag, or pastry bag, replaced the paper cornet, a technology invented by a Bordeaux *pâtisserie* for embellishing meringues, almond paste, and sweets. Carême recommended the use of the cornet "to form sponge fingers, *croquettes à la reine*, and *biscottes à la parisienne*." (Montagné 1977, 276) Refinements of the original cornet included the addi-

tion of nozzles of various sizes and shapes to produce decorative designs and the use of a syringe to extrude firmer substances. One variation, the *purée presser*, was a two-part device consisting of a wood-handled plunger that forced fine streams of fruit, vegetable, or meat fiber through a series of holes out the side of the barrel.

In 1900, while culinary lecturer-demonstrator Sarah Tyson Rorer, founder of the Philadelphia Cooking School, was giving a stage presentation, she found her forcing bag missing from the model kitchen. Deftly, she folded a tea towel into a three-cornered receptacle, pinned one edge, and forced the tube end through a hole at the corner. The audience reportedly burst into applause.

A cake decorating set patented in 1925 applied the concept of the forcing bag to a metal plunger and glass syringe that forced icing out a variety of tin tips. Packed in the carrying case were the tube and plunger, a dozen tips, and an instruction booklet, which bore the seal of approval from the Good Housekeeping Institute. The text explained how to make swirls, edging, birds, rosettes, leaves, and frills and how to letter names and holiday and birthday greetings on family desserts.

Forcing bags or similar implements have been used in traditional cookery in many countries. In Holland, bakers created holiday cookies called *sprits* by piping the dough onto baking sheets; German cooks used pastry tubes to squeeze jam or jelly into Fastnacht pancakes and the doughnuts called Bismarcks after Otto von Bismarck, founder of modern Germany. Swedish cooks piped Lenten or Shrovetide buns called *semla*, emulating a German original from the 1700s. Mexican cooks pressed *albundigas* (hot ground meat) through a ring over boiling stock and cut lengths to resemble sausages. In a 1950 article for *Vogue* magazine entitled "Food, Artists and the Baroness," Alice B. Toklas explained how she had once decorated a poached fish with mayonnaise-and-tomato juice icing to serve to a guest, the artist Pablo Picasso.

French cooking of the twenty-first century incorporated additional *couché* (extrusion) techniques for stuffings and galantines and for piping pâtés, lady fingers, and purées onto baking sheets. Forced substances were also integral to many other dishes—meatballs, mousse, molds, canapés, tarts, and decorative borders. In Arlésienne cooking, meat platters were often accompanied by garnishes of tomatoes stuffed with rice mix or large olives piped with chicken forcemeat. In Italian kitchens, the forcing bag shaped gnocchi, small doughy flour or potato dumplings dropped into boiling water. Replacing an earlier generation of forcing bags made from leather or canvas were bags made of a washable polyurethane-coated fabric fitted with a nylon coupler that attached to a variety of screw tips.

Further Reading

Greenspan, Dorie, "The Pastry Bag," *Bon Appétit*, April 1999, 50.

FORK

The fork is a pronged dining utensil used to pick up pieces of food. Historical documentation attests to early use of a precursor of the table fork. In biblical times devout Jews removed morsels from metal pots with a two-pronged implement as offerings to Jehovah. In Byzantium around 1050 CE, householders employed forks solely for serving suckets, or sweetmeats. The Dogissa Maria Argyra, a Greek-born Venetian, is the first diner known to have eaten with a two-tined gold fork, which she called a prong. According to her contemporary, Peter Damiani, the Bishop of Ostia, a stern critic of ostentation and vice: "Such was the luxury of her habits…[that] she deigned [not] to touch her food with her fingers, but would command her eunuchs to cut it up into small pieces, which she would impale on a certain golden instrument with two prongs, and thus carry to her mouth." (Wright 1999, 82) Perhaps because of the fork's provenance, to the English it remained for some centuries an effete "Italianism," an affectation to be avoided.

The fork apparently served a central purpose in Mongolia. In a report on his mission to Central Asia, Friar William of Rubruck wrote to Louis IX of France in 1255 about a huge meal of boiled meat cut into small cubes: "With the meat of a single sheep they feed fifty or a hundred men: they cut it up into tiny pieces…then on the end of a knife or a fork made specially for the purpose—the sort with which we usually eat pears and apples baked in wine—they offer each of the bystanders one or two mouthfuls." (Lysaght 1994, 132) This testimony refutes the assertion of some culinary historians that the European fork was a Byzantine invention of the 1400s limited to use by nobles and royalty.

In western Europe, straight, two-pronged *râbles* or *roables* (fire rakes), a domestic version of the twin-pronged battle spear, served kitchen duty but were not considered graceful or elegant enough for the table. They evolved into serving pieces in the 1400s and into a smaller version for individual use the next century in Italy. Eustachio Celebrino da Udene, a *scalco* (head waiter) and book illustrator, lauded the shift in table etiquette in his book *Opera Nova Che Insegna Apparechiar Una Mensa a Uno Convito* (New Book That Teaches the Use of Banquet Table Implements, 1526). His acceptance of the *pirone,* or dinner fork, appears in his instructions for table setting, which place the knife and fork alongside plates and servings of bread and crackers.

The use of the fork became widespread during the high Renaissance. By the death of Henry VII of England in 1509, when the reading of his will noted a case containing twenty-one knives and a crystal and chalcedony fork, the implement had become valuable but not common to any but the nobility. The first to use the implement at the French table was Catherine de Médicis upon her marriage to Henry II in 1533. The Italian painter Jacopo Bassano included a fork in a depiction of the Last Supper in 1599. In Spain, Charles V owned a set of the newly introduced eating implements, but at the court of Henry III of France, diners at the king's table rejected the fashion for table forks, which he had purchased in Venice.

In the Elizabethan age, English diners began replacing the knife with a curved fork suited to spearing and scooping up foods; the Spaniards, England's rival on the seas, carried only straight-tined forks on the vessels of the Spanish Armada. Relics retrieved from the Spanish warship *Girona,* which shattered on rocks off Lacada Point, Ireland, on October 26, 1588, included silver forks, the dining implements of gentlemen. Their handles long eroded by the time they were recovered, these utensils bore metal heads that varied in the number and length of the tines. By 1589, the French court had accepted the use of forks at table.

In his play *Volpone* (1606), the English poet and dramatist Ben Jonson wrote that a fork ended diners' dependence on a napkin, presumably by freeing the fingers from manipulating sticky, greasy foods. Thomas Coryat, perhaps England's first fork user, mused on the fork in *Coryat's Crudities Hastily Gobbled Up in Five Months Travels in France, Savoy, Italy, &c.* (1611). To his way of thinking, the Italian use of forks represented an advancement in sanitation. He described the innovation as a small iron, steel, or silver implement that kept foods free of the impurities of servants' hands. His commentary drew scorn for its Continental pretensions and earned him the nickname "Furcifer," a Latinate neologism meaning "fork-bearer" and sounding suspiciously like Lucifer, a common name for Satan. In 1616, Jonson took up Coryat's campaign for a more salutary table in *The Devil Is an Ass*, in which he surmised that the Italians used forks to keep their hands clean and spare the host soiled napkins.

London's Victoria and Albert Museum houses England's oldest fork, a two-pronged, crested implement belonging to John Manners, eighth Earl of Rutland, and made by a silversmith in 1632. Nobles and imitators followed the dainty example of royal fork users and adapted the use of the knife and fork, thus setting a new trend in etiquette. Travelers carried their own table settings, sometimes selecting folding knife and fork for ease of packing. At hearthside, cooks used a kraut fork, a short, stubby wood fork, to fluff cabbage flakes. For display at table, carvers preferred more ornate meat forks, often adorned with curved wrought iron detailing and a brass medallion.

When the Pilgrims landed at Plymouth Rock in 1620, they brought knives, spoons, and a few long-handled kettle forks but no table forks. The toasting fork, a common item in colonial kitchens, enabled the cook to brown a piece of bread without overheating the fingers. The slow turning of bread on the tines required patience and a careful study of heat and its effect on crust and crumb.

In 1633, the table fork debuted in New England in the possession of Governor John Winthrop, who stored it along with a knife and bodkin, or skewer, in a leather case. Up to that time, all colonial diners had depended heavily on linen napkins to wipe away grease and sticky residue left on their fingers. The use of the fingers remained the norm, however, until the end of the century, when two-tined silver and iron forks joined other items of flatware on tables in Massachusetts, New York, and Virginia. Matched with spoons, forks sported decorative bone, ivory, or wooden handles; artistic versions featuring enameling and set with precious stones served notables and aristocrats.

In status-seeking European households, the placement of utensils became a means of advertising the family's wealth and prestige. The presence of a crest on tableware attested to the owner's noble genealogy. At the table of Louis XIV, the lord pantler, taster of the king's food, also presided over the arranging of his knife and fork. The pantler's coat of arms bore an image of the lidded *nef*, a gold or silver container that held knife, fork, and salt cellar.

Unlike cooking forks or wrought-iron toasting prongs, the table fork served the diner solely as a mealtime implement. When the four-tined version came into use in the 1880s, eating from a knife became passé. Specialty forks appeared in many varieties, among them the following:

Blending fork—a beater, blender, and dough mixer shaped like a large meat-turning fork and equipped with wide-spaced tines and knifelike edges at back for incorporating shortening with flour or meal, creaming fat with sugar, smoothing gravy, tossing salad, and mixing pastry
Cold meat fork—a serving piece used for lifting bacon, chops, cold sliced meat, fish, and salad
Dipping fork—a long-handled two- or three-pronged wire fork for submerging bread and candies into coatings

Flesh fork or granny fork—a large two-pronged meat server and tester of cooked vegetables
Lemon fork—an ornate piece with slender tines bent outward to maneuver citrus slices
Olive fork—a small serving piece with slender tines for selecting olives from a bowl or tray
Pickle fork—a serving piece with slender tines bent outward to lift olives and pickles
Pot fork—a sturdy, long-handled implement that enabled the cook to turn meat without risking a burn from steam or popping grease
Raclette fork—the implement that Valaisian shepherds used to melt cheese for scraping over a plate of boiled potatoes
Serving fork—a jointed device that resembles two forks turned face to face and used to grasp large pieces of meat, vegetables, and snack foods
Sucket, or sweetmeat, fork—a diminutive implement with prongs at one end and bowl at the other for serving candied or crystallized fruit

Humble homemakers kept a box of sand layered with grass or straw for scrubbing forks. In more affluent kitchens and restaurants, a unique device for cleaning forks was the wire or fiber fork cleaner, a metal frame holding stiff brushes, into which the dishwasher plunged the implement to remove stains and dried bits between the tines.

At the beginning of the Gilded Age, the U.S. First Lady Caroline Scott Harrison compiled *Statesmen's Dishes and How to Cook Them* (1890), a series of White House recipes. In her directions for homemade mayonnaise, she specified that a silver fork be used to stir the egg yolks into the olive oil—the unspoken implication being that pewter might mar the delicate taste of the dressing by interacting with the acidic lemon juice used to thin the emulsion.

By the late 1800s Continental manners had made a bold shift away from fork-centered dining. In previous times, the eater had held the fork in the dominant hand when eating and exchanged it for a knife when cutting foods. The knife was set to rest when not in use. The change in dining style called for holding a shorter-bladed knife in the dominant hand and using the other hand to hold the fork, tines-down, to spear food and lift it to the mouth. In the Western Hemisphere, the persistence of the earlier fork-dominant style set most Americans apart from their European cousins.

In the twentieth century, new materials yielded such innovations as ergonomic resin handles and beveled prong tips. A battery-operated barbecue fork contained a built-in instant-read temperature gauge and preprogrammed temperature scale for assessing levels of doneness.

Further Reading

"Knives, Forks, and Spoons," *Aramco World*, March 1960, 16–19.

FRANCATELLI, CHARLES ELMÉ

Although he was Victorian England's most famous chef, preparer of meals for peers of the realm and even the Queen herself, Charles Elmé Francatelli nonetheless understood the plight of the downtrodden. In an era when the upper class dined with lavish excess, he compiled a cookbook—*Plain Cookery Book for the Working Classes* (1852)—expressly for working families struggling to put food on the table.

Francatelli was born of Italian ancestry in London in 1805. Educated in France by the esteemed chef Marie-Antoine Carême, he worked his way up to the status of *chef de cuisine*. Among the aristocrats whose tables he stocked were the Earl of Chesterfield, Viscount Ednam, the Earl of Dudley, and Baron Kinnaird. Francatelli also served England's discerning gourmets during seven years on staff at the Reform Club, Coventry House Club, Freemason's Tavern, and the prestigious St. James Hotel, which he managed. In 1840,

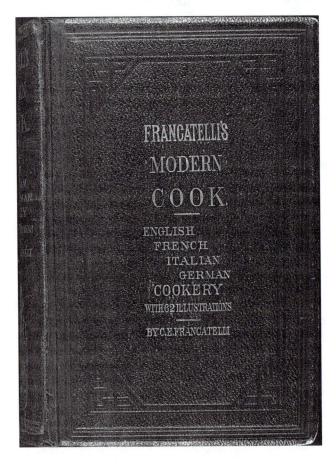

Cover of *The Modern Cook* (1860).

he advanced to Queen Victoria's chief cook and *maître d'hôtel*.

Accustomed to catering to the appetites of the privileged, Francatelli was able to coordinate a sumptuous meal that might include as many as thirty different dishes, an accomplishment that elevated his reputation during an era marked by conspicuous culinary consumption. Superintending two dozen undercooks and two deputy chefs, he created such elegant repasts as this winter spread for twelve diners:

First Course

Soups
Macaroni clear soup
Purée of carrots à la Crécy

Fish
Fillets of whiting à la Royale
John Dory with Dutch sauce

Removes
Braised beef à la Polonaise aux choix rouges
Poularde à la Périgeux

Entrées
Boudins of pheasant à la Reine
Fillets of pigeon à la duxelle
Mutton cutlets, à la Bourguignotte
Marrow patties with fine herbs

Second Course

Roasts
Teal
Hare

Removes
Brown bread soufflé
Ramequins à la Sefton

Entremets
Salsifis à la crème
Vol-au-vent of greengages
Potatoes au gratin
Noyeau cream
Lemon jelly
Pithiviers cake
(Berriedale-Johnson 1989, 12)

Because the queen and her family set the tone and style of the age for England, Francatelli's lavish meals became the fashion for the upper classes, requiring extensive shopping for rare food items and the employment of a disciplined kitchen team.

When critics mocked him for producing a cookbook aimed at the laboring classes, Francatelli retorted that he could feed 1,000 families on the food wasted in London in a single day. In the book's introduction, he inventoried—and specified the exact cost of—the necessary equipment for a kitchen, beginning with a stove with workable draft and a boiler for heating water. He specified one oval pot, two lidded saucepans, potato steamer, fry pan, gridiron, brewing copper, mash tub, and a cooler, which the thrifty household could make from a recycled beer cask.

In 240 recipes, he explained in a chatty if somewhat condescending style how to melt jelly into sauce, boil beef, and stuff and roast a goose. His compendium incorporated traditional English dishes such as Christmas plum pudding and working-class fare such as "toad-in-the-hole" (sausages cooked in batter), and the potato-and-cabbage hash dubbed "bubble-and-squeak." In describing the preparation of a freshly slaughtered pig, he spoke with authority on removing the bristles with burning straw, scraping the surface dry with a knife, and cleansing the gut before removing pluck, fat, and chitterlings. His instructions for curing included precise measures of salt, treacle, saltpeter, herbs, and spices.

Francatelli introduced his readers to the French *haricot vert* (green bean), which he described as "a principle part in the staple articles of food for the working-classes, indeed for the entire population." (Francatelli 1999, 75) For the many cooks who had no ovens of their own, he advised: "You can easily roast your potatoes by placing them on the hobs, bars, and under the fire-grate; and if you are attentive to their being well roasted, by turning them about now and then, so that they may be done all over alike, you need not be deprived of a baked potato for the want of an oven." (Ibid., 71)

A separate section on sickroom cookery suggested beef tea and chicken or mutton broth strained through a clean cloth as a suitable diet for invalids. Francatelli's list of ingredients offered variety for the recovering patient, whom the cook might tempt with oatmeal, groats, blancmange, and Iceland moss jelly. Advice on a single-serving bread pudding concluded reassuringly that any pudding constituted safe food for even the most delicate patient.

In addition to his classic cooking manual, Francatelli compiled *The Modern Cook: A Practical Guide to the Culinary Art in All Its Branches* (1845), containing 1,462 recipes, including French, German, and Italian dishes and Indian curry. This publication was followed by *French Cookery* (1846) and *Cook's Guide, & Housekeeper's & Butler's Assistant: A Practical Treatise on English & Foreign Cookery in All Its Branches* (1864). *The Royal Confectioner: English & Foreign. A Practical Treatise on the Art of Confectionary*

in All Its Branches (1862) he illustrated lavishly with wood carvings and chromolithography.

After a half-century career of cooking and food, Francatelli died on August 10, 1876 at Eastbourne. His sensible cuisine and emphasis on culinary economy influenced many other chefs, notably, Elena Burman Molokhovets, author of the classic Russian cookbook, *A Gift to Young Housewives* (1861), which included her version of his Calf's Feet Soup à la Windsor.

Further Reading

Francatelli, Charles Elmé. *A Plain Cookery Book for the Working Classes*. London: Bosworth & Harrison, 1999.
Zlotnick, Susan, "Domesticating Imperialism: Curry and Cookbooks in Victorian England," *Frontiers*, 1996, 51–58.

FREDERICK, CHRISTINE McGAFFEY

A pioneer in the science of home economics, Christine McGaffey Frederick contributed to the streamlining of the kitchen for greater efficiency. She was born in Boston on February 6, 1883. After graduation from Northwest Division High School in Chicago, she earned a B.S. from Northwestern University.

As a homemaker and the mother of four, Frederick began a serious study of domestic management. She adapted rooms in the family's Greenlawn, Long Island, home to function as the Applecroft Home Experiment Station, a laboratory laundry and kitchen where she tested household equipment and products. She wrote recipes, compiled pamphlets on household goods, filmed housekeeping procedures, charted food values, and lectured on household efficiency. Before engrossed audiences, she demonstrated how to label drawers and canisters, inventory kitchen and laundry items, plan meals, and schedule work by the week, month, or season.

In 1912, the publisher Edward Bok hired Frederick to write a household column for *Ladies' Home Journal*, then the leading U.S. women's magazine. From a series of articles on home economics she developed a domestic classic, *The New Housekeeping: Efficiency Studies in Home Management* (1913), the first home economics manual for housewives. Her approach to housekeeping grew directly from her own understanding of the complexities of running a home: "In a factory the workers do just one thing. . .and it is easy to standardize one set of operations. But in a home there are dozens, yes, hundreds, of tasks requiring totally different knowledge and movements." (Molesworth 1998) Eager to break with the drudgery of earlier generations of homemakers, she formulated the motto,

"The ideal home life of today unhampered by traditions of the past." (Ibid.)

Frederick broke new ground with *Household Engineering: Scientific Management in the Home* (1915), a study of time and motion that adapted for the home environment the principles of labor crusader Frederick Winslow Taylor, the author of *Principles of Scientific Management* (1911). Among her recommendations for efficiency were small, compact work spaces free of unrelated clutter and arranged for a single task. To reduce wasted motion in the kitchen, she introduced the continuous counter top. To ensure an immaculate, sanitary kitchen, she demanded linoleum flooring and smooth, nonporous tiled wainscoting. For kitchen furniture, she preferred a stove on legs, porcelain- or metal-topped cabinet, wood or enamel table, icebox, and a sink of iron or enameled iron, slate, or soapstone. She emphasized that the cook should work at the center of the room at a well-lit tabletop of enamel, porcelain, or zinc. Unlike traditional wood surfaces, these materials did not absorb grease, contaminants, or odors nor were they flammable.

Frederick's fresh approach impressed the Austrian architect Grete Schütte-Lihotzky and the other European designers who created the mass-produced Frankfurt Kitchen. Her work also influenced the efficiency experts Frank and Lillian Gilbreth, who helped liberate housewives from repetitive tasks. In addition to appearing on radio programs and European tours, Frederick traveled the United States throughout 1917 as a star orator of the Chautauqua circuit.

In Germany, after a translation of *The New Housekeeping* in 1922, many industrial designers followed her lead. Lihotzky and Walter Dexel published *Das Wohnhaus von Heute* (The Dwelling of Tomorrow, 1926), Ludwig Neundörfer brought out *So Wollen Wir Wohnen* (This Is How We Want to Live, 1931), and Bruno Taug, *Die Neue Wohnung: Die Frau als Schöpferin* (The New House: The Woman as Creator, 1928). Manufacturers immediately saw an opportunity to mass-produce residences, furniture, and domestic wares based on the Frederick model.

In addition to writing for *The Delineator, The American Weekly,* and the advertising departments of home products marketers, in 1912 Frederick organized the League of Advertising Women for the purpose of studying false advertising claims. Her study of women's buying habits, *Selling Mrs. Consumer* (1929), advised manufacturers and marketers to provide women with reliable brand-name goods.

Frederick represented women's interests during her inspection of housing projects and efficiency apartments. She collected her thoughts and suggestions in *Efficient Housekeeping or Household Engineering—Scientific Management in the Home* (1925), a publication of Chicago's American School of Home Economics, and *The Ignoramus Book of Housekeeping* (1932). In the former, she set up criteria for purchasing kitchen equipment that included multiple uses, comfort, sound construction, and easy care. One item she considered indispensable was the wheeled tray or tea cart, a versatile piece of equipment that could be placed at right angles or parallel to tables and workstations.

As the study of home economics grew into a science taught at secondary schools and colleges, Frederick reinvented her career numerous times to keep pace with trends and demands. In later years, until retiring at age sixty-four, she worked as a decorating consultant and interior designer. She died in Newport Beach, California.

See also **Home Economics**

Further Reading

Coppens, Linda Miles. *What American Women Did, 1789–1920.* Jefferson, N. C.: McFarland, 2001.

Hoy, Suellen. *Chasing Dirt: The American Pursuit of Cleanliness.* New York: Oxford University Press, 1995.

Sicherman, Barbara, and Carol Hurd Green, eds. *Notable American Women: The Modern Period.* Cambridge, Mass.: Belknap Press, 1980.

FRONTIER KITCHENS

On the world's frontiers, care in gathering, storing, and preparing food is essential to survival. Long before the pioneer era, the first woodsmen and expeditioners made the trek west across the Americas over trailless routes. As military families, civilian guides, wagoneers, and settlers traveled from the urban East Coast to the American West, they left behind settled kitchens, fresh produce, herbs, and dry goods stores. On these long journeys, stocking foodstuffs required foraging, hunting, fishing, and trading. In preparation, they nailed kegs to the wagon bed to hold grease and attached tools to hooks and railings. Along with foodstuffs and bedding, there had to be space for extra oxshoe nails, bolts, tar, turpentine, chain, files and saws, and extra yokes and oxbows to repair the huge hoop-topped Conestoga wagons. Mormon hand-carters, who arrived in the Americas from Britain and Scandinavia, bore their loads in smaller topless vehicles on the great migration between 1856 and 1860.

In addition to homesickness and the jostling of constant travel, pioneers acclimated to campfire cookery and uncertain menus. Most cooked over open fires. According to Dee Brown, women discovered that eggs boiled slower at high altitude and that cooking under a wagon bed in a squall worked best in a closed dutch

Frontier kitchen with cauldron and kettles on an open hearth.

oven. Some kept a johnnycake board for rapid cooking of corn gruel into thin cakes. On dry days, they let down the wagon tailgate, which a single drop-down support held level for cooking and serving meals. Esther Hanna, the eighteen-year-old wife of a minister, complained that such outdoor cookery was trying, especially when cold wind chilled her and blew smoke in her eyes.

Mountain men, who made a living hunting, guiding, trapping, and trading, earned a reputation for uncivilized cookery. Osborne Russell, the author of *Journal of a Trapper or Nine Years in the Rocky Mountains 1834–1843*, described the hot-ash roasting of "a ponderous mass of Buff beef." (Russell 1921, 239-240) The firekeeper struck the amorphous cut of meat with a club to dislodge ash, then hacked out individual servings for diners. As provisions became available, he also served salt pork and hardtack to round out a diet heavy in elk ribs, buffalo tongue and boss-meat from the hump, beaver tail, bear stew, jerky, and pemmican, a native American trail meat preserved in animal intestines.

In the bestselling *The Prairie Traveler: A Hand-Book for Overland Expeditions* (1859), containing advice, maps, and intineraries over the principal routes between the Mississippi River and the Pacific Ocean, army captain Randolph Barnes Marcy lectured wagon train members about the importance of careful planning and packing. He admonished, "It is a good rule to carry nothing more than is absolutely necessary for use upon the journey. One can not expect with the limited allowance of transportation that emigrants usually have,

to indulge in luxuries upon such expeditions." (Marcy 1978, 32)

Marcy's advice spoke graphically of what to expect and how to prepare for it. For cooking, he enumerated staple items needed for the crossing: "150 lbs. of flour, or its equivalent in hard bread; 25 lbs. of bacon or pork, and enough fresh beef to be driven on the hoof to make up the meat component of the ration; 15 lbs. of coffee, and 25 lbs. of sugar; also a quantity of saleratus or yeast powders for making bread, and salt and pepper." (Ibid., 36)

His choices varied from that of Canadian Quaker pioneer Joel Palmer, author of *Journal of Travels over the Rocky Mountains* (1847), who had enumerated a more varied stock of essentials twelve years earlier: "20 lbs of flour, 30 lbs. of pilot bread [hardtack], 75 lbs. of bacon, 10 lbs. of rice, 5 lbs. of coffee, 2 lbs. of tea, 25 lbs. of sugar, 1/2 bushel of dried beans, 1 bushel of dried fruit, 2 lbs. of saleratus [baking soda], 10 lbs. of salt, 1/2 bushel of corn meal; 1 small keg of vinegar." (Williams 1992, n. p.)

To prevent scurvy, Marcy advised travelers who bought no vegetables to carry antiscorbutics, a form of citric acid that was portable, shelf stable, and effective against a potentially deadly weakening of the body's connective tissue from lack of vitamin C. He explained how the user could add sugar and water to the powder to make lemonade. In lieu of prepared citric acid, wild onions, greens, wild grapes, and hemlock leaves were alternatives. Another method mentioned by Dee Brown was the dehydration of fruit leathers, a thin paste of wild plum, apple, or berry purée sieved and dried on platters at a campfire and suspended from wagon beams until needed. Children chewed the sweet pulp like jerky. Reconstitution with water and brown sugar returned the dried fruit to a usable texture for turnovers or a fruit sauce to accompany venison or pork.

To the heavy burden of kitchen staples, Marcy listed the minimum of kitchen ware that should accompany each family's wagon. For six to eight persons, he specified two wrought-iron kettles for boiling meat and making soup, tin plates and a heavy tin coffee-pot and cups with riveted handles, a heavy tin or iron mess pan for mixing bread, and wrought-iron frying and baking pans for roasting coffee and baking bread. For the table, he listed knives, forks, and spoons plus a tin or gutta percha water bucket rather than less reliable wood. Tool kits had to include an ax, hatchet, spade, and mallet for driving picket-pins and slaughtering and disjointing large game. He warned cooks to cork their matches in a bottle to keep them dry.

Daily menus varied with speed of travel, comfort, weather, and the cook's experience with campfire cookery. For rapid departure, pioneers often baked a quick round of biscuits in a dutch oven, filled them with bacon, and tied them in a sack to snack on during the endless roll of the wagons. For maximum use of supplies, the cook could dip dry or hardened bread in pan drippings for hot evening meals. When bacon supplies sprouted bugs, a deep smoking over the fire removed vermin.

For simple meals, trail-side cooks relied on corn meal and parched corn that retained its flavor over the long haul. Corn kernels crushed in a mortar to a coarse consistency and blended with cinnamon, sugar, and water made a tasty mush or porridge. For those travelers fortunate enough to lead a fresh cow behind the wagon, mush and milk nourished children, the elderly, and those convalescing from hard traveling and disease.

For pioneers willing to learn from an alien culture, substitution of Indian foods extended supplies that ran dangerously low on the last leg of the journey. Presbyterian missionary Narcissa Prentiss Whitman, who published *My Journal, 1836*, acquiesed to camas root, the staple northwestern root crop resembling the color and shape of onions and tasting like a sweet roasted fig. In Thomas Jefferson Farnham's *An 1839 Wagon Train Journal*, he reprised the misery of living on hardtack and water and of cooking "trapper's butter," the trail name for marrow boiled in blood and water, and of stuffing animal intestines with tenderloin strips to make "boudies," a prairie sausage that he impaled on twigs to roast over a campfire. (Snodgrass 1997, 276)

Making-do did not stop when the wagons came to rest. In the outback, builders of agrarian cabins, outfitted with corn crib, lean-tos, and poled chicken coop,

made up in fresh goods what they lacked in convenience shopping at local grocery stores and dry goods dealerships. Yet, life in cabins, ranch houses, and forts was little better than the gypsy existence on the trail. As chronicler William Worthington Fowler observed in *Woman on the American Frontier* (1876), "Everything ministers to the useful; nothing to the beautiful." (Fowler 1976, 187).

See also **Mining Camp Kitchens; Oilcloth; Pemmican**

Further Reading

Fowler, William W. *Woman on the American Frontier.* Williamstown, Mass.: Corner House Publishers, 1976.
Russell, Osborne. *Journal of a Trapper or Nine Years in the Rocky Mountains 1834–1843.* Boise, Ida.: Syms-York, 1921.
Williams, Jacqueline, "Food on the Oregon Trail," *Overland Journal*, Vol. 11, 1993.

FRUIT

The preparation and preservation of fruit permeate kitchen history, whether for use as a staple food, snack, recipe ingredient, or propitiatory gift to the gods. Evidence from Ch-k'ou-tien, China, indicates that Peking Man cracked nuts and consumed berries during the Pleistocene Age, some 1,600,000 years ago.

Fruit may have been a serendipitous find for prehistoric humans, who valued it as a food in much the same way as their fruit-eating simian ancestors. Wild berries grew in juicy, tantalizing clumps ripe for the taking and ready to eat without preparation or cooking. The edible varieties ranged from the more common strawberry, raspberry, blueberry, and blackberry to the serviceberry, chokecherry, hawthorn, currant, haw, rose hip, buffaloberry, and bilberry. In a time when food supplies were precarious, even children and the elderly were capable of picking berries, thus contributing to the group's survival.

Versatile Food

The early written record of kitchen history documents the versatility of fruit as a foodstuff. Around 8000 BCE, Mesopotamians revered the date palm as a magical tree of life. They ate its fruit compressed into patties, dried, and fermented into wine and crushed the pits to extract oil or to stir into a hot drink. The Mesopotamians also cultivated pears and apples, which later grew in the gardens of the Egyptians, Chinese, Indians, and early Swiss and Celts. The Hittites planted pear orchards. The Chinese began growing apricot and jujube stock in 2200 BCE and peaches even earlier.

Boxes of freshly harvested oranges line the space between orange trees. [© *Courtesy of Agricultural Research Service, USDA. USDA Photo, Charles O'Rear.*]

From the East, these succulent fruits spread west to Persia, Assyria, Babylonia, and the Mediterranean basin. Dates appear to have originated in Assyria and Babylonia and appear in the Ur writings of 2050 BCE and were depicted in a later palace frieze. The Anatolians and early Swiss favored the wild grape, which graced the Western Hemisphere garden by 1800 BCE.

Along the eastern end of the Mediterranean, fruit took on a lasting domestic and social significance. Dried fruit, since prehistoric times a treasured food and source of sweetener and juice, was one of the area's lasting food industries. Tutankhamun, who ruled Egypt from 1370 to 1352 BCE, appears to have enjoyed grape juice and went to his tomb with a jar of it among his burial treasures. After 1304 BCE, Ramses II's garden sported pomegranate trees. Egyptian tomb urns contained cherries and mulberries to nourish the dead on their long journey to the underworld. Early Palestinians dried grapes into raisins for snacks and adding to cooked grain.

The Romans dried and preserved grapes in fig leaves and reduced grape and raisin juice into *caroenum, defrutum, passum,* and *sapa,* essential culinary syrups and sweeteners that were shipped around the Mediterranean world in amphorae. For its Armenian origins, they called the peach the *armeniaca.* According to the Roman encyclopedist Pliny the Elder, author of *Natural History* (ca. 77 BCE) in 74 BCE, Lucullus introduced the pontine cherry as a spoil of war. Up to that time, it had been the private stock of the Scythians who considered the cherry tree a prized personal possession and the source of *aschy* (cherry juice).

The variety and abundance of fruit in ancient times is obvious from its frequent mention in anthropological studies and folklore and depiction in murals and mosaics.

Australasian fruit fanciers appear to have domesticated the banana, which had previously been too seedy for eating. It recurred as food in Malaysia, where Pacific islanders added bananas to local gardens. Anatolians at Catal Hüyük (or Hoyük) cooked apple dishes around 6500 BCE. At other Turkish sites plum trees were common.

Citrus fruits, late arrivals to the Old World's fruit stock, grew in eastern Asia as early as 2400 BCE. Lemons and limes grown in India were kitchen garden fruit; Arabians transported citrons overland from the Medes and dwellers on the Fertile Crescent to Greece. Oranges were a Chinese favorite and served as an ambassadorial entrée in Burma after 300 CE. In the Roman Empire, where actual citrus fruit was a rarity, depictions of the fruits often appeared in the decorative friezes of dining rooms. Also late to arrive in Rome were quinces and peaches, which traveled from the Orient to Italy, where they flourished after 100 CE. After 618 CE, the beginning of the Tang dynasty, the pharmacologist Meng Shen began a trend toward imperial hothouses and orchards to add to the royal diet fresh ginger, kumquats, loquats, persimmons, star anise, winter melon, calamondin, and star fruit.

The notion that all tropical islands produced ample varieties of fruit is a misconception. When Chief Hawaii-Loa led the first settlers 2,400 miles from the Marquesas to the Society Islands in 450 CE, they found Hawaii blessed with fish, seaweed, birds, and foliage but no fruit or carbohydrates. The introduction of stock from Polynesian islands to the west was a propitious marriage with a temperate climate and fertile land. It was from these Marquesan voyagers that the Hawaiians acquired stock of taro and breadfruit, coconut palms, yams, sugarcane, mountain apple, pineapple, candlenut, arrowroot, and *awa* or *kava*. To these, they added the sweet potato from South America. In the first quarter of the nineteenth century, the amateur agronomist Francisco de Paula Marin planted a host of additional vegetables, orchard fruits, and grapes to the island through slips he obtained from friendly ships' captains calling in at island ports.

Around most of the eastern Mediterranean, the fig found favor in palace grounds, oases, and humble gardens because of its versatile food uses. Like dates and grape must, figs were a popular trade item of North African and Syrian sailors. Among the Saharan Berbers of Algeria and Niger, nomads and their mounts subsisted on desert grasses, vegetables, and fruits, including mulberries, dates, and dwarf palm fruit. At the Qafsah (or Gafsa) oasis north of the Shore of Palms in southern Tunisia, in the 1400s, the caliph of Egypt irrigated gardens and planted apricots, dates, figs, lemons, oranges, peaches, and pomegranates to supply his kasbah, the far western outpost of the Hafsid realm.

In the Western Hemisphere, the cave dwellers of Tamaulipas, Mexico, gathered sweet red cactus fruit called prickly pear or tuna in 7000 BCE. Peruvian gatherers prized guava, avocado, caigua, pineapple, wild plums, juicy *pepino*, globular papaya or pawpaw, sweet *algarroba* pods, *pacae* seeds, and a pome fruit know as *lucuma*. Navaho cooks prepared cactus fruit by boiling, drying, jelling, pickling, pulping, roasting, and serving raw as chewing gum. The Cheyenne cooked a gravy from wild sand plums and chokecherries, which they split, crushed, and pounded for sun-drying in patties. To simplify the job of gathering cactus fruit, the Tohono O'odham of the Sonoran Desert carried *kuibits*, harvest sticks that they used to dislodge fruit from the tall saguaro.

Raw and Cooked

The formal addition of fruit to cuisine introduced new flavors, aromas, and textures to meals heavy in grains, fish, and red meat. In addition to barley, semolina, and other grains, cooks varied the medieval Islamic diet with dates and other dried fruit, especially in wealthy households. Late in the eleventh century, Abu'Ubayd al-Bakri, a Cordoban geographer and minister at the court of Seville, described the Arab Mediterranean lifestyle in *Kitab al-masalik wa'l-mamalik* (Book of Highways and of Kingdoms, ca. 1090). Writing of the diet of Ifriqiya, the period name for Tunis, he names fine table fruits — black figs, citrons, grapes, sugar cane, pomegranates, quince, jujubes, and oranges, all fertilized with night soil (human waste). A favorite in Morocco, Algiers, and Tunis was the preserved lemon,

a cooking staple prepared by cutting lemons into wedges, immersing them in a solution of lemon juice, olive oil, and salt, and sealing them in a jar.

Europeans were fermenting fruit juice into *bjórr* in eleventh- and twelfth-century Scandinavia, Iceland, Greenland, and England. Viking servers refilled wood and pottery cups with fruit beverage as a symbol of hospitality. To the south, the Italian food writer Platina's *De Honesta Voluptate et Valitudine* (On Right Pleasure and Health, 1475) devoted much space to fruit cookery. Drawing on Apicius, Pliny, Columella, and other Roman authorities, Platina wrote, "There is an order to be observed in taking food, since everything that moves the bowels and whatever is of light and slight nourishment, like apples and pears, is more safely and pleasantly eaten in the first course." (Platina 1999, 17) He was particularly fond of grapes, of which he said, "Preserved in jars and taken out to eat, they arouse appetite in the stomach." (Ibid., 28)

According to the English antiquarian Thomas Wright's *Domestic Manners and Sentiments in England during the Middle Ages* (1862), the medieval English depended on fruit, especially cherries. Their taste for fruit is obvious in the number of recipes found in early cooking manuals and still room books. In some recipes, apples and pears were the highlights of the dish; in meat stuffings and casseroles, fruits such as currants and raisins added flavor, nutrients, and texture. For dried fruits, cooks purchased stock imported from the Middle East. Pears provided the basis for perry, the equivalent of pear cider; sloes and plums could be fermented into *prunellé;* murrey, or *muré*, was the fermented juice of blackberries or mulberries.

The main problem in keeping the table supplied with fruit was its rapid desiccation and spoilage occurring during transport, sale, and storage. In the 1700s, while the Tepehuan of Chihuahua, Mexico, saved their apple crops in crude log bins topped with loose timbers, Europeans were building glass-paned hothouses for the cultivation of exotic fruits from warmer climates. The development of greenhouse culture provided a supply of oranges, grapes, cherries, strawberries, and nectarines where previously only apples and hardy pears had been available.

New World Orchards

In the early days of the United States, the immediate establishment of apple orchards from seedlings in New England and the mid-Atlantic states assured the apple a place of distinction in the American kitchen. Children busied themselves gathering baskets of fruit and pushing cloves into apples and rolling them in ground nutmeg and cinnamon to make fragrant pomanders for deodorizing musty closets and pantries. To provide the household with cider, families erected mills on a steep incline so the apples entered the top story on the upper side and departed in liquid form into a wagon on a lower floor. After pressing and sealing the amber liquid in barrels, the beverage maker listened for the bubble and hiss of fermentation, called the "singing of the cider." (Ulrich 1991, 23) Table and cooking quality cider reached the height of alcoholic content at five percent; alehouses served a headier, seven-percent brew.

In addition to inexpensive cider, which cooks served in homes and at church socials, schools, and colleges, daily fare abounded with apple dishes such as apple slump, apple pan dowdy, apple dumplings, apple tart, apple cider boiled with mash to make apple butter, and mess, or puff, apple pie. For a "stirring" of apple butter, Illinois women worked over a communal copper kettle set up outdoors atop a log fire. (Algren 1992, 32) They boiled cider, dropped in peeled apple chunks, and took turns stirring with huge ladles as long as timbers. When the mix was ready for storage, they topped it off with clove oil, then sealed it in sterile jars for storage in fruit cellars. As demonstrated in *The Farmers' Cabinet: Devoted to Agriculture, Horticulture and Rural Economy* (1839), a compendium published by John Libby of Philadelphia, apple recipes characterized the neighborly custom among Pennsylvania Dutch of hosting an apple butter party to make a table spread "very much superior to any thing that comes under the name of apple sauce." (Franklin 1997, 8)

In the nineteenth century, several published kitchen guides assisted homemakers in storing fresh fruit. One method of preserving apples appears in Dr. Anthony Florian Willich's *Domestic Encyclopedia* (1804), a familiar English home and farm handbook that Philadelphia editor James Mease adapted for American readers. The text advises drying a glazed crock and lining the bottom with pebbles. By layering apples and mortaring a headboard into place over the mouth, the householder could keep out light, air, mold, and insects, while juice collected at bottom.

Elena Burman Molokhovets, author of the classic Russian cookbook, *A Gift to Young Housewives* (1861), offered numerous methods for storing plums, fruit drinks, and preserved lemons in icehouses and sand pits. She nestled apples into oakum or tow fiber and kept bunches of grapes sealed in glass jars of water in a second-floor room she turned into a storage space for the purpose. The method necessitated constant monitoring and immediate removal of any moldy grapes to keep rot from spreading. To address the problem of moisture in the storeroom, she brought in barrels of quicklime or slaked lime, a compound that removed humidity from the air. A simpler method used

a century later in Bulgaria, according to food ethnologist Lilija Radeva, the author of "Traditional Methods of Food Preserving among the Bulgarians" (1988), consisted of harvesting grape clusters, hardening their cut ends with beeswax, and hanging the bunches in a cool draft.

As the American Civil War and its aftermath wrought chaos on markets, many Americans sought to grow their own fruit. The novelist Harriet Beecher Stowe retired to Mandarin, Florida, to raise oranges, which some homemakers, comparing their bitterness to that of quinine, purchased to treat malaria. On the treeless plains, families treasured creek banks thick with wild plums and spent much of the year yearning for native fruit. To establish their own fruit gardens, they planted spindly fruit stock. Longing for the fruit pies of the East Coast, settlers in Illinois invented the vinegar pie. The filling, a custard blended from cider vinegar, molasses, water, nutmeg, and flour, was a springtime favorite until new orchards began setting apples.

Parallel fruit traditions permeated Europe. In Italy cooks fermented pomegranate and grape juice into wines and vinegars. Before Zadar, Dalmatia, became Zara, Italy, its cherry brandy carried the Italian name *maraschino*. To the northeast in Bulgaria, Yuletide delicacies consisted of sponge fingers served with cherry, raspberry, and apricot compote laced with dessert wine or sauterne. The Yugoslavian variation topped strawberries and peaches with white or red wine. French cooks prepared *fruits confits au vinaigre* (fruit preserved in vinegar), a popular condiment served with meats.

In the late nineteenth century, American homemakers began to learn of exotic new fruits such as coconuts, bananas, and pineapples. The selection of fresh fruits in grocery stores increased as transportation and packaging improved and advertising built demand. For the elite and the social climber, fruit became a symbol of luxury. In F. Scott Fitzgerald's novel *The Great Gatsby* (1925), the narrator, Nick Carraway, observes the preparations for one of the lavish weekend parties hosted by his mysterious millionaire neighbor, Jay Gatsby: "Every Friday five crates of oranges and lemons arrived from a fruiterer in New York—every Monday these same oranges and lemons left his back door in a pyramid of pulpless halves. There was a machine in the kitchen which could extract the juice of two hundred oranges in half an hour, if a little button was pressed two hundred times by a butler's thumb." (Fitzgerald 1992, 43–44)

To meet the needs of this growing appetite for fruit, a huge U.S. market developed for native stock. Just as Nellie Aldridge had boosted the citrus groves of San Bernardino, California, with *Nellie Aldridge's*

FRUIT

National Orange Show Cookbook (1928), four years later, Jack Shepherd promoted the avocado, a strange fruit that puzzled home cooks but had at one time provided sailors with a creamy spread for sea biscuit that the men dubbed "sailor's butter." To replace the peculiar name by which Floridians knew the fruit—avocado—California growers held a contest to come up with a separate label for West Coast varieties. Chosen as the winner was "calavo," a moniker that preserved some of the Latino mystique of a fruit introduced to North America from Central America. The California cooperative issued a pamphlet, *The New Calavo Hostess Book* (1932), which touted such dishes as calavo on the half-shell, calavonnaise, calavo-strawberry pie, and calavo ice cream.

Women's magazines of the 1920s and 1930s cited fruits by brand name, e.g., Dole pineapple, Chiquita bananas, Sealdsweet Florida oranges and grapefruit, Sunsweet prunes, and Sunkist lemons, oranges, and grapefruit. In an era obsessed with vitamins and health regimens, Sunkist's advertising cited medical authorities, who testified that citrus fruit was the best source of vitamin C and remedy for acidosis. Full-color ads fattened the cook's stock of recipes with cooking and serving ideas, such as Ocean Spray cranberry sauce sliced and cut into hearts and flowers for bridge luncheons, bridal showers, and wedding receptions.

In the late twentieth century, the fruit industry established in Hawaii a century before continued to thrive. Island farms grew more than 360 different varieties of fruits. One plant grower and breeder, Frank Sekiya, credited the beginnings of his interest in fruit propagation to the avocado tree growing in his mother's yard in 1970. As an agronomist in adulthood, he propagated and grafted fruit at his nursery in southeastern Oahu. His stock ranged from the familiar lemon, mango, guava, tangerine, papaya, banana, and pineapple to exotica such as the lychee, sapodilla, jackfruit, rambutan, kasturi, durian, and Indonesian *gnetum*. A favorite of Filipino- and Vietnamese-descended islanders was the longsat; Hawaiians of Chinese ancestry preferred its kin, the longan. To increase his production of Asian specialties, Sekiya made annual trips to Thailand, Indonesia, Taiwan, Brunei, Sumatra, or the Philippines in search of stock.

Improving on Nature

In the 1980s and 1990s, horticulturists and growers introduced new strains of fruits that offered consumers more sweetness and juice, crisper texture, and longer storage life. Genetic advances armed fruit-bearing trees and plants with resistance to many pests, among them brown rot, fire blight, fusarium wilt, red stele

fungus, and anthracnose. Hybridizers developed varieties of citrus fruits, grapes, peaches, blueberries, raspberries, and strawberries that grow in colder climates. New varieties of oranges and grapefruits can be pre-peeled with food-grade enzymes, which remove the bitter white portion and shorten preparation time. Commercial fruit processors have enhanced the levels of beta carotene and vitamin A in citrus fruits and created a cold water bath with citric acid to protect ready-to-eat varieties during marketing. One innovation, the Charleston gray watermelon, had a harder rind than others on the market and a more uniform oblong shape that stacked and shipped more easily.

In 2001, Japanese fruit growers offered homemakers a new convenience: cube-shaped watermelons. To suit their produce to the average home refrigerator, farmers in Zentsuji on the island of Shikoku began forcing melons into a boxy shape in glass molds, which admitted sunlight to enhance sweetness. The unusual fruit, which Japanese markets sold at $82 each, or more than five times the normal price, solved the problem of refrigerating an awkward oblong fruit without wasting space.

Around this same time, fruit growers in Jiangxi Province in eastern China produced a strain of miniature watermelons that were much in demand. Using cultivation technology from Guangdong Province, they produced the small fruits by a labor-intensive method—suspending each green ovule in a string bag to reduce contact with the ground. The wee striped watermelons—which cost less to ship than ordinary ones but brought double the price—decorated tables and platters at business luncheons and receptions in Guangdong, Hong Kong, and Macao.

While plant breeders and growers in Asia were busy re-making the melon, scientists in New Zealand identified seedless varieties of apples, including the Wellington Bloomless, Spencer Seedless, and Rae Ime. Although small and low in quality, these seedless fruits earned greater returns for growers because consumers were willing to pay more for them.

An Appetite Undimmed by Time

Twenty-first century households keep fruit handy for snacks, cooking, jams and jellies, and the pleasure of seeing their opulent colors in a glass compote dish or basket. Kitchen gardeners in Japan grow *kaki* (persimmon), a tasty but astringent fruit, as well as *nashi* (pear). Sicilians often serve *granita di lemone* (lemon ice) in hollowed out orange or lemon peels. Italians enjoy the colorful end-of-meal *macedonia di frutta*, know to the French as *macédoine*, an attractive arrangement of sliced fruit dotted with berries and grapes, sweetened with raisins and steeped in natural fruit juices during brief refrigeration. For impact at presentation, they serve the melange in a glistening crystal or cut-glass bowl and topped with wine and a sprinkle of sugar. The dish takes its name from the medley of cultures that permeated Macedonia during the residency of Alexander the Great. In South Africa, fruit often comes to the table in the form of kabobs, consisting of fresh melon, pineapple, lime, and papaya spiked on acacia thorns or twigs.

Innovative gadgets continued to aid cooks in preparing fruit. In the late 1990s, one manufacturer introduced a storage system composed of washable polyester pouches designed to cradle individual pieces of fruit until they were ready to be eaten. Free circulation of air prevented spoilage as the fabric column hung in kitchen or pantry. To the delight of pie makers and eaters, a hand-operated cherry stoner with spring-loaded steel plunger, quickly separated pit from fruit, retained pits in a plastic cup, and ejected the pulp into a bowl. Electric dehydrators sped the natural drying process.

See also **Bananas; Canning; Coconut; Parers; Pineapple**

Further Reading

Jenkins, Virginia Scott. *Bananas: An American History.* Washington, D. C.: Smithsonian Institution, 2000.

Marsh, Dorothy B., "Simple Ways Are the Best Ways of Cooking Fresh Fruits," *Good Housekeeping*, October 1930, 92–93, 288.

McPhee, John. *Oranges.* New York: Farrar, Straus and Giroux, 1967.

Yim, Susan, "Bearing Fruit," *Islands*, November 2000, 50–56.

FRYING

A late addition to kitchen technique after the advent of barbecuing, roasting, boiling, and stewing, frying is a traditional method of adding flavor to foods. As described by the French writer on gastronomy Jean Anthelme Brillat-Savarin in his classic *Physiologie du Gout* (The Physiology of Taste, 1825), deep frying in fat or oil forms a casing or shell around food. While sealing out the cooking fat, the shell seals in juices and flavor and allows the interior to cook to doneness.

Once discovered, the flavor secret of frying augmented the blander taste of boiled meals in the ancient world. In pharaonic Egypt, cooks fried white lotus and possibly papyrus root. According to the book of Leviticus, around 600 BCE Hebrew cooks pan-fried foods in vegetable oil. In Roman kitchens, the *sartago,* or fry pan, offered a flat surface for general sautéing but the technique never gained favor among cooks, who preferred saucing to crispy exteriors. In the Republican era, cooks developed the asymmetric *scriblita* (fritter), a free-form doughnut that Cato mentioned in the second century BCE. A specialized Roman egg fryer contained indentations for cooking four eggs simultaneously.

Four Chinese Styles

Chinese culinary records from the Han dynasty (206 BCE to 220 CE) credit native cooks with evolving four styles of frying: (1) *chao* (stir frying), frying at high temperature in little oil while stirring constantly, a technique that demanded the most skill and diligence, as timing, proportions, and maintenance of even heat were crucial; (2) *chien,* or sautéing—gently browning

Man frying food in Pushkar, India.
[© Vittorio Sciosia.]

251

Medieval trivet for a frying pan.

in oil—was the traditional method of readying *jin dui* (sweet rice dumplings) for New Year's Day; (3) *pon*, frying with sauce, was a variation of *chao* with sauce replacing oil; and (4) *tsa* (deep frying), the searing of dry ingredients in two inches of very hot oil, a method that crisped meat, poultry, and shrimp that had previous been steamed or simmered.

The *chao* style, which influenced European, African, and American cookery in the late twentieth century, was originally a thrift measure. In China, where fuel was scarce and expensive, rapid frying over high heat saved time and fuel while preserving the maximum amounts of nutrients and flavor of delicate vegetables, seafood, and meats. It made its first inroad into American cookery in 1900, when Viceroy Li Hung Chang cooked chop suey for visitors to his embassy home in Washington, D.C.

Stir-frying was a dramatic art requiring skill at organizing foodstuffs by density and size. The cook first seasoned a round-bowled wok, heated plain or salted oil or broth, and quickly placed uniformly cut bite-sized pieces of food into a single layer at the center of the wok for sautéing. Cooks blanched clams and mussels to open them before frying. Vegetables had to be dry but not desiccated; a modicum of liquid was necessary, as it gradually turned to steam and enhanced the cooking process. The development of *wok hei* (wok air), the rhythms of rocking or maneuvering the wok on its steel ring, indicated command of Asian cooking technique and assuredness in quick cooking over high heat.

Fried Treats of Earlier Times

Frying methods and recipes were among the world's most common trade items. The geographer and encyclopedist 'Ali al-Masu'di, well-traveled in India and China and the author of *Muruj al-Thahab wa al-Ma'adin al-Jawahir* (Meadows of Gold and Mines of Precious Stones, ca. 946 CE), praised *sanbusaj*, a pastry fried in oil and smeared with mustard. The Ottoman Turks acquired the *börek* (fried pastry) before 990 CE from Bugra Khan, who ruled in Turkistan. The khan made his savory pie from eggs fried inside leafy-thin sheets of dough similar to Chinese wonton wraps. The Algerians, Tunisians, and Moroccans adapted the pastry, substituting their own ingredients. Similarly, other foods migrated across national boundaries. The deep-fried Arab *sifanj* (doughnut) was the origin of the Sicilian *sfinci*, hawked in the streets of Palermo around 1298, according to the public registrar Adamo de Citella.

In Renaissance times, English cooks made *cryspeys*, a kind of funnel cake, by streaming a runny yeast batter from their fingers into hot fat; the cooked pastries, still hot, received a sprinkle of sugar. In Sicily, the creation of *scuma* (foam), a super-light pasta, demanded controlled temperature. After cooking the delicate strands for an instant in boiling water, the pasta maker wound them on a fork, dipped them in an egg and crumb batter, and fried them in boiling lard. A holdover from the *cucina baronale* (baronial kitchen), crispy *scuma* paired well with chopped pistachios and orange blossom honey. The *scuma* nests also made handy baskets for serving tidbits of chicken, a seventeenth-century specialty revived by Giovanni Messina, chef to the Conte Tasca d'Almerita.

Platina, author of *De Honesta Voluptate et Valitudine* (On Right Pleasure and Health, 1475), opened Book IX of his compendium with an explanation of the etymology of the word *fritter*, which he claimed was a derivative of the Latin *frictus* (fried). His recipes for fried bits made from elderberry, cheese, sour milk, rice, sage, apple, laurel, and almond suggest his delight in frying. The text description of sweet almond and

FRYING

raisin fritters concludes with putting the dough in a fish-shaped mold and frying the fritter-fish in hot oil.

The European version of *tempura*, an eighteenth-century Japanese frying style requiring a light coating, apparently originated in the Florentine kitchens of the Italian gourmet Catherine de' Médicis, who introduced fried foods in France. The technique passed to Japan through Portuguese traders.

In the open-hearth cookery of Europe, meats were typically grilled or fried, but the cooking method did not become widely popular until the advent of cast iron cooking pots, skillets, and griddles. To facilitate monitoring of fried foods for doneness, the Spanish devised the *sartén*, a terra cotta fry pan. The French invented the *grille,* a meshed holder that the cook could lift partially or completely from hot fat for visual evidence of crispness. One French recipe called for *choucroute* (sauerkraut) to be fried in rendered duck or goose fat, a local specialty that added savor to the vegetable. The first British fry pan was patented in 1839, long after the invention of a Continental model.

American Fries

In the Americas, native cooks used the fat of passenger pigeons for deep frying. Father Jacques Marquette, who visited the Peoria of the Mississippi Valley in 1673, relished the native cooking of *sagamité*, a cake of cornmeal blended with berries and fried in bear grease. A favorite fritter for early plains and desert Indians was a batter of piñon or pinyon nuts and water patted into cakes and fried on a duma, a heated cooking stone. The Inca of western South America and the Caribbean Taino enjoyed fried *batatas* (potatoes).

The fry pan accompanied settlers on their westward journey. In *America Eats* (1992), the U.S. writer and food historian Nelson Algren related a legend concerning a wagon train crossing Kansas in frontier days. The travelers decided to split into two groups but did not have enough cookware to supply both companies with a pot and a frying pan. To divvy up the implements, they counted off people who preferred ashcake to boiled dumplings. Those choosing the former left with the skillet. The remainder continued on their way with the dumpling pot.

The frying pan was a treasured item for troops in the American Civil War. As Union veteran Charles E. Davis, Jr., explained in *Three Years in the Army: The Story of the Thirteenth Massachusetts Volunteers* (1894), the one-dollar cost of a frying pan was more than most soldiers could afford. To purchase such an extravagance, five men contributed 20 cents each toward a single pan and shared its use. For those who had no cash, half of a discarded canteen fitted with a whittled wood handle had to suffice. In 1864, the U.S. Patent Office registered the first American model, which featured ridges on the cooking surface to separate meat from pan drippings. When food supplies ran low, Union cooks specialized in skillygalee, a mush of water-soaked hardtack fried in pork fat.

Manufacturing innovations in the late nineteenth century added to the assortment of frying vessels on the market. An ingenious item described in the F. A. Walker Catalog around 1875 was the bouche iron, a turned wood handle attached at right angles to a crimped, fluted, corrugated, or cylindrical iron form. By dipping the form into hot fat and plunging it into batter, the pastry maker could shape and cook individual pastry cups, called coffins, to be filled with custard, curd, or fruit purée.

A more demanding task than pan searing was the frying of crullers, potatoes, fritters, or doughnuts, also called *oly koeks* among the Dutch settlers, according to Washington Irving's *Knickerbocker's History of New York* (1809). These treats needed careful minding while they simmered in deep fat in a frying kettle or Dutch oven. In place of the long-handled turning fork, which pierced the exterior of cooking foods, some cooks chose a bird's nest basket, a pair of long-handled nested baskets, or a deep-fat fryer, an open wire or slotted tin basket that fit into a stovetop or electric fry pot.

Invented in the 1940s and marketed as the Dormeyer Fri-well and Dula's Fryryte, the thermostatically controlled stovetop fry-cooker put an end to the problems of flame-ups and overdone food. These devices also allowed cooks to save and re-use their cooking oil. In 1953, the Sunbeam aluminum automatic fry pan removed the process from the stovetop to the kitchen counter, thus freeing a burner for other dishes. The introduction of nonstick coatings in 1956 simplified the messy job of removing burned-on crust from steel and aluminum frying pans.

Ethnic Favorites

For both flavor and speed, frying remains a standard culinary cooking method in kitchens worldwide, from the island of Kiribati in the western Pacific Ocean, where fritters are a popular dish, to the fish-and-chips pubs of England and Wales. Fried foods are menu staples throughout the West Indies. Street cooks serve up fried jack fish on St. Vincent, shark slices in a puffed fritter in Trinidad, *pastelitos* (filled pastries) in the Dominican Republic, breakfast slices of flying fish on Barbados, and plantain chips throughout the Caribbean. Chinese and Japanese cooks value starch derived from the kudzu vine, which produces an alkaline flour for dredging foods for deep frying, resulting in a crisp, snowy crust. On the Trans-Siberian Railway, Chinese dining-car cooks quick-fry meat, fish, and vegetables to add to low-cost meals of fried rice.

Kashmiri cooks collect fresh lotus root from lakes and grate it to make spicy balls deep-fried in a wok. Bulgarian cooks make *kufteta* by frying a patty made of minced meat and breadcrumbs. Guatemalans enjoy fried plantains served with honey and cream. In Botswana, families dine on tea and cakes of deep-fried dough at breakfast and lunch. Uruguayan cooks deep fry *arepa*, thick corn pancakes that they serve with meat and cheese or butter. Another variety holds minced meat stewed with olives, raisins, and potatoes. Gabonese eat *beignets*, French doughnuts also popular in New Orleans; Chileans make *sopaipillas* (fritters), a similar treat, from deep-fried pumpkin dough and a sprinkle of sugar. In addition to breakfast porridge, Gambians like an early morning fry of *accara* (bean flour).

State of the Art

Early in the twenty-first century, frying pans, along with woks, griddles, tongs, and basket-shaped spider ladles, continued to command much of the kitchenware market. Manufacturers introduced pans in cast iron and cast aluminum designed expressly for omelet making and sautéing. The Teflon-coated fry pan put an end to centuries of scrubbing. Innovations in design and materials made deep fryers easier to clean and less messy to Use than previous generations of kitchen equipment. One kitchenware manufacturer even introduced an appliance that deep fried without oil.

See also **Cookware; Kitchen Business; Maillard Reaction; Street Food; Teflon**

Further Reading

Aubaile-Sallenave, Françoise, "Frying," *Slow Food*, April–June 1997.

Derven, Daphne, "Cooking with Fire," *Whole Earth*, Winter 1999, 50–52.

"Focus on Frypans," *Consumer Reports*, February 2001, 52–53.

G

GALLEY

The galley, or kitchen of a ship—and later, of an airplane and space craft—which is the source of meals for both passengers and crew, has evolved over the centuries into a streamlined space. Although confined, it may be equipped with as many or more conveniences as the most efficient home kitchen. It was not always so, however. In fact, early ships had no cooking facilities, and the amenities of travel by water were few.

Ancient Galleys

Transportation by ship began in Egypt and Mesopotamia before 3000 BCE. According to the *Argonautica* (235 BCE), a Greek journey legend by the poet Apollonius of Rhodes, the sailors who accompanied Jason to the Black Sea in search of the golden fleece rowed in an open boat for days at a time. The crew got a two-day respite when they beached the ship, built fires on shore, and roasted meat. A later work, Fa-Hsien's *Travels* (406 CE), described how Chinese sailors grew fresh ginger in pots on deck to stir into their cook pots and steep into hot beverages.

In classical Greece and Rome, ships' crewmen were obliged to fend for themselves. Thirsty sailors obtained small amounts of drinking water by holding a sponge over a pot of boiling seawater. In Roman times, passengers booking space aboard freighters received no provisions other than fresh water, which the captain rationed. Travelers slept on the open deck and brought their own slaves to prepare food on the galley hearth,

which might include a firebox and an iron grill encased in tile to limit the hazard of deck fire.

More completely outfitted was the galley of a Byzantine ship that sank after striking a reef off Yassiada Island between Turkey and Cos. Exploring the wreckage, archaeologists noted that the cook stored provisions in terra cotta pantry canisters and drew water from *pithoi* (jars) located on the opposite side of the deck from the kitchen. At a tiled hearth under the vented roof, they found mortar and pestle, twenty-one cook pots, two cauldrons, and a copper baking pan. A store of copper and bronze pitchers, ceramic amphorae, and fine redware plates and dishes attested to the quality of food service at sea.

When Danes from Scandinavia and northeast Germany swept westward into Britain and Labrador, they rowed open boats that lacked galleys. The sailors' wives supplied the craft with butter, cheese, herbed mead, and fermented whey drinks. In England seagoing insurgents against the Danes built so-called Dane towers, square stone keeps constructed near the shore and fitted with rough shelving to hold ships' provisions such as grain, smoked beef, and rashers of wild pig.

Limited Fare

During the Crusades, armies punctuated the lengthy round trip from Venice to Joppa with frequent stops for the loading of fresh water, meat, and bread. Captains promised travelers wine and water twice daily along with hot meat and *bizcocho,* or ship biscuit, a

GALLEY

coarse, flat wafer later called hardtack, sea bread, or pilot bread. The purser allotted two barrels of wine and one of water per passenger. Supplementing the limited galley fare were travelers' own stores of cheese, eggs, figs and raisins, ginger, bacon, pepper and saffron, cloves and mace, and wine. They kept food in a chest that could also hold a small cauldron, fry pan, and grater, along with platters, dishes, and cups. A favorite cooking device was the conjurer, a tiny stove fueled by small amounts of oil. The lucky traveler would also manage a deck-top cage of hens and enough seed to feed them until landing.

The Dominican friar Felix Fabri of Ulm, author of *The Wanderings of Felix Fabri* (1483), described the food service on a Venetian cargo ship bound for Palestine. According to Fabri, ships' captains agreed to twenty-four articles of good faith, including the pledge to provide passengers with two meals a day. One article listed the specific foods to be provided: bread and sea biscuit, wine and pure water, meat, eggs, and other foodstuffs. Writing of his second pilgrimage from Germany to Mt. Sinai, Fabri confided that he pitied the ship's four ill-tempered cooks, who had to suffer the miseries of a narrow kitchen where many dishes had to fit over one small flame.

Renaissance-era sailing came at a price for the sailor who liked to eat well. Aboard the *Pinta, Nina*, and *Santa Maria* in 1492, Christopher Columbus's crew received the barest minimum of cooking space at a simple firebox topped with a hood to shield it from the wind. On a pilgrimage two years later, Peter Casola, author of *Viaggio a Gerusalemme* (Voyage to Jerusalem, 1494), noted that cheese makers in Candia, Crete, supplied galleys with feta cheese, a Greek staple, to provide a quick, uncomplicated source of protein during long sea trips when meat was scarce.

That the diet of the English sailor improved in the seventeenth century may be presumed from the writings of Henry Teonge, ship's chaplain on the HMS *Assistance,* who celebrated Twelfth Night at sea in 1676. He described the enjoyment with which the crew dispatched the traditional king cake that the ship's cook made in honor of the holiday.

On the early voyages that brought European settlers to North America, shipboard meals simmered at an open iron hearth that occupied a fireproof brick surface on deck. Food cooked and water heated in a huge kettle on an iron tripod. Some ship builders outfitted crafts with a cruder version of the brick hearth, a sand bed in a wood frame, which held a charcoal fire. When Governor John Winthrop sailed aboard the *Arabella* in 1630, the cook room dispatched food to the quarterdeck for Lady Arabella John and her gentlewomen and delivered officers' provisions to the roundhouse. The rest of the passengers ate wherever they could find space and protection from the weather on main deck or spar deck. On the most cramped vessels, quartermasters distributed rations to each family or group, which dined on cold food washed down with beer.

Provisions for passengers on the high seas remained sparse over the next 130 years. In 1760, the diarist Jacob Bailey of Rowley, Massachusetts, sailed from Boston to London in the *Hind*. He described food service from the galley, which produced enough stew to fill a wood tub as large as "half of a quarter cask." (Dow 1988, 163) The inelegant tableware consisted of two pewter places, one holey and the other half melted, a broken fork, a bone-handled knife, and two spoons. A heavy gale soaked Bailey's private food stores in seawater and spoiled the galley's stock of neck beef, herring, oatmeal, and potatoes. To keep the salt beef fresh, the cook hung it over the side of the ship on a cord.

In an era short on comfort, one historic seaman took an active role in galley matters. In the late 1760s, Captain James Cook set out aboard the HMS *Endeavour* for the South Seas with the intention of remaining at sea for long periods while he explored the Pacific. Cook knew of the writings of James Lind, a Scottish naval physician, on the prevention of scurvy, a nutritional deficiency that plagued sailors deprived of fresh fruits and vegetables during lengthy voyages. The Chinese had solved this problem in the fifth century CE by adding ginger to the shipboard diet. To protect his own crew, Cook stocked the galley and hold with foods believed to prevent scurvy—fresh fruit, an herb known as scurvy grass, wild celery, eighty bushels of a prepared malt additive, and "sour krout." (Villiers 1971, 328) The captain ordered sauerkraut on the menu at the rate of fourteen pounds per week, either as a vegetable or in soup, but the crew initially rejected it. Cook responded by insisting that his staff eat sauerkraut regularly and pretend to like it. A week later, the common sailor was demanding the same food that was being served to officers. (Gray 1984).

In the English navy, the ship's galley or cookhouse—called a cuddy, camboose, or caboose in small vessels—was traditionally a close area well fitted with necessary work implements and limited in staff to a cook and a galley helper. In the early coaster, fishing boat, or small merchant ship, the caboose was a wooden casing built on deck around the chimney. Condensate from the flue supplied fresh water for shaving or treating injured sailors in sickbay. The presence in shipboard meals of "galley pepper"—ash that sifted onto cooked food—bore witness to the cramped nature of the cook's quarters.

The ship's cook was often a pensioner or an injured sailor who could no longer walk the decks or climb rigging. To provide meals round the clock, he worked constantly. His helper, the cook's boy, stoked the fire-box with wood splits stored in the forward hold. Ship-board kitchen labor benefited from Europe's first encounter with *lignum vitae*, the world's densest wood, which grows in South America. Rolling pins, pestles, and other implements carved from *lignum vitae* survived hard daily wear; heavy wooden bowls withstood the ship's gyrations without tipping. During gales or high seas, the cook fed the crew all of the cooked food on hand and put out the embers to prevent fire. Both cook and helper manned buckets with bailing or falling handles to dip water from a flooded galley. In his spare time, the cook made a seawater-soluble dishwashing soap by pouring oil, resin, fish glue, soda, and oxalate of potash through soapwort in a perforated tray into a tub.

In most sailing vessels, the duty mess cook served meals at a folding table. Assistants laid out wooden trenchers or bowls and spoons. The crew dined in groups of eight to twelve men, who were called mess-mates. Before the advent of canned foods, supplies of beef and pork aboard ship were preserved in brine. The cook boiled off fat from salt beef to produce bully beef and collected the residue, known as "slush," for the grease tub, which the purser bought for making candles.

A favorite dish of sailing crews was lobscouse or 'scouse, a hash of minced meat, biscuit crumbs, potato, onion, salt, and spices. A standard menu item was sea pie, a catch-all pot pie made from vegetables or dried peas, fish, and meat layered with dough or biscuit. A thin sea pie was a two-decker; deeper pies were three-deckers.

In the case of so-called hen frigates—ships with the captain's wife on board—both officers and crew might have been treated to home-style meals prepared by this lady herself. A woman's shipboard presence inclined the captain to call into port more often to lay in fresh supplies, thus guaranteeing better than usual food service. On standard womanless voyages, however, ordinary fare prevailed. For breakfast, the cook often served burgoo, a gruel made of oatmeal with butter, salt, and sugar. It was an easy, if tasteless porridge that could be boiled in rough seas and held over for an evening meal. Poor quality food made for a disgruntled crew, a situation that sometimes resulted in a mutiny at mess or throughout the ship. By 1832, the British Royal Navy had established a victualling board to manage provisions and prevent such shipboard rebellions, but this body earned an unsavory reputation for graft and substandard goods.

On substantial vessels ample stores were in the galley fitted below the upper deck. On Lord Horatio Nelson's flagship, the HMS *Victory*—the most famous warship of the Royal Navy, which he first commanded in May 1803—an iron stove, Brodie's Patent Galley offered space for baking, boiling, and roasting to serve a crew of 821. A list of rations from the *Victory* reveals that the men received a daily allotment of one gallon of beer or wine and one pint of grog, which was one part rum cut with three parts water. Staff issued it before breakfast and dinner. Traditionally, grog, beer, and wine were favorites because they withstood contamination during long periods at sea. Once emptied, sailors knocked the casks in which the drink was shipped into staves and hoops to ease crowded spaces.

Strong drink helped ease the tedium of solid food, which was repetitive and unappetizing. Each crewman received a ration of preserved meat and a bread loaf or pound of hard sea biscuit. The palatability of the salt meat may be inferred by the seamen's nicknames "salt junk," "pork slush," "salt horse," and "Irish horse." An additional distribution of two pounds of salt pork on Sunday, Tuesday, Thursday, and Saturday and cheese and oatmeal on the remaining three days supplied each man.

The ordinary seaman echoed the same complaints for centuries, notably, "Unwholesome and stinking victuals, whereby many of them are become sick and unserviceable, and many are dead." (Hartley 1964, 149) Sailors' letters and journals mentioned cheese hard enough to carve into ornamental boxes and buttons or spliced into broken masts, casks of horsemeat complete with hooves and harness, beef foul enough to cause illness, rancid oatmeal, beer reeking like sewage, ditchy drinking water, and butter more suited to lubricating rigging than serving at mess.

Exacerbating a sense of deprivation was the matter of preferential treatment. Sailors were all too aware that officers pooled private funds to enhance the wardroom pantry. They also had their own cooks, who drew on supplies of fresh fruits and vegetables as well as eggs, meat, butter, and milk, often produced by dairy cows and sheep or by goats and poultry penned on board. Pigs, butchered on long voyages, provided fresh pork. To protect the privileged from prying swabbies, the cook staff served officers in private dining quarters.

Improving Galley Rations

Technological advances in the early nineteenth century made cooking at sea safer and more convenient than in earlier times. By 1815, the iron cook stove had replaced open-hearth cookery, thus decreasing the risk of galley fires. After 1814, Nicolas Appert's invention of canning increased the availability of seasonal foods.

With improvements to galley service, the mid-nineteenth century saw the reduction of complaints and the recruitment of a higher grade of sailor, one likely to think of the navy as a career. A variety of canned foods augmented the English sailor's traditional seaboard diet. Provisions began to include fresh produce, oatmeal, cheese, olive oil, rice, and wine, and, from the early eighteenth century, vinegar and cocoa. Tea with sugar was available, if not for the general roster, at least for those in sick bay. Merchant seamen received the first citrus juice allotment in 1844, the beginning of a decline in scurvy.

By English law, victualling changed in 1906, when the British Merchant Shipping Act specified exact measurements for the daily "whack," a slang term for a food ration weighed on a scale. (Kemp 1988, 932) Meat regulations guaranteed three pounds of salt beef and two of salt pork, thirty-six ounces of tinned meat, twelve ounces of fish, and four ounces of suet. Grain rations included four pounds of biscuit and three of bread and eight ounces of oatmeal. Beverages called for 1.75 ounces of tea, four ounces of coffee, twenty ounces of sugar, and a third of a pound of condensed milk. In addition, the sailor could count on eight ounces of butter, a pound of jam or marmalade, and eight ounces of syrup or molasses. German and Scandinavian sailors received less than the British; seamen in the U.S. and Canadian navies received more.

Meals in the Air and Undersea

Pioneering airlines and company-owned planes began imitating the efficiency of ship's galleys with miniature kitchens capable of heating food for in-flight service. On a May 1, 1930 flight aboard Ford Motor Company's private plane, passengers ate hot chicken consommé, cheese wafers, jellied pineapple-mint salad, crudités, bran muffins, macaroons, and coffee, all prepared in a "sky kitchen" equipped with sink and drainboard, hot plate, ventilator and fan, and storage drawers. Later in the decade, airlines inaugurated regular meal service. In part to keep passengers content and occupied, airlines introduced table service and white-jacketed stewards, who brought trays and poured wine. After World War II, the whole system metamorphosed into a miniaturized restaurant serving full-course fare. On the ground, airline cooks served up alternate *à la francaise* menus for maximum choice for first class, business, or economy passengers and offered vegetarian, children's, and dietetic meals to those who phoned in an order ahead of takeoff. For the transportation of plates from kitchen to cart to plane, food workers covered dishes with plastic wrap and bundled cutlery, swizzles, napkin, salt, pepper, and condiments in hygienic sealed packages.

Throughout World War II, submarine designers on both sides of the conflict compressed even further the workings of the standard ship's galley to assure safety from onboard fires. The USS *Cod*, which housed 100 men, was among a fleet of U.S. vessels pioneering the all-electric kitchen, including a Hobart mixer. In the tiny galley space, which admitted only one cook, storage racks above the appliances accommodated staple foods and cooking implements.

Modern Technology

During deployment in the Arabian Gulf from November 1, 1998 to May 30, 1999, the USS *Rainier* volunteered for SMARTSHIP, a program designed to save on kitchen labor by reducing preparation and cleanup time. The galley bore some 1,500 cases of cook/freeze products. By instituting cooking on demand, the galley staff reduced food waste. A parallel program aboard the USS *Vinson* loaded pantries and freezers with 141,000 pounds of cook/freeze products such as frozen bread dough and frozen sandwiches. Cooks aboard the USS *Tarawa* experimented with no-prep pasta, rice, and vegetables that cooked in as little as ten minutes. Although more expensive, the new system had definite benefits: the food was easier to prepare and the sailors liked the meals.

In an effort to upgrade food service, the navy also updated its galleys with state-of-the-art multifunctional commercial food service equipment. Galley workers received instruction from professional chefs on new inventory-management systems for ships' messes. The application of commercial business practices to shipboard food service decreased the amount of work involved while producing more nutritious and varied meals and improving sailors' satisfaction ratings.

Vessels of the early twenty-first-century displayed the stainless steel surfaces and serviceable appliances of institutional kitchens. The well-equipped kitchen of the Swedish submarine *Gotland*, built in 1995, boasted cookers, freezers, and adequate counter space for food preparation. A dumbwaiter ferried prepared dishes from the kitchen situated below the tower to serving areas above. A garbage chute jettisoned vegetable waste and plate scrapings into the sea

In the 1990s, to ensure production of hot, nutritious meals in the wake of staffing shortfalls, military designers for the U.S. navy began creating clean, well-appointed mess decks and more efficient galleys offering the latest food technology. A staff of three registered dietitians, aided by the navy surgeon general, planned healthful menus and promoted a healthy shipboard lifestyle. To simplify labor-intensive food service, supply ships replenished galleys with a variety of prepared foods—ground turkey and turkey breast, boneless, skinless chicken breasts, low-fat salad dressings, bran cereal, lasagna, precooked bacon, and frozen bread dough. Cooks relied on soups, sauces, entrées, meats, and salads that remained shelf stable for up to forty-five days. Frozen products were edible up to twelve months. In addition to their professional cooking instruction, galley personnel learned the importance of nutrition for military preparedness.

See also **Biscuit; Grog**

Further Reading

Casson, Lionel. *The Ancient Mariners*. Princeton, N. J.: Princeton University Press, 1991.

Druett, Joan. *Hen Frigates: Wives of Merchant Captains Under Sail*. New York: Simon & Schuster 1998.

Fabri, Felix. *The Book of the Wanderings of Felix Fabri*. London: Palestine Pilgrims' Text Society, 1896.

Fisher, Katharine A., "Luncheon a Mile Up," *Good Housekeeping,* July 1930, 84, 223.

Kemp, Peter, ed. *The Oxford Companion to Ships and the Sea.* Oxford: Oxford University Press, 1988.

Svensson, Sam, ed. *The Lore of Ships*. New York: Barnes & Noble, 1966.

GARBAGE

Kitchen waste, the normal accumulation of husks, shells, plate scraps, and spoiled food, is an inevitable byproduct of home and commercial food preparation. Until the invention of crushing and grinding devices to reduce garbage to a manageable slurry, waste removal was a cumbrous and unenviable task. Families and communities devised various strategies for covering, removing, and disposing of trash, either by burying or burning it or abandoning it to nature.

A serious hindrance to medieval kitchen efficiency, the accumulation of parings, peelings, and meat scraps required creative methods of disposal. To minimize odors and unsightly accumulation, the kitchen scullion regularly dumped waste water and slops into the midden, or refuse heap. Cleaners scooped up the refuse and hauled it to a distant dump site, often a river bank. In towns, stringent laws governed the removal of waste to keep citizens from dumping dead animals, excrement, and kitchen scraps in the kennel, the drainage ditch that ran down the center of the street. When refuse backed up, especially during epidemics, magistrates hired street cleaners to remove the growing heaps of offal.

The industrial revolution and the advent of mass production created an unending stream of goods, which, in turn, produced an unending stream of used

and broken items and discarded packaging. In the April 1878 issue of the *American Agriculturist*, an essay entitled "The Tin Pan Nuisance" called attention to the problem of disposal of obsolete or nonfunctional domestic goods. The author complained about unsightly roadside dumps littered with "a mélange of old tin ware—coffee and tea-pots, pans, cups, watering pots, innumerable fruit and vegetable cans, and broken crockery." He commented on the difference between urban and rural practices: in cities, housemaids tossed refuse into the ash barrel, while in the country, disused kitchen items cluttered porches, cellars, and shrubbery. The solution proposed in the text was "a well dug for the purpose—one which has a cover, and which, when full, can be earthed and grassed over," a fair description of the modern landfill. In 1925, advertisements in *Good Housekeeping* touted the Majestic Underground Garbage Receiver, a commercial improvement on the very same in-ground waste systems described nearly fifty years earlier.

In industrialized nations, small advances in technology gradually upgraded the task of trash handling in the home. A humble but efficient product for the kitchen invented by efficiency expert Dr. Lillian Moller Gilbreth in the 1920s, the hands-free pedal bin enabled the cook to dispose of garbage without touching the lid of the trash can. A later model, the Vipp pedal bin from Denmark, featured sleek European design in stainless or enameled steel. An internal mechanical air brake lifted the top, then lowered it gradually to engage the lip with a rubber gasket, which kept odors from leaking into the cooking area. A lift-out galvanized steel liner with a rubberized bottom simplified the task of emptying, cleansing, rinsing, and air-drying.

Garbage Disposers

The architect John W. Hammes pioneered the kitchen garbage disposer at his home in 1927; his invention evolved into the In-Sink-Erator, a brand that led the domestic market. In 1935, General Electric challenged the front-runner with a kitchen disposer similar to the ones used in hospitals and sewage plants. Initially a slow seller, after World War II the home disposer came into its own. In 1949, Avco advertised the disposer as the way of the future, claiming that garbage cans were "as out-moded as outhouses." Although laws in Boston and New York City banned disposers, the growing number of all-electric homes encouraged builders to install them as a selling point. By the 1960s, they were familiar items in most kitchens and evolved from batch-fed to continuous feed systems, which operated under cold running water to solidify fats and cool overworked motors. Updated domestic garbage disposers, which updated 80 percent of new homes in 1994, improved waste removal by sparing septic tanks and landfills the containment of table and kitchen scraps, which averaged 1.2 gallons a day per household.

In 1999, Donald Sullivan of Draper, Utah, came to the aid of owners of older homes and cabins, patenting the HydroMaid hydraulic garbage disposer. The device contained a valve that increased home water pressure to a level necessary to turn the blades that grind food waste. For the more than 50 million U.S. homes that lacked an available kitchen electrical outlet, the device revolutionized in-sink disposer technology, reducing energy usage, cutting refuse into small particles, eliminating drain clogs, and promoting rapid decomposition of biodegradable substances.

Trash Compactors and Incinerators

The creation of trash compactors by General Electric, KitchenAid, and Whirlpool in the 1960s applied an industrial bulk-waste reduction method to kitchens. By thrusting a ramming device against plastic, glass, and paper containers, the machine reduced kitchen waste to a rectangular bale packaged in a heavy-duty bag. A mechanism above the bag sprayed deodorizing and sanitizing mist over the finished cube of trash. Because of the compact size of domestic models, they fit easily under a kitchen counter and blended in with standard appliances.

Waste-reduction systems that cut the volume of trash aided kitchens in hospitals, navy carriers, cruise ships, and restaurants were themselves smaller in 1993. For small restaurants and fast-food chains, slimmed-down units lessened the need for frequent dumping and daily garbage pickup. Unlike standard compactors, one waste reducer ground waste into particles, mixed them with water, and passed the slurry through a screw press that squeezed out the water to produce damp cardboardy lumps. The savings were significant: reduction by three to one for compactors increased to eight to one for waste reducers.

One time-honored method of dealing with garbage is incineration, which once lit up open fields, backyards, vacant lots, and burning barrels. The enclosed incinerator, a technological improvement on open burning, removed some of the danger of wildfire, but emitted hazardous ash and carbon monoxide fumes, smoked up the skies, encouraged acid rain, and created new problems with air, water, and land fouled by dioxins, furans, metals, and fine particulates.

Recycling

Although burning can remove up to 90 percent of refuse, it did not satisfy the demands of environmental activists. In the mid-1980s, pro-incineration forces urged cities to turn burnable refuse into energy; they also proposed mulching of kitchen waste and for-profit recycling of aluminum, glass, motor oil, paper, and yard clippings.

Public outcry against overstuffed landfills prompted more industrialized nations to recycle, reuse, and compost. Between 1988 and 1992, the number of city recycling programs in the United States grew from one thousand to 7,500 and involved 120 million citizens, or 48 percent of the total population. By stripping plastic caps from glass bottles, breaking down boxes, and separating trash for curb pickup into aluminum cans, glass, paper and cardboard, and plastics, citizens carried out the first step of the recycling process. Aluminum cans went to chippers and ovens for melting into aluminum bars to be pressed into sheets for the canning industry. Crushing machines remelted and reshaped discarded glass into new bottles and jars or into asphalt for paving. Bundles of newspaper and bales of cardboard traveled to paper mills, where processing pulped, de-inked, and remanufacured waste as paper towels, napkins, grocery bags, and wrapping for bakery goods. Plastic bags and containers got a cleaning, then journeyed down a conveyor belt to a chopper and melting oven for remolding into containers. Old tires returned to life as tire-tread doormats. These processes saved time, energy, and natural resources by sparing trees, metal ores, and petrochemicals that would have gone into new goods. However, the vision of a trash-free society, such as that launched in Spokane, Washington, disappointed idealists, who had failed to consider costs of startup, export of ash and nonburnables, toxic waste removal, and landfills.

In 1999, *Mother Earth News* applauded the introduction of biodegradeable picnic utensils made from corn starch. Because landfills were absorbing 90 billion pieces of nonbiodegradable plastic utensils yearly that would survive unchanged for a century, the California-based Biocorp USA pioneered a line of eating utensils for use in school lunchrooms, zoos, playgrounds, and fast-food restaurants. Items broke down into absorbable, earth-friendly components in less than six weeks. Field-tested in April 1999 at Chicago's Brookfield Zoo under the trade name "reSourceBags" and "reSourceWares," the items decomposed in around forty days before returning to the ground as odor-free fertilizer. European diners were using similar nonpolluting goods at the World Ski Championships in Austria and at McDonald's restaurants in Austria and Sweden.

Composting

Other methods of ridding the planet of kitchen waste include worm-farming and composting. For householders interested in producing friable soil in kitchen gardens and flower beds, vermicomposting—the feeding of worms on scraps, tea bags, eggshells, coffee grounds, paper filters, and shredded yard waste—turned refuse into top-grade fertilizer at the same time that it saved carting, separating, burning, and burying trash. Through the dual action of worms and anaerobic micro-organisms, within three to six months, vermicomposting turned out a richer product than simple composting by supplying worm castings, a super-nutritious plant food rich in nitrates, phosphorus, and potassium. By mulching and enriching kitchen and herb garden beds with humus, the home recycler reaped a harvest of fresh greens and vegetables from what was once garbage.

Further Reading

Cozic, Charles P. *Garbage and Waste.* San Diego, Calif.: Greenhaven Press, Inc., 1997.
Cozic, Charles P. *Pollution.* San Diego, Calif.: Greenhaven Press, Inc., 1994.
Martin, Sam, "Cornstarch Cutlery," *Mother Earth News,* August 1999, 14.
The Plastic Waste Primer. New York: Lyons & Burford, 1993.
Watkins, Yoko Kawashima. *So Far from the Bamboo Grove.* New York: Puffin Books, 1986.
Wolf, Nancy, and Ellen Feldman. *Plastics: America's Packaging Dilemma.* Washington, D.C.: Island Press, 1995.

GARUM

An essential to the diet of ancient Rome as well as Bithynia and the Far East was garum, or liquamen, a strong-flavored, odoriferous processed sauce of fatty fish similar to the Swedish *surströmming,* Thai *nam pla,* Vietnamese *nuoc mam,* Mediterranean anchovy and sardine paste, and English Worchestershire sauce. Based on a Greek condiment called *garos,* from around 500 BCE, the Roman version of fish-pickle differed in the addition of mackerel blood, gills, and guts. Cooks layered the fish offal in a vat with salt, vinegar, parsley, wine, and sweet herbs to produce a thick condiment paste, with which they seasoned oysters and flavored cooking oil. The satirist Martial characterized garum as "proud" because it was "made from the first blood of a still breathing mackerel." (Edwards 1984, xxiii)

Reputedly perfected by the Roman cookery specialist Marcus Gavius Apicius in the first century CE for his gourmet dishes, garum went through a lengthy processing—including boiling, liquefying, and fermenting—to break down oily blends of offal from anchovy, herring, mackerel, scomber, red mullet, shellfish, sprat, and tuna. Cooks strained the garum through a long-handled basket sieve and retained the *allec* (also *allex* or *hallec*), the residue or dregs, a fish paste used for other purposes. Before straining and bottling, the Roman mixture aged in the sun in a sealed amphora for two or three months; the Bithynians, who developed their own garum recipe, preferred ripening in clay vats. Sauce makers bottled the salty garum liquid and sealed it for later distribution at table and as a side dressing on platters for meats, crudités, and leafy greens.

The garum-making process also sufficed for the making of *muria* sauce, a cheaper table condiment composed of pickling brine, oregano, and less expensive tuna. The cook reduced the ingredients over heat until the bones dissolved, added boiled wine, and strained the mix for kitchen or table use. Less ambitious households bought imported sauce, primarily from Spanish warehouses. Professional garum makers in Hispania offered amphorae of the sauce in different forms—water-based *hydrogarum,* wine-based *oenogarum,* oil-rich *oleogarum,* peppered *piperatum,* and vinegar-based *oxygarum*—which they began exporting near the end of the first century BCE as far east as Palestine, south to Egypt, and north to Gaul and Britain.

A garum aficionado, the encyclopedist Pliny the Elder, author of *Natural History* (ca. 77 CE), described the netting of scomber for pickling off the straits of Gibraltar, where the Atlantic Ocean meets the Mediterranean Sea. It flavored the best of food seasonings; according to Pliny, "No liquid, except unguents, fetched a higher price." (Clarke 1847, vol. ii, 82) Less particular cooks made the more common *allec* of creamed anchovies. A higher grade melded the flavor of mullet liver, oysters, sea urchins, and sea nettles. Marcus Apicius's own brand of garum included red mullet liver.

Apicius gave the condiment a sassy name, *garum sociorum* (sauce of companions). A later Apicius, Caelius Apicius, author of *De Re Coquinaria* (On Cooking, late 300s CE), offered advice on rejuvenating stale fish pickle by smoking the vat with burning laurel and cypress, two evergreens whose fragrance removed the rancid odor of past batches. Roman food containers found at archeological sites and in shipwrecks in the twentieth century still contained residue of garum.

See also **Amphora; Roman Cookery**

Further Reading

Edwards, John. *The Roman Cookery of Apicius*. Point Roberts, Wash.: Hartley & Marks, 1984.

Hanson, K. C., "The Galilean Fishing Economy and the Jesus Tradition," *Biblical Theology Bulletin*, v. 27, 1997, 99–111.

GAS

A colorless, odorless hydrocarbon prized for its flammability, natural gas is a multipurpose fuel used to power stoves, furnaces, hot-water heaters, air conditioners, clothes dryers, refrigerators, incinerators, and garbage disposers. Derived from decaying plant matter and aquatic organisms found in sandstone, Devonian shale, and coal seams, it liquefies at the Earth's surface as gas condensate, natural gasoline, or liquefied petroleum gas. In comparison with other fossil fuels, natural gas is nearly pollution free. It burns completely and leaves no sulfur dioxide and little carbon, carbon monoxide, or nitrogen oxide.

Discovery

Iranians discovered the first natural gas in seeps, or aboveground pools, from 6000 to 2000 BCE. Such pools were common to the eastern Mediterranean as far inland as Azerbaijan. The discovery of gas seeps launched the worship of Apollo at Delphi, where the fumes from leaking deposits dizzied the Pythian oracle, causing her to babble cryptic answers to seekers' questions. Possibly ignited by lightning, perpetual flames impressed the Persians, who worshiped them as evidence of divinity at the temple of Zoroaster near Baku on the Caspian Sea.

Around 900 BCE, the Chinese were burning natural gas as a fuel. Fitting bamboo to drill bits, they sank the first gas well in 211 BCE west of Chungking as a means of drying rock salt in limestone. In 615 BCE, Japanese surveyors began to exploit natural wells as sources of combustible fuel. Gas appears to have been in domestic use around 120 CE in Iran. A Greek text describes how the king of the Medes in Psittakos, Persia, erected a kitchen alongside a clear flame, which burned constantly.

The Chinese remained in the forefront of turning natural gas to practical use. To aid in salt manufacture, around 300 CE, they heated vats of brine with natural gas. The geographer Ch'ang Ch'ü, author of *Records of the Country South of Mount Kua* (347 CE), described how gas piped through bamboo tubing made an ashless fuel that produced both brilliant light and home heat.

Mass distribution of natural gas was slow to develop. Europeans, who depended on "town gas" from carbonized coal for home heating and lighting, made no advances in harnessing natural gas until the mid-seventeenth century.

Evolution of a New Technology

Householders wearied with daily hauling of wood ashes and constant tending and cleaning of oil lamps and sooty wall sconces sorely needed gas technology. In 1784, the Belgian chemist Jean Pierre Minckelers educated students at the University of Louvain on the flammabililty of coal gas, which did not evolve into a major domestic fuel until the nineteenth century. In Cornwall, England, William Murdock became the first gas producer to light his home with gas in 1792. He also applied gas technology to lighting the factory of the Scottish engineer James Watt, inventor of the steam engine. For all their promise, however, Murdock's ventures did not launch a major shift to gas as a domestic fuel.

In 1799, the public observed the first demonstration of lighting with natural gas, about the same time that the engineer-inventor Philippe Lebon, professor of mechanics at the Paris School of Bridges and Highways, lighted his own home and yard in Angoulême, France. Two more breakthroughs brought gas to the public's attention: the Austrian chemist Zachaus Andreas Winzler pioneered gas cookery, and the German inventor Frederick Albert Winsor of Braunschweig, Germany, used natural gas to cook the food for a dinner party in his own home in England in 1802. The technology slowly advanced from experimental to home use.

Natural gas began piquing commercial interest in the early nineteenth century. On May 18, 1804, England issued a patent for gas production to Winsor, who lighted Pall Mall in 1807. After reports of gas seeps in Charleston, West Virginia, the United States made its first use of natural gas in 1817, lighting the streets of Baltimore three years before Paris's public works began the practice. It was not until 1885, when the Austrian chemist Baron Karl Auer Von Welsbach synthesized a flameproof incandescent mantle, that gas illumination reached a majority of homes.

Cooking with Gas

The gas cooker began as a simple compartment fitted with a meat hook at top and burner below. Homemakers saw the first commercially marketed gas cooker in Liverpool in 1824. Two years later, the English engineer James Sharp designed for his own use the first gas stove, which the English firm of Smith and Phillips began marketing in 1828. Consumers were hesitant to invest in an appliance considered hazardous, but a trusted spokesman, Alexis Soyer, chef of London's Reform Club, boosted acceptance of the new technology. In 1841, Soyer proclaimed gas cookery economical because the flame burned only when the stove was in use; coal ranges, on the other hand, remained lit most of the time as a source of heat. Formal launching of the gas stove came at the demonstration of a gas cooker at the Great Exhibition of 1851 at London's Crystal Palace. Because the English gas utilities were state-owned, the price of fuel there remained low, in contrast to expensive supplies in the Americas. Thus, English homeowners could easily afford to make the switch to a cleaner, more efficient method of cooking, which spread rapidly in the 1880s.

The late nineteenth century saw the profitable production of gas cookers and stoves, led by Schulze & Sackur's Wobbe-Brenner serviceable cooker in 1878 in competition with the German Continental Gas Company. Because of its flexibility, the gas stove quickly replaced the hot, sooty coal stove, which overheated kitchens in summer and required storage space for its bulky fuel. On the down side, cooks missed the ease with which they could heat water on coal stoves and the burnerless cook top on which vessels could be set in variable positions. Engineers at Schäffer & Walcker in Berlin designed models with more ducts for circulation of heated air. Costly and oversized, the new stoves found no kitchen display area at the 1873 Vienna World Exhibition and made slow progress against coal until the advent of a common rival—electricity.

In 1890, the development of a tight coupling for pipes ushered in delivery systems reaching as far as 100 miles from the gas source. To assist home cooks with the new technology, utilities' promoters hired women spokespersons to answer housewives' questions and reassure them of the safety and value of gas as a home fuel. To promote her father's cookers, the food demonstrator-lecturer Hannah M. Young of Birmingham, England, issued *Domestic Cookery, with Special Reference to Cooking by Gas* (1886); London gas distributors hired Marie Jenny Sugg, the wife of the manufacturer of the Westminster Gas Kitchener, to write *The Art of Cooking by Gas* (1890). In Philadelphia, Lucy C. Andrews compiled *Choice Receipts Arranged for the Gas Stove* (1893), a compact pamphlet endorsed by *New England Kitchen Magazine*.

At the Philadelphia Cooking School, Sara Tyson Rorer, a pioneer home economist and dietitian, championed gas cookery as a labor-saving technology that freed women from the drudgery of stoking and cleaning coal stoves. In an 1890 column in *Table Talk* magazine, she declared, "It is impossible for any human being

during the hottest months to serve a daintily prepared meal if a large coal range is the only apparatus provided." (Weigley 1977, 113) Rorer assured housewives that gas stoves turned out quality meals with less waste of food and energy than coal-fired models.

The increasing availability of gas and subsequent drop in price combined with improvement in energy-saving equipment to boost public acceptance of gas cookery. In 1908, the gourmet and artisan Albert Dupuy, founder of the La Cornue stove factory in St. Ouen L'Aumone, France, began marketing the first circulating hot-air gas oven, which is still sold as Cornuchef, one of the prized cook stoves for professional and commercial use. In 1915, the American Stove Company further streamlined gas cookery by equipping gas ovens with a fuel regulator.

The 1920s saw interest in gas cookery piqued through clever promotions. To win over younger housewives, Hungary's gasworks opened a downtown appliance showroom and offered free cooking classes. By the end of the decade, Germany was experiencing a boom in modernization, evidenced by the success of the Austrian architect Grete Schütte-Lihotzky's modular Frankfurt Kitchen. To promote gas technology to Frankfurt homeowners, Franz Tillmetz, the director of city utilities, and the architect Adolf Meyer established a permanent exhibition, remodeling the Kaiser-Wilhelm Passage in the heart of the city into the Gaspassage, a venue for demonstrations of gas ranges, ovens, water heaters, and home heating.

In the United States, companies formed to supply natural gas via an expanded network and offered gas cook stoves for home use. With improvements in welding technology in 1931, ten systems of twenty-inch pipe crisscrossed the United States, supplying homes with abundant cheap fuel. The pipe gauge was increased in the late 1940s to service the housing projects springing up to accommodate soldiers returning from overseas and establishing families.

Winning over Consumers

As gas delivery systems improved, so did gas appliances. The ECFM gas company lured French housewives with a display of gas ranges at the 1938 Ideal Home Show in Paris. In the United States, the Tappan gas range of 1939 incorporated the "Visualite" oven, a pane of tempered glass in the front panel that enabled cooks to view the heating process and thus obviated the need for repeated opening and closing the oven. A few years later, the Harp-Wyman gas range featured a special simmer burner, which heated large containers with its outer ring or small containers with a smaller inner ring. The inner ring could also be used to keep food warm on a low flame, conserving gas and reducing kitchen heat.

New stove models continued to offer innovative features. In the October 1947 issue of *Woman's Home Companion,* the magazine's home equipment editor Elizabeth Beveridge surveyed twelve gas ranges and pointed out such advances in engineering as a deep broiler, pull-out drip trays, safety shut-off, and glass plates over burners to steady wobbly pans, protect the units from spills, and provide places to warm baby bottles.

In 1953, the Cribben and Sexton Company of Chicago brought out an unusual appliance—the Universal gas range-dishwasher. The bottom compartment on the left side of the stove pulled out to reveal a glass-topped cabinet that held 100 soiled dishes. To activate the washer, the user rolled it out of the stove cabinet to the sink and attached a hose to the faucet. The machine heated and softened water automatically, then washed, rinsed, sterilized, and dried dishes.

By the turn of the twenty-first century, stove manufacturers were offering an entirely new generation of conveniences. One of these was an enameled cast-iron plate placed between pot and flame to diffuse heat and protect foods from sticking or burning. For backyard cookery, gas grills were providing stiff competition to the traditional charcoal-burning barbecue.

See also **Brereton, Maud Adeline; Stoves; Victorian Kitchens; Young, Hannah**

Further Reading

Beveridge, Elizabeth, "There's News in Gas Ranges," *Woman's Home Companion*, October 1947, 104–106.
Giles, Bridget, and Anne O'Daley, eds. *Inventions and Inventors*. Danbury, Conn.: Grolier, 2000.
Weigley, Emma Seifrit. *Sarah Tyson Rorer*. Philadelphia: The American Philosophical Society, 1977.

GILBRETH, LILLIAN MOLLER

Perhaps the best-known female engineer of the twentieth century, Lillian Evelyn Moller Gilbreth applied the principles of motion study to the design of kitchens and common domestic objects. Although she obtained a Ph.D. in literature from the University of California and another in psychology from Brown University, in her early career, she collaborated with her husband, Frank Bunker Gilbreth, who introduced worker-centered studies to the marketplace. Their contributions streamlined industrial processes and improved workplace layout.

After her husband's sudden fatal heart attack in 1924, Lillian Gilbreth took over Gilbreth Inc. while at the same time managing a family of twelve children. She sent them to college from her earnings as a consultant and a world-renowned expert on workplace enhancement. Based on their experiences growing up in their unusual family, her son and daughter, Frank Bunker Gilbreth, Jr., and Ernestine Gilbreth Carey, wrote two humorous memoirs, *Cheaper by the Dozen* (1949) and *Belles on Their Toes* (1950).

In collaboration with her husband, Gilbreth published two monographs, *A Primer of Scientific Management* (1912) and *Applied Motion Study* (1917); on her own, she issued *The Psychology of Management* (1914), the touchstone for a new field of study. She patented an electric mixer, home lighting fixtures, and a domestic trash can equipped with a treadle that lifted the lid, thus saving the housekeeper repeated hand washings. Her labor-saving kitchens, designed for the Brooklyn Gas Company and featured at an international training center at New York University, aided homemakers, particularly the disabled, whose special needs she studied at the Institute of Rehabilitation Medicine.

Based on concepts she and her husband developed for industry, her text *Management in the Home* (1954, coauthored with Orpha Mae Thomas and Eleanor Clymer) suggested methods for expediting culinary work by organizing work centers for activities such as baking, vegetable preparation, and roasting. To save labor in a servantless house, Gilbreth urged the housewife with an outside job to think beyond restrictive designations such as "dining room" and "attic" and to put space to work for a variety of uses. To accomplish this goal, she instructed the reader to "draw a floor plan to scale . . . [with] two-dimensional scale models of your furniture out of cardboard so you can move them about." (Gilbreth, Thomas, & Clymer 1954, 159)

Gilbreth suggested methods for visualizing work plans, for example, by putting push pins at stopping places on the floor plan and attaching string to show the length of trips between chores or by creating a flow chart that divided distance traveled during normal tasks into categories such as operations, transportation, inspection, delays, and storage. More sophisticated studies of micro-motion and simultaneous motion enabled her to divide tasks into identifiable units for decreasing the amount of time needed, lightening the load, and eliminating wasted motion. She proposed storing food in the quantity used and assembling complete meals in a single freezer container. For cleaning a room, she advised moving from right to left and top to bottom rather than crisscrossing the space in random directions.

Dr. Lillian M. Gilbreth, left, with Col. Arthur Woods.
[© *Library of Congress, Prints and Photographs Division (LC-USZ62-101773)*]

To alleviate congestion and accidents, Gilbreth instructed kitchen planners to minimize wall and furniture obstacles, for example, by placing the telephone away from the traffic pattern. To simplify receipt of mail, laundry, dry cleaning, and groceries, she suggested the establishment of a receiving center with shelves, pad and pencil, and places for incoming and outgoing mail. For easy access to garden equipment and efficient disposal of trash and fireplace ash, she proposed a separate basement door and a covered walk from house to garage.

In assessing kitchen layout, Gilbreth instructed the planner to think through the steps necessary to make an average meal of meat, potatoes, vegetable, salad, dessert, bread and butter, and milk. She predicted that by enumerating the number of trips to sink, stove, refrigerator, preparation center, and dish storage, the housewife would recognize a pattern of priorities—sink first, stove second, and preparation center, refrigerator, and dish storage third, fourth, and fifth. Her suggested floor plans included a U-shaped kitchen with the sink at center, which she identified as the best choice, an L-shaped room with sink at the angle, her second choice, and a strip or corridor-style kitchen with sink on one wall and stove and refrigerator opposite, which she deemed the least efficient of the three.

Among her many accomplishments, Gilbreth served on the President's Emergency Committee for Unemployment Relief in 1930, advised the Office of War Information, lectured at the Dartmouth College Conference on Scientific Management, taught engineering at Purdue University, and wrote learned articles and a woman-centered book on home engineering, *The Home-Maker and Her Job* (1927). Her honors included the Hoover Medal from the American Society of Civil Engineers, an award from the National Institute of Social Science, and membership in the Society of Industrial Engineers, National Academy of Engineering, and the Women's Hall of Fame. The Frank and Lillian Gilbreth Industrial Engineering Award honors contributors to human welfare through industrial engineering.

Further Reading

Gilbreth, Lillian M., Orpha Mae Thomas, and Eleanor Clymer. *Management in the Home.* New York: Dodd, Mead & Co., 1954.
Yost, Edna, and Lillian M. Gilbreth. *Normal Lives for the Disbled.* New York: Macmillan, 1945.

GILMAN, CHARLOTTE PERKINS

A prominent socialist lecturer, critic, writer, and forerunner of the women's movement, Charlotte Anna Perkins Gilman espoused feminism and benevolent capitalism a century before they became popular. Born on July 3, 1860, in Hartford, Connecticut, she modeled her life after that of a well-known relative, the writer Harriet Beecher Stowe. After completing a two-year course at the Rhode Island School of Design in Providence, she worked as a commercial artist, art teacher, and governess.

Following marriage and motherhood, Gilman suffered an emotional breakdown. She abandoned domesticity to travel the American West and write verse and essays for the *Pacific Monthly* and *Pacific Rural Press.* Of her many accomplishments, she is best remembered for her short story "The Yellow

Charlotte Gilman, portrait.
[© *Library of Congress, Prints and Photographs Division (LC-USZ62-106490)*]

Wallpaper," an autobiographical account of mental illness published in 1892 in the *New England Magazine.* After creating a public scandal by denouncing the inequality of the sexes, divorcing her husband, and returning her daughter to him and his new wife, Gilman devoted the rest of her life to improving the lot of women.

For the Women's Congress at the World's Columbian Exposition of 1893, Gilman and Helen Campbell formed the Chicago Household Economic Society, which advocated the formation of neighborhood cooperatives to manage cooking, laundry, and child care in much the same way as businesses. Basing their idealism on Ellen Swallow Richards's New England Kitchen and the Rumford Kitchen displayed at the 1893 Chicago World's Fair, Gilman and Campbell envisioned committees that would plan methods for simplifying housework.

Gilman wrote for the *American Fabian* and published her first remunerative work, *Women and Economics: A Study of the Economic Relation between Men and Women as a Factor in Social Evolution* (1898). An international bestseller translated into seven languages, the book challenged androcentrism and women's domestic slavery and sexual repression. In 1906, Gilman wrote and edited a women's rights forum, *Forerunner* magazine, in which she denounced patriarchy as a producer of poverty and advocated eugenics and forced sterilization of people unfit for parenting. She pursued additional radical subjects in *Concerning Children* (1900), *The Home: Its Work and Influence* (1903), *Human Work* (1904), *The Man-Made World; or, Our Androcentric Culture* (1910), *His Religion and Hers* (1923), and articles for, among others, *Saturday Evening Post, Harper's, Scribner's, Appleton's, Forum, Nationalist,* and the *American Journal of Sociology.*

In *The Home,* Gilman challenged the notion that the institution of the home was sacrosanct and stripped "home cooking" of its long-cherished implications of maternal love. Expressing her frustration with gender inequities, she described men as "specialising in a thousand industries," while woman was "limited to her domestic functions." She rejected the notion that a loving wife and mother felt herself adequately rewarded by family affection

Gilman lauded home economics as a field of scholarly study and praised the invention of new kitchen implements, but she deplored the amount of time spent preparing "ordinary meals." She calculated that half the world's population spent half their work hours preparing food. She criticized the traditional home design, which imprisoned and isolated women in kitchens and parlors like snails in their shells, and challenged architects to build houses with as much

thought for the comfort and convenience of the female inhabitants as for the men. Perhaps her most controversial proposal was the socialization of cooking through communal kitchens run by hired staff. To remove the "thousand superfluities" of individual homes, she foresaw houses grouped into organized blocks. (Hayden 1985, 194) Through connected walkways, each could access a communal dining hall or have meals delivered. She also projected that freeing women of domesticity would encourage self-fulfillment through civic and political involvement and jobs.

Faced with the death of her second husband, George Houghton Gilman, and the prospect of her own death from breast cancer, she killed herself with chloroform on August 17, 1935. She left behind an autobiography, *The Living of Charlotte Perkins Gilman* (1935). The Feminist Press revived the feminist utopia *Herland* in 1979.

Further Reading

Degler, Carl. *At Odds: Women and the Family in America from the Revolution to the Present.* New York: Oxford University Press, 1980.
Gilman, Charlotte Perkins. *The Home: Its Work and Influence.* New York: McClure, Phillips & Co., 1903.
Hayden, Dolores. *The Grand Domestic Revolution: A History of Feminist Designs for American Homes, Neighborhoods, and Cities.* Cambridge, Mass.: MIT Press, 1985.
Upin, Jane S., "Charlotte Perkins Gilman: Instrumentalism beyond Dewey," *Hypatia,* Spring 1993, 38–43.

GLASS

An offshoot of pottery, glass is a product of silica, soda ash, wood ash, and lime. The first glass makers in Egypt and Mesopotamia may have formed glass to emulate gemstones. The technology of glass bead making grew into a valuable skill around 3000 BCE. In 1500 BCE, Egyptian, Phoenician, and Greek glass workers shaped containers by dropping a bag of sand into melted glass to create a hollow vessel. Three centuries later, manufacturers pressed glass into bowls and cups.

Early Technology

The Phoenicians pioneered the creation of round glass objects in 300 BCE with their invention of the blowpipe. In addition to increasing the repertoire of shapes, glass blowing took less time than molding. In 100 BCE, Syrian glass blowers made bottles and jugs from a bubble of molten glass shaped at the end of the pipe. By the first century CE, advances in technology had lowered the cost of producing glass, and domestic glassware, formerly a symbol of wealth, had become an inexpensive household commodity. Homemakers preferred glass vessels to those made of wood and metal because they did not alter the taste or smell of food. About this same time, refinements in processing produced the first transparent glass, a boon to homemakers, who were able to store kitchen staples in see-through containers.

As described in *Natural History* (ca. 77 CE) by the Roman encyclopedist Pliny the Elder, glass blowers were able to create fancifully shaped cups and dishes by forcing molten glass into reusable molds. One handy carry-all, a two-sided clay *incitega* (liquor basket), bore individual glass vessels on each side like a cruet set. Other implements recovered from this era include a glass funnel and a bird-shaped siphon with a long tail through which the wine taster drew up a sip of wine for sampling the vintage. It was not until the 1600s, however, that vintners trusted wine fermentation to glass bottles.

Ordinary—and Extraordinary—Objects

In Europe, traditional glassmakers crushed ingredients in a crucible and heated the blend to melting. The artisan blew molten glass into a bottle shape in a mold or shaped it externally at the end of the pipe with a wooden paddle called a battledore. For shaped pieces, glassmakers gathered a melted blob on the blowpipe and rounded it against a marble or iron marvering table or board. Once the bubble assumed a useful shape, the worker cut or marked the soft vessel with a pontil rod. The *verrer* (glazier) joined multiple shapes with seams that smoothed from heat and manipulation of shaping tools. Finished pieces went to a lehr oven for cooling and tempering. (Hartley 1979, 294)

In Italy and France, weavers covered with plaited wicker the bulbous body of the demijohn, a common glass or clayware bottle. Woven casings made of materials such as straw or rushes protected the bottom of the bottle during shipping and pantry storage and made an attractive variation on a mundane molasses or vinegar jar. For elegant entertaining, hosts brought out the Venetian *tazza*, a long-stemmed shallow drinking bowl similar to the Roman *crater*. Shaped like a saucer, it required balance and caution for pouring and sipping without spilling the contents on fine banquet linens and clothing.

Starting in 1639, glassmaking thrived in colonial Salem, Massachusetts. The first products were brownish-black bottles and beads, which colonists used like coins for trading with the Indians. In 1739, Alexander Middleton of Boston was selling crown glass, either uncut or in squares, as well as sheet lead and glass bottles in pints and quarts. In August 1745, Gershom

Flagg of Hanover Street, Boston, advertised in the *Boston Gazette* his stock of "fine Jelly Glasses" and "Crewits of double Flint." (Dow 1988, 129)

In 1752, three hundred Germans arrived by ship from Holland and settled at Germantown, a section of Braintree, Massachusetts, with the intention of establishing a glass factory. A year later, their manufacturing operation was such a popular attraction that the artisans complained of damage from onlookers and charged a shilling to any wishing to observe the glassmaking process. The observers were such a nuisance that staff ordered them to limit their questions to the artisans. (Ibid., 130)

Those who could afford glass preferred it for storing medicines and herbal concoctions. They bought and traded for wide-mouth containers for syrup and brandied fruit, small mortars and pestles for grinding powders or crushing herbs, drinking glasses and decanters, and dessert epergnes. Those who traveled by land, water, or horseback needed case bottles, two-stage cylindrical holders for liqueurs and spirits that slid neatly into wooden or leather cases for safe transportation and storage.

After 1810, when *service à la russe* replaced large displays of dishes with presentation of servings plated and sauced in the kitchen, the European homeowner shifted from pride in fancy plates to the display of fine glassware. Under *service à la francaise,* waiters proffered sips of wine in glasses extended to diners on a tray; no glasses remained on the table. After the change in presentation during the Napoleonic era, hosts began to decorate their tables with sparkling glassware specifically designed for *aperitifs,* sipping during meals, dessert accompaniment, and after-dinner champagne. In addition, table servants placed carafes and decanters on coasters to allow diners to serve themselves.

During the homey, bourgeois Biedermeier period in central and eastern Europe, housewives purchased glass bowls and beverage sets made in Osredek and decorated in a variety of techniques, including grinding, cutting, matting, engraving, coloring, painting in transparent hues, overlaying, or adorning with small glass beads. Most popular around 1850 were thick glass bilicums, or welcome mugs, and tumblers with nationalistic mottoes, medallions, engraved symbols, texts and verses, monograms, or Illyrian crests. On memorable occasions such as wedding feasts and baptismal dinners, some families gave the guests commemorative glasses as souvenirs. The Biedermeier style was short-lived, however. Heavy competition from mass-produced goods ended the Croatian dominance of glassmaking. A fire in 1846 wiped out Joseph Lobmeyer and Dragutin Sigmund Hondl's Zveèevo glassworks. In 1847, Baroness Kulmer sold her factory to an Austrian, Franjo Pann. Eventually, the specialty glassworks went out of business.

During the rise of French *haute cuisine,* glass implements and vessels served special needs that wood or clay could not accommodate, such as the presentation of a mound of *granita di limone* (lemon ice) at meal's end or the potting of chutney and caviar, both strong in flavors and odors that penetrated porous vessels. Glass cloches covered plated foods to keep them warm or sheltered cheese to keep it from drying out.

In ordinary households, glass served daily needs. One special vessel, the flip glass, held a blend of rum, water, sugar, lemon, and egg. The server plunged in a heated toddy stick, then stirred the beverage with a swizzle or flat spoon. The serving of a communal flip glass or punch bowl welcomed guests with both warmth and a quenching of thirst. Humbler drinking glasses or tumblers replicated the round bottoms of the treen, the wooden originals. A common domestic object, the glass washboard, replaced the corrugated wood and zinc model for rubbing heavily soiled garments or delicate items over a wash tub.

Mass Production

By the twentieth century, glass items featured in the 1900 Sears, Roebuck catalog augmented a long list of tin and cast iron kitchen implements and containers. Most cooks preferred glass juice extractors to those made from other materials. Attractive sets included pitcher, glasses, serving bowls, celery glass, cake stand, and lidded butter dish, all for as little as a nickel per item.

Glass entered its most functional phase after manufacturers learned how to treat it to tolerate broad ranges of temperatures. In 1908, Eugene Sullivan of Leipzig, Germany, director of research at Corning Glass Works, invented Nonex, a low-expansion material. He built on the formulations for borosilicate invented by Otto Schott of the Jena Glass Works, a Germany glass chemist and maker of optical equipment, for use as unbreakable lantern globes and battery jars. In 1909, in Massachusetts, two sisters invented the Silex vacuum drip coffeemaker, which the Frank E. Wolcott Manufacturing Company made and marketed.

The 1923 Sears, Roebuck catalog displayed a variety of glass goods to enhance the decor of the ordinary kitchen. For as little as $1.57 per dozen, homemakers could purchase sets of stemware, including footed sherbets, water goblets, and tumblers in varying sizes, in a variety of different patterns. An ornate iced tea set featured six glasses and matching lidded pitcher with cut floral design plus matching spoon sippers and mahogany tray for $6.75. The mail-order giant also offered occasional pieces—salad bowl and plate, jelly bowl, lidded jam jar and spoon, bonbon dish, salt- and pepper-shakers in a silver rack, sherbet set, and bud vase—at prices ranging from 69 cents to $1.95.

Women's magazines featured glass as a focal point of stylish table settings. A 1925 advertisement by the Fostoria Glass Company of Moundsville, West Virginia, showcased its line of popular, affordable glassware and crystal. More radiant and elegant than dime store glassware, the lace-etched pitchers, glasses, dessert dishes, and vessels promised gracious service of salads, compotes, and bonbons. To assist the homemaker in correct table decoration, the company offered a brochure, "A Little Book About Glassware."

In Finland, the designer Aino Marsio Aalto contributed a gentle undulation to her glass vases, plates and platters, bowls, pitchers, and stackable beverage tumblers, all examples of the esthetic shift from classicism to functional urban modernism. The handmade pieces, which required the skill of master glassmakers, answered a demand for glassware when Finland ended its thirteen-year prohibition of alcohol in 1932. Although mocked by traditionalists who compared the modern-style glassware to laboratory vessels, the practical, easy-to-grasp pieces earned the Milan Triennale's gold medal. For the 1939 New York World's Fair, Aalto designed a unique vase composed of glass petals; her husband-collaborator, the architect Alvar Hugo Henrik Aalto, produced a free-form serving tray in clear, white, or blue glass, all made by their company, Artek, which began manufacturing glass decanters and goblets, serving carts, wood tables, and chairs in 1935.

During the Depression era, U.S. dime stores offered sets of glass dishes, beverage sets, platters, bowls, spice jars, and vases for less than two dollars. Some individual pieces sold for less than a nickel. Uniquely American, the practical shapes were the first kitchenware mass produced by machinery. "Depression glass," as it later became known, was available in light pink, yellow, green, blue, and lavender and also in darker hues of amber, amethyst, and cobalt. Distinctive patterns featured thumbprint indentations, flowers, birds, fruit, and snowflakes. Abstract swirls, bubbles, diamonds, cubes, rings, blocks, and ribs enhanced an essentially unadorned food-service necessity.

In production from 1928 into the 1940s and, in some cases, into the 1960s at factories in Ohio, Pennsylvania, and West Virginia, these popular styles of glassware became coveted collectors' items. Easily found on the East Coast, Depression glass is less common in the plains and western states. It is distinguishable from copies and fakes for its crude shaping and flaws.

Unlike higher quality pressed glass or crystal, which was sold in jewelry and department stores, the standard from the Depression era allowed mold marks, uneven edging, and bubbles.

After World War II, when the military's need for glass eased, glass cookware gained in popularity. Club Aluminum Products of Chicago updated the image of glassware with Club Glass Cookware, a matched set to suit the sleek decor of 1940s kitchens. A complete line including matching double boiler, sauce pan, teapot, whistling kettle, percolator, vacuum pot, and drip pot with Melamine insert appealed to a nation of enthusiastic homemakers. The company's ads in *Woman's Home Companion* touted the convenience, balance, and easy cleaning of see-through vessels.

In this same period, the Danish glassmaker Peter Bodum, who established the Bodum firm in 1944, marketed the sleek Santos coffeemaker, the design of Kaas Klaeson. In the 1950s, production of Pyrex in bright crayon colors revived a kitchenware industry that had begun in 1915. Corning unveiled a new generation of oven-to-table glassware called Pyroceram in 1953. Made from the same substance applied to the nose cones of guided missiles, it was the forerunner of popular bowls that doubled as cook pots, which dominated the market into the 1970s. Toward the end of the twentieth century, the company expanded into the manufacture of stove tops and electric kettles.

With the establishment of commercial canning, mineral water became available in handy bottles produced on a rotary bottle-making machine pioneered in 1889. More than one hundred years later, at Source Perrier in France, the company's trademark bottle—perhaps the most familiar glass container in mineral water history—took shape in a robotic factory process. After workers recycled broken bottles at high heat, a mechanism similar to a gatling gun shot the green blobs onto the assembly line, where they cooled and passed beneath automatic detection lights during the filling process. Late in the 1990s, tourists could watch from an upstairs gallery and slip francs into a vending machine for a chilled bottle of the bubbly water.

See also **Pyrex**

Further Reading

Mauzy, Barbara. *Pyrex: The Unauthorized Collector's Guide.* Atglen, Penn.: Schiffer Publications, 2000.

GLASSE, HANNAH

Although she was strongly anti-French, Hannah All-good Glasse, England's first kitchen guide writer, influenced cooking styles and recipes on both sides of the Atlantic. She was born in London in 1708, married at age seventeen, bore eleven children, and worked as a milliner and dressmaker for the Princess of Wales and made medicinals for sale in her kitchen.

Claiming to write from her own kitchen experience, Glasse produced her first written work, *The Compleat Confectioner: or the Whole Art of Confectionaery Made Plain and Easy,* in 1742. The book included text lifted verbatim from a volume by Edward Lambert. She followed with a culinary landmark, *The Art of Cookery Made Plain and Easy: Excelling Any Thing of the Kind Ever Yet Published* (1747), which was published anonymously, attributed simply to "a Lady." Among the contents were instructions for shaping gelatin into a pond, hen's nest, mousetrap, fish, and moon and stars. Her compilation of forty-five recipes for boiled beef, thirty-six for roasts, and numerous recipes

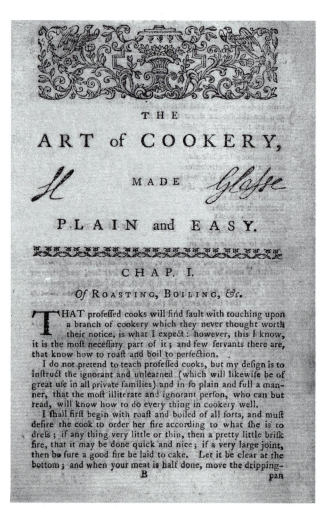

Page from *Art of Cookery* (1912).

for stews, fricassees, and braised and fried meats attest to her readers' fondness for meat dishes, especially large roasts. In her specifications for cooking times, she listed the requirements for ten- and twenty-pound roasts.

Alhough Glasse claimed authorship, remarking that her intent in compiling the volume was to "gain the good opinion of my own Sex." (Blain & Grundy 1990, 432), some of her contemporaries insisted that a Dr. Hill was responsible. The critic and grammarian Samuel Johnson disputed that attribution by pointing to spelling errors that a learned gentleman would not have made. Glasse marketed the book at Mrs. Ashburn's china shop on Fleet Street, an address chosen for its patronage by members of the moneyed elite. A later work, *The Servant's Directory, or Housekeeper's Companion* (1760), published a decade before her death at Newcastle, provided advice on domestic staffing as well as blank pages for keeping kitchen accounts.

Glasse's influence on cookery crops up constantly in kitchen history as a period touchstone. Drawn from some ninety sources, including an anonymous work, *The Whole Duty of a Woman* (1737), her first book targeted "every servant who can but read." (Graham 1969, 17) She promoted the making of cold desserts, which prefigured the introduction of ices and home-cranked ice cream. Before Louis Pasteur elucidated the dangers of microbes in food, Glasse explained how to seal jam jars with animal bladders to assure purity. She also raised the alarm over the potential toxicity of brass cooking and serving vessels. From her writings came many English cookery firsts, including the first appearance of the clam in written recipes, the coinage of the terms *kickshaw* for a small fruit turner and *lover's knots* for doughnuts, and the technique of roasting meat in butter paper.

In a classic eighteenth-century literary tiff—evidently underpinned by a family feud—Glasse's expertise came into question. Ann Cook, an innkeeper and rival, who wrote *Professed Cookery* and signed herself "Teacher of The True Art of Cookery" deemed her recipes "impracticable." (Ibid., 19) Cook warned that recipes from *The Art of Cookery Made Plain and Easy* endangered health and finances. She ridiculed Glasse's recipe for Portuguese rabbit, claiming that it mistakenly treated a four-legged mammal as if it were poultry.

Glasse's classic *The Art of Cookery* returned to press in Alexandria, Virginia, in 1805 and became a standard reference work in Williamsburg for professional cooks and housewives. Her preference for hearty family-style cookery over table showpieces endeared her to women who cooked to satisfy husbands and children rather than to please nobility. Despite Mary Cole's accusations of recipe thievery in

The Lady's Complete Guide; or Cookery in All Its Branches (1788), Glasse's cookbook remained a favorite culinary source for those seeking to prepare unassuming, filling meals. She earned her own comeuppance in 1807 when John Farley stole her recipes and published them in *The London Art of Cookery*.

Further Reading

Graham, Frank. *Famous Northumbrian Women*. Newcastle, Scotland: R. Ward & Sons, Ltd., 1969.
Wolf, T. H., and R. J. Byrd, "Once Upon a Time a Cookbook Was a Recipe for Excess," *Smithsonian*, November 1991, 118–126.

GOURD

A hard-shelled bulbous ornamental fruit of the cucurbit family (*Cucurbitaceae*), the gourd is a relative of cucumbers, melons, squash, and pumpkins, which may have been the first domesticated food in the Americas. It is an annual vine easily grown over a back fence, on a trellis, or in a sunny kitchen garden. Of its 750 types, common species include *Lagenaria siceraria*, the bottle gourd or calabash, which householders have grown since 7000 BCE in Mexico and since 6000 BCE in Peru for use as dippers or bird houses for martins, avian eaters of garden pests. Also valuable are the calabazilla, or wild pumpkin; *Luffa cylindrica,* the dishrag, sponge, or luffa (loofah) gourd; and the snake gourd, teasel gourd, and wax gourd, or Chinese watermelon. The first baskets may have evolved from gourd carriers made of woven vines.

Woman carrying a Gourd vessel, Mopti, Mali.

Because of the decorative qualities of the gourd's warty surfaces, mottling, bands, or stripes, it is a valued ornament and common table decoration for fall holidays. It adapts to use as a dipper, bottle, or storage container and shaping into a whistle, pipe, or lamp. The luffa gourd produces an interlaced vascular bundle that creates a natural sponge, dishcloth, strainer, or filter.

The gourd's ubiquity in India, Egypt and other parts of Africa, and the Western Hemisphere has puzzled naturalists. It may have evolved in Africa, where Kenyans used it for brewing *pombe* beer, and floated to the New World long before the arrival of Columbus. The Las Vegas people of Ecuador, who lived between 8000 BCE and 4600 BCE, cultivated gourds and squash. The Mexica appear to have grown gourds in 7000 BCE and the Peruvians some 2,000 years later. By 3000 BCE, the gourd joined the squash, sunflower, goosefoot, and marsh elder as essential plants to the natives of eastern North America. The pre-Hispanic villagers in Joya de Cerén, El Salvador, which succumbed to volcanic ash from Laguna Caldera in August 595 CE, used painted gourds as containers for beverages, food, and other substances. Polynesians who settled the Society Islands in 400 CE introduced gourd seeds to Hawaiian agriculture.

Even after the advent of pottery and glass, gourds continued to be valuable to the Mediterranean cook. Greek and Roman connoisseurs speak of preserving fragrant waters and wines in calabashes. The Roman Caelius Apicius, author of *De Re Coquinaria* (On Cooking, late 300s CE), used the gourd as a food in appetizers blended with wine, vinegar, pepper, and herbs. One of the recipes, *cucurbitas more alexandrino* ("Gourds Alexander"), reflects the cuisine of Egypt, where gourds were a staple of vegetable cooking during the tenure of the Greek invader Alexander the Great. During the Middle Ages in Walata, west of Timbuktu, Africa, the Muslim traveler Ibn Battuta, author of *Tuhfat al-Nuzzar fi Ghara'ib al-Amsar wa'Ajaib al'Asfar* (On Curiosities of Cities and Wonders of Travel, 1354), formed a low opinion of Malian hospitality, which provided him a mere calabash filled with pounded millet blended with milk and honey.

Among native American peoples, the gourd or calabash was prime kitchen ware for storing foodstuffs and medicinal ointments. The gourd functioned as cup, dish, pot, and eating utensil; when used as a container, it could be plugged with a corncob or a carved wooden stopper. In the Carolinas, the gourd aided bottling, fermenting, storing, and pouring such valuable liquids as passenger pigeon oil. The netted inner fiber of the luffa gourd was a valued pot scrubber or dish cloth.

Gourds also stored strong drink. The Carib, who migrated from the Orinoco Basin north throughout the West Indies, extracted cane sugar to blend with grated cocoa to make cocoa milk, a treat that cooks distributed in calabash cups to guests. From gourds, Southwestern desert cooks poured pinole, a drink made from ground maize or cactus seeds and water. The Aztec fermented maguey juice into pulque, a ceremonial beverage they regarded as a gift from the feathered serpent-god Quetzalcoatl. Ritual gourds of pulque joined other gifts to the god at pathside altars. The Potawatomi turned maple sap into vinegar and stoppered it in gourds for daily use.

With similar ingenuity, the early Guarani of the South American rain forest, the Jesuit missionaries in Paraguay and Brazil, and the gauchos of Paraguay used the calabash for brewing *yerba maté,* a bracing tealike beverage made by steeping shoots and leaves from a wild relative of holly (genus *Ilex*) and serving it in a gourd with a *bombilla,* or filtering straw.

Hawaiian cooks used the ipu, or canoe gourd, for storing shark bait, dyes, and fresh water. Captain James Cook, English voyager to the Pacific Ocean in 1768, reported in his log that Hawaiians stored up to twelve gallons of liquid in the *ipu nui,* a gourd that grew as long as three feet. Hawaiians also shaped gourds into drums, shakers, and whistles.

In nineteenth century Hawaii, crafters shaped gourds, like coconut shells, into storage vessels and tableware. They accompanied native sailors from Honolulu and Lahaina as lightweight water canteens. After harvesting taro in wet, mucky fields on foot and by raft, workers sat at long boards to pound the root with mallets into a purplish pulp called *poi*, a dietary staple. They served it in oversized calabashes or wooden bowls, sometimes devouring five pounds each at a single meal.

On the American frontier, where practical pioneer women rejected delicate china and crystal as wasteful and too much trouble to pack for the bumpy westward wagon journey, calabashes served as faithfully as clay jugs and pewter dishes. According to William Fowler's *Woman on the American Frontier* (1876), when gourds were scarce, cooks stored liquids in hard-shell winter squash, also a member of the cucurbit family. In the Appalachians, settlers valued gourds as disposable drinking vessels, which they carved and hung on thongs by communal water buckets or at springs.

During his sojourn on Fatu-Hiva during the 1970s, the Norwegian expeditioner Thor Heyerdahl found implements and containers made from natural materials. Of drinking vessels, he wrote: "Water was fetched in a jar-shaped container made from the rind of bottle gourds scraped empty and smoke-dried over a low fire." (Heyerdahl 1974, 45) He concluded that the use of gourds by the islanders proved the Swedish ethnologist Erland Nordenskiöld's theory that there was communication between Oceania and the Americas before the voyages of Columbus.

The gourd adapts readily to a variety of uses. It dries naturally into a rattle or can be pierced and filled with grains or stones to produce a unique sound. In India, crafters turn it into a sound box for the sitar. In Africa, cooks pass grain from one gourd to another to separate kernels from chaff. In Nicaragua dried gourds are fashioned into spoons. In Mbale in southern Uganda, where families depend on the banana as a dietary staple, the hourglass gourd is a natural fermentation vessel for banana beer. Among Karamojong stockmen, gourds hold the blend of milk and blood from zebu cows for easy sipping. In Nigeria, Fulani women distribute yogurt mixed with millet balls in calabash bowls.

Because of its whimsical shape, varied sizes, and long, tubular neck, the gourd serves homemakers as a kitchen scoop and ladle as well as a birdhouse, fish float, and a *kimbung*, a penis sheath worn by Chimbu men of New Guinea. Among the lake-based Intha living in stilt houses in Inle, Burma, gourds become water wings for toddlers who occasionally fall from work platforms to the water below while their mothers prepare the daily meal of rice and fresh fish. In Japan, strips of fish and *kampyo* (gourd) garnish *maki-zushi*, a serving of rice placed on seaweed.

Across Africa, gourds are standard features of worship and celebration. The Wodaabe of Niger present a collection of calabashes to a bride as home adornments and symbols of abundance. Among the Fulani of Chad, gourds are a housewife's most prized possessions, a symbol of wealth and womanhood that she etches and decorates with milk paste before stacking them on her head for public displays of housewifely skill. Farther north, the Surma of Ethiopia share enormous calabashes of *borday*, a ceremonial drink brewed from sorghum and corn and borne on the heads of females in somber procession. At the gravesite, the officials anoint the ground with a calabash of milk, which blesses and consecrates it. At the oxen blessing ritual that follows, women fill calabashes with *borday* for sprinkling on the oxen.

At the bull-jumping ceremony celebrated by Omo herders of Ethiopia, women prepare a ritual coffee drink and ladle portions into huge calabash bowls with a gourd-spoon attached to a long pole. The Basuto of South Africa honor their chief with a ripe gourd, a symbol of first fruits. In Swaziland, before anyone cooks from the harvest, the king throws a green gourd to his men, who must not let it fall to the ground lest the tribe's food be cursed.

See also **Leaves; Taro**

Further Reading

Beckwith, Carol, and Angela Fisher. *African Ceremonies*. 2 vols. New York: Harry N. Abrams, Inc., 1999.
Dickason, Olive Patricia. *Canada's First Nations*. Norman: University of Oklahoma Press, 1992.
Maui, Dove White Hana, "Canoe Plants of Ancient Hawai'i: Ipu," *Pacific American News Journal*, April 1997.
Wise, James, "The Art of Gardening," *Archaeology*, January–February 1998.

GRAHAM, SYLVESTER

A nutrition theorist, social reformer, and early health food advocate, Sylvester Graham created the graham cracker, a popular ready-to-eat snack food favored by infants and children. Graham's lifelong interest in healthful habits evolved from events of his early childhood. A native of West Suffield, Connecticut, he was born on July 5, 1794. After his father's death and his mother's breakdown, the two-year-old boy passed among the households of kin. He lived with a tavern keeper, suffered insecurity and rejection, contracted consumption, and developed exaggerated fears of insanity and alcoholism.

After a checkered academic career, Graham sought private tutoring in theology and ordination as a minister. His personal goals extended from saving souls to upgrading asylums, freeing blacks, uplifting prostitutes, and eliminating corsets. Under the influence of William Metcalfe's *Abstinence from the Flesh of Animals* (1823), Graham evolved a personal philosophy of vegetarianism and sexual abstinence based on his notion that enjoying meat was a carnal act.

After failed attempts at business and the ministry, he worked for the Newark, New Jersey, presbytery and, in 1830, for the Pennsylvania Society for Discouraging the Use of Ardent Spirits before beginning his career as a health and temperance lecturer. His topics included "The Young Man's Guide to Chastity" and "Epidemic Diseases." Although he had scant scientific understanding of disease, he exploited a cholera epidemic in 1832 with histrionics denouncing lewd behavior and chicken pie. He edited Luigi Cornaro's *Discourses on a Sober and Temperate Life* (1832) and published *A Lecture on Epidemic Diseases Generally and Particularly the Spasmodic Cholera* (1833) and *The Young Man's Guide to Chastity: The Aesculapian Tablets of the Nineteenth Century* (1834).

Of all Graham's controversial opinions and pronouncements, the one that caused the most uproar was his vilification of white bread and advocacy of a diet rich in coarse homemade loaves called "dyspepsia bread." His opinions on baked goods were specific: the most healthful should be at least a half-day old and made from coarse, unbolted flour. He claimed that this wholesome foodstuff would stem anger, violence, and drunkenness and stave off premature death. His pamphlet "Treatise on Bread and Bread Making" (1837) incited Boston bakers to riot and, with its allegation that meat products were to blame for premature aging and disease, aroused the ire of butchers. When locals marched on the hotel where he was speaking, "Grahamites" dropped bags of lime from the roof and scattered the mob.

Issuance of the weekly *Graham Journal of Health and Longevity* from 1837 to 1839 paralleled the reformer's mounting influence on American diet. Graham earned the praise of the publisher Horace Greeley and abolitionist William Lloyd Garrison. One of the causes he embraced was the promotion of unsifted whole-wheat flour, which acquired the name "graham flour." To accompany it, he devised Graham butter, a creamy milk thickened with brown flour. As a commodity, graham flour was the start of the multibillion-dollar breakfast cereal industry and laid the groundwork for the health foods movement of the late twentieth century. Graham crakers, first marketed in 1829, were still in production from Nabisco in the twenty-first century.

Graham earned the reputation of crank and hypochondriac for advocating therapeutic Bible reading, vegetarianism, a high-fiber diet, firm beds, open windows, pure drinking water, cold showers three times a week, dancing for exercise, and nonrestrictive clothing. He believed that the individual should exercise the jaws, teeth, and digestive system by eating nuts and raw vegetables rather than processed, refined foods. In addition to denouncing tobacco, whiskey, wine, and opium as debauchery, he demonized slaughterhouses, animal fats, spices, food additives, refined sugars, butter and cream, carbonation, tea and coffee, and reliance on the medical profession, which, he believed, resorted too readily to calomel purgatives. To the consternation of the delicate-minded, he illustrated his talks with drawings of the digestive tract. Newspapers called him "Dr. Bran" and labeled his notions quackery; Ralph Waldo Emerson called him a "prophet of bran bread and pumpkins." (Bee 1999, 41)

Abstemious Grahamites sampled communal living at Brooke Farm and opened college cafeterias and Graham boardinghouses in Boston. As Graham increasingly came to picture himself as a Christian martyred by the rabble, his intellectual interests turned from healthful dietary practices to phrenology and prevention of premature burial. His alliances brought him into the company of Quakers, Shakers, temperance groups, John Harvey Kellogg, and other crusaders for a healthful lifestyle. Graham's doctrines influenced the diet of the social theorist Charles Fourier and his followers, Mormon Church founder Joseph Smith, and essayist Henry David Thoreau, all of whom tried vegetarianism. An amused public tended to focus on his nutritional advice to the exclusion of his theories on physiology, causes of cholera, personal hygiene, alcoholism, and sexual abstinence. He died at home in Northampton, Massachusetts, on September 11, 1851. Of his many articles, books, essays, and varied interests, graham crackers survived, making his name a household word.

Further Reading

Bee, Wilson, "Bread and Nutter," *New Statesman*, January 1, 1999, 41–43.
Farmer, Jean, "The Rev. Sylvester (Graham Cracker) Graham: America's Early Fiber Crusader," *Saturday Evening Post*, March 1985, 32–36.
Gordon, John Steele, "Sawdust Pudding," *American Heritage*, July–August 1996, 16–18.
Klaw, Spencer, "Pursuing Health in the Promised Land," *Horizons*, Spring 1976, 24–29.

GRATER

A grater is any of a large and diverse group of perforated kitchen implements, usually made of metal, used for shredding such foods as cabbage and coconut or crumbling hard substances such as cheese, chocolate, and nutmeg. Grated foods have influenced menus throughout culinary history. The Taino, whom Christopher Columbus encountered in San Salvador, grated yuca tubers and formed the fiber into cakes to roast on terra cotta baking dishes. In the Middle Ages, the French grated nutmeg and cheese to flavor crusts. Irish kitchens required a grater for making boxty, a potato pancake served on All Saints' Day each November 1. The ingredients consisted of milk, eggs, flour, and grated raw potato. For a soupier version called dippity, the cook increased the proportion of milk. Japanese cooks used a grater to break down a woody hunk of dried bonito into powdered meat to season and thicken soup.

Early American tinsmiths purchased grater blanks that they could puncture to the tastes and needs of their customers. Uncomplicated tin grating columns or cylinders were handy for shredding cabbage for sauerkraut, potatoes for latkes, and citrus peel and nutmeg for use as flavorings. The smaller cucumber slicer was a miniature of the cabbage shredder and identical in design. An oval grater with hooped handle slid easily over stale, dry bread to make crumbs to thicken a gravy, sauce, or pudding or to top a casserole. For convenience, box graters of tin and wood positioned a grating surface above a drawer-like compartment for easy collection and removal of shredded foods. For smaller jobs, the bread rasp, shaped like an iron file, scraped the bottoms of blackened muffins and loaves and grated crumbs over the surface of soup or broth.

Devised in the 1890s, the combination box grater, cucumber slicer, slaw cutter, and kraut cutter improved on the columnar grater. It offered a wooden frame to hold peeled vegetables or chunks of cabbage while the hand pushed them back and forth over a cutting blade secured within the larger wooden frame. To create different kinds of slices, the user adjusted the angle of the blade or removed the straight-edge blade and replaced it with a fluted or serrated edge. In1897, Robert M. Gardiner carried ingenuity to extremes by patenting a "combined grocer's package, grater, slicer, and mouse and fly trap." (Breeden 1971, 158) Another invention of the period, the drum grater, which was pierced on one side for grating and slotted on the other for slicing, also accommodated a cone-shaped screen that allowed vermin to enter but prevented their escape.

Into the 1900s, these tools eased kitchen drudgery for Caribbean cooks preparing fibrous cassava, yam, and coconut. For sweet potato pudding, the Grenadine cook assembled pumpkin, tannia corms, and green banana for grating with coconut into a thick slurry. Blended with flour, spices, and raisins, the mix baked into a wholesome dessert. For a serving of planter's punch, a nutmeg grater created a fine dusting of the pungent spice. The grating of cones of *papelón,* a by-product of sugaring, added the flavor of a raw native sweetener.

More difficult to label by date and place is the invention of the mandoline, the professional cook's grater, an expensive hand-held rectangle with an opening for a variety of blade shapes and sizes and a handle for steadying the frame and guiding solid pieces through the openings, which slice and ruffle as well as shred. It may have been a nineteenth-century invention from Alsace, France, for sauerkraut making. Whatever its origins, it became a kitchen and restaurant classic for slicing garnishes and gaufrette potato chips and for julienning vegetables.

By the end of the twentieth century, culinary supply stores offered a variety of specialty graters, each adapted for a particular task. Among the many variations were the lemon grater, a hand-held implement with small perforations to rend citrus zest into fine shreds; the microplane rasp, a light-weight short-handled tool with a broad, flat perforated surface for grating ginger, chocolate, and nutmeg or mincing shallot or garlic directly over dishes; the nutmeg grater, a conical device with raw metal edges that both stored and grated a nutmeg; and the revolving grater, a hand-cranked or clamp-on grater of tin or cast iron formed with a rotating grater drum that intersected with nut

meats or chunks of chocolate, carrot, potato, or hard cheese pressed into a hopper by a lid or tamper. A simple hand grater enabled the Swiss cook to pare potatoes to blend with chopped onion for *rösti,* a large, flat potato pancake. The grater remained a kitchen necessity into the twenty-first century, despite the existence of other, more elaborate appliances such as food processors and blenders, designed to ease the task of reducing solid pieces of fruit and vegetables into fine shreds or pulp.

Further Reading

Breeden, Robert L. *Those Inventive Americans.* Washington, D.C.: National Geographic Society, 1971.

GREENS

Abundant and nutritious, the green leaves of plants have served humanity as a food source from prehistory. Ancient authors, who thought of the hearth and the kitchen garden as household yin and yang, described the plucking, rinsing, and mixing of salad greens, which ranged from mundane beet tops, mustard, cabbage, and dandelion leaves to seaweed, bryony, lichens, colewort, fleabane, baobab leaf, and fennel. The ayurvedic diet of Indian vegetarians promoted greens to cleanse the body of impurities. The Egyptians considered lettuce milk a stimulus to romance. Roman food writers Apicius, Cato, Pliny, and Columella mentioned the use of vinegars and garum as dressings and dips for leafy vegetables. Cooks in Nepal began seeding their gardens with spinach in 647 CE. In Lebanon, at the end of a Ramadan fast, Muslim cooks readied *fattoush* (mixed salad) from standard garden vegetables, parsley, mint, and purslane gathered in the wild.

Early Salad Enthusiasts

In the early Middle Ages, the absence of greens in late winter left only dried peas and parsnips to break the monotony of bread, cheese, and meat. A hearty meal of the first greens of spring produced a laxative effect that cooks valued as a tonic and appetite stimulant. Platina's *De Honesta Voluptate et Valitudine* (On Right Pleasure and Health, 1475), a classic food text from the Italian Renaissance, gave fair analysis of greens as healthful food, especially spinach and chard, which he advocated served with their natural juices. Gervase Markham's compendium *The English Hus-wife* (1615) offered instructions for making spinach pie, a laborious process requiring finely minced greens cooked down in wine, cinnamon, sugar, and rosewater. The baker poured

Lettuce in the produce section of a Virginia supermarket.

the jelled green filling into a *coffin* (pastry shell) to cool before garnishing it with caraway comfits.

An avid proponent of the salad, the English diarist and oft-cited kitchen gardener John Evelyn, who compiled *The Compleat Gardner* (1693), lauded lettuce as a cure for fever, thirst, sleeplessness, vapors, intemperance, lust, and pain. From his observations of Continental cuisine over a two-year journey in France and Italy in 1652, he listed among the 300 recipes in his masterwork, *Acetaria, A Discourse of Sallets* (1699), preparations of vegetables and greens. His directions for cleaning salad vegetables describe a process that has changed little since the late Renaissance: "Let the herby ingredients be exquisitely cull'd and cleans'd of all worm-eaten dry-spotted leaves. Then discreetly sprinkled with spring water, let remain for a while in a cullender, then swing gently in clean napkin." (Beard et al. 1975, 32)

Meals from the Wild

American Indian cookery featured greens as a balance to meat-heavy meals. In Mexico and the southwestern

United States, the Tohono O'odham foraged for greens and mescal. The Miwok of San Francisco Bay, California, attached cone-shaped baskets to their foreheads by tumplines to hold their gleanings of columbine, clover, larkspur, milkweed, and miner's lettuce to vary a diet of fish, meat, game, nuts, and seeds. Forest Indians valued chickweed for stone boiling and made salads of sorrel, purslane, and cress, a common green that flourished on waterways and in damp lowlands. The Maliseet of New Brunswick, Passamaquoddy of New England, and Cherokee of the Carolinas and Tennessee prized immature fronds of fiddlehead fern, which they gathered near waterways and cooked for a spring vegetable or made into soup.

Frontier cooks contributed to the world's knowledge of gathering and cooking greens. In Moreton Bay, Australia, settler Constance Petrie wrote about the roasting of bungwall, a semi-aquatic fern found in Australian swamps. Newcomers to New Zealand discovered the Maori love of ferns, particularly the hen and chickens (*Asplenium bulbiferum*). When Captain James Cook sailed the *Endeavour* to New Zealand in 1770, he chose Botany Bay greens (genus *Tetragonia*), a wild spinach, as a source of the nutrients needed to prevent scurvy and instructed his cook to add the leaves to vegetable stew and salads. His botanist, Sir Joseph Banks, later the president of the Royal Society and author of *The Endeavour Journal 1768–1771*, transported the greens to England. From there, the plant spread to England and the Americas, where it thrived in kitchen gardens.

In *The Countryman's England* (1935), the social historian Dorothy Hartley mentioned numerous wild greens gathered for food, including samphires, which grew in sand dunes; charlock, a weed found in grain fields; and sloke, a Welsh sea spinach. She described a Devon waterweed, laver—"like thin brown silk clinging to the rocks between tide-marks"—a delicacy traditionally sold in the streets of Bath by the "laver woman." (Hartley 1980, 109) Served boiled, laver was typically the first course of a low country meal rounded out with marsh mutton. Hartley contrasted the simple goodness of laver, eaten cold or hot, with Ireland's carrigean (or carrageen), also called Dorset weed or white weed, Irish moss, Iberian moss, or Dorset moss. This plant was the source of a vegetarian gelatin and suitable to the making of cough drops, blancmange, custard, and jelly.

A popular song during the U.S. Civil War, "Bacon & Greens," evoked fond table memories for hungry soldiers who missed home cooking. The last stanza described how to eat the hearty dish: "Stick your fork in the fat; wrap your greens round the bacon/And you'll vow there's no dish like good bacon and greens." (Weaver 1989, 12) For slaves, however, the dreary daily diet of bacon and greens was not a source for celebration, nor did their reliance on this humble fare end with emancipation. During Reconstruction and after, black laborers entered quasi-slavery in Southern work camps under the guise of contract labor. Camp cooks set up shanty kitchens that served little more than greens and hog jowl, a diet that generated a tradition of anemia and rickets among the region's poor.

Place in the Modern Diet

Cooked greens are a tasty contribution to a nutritious meal. Meal planners value them as roughage and the touch of color they add to the table. In the 1960s wild greens increased in popularity as a result of the writings of Euell Theophilus Gibbons, an enthusiastic proponent of foraging who earned the titled "father of modern wild foods." As a child, Gibbons had scoured New Mexico's hill country for piñon nuts, mushrooms, prickly pear fruit, and edible greens to supplement the family's table while his father searched for work. His first bestseller, *Stalking the Wild Asparagus* (1962),

preceded articles in *Organic Gardening and Farming, National Geographic,* and *National Wildlife Magazine.* To encourage the collecting and cooking of native plants, he organized the National Wild Food Association and Foraging Friends and promoted his interest in nature on popular television programs. After his death in 1975, Boston University archived his journals and notes, which have served camping enthusiasts as a cache of information on camp cookery and wilderness survival.

In "The Common Stinging Nettle," an essay reprised in the spring 1998 *Vermont Weathervane,* Gibbons promoted this despised weed—a common sight on roadways and in vacant lots—as a free source of protein, trace minerals, and vitamins A and C. He claimed that "a good French cook can make seven delicious dishes of nettle tops." (Gibbons 1998) He explained that the tender greens were edible in early spring and advised using a long-handled spoon, shears, and tongs during preparation of creamed or puréed nettle greens and added an Old English recipe for hearty nettle pudding.

The English food writer and traveler Patience Gray saluted greens in *Honey from a Weed: Fasting and Feasting in Tuscany, Catalonia, the Cyclades, and Apulia* (1986). Experience of the late winter dandelion and daisy harvest on Naxos sparked her interest in wild herb cookery. Among the *radici* (roots), she listed succulent and healthful chicory, endive, hawkweed, sowthistle, marigold, and chamomile. She described how Greek islanders cut stalks free from the root, rinsed them at a fountain, and boiled the leafy mass before plating them along with an oil and lemon juice vinaigrette and hard-boiled eggs.

In kitchens worldwide where cooked greens are a staple, purées of nettles, chervil, mallow, or spinach take on new flavor possibilities from the addition of sieved boiled eggs, chopped peanuts, sliced mushrooms, and anchovy paste. As a winter source of vitamin A, European cooks grow kale and Swiss chard long after the first frost. Middle Easterners flatten cabbage and grape leaves as wrappers for mixtures of meat, rice, and seasonings. Cooks in Papua, New Guinea, steam fresh greens in bamboo tubes, stuffing in more as the greens shrink from evaporation and flavoring them with salt and meat drippings. Another class of greens, water plants and their rhizomes, are popular in Asia. Malaysian cooks favor mustard greens and *kang kong* (Asian spinach) for stir-frying. The Japanese prefer seaweed.

In Africa, greens provide a traditional source of nourishment. Harvesting of *morogo,* a general term for edible leaves of buffalo-thorn, pumpkins, silver beet, or sweet potato, requires careful selection of tender shoots and the peeling of tough stalks. Tanzanian women pluck greens at their height of flavor during the rainy season and sun-dry them for later use. To make the most of garden produce, Zambians chop and simmer beet tops and cook *lupusi abuntele* (pumpkin leaves with peanuts) for feasts. Kenyans prize stands of wild leafy vegetables and amaranth root to make *supa ya mchicha* (red root soup); as a staple additive, they tenderize the greens known as *sukuma wiki* to eat with grain porridge. South African cooks simmer root, sow thistle, chard, spinach, pumpkin leaves, or lamb's quarters with garlic, onion, and cornmeal into *imifino*, a one-dish meal.

Further Reading

"Euell Gibbons: The Father of Modern Wild Foods," *Wild Food Adventurer*, November 1998, 1.
Gibbons, Euell, "The Common Stinging Nettle," *Vermont Weathervane*, Spring 1998, 1.

GRIDDLE

The griddle, also called girdle, is a flat, polished baking surface used for cooking small cakes made from batter, such as Japanese *mochi* (rice cakes) and Scandinavian apple pancakes. Among the Berbers, who roast pounded barley over a flame on a *ghana'a* (griddle), the result is *dashisha*, a dish similar to the Arab couscous and grits, a regional specialty of the American South. For open-hearth cooking, the griddle traditionally sports long handles or a bail for use in attaching it to an overhead chain or bar.

The molding of sacral griddlecakes has a long history in India, where the temple cook pressed out flat cakes on an earthenware plate. For making sacrificial meals, cooks chose an open grilling pan with hollows in shapes that produced varied motifs in the cakes. Griddle cuisine appears in the Sutras, the sacred books written from 800 to 350 BCE.

In Aztec and Latino kitchens, a hard-clay cooking slab or iron or copper griddle called a comal, or comali, suits the quick cooking of flat breads or tortillas. Among the Tepehuan of Chihuahua, Mexico, preparation of pinole gruel, a traveler's campsite staple, began with the toasting of maize grains either in an olla or a comal before cooks ground them into flour and blended them with molasses. Cooks also fried squash, squash blossoms, and mashed beans or peas on the comal. When a supply of seeds sufficient for planting accrued, homemakers dried extra squash seeds or acorn meats on the hot surface as a delicacy. Originally, the comal's cooking surface rested on three small stones, which elevated it above a small fire fed from the side with mesquite twigs, grass, and husks. The cook applied a paste of corn and water to the hot surface, which instantly dehydrated the batter into a flat bread called *tlaxcalli* in the Nahuatl language.

In the American colonies, the griddle, paired with a stewpot of grease for lubricating its surface, served at each meal as the hot surface for quick-cooking plain foods. The corn dodger, a compact pone, was a test of the cook's skill. To kiss the hot griddle in a spot no larger than a quarter, the batter had to be stiff enough to stay in one spot without spreading out as pancake batter would. The griddled dodger made excellent food for traveling. Packed hot in a sack or leather bag, it warmed the rider's body. When the horseman was ready to dismount and eat, he reheated the pone at the fire or toast it on a portable griddle.

In 1848, *The American Lady's System of Cookery*, by Mrs. T. J. Crowen, made specific reference to the use of the griddle for cooking corn. She instructed the cook to shuck fresh ears and roast them directly on the "gridiron." (Fussell 1999) This laborious task involved regular rotation of the ear to make sure every part of it came into contact with the hot oiled surface. An alternate method suggested laying the ear on a clean hearth in front of the fire. This same primitive roasting tradition, which American colonists learned from observing Indian cooks, was still in use a hundred years later, as described in the 1943 classic *Joy of Cooking*.

In nineteenth-century Europe and the Americas, specialty griddles offered numerous features. A cast iron gridiron with a slotted or perforated grate cooked steak or fish. Melted fat dripped through the perforations into the fire, leaving the meat less greasy and more flavorful than if it had cooked in a skillet. Deluxe models, which resembled the backyard charcoal grill, offered folding legs. Griddles made of soapstone, a natural substance, cooked flat cakes or held rings in which muffins baked. Soapstone provided an unusual baking surface in that it required no fat to keep foods from sticking. In 1904, Duparquet, Huot & Moneuse of New York City marketed a range fitted with a built-in griddle, a long heated surface that allowed for extensive frying, steak cooking, or pancake making.

Neat and compact, the griddle was ideal for street vendors operating their own kitchen businesses. In Djemaa El-Fna, the *suq* (market place) of Marrakech, Morocco, on-the-spot grilling at food stalls and on umbrella-shaded push carts supplied shoppers with quick lunches into the 1990s. Lighting their wares with gas lanterns after sundown, the street cooks enticed diners with grilled kidney and sausage on skewers.

Griddle cookery retains its importance for breakfast foods, sandwiches, crêpes, and meats. The most primitive flat-bread cooker, the heated rock, a forerunner of the griddle, still serves the Bedouin of Jordan and the Hopi of the southwestern United States. Pakistani cooks, whether in Asia or the Caribbean, heat rounds of dough for *roti* on a *tava*, a flat metal disk set over a fire. In home settings, military camps, or market stalls, Moroccan, Kurdish, Armenian, Syrian, Lebanese, and Qashqai cooks place a fuel-efficient concave griddle over a controlled fire in a portable hearth. In Kyrgyzstan, a double griddle produces a concave flat bread. By setting dough in the bottom griddle above a fire and nesting the second griddle on top, the baker can fill the upper dome with coals and cook both sides of the bread at one time. Ethiopian griddle bread begins with a sour batter of teff flour and cooks on a clay *injera* into a large, flat loaf that doubles as a plate or food wrap. Into the twenty-first century, Latino cooks continued to use the comal for crisping maguey worms (an aphrodisiac) and for baking balls of corn dough called *testales* into *tlaxcalli, yet,* or *wej,* the Nahuatl, Zapotec, and Mayan words for tortilla. Diners then used the finished flat bread to wrap meat, onion, and tomato fillings. Another application of the comal in Mexican kitchens is for blistering chiles, charring tomatoes, and toasting the spices that form the key ingredients in adobos, moles, pipianes, recados, and salsas. To prevent hot spots or sticking, cooks brush the surface of the clay comal with lime (calcium oxide).

Twenty-first-century griddles are available in a variety of styles and offer such amenities as an anodized aluminum body, ridged and/or nonstick surfaces, and a pouring lip for draining off fat. A small portable grill, notched to fit a stovetop burner, heats food rapidly and drains fat into indentations in the surface. Oversized electronic griddles augment stovetop space by supplying large heated cast surfaces that heat up to 425 degrees Fahrenheit. Immersible when the heating element is removed, they clean quickly and can be stored out of the way when not in use. Another variant, a combination fajita skillet and oval griddle with wood underliner, offers convenience while preserving the traditional Tex-Mex style of cooking.

See also **Cooking Stone**

Further Reading

Alford, Jeffrey, and Naomi Duguid, "On the Flatbread Trail," *Amsco World*, September–October 1995, 16–25.
Fussell, Betty. *The Story of Corn.* New York: North Point Press, 1999.
Werner, Louis, "The Magic Circles of Djem El-Fna," *Aramco World*, July–August 1993, 40–47.

GROCERY STORE

The public sale of food began with individual vendors delivering goods, selling door to door, or setting up stalls in public markets. Around the Mediterranean and in the Orient, market days brought into an area goods from distant places, delivered by sea or packed overland by camel, mule, and horse-cart. In ancient market cities, shoppers could choose from a wide variety of goods that promoted cosmopolitan tastes in wines, fruits, and vegetables. Shopkeepers tabulated purchases on their fingers or with tally marks drawn in the dust or incised on a wax tablet. Counting devices increased the efficiency and speed of commerce. Perhaps the best known is the abacus.

A Fledgling Trade

In Medieval England, farmers who had extra eggs, poultry, or other goods could commission them to a sales agent, but had to claim unsold goods before the closing of the market or forfeit all to the agent. Forestallers, contractors who bought up goods before the market opened, incurred a penalty for raising prices above normal supply and demand. A major injunction of the Magna Carta, the cornerstone of English liberty, referred to the rights of the domestic merchant and importer: "Let all merchants have safety and security in exiting Anglia and coming into Anglia to stay or pass through Anglia, on land as well as on water, for the purpose of buying and selling." Nonetheless, middlemen who bought up butter, cheese, bacon, wax, honey, and poultry caused prices to rise. Gradually, trade in baskets of fruit and clutches of chicks expanded into full-scale, sophisticated sale of groceries where buyers had to put up coins, wine, spice, silk, or other nonperishables.

The freedom of food distribution ended in the Middle Ages, when flagrant violations of the public trust prompted bureaucratic action. In 1328, London's pepper mongers formed an alliance, the *grossarii*—hence the origin of the term *grocer*. (Davidson 1999, 595) In Paris, members of a butchers' guild turned out at Les Halles on June 22, 1351, to see a shop worker executed for endangering customers with spoiled goods. In 1399, regulations forced dealers to sell perishables within forty-eight hours in winter and thirty-six hours in summer. To halt the commerce in rancid, discolored meats, the law limited sales to full daylight. By 1431, stiffer directives condemned deceitful sellers for substituting cat meat for hare and forced culprits to stand at the Seine at midday to toss foul meat into the river

Interior view of grocery store, Washington D.C. 1920.
[© *Library of Congress, Prints and Photographs Division (LC-USZ62-114699)*]

and to call out a public apology. Additional pressures on dealers forbade selling pigs fed on human remains or reheated leftovers.

British grocery stores got their start during the Industrial Revolution. In 1777, when James Fitch entered the business of food merchandizing in London, he found practices not much changed from the medieval guild system. Bakers, butchers, fruiterers, grocers, and poulterers maintained proprietary claims to their specialties. Gradually, the grocers expanded from trade in imported spices and dried fruits to include tea, coffee, chocolate, and sugar; eventually they encompassed the trade of the other specialists. In 1844, Rochdale Pioneers, a food cooperative, launched a successful commercial venture, which developed branches in numerous communities where workers' incomes were rising. In 1872, Thomas Lipton opened a general grocery concern in Glasgow that grew into a merchandising phenomenon of the British Isles. By the 1930s, when Allied Suppliers and Unigate flourished,

multiple outlets were taking advantage of British standardized packaging, name brands, and national advertising.

Tradition of the General Store

In many locales, shoppers relied on the country or general store, with its cozy assortment of brooms, tools, lanterns, oversized coffee grinder, and kitchen staples. Barrels and baskets held assortments of fruit, eggs, and soda crackers, crisp leavened or unleavened biscuits or wafers sold loose since the 1870s. Town dwellers shopped regularly; a woman might lead children pulling wooden wagons to haul home the family groceries. Countrywomen got to town less often, usually when a wagon was passing that way or a kitchen emergency forced them to halt work and make a special trip. Storekeepers enticed children with glass jars of penny candy and entertained them by demonstrating how they could reach items on the top shelf with elongated tongs.

When buying staples, shoppers served themselves, selecting from bins the meal, flour, sugar, raisins, molasses, spices, and salt necessary to restock dwindling home supplies. Barrels held brined pickles and dry crackers; bushel baskets contained dried peas and beans, purchased by the scoop. The advent of railroads helped keep the grocer stocked and introduced produce and items from distant communities, while expanding to new venues the market for locally produced herbs, canned goods, and homemade candies, pies, and bread.

In the Australian gold fields, where a full range of groceries was a rarity, merchants brought in goods to sell in tent emporiums. Merchants marketing native produce, potatoes, and flour, baking powder, tea, chicory, jams, condiments, and grog easily earned more than miners. In Gulgong, New South Wales, a female grocer in her small wood-frame store stocked fresh vegetables and fruit, fuel, matches, pots, and expensive canned goods and mining equipment. Not until the 1880s did a road system link the outback with port cities. With the coming of civilization, Australian butchers, who began business in unsanitary open-air stalls, became one of the first trades to organize.

On the American frontier, the problem of provisioning was endemic. Westward travelers who lacked stalking and shooting skills hired professional hunters to accompany the wagon train. Wives scavenged berries and herbs and stretched their meager staples as far as they would go. When supplies ran out, they bartered with Indians for fish and game. By the time the train reached a trading post or town large enough to support a grocer, pioneer cooks were willing to pay dearly for fresh food, regardless of its quality.

Rise of Chain Stores

In the United States, the budding field of domestic science educated the home cook on the necessity of a well-stocked pantry, which encouraged patronage of full-service grocery stores. By the early twentieth century, the grocery business was rapidly moving toward a full range of goods under one roof. In 1911, to attract a new class of licensed drivers, the first self-service stores, Alpha Beta Foods in Pomona, California, and Ward's Groceteria in Ocean Park, wooed shoppers with the promise of convenience. In Memphis, Tennessee, in 1916, Clarence Saunders founded Piggly Wiggly, the first supermarket chain, which offered 605 items. Part of his merchandising strategy was to organize the goods in a series of aisles that forced the customer to walk the entire store before checking out.

As more women shopped for themselves, fewer stores delivered purchases.

In the February 1925 issue of *Good Housekeeping*, Arthur E. Albrecht distinguished the different choices in shopping open to urban housewives. He reminded them that, "In cities having large foreign populations, pushcart peddlers and wagon vendors supplement retail dealers in the distribution of food and other commodities." (Albrecht 1925, 136) He noted that although door-to-door vendors' prices were low, shoppers had to walk long distances and pay cash for foodstuffs that might be inferior in quantity and haphazardly weighed and measured. He concluded, "Furthermore, unsatisfactory food can not be exchanged." (Ibid.) A follow-up article the next month urged, "Consistent cooperation with your grocer will in time do much in influencing the reduction of some of your food costs." ("You and Your Grocer," 1925, 274)

Ads in *Woman's Home Companion* reflected a similar market strategy at A&P, a chain launched in the 1850s as the Great Atlantic and Pacific Tea Company. The company banked its success on volume, great values, and small profit margins. It invented a house brand, labeled "Ann Page"—a clever scheme for implying that a female presence supervised the preparation of the staples marketed in her name. This use of branding as a guarantee of quality extended to 750,000 trademarks by the twenty-first century.

At the beginning of the Great Depression, A&P's 15,000 U.S. stores sold $1 billion in goods. The chain drove down prices through cutthroat competition with mom-and-pop stores and farmer's markets. To counter the chain's advantages of bulk buying and sweetheart deals with distributors, Chicago accountant Frank Grimes organized independent grocers under the IGA banner.

Around this time Michael Cullen opened King Kullen, a warehouse grocery emporium, in Jamaica, Long Island. He bolstered sales with bold, flashy ads for unusually attractive bargains sold at low margin. In 1932, small, vulnerable New Jersey grocers banded together to fight Cullen and his competitor, Big Bear supermarkets, by forcing the media to reject their advertising and coercing the state legislature to ban the sale of food at or below cost. These strong-arm methods failed, however, and Bull Market, Great Leopard, Great Tiger, and other giant food distributors emerged. Within a year, A&P's 18,000 stores commanded 11 percent of grocery sales. In Los Angeles, a small group of farmers took a stand against West Coast chains, uniting to form the signature Farmer's Market, a city landmark.

In 1937, Sylvan N. Goldman made an extraordinary impact on grocery shopping when he introduced the folding wheeled "basket carrier" for use in his self-service markets in Oklahoma City. (Powell 1997)

Goldman worked with mechanic Fred Young to build the first grocery cart from a folding chair on wheels equipped with removable upper and lower level wire baskets to replace the woven baskets his customers had been carrying. The cart prompted a new approach to shopping, encouraging consumers to buy a week's goods at a single store visit. Goldman's invention also revolutionized the way foods were packaged, shelved, marketed, and stored.

Initially, customers were leery of the cart. The idea did not catch on until Goldman hired people of varying ages and physical condition to pose as shoppers and demonstrate the value of having hands free for examining items. The innovation soon attracted more people to the store and encouraged them to buy more at each visit. He formed the Folding Carrier Company, forerunner of Unarco of Wagner, Oklahoma, to market the carts to other retailers, whose demand soon caused a seven-year backlog of orders. By 1947, Goldman had invented the nesting cart with baby seat. The Smithsonian Institution put his grocery cart on display as a model of American ingenuity and commercial savvy.

Buying from one of the new emporia had its advantages. In Samuel Chamberlain's *Clémentine in the Kitchen* (1943), a light-hearted recipe collection and story of a French cook serving an American family, he observes: "Of course, it's fun to buy dried peas and lentils and beans encased in cellophane, as we now do in our New England town. It's a great convenience to order by telephone—sometimes. It's nice to have a date on your coffee, a slogan stamped on your oranges, a chance to add twenty-five words or less to your soap wrapper and thus win a fortune." (Levy 1997, 153) But the old habit of sparring with the grocer and watching as familiar hands scooped meal into the hanging scale, poured it into a brown bag, and tied it with grocery string died hard.

Luring Customers

The introduction of shopping carts and self-service aisles marked the beginning of a concerted effort by merchandisers to lure customers. In 1938, Curtis Leroy Carlson, an entrepreneur from Minneapolis, Minnesota, launched Gold Bond Trading Stamps, a series of coupons that customers collected to exchange for premium items, such as dishes, linens, grills, and small appliances. The idea of a buyer's premium, which had debuted among grocers in 1890, reached Denver in 1950 with the introduction of S&H Green Stamps, the nation's most popular premium stamp, which Thomas A. Sperry and Shelly B. Hutchinson had initiated in 1896 in Jackson, Michigan. Kroger brought out its Top Value Stamp in 1955. By 1966, 83 percent of American households were saving stamps, pasting them into books, and stockpiling them toward a valued domestic item. Another type of premium assisted the poorest shoppers. In 1938, the U.S. Department of Agriculture printed and distributed the first food stamps to low income families in Rochester, New York.

Markets opened bigger and better than ever before in the post-World War II years; the offerings expanded with the addition of self-serve delis and home products such as kitchen linens and gadgets. In 1950, J. Sainsbury, the self-service British grocery store, brought the American system to London, where customers proved equally eager to help themselves. By 1959, U.S. consumers were making 69 percent of food purchases in supermarkets. The smiling local grocer and neighborhood food specialty shop rapidly disappeared as the chain store offered more selection but a smaller staff.

From mid-century into the late 1990s, the height of supermarket dominance of food shopping, distributor buyouts consolidated food marketing. In 1956, Procter & Gamble bought Duncan Hines and Consolidated Foods bought Sara Lee. The following year, soft drink marketer Coca-Cola purchased Minute Maid. The trend picked up speed in the 1980s, with R.J. Reynolds acquiring Nabisco, Philip Morris acquiring General Foods and, later, Kraft. Control of major brand names passed from small entrepreneurs to the growing conglomerates, moving farther from the consumer and requiring more advertising to assure buyers of quality.

The application of electronic technology to the marketplace speeded up the weekly trip to the grocery store with the price scanner, introduced in 1974 at Marsh Supermarket in Troy, Ohio. From clerk-controlled scanning to shopper scanning, the use of electronic reading of prices allowed the consumer more freedom and faster and more accurate totals of their purchases. Itemized bills listed by name, price, and quantity the consumer's goods, simplifying comparison shopping and household accounting. Also popular in the late 1970s and 1980s in New York, Seattle, San Francisco, Berkeley, and Cambridge, Massachusetts, were grocery cooperatives, a group purchasing method that reduced prices on staples easily warehoused and distributed to members.

Over much of Asia and Europe, the neighborhood grocery store remained small and intimate enough for grocers to call shoppers by name. Rural Laotian women rose before sunup to reach the open-air market in time for the best selection of produce. Late risers had to content themselves with leftovers. In Germany and France, hometown bakeries and greengrocers were the norm. In string bags, shoppers placed small amounts of staples, enough for no more than a few days. Such timing of purchases assured the freshest ingredients available.

Changes and Challenges

In 1975, as grocery discounting flourished in the United States, A&P, a bellwether chain, began to close warehouses, distribution centers, and almost half of its 3,500 stores. In a shift of pricing control from distributor to retailer, in 1978, David Nichol introduced the President's Choice name brand, a private label that competed with established market leaders. That same year, Jewel Food Stores launched a line of generic foods. By the late 1980s, the average supermarket struggled to accommodate up to 12,000 brand-name and generic items in 22,000 square feet of space. Managers kept watch on trends, reducing stock in items that went out of fashion or lost market share to competitors, and eliminating some brands altogether.

In 1991, K-Mart opened its first Super K in Medina, Ohio. The chain, which Sebastian Spering Kresge began as a variety store in 1899, advanced in competition with Wal-Mart by exploiting the F. W. Woolworth model of the self-service dime store. By 1962—the same year Sam Walton opened his first store in Rogers, Arkansas—it had evolved into a discount department store, with its first outlet in Garden City, Michigan. The progression to an all-encompassing super mart challenged local mom-and-pop stores with a broad range of low-priced goods, including housewares, clothing, gift items, groceries, and deli foods. Open night and day, these stores suited the needs of singles, families with small children, and second- and third-shift workers in need of a shopping headquarters that kept unconventional hours but offered the same stock as standard grocery stores. In the early 1980s, Walton launched a wholesale chain, Sam's Club, where shoppers who paid a membership fee could save money on a wide range of merchandise—including food—by buying in large quantities.

In the twenty-first century, grocery stores continued to revamp displays and offerings to suit changes in consumer lifestyle. Headaches for managers kept pace with advances. They hired staff to keep transients and children from stealing and defacing carts. To keep carts in the lot and not out in traffic or in gullies, some stores added electric systems that tripped a wheel lock when the carts reach property bounds. They also added mobile carts for the handicapped or elderly shopper, oversized carts for families with more than one toddler, and child-size carts for youngsters referred to as "customers in training." A Salt Lake City inventor, Paul G. Begum, introduced a shopping cart that dispensed coupons electronically. From an LED screen in the handle, the pre-programmed device informed shoppers of specials and mark-downs in the aisles they were cruising.

To maintain their typical 2 percent profit margin, grocers had to find new ways to attract consumers. Many stores added home meal replacements—prepared dishes designed for those too tired or harried to cook. Frequent-shopper cards attracted consumers via clipless coupons that automatically deducted a given amount from the standard shelf price. In addition to encouraging regular shopping at the same store, the card enabled management to track shopper demand and loyalty and to reorganize item mix and shelf placement to improve turnover and profits. The date provided by these electronic systems helped shape retail grocer strategy. The collapse of some promising online grocery shopping services in mid-2001 disproved predictions that American consumers were abandoning personal grocery-buying trips to allow warehouse agents to fill their orders and deliver goods to the kitchen door.

Search for the Freshest and Finest

In New York City, a yearning for the kind of European-style shopping that city-dwellers enjoyed before World War II inspired Barry Benepe to open Greenmarket, a farmer's market set up four days a week in Union Square. Urban homemakers and restaurateurs shopped for strings of peppers, sorrel and dandelion greens, mesclun, fresh apples and pears, pumpkins, snap peas, and fingerling potatoes displayed in tented stalls. The largest open-air market in the United States, Greenmarket connected home cooks with organic orchardists, kitchen gardeners, herbalists, artisanal cheese and bread makers, and small rural farms, offering a venue for producers too small to compete with agribusiness.

Metropolitan Atlanta shoppers thrived in the multicultural environment of Harry's Farmers Markets, entrepreneur Harry Blazer's suburban megastore with outlets in Roswell and Marietta, Georgia. In addition to flowers, spices, and condiments from around the globe, the grocer supplied vegetables, fruit, smoked and fresh fish, poultry, and meats catering to a variety of ethnic tastes. Wines and rice came from every producing country, and coffees from Zimbabwe, Sumatra, Ethiopia, Tanzania, and Colombia were roasted fresh daily. Sophisticated shoppers in search of special ingredients found chipotle peppers, shiitake mushrooms, tandoori paste, cornhusks for tamales, yam flour, French crème fraîche, and live fish, cleaned and filleted on the spot.

See also **Weights and Measures**

Further Reading

Albrecht, Arthur E., "Food: Its Journey to Your Table," *Good Housekeeping*, March 1925, 73, 136.

Coppens, Linda Miles. *What American Women Did, 1789–1920.* Jefferson, N. C.: McFarland, 2001.

"You and Your Grocer," *Good Housekeeping*, March 1925, 77, 274.

GROG

Grog, a blend of rum and water, was a staple drink for British sailors from the seventeenth through the nineteenth centuries. Alcoholic beverages were a necessity on shipboard, where supplies of fresh water quickly spoiled due to pollutants and bacteria. Mixtures of rum with water were one answer to the problem of grumbling and lost man-hours as a result of compromised drinking water. Some ships provided rations of a weak beverage called toddy, which consisted of four or five parts hot water to one part spirits, plus sweetening. Another hot drink, cider flip, involved heating cider at hearthside with an iron flip dog or loggerhead and adding sugar, rum, and lemon.

Prior to the British conquest of Jamaica—and ready access to rum—brandy had been the navy's drink of choice. Grog became the standard in 1687 as a substitute for brandy. Under the purser's watchful eye, an assistant doled out servings twice daily. Officers supervised dispersal to assure each crew member his fair portion. Individual messes collected their ration in a monkey, a small cask or metal kettle, and carried it to the table for service.

Cutting rum with water was the policy of Admiral Edward Vernon, a naval hero who seized the Spanish stronghold of Porto Bello, Panama, in November 1739. In 1740, he insisted on dilution to stem shipboard drunkenness on daily rations of a pint for men and half that for boys. Issued from a half-cask, called a scuttlebutt or grog-tub, the drink took its name from Vernon's nickname "Old Grogram" or "Old Grog," a snide reference to his all-weather grosgrain cloak. (Kemp 1988, 357) Cook's boys poured leftover grog, known by the slang term "plush," into the scuppers, drain lines that channeled it across the deck and over the side to keep unscrupulous cooks from getting more than their share. Overindulgence was known as the "groggies" or "grog-blossoms," terms, respectively, for intoxication and inflammations of the nose and cheeks. Punishment was "six water grog," a daily portion of rum diluted with twice the usual amount of water.

In the 1760s, as English explorer Captain James Cook made for Mauna Loa, Hawaii, the crew rebelled over the issue of their drink allotment. The captain had read up on methods of avoiding scurvy, a nutritional deficiency that could decimate an ill-fed company in short order. Cook ordered the galley crew to brew shipboard beer, using sugarcane the vessel had taken onboard. When Cook replaced the grog ration with the home brew, his men mutinied, complaining that the drink was unhealthful. In its stead, they demanded grog, the sailor's right.

Under Lord Nelson, in 1795 the English navy issued each vessel a supply of lemons, which provided the vitamin C necessary to prevent scurvy, and posted a guard over water supplies kept in the scuttlebutt. As the incidence of scurvy diminished and the purity of water supplies improved, the demand for alcohol lessened. By 1824, the Royal Navy had cut the ration to the noon issue only. In 1850, allotment sank to one gill (five ounces). Rum distribution to common sailors ended in 1881 and to warrant officers in 1918. Petty and chief officers continued to take a daily half-gill of rum until the end of distribution in 1970.

Further Reading

Kemp, Peter, ed. *The Oxford Companion to Ships and the Sea.* Oxford: Oxford University Press, 1988.

H

HALE, SARAH JOSEPHA

Sarah Josepha Buell Hale, author of *The Good House-keeper: or the Way to Live Well and to Be Well While We Live* (1839), influenced the domestic tastes and tenets of American women for a half century. She was born on October 24, 1788, in Newport, New Hampshire. Her older brother Horatio assisted her home education by sharing his notes and texts from Dartmouth. Before her marriage, she taught at a private school and assisted the innkeeper at the Rising Sun, a Newport hostel.

In 1822, Hale found herself a widow with five children to support. She earned a comfortable income with the publication of a novel, *Northwood: A Tale of New England* (1827). The accomplishment brought her the editorship of John Laurie Blake's Boston-based *Ladies' Magazine*, the first successful U.S. periodical for women. It attracted housewives with a mixture of essays, book suggestions, travelogues, short fiction, and verse. In defiance of those advocating women's liberation, Hale used the magazine as a forum to promote a conservative view of women as molders of refined, high-minded families.

When Hale sold the journal to Louis Antoine Godey in 1837, he altered the name to *Godey's Ladies Book*. She continued to contribute to the magazine as well as to edit it in compliance with Godey's intent that it be "a beacon light of refined taste, pure morals, and practical wisdom." By 1862, the magazine's subscribers numbered 150,000.

Hale used her position to broaden opportunities for women writers, publishing the works of Harriet

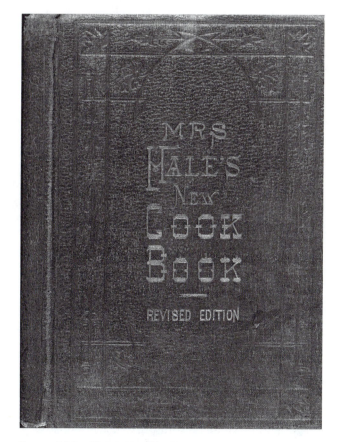

Cover of *Mrs. Hale's New Cookbook* (1873).

Beecher Stowe, Lydia Sigourney, Eliza Leslie, Ann Stephens, and Lydia Maria Child, along with submissions from Nathaniel Hawthorne, Washington Irving, and Henry Wadsworth Longfellow. Her most effective pieces appeared in "Literary Notices" and "Editor's Table," where she promoted courtesy, civic responsibility, and public charity.

The contributions of *The Good Housekeeper* to kitchen history are the sincerity and pragmatism of its author. To produce a guide to healthful living, Hale adopted and refined ideas from William Kitchiner's *The Cook's Oracle* (1831) and Lydia Maria Child's *The American Frugal Housewife* (1832). She encouraged the affluent to preserve their health and explained to the poor how frugality could increase their meager comforts. Like others of the era who connected domestic morals with home cooking, Hale advocated hearty bread from country kitchens and warned haughty sophisticates that "Italian and music are worthless accomplishments compared with the knowledge of bread-making." (Hale, 1966, 31)

Hale's kitchen advice was both practical and detailed. She listed the best cuts of beef for roasting and boiling and warned that raw pork and mutton endanger digestion. Of all meats, she found poultry the most delicate and delicious and the easiest to digest, especially for invalids. Hale compared the sauces that drown food to the periwig, a head covering that she denounced as a violation of natural beauty. Following her application of religious principles to diet, she denigrated pies and puddings, but exalted fruit as the original food of humankind. She wrote that "the Eden taste still lingers in our race, for in childhood there is no food so eagerly sought and relished." (Ibid., 87) She placed the strongest injunction against seasoned dishes for children.

In service to household economy, Hale listed foods that she considered inexpensive. At the head of her list was anything made of corn meal. She also cited various plain puddings, boiled rice, pork and beans, stew, and hash. On the subject of alcoholic beverages, she adhered to the rule of temperance, pronouncing, "No *woman* should violate [the rule]—never make any preparation of which *alcohol* forms a part for family use!" (Ibid., 110)

On the perennial issue of finding good kitchen servants, Hale stressed the difference between Continental standards and those maintained in America. She asserted that servants worked for money rather than professional satisfaction. Of the much castigated Irish kitchen maids, she believed them capable but ignorant. Their only hope, she opined, was education by a kind mistress to make them worthy wives and mothers.

In addition to *The Good Housekeeper,* Hale wrote *Ladies' New Book of Cookery: A Practical System for Private Families in Town and Country* (1852), *Mrs. Hale's New Cookbook* (1857), *The New Household Receipt Book* (1852), *Mrs. Hale's Receipts for the Millions* (1857), and *Manners: or, Happy Homes and Good Society All the Year Round* (1868). She introduced U.S. cooks to the English food writer Eliza Acton with *Modern Cookery in All Its Branches* (1848), an American version of Acton's *Modern Cookery for Private Families* (1845). Her writings, popular on both sides of the Atlantic, remained in print through thirty editions.

Hale relinquished the editorship of the magazine in 1877 and died two years later. She earned fame for two other accomplishments: publishing "Mary Had a Little Lamb" in *Poems for Our Children* (1830) and establishing Thanksgiving as a national holiday. In addition, she launched the Seaman's Aid Society, supported the preservation of Mount Vernon, and co-founded Vassar College.

See also **Women's Magazines**

Further Reading

Hale, Sarah Josepha. *Early American Cookery: "The Good Housekeeper, 1841,"* Mineola, N.Y.: Dover Publications, 1966.

Tebbel, John, and Mary Ellen Zuckerman. *The Magazine in America, 1741–1990.* New York: Oxford University Press, 1991.

HARTLEY, DOROTHY

Through her writings on traditional English cookery techniques and equipment, the cultural historian Dorothy Rosaman Hartley preserved a vital record of Britain's culinary past. A native of Skipton, Yorkshire, Hartley was born on October 17, 1893. After attending high school in Loughborough, Leicestershire, where her father was headmaster, she began writing and teaching art at age eighteen. During World War I, she worked in a munitions plant and attended classes at Regent Street Polytechnic, studying scholarly writing, art, and journalism.

Along with Margaret Mary Victoria Elliot, Hartley co-produced the six-volume *Life and Work of the People of England: A Pictorial Record from Contemporary Sources* (1925), a rich, multilayered work on English customs and lifestyle. With numerous illustrations and short, informative paragraphs, the compendium brought to life daily activities of the sixteenth century. Kitchen work was described in rich detail—for example, how cooks boiled a boar's head in vinegar to tenderize it before baking.

During a span of years in which she wrote for the *Daily Sketch*, Hartley published *How Medieval Folk Lived* (1930, also co-written by Elliot); *The Old Book: A Medieval Anthology* (1930); *Thomas Tusser: His Good Points of Husbandry* (1931); *The Countryman's England* (1935); *Holiday in Ireland* (1938); and *Made in England* (1939). During this time she also biked and drove throughout the British Isles, sketching, photographing, and capturing the essence of rural life. Between interviews with eelers, tinkers, herders, and whittlers, she cooked meals gypsy style over a twig fire and slept in the wild.

A delight in rural industry permeated Hartley's writings, as in her characterization of fine English and Welsh cheeses and her description of the Irish churner who lifted and plumped the dasher in time to a Hail Mary. Of dairying she commented: "It is a pleasant sight watching milk being skimmed, the rich cream gathering up into thick leathery folds before the edge of the shell, and falling in heavy soft blobs into the cream pan." (Hartley 1980, 49)

Hartley's masterwork, *Food in England* (1954), got its start in 1939, when she produced a monograph, *For Those Who Work on the Land,* illustrated with her own artwork, for the League of Nations. The text included such minutiae as the cooking technique of a bargee on the Bingley-Shipley canal, who filled a seven-pound jam jar with layers of pork, parsnips, carrots, pastry, potatoes, and applesauce, a one-pot meal cooked in a bucket of boiling water. At the time of the book's publication, she was a scriptwriter for the British Broadcasting Corporation, a television personality and program adviser, and teacher of domestic economy. Her lectures at the University College of London and Goldsmiths College earned a journalism award. Upon release of the seventh edition of her classic kitchen history, the London *Times* praised her vigor and embrace of all things English, even the arcane.

In her characteristically evocative style, Hartley continued to document domestic life in *Water in England* (1964), *The Land of England* (1979), and *Lost Country Life* (1980), and in articles for *Harper's* and the *Manchester Guardian.* Hartley died on October 22, 1985 in Froncysylte, Wales. Her will bequeathed valuable letters and photos to the Reading Museum of English Rural Life.

See also **Greens**

Further Reading

Hartley, Dorothy. *The Countryman's England.* London: Jill Norman Ltd., 1980.

HAY-BOX COOKERS

The hay box, or fuelless *marmite norvégienne* (Norse cooker), encases a hot short-handled cook pot or Dutch oven in a box insulated with a weak heat conductor to hold high temperatures in the vessel. As the internal temperature drops to 158 degrees Fahrenheit, the inner chamber maintains that level for up to six hours of unsupervised, flameless cooking. The device first became popular as a consequence of the fuel shortages of World War I. Later, because of fuel rationing in Britain during World War II, the ministries of agriculture and food encouraged families to rely on the cooker for meal preparation much as they had relied on the thermos to cook beans for factory workers' lunches.

Revived by missionaries and Peace Corps workers, the hay box improved domestic efficiency in third-world communities. In Swaziland, activists made "wonder boxes" out of cardboard and styrofoam-stuffed cushions. (Schlabach 1991, 173) The box encouraged environmentally minded Fijians attending the 1995 United Nations Conference on Women in Beijing, where they sought answers to domestic needs of working women. In the twenty-first century, the boxes applied the principles of fuel conservation and solar energy in South African shantytowns and Tamil communities in Indonesia. In Zambia, cooks wove their own basket cookers and insulated them with linings of hay or wild cotton.

In *Simply Living, the Story of Compassion and the Wonderbox* (1989), Anna Pearce of Saffron Walden, Essex, described Box-Aid, a Quaker-sponsored project among the poor in Africa, Brazil, Bangladesh, and India. To reduce dependence on wood- or paraffin-burning stoves, the group supplied the Wonderbox, a nest formed from two cushions filled with polystyrene beans to shelter a hot cook pot hay-box style. Encouragement of such fuel-efficient cooking methods spared Africa's vanishing tree cover and helped to curb the greenhouse effect and desertification, a loss of green land that forced women farther from home each season to glean fuel for their kitchens. One application of the box was for bread making. The raised dough rested in boiling water for twenty minutes before placement into the Wonderbox. After an hour's cooking, the bread was done.

The Quaker workers also developed the hay box into a drink cooler, yogurt maker, dye cooker, and foot warmer. They taught African women to knit scrap carpet yarn into linings for ovens built from wood crating and chicken wire, which they covered with plastic and cement. Another type of box, the wide-cone Anahat, a cardboard-box solar cooker, encased food in aluminum foil and cooked it with solar heat.

The Vajra Foundation, established in Utrecht in 1997 to fight poverty and preserve the environment, premiered a solar hay box cooking project to serve 100,000 Bhutanese refugees at seven camps in southeastern Nepal. The cookers saved on kerosene, did not dirty or overheat the kitchen, and performed as well as or better than conventional cooking methods. User-friendly and easy to build from scrap, the cooker satisfied the needs of the refugees, who added some improvements to maximize its performance—for example, painting each pot black to absorb heat, topping the box with glass, placing it on the roof in full sun, sealing cracks, and adding a dish-shaped, deep-focus reflector to concentrate solar energy.

Construction guidelines for self-made hay boxes explain how from otherwise useless materials, the builder can form a cover or casing from bamboo, cardboard and duct tape, discarded crating, plastic, styrofoam sheets, or scrap wood planks. Insulation can include paddy (unthreshed rice), wheat straw, fur, wool, blankets, styrofoam peanuts, rice or corn husks, sawdust, newspaper, or rags. Because the insulation is loose fill, air pockets hold heat. An alternate plan suggests burying a blanket-wrapped pot in ashes and soil. The finished box requires no fuel and little tending or pot watching while it cooks nutritious food without scorching, dehydrating, or burning.

Further Reading

Matthess, W. R., "The Hay Box: The Original Slow Cooker," *Countryside & Small Stock Journal*, July 8, 1998.
Pearce, Anna. *Simply Living, the Story of Compassion and the Wonderbox*. Essex, Eng.: self-published, 1989.

HERBS

As the flavorings indigenous to a geographic area, herbs define regional cookery as certainly as do the local cereal grains, fruits and vegetables, fish, or meat. To recreate the taste and aroma of a regional or national style of cooking, the cook must master the herbs.

Early civilizations left records of their herbal lore. Babylonian clay tablets from 3000 BCE contain recipes for home curatives and lists of the trade in imported herbs. Subsequent written herbals appeared in Assyria, China, Egypt, and India. The emperor Shên Nung (also Shen Nunn or Shen Nong), the second of the Five Sage Emperors, compiled the *Canon of Herbs* (ca. 2700 BCE), a record of his personal experience with taste tests of 252 plants to determine which were toxic. Huang Ti, the legendary Yellow Emperor of the twenty-fifth century BCE, compiled the *Nei Ching* (Canon of Medicine), a forerunner of the modern pharmacopoeia. Egyptian herbal lore from 1550 BCE covered aromatics, cosmetics, and ritual uses of herbs.

The Mediterranean housewife found a broad range of uses for herbs. Roman women followed the advice of Citro, a first-century CE compiler of beauty secrets, such as using herbs to combat wrinkles, smooth hands, and sweeten underarms. Around 160 CE, the physician Galen offered a recipe for an herbal face cream. A more citified writer, Caelius Apicius, author of *De Re Coquinaria* (On Cooking, late 300s CE), transferred herbal lore from the sickroom, boudoir, and altar to the kitchen. Second only to pepper in his estimation was lovage, a local herb in the celery family. He valued its leaves, roots, and seeds, which gave a distinct, refreshing taste to dishes. Third on his list of favorites was rue (*Ruta graveolens*), a bitter flavoring that counterbalanced the sweetness of honeyed meats and raisin wine. The remainder of Apicius's favorites, listed in order of preference, were coriander, cumin, oregano, celery seed, parsley seed, bay leaf, aniseed, fennel, mint, caraway, mustard seed, wormwood (artemisia), chervil, colewort or rocket, saxifrage or sweet cicely,

Herbs for sale at the Crescent City Farmer's Market in New Orleans, Louisiana.
[© *Courtesy of Agricultural Research Service, USDA. USDA Photo, Bill Tarpenning.*]

thyme, sage, pennyroyal, pellitory, elecampane, saffron, and mastic. (Edwards 1984, xxi)

A less familiar seasoning, laser, earned the praise of the encyclopedist Pliny the Elder, author of *Natural History* (ca. 77 CE), who called it "the most extraordinary of nature's gifts." (Ibid., xxiv) A giant fennel related to *Ferula tingitana*, laser grew wild in North Africa, where traders profited by gathering it for transport to Egypt, Greece, and Rome. Cooks slit the stems and roots to extract laser sap, which the Greeks called *silphium* and Indians referred to as *heeng*. Apicius generously seasoned with laser his relish, turnips, sausage, peas, barley soup, seafood, chicken, pigeons and doves, cracklings, and knuckles. He ground the herb with pine nuts to make a pine meal powder, a prepared dressing that he stored with whole nuts in a cask to keep the taste lively. After overpicking destroyed the African stock of laser, purchasers sought supplies from Iran, Iraq, and Syria. Centuries later, the plant flourished once more on the southern Mediterranean shore.

Medieval cooks relied on stores of spices from exotic markets and paid a high price to add cloves to piquant meat dishes, pepper and grains of paradise (*Aframomum melegueta*) to pork and fish, and nutmeg and saffron to desserts. Thomas Fromon compiled a kitchen list, *Herbys Necessary for a Gardyn* (1535), which guided the gardener in selecting and propagating thirty species valued for beauty and aroma. Late in the Renaissance, householders seeking health benefits from a kitchen garden studied John Gerard's *The Herbal* (1597), a compendium listing plants with curative powers.

Herbs proved an aromatic addition to housekeeping aids. British laundries bore the scent of lavender and bergamot during the final rinse and preparation of fragrant starch, which protected linens during long storage. Dried marjoram scented homemade beeswax-and-turpentine furniture polish; a simpler application of ground sweet cicely brightened dull wood and wainscoting. Horsetail made a metal polish; burned angelica root and seed disinfected a room.

Herb gardens were decorative as well as useful. Laid out in careful geometrics, in the form of circles, squares, diamonds, wheels, or more elaborate patterns such as interlocking diamonds, they displayed contrasts of color and texture derived from such artistic pairings as red bergamot with lavender or mint. Kitchen gardens varied according to the available space and light. In small kitchen beds, nasturtiums grew well in urns, bay tree in pots, and basil in window boxes. Where there was limited space, cooks raised sage in a window basket, trained creeping thyme and chamomile over rock walls, and grew pots of tarragon for vinegar and rosemary for poultry seasoning. Children created their own plantings in beds of primrose,

fennel, spearmint, angelica, sweet cicely, pennyroyal, and tall sunflowers. By the seventeenth century, the drift toward enlightenment had begun to reduce dependence on herbs for healing. The term *herb* remained so valuable to cookery, however, that it characterized vegetables (pot herbs), salad greens ("salet" herbs), and flavorings (sweet herbs). The kitchen gardener John Evelyn, author of *Acetaria: A Discourse of Sallets* (1699), characterized the bud, flower, seed, leaf, stalk, and root of seventy-three salad plants and determined whether to chop, steam, blanch, or pickle each.

Around 1800, the importation to England and the Americas of the Chinese herb boat, also called a ship grinder, ship mill, sow-and-pig mill, or go-devil, applied the technology of the mano and metate to the crushing of herbs. A boat-shaped wood base set on bootjack legs accommodated a cast-iron wheel pierced by a pair of dowel-shaped wood handles. By leaning forward and rolling the wheel back and forth in the groove of the trough, the user could rapidly reduce stems, roots, and leaves to fragments. The Chinese powered the Asian version with their feet.

When Juliet Corson, an editor for *Household Monthly* and home demonstration lecturer, published her concise homemaking manual, *Cooking School Text Book and Housekeeper's Guide to Cookery and Kitchen Management* (1879), she singled out an herb pouch, the *bouquet garni* (flavor bundle), in the first chapter as a cooking essential. To collect herbs for these bundles, which flavored soups and stews, she instructed the cook to seek a German grocery or drugstore, where a stock of herbs lasting several months could be had for a nickel.

The first successful New World kitchen herb business began at the Shaker commune in New Lebanon, New York. From tentative kitchen gardens, the industry grew to fifty acres of physic garden. In addition to 200 local varieties, growers introduced around forty varieties from the Southwest and Europe. They gathered wild pennyroyal, spearmint, peppermint, catnip, wintergreen, throughwort, sarsaparilla, witch hazel, and dandelion from fields outside their farm. By 1861, the commune was bottling extracts in glass vials; shaping wintergreen lozenges; sewing moth-repelling herbs in bags; and pressing leaves and pulverizing roots. The success of New Lebanon's herb business encouraged parallel endeavors at communes in Watervliet, Harvard, Enfield, New Gloucester, Canterbury, and Union Village.

The 1960s saw a revival of interest in herbal cures as part of a natural foods movement. There was an increasing use of herbs in cooking to create flavorful, low-fat dishes during the health-conscious 1980s and 1990s. In the late twentieth century, families began combatting pollutants and threats to health by doing what their medieval ancestors did: returning immunity and longevity concerns to the kitchen. A thriving industry in herb handbooks, essential oils, and packaged nostrums provided the cook with the additives and recipes to strengthen the body, treat allergies and indigestion, fight stress and depression, slow the aging process, and ward off cancer and heart disease. The kitchen pantry offered echinacea tea to lessen the impact of the common cold, rhodiola for heart health and weight control, soy snacks for the symptoms of menopause, ginkgo for concentration and alertness, and lavender and tea tree pillows to heat in the microwave oven and apply to neck or forehead to relieve migraine and sinus headache. Into the twenty-first century, the media offered advice on which herbal preparations, antioxidants, and additives show promise against a host of ills, from prostatitis and irritable bowel syndrome to AIDS and SARS. Worldwide, ambitious kitchen gardeners began turning patches of fresh herbs into businesses by raising herb plants for sale, supplying restaurants and bakeries with fresh herbs for cooking and baking, or collecting, seeding, and drying plants in their ovens to sell to large distributors.

See also **Dyes and Colorants; Kitchen Cures; Kitchen Gardening; Witches' Kitchens**

Further Reading

Andrews, Edward Deming. *The People Called Shakers: A Search for the Perfect Society.* New York: Oxford University Press, 1953.

_____, and Faith Andrews. *Work and Worship: The Economic Order of the Shakers.* Greenwich Conn.: New York Graphic Society, 1974.

Dragland, Steinar, et al. "Several Culinary and Medicinal Herbs Are Important Sources of Dietary Antioxidants," *Journal of Nutrition*, Vol. 133, No. 5, May 2003, 1286–1290.

Pliny. *The Natural History of C. Plinius Secundus.* New York: McGraw-Hill, 1962.

Tucker, David M. *Kitchen Gardening in America: A History.* Ames: Iowa State University Press, 1993.

HINES, DUNCAN

As one of America's legendary food critics, Duncan Hines sold millions of copies of his landmark restaurant guide and became a trusted advisor to a generation of American motorists. Hines was born in Bowling Green, Kentucky, on March 26, 1880. In his formative years, he admired the ample table of his grandmother, who helped raise him after the death of his mother. After living in the southwest and Mexico for many years, he accepted a position in printing and advertising in Chicago, where he remained until 1938.

That year, Hines published a classic pamphlet, *Adventures in Good Eating*, a directory to the country's best restaurants, which he developed from a list he sent to friends in lieu of Christmas cards. Astonished by its popularity among motorists after a boost by *Saturday Evening Post,* he retired from advertising to write *Lodging for a Night* (1938) and *Adventures in Good Cooking* (1939), an anthology of recipes. Encouraged to market his own specialties, he returned to his hometown to open a business in hickory-smoked ham. With the proceeds, in 1943, he established a philanthropic foundation to aid future hoteliers and restaurateurs studying at Cornell and Michigan State universities.

Along with his wife, Florence, Hines traveled 50,000 miles annually, sampling food from a variety of restaurant kitchens. He employed a network of culinary critics and a staff to winnow out the best food commentary from the 50,000 letters he received per year. He promoted cleanliness over ambience and was more impressed by fresh local produce than by French names on the menu. In 1949, he collaborated with Roy H. Park to license his name as a brand for a line of boxed cake, brownie, and muffin mixes, as well as jams, bread, appliances, pottery, and stainless steel cookware. In addition to Hines-Park Foods, Inc., which Procter & Gamble acquired, he launched the Duncan Hines Institute, which issued *Duncan Hines' Vacation Guide* (1948).

Continuing to revise his original pamphlet, Hines embodied the public's interest in fine dining in an era that elevated chefs such as James Beard to national prominence. Hines's ratings of the best foods and service influenced radio broadcasts and print media. His chief criticism of American cooks was that they overcooked meats and vegetables. He balanced his complaints against chain restaurants with praise for such regional fare as apple pie, chicken and dumplings, black bottom pie, baked clams, buckwheat cakes, and buttermilk biscuits. An annual festival in his hometown honors him each June with a brownie-baking contest.

Further Reading

"Duncan Hines: Restaurant Critic," *American History,* February 2000, 14.

Schwartz, David M., "Duncan Hines: He Made Gastronomes out of Motorists," *Smithsonian,* November 1984, 86–91.

HOME ECONOMICS

Although the discipline of home economics—a scientific approach to domestic management—was not introduced until the nineteenth century, the idea of educating girls in the domestic arts has been present in cultures around the world. In colonial America,

A home economics class at McKinley High School, Washington, D.C., gets a practical lesson in home canning of fruits and vegetables, looking toward supplementing the limited allowance of canned foods available to holders of war ration book two (1943). [*Library of Congress, Prints and Photographs Division (LC-USE6-D-008751)*]

young girls learned cookery, candle dipping, and sewing under the supervision of their mothers and grandmothers. In *Good Order Established in Pennsylvania and New Jersey: Being a True Account of the Country; with Its Produce and Commodities There Made* (1685), the Quaker author Thomas Budd proposed establishment of public girls' schools to educate women in flax spinning, sewing, needlework, knitting of gloves and stockings, and the plaiting of straw for use in hats, baskets, and mats.

Establishment of Domestic Science Curricula

In 1841, the U.S. feminist and educator Catharine E. Beecher published her *Treatise on Domestic Economy for the Use of Young Ladies at Home and at School,* a scientific home management text for women. After the passage of the First Morrill Land Grant Act of 1862,

which set aside federal land for colleges teaching agriculture and mechanical arts, Beecher and her sister, the novelist Harriet Beecher Stowe, produced the groundbreaking *The American Woman's Home, or Principles of Domestic Science* (1869). Beginning with Catharine Beecher's charge that "women are not trained for [home] duties as men are trained for their trades and professions," they go on to state that amateurish attempts at home management had produced "family labor [that] is poorly done, poorly paid, and regarded as menial and disgraceful." (Ibid.) To remedy this situation, the sisters compiled their monumental handbook, complete with diagrams and advice on the complete gamut of homemaking topics. Their advice on how to arrange a root cellar or cook nourishing dishes for an invalid, where to plant fruit trees, and how often to launder dish cloths provided housewives with practical, immediately applicable information. The Beechers' example supported the efforts of fledgling women's unions and cooking schools, especially Mrs. Elizabeth Goodfellow's Cooking School in Philadelphia, the nation's first. Treasured by Quakers for the staff's emphasis on wholesome food, the school produced the cookbook writer Eliza Leslie.

Across the Midwest, fledgling domestic programs took root. Educator Mary Beaumont Dudley Welch, the initiator of the first organized extension work in home economics in the United States, headed Iowa State's pioneering home economics course, initiated in 1871 after a vote of four to three in favor of admitting women. Kansas State established a department of domestic economy in 1873, and Illinois Industrial University's homemaking curriculum took shape the following year. In Boston, the Women's Educational and Industrial Union opened on Boylston Street in 1877. The purpose of the institute was to help unsophisticated country girls find work in the urban area. It also marketed foodstuffs and women's handicrafts, offered lectures on preventive health care, served nourishing lunches, and made lunch-hour appointments for working women to consult with female physicians. The union's president, Abby Morton Diaz, and director, Mary Morton Kimball Kehew, expanded the curriculum with vocational training classes and placement and legal services. In the 1880s, Mary Welch opened a cookery school in her own kitchen and developed a home economics curriculum. Another altruist, Mary Porter Tileston Hemenway, opened a public school in Boston teaching cooking and sewing. She started the Boston Normal School of Cooking, later named the Mary Hemenway Department of Household Arts at Framingham in her honor.

In 1890, the educator and nutritionist Abby Lillian Marlatt founded a domestic science department at Utah Agricultural College. Four years later, she created a second curriculum at the Manual Training High School in Providence, Rhode Island. A participant in the Lake Placid Conferences on Home Economics and charter member of the American Home Economics Association, she continued her support of domestic science in 1909 at the University of Wisconsin as chair of the department of home economics in the agricultural college. She specialized in nutritional problems and furthered techniques for preserving the vitamin content in prepared foods.

Women's groups of the period joined forces to pressure the U.S. Congress for legislation regulating the food, beverage, and drug industries. In the South, the Mother's Circle of Montgomery, Alabama, was an early proponent of monitoring foods that housewives bought for their pantries. The movement held firm until 1909, when President Theodore Roosevelt negotiated passage of the Pure Food and Drug Act.

Publication of a Pivotal Text

In 1879, Juliet Corson, superintendent of the New York Cooking School, published a pivotal work, *Cooking School Text Book and Housekeeper's Guide to Cookery and Kitchen Management*. In the preface, which she wrote in November 1878, she stated her intent to "[offer] our special plan of instruction for the guidance of societies or individuals who wish to establish similar institutions elsewhere." (Corson 1879, iii) For advanced students, she taught how to classify foods according to nutritional value and how to detect adulterants and food deterioration. Typical of the times was an introduction to the kitchen itself—its weights and measures, sanitation, stove maintenance, fire-tending, temperature control, and purchase and upkeep of utensils. Regarding the importance of domestic science to health, she concluded, "The object of cooking is to prepare food so that its nutritive elements may be changed by the process of digestion into healthy blood." (Ibid., 234)

Corson produced *Family Living on $500 a Year* (1887), subtitled "A Daily Reference-Book for Young and Inexperienced Housewives" and based on a series of articles she had published in *Harper's Bazaar*. Corson detailed such essentials as the making of candles and soap, cleanliness in the kitchen, and the "Second Serving of Food," her euphemism for leftovers. (Corson 1888, 184) In lieu of the German method of placing daughters "in the household of some notable *Hausfrau*," she suggested that the best way for a young woman to learn these basics was service in an upscale kitchen. (Ibid., 290)

Corson's cooking school and others in Philadelphia and Boston led the way toward an established home economics curriculum. Mary Hemenway headed a philanthropic consortium that set up experimental school kitchens in five Boston schools in 1885. The concept fueled interest among educators, who toured the premises to take notes on layout and instructional method. Student cooks, outfitted in white caps and aprons, completed their studies by serving a meal to notables as evidence of the value of domestic training. Proponents opened six more school kitchens, from which some 1,600 pupils could purchase dishes to serve their families.

Sarah Tyson Rorer, nicknamed the "Queen of American Cookery," was the compiler of fifty-four domestic handbooks, among them *Mrs. Rorer's Philadelphia Cook Book* (1886) and the classic *Mrs. Rorer's New Cook Book; a Manual of Housekeeping* (1902). For the emerging domestic science, she composed a first-person position statement, "How I Cured My Own Ill-Health," which appeared in the June 1905 issue of *Ladies' Home Journal*. She wrote: "The great possibilities of domestic science—from a practical standpoint, the uplifting of the homes—are always before me. I should like to teach every woman to cook, teach her how to live." (p. 38)

Rorer formulated exacting principles for cookery. In the absence of oven thermometers for precise control of baking and roasting, she taught her students the time-honored method of testing temperature by throwing flour on the oven floor and observing how long it took to brown. She also suggested holding a hand in the oven to the count of twenty to determine when it was hot enough to brown bread or cake.

Boston cooking instructor Maria Parloa envisioned the science of home economics and the invention of labor-saving devices as a means of transforming women's lives by simplifying kitchen work. To disseminate her ideas on economical cookery, she wrote *The Appledore Cookbook* (1872) and *Miss Parloa's New Cook Book and Marketing Guide* (1880), which featured a recipe for pancakes made with snow and such domestic instruction as how to make starch, mend plaster and picture frames, and concoct furniture cleaner and polish at home. After launching the Boston Cooking School in 1879, she promoted distribution of food from the school's food labs at cost to the poor.

Mary Lincoln, a teacher at the Boston Cooking School, issued *Mrs. Lincoln's Boston Cook Book* (1884), a public school textbook drawn from her course outlines and classroom methods. In the commentary on public education for women, she championed the importance of stove blacking, tin scouring, and meal preparation and placed them on an intellectual par with geometry proofs. Lincoln advanced to a staff position at the Lasell Seminary in Auburndale, Massachusetts, and wrote *The Peerless Cook Book* (1886), *The Boston School Kitchen Textbook* (1887), and *Carving and Serving* (1887), as well as lectures and a culinary column for the *American Kitchen Magazine*, which she served as food editor in 1895. She joined Lida Willis, Sarah Rorer, Helen Armstrong, and Marion Harland in compiling a home economics text, *Home Helps: A Pure Food Cook Book—A Useful Collection of Up-to-Date, Practical Recipes by Five of the Leading Culinary Experts in the United States* (1910). With public educator Anna Barrows, Lincoln also founded and edited the *New England Kitchen Magazine*, in which she tailored advice to meet individual needs, including those of girls learning to cook on Indian reservations. One menu plan proposed a washday lunch of potato salad that yielded sufficient leftovers for mashed potatoes at dinner.

The Movement Overseas

In the Edwardian era, the goals of step-saving and organized shelving preceded the formalization of the field of home economics. In England, the establishment of Agnes B. Marshall's National Training School of Cookery in 1883 introduced girls to scientific food preparation and prepared them for service at aristocratic tables.

The advance of home economics training in Scandinavia elevated domestic experts as authorities on appliances and food preservation. At the Finnish home economics school in Tampere, in 1893, working-class pupils and farm wives learned from school principal Sofia Soininen the value of the icebox. The school's institutional-size box, provisioned with ice from the Pynikki brewery, was located in a cold cellar. It served as a model of refrigeration to extend the storage life of perishables. A local journalist concluded that the time was right for manufacturers to supply all homes with a similar chilling system. For more than thirty years, iceboxes received ongoing promotion in the home-making magazine *Kotiliesi*, which ran its last icebox ad in 1927.

In Germany's Weimar Republic between 1890 and 1918, feminists demanded social and political equality at a time when women were moving beyond the home in great numbers and into jobs and university faculties. While revolutionary activists such as Clara Zetkin and Rosa Luxemburg worked to transform society and redefine woman's role, the picture of a complex, multi-dimensional modern German woman began to emerge from the stereotypical *hausfrau* (housewife). As the dwindling availability of servants forced more menial tasks on the "new woman," housewives clamored for a more scientific approach to domestic chores, rendering the "new housekeeping" an equivalent to men's professions and factory organization. (Henderson 1996, 224)

The purpose of the restructuring of gender roles, in Zetkin's view, was to reward the home worker with a richer circle of influence and a place beside her husband "as a companion in his struggles, as a comrade in his efforts and his exertions, giving and receiving intellectual and moral support." (Ibid. 225) Applying principles of ergonomics, time-and-motion consultants sought to quantify kitchen work, increasing productivity and eliminating wasted effort. Domestic experts agreed that the professionalization of housekeeping was possible only through simplified home design and re-engineering of appliances.

First Conference at Lake Placid

In 1899, the educator and chemist Ellen Swallow Richards, aided by librarian Melvil Dewey, convened the first of ten Lake Placid conferences, a forum for discussing the problems and future of household science. Among the questions considered by the eleven participants was the choice of a name for their science. They rejected the terms *domestic economy, domestic science,* and *household administration* in favor of *home economics.* A decade later, Richards co-founded and headed the American Home Economics Association, set goals for public school instruction in cooking and the household arts, and supported publication of the *Journal of Home Economics.* She worked with experts to write curricula and supervised teacher education. She established a housekeeping school at Boston's Woman's Educational and Industrial Union, the forerunner to Simmons College's department of home economics.

To assure credibility among the sciences, Richards sought consensus at the Lake Placid conferences, where attendees thrashed out differences between academics on the left and supporters of women's traditional roles on the right. Richards had as backup six learned lecturers, teachers, and writers: Anna Barrows, editor of *New England Kitchen Magazine;* Maria Daniell, lecturer and cooking demonstrator; Emily Huntington, pioneer of housekeeping education for children via the Kitchen Garden method; Louisa A. Nicholass, curriculum founder at the State Normal School in Framingham, Massachusetts; Alice Peloubet Norton, domestic science director for the Brookline, Massachusetts, public schools; and Maria Parloa, creator of the Boston Cooking School.

In 1902, Marion Talbot summarized the evolving mission statement as progressive reform—a general social system in which men and women mastered the "processes, activities, obligations and opportunities which make the home and family effective parts of the social fabric." (Ibid., 28) Her vision proved true to the spirit of the American Home Economics Association as stated at its founding in 1908. Within eight years, 20 percent of U.S. high schools offered homemaking courses. In colleges, enrollment rose to 17,000.

Inclusion of Minorities

In 1881, Booker T. Washington, founder of the Tuskegee University in Alabama, assembled a vocational curriculum based on societal need for plumbers, carpenters, coopers, seamstresses, housekeepers, food processors, and cooks. Washington is often overlooked in histories of home economics. He initiated domestic courses immediately, appointing as teacher his first wife, Fanny Norton Smith Washington. In his second textbook, *Working with the Hands* (1904), he included a chapter entitled "Lessons in Home-Making." When guests arrived on campus, they could take meals in the dining hall and taste foods grown, harvested, canned, cooked, and served by students. The menu offered a breakfast of ham, pancakes and syrup, butter, milk, and fruit. For lunch and dinner, the visitor enjoyed roast beef and ham, rice, green beans, tomatoes, potatoes and yams, corn bread, and buttermilk. In his opinion, such a display of success taught "dignity of labour" while helping needy students pay their educational expenses. (Washington 1904, 80) Washington regarded the contribution of the homemaker as "[supplying] and [guarding] the health, strength, morals, and happiness of the family." (Ibid., 98) His restriction of woman's sphere to home and hearth was typical of the era and paralleled the gender-specific role attitudes of early twentieth-century Christian pietists. He declared that personal and spiritual uplift "must begin with [the negro's] home and its surroundings." (Ibid.)

Washington's third wife, Margaret James Murray Washington, helped to disseminate her husband's views on cleanliness and order, which he considered woman's work. She broadened her outreach through rural health clubs, the National Federation of Afro-American Women, the National Association of Colored Women, and the Alabama State Federation. She opened a Saturday school at an old fire-engine house in town to make use of women's time while their husbands traded and bought goods. A hundred interested women, some traveling more than ten miles to class, studied the use of cook stoves and laundering at a tin tub.

From the success of Tuskegee came new black academies, some founded and managed by students of Washington. In Columbus, Georgia, a new course of study in cooking and sewing began in 1899 with Tuskegee graduates planning the curriculum. In 1898, Margaret Washington extended classroom work to "missionarying" at the Russell plantation school eight miles from Tuskegee and modeled its program on urban settlement houses. (Thrasher 1969, 154)

New Science in a New Century

In the first decade of the twentieth century, women streamed into home economics teaching positions and research posts created by the Department of Agriculture with funding provided by the Smith-Lever Act of 1914 to upgrade rural life. The teacher Marie Cromer founded the first girls' tomato club in 1909; South Carolina dispatched its first two home demonstration agents in 1912. In the Southwest, Dora Edna Ross, a dairy extension agent, taught farm women how to establish remunerative kitchen businesses from butter making and marketing.

The food conservation campaigns, canning clubs, and victory gardens of World War I served as an added impetus toward increased training of young women in home skills. During the period 1917–1919, when shortages made food shopping difficult, the Cooperative Extension Services promoted nutrition and economy. With the assistance of extension agents, homemakers learned that brown bread could replace white and beans substitute for meat.

The war helped to advance the careers of female professionals of all kinds. Home economists gained employment in the private sector as dietitians and food demonstrators and in institutional management of dining halls and public and military hospital kitchens and cafeterias. In 1917, dietitians meeting at Cleveland, Ohio, discussed their obligation to hospitals and rehabilitation centers treating war veterans. As a result of their sessions, Lena Frances Cooper, a Kansan graduated from Philadelphia's Drexel Institute and dean of John Harvey Kellogg's Battle Creek College, founded the American Dietetic Association.

Despite advances in domestic science, the elite Eastern women's colleges known as the Seven Sisters—Barnard, Bryn Mawr, Mount Holyoke, Radcliffe, Smith, Vassar, and Wellesley—with support from the American Collegiate Association, rejected domestic science as unworthy of a place among academic disciplines. Supporting their denigration of household arts was the Smith-Hughes Act of 1917, which further typified domestic science as a teacher-training field in vocations rather than pure science. Nonetheless, the creation of the title "home economist" preceded numerous new posts at the U.S. Department of Agriculture and U.S. Food Administration. By 1920, to meet the growing demand, thirty states had added domestic vocational training to their public school curricula.

As women grew in political influence following their enfranchisement in 1920, home economics began to reflect the new status of women as citizens and activists. In the 1920s, the upsurge in U.S. home economics education programs paralleled a rise in women's liberation through additional schooling and career planning, led by Columbia Teacher's College in New York City and advanced by the work of Margaret Comstock Snell, head of home economics at Oregon Agricultural College. An uncompromising proponent of domestic training, Snell applied her skills to designing an idealized home with a retractable canvas roof over the kitchen to admit light and fresh air. She insisted that sanitary living was the only guarantee of happiness and success.

In New York state, a dynamic advocate of domestic science, Martha Van Rensselaer, applied her experience educating women in rural Cattaraugus County to the organization of extension courses from Cornell University. In 1903, the university offered the first home economics course; the next year, New York State College of Agriculture included coursework for women in its curriculum. After assisting the U.S. Food Administration during World War I and serving as editor of the popular women's magazine *The Delineator,* Van Rensselaer headed Cornell's department of home economics and, in 1925, directed the New York State College of Home Economics. President Herbert Hoover appointed her to chair a committee on homemaking, housing, and family life. She was named among the twelve most distinguished women of the United States.

To legitimize the place of domestic science in agricultural reform, women wrote scenarios for such teaching films as *The Happier Way* (1920) and *Helping Negroes to Become Better Farmers and Homemakers* (1921). With the aid of such field workers as Mary Engle Pennington and Margaret H. Kingsley of the Household Refrigeration Bureau, rural women studied domestic science under the Home Bureau, a curriculum in sewing and decoration, child care, and nutrition set up at Cornell. Like the Grange, Ladies' Aid Societies, and the Women's Christian Temperance Union, the extension service offered intellectual stimulus and practical education to farm wives who lived too far from colleges to obtain degrees or who lacked the funds, English language skills, or ambition to apply to a university. From tentative beginnings, extension agents helped farm families cope with the Great Depression by publishing suggestions on preventing nutritional deficiency and disease in children through wholesome meals and sanitary homes.

Expanding Professional Opportunities

Throughout the period of women's liberation from housework to home economics careers, American domestic professionals moved into jobs outside the classroom, including research, product development, sales, and advertising. Companies such as Ball Brothers Manufacturing Company, Kraft-Phenix Cheese Company, Piggly-Wiggly Stores, and Sears, Roebuck hired their own home economists. Mary Barber, director of home economics for the Kellogg Company, found an unusual use for her talents as an air hostess aboard the Ford Motor Company's private plane. Ads in *Good Housekeeping* lured women from domestic work into careers as hotel hostesses, apartment managers, and restaurant and institutional cooks.

Another source of employment for home economics graduates outside of education was government service in the military and extension agencies and in school and institutional dietetics and domestic design. In Hawaii, home economists analyzed the nutrient content in local foodstuffs, assessed the Asian-American diet, and charted basal metabolism for peoples of the Pacific rim. Their publications initiated interest in island staples.

The kitchen designer Christine McGaffey Frederick described the field of household engineering in *Efficient Housekeeping or Household Engineering—Scientific Management in the Home* (1925), a publication written for a correspondence course offered by Chicago's American School of Home Economics. A leader in domestic management and a syndicated columnist, Frederick, who was also a collaborator with time-and-motion expert Lillian Gilbreth, advanced home economics by demonstrating how scientific principles could simplify household tasks in the same way that they streamlined work in factories and offices. A widely published author and editor for *Ladies' Home Journal* and *The Delineator*, in 1912, she opened and managed the Applecroft Home Experiment Station at her residence in Greenlawn, Long Island. By examining appliances, analyzing new products, and working out sequential tasking procedures, she precipitated serious thought about the complications and frustrations of running a home. To correct faulty merchandizing practices for domestic goods, in 1912, she organized the League of Advertising Women. She summarized women's needs and outlook in *The New Housekeeping* (1913), *You and Your Laundry* (1922), and an advertising classic, *Selling Mrs. Consumer* (1929).

In Europe, Frederick's message resonated with forward-looking women in Germany and Holland. *De Denkende Huisvrouw*, the Dutch translation of Frederick's *The Thinking Housewife* (1928), contrasted the stylish modern housewife with the frazzled soul who once labored slavishly at the hearth. Trim, neat, and organized, the new woman had panache and optimism. Frederick's model inventories, time charts, and menus turned the home into a work center, but it did nothing to relieve the homemaker's isolation.

To better their lot, women reformers unified under the banner of *Mütterliche Politic* (motherly politics), a pro-woman activist movement that resulted in compulsory home economics courses for elementary school females and in vocational courses for working-class girls in sewing, laundry, and child care. The publication of *Die Küche der Klein- und Mittelwohnung* (The Kitchen of the Working- and Middle-Class House) in the late 1920s focused on such concerns as kitchen layout. Collaborative efforts among city planners, women's clubs, and housing boards resulted in higher standards for domestic equipment and products. One of the vocal leaders of this alliance, Marie Elisabeth Lüders, advised the industrialists and architects who established the Bauhaus, an experiment in modern living. Another, writer Erna Meyer, author of *Das Neue Haushalt* (The New Household, 1926) and *Siedlung und Wohnungen* (Settlement and Housing, 1927), critiqued home furnishings, flooring, plumbing, and cooking equipment.

In 1927, the Deutscher Werkbund (German Crafts Federation) Exhibition in Stuttgart crystallized for attendees the new philosophies of German home economics. Aided by architect J. J. P. Oud, Meyer set up two kitchens at the city's Weissenhof settlement, a model complex of livable apartments and residences for which Mies van der Rohe and Lilly Reich designed interiors and furnishings. The concept of the kitchen workstation imitated the factory model, where decreases in time and motion freed the worker of tedium while boosting productivity and profit.

The success of the Austrian architect Grete Schütte-Lihotzky's Frankfurt kitchen, a prefabricated unit ergonomically designed for a single operator, led to more design opportunities. In a 1929 issue of *Das Neue Frankfurt* (The New Frankfurt), Lihotzky wrote that instruction in domestic skills was the only way to transform the kitchen and, by extension, women's lives into a modern era of equal opportunity.

"Why Study Homemaking?"

In *The Girl and Her Home* (1932), a textbook in the Riverside Home Economics Series edited by Mabel B. Trilling and Florence Williams Nicholas, the answer to the question "Why study homemaking?" outlined an emerging feminism. The two domestic writers assured readers that homemaking was too complicated to be treated as anything but a science. They stressed that research would benefit various domestic areas. Homemakers, they concluded, should think of themselves as professional businesswomen.

Competency in home cleaning and comforts became a goal of the middle class in the 1930s. In the United States, home economics emerged as a popular course in high schools and colleges. Domestic experts marshaled data from laboratory science to focus on hidden microbes and sources of food poisoning.

For the Temporary Emergency Relief Agency, home economist Flora Rose outlined quality nutrition on a limited food budget, an influential scheme popularized by first lady Eleanor Roosevelt, who instituted Rose's program at the White House kitchen. To spread the word, the *New York Times* published daily updates on food service to the president; Mrs. Roosevelt issued her own sample menus in a book, *It's Up to the Women* (1933), a text that honored home kitchen work as a scientific occupation. Home economist Lorna Barber lectured in eighty-two towns and cities at such venues as the American Legion, Grange, Home Bureau, and PTA on methods of avoiding malnutrition and on preserving and canning to make garden produce available throughout the year. Agents distributed farm surplus and, with volunteer help, sponsored community gardens and canning kitchens to bolster emergency diets.

World War II produced new challenges in the form of food rationing and shortages. The home economics curriculum of the day called for specific plans for emergency rations. In 1941, President Franklin D. Roosevelt appointed to the First Nutrition Congress the researcher and food writer Agnes Faye Morgan, the home economics department chair at the University of California at Berkeley and a proponent of the science of dietetics. At the end of the war, she became the first female to administer research grants for state agriculture experiment stations, a post she held until 1950. Ava Bertha Milam Clark, the author of *Adventures of a Home Economist* (1969), applied her considerable experience to bolstering college training programs and establishing high standards for instruction. Another wartime appointee, Sarah Gibson Blanding, the director of the New York State College of Home Economics at Cornell University, promoted food and nutrition education, child-care, conservation of rationed materials, and mass feeding for the New York Human Nutrition Division of the State Emergency Food Commission and also coordinated volunteer programs.

After decades of experience at home and neighborhood domestic work, directing war era food conservation, and lecturing women's tomato clubs for the Farmers' Institute in Raleigh, North Carolina, Jane Simpson McKimmon, the author of *When We're Green We Grow* (1945), promoted home economics as a profession. In addition to lobbying county commissioners to fund local programs for housewives, she dispatched home demonstration agents to churches, curb markets, schools, courthouses, and fairgrounds to educate women on balancing meals, growing vegetables at the kitchen door, and making linens, aprons, and house dresses from feed sacks. From an understanding of women's longstanding financial dependence, she focused on ways for them to raise money, network, and improve their situations.

A Permanent Record

In 2000, the staff at the Albert R. Mann Library at Cornell University collected 1,500 seminal domestic science documents published between 1850 and 1950 and made them accessible online at a Web site called Home Economics Archive: Research, Tradition and History, or HEARTH (http://hearth.library.cornell.edu/h/hearth/). The mission of the site was to organize and conserve primary sources from a vital period in the history of home economics, many of which were in danger of being lost to future students of the discipline. The materials were chosen by experts in the field on the basis of their historical significance. Among the documents available are Maria Parloa's *Home Economics: A Guide to Household Management* (1898), Henriette Davidis's *German National Cookery for American Kitchens* (1904), Martha Van Rensselaer's *Manual of Home-Making* (1919), *Home Economists: Portraits and Brief Biographies of the Men and Women Prominent in the Home Economics Movement in the United States* (1929) from the American Home Economics Association, and Ola Powell's *Successful Canning and Preserving* (1930).

See also **Akabori, Minekichi; Beecher, Catharine Esther; Beeton, Isabella; Brereton, Maud Adeline; Clark, Ava Milam; Corson, Juliet; Farmer, Fannie; Frederick, Christine McGaffey; Gas ; Gilbreth, Lillian Moller; Kellogg, John Harvey; Leslie, Eliza; Lihotzky, Grete Shütte; Maltby, Lucy; Marshall, Agnes; Refrigeration; Rorer, Sarah Tyson; Thermometers; Women's Magazines; Young, Hannah**

Further Reading

Bancroft, Hubert Howe. *The Book of the Fair.* Chicago: The Bancroft Company, 1893.
Clark, Ava Milam, and J. Kenneth Munford. *Adventures of a Home Economist.* Corvallis: Oregon State University Press, 1969.
Coppens, Linda Miles. *What American Women Did, 1789–1920.* Jefferson, N.C.: McFarland, 2001.
Corson, Juliet. *Cooking School Text Book and Housekeeper's Guide to Cookery and Kitchen Management.* New York: Orange Judd Co., 1879.
Goodwin, Lorine Swainston. *The Pure Food, Drink, and Drug Crusaders, 1879–1914.* Jefferson, N.C.: McFarland, 1999.
Henderson, Susan R., "A Revolution in the Woman's Sphere: Grete Lihotzky and the Frankfurt Kitchen," in *Architecture and Feminism.* New York: Princeton Architectural Press, 1996.
Marsh, Dorothy B., and Helen W. Kendall, "One Thousand Women Meet to Discuss Home Problems," *Good Housekeeping,* October 1930, 94–95.
Peiss, Kathy L., "American Women and the Making of Modern Consumer Culture," *Journal for MultiMediaHistory,* Fall 1998.

Stage, Sarah, and Virginia B. Vincenti, eds. *Rethinking Home Economics: Women and the History of a Profession.* Ithaca, N.Y.: Cornell University Press, 1997.

Thrasher, Max Bennett. *Tuskegee: Its Story and Its Work.* New York: Negro Universities Press, 1969.

HOMINY

Hominy—corn kernels that have been soaked in a caustic solution and then rinsed—has a long history from its development by native American cooks through Hispanic versions and commercially canned hominy, also called *posole* or *pozole.* The term *hominy* is derived from the Algonquian word *rockahominie,* meaning parched corn kernels.

In prehistoric Teotihuacán, Mexico, *nixtamal,* a low-nutrient hominy made from corn soaked in lime water, was part of the daily diet. New England Indians prepared a forerunner of hominy called *samp,* a hot mush named for the Narraganset term *nasaump* (corn gruel). After sifting coarse meal, they cooked it in water and pounded it in a mortar to create a nourishing hot cereal similar to grits.

The early Mohawk turned dried corn into fluffy grains by soaking dried maize kernels and boiling them in an alkaline solution made from blackjack, or scrub oak ash. The next stage required twirling and massaging kernels in a rawhide hulling bag. In 1664, Father François du Creux, the author of *Historiae Canadensis seu Novae Franciae* (The History of Canada or New France), made a sketch of two Huron women stirring corn in a cylindrical container and removing husks in small batches with a hulling bag. After separating kernels from their outer shells, they had to rinse them several times to rid the resulting hominy of an ashy taste.

Colonial settlers of North America imitated the native method of transforming corn into hasty pudding, or corn meal pudding. After hollowing a small tree trunk ten inches deep, they applied a pestle to pound macerated kernels. Stirring with a crook-handled hasty pudding spoon, they slowly turned the mass into hominy or baked it on a wooden bannock board into ash cakes. When Southern cooks created a method of baking such cakes on the blade of a hoe, they called their corn pones "hoecake."

During the hard winter of 1777–78 at Valley Forge, General George Washington and the Continental Army knew hunger and despair. To economize, Martha Washington made a kind of griddlecake from hominy and cornmeal, mixed with milk, butter, and eggs. She served the finished cakes with honey or syrup.

According to Eliot Wigginton's *The Foxfire Book* (1968), the first of a successful series of interviews and photos on the lifestyle and cookery of mountaineers in the southern Appalachians, homemade hominy survived among hill people long after it had become available in cans on the grocery shelf. To make the fluffy kernels, cooks put a gallon of lye in a large wash pot, shelled twelve to fifteen ears of yellow or white large-kernel corn into the pot, and cooked it for up to nine hours at an outdoor fire or in a fireplace. The swollen, softened cooked kernels required lengthy rinsing to remove the husk and germ. After a dozen rinsings, removal of the skins from the kernels, and neutralization of the lye, the hominy was ready to be cooked all night in ample water or broth before serving or canning.

See also **Ollas**

Further Reading

Dickason, Olive Patricia. *Canada's First Nations.* Norman: University of Oklahoma Press, 1992.

Fussell, Betty. *The Story of Corn.* New York: North Point Press, 1999.

_____, "Translating Maize into Corn: The Transformation of America's Native Grain," *Social Research,* Spring 1999, 41–65.

HONEY

Honey, a pure sugar, energizes the body and satisfies the desire for sweet tastes shared by humans and other primates. Europeans and Americans prized it as a table sweetener; in Asia, it was traditionally valuable as a medicine; and in Africa, it was the basis for an alcoholic beverage. Pictorial and archeological evidence from Altamira, Spain, dating to 15,000 BCE, documents early interest in honeycombs. A wall painting of a comb at Catal Hüyük, Anatolia, suggests that apiculture, or beekeeping, thrived as early as 6600 BCE. Later proof of the use of honey in ancient cultures includes honey-based medicines recorded in Babylonian recipe books, storage jars found at Thebes, evidence of hive tending in classical Greece and Cyprus, rock honey chambers carved by Sicilian farmers in the Hyblaean Mountains of Syracusa, and the smoking of bees in Egypt, where favor-seekers courted Ramses III with pots of honey. Like the early Egyptians, Australian aborigines trailed bees to their hives and subdued them with smoke in order to gather the combs.

Ubiquitous Food

As a food, honey was ubiquitous in the ancient world. The paintings on the burial monument of Rekhmire, vizier to the fourteenth century BCE pharaoh Thutmose III, depict the frying of honey cakes. Clearly

Honey bee frame of artificial hive showing cells where bees store honey (Illinois, USA).
[© *Nature Picture Library / Alamy.*]

visible among the culinary equipment and supplies is a honey jar. A surviving honey cake from Luxor, dating to around 1400 BCE, bears decorative human figures similar to gingerbread men. In 1000 BCE, Persian suppliants served honey as a substance sacred to Zoroaster. Similarly, devotees of Buddhism, Jainism, Judaism, Confucianism, Taoism, Shintoism, and Sikhism considered honey a holy substance. Worshippers, priests, and sacred animals ate it and burned it at altars.

Sacred texts, lore, and art are replete with references to honey cookery and trade. The Indian *Vedas,* compiled around 1000 BCE, proclaimed the benefits of honey to followers of the faith. One passage of scripture proposes, "Let one take honey along with our valued diets to beautify his appearance, develop his brain faculty and strengthen his body. With honey he would digest properly all the foods." (Crane 1999, 503) Nepalese Buddhists revered honey as a sacred nectar, sharing honors with milk and water. The book of Genesis 43:11 records that Jacob's brothers traded for Egyptian corn with honey, myrrh, nuts, and spices; Psalm 81:16 recounts how God fed Jacob with honey from a rock nest. To the Hittites, honey and sweetness were synonymous. Muhammad sanctioned bees in Sura 16:68 of the Koran, proclaiming that Allah bestowed upon them their nesting instincts. Muslim cooks valued honey, into which they plunged a clay casserole of semolina and butter for a dish called *tomina.* The Maya worshipped the honey bee (*Apis mellifera*) and offered a tribute of honey to the Aztec monarch Montezuma in the 1400s, much as Corsicans paid tribute to Etruria and Ethiopians paid property leases with wax and honey. The Lacandon of Chiapas, Mexico, perpetuated ancient Mayan reverence for balche, a fermented mead that conferred honor on the brewer, whom they called the "Lord of the balche," an earthly manifestation of Bohr, the drinker's god. (Andrews 2000, 15) A honey-hunting song from the Bantu of Tanzania petitioned God for sweet roots and honey.

Throughout the Greek world, honey equated with the sweet love of the goddess Aphrodite. When Daedalus, the mythic engineer and wing-maker, fled Crete for Sicily, he thanked the goddess for safe landfall with a golden replica of a honeycomb. About 530 BCE, Pythagoras claimed that he owed his longevity to regular consumption of honey. In the *Deipnosophistae*, the food writer Athenaeus attributed the good health of Pythagoreans to the eating of bread with honey and characterized Plato's sweet words as the result of honey placed in his mouth in infancy. Athenaeus also supported his case for honey's nutritional value by describing how serving women kept the aged philosopher Democritus alive in his last days by feeding him only honey. During the Greek colonization of Sicily, cooks celebrated the Thesmophoria, an annual feast of Demeter and Persephone, by shaping honey and sesame seed cakes in molds resembling *mylloi* (female pudenda), a treat that Athenian satirist and rhetorician Alciphron relished in the early third century CE.

As Athenaeus's recipes and Alciphron's witty letters demonstrated, honey was a common element in nature and food writing. Because sweets were the standard conclusion to the Roman meal, the poet Marcus Terentius Varro considered honey a dual substance, worthy on the altar of the gods and at the human table. The *apiarius,* or beekeeper, devoted himself so completely to the task that he built his residence among the hives.

The Roman Caelius Apicius, author of *De Re Coquinaria* (On Cooking, late 300s CE), listed honey and grape pulp as food preservatives, He recommended a honey glaze for ham or roasted crane or duck and honey as a sauce for boiling ostrich and for frying wine cakes and bread. He also explained how to use honey to preserve apples, cherries, figs, pears, and plums, to mix in a sweet-and-sour marinade for steeping turnips and myrtle berries, and to keep meat fresh without salting. More detailed are the writings of Columella, who explained how to store quinces in jars under a bath of honey. For an everyday custard, Roman bakers simmered eggs, milk, and honey in a clay pot.

Extraction of honey from the comb challenged the creativity of the Roman honey collector. In the early years of the Roman Empire, the poet Virgil compiled most of the scholarship on apiculture and the use of honey as food. In his fourth *Georgics*, he wrote of the smallholder's dependence on apiculture. Writing of the Sabaei, the historian Pliny the Elder, author of *Natural History* (ca. 77 CE), identified them as a nation rich in honey and wax, two valuable trade commodities.

Because of the health benefits of honey-laden medicines, compotes, lozenges, and mead, humans hunted and traded honey for thousands of years. Arab traders traversing West Africa in 1067 CE cited honey as an item of Senegalese wealth. Nearly three centuries later, the Muslim traveler Ibn Battuta journeyed to Mali and found edible honey from combs in rotted trees along the Sahara Desert. The Portuguese expeditioner Vasco da Gama discovered a honey hunter at the Cape of Good Hope in 1497. The practice continued among the Mbuti, hunter-gatherer pygmies of Zaire as well as among the Hottentot, Maasai, Zulu, and Babinga of Central African Republic, where stouthearted climbers robbed bees' nests high in the trees and deposited the sweet reward in bark baskets. The Wkamba of Kenya preferred to store their cache in a honey bag stitched from the stomach of a cow.

Europeans intent on gathering honey built niches in stone cottage walls and laid out kitchen gardens that attracted bees to the straw skep, a dome-shaped basket that fit over an eke, or imp, a cylinder placed inside as a reservoir. Essentials included clusters of fragrant herbs, hedges and windbreaks to protect insects from gales, and nectar- and pollen-producing plants such as viper's bugloss and allium for nourishing a hive. Hardy apiculturists made bee traps; Hungarians, Slovaks, and Romanians shaped sections of horn with sliding lids. In Sweden farmers removed a section of a tree trunk containing a hive and placed it in the garden for apiculture. English apiarists mastered beekeeping as much for the beeswax, used for candles, as for the honey. Recounting a day's activities, one twelfth century English chronicler wrote, "Me ligtede candles to oeten bi" (I lit candles to eat by). (Jekyll & Jones, 1939, 83)

Honey appears in dietary information from the Middle Ages, especially after Crusaders adapted recipes for confections from Arab lands to ingredients found in Europe. The encyclopedist Thomas of Cantimpré compiled existing honey lore and recipes in *Liber de Apibus* (Book on Bees) in the mid-twelfth century. Both Agnes Sorel, mistress of Charles VII, and arts patron Margaret of Navarre, sister of Francis I, valued honey-based cosmetics and enjoyed the French *pain d'épices* (spiced cakes), forerunners of gingerbread that later became popular at the court of Louis XIV. The recipe influenced the Belgian *coques de Dinant*, Slovenian and Czech gingerbread, and Swiss *lebkuchen*, all confections implying love when given as a gift to sweethearts. A French etiquette guide from the fourteenth century noted that sticky fingers were an inevitable consequence of eating honeyed comfits.

Honey-sweetened beverages were popular in eighteenth-century Russia. *Sheeten*, a hot drink of watered, spiced honey, revived energy on cold winter nights. *Sbitien*, a hot, spiced honey beverage that remained popular for two centuries, was the center of flourishing kitchen businesses. At outdoor markets, brewers set up woodsheds to house their copper samovars. Careful mixing of honey with caraway, cinnamon, clove, ginger, and nutmeg and proper stoking of the pot with charcoal produced the best flavor. In this same era, Russian cooks mimicked the Tartar use of honey to preserve root vegetables, a technique applied to lettuce stalks in Elena Burman Molokhovets's classic Russian illustrated cookbook, *A Gift to Young Housewives* (1861).

Apiculture Through the Ages

Honey became a hobby and research topic in the Renaissance. In his masterwork, *De Honesta Voluptate et Valitudine* (On Right Pleasure and Health, 1475), the Italian cook and culinary writer Platina differentiated between early and late honey. For curative and preservative use, he preferred summer caches to those of autumn. Of the culinary use of honey, he wrote, "Cooked honey is considered better than raw, for it does not bloat one so much or increase pains in the midriff or bile." (Platina 1999, 37).

Bee culture varied according to the ingenuity of the apiarist. From the Middle Ages into modern times, French and English beekeepers coiled straw into a skep. As drawn by Samuel Linnaeus, the brother of naturalist Carl Linnaeus, in 1768, Swedish skep builders created a stacking system for six storied hives capped by a knobbed lid. Hive workers also wove straw within a wood frame as an encouragement for cell building. In Manisa, Turkey, a series of horizontal boards kept the nests growing, much as they did in Italy in the late sixteenth century. In Australia, bee-keeper James Carol developed shelters with movable frames and bell jars on top in 1870. Within three years, he was cultivating eighty-seven colonies. Moroccans at Gharb formed clay hive holders, which resembled the bottle-shaped pipe joints favored in Malta. Cottage hive stands in colonial America held conical skeps coiled from grass or hay, which they covered with clay baskets to keep them warm and dry.

Various strainers eventually replaced the cloth honey bag. A scientist and member of the Royal Society, the English apiarist Sir Jonas Moore suggested using a sieve called a ridder. In 1759, John Hill's *The Virtues of Honey* contrasted honey that drained naturally from a strainer to that extracted by heat and concluded that the natural method produced the best flavor. A Polish potter created a ceramic honey strainer, a two-handled jug pierced with holes over the bottom half of the container.

Around 1850, the Philadelphia inventor L. L. Langstroth's moveable frame hive stimulated beekeeping in the United States. In the 1860s, inventor Thiphena Hornbrook patented an enclosed hive shed that allowed the bee tender to remove a collection tray from the bottom and feed the bees through a trough without touching the hive.

By the twentieth century, the study of bees and their habits, once the province of observant hobbyists and naturalists, had become a serious branch of the science of entomology. In 1953, *The Dancing Bees: An Account of the Life and Senses of the Honey Bee* summarized a forty-year study of bee behavior by the Nobel laureate Karl von Frisch, a Viennese entomologist. He decoded bee body language indicating sources of food, useful knowledge for keepers trying to locate a swarm.

Ritual and Table Favorite

Honey remains a ritual and table favorite around the world. Ceremonial practice governs the gathering and use of honey in Arabia, Burma, India, Indonesia, Malaysia, and Thailand. In the Cameroons, before breaching a nest, gatherers suit up in straw armor with a pierced facemask providing woven peepholes. Out of respect for nature, they never rob a comb of its entire contents.

The Kikuyu of Kenya honor a wedding tradition that calls for gifts of honey from the prospective groom to his future mother-in-law to brew beer for the bride's father. Italians make *torrone,* a nougat blended from egg whites, ground almonds, and honey in the style of *turrón,* a sweet that Islamic immigrants introduced in Spain after 711 CE. In Yemen, festive diners top bread with warm honey and clarified butter. Hosts in Lithuania welcome guests with *Krupnikas,* a honey liqueur. In the Caribbean, honey cutters on the island of Nevis wield a cutlass and bucket to gather nectar from the tropical coconut, coralita, gliricidia, guenip, logwood, mango, and orange. Honey made from the nectar is a prized ingredient for desserts. The Guayaki of Paraguay consider honey the mainstay of their diet.

Both ancient and modern methods of gathering honey persist. Although apiarists in Nepal continue to extract honey by hand-squeezing the comb, professional apiarists in industrial nations use centrifugal force to empty the cells of their contents.

See also **Candy; Kitchen Cures; Mead; Sweeteners**

Further Reading

Bendure, Glenda, *et al. Scandinavian & Baltic Europe.* Melbourne: Lonely Planet Publications, 1999.
"Honey Bee," *Aramco World*, March 1960, 9–11.
Nicolet, Gilles, "Suiting Up for the Honey Wars," *Smithsonian*, August 2001, 79–83.
Platina. *On Right Pleasure and Good Health.* Asheville, N.C.: Pegasus Press, 1999.
Roosevelt, Priscilla. *Life on the Russian Country Estate.* Hartford, Conn.: Yale University Press, 1995.
Rubin, Barbara Blatt, trans. *The Dictionarius of John de Garlande.* Lawrence, Kans.: Coronado Press, 1981.

HORN

Since prehistoric times, householders have shaped domestic items from the horns or antlers of cattle, oxen, sheep, goats, and antelopes. In *Anabasis* (ca. 400 BCE) the Greek historian Xenophon described a Thracian banquet at which guests quaffed wine from horn cups. Roman architects covered windows with thin sheets of hide, animal bladder, or membranes, all of which were forerunners to the later use of horn plates for the same purpose. Pliny the Elder, compiler of a Roman encyclopedia, *Natural History* (ca. 77 CE), referred to horn plates in lanterns, which Romans may have used in inclement weather.

Anglo-Saxon drinkers of the seventh century are stereotypically depicted with horn beer cups made from a full cow's horn sawed level and fitted at bottom with a circle of flat horn wedged inside the narrow end. Unlike wood, horn did not swell as it became water logged. The pointed shape of the horn cup forced drinkers to drain the contents before setting cups on the table. Archeologists located examples of these horn cups and other table implements at the Sutton Hoo dig at Taplow Court, Buckinghamshire, in 1883 and 1939 at a chieftain's grave near Woodbridge, Suffolk. Remains include drinking horns carved and edged in gold for the serving of ale or mead to a monarch. Metal bands at center and a metal tip provided weight for a balanced vessel.

In the late Middle Ages, hosts made a show of providing clean, safe flagons and cups for banquets. In addition to the ceremonial cup washing at table, the thoughtful host set out assay, or anti-poison, cups of horn. House staff tested assay cups by poisoning the contents, then setting the vessels near a columbarium for pigeons to sample. If the birds survived, the cup proved its use as a deterrent to intentional poisoning.

In England, the splitting of a sheep's horn produced a common pair of table spoons or kitchen fork and ladle, each with the characteristic curve of the original material. Another application was the stable lanthorn, a safe candle-carrier that lighted the way from kitchen to stall for birthing calves and lambs and for egg gathering and early morning milking.

In the Americas, Indians chose horn, along with bone, antlers, teeth, and tusks, as a sturdy raw material. Northeastern and Plains Indians, who recycled all parts of bison, often turned the horns into spoons, ladles, drinking cups, and stirring sticks. The northern Algonquian used the horn of mountain sheep and goats for similar implements and vessels. For the Alaskan Tlingit, horn was the main source of spoons, dishes, and food storage containers.

The Havasupai, who lived near the Grand Canyon, prized the horns of bighorn sheep for fashioning large-bowled spoons for baking and cooking. For smaller spoons, they used horn from the pronghorn. As described in the autobiography of Mourning Dove, a Washington state Salish, the fashioning of eating implements from mountain sheep horn required some skill: "The horns were soaked in hot water until they were soft enough to cut and shape on round stones to form the bowl. They were tied tightly in place on the curved stone with buckskin cords, leaving the untouched portion as the handle. These spoons, serving as both ladle and soup bowl, were used in turn by the family members while eating." (*Mourning Dove* 1990, 62) She added that spoons were gender specific: men ate from designated horn implements to spare them using a spoon intended for women.

The traditional horn bowl of the Eskimos at Hudson's Strait struck the fancy of the Arctic navigator Sir William Edward Parry, who sailed in search of a Northwest passage in 1820. It was hollowed out of the root of the *oomingmuk*, or musk-ox, horn. The smaller end of the horn supplied the Eskimos with spoons and drinking cups, which they notched with knives to make them easier to hold.

Horners, or hornsmiths, prized the European alpine goat and Mediterranean sea turtle, both of which produced natural layers of horn. These materials—forerunners of gutta-percha, rubber, and plastic—could be heated and steeped in liquid, delaminated, and shaped around hot irons into buttons, combs, knobs, and handles in natural colors that imitated pearl and ivory.

American colonists often relied on horn for stirrup cups, mirror frames, knife handles, salad sets, and other daily needs. At the home of the Reverend Jonathan Ashley, the Puritan minister who supplied the pulpit of Deerfield, Massachusetts, the family ate at a drop-leaf table from humble wood plates and horn spoons. A silvered horn cup used on Long Island held a quince drink, a heady blend of rum toddy, quince preserves, and sugar. For the hunter and soldier, the trusty powder horn kept powder dry for charging a flintlock rifle.

In seventeenth-century England, horn was the chosen material for making scrapers to remove the leftovers in mortars and basins and the sticky candy makings on marble slabs. As flatware gained popularity, iron knives, forks, and spoons sported horn handles. One horner of the era, John Osborne, specialized in molding liquified horn into useful objects. London became a horn-molding center in 1725, when factories produced die-molded snuff boxes, napkin rings, and combs.

An 1845 issue of *Scientific American* published a detailed description of the making of knife and razor handles from molded horn. The process began with sawing pieces of horn to a usable size and shaping heated pieces with a spoke-shave or knife for fitting into metal molds to produce straight, curved, twisted, rounded, and beveled shapes. Next the horn, clamped in dies screwed tightly shut, went into a boiling water bath before finishing. The handles of some implements resulted from the joining of two pieces of horn.

Further Reading

Insoll, Timothy A., "The Road to Timbuktu: Trade & Empire," *Archaeology*, November/December 2000, 48–52.

"Making Articles in Horn," *Scientific American*, August 28, 1845.

Paunov, Evgeni, "Thracian Treasures from Bulgaria," *Athena Review*, Vol. 1, No. 4, 76–82.

HORNO

The horno is a conical outdoor oven resembling a beehive. Native Americans living in the pueblos of the Southwest shape hornos from adobe. To make the free-form oven, the builder sun-dries bricks fashioned from clay mixed with gravel, sagebrush ash, and straw. Usually thigh-high, the horno allows the cook to bake, steam, and stew foods outdoors, thus keeping residences cool and free of fumes and smoke. From cooking aromas seeping from minute cracks in the oven, cooks are able to judge the stage of doneness of dishes and baking.

Cooks of the San Ildefonso use the horno for baking corn loaves; the Taos bake honey cookies and bread for sale to tourists. The Hopi use a wood paddle to form *chukuviki*, a cornmeal loaf, which they wrap in cornhusks and bake in a horno on a grate. In Paraguay, cooks shape *chipa guazú* (scalloped corn) into cakes and brown them in hornos to serve as a side dish, a favorite during the corn harvest.

Like Hispanic versions in New World *estancias*, the horno survives in twenty-first-century versions and in the name of a Chilean dish, *empanadas de horno,* which are oven-baked meat turnovers. Argentine baker Violeta Balhas, originally from Buenos Aires, honored her mother in 1999 by building an authentic adobe bake site at her home in Australia. Balhas and her husband used firebrick, refractible concrete, aluminum flashing, and a second-hand flue for hardware. After choosing a front chimney design to circulate air from the door to the flame, they created a template from a tub-shaped basket.

For a durable adobe, Balhas obtained straw and made plaster from sticky, red adobe dirt mixed with white clay from a gravel pit. After concreting stacked fire brick, they shovel-mixed dirt and straw with water by guess, removing stones and lumps larger than a walnut. They cut the flue to suit and angled the bottom to attach to the firebox. For maximum heat retention, they crafted the door out of adobe and concrete and air-dried the finished panel. Final adjustment involved setting a curing fire fueled with cane and eucalyptus wood and sealing cracks with adobe.

Use of the horno begins with four hours of firing—or three hours if heat remains from a previous day's baking. Balhas established a timetable for horno cookery: fish, ten to twenty minutes; vegetables twenty to sixty minutes, baked yams and potatoes nearly ninety minutes, chicken up to ninety minutes, turkey or leg of lamb two hours, and rib roast around two hours and thirty minutes.

Baking in a horno demands its own process and timing. Balhas began with coal removal and a wet mopping or hosing of the bare floor to remove ash and generate steam to promote crusting. A generous sprinkle of corn meal or semolina on a peel and on the oven floor created a gritty sliding surface for removal of pots of baked beans, loaves, pita, or pizza. Bread took around a half hour, pizza only five minutes. Beans and grain could cook overnight in a cooling oven.

The concept of cooking in an earthen dome is not unique to the New World. In Jordan, homemakers have traditionally baked at a *tabboun,* a thick mud-and-chipped-flint dome covering a mud-and-stone baking surface. Above a fire trench fueled with wheat chaff, the flame is usually fragrant with oak sticks, olivewood, or a mix of the two. Still in use by local bakers and take-out restaurants, the *tabboun* maintains heat for baking a series of madaba wheat loaves, casseroles, stuffed chickens, and whole lambs.

Further Reading

Fistere, Isobel, "Jordan's Legendary Musakahan," *Aramco World*, November–December 1975, 26–27.

I

ICE

Before refrigeration, the use of natural ice as a food preservative presented logistical problems of time, transportation, and cold storage. Glaciers may have been the forerunners of ice chests and icehouses. One supposition about Ice Age food harvesting suggests that early humans hacked through glacial ice into the carcasses of mastodons that may have been frozen for millennia. Later technology involved the shaping and placement of ice onto food. Zimri-Lin, an Iraqi monarch, constructed an icehouse near the Euphrates River in 1700 BCE. As early as 1000 BCE the Chinese cut ice for kitchen use and for preserving melons and fruit in ground caches. At Yongcheng in Shensi Province, a palace ice pit survives from around 600 BCE. Insulated with rice husks, cached foodstuffs were accessible through sluice gates. Melted ice drained away through a channel to the river.

Ancient Source of Refreshment

As recorded in the *Shih Ching* (Classic of Poetry), China's first poetry anthology, edited by Confucius around 475 BCE, icehouse management required periodic cleaning and restocking. Ice harvesters in Beijing sliced pieces from ponds and lakes and stored them in deep ground caches lined with hay. These cold-storage caches kept fruits and vegetables fresh for the court kitchen. A house staff of ninety-four provided ice for the Chou emperors around 300 BCE for chilling beverages and as a preservative of corpses. As early as 221 BCE, the emperor Shih Huang Ti ordered the construction of a permanent ceramic ice pit at Hsien-yang, perhaps to improve sanitation. Formed of interlocking ceramic collars, it lined a column forty-three feet high and five and half feet wide. As demand increased, the Chinese began gathering and storing ice blocks from northern Asia during the Tang dynasty, which started in 618 CE.

Roman refrigeration systems emulated the wine coolers made by potters at Vulci, Etruria, around 500 BCE and the refrigeration pits topped with oak limbs built at the direction of Alexander the Great around 330 BCE. In the first century CE, Nero demanded ice at the Roman imperial palace. For his use, slaves harvested snow in the Alps and stored it in icehouses. The emperor's wine bottles arrived at the table nestled in an ice-filled wine bucket. At banquets, guests heaped bronze strainers with ice chips and drizzled icy runoff over their wine cups, a practice denounced by Seneca, a social critic who despised the empire's frivolous fads.

To Roman shoppers, merchants sold snow from ice dispensaries. By storing quantities of ice in pits insulated with straw, they made use of alternate thawing and refreezing, which hardened the bottom layer, thus increasing its value above that of the wine it chilled. In the coastal city of Pompeii, slaves ventured by donkey cart to Apennine peaks to cut and load ice for freezing *sorpata* (sherbet) and *gelata* (ice cream). At any of the city's more than 200 wine counters, where travelers could stop for refreshment, snow keeps stored beverages cool.

In Arab kitchens, ice was essential for diluting sweet fruit syrups for *sarbat,* the forerunner of sherbets, sorbets, and snow cones. The elite of Istanbul received snow by barge for kitchen use. During the Mamluk dynasty that ruled Egypt and Syria from 1250 to 1517, postmen doubled as snow deliverers on their way from Lebanon to Cairo. At Oran, snow for beverages arrived by sea; on Malta, carters brought straw-wrapped bales of Neapolitan mountain snow to the stronghold of the Knights Hospitallers for use in the kitchen and clinic. Syrian shops in Tripoli sold snow water and, from the harbor, marketed bags of snow to pilgrims, according to the traveler Peter Casola's *Viaggio a Gerusalemme* (Voyage to Jerusalem, 1494). Syrian traders carried snow overland on horseback to Egypt.

Drawing on Egyptian technology dating to 100 CE, Turkish hosts chilled water for guests in a *bardak,* a porous, unglazed carafe suspended in a breezy area out of the sun. As liquid oozed from the pores and evaporated, the contents chilled. The hotter the atmosphere, the cooler the drink. In 1527, when the sultan had a staff of more than 5,000 at the Topkapi palace in Constantinople, he numbered among them stewards of ice and snow. Some diners sprinkled snow onto foods as a condiment.

In Europe, the *lednik* (icehouse) got its start in Russia in 1481. In the 1660s, the czar's kitchen staff expanded the nation's considerable icehouse technology to fifteen meat-and-fish cellars and thirty in-ground beverage chillers. As an adjunct to controlling temperature of dishes, in 1660, Italian Galileo Galilei created the first thermometer, a vapor tube that measured temperature by the rise and fall of liquid, replaced with alcohol. Two years later, Charles II of England erected an icehouse in Greenwich. In 1667, his brother James, the Duke of York, equipped St. James's Palace with a straw-lined snow well that became the model for other in-ground storage chambers.

Supplying the Home

The icehouse became a household standard late in the seventeenth century. Builders often sheltered a family's ice supply below a copse on the grounds of a great house, within a brick chamber in a hillside or moat, or in a thatched shed. Built like caches or in-ground wells, they tended to face north and needed a vestibule air lock and stone dome or shingle roof for maximum cooling. Some held ice chunks sawed from ponds or lakes, others contained dry snow rammed into place on straw or marsh grass flooring with a wood tamper. The English cultural historian Dorothy Hartley, the author of *Water in England* (1964), found a Yorkshire estate igloo, a rounded affair set over a deep stone-lined pit and covered in turf. The filler maneuvered ice chunks into place on an oak timber slide; an overhead pulley

fitted with ice tongs lifted them to the level of a wheeled dolly for pony transport to the kitchen.

By 1676, French diners were drinking wines iced in a *glacière* (ice chest). In English cities, supper tables bore blocks of ice, which servants obtained from a fishmonger, butcher, or ice dealer and carved to create a centerpiece. Ice chips filled butter containers and finger bowls, chilled puff pastry, and set creams and jellies.

When the British colonized the Indian subcontinent, they expanded on native ice-making methods and snow retrieval from the mountains near Kasauli. In 1775, a judge described an Allahabad ice works where workers made ice during the winter months. They poured boiled water into shallow pans in depressions insulated at the side and bottom. The next morning, they collected a year's worth of ice to store in pits. By 1875, the ice works was producing up to twenty-nine tons per night.

In Sicily, the bishop of Catania claimed a considerable revenue from snow and ice harvested from Mount Etna's slopes. Patrick Brydone in his travel journal *Voyage en Sicile et à Malthe, Fait en l'Année 1770* (A Tour Through Sicily and Malta in 1770), published in 1773, wrote, "There is no entertainment given by the nobility of which these do not always make a principal part: a famine of snow, they themselves say, would be more grievous than a famine of either corn or wine." (Simeti 1989, 283) However, ice hunters needed more than a winter's snowfall. To keep ice throughout the hot Mediterranean summer, according to the painter-engraver Jean Houel's *Voyage Pittoresque en Sicilie* (Picturesque Journey in Sicily, 1784), the Order of Malta established a lava-roofed grotto on Mount Etna consisting of double carved wells into which workers compressed snow. They loaded the frozen chunks onto mules for delivery to boats carrying them to kitchens on the shore.

In the American colonies only the wealthy could afford to maintain icehouses. One model still standing in the twenty-first century was that of the Wayside Inn, America's oldest operating inn built by David How in 1702 in Sudbury, Massachusetts. To stock up, the innkeeper had servants or slaves cut the frozen surface of lakes and ponds in winter and store the blocks in hay and wood shavings deep in the flooring. They mounded the upper portion of the Chamber to keep it cool and to impede melting and evaporation. Common icehouse utensils included the ice pick, galvanized iron ice hatchet and chisel, wood or metal scoop, and ice chipper, such as the Lightning and Crown models manufactured by North Brothers of Philadelphia for home and professional kitchens. The food writer Sarah Tyson

Rorer promoted ice tools in *Dainty Dishes for All the Year Round: Recipes for Ice Creams, Water Ices, Sherbets, and Other Frozen Desserts* (1890), a source of recipes for Delmonico, English, Neapolitan, and plain ice cream. To make fine-textured ice chips for desserts, cold drinks, or the lining of a butter bowl or shrimp cocktail glass, the ice shaver, consisting of a cup on a handle, applied a serrated blade on the cup bottom to shred ice into the container.

At Monticello, Thomas Jefferson's country estate outside Charlottesville, Virginia, the superintendent, Edmund Bacon, attended to ice preservation to reduce the amount of fresh meat demanded by a constant round of entertainment. Jefferson wrote in 1809, "It would be a real calamity should we not have ice." Beginning in 1803, during Jefferson's first presidency, the Monticello staff kept wagons on alert for the first hard freeze on the Rivanna River. They layered the bottom of the icehouse with non-potable river ice as a food preserver, bedding it directly onto a lattice of boards and straw lining and a sealing of wood shavings. After tamping the ice into place, workers topped it with edible snow, which chilled drinks. The whole process took four days. Filling a bucket with ice for the table was the work of a slave, who climbed down a ladder, swept away the sawdust, and cut out a large chunk with an ax. A pump installed in 1807 removed the water created by melting ice, which slaves collected and conveyed to Wanscher, Jefferson's German plasterer. When a blaze broke out in the north pavilion in 1819, they hoisted snow from the icehouse to the terrace to stop the fire from spreading.

Birth of a New Industry

In the first half of the nineteenth century, the shipping of frozen foods packed in ice made perishable goods available over a wider area. In 1806, Frederic Tudor, a risk-taker who dreamed of a global ice business, began harvesting ice from Walden Pond and Wenham Lake, Massachusetts, making his first sale in the Caribbean on the island of Martinique. Although he experienced problems with shipping and agents, along with an unseasonably warm New England winter, he continued to pack ice in felt and pine sawdust to ship to the West Indies, South America, and Asia, a major purchaser. By 1834, Jacob Perkins, a Massachusetts inventor, was manufacturing ice with a steam ice-maker, later developed in Florida by John Gorrie into a large commercial ice machine for supplying treatment centers for yellow fever victims. English entrepreneurs were experimenting with artificial ice from an absorption process that used sulfuric acid to lower temperatures.

In the 1820s, an ice-harvesting industry flourished in Norway, providing refrigeration for breweries, grocery stores, and fish houses. Scottish fisheries built icehouses to assure the quality of their salmon catches, and Russian poultry and veal packers used snow to chill meat shipped from Archangel to St. Petersburg.

In 1860, New York entrepreneur James Cheeseman launched an ice business from Kennebec, Maine, and shipped 30,000 tons in a decade before selling his interest to the Knickerbocker Ice Company. His method was tedious, as well as hazardous to the workers. First, the surface of the ice along the Kennebec River was scraped clear of snow and debris; using a snowplow, workers gouged a line, which the groovers then deepened. Sawyers used a five-foot handsaw to separate blocks, which they removed with chisels. With the aid of a chain-driven escalator, large chunks were lifted into freezer lockers, where they were planed to a uniform twenty-two inches by thirty-two inches. From there, loaders forced the blocks onto wood runners into the holds of transport vessels. Cheeseman erected twelve freezer lockers along the river holding a total of 70,000 tons of high-grade natural ice.

In the winter of 1854, a team of ice harvesters at Walden Pond in Concord, Massachusetts, removed 1,000 tons daily over a one-acre surface, prompting the essayist Henry David Thoreau to comment that the same water he used for drinking cooled diners in Charleston, New Orleans, Bombay, Calcutta, and Madras. The ice harvested in New England and shipped across the American continent and to ports in Europe, Asia, and the Caribbean enabled cooks in isolated places to serve delicacies never before available.

New technology replaced the tedious labor of slicing and freezing ice chunks from impure lakes and ponds. In 1850, the Scottish inventor James Harrison, an immigrant to Australia, constructed the first ice-maker by reducing temperature with ether, a cooling system upgraded by the French inventors Edmund and Ferdinand Carré, who replaced ether with ammonia. They applied Michael Farady's ammonia coolant and the steam engine to an automatic chiller and ice-maker displayed at the 1862 World Exhibition in Paris. The creation of the ice saw in 1860 and the subsequent manufacture of icebreakers replaced the ice pick and chisel with steam-powered rigs. By 1876, French shoppers could buy South American beef shipped from Argentina to Rouen aboard the S.S. *Frigorifique*. In 1880, the S.S. *Strathleven* made the first major cargo haul from Melbourne to London, the beginning of a world market in frozen meat.

In 1874, entrepreneurs in India began manufacturing ice locally by steam processor at the International Ice Company in Madras. The idea spread to Calcutta in 1878, marking the first time that ordinary kitchen workers were able to duplicate the frozen delights molded in the sixteenth century in the royal kitchen of the emperor Akbar. From the introduction of artificial cooling grew a demand for cabinet refrigerators, which replaced the open-back window ice saver, a box fitted into an open window that used outside air to chill foods during the cold months of the year.

In Scandinavia, iceboxes replaced the haphazard dependence on springs or icehouses for chilling perishables. Swedish merchants began selling the containers in 1870. In 1882, Helsinki-based importer Carl Jakobsen issued a catalog offering twelve sizes of Swedish iceboxes. The Swedish inventor Christian Fredrik Madlung patented a partitioned icebox in 1896; in Finland, a machinist, Birger Serlachius, improved on the icebox by adding double walls separated by a slab of insulation and by circulating water through tubes in the walls. Within a short time, the firm of Auran Rautateollisuus Oy in Turku, Finland, began manufacturing American Temperator iceboxes with glass shelves. The devices functioned so poorly in hot kitchens that homemakers removed them to foyers, basements, attics, or food cupboards.

Cold Convenience

In the United States, a host of new kitchen implements followed the success of iceboxes. *Delineator* magazine touted the ice cuber, a compartmentalized metal tray that pressed on block ice to form cubes. The user lifted the cuber from the block with a three-pronged ice fork. The 1908 Sears, Roebuck catalog featured steel ice tongs for 51 cents and a double-walled galvanized iron water cooler for as little as $1.39. The two-, four-, or eight-gallon cylindrical reservoir, covered by a painted surface and topped with a fancy lid, dispensed water through a nickel-plated faucet.

The National Association of Ice Industries placed ads in women's magazines reminding homemakers to patronize grocers who secured vulnerable fruits and vegetables in crushed ice. The photos showed lush-colored vegetables—green lettuce, creamy cauliflower, red tomatoes and radishes, and orange carrots—emphasizing the protection ice afforded against wilting and browning. The ad copy cited scientific research attesting that crispy-cold produce retained its vitamins and flavor better than produce stored at higher temperatures.

By the mid-twentieth century, ice was an accepted kitchen staple for cooling beverages, serving around

chilled dishes such as shrimp cocktail, and making home-cranked ice cream. For quick reduction of chunks, Dazey manufactured a hand-cranked ice crusher that fastened to the wall. The user released the rocket-shaped chamber and poured crushed ice as casually as water. Within another two decades, a new generation of refrigerators appeared boasting such conveniences as automatic ice-makers—eliminating the need to fill trays at the kitchen sink—and exterior dispensers from which a person desiring ice could remove it without opening the appliance door. Later models dispensed water and a choice of ice cubes or crushed ice in the same manner.

Into the twenty-first century, iced treats retained their appeal, especially to beach-goers, campers, and vacationers. *Raspado* (snow cone) vendors conducted a lively kitchen business in Panama; the same treat flourished in Costa Rica as the *piragua* and in Puerto Rico as a *frio-frio*. Summoning customers with a bell or horn, the vendors peddled their bicycles or wheeled carts to likely spots, then halted to scrape servings of ice and mix them with syrup. Metal hand shavers reduced block ice to slivers for fluffing into snow. Over plastic cups of ice, they poured the customer's choices of fresh pineapple, strawberry, mint, anise, kola, or orange *miele* (syrup) and topped cones with honey and condensed milk. In Mexico, *raspado* vendors made their own purée from a variety of fruits, including apricot, grape, lemon, mango, papaya, pineapple, and tamarind.

See also **Amanite Kitchens; Amish Kitchens; Ice Cream; Marshall, Agnes; Refrigeration; Tudor, Frederic**

Further Reading

Bryan, John M. *Biltmore Estate: The Most Distinguished Private Place.* New York: Rizzoli, 1994.

Crowe, Mike, "Kennebec Ice," *Fisherman's Voice,* May 2000, 1–2.

Hamilton, Neil A., "The Ice King," *American History,* October 2000, 30–34.

Marshall, Agnes B. *Mrs. A. B. Marshall's Cookery Book.* London: Simpton, Marshall, Hamilton, Kent, & Co., 1894.

_____. *Victorian Ices & Ice Cream.* New York: Metropolitan Museum of Art, 1976.

McLaughlin, Jack. *Jefferson and Monticello: The Biography of a Builder.* New York: Henry Holt & Co., 1988.

Nagengast, Bernard, "The History of Sealed Refrigeration Systems," *ASHRAE Journal,* 1996, 37–38, 42–46, 48.

Shenoy, Sudha, "Freezing History for Posterity," *The Hindu,* April 17, 2000.

"Spirit of Enterprise by Mohammed Bah Abba," *Scientific American,* December 2000, 9.

Soda jerker flipping ice cream into malted milk shakes (Corpus Christi, Texas, 1939).
[© *Library of Congress, Prints and Photographs Division (LC-USF34-032264-D)*]

ICE CREAM

The creation of flavored ice and frozen desserts began in China and passed west to India, Persia, and Arabia. One method of freezing sweet mixtures was to agitate a sweet liquid against the side of a metal container, which sat in a vessel filled with ice. Constant stirring kept the mix light and airy and prevented formation of hard, tasteless ice chunks. After Nero came to power in the Roman Empire in 54 CE, he dispatched an ice patrol to the Apennine Mountains to retrieve snow and ice for mixing with fruit, honey, and juices. The Roman taste in chilled desserts shifted from fruit slush to *mecla* (ice milk) in the second century CE.

After 900 CE, Arab sherbet makers established businesses in Sicily chilling fruit syrup into *sarbat,* the forerunner of sherbet. They explored the heights of Mount Etna for ice, which supplied kitchen innovators creating ice creams, ice puddings, and *granitas* (flavored ices), a confection made by a tedious process of repeated scraping of ice chunks into a flaky slurry. From the Sicilian fondness for sweet chilled desserts came a progression of treats — *gelato* (iced confection), *gramolata* (granular ice), *spongata* (frozen cream), *spumoni* (ice cream layered with fruit and nuts), and *zabaglione ghiacciato* (egg-based ice cream). In 2000, Sicilian barkeeps were still following the tradition of topping glasses of cold tea with flaky mounds of *granita di limone* (lemon ice).

In the late 1200s, the legendary traveler Marco Polo returned to Venice from his sojourn in China and wrote his account of the journey, *The Travels of Marco Polo* (ca. 1299). He published a recipe for sherbet, the origin of the fruity Italian *sorbetto* (frozen beverage), another confection still sold on street corners and made in home kitchens at the turn of the twenty-first century.

Frozen Desserts Conquer Europe

In the mid-sixteenth century, Catherine de Médicis, wife of Henry II of France, brought to her new homeland a cadre of Italian pastry cooks and Sicilian ice cream specialists. Her enthusiasm for tasty nonalcoholic drinks introduced the nation to the custom of *'a pigghiata di gelati* (the taking of an ice) and the enjoyment of chilled orangeade, lemonade, citron bitters, frangipane water, and sherbet. (Simeti 1989, 299) The Tuscan architect Bernardo Buontalenti devised a way to churn milk, sugar, and egg yolks into *gelato* for the marriage of Catherine's kinswoman, Marie de Médicis, to Henry IV of France in 1600. At the Salone dei Cinquecento (Salon of the 500) in Florence's Palazzo Vecchio, Buontalenti astonished 300 guests with a honey and milk *cherbert* (sherbet).

Ice cream flavored with fruit and rose petals became the rage during the Renaissance. In 1600, the Sicilian dessert-maker Francisco Procopio de' Coltelli, inspired by the Caffé Florian in Venice's popular Piazza San Marco, introduced sorbet and ice cream to Paris. Within a decade, he popularized cold, sweet treats each summer at the Café Procope on the Rue des Fossés-Saint Germain. His success spawned the Café Napolitain on the Boulevard des Italiens and a tribe of *limonadières,* shopkeepers specializing in soft drinks who eventually worked under a licensing system to regulate trade. In 1672, Elias Ashmole referred to a dish dispensed at Windsor at the Feast of St.

George as "ice cream," the first recorded use of the term. In 1750, a dealer named Buisson increased the sale of cold sweets to a year-round commerce.

During the rise of *bourgeois cuisine* (middle-class cookery) in the eighteenth century, recipe books such as *L'Art de Faire des Glacés* (The Art of Making Ices, 1700), *Mrs. Eales' Receipts* (1718), by Queen Anne's confectioner, and Hannah Glasse's classic *The Art of Cookery Made Plain and Easy* (1747) expanded the variety of chilled desserts for home replication to include apricot, violet, rose, chocolate, and caramel. Makers improved the delicacy and consistency of iced treats molded into *fromage glacé* (iced cheese) or *fromage bavarois* (Bavarian cream). By the 1790s, the French acclaimed the *bombe glacée*, a specialty that confectioners shaped in a bombe mold with a tight-fitting lid. Neapolitan connoisseur F. Vincenzo Corrado, author of *La Manovra della Cioccolata et del Caffé* (The Making of Chocolate and Coffee, 1794) detailed a recipe for chocolate sorbet, which the maker buried in snow layered with salt for freezing. In later developments, cooks added egg yolk and syrup to firm coupes, mousses, neapolitans (layered flavors), and parfaits. They froze fruit in ice cream topped with browned meringue in a concoction known as *omelette à la norvé gienne* (Norse omelet). The spoom, or Italian meringue, blended wine or fruit juice that cooks froze into a sherbet and served in a glass.

Popularity in the New World

In the Americas, a form of ice cream was a staple among the Ingalik of western Canada's Lower Yukon River. Dessert-makers mixed cottonwood pods, berries, and oil with snow to create a ceremonial dish. The Inuit made *a-gu-tuk* by blending fish oil or fish liver, snow, berries, and sweetener with pounded caribou fat. Protestant missionaries referred to the frothy mix as "Eskimo ice cream." (Patterson & Snodgrass 1994, 3)

Colonists in North America quickly added iced foods to their menus, most likely as a result of French or Italian culinary influence. In 1744, William Black reported that the French wife of Thomas Bladen, governor of Maryland, served ice cream made in her Annapolis kitchen. A sudden hailstorm in Williamsburg, Virginia, in July 1758, provided Governor Francis Fauquier with enough ice to make his own ice cream and chill his wine. Ice creams became so popular that confectioner Philip Lenzi advertised his wares on May 12, 1777, in the *New York Gazette;* Joseph Corre did likewise in the *New York Post Boy.* Victor Collet's ice cream ad appeared in both English and French. In 1784, George Washington reported buying a pewter ice cream churn in Philadelphia for his Mount Vernon residence.

The flight of chefs, bakers, and confectioners from France following the French Revolution in 1789 was a boon to New World culinary traditions. The arrival of these emigrés preceded investments in a host of ice cream parlors, pastry shops, bistros, and cafés, all featuring European recipes. Bosse, a cook at Philadelphia's New Caveau Hotel, introduced ice cream in 1800. A black cook, Augustus Jackson, learned to make ice cream in the White House kitchen, where Dolly Madison added the dessert to the menu for President James Madison's second inaugural ball in 1812. By 1828, when vendors were hawking ice cream on New York City streets, the treat had become more egalitarian.

Between 1790 and 1873, some sixty patents were issued for ice cream freezers and *sorbétières* (also *sabbatiers*); these devices simplified the cumbrous job of making frozen desserts. A popular item of the era was the wooden ice cream freezer invented in 1843 by Nancy M. Johnson; nested tubs held the frozen dessert mix in the inner tin compartment, while the user packed ice and coarse salt into the space between the two container walls. A tight lid held a wooden dasher in place in the mix. The user turned a crank that rotated meshed gears to stir and blend the ice cream with a stationary paddle. When the mechanism stopped turning, the ice cream was frozen and ready to eat. Johnson did not legally protect her design, however, and in 1848 William G. Young began marketing the Johnson Patent Ice-Cream Freezer.

A Treat for the Masses

Ice cream reached fad proportions on the Atlantic seaboard. Schall & Co., Eppelsheimer & Co., J. Ernst, T. Mills & Bros., Fr. Krauss, and Valentine Clad & Sons of Philadelphia began marketing confectioner's tools, copper saucepans, and molds shaped in various shapes—Napoleon, flags, George Washington, American eagles and flags, Uncle Sam, the Statue of Liberty, Civil War soldiers, artillery, Abraham Lincoln, Theodore Roosevelt, sports figures, tennis rackets, Halloween pumpkins, Thanksgiving turkeys, Christmas trees, Easter bunnies, cupids, Elk's heads, Masonic symbols, and Odd Fellows' emblems. Recipes for ice cream appeared in the mid-nineteenth century in *Godey's Lady's Book* and cookbooks. In Baltimore, Jacob Fussel, the father of ice cream merchandizing, founded a chain of establishments in Boston, Chicago, Cincinnati, New York, Philadelphia, St. Louis, and Washington.

For those homemakers lacking ice cream churns, Mrs. A. P. Hill's *Mrs. Hill's New Family Receipt Book*

(1870), explained how to set a bucket in a wood tub of salted ice and jostle the inner container while keeping the contents free of salty slush. By 1865, an ice factory in New Orleans was supplying Southern cooks with an endless source of cooling for chilled foods and ice for ice cream churns. In 1872, *Harpers* carried an advertisement for Charles G. Blatchley's horizontal ice cream freezer, a cedar churn set on an oak sawbuck. An updated home model, the Jack Frost, advertised in the July 1891 issue of *The Housewife* reduced the crank time to minutes. Its unusual arrangement of a cylindrical mix holder placed in a wood box of salted ice and rotated with a side-mounted handle applied quality engineering but did not revolutionize ice churn design.

In England, the demand for ice for desserts and beverages produced a boom in Norwegian imports. Promoted by Agnes B. Marshall, who began directing the National Training School of Cookery in 1883, the use of ice spawned a sub-industry of gelatins, tin molds, ice cream freezers, and ice caves. Marshall published *Ices Plain and Fancy: The Book of Ices* (1885), a compendium of 177 recipes that encouraged the purchase of ice as well as of food supplies and equipment sold under the trademark of her London warehouse.

Those who wished to skip the task of scraping down the sides of a mold with a wooden paddle could purchase ices and sorbets ready-made from Gunter's of London, the city's top name in frozen desserts. The home cook could also consult *Gunter's Modern Confectioner: A Practical Guide—Designs for Preparing and Laying out Desserts* (1867), written by William Jeanes, confectioner to Queen Victoria. In Russia, the food writer Elena Molokhovets, author of *Classic Russian Cooking* (1861), was familiar with the home ice cream churn, but continued to advise that cream for desserts be stirred by hand. Her rejection of technological advances suggests that the churn may not have been readily available.

In the United States, Delmonico's and Sherry's were the most famous restaurants to offer frozen specialty items on the menu. The master chef Ranhofer concocted ice cream desserts at Delmonico's for three decades. In 1867, at a gala banquet honoring the novelist Charles Dickens, Ranhofer served a mid-meal palate-clearing *sorbet à l'américaine*, a delightful citrus base spiked with champagne, kirsch, and prunelle. He also invented the baked Alaska, which he described in his cookbook *The Epicurean: A Complete Treatise of Analytical and Practical Studies on the Culinary Art, Including Table and Wine Service* (1894). The specialty honored the 1867 purchase of Alaska by William Henry Seward, then secretary of state, who endured public ridicule for spending tax dollars to acquire a snowy wasteland dubbed "Seward's Folly." After freezing banana and vanilla ice creams in a cone atop a firm cake base, Ranhofer piped on meringue at the last minute, browned it under the broiler, and served up a unique hot-and-cold taste sensation.

The Sundae and Other Innovations

Robert M. Green may have inadvertently made the first ice cream sundae by clandestinely replacing soda with vanilla ice cream after running out of supplies at the 1874 Franklin Institute of Pennsylvania bicentennial. In 1881, Ed Berners, an ice cream parlor owner in Two Rivers, Michigan, presided over the more deliberate creation of an ice cream sundae. When George Hallauer ordered his ice cream with a topping of chocolate syrup, he started a fad that extended to cider-topped ice cream and other variations. George Giffey of Manitowoc, Michigan, introduced the term *sundae* by offering the concoction as a Sunday special. Glass manufacturers capitalized on the sundae craze by designing a boat-shaped pedestal glass, the style that eventually cradled the banana split.

Several accounts of the origin of the ice cream cone have circulated in culinary history. An Italian-American pushcart vendor, Italo Marchiony, claimed he had invented the edible holder for his Wall Street clientele on September 22, 1896, and patented it seven years later. In 1904, a Syrian-American waffle-maker, Ernest A. Hamwi, shaped a *zalabia* (pastry) into a cornucopia to hold ice cream at a World's Fair booth that ran out of dishes. His Cornucopia Waffle Company developed into the Missouri Cone Company. An alternate legend claims that the unidentified girlfriend of concessionaire Charles Robert Menches invented the ice cream cone from a waffle at the 1904 Louisiana Purchase Exposition in St. Louis as a convenient method of holding her rapidly melting ice cream.

For home use, conical ice cream servers, also called cornet dishers, scooped ice cream in shapes intended to fall easily into the cup. Some tin dishers came equipped with a key scraper, an internal knife blade that scavenged every speck of ice cream from inside the server; the more familiar type had a thumb lever that ejected a perfectly formed scoop onto the dish. The ice cream cone fryer, offered in the 1910 Hueg catalog, consisted of five cast-iron cones attached to a central knob. The user dipped the cones into hot oil and then into batter. Five cones could thus be baked at one time. A sharp rap caused the finished cones to slide off the lubricated irons.

Many families bought tins of Inexhaustible Freezing Crystals for quick freezing ice cream at home. The 1908 Sears, Roebuck catalog offered the three-quart, galvanized steel Alaska model for $1.92. The advertiser claimed that it "makes better cream, freezes quicker, and requires less ice and salt than any other freezer made." (Schroeder 1971, 469) The paraffined Northern pine tub and a mechanism with fewer moving parts than its predecessors were selling points at a time when families were just acquainting themselves with home-churning their own ice cream. The Alaska featured tin plate with re-tinned iron top and bottom for long life and internal action that scraped the sides and channeled the mix to the center for thorough beating and aeration. The churn came in eight sizes, up to twenty quarts, and could be mounted with a fly wheel for cranking large batches. A tin ice cream disher with revolving knife was available for 10 cents. The heavy metal scoop divided each quarter into eight equal portions. An exotic item out of the mainstream, the Imperial noiseless milk shake machine, either freestanding or countertop, agitated glass-capped tumblers on a level platform by the hand-cranked action of a flywheel and pulley mechanism.

Adjuncts to ice cream making included fancy tin, lead, or pewter ice cream molds, some flat on the open side and others hinged to form two sides of a bombe. One advanced model server was spring-loaded to force a moveable bail across the bottom of a hemispheric scoop to dislodge the ice dream in globular dollops.

Ice cream was a popular food in the 1940s. In England, the Wall's Ice Cream vendor peddled a three-wheel cart house to house, stopping at residences displaying the W card in the window. His placard advertised ice cream in bricks, brickettes, tubs, and bars, as well as a frozen specialty called "Snofrute." (Schärer & Fenton 1998, 293) The company, a division of Birds Eye frozen foods, claimed to dispatch 1,500 tricycles daily dispensing high-quality goods "attested by the Institute of Hygiene." (Ibid.)

Writing in *The Sealtest Food Adviser* (1945), H. A. Ruehe, a food scientist, claimed that ice cream was so ingrained in the American psyche that its availability to U.S. troops had contributed to victory in World War II. As Ruehe described it, the army, recognizing the morale-building value of this familiar treat from home, invested in prepared mixes and portable equipment so front-line cooks could provide dishes of ice cream directly to battle-weary soldiers in foxholes.

In the second half of the twentieth century, manufacturers of upscale kitchen equipment such as Krups, Cuisinart, and Delonghi introduced home ice cream makers that reduced a traditionally laborious and time-consuming process to the touch of a button. Once filled with fresh ingredients and flavorings, these machines mixed, blended, and froze automatically.

See also **Ice; Marshall, Agnes; Molds; Refrigeration**

Further Reading

Ballerini, Luigi, "Catherine de' Medici," *La Cucina Italiana,* June–July 1999, 90–91.

Lysaght, Patricia, ed. *Milk and Milk Products from Medieval to Modern Times.* Edinburgh: Canongate Press, 1994.

Marshall, Agnes B. *Victorian Ices & Ice Cream.* New York: Metropolitan Museum of Art, 1976.

Taylor, George, "The Street Cries of Damascus," *Aramco World,* September–October 1971, 12–15.

Wu, Esther, "Filipino Fest Savors Taste of Tradition," *Dallas Morning News,* June 1, 2000, 22A.

INSECTS, REPTILES, AND WORMS

Insects, reptiles, and worms have figured in kitchen history not only as pests, but also, in many parts of the world, as valued foods and even as delicacies. The list of creatures prized in some cultures—although regarded as inedible in many others—ranges from the common honey bee and house fly to the pine borer, rhinoceros beetle, weevils, pandora moth, silkworm, ox warble, and maguey worm. In Thailand and the Philippines, coastal diners have traditionally favored the ship worm, a long segmented creature (technically a mollusk rather than a worm) found in floating logs, driftwood, and trunks, eaten pickled, fried, or simply swallowed alive. Chinese cooks in Peking developed recipes calling for sautéing worms in sesame oil. Locusts were a delicacy at the royal table of Ashurbanipal in Ninevah and figure in the Hebrew dietary laws of Leviticus.

According to the writings of early authors, insects, reptiles, and worms were valued foods in numerous places and situations. Arab cooks sun-dried locusts for several days, then stored them in bags for later pulverizing in mortars and blending with water to form a dry pudding. The Parthians and the Israelites consumed grasshoppers, which King Solomon fed to his harem to boost their alertness.

Recipes and Storage

Greek eyewitnesses corroborate additional use of insects as food. As described by Herodotus around 450 BCE, Libyan cooks sun-dried locusts to serve with milk. The philosopher Aristotle lauded the sweetness of the cicada, especially the egg-filled female. Around 50 BCE, the historian and traveler Diodorus of Sicily reported that Ethiopians made the most of swarms of locusts by building a smoky fire to kill them, then seasoning them with salt for storage. The Romans, too, ate insects and larvae. They especially valued oak grubs, which they preserved as delicacies.

Native Americans living in the Ozarks also appear to have eaten beetles and grasshoppers, as did the Washo of Utah, Jamaican natives, and Venezuelean tribes. The Ozark stampeded grasshoppers into a pit fire, where the insects roasted. The Pomo of San Francisco Bay parched caterpillars over open flame. The Yurok, Cherokee, Snake, Ute, Montagnais, and Eskimo removed body lice and ate them on the spot. On the Baja peninsula, the Tipai-Ipai supplemented a diet of beans, seeds, nuts, cactus, fish, and birds with lizards, snakes, insects, and larvae, which they stored in baskets; the Wintun and Yana of northern California added grubs and grasshoppers to stores of acorns, seeds, and greens foraged in the wild.

The Aztec preferred water bugs, which they netted from boats, ground and shaped into balls, and cooked in corn husks. With twine, they scooped the insect's eggs from the water to add to tamales or tortillas. The Dominican monk Thomas Gage observed the Maya relishing cakes of water bug eggs in 1625 and described the food as cheese. The Tepehuan of Chihuahua, Mexico, roasted grubs and insects; other Mexican groups fermented a beverage made of water or alcohol mixed with pulverized tiger beetles. The Mexica favored bees, wasps, and mites.

Aboriginal cooks used a variety of cooking methods—coating insects with paste and roasting them, grinding them into flour, or impaling them on stakes to be eaten as snack food. The Wongapitcha of Australia preferred witchitty grubs and caterpillars, which they retrieved from trees with hooked sticks and relished for their nutlike taste. For robbing wasp larvae, they held burning grass clumps at the nest, then picked out morsels to eat raw. In *The Passing of the Aborigines: A Lifetime Spent among the Natives of Australia* (1938), the journalist and pioneering expeditioner to the Murray River Basin Daisy O'Dwyer Bates commented on the aboriginal taste for *mawgu* (white grub) but added, tongue in cheek, that "it was eaten sparingly by the wise, who found it rich to biliousness." (Bates 1967, 209)

During the California gold rush of 1849, miners observed Miwok women gathering insects. According to *Hutching's California Scene*, a newsletter dated 1854, to secure grasshoppers, the women first dug a hole deeper than the height the insects could jump. Making a wide circle, they either set the bracken on fire or beat it with brush and drove the insects toward the basin. To make their catch into loaves, they used flat stones to grind acorns, berries, and flower seeds into flour and pound the insects into paste. They also cooked insects or small game with acorn meal in mocucks by the stone boiling method. Another mode

of cooking grasshoppers involved soaking them in salt water, then pouring them into a trench and placing heated rocks on top for fifteen minutes. The Miwok then ate the cooked insects in the same way as shrimp.

Flying insects harassed families cooking over fires at tent flaps and thrived in the walls of unfinished log cabin walls. In 1855, an inundation of grasshoppers overcame settlers in the Dakotas and Utah, where farm families had to eat the insects in lieu of their destroyed crops.

In *Lizard Hunts on the North Coast* (1957), Allen R. Holmberg described the Peruvian yen for small lizards, a staple dried meat that Spanish adventurers found warehoused on a coastal isle in 1532. In underground lairs beneath gurango trees, the lizards survived solely on its fruits. When the tree bore fruit in November, the lizards ended their seven-month hibernation to climb the trunks and eat their fill. Locals snared and immobilized them, then tossed them onto hot coals. After the skins toasted, cooks could strip the lizards and spread their carcasses in bake holes in the sand. Roasting consisted of a covering of glowing embers for ten minutes. The meat could be eaten fresh or stored for meals during the year.

A Solution to Famine?

Late in the twentieth century, scientists studying non-industrial cultures made peace with the presence of insects in the diet. In 1971, when anthropologists and journalists from *National Geographic* first visited the twenty-five remaining Tasaday of Mindanao in the Philippines, they found a Stone Age people living in caves. Their simple diet consisted of palm fruit, wild bananas, nuts, fish, frogs, tadpoles, and grubs. A year later, the U.S. writer John Gunther published his book *Inside Australia*, in which he reported on the scarcity of meat in New Guinea. He described how, in order to supplement the meager sources of protein in their diet, locals burned areas of kunai grass and ate the charred remains of lizards and mice.

It was only a matter of time before scientists suggested that the population of industrialized countries should follow suit. Ronald L. Taylor's *Butterflies in My Stomach: Or Insects in Human Nutrition* (1975) and David George Gordon's *The Eat-A-Bug Cookbook* (1998), corroborated the thesis of Vincent M. Holt's *Why Not Eat Insects?* (1885), a treatise proffering entomophagy as a solution to famine in the British Isles. Although the idea of enriching the human diet with bugs repulsed most readers, Gordon, the author of *The Compleat Cockroach* (1996), touted them as a source of protein. He pointed out that insect raising required less space, labor, time, and resources than the raising of livestock. From a study of the world's kitchens, he recommended the best oddities for cooking. For nutrition, he extolled the protein-rich alga, which Taiwanese feed their pigs. He asserted that crickets contained calcium, and termites, iron and protein, which made up more than 45 percent of their body weight.

Cooking instructions for insects were much like those for meat and fish preparation. In Dr. C. Louis Leipoldt's *Leipoldt's Cape Cookery* (1976), the touchstone of Cape-Dutch cooking, the inclusion of locusts substantiated their use as a meat substitute. His instructions called for immersion in boiling water before beheading and removal of appendages. For cooking the trunk meat, he advised a sprinkle of salt, pepper, and cinnamon and a quick fry until they were brown. He compared the flavor to whitebait, a minnow popular in England.

Investigative journalist Jean-Pierre Hallet, the author of *Congo Kitabu* (1974), wrote about the starving Ebuya, a Pygmy tribe of central Africa. In their search for protein, they scouted for termitaria, dug moats around them, and then trapped the juicy insects. Whole tribes worked at filling wicker baskets with insects for grilling over hot coals. In the case of severe famine, they ate the insects raw. Joetta Handrich Schlabach's *Extending the Table: A World Community Cookbook* (1991) recorded a similar hunt in Zaire, where cooks relished the *masenda* (white grub). A day of hoeing crusty soil and digging by hand for grubs concluded with the snapping of the tail and gutting by sliding the finger into the carcass, a smooth hand action similar to cleaning shrimp. On a photographic shoot for *National Geographic* early in 2001, Peter Godwin's team found the bushmen living near the Nyae Nyae Conservancy of Botswana foraging for *mangetti* nuts and beetles. They stripped the wings and roasted the insects only a few seconds over flame for immediate crunching.

At the 2000 Olympics in Sydney, Australia, Japanese athletes touted hornet juice as the latest adjunct to the training table. Before competing, Naoko Takahashi, a gold medal-winning women's marathoner, consumed drinks made from *suzumebachi* (yellow hornet). The all-natural supplement, extracted from larvae and sold under the brand name Vaam was a $50 million-a-year business in Japan. A biochemist at Tokyo's Institute of Physical and Chemical Research corroborated the effectiveness of the substance after discovering that the extract boosted the performance of mice by 50 percent.

Local Delicacies

Insects, reptiles, and worms, either raw or cooked, remain the food specialities of various parts of the world. In Gabon, termites and palm grubs are common foods; *phane* worms are a delicacy in Botswana, where foragers gather them from the *mophane* tree and dry them in hot embers before eating. Among the Vietnamese of Tam Dao, restaurant cooks skin and gut snakes alive and harvest their blood, heart, and genitals for special dishes purported to boost virility.

Larvae, grasshoppers, termites, and sugar ants of various types nourish aboriginal diners in Australia, Venezuela, Uganda, Tanzania, Madagascar, Malawi, and the Congo. The Pedi of South Africa roast and stew locusts and serve them as relish on porridge. West Africans fry termites in palm oil, and Malawians and Congolese sun-dry the insects. In Indonesia, Mandalay cooks sell *payit-kyaw* (fried cricket) on the street, where the Burmese buy them to offer to Buddhist mendicant monks. Balinese cooks wrap crickets in banana leaves to make *pesan* for steaming or roasting over embers. Balinese children use a sticky pole to attract and capture *mang por* (dragonflies), which they fry in coconut oil along with spiced vegetables and shrimp. Thai cooks value cockroach and praying mantis eggs and adults; in Papua, New Guinea, fry-cooks heat them them over an open flame.

In Central and South America, the Yukpa (or Yuko) net the caddis fly and capture grasshoppers in their hands or organize a fire-drive. Women await the arrival of the harvested insects and dry them by communal fires. They carry baskets of insects home to wrap in leaves and roast or toast on skewers. In Mexico, maguey worms have been standard menu items since ancient times. Mexican Indians also scrape stinkbugs from trees to sell at market in paper cones. Cooks drop them into stew as a garnish or toast them for grinding with chilies and mixing with tomato puree as a condiment for pancakes and tortillas. Another delicacy around Lake Texcoco are cakes mixed with water bugs, which are also considered delicacies in Japan, China, India, New Guinea, and Egypt.

See also **Vermin**

Further Reading

Billard, Jules B., "Macao Clings to the Bamboo Curtain," *National Geographic*, April 1969, 520–539.
"First Glimpse of a Stone Age Tribe," *National Geographic*, December 1971, 880–884.
Godwin, Peter, "Bushmen," *National Geographic*, February 2001, 90–117.
McCrae, Michael, "Tam Dao: Vietnam's Sanctuary Under Siege," *National Geographic*, June 1999, 82–97.

Morgan, Elaine. *The Descent of Woman*. London: Souvenir Press, Ltd., 1972.

Taylor, Ronald L. *Butterflies in My Stomach: Or Insects in Human Nutrition*. Santa Barbara, Calif.: Woodbridge Press, 1975.

van Gelder, Geert Jan. *God's Banquet: Food in Classical Arabic Literature*. New York: Columbia University Press, 2000.

IRONWORK

Iron, a malleable, ductile, and adaptable silver-white metal, was first worked in 1200 BCE, the beginning of the Iron Age. Cast iron, an alloy formed with silica and carbon, derives from the melting of ore, pig iron, ferric alloys, and steel or foundry scraps. Workers pour the molten substance into wooden or metal molds lined with sand and clay. Processing results in a variety of end products, including gray iron, used in the manufacture of kitchen stoves, and wrought iron, which—because it resists corrosion and metal fatigue—has survived more than 3,000 years as the oldest form of iron. Inexpensive to manufacture and easily alloyed with steel, wrought iron is a common material used for making pipes, rails, and farm equipment.

Versatile Material

In early times, iron served the needs of the armorer, rifle maker, scientist, sculptor, architect, and cook and provided the home with ash shovels, surface-mounted oven hinges, hasps and locks, door knockers, lever handles, latches, keyhole escutcheons, casement supports, chimney cranes, chains and hooks, and holders for rush lights. Attached to the primitive fireside, iron frames held skewers at the ready for pinning fowl and securing meats to the spit. Roman ironworkers hammered heavy meat hooks from iron for lifting boiled meat from cauldrons. The embossed iron cask dates to the Crusades as a symbol of family pride, order, and security.

Humble ironware served homes in many parts of the world. Among nomadic Baluch of the highland Sarhad region of southeastern Iran, cooks heated dough for *galfach* on concave iron dishes set over triangular stands above twig fires.

In medieval Europe, objects made of iron replaced those of flimsier materials. Heavy cooking vessels had traditionally swung from pothooks or trammels attached to a lug-pole made of green wood, which charred slowly. Occasionally, poles collapsed, causing the contents of a boiling cauldron to splash on unwary cooks. In time, the iron backbar and the L-bracket supplanted these wooden beams.

For butchering, the householder needed iron ax heads and meat saws; iron bands secured the staves in rendering tubs and barrels. More delicate ironware included small mortars and pestles for grinding powders and crushing herbs, sugar nippers and cutters for kitchen and table, and bean roasters and grinders for coffee. The waffle iron combined metal work with artistry, enabling cooks to turn out light batter cakes embossed with patterns or letters. In 1358, an English congregation chose one Sunday in Lent as Mothering Day, when youth made wafers for their mothers. The custom existed in Sweden, where the waffle maker baked the tokens for distribution to parents. In France, the *oubleyeur* (pastry chef) was named for the *oublie*, a wafer cooked at the end of an iron *gaufre* (waffle maker) dipped into hot fat. The Welsh cook valued a thin iron *planc* as a baking sheet for oatcake, a daily staple.

At Renaissance fireplaces, iron fretwork in decorative patterns directed heat outward rather than up the chimney. Stout chimney cranes evolved from basic L-shaped brackets into the more ornate pot cranes bearing scrolled details or wrought-iron leaves, trees, and family crests. The pots, which weighed as much as forty pounds unfilled, swung from pothooks and slotted hangers that allowed cooks to vary the vessel's distance from the fire below.

One-pot cookery required the simultaneous boiling of all vegetables, which the knowledgeable cook added in sequence, beginning with dense root vegetables such as carrots and parsnips and finishing with delicate herbs. The user submerged wrought iron or wire potato boiler, shaped like a globular bird cage, in the broth but kept potatoes separate so they could be tested for doneness with a skewer and removed at the appropriate time. Also suspended from the pot arm were the fry pan and girdlepan, a round or oval brace into which the cook fitted a pot, griddle, or *galettoire*, the flat, rimless iron plate on which pancakes and scones heated. A handy device that saved burned fingers was the idle-back, or lazy-back, a levered frame that allowed the cook to pour water by tipping the kettle in its bracket without touching its handle. Below, long-handled frying pans and spiders on legs heated foods on a pebbled surface suited to bacon, sliced ham, and fish. For the table, iron serving pieces, spoons, forks, and knives were sturdy, dependable tableware for those who could not afford pewter or silver.

Nambu Tekki, the traditional Japanese ironware made on the main island in Morioka City and Mizusawa City, originated in the 1600s. With a casting method developed in the twelfth century, metal crafters from Kyoto used volcanic ferrous sand to produce weapons and armor, Buddhist temple bells, and griddles, kettles, and other cookware. Working over charcoal braziers, the ironworkers perfected a signature hobnail surface that produced a ringing tone when tapped.

They topped the finished pieces with brass, bronze, or copper lids. Iron that leached from the cooking surfaces of these implements had a beneficial effect, preventing anemia in the populace. Importers in the United States in the twenty-first century offered Nambu pans, ashtrays, bottle openers, and wind chimes.

Domestic Implements in the New World

In 1642, Joseph Jenks, an ironworker in Lynn, Massachusetts, fabricated the first cast iron kettle in the New World. From a one-man forge specializing in production of the mundane three-legged quart pot, Jenks built a family business that passed to his son, who settled in Rhode Island.

American colonists depended on domestic implements forged from iron, in particular, meat forks and long turning forks for open-hearth cookery, ladles and skimmers, spoons and spatulas, griddles, fruit stone crushers, and grate baskets or firedogs to hold spits for roasting rabbits, beef cuts, pheasants, quail, and domestic fowl. Tongs had multiple uses, including rotating pots and dishes cooking in embers, removing ramekins and other small items, and steadying meat and bread during cutting. Prized items of ironware passed from generation to generation, sometimes detailed in wills. The scarcity of iron goods on the Atlantic seaboard changed only after coke and anthracite replaced charcoal in the process of ore reduction.

Those living on the frontier far from civilization's conveniences had no choice but to heat and hammer their own metal cooking vessels, to mend split seams and holes, and to stop leaks with metal slugs. Military-issue tableware provided the Revolutionary War soldier a fork twisted from wire. For the traveler, the handy pocketknife suited all tableware purposes by offering a flat blade and forked end. A cast-iron cherry pipper invented in 1860 simplified the job of extracting stones by driving a rod through each fruit. By 1873, Messrs. Landers Frary & Clark of Boston were marketing a forged fruit corer and peeler, a bladed device with cogwheels fitted on a base that clamped to a tabletop. The English raisin stoner fed damp fruit through a serrated roller that removed tiny seeds before channeling flattened raisins down a chute.

Small utensils of cast iron served numerous special purposes, for example, pitting olives, stretching game for drying, and shaping batter on the end of a fritter baker, patty iron, or Vienna cake mold. An apple cutter comprised of a two-handled circle of iron around a wheel of blades cored and sliced fruit in one operation. For open-hearth cooking, a metal stand or trivet, the brandelette, also called brandise, supported pots in hot ash. Trivets came in fixed and revolving models and varied by weight and height to suit the size and shape of a variety of open-hearth vessels. The iron dough kneader lessened the labor involved in preparing dough for baking. It consisted of a pot that held nickel-plated rollers that cranked dough inward and out the other side until it reached the appropriate consistency. Another useful gadget, the sugar auger or fruit lifter, a T-shaped shaft ending in twisted prongs, loosened granulated sugar or fruit packed in a crock or barrel. The cast iron corn bread pan shaped batter into flat lengths indented to resembled ears of corn. A less common alternate was the hinged corn bread mold.

Cooks prepared new ironware by seasoning it, a process that readied the metal to come into contact with food without sticking, rusting, or spoiling the flavor. One late nineteenth-century seasoning method involved boiling ashes in the new container, then scrubbing with grit and detergent. The final step was boiling with several changes of water, until all evidence of scouring disappeared from the rinse water. Other formulations for seasoning have included hay, grass, and potato peelings boiled in water or a thorough rubbing with fat and heating in the oven.

For stovetop cooking, cooks placed flat, one-handled adapter rings on stove eyes to support handleless pots, which sank into the center and protruded downward so only the lid showed above stovetop level. Thus, a shift of the handle resituated the container and allowed the user to lift the pot without risking a scald, burned-on mess, or wasted food. Cast iron plate warmers enabled hosts to ensure that food arrived warm at the table.

Iron cookware and kitchen equipment entered a period of innovation in the late nineteenth century. In the 1850s, manufacturers introduced enamel surfacing, which added decorative appeal to kitchen necessities and reduced the drudgery of scraping off rust and corrosion from unadorned ironware. Two decades later, pressed steel and aluminum cookware made inroads against iron, which had set the standard for kitchenware since the Iron Age.

Quality, Durability, Good Design

Into the twentieth century, cookware and utensils that originated in the early Middle Ages appeared in improved iron versions. The 1908 Sears, Roebuck catalog displayed a number of handy iron items for kitchen and home at low prices, such as grinders and home tools. An iron foot scraper at three for 14 cents kept mud out of the kitchen. Handy iron chain at 5 cents a yard fell short of the usability and strength of steel coil chain, which cost a penny more per yard.

Quality brands in iron mongery attracted investors in kitchen goods. The Griswold ironworks of Erie, Pennsylvania, established in 1865, became America's longest-lived brand name. The company tapped into period nostalgia in 1910 by inventing a three-compartment iron skillet for cooking hash browns, eggs, and bacon. In 1925, at Fresnoy-le-Grand, France, Le Creuset began producing a weighty porcelain-enameled cast-iron cookware that suited fashionable kitchens for decades to come. To accommodate acidic foods, the company toughened the double-coated surface by firing it at approximately 1,450 degrees Fahrenheit and issued a limited warranty of 101 years. Available in bright primary colors, the sets added chic, sturdiness, and flair by melding beauty with performance in slow-cooking, simmering, deglazing, and blackening. In 1998, Björn Dahlström created a professional-quality cast-iron pot for braising, browning, and stewing. Crafted of seasoned metal with gently sloped lid and bold handles, it was a feature in the catalog of New York City's Museum of Modern Art.

Cooks at the turn of the twenty-first century continued to rely on iron skillets, trivets, and casseroles. A popular item in many cookware catalogs was a cast-iron stovetop skillet with a ridged cooking surface that enabled grease to drain away from cooking foods. A useful addition for Tex-Mex and New Orleans-style stovetop cooking, the iron hand press flattened beef and chicken for blackening of *alla diavola* dishes.

See also **Stoves**

Further Reading

Batey, Colleen, Helen Clarke, R. J. Page, and Neil S. Price. *Cultural Atlas of the Viking World*. Abingdon, Oxfordshire: Checkmark Books, 1994.
Kondoleon, Christine. *Antioch: The Last Ancient City*. Princeton, N.J.: Princeton University Press, 2000.
Salzman, Philip Carl. *Black Tents of Baluchistan*. Washington, D.C.: Smithsonian, 2000.

J

JAPAN WARE

Japan ware is a category of objects covered in a characteristic, multiple-coated hard black lacquer finish. The process of layering this finish is known as japanning. Objects made from a variety of materials, including papier-mâché, leather, wood, tin, and iron, accept japanning.

Imitation lacquer ware originated in Europe in the late 1600s, when manufacturers began simulating items imported from Japan. *Tôle peinte* (tablet paint), a decoration of japanned tinplate or pewter, derived from factories in Monmouth, Pontypool, and Usk, England; Paris; Hoorn and Zeist, Holland; and parts of Pennsylvania. The craft involved dipping tinplate into melted tin or pewter. After japanning with varnish, the items—boxes, screens, canisters, caddies, furniture, trays, teapots, candlesticks—bore a patinated surface that protected elaborate drawings, feathering, graining, sponging, and edging. Metal surfacing required hardening in the oven. Black japanning, the most common method, blended varnish, oils, and turpentine with melted asphalt to yield a brown undercoat.

With the introduction of tôle painted japanning, tinsmiths continued the industry into the eighteenth century, producing chafing dishes, toast carriers, tea caddies, condiment and cutlery trays, and cheese cradles in yellow and ochre, orange, deep reds, chocolate brown, prussian blue, black, metallic striping, and imitation tortoise shell. Among kitchen implements professionally surfaced with baked japanning were pincer meat tenderizers, nut crackers, housemaid's boxes, utensil holders and organizers, spouted molasses cans or dispensers, and fish scalers shaped like hairbrushes. James Smith's *The Dictionary of Arts, Sciences and Manufacturers* (1854) explained how the homemaker could protect "ironmongery" from rust by applying lampblack mixed with linseed oil. After heating in a stove at low heat, items took on a black gloss that needed no polishing. They were especially useful as protective containers for storing candles, salt, spices, and knives, which remained dry and rust-free.

Japanned items featured in the 1908 Sears, Roebuck included a two-handled aluminum lemon squeezer, a clothesline hook, iron sausage stuffer, coffee mill, and two grades of carpet sweeper cases. A flour bin and sifter holding twenty-five pounds could be purchased for $1.57. The advertising copy promised convenience and added that the rust-proof cylinder "keeps dust, insects and disease germs out and is the most sanitary method of handling of flour." (Schroeder 1971, 464) The system worked so well that the U.S. military supplied pocket-sized japanned tins of emergency rations containing powdered beef and wheat and chocolate.

The 1938 Cussins and Fearn catalog featured an entire kitchen in matching white japanned surfaces enhanced with red trim and "les fleurs" decals. The style-conscious homemaker could collect dust pan, canisters, cake tin, tray, and waste basket and extend the decorative theme to matching kitchen chairs, a floor-model vegetable bin, and a step-on galvanized garbage can, a popular item in the fashionable sanitized kitchen. In the second half of the twentieth century, despite competition from new materials such as

319

metal alloys and plastic, japanned goods—decorative, lightweight, and portable—retained their appeal.

Further Reading

Franklin, Linda Campbell. *300 Years of Kitchen Collectibles.* Iola, Wisc.: Krause Publications, 1997.

JONES, AMANDA THEODOSIA

The U.S. inventor Amanda Theodosia Jones alleviated much of the drudgery associated with innovations in home canning and preservation of foods. Jones, born in 1835 in East Bloomfield, New York, had a brief career as a teacher at Buffalo High School. She was writing for a newspaper in 1872 when she had a sudden inspiration: with no prior experience in engineering, she created a method of ridding glass jars of air with a valve mechanism dubbed the "Jones exhauster." It removed the remaining air from newly filled jars and replaced it with hot water or sugar syrup. The speed of the method allowed food to process quickly without becoming overcooked. The application of steam to jars of food in a boiling water bath created the vacuum that instantly sealed the opening, ending the necessity of salt curing, wax seals, or other cumbrous, taste- and texture-destroying food preservation methods.

With the aid of her cousin, Leroy C. Cooley, Jones obtained seven patents in hopes of generating a food preservation industry. After failing to launch her own canning factory, she turned her ingenuity to heating technology after a northern Pennsylvania oil producer requested a burner that would adapt crude oil as a home fuel. The valve she devised to control the flow of oil from a reservoir earned her three patents and kudos from the U.S. Navy, which applied her technology to transform coal-burning ships to oil. Because of her lack of experience at finance, she failed to profit from the invention.

At age fifty-five, Jones focused once more on the canning venture. At the height of the women's suffrage movement, she envisioned an industry that would welcome women as laborers and investors and treat them fairly. She settled in Chicago near the center of the meatpacking industry and, in 1890, opened the U.S. Women's Pure Food Vacuum Preserving Company, which marketed luncheon meat, fruit preserves, and rice and tapioca puddings. Except for her cousin and a man who tended the boiler, it was a women-only business that thrived for thirty-one years.

Jones opened plants in Illinois and Wisconsin. According to the account in her memoir, *A Psychic Autobiography* (1910), the company's success waned after a consortium of men ran the factory and sold its stock. Within three years, the business failed. Jones's contributions to the food industry and women's rights earned her a place in *Who's Who in America.*

Further Reading

Vare, Ethlie Ann, and Greg Ptacek. *Mothers of Invention.* New York: Quill, 1987.

K

KEICHLINE, ANNA WAGNER

The first female architect registered by the states of New York and Pennsylvania, Anna Wagner Keichline distinguished herself by inventing the K brick, a forerunner to the concrete block. She also invented the compressed air radiator-dryer, as well as kitchen appliances and devices, a wall-mounted folding bed, and toys. Born in Bellefonte, Pennsylvania, on May 5, 1889, she began making furniture for her family before completing studies at the Cornell School of Architecture in 1911.

A contemporary of the time-and-motion expert Lillian Gilbreth during the rise of home economics as a science, Keichline patented a design for an innovative, efficient kitchen in 1926. An attendee at the White House Better Housing Conference, she worked at a home industrial arts studio to create a time- and motion-saving kitchen. To reduce steps for the cook, she equipped counters with a motor shaft that attached to a coffee grinder, eggbeater, and vegetable peeler.

Keichline knew from experience what women needed to expedite their work. The counters in her design were sloped to make cleaning easier, and the stove was flush with the floor to eliminate the labor of mopping under it. Her plan called for fewer ceiling-level cabinets, thus obviating the need for a step stool, and glass-fronted cabinet doors that allowed the cook to view the contents without opening the door. One handy device she developed was a finger valve that let the cook measure out small amounts of staples without opening the canister lid and scooping from the contents. The device helped to preserve freshness and purity in stored meal, flour, and sugar by reducing the number of exposures to kitchen air, particulate, and insects.

KELLOGG, JOHN HARVEY

A surgeon, proponent of dietary reform, and health fanatic, John Harvey Kellogg gave his name to a major force in the U.S. cereal industry. Born in Tyrone, Michigan, on February 26, 1852, he grew up in Battle Creek, a Seventh Day Adventist stronghold. In addition to learning the broom-making trade and apprenticing as a printer's devil, he developed a life-long interest in vegetarianism.

After recovering from tuberculosis in his teens, Kellogg studied the precepts of the diet and health reformers Dio Lewis—the author of *Our Digestion; or, My Jolly Friend's Secret* (1872)—and Sylvester Graham, the inventor of the graham cracker. Kellogg evolved his own philosophy of natural medicine and eventually studied medicine at the Hygieno-Therapeutic College in New Jersey and University of Michigan Medical School. On the basis of his practical experience at New York's Bellevue Hospital Medical College, Kellogg edited the Adventist *Health Reformer* and began to conduct independent research on the body's natural defenses.

A devoted essayist, Kellogg spent his life educating people about practices for maintaining wellness. At age twenty-four, he superintended natural treatments at Battle Creek's Western Health Reform Institute, where he served as staff physician and adviser on diet.

He changed the establishment's name to the Battle Creek Sanitarium, which he dedicated to wellness through biologic living.

Kellogg added schools of nursing, physical education, and home economics and promoted eugenics. He appointed his wife, the dietitian Ella Eaton Kellogg—a champion of the Women's Christian Temperance Union and author of *Science in the Kitchen* (1892) and *Every-Day Dishes* (1898)—to teach cooking in the domestic science division. From the sanitarium's outreach came cadres of doctors, nurses, physical therapists, dietitians, and medical missionaries. Kellogg's crusade against self-defeating habits encouraged people to reject drugs, medicines, alcohol, tobacco, tea, coffee, chocolate, meat, and condiments.

The Kellogg diet focused on nuts, beans, and whole grain plus small amounts of yogurt, tofu, milk, eggs, and sugar. His daily regimen called for fresh air, sunshine, correct posture, and exercise. For the sick, the sanitarium offered massage and water treatments, copied in part from therapies Kellogg had studied in Europe. His surgical patients practiced bed exercise to prevent complications and infection. With the proceeds from some 22,000 operations, he financed his wellness literature and treated the poor.

In his laboratory, Kellogg developed imitation coffee and the meat substitutes Nuttose and Protose. He also concocted granola, peanut butter, zweiback, and cereal flakes made from wheat paste rolled thin, baked, and scraped from the baking sheet with a bread knife. His brother, Will Keith Kellogg, distributed the flakes as an early entry in the growing breakfast cereal market. Central to the digestion of these foods was a method of eating based on the nutritionist Horace Fletcher's treatise *Nature's Food Filter: Or When and What to Swallow* (1899). Fletcher recommended that each mouthful of food be chewed until it was liquefied—for example, thirty chews for toast and eighty for brown bread.

After parting company with the Adventists, Kellogg was excommunicated in 1907 and had to fight the church for control of the sanitarium. Into the 1920s, it prospered, drawing hundreds of patients for hydrotherapy, internal and external cleanliness regimens, aerobic exercise, treatment in electrified pools and vibrating chairs, naps, and a controlled diet. Kellogg flaunted the names of the prestigious individuals who practiced his health-affirming regimen—Henry Ford, Charles William Post, J. C. Penney, George Bernard Shaw, Johnny Weismuller, Carrie Chapman Catt, S. S. Kresge, Sarah Bernhardt, Richard Byrd, Thomas Edison, Harvey Firestone, William Howard Taft, and Amelia Earhart.

The Great Depression bankrupted the sanitarium. Kellogg's brother Will succeeded in marketing the innovative foods John had initiated during his years of research. The key to their campaign lay in selling healthful food to healthy people rather than to invalids and hypochondriacs. A Kellogg advertisement in the October 1930 issue of *Good Housekeeping* extolled the tonic effect of Savita bouillon cubes and the blood-building capability of Food Ferrin, a tonic the company claimed to be a better source of iron than green vegetables. The company also offered "Healthful Living," a booklet with advice on improving the family diet.

In retirement from medical practice, Kellogg lectured, served on the Michigan State Board of Health, founded Chicago's American Medical Missionary College, and issued monographs and books on health, including the best-selling *Sunbeams of Health and Temperance: An Instructive Account of the Health Habits of All Nations* (1887), *How to Have Good Health through Biologic Living* (1932), and *Rules for "Right Living"* (1935). Kellogg's name survives mainly in his contribution to the American breakfast, which he revolutionized by introducing cereal that required no preparation.

See also **Kellogg, Will Keith; Post, Charles William**

Further Reading

Carson, Gerald. *Cornflake Crusade*. New York: Rinehart & Co., 1957.

Goodwin, Lorine Swainston. *The Pure Food, Drink, and Drug Crusaders, 1879–1914.* Jefferson, N.C.: McFarland, 1999.

Klaw, Spencer, "Pursuing Health in the Promised Land," *Horizons*, spring 1976, 24–29.

KELLOGG, WILL KEITH

The younger brother of physician John Harvey Kellogg, the creator of dry breakfast cereal, Will Keith Kellogg put into practice the theories of vegetarian Sylvester Graham by marketing and popularizing grain flakes. Born in Michigan on April 7, 1860, Will Kellogg received little education. At age fourteen, he began supporting himself under the name W. K. Kellogg, broom salesman. After managing a Dallas broom factory, he moved to Battle Creek, Michigan, to study bookkeeping at a school run by Seventh Day Adventists.

At age twenty, Will Kellogg was working at his brother's sanitarium promoting healthy living and managing John's Sanitas Nut Food Company. Although he ridiculed "The Doctor" and his regimen at "The San," Will oversaw the production of John's monthly medical journal and assisted in his experiments on vegetable protein. The two devised baked wheat flakes, source of the economic boom that drew national attention to Battle Creek and to John's theories of healthful living. After Charles William Post pirated their technology and successfully dominated the wholesale dry cereal market, Will devoted himself to perfecting Kellogg's corn flakes, created in 1902.

The Kellogg brothers remained in partnership for the next three years, during which sales of cereal flakes rose to 1,000 cases a day. Charles D. Bolin, a St. Louis insurance agent and speculator, influenced Will to launch the Battle Creek Toasted Corn Flake Company in 1906. As manager, Will distributed the cereal, basing his product promotions on the connection with John's name and research. The company introduced another product, All-Bran, after 1910.

Shrewd advertising boosted cereal sales in a thriving world market. John Kellogg contested Will's abandonment of the original partnership. Will won the right to call his cereal a Kellogg product and to publish the claim, "None genuine without the signature of W. K. Kellogg." He also set up the W. K. Kellogg Foundation, a consortium that sought to alleviate domestic problems through programs in agriculture, education, and health.

See also **Kellogg, John Harvey**

Further Reading

Carson, Gerald. *Cornflake Crusade*. New York: Rinehart & Co., 1957.

KETTLE

The kitchen kettle, which takes its name from the Old English *cytel,* is perhaps the most familiar cooking container of folk origin. Throughout history kettles have adapted to meet a list of needs, from heating water and broth to boiling soup stock, cooking fruit for jelly, heating milk for cheese making, and providing a water bath for sterilizing canning jars. Early kettles, used for open-hearth cooking, were footed so that they could be placed in hot embers. A useful invention was the kettle lifter, a hinged connector attached to a crane or overhead bar for tilting heavy kettles to decant or pour out their contents.

A Versatile Implement

The kettle's prominence in archeology has allowed experts to surmise much about the social structure, living arrangements, and population of prehistoric peoples. From the large size of Owasco kettles, Dean Snow, chair of the department of anthropology at Penn State, concluded that these forest-dwelling ancestors of the Iroquois, who migrated from Pennsylvania to

Kettle over hearth fire.

New York state around 900 CE, lived in extended families. Such an oversized cooking vessel suggested how the people organized for war, commerce, or building projects.

Over time, the kettle retained its round shape, lid, and falling handle, but varied in style with spouts and pouring lips and in composition from iron and tin to enamelware, bell metal, bronze, copper, brass, and steel. The Bedouin chose tinned copper for their *jidda* (kettle), the standard stewing pot for freshly butchered meat. The Roman *cacabus* (cooking kettle) differed from the *ahenum* (water cauldron), a broad-mouthed vat for scalding, boiling, and heating water for laundry. A hemispheric vessel fitted into an iron tripod, the *cacabus* narrowed to a small mouth and wire handle for enclosed cookery that held in flavors. Cooks tasted their bubbly stews and removed portions with long-handled *simpula* (ladles), which ended in rounded bowls or flat-bottomed cups.

Kettles designed for specific chores include the butter kettle and the keeler, or kelfat tub, a shallow kettle intended for cooling hot broth. The medieval cook chose a muller kettle, a cone on a handle, to thrust into embers rather than set it on a hot surface. Among the Irish, the copper kettle graced the hob to keep water hot for tea. In the colonial Americas, two large household necessities were the maple sugar vat and the laundry boiler, a kettle used in the yard or in a wash house rather than inside on the home hearth. For meticulous French cooks, the asparagus cooker offered an appropriate tall, cylindrical shape and inner basket for lifting delicate spears from boiling water.

Among settlers of the St. Laurence and New England colonies, the dependable iron kettle formed a substantial portion of each newcomer's pack. In 1634, colonist John Wynter wrote a description of his ample, adaptable cooking vessel: "The Chimney is large, with an oven at each end of him: he is so large that wee can place our Cyttle within the Clavell-piece [fireplace]. Wee can brew and bake and boyl our Cyttle all at once in him." (Earle 1975, 54)

The kettle became the vessel of choice for innovative cooks. In roomy pots, French cooks prepared meat *à la flamande* (in a hotpot), garnished with braised vegetables and pork. On the French coast, the *poissonière* (fish poacher) suited the shape and delicacy of fish cookery. The cook lifted the grid with handles to drain excess liquid while keeping a whole fish intact. For larger flatfish, the oblong *turbotière* (turbot kettle) preserved the entire length. The lidded *jambonnière* (ham poacher), shaped like a ham, allowed the cook to simmer a salted chine before skinning, encasing in pastry, and glazing. Hungarian cooks cubed beef, mutton, or pork and heated it in an iron kettle to evaporate fluids. They sun-dried the meat and stored it in sheep's stomachs for a travel food known as *gulyas,* the forerunner of goulash. In the India of writers Rudyard Kipling and E. M. Forster, the traveler packed a quick-boiling spirit kettle for brewing tea in train carriages.

Communal Cooking

During the Civil War, Union army camps, barracks kitchens, and messes were visited daily by company officers. To prevent epidemics of enteritis and other communicable diseases, they regularly inspected the tin-lined copper or brass kettles. The commanding officer of the regiment observed scouring of kettles and washing and rinsing of utensils under sanitary conditions in clean water.

In the English writer Flora Thompson's trilogy *Lark Rise to Candleford* (1945), an account of growing up in Oxfordshire in the last decades of the nineteenth century, she vividly described an afternoon of communal kettle cookery. An evening meal of bacon, garden vegetables, and roly-poly (a flour pudding or jam roll) cooked in single three-legged kettle hooked to a trammel chain and swung over the grate. The meat simmered in one net bag, vegetables in another, and the

roly-poly in a kitchen towel. Through expert timing, the cook brought all to doneness at one time while keeping the ingredients whole and appetizing.

In Rumania cooks made *mamaliga,* a flavored corn mush resembling the Italian polenta, in the traditional iron *ciaun* (kettle) with the aid of the carved *facelet* (wood stirrer), a family heirloom bearing the family name. After grinding meal in a handmill, the peasant cook set the pot to boil over an open fire, either outdoors or in the home fire pit. After three hours of simmering, the stirrer held the pot between her knees and continued smoothing the mass. Returned to the flame, the kettle dried the mush. Once solidified into a kind of loaf, it required turning out on the table and slicing with a taut thread held between two hands. Like polenta, it filled diners either warm or cold, reheated, or fried.

Improvements

In the mid-1800s, a Michigan woman, Clarissa Britain, principal of the Niles Female Seminary, resettled in South Carolina. During the Civil War, when schooling ended for most students, she turned to inventing as an outlet for her skills. After patenting a floor warmer, she improved the potato boiler, a two-stage steam kettle that allowed cooks to lift the inner pot from the heat source, thus saving hands from burns.

The electric kettle, which had a metal wire around the inner circumference, made its debut at the Crystal Palace Great Exhibition of 1851. In England, the Crompton Company sold a remarkably slow version that required up to twenty minutes to heat three pints of water to boiling. When Carpenter Electric Company of St. Paul, Minnesota, marketed its first electric kettle in 1891, it functioned on heating elements with a limited life span.

German pot makers made notable alterations to kettle design. In 1907, the electronics designer-inventor Peter Behrens took over development at Allgemeine Elektrizitäts-Gesellschaft, one of the world's largest manufacturers, which Emil Rathenau established in Berlin in 1883. Behrens molded his vessels on round, oval, or eight-sided bases to produce thirty variants.

Early electric kettles left room for improvement. In 1922, inventor Leslie Large ended the problem of suspending the heating element by creating a copper-clad wire that could touch liquid. Because it accumulated lime deposits, the wire came with a wire scrubber for descaling its length. In 1931, Bulpitt & Sons came up with a novel idea—a plug that disengaged itself if the kettle boiled dry. It was not until 1955, however, that Bill Russell and Peter Hobbs created a fail-safe automatic shut-off.

Although the electric kettle offered efficiency, it was useless to those in rural areas lacking electricity. In the late 1800s, crofters in western Ireland invented the copper storm kettle, or kelly kettle, a portable two-stage water heater. The device, comprising a boiler and a base, resembled a thermos bottle with firebox in the bottom, central chimney, and wire handle. To heat liquids rapidly, the user filled the chamber surrounding the flue with water and stoked a small fire in the base using twigs, grass, newspaper, or other found tinder. As funneling drew the heat and concentrated it along the cylinder, the kettle heated more than three pints of water in three minutes. Marketed in an aluminum version by John Grindlay in the 1970s, the storm kettle remained a favorite of fishermen, hikers, and campers.

At the turn of the twenty-first century, the preponderance of the world's cooks still depended on kettles. In Scotland, homemakers stoked the oatmeal pot with a hearty, nourishing breakfast to get families through cold mornings. In Namibia, a *potjiekos* (pot foot) meal encompassed anything cooked in a three-legged cast iron kettle over open flame. St. Lucians referred to their one-dish kettle as a coal pot, used to prepare vegetable and meat or seafood ragouts. For trekkers on safari, or *mokoro*, in Botswana, licensed polers provided advice on fishing, hunting, and birding and carried along kettles, mealies, and rice for lunch. Travelers were expected to provide their own utensils, vegetables, and tinned curry or stew.

American and European cordless kettles fit tidily on a plug-in base for tableside service. An automatic shut-off keeps the electric coils from overheating. In institutional kitchens, the steam-jacket kettle is a necessity for making stock and soup and cooking sauces, pasta, seafood, rice, meats and vegetables. The professional-size kettle easily manages from one quart to 160 gallons or more of food at a time. A vertical dynamo with a small footprint, the steam-jacket kettle comes in steam-powered as well as electric and gas models and mounts on legs or a pedestal.

See also **Cauldrons; Hay-Box Cookers**

Further Reading

Bensky, Gary, "Fine Kettle of Fish: Steam-Jacket Is the Heart of the Kitchen," *Nations Restaurant News*, August 7, 2000.

KIMCH'I

In North and South Korea, since the seventh century CE, cooks have made *kimch'i* or *kimchee*, a fiery cabbage pickle soaked in salt water and spiced with red peppers or onions and garlic. The process of marinating vegetables first appeared in print in the *Book of Si-Kyong,* a Chinese anthology written after 1000 BCE, when Koreans resided in Manchuria and preserved vegetables to sustain their health during hard winters. A court record, *The Three Kingdoms Period,* compiled after 57 BCE, describes the Korean peasants as adept at brewing and pickling, the latter kitchen method apparently common to their cuisine. After 918 CE, recipes show the evolution of brined vegetables into a pickle flavored with garlic and spiced fish paste.

The term *kimch'i* appears to derive from *jimchae,* or *dimchae,* meaning vegetables in salt water, or from the Chinese *cham-tse* (also *kam-tse,* pickled vegetables). The concept of pickling in brine derived from the farmers' practice of soaking cabbages in seawater to produce a hearty flavor. Variant pickling ingredients can include chopped turnip, cucumber, or radish and a full range of seasonings. The early thirteenth-century poet Lee Kyu Bo recorded the pickling process. At that time, the recipe began with twenty cabbage heads per person. By 1700, with the availability of dried or powdered red pepper, *kimch'i* had evolved into a hot pickle.

During fermentation, traditional *kimch'i* makers placed the vegetables in a barrel or buried the mix in the ground in a clay pot. During months when fruits and vegetables were scarce, *kimch'i* added sufficient vitamin C to the peasant diet to prevent scurvy. The pungency of condiments also complemented bland foods during winter months. Modern *kimch'i* strayed from the simple peasant recipe with the addition of shallots, carrots, leeks, ginger, sesame seeds, pears, oysters, chestnuts, pine nuts, seaweed, shrimp, and abalone.

By the end of the twentieth century, commercial picklers were providing *kimch'i* for home cooks who no longer had time for the laborious process of chopping and seasoning or access to a yard for burying a *kimch'i* pot. Factory owners in Korea offered to pay *kimch'i* bonuses for ingredients for the winter pickle. Samsung-dong features a *Kimch'i* museum, which offers samples of *possam kimch'i*, made from salt-soaked cabbage leaves encasing a filling of minced turnip, red pepper, and garlic plus chestnut, black mushroom, parsley, ginger, onion, pear, apple, cucumber, pine nut, salted baby shrimp, and raw oyster.

See also **Pickles**

Further Reading

Frongillo, Edward A., "Acculturation and Diet-Related Factors Among Korean Americans," *Nutrition Research Newsletter,* January 1, 2000.
Skabelund, Grant P., man. ed. *Culturgrams: The Nations Around Us.* Vols. I & II. Salt Lake City, Utah: Brigham Young University, 1997.

KITCHEN BUSINESS

Around the world, the extension of kitchen arts to entrepreneurial ventures has occurred in much the same way—as a natural progression from food prepared for family consumption to edible goods sold for extra income. Kitchen businesses flourished throughout much of culinary history. Throughout Turkey, sellers of dairy goods made from the milk of water buffalo have hoisted containers of yogurt and *kaymak* (clotted cream) on poles to market in the streets. In medieval China, as described in *Jane Grigson's Fruit Book* (1982), the street was alive with the call of the candied *kaki* (persimmon) seller. In the 1100s, European waffle-makers set up at church doors on feast days and heated the embossed plates of their hinged irons for shaping *gaufres* (waffles) on the spot.

Source of Supplemental Income

The fresh, cooked, or baked foods peddled in marketplaces or displayed in barrows and wagons replicated the foods found on home tables. In northwestern Europe, the medieval householder supplemented farm income by baking extra loaves or pasties or by donning a shoulder yoke to balance pails of milk for sale to local buyers.

Along the waterways of Russia and the Danube delta, small, reeking sheds housed modest caviar operations. One person could grasp live sturgeon ten to twelve feet long, probe for roe, and strain the viscid ova through a sieve. After salting and pressing the cache in a tin, the vendor was ready for customers.

Householders trained in confection, chocolate making, butchery, and pastries often filled a gap in standard guild service, such as catering to workers and prisons. Enterprising housewives at times operated illegal drink shops out of the home as a hedge against desertion or widowhood. Around 1268, Etienne Boileau, the provost of Paris, summarized the procedures of the cooks' guild in his *Livre des Métiers* (Book of Skills). First, he declared that sellers of cooked dishes should know how to dress meat and should hire only apprenticed journeymen with two years' experience. Essential to the public's health was the injunction to sell only decent, edible, fresh meats and forcemeats. Boileau's regulations therefore banned blood sausage, which he considered *perilleuse* (dangerous). (Ibid., 237) If cooks were caught selling adulterated goods, guild authorities condemned and burned their stock and applied the collected fines to a fund for indigent retired guild members. Another stipulation forbade inappropriate competition or disparaging of the goods served by a fellow cook. Despite the restrictions, kitchen business thrived in this period.

Women emigrating to the New World took their entrepreneurial spirit with them. In colonial Salem, Massachusetts, Elizabeth Haskett ran a bakery near the North River and sold spitted meat from her washhouse and soap from her cauldron. Nantucket fishwives earned the admiration of observer Hector St. John de Crévecoeur, author of *Letters from an American Farmer* (1813), in which he commented that women in the new nation had to step beyond the confines of kitchen and mundane woman's work into the roles of trader and accountant.

Into the nineteenth century, country women traded eggs, cheese, and butter and gathered cress, bittersweet, dandelions, valerian, hedge mustard, and scurvy-grass for sale. In 1822, Sarah Snell Bryant of Cummington, Massachusetts, widowed mother of the poet William Cullen Bryant, recorded in her diary the value of cheeses she had sold for profit. For 602 pounds, she earned only $36—or 6 cents per pound.

In the absence of ready money, kitchen businesses provided the means to acquire cash or goods. Poorly paid Hawaiian missionaries, mostly from New England, found themselves in difficult straits in an unfamiliar land producing taro and living on seafood. Ministers' wives, desperate for fresh food and cash to buy produce, offered meals to sea captains and their officers in port. In exchange, they received butter, molasses, oil, wine, and brandy.

From food stalls and barrows, English costermongers offered raw produce, meats, and fish. Hawkers shouldered trays of goods to carry to Leadenhall Market and into upscale neighborhoods. A stroller could sip coffee and eat bread and butter and "block ornaments," the cheap bits of meat that butchers heaped to the side while cutting larger portions. Hardier fare—kidney or mutton pasties, rhubarb or currant tart, sausages, oysters, fried eels, ham rolls, ginger nuts, buns, crumpets, rice milk, and strawberry cream—was available for a few pennies.

Recording his impressions of a visit to Sicily in 1798, the travel writer Thomas Bingham Richards described a cacophony of merchandising produced by bawling street sellers and stall-keepers. From roast chestnuts, cones of *semenza e càlia* (seeds and chickpeas), figs, olives, melon slices, and citrus fruit plus the potherbs of country folk, buyers could select a kitchen-fresh morning meal. One enterprising vendor, the seller of prickly pears, also stocked iron tweezers at a half cent each.

In the same era, Turkish street traders prepared their wares—rice dishes, soup, meatballs, pastries, breads, fritters, and the anise-flavored liqueur, raki—at night in home kitchens. Wandering thoroughfares in search of the best venues, they stopped at gardens, schools, athletic fields, and the market place to sell hot foods, some fried or heated on charcoal stoves. Along the shores of Istanbul, fishermen sold fresh catch floured and fried in hot oil over charcoal to crowds on the quays.

The Entrepreneurial Spirit

On a colonial Charleston plantation, horticulturist and nursery owner Martha Daniel Logan, author of *The Garden Calendar* (1752), became one of the first American kitchen gardeners to go into business. In 1753, she advertised in the South Carolina *Gazette* packets of seeds, roots, and fruit pits, which she marketed on the green near Trott's Point. Respected for her knowledge of plant propagation, she increased her business through a trade in seeds and cuttings, which she shipped between Philadelphia and South Carolina.

A model entrepreneur from the Mennonite culture was Ruth Hershey, a late nineteenth-century cook at a homestead outside Paradise, Pennsylvania. Without electricity, she chilled dairy goods in her springhouse and heated kettles on a two-hole furnace for laundry. In addition to growing and preserving food from her kitchen garden, she made extra portions of cup cheese from sour milk for distribution in local factories. When asparagus, strawberries, and sugar peas grew well in her garden, she sold them to neighbors. Her sale of homemade potato chips and doughnuts to her children's schoolmates also added to the family's income.

After the enfranchisement of women in 1920, increasing numbers of women found outlets for talents they had honed while feeding, clothing, and tending families. In the 1930s, women's magazines carried discreet advertisements for training schools and jobs that transformed kitchen skills into saleable sevices. A thirteen-line ad for the Lewis Tea Room Institute in Washington, D.C., entitled "Pouring Tea for Profit" boasted excellent salaries and great opportunities for interesting jobs in the coffee shop and tearoom business.

An ad from the American School of Home Economics in Chicago in the September 1930 *Good Housekeeping* attracted aspiring female entrepreneurs with promises of profit from candy making, attested to by prolific food writer Alice Bradley, dean of the Boston School of Cooking and author of *The Candy Cook Book* (1922). The ad promised that women who bought the necessary kitchen equipment and adhered to approved selling plans would make money the first week in business. A similar ad for the Capitol Candy School of Washington, D.C., claimed that candy makers could work in their spare time and sell products at four times their cost.

Throughout the twentieth century, peasants organized co-ops and maximized kitchen skills by selling their wares, either from home or in public markets. In Leh, Ladakh, a Himalayan city, women baked flat bread in portable cylinder ovens for sale to passersby. In Ilha de Luanda, Angola, the enterprising African cook of the late 1990s set up street stalls serving dishes of fish with rice and goat with corn; in Cotonou, Benin, the street stall cook tended toward avocado salad and egg sandwiches, both based on indigenous foods. In the streets of Damascus food vendors offered a range of home-cooked fare. Housewives shopping in person had replaced the traditional female shopper who, immured in an upstairs latticed apartment, had lowered a *sallah* (basket) to a hawker on the pavement below.

Success Stories

In a memoir of her family's struggles in the Dakotas, Carrie Young, author of *Nothing to Do but Stay* (1991), paid tribute to her mother's determination to turn food sales into a livelihood. Each week, she transported eggs into Williston to trade at the grocery store for staples. She took no more than her goods would buy. Young salutes her mother's self-reliance: "My mother churned her own butter, rendered her own lard, made her own bread, and canned whatever she could glean out of the summer's parched garden." (Young 1991, 39) In addition, she sold cream from a dozen cows for shoes and fabric to outfit "the child in college who needed it most." (Ibid., 38-39)

Ramona Acosta Bañuelos, who was eventually appointed U.S. treasurer by President Richard M. Nixon, turned domestic work into a thriving business. Born to illegal Mexican immigrants in Arizona in 1925, she settled in El Paso, Texas, worked as a laundress and dishwasher, and opened a small kitchen business that became Ramona's Mexican Food Products, Inc. From a $400 investment in tortilla-making machines, she built the trade in Hispanic foods into a $12 million corporation employing 400 workers.

Kitchen businesses continued to thrive into the twenty-first century. Chadians supplemented their income by brewing *bili-bili*, a millet beer; in Sierra Leone, women sold roasted peanuts on the street along with homemade cookies and candy. Street cooks of Tana, Madagascar, simmered a *soupe chinoise* (Chinese soup) of noodles and vegetables spiced with coriander. In Ouagadougou, Burkina Faso, women made extra cash at sidewalk stalls frying yam and bean balls for evening snacks; those of Maseru, Lesotho, marketed grilled meats with curry and rice.

In Malaysia, food stalls and pushcarts distributed a broad selection of ethnic street foods. Soup vendors amazed tourists by balancing kettles of hot *soto* (soup) while riding bicycles. (Rajah 1996, 18) Fishball soup hawkers called *tok tok* men banged bamboo sticks together to draw trade; Indian Muslim *mamaks* (traders) carried small portable kitchens to cook *mee goreng,* a popular dish of meat, vegetables, and noodles. The operators of stall kitchens slept on the premises, sometimes remaining alert into the wee hours to serve late-night strollers.

See also **Kitchen Gardening; Marshall, Agnes; Raffald, Elizabeth; Randolph, Mary; Young, Hannah**

Further Reading

Brill, Betsy, "Merlinda Sedillo Welch," *New Village Journal,* Issue 2, 2000, 34.

Good, Phyllis Pellman. *A Mennonite Woman's Life.* Intercourse, Penn.: Good Books, 1993.

Hufton, Olwen. *The Prospect before Her: A History of Women in Western Europe, 1500–1800.* New York: Vintage Books, 1998.

Keatinge, Hilary, "The Road to Leh," *Aramco World,* July–August 1993, 8–17.

"The Pushcarts of Beirut," *Aramco World,* January–February 1971, 2–11.

Rajah, Carol Selva. *Makan-Lah!: The True Taste of Malaysia.* Sydney, Australia: HarperCollins, 1996.

Taylor, George, "The Street Cries of Damascus," *Aramco World,* September–October 1971, 12–15.

KITCHEN CURES

Early writers on food were as much concerned with curative properties as with taste and nutritional value. In classical times, for example, honey, a food long known to have medicinal uses, surfaced in the writings of Zenon, Herophilus of Alexandria, Celsus, Pliny the Elder, Galen, Charak, Marcellus Empiricus, and Dioscorides. The Vedas proclaimed its usefulness as a laxative and digestive. Ancient Egyptian papyri list 147 medicaments featuring honey and characterize it as a treatment for cough and asthma, while in the third century CE, Aelian relied on honey as an anticonvulsant. Although many of the compendia on healing were written by men, through the centuries, the task of preparing home remedies was a womanly chore closely allied with cooking.

Eastern Remedies

In prehistoric India, cooking and healing merged into one art. As early as 3000 BCE, India developed the holistic science of Ayurveda, an alliance of cooking and diet with physical well being and vitality. To maintain *prana,* or energy, home cooks stressed a diet of grain, fruits, vegetables, seeds, beans, roots, herbs, yogurt, and ghee, a clarified butter, all carriers of strength and nutritional balance. The *Upanishads*—the most metaphysical of Vedic literature, a mystical teaching text that Brahman encyclopedists began compiling in 2100 BCE from the lore of wandering ascetics and forest hermits—explained therapeutic methods of cooking. They regarded *sattvic* foods, the fresh elements of the vegetarian diet, as health promoting. The ten principles of cookery coordinated complementary foods, easily digested, served hot in appropriate amounts in pleasant surroundings, and eaten slowly and thoughtfully to promote digestion. Susruta, a practitioner of Ayurvedic healing around 1400 BCE, compounded a honey-and-butter salve, a homemade dressing that prevented infection in incisions. In 1000 BCE Ayurvedic medicine offered recipes for rejuvenating foods, a category that included greens.

Parallel to Indian methods, healing practices in the Far East focused on herbs and curative foodstuffs. Around 2700 BCE, Shên Nung (also Shen Nunn or Shen Nong), the second of the Five Sage Emperors, organized weekly marketing, taught agricultural management, and studied the nutritional value of herbs and foods. Legend describes his roadside search for edible and medicinal plants, which he tested first on a dog, then on a slave, and finally on himself. In addition to peas, wheat, and rice, he identified seventy toxic plants in a compendium, *Canon of Herbs.* Two millennia later, the court physician Sun Simao was still advocating that patients eat healing foods before turning to pharmaceuticals.

The Tao-te Ching, a compendium of Chinese folk beliefs and occultism dating to Huang Ti, the legendary Yellow Emperor of the twenty-fifth century BCE, recorded the food lore of the sage Lao-tse (also Lao-Tze or Lao Zi) from 300 BCE. His concept of a healing diet included raw and steamed vegetables blended with plants, herbs, mushrooms, seeds, and sea vegetation.

Chinese herbalism expanded during the Middle Ages. In the 1200s, Chia Ming published *Essential Knowledge for Eating and Drinking,* another in a long line of guides to eating for health. Another Chinese herbalist, Li Shizhen, summarized the knowledge of the day in *Compendium of Materia Medica* (1578), which listed 11,000 herbal recipes. Traditional Chinese practitioners consulted the Chart of the Five Elements, which connected flavors with organs, senses, and tissues.

Taste Associations from the Chart of the Five Elements

Taste	Organs	Senses	Tissues
sour	liver, gall bladder	vision	tendons
bitter	heart, small intestine	taste	blood
sweet	pancreas, stomach	taste	flesh
spice	lungs, colon	smell	hair
salt	renal system	sound	skeleton

Regimens based on the chart balanced dietary intake to promote health and well being. Into the twenty-first century Chinese kitchen cures continued to depend on such natural medicines as mahuang tea, a source of ephedrine, used to relieve asthma, colds, and sinus and chest congestion.

Advice from Mediterranean Healers

In the Mediterranean world, religious and domestic advisories lauded the medicinal properties of herbs. In 1550 BCE, Egyptian healers recorded herbal compounds and incantations in the Ebers papyri. The Assyrians trusted lettuce as a cure for flagging libido; the Malagan healer Ibn el-Beithar preferred honey. The first Greek medical texts addressed the efficacy of properly prepared foods and herbs for wellness. Around 550 BCE, the mathematician Pythagoras of Samos made nutritious snacks of herbs, sesame and poppy seeds, mallow leaves, onion skin, barley, and peas, which he blended to a paste in honey. Hippocrates of Cos, the father of medicine and author of *De Diaeta* (On Diet, ca 410 BCE), recommended health-promoting cooking techniques: "Take away power from strong foods by boiling and cooling many times; remove moisture from moist things by grilling and roasting them; soak and moisten dry things, soak and boil salt things, bitter and sharp things mix with sweet, and astringent things mix with oily." (Flandrin & Montanari 2000, 144)

The Greek physicians taught their Roman followers that fragrant oils eased muscle cramps and that ox liver cured night blindness and other eye afflictions. Roman cooks listed watercress dressed with vinegar as a restorative to the mind. Another Roman who trusted healing foods, the emperor Nero, had his cook prepare a daily portion of leek soup to protect and deepen his voice for singing and oratory.

The Roman encyclopedist Pliny the Elder, author of *Natural History* (ca. 77 CE), made his own recommendations concerning plants that improved health. He declared that rocket seed could cure a scorpion's sting, remove facial blemishes, and reduce scarring. Pliny also recommended wild mint tea to cure leprosy, gout, scrofula, jaundice, and dandruff, among other ailments. His herbal advice centered on such kitchen garden staples as pennyroyal and purslane. He suggested citron for morning sickness and an antidote to poison and lauded the herb laser, a North African member of the fennel family, as a panacea for edema. He valued rue as an antidote to toxic mushrooms and a remedy for angina pectoris, indigestion, hangover, cough, and failing vision. In accounting for the herb's efficacy as an antivenin, he explained, "When weasels are about to fight with snakes they first fortify themselves by eating rue." (Edwards 1984, xxv) For those about to be flogged, he advocated drinking wine fortified with colewort *(Eruca sativa)*, a desensitizing agent.

Monastic Lore

In medieval Europe, monasteries were a source of kitchen cures based on the nuns' and brothers' knowledge of healing plants and minerals. Monks lauded aloe and rhubarb as purgatives, dandelion as a diuretic and astringent, and meadowsweet, the medieval cure-all, as a fungicide and fumigant. Works such as St. Benedict's *Regula Monachorum* (Rules for Monks, ca. 515 CE) and Walafrid Strabo's *De Cultura Hortarum* (On Gardening), also known as *Hortulus* (The Little Garden, ca. 840 CE) encouraged the planting and drying of curative herbs and flowers, which he studied at the abbey at Reichenau on Lake Constance. St. Gall of Leinster, a late sixth-century Christian missionary and evangelist, settled at Lake Zurich, where he cultivated coriander, dill, parsley, chervil, mint, sage, rue, pennyroyal, cumin, lovage, as well as poppies, the source of a sleep-inducing substance. Gall's scriptorium produced herbal handbooks containing healing pharmaceuticals based on time-honored recipes.

The distillation and concoction of medicines was a womanly skill widely practiced in home kitchens and in livestock pens and barns, where animals, too, required treatment for ills. As a preventive for fainting, women gathered summer roses and distilled a rosewater suitable for reviving the heart. During epidemics, housewives scented water and oils and made aromatic pomanders, wreathes, sachets, and nosegays, later called tussie-mussies, to cleanse and disinfect the air. During the plague years in England, housewives frantically sought rue, marigold, and fresh eggs for one preventative that could be cooked on the home hearth and served to family members to prevent infection. Throughout Germany, the female members of the Teutonic Knights, forerunners of public health nurses, began carrying treatment and advice to homes, where they tended the sick and dosed them with herbal simples compounded from their kitchen gardens.

The height of monastic healing came from St. Hildegard of Bingen, abbess of the Benedictine cloister in Disibodenberg (Diessenberg) and a practitioner of herbal medicine, which she described in *Liber Simplicis Medicinae* (Book of Healing Herbs, ca. 1158) and *Liber Compositae Medicinae et Causae et Curae* (Book of Medical Treatment and Causes and Cures, 1163). She professed a belief in mind and body cures and advocated foods and health practices that encouraged wellness through harmony with God.

Cooking Up Cures

The preparation of dishes for the sick placed a heavy responsibility on cooks. Recipes for fever-reducing tisanes and barley water were valuable. Master Chiquart Amiczo, master chef to Duke Amadeus of Savoy, author of *Du Fait de Cuisine* (On Cooking, 1420), compiled recipes for seventeen sick-dishes and restoratives made from wheat, semolina, oatmeal, barley, chickpeas, almonds, spinach, parsley, quince, pears, applesauce, beef marrow, partridge, chicken, and capon.

Into the Renaissance, kitchen gardens were a source of cordials and salves, tooth polish, and cures for nightmares. They supplied betony, tormentil, cowslip, borage, lemon balm, and other herbs. One of the duties of a lady of the manor was to make and distribute potpourri and nosegays throughout the house, especially in the laundry, pantry, sickroom, and privy. She also had a responsibility to treat local peasants in her domain during epidemics.

For the sixteenth century woman, whether farm wife or aristocrat, a book of simples, or herbal remedies, was a kitchen partner to collections of recipes. Referring to such works in his *Description of Elizabethan England* (1577), the historian William Harrison proclaimed, "For my part I doubt not if the use of outlandish drugs had not blinded our physicians of England in times past, but that the virtues of our simples here at home would have been far better known, and . . . thereunto be found more profitable for us than the foreign either are or may be." A corroborating opinion came from Harrison's contemporary, the Dutch agronomist Conrad Heresbach, author of *Rei Rusticae Libri Quattuor: Universam Agriculturæ Disciplinam Continentes* (The Whole Art and Trade of Husbandry, Contained in Four Books, 1577). At the heart of Heresbach's philosophy was his belief that nature supplied a remedy for each disease, which any gardener could grow at home.

Sir Hugh Platte's *Divers Chimicall Conclusions Concerning the Art of Distillation* (1594) provided instructions for setting up a home still, comprising a brass vessel for cooking liquids and a pewter alembic to cool vapor, which flowed into a glass receiver to form cordials. Readers could learn the best selection of restorative herbs from John Gerard's meticulous 1,400-page plant catalogue, *The Herbal or Generall Historie of Plants* (1597), and from Thomas Hill's *A Most Brief and Pleasant Treatise Teaching How to Dress a Garden* (1563), which listed the best stock for making medicines and explained how to use natural substances as repellants for vermin. According to his advice, a sprinkling of artemisia—commonly called wormwood in England and *chernobyl* in Russia—protected the ankles from fleabite; tansy and yarrow rid the mattress of bedbugs.

Because housewives concocted medicines and foods in the same kettles and crocks, the concepts of nutrition and preventive medicine worked holistically. Thus, flavoring for a soup recipe strengthened the heart and liver, while it settled the belly and cleared the head. The list of such correspondences was lengthy: violets for headache, rosemary for melancholy, basil or peony for childbirth, valerian for rest, and lily of the valley or foxglove for stimulating the heart. One stovetop recipe for a soothing treatment for the winter blahs called for mixing hollyhock, mallow, fennel, danewort, St. John's wort, centaury, ribwort, chamomile, smallage, speedwell, bugloss, and wild flax with other potherbs. The sufferer was to sit over the vapors under cover to steam away upper respiratory discomfort. A sleep sponge mixed from hemlock, opium, mandragora, ivy, mulberry, and lettuce restored an insomniac's nighttime rest.

Gervase Markham's compendium *The English Huswife* (1615) was the most popular household book of the period. According to Markham, the housekeeper could concoct kitchen "bitters and simples" from herbs and oils. (Gould 1962, 163) He recommended sugar, spice, and treacle for decoctions and the distilling of medicinal waters. Common kitchen remedies ranged from mint and bicarbonate of soda for indigestion, licorice for sore throat, rattlesnake root for gout, and wild cherry bark for coughs, to ipecac for poisoning, blackberry juice for inflamed kidneys, and digitalis, or foxglove, for regulating heartbeat. With basic kitchen tools, the cook could also remove splinters, open wens and blisters, set broken bones, and draw rotted teeth. The burning of citronella helped to remove gnats and mosquitoes and the burning of sulfur and the spreading of lime and coal dust supposedly cleared the air of contagion.

Cookbooks often paired recipes and nostrums, as was the case in a volume entitled *A Choice Manuall, or Rare and Select Secrets in Physick and Chirurgery: Collected, and Practised by the Right Honourable, the Countesse of Kent, Late Deceased* (1653). Hannah Wooley's *The Gentlewoman's Companion: Or, a Guide to the Female Sex* (1675) enlarged on the homemaker's sickroom responsibilities by listing associated problems and symptoms, for example, foul breath, laboring in childbirth, and insufficient lactation. In the section entitled "An Introduction to Physick and Chyrurgery," she enumerated healing spices, beginning with pepper, which "cutteth gross stegh (stomach fullness), dispelleth Crudities, and helpeth Digestion." (Wooley 1675, 161) She defers to the more complete knowledge of Nicholas Culpeper's *The English Physician Enlarged, or the Herbal* (1653).

The shipping trade carried medicinal substances around the globe. In 1723, a British captain listed the goods shipped from the Arab harbor of Mocha, which included "petrea [trading coffee] and some Drugs, such as Myrrh, Olibanum or Frankincense from Cassin, and Alloes Soccatrina from Socotra, liquid Storax, white and yellow Arsenick, some Gum Arabick and Mummy; with some Balm of Gilead, that comes from the Red Sea. (Ward 2000, 17) Likewise, sailors disseminated to other lands home remedies that for centuries had remained localized.

A London healer, Mary Kettilby, compiled *A Collection of Above Three Hundred Receipts in Cookery, Physick, and Surgery* (1734), an indexed handbook subtitled "for the use of all good wives, tender mothers, and careful nurses." Her collection of main dishes, desserts, and home remedies contained advice for the treatment of palsy, consumption, and rickets. Unlike less forthcoming editors of her day, she attributed some of her learning to housewives who contributed to her collection.

Another collector of healing recipes, the English farmer William Ellis, compiled the eight-volume *The Modern Husbandman* (1750) and *The Country Housewife*, first issued in 1772. A long-lived observer and journal-keeper, he knew enough about cures to dose himself and his family and animals to combat sprains, lice and worms, pink eye, sore throat and cough, cramp, chilblains, indigestion, toothache, and edema. He himself referred to *The Ancient Physicians Legacy* (1733), by London physician Thomas Dover, and Dr. Quincy's *Pharmacopoeia Officinalis* (1749) and accepted the advice of local gentry, who circulated treatments and herbal tonics that he concocted in his kitchen. Ellis's ingredients were the standard household nostrums—nettle, plantain, pepper, butter, molasses, honey, tobacco, spirits, and beer. A volume from the next century, the anonymous *Ladies' Indispensable Assistant: Being a Companion for the Sister, Mother, and Wife* (1850), clearly placed the responsibility for home cures on females. The book's unusual range of topics included medicine, herbal cures, cookery, etiquette, ladies' toilette, care of canaries, letter-writing, embroidery, and fabric-dyeing, along with lists of edible animals.

Nostrums in the New World

When Europeans settled the Western Hemisphere, they encountered American Indian healers with a thorough knowledge of healing plants. Cherokee healers found that bitters mixed with cooking oil soothed arthritis if administered to the ear. For relaxing the body, they steeped mint and chamomile into tea. The Creeks relied on willow bark to cure malaria, fever, nausea, and rheumatism and applied snakeroot to the treatment of neuralgia, snakebite, malaise, and kidney disease. Navaho healers tenderized prickly pear pads and bound them to raw flesh as a natural wound dressing. Native cooks and herbalists refined these and other plant substances as foods, veterinary medicine, tonics, teas, and potions and taught them to European immigrants, to whom New World biota were unknown.

Many native American dishes served double duty as food and strengthening agents that guaranteed long life as well as nutrition. Examples include agrimony tea and ground tule as a tonic and fever reducer; arbutus, or black ash, tea to improve digestion; basswood tea as an antidote for hangover or heartburn; bittersweet tea to relieve infant colic; chinchona or Peruvian bark to revive the spirits; juniper tea for flatulence; and witch hazel for skin eruptions.

Spanish colonists learned from South American tribes the value of coca, ipecac, and Peruvian bark, the source of quinine. In Mesoamerica, women fermented pulque, or Indian beer, from the *aguamiel* (honeywater) excised from the heart of the agave plant; it was a standard treatment for pain and illness. In Hidalgo, Tlaxcala, Puebla, and Oaxaca, Mexico, pulque-making was the work of huge haciendas. For the Otomi, the drink was a source of hydration in the desert. In the post-Columbian era, pulque bars, called *pulquerías,* evolved kitchen brewing into a social institution among the laboring class.

In the American colonies, "doctoring" was woman's work. Catherine Clinton's *The Plantation Mistress* (1982) explained, "The female head of household acted as doctor or nurse . . . for it was her task to supervise the medical care of her families, white and black." (Clinton 1982, 143) Women's home remedies typically derived from kitchen vessels and utensils. Favorite ingredients included fireplace ash, milk, butter, eggs, meat fat, vinegar, cloves, baking soda, whiskey, syrup, tea, and brown sugar, as well as herbs, leafy plants and roots, and minerals. Supervision of healing involved collecting herbs, drying them, and dispensing medicines to the sick as well as advice on diet, hygiene, rest, and exercise.

One of the stalwart nurse-midwives of the New England frontier, Martha Ballard kept house and tended the sick of Kennebec, Maine. Laurel Thatcher

Ulrich's book *A Midwife's Tale: The Life of Martha Ballard, Based on Her Diary, 1785–1812* (1990) characterizes the homemade simples that Ballard carried in her kit to ease parturient women and to treat burns, broken bones, and infectious disease. When she had no calls to make, like other New England housewives, she distilled vinegar, carded flax, and planted vegetables, fruit, and herbs in a kitchen bed.

On the move west, pioneers who made do without proper pharmaceuticals scouted herb patches and used common vegetable cures, such as sliced potato for sore eyes. At their campfires, they mixed onion syrup for croup and compounded a hot salt and whiskey gargle for raw throats. Peppermint and whiskey aided burns and cleansed contusions and cuts. Straight whiskey or brandy and chamomile tea treated menstrual pain and eased the hard labor of childbirth. As late as the mid-1860s, the Andrew Johnson family stocked elderberry tea, a pioneer favorite, at the White House to serve with honey or sugar as a refreshing tonic, blood purifier, and cold preventative.

Eliot Wigginton's *The Foxfire Book* (1968), a collection of lore from the southern Appalachians, recorded some of the home remedies relied upon in isolated coves where physicians and hospitals were nonexistent. The list of cures ranged from herbal remedies with a sound scientific basis—e.g., mullein tea for cough—to those grounded in superstition—wearing scissors around the neck as a cure for nosebleed.

One of the most famous inventors of kitchen-brewed potions was Lydia Estes Pinkham of Lynn, Massachusetts, who developed Lydia Pinkham's Vegetable Compound in 1875. Forced by penury to bottle the concoction, she claimed that her formula targeted an unspecified list of women's disorders and ailments. Her advertising system consisted of handbills that her sons distributed door to door. She patented her nostrum the next year and gained rapid credibility after posting an ad in the Boston *Herald*. Within two decades, her formula was the most widely advertised patent medicine in the United States.

Ongoing Trends

Into the twenty-first century, healing foods and restorative beverages reflected the character and style of native cooks, such as the Japanese reliance on *ukeboshi* (salted plums) to ease a chill or settle a colicky digestive tract. In Latvia, the health-conscious take drafts of dark, viscid *Rigas Melnais Balzams* (black balsam), a strong tonic mixed with vodka or coffee. Italians value *grappa*, a wine made from grape seeds that purportedly cured numerous ills, including menstrual cramps. British hosts serve Pimm's, a light, summery

alcoholic drink decorated with slices of citrus fruit, apple, strawberry, or cucumber or mint sprigs. James Pimm concocted it in the 1820s as a digestive aid and sold it in his London oyster bar. Twenty years later, local support for gin and vodka-based Pimm's influenced him to distribute his drink more widely.

In the United States, a growing interest in alternative medicines and, simultaneously, increasing skepticism about the medical establishment were among numerous trends that contributed in the late twentieth century to a renewed enthusiasm for dietary therapies and healing foods. Selene Yeager's *The Doctor's Book of Food Remedies* (1998) from Rodale Press was one of many texts offering cooks suggestions for improving family health, boosting energy, staving off disease and premature aging, and treating illness. U.S. physicians, not previously a profession well trained in principles of nutrition, became knowledgeable about the health benefits of foods such as soy and fish oils, while medical researchers explored the potential disease-preventing properties of such mundane foods as tomatoes and broccoli.

See also **Alcohol; Evelyn, John; Francatelli, Charles Elmé; Herbs; Kitchen Gardening; Monastery Kitchens; Water; Witches' Kitchens**

Further Reading

Bremness, Lesley. *The Complete Book of Herbs*. New York: Penguin Studios, 1994.

Clinton, Catherine. *The Plantation Mistress*. New York: Pantheon Books, 1982, 143.

Ellis, William. *Country Housewife's Family Companion*. London: Prospect Books, 2000.

Johnston, William M., ed. *Encyclopedia of Monasticism*. Chicago: Fitzroy Dearborn Publishers, 2000.

Magic and Medicine of Plants. Pleasantville, N.Y.: Reader's Digest, 1986.

Morningstar, Amadea, and Urmila Desai. *The Ayurvedic Cookbook*. Twin Lakes, Wisc.: Lotus Press, 1990.

Tucker, David M. *Kitchen Gardening in America: A History*. Ames: Iowa State University Press, 1993.

Ulrich, Laurel Thatcher. *A Midwife's Tale: The Life of Martha Ballard, Based on Her Diary, 1785–1812*. New York: Alfred A. Knopf, 1990.

KITCHEN GARDENING

Kitchen gardening is the cultivation of vegetables, fruits, and herbs for use in the family kitchen. Although the size of a kitchen garden plot can vary considerably, most are located in close proximity to the house and, indeed, often near the kitchen door, where the cook can gather fresh ingredients only a few steps from the food preparation area.

From *The Grete Herball*. Earliest of the numerous herbals which appeared in England, the Grete Herball, founded on the French *Grand Herbier*, was printed by Peter Treveris at Southwark in 1526.

Villas, Castles, and Monasteries

At early Egyptian villas near the Delta and the rich al-Fayyum district west of the Nile, the focus on a contented existence required a kitchen garden equal to the demands of the owner's table. In addition to herbs, the meticulously designed grounds offered fig and date trees espaliered along walls. Universally, the householder trained an array of grapevines to poles, pergolas, or trellises. Handy to the kitchen, patches of onions, leeks, beans, lentils, garlic, pumpkins, gourds, melons, cucumbers, radishes, spinach, carrots, lettuce, and turnips provided variation in the mundane grain- or meat-centered diet.

During the early years of the Roman Empire, kitchen gardens produced varied salad crops, including Egyptian romaine and Greek and Spanish pink lettuce, which kitchen workers pickled in vinegar and honey. To extend the growing season, gardeners topped tender plants with translucent stone cloches and added wheels to pot beds for quick removal to a sheltered area when frost threatened. During the late Roman Republic and early Empire, three writers issued handbooks to kitchen gardening. Consul Marcus Cato extolled the simple rural life in recipes compiled in *De Agricultura* (On Agriculture, ca. 149 BCE). A century later, the soldier and author Varro wrote *De Re Rustica* (On Country Life, 40 BCE), which preceded the poet Virgil's *Georgics* (29 BCE). The first major volume of gardening advice during the empire came from the agronimist Columella, the author of the twelve-book *De Re Rustica* (60 CE), followed by a scientific hallmark of the era, the encyclopedist Pliny the Elder's *Natural History* (ca. 77 CE).

Roman kitchen gardens produced valuable herbs and plants used in the making of restoratives and medicines. When Augustus, the first emperor, languished from crippling arthritis, respiratory illness, and insomnia during a period of political upheaval, he received care from the freedman Antonius Musa, a Greek herbalist recommended by poets Virgil and Horace. Musa, who wrote a learned treatise on forty-seven diseases cured by the plant wood betony, quickly earned the frail emperor's respect and trust. Musa set him in a tub of cold water and fed him lettuce, the wonder cure of the day, until he was restored to health. According to the historian Suetonius, this accomplishment earned Musa a memorial statue at the temple of Aesculapius, fount of healing.

In his advice on horticulture, Pliny determined that good soil was the essence of the successful kitchen bed. He explained that the best way to test the soil was by smelling and tasting it, especially after a rain: "The earth will send up a vapor and exhalation so heavenly and divine, as no perfume is comparable to it." (Pliny 1962, 159)

Caelius Apicius, the author of *De Re Coquinaria* (On Cooking, late fourth century CE), the world's first cookbook, valued blossoms for the making of fine table wines and aperitifs. His text offers recipes for berries preserved in grape must and pulp and delicate drinks fermented from the petals of roses and violets. Contributing to the quality of his vintages was a careful drying of dew from flowers and appropriate filtration of flower parts from fragrant liquids.

Miniaturists, engravers, and illuminators of the Middle Ages left graphic evidence of the layout and planting of manorial kitchen plots, which usually adjoined the castle kitchen. In addition to espaliered fruit trees and vines trained on whitewashed walls, kitchen staff cultivated pots of herbs and fragrant flowers. A pond located in the courtyard supplied the table with fresh trout, pike, and dace. In Palermo, Sicily, bright green *viridaria* (courtyard gardens) were productive, aromatic, and decorative. During quarantines to halt outbreaks of plague, families relied heavily on the fruits and vegetables that grew in the walled plots outside their kitchen doors.

At the vanguard of medieval agriculture were Cistercian and Benedictine monks, who developed into model kitchen gardeners, cooks, herbalists, and healers. Monastery kitchen beds produced enough fresh vegetables for feeding residents, guests, and beggars. The monks experimented with crop strains, soil enhancement, drainage schemes, and land reclamation. A German nurse and herb grower, St. Hildegard of Bingen, became abbess of the Benedictine cloister in Disibodenberg (Diessenberg) in 1136. From her study of herbs and training of a cadre of followers came two valued handbooks—*Liber Simplicis Medicinae* (Book of Healing Herbs, ca. 1158) and *Liber Compositae Medicinae et Causae et Curae* (Book of Medical Treatment and Causes and Cures, 1163).

Another source of information, the grammarian and lexicographer John of Garland's *Dictionary* (1220) lists the varieties in his own kitchen garden—sage, parsley, dittany, hyssop, celandine, fennel, and chamomile—and a series of medicinal plants, namely, mercurialis, mallow, agrimony, bittersweet, and heliotrope, a cure for insect bites and stings. For his table, he grew cabbage, borage, spinach, chives, garlic, mustard, leeks, onions, and scallions. Beyond his kitchen beds, he planted cherry, pear, apple, plum, medlar, quince, peach, and chestnut trees and established a grove of almonds, filberts, and figs. His text saves until last his "vine branch, grapes and tendrils, the young shoots of the vine both in rows and ordered ranks," and comments that "without all these the table of rich men has been reduced to beggary." (Rubin 1981, 79)

In Polsloe, Devonshire, England, the local nunnery was built around 1250 and expanded in the 1300s to admit more young women whose families wanted them to gain an education or commit to a religious life. The allocation of space suggests the importance of kitchen gardening to priory self-sufficiency. To the north, the church, encompassing a third of the grounds, anchored the complex. The living compound, situated on the middle third at center, walled in inmates according to the dictates of cloistering. The southern third of the property contained a spacious rectangular garden capable of supplying vegetables and herbs for the sisters' private kitchen and refectory and for feeding guests and the poor.

In Italy and Sicily, grain fields, orchards of sour oranges and almonds, groves of date palms, and market gardens dominated coastal cities. In the period of Muslim rule during the tenth and eleventh centuries, impressive royal gardens featured ornamentals and espaliered trees, both beautiful and fruitful. When the Normans overthrew the Arabs, they perpetuated the kitchen garden as a source of exotic fresh foodstuffs for the discerning gourmet. In the kitchen gardens of the peasantry, the largest section offered cabbage and onions, the basis for minestrone. With the addition of fava beans and chickpeas to soup and stale bread, cooks established a regional Mediterranean cuisine still respected and emulated. The arrival of hardy garden seeds and tubers from the New World altered the feast-and-famine cycles that stalked western Europe, greatly reducing the toll of malnutrition and infectious diseases and doubling the population in the 1700s.

"It Must be Weeded…."

As depicted in William Harrison's *Description of England* (1587), kitchen or cook's gardens took on added importance during the English Renaissance with the planting of lime trees, roses for making jelly and rosewater, and chives, cauliflower, and purslane, all new to the British Isles. In *The Book of Husbandry* (1523), the Renaissance moralist John Fitzherbert offered a month-by-month advisory for the kitchen gardener: "And in the beginning of March, or a little afore, is time for a wife to make her garden, and to get as many good seeds and herbs as she can, and especially such as be good for the pot, and to eat, and as often as need shall require, it must be weeded, for else the weeds will overgrow the herbs." To create a rich, organic humus, the housewife tossed kitchen scraps, dishwater, spoiled straw, and barn waste into the compost heap. A handful of manure stirred into water from the rain barrel darkened into manure tea, a nourishing, safe liquid fertilizer.

In the French royal gardens of Versailles, the pomologist, or fruit grower, Jean de la Quintinye, gardener for Louis XIV, enriched a twenty-five-acre kitchen garden with imported soil. His book, *Instruction pour les Jardins Fruitiers et Potagers, avec un Traite des*

Orangers, et des Reflexions sur l'Agriculture (Instructions on Fruit and Vegetable Gardening with a Treatise on Orangeries and Some Reflections on Agriculture), was published in 1697. In admiration of Quintinye's skill and generosity to ordinary gardeners, the American essayist Ralph Waldo Emerson credited him with teaching all people to value growing things. The humanist John Evelyn, author of *Acetaria: A Discourse on Sallets* (1699), provided the home gardener with a pullout plat for a vegetable patch. He coordinated month-by-month explanations of what to plant, how to cultivate, when to harvest, how to cook and preserve produce, and what healing qualities each dish contained.

On estates, chores for servants included the pickling of winter "salat," which involved marinating marigolds and dianthus in a sweet-sour sugar-and-vinegar solution. Intricate knot gardens and walkways needed constant edging and weeding. Enclosing of the garth, the Anglo-Saxon term for a walled garden, began with wattle, a screening of interwoven branches and limbs used as a barrier before the creation of paling fences and cemented stone and brickwork walls. By planting fruit trees, nut bushes, and berry vines against the walls of the enclosure, gardeners made maximum use of reflected heat to protect the plants and speed ripening of fruits.

In colonial America, the kitchen garden satisfied meticulous cooks, who valued grape and nut arbors and orchards for a ready supply of table food, nuts, and fruits for drying. In addition to their culinary uses, common herbs such as parsley, rosemary, sage, and thyme were household essentials, valued as deodorants for closets and kitchens, vermin repellants, and medicines. Bottlebrush and horsetail provided pads for scouring metal, cleaning woodwork, and polishing pewter. To assure sweet soil for these plants, in 1723, two lime kilns in the Boston area sold lime in liquid and granular form for distribution over gardens.

By 1760, a steam-fed hot wall—a brick garden wall warmed with horizontal flues—sped the maturing of garden produce at estates such as Thoresby, in Nottinghamshire, England. The stores of fruits and root vegetables in home cellars became so important that executors of estates in the eighteenth century listed baskets of cabbages and barrels of medlars along with jewelry, musical instruments, cottages, and deeds.

In this era, the rural English kitchen garden was the housewife's hedge against boring menus. Herbs, fruit, and vegetables enhanced smallholders' diets, which tended heavily toward bacon and mutton. Estate gardeners experimented with chemical fertilizers and imported espaliering techniques for the cultivation of lush, oversized tree fruit.

So that they could pass between the vegetable rows, arbors, and blocks of fruit trees, gardeners followed the advice of *The Gardener's Dictionary Containing the Methods of Cultivating and Improving the Kitchen, Fruit and Flower Gardens* (1731), written by florist and horticulturist Philip Miller, curator of the Chelsea Physic Garden. They laid planking or brick paths, gravel or sandy lanes, or, in coastal regions, walkways surfaced in crushed shells. In addition to increasing access for regular tending of plants, these footpaths freed clogged feet of mud and eased passage of wheelbarrows.

Utilitarian Beds of the Americas

In the Americas, around 5000 BCE, as a multidimensional dietary staple, growers developed five families of corn—dent, flint, flour, popcorn, and sweet corn. They served it fresh, dried, cooked as samp, or gruel, ground into coarse or fine flour for tortillas and cornbread, soaked in ash water for hominy, cooked with chestnuts and maple sugar for porridge, or popped into an airy snack. Near their homes, the Valdivia of Ecuador grew corn, manioc, squash, beans, and achira or canna lily bulbs as early as 3000 BCE. In their dooryards, utilitarian beds nourished fruit and herbs as sources of food, fragrance, and healing. The focus on preparation of stew, grinding of nuts and herbs, and tending of an open hearth greatly contributed to stabilization, rooting family and clan to a permanent home. As herds of animals diminished in the Southwest, the men of the Navajo and Pueblo, formerly the meat-providers, took over gardening from the women and elevated seed viability to the level of deity.

Farther north, males superintended swidden systems, by which rotation farming left some fields fallow for a year or more. Burning reduced undergrowth to stubble, renewed the soil with ash, and readied the replenished loam for furrowing and hilling. The Huron of Canada discovered that sowing squash seed in rotted stump pith in bark mocucks over a fire warmed them for early germination, thus making the most of a short growing season. Chance discoveries demonstrated that hilling the soil into mounds—a forerunner to the system of raised beds—spared seeds from cold and wet and helped prevent soil compaction.

South of the Great Lakes, the Iroquois and Shawnee established mathematical matrices—six hills of corn and a seventh planted with beans after the corn emerged. The prosperous union of the two presaged the kitchen marriage of corn with limas for succotash. The system reflected a basic nutritional principle—that beans compensated for the protein and lysine lacking in corn. The cucurbits, the third plant group of the native triad, produced varied types of squash and pumpkins. To the outer edge of the kitchen plot, native kitchen gardeners added sunflowers for oil and seeds and sunchoke, which Europeans called Jerusalem artichoke, a crunchy tuber rich in potassium and vitamin C.

Kitchen gardening demanded labor and cooperation. Gardeners hand plucked hornworms, stem borers, and squash beetles. To ward off scavenging birds, rabbits, and other animals, families teamed up to build lookouts, snares, and deadfalls, the weighty logs propped on sticks and baited so that opossums and raccoons would meet a swift end. Men cultivated the beds using hoes made from clamshells, wood chunks, or the shoulder blades of deer attached to wood handles; harvesting was primarily woman's work. The gardens produced two-thirds of the forest Indian diet.

Settlers and Seeds

European settlers in North America relished the fresh goods of the kitchen bed as food, flavoring herbs, and healing plants as well as cut flowers and greenery for table decorations, dried arrangements, and holiday swags. They looked forward to the ripening of corn for its many uses as roasting ears, hominy, grits, and corn bread; sweet potatoes, baked or roasted or used in fillings for pies, were another versatile crop. They grew butter beans, limas, navy beans, and peas from seed; Irish potatoes, on the other hand, required imported stock. The most prolific crop in the South was the turnip, which cooks, both slave and free, planted late in the season for a fall supply of greens and turnips in a season devoid of most green vegetables. Cowpeas were a double delight for cooking and for replenishing beds as a green manure.

By 1795, American seed merchandising, begun by the Shakers of New Lebanon, Ohio, prefaced a deluge of direct sales through the mail rather than through seed outlets. Of a field of 800 distributors, the most successful mail order tycoon, Canadian horticulturist Washington Atlee Burpee, publisher of the *Burpee Farm Annual,* trumped them all with a gardening contest. He tempted kitchen gardeners with the offer of a $50 award to the three who raised the largest fruit from his Cuban Queen watermelon seed. His catalog's straightforward representation of plants and vegetable size and weight built consumer trust that survived over a hundred years.

Frontier families kept vegetable beds and orchards as their primary source of fresh produce. In *The Colonel's Lady on the Western Frontier* (1989), Alice Kirk Grierson collected letters from her sojourn at an army outpost in Texas. Chief among her longings for domestic contentment was a shipment of garden seeds. In

unfamiliar terrain, planters like Grierson learned how to irrigate and tend familiar vegetables from seeds they brought from home. Shielding prairie gardens from strong winds required immediate windbreaks constructed from scrub or cedar boughs thrust into the ground and hedges or rows of trees as permanent protection. One planter grew so enraged at a rooster that followed her up a corn row, gobbling her seed, that she chopped it open and retrieved the kernels from the craw and continued sowing her furrows. For healing, the gardener also nurtured herbs, particularly sage for tea, mustard for plasters, onions for poultices and soothing aching ears, onion and lard salve for frostbite, and peppermint, one of the most valuable cures and carminatives in the family medicine chest. (Brown 1958, 205)

The nineteenth century produced strong advocacy for kitchen gardening. A determined spokesman for vegetables grown at home, the Reverend Timothy Dwight, a Congregationalist chaplain and president of Yale College, maintained that eating too much fish and red meat compromised the nation's nutrition. He supported gardening as a source of nutrients and as exercise, particularly to alter urban women's sedentary habits. Additional promotion came from Dr. Shadrack Ricketson's *Means of Preserving Health and Preventing Disease* (1806) and Catharine Esther Beecher's *A Treatise on Domestic Economy for the Use of Young Ladies at Home and at School* (1841). A new impetus derived from America's first "health food" store, opened in Boston by Dr. William A. Alcott, author of *The Young House-Keeper; or Thoughts on Food and Cookery* (1838), and from catalogs distributing seeds of European varieties.

In the 1880s, home gardeners abandoned the English enclosed bed for an American-style row planting that suited larger home lots and wheeled hoes, forerunners to the gasoline-powered rotary tiller. The availability of patent medicines caused a decline in the cultivation of herbs. The era's gardeners tended to value summer savory and basil for their varied foliage and fragrance rather than for medicinal and nutritional value. In the suburbs, the American ideal of a spacious green lawn deflected attention from the growing of edibles. In cities, vacant-lot gardens spawned delight and nostalgia in immigrants, who recreated the joys of vegetables from the mother country.

Urban and Suburban Plots

In New York City, a groundswell of interest in park and vacant-lot gardening fueled a rush for soil testing and plot staking. In 1917, Oklahoma City hired a gardening adviser to aid inexperienced urbanites in growing their own kitchen produce. As part of the Progressive Era's war garden campaign, President Woodrow Wilson promoted home tillage and sowing by declaring kitchen gardening a step toward victory. Boys joined corn clubs, and girls formed canning clubs, quadrupling the amount of produce grown and preserved before the entrance of the United States into the war. A romanticized image of a uniformed female volunteer demonstrating sanitary canning techniques graced the cover of a 1918 issue of *The Country Gentleman*.

Louisa King, a co-founder of the Garden Club of America in 1913 and author of *The Well-Considered Garden* (1915), presided over the Woman's National Farm and Garden Association during World War I. As a result of her advocacy, women in the Carolinas adopted the slogan "A Garden for Every Home the Year Round." (Smith & Wilson 1999, 212) For her promotion of kitchen gardening, King joined Britain's Royal Horticultural Society and became the first woman to receive the George White Medal of the Massachusetts Horticultural Society, the nation's highest gardening award.

The publication in 1962 of naturalist Rachel Carson's *Silent Spring* initiated a revolution in the way people thought about the environment. In place of toxic sprays and powders, garden centers began stocking such bio-friendly goods as insecticidal soaps, diatomaceous earth (a natural slug deterrent), and fish emulsion fertilizers. In the United States, the counterculture movement of the 1960s, harking back to an earlier peaceful, agrarian existence, revived interest in kitchen gardening. From the drop-out mindset arose new publications—*The Great Speckled Bird, Mother Earth News*, and various editions of the *Whole Earth Catalogue*—and a new devotion to reclaiming the land through apiculture, home gardening, and energy conservation. In 1972, the Environmental Protection Agency banned DDT. Canada, Sweden, and Denmark passed similar laws restricting the sale and use of nonbiodegradable pest control for agribusiness and home use.

In the United States and Canada, the 1980s exhibited increasing culinary sophistication, coupled with a growing interest in exotic vegetables. Inspired in part by immigrants from Asia, kitchen gardeners began reading up on *wong nga baak* (Peking celery cabbage), *bak choy, seut choy* (Shanghai cabbage), *choy sum* (flowering bok choy), mung beans, and *daikon*, the Japanese radish. One impetus to the addition of these plants to old standbys was the publication of Geri Harrington's *Grow Your Own Chinese Vegetables* (1978); another was the appearance of Asian vegetable seeds among the stock of Shepherd's Garden Seeds in Felton, California, and Kitasawa Seed Company in San Jose.

Adventuresome gardeners, particularly those battling short growing seasons, developed hydroponic systems. They constructed lightweight growing frames, sowed seeds into cups of perlite and vermiculte, then transplanted seedlings into cups or jars fed by a nutrient-containing liquid pumping system. Practiced under grow-lights, on patios, and in greenhouses, the soilless garden technique produced greens, tomatoes, peppers, and kohl vegetables without the traditional tilling, cultivating, weeding, and battling of soilborne pests.

Into the twenty-first century, the kitchen garden enriched diets in much of the world. In South Africa, gardeners protected the home *shamba* (vegetable patch) from invasion by baboons and hippos. To drive away monkeys, chefs burst from the kitchen banging pot lids together. Gardeners choosing organic methods of vermin control blended garlic with soap and water to spray on infested leaves. At the Japanese imperial palace in suburban Tokyo, 620 acres of lush black soil produced leeks and other vegetables for the royal family. In Kenya, the Kikuyu expected travelers to stop at any garden for a snack of bananas, sugarcane, or sweet potatoes. They stated their logic in a proverb: "Hunger is not questioned." (Schlabach 1991, 92) Thus, families welcomed all to a meal, but considered anyone who took away produce to be thieves.

In some countries kitchen gardening became a key to health. For retired Russian families living in rural dachas, the kitchen *ogorod* (garden), berry bushes, and orchard were sources of quality nutrition in a country where grocery stores often stocked inferior goods. The wise dacha owner canned some of the homegrown produce to vary a winter diet dominated by root vegetables.

Rural islanders of St. Lucia relied on the kitchen garden for fresh herbs and "ground provisions," a local term for root vegetables. To Antiguans and Barbudans, whose diet was meager and limited by drought, the kitchen garden supplemented foodstuffs largely imported from Europe and the rest of the Caribbean. Like European kitchen gardens, Japanese household beds produced everyday favorites—*butterbur* (Japanese taro), *dasheen, mizuna* (greens), *daikon, gobo* (burdock), and *shiso* (beefsteak plant).

See also **Amanite Kitchens; Beecher, Catharine Esther; Herbs; Kitchen Cures**

Further Reading

Dabars, Zita, and Lilia Vokhmina. *The Russian Way.* Lincolnwood, Ill.: Passport Books, 1996.
Gardiner, Anne Gibbons. *Mrs. Gardiner's Family Receipts from 1763.* Boston: Rowan Tree Press, 1989.

Platt, Colin. *The Abbeys and Priories of Medieval England.* New York: Barnes & Noble, 1996.

Rubin, Barbara Blatt, trans. *The Dictionarius of John de Garlande.* Lawrence, Kans.: Coronado Press, 1981.

Stow, Josie, and Jan Baldwin. *The African Kitchen.* Brooklyn, N.Y.: Interlink Books, 2000.

Tucker, David M. *Kitchen Gardening in America: A History.* Ames: Iowa State University Press, 1993.

KITCHEN MURDERS

The tradition of homicide via food or drink has a long and curious history. Kitchen murderers have employed both natural toxins—most famously, poisonous mushrooms—and synthetic chemicals, served up to unknowing victims in many cunning guises. The notorious French murderer Madame de Brinvilliers baked a toxic pigeon pie; Cordelia Botkin added lethal poison to bonbons, and pesticide-laced chocolate truffles were the weapon of choice of the German-born poisoner Christa Lehman. An Italian barrel-maker, Luigi Carigiola, eliminated his rivals for the inheritance of his uncle's factory by inviting all of them to dine on pasta topped with strychnine-laced sauce.

Treacherous Cooks

The earliest toxins known to humankind were valuable not to eliminate personal enemies but rather to stun or disable animals valued as food. In the Americas, indigenous peoples found that certain harmful substances, when applied to arrowheads and spear points or added to water in pools, would stun fish for easy netting. To deoxygenate water, they used toxic solutions made from poisonous plants: in North America, California buckeye, dove weed, smartweed, soap plant, or turkey mullein; in South America, barbasco, cubé, and devil's shoelace. Ergot, the toxic product of a grain fungus, has a lengthy history, as documented by inscribed tablets from the Fertile Crescent and the writings of the Greek physicians Hippocrates and Galen, the Arab healer Muwaffak, and the scientists Theophrastus and Pliny the Elder.

Ancient Rome produced several legendary murderers who used poisonous mushrooms to dispatch those who stood in their way of their ambitions. Livia Drusilla, third wife of Augustus, Rome's first emperor, so yearned for the accession of her son Tiberius that she poisoned the emperor's son-in-law Marcellus and his two sons. Agrippina the Younger, the mother of Nero, appears to have killed her second husband, the emperor Claudius, with a serving of muscarine mushrooms, a crime corroborated in Book IX of Platina's *De Honesta Voluptate et Valitudine* (On Right Pleasure and Health, 1475). A twelve-hour agony of vomiting and diarrhea, pain, falling blood pressure, and respiratory failure ended the emperor's life in 54 CE, when Agrippina announced her ascendance to the role of imperial matriarch.

Poisoning was a source of concern for Muslim princes, who could not easily distinguish murder from accidental death due to bacterial food contamination. The ruler worried constantly about poisoning. To ensure that the prince's master cook and kitchen staff were trustworthy, court officials paid high prices for the best slaves and turned court cooking into a political job.

The precautionary practice of tasting of items before their presentation to an important personage cropped up at many moments in history—at the court of France's Louis XIV, for example, and in more recent times, during Rumanian dictator Nicolae Ceaucescu's state visit to Elizabeth II of England in 1978. In Africa and Papua, New Guinea, it was the custom for the host to sample water and food before serving them to guests. Hirohito, the emperor of Japan from 1926 to 1989, replaced food tasting with chemical analysis and sterilized dishes. When his son Akihito came to power, he ended the practice of food tasting.

The cozy image of the home kitchen belies the number of creative homicides perpetrated in the family food center. Although certain killers have used kitchen implements such as knives or cleavers or invented novel means—the Earl of Conway, for example, who, in 1234, drowned Viking invaders of the Orkneys in barrels of mustard—the majority of kitchen murders involve poisoning. In the Middle Ages and Renaissance, witch hunts often relied on allegations of poisoning as the justification for persecuting women. Francesco Maria Guazzo's *Compendium Maleficarum* (Anthology of Evils, 1608) corroborated the presumption that female witches used toxic plants, animals, stones, and metals in powdered inhalants, food, or drink.

In 1851, Charles Mackay's *Extraordinary Popular Delusions and the Madness of Crowds* cited the example of Pope Alexander VII, who was so shocked to learn of a ring of murderous wives during a rise in poisonings in Rome in 1659 that he had the leader, Hieronyma Spara, arrested and executed along with her "infernal sisterhood." Mackay's text dispelled the stereotype of the female poisoner as a glamorous aristocrat. According to him, peasant women typically concocted murderous meals to end wretched marriages and to collect the burial savings. In the words of Ann Jones, author of *Women Who Kill* (1980), "For the wife whose duty it was to cook the meals and nurse the ailing, what could be simpler than poison?" (Jones 1980, 76)

Domestic Dramas

The annals of kitchen murders are replete with tales of domestic strife. Lucretia Chapman, a married woman living in Andalusia, Pennsylvania, was the quarry of a dashing Spaniard of apparent wealth and aristocratic ancestry. After her husband became ill from a dinner of pork and smearcase, Lucretia made him a soothing bowl of chicken soup. He died suddenly. Twelve days later, Lucretia married her suitor, who turned out to be an impostor and a fraud. A trial found her innocent—he was hanged.

When Hannah Hanson Kinney's husband, Bostonian George T. Kinney, died of arsenic on August 9, 1840, evidence suggested that, in revenge for having contracted venereal disease through his mistress, Hannah sought a homemade punishment. Testimony connected her with cups of sage tea bearing a white sediment and unusual sweet flavor. On November 7, 1849, Ann Simpson of Fayetteville, North Carolina, used the same method to rid herself of her husband. Not only did she pass him a cup of the suspect tea in front of boarders, she insisted that the cup go to him alone, then read his fortune in the lees, predicting sickness and death.

The reputed queen of poisoners, Marie Davaillaud Besnard of Loudon, France, slew thirteen victims, including husbands, cousins, in-laws, and parents. Despite the blatant nature of her crime, the court failed to convict. At her third trial in 1961, after a confession and recantation, she went free. So, too, did suspected caretaker Edith Bingham, who was acquitted in 1911 of multiple killings at Lancaster Castle in England. Other notorious kitchen poisoners, including two Americans, Rhonda Bell Martin of Alabama and Velma Barfield of North Carolina, and the South African killer Daisy de Melker, were executed for their crimes. A Russian murderer, Madame Popova, who "liberated" women from unpleasant husbands, died before a firing squad in 1909. The notorious Vera Renczi, the Hungarian killer of thirty-five men, survived to show investigators thirty-five zinc coffins in her basement and died in prison while serving a life sentence.

Tools of Mayhem

Several notorious incidents of kitchen homicide have involved everyday implements and utensils—among them, soup ladles, carving forks and knives, can openers, machetes and cleavers, crockery shards and bottles, flatirons, candlesticks, fire tongs, washboards, and pestles. In 1740, two English women, Elizabeth Branch and her daughter Mary, who had a history of assaulting household staff with cooking implements, used a broom to beat to death a servant who returned late from shopping. In the mid-nineteenth century a groom at a farm near Windsor, England, angered that the housekeeper had brought him only a half glass of ale with his supper, struck her with a lard beater, then finished the job with a fireplace poker. An attempt to cover the crime with arson failed. In a notorious 1980 incident in Florida, a woman bludgeoned her husband with a frying pan after poison failed to kill him. These crimes were discovered and the perpetrators prosecuted, but many more such murderers have undoubtedly been successfully hidden behind the kitchen door.

See also **Banquets; Witches' Kitchens**

Further Reading

Cooper, George. *Poison Widows*. New York: St. Martin's Press, 1999.
Jones, Ann. *Women Who Kill*. New York: Holt, Rinehart and Winston, 1980.
Kieckhefer, Richard. *Magic in the Middle Ages*. Cambridge: University of Cambridge Press, 1989.
Nash, Jay Robert. *Encyclopedia of World Crime*. Wilmette, Ill.: Crime Books, Inc., 1990.

KNIVES

The knife, a sharp-bladed cutting tool, is a standard item of cutlery dating to prehistory, possibly to human ancestors who used sharp-edged stones, volcanic glass, and shells for cutting meat. Among primitive peoples living in India and Africa around 200,000 years ago and cooking at fire pits, a chipped flint, obsidian, chert, or shell knife, hand axe, or chopper was the primary—and sometimes only—cooking implement. Along the coasts of Ireland and Norway, around 5000 BCE, Neolithic fishermen carried slate knives for dismembering fish and other seafood. From 3000 BCE, farmers in Lung Shan and Yang Shao, China, and Togaruishi, Japan, were flaking reaping knives for use in harvesting grain.

In the absence of plates, the cutting of food apparently occurred at the mouth. The diner held a large chunk of meat in the teeth and sliced away the portion that was too large to chew and swallow. The Syrian travel writer Poseidonius observed this style of eating among the Celts of Gaul in the mid-second century BCE. Each male carried a table dagger in a small sheath attached to his sword.

Evolution of the Handled Knife

The handled knife represented the next stage in the development of cutlery. In north-central Ohio, paleo-Indians at Sheriden Cave south of the Laurentide Ice Sheet honed and flaked fluted chert scrapers, gravers, and bone cutting tools. The stone was crosshatched at one end, where it could be hafted to a handle or pole. The Ice Age knife appears to have served its maker in preparing meals of long-nosed peccary, vole, porcupine, and caribou. This early knife-making technology flourished in Eurasia, Alaska, Saskatchewan, Washington, Oregon, Montana, Wyoming, New Mexico, and Florida. Among the Thule people of Greenland, the snow knife, formed from sharpened whalebone, was the essential tool for slicing building blocks of snow for an igloo.

In 2000, Albert C. Goodyear, an archeologist and director of research at the University of South Carolina, discovered small stone blades and scrapers at Topper on the Savannah River. These cutting tools date to the period when humans first inhabited the eastern coast of the United States. Into the mid-twentieth century, similar primitive food choppers remained in use among the Biami of Nomad River, New Guinea, giving anthropologists a glimpse of the difficulty of hand-grinding an adze or blade, stone against stone, a time-consuming procedure the tool maker performed in a squatting position.

At Barton Gulch, a valuable archeological site in Montana, early people living in portable shelters depended on knives, scrapers, flaked-edge stones and other primitive implements—bone needles, grinders, mallets—to cut into bite size pieces the plant and animal foods they cooked in an earth oven. At the Shawnee-Minisink site in the upper Delaware Valley of Pennsylvania, a cache of implements yielded a Clovis point knife as well as other knives and scrapers. Australopithecines of southern and eastern Africa fashioned knives and blades from the lower jaws of antelopes, scrapers from upper jaws, picks from horns, and smaller cutting edges from flakes of split bone. By striking and twisting long bones longitudinally, they fashioned a spiral knife blade.

The domestic knife suited multiple demands in the kitchen because the cook split tinder for the fire and reduced fish and animal carcasses into edible portions. Early native Americans of the northwestern coast and Arctic regions used a flensing or stripping knife to flay and rip blubber from walrus and whale carcasses. The Copper Inuit of Labrador formed their utility blades of bone or copper. Whalers removed blubber with an iron flenser, winch, and tackle. At sea, the work progressed on the flensing deck. Another use of the flaying knife was the removal of horn plate or shell from turtles to uncover edible meat. The use of a flensing spade survives among St. Lawrence Islanders, who strip raw skin and blubber to make *muktuk,* an Eskimo delicacy.

Indians used the sharpened shin bones of animals to rip fat, membrane, and edible tissue from the inner side of a deer or buffalo hide. When the French *coureurs de bois* (woodsmen) arrived among the Chippewa, they presented their hosts with gifts of steel knives, the first in the Indians' possession.

As the availability of metal blades freed the Indians from dependence on easily dulled stone, shell, and bone tools, a standard Indian blade, the crooked knife, became a favorite utility or craft knife. Among the Maliseet of New Brunswick, it served as a paring knife or a gouge for shaping wooden bowls, cups, boxes, storage canisters, and trenchers as well as for cutting babiche (thongs), cording, and materials for basket-weaving. The Chipewyan and the Penobscot of Maine and the Naskapi of the St. Lawrence Valley made the knives by lashing a curved steel blade to an antler, bark, bone, or carved wood handle.

In settled parts of the globe, later versions of bronze and iron knives were ubiquitous for the dismemberment of joints and slicing of meats and tough vegetable leaves and tubers, for example, cabbage and kale in Peloponnesian communities, bistort in Denmark, beetroot in Belgium, water chestnuts throughout Europe, and scirpus bulbs in Catal Hüyük (or Catal Hoyük), an Anatolian community dating to 6800 BCE. From the same period at Jericho, a variety of types and sizes of metal blades were unearthed. Villagers at Joya de Cerén, El Salvador, which succumbed to volcanic ash in August 595 CE, valued obsidian cutting tools, which they stored overhead in thatched roofs to keep them out of the reach of children or thieves.

Honed blades were essential to the culinary refinements of the late Roman Empire. In Roman Gaul, one-piece bronze knives served diners whose primary nourishment was meat. To suit a sophisticated and demanding populace of aristocrats in urban Rome, cooks learned to bone fish and quadrupeds without raising a ripple on the skin. In "Trimalchio's Feast," a chapter in Petronius's *Satyricon* (mid-first century CE), the host ended a night of lavish feasting by presenting food "sculptures" that his cook carved from a pig: "a fish out of a sow's belly, a wood pigeon out of bacon, a turtledove out of a ham, or a chicken from the pig's knuckle." (Edwards 1984, 302) In thanks, Trimalchio made a public presentation of a carving set forged from Norican steel and allowed guests to test their sharp edges.

Pointed, finely honed cutlery stored in *nefs* remained in use into the Middle Ages, when cutlers crafted steel blades to fit hafts of crystal, carved antler or ivory, ebony, or silver. (Hartley 1999, 26) The poor made do with wood- or bone-handled knives. The wealthy carried their own paired meat and bread knives in leather cases or sheaths for table use as well as for any occasion of violence that might break out during a meal. Diners would habitually sharpen their blades on a whetstone before entering a banquet hall, both as an aid to dining and protection from attack.

Medieval knights ate with hunting knives and daggers, which became prime commodities for sale or trade. In 1220, John of Garland reported in his Latin *Dictionarius:* "Vidi hodie institorem habentem ante se cultellos ad mensam, mensaculos, et artavos, vaginas parvas et magnas, stilos, et stilaria." ("Today I saw a huckster peddling table knives, carving knives, and daggers, scabbards small and large, styli, and stilettos.") (Rubin 1981, 22–23) By the 1300s, steel blades offered cutlery buyers a sharper edge.

In medieval France, *couteaux de cuisine* (kitchen knives) included such specialty tools as the long-bladed *minchoir* (slicing knife) for the paring of fat. A tradition of reserving pig offal for large and small sausages called *andouille* and *andouillettes* required extensive chopping of meats for filler. The cutting of tripe into strips for dicing or mincing preceded the stuffing of forcemeat into the intestines, which the cook used for casings. A deft turn of the knife during grilling slit open the skin to allow the filler to expand. A more delicate medieval implement was the ivory knife, a salt-serving implement that accompanied salt crushing tools on the sideboard. Unlike metals, ivory was impervious to corrosion by salt.

Cutlery as Status Symbol

In the fifteenth century, John Russell, author of *The Boke of Nurture* (ca. 1450), summarized the types of cutlery the butler or pantler should have on hand. In addition to a sharp bread knife, there should be a smooth-edged knife for squaring the sides of trenchers, which were thick slabs of four-day-old bread that served as meat trays. Platina, author of *De Honesta Voluptate* (On Right Pleasure, 1475), spoke directly to the kitchen staff on the matter of readying cutlery for the table: "Let a servant scrub the knives and sharpen their points so that diners will not be delayed by dullness of iron." (Scully 1995, 173) The wealthy host augmented the standard items of tableware with a *présentoir,* a decorative knife consisting of a broad silver or steel edge and firm handle for selecting choice slices to present to guests at table.

Wynkyn de Worde's *Boke of Keruynge* (Book on Carving, 1508), published from his Fleet Street print shop in London, documented the importance of presentation in food service for royalty. The text opens with a call to the kitchen staff to sauce the capon, dismember the heron, and wing the partridge. Having established meat as the *sine qua non* of the feast, he

addresses butler and pantler, who are beginning on-the-job training with "the pantry knyves, one knyfe to square trencherous loves, an other to be a chyppere, the thyrde to shape to make smothe trenchours." Worde also commands kitchen workers to keep the knives well polished. His concern for shiny cutlery suggests that knives were both implement and adornment to the noble hall. His commentary resurfaced in 1661 in domestic writer William Rabisha's *The Whole Body of Cookery,* which established that the classic carving method from his predecessor's day had remained unchanged.

Knives so completely symbolized manhood and honor that those swearing oaths handed over their implements as a testimony of good faith. Such an exchange occurred in Paris when a landowner donated the site on which Notre Dame Cathedral was built. The knife also served the young courtier as a betrothal gift to his lady. An exchange of carving knives at the altar called for graceful inscriptions and initials on the handle.

Carving became the height of food presentation. In 1581, the Renaissance courtier Vincenzo Cervio's *Il Trinciante* (The Carver) explained how to lift a whole turkey on a fork for a dramatic mid-air carving. By the Tudor era, hosts stocked table service with cased knife sets. The inventory of Henry VIII's utensils described the knife case as "garnished with sundry emeralds and pearls and rubies about the neck and divers amethysts, jacynths and balases upon the foot thereof furnished with knives having diamonds at the ends." (Wilson 1991, 70)

Into the late Renaissance, as more refined table manners replaced the rough cutting and stabbing of food, gentlefolk acquired various styles of domestic cutlery for meals. The practice of wearing personal dining tools in a sheath continued into the time of Louis XIII, a fastidious French monarch who banned weaponry at table after his accession in 1610. To put an end to diners' habitual picking of teeth with sharp pointed knives that might also serve as killing blades, Louis's adviser, Cardinal de Richelieu, offered in their place the forerunner of the modern table knife with rounded end. Some table knives bore a trough in the blade, an adaptation that blurred the distinction between knife and spoon. At the Château de Chantilly as head cook to Louis XIV, the *maître de hôtel* François Vatel spoke highly of the importance of cutlery and stylish carving to the kitchen and serving staffs. He defined the carver as a ranking servant who displayed civility, breeding, and amiability.

Each cutlery user sharpened edges with some type of grindstone or emery wheel, which fit in the hand or on a clamp at the table. A simple knife scouring box packed with straw or grass in oiled sand or pumice offered a sharp edge and no rust in exchange for a daily plunge into the abrasive surface. A variant, the wood knife board, offered a narrow surface covered in brick dust for stropping a kitchen knife up and down. A kitchen steel, like a barber's strop, presented a cross-hatched steel column for toning up a dull edge in the midst of cooking maneuvers. Travelers carried pocket whetstones for improving the edge on multipurpose hunting and utility knives. A grinder in a frame turned by hand or rotated with a treadle to sharpen kitchen knives as well as axes, froes, hoes, and scissors. The knife-cleaning machine, consisting of a frame holding brushes against a drum, produced enough abrasive action against inserted blades to end the tedious and tricky job of sharpening each blade by hand with a whetstone. For city dwellers, cries of the scissors grinder and the tinkle of his bell signaled the approach of a portable grinding wheel and a professional who could bring a new edge to all household cutting tools.

In the Western Hemisphere, cutlery was more rudimentary than its European counterpart. Households in colonial New England survived on two mundane forms of cutlery—the jackknife and the butcher knife. Table etiquette set the standards for carving fish, meat, and fowl. In colonial Quebec, the cutting of bread was a magic moment in family life. With great respect, the head of the household faced the loaf and blessed it by crossing it with the tip of the bread knife, to assure an ongoing supply of bread for the family's well being and survival. Cutting rather than breaking the bread honored the family's integrity and traditions.

One decorative element in the American colonial kitchen was the knife or cutlery box or knife tray, a wooden box with slots for holding cutlery of various sizes and shapes. The lid fastened with a hasp that accommodated a lock for safekeeping. Elaborate versions of the knife box featured marquetry and ivory inlays, family crests and initials, and velvet, silk, or satin linings.

In the late eighteenth and early nineteenth centuries, artful carving of a joint of meat was a skill displayed by the well born. Men taught their sons to slice meat and disjoint poultry at table with panache. After *service à la française* dining came to an end with the introduction of precut servings in the *à la Russe* manner in 1830, carving passed from the host's responsibility to that of the *maître d'hotel*. One of the most famous French carvers, Joseph Dugnol at Taverne Joseph, earned a reputation for understanding how to slice with the grain to produce an elegant, delicate serving. At Tour d'Argent in Paris, Frédéric Delair mastered the carving of poultry, specializing in Rouen duckling.

Carbon steel, with its comparatively soft and easily sharpened edge, replaced lesser metals for knife blades. In 1812, a French cutler named Sabatier registered the trademark for his classic chef's knives, which featured long-lasting steel blades and three brass rivets that secured the pistol-grip handles. More than a dozen firms began to manufacture the gently curved Sabatier-style cutlery. Some imitated the shape and oval logo but cheapened the product.

In pre-industrial societies, the knife retained its importance for domestic duties. On a visit to the Inuit of Cumberland Inlet, Greenland, Captain Charles Francis Hall, author of *Life with the Esquimaux* (1862), commented on the centrality of the knife to Inuit survival. He observed how Inuit men, using snow knives, sliced segments from blocks of ice for shaping into an igloo. In a hot, steamy tent interior crammed with a dozen natives, Hall found each wielding a knife. At first fearful, he realized, "There was no cause for alarm. The knives were not for any warlike or evil purpose. They were being used simply for cutting off strips of seal, to be shoved into the widely-extended mouths of the hungry people before me." (Hall 1970, 139)

When Inuit hunters killed a deer, they used saw, hatchet, and axe to dismember it and returned the venison and moss from the stomach to the kitchen. If the carcass overloaded their *kia* (hunter's boat), they hacked at the saddle, hide, hooves, horns, and skull and bore them home as the most useful parts. When they located an infant seal, they used their knives to remove the milk in its stomach and served the liquid as a delicacy. In a gesture of reverence, they left behind bits from various parts of the animal buried under sod or moss as a gift to nature.

Advent of the Stainless Steel Blade

A major contributor to the cutlery of industrialized nations, Friedrich Krupp launched a family steel-making operation in Essen, Germany, in the late eighteenth century. His son Alfred Krupp entered the business in 1826 at age fourteen after his father's untimely death. In 1912, he produced the first stainless steel for knife blades, simultaneous with the steel process devised by inventor Harry Brearley of Sheffield, England. Brisk sales enabled Krupp to expand his operation to other steel goods.

The demand for well-sharpened implements spawned a host of new products. Introduced in the late 1800s, Knight's patent knife cleaner consisted of a rubber roller inside a mangle-shaped box. Up to eight knives could be accommodated within the hand-cranked whirling device, which purported to revive silver cutlery without harming handles or wearing off the shine. In 1882, Kent's knife cleaner, a wood drum anchored to an iron stand, sold briskly. Cheaper models, including the Davis Excelsior and Spong's, offered a revolving wheel in which the user inserted knife blades. The turning of the crank caused leather inserts to strop the blades. For maximum sharpening, some users added emery powder.

In the domestic boom that followed World War II, homemakers began to think of knives as a serious kitchen investment rather than a mundane necessity. Ads in women's magazines recommended that the buyer of a knife seek out quality from tip to heel. Ekco Products of Chicago advertised high-arc, hollow-ground cutlery for carving and cutting in the kitchen or at the table. Their blades of chrome vanadium steel with hardwood handles gave the cook the appearance of a serious food handler. Various bladed instruments, including the three-bladed, spring-action chopping knife and the multisection pear slicer, allowed homemakers to reduce to a single stroke messy, complicated jobs like dicing, coring, and sectioning. The magnetic knife holder, introduced by R. E. Phelon company in 1947, allowed the homemaker to arrange knives and scissors on a wall-mounted metal strip within convenient reach of work stations.

Late in the twentieth century, African tribes maintained ceremonial knives for special occasions. Among the Maasai of Kenya, slaughtering was a religious and tribal ritual. After fattening cattle on beer, milk, and herbs, they led the chosen bull to a sacred glade out of the eyes of women for slaughter. Before flaying and disjointing, a chosen participant smothers the beast in a blanket. With skilled turns of the knife, the sacrificer channeled the sacred blood into the dewlap for sharing among warriors. For each man, an elder sliced a share of meat and bestowed a blessing. To the south, the Himba of Namibia prepared for a wedding by standing on the throat of a sacrificial beast to choke it before spilling blood and slicing the meat. The bride and other women received the stomach membrane for draping on their heads; other choice cuts went to the community. It was the groom's job to scrape, tan, and trim the hide as a gift to the bride and her mother.

Cutlery manufacture took a new turn toward the end of the twentieth century. Featured in the May–June 1999 issue of *Kitchenware News* was a set of ceramic-bladed folding knives from Boker Baumwerk of Solingen, Germany. Available in three lengths, the blades of these knives come guaranteed to be free of metallic taste and impervious to corrosion, rust, and stains.

Into the twenty-first century, kitchens feature bagel- and egg-slicers, knife holders, magnetic knife strips, sharpening steel, and cutting board surfaces on counter, island, and appliances. An aid to the mutton carver, the *manche de gigot* (mutton sleeve), screws or clamps to the end of the shank to hold it steady during slicing. A Swiss mini-chopper, pumped by hand, minces onions, nuts, and herbs directly into the attached storage container. A multi-purpose blade, the retractable utility cutter from SilverStone, resembles the hemispheric ulu. It features safe inner storage or a nonstick coated blade that minces nuts and herbs and slices pizza and foccacia. The Farberware Farber Peel robo-peeler rapidly strips low and high density vegetables, including tomatoes. German-engineered knives from Böker offer long-lasting precision blades of titanium, which hold their edge six times longer than stainless steel. Lightweight and balanced, they resist bacteria and never rust or stain.

From *Abbate* to Zester

Cutlery continues to star in many kitchen roles, particularly the ubiquitous paring knife, the workhorse implement used for peeling vegetables, skinning peaches, chopping herbs, boning poultry legs and wings, carving garnishes, and segmenting oranges and grapefruits. Special bladed instruments with specific uses abound, from the *abatte* (beater), the thick, double-edged French knife prized for flattening meat, to the zester, a small scraper with scalloped blade for removing the thin outer skin of oranges, limes, and lemons for flavoring salads and desserts.

The baker's bench knife, a rectangular blade topped with a wood grip, is used for dividing yeast dough and scraping wood surfaces. The boning knife, a short, extremely sharp-pointed knife with a narrow blade and a finger guard, is designed for boning or removing waste, fat, or silverskin from meat, poultry, and fish. Related to the boning knife is the Finnish filleting knife, a thin, pliable, extremely sharp blade curved slightly upward for gutting and boning delicate fish and for slicing vegetables and fruits for garnishes.

The long, blunt-ended bread knife, with its fluted, pinked, beveled, or scalloped edge, is meant to cut evenly through hot loaves, cake, and phylo dough with a minimum of crumbling. A version favored for tea in Victorian England is the tea bread knife, a framed blade similar to a hacksaw, which guided slices of bread or cake smoothly through the opening. Another variant, the cake knife, is intended to slice individual servings from a cake without undue crumbling. The butter curler, a serrated knife curled into a tight arc, forms a decorative ribbed butter ribbon from a solid slab of butter. The shovel-shaped slotted cheese slicer shaves thin slices of cheese or form cheese curls for garnishes. Another tool for making garnishes is the garnishing or fluting knife, a thin corrugated or serrated knife prized for segmenting fruit or carving embellishments from vegetables, melons, and other fruits.

One of the most indispensable kitchen tools is the chef's knife, a stocky, medium-sized knife with a broad blade rapidly tapering to a keen point. It peels and slices onions or pineapples and juliennes citrus zest, herbs, potatoes, carrots, celery, leeks, cucumber, radishes, peppers, and the like. The chef's knife peels chestnuts, minces herbs and garlic, and cuts *brunoise*, a mixture of vegetables cut into tiny cubes or shreds. A variant, the Asian chef's knife, curves slightly upward to a sharp tip.

The clam knife, a thick, stubby knife with a three-inch wedge-shaped blade and a rounded end resembling a putty knife, forces open clams at the hinge. Another seafood implement, the crab knife, has a heavy handle for cracking claws and shells and a sharp-pointed blade for routing out the meat. The oyster or clam shucking knife is a sturdy short-bladed knife with a grip handle, heavy bolster or guard, and thumb rest to give the user leverage when forcing the blade into a bivalve's hinge to pry the top shell upward. The operation concludes with running the tip of the blade along the top shell to sever the meat from its ligature without wasting the liquid. Atlantic Coast versions include the steel oyster knife shaped like a chisel, the Boston blade with ovule wood handle similar to an awl, the New Jersey blade resembling an ax mounted on wood, and the New York knife smoothed like a tongue depressor.

The *hachoir* (mincer), or hashing knife, is a broad, sturdy chopping blade of iron or steel, sometimes augmented with multiple blades formed with parallel cutting edges attached by one or two tangs to a wood or tubular steel handle. The ulu, an Eskimo version, resembles the Italian *mezzaluna* (half-moon), a curved blade that rocks or pivots against a curved bowl or tray for chopping vegetables and herbs. The practice of hashing corned beef got its beginning in the 1600s with a variation of the curved French *hache-viande* (meat chopper). A German model pairs stainless steel blades with wood handles.

The electric knife has been a popular kitchen utensil since its invention in 1963. It scores the skin of an uncooked ham, splits cakes into layers, and slices appetizers, roast meats, and layered foods such as quesadillas, phyllo pastry, and roulades, which might be damaged by the pressure of a regular knife.

Significant to the cost and life span of a knife are the length of the tang within the handle, the quality of wood or resin used to fabricate the handle, and the technology for bradding, or fastening the pieces together. Another consideration is the style of the cutting edge, whether an arched bevel or wavy, convex serrations.

A necessary adjunct to an assortment of kitchen cutlery, the cutting board, made of wood, tempered glass, or a rubberized composite material, is a stable, multipurpose surface for all cutting activities, from fine mincing of herbs to cleaving spareribs, fish, and whole poultry. For the sake of proper sanitation, the cutting board should feature a material that can be scoured clean and free of bacteria while maintaining its seasoning. To prevent the flavors and odors of foods cut on the board from lingering and accumulating, cooks scrub it with hot water and antibacterial detergent or bleach solution and rub it down frequently with coarse salt or hydrogen peroxide.

See also **Cleaver; Krupp, Alfred; Parers**

Further Reading

Dart, Raymond A., "The Bone Tool-Manufacturing Ability of Australopithecus Prometheus," *American Anthropologist*, vol. 62, 1960, 134–137.
Erlandson, Keith. *Home Smoking and Curing*. London: Barrie & Jenkins, 1977.
Gentry, Patricia. *Kitchen Tools*. San Francisco: 101 Productions, 1985.
Haedrich, Ken, "Kitchen Companion: Tools of the Trade," *Kitchen Garden*, December 1998/January 1999, 76–77.

KNOX, ROSE

A determined businesswoman and prolific recipe developer, Rose Markward Knox made an enduring contribution to kitchen convenience by marketing and promoting powdered gelatin. Born on November 18, 1857, she was educated in her hometown of Mansfield, Ohio. In the late 1870s, she went to work as a sewer in a glove factory.

Her life took a different direction after her marriage to Charles Briggs Knox, who took an interest in his wife's preparation of calf's foot gelatin. In 1890, the couple used their savings of $5,000 to launch a gelatin business in Charles Knox's hometown of Johnstown, New York, whose tanneries supplied the raw materials essential for making gelatin. Rose Knox occupied herself in the marketing of their product, Knox Sparkling Gelatine, emphasizing its worth as an invalid food and a versatile pantry staple.

To educate cooks on the versatility of gelatin, she compiled *Dainty Desserts for Dainty People* (1896), a forty-one-page pamphlet of recipes from her own kitchen, and distributed a million copies per year. Charles Knox added to their original investment by acquiring the *Morning Herald* and Spim Soap, Ointment, and Tonic. In the early 1900s, he sought out novel ways to promote Knox gelatin, including a company blimp, racehorses named Gelatine Lad and

Gelatine Queen, and ads on the sides of New York state's first horseless carriages—all venues geared to attracting male customers.

A widow at fifty-one, Rose Knox chose to manage the family holdings personally as a means of preparing her sons for the business world. Operating under the name of her son Charles Markham Knox, who was still in school, she revamped the marketing effort, focusing on female rather than male customers.

To expand the business, Knox established laboratory kitchens at her home and at the Mellon Institute in Pittsburgh. Recipes developed in the test kitchens appeared on boxes of gelatin. Knox also issued a series of advertisements, "Mrs. Knox Says," in the guise of advice and published two cookbooks, *Food Economy: Recipes for Left-Overs, Plain Desserts, and Salads* (1917) and *Knox Gelatine Dainty Desserts, Salads, and Candies* (1927). Her emphasis on high nutritional value, low-cost, kitchen convenience, and a sanitary product appealed to U.S. homemakers.

In 1929, Knox, by then a noted business leader and philanthropist, became the first woman to join the American Grocery Manufacturer's Association, of which she was twice a director. After buying half of the distributor Kind and Landesmann in Camden, New Jersey, she organized the Kind and Knox Gelatine Company in 1930. Within six years, she opened a new factory making flavored Knox Jell from the shin bones of Argentine cattle.

Knox was famous for her progressive labor policies, including the forty-hour work week and two-week paid vacations. She earned the respect of the people of Johnstown, many of whom worked for the company. On the proceeds from the business, she purchased a swimming pool for the YMCA, bells and chimes for local churches, a public athletic field, and a home for aged women. She also endowed research into industrial and medical uses of gelatin. In the three years after retiring in 1947 and turning over the business to her son, she continued to play an active role in management. She was still writing new recipes for gelatin at the time of her death on September 28, 1950.

Further Reading

Lovegren, Sylvia. *Fashionable Food: Seven Decades of Food Fads.* New York: Macmillan, 1995.

KOSHER KITCHENS

Kosher, derived from the Hebrew *kasher* (fit, proper), is a term that describes foods prepared according to *kashruth,* or *kashrut* (literally, "fitness"), the Jewish code of dietary laws. A kosher kitchen is one in which *kashruth* is observed. Leviticus, the third book of the

For Passover, observant Jews through the ages have performed a ritual search in kosher kitchens for the crumbs of leavened bread.

Bible, explains the rationale for the dietary laws in terms of obedience: "You shall distinguish between the clean animal and the unclean, and between the clean bird and the unclean....You shall be holy for me, for I, Hashem, am holy; and I have separated you from the peoples to be mine." (20:25–26) To be devout, the orthodox Jew accepts the dietary laws as an essential part of living a sacred life. The Hasidim, the strictest of the faith, insist on *glat* kosher, a particularly fastidious observance of the laws.

Ensuring Food Purity

The dietary laws are set down in the Talmud, the compilation of all Jewish law. A basic precept is that all goods must set aside a tithe. Cooks must separate edible foods from *terefah* (forbidden foods) according to the biblical concept of purity, which is explained in the text called *Hullin* (unhallowed things). Professional food preparers, especially slaughterers, must be devout, clean-living individuals respected in their communities. Dairy products must come from kosher animals.

To assure purchasers of pure food—whether in Israel, Europe, or the Americas, or among the Baghdad Jews, the Ben-Israel community of Bombay, or the Cochin Jews of Kerala, India—rabbis supervise *shechitah* (ritual butchering), which requires a single, quick, painless draw of the knife over the throat of the animal; the law applies to livestock, poultry, wild fowl, and fish with fins and scales. The Torah (the first five books of the Bible) declares swine unclean for two reasons: because they are not cud-chewing animals and because, unlike the herbivorous cattle, goats, and sheep, pigs eat carrion. Scripture also removes from consideration as food horses, donkeys, camels, rodents, carnivores, water mammals, rabbits and hares, cats, sharks, swordfish, eels, rays, sturgeon, predatory fish, reptiles, amphibians, mollusks, crustaceans, and insects. Such forbidden food cannot touch edible food. Inspectors also reject carcasses of kosher animals that fail the test for purity, including animals that were diseased or injured at the time of slaughter, contain defects that violate rules of cleanliness, such as perforated lungs or loose tissue, died a natural death, or were killed by other animals.

Because blood equates with soul, as stated in Leviticus 17:11, any slaughtered animal must be drained of venous fluids before the meat is fit for consumption by the devout. The kosher carcass then receives tags denoting date of slaughter and the identification of a licensed butcher. Meat and dairy foods have to be cooked and served in separate sets of dishes, a procedure observed in kosher kitchens of factories, schools, airlines, hotels, restaurants, and catering kitchens throughout the world.

Foods that pass inspection receive a recognizable seal of approval. In addition to avoiding nonkosher goods, according to *kashruth*, obedient Jews cannot share bread or pastry, milk, cheese, oil, honey, or wine with gentiles, nor can they drink milk or eat dairy products from kosher dairy animals that have been milked by a non-Jew.

Cooks' Responsibilities

Cooks preparing uninspected foods must observe regulations regarding rinsing and soaking non-kosher meats. To purify joints, cooks place the meat in cool water in a pan that has no other purpose than removing blood from meat. The second stage of preparation covers draining the meat, placing it on a perforated board, sprinkling coarse salt on the meat, and allowing blood to drain. Two hours of draining precede three rinses under running water. These strictures are postponed during freezing but must be observed immediately upon the thawing of unkoshered meats.

Meat by-products also come under strict regulation. Cooks must keep bloody bones separate to avoid contaminating koshered portions. Livers are unfit for normal draining. The user must rinse, segment, or score them with a knife before salting and grilling.

The clean kitchen demands meticulous attention to detail, such as inspection of dishes for cracks and chips, of fruit and vegetables for worms and blemishes, and of eggs for blood spots and embryos. Eggs that come from roosterless farms are always edible; eggs from gentile-operated farms are unfit. For the sake of sanitation, food preparers must discard cracked eggs, peeled garlic and onions, and liquids left overnight.

Storage of foods comes under strict rule. One refrigerator may store both kosher and nonkosher foods but only in separate places where containers do not touch. The most discerning kosher cooks may choose to separate fish from dairy and may use a third set of dishes for *pareve* (neutral) food that is neither milk nor meat, such as vegetable oil, honey, cake, cereal, fruit, pastry, dessert, and nondairy beverages. Dishwashing requires separate dishpans, wash cloths, and towels—and, in some households, separate dishwashers—for dairy and meat dishes. Observant Jewish travelers drink from glasses or disposable cups rather than crockery, which may be contaminated.

Precise preparation and consumption, like carefully monitored sacrifices to Yahweh, demand compliance in every detail. Standard preparation of the *challah*, a braided loaf symbolizing the mystical manna that sustained the Israelites during their exodus from Egypt, begins with separating dough into three, six, or twelve lengths for plaiting into a single loaf. If the Hasidic housewife discerns even a drop of water leavening flour or finds matzoh stored with ordinary bread, she discards the ritual bread as useless.

In biblical times, the strictness of kosher kitchens set the Jews apart from their pagan neighbors. The task of keeping kosher was part of the Jewish housewife's unvarying role. The kosher cook allowed no gentile servant to contaminate food. She honored the Sabbath as well as *Rosh chodesh,* the beginning of the month. Sabbath meals beginning late on Friday required that food be cooked in advance for the day of rest, when no fire might be lit in the stove.

Local Traditions

In Ashkenazic tradition—the customs of the Jews of central and eastern Europe—potters marked kitchenware with F for *fleishig* (flesh) and M for *milchig* (milk) to simplify identification of containers used for milk and meat. In Syria, Jews cooked their Sabbath meal in hollow squashes or pumpkins. From Sicily, Jewish exporters introduced Italian cooks to the eggplant, a staple of traditional mainland dishes. From Izmir, wayfarers settling in Venice brought a quick kosher dessert—a fig stuffed with a walnut half.

Sephardic culinary tradition, that of Jews in the Iberian peninsula and Jewish immigrants to Turkey and Greece, relied heavily on puls, rice, lamb, olive oil, and spices. During the late Middle ages, Spanish Marranos, Jews forced to hide their faith to prevent persecution, established a tradition of slow-cooking a Friday night *adafina*, a stew of veal, potatoes, and chickpeas to sustain them during the Sabbath. To identify devout Jews, Catholic Inquisitors forced cooks to add pork or pork grease to the dish as a test of their claims of conversion to Christianity.

During the era of unified Jewish communes in Prague and other European ghettoes, cooks reserved an earthenware pot of *cholent,* or *schollet*—barley with peas or beans and turkey or goose meat, which stayed warm in the municipal house oven for the next day's meals. At noon on Saturday, each family extracted a pot of the mix, wrapped it in a quilt or cozy, and hurried home to serve it hot at the family table.

Ancient Laws in Modern Times

In 1923, the H. J. Heinz Company established purity standards that conformed to the dietary laws. With the assistance of the Orthodox Union, the factory began processing kosher foods, which it stamped with the "Circle U" symbol. The insignia assured buyers that the prepared followed kosher dietary laws. The purity controls extended from items for adult consumption to a line of Hebrew Strained Foods and Hebrew Junior Foods for infants and toddlers. According to data from the Kosher Overseers Associates of America, the oldest U.S. certifying agency, by the late 1990s kosher food service was a $33 billion industry.

The kosher tradition continued into the twenty-first century. In September 2001, Dartmouth College opened a new dining hall observing the dietary restrictions of the Torah for Jewish students—as well as those of the Qu'ran for Muslims. The new arrangement copied programs that accommodated Jewish and Muslim diners on the campuses of Stanford, Syracuse, Brown, and the State University of New York.

See also **Pomiane, Édouard de**

Further Reading

Hautzig, Esther. *The Endless Steppe.* New York: Harper & Row, 1968.
Krekulová, Alena, and Jana Dolezalová. *The Jewish Kitchen.* Edison, N. J.: Chartwell Books, Inc., 1996.
Terry, Michael. *Reader's Guide to Judaism.* Chicago: Fitzroy Dearborn, 2000.
Yossef, Ovadia. *The Kosher Kitchen.* New York: Aharon HaCohen Institute for the Publication and Dissemination of Torah, 1996.

KRUPP, ALFRED

The German metallurgist Alfred Krupp turned a family business into Europe's most respected forge and devised tools for the mass production of tableware. His father, Friedrich, a major contributor to European cutlery launched a family steel-making operation in the factory center at Essen, Germany, a forested area that had supplied iron smithies with charcoal since the earliest days of the industry. Central to his success was the steel-casting method invented by the Sheffield, England, watchmaker Benjamin Huntsman in 1740. Krupp (firm of Friedrich Krupp) flourished in a time of protracted warfare, which created a constant demand for crossbows and arrows and guns.

Alfred, Friedrich's oldest son, entered the business in 1826 at age fourteen after his father's untimely death. Poverty forced Alfred to quit school and forego the usual beginner's apprenticeship. Aided by his mother, Therese, he learned firsthand at the forge. To succeed where his father had failed, he hardened himself to the demands of the business world.

As Prussia thrived economically and militarily, so did Krupp's fortunes. With a staff of seven, he applied a new steam engine to the manufacture of metal implements and specialized in scissors and cutlery. To speed the process of making utensils, he invented the spoon roll, a cast-steel cylinder that stamped out 150 spoons and forks a day. He sold the patent to the Berndorf spoon factory in Vienna and moved on to master the fabrication of metal wagon wheels. In 1912, he produced the first stainless steel for knife blades, which he perfected by surreptitiously studying the steel process devised by the inventor Harry Brearley, also of Sheffield.

Brisk sales enabled him to expand his operation to the manufacture of screw propellers, crankshafts, axles, and other steel goods. Despite a troubled home life—he was abandoned by his wife, Bertha—and a reputation as a poor father, Krupp was a responsible employer who provided his 21,000 workers with pensions, sanitary housing, hospitals, churches, and schools. He was also a public benefactor, establishing soup kitchens to feed the poor. He died of heart failure in 1887. During World War I, his firm's production of rails, switches, and munitions earned him the epithet "cannon king." The firm's oversized cannon acquired the nickname "Big Bertha."

Further Reading

Manchester, William. *The Arms of Krupp*. Boston: Little, Brown & Co., 1968.

Muhlen, Norbert. *The Incredible Krupps*. New York: Henry Holt & Co., 1959.

L

LA VARENNE, PIERRE FRANÇOIS DE

The seventeenth-century French chef Pierre François de la Varenne, the first cookbook writer to achieve an international reputation, introduced the tradition of classic French cuisine. For members of the French upper class during the reign of Louis XIV, dining in a lavish, luxurious style was integral to the display of wealth and privilege. La Varenne was the most renowned and imitated chef of the period. With information and expertise they obtained from the market stalls and vendors of Paris's Les Halles, men such as La Varenne and Nicolás de Bonnefons, the king's *valet de chambre* and the author of *Les Delices de la Campagne* (The Delights of the Countryside, 1654), codified kitchen techniques that have been preserved and passed on by subsequent generations of culinary innovators.

Despite La Varenne's enduring reputation, the details of his life—from his birth in 1618 to his death in Dijon seventy years later—are sparse. He got his start as a *marmiton,* or kitchen servant, in the household of Catherine de Bourbon, the Duchesse de Bar, sister of King Henry IV. By age twenty-two, La Varenne was serving as *écuyer de cuisine* (head cook) to the *maréchal de France,* Chalon du Bled. A serendipitous alliance of La Varenne's genius with opportunity came during the reign of Marie de Médicis, cousin of Catherine, the founder of France's *grand cuisine,* who arrived at the French court in 1533. La Varenne apprenticed in Florence and cooked for the Marquis d'Uxelles, whose name lives on in one of his

chef's creations, duxelles of mushrooms, a seasoning still in use for vegetables and fish.

La Varenne was the first food writer to unify tone and style and the first to speak of his opinions and experience in first person. He pioneered systematizing recipes in cookbooks and added to French cuisine foodstuffs from the New World. A departure from the inexact food writing of the Middle Ages, his *Le Cuisinier Français* (The French Cook), also called *Le Vrai Cuisinier* (The True Cook, 1651) was the first compendium to spell out rules and principles of cooking. The book contained the first French recipe for roux, the fat and flour mix used to thicken sauces. La Varenne flavored his roux with onions and stored it in an earthenware pot.

La Varenne was well known for creating recipes that relieved the dreariness of the meatless meals authorized by the church for Fridays, holy days, and some Wednesdays. He devised popular dishes such as artichokes with hollandaise sauce. He also published *Le Pâtissier Français* (The French Pastry Chef, 1653), the first comprehensive guide to pastry making, which provided additional meatless egg recipes and introduced waffles, *petits fours*, darioles (cream tarts), and puff pastry to the French kitchen. He followed this successful publications with *Le Confiturier Français* (The French Confectioner, 1664) and compiled *L'École des Ragoûts* (The School of Stews, 1725), published posthumously.

Although La Varenne influenced French cooks to abandon over-spicing and parboiling of meats and to return to the fresh herbs of their kitchen gardens, he profited little from a dual career as chef and food writer

Title page to *Le Pastissier François* (1655).

Roman lamp stands and lamps.

and died in poverty. Over time, his classic works remained in circulation, influencing subsequent generations of cooks, including Elena Burman Molokhovets, author of the classic Russian cookbook, *A Gift to Young Housewives* (1861), which included her adaptation of his potage de pigeons aux pois verts (pigeon stew with green peas). In particular, he inspired the English chef Anne Willan, a London Cordon Bleu graduate and author of *La Varenne's Paris Kitchen* (1981) and *My Château Kitchen* (2000). In 1975, she founded L'Ecole de La Varenne (La Varenne Cooking School) in Paris. His legacy lives on in his continuing influence on chefs and in his printed works.

Further Reading

Ballerini, Luigi, "Catherine de' Medici," *La Cucina Italiana*, June–July 1999, 90–91.

Willan, Anne. *From My Château Kitchen*. New York: Clarkson Potter, 2000.

LAMPS AND LIGHTS

Since prehistoric times, humans have sought sources of illumination for domestic tasks that had to be performed after dark or in enclosures lacking natural light. Cave dwellers may have deduced the value of hand-held sources of light when they observed the inadvertent kindling of slivers of wood soaked in animal fat. They applied the technology to the creation of ledge lamps, natural depressions in stones or shells, which they filled with oil, grease, or tallow topped with pieces of tinder lighted with spills from the cook fire. Along the west coast of North America the Tillamook of Oregon lit their homes with fish-head or whale-oil lamps or pitch torches. The Carib, who migrated from the Orinoco Basin into the West Indies, valued the sap of the gommier tree (*Dacyrodes excelsa*) for making torches.

Early Sources of Illumination

At open-air caves and rock shelters, lamps from the Upper Paleolithic era survive in France, Spain, Czechoslovakia, and Germany. The earliest, found in the Grotte de la Mouthe in Dordogne, France, are largely unadorned; only a few have carved handles, perhaps an indication of ritual use. In the third millennium BCE, the Mesopotamian lamp, a simple slipper-shaped holder, burned sesame seed oil with a wool or reed wick.

Around the Mediterranean region from about 1500 BCE, tapering oval lamps, the standard for interior

Lighting the dinner table.

illumination, gave off a weak, unsteady light. Fashioned from pottery or bronze, depending on the household's economic resources, they featured single handles and flattened tops. Users could place lamps on a tripod or suspend them from a wall bracket.

When molding replaced hand throwing around 45 BCE, lamps became more affordable. As described in the architect William Clarke's *Pompeii: Its Past and Present State* (1847), Pompeiians imported the best mass-produced lamps from the island of Aegina: "Bronze lamps, dependent from chains of the same metal, or raised on richly wrought candelabra, threw around the room a brilliant light. Slaves, set apart for this service, watched them, trimmed the wicks, and from time to time supplied them with oil." (Vol. II, 14–15) An improvement over torches and floating-wick pan lights, the molded lamp spread to Gaul and Britain.

In Greek households from around the sixth century BCE, the terra cotta lamp filled with olive oil and fitted with a floating wool or reed wick was the standard for home lighting. For general purposes, the user could mount the lamp on a tall stand to spread light over a large area. In Etruria in the same period, technology produced a bronze candleholder that could be adjusted to suit the position of the user, whether seated or standing.

Around 300 BCE, the Chinese achieved sophisticated lighting technology with the evolution of the first whale oil lamp equipped with a wick made of asbestos, a soft rock that shredded into long-lasting fibers. During the reign of Chao of Yen, coastal people extracted oil from whale blubber and, as a gesture of fealty, donated it to the king for lamp fuel.

In Roman Britain, householders relied on candles and oakum- and flax-wicked oil lamps, which burned vegetable oil. As described by the first-century BCE Roman architect Vitruvius, oil lamps soiled wall hangings, statuary, and cornices. In return for the meager amount of light they shed, they required continual tending by slaves, who were kept busy filling the lamps, trimming wicks, and removing the oily soot.

Light from Oil

Petroleum technology developed much later than candles, rush lights, and vegetable oil lighting. The Roman encyclopedist Pliny the Elder, in *Natural History* (ca. 77 CE), makes the first mention of crude oil as a light source. In Roman settlements at Antioch, the wealthy could afford to light evening banquets with hanging fixtures called polycandelons, circular brass or iron frames that supported multiple conical oil holders. After slaves lit the oil, they suspended polycandelon from a ceiling mount with a tripartite harness. In the late eighth century at the height of the Islamic kingdom during the reign of Harun ar-Rashid, homemakers threaded oil lamps with asbestos, which they called *hajar al-fatila* (wick-stone). The use of petroleum oil as fuel reached China in the Middle Ages, when homeowners soaked straw in gasoline and burned the mass in lamps.

The Irish valued cod, seals, sharks, and whales for liver oil, a smelly source of lamp fuel. Along the west coast, they salted the livers and sun-dried them to extract the oil, which they bottled and corked. To light kitchen chores, they placed lamps on the fireplace hob or fitted scallop shells in wall boxes to hold burning

LAMPS AND LIGHTS

lamp fuel. When moving about the house, they dipped peeled rushes into liver oil and carried them aloft.

For the English in the Middle Ages, the availability of good sources of lighting determined how much people strayed from home in the evening and how safe they felt returning home after "day dapple" from the barn- or hen yard. (Wolkomir & Wolkomir 2001, 40) In hard times, homeowners made frequent turns about the lean-to keeping watch for firewood thieves. On a foggy night, tow bound with flax trimmings and hemp and soaked in resin or beeswax produced a torch or flambeau set in an iron holder. Hemlock stems, reed mace, or cow parsley also served as torches.

In the homes of wealthy landholders, a large central cook fire also illuminated the great hall. Down long corridors and into courtyards, torches on iron spikes or cressetts (iron baskets) burning oil or pitch added brightness, particularly during increased nighttime activity. A precursor to the brass candelabra was the candle beam, a hanging wooden bar on which homemakers set wax tapers.

The poor made do with rush lights formed of porous peeled rushes dipped in grease pans or in tallow mixed with beeswax for firmness. Even after air drying to reduce moisture, these produced a sputtering, unsteady light. The frail quality of light greatly limited work during the short daylight hours of winter. Poor women sometimes coordinated their spinning time to make the most of shared illumination. Friends working at a sewing circle could turn the rotating rush light toward their work as they searched for a dropped needle or gathered threads into fine French knots. In churches and manor houses, candles, called wax lights, provided illumination for worship and social engagements. For less affluent homes, itinerant candle-dippers molded a lower quality candle from the clarified cooking fat collected by thrifty householders.

Off the California coast, the Catalina Island Indians quarried soapstone and carved it into lamps. The early Eskimo and Chinook filled a *qulliq* or *koodlik,* an oval soapstone (or steatite) lamp, with oil extracted from whale or seal blubber or from beluga or caribou fat. The oil illuminated and heated an igloo, dried clothes, and cooked. To slow the flame, the user suspended blubber overhead, allowing drops of oil to ooze onto the grass or moss wick, or adjusted the wick's air supply. While the lamp burned, the user could place above it a layered rectangular frame that held a cook pot and, on the tier above, damp clothing.

Lanterns, Candle Holders, and Chandeliers

In sixteenth-century England, while the poor tolerated fish oil lamps, the homes of the privileged displayed candles borne in silver sconces and brass candlesticks. During the next century utilitarian candleholders evolved into art objects as craftsmen emulated Holland's multibranch candelabrum of brass, wrought iron, or gilded wood. High-quality candelabrum came with matching candlesnuffers and shades of horn.

In late seventeenth century Europe, flaming pieces of wood—hornbeam, fir, and pitch pine (*Pinus rigida*)—lit the nighttime hours. Subsequent decades introduced further embellishment of candleholders, girandole wall brackets, and looking-glass wall lights and decorative lanterns with horn panels to shield the flame from drafts. Fragile Venetian glass provided tiers of candleholders bedecked with faceted pendants to enhance the glow. Outdoors, iron lanterns required constant care and cleaning to assure illumination along paths and between hedges. In ballrooms and foyers of large estates, sparkling chandeliers adorned social gatherings. These too required constant care; house servants lowered the fixtures for soaking in hot water, scraping of spilled wax, and polishing.

Not-So-Romantic Candlelight

For colonists in New England and Virginia, slices of pinewood augmented candles and rush lights but exuded a messy trail of pitch. To make the most of light and minimize tar droplets and smoke, the user positioned the pine knot on a flat stone and set it in the fireplace. Some table tops held boxes or balconies on which householders stored rushes for replenishing house lights.

Throughout the American colonies, the only light available for kitchen chores was daylight, thus limiting the workday to the hours between dawn and dusk. Candles, too precious to be used for everyday tasks, illuminated entertaining. To augment light from the fireplace, the householder might shape tin into a sconce or wall bracket to which a candleholder attached. Mirrors and reflectors further spread light from the source. Candle stands crafted from wrought iron in the late 1600s allowed the user to move the light source and raise and lower the candle as it burned down. The poorest, smelliest, and least dependable light came from the standard rush lights, made from tules or rushes dipped into cooking fat.

When the whaling industry flourished, comfortable middle-class families in late-Regency England and the Americas relied on whale oil lamps, formed of a tin, pewter, or brass base topped with a globe that enhanced

352

the light, channeled smoke and heat upward, and protected against fires. The change in technology came at a stiff price, however, as whale oil cost two dollars per gallon. Lamps burning spermaceti oil were available in Boston near the North Battery in 1758. These lights had numerous shortcomings: sperm oil was tricky to light and required a short wick to heat the viscid oil, which tended to thicken quickly as it cooled. Another room brightener was the lacemaker, or shoemaker's lamp, in which a water-filled globe intensified the light and cast shadows on walls and furnishings.

On the frontier, pioneers resorted to candles, pine knots, lard-oil lamps, or saucer lamps, dishes of cooking fat or coon oil topped with a twisted rag or rush wick. With this meager, oily glow, housewives completed kitchen chores and sat down after supper to mend clothing, knit mittens or dish cloths, and repair tarps and leather harnesses. Lanterns were less drippy but required daily washing and rewicking. Moreover, a person carrying a lantern to a window or door ran the risk of injury from flying glass if a gust of wet air or rain struck the hot globe and caused it to shatter.

For the poor, the lard or fish oil Argand lamp, invented in 1782 by the Swiss engineer Francois-Pierre Aimé Argand and manufactured by Matthew Boulton of Birmingham, satisfied ordinary household needs. The Argand light consisted of a substantial reservoir, central draft, and glass chimney shading steady, smoke-free illumination from a hollow wick, which maximized the amount of oxygen feeding the flame. Argand's lamp assured even combustion of lard, fish oil, vegetable oil, and mineral oils.

Several other affordable innovations of the mid- to late 1800s, as well as new styles and fuels for the wealthy and upper middle class, rapidly changed home illumination. In 1850, the same year that James Young invented an oil lamp fueled by liquefied paraffin, the kale oil or rapeseed oil lamp, called the party light or Colza lamp (from the French and Italian name for rapeseed) came on the market. The lamp held a vinegar-soaked cotton wick dipped in a bright-flamed vegetable oil. One flexible version, the peg or socket lamp, could be moved from room to room and set into a candle socket.

Gaslight Comes of Age

Gas lamp fuel began illuminating London homes by the 1850s, when gas chandeliers graced parlors and front halls. Servants raised and lowered them by means of a water-slide or counter-weighted rise-and-fall system, which permitted easy cleaning. The most ornate attached to a hollow gas pipe that emerged from a circular ceiling medallion. Globes and shades mimicked the shapes of those on Regency-era oil lamps, but the new gas lights required no bulky fuel reservoirs.

Following the discovery of petroleum in Ontario in 1857 and the drilling of the first commercial oil well in Titusville, Pennsylvania, fossil fuels began to supplant animal and vegetable oils. Gaslight was economical, and householders liked the clean, bright, odorless combustion, which enabled cooks to continue working on winter afternoons when natural light faded early. Cities sprouted oil lamps and gas lamps, which were twelve times stronger than earlier sources of light, and hired more police to replace the traditional night watchman.

In Catharine E. Beecher and Harriet Beecher Stowe's *The American Woman's Home, or Principles of Domestic Science* (1869), the text advises, "It is poor economy to use a bad light." (Beecher and Stowe 1994, 362) They listed different types of fuels and commented on each, noting that gas was cheapest, but an Argand lamp burning sperm oil was the best. They conceded that kerosene lamps would suffice where mediocre light suited household needs.

To ensure proper lighting for various needs, they recommended that homemakers keep a shelf of lamps, including a reading lamp, lamps with handles for carrying, and broad-bottomed metal kitchen lamps that did not tilt. They warned that kerosene lights were a mixed blessing—along with providing a strong flame, they were a source of explosions. For safety's sake, they suggested that homeowners test the oil: "Pour a little into an iron spoon, and heat it over a lamp until it is moderately warm." (Ibid., 363) If the vapor ignited readily, it was too volatile for safe use.

Thomas Fell and John Ulrich's standing or hanging angle lamp, which replaced center draft lighting in 1893, created no shadow as it replaced the top-mounted burner above the font with a movable burner set on a hinge. The user could lift off the bowl and refill it without extinguishing the flame. In 1895, Louis Comfort Tiffany, an interior designer and painter, began production of bright-hued glass shades, to which he added shimmer by injecting dye into molten Favrile glass and setting it at an angle within a lead matrix.

Relief from the smoky, sooty lamp and its wayward wick and breakable fuel chamber finally arrived with the advent of electric lighting. The U.S. inventor Thomas Edison pioneered the carbonized cotton filament at his laboratory in Menlo Park, New Jersey, in 1879. From a light with a forty-five-hour life span, Edison's staff moved on to bamboo filaments lasting more than twenty-two times as long. The English chemist Joseph Wilson Swan, patented his own version in 1880, an incandescent bulb lighted by a nitro-cellulose carbon thread. The two inventors gave up fighting for rights

LAMPS AND LIGHTS

in the courts and established Ediswan, the logo for the Edison and Swan United Electric Company, established in 1883. The first electric station, built in New York City on Pearl Street in September 1882, provided service to one small neighborhood, enabling homeowners to illuminate their residences with flame-free, clean, odorless, and controllable lighting.

Illuminating the Twentieth Century

By 1900 the Sears, Roebuck catalog was advertising a full line of home lighting devices, from their floral-decorated bowl and globe at $6.95 to a glass hand lamp for 23 cents. There were desk lamps, kitchen fixtures, and light sources for the dining room. In the latter category, a patented four-lamp bronze chandelier with automatic extender bar offered gas burners that the user could light and trim with an adjustment to the globe or chimney, thus lessening worries about breaking the glass components. Highlighted among some forty-four catalog models was the Juno Store and Hall Lamp, a 400-candle power shaded lamp with bowl and chimney set in a brass or nickel frame on an automatic spring extension for a $3.75.

Rapid development of the home lighting market resulted in such innovations as the rheostat light dimmer, a feature of Frank Lloyd Wright's Robie House, built in Chicago in 1908. The following year, General Electric began producing Osram bulbs, a German invention employing tungsten filaments. These economical globes used at least 50 percent less electricity than bulbs with carbon filaments. By the 1920s, electric homes had become common in industrialized nations. For the rural poor living far from power plants, however, oil lamps and lanterns remained in service.

Advice on home lighting became a standard subject in U.S. women's magazines. An article in the February 1925 issue of *Good Housekeeping,* explained the desirability of kitchen lighting that did not cast shadows on work surfaces. Where ceilings were low, the author advised placing small lights with shades over sink, cabinet, and range to augment the central ceiling light.

The marketing of phosphor-coated fluorescent bulbs, invented in 1859 by a French physicist Alexandre Edmond Becquerel and perfected by the German glassblower Heinrich Geissler and the English chemist Sir William Crookes in the late 1930s, further diversified lighting choices for the kitchen with a bulb up to five times more efficient than the Edison bulb. For large spaces, plastic sheets mounted in frames covered fluorescent fixtures, creating a luminous ceiling. An

icon of modern lighting design, George Nelson's 1956 vinyl bubble lamp, manufactured by Howard Miller Clock Company, consisted of a utilitarian bullet-shaped shade supported on wrought-iron legs. Over work spaces and tables, bubble lights suspended from the ceiling could be raised and lowered easily by a counterweight system and spared surfaces below from the clutter of lamps.

Following World War II, the issues of proper home lighting continued to occupy the pages of women's magazines. Anne Landor, staff interior designer for *Woman's Home Companion*, made specific recommendations for improvements. Over the food preparation area, she suggested a louvered fixture housing two fluorescent tubes, which would shed bright, unshadowed light. Under the cabinet at the baking area, she proposed an under-cabinet fixture. For maximum illumination for rinsing vegetables and washing dishes, she chose shaded lamps attached to cabinets at either side of the sink. The halogen lamp, pioneered in the 1960s, cast brighter light than its predecessors but was more fragile.

Brighter Tomorrow

Advances in lighting in the 1980s and 1990s improved the cooking environment by illuminating work surfaces and control panels without glare, a major cause of eye fatigue and headache. Cool fluorescent overhead lights and panels maintained excellent light without the heat generated by conventional electric bulbs. Another improvement, incandescent bulbs in exhaust fans over stoves, illuminated the burners and helped cooks avoid spills, splashes, and burns. Under-cabinet lighting in the form of strips or panels contributed to the brightening of countertops, providing cooks with increased visibility for chores such as slicing, cutting, and chopping.

At the turn of the twenty-first century, the lighting industry focused on combining high performance with energy conservation. One innovation, the compact fluorescent lamp, burned brighter than traditional bulbs without producing more heat, required less electricity, and outlasted other bulbs. It was considerably more expensive, however. Because of growing concerns about the costs of energy, along with anxiety over supply and possible shortages, this type of product seemed likely to light kitchens of the future.

See also **Candles; Electric Cookery and Appliances**

Further Reading

Bilkadi, Zayn, "The Land of the Naphtha Fountain," *Aramco World*, September–October 1995, 26–33.

Howard, Bryan P., "Piercing the Darkness: Terracotta Oil Lamps in Roman Gaul," *Athena Review*, Vol. 1, No. 4, 83–85.

Wolkomir, Joyce, and Richard Wolkomir, "When Bandogs Howle & Spirits Walk," *Smithsonian*, January 2001, 38–44.

LAUNDRY

When early humans began protecting their bodies with garments, they produced a demanding chore—cleaning the clothes that became soiled in the course of everyday activities. The first clothes washers were deep freshwater holes formed in streams where water tumbled from rocks into depressions in the sandy streambed. Grit became a natural washboard for launderers who stood knee-deep in water for scrubbing and rinsing. Roman house servants took laundry to the *fullonica* (wash house), where launderers applied fuller's earth, a fine-grained detergent clay, and aluminum silicates that removed grease and soil from household linens and clothing. The poor washed at home in buckets and draped their clothes in sunshine to dry.

Tubs and Paddles

Before laundry moved to the kitchen, washing was often inconvenient. In France, washerwomen usually worked over the communal battling stone in a shed at the village wash place; Dutch and British clothes washers scrubbed their laundry at the farmstead well or pump. The process of clothes washing, called "bucking the laundry," may have moved into the home when the first coopers shaped iron hoops to bind wood staves. In the same type of tubs and barrels they used for food storage, housekeepers dyed, soaked, and laundered their linens. Heavy tablecloths, covers, and towels went to the wash tub in a buck basket and from there into a buck tub. The dirtiest went in first, with the least soiled capping the stack.

In England, as described by the domestic historian Dorothy Hartley, the cottage housewife poured water into the laundry tub and agitated the soaking mass of cloth with a buck stick or a posser, a cone on a stick that produced suction in the manner of a drain plunger. The Irish launderer trampled dirty clothes underfoot or beat them with a *slis* (bat or battledore), the forerunner of the dolly pin, a stir stick for laundry tubs that removed stains, odors, and creases. The water extractor, a Welsh device invented in 1669, wound clothes onto a wood roller to squeeze out moisture. Scandinavian models often bore painted images and carved handles. The Irish *ley*, or soaking solution, of bran cleaned chintz hangings by swelling the underfibers and lifting the dirt. A stronger *ley* of soda removed embedded grease from linens. A *ley* composed of an acid plant, wood ash, and urine removed stains from sheets, which required boiling for maximum cleaning. A tap at the bottom of the buck tub let the water drain into the underbuck. From there, the launderer recycled the wash water over the wet wash. The process ended with the launderer vigorously pummeling the wet cloth over a batting stool with an ash stick or paddle before hanging pieces to dry with pins, which were either whittled at home from wood scrap or bought from gypsy peddlers.

Special goods called for individual handling. Wine stains on tablecloths and ink or dye in kitchen towels whitened in buttermilk or skim milk mixed with vinegar and sorrel. Butchers' aprons steeped clean in

Laundry wash tub and wash board
right of fireplace

Wringing Laundry, 1941.
[© *Library of Congress, Prints and Photographs Division (LC-USF34-039081-D)*]

salted water. Bedding, too, demanded the drying of feather ticks in the oven.

The job of the whitester (or whitster) was to rinse linen in running water and a whitening agent, such as buttermilk, chloride of lime, or sulfur fumes. Because wet linen was stiff and heavy, the task required the strength of at least two people. After a "firsting," a "rench," and "seconding," they took the wet linen outdoors and spread it flat on grass to dry and bleach in the sun. Linen ruffs and the caps and bonnets worn by kitchen staff needed wood, bone, or steel poking sticks—also called peck-a-dillers, piccadillas, and piccadillies—to hold their shape during drying. Instructions for fabric care dominated the text of domestic handbooks of the thirteenth and fourteenth centuries, such as John of Garland's *Dictionary* (1220) and the anonymous *Menagier de Paris* (The Goodman of Paris, ca. 1394).

Launderers left kitchen towels and table napery to soak in a wood trough in a solution of water, wood ash, and caustic soda. Essential tools for the task

included an iron beater, lye mixed with grease for soap, and a lye tub, washboard, and slick stone for smoothing linens, which were bleached separately from other clothes. Housewives developed kitchen recipes for starch or adapted existing formulations based on available stiffening agents. Early applications of potato, rice, milk, gum arabic, anatto, and glue starches proved unsatisfactory. One English inventor and dressmaker, Anne Turner, concocted a yellow starch, which she cooked over the stove. The quality of her work fostered a steady kitchen business. For her complicity in the 1613 murder of Sir Thomas Overbury, she was hanged four years later wearing one of her impeccably starched ruffs.

In Restoration England, several times a year, house staff performed a bucking, a general washing of linens. Where family finances permitted, the mistress hired a laundress for the occasion; in poorer homes, the lady of the house joined her maid and daughters for a job that filled the kitchen with steam and the fragrance of laundry soap. Workers pinned clean linens to clotheslines or

LAUNDRY

dried them on fragrant shrubs planted by the kitchen door specifically for their fresh scent.

In the United States, housewives followed a weekly wash schedule rather than the once a month or once a quarter wash style of Europeans. The invention of the scrub board in 1797 and the mechanical wringer in 1847 eased some of the drudgery and enabled housewives to work in the tight space available in small kitchens.

In American colonial and frontier times, laundry might be done indoors by the fireplace in winter. In warm weather, the task usually required extending kitchen work to the yard, where an iron kettle suspended over a fire heated water for the wash tub. The housewife added kitchen-made soft soap and bleach, concocted of birch ash and water, and stirred clothes with a pole. Heavily soiled items needed boiling. Harder rubbing called for a scrubbing stick, a wood slab that preceded the wooden washboard, which offered a wide panel of ridging for lightly soiled clothes and narrow ridging on the opposite side for the dirtiest clothes. Above the rising heat from the kitchen fireplace, stout poles supplied the launderer with an indoor drying rack that doubled as a place to dry pumpkin rounds or festooned beans and apple slices.

The screw press and box mangle applied the screw, rachet wheel, and rolling pins to the job of smoothing linens and opened a new field of endeavor for the professional launderer. Inventor Rodger Rodgerson patented his washing machine in England in 1780; in 1797, an American slave trader, Nathaniel Briggs of New Hampshire, sought his own patent for a laundry scrubber.

In England, Harrods department store offered a refurbishing service for worn mangles. At Shugborough Hall, Staffordshire, in 1810, the staff launderer cranked a mangle purchased from Baker of London. The device remained serviceable for more than a century. During this period of shift from hand labor to machines, the Royal Navy continued to issue mangle bats for smoothing uniforms.

Laundry exertion changed little after the invention of the Cataract paddle-wheel washer, which the U.S. engineer John Schull of Moreland, Pennsylvania, pioneered in 1831 and J. Picken of Birmingham, England, sold in 1858; in 1860, Torpedo Washers of Huddlefield, England manufactured a conical churn washer. However, as standards of hygiene rose during the Industrial Revolution, so, too, did the techniques for cleaning and deodorizing linens with purer water and more efficient soaps and detergents.

In Ireland, the chore became a test of respectability for the housewife, who ferried wash water to the kitchen tub from a community cistern or standpipe and

rinse water from a rain barrel. The job was woman's work, shared by their sons until they reached their teens. Washing in the family's zinc bathtub set on kitchen chairs necessitated the heating of pots of water on the stove and the boiling of sheets and towels. In the poorest neighborhoods and tenements, women passed on their used wash water to the less fortunate. The real drudgery of washing came with lifting, hand wringing, spreading or stretching, and drying. Given Ireland's climate, evaporation of moisture from wet laundry could take days in a peat-heated kitchen. In warm, breezy weather, clothes dried in an afternoon. When the weather turned damp or rainy, women set up chairs near the fire for spreading linens, hung them across the kitchen on clothes horses at ceiling level, or strung them on lines attached to pulleys over the heat of the kitchen stove.

In 1858, a Shaker inventor, David Parker of the Canterbury commune devised a wash mill, an improvement on the washing machine invented by Nicholas Bennett of New Lebanon. The device connected six tubs in a row. At the center, a water-powered handle agitated dashes. The mill won a gold medal at the 1876 Philadelphia Centennial Exposition. Prized for the quality of its workmanship, it was a favorite at schools and orphanages and sold to hotels in Boston, New York, Philadelphia, and Washington, D.C. Yet, for all its ingenuity, hand filling and emptying, and positioning clothes in the water and removing them for drying involved considerable effort. Simultaneously with the invention of the wash mill came the bottling of household ammonia, which enhanced laundering and dishwashing by cleaning brushes, glass, and silver.

Rural and poor launderers heated brass vats of water on the kitchen hearth over a low charcoal fire. Into the soaking clothes, the housewife or laundry servant inserted a posser or posher cone on a handle, T-handled wash punch with cylindrical base, or a dolly pin, a more effective four-legged pegged staff that was the forerunner of the spiral agitator. Shaped like a club, the wooden shaft, rotated from above by a crossbar, applied a grooved end to the clothes for mangling and twisting. Draining the water through a bottom spout preceded boiling in a copper wash tub and three more rinses to remove harsh residue. An end to washday arrived after stain removal with scouring balls, draining, wringing, and draping clothes on bushes, in grass, or across hemp rope. A photo of a Detroit tenement district revealed so many wash lines extending from kitchen windows to flats across the alley that the area seemed decked with a variety of flags. Some items profited from tie-drying, which creased the length naturally to give a crepe effect.

Vendors of clothes props recycled poles from the shipyard or timber works and hawked clothesline supports made of deal or pine. Those who could not afford props relied on the crotched stick, which fit into a slot in the floor for support. The clothespeg, or clothespin, developed from a home-whittled U to a turned peg, either bound with a thong or length of tin or fitted with a metal spring for tighter hold and into a high-tech spring clip.

The first mechanized washing machines had levers that forced a conical plunger into the wash tub. According to Ross Murray's *Modern Householder: A Manual of Domestic Economy in All Its Branches* (1870), advertisers of the mangle, invented around 1850 and patented as the Home Washing Machine & Wringer, assured home launderers that the device was a cheap and pleasant way to do the wash at home rather than risk infection by sending clothes and linens out to a professional laundry. The wringer device applied a series or parallel rollers, which forced dirt from clothes as the user cranked them through. Such strenuous labor taxed even the most robust launderer and worsened upper respiratory diseases already exacerbated by coal-fired water boilers. Clamped to washtubs, Scandinavian mangles were no harder on garments than pounders, the long corrugated clubs on poles that worked the clothes up and down by means of suction. Mangle makers increased the action by boring holes into the surface of the club. The first poleless and clubless washing machines were the invention of tinkerers who added baffles to a square box to hold clothes while the washer applied a mangle or dolly. A variant was the cradle, a tub on legs that the washer rocked back and forth to agitate the contents. The centrifugal drying machine introduced new technology to the process. A cylinder attached to a hand crank, the updated drying machine forced water from the circling wash in the style of a cream separator.

The smoothing board preceded metal irons as a means of taking wrinkles from clothing. A long scalloped or ribbed and slightly arched board with a handle or grip at one end, it allowed the laundry worker some leverage against stiff sheets, towels, bed testers, and curtains. After furling clothing on rods, the user rolled the smoothing board over items in a laborious pressing of damp cloth. The friction dried pieces as it compressed them.

During the California gold rush of 1849, males had to fend for themselves in domestic matters. For washing the grimy work clothes in which they lived and slept, they carried heaps of pants, vests, longjohns, and shirts to streams and rivers, where they scrubbed both garments and themselves. Probably from Indians or Latinos, they learned to dig a native lily bulb, possibly camas root or bear grass, as a natural laundry soap.

For drying, they spread wet garments over bushes or draped them beside campfires. One enterprising miner turned to a donkey-powered machine in 1851. His crude laundromat could wash twelve shirts per load. For ironing, they filled copper braziers with charcoal, in which they heated flatirons or sadirons.

Nineteenth-century drying techniques entailed erecting frameworks fitted with tenterhooks for stretching wet fabrics back to their original shape, a system that consumed kitchen space. The application of weights to each piece completed the smoothing process without ironing. Pieces that did not fit on the frame had to be smoothed with a flat iron heated on the kitchen stove.

For those who could not afford servants, laundry continued to demand hard kitchen labor. Only the wealthy could pay such exorbitant prices as those demanded by the Old City Laundry of Bridgeport, Connecticut, in 1878–79, where a tablecloth cost between 5 and 10 cents to launder and napkins, 2 cents each. (Cowan 1983, n. p.)

Primitive Machines

An Indiana manufacturer of corn planters, Bill Blackstone, made the first geared washing machine in 1874. To a wood tub, he added six peg legs and equipped it with a hand-cranked mechanism that agitated clothes in soapy water. On his wife's recommendation, his company, the Blackstone Corporation, built more models and sold them for $2.50. The new device spawned 2,000 imitations within the year. Users stored the heavy machines on the porch or in a lean-to and ferried them into the kitchen for weekly laundry.

In 1882, the electric iron divorced the last step of the laundry process from the kitchen stove or fireplace. Invented by New York electronics expert Henry W. Seely, the electric iron contained two carbon rods that carried current. Because it operated on the principle of arcing, the sizzling spurts of energy terrified users, even though the wood handle attached to the cast iron base protected them against burns or electrocution. The balky appliances also drizzled smoldering bits of carbon that burned pinholes in cloth. Alternatives to Seely's iron included the gas iron, equipped with a smoking chimney, or one of several heavy electric models from Germany.

The primitive washing machines offered in the 1900 Sears, Roebuck catalog characterized the state of laundry work at the beginning of the twentieth century. The eighteen different models varied from the Anthony Wayne tub and flywheel, the Virginia Rotary Washer with circling pin wheel, and the St. Louis Washer with cylindrical crank shafts to a white cedar electric washer with galvanized gears, the only plug-in model on the two-page spread. The washing machine offered multiple applications in addition to simply washing clothes—soaking, stain removal, deodorizing, and dyeing.

In 1904, Adolf Schulthess expanded the productivity of his Zurich plumbing business by manufacturing a washing machine. The first model failed due to its primitive design. Three years later, the company pioneered Europe's first hand-operated spin-drying model, which used centrifugal force to remove water from wet clothes. The firm moved away from domestic laundry devices to produce heavy-duty machinery for commercial use, including a single unit washer-dryer.

In 1908, when washing machines were still out of reach of lower-middle-class and poor women, Sears, Roebuck featured a host of items in their catalog to simplify and streamline hand laundry chores: solid copper-lidded wash boilers for heating on the stove, reinforced brass washboards, nickel-plated flat irons sold; charcoal-stoked irons; and frames for heating irons. A five-part set at 96 cents grouped three polished nickel-plated sad irons and detachable handle and sturdy stand. More expensive offerings included a ball-bearing Superba drum washing machine for $6.38. The catalog featured schematic drawings of the tub interior and agitator and a line drawing of a prim, curly-mopped child operating the machine with one hand.

In 1912, environmental chemist Ellen Henrietta Richards and her coauthor Sophronia Maria Elliott emphasized the importance of effective home cleaning in *The Chemistry of Cooking and Cleaning*. Concerning water for laundry, the text warns that cistern water tends to be softer than well water but carries contaminants from shingles, paint, and mossy roofs. They also explained how ground water, hardened with lime and magnesia compounds, formed hard curds on hands and fabrics and wasted soap.

The American Heating company in Detroit brought out a chrome-plated iron in 1912 that sold well on both sides of the Atlantic. After the invention of the variable thermostatic control, Proctor-Silex began marketing an improved iron in 1926. That same year, the Eldec Company developed a steam iron, forerunner of the popular Steam-O-Matic, which came on the market in 1938 and quickly sold to women who hated the hot, miserable job of sprinkling and smoothing cotton clothes and linens. In larger homes, restaurants, and institutions, domestic servants operated electric ironers, pressers, or roller ironers, which cranked fabrics across a hot cylinder.

Introduction of Automation

The automatic washer freed the homemaker from drudgery and improved the supply of clean clothes and fresh linens to people at all economic levels. The first electric model was the invention of engineer Alva John Fisher in 1907 and appeared on the market under the Thor logo produced by Chicago's Hurley Machine Company. His chain-driven apparatus with galvanized drum and power wringer spelled the end of hand, steam, and gas-powered models as well as washer treadmills turned by dogs, sheep, or ponies. In 1911, Upton Machine Company, forerunner of Whirlpool, began producing electric wringer washers, which took up less kitchen space and human energy than hand-cranked models. Simultaneously, Maytag of Newton, Iowa, and Winnepeg, Canada, founded in 1893, replaced its hand-cranked Hired Girl and Pastime washers with the company's first electric model and perfected a gasoline model four years later. In 1922, the company's engineers devised a streamlined rectangular aluminum model, the Gyratator, fitted with a paddle agitator. The establishment of commercial laundries equipped with large electric washers and ironers offered employment to women during the boom years before home washing machines replaced professional services.

A two-page spread in the 1923 Sears, Roebuck catalog introduced the electric washer, which came in a variety of sizes and shapes. The boxy Allen washer with swinging wringer, selling for $89.50, featured an oscillating wood cylinder for rocking clothes clean without staining them. For $59.95, the customer could choose a wood tub dolly type Liberty washer, which updated an antique apparatus by attaching it to an electric motor with external belts that powered drive wheels. At an investment of $117.50, the homeowner could choose an engine-driven power washer, a two-tub model with appended wringer and motor out of the way beneath the frame. Line drawings picture a kitchen worker pulling the strap starter, wringing clothes as they passed from one tub to the other, wringing the wash once more into tubs set on a folding frame at the back, and completing the wash with another wringing as clothes moved from rinse to bluing water.

In March 1925, Katharine A. Fisher, the director of the Good Housekeeping Institute, compiled a detailed five-page spread on scientific methods of laundering. The text summarized labor-saving advancements and fabric-sparing methodology for delicate garments. Schematic drawings pictured oscillating and cylinder washers, suction cup machines, paddle-driven action, and an electric stick washer lowered into the home laundry tub. She urged homemakers to buy flexible rubber hose and wringers with safeguards, to keep machinery lubricated, and to use flake or jellied soaps that dissolved immediately.

Many products touted during the Great Depression were humble laundry aids, such as Fels-Naptha, a laundry whitener and grease remover in bar form that women chipped with a paring knife directly into the wash tub. To increase use of the product, Fels & Company of Philadelphia offered a bladed chipper for the price of a two-cent stamp to cover postage. The Perco clothes washer, made by PercoSteril Machine Corporation of New York City, featured a stovetop clothes boiler with percolating action through a central column as an alternative to expensive washing machines. The Silver Lake Company of Newtonville, Massachusetts, distributed clothesline, a necessity for backyard, basement, or kitchen drying. Specializing in unadulterated cotton to assure stain-free laundry, the company guaranteed a soft, pliant braided product that avoided the chafing and tearing of twisted line or wire. As enticements to buyers, the company affixed a handy loop secured at one end for slipping over a kitchen wall hook and offered a sample length suitable for making a kitchenette clothesline or jump rope.

In November 1930, *Good Housekeeping* summarized the current state of laundry in America as reported by subscribers' letters. The magazine found that 49 percent did laundry in home kitchens, 39 percent relied on electric washers, and 29 percent did laundry both by hand and by machine. Some 18 percent sent their laundry out to a professional service. Only .02 percent washed entirely by hand. (Kendall 1930, 87).

A decade after the invention of the Easy Washer, Bendix debuted the Model S, the first automatic washer, invented by John W. Chamberlain and Rex Bassett and demonstrated at a Louisiana fair in 1937. With a single setting of the controls, it put nine pounds of wash through an automatic soaking, agitation, triple rinse, and spin. *Consumer Reports* applauded the development of the Bendix dial-controlled wash cycles.

To keep up with the competition, in the late 1940s, major manufacturers upgraded their products. Thor marketed a unique clothes washer that shifted to dishwashing with the insertion of a different drum. Ad copy in the April 1947 issue of *Woman's Home Companion* emphasized that this amazingly versatile washer took up only two square feet of floor space. General Electric added the soap dispenser to the top-loading washer; Bendix featured a soap injector on its Gyromatic. Westinghouse introduced a drop-front laundromat, the beginning of the end for wringer mechanisms. Known for reliable appliances, Maytag took an extra decade to produce its own legless automatic washer, intro-

duced in 1949, and another five years to pair it with an automatic dryer.

The changes in home laundry equipment answered the demands of women who were liberating themselves from kitchen toil. Elizabeth Beveridge, the home equipment editor for *Woman's Home Companion,* summarized the best in washers in an article for the magazine's June 1947 issue. After surveying nine types, she advised inexperienced shoppers on differences between portables, wringer washers, and spinners. She concluded with the unveiling of the Universal wringer washer that offered two speeds and a safer wringer that prohibited the mangling of the user's hand or arm. Bendix continued to lead the market with its Duomatic washer-dryer, launched in 1953. An innovation in kitchen decor of the 1950s was the shift from hygienic white to colored enamel surfaces, which plastics manufacturers matched with coordinated clothes pins, laundry basket, and clotheslines.

Along with the new washers came more products to simplify laundry chores. General Electric brought out a four-pound automatic steam and dry iron that shut off automatically when set on its heel rest. The Thor Automagic Gladiron claimed sit-down ease at the electric clothes press, a sleeve roll for shirts, and fold-down efficiency for a unit that fit on 1.75 square feet of floor space. Linit and Quick Elastic introduced prepared starch that required no cooking and no straining.

Electrolux introduced America's first household electric clothes dryer in 1951, which used centrifugal force to remove the water from wet laundry. Within a few years, the principle passed from the spin dryer to a separate appliance that heated and spun clothing dry enough for immediate hanging or wearing, often bypassing any need for ironing. Marketed by Whirlpool and Maytag, the tumble dryer came in both electric and gas models and included a lint-removal system.

In Europe, where innovation was slower to change women's lives, laundry continued as a one-woman kitchen operation in 88 percent of French households and 73 percent of English homes. In Switzerland, in 1987, Schulthess, maker of the first European domestic washing machine, pioneered the microprocessor for washing machines, revolutionizing control technology. A touch pad at the top of the front-loader simplified the programming of numerous choices in soaking, washing, and spinning.

The manufacturers of soaps and fabrics kept pace with the need of consumers by producing low-suds cleaners and chlorine-free brighteners and no-iron synthetics. Programmable controls on machines offered more choices for delicate items, bulky work clothes, and linens. The installation of microchip controls in the 1980s further automated machines, enabling them to sense size, texture, and weight of wash loads and choose the appropriate water level, temperature, and wash time.

Early in the twenty-first century, laundry was less a kitchen chore than a domestic specialty. Homemakers in industrialized countries were less likely than those of earlier generations to wash and iron in the kitchen, except in apartments and condominiums where space was at a premium. Among the poor of Macao, portable bamboo rods exposed wet laundry to fresh air. In working-class neighborhoods in Spain and Italy, looped laundry wire on tandem pulleys from kitchen to alleyway made use of air and sunshine to dry clothes and linens attached one by one at an upstairs window and pulled by hand across the expanse.

Homeowners seeking ways of lifting the humdrum house into the twenty-first century hit upon the dreary laundry as the room most in need of a makeover. Instead of a dark, dank corner cluttered with plastic clothesbaskets, they painted laundry areas in bright colors and fitted them with attractive, functional counters, shelving, baskets, hampers, racks, hangers, and other items intended to maximize space.

See also **Detergent**

Further Reading

Beveridge, Elizabeth, "Here's the Line on the New Washers," *Woman's Home Companion*, June 1947, 98–100.

Coppens, Linda Miles. *What American Women Did, 1789–1920.* Jefferson, N.C.: McFarland, 2001.

Fisher, Katharine A., "The Institute Develops Methods in Laundry Work," *Good Housekeeping,* March 1925, 82–85, 110.

Kendall, Helen Whitson, "The Way We Wash," *Good Housekeeping*, November 1930, 86–87.

Hoy, Suellen. *Chasing Dirt: The American Pursuit of Cleanliness.* New York: Oxford University Press, 1995.

Naether, Carl A. *Advertising to Women.* New York: Prentice-Hall, Inc., 1928.

Osband, Linda. *Victorian House Style.* London: David & Charles, 1991.

LEATHER

From early times, leather and rawhide have figured in numerous peripheral aspects of cookery. For example, Egyptian cheese makers stored curds in leather bags. European cooks and butchers often carried their cutlery in wood cases bound in leather, and diners sheathed personal table knives in leather scabbards attached to belts. In India in the first century CE, leather-workers shaped spoons from hide and constructed bags for transporting ghee, or clarified butter, to Rome, where the wealthy bought it for home cooking and temple sacrifices. Saffron arrived at Mediterranean trade centers wrapped in linen and secured in

Leather tannery, Morocco.
[© *Anton Art / Alamy.*]

leather bags, which cooks hung at their worktables to guard the costly grains from waste or pilferage. Farther west, Sicilian and Sardinian dairy workers used a leather *tulum* (pouch) for storing cheese.

In 1255, Friar William of Rubruck enlightened the Western world on Mongolian practices and customs after his mission journey to Central Asia. In a report to Louis IX of France, Rubruck described the ceremonial serving of *koumiss,* a fermented mare's milk. Near the entrance to the chieftain's tent, cooks stored huge quantities of the beverage in a *saba,* or vat, made of ten horse hides sewn together. It was considered good manners for visitors to use one of the carved wooden ladles to agitate the milk upon entrance to the tent to encourage fermentation.

As explained by the English domestic historian Dorothy Hartley, in the late Middle Ages, European smallholders tanned their own leather by a laborious process. First, they soaked newly cut hide in meadow streams and trod the pieces under foot. They loosened hair still clinging to the hide by steeping it in lime. With a quern, the householder pulverized the bark of beech, oak, or willow, then immersed rawhide in a vat of crushed bark and water, which formed a strong acid.

Artisans used the resulting leather for screening, coffers, chair seats, pouches, tool belts, *bougets* (yoked water bags fashioned by *bougemen*), and tops for dredges, pierced shakers used for sprinkling meal or flour over roasting meat. Prize pieces of leather covered the fronts of fortified food chests. Of particular importance to the housewife was the yard apron, a stiff leather shield used to protect clothing during messy jobs, such as cramming poultry to fatten them, slaughtering pigs, and dyeing cloth.

The applications of leather to domestic use have typically answered specific needs, for example, the Welsh shepherd's leather bottle of whey or buttermilk and the traveler's leather hoggin slung over a saddle until time to make camp, unpack, and cook dinner. At the hearth, a pegged or dovetailed wood salt box hinged with leather kept crystals clean and free of the corrosion that would ruin iron or copper fastenings. Throughout dairy country, milkmaids slung leather stoupes, or wooden buckets, from leather straps that hung from the ends of shoulder harness for ease of carrying brimming pails from dairy to kitchen. A similar counterbalancing system weighted two ends of a *cowstal,* or shoulder stick with paired *bougets* sewn from animal hides and filled through leather funnels. English spit roasters connected leather pulleys to treadmills, which small, bowlegged dogs turned with their steady pace.

In the Americas, hide and leather, natural by-products of hunting, provided indigenous peoples with dependable materials for bags and cords. The Maya used tubing fashioned from leather in the distillation of mead. The western Apache stitched storage bags from buckskin to hold nuts, seeds, berries, fruit, wild onions, and potatoes. American Indians also used leather and babiche, a hand-cut coil of rawhide, for numerous kitchen tasks, including making tumplines and handles for burden baskets and attaching animal stomachs to a wood frame for stone boiling. Early Plains Indians made a parfleche, or portfolio, by softening and forming a whole, unseamed hide into an envelope or traveling bag. Inside a dwelling the parfleche lashed to a beam provided extra storage space. Decorated with designs and tribal symbols, it was handy for transporting food, medicinal plants, and tools. The Shoshone of the Great Basin fashioned leather parfleches into expandable food canisters for storage and, after Hispanic explorers introduced the horse, for transporting rations on horseback. To secure it to the back or to a pack animal, the designer pierced it with a bone awl and laced it with babiche that could be tied to a saddle.

Colonial Americans often shaped domestic items from leather, including hinges and handles for doors, cabinets, and food chests and the straps for maple sap buckets. As early as 1635, a resident of Lynn, Massachusetts, had set up shop as a fellmonger, or dealer in hides. Common leather farm and home items included harnesses and straps for dray animals, nosebags for feeding horses and mules, buckets, bottles and urns waterproofed with pitch or rosin, and meal bags.

Waxed jack mugs, also called giskins or blackjacks, were adaptations of Elizabethan drinking mugs crafted from leather and waterproofed with pitch. Another vessel, the bombard, a larger size of blackjack, held large drafts of ale, beer, or metheglin. They were so artful and attractive that a French visitor to the colonies mistook the stitched cylinder for a boot. Even when pegged or bradded with metal studs or mounted and banded with silver, the leather required regular dressing with lard or buttermilk and frequent repair with awl and stylus, which forced a waxed thread through connecting pieces.

Leather made a hand guard for broom makers, who were typically slaves, cripples, or children. After the broom corn worker scraped seed from "Guinea wheat" panicles and rippled the stalks with a comb, the stiff bristles were ready for shaping around a wooden dowel or straight limb. To protect their hands while forcing a threaded bodkin through the mass of bristles, broom makers wore a leather palm shield. Another use of leather was as a contamination-proof covering for jars. The food writer Hannah Glasse, author of *The Art of Cookery Made Plain and Easy: Excelling Any Thing of the Kind Ever Yet Published* (1747), topped her jam jars with an animal bladder and leather to assure an airtight seal and to keep out mice and insects.

Into the twenty-first century, leather remains useful for domestic purposes. The nomadic Sarhadi of Baluchistan in southeastern Iran depend on sheep- and goatskin bags for packing fresh and dried dates during travel. The Vermont Country Store catalog, *Voice of the Mountains*, continues to stock an Amish-design leather flyswatter. Washable leather potholders in a variety of colors protect the hand from burns. A chamois sponge leaves freshly washed glass-front appliances, refrigerator shelves, and counters streak free.

See also **Babiche; Stone Boiling**

Further Reading

Catlin, George, *North American Indians*. New York: Penguin, 1989.
Sloane, Eric. *A Museum of Early American Tools*. New York: Ballantine Books, 1964.

LEAVES

The use of leaves to wrap food for cooking and serving is an ancient practice. Evolved around 25,000 BCE, leaf wrappings allowed cooks to heat succulent foods without scorching them. Through experimentation, cooks learned to select leaves that not only protected ingredients but also added flavor and aroma.

Since the time of the domestication of chickens in China around 1000 BCE, cooks have created traditional poultry recipes such as baked chicken wrapped in lotus leaves and topped with handfuls of hot salt. Columella, the Roman gourmand, recorded a recipe that called for combining figs with cumin, fennel seed, anise, and sesame and wrapping the mixture in fig leaves for drying and storing in clay amphorae. The Sanskrit prose of master Dandin, the author of *The Adventures of the Ten Princes* (ca. 600 CE) described the presentation of boiled rice, *ghee* (clarified butter), and condiments on a green plantain leaf, a humble meal that appealed to the diner's senses of touch, taste, sight, and smell. According to Hindu tradition, the choice of leaves as vessels emulates the dining style of Lord Krishna, who sat at a picnic with the devout eating from palash leaf plates. Indian cooks therefore made plates and cups of banana leaves or stitched palash and banyan leaves with cane or hay slivers to make disposable dishes, a means of setting a clean table.

Ibn Battuta, author of the memoir *Tuhfat al-Nuzzar fi Ghara'ib al-Amsar wa'Ajaib al'Asfar* (On Curiosities of Cities and Wonders of Travel, 1354), described the chewing of betel leaves after a meal to "sweeten the breath, remove foul odors of the mouth [and] aid digestion." (Bullis 2000, 20). The age-old custom is still in use around the Indian Ocean and among Indians and Pakistani worldwide.

Leaves are disposable containers in kitchens worldwide. In the Pacific isles from early times, stiff banana sheaths have doubled as dishes. Woodcuts from the 1500s show American Indian women wrapping tamales in leaves. In the 1760s the English explorer James Cook described a traditional Tahitian meal served in Papeete, capital of French Polynesia: "Raw fish marinated in lime juice and served in coconut milk, chicken cooked with taro leaves." (Gray 1981, 56) With disposable cookware lying so easily at hand, Tahitian cooks had no need to make clay pots or baking ovens. The Hawaiians perpetuated their traditions and set up extended tables for *poi* suppers, at which they chose whole ti leaves for steaming coconut into *kulolo*, wrapping mullet for baking, steaming pork and salt fish into *laulau*, or tenderizing taro root.

The French furthered the use of edible leaves, flavoring pickled gherkins with grape leaves. For game cookery, they selected tender vine leaves along with bacon and pork strips to bard fresh game. For a replication of Turkish *dolmas* (meat balls), they wrapped each in a leaf. They also minced nasturtium leaves and blossoms for green salad and added them to fritters.

In early twentieth-century Ireland, farm families shaped ash cake from maize meal, which came in fine, medium, and coarse grade. To make Ingan cake, cooks poured meal into a bowl, scalded it with a kettle of boiling water, salted it generously, and shaped up a dough. Before baking, they wrapped the lump in cabbage leaves to shield the loaf from contaminants causing an ashy taste. After a half-hour, the leaves scorched, indicating that the baking was complete.

In the twenty-first century, leaves continue to play a part in the cuisines of many cultures, especially in the *dolmades* of Greece and the *dolma* of Turkey, stuffed grape leaves favored as *meze* (starters) for banquets and heavy meals. American Indians have retained the tradition of boiling corn in the husk, and Mexican cooks wrap tamales in cornhusks just as their ancestors have for millennia. Similarly, Panamian cooks secure *bollo* (corn mush) in husks for boiling.

A preference for leaves as dishes and food wrappings remains a standard among the people of Tanna in the New Hebrides. For gift giving at a family social, guests still present *laplap*, a paste of yam or taro, encased in leaf wrappings and bound with a liana. Samoans bake *palusami* (coconut cream) in taro leaves; Papuan peasants of New Guinea and some Singaporeans dish up meals on banana leaves. Niue islanders pick broad leaves for plates and bake taro and papaw slices in leaf wrappings. Tongans enjoy taro leaves with *lu pulu* (corned beef) and coconut cream. French Polynesians choose only banana leaves for binding oven-roasted dishes. In Malaysia, banana bracts combine with snake beans and chilies in jackfruit salad; banana leaves softened in hot water enwrap fish balls and prawns before grilling. Pandau leaves chopped into *chendol*, a coconut-flavored dessert, add an unusual chewy texture.

Leaves provide flavor and texture in many traditional dishes. In Laos, the banana leaf is essential for making *mok paa* (cooked fish) or *mok kayx* (cooked fowl). Cabbage, too, doubles as binder and flavoring: in the Ukraine, cooks prepare *holubtsi* by encasing a mixture of ground meat and rice in cabbage leaves and in Russia the traditional dish called *golubtsy* consists of stuffed cabbage leaves served with tomato sauce and sour cream. Lithuanian *balendelai* requires a blend of meats and vegetables to roll in cabbage leaves. Similarly, in New Zealand, the Maori line wire racks with cabbage leaves for the cooking of *hangi*, a blend of meat and seafood with potatoes, carrots, and sweet potatoes steamed in an *umu* (earth oven).

Africans, too, make daily use of leaves in the kitchen. The people of Equatorial Guinea drink from leaf cups and bundle peanut paste and sauce into banana leaves and secure them with melango fiber. Cooks in Equatorial Guinea roll peanuts in leaves for roasting. In Sierra Leone, cooks serve rice with *plasas,* a sauce of potato and cassava leaves fried in palm oil; the popular additive in Cameroon and Gabon is manioc greens, described in French on restaurant menus as *feuilles* (leaves). The popular snacks of the Central African Republic are *mangbele* (boiled cassava dough) and *kanda* (steamed meat, fruit, or termites), both rolled and cooked in leaves. Local cooks also plate *gozo* (cassava root paste) with ground cassava leaves as a condiment called *ngunza,* thickened with peanut butter and tomato paste. In Nigerian kitchens, baobab leaves are a necessary part of a sauce compounded with okra, peanuts, and tomatoes. For American-style imitations of African grilling, wrappings of maple, grape, or banana leaves inject unusual flavors.

Further Reading

Gray, William R. *Voyages to Paradise: Exploring in the Wake of Captain Cook.* Washington, D.C.: National Geographic Society, 1981.

Rajah, Carol Selva. *Makan-Lah!: The True Taste of Malaysia.* Sydney, Australia: HarperCollins, 1996.

Read, Kenneth E. *The High Valley.* New York: Charles Scribner's Sons, 1965.

Reader, Ted, and Kathleen Sloan. *Sticks & Stones: The Art of Grilling on Plank, Vine and Stone.* Minocqua, Wisc.: Willow Creek Press, 1999.

Skabelund, Grant P., man. ed. *Culturgrams: The Nations Around Us.* Vols. I & II. Salt Lake City, Utah: Brigham Young University, 1997.

Stuart, George E., and Gene S. Stuart. *The Mysterious Maya.* Washington, D.C.: National Geographic Society, 1977.

LESLIE, ELIZA

Eliza Leslie, the first U.S. woman to earn a living from writing cookbooks, was also a forerunner of the home economics movement. She compiled *Miss Leslie's Directions for Cookery* (1837), America's most popular cookbook of the 1800s, which remained in print through thirty-eight editions. Born on November 15, 1787 in Philadelphia, she lived in England from age five to eleven. Upon the family's return to Philadelphia, her father died, leaving her mother too poor to send Eliza and her brothers to school.

A self-motivated scholar, Leslie learned music and French, mastered needlecraft, and studied cookery at the school of Mrs. Goodfellow. From girlhood, Leslie collected recipes, which her brother suggested she

Portrait of Eliza Leslie.
[© *Library of Congress, Prints and Photographs Division (LC-USZ62-103454)*]

publish in a collection. Along with the classic *Seventy-Five Receipts for Pastry, Cakes, and Sweetmeats* (1837), she produced a series of cookbooks that established her credibility with American housewives. Among her innovations was the first recorded recipe for beet root.

In addition to writing a young adult collection known as the Mirror Series and the novel *Amelia, or a Young Lady's Vicissitudes* (1848) and contributing prize-winning fiction and social satire to *Godey's Lady's Book* and *Graham's Magazine,* Leslie turned out cooking and home economics manuals as her chief source of income. These works included *200 Receipts for French Cookery* (1832), *The House-Book; or, A Manual of Domestic Economy* (1840), *The Lady's Receipt Book* (1846), and *Miss Leslie's Secrets: What Every Bride Should Know* (1854), a reprise of 1,011 recipes from her earlier cookbooks. During her residence at the United States Hotel, both American and European visitors came to meet and praise her works, including an autobiography she published in 1852.

Leslie compiled handy domestic works that enjoyed wide circulation. Eclectic in style and interests, she valued French methodology as well as American regional recipes made from native ingredients. In *The Indian Meal Book* (1846), she summarized recipes for such dishes as cornbread, Johnny cake, griddle cakes and pancakes, muffins, cupcakes, biscuits, dumplings, hominy, and succotash. Her intent was to introduce British cooks to maize as an alternate to oats. To assure understanding, she wrote precisely, specifying measurements and methods for turning out no-fail dishes.

Leslie's expertise encompassed a diverse range of dishes, Moravian sugar cake to West Indian coconut pudding. She mastered the details of entertaining and wrote confidently on etiquette and food service, describing for her readers the refined behaviors of Philadelphia gentry. For the homemaker, she compiled tables of weights and measures and provided instructions for compounding ink, soaps, perfume and fragrant oils, and domestic solvents. Among treasured Civil War recipes was her capillaire, a refreshing drink made from orange flower water, sugar, and eggs. Leslie died on January 1, 1858, in Gloucester, New Jersey.

See also **Home Economics**

Further Reading

Daniels-Zeller, Debra, "Beet It!," *Vegetarian Resource Group,* September 2000.

Fitzgerald, Vickie, "The Century of the Sandwich," Quincy, Massachusetts, *Patriot Ledger,* February 4, 1998.

LI, HUNG CHANG

According to folk myth, Li (or Lee) Hung Chang invented chop suey, the first Chinese dish introduced to American diners. Li was a foreign minister for the dowager empress Tz'u Hsi and China's most revered dignitary during the opening of China to world diplomacy. A native of Hofei in Anhwei Province, he was born on February 15, 1823. Under the tutelage of diplomat Tseng Kuo-Fan, Li pursued academic credentials at Hanlin Academy. During more than a quarter century of service until his death in 1901, he urged the nation to embrace foreign trade and economic development. After China's defeat by Japan, Li personally signed the Treaty of Shimonoseki in 1895. He attended the coronation of Russia's last czar, Nicholas II, in 1896 and made state calls on Otto von Bismarck, Germany's modernizer, and on William Gladstone, the English prime minister.

It seems unlikely that so prestigious a national figure would have had an impact on kitchen history, especially during a visit in a foreign land. The event that connects Li's name with cuisine occurred in 1896, when he met with U.S. officials to win their support during the Sino-Japanese War. The Americans wondered why he rejected such elegant banquet fare as *filets de kingfish à la Tourville* and *ris de veau à la Daubigny* and had his own cooks prepare traditional Chinese foods. His diet perplexed the chef at the Waldorf-Astoria and writers for the *New York Times.* When Li invited guests to the Chinese embassy in New York City on August 29, he had his kitchen staff mince meat, celery, and bean sprouts for *chop suey* (mixed pieces), a sauced specialty similar to hash that his cook served over steamed rice. From this historic meeting of East and West grew an American fascination with Chinese cuisine, at that time largely unknown in the West. Chop suey restaurants flourished in New York and San Francisco, both cities with sizeable Asian populations. To enhance the dish, restaurant managers dubbed it Viceroy Li Hung Chang chop suey.

In the Kitchen of the Waldorf-Astoria Hotel.
[© *Library of Congress, Prints and Photographs Division (LC-USZ62-115185)]*

RESEARCHES

ON THE

CHEMISTRY OF FOOD.

BY

JUSTUS LIEBIG, M.D.,

PROFESSOR OF CHEMISTRY IN THE UNIVERSITY OF GIESSEN.

EDITED FROM THE MANUSCRIPT OF THE AUTHOR,

BY

WILLIAM GREGORY, M.D.,

PROFESSOR OF CHEMISTRY IN THE UNIVERSITY OF EDINBURGH.

LONDON:

PRINTED FOR TAYLOR AND WALTON,

UPPER GOWER STREET.

1847.

Title page from Researches on the Chemistry of Food (1847).

LIEBIG, JUSTUS VON

Baron Justus von Liebig, a noted German chemist, advanced empirical science and its application to biochemistry and human nutrition. The second of ten children, he was born in Darmstadt, on May 12, 1803, and learned chemistry from training at his father's dealership in dyes and pharmaceuticals. A government grant paid his tuition at the University of Bonn where, at age seventeen, he studied under Karl Wilhelm Kastner, a chemical analyst who tutored him privately at Erlangen. He earned a doctorate in 1822. From the Grand Duke of Hesse-Darmstadt, von Liebig gained another study grant and journeyed to Paris in November 1822, to apprentice under Joseph Gay-Lussac, who mastered gas laws. After completing his survey of fulminates at a private laboratory, at age twenty, von Liebig addressed the French Academy and landed an assistant's post at the University of Giessen where he introduced experimental teaching of qualitative and quantitative analysis of organic compounds. His revolutionary classroom method drew pupils from both sides of the Atlantic and earned him the title of baron in 1843.

In collaboration with Fried Wöhler, von Liebig discovered the benoyl and ethyl radicals, the beginning of research that produced ether, chloroform, chloral, and hippuric acid. His analysis of plant matter proved the importance of minerals to flora. His instructions on extracting nourishing elements from beef gravy soup preceded testing on the sick and malnourished, who profited from a nourishing *extractum carnis* (meat extract), commonly known as beef tea. Such patent foods as *bouillon* and pocket soup made warehousing and transportation of a protein-rich soup base practical for the military and humanitarian groups.

In addition to publishing *Organic Chemistry and its Application to Agriculture and Physiology* (1840), *Animal Chemistry* (1840), *Organic Chemistry in Its Application to Physiology and Pathology* (1842), *Familiar Letters on Chemistry* (1843), and *Researches on the Chemistry of Foods* (1848), von Liebig began researching methods of improving agricultural yield and preventing famine. He warned about adulterated flour, attempted to produced a marketable baking powder, and promoted whole-grain baking and methods of turning sprouted grain into bread. When his daughter failed to lactate after giving birth, he created *suppe für saüglinge* (sustenance for the nursing baby), an imitation of human milk that frauds emulated and marketed under his name.

In 1862, von Liebig went into business with Georg Christian Giebert to manufacture food in Fray Bentos, Uruguay. By recycling cattle killed for their hides into a brown meat powder extracted under pressure, the firm produced a valuable product from otherwise wasted meat. The food, later marketed as Lemco and Oxo, received recognition for sustaining explorers Dr. Henry Morton Stanley, Roald Amundsen, Robert Scott, and Ernest Henry Shackleton. In 1866, Florence Nightingale thanked Liebig's company for sending a sample of the extract, which she approved for invalid feeding. At the 1867 Paris Exhibition, von Liebig won gold medals for his beef extract. At his death in Munich on April 18, 1873, he led the field in organic chemistry with hundreds of monographs, the pioneering of research universities, and the study of nutritional chemistry.

Von Liebig's powdered soup concept spread to factories in Argentina, Australia, New Zealand, and North America. In 1874, competitor John Lawson Johnson, a Scottish butcher, began processing Johnston's Fluid Beef from a factory in Quebec. He shifted his operation to London and renamed the soup Bovril, a trade name made up from "life force of the ox." Subsequent beef teas flooded the market under the names Beefex, Bonovin's Exox, Borthwick's Fluid Beef, CWS Silvox, Foster Clark's Ju-Vis, Hipi Mutton Essence, Hugon's Torox, Valentine's Meat Juice, Vigoral, Vimbos, and Viskor. The November 1930 issue of *Good Housekeeping* touted Lemco as a genuine Liebig bouillon for stirring into gravy, fish and meat, sauce, stew, soup, salads, and vegetables. In a 1968 merger with Brooke Bond, von Liebig's formulation survived as Brooke Bond Oxo.

Further Reading

Harper, Alfred E., "Nutritional Essentiality: Evolution of the Concept," *Nutrition Today,* November 1999, 216–222.

Landau, Ralph, "The Chemical Industry: From the 1850s Until Today," *National Association for Business Economics*, October 1999.

LIHOTZKY, GRETE SCHÜTTE

One of twentieth-century Europe's visionaries, the architect Margrete "Grete" Schütte-Lihotzky incorporated the rational housekeeping revolution into boldly minimalist design. Born January 23, 1897 in Vienna, she enrolled at eighteen at the Wiener Kunstgewerbeschule am Stubenring (Vienna School of Arts and Crafts), where she specialized in practical domestic design. Following the advice of her teachers, the architects Oskar Strnad and Heinrich Tessenow, before entering a competition to design new public housing, she observed firsthand life in working-class tenements. Her design earned the Max Mauthner Award, followed in 1919 by the Lobmeyr Prize (named for the Viennese industrialist Ludwig Lobmeyr).

At a time when Walter Gropius and other architects in Austria and Germany were studying ways to simplify domestic work through innovative design and streamlining, Lihotzky collaborated with Adolf Loos, head of the Vienna Housing Authority, on behalf of the Siedlungsbewegung (Settlers' Movement), sponsored by local Social Democrats. With several other architects, Lihotzky and Loos began work on the Winarsky-Hof housing project, which replicated some of the spare functionality of Gropius's L-shaped kitchen, an element of the Bauhaus style. In 1922–23 she designed four houses in the Werkbundsiedlung, an experimental project to create affordable single-family residences for working people.

In 1926, at the height of German feminist influence on home economics, Lihotzky went to Frankfurt am Main to work for Ernst May, head of the Schlesische Heimsttäte (Silesian Rural Housing Authority), on a revolutionary ideal—to contribute her expertise to *Wohnkultur* (domestic culture) and to develop a domestic movement known as the *Neues Leben* (New Life). The previous year, for May's journal *Schlesisches Heim* (Silesian Home), she had proposed a modular concrete kitchen assembled in a factory and lowered onto the home site by crane. He was so impressed by her bold, fresh minimalism that he offered her a post on his design team to complete the nation's largest housing initiative.

Following the building of the Weissenhof Settlement, a modern housing complex erected at the Werkbund Exhibition in Stuttgart in 1927, Lihotzky and May labored in tandem. In *Das Neue Frankfurt* (The New Frankfurt), he published his research on the positive effects of color, smooth-edged materials, and enamel surfacing. She created the Frankfurt Kitchen, a model work space for small, low-cost apartments to house war widows, handicapped homemakers, and renters on limited pensions. The plan reduced appliances to a sink, gas range, and *Kochkiste* (warming chamber).

On the basis of time-and-motion studies of kitchen operations, Lihotzky determined that sixty-five square feet of floor space would suffice. She fitted each rectangle with clean metal surfaces and fittings that were functional, easily maintained, and visually engaging. To integrate the kitchen with the rest of the living space, she placed pocket doors between kitchens and living rooms, a concept repeated in the U.S. architect Frank Lloyd Wright's modern kitchen designs. The design process took into consideration suggestions from *Hausfrauvereine* (housewives' clubs) and from Georg Grumbach, a manufacturer of kitchen fittings and cabinetry. Her ergonomically sound design made the kitchen more efficient and functional; prefabricated units contained costs.

Like railway dining cars, ships' galleys, or lunch wagons, Lihotzky's compact, one-cook kitchen ran on gas and electricity and required no additional furniture. She designed flour canisters that discouraged mealworms and beech wood tabletops that resisted acid, burns, and cuts. Tile, glass, and metal surfaces contributed the sanitized ambience of a laboratory. A fireless cooker heated food; a refuse chute received kitchen waste and guided it into the garbage pail. A revolving stool on rollers enabled the homemaker to perform many kitchen tasks without standing. Windows provided natural light; glass-fronted cupboards made it easy for the cook to find stored items. Newly washed dishes air-dried in a wooden plate rack over a drain board, thus obviating the need for towel drying. Staple foodstuffs fit into eighteen labeled drawers.

Lihotzky married architect Wilhelm Schütte in 1927 and settled into her own Frankfurt Kitchen, where she demonstrated her design to visiting international teams of experts and survived critiques that lambasted her for treating housewives as if they were cogs in a machine. May constructed 4,000 of the apartments, which set a standard throughout Europe. In 1928, the French labor minister Louis Loucheur, bought 200,000 prefabricated units for a housing project; Swedish designers drafted their own version of the Frankfurt Kitchen. The German Department of Standards rated the design unique. Frankfurt's Gaspassage, a showcase for gas-fueled appliances created by the architect Adolf Meyer and city utilities director Franz Tillmetz, featured a demonstration kitchen designed by Lihotzky. Belgian firms copied the style for their cubex kitchens; Dutch architect Pieter Zwart of the Bruynzeel company put her units into mass production by 1936.

European abhorrence of Adolf Hitler and his extremes of social regimentation ended public enthusiasm for the slick, Germanic functional kitchen. With a world war threatening, Europeans returned to the homey clutter of the family kitchen-dining room complex, a symbol of safety, warmth, and tradition.

In 1986, Lihotzky's work for the resistance movement was the subject of a television film, *Eine Minute Dunkel Macht uns Nicht Blind* (One Minute of Darkness Does Not Make Us Blind). Still a fervent anti-Nazi, in 1988 she refused to accept Vienna's Award of Honor for Science and Art from President Kurt Waldheim, a former SS officer. When she died at nearly 103, she had earned a place among the idealists of the century.

See also **Design; Home Economics**

Further Reading

Coleman, Debra, Elizabeth Danze, and Carol Henderson, eds. *Architecture and Feminism*. Princeton, N.J.: Princeton Architectural Press, 1996.

Dawson, Layla, "Margarete Schütte-Lihotzky, 1897–2000," *Architectural Review*, March 2000, 23.

LINENS

Since the origin of the art of weaving, linens have been a substantial part of the domestic fiber production. Native peoples of the Americas turned hemp, reeds, and other fibers into mats that served as place settings, as was the dining custom of the Wyandotte of the St. Lawrence Valley. Among the Washington state Salish as well, homemakers rolled out mats of grass or hemp fibers or laced cedar slats at meal times.

Around the world, the standard set-up of the loom accommodated the arm-span of the weaver, thus limiting fabrics to a single width equivalent to about a yard; a two-person loom produced a double-width cloth equal to seventy-two inches. In medieval farmhouses, housewives cut lengths for towels and wrapped hams hung from pegs in ceiling joists. A length of cloth accompanied the ewer and basin for hand-washing. A length of toweling used to encircle the cook's middle evolved into the apron.

Evolution of the Napkin

According to the domestic historian Dorothy Hartley's *The Land of England* (1979), the medieval table on a dais in the great hall required a frontal drape as a decorative covering for diner's legs and also as protection from drafts. A long tabletop covering draped both ends of the table to complete the concealment of raw wood. A top covering, or draw cloth, concealed the joint of the first two cloths to produce a finished surface. For lengthy banquets, the staff placed several top cloths and removed the upper layer at the end of each course to rid the table of stains and crumbs. Along the side where the guests sat, a *sauve-nappe* (tablecloth saver) caught the spills and grease from hands.

Until the 1400s, diners wiped their fingers on the *doublier*, a cloth used like a towel, and covered their laps with a *longière*, or runner, during meals. Essential to sanitation, the *longière* served as a communal napkin. It appears to have enjoyed centuries of use, as demonstrated by an artistic representation on the Egbert Codex at Trier from 980 CE and on Dirk Bout's altarpiece in St. Peter's at Louvain, completed in 1468.

Table servants and kitchen staff wiped their hands on dining towels attached to the wall. These cloth rectangles developed into personal napkins, which the right-handed user first draped over the left arm and later tied around the neck for convenience during two-handed cutting with knife and fork. Royalty received napkins twined around cutlery and offered at the time of food tasting. To assure the user that the cloth was untainted by poison, the servant kissed it before spreading it in place on the diner's lap. Women collected linens from girlhood as a basis for endowing their future households. The stock of linens had to be substantial to outfit a home where laundry might be performed twice a year or no more than four times annually.

Platina, the Renaissance arbiter of taste and author of *De Honesta Voluptate* (On Right Pleasure, 1475), instructed: "Napkins should be white and the tablecloths spotless, because, if they were otherwise, they should arouse squeamishness and take away the desire to eat." (Scully 1995, 173) The groom serving bread held loaves in a napkin furled into a pouch and borne over the shoulder. The lord of the house received his serving wrapped neatly in cloth. The sharing of linens as well as flagons, bowls, and loaves indicated acceptance into a group. Those not in the lord's favor received no invitation to share. At the "drawing of the cloth," servants removed dishes and leftovers to the kitchen and left the tabletop clean for dessert, wine, and socializing.

In Renaissance Italy, the lavishness of table napery determined the householder's reputation for hospitality. Florentine hosts prepared for five-course meals with exotic table settings and fragrant fruit-and-flower arrangements. The household staff set up banquet tables in advance, sometimes taking days to work out a symbolic shape for *touailles* (napkins). The folding was the job of specialists, who followed schematic drawings created by sculptors. The height of napery was the enfolding of a small bird, which flew upward when the guest unfurled its cloth cage.

Uses of Cloth in the Kitchen

It was not until the mid-fifteenth century that kitchen linens gained importance. The linen or cotton kitchen towel began as a coarsely woven rectangle called a crash. The absorbent glass towel served the washer and dryer of dishes. The same materials suited molding cloths to shield holiday cheeses from dust and insects and drawstring bags for straining fruit pulp for jelly. In tropical regions, a length of mosquito netting recycled from a bed cover made a functional meat safe. To give it shape, the homeowner suspended it from a beam, erected a frame of twigs, and draped the netting over all before tying it neatly at the bottom. As kitchen managers began to concentrate on organization and cleanliness in the 1600s, they welcomed cloth goods as necessities to well-ordered food service.

Linens received hard wear in the kitchen, often functioning as strainers or draining bags. Bartolomeo Scappi, private cook of Pope Pius V and author of *Libro Nuovo nel Qual s'Insegna a Far Ogni Sorte de Vivande* (New Recipe Book for All Sorts of Foods, 1549) and *Opera dell'Arte dell Cucinare* (Compendium on the Art of Cookery, 1570), collected recipes for the latest in chic dining. In his instructions for morello cherry cake, he explained how to cook the fruit in white wine and pass the pulp through muslin. The cook mixed the strained fruit with sugar, grated cheese, cinnamon, pepper, butter, and eggs.

For difficult sieving processes, such as straining jelly or consommé, steaming couscous, and separating fat, cookbooks of the period specified white, closely woven cloth, often tied into place over a vessel with kitchen string or cording. To drain boiled vegetables,

experts suggested suspending them in a cloth after sieving to wick away the last of the moisture. To make hypocras, a spiced after-dinner wine, servants poured wine through bags containing cinnamon, clove, or lemon peel. If the flavor seemed weak, the liquid received another pouring through one or more of the bags until it reaches the required strength.

Seventeenth-century hosts enhanced their status and reputation for tidiness by providing individual diners with their own napkins, which they kept in a press screwed tight to preserve the tidy pleats and folds of such elegant shapes as the double cockleshell, a triplex pleated fan. A clever groom might serve the bishop's bread in a mitre-shaped cloth, a lady's share in a napkin pleated like a lily, and the traveler's crust in a napkin folded like a shoe. In 1682, Giles Rose, head chef of England's Charles I, translated the French *L'Escole Parfait des Officiers de Bouche* (1676) as *A Perfect School of Instruction for the Officers of the Mouth*. He characterized the importance of linen folding to a well-run royal kitchen and table. He marveled at the intricacy of twisted, folded, and creased napkins transformed into beasts, birds, fish, and fruit. At Versailles, the most famous folders of *serviettes* (napkins) produced creations resembling chickens, boats, frogs, peacocks, and swans. When the Duc de Lorraine came to call, a four-cornered showpiece in the shape of the Cross of Lorraine ensconced a dinner roll. The shapes so delighted diners that they received plain napkins for use at table and saved the fanciful linens as favors.

Another standard piece of linen to derive from this era was the doily, named for a London linen draper named Doily (or Doyley), who operated a business in the Strand in the 1600s. From his name came a term originally applied to the doily-napkin, which Irish-born satirist Jonathan Swift named in 1711 in a comment on service of after-dinner drinks. Etiquette books instructed diners to wipe their greasy fingers on the doily-napkin rather than on bread, clothing, or tablecloth. Initialed or individualized tin or bamboo rings identified each napkin, which diners used several times before laundering.

The domestic adviser Jonathan Periam, author of *The Home & Farm Manual: A Pictorial Encyclopedia of Farm, Garden, Household, Architectural, Legal, Medical and Social Information* (1884), summarized the most useful methods of creasing and folding napkins and mitering corners. During Japan's introduction to Western customs, proper diners shunned the practice of wiping greasy hands on napkins. Instead, kitchen staff heated water to boiling and wrung out small hand towels to pass around the table.

By the mid-nineteenth century, the term *doily napkin* had been shortened to *doily* but occasionally took on airs, as in an 1868 advertisement for needlework

"D'Oyleys." (Wilson 1991, 136) It shifted in purpose from a cloth for wiping hands to a decorative cloth placed under dishes. Gradually, paper doilies stamped in lacy patterns took the place of cloth under ice cream sundaes, fruit and soup cups, and plates of macaroons and *petits fours*.

In New England and on the American frontier, cloth was a precious commodity. Homemakers recycled sails as floor cloths and old curtains and tablecloths as aprons and polishing cloths. A precious piece of resilient cloth came from commercial flour sacks, which families sewed into toweling, straining cloths, aprons, and bibs and diapers for babies.

As settlers struggled to preserve remnants of refinement on their way West, the presence of clean, folded table linen reminded them that home could be a wagon or a cabin in the wild. Eliza McHatten Ripley, the author of *From Flag to Flag: A Woman's Adventures and Experiences in the South during the War, in Mexico, and in Cuba* (1888) characterized the value of a single towel to a pioneer company that shared it: "Our ablutions were performed habitually in the horse-bucket, and the towel—we were reduced to one, the others having been ruined or blown away while camping out—the precious towel, . . . flapped in the breeze and dried as we rode along. (Ripley 1888, 12) Forced to reuse cloth, women on the frontier took great delight in new fabric. Susan Shelby Magoffin's *Down the Santa Fe Trail and Into Mexico* (1846) remarks on the excitement of Southwestern women after her husband opened a bale of forty-five pieces of calico and spread them out for sale.

Era of Synthetic Fabrics

In the February 1925 issue of *Good Housekeeping*, Standard Textile Products advertised a new fiber, "linenette," from which minor spills could be removed simply by wiping. Homemakers could choose from floral and geometric designs in blue on white and could trim the attractive covers to suit round or square tables. The October 1930 issue featured an ad for Startex kitchen towels, made from a cotton-linen fiber that dried clean and left no lint. For a dollar, the company offered a sixteen-piece trial set edged in blue, gold, green, or red to coordinate with kitchen decor. As the textile industry replaced home spinning, weaving, and dyeing, women began to think of yarn and fabric as a domestic purchase rather than a home chore.

Cloth continues to serve many purposes in the kitchen, such as covering rising dough and enclosing herbs and seasoning in a *bouquet garni* (flavor bundle). Invented by Pierre de Lune, chef of the Duke of Orleans in the mid-1600s, the *bouquet garni* imparts flavor and aroma to dishes such as stews and soups. For cheese making, a loosely woven muslin fabric shaped like a jelly bag or jelly strainer drained the watery liquid from curds. For makers of vinegar, cheesecloth filtered out mother, the gelatinous white mat of cellulose and bacteria that forms on fermenting vinegar. In Guadeloupe and Dominica, cooks completed the peeling, grating, and juice and pulp extraction of manioc with a final squeeze through cheesecloth. Another domestic muslin bag was the *nouet*, a receptacle for any food to be cooked, flavored, or infused in liquid without leaving particles behind. A more complex use of fiber was the kitchen work glove interwoven with stainless steel thread to prevent cuts while slicing, grating, and chopping with sharp blades. On the Caribbean island of Dominica, cheesecloth was the essential calabash covering for cooks grating coconut to remove the milk. After they squeezed handfuls of the gratings, they collected the juice for straining through the cloth and squeezing and twisting the pulp to extract every drop of the flavor.

Low-tech uses of kitchen linens persist in modern times. The tea towel folded numerous times becomes a potholder or trivet. Wound around ramekins in a baking pan, it secures them in place during transfer to the oven. Placed between rice steamer and lid, it absorbs liquid during the final moments of processing. A sturdier fiber, natural canvas or duck cloth, is still used as a pastry cloth and *couche* for baguettes.

LINOLEUM

Linoleum quickly became a favorite flooring for kitchens because, unlike wood, it resisted flame, scratches, and dents and did not collect cooking fat, oil, or grease. And unlike rugs and carpets, the new material did not require outdoor sweeping, airing, napping, or beating over a clothesline or fence. Soft, cushiony, cheap, and durable, linoleum began to replace heavier floor coverings such as stone, marble, and hardwood parquet. It took its strength from sturdy jute or canvas heat-bonded to an oxidized linseed oil surface pressed from flaxseed.

An innovative flooring product that developed out of the floor cloth industry, linoleum originated in Britain. The English rubber manufacturer Frederick Walton invented it in 1863 to replace the more expensive rubber Kamptulicon flooring. Walton coined the term *linoleum* from the Latin for "flax oil," a common coating for oilcloth. The first linoleum was the product of Walton's Linoleum Manufacturing Company in Staines, Middlesex, England. The process involved air-drying thin films of linseed oil into a springy mass, which workers ground up, blended with wood dust,

Linoleum advertisement created by the the Office for Emergency Management, Office of War Information, Domestic Operations Branch. 1941-1945.
[© *Courtesy of National Archives and Records Administration.*]

and rolled over a burlap foundation. After they seasoned the "dough" in a dry room, they built it up with colored pigments and topped it with a surface coat of pyroxylin lacquer.

Michael Nairn, a Scottish weaver and flooring maker, altered the standard linoleum width from two to four yards. He moved his company, Nairn Linoleum, to Newark, New Jersey, in August 1886. In addition to the Newark facility, he had seventeen other factories, in Glasgow, London, Manchester, and Paris, which made linoleum, floor cloth, canvas, baize for table coverings, and cork carpet. In 1895, he introduced inlaid patterns via screen printing on linoleum with colored granules dropped through a perforated zinc tray. Within five years, he opened factories in France and Germany and dispatched agents to Holland, Denmark, Norway, Sweden, Spain, Portugal, Canada, South America, South Africa, Australia, and New Zealand.

Linoleum brought out imagination in designers. In the first decade of the twentieth century, most homeowners preferred mosaic or encaustic patterns, readily available from the Congoleum Corporation. The next decade saw a revival of colonial motifs as well as the

introduction of art deco and art moderne designs. In 1928, linoleum manufacturers formed Continentale Linoleum Union, an informal consortium of five manufacturers: DLW in Germany, Krommenie in Holland, Forshaga in Sweden, Giubiasco in Switzerland, and Sarlino in France. In Britain, Walton's company merged with the Barry Staines Group of Scotland in 1930 and remained in business until 1973.

Armstrong, North America's leader in linoleum production, got its start in Pittsburgh as the Armstrong Cork Company; it was still thriving in the twenty-first century with sixty factories in fifteen countries. In 1860, Thomas Armstrong, son of immigrants from Londonderry, Ireland, launched a two-man cork-cutting operation. They loaded the product into burlap sacks and delivered it by wheelbarrow. Four years later, he instituted a customer-centered business with the Armstrong name stamped on every cork. The company diversified, producing brick, insulating corkboard and fiberboard, cork tile, flexible support for hardwood and ceramic floors, and, at its Lancaster factory in 1906, linoleum.

In the 1930s, Armstrong became the largest linoleum manufacturer in the United States. Its pattern book listed 294 selections, including flagstone, faux carpet, geometric patterns, and customized designs in stark color contrasts. Whole-page advertisements in women's magazines pictured inlaid marble designs and broken stone patterns for entranceways. To assist consumers with selection, Armstrong issued a booklet, "New Ideas in Home Decoration," written by Hazel Dell Brown, the author of *Portfolio of Room Interiors* (1946). Sealex Linoleum, sold by Congoleum-Nairn, Inc., Kearny, New Jersey, also offered a free booklet, "Color and Charm in Home Interiors," promising to assist the homemaker in choosing tasteful flooring to harmonize with the rest of the decor.

The linoleum flooring industry spawned a host of new businesses built around cleaning and caring for linoleum. In the 1930s, Beckwith-Chandler Company, of Newark, New Jersey, advertised its B/C Lacquer, a linoleum dressing that sealed surfaces to protect gloss and to keep out stains and ground-in dirt. The concept made sense: by halting these pollutants at the surface, the homemaker had an easier task of cleaning the kitchen floor with a swish of the mop. A competitor, 61 QDV from Patt & Lambert of Bridgeburg, Ontario, and Buffalo, New York, promised safe, nonslippery linoleum that was mar proof, waterproof, and impervious to black heel marks.

In the post-World War II era, when American linoleum makers such as Armstrong, Congoleum, and Pabco were turning kitchens into showplaces, advertisements for Johnson's Wax, a product of Johnson & Son, Racine, Wisconsin, filled women's magazines with full-color pictures of chic kitchens with gleaming linoleum floors. Its most familiar product, Glo-Coat, promised a lasting sheen for linoleum as well as for wood floors. Armstrong competed with a similar strategy, featuring new kitchens with the latest equipment, decor, and a kitchen floor that tied together colors and motifs.

Linoleum suffered an undeserved reputation for poor quality in the mid-twentieth century because workers often applied it to a damp subsurface. U.S. factories abandoned linoleum manufacture in the 1970s; at its closing in 1975, Armstrong's Lancaster, Pennsylvania, plant was the last holdout. Toward the end of the twentieth century, however, linoleum experienced a resurgence in popularity. After decades of vinyl and plastic flooring and indoor-outdoor carpeting, acrylic-topped linoleum returned to favor for its formatting from renewable natural substances. In contrast to the chlorine, plasticizers, and petrochemicals used in the manufacture of synthetic surfaces and carpet fibers, linoleum's natural ingredients included linseed oil, cork flour, pulverized limestone, pine rosin, wood flour—recycled waste from the lumber industry, and organic, nontoxic color pigments, and a backing of natural jute fiber.

As explained in *Environmental Building News,* linoleum was a preferred flooring for kitchens, nurseries, basements, and health-care institutions because it was naturally bactericidal. As it oxidized, it subdued bacterial colonization, a concern of mothers with children young enough to play at floor level. In addition, its anti-static properties repelled dust and dust mites, both of which contribute to upper respiratory illness. Although it is more difficult to lay than carpeting or tongue-and-groove wood, the size of linoleum sheets reduces the need for heavy seaming, thus more thoroughly sealing out air and moisture. Maintenance of modern linoleum consists only of washing with a mild cleaner and water. As an added advantage over non-biodegradable, synthetic flooring materials, when homeowners decide to remove linoleum—after its thirty to forty years of service—it can be placed in a landfill or incinerated with no danger to the environment.

See also **Oilcloth**

Further Reading

Ingersoll, John H., "Linoleum, Anyone?" *Country Living*, February 98, 52.

Jordan, Steve, "Faux Linoleum," *Old House Journal*, January/February 1996, 34–37.

"Planned by Hazel Dell Brown," *Good Housekeeping*, August 1930, 167.

Wilson, Alex, "Linoleum, Naturally," *Architecture*, May 1999, 161.

M

MAILLARD REACTION

The Maillard reaction is the chemical process that is responsible for changes in the flavor, color, and nutritive value of foods upon cooking. It is also the process by which mutagenic compounds form. In 1912, at the University of Nancy, French biochemist Louis-Camille Maillard, building on the work of the German chemist Emil Fischer and the brewing expert Arthur Robert Ling, discovered the reason why cooked food tasted good to human diners. The most common methods of heating foods not only raised temperature, but also produced flavor changes:

- The main method of browning was grilling, which altered the surface by infusing smoke and flavor and developing a crisp crust.
- Roasting also encrusted the upper layer of food while sealing in moisture.
- Sautéing and stir-frying, similar quick heating methods, applied high heat and constant agitation in a minimum of fat to produce crisp and tender food.

To analyze these changes scientifically Maillard studied the unknown chemical change in the presence of heat that generated the flavor and texture enhancements.

To reproduce the metamorphosis of food from raw to cooked, Maillard heated sugar and amino acid in a test tube, where the mix slowly browned. The nonenzymatic browning that occurred in cooked food was a chemical change that darkened the color, depending on the amount of water in the tissue, temperature, and food pH. As glucose attached to proteins during cooking, Maillard perceived that it browned the surface.

Maillard reported his findings to the French Academy of Sciences, stating that the reaction affected humans, plants, humus, and combustible minerals. In 1921, he took a faculty post in biology and chemistry at the University of Algiers. After he died in 1936 in Paris, his work was largely forgotten until World War II, when the U.S. military studied unappetizing chemical changes in powdered eggs cooked for soldiers.

In 1946, biochemists H. M. Barnes and C. W. Kaufman of General Foods studied the Maillard reaction to enhance bread crusts, roasted coffee, beer, maple syrup, chocolate, soy sauce, and cooked meat. Subsequent work resulted in artificial maple flavoring and osmazome, the characteristic flavor of meat, which Lever Brothers patented in 1960. By 1963, some five hundred food flavorings and aroma compounds were identified by chemical makeup; in two decades, the number rose to 4,300 and has since nearly doubled.

In 1999, Red Arrow Products of Manitowoc, Wisconsin, reproduced Maillard's reaction with a sugar derivative browning agent appropriately named Maillose. Whether atomized, dipped, rubbed, or sprayed on the surface, the liquid supplied uniform color from a caramelization process that increased with rising temperatures, longer cook time, or additional application of the agent. Cooks were, for the first time, able to produce the bite, chewability, and tenderness in microwaved meat and poultry that had been lacking since microwaves entered the kitchen market. European food processors coated skinless chicken parts with the dry form of Maillose; the agent also browned the casings of sausage and wieners.

Further Reading

Austad, Steven N. *Why We Age*. London: John Wiley & Sons Inc., 1997.

Labell, Fran, "Agent Speeds Controlled Browning," *Prepared Foods*, January 1999.

McGee, Harold. *The Curious Cook*. New York: HarperCollins, 1992.

Ohr, Linda Milo, "Recreating Culinary Trends" *Prepared Foods*, October 2000.

MALTBY, LUCY

During the rise of home economics as a professional field, Lucy M. Maltby made a career at Corning Glass Works, a leading cookware manufacturer, advising the company on design improvements and marketing techniques. A native of Corning, New York, she was born in 1900 and studied home economics with pioneering teachers Flora Rose and Martha Van Rensselaer at Cornell University. At Iowa State College, Maltby earned a master's degree in extension service, family life, home management, and science, with specialties in housewares engineering. On leaving the academic realm in 1929, she joined the staff of Corning, a hometown company manufacturing Pyrex glass bakeware.

As a student in Iowa and later a professor of home economics at Pennsylvania's Mansfield State Teachers College, Maltby had ample experience using Pyrex products. As head of Corning's home economics department, she instituted a systematic approach to market research, product design and testing, and promotion. She advised industry specialists that cooking pans should conform to recipe and oven sizes and that glass cookware needed easy-to-grip handles; she accompanied her suggestions with drawings. From a study of homemakers' comments about Corning cookware, she recommended ways the company could create more desirable products. Maltby also recognized the need for attractive styling to accommodate oven-to-table service, thus reducing the burden of dirty pots and pans.

Under the direction of Pyrex division sales manager James L. Peden, she established a consumer liaison service consisting of a company laboratory kitchen and field testing operation. More than a sales promoter, she answered consumers' letters, provided precise product instructions, and invented utensils, containers, and recipes that made cooking and cleanup easier.

Maltby further educated herself by completing a doctorate at Syracuse University. Her insistence on scientific principles and accountability enhanced the credibility of the work of Lilla Cortright, Helen Martin,

and June Packard, all members of her staff. Using a variety of wood, gas, and electric stoves, they built corporate expertise in cookery for the home, military, and institutions. During her years at Corning, Maltby maintained a collegial relationship with General Foods, Kraft Foods, the Meat Board, Poultry and Egg National Board, and Wheat Flour Institute. She appeared at trade shows and conferences, distributed recipe cards, and compiled *It's Fun to Cook* (1938) and *Pyrex Prize Recipes* (1953) to stress economy, reliability, and versatility of Pyrex products.

Maltby set up course work to train male colleagues in household chores; such training enabled them to increase sales and enhance the Corning image. She provided Corning cookware to field agents and cooking demonstrators, thus increasing the visibility of company products with free publicity. The Meat Board donated the goods Maltby's staff used for demonstrations to schools and public utilities. By the mid-1940s, Corning had secured its place in the kitchenware market. Maltby retired in 1965 after more than three decades devoted to promoting corporate responsibility to consumers and solidifying the place of Corning Glass Works in kitchen history. She died in 1984.

Further Reading

"'Cooking Up' a Double Boiler," *Corning Glassmaker*, April–May 1953.

Stage, Sarah, and Virginia B. Vincenti, eds. *Rethinking Home Economics: Women and the History of a Profession*. Ithaca: Cornell University Press, 1997.

"Where Mrs. Homemaker Is Never Forgotten: Consumer Products Division's Proving Ground for Corning Glassware," *Corning Glass Works Gaffer*, October 1946, 3.

MANIOC

Like the potato and yam, manioc (also called cassava or yuca), has fed natives of the Americas for centuries. The root is poisonous in its raw state and requires heating to remove toxic hydrocyanic acid. As explained in Evelyn Reed's *Woman's Evolution from Matriarchal Clan to Patriarchal Family* (1975), women learned to cook manioc to remove the poisons by converting the tuber from its natural state into food. By squeezing the toxins from the root in a basket press and neutralizing the residue, the cook turned manioc into a staple meal.

Evidence of manioc's fibers survives from as early as 7000 to 5000 BCE in Panama and 2300 BCE in Mexico's Tamaulipas cave region. The easiest way to cook the tubers was hot coal roasting for peeling and eating. Preparation of flour began with grating raw tubers and multiple rinsings to leach out toxicity, which gave hunters a by-produce to use as spear and

Caribbean worker grinding manioc. [© *Original illustration by Dan Timmons.*]

arrow poison. Cooks fashioned manioc dough into loaves, tortillas, and tapioca, a bland food suited to children and invalids.

For the manufacture of beer, Maya brewers preferred corn or the starchy manioc. To ready the fibers, women chewed them and spit the mass into calabashes. Warmed by sunlight or at the hearth, the slurry fermented in the presence of oral bacteria and agents remaining in the gourds from previous batches. The drink found favor with the Cario, Chaco, Gêm Tupí-Guarani, Botocudo, and Charua of South America before Africans brewed it during the Renaissance.

Manioc remains a peasant staple, particularly in Equatorial Guinea, where fermented sticks are daily fare, and Gabon, where cooks form manioc into a paste called *bâton de manioc*. Nigerians balance manioc consumption with servings of yams and rice; Ghanaians have a wider selection of starches, including manioc, millet, rice, corn, and plantain. As depicted in the Lonely Planet guide to Africa, tasty menus on the Ivory Coast accompany chicken or fish entrées with *attiéké* (grated manioc), a specialty served with cold beer. In Fiji, cooks boil manioc with taro plucked from the kitchen garden.

In the slave-influenced cuisine of Cuba and the Dominican Republic, *yuca* (manioc) accompanies rice, sweet potatoes, plaintain, and potatoes. In Guyana, *casareep* (manioc extract) flavors a popular pepper pot stew. Jamaican cooks, also reflecting African heritage, bake manioc dough into *bammy* bread, which they fry and serve with salt fish, the national dish. In Guadeloupe and Dominica, manioc growers follow a labor-intensive task of peeling, grating, extracting juice and pulp, then squeezing out excess water through cheesecloth. After stirring the drying solids on hot griddles, they grind the hardened block into farine, which they

toast as a base for salt fish dishes. Cassareep, the liquid by-product cooked down to a syrup in a *canaree* (clay pot), is a useful meat preservative.

Further Reading

Mason, Otis Tufton. *Women's Share in Primitive Culture*. New York: Appleton, 1911.

Mintz, Sidney, "The Old And New World Exchange," *Nutrition Today,* May 1, 1998, 1–5.

Zimmerer, Karl S., "The Ecogeography of Andean Potatoes: Versatility in Farm Regions and Fields Can Aid Sustainable Development," *BioScience*, June 1998, 445–454.

MANO AND METATE

The mano and *metatl,* or metate, are paired grinding implements with a long history in human food preparation. The original mano was a hand-sized stone roller or cylindrical millstone that crushed berries, grain, nuts, and roots against the concave metate, or grinding board. One of the earliest kitchen implements, it survives at archeological digs as evidence of ancient grinding and milling technology. The archeologist George Carter claims that grinders from California may date to 78,000 BCE, although this date is 68,000 years earlier than the accepted date for aboriginal residency in the Americas. Another pair of grinding stones from Florisbad, Orange Free State, South Africa, appears to have been in use in 46,900 BCE. A set uncovered at Bushman Rock Shelter in Transvaal may have crushed ochre dye around 45,000 BCE. More examples found at Olieboomspoort Cave, Transvaal, and Cuddie Springs, New South Wales, testify to the use of grinding stones by the earliest human inhabitants. From skeletal deformities and signs of wear on female toe, knee, and shoulder bones in northern

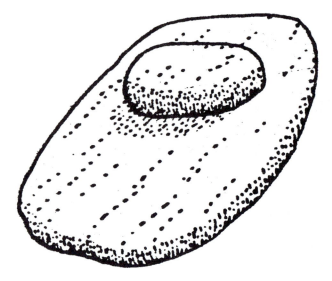

Metate.
[© *Original illustration by Dan Timmons.*]

Mesopotamia, anthropologists have deduced that female cooks daily engaged in chores that required kneeling and exerting arm pressure against a grindstone.

The pre-Hispanic villagers in Joya de Cerén, El Salvador, a settlement destroyed by volcanic ash in 595 CE, positioned large metates on *horquetas,* forked stands similar to modern models. Smaller versions of mano and metate ground pigments for paint and cosmetics. The Mogollon Indians adopted the trough metate after 650 CE to speed the preparation of corn dishes; so, too, did the Nambé Pueblo, who settled north of Santa Fe, New Mexico.

Although use of the paired grinding stones increased nutritional yield, wielding the two-handed mano forced women to spend long periods of time in an uncomfortable crouching position. The perpetual back-and-forth rocking motion of the grinding operation, especially difficult for pregnant women and the elderly, stressed the arms, shoulders, knees, and neck at the same time that it developed strong abdominal, back, and thigh muscles. Anthropologists surmise that women labored at the grinding process for three hours daily during their entire adult lives. A relocation of grinding sites from home hearthside to rooftops and outdoor plazas around 1300 CE suggests a shift from individual to communal labor.

The uses of foodstuffs ground into small particles varied among tribes. Pictures on the Codex Mendoza (ca. 1549), an Aztec history commissioned by the Viceroy Antonio de Mendoza for Charles V of Spain, show very young Aztec girls at work grinding corn for tortillas. To demonstrate their readiness for matrimony, they made *atole* (corn mush), a maize-based pap, from scratch. Using stone grinders on top of carved, four-legged bases, Aztec cooks pulverized cacao beans for

sacred ritual drinks and ground amaranth into flour for cooking as a hot cereal or forming into loaves and cakes. Aztec priests stirred amaranth meal into the blood of human sacrifices, whom they had also fattened on amaranth. After his arrival in Yucatan in 1519, the Spanish explorer Hernán Cortés forbade the use of sacrificial meal and burned the *chinampas* on which farmers grew the plant.

On the Pacific Coast of North America, the Hupa and Pomo wielded a mano or pestle in an oblong basalt metate that they hollowed for the grinding of purified acorn pulp into a floury paste. The acorn meal thickened soups and stews or suited flat bread, cakes, and loaves. The laborious task of grinding and moistening corn removed the pericarp layer to reveal the kernel, the source of corn oil for frying and flavoring foods. The friction also homogenized and gelatinized starch while dehydrating it. The development of corn flour, which stored more easily than fresh corn, greatly augmented seasonal diets and improved the nutrition and general health of people in maize-based cultures. The Havasupai, who resided near the Grand Canyon, valued a hard hand-grinding stone that, unlike the manos of the Hopi, did not spoil seed meal with grit. Ground seed moistened with water formed a butter that cooks spread on bread. For the Hualapai (or Walapai) of Arizona, flat pounding stones and querns (rotary grinders) reduced mesquite beans, piñon nuts, and corn into meal for daily dishes.

Among West Coast Indians and the Tepehuan of Chihuahua, Mexico, the mano and metate, either alone or supported on a wood stand, were a necessity for making *atole,* a traditional finger food that the diner hand-dipped or ladled with a mush spoon or paddle from a communal pot. Cooks also used the creek stone roller to grind corn stalks to extract juice for cooking or fermenting into a drink or to refine rock salt or hard clay for pottery. The soft volcanic basalt of the grinding implements gradually crumbled into the corn meal, producing even grains and simultaneously cleaning diners' teeth and gums through the friction of abrasive particles. The Hopi kept different grades of metates to produce grains varying from coarse to fine.

The grinding of maize homogenized, gelatinized, and dried the starch, protein, and germ, an essential step in the process of making tortillas. The mano and metate were fundamental hearthside tools among the Aztec, who used tortillas daily as both scoop and bread. For this reason, the Aztec maiden had to demonstrate to potential husbands her skill at reducing meal to the correct consistency for tortillas. Mesoamericans pulverized cacao beans with mano and metate and mixed the resulting powder with maize flour, sugar, cinnamon, and vanilla and shaped the mass into a paste for cakes.

When the Spaniards introduced cacao beans into Europe, they imported the mano and metate as the correct tools for preparing chocolate. In 1687, Nicolas de Blegny, the author of *Le Bon Usage du Thé, du Caffé, et du Chocolat* (The Service of Tea, Coffee, and Chocolate), illustrated his text with a picture of a male kitchen servant kneeling behind a metate heated underneath by a box of coals. The European concept of the mano and metate persisted in line drawings in Denis Diderot's *Encyclopédie* (1751–72), which showed how cooks shaped chocolate confections from ground and melted cacao. A nineteenth-century drawing of Italian chocolate workers depicted the chocolate-making at each stage, including an image of a grinder hard at work over a metate that sloped directly into a trough for easy transference of chocolate powder to the cookpot.

On the American frontier, pioneers learned firsthand how to use the mano and metate. In her diary, published as *Down the Santa Fe Trail and Into Mexico* (1846), Susan Shelby Magoffin described a cooking lesson she received from guests, a Hispanic woman and her daughter. After placing a handful of pre-soaked grain on the hollow at the stone's center, the visitors knelt in "a position most fatiguing to the back and indeed the whole frame to rub the corn up and down on the other till it was ground to a paste." (Magoffin 1962, 168) Repeated grindings and wettings produced a fine quality pulp. Placing biscuit-sized lumps on a griddle, the women cooked tortillas over the fire.

In the mid-twentieth century, the mano and metate had not lost their centrality to the Maya kitchen. In parts of Yucatán, each man sought a woman for whom to raise corn. The woman pledged herself to a lifetime of pulverizing grain. Midwives offered newborn females a mano and metate.

See also **Chocolate; Corn; Ollas; Salt**

Further Reading

Coe, Sophie D., and Michael D. Coe. *The True History of Chocolate*. London: Thames & Hudson Ltd., 1996.

Pennington, Campbell W. *The Tepehuan of Chihuahua: Their Material Culture*. Salt Lake City: University of Utah Press, 1969.

Stuart, George E., and Gene S. Stuart. *The Mysterious Maya*. Washington, D.C.: National Geographic Society, 1977.

Weber, Steven A., and P. David Seaman, eds. *Havasupai Habitat*. Tucson: University of Arizona Press, 1985.

MAPLE SUGAR

Like corn, pecans, potatoes, tomatoes, and blueberries, maple sugar is an American original, unknown to the rest of the world before the arrival of European explorers.

The Massachusetts Pilgrims learned how to tap the tall sugar maple tree (*Acer saccharum*) from local Indians, for whom sugaring carried mythic significance.

The Huron and Iroquois drained the sap from sugar maples into mocucks (bark vessels) to make into sugar. Sap collection in March was the occasion for an annual pilgrimage to the sugar bush, a grove where the same families returned season after season. The Indians regarded the flow as a renewal of life and the syrup as a life force rich in health and energy. Sap collectors erected sugar wigwams, where they stored birch bark mocucks and built a fireplace for boiling the sap into a thick liquid to evaporate into granular sugar.

Sap rises in the tree trunk during the first stirrings of spring while nights are still cold. In trees larger than ten inches in diameter, the process of sugaring began with making horizontal slashes three or four feet above the roots, boring holes for the spouts, and collecting sap in watertight mocucks set to catch the flow. The liquid eased from the trunk at a steady rate of sixty-six pounds per day, which yielded 4.5 pounds of sugar. Stone boiling reduced the liquid to a stringy consistency; boiled down, thirty-two to fifty gallons of sap yielded one gallon of dark, sweet syrup.

Sugar makers next passed the liquid syrup through strainers or mats made of cloth or basswood fiber and then into a wooden trough for granulation and packing into molds, shells, or wooden hoops. Using wooden paddles, they worked the mass into sugar loaves for storage. At the end of sugaring season, they polished the kettles with wood ash and a stone, folded the wigwam, and stored it for the next year's sugaring. Throughout the year, to make a grainy confection and all-purpose sweetener, they pounded the sugar cakes and loaves in mortars. Maple sugar served as a treat for children and sweetener for banquet dishes and ritual foods. According to the French *coureurs de bois* (woodsmen), the Chippewa of the Great Lakes region seasoned fish heads with maple sugar and fed them to their babies; the Mahican mixed maple sugar with meal of dried corn for a snack or trail food. The traditional practice of pouring maple syrup over popcorn to form balls was the origin of an American invention, Cracker Jacks, first marketed in 1893.

The culinary technique of preserving foods with sugar, discovered around 1600, enabled settlers in America to store fruit, ham, and other foods by curing them in sucrose, a process called sugaring or sugar curing. Enthralled with the productivity of the sugar maple, Sir William Berkeley, governor of Virginia, reported in 1706 on the Ojibway method of wounding the tree trunk and placing a receptacle under the slash to catch the sap. He estimated that natives made a pound of sugar per eight pounds of liquid. He described the maple sugar as "bright and moist with a full large Grain, the Sweetness of it being like that of good Muscovada [sugar]." (Earle 1975, 111) When barter enlarged the colonial economic system, families valued cakes of the purest white maple sugar as a trade item. For newcomers in Quebec, Ontario, New Hampshire, Vermont, and New York and as far west as Minnesota and Wisconsin, maple sugar surpassed cane sugar in importance as a food additive.

In colonial times, the sap collection method was crude, and the slashing of the bark killed many maple trees. Over time, however, workers refined the process. The collecting season started with reopening of the sugar shack, a staging area that doubled as a work station and temporary residence during chill nights when the sap was high. Before tapping the trees, sap collectors burned the pith from spiles, or spouts, whittled from elder, basswood, or sumac limbs. Tapping consisted of driving the spouts into holes bored into the lower trunks and suspending rough-hewn buckets to catch the sap, which ran clear until April, then turned milky. The greatest runs came from trees more than forty years old, which old hands called "sap cows." (Garbers, 2000)

Into the night, sugaring proceeded at a steady, unhurried pace. Workers made the rounds of spiles to pour the liquid into sap carriers, staved buckets pierced on two sides to accommodate a dowel for a handle or to attach to a wood-and-leather shoulder yoke. In heavy snow, tappers carried the paired buckets to the processor on an ox-drawn sled called a scoot. Larger operations replaced sleds with a gathering tank drawn by horses. Sugars kept the fresh sap cool to halt molding or turning rancid.

At the sugar house, workers heated large potash kettles suspended over the fire from horizontal poles. They stirred the sap with long-handled scoops and skimmed it to remove residue. After cooking for three days, the sap reached the desired consistency, flavor, and color, varying from a dark tan to a dark brown. Sealed in jars, the varying grades of syrup had different uses; some for candy or maple butter, others for baking and canned goods or adding to tobacco.

The maple was not the only tree that produced a flavorful sap. In sub-Arctic Canada, native cooks collected birch sap to boil down into syrup for pouring over dry fish meal. A subtle flavoring made from black birch or cherry birch was a similar food additive prized by the Ojibway. Birches, tapped in early spring, yielded a gallon an hour of lightly sweet liquid. It tasted mildly minty and refreshing but lost its wintergreen flavor during processing. Lengthy boiling reduced it to a syrup as thick as molasses, which cooks valued as a preservative for vegetables, fruit, and berries. In Poland, cooks fermented birch sap into *oskola*,

a beverage consumed during haymaking and harvesting.

In the late 1800s to 1900s, sugaring in the United States ceased to be a family operation; farmers abandoned collection sheds, wooden implements, and sleds. Instead, sap collection became an industrial process, and companies opted for galvanized metal spiles and vats, factory-made collection tanks, and, eventually, networks of plastic tubes that carried the sap downhill or by pump to a central collection point and enclosed evaporator. In her 1955 painting *Sugaring Off,* the twentieth-century U.S. artist Anna Mary Robertson "Grandma" Moses, known for her images of country life, depicted the traditional process as she remembered it from her childhood. In a broad overview of a snowy landscape, members of a rural community perform all the tasks associated with syrup making—hauling logs, building the fire, tapping trees, and stirring the boiling cauldron. She captures the energy and unity aroused by the finished product.

Further Reading

Ball, Jeff, "The Savory Sugar Maple," *American Forests,* Winter 2001, 44–46.

Garbers, Alan, James, "Ambrosia," *Mother Earth News,* February 2000, 74–79.

May, Stephen, "Grandma Moses Country," *Smithsonian,* April 2001, 68–78.

McCarry, Charles, "Home to the Enduring Berkshires," *National Geographic,* August 1970, 196–221.

Papanek, John L., ed.-in-chief. *Hunters of the Northern Forest.* Alexandria, Va.: Time-Life Books, 1995.

Williams, Jacqueline, "Food on the Oregon Trail," *Overland Journal,* Vol. 11, 1993.

MARGARINE

Margarine, a vegetable-oil product sometimes containing dairy products, is a butter substitute. Like the technology of canning, wartime food scarcities and market fluctuations spurred the development of margarine. In 1869, during an economic downturn preceding the Franco-Prussian War, the Emperor Napoleon III offered a reward to anyone who could invent a cheap, stable substitute for butter to feed the French navy and the nation's poor. Only one inventor entered the competition. The French chemist-food technologist Hippolyte (sometimes given as Henri) Mège-Mouriés synthesized margarine after earlier failed attempts to create a spread from beef fat and udder tissue blended with milk and water. By congealing curds from skimmed milk, water, and oleo, the oil in beef suet, at the emperor's farm at Vincennes, Mège-Mouriés produced a white substance remarkably like butter. He named it for the Greek *margarites* (pearl) because he incorrectly assumed that the fat congealed through the action of margaric acid, a nonexistent substance.

Mège-Mouriés produced margarine in Paris at his own factory, but his invention came to nothing after Napoleon fled during the war. In an era of high demand for milk products, a Dutch dairy firm picked up the option and began manufacture. Patented as oleomargarine in the United States in 1873, the product appeared in English markets in 1887 as butterine. It was an oleaginous substance flavored with butter, which, according to standards later set by the U.S. Food and Drug administration, contained 40 percent margarine and 60 percent butter. The Paris Council of Hygiene authorized the sale of margarine so long as it did not appear under the name *butter*. Sold under both names, margarine and butterine, the spread gained popularity for its long shelf life and similarity to home-churned butter.

As controversy grew over the purity and dietary value of butterine, throughout the United States, angry dairy owners sought a competitive edge for their own product. They demanded an outright ban on margarine sales, a high tax on the yellow die used to make it look like butter, or the addition of a green tint to make it easily distinguishable from butter. Nonetheless, ads and question-and-answer columns in women's magazines such as "What Is Margarine Good For?" in the April 1929 issue of *Good Housekeeping* continued to educate housewives about butter substitutes. Dr. Walter H. Eddy, a regular columnist for the Good Housekeeping Institute, declared that oleomargarine was safe and nutritious, although it lacked the vitamin A found in butter.

Alterations in content brought added vitamin A in 1933 and a replacement of coconut oil in 1934. After the invention of the chemical process of hydrogenization, in the 1930s, German processors created margarine from cottonseed, soybean, safflower, canola, sunflower, palm, peanut, and other vegetable fats, thus making a product that was acceptable to vegetarians. By World War II, at a low point in margarine's history, sodium benzoate lengthened margarine's shelf life. In 1947, margarine manufacturers replaced coal-tar dyes with beta carotene from carrots, a colorant that received homemakers' approval.

By law, margarine marketed in the United States had to contain no more than 16 percent water and at least 80 percent fat. By 1950, margarine marketers were luring consumers with bucolic-sounding brand names such as Blue Bonnet, Cloverbloom, Farm Belle, Sunnyland, and Table Maid. In mid-century, when margarine was outpacing butter in sales, manufacturers introduced soft margarine packaged in tubs. In 1998, the Raisio Group of Finland developed Benecol, a costly margarine made from pine extract, which lowered users' cholesterol levels. Imitators quickly introduced competing products. A short time later Olivio, a butter-olive oil blend developed in Italy, went on the market in England. In April 2000, the Big Idea, an exhibit dedicated to invention and creativity in Irvine, Ayrshire, Scotland, honored the original stick margarine as a significant modern idea.

See also **Sailland, Maurice Edmond**

Further Reading

Eddy, Walter H., "Dr. Eddy's Question Box," *Good Housekeeping*, November 1930, 114.
_____, "What Is Margarine Good For?" *Good Housekeeping*, April 1929, n. p.
Mencken, H. L. *The American Language*. New York: Alfred Knopf, 1937.
Wilson, Bee, "A Wonder of the Modern World," *New Statesman*, March 27, 2000, 50–51.

MARKHAM, GERVASE

A late Renaissance author of verse and drama, Gervase (or Jervis) Markham produced a classic of domestic advice, *The English Hus-Wife* (1615), which he subsequently incorporated into *A Way to Get Wealth* (1639). The latter became one of the era's most popular practical guides to housewifely skills and cookery. His compendium on household work spoke of the day-to-day tasks of peasants and middle-class women. Above all, he championed mastery of cooking as the womanly duty upon which marriage was based. Born around 1568 in Nottinghamshire, England, he served in the military in Ireland and Holland before becoming a professional writer. Markham also wrote books on veterinary care, horsemanship, and the farrier's trade.

At a time when home brew was a common beverage, Markham provided detailed directions for the brewing of beer, ale, mead, metheglin, and perry, or pear cider. Writing on kitchen design, he advised that homeowners erect the brew house close to the kitchen to make double use of the heat in the house while preventing smoke from entering the private rooms. A stickler for purity and cleanliness, he explained the importance of proper ventilation, lest smoke taint the beverage, and chose copper over lead utensils and containers and impeccably clean tubs for "worts and liquors." (Markham) Surviving long after his death in 1637, his domestic handbook proved so valuable that it accompanied colonists to the New World and influenced the approach to housekeeping in Canada, the United States, and the Caribbean.

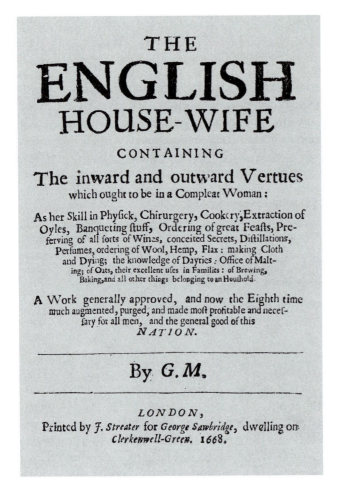

Title page of *The English Housewife* (1668).

Agnes Marshall from *A. B. Marshall's Larger Cookery Book of Extra Recipes* (1891).

Further Reading

Baugh, Albert C., ed. *A Literary History of England.* New York: Appleton-Century-Crofts, Inc., 1948.

Wolf, T. H., and R. J. Byrd, "Once Upon a Time a Cookbook Was a Recipe for Excess," *Smithsonian*, November 1991, 118–126.

MARSHALL, AGNES

The Victorian era's most enthusiastic proponent of iced desserts, Agnes B. Marshall had a successful career as a teacher of cooking, cookbook writer, and promoter of her own line of kitchen equipment. Born Agnes Bertha Smith on August 24, 1855, at Walthamstow, Essex, she learned to cook from home experience and work under skilled Parisian and Viennese chefs. In 1883, she purchased the National Training School of Cookery on Mortimore Street in London, which had been operated by Felix and Mary Anne Lavenue since 1857. The curriculum, a forerunner of home economics education, offered specialty instruction in cooking, including lessons in curry from an English colonel who had served in India and classes in French *haute cuisine*

taught by a Cordon Bleu graduate. Within two years, Marshall built her clientele to forty pupils; they included both professional cooks serving aristocratic families and middle-class women who wanted to set a respectable table. Annual attendance soon numbered in the thousands for day-, month-, semester-, or year-long courses. All students paid the standard tuition of £22 for a three-month enrollment, the equivalent of a cook's annual salary.

Marshall expanded her culinary empire to an employment registry, kitchen shop, and warehouses. Among the items stocked under her own name were specialty foods, utensils, cutlery, cast-iron equipment, and cooking supplies including baking powder, flavorings, vegetable food colorants, leaf gelatin, and in 1888, an edible *cornet à la crème* (ice cream cone) made with ground almonds. Her 1,000 varieties and sizes of tin ice cream molds ranged in motif from Turk's cap, flutes, and geometric towers to fruit, vegetable, and flower shapes. She was noted for encouraging the molding of ice cream into decorative shapes rather than serving it as a crude slab or scoop. In print and in person, she promoted shallow freezers, ice caves (forerunners to the thermos), and refrigerators, which she invented and marketed. With coupons from her products, customers could obtain copies of her cookbooks.

Marshall compiled and illustrated a self-published guide, *Ices Plain and Fancy: The Book of Ices* (1885), later issued as *Victorian Ices & Ice Creams* and subtitled *Cream and Water Ices, Sorbets, Mousses, Iced Soufflés, and Various Iced Dishes with Names in French and English, and Various Coloured Designs for Ices.* The compendium offered sepia photos, line drawings of molds, and 177 recipes for wine and spirit ice creams, jam-flavored frozen desserts, coffee and curry soufflés, nesselrode custard pudding, spinach and cucumber ices, and praline, filbert, and chestnut creams.

Marshall encouraged the placement of *glaces assorties* (assorted ices) in varying colors and flavors in chilled dishes lined with tiny lace paper doilies and cups she called "dish papers." The papers were more than a decoration; they stabilized cold scoops, preventing them from skidding off the plate. They also simplified the mess of washing up after a sticky serving of sweet creams and custards. For a dessert both beautiful and flavorful, Marshall lauded the Neapolitan, an ice called *crème panachée* (stylish cream). To make it, she layered a variety of different flavored creams and ices in a metal box; the chilled confection was sliced like a cake and served on paper lace. Despite her great fondness for creams and ices, Marshall acknowledged their place as special treats "in no way either suggestive of nourishment or solidity." (Marshall 1976, xiv)

Marshall never missed an opportunity to promote her enterprises. In the first chapter of her book she reminded readers that lessons in ice making were regularly scheduled at her London school. Prominent in each recipe and the lengthy appendix were food supplies carrying her brand name. She boasted in an ad for the London *Times* that her freezer could solidify a dessert in three minutes and her ice cave could maintain the temperature for twelve hours.

In 1886, Marshall initiated a weekly newspaper, *The Table,* to which she contributed popular recipes and articles for the remainder of her life. In first-person editorials, she championed the cause of kitchen staff in aristocratic homes, where, she remarked, cooks received less training and respect than carriage horses. Her outspokenness incurred the wrath of financier and newspaper magnate Horatio Bottomley. To maintain stature with readers, she dropped her contract with a printer who refused to publish her sharp remarks.

In 1888, Marshall completed *Mrs. Marshall's Cookery Book,* a compendium based on her classroom and home kitchen experience, which sold more than 60,000 copies. The book, intended for upper-class ladies and their staffs, offered dishes under their English and French names and flourished through fifteen editions. Not all of the text was original—Marshall drew whole passages of recipes from *Gunter's Modern Confectioner* (1867), composed by William Jeanes, confectioner to Queen Victoria, and cribbed menus from *Kettner's Book of the Table* (1877), an encyclopedia compiled by Soho restaurateur Auguste Kettner.

To assure the public's understanding of her procedures, Marshall launched a series of Saturday lecture-demonstrations for aristocratic ladies and their cooks entitled "A Pretty Luncheon." On a schedule of six talks per week, she traveled Birmingham, Glasgow, Leeds, Manchester, and Newcastle; a second tour went to twelve additional cities. Her most publicized live demonstration series, held on consecutive Saturdays in London, drew rave reviews from the *Times*. She took her lectures to the United States in the summer of 1888, but received scant acclaim from the *Philadelphia Evening Bulletin,* which compared her to the well-known U.S. cookbook writer and teacher Maria Parloa.

Toward the end of Marshall's career, she turned from education and writing to charity. She initiated Yule dinners for the poor and maintained winter soup kitchens. In 1891 she issued *Mrs. A. B. Marshall's Larger Cookery Book of Extra Recipes,* a general-purpose compendium dedicated to Helena, daughter of Queen Victoria. The text included American recipes for Philadelphia and Chicago doughnuts, Saratoga potato chips, flannel cakes, and corn on the cob. She retired to Pinner, her estate on the River Pinn, and wrote one more dessert book, *Fancy Ices* (1894), which stimulated the importation of ice from Norway for culinary projects. She died at Brighton on July 29, 1905, while convalescing from injuries received in a riding accident.

Marshall's newspaper, company, and school survived well into the twentieth century, but her influence and opinions endured even longer. She denounced canned food and the substandard meals served in railway cars and depots. She campaigned for the availability of fresh produce and trained kitchen staff. Her prognostications foresaw the acceptance of dishwashers, the expansion of automobile travel, the advent of supermarkets, fad diets, chemical purification of water, refrigerated trucks, and the popularization of the ice cream freezer.

Further Reading

Marshall, Agnes B. *Mrs. A. B. Marshall's Cookery Book*. London: Simpton, Marshall, Hamilton, Kent, & Co., 1894.

_____. *Victorian Ices & Ice Cream*. New York: Metropolitan Museum of Art, 1976.

MASTERS, SYBILLA RIGHTON

America's first patented inventor was Sybilla Righton Masters (also Sabella or Isabella), a Quaker from the western end of the New Jersey colony. Her birth date is uncertain; she was second of the seven offspring of Sarah and William Righton. She may have been a native of Bermuda reared on the Delaware River. As an adult living in Philadelphia, she improved the labor-intensive job of cleaning and curing dried corn into grits, which she valued as an antidote to tuberculosis. She intended to market native American food in Europe as a restorative for invalids.

Because Pennsylvania issued no patents, in 1712, Masters journeyed to London to register her first invention, a stamper for corn. The device operated on horse or water power, which her husband, attorney and landowner Thomas Masters, mayor of Philadelphia, intended to harness at Governor's Mill. She presented the English patent office with drawings and annotations in her handwriting. Under the aegis of King George I, on November 25, 1715, the royal court issued two patents in the name of Masters's husband. The documents credit her with the declaration of a "new Invention found out by Sybilla, his wife." (Vare & Ptacek 1987, 31)

Masters's most important contribution to kitchen work was English Patent No. 401, a design for a system of clubs or hammers dropped into a mortar, a method of refining dried corn into hominy meal that emulated the native American mortar and pestle. The device replaced the grinding wheel. She called the finished meal "Tuscarora rice" after the North Carolina nation who lived among tobacco planters and shared native foods with European settlers. A year later, Masters devised a method of weaving straw and palmetto chips from the West Indies to make chair seats, table mats, infant bedding, baskets, and headwear and sold original hats and bonnets at her shop in London. On the couple's return to Philadelphia in 1717, the Provincial Council of the Pennsylvania colony validated her initial successes.

Further Reading

Vare, Ethlie Ann, and Greg Ptacek. *Mothers of Invention*. New York: Quill, 1987.

MATCHES

The match, or fire lighter, had its origins in prehistory, when early humans first learned how to preserve hot coals and transfer flame from one spot to another by means of a sliver or spill (twist) of a slow-burning substance such as heartwood, pine cones, coconut shells, or palm tow fibers. The Achumahi a woodland tribe of Mount Shasta, California, made fires with juniper whorls and lit them with matches made of slow-burning cedar rope. The Paiute of the Great Basin made their smoldering matches from wood fiber rolled into a cigarlike shape.

Since the Middle Ages, matches have saved the fire builder time, effort, and frustration. The first record of instant lights dates to Tao Ku's *Records of the Unworldly and the Strange* (950 CE), in which he explained in detail how women at the Ch'i court hurried the slow process of striking a light with flint by using pine sticks impregnated with sulfur.

Around 1530, English cooks were using sulfur matches, or spunks, made from wood splits, cording, or paper spills. To enhance flammability, matchmakers dipped the material into melted sulfur, which burned with a blue flame and gave off an acrid odor. They stored matches in a tightly sealed box, which kept them moisture free. Selling matches on the street was a source of income for the poor, who engaged in the risky process of procuring waste wood from woodworking shops, cutting the pieces into splints, and coating the tips in melted sulfur.

In 1786, an Italian inventor touted the first "instantaneous light contrivance," a phosphorus box containing sulfur-tipped matches to be dipped into a vial of phosphorus, a nonmetallic element discovered by the German alchemist Hennig Brand in 1669. Another version of the sulfur match, patented in 1810, consisted of a wood spill coated with a paste of potassium chlorate, gum, and sugar for immersion in a vial of sulfuric acid. A patented tin box placed the matches alongside an inner ring designed to hold the bottle of acid. Inventors experimented with other chemical fire starters, but these failed because of inconvenience. Introduced in 1825, the eupyrion, a matchstick soaked in chlorate of potash, was accompanied by a bottle of sulfuric acid. A quick dip of the matchstick into the bottle produced flame, but the process worked only when the wood was dry.

Yard-long friction fire starters, called sulfurata hyperoxygenata frics or sulfuretted peroxide strikables, and nicknamed "Congreves" after rocket-maker Sir William Congreve, originated in 1827 in the laboratory of John Walker, a chemist and inventor from Stockton-on-Tees, England. The discovery was accidental: Walker inadvertently produced flames when he rubbed a stick that was coated with potassium chlorate and antimony sulfide. Intrigued by the commercial possibilities, he set children and homeless people to work manufacturing his fire starters. At a cost of a shilling for fifty, the wood slivers or cardboard twists holding a dab of yellow sulfur at the tip needed only a quick swipe on "glass-paper" (emery) to produce instant flame.

Walker sold his invention to Samuel Jones, who renamed his matches "Lucifers," from the name of Lucifer, the fallen angel and forerunner of Satan. (*Lucifer* is Latin for "light-bearer.") Jones sold only 250 boxes in the first thirty months of production before the concept gained a loyal following. In 1830, the French chemist Charles Sauria introduced matches made with white phosphorus. These lacked the unpleasant odor produced by Lucifers but emitted poisonous fumes that caused a serious disease, dubbed "phossy jaw," in both workers who made matches and users of matches. In 1834, two years after German factories first began making matches, an American version went into production in Springfield, Massachusetts, at the factory of Daniel Chapin and Alonzo Phillips, who concocted the igniting end from phosphorus, sulfur, chalk, and mucilage. When a Boston firm bought them out, Lucifers took the name "Boston matches." Because a mere jostling of the container could cause one match to ignite another, safety-conscious users kept them in clay-lined tin or enamelware boxes called match safes or alumettes, which sometimes had a steel striker on one edge. Another purpose of the box was to keep rodents from chewing on the matches, which could cause the entire bundle to ignite.

In the wake of numerous incidents of accidental house fires and burned hands and eyebrows, an article in the 1858 *Scientific Artisan* alerted homemakers to the danger of allowing matches to rub together. The author suggested that homemakers keep an earthen or metal box for storing matches rather than leaving them loose on shelves or in closets "where a careless servant, or an unthinking child or a mischievous mouse, may produce disastrous results." (Franklin 1997, 383) The 1885 edition of *Practical Housekeeping* warned that match heads could poison children who put them in their mouths and could set fire to the skirts of women who inadvertently stepped on them.

In 1855, the Swedish inventor Johan Edvard Lundstrom's patented safety match replaced the Lucifer. Lundstrom removed the phosphorus from the match head and placed it in the crushed glass or ground silica striking area on the box. Streamlined matchbooks or packets, which Pennsylvania attorney and inventor Joshua Pusey called "flexibles," passed to the Diamond Match company in 1896 after a messy patent infringement battle. In 1897, Pusey gained his first advertisement

order when the Mendelsohn Opera Company contracted for 200 book matches with photos of singing stars and hand-written announcements of their opening. Thirteen years later, the company patented a nonpoisonous match made from sesquisulfide of phosphorous, which was harmless to children. In 1902, Pabst Brewing Company launched a major ad campaign, distributing ten million matchbooks with its logo on the cover. A common kitchen item around 1910, the nickel-plated Lusk match safe featured a spark guard and striker that protected woodwork and wallpaper from becoming marred.

By 1930, annual match sales numbered more than 8.5 billion. They were more expensive in isolated areas, particularly on the frontier, where pioneers resorted to cheaper "China matches," a block of treated wood splits from which they stripped off one match at a time. Delcie David Bean and his sons D. D. Bean, Jr., and Vernon Bean went into the match business near Mount Monadnock in Jaffrey, New Hampshire. By promoting the popular book match as a source of print advertisement, they launched a vast distribution network. From their initial factory in an abandoned textile mill, they soon expanded to facilities in Winston-Salem, North Carolina, and Oxnard, California, and marketed their goods throughout the United States and Canada.

See also **Fireplace**

MEAD

Mead, a drink made with honey, may be humankind's oldest fermented beverage. It has borne many different names and a variety of forms in different parts of the world, including cyser (honey with apples), hippocras or hypocras (spiced honey with grapes), and metheglin (spiced honey), to list only a few. The word *mead* occurred in Holland as *mede*, in Latvia and Lithuania as *midus*, in Germany as *medu* or *med*, in Bulgaria and the Ukraine as *med*, and in Poland as *miòd*. Czechs and Slovaks said *medovina*; Russians, *medovukha*. The Anglo-Saxons called it by the name *meodu*, the Welsh *myddyglyn*. Around western Europe, the drink was known as *hydromel* (France), *idromele* (Italy), and *hidromel* (Portugal); in Spain, the name was *aquamiel*, which preserved the original Latin combination of "water" plus "honey."

According to *Water in England* (1964), by the English domestic historian Dorothy Hartley, the first mead resulted from the steeping of straw skeps, broken honeycomb, and the filtering bag from which the beekeeper dripped clear honey. Natural fermentation from spores in the rye straw in skeps mellowed mead as a by-product. The water that soaked clean sticky spoons

383

and dishes became ordinary barrel mead for family use. Lightly foamy, it took its sweet aroma from a bush of scented herbs that the brewer stirred into the mix. After air-drying, the fungi thrived, making the herbs reusable in the next batch of mead.

References to mead permeate many ancient texts, including the Vedas, Ramayana (ca. 300 BCE), and Greek myths. The Picts guarded the mead-making process so closely that the last priest to know the secret leaped from a cliff, taking along the Scottish monarch who forced him to divulge it. As ritual, Scots fermented mead from heather honey to honor a sea god. The ceremony occurred each June 9, the feast day of St. Columba, the Ionian monastic and Christianizer of Scotland who built a leprosarium and treated sufferers with *aquavit* and *uisgebeatha* (water of life), the original Irish whiskey.

Mead making has taken numerous forms, depending on the natural resources at hand. The Maya fermented a sacred drink called *balche*, a quinine-laced vermifuge (remedy for worm infestation) that purified the digestive tract. Another category, called bracket, bragget, or bragot, made by the Celts of Wales, featured honey as an additive of ale. At the end of the tenth century CE, Russian bee stalkers in Vasil'ev collected honey as the base for a mead drink. Other variants include a yeast-fermented Sudanese beer called *duma*; *mádhu* in India; a honey beer fermented with *nggign* (fern) among the Caingang of Brazil; Australian Grevillea nectar; fermented *poull*, or honey water, in New South Wales; an Ethiopian barleyed honey water called *tej* or *t'edj*; *pure* or hop-brewed mead; *borgerastre*, or herb-tinged honey; a doubly sweet sack mead; and honey ale or honey beer.

Mead is the featured beverage in *Beowulf* (ca. 700 CE), the Anglo-Saxon folk epic; Aneirin's *Y Gododdin* (ca. 500), a Welsh chronicle featuring the toasts that preceded the battle of Cattraeth; the *Kalevala* (ca. 1100), the Finnish epic; and the *Edda* (ca. 1200), Iceland's literary epic. The latter links consumption of mead with the bravery of Viking warriors, who also consumed their favorite beverage in the afterlife at Valhalla.

Mead originally refreshed the mighty and prestigious. The aristocratic Roman imbiber preferred wine, but enjoyed occasional *mulsum*, a wine beverage sweetened with honey. In Wales, a thirteenth-century law established the biennial *gwestfa*, an entertainment tax that supported the royal table and cellar. Each township offered the king a tun of mead deep enough to bathe in, perhaps in token of good wishes for his health. In Mongolia at the court at Karakorum in 1254, a decorative four-sided fountain dispensed saki, *koumiss*, or fermented mare's milk, wine, and *bal* (mead) into huge hemispheric bowls.

In his *Description of Elizabethan England* (1577), Chaplain William Harrison writes at length of beverages. He speaks well of fruit drinks, notably cider, pomage, and perry, but of homemade mead, he sneers: "There is a kind of swish-swash made also in Essex, and divers other places with honeycombs and water, which the homely country wives, putting some pepper and a little other spice among, call mead. . . . Truly it is nothing else but the washing of the combs when the honey is wrung out, and one of the best things that I know belonging thereto is that they spend but little labour, and less cost, in making of the same." (Harrison, 1577) Written long after Italian, Spanish, Portuguese, and French wines had consumed the European imagination as the drink of choice, his commentary comes after centuries of table service when hosts had little more to offer guests than fermented cider, perry, ale, or mead.

In the 1700s, Russian mead evolved from plain fermented honey-water to a treacly raisin wine, to which home brewers added barm. The purpose of raisin mead was to extend wine making to a year-round activity. In the absence of suitable sacral wine, it became a standard Passover drink for Ashkenazic Jews of eastern Europe. In Elena Burman Molokhovets's classic Russian illustrated cookbook, *A Gift to Young Housewives* (1861), a recipe for a small barrel of raisin wine calls for ten pounds of fruit and the pulp and zest of five large lemons. After twelve days' fermentation on ice, the beverage was ready for bottling.

In 1984, an archeological dig on Rhum Island west of Scotland turned up a pot of dried mead dating to 2500 BCE. Chemists separated the dregs into the original ingredients—heather honey, oats, barley, royal fern, and meadowsweet. Distillers William Grant and Sons of Scotland attempted a revival of the Celtic brew, but failed to produce a drinkable mead.

See also **Digby, Kenelm; Honey; Markham, Gervase**

MÉDICIS, CATHERINE DE

An influential figure in European food history, Catherine (or Caterina) de Médicis, mother of two queens and three kings, originated France's *grand cuisine*. Born on April 13, 1519 to Madeleine de La Tour d'Auvergne, a Bourbon countess, and Lorenzo de Médicis, Duke of Urbino, she lost her parents in childhood and came under the care and tutelage of Florentine and Roman nuns. In contrast to the monastic austerity of these later years, her earlier years among the splendid Médici villas introduced her to court dances and banquets that were the hallmark of Flo-

Jean Nicot presenting the tobacco plant to Queen Catherine de Médicis and the Grand Prior of the House of Lorraine.
[© *Library of Congress, Prints and Photographs Division (LC-USZ62-116155)*]

rentine society. At age fourteen, Catherine agreed to a marriage with Henry, Duc d'Orléans, that her uncle, Pope Clement VII, arranged.

After Henry was crowned Henri II in 1547 and took up with a mistress, Diane de Poitiers, he began to emblazon double D's on buildings and monuments. Catherine, less trim and stylish than her rival, turned her energies to the education of the seven survivors of her ten children and their preparation for royal duties. In addition to building the Tuileries and designing Chenonceaux, the country estate that she left incomplete, she introduced her subjects to Renaissance Italian cuisine, thus establishing the basis for French dominance of gastronomy for centuries to come.

Catherine did not arrive in France empty handed. A hearty eater, she brought with her olive oil, recipes for ricotta cheese, and the seeds of New World beans, artichokes, savoy cabbage, spinach, broccoli, peas, and haricot beans, all relatively new to the French. In addition to importing Italian cosmetologists, artists, musicians, tailors, dancers, and perfumers, she brought

chefs to enliven culinary arts. To kitchen procedures, her Italian staff introduced deep frying, *béchamel* sauce, crêpes, and the *bain-marie*, the water bath that refines and gentles foods that would otherwise dry out in baking. For a wedding celebration, one Sicilian specialist in ices produced a series of *granitas*, a different flavor for each day of festivities.

Catherine liked gaiety. Her staff busied about the kitchen preparing *fêtes*, which she labeled "magnificences." (Visser 1991, 28) Her dinners, ballets, and costume balls promoted political harmony. While she spent two years introducing her son Charles IX to his future subjects, the French reciprocated with castle banquets and humbler repasts at inns and private homes, prepared with the aid of her traveling cook staff. The demonstrations of professional cookery helped disseminate her imported cuisine to the masses.

To the cultivated table Catherine introduced Italian etiquette, porcelain plates, and Venetian crystal. To the court menu she introduced sweetbreads, aspic, truffles, macaroni, ice cream, sherbet, and zabaglione. Her personal recipe collection included herbed sea skate, eel, shrimp, *garmugia* (artichoke soup), and innovative spicing. She valued piquant flavors to enhance foods rather than to conceal the taint of spoiled meat. When Europe suffered famine during poor harvests, in 1565, she reduced extravagant and wasteful dinners to three courses. On behalf of the women of France, she rescinded rules dating to Charlemagne that brought them to meals only rarely and established equality of men and women at table. Catherine died at Blois on January 5, 1589. A decade before her death, primarily because of her influence, Italian cooking dominated the kitchens of Europe.

Further Reading

Ballerini, Luigi, "Catherine de' Medici," *La Cucina Italiana*, June–July 1999, 90–91.

MEDIEVAL KITCHENS

During the Middle Ages (400–1450 CE), social class largely determined the quantity and quality of foods available to people. For the poor, meals were simple, food preparation was minimal, and hunger was constant. Kings and landed nobility enjoyed elaborate menus featuring a variety of ingredients prepared in well-staffed kitchens.

Struggle for Sustenance

In Byzantium, the peasantry ate cold work-a-day meals consisting of bread and cheese, fruit, and olives. Lower-class European peasants and cotters suffered extensive periods of hunger, brought on by epidemics, invasions, taxes and tariffs, crop failure, and vicissitudes of marketing and transportation. The struggle for sustenance was ongoing, particularly in winter and during crop shortfalls. Under the principles of feudalism, during periods of danger from insurgents, drought, or epidemic, the lord could call his tenants to perform *boons* or *benes*, voluntary work for the estate. In exchange, he rewarded the faithful from his kitchen or larder sufficient water, ale, bean or pea gruel, bread, cheese, and meat or fish to express his thanks and keep them alive and vigorous for future labors.

John de Garland's *Dictionary* (1220) summarized the needs of a worthy man's household as a demountable table with trestles and white tablecloth, hemmed towel, three-legged stools, firebrands, a hearth and fireplace crane, candlesticks, benches, armchair, bedstair, folding chairs, quilt, bolster, cushions, two sieves, bucket, milk pail, cheese vat, and mouse traps. In his description of dishwashing, Garland names the dishes that were most frequently scrubbed: cauldrons and *becdasne* (spouted pots with handles), pitchers, plates, frying pans, basins and *fèrals* (water jugs), mortars, trenchers, saucers, vinegar bottles, bowls and spoons, gridirons, graters, meat hooks, and chafing dishes.

Families had primitive sanitary arrangements—plumbing was nonexistent and pigs, goats, geese, and hens wandered at will about kitchen and larder. Kitchen furniture consisted of little more than flat wood circles and rectangles pegged with splints for legs or "the board," a collapsible dining surface mounted on trestles. Families huddled in inglenooks and niches inside the fireplace as sources of warmth and places to dry clothes, cook pastry on bake stones, and toast the typical oat or wheat loaf.

This bleak domestic model advanced to hearth and chimney in the half-timber stucco cottage that merged residence with cow barn. High-backed settles offered a draft shield for fireside seating and storage room below its seat. Windmills pumped water that householders had formerly been obliged to haul from streams and springs; wells brought underground water closer to the cook, who accessed the supply with a wooden well bucket lowered on a windlass or sturdy capstan.

For convenience, the cook or servant often washed dishes on a wood bench by the well and pulled handfuls of soapwort planted nearby to facilitate removal of grease. For washing dishes closer to the kitchen, the householder positioned a water butt, a barrel mounted on a brick plinth to keep the wood from rotting. Another source of kitchen water was the garden cistern placed at the corner of the roof to catch rainwater. A tap near the bulge simplified the matter of filling firkins and basins.

Water- and dray-powered mills eased the chores of grinding grain and pressing apples and pears for fermentation. The predominance of meat, seafood, grain, and dairy goods created hearty fare, rounded out with the sweet-sour sauces combining for example, raisins and vinegar into *agradolcie* to balance body humour.

Grand Kitchens of the Gentry

For gentry, aristocrats, and royalty, meals ranged from breakfast and lunch to a late-night supper; the latter, according to Chaplain William Harrison's *Description of Elizabethan England* (1577), was the invention of Hardy Canute, who ruled England in the early eleventh century. The kitchens of the upper classes, like their great halls, displayed elegant appointments and functioned on a grand scale. At Chepstow Castle in Monmouthshire, Wales, adjacent to the high-ceilinged great hall lay a sumptuous food storage and preparation space in a buttery, where the butler poured beverages from butts and bottles. The buttery originally contained a sink and drain that directed waste to the river. An adjacent pantry served for readying bread for the table. For grand meals, additional kitchen rooms supplemented food preparation areas.

To the rear of the main hall near the great eastern gatehouse and guard room, builders erected an oven and serving complex, which retained cooking odors and heat to keep them from destroying the pleasure of diners. A screened passage allowed cook and serving staff to move about without disturbing the progress of the meal. Near the slaughtering area, an outdoor scullery contained utensils and basins for washing dishes. For unusually large meals, such as the banquet held for the crowning of Edward I in 1273, householders set up auxiliary kitchens to accommodate spits and cauldrons.

Carpenters, smiths, stone masons, and painters applied Gothic touches to furnishings, wainscoting, and wood and iron architectural elements. Flooring ranged from stone slabs or geometric tile or brick patterning to pegged oak or elm boards.

Staffing, which was more than generous, followed a carefully delineated hierarchy of status. The Earl of Northumberland once employed 166 servants at the kitchen, scullery, larder, bakehouse, brewery, and dairy. From medieval times, Windsor Castle resembled a small town. Even an abbey might have close to 1,000 dependents. In 1206, during the reign of King John of England, royal carpenters added a roof to Clarendon Hall, along with two new kitchens large enough to manage the roasting of three oxen and a Yule feast consisting of twenty oxen, 100 each of hogs and sheep, 1,500 hens, and more than 416 dozen eggs. As of 1350, the staff of Thomas, Lord Berkeley, daily fed a household of 300. At its largest, in 1420, the household of the Earl and Countess of Warwick numbered 125; for the Duke of Buckingham in 1507, the number could fluctuate from 100 to 200 on major holidays.

To meet the dining needs of such huge households, architects simplified food preparation by elevating kitchen ceilings and ventilating the roof with louvres or chimneys to accommodate the teamwork of five to fifty kitchen laborers in a dimly lit atmosphere. An ample supply of pots, tripods, mortars and pestles, hatchets, stirring sticks, baking pans, meat hooks, and griddles complemented table necessities of round or square *tailloirs,* or *tranchoirs,* trenchers of bread that served as plates or platters. The head cook, according to the food historian Isabella Beeton, sat on a high chair and directed proceedings with a wood spoon, which also served for tasting dishes and drubbing idlers and incompetents. Next in importance in great manor kitchens was the master *saucier,* the cook most responsible for creating good flavor and aroma. Lesser workers performed the more routine kitchen tasks.

Because of the bustle, noise, odor, heat, and danger of fire, floor plans separated kitchen from main house. The grandeur of these vaulted, shuttered work spaces survived into the twenty-first century at Raby Castle, Durham, a gray stone residence built by the Neville family in the fourteenth century, and at Stanton Harcourt, Oxfordshire, where the elaborate kitchen design paralleled the magnificence of the great halls themselves.

For the privileged, meals consisted of two formal presentations. The first, dinner, occurred in late morning and sufficed as the most important meal of the day. The foods, too, took a pre-determined order, starting with an aperitif or posset, light fruit, and salad dishes, followed by eggs and sweets. A phalanx of liveried servants made a steady pilgrimage from fireside to table, holding heads high and stepping lively to keep food from cooling before it arrived at the plate. The meal concluded with the passing of a decorated box of *dragées* (hard spiced candy) and the pouring of hypocras or mulled wine.

Daily readying of the great hall for a meal necessitated the removal from the floor of old straw or rushes, excrement, grease, ale, and the fish heads, gristle, and bones chewed by the family's dogs. Sweepers scrubbed wood floors with succulent leaves to stain the grain before polishing them with wax. They strewed fresh rushes or plaited mats and fragrant herbs on the floors. In the most elegant of castles, the lord's *table dormant* (permanent table) was a sturdy wood piece on legs, set on a dais of wood or stone under a canopy in a prominent place at the head of the chamber.

For all the advancements in fireplace technology up to this time, the kitchen work generated in these large households was laborious and heat intensive. The year had its busy seasons, in particular the arrival of the first frost, the time for the slaughter and salting or smoking of beef and preparations for Yuletide and New Year's feasting.

An important task for the cook was grinding and melting gelatin, a tasteless, odorless collagen extracted from animal carcasses by boiling bones, hoofs and other connective tissues. The gelatin freshened fish and pork and chicken stews. In Ireland, cooks used carrageen, or Irish moss, a purplish seaweed, to produce a similar clear aspic or thickener. Because of the complexities of preparing and applying of gelatin, these skilled tasks were accorded to the more experienced cooks. Galantine, another coagulated protein jelly, derived from boiled fish or meat. Cooks stirred it into a specialty sauce spiced to the tastes of the individual chef and used as a preservative. In addition to cooking and dressing foods, cooks obscured the odors of less-than-fresh ingredients by sprinkling dishes with expen-

MEDIEVAL KITCHENS

sive peppers, musk, or blossoms of hawthorn, iris, primrose, rose, or violet from the kitchen garden.

Under the vassalage system, laboring families were obliged to put the welfare of nobles over their own needs or ambitions. Work in their own behalf began only at nightfall, after a day spent gathering the lord's walnuts, cultivating his arbor, threshing his grain, stabling his livestock, brewing his ale, and carrying wood tankards of water from conduits to fill the master's bath. In a bleak one-room home, the peasant cook dried fruits and vegetables by the fireside, the family's source of heat and light, and suspended braided onions and garlic from the ceiling beam. The rare bird or hare roasted on an oak stick.

For major victualling, the lord's provisioning staff looked to local goods to stock the larder and may have bartered for commodities when coins were scarce. Weights and measures were standardized. Cooks supervised weighing and dispersal during major expenditures for local meats, annual vintages, additions to equipment and storage vessels, and repairs. Keeping track of financial transactions was a challenge for kitchen workers, who were largely illiterate.

The vast estates of kings and feudal seigneurs supplied their tables with wealth of the land, including game of all sorts. Charlemagne expected the royal larder to contain bacon and salted meat, smoked ham, sausage, cheese and butter, mustard, honey, mead, malt, and beer. He listed the skilled underlings necessary to the smooth running of the manor: "blacksmiths, a goldsmith, a silversmith, shoemakers, turners, carpenters, sword-makers. . .men who know how to make beer. . .bakers to make pastry for our table," all superintended by *missi dominici* (the lord's emissaries), who inspected all on the king's behalf. (Severy 1977, 57) Castle and estate management was the job of the steward or seneschal, who superintended the lord's fiefs, lands, livestock, servants, taxes, and rents. Better educated than a cook or provisioner, he knew the amount of meat, fruit, and vegetables to expect from the flocks and herds, hives, warrens and rabbit runs, fishponds, dovecotes, barns, orchards, and gardens.

The palace kitchen hummed with constant labor, beginning long before sunrise with the soaking and rinsing of salt-cured meat, the stoking of the bake oven or bake house, and the crusting of loaves with spices and herbs. Workers eviscerated, dressed, scalded, and plucked freshly slaughtered fowl before roasting or storing them in brine tubs. At fireside, assistants turned broaches that fit into elevated andirons and basted sides of beef, legs of mutton, joints of pork, and spitted birds. Work extended over so much of the day that workers typically slept at the hearth. To add to the confusion of the busy castle kitchen, visiting royalty and important dignitaries brought their own cooks and serving staff, who expected the best of foodstuffs and demanded separate hearths and quarters and the obeisance of locals.

Cooking and formal presentation challenged cooks to create wholesome, fragrant, attractive entrées. For these displays, cooks maintained the shine on house plate and serving pieces with polishing paste and carefully guarded their secret techniques for producing crispy duckling skin, flamed pudding, crusted breads, sparkling wines, and savory herb-roasted vegetables. Labor-intensive kitchen procedures included the making of *mortrews*, a meat or fish dumpling, and the formation of a loaf-style dessert called a leach, or the mounding of a succulent *blancmange*, a semi-solid custard. Kitchen artistry called for the application of laurel leaves to meat aspic and the stuffing of pies with meats, egg, and fish seasoned with dried fruit. Colored aniseed comfits in contrasting colors adorned pottages; pastry points stood upright in the *flampeyn* (tart).

To satisfy the discerning mistress, the *officier de bouche* (head chef) mastered subtleties of cuisine: the stewing of chickens with claws, heads, and viscera intact, the boiling of eels in wine, the sculpting of sugar figures. The boar's head came to table with garlanded ears and fruit in mouth; fish, rabbits, and pigs cooked whole on a rotating spit. The most difficult to preserve, peacocks, cranes, curlews, and herons, had skin and feathers removed for cooking. Cooks redressed them to preserve the grandeur of the living bird. As a last-minute refinement, their beaks and combs were gilded.

After all diners took their seats, servants lifted trays high overhead in a formal promenade led by the hall marshall, who wielded a white staff of office on his emergence from the carved screen at the end of the hall. A memorable *entremet*, or specialty presentation, mimicked the children's rhyme "Old King Cole" by topping a huge pie tin with crust so the master could make a stir by slicing it open to release live songbirds. In the mid-1400s, Olivier de La Marche, head steward of Charles the Bold, presented an *entremet* with himself seated on an elephant led by a huge servant in Saracen costume. In the main hall, liveried table servants set places with wood or metal trenchers, knives, and spoons and served slices of meat, grilled fish, and bread while the wine steward poured fresh drink. The cook's perquisite was first choice of leftovers; assorted kitchen varlets claimed scraps and scrapings and any remaining crumbs went to the poor, who turned scavenged bits of bread into bread soup.

See also **Alcohol; Banquets; Cabinets and Cupboards; Etiquette; Kitchen Gardening; Knives; Linens; Servants; Spices; Tables; Wine**

388

Further Reading

Furnivall, Frederick J., ed. *Early English Meals and Manners: John Russell's Boke of Nurture.* London: Kegan Paul, Trench, Trübner & Co., Ltd., 1868.

Girouard, Mark. *Life in the English Country House: A Social and Architectural History.* New Haven, Conn.: Yale University Press, 1978.

Negrin, Micol, "Medieval Magic," *La Cucina Italiana,* March–April 1999, 46–51.

Pelner-Cosman, Madeleine. *Medieval Holidays and Festivals: A Calendar of Celebrations.* New York: Charles Scribner's Sons, 1981.

Toy, Sidney. *Castles: Their Construction and History.* New York: Dover Publications, 1985.

METALWORK

Unlike earlier materials used in the kitchen—natural fibers, wood, clay—metal alloys allowed makers of cookware some leverage in matters of heat distribution, shaping, and tempering surfaces. In contrast to the problems posed by combustible baskets and breakable ceramics, the drawbacks of metal cookware were few, although critical to performance. Warping caused by exposure to high temperatures, loose handles and rivets, discoloration upon contact with acid foods, and scratched cooking surfaces compromised some vessels, rendering them unsightly, hazardous, or useless.

Another source of concern was toxicity. The danger was widely recognized, but the unwary cook needed reminders. Elena Burman Molokhovets, author of the classic Russian cookbook *A Gift to Young Housewives* (1861), advised against using copper vessels for soup-making and urged the cautious housekeeper to re-tin copper cookware every two months. The hazard persisted in the twentieth century. In the Tyrol province of Austria from 1900 to 1974, some 138 infants and small children died from cirrhosis of the liver due to exposure to toxic metals. The source was milk boiled in untinned copper and brass cookware.

Early Alloys

The first use of copper in cook pots occurred in Asia. Bronze, a blend of tin with copper, was a Chinese invention around 3500 BCE, when smelters used the new material to shape harder weapons and more durable tools and cook pots than the traditional stone implements and clay vessels. By 2000 BCE, the Shang advanced technology with bronze casting. At a foundry in Hsiao-t'un, near Anyang, China, the industry flourished as early as the thirteenth century BCE, producing cookware, ritual and ceremonial vessels and bells, serving dishes, and utensils. A specialty, the three-legged *li*

(cook pot), heated directly on top of embers and accommodated a *hsien* (basket) to form the first two-stage steamer.

The *acquamanile* or *aquamanile,* a medieval ewer that held water for hand washing, often took the form of an animal. One bronze piece, inlaid with copper and silver and dating to eight-century CE Persia, resembled a bird of prey. An Arabic inscription on the neck quoted the Koran: "in the name of God the Merciful the Compassionate, Blessings from God." ("Oriental Art") The artisan who created this pitcher, the earliest datable Iranian bronze object, signed himself Master Suleiman.

So-called bell metal, a blend of copper and tin, resembled brass, but altered the standard mix of two parts copper to one part tin to a mix of three- or four-to-one. In addition to bells, the resulting metal suited the shaping of kettles, skillets, spiders, and mortars and pestles. Among the Bedouin, the tinned copper *jidda* (kettle) became the standard stewing pot for freshly butchered meat. Greek cooks relied on the bronze *teganon* (stew pan), which they placed on a tripod to lift it above the hearth flame.

Plating a metal with a thin covering of another type of metal was a skill that originated prior to the Middle Ages. In 1220 the English grammarian John de Garland reported in his *Dictionary,* "Craftsmen who cover vessels with golden and silver encrustations are called cup-makers, and they put feet under bowls which they encircle with hoops that they may be more beautiful and more durable." (Rubin 1981, 39) His comment suggests that plated vessels primarily adorned the tables of the rich and privileged. The same was true of enameled vessels. Enameling—the coating of metal with molten glass—developed in the 1600s in Europe and in China during the rule of emperor K'ang-hsi for the enhancement of incense burners.

Among the Lambayeque or Sicán peoples of coastal Peru, in the thirteenth century, metalwork in gold, copper, and gold alloy employed whole families. In workshops at Cerro Huaringa, specialists adapted the familiar kitchen mano and metate as the stone *batán* and *chunga,* a pair of grinding implements requiring the same rocking motion used when grinding corn for tortillas. Families worked together—man, woman, and children—to complete metalwork projects, from the crushing of slag and extraction of prills (pellets of solidified molten metal) to the completion of domestic duties that supported craft workers. Bronze casting survived in southwestern Ecuador into the twenty-first century, when laborers still fueled and tended stone-mounded home forges.

Industrial Metals

Within seven centuries of the invention of metalworking technology, ironworkers expanded their manipulation of ores to the making of carbon steel, a strong material suitable for shaping weapons and kitchenware. By the 1700s, English blast furnaces at Coalbrookdale were turning out iron for machines, tools, and home products.

Factory-made copper in the 1800s came with a tinned interior to keep acid food from releasing copper acetate. Preparing the carpet-wrapped copper or zinc foot warmer for use on footstools and in chilly beds was often the last duty of the cook, who filled it with the remaining hot water from the copper water boiler or kettle in the kitchen. In the morning, the staff stoked the hearth and set water boilers again to heat. Invented in 1854, one model offered a projecting tapered spigot mounted at the bottom of the pot for the user's convenience.

In her *Cooking School Text Book and Housekeeper's Guide to Cookery and Kitchen Management* (1879), the U.S. domestic authority Juliet Corson emphasized the importance of copper utensils. In Chapter One, where she listed the criteria for a functional kitchen, she wrote, "There can be no questions of the superiority of copper cooking utensils over those composed of any other metal, providing they are used with care." (Corson 1879, 21) She acknowledged that copper vessels were more costly than those made of iron or tin, but she noted that copper pieces survived high heat without wearing out. She reminded the thrifty cook that old copper had a higher resale value. On the matter of cleaning copper cookware, she cited the New York Cooking School's best chef, who washed utensils in soda water and scoured them with a blend of soft soap and sand.

Common nickel- and chrome-covered objects included wood and steel fruit ballers or bezel scoops, which shaped and crimped melon pieces for fruit compote or table decoration. Block tin or retinned ware, a sheet coated with refined tin, was lower in quality than grain tin or stream tin. In 1825, Isaac Babbitt blended antimony, copper, and tin into a white alloy dubbed Babbitt metal. Similar to Britannia metal, it was a cheap imitation of silver or pewter. Chrome also coated inexpensive kitchen furniture. The ChromCraft Dinette set, made in St. Louis by the American Fixture and Manufacturing Company, was a favorite of economical U.S. housewives. In 1877, the International Nickel Company in New York City began making common culinary implements from monel, a noncorrosive alloy patented in 1905, which blended nickel and copper with minor amounts of carbon, iron, manganese, and silicon.

One of the giants of the kitchenware industry, the S. W. Farber Company, got its start in a Manhattan tin workshop in 1900. From there, the company pioneered Farberware, plating table goods in chrome and silver and manufacturing high-quality pots, pans, broilers, and automatic coffeemakers. In midcentury, the company turned to aluminum and stainless steel goods and, in 1954, engineered the first stainless steel electric fry pan.

Innovation in metals during this period greatly changed the appearance and efficiency of kitchens. Early twentieth-century workspaces featured wipe-clean block tin as a sturdy, thrifty covering for counters and cabinets. In 1921, Giovanni Alessi Anghini, an Italian metalsmith, electroplated metal with brass, chrome, nickel, and silver. From coffee services and table utensils, the family-operated Alessi Company developed vessels both practical and beautiful. Within a half-century Ettore and Alberto Alessi wed design to art to produce a wire fruit basket in stainless steel as well as kettles, beverage sets, and other table objects.

Women's magazines were enthusiastic advocates of metal cookware and utensils. In the mid-1930s, *Good Housekeeping* carried ads for a nickel-plated brass thermos that could keep cold foods cool for seventy-two hours and maintain heat in hot foods and beverages for twenty-four. Other innovations in metal tackled the basics of domestic work. The Chore Girl knitted-copper sponge offered the homemaker a rinsable pot scrubber that did not shed splinters like other metal scouring pads.

In 1939, the U.S. Revere Copper and Brass Company, founded in Rome, New York, in the 1890s, introduced an American staple—the Revere-ware copper-bottom steel pan, valued for even heat distribution. Because of its malleability and appealing color, copper became a common additive to metals used in the manufacture of molds, funnels, kitchen utensils, and cookware. It conducted heat well and distributed it evenly for a thorough cooking, as demonstrated by the French *plafond,* a tinned-copper baking sheet used for browning meat chunks. For these reasons, copper was an element in Babbitt metal, bell metal, brass, Britannia, Muntz's metal, and German and nickel silver. One item, the ham or turkey boiler, featured tin-lined copper in a large oval shape with removable tray. Another, the untinned copper jam cooker, stabilized the intensity of heat for evaporating moisture from fruit.

In the post-World War II era, tubular chrome was the top seller in dinette sets. An ad for Daystrom Corporation's kitchen furnishings depicted a new kitchen with a chrome-banded, plastic-topped table and lightweight chairs, with tubular legs matching those of the table, boasting cushioned seats in wipe-clean plastic.

Enhancing the metallic theme was the Aristo appliance mat, a chrome utility pad designed to fit the workspace on large kitchen ranges, providing a safe place to set hot dishes and coffee carafes. As a guide to homemakers, the master chef James A. Beard and his colleagues compiled *The Cook's Catalogue* (1975) with detailed information on the best metal implements and vessels to purchase for outfitting a kitchen.

Into the twenty-first century, metalwork offered cooks quality utensils with a longer life and more advantages than the original ironware and alloyed pieces. A premium line of cake pans, cookie sheets, and jellyroll pans with a unique five-ply construction was durable at high heat, dishwasher safe, and impervious to chipping, flaking, staining, warping, or bending.

Although expensive, titanium kitchenware had advantages over other metal items. Heavy-gauge titanium cookware from Denmark offered glass tops and resin handles that were ovenproof to an unprecedented 500 degrees Fahrenheit. Titanium knives held an edge much longer than those crafted of stainless steel and weighed half as much. In addition, the titanium blade was bacteria-resistant and did not stick to foods such as cheese.

Copper cookware remained popular, although manufacturers were still combating its earlier associations with toxicity. The Copper Development Association of England assured consumers that coatings on copper kitchenware protected foods from metallic taste, but the organization did not guarantee safety from toxicity. Moroccan *suks* (markets) showcased polished brass and chased copper goods for kitchen and table. In Majorca, off the eastern coast of Spain, paella houses displayed braising pans nearly two feet wide in which cooks combined the sausage, shellfish, chicken, vegetables, and saffron rice that constitute their national dish. In Turkey, the traditional cook relied on the *djindjère,* a hemispheric dish of beaten copper. A similar vessel from Portugal, the hinged, tin-lined copper *cataplana,* used for steaming seafood and sausage, imitated the shape of a clamshell.

See also **Aluminum; Brass; Flatware; Monel; Pewter; Precious Metals; Tinware**

Further Reading

Corson, Juliet. *Cooking School Text Book and Housekeeper's Guide to Cookery and Kitchen Management.* New York: Orange Judd Co., 1879.

MICROWAVING

Microwaves provide a technological advancement in satellite broadcasting, long-distance communication, aircraft spotting, surgery, rubber curing, metal and laundry drying, sewage disposal, and industrial and home food processing. As a sideline to weightier applications, microwaving expedites thawing frozen foods, reheating leftovers, and preparing frozen meals and snacks such as popcorn, nachos, and egg rolls.

The first electronic tube that produced microwaves was the magnetron, invented for use in radar during World War II by Sir John Randall and H. A. Boot. In 1946, the physicist Percy le Baron Spencer of Howland, Maine, created the first microwave oven. His idea came after accidentally melting chocolate in his pocket while standing in front of a magnetron. He tested his theory that microwaves could cook food by popping corn in a brown paper bag.

Raytheon of Waltham, Massachusetts, first marketed an institutional microwave oven in 1947, but did not begin manufacture of home ovens until 1967. The premiere model, made by Tappan in 1952, stood five feet tall and weighed 750 pounds. It sold for $5,000, but the price quickly dropped as the appliance shrank in size. In 1975, sales of microwave ovens outpaced those of gas ranges. Within two decades of the invention of the microwave oven, more than 12 million units were in use. By 1988, nearly 1,000 microwavable food products were available in grocery stores.

Microwaves take numerous forms. Long electromagnetic waves transmit radio signals; the shortest carry light. Microwave cooking applies electromagnetic radiation, which causes electrons to undulate like electricity coursing through wire. An oven's tubular magnetron produces medium-length waves of about five inches that activate water molecules in food in a wave pattern at billions of impulses per second. The rapid motion causes friction that heats the substances it penetrates. A front panel of tempered glass protects the kitchen and the cook from microwaves emitted by the oven.

In comparison to the longer cooking times of electric and gas ranges and ovens, the microwave oven thaws and cooks meat and baked potatoes and warms soup in a fraction of the time without a direct source of energy. Because the waves heat the food but not the container, users need only simple cooking vessels—often the packages in which prepared microwavable foods are sold. The New Jersey inventor Stanley I. Mason, Jr., the designer of the squeezable ketchup bottle, granola bars, and heated pizza boxes, devised a special line of heatproof plastic microwave cookware. Tupperware also brought out containers suited to transfer of frozen foods directly to the microwave oven.

Although for the first time in the human exploitation of energy, microwave generation no longer depended on skill in fire building, the ovens produced a new set of problems. If the waves clashed at just the right intervals, they cancelled each other and caused disparities in heating. To avoid cold spots in microwaved foods, manufacturers began equipping ovens with carousels that rotated dishes to maximize the waves' heating capacity. Because porous earthenware, polyethylene, glass, wood, and paper lack water, they remained unaffected by the generated energy. They became hot only through contact with heated contents. Metal and foil, however, sparked and burned in the presence of microwaves.

In the 1970s, the microwave phenomenon generated a change in home cookery. Inexperienced cooks and even children were able to take charge of heating and preparing simple dishes without fuss or complicated instructions. After Hitachi, Panasonic, Sanyo, and Sharp began marketing countertop models, these new appliances set the style of the postmodern kitchen, which was cooler and more fuel efficient than its predecessors thanks to microwave cooking.

Not everyone was satisfied with the quality of food prepared in the microwave oven. Some critics cited loss of texture, color, and aroma through faster preparation. The addition of a browning unit addressed the complaint that microwaved dishes were bland and unappealing. By 1990, some 80 percent of households in industrialized countries had microwave ovens, as compared with only one percent of Chinese kitchens.

Subsequent engineering reduced the microwave's size, trimmed energy consumption, and solved technical problems, all while significantly cutting the price. The availability of sleek, built-in ovens encouraged builders to add microwaves to new homes and condominiums as a selling point. By 1993, when 90 percent of American and 85 percent of Canadian kitchens had microwave ovens, a byproduct of research into semiconductors in Fremont, California, produced Flash-Bake ovens, which combined visible and infrared light to deep-heat and brown foods. Equipped with five to twenty-five quartz bulbs and an air blower, the new oven cooked with radiant energy, which was up to ten times faster than conventional means.

Into the twenty-first century, microwaving made itself even more attractive to homeowners. It lessened concerns about salmonella, *Escherichia coli*, and other foodborne bacteria, which are killed by high temperatures. The latest microwave ovens, countertop units as well as built-ins, are more stain resistant and easier to clean than conventional ovens and cook tops. Combination microwave-convection ovens offer multiple cooking operations, and a high-wattage model defrosts twice as fast as others on the market and cooks evenly in less time than conventional microwave ovens. Some models list preprogrammed settings for the most commonly microwaved foods.

See also **Maillard Reaction**

Further Reading

"Complete Guide to Microwave Ovens," *Good Housekeeping*, December 1982, 196–201.
Gunther, Judith Anne, "The Microwave Oven," *Popular Science*, October 1997, 122.
"Microwave Ovens: Friction in the Kitchen," *Today's Science*, January 1998.
Scott, Christopher, and Tori Scaduto, "Wave of the Future," *Popular Electronics*, November 1997, 26.

MILITARY KITCHENS

In the beginning of organized armies, there were no central kitchens, no mess halls, not even an appointed provisioner or cook. Soldiers scavenged for meals, stealing from gardens, pantries, and tables and coercing area

Making biscuits on a naval vessel.
[© *U.S. Navy Imagery used in illustration without endorsement expressed or implied. U.S. Navy Photo by Chief Journalist Al Bloom.*]

people to supply meat and grain free of charge on pain of rape, plunder, and death. Improvisation followed the exigencies and supplies at hand. For example, for Turks in the field, outriders carried mutton or beef haunches under their saddles. The combination of hard riding and horse sweat preserved and tenderized the meat for field rations. When Xenophon made Greek provisioners distribute watercress, it was as a tonic rather than a mess treat.

Far on Rome's Gallic border, Roman troops kept the peace and assured a steady influx of slaves and captured goods while dining simply at a soldier's mess. In addition to sword, pick, and shovel, each legionary bore his own mortar and pestle for crushing a three-day supply of nuts and grinding grain for gruel. If he could afford it, he carried a single-nozzled clay lamp fueled with vegetable oil for lighting late-night meals and dice games. His *salarium* (soldier's pay) bought him meat and provincial wine, the standard military beverage shared over a campfire and prized as a restorative and cleanser of wounds. For officers, kitchen servants packed a wider range of choices, for example, squill vinegar for dressing salad greens and cooked cabbage, which was a recommended cure for inebriation. A popular campaign bread, the *biscotto*, literally "twice baked," provided packable nourishment that remained edible over a long period.

The individual soldier's pack food varied widely over military history. According to Strabo's *Geography* (ca. 20 BCE), soldiers in Celtica subsisted primarily on milk and pork, which they ate fresh and salted. In 1255, when Friar William of Rubruck reported on his observations in Mongolia to Louis IX of France, he described the churning of *koumiss*, a fermented mare's milk. In addition to this staple, Genghis Khan and his horsemen lived on dried beets and bags of dried milk and curds. The Irish mixed porridge meal with butter to make *meanadhach*, a ready-to-cook dinner that campaigners accepted in lieu of cash pay. They packed meal stores with their saddle gear. To discourage mealy worms, they mixed in garlic, a known vermifuge.

In comparison to the British infantryman, who rode hard and who stopped to eat stale loaves soaked with horse sweat and wash it down with branch water, the Scotsman was far better fortified for fighting on the move. His love of oatcake kept him going at Mafeking, South Africa, during the Boer War, according to F. Marian McNeill's *The Scots Kitchen* (1929). Under siege from Oct. 12, 1899, to May 17, 1900, when Robert Baden-Powell heroically held off Boer forces, the camp cook supplied the garrison with sowans, an oat gruel made with the scrapings of the stable feed box.

In the late thirteenth century, when Marco Polo made his way east to Cathay, he was intrigued by the provisioning of the 100,000 cavalrymen of the Tartar army. In *The Travels of Marco Polo* (ca. 1299), he reported that they traveled without luggage and packed two leather flasks of milk and a small pot for cooking meat. They were so inured to hardship that they could travel ten days without provisions or fire by piercing the neck veins of their horses to drink from on the move. They sun-dried milk for mixing with water for a breakfast drink.

Provisions for Garrisons

Throughout the Middle Ages, it was the job of the steward or seneschal to provision the castle garrison out of house stores collected from surrounding manors and fiefs. Armies on the march carried their kitchen supplies in four-wheeled carts fitted with nail-studded wheels for traction in mud, ice, and snow. Inside, they stacked helmets and hauberks; outside, they hung cook pots and kettles in a space-saving style later emulated by the pioneers who settled the New World and by the cooks on chuckwagons during cattle drives.

An example from Japan, the Matsumoto Castle, built in 1596, illustrates the strategy of separation of the kitchen from main reception areas. The castle placed cooking in two areas—at the inner wall and away from the main structure, and a second kitchen in the main keep near officers' and soldier's quarters. In the event of a successful attack and breach of the outer wall, the second kitchen maintained food service to the residential militia.

In the 1500s, when Muslims controlled Istanbul and much of the Mediterranean Sea, Spain under Ferdinand V established presidios along the Barbary Coast as military outposts, such as Melilla and Ceuta, and over three hundred watchtowers as guardians against piracy. Primarily shore defenses, the posts looked outward toward the sea from north Africa, holding the Turkish navy at bay. Crucial to the plan to stop the advance of Islam into western Europe was the provisioning system that channeled wheat from Sicily and wine and vinegar from Naples to military kitchens.

In heavily contested sea lanes, Spanish ships dispatched from headquarters at Málaga imported the chickpeas, fish, and water that sustained land forces. A fortuitous engagement with a Turkish corsair gave Ferdinand goods to use or resell. Against this constantly shifting balance of power, in 1569, men guarding the coast of Libya, Morocco, Tunisia, and Algeria sufficed on stew and soup, the unassuming fare of the army kitchen made from irregular supplies of tuna and salt meat, flour, chickpeas, olive oil, and wine and from goods snatched on raids of outlying Muslim farms and villages.

During the American Revolution, the military evolved an initial rationing program, which covered provisions, soap, and candles. In 1775, the Second Continental Congress set up the first national standards of nutritional health and diet for soldiers. Cooks worked within weekly limitations of a garrison ration to feed one hundred men: 100 pounds of beef, 75 pounds of pork, or 100 pounds of salt fish; 75 gallons of peas or beans; 6.25 gallons of rice or 12.5 pints of corn meal; 100 pounds of flour or hardtack; 77 gallons of milk; and 175 gallons of spruce beer or cider. Donations of fresh goods supplied the only fruits, vegetables, and baked items the men enjoyed during a hard-fought war of independence. Kitchen help came from outside sources, including local volunteers.

Immediately after the war, when the commissary general reduced the issue of meat and fresh food, the surgeon Benjamin Rush charged that poorly fed men were predisposed to illness and slow healing from injury and wounds. Army messes improved on the frontier after 1796, when Congress increased allotment of supplies to camp and post kitchens. After the War of 1812, the military sought solutions to the need for better, fresher, and more appetizing food by establishing kitchen gardens at posts. In 1832, President Andrew Jackson, an experienced soldier, halted the distribution of brandy and rum, which he replaced with coffee and sugar.

Food for Navies

In Lord Nelson's navy, precise organization of supplies by a victualling board resulted in less waste and better meals for some 145,000 sailors. At a Plymouth cooperage, naval supply stored staples in casks. A shore-based kitchen staff of 436 commandeered the services of a foreman, forty bakers, three assistant bakers, a granary man, a miller and assistant, four pastry cooks, five warders, a gatekeeper, master brewer, clerk and three assistants, seven apprentices, six coopers, sixty-six block coopers, and two millers' aids. Supply stations awaited ships in Gibraltar, Malta, Cape Horn, Rio de Janeiro, and Heligoland in Lisbon.

For shipboard food service, officers divided into mess units and collected from all participants a fee to supplement the navy pantry. The choice of what, when, how, and how much to upgrade the standard diet caused disputes that each mess handled in private. Each man brought his own utensils. Staff erected tables between guns on the lower deck on a two-decker and moved below during high seas and inclement weather.

Most men kept a knife, spoon, and personal hook pot in the galley for cooking private stock of food. Rough weather threatened tableware. When heavy seas destroyed the platters and earthenware of the *Boston*

in 1794, the staff returned to wood vessels. The hierarchy respected the morning meal as the men's right. After being piped to breakfast, the men dined in peace except in emergencies.

For Nelson's sailors, cooking and serving followed a strict protocol. Holders—staff supervising the hold—brought casks of food to the steward's room for daily distribution to the forecastle galley for cooking in two large kettles. In place of burners, the regulation navy stove had two deep lidded compartments, an oven door to the left, a rack to hold a grill, and a funnel and turnspit to the right. In port, regimentation relaxed. In addition to standard issues of hardtack and salt meat, the men could look forward to fresh meat, loaves of bread instead of biscuit, and vegetables.

Feeding Sick Soldiers

At the Crimea, chef Alexis Benoît Soyer joined nursing supervisor Florence Nightingale in improving the quality of food fed to sick soldiers. She found the special diet kitchen at Scutari's Barrack Hospital clean, orderly, but cramped and ill-equipped. To the detriment of the soldiers, nurses fed one ward from a single pail, used for beef broth, negus, arrowroot, and water. The men, who had abandoned their implements in knapsacks left at the Alma battlefield, had to share spoons.

Soyer disapproved of the state of the copper pots and utensils, the condition of the premises, and the cooks' methods. He found joints of meat tied to wood skewers before being boiled in pots. The bindings were so tight that the meat cooked unevenly. The simple loosening of the ties and the addition of salt and pepper greatly improved meals. Soyer also scolded orderlies for tossing out the broth, which contained nutrients that shouldn't be wasted. As to plate service, he explained that pouring soup over meat was a means of supplying the food in one bowl so that the meat would remain hot while the patient drank the soup.

Soyer halted the waste of fuel by devising a stove to use forty-seven pounds of wood instead of the unnecessary 1,760. He insisted on order, much as he had established in his civilian kitchen. He systematized the use of boilers to hold rations for 150, appointed a permanent supervisor, and posted recipes and instructions in the food preparation area for ready reference. In place of a wad of tea leaves bound in a rag and boiled haphazardly in a soup kettle, he invented a Scutari teapot, a kettle fitted with a tea filter to allow boiling water to infuse each leaf, thus reducing waste. Before departing, he had the copper pots retinned, ordered partitioning of the larder and pantry, oversaw the fitting of chopping blocks and dressing tables, and supervised construction of an oven and charcoal stove.

At Balaclava, Turkey, with Florence Nightingale, Soyer inspected the kitchen at the Sanatorium on the Genoese Heights. He found meals cooked in open-air mud huts. These cookhouses wasted so much fuel and produced such poor results that he replaced them with a central kitchen. For government bakeries, he invented a hard biscuit made palatable by soaking in coffee, tea, or soup. He reorganized the compression of vegetables into cakes partitioned like scored chocolate blocks to be broken apart day by day for a single ration.

Nineteenth-Century Rations

For many of nineteenth-century English mess cooks, the preparation of bully beef produced a limp, defatted corned beef. The resulting *boeuf bouilli*, called "bully beef" by the English, lacked flavor. In the Royal Navy, the term carried over to the first tins of meat, a process devised by chef Nicholas Appert and made available through suppliers Donkin and Hall in 1813. During World War I, bully beef remained a staple of the military at Gallipoli, where it was the main source of protein for trench soldiers who were too far from the cookhouse for caterers to deliver hot meals. For the Prussian army cook, the menu varied little from pea soup, meatballs, pork with sauerkraut, potatoes, and bread.

During the American Civil War, military food service cranked rapidly into action after the firing on Fort Sumter, South Carolina. Confederate troops enjoyed the abundance of the agrarian South, which supplied military kitchens irregularly between harvests. Hampering a steady provisioning of goods the rest of the year was the lack of railroads, open roads, and regular provision wagons as well as noncombatants to farm the land and staff warehouses. Although Tennessee and Virginia farmers supported the cause, undependable food delivery became a major cause of the rebellion's failure.

A necessity to the success of the campaign, hygiene and quality camp cooking, in the estimation of Winfield Scott, general in chief of the U.S. Army, warded off scurvy, dysentery, pneumonia, typhoid, malaria, and diarrhea. These standard wartime scourges could rapidly decimate a fighting force, causing 400,000 of the 600,000 deaths reported. In traditional fashion, soldiers on both sides also foraged for fuel and supplies, from innocent berrying and herb-picking to thieving and intimidation of owners of pantries, apiaries, orchards, dairies, henyards, and stores.

Procurement placed tremendous burden on the Union's Subsistence Department, headed by Commissary General Colonel Joseph P. Taylor. He dealt indirectly with merchandisers through inexperienced contractors and supply officers and dispatched goods via wagon, steamships, barges, and rail cars. According to the U. S. Surgeon General, Union issue from the regimental commissary allotted each cook per day for one hundred men: meat, 75 pounds; bread or flour, 137.5 pounds; hardtack, 100 pounds; corn meal, 125 pounds; potatoes, 30 pounds; legumes, 15 pounds; rice or hominy, 10 pounds; green coffee, 10 pounds; roasted coffee, 8 pounds; tea, 24 ounces; sugar, 15 pounds; vinegar, 1 gallon; molasses, 1 quart; salt, 3.75 pounds; and pepper, 4 ounces.

On March 1, 1863, from the Medical Director's Office at headquarters for the Army of the Potomac near Falmouth, Virginia, the surgeon Jonathan Letterman summarized the causes of disease as cold, fatigue, exposure, low quality foodstuffs, and poorly prepared meals. His recommendations included ample supplies of fresh onions, potatoes, and other vegetables for fourteen days and at least twice a week thereafter. He sanctioned pickles, sauerkraut, and dried apples and peaches and called for floating ovens and permanent cooks to supply fresh bread three times a week. As an antiscorbutic to prevent scurvy and night blindness, the government issued pressed sheets of desiccated vegetables.

When soldiers ate with their units, officers appointed camp cooks and their assistants from the ranks. When supplies ran low, the men poured a thin batter of flour and water into grease for "coosh" or "slosh," a thin pancake. When luck ran out, troops marched and fought on empty stomachs. If they met up with opportunities to rummage through the haversack of a dead enemy soldier or overrun the enemy's camp, there were no rules forbidding their expropriating edibles.

The kitchen staff gained one privilege—to ride in wagons rather than march. They assigned off-duty helpers to carry water and round up firewood and loaded equipment on mules. At the camp kitchen, they arranged boxes and barrels into make-shift work space for slicing meat and quartering potatoes. Neatness required them to scrape each kitchen surface clean, but sanitizing was not a camp standard. With no training or background in food service, they set up at open-air stoves, covered by tarps in wet weather, or made do at local fireplaces. For coffee roasters, they spread green coffee beans in a mess pan, set it over a camp fire, and stirred with a stick to produce an even product.

Each camp's hearth consisted of crotch sticks to hold the poles on which to swing camp stew kettles and sheet-iron pails for cooking meat and potatoes. Cook staff poured ingredients into sheet-iron pans with flared sides for frying pork and filled them with water for washing dishes. The cooks ladled out portions, sliced hunks of bread, then put coffee on to boil in kettles. After dinner, the stewing and coffee-making pot doubled as a laundry kettle for boiling dirty clothes.

For individual purchases beyond government issue, Union soldiers spent their monthly salary of thirteen dollars at commissaries and sutleries, the traveling groceries that followed the troops. These government-approved profiteers drove wagons filled with more palatable goods than army-issue hardtack and salt pork. In exchange for cash, vendors sold pies, molasses candy, raisins, crackers, sugar, flour, butter and cheese, eggs, bacon, salt mackerel, citrus fruit, apples, and soft drinks as well as tobacco and liquor. Men grumbled, but looked forward to the moldy, rancid, and overpriced goods that they could cook in a tin dipper, a tin can with wire bail, or a makeshift fry pan fashioned from half a canteen with a stick handle.

Although the Civil War was the beginning of the military's concern for the ordinary soldier's acceptance of food, soldiers from varied backgrounds ate in messes of up to twenty soldiers and accepted spartan fare as part of the heavily masculine atmosphere demanded by field operations. Officers carried their own place settings. In the rebel camp, Robert E. Lee, whom Confederate soldiers admired for sharing the daily fare ladled out by an army cook, sat and ate with the folding ivory-handled knife, fork, and spoon he stored in a personal leather envelope throughout his military career. At the end of a meal, each soldier washed his own dishes and stored them in a haversack, a single-strap canvas bag slung over the shoulder.

After the battle of Kernstown, Virginia, on March 23, 1862, kitchens of the U.S. Army quartermaster department established a routine of feeding one thousand military prisoners at a time on standardized rations distributed from a mess table. In addition to an allotment of three twelve-inch candles per day, each inmate received a pound of fresh beef, a pound of salt beef, twenty ounces of flour, ten ounces of green coffee, and twelve ounces of sugar. In contrast, farm wife Emily Harris living near Spartanburg, South Carolina, reported in her diary that her husband, David Harris, drew from the Confederate supply six quarts of meal, one quart of flour, three quarts of rice, twenty-four ounces of meat, and a teacup of salt every five days for himself and one other soldier.

When U.S. combat shifted to the frontier during the Indian Wars, the army expected soldiers to live off the land and to accommodate their diet to Southwestern pemmican, jerky, and pinole. To standardize rations, in 1896, the commissary general issued a manual for camp cooks composed of recipes tailored to feeding one hundred men. Standard operating procedure for a camp kitchen called for stewing and boiling; army regulations considered roasting, broiling, and frying too labor-intensive, too wasteful of rations, and less suited to the digestion of men under stress. Regulations specified the boiling of soup at least five hours and the cooking of vegetables to a soft and digestible state. In accordance with beliefs that hot bread damaged the body, cooks served loaves and biscuits only after they had cooled. Army surgeons and camp officers inspected kitchens daily to assure the men received quality food free of decay and insect infestation.

Military Mess, Central Supply

During the Spanish-American War, the first military war that the U.S. fought beyond its shores, the inspection, preservation, and transport of provisions created the first collaboration of army and navy. Caribbean heat spoiled meat. As a result, men weakened and collapsed at an alarming rate, jeopardizing the Cuban campaign. Unlike post kitchens, which received fresh foodstuffs from rail lines, cooks in Cuba served deficient rations that caused food poisoning and precipitated intestinal upset. The brief, but costly war proved to the military that emergency measures in buying, storing, and cooking wholesome, sanitary foods were advantageous to prevent deterioration of the fighting force. To raise standards, officials upgraded the pay of cooks and stocked quality utensils, vessels, field ranges, and mess gear. After ending the system of campfire cookery, in 1902, the army founded its first military cooking school; the navy compiled a *General Mess Manual and Cookbook* (1902). Additional changes included supplying kitchens with corned beef, more processed foods, and chicken and turkey for holidays.

World War I

The U.S. army further differentiated military cookery for troops at home and abroad and for European allies, civilian home front, and European civilians. In 1917, food commissioner Herbert Hoover controlled pricing of provisions and countered hoarding and profiteering. The next year, the army replaced the one-man office with the Subsistence Department of the Office of the Quartermaster General and a Food Purchase Board to supply and equip kitchens for army, navy, and allies. To assure a regular receipt of goods, they shipped from the U.S. and European markets and from army factories that manufactured macaroni, bread, and candy specifically for military kitchens.

A standard source of protein in field kitchens during World War I was bully beef, tinned corned beef that England's 300,000 field suppliers and cooks could grind into hamburger. Each soldier carried a reserve ration, an individual two-pound packaged meal of corned beef, hard bread, sugar, coffee, and salt secured in each man's haversack in event of extreme separation from camp kitchens. The trench ration for twenty-five men, comprising a day's allotment of canned beef, salmon, or sardines and hard bread, salt, sugar, instant coffee, solid alcohol, and cigarettes, came to the field in galvanized containers that protected perishables from poison gas. Although nutritionally unbalanced, bulky, and heavy, these early military convenience foods could be eaten cold or heated. The emergency ration, a subsistence packet of three three-ounce cakes of beef powder and wheat and three one-ounce chocolate bars, fit into a pocket in a lacquered can to nourish a man in the most extreme conditions. As a food supplement, the Ovaltine company supplied its chocolate milk additive.

By 1916, the burden of feeding soldiers forced cooks to limit meat rations to a daily serving of six ounces, which maintained nutrition at 3,574 calories per day. Men at the front continued to receive twelve-ounce tins of bully beef; those behind the lines ate meatless meals twenty-one days out of the month. Kitchen workers depended on buying local vegetables and collecting nettles for stew. To extend army issue, they mixed ground turnips into bread and provided pork and beans and a few chunks of horsemeat in pea soup, which each battalian cook made in two huge lidded iron vats called dixies. They supplemented with bacon fried in the dixie lids and with Manconochie Rations, a watery tinned Irish stew or soup of sliced carrots and turnips heated over charcoal braziers.

When supplies were available, camp cooks issued dehydrated vegetables and canned boneless beef in standard garrison rations. U.S. soldiers complained of fieldhouse "slumgum" or stew and "monkey meat," a mixture of beef and carrots imported in tins from South America. For doughboys in the trenches, for the first time in U.S. military history, cook staff organized a delivery service of potable water and hot food secured in milk cans and slung over poles for a two-man carry. To boost morale in wretched conditions, suppliers also distributed to the front tobacco and eight ounces of candy per man every ten days.

German field cooks relied on the Gulasch-Kanone or "stew gun," a field kitchen on wheels. From the English cookhouse, field servers conveyed foodstuffs into combat in recycled jam jars, petrol cans, and boxes lined with straw. Because of rough terrain and distance from the fighting, food usually arrived cold. Soldiers kept their own primus stoves and heated food and water for tea. Australian soldiers called their cookpots "billies." They augmented their rations by crumbling stale "dog biscuit" in saucers and soaking the powder in condensed milk or by boiling crumbs in a sandbag with onions, potatoes, or sultanas.

On advances into enemy territory, each man carried a stock of iron rations, composed of bully beef, biscuit, tea, and sugar. They used their emergency store only with officers' permission. When the food ran out, they had to cede territory to the enemy and move closer to supplies in the rear. Foot soldiers wrote 200,000 letters to army headquarters complaining that the cook staff provided substantial hot meals for officers only. A letter from a Major Graham confirmed the difference by declaring that he received bacon, tomatoes, bread, jam, and cocoa for breakfast. At lunch, he ate shepherd's pie, potted meat, potatoes, and tea with bread and jam. His dinner consisted of ox-tail soup, roast beef, leeks, rice pudding, coffee, and whiskey with soda. He added that Harrods sent weekly grocery parcels.

Between World Wars

After the war, the army reengineered combat food by redesigning the container, separating trench provisions into individual servings, and adding chocolate and a better grade of coffee. In 1922, the Quartermaster Corps Subsistence School standardized slender tin cans holding four main components: three ounces of corned beef or chocolate, one pound of dried sliced beef, fourteen ounces of hard bread, and tablet sugar. Three years later, provisioners altered meals once more by reducing bread and corned beef and replacing dried beef with pork and beans.

In 1935, the U.S. Quartermaster Subsistence Research and Development Laboratory, headed by Colonel Paul Logan, added choice to its field rations by offering both a corned beef meal and a pork and bean meal. When trench warfare gave place to tank and air combat, the rapid deployment of troops called for the rethinking of field rations, including additions of chocolate, sugar, and peanut butter. Further development blended oat flour, sugar, chocolate, cacao, milk powder, and artificial flavor into the high-energy, aluminum-wrapped Logan bar.

Major W. R. McReynolds, the first director of the Subsistence Research and Development Laboratory, invented the C ration in 1938. A complete twelve-ounce field meal of beef stew, beef and noodles, lamb stew, or Irish stew with bread, it evolved into ten menus upgraded to a full pound per can. Because of manufacturing problems, in 1939, the army reduced choices to meat and beans, meat and vegetable hash, and meat and vegetable stew. Field testing found the cans awkward and the food dull, but nutritionally sound. Redesigned in twelve-ounce cans with reductions in bread, coffee, and chocolate and the addition of hard candy and chocolate caramel, the C ration was already in production in August 1941, four months before the United States entered World War II.

World War II

The U.S. military food complex developed its kitchen supply during World War II to provision the European and Pacific theaters. The logistics challenged planners to reduce the weight and upgrade nutrition and survival rations for army and marine field units, air corps, and sailors. By collaborating with universities and the food industry, cooking supervisors devised twenty-three forms of rations and supplements that followed standardized recipes created from precise measures of ingredients and controlled kitchen techniques. To bolster a heavily taxed fighting force, cooks received as much fresh fruit, vegetables, and meats as the military could store. Supplements of canned food, dried fruit, and powdered eggs and occasional holiday treats kept men at the front content and well fed. Distributors of Ovaltine again supplied troops with its food supplement as it had during World War I.

American GIs carried mess kits containing basin and utensils. Those on the move beyond kitchen wagons dined on C rations, a series of six cans of food for a day's three meals. The contents varied from baked beans, meat chunks, and vegetables to candy and crackers. The lucky soldier who had a supply of chocolate bars from home could use them to barter in European venues.

The military added emergency food packets and supplements throughout the war for a total manufacture of one billion special rations costing $675 million. A more varied unit of B rations, containing six meals for two days offered stew, spaghetti, meat and beans, ham and eggs, meat with noodles, pork and rice, franks and beans, pork and beans, ham and limas, or chicken and vegetables plus biscuits, cereal, candy-coated peanuts or raisins, coffee, sugar, jam, cocoa powder, lemon or orange drink mix, hard candy, and caramels. By the end of World War II, packaging of fudge and sandwich cookies replaced peanuts and raisins.

Army kitchens also devised lightweight K rations, emergency D rations, and food-for-a-day combat or C rations for specific climatic needs in mountainous, jungle, and desert regions. Used for assault and combat missions, the K ration, packed in Chicago in 1943 by the Wrigley Company, was compact and upgraded from pemmican, biscuit, peanut bar, raisins, and bouillon to a paratrooper's meals for a day, containing ham spread, bouillon cubes, sausage, chocolate bar, malted milk tablets, canned veal loaf, instant coffee, sugar,

dextrose, and lemon powder. A new design called for replacement of thermoplastic and waxed paper covering to a crepe rubber and wax that survived -20 to 135 degrees Fahrenheit. Changes in foods added a fruit bar and a wood spoon wrapped in cellophane.

To extend the best possible food service in extreme conditions, designers considered the exigencies of flight crew lunches, paratrooper emergency packs, in-flight combat meals, and sea survival in lifeboats. For mountain rations, the military food laboratory devised a high-altitude, high-roughage ration under forty ounces in weight to feed four men for one day. It consisted of meat and beans or rice, potatoes, butter substitute, instant coffee, dry milk, biscuits, hard candy, cereal, dehydrated cheese, energy and fruit bars, gum, lemon powder, dehydrated soup, salt, sugar, tea, cigarettes, and toilet paper. Jungle rations suited to the tropics added peanuts, cooked cereal, gum, cocoa powder, and raisins in a fiber carton.

The five-in-one ration, introduced in 1942, supplied motorized combat forces in desert regions with a day's food for five soldiers. The packet, consisting of spread, vegetables, meat, evaporated milk, fruit juice, fruit, dehydrated soup, cereal, beverages, biscuits, hard candy, salt, sugar, and toilet paper, required a minimum of cooking equipment. Kitchen labs replaced the successful five-in-one with a ten-in-one, a double five-in-one modeled on the British "compo" or fourteen-in-one ration issued in 1942 during the North African campaign. Wrapped in cellophane, it varied a day's selections to feed ten men and added instant coffee, pudding, and jam plus cigarettes and matches, can opener, toilet paper, soap, towels, and water-purification tablets.

For commercial airliners, the Quartermaster Corps produced a bulky four-pound hard candy, vitamin pill, and gum ration high in carbohydrates for sustaining life under restricted water intake. Manufactured for the Coast Guard and the merchant marines, a more substantial survival packet offered C biscuits, pemmican, chocolate tablets, and milk tablets. By 1943, a hospital supplement for the kitchens of evacuation and base institutions provided canned fruit and juice, evaporated milk, coffee, sugar, and dehydrated soup. The kitchen spice pack, a supplemental ration for aid stations and hospitals, did not come into being until 1944.

In 1944, the U.S. army laboratory was producing an X ration, an invasion-force meal packed in a wax carton. It supplied meat, biscuits, chocolate, fruit or energy bars, bouillon powder, instant coffee, sugar, gum, hard candy, and multi-vitamin tablets. The assault lunch boxed prepared food suited to the amphibious Pacific campaign in 1944. Packed in the Hawaiian Islands, it included hard candy, chocolate bars, caramels, dried fruit, gum, peanuts, salt and water-purification tablets, and cigarettes and matches for a 1,500 to 2,000-calorie snack suited to temperatures varying from -60 to 130 degrees Fahrenheit. The AAF combat lunch, a packet of unprepared and dehydrated items, required that crew reconstitute and cook for three meals a selection of dry milk, chili powder or tomato paste, bouillon cubes, rice, hard candy, gum, salt, and tea tablets, packaged in a waxed fiberboard box with a can opener. Because crew members preferred prepared soup, a thermos of coffee, meat or cheese sandwiches, oranges, and candy bars, the AAF combat lunch quickly became obsolete because of the demands it placed on personnel and equipment. In addition, food preparers reduced nutrients to liquid diet packs for aid-station and hospital patients and casualties at advance medical posts and planned a kitchen spice pack for mobile kitchens. The airborne lifeboat ration, developed in 1944, stowed aboard boats enough food for breakfast and supper. Containing meat, condensed soup, matches, and toilet paper boxed in a fiberboard container, it remained in production until 1949.

For casualties, the battle casualty pack evolved into the aid-station beverage pack. It boxed coffee, tea, cocoa powder, evaporated milk, and sugar plus plastic straws, can opener, and toilet paper. The liquid selections suited maneuvers, airplane crews, rescue craft, and isolated units supplied by parachute. A twelve-pound Red Cross prisoner-of-war packet manufactured in 1945 coordinated plied meat spread, canned bacon, lunch meat, salmon, dehydrated corned beef, canned cheese product, instant coffee, powdered milk, and chocolate bars along with tobacco, salt, vitamins, toilet paper, soap, paper towels, can opener, buttons, needle and thread, and patching cloth. The army ceased producing the kit in 1949.

At war's end, kitchen staff had completed an assault packet, a quick-energy boost for the combat force. Stockpiles of D rations in six hundred-calorie and three hundred-calorie units in 1945 led to extended discussions of use for civilian emergencies or repackaging for prisoners of war. Because of overdependence on short rations for weeks rather than a few days, in 1946, army food handlers discontinued the unpopular K rations, which field workers distributed at overseas civilian feeding stations. During the Korean War, the air crew ration, a World War II snack intended for pilots, parachutists, crew, passengers, long-range missions, and survivors of crashes, contained loose candies, candy bars, chocolate drops, fondant, gum drops, licorice, peanuts, and gum packaged in a two-compartment box. Parachute emergency rations, an emergency pack the Air Force prepped in 1942, offered energy and fruit bars, hard candy, lemon-juice powder, and K biscuits as survival food. It evolved into a pocket pack limited to chocolate, hard candy, dehydrated cheese and crackers, bouillon cubes, sugar, cigarettes, water-purification tablets, instant coffee, and gum, a popular item that remained in supply until 1952.

Among the Allies during World War II, Aussie soldiers carried an individual billy can for cooking and a K-ration kit outfitted with camp pie, soup mix, sweets, and a hard biscuit. The varied menu met the body's requirements. As explained by Chris Forbes-Ewan of the Physiology and Nutrition Department of Defence Materials Research Laboratory in Scottsdale, Tasmania, to keep up morale, service kitchens served up good food. One day's menu began with ham and eggs and included beef, vegetables, freeze-dried rice, peaches, biscuits, plum jam, cereal, cheese, chocolate, curry powder, chewing gum, butter concentrate, butterscotch, condensed milk, tea bags, sugar, salt, and powdered fruit drink. Kits also carried matches, can opener, rubber bands, soap, scouring pad, and toilet paper. Similar to the American army's MRE (Meal Ready to Eat), the Vietnam War era C Rations, Aussie field rations come in lightweight plastic and foil pouches. Freeze-dried fruits and vegetables hold down packet weight.

Post-World War II

To further strengthen cooking and food service, in 1946, the army replaced the outmoded research and development laboratory of the Subsistence Department with the Quartermaster Food and Container Institute for the Armed Forces, established in Chicago. Eight years later, Quartermaster Research and Development Command opened a new facility in Natick, Massachusetts, which it renamed the U.S. Army Natick Laboratories in August 1963. In the twenty-first-century the food lab, called the Natick Research, Development and Engineering Center (NRDEC), refined 1,500 one hundred-portion recipes for all branches of the service and issued them on five by eight-inch note cards.

Military issue offered foods that met the demands of one day's strenuous activity as well as food that suited the tastes of men and women far from home, particularly those in hospitals and rehabilitation centers. Criteria for recipe write-ups covered portion size and weight, military cooking terminology, feasible cooking procedures within the scope of allotted equipment, reduced fat and cholesterol, and maximum complex carbohydrates. Cooks learned methods of optimizing fragrance, texture, color, and taste of traditional foods plus trendy meals and ethnic, regional, and personal preferences, such as vegetarian and kosher meals. In the field, T rations or meals ready to eat (MREs) supplied by the Army Field Feeding System were successful during brief modern wars for which host nation support and the Logistical Civil Augmentation Program came too late.

A cardboard box held the British Army's modernized twenty-four-hour "ratpack" (ration pack). Weighing 4.5 pounds, it came with folding stove and hexamine solid fuel tablets or a sterno cooker. Foods included oatmeal, bacon or baconburger, biscuit, meat spread, chocolate bar, hard candy, dextrose tablets, instant soup, fruit dessert, tea bags, instant drink, gum, salt, and cocoa plus toilet paper, matches, can opener, and water purification tablets. A menu card guided the breakdown of high-energy elements into breakfast, main meal, and snack.

Military kitchens continued reducing size and bulk as they planned for future wars. One U.S. military feeding program looked to technology to create a micronutrient wafer for use in 2025. After entering the digestive tract, the gold-capped disk would estimate bodily need and release vitamins and minerals as well as nutraceuticals, foods impregnated with pharmacopia to bolster the autoimmune system, combat stress, and enhance performance.

See also **Biscuit; Borden, Gail; Galley; Soyer, Alexis**

Further Reading

Betz, Virginia, "Bread, Wine, and Villas: Agriculture in Roman Gaul," *Athena Review*, Vol. 1, No. 4, 51–55.
Froissart's Chronicles. London: Penguin, 1978.
Hermann, Captain I. *Memoirs of a Veteran.* Atlanta, Ga.: Byrd Printing Company,
Lavery, Brian. *Nelson's Navy.* London: Conway Maritime Press, 1989.
MacDonald, Fiona, David Antram, and John James. *A Samurai Castle.* New York: Peter Bedrick Books, 1995.
McCarthy, Carlton. *Detailed Minutiae of Soldier Life.* New York: Time-Life Books, 1982.
Morris, Helen. *Portrait of a Chef: The Life of Alexis Soyer.* Cambridge: University Press, 1938.
Worsham, John A. *One of Jackson's Foot Cavalry.* New York: Neale Publishing Co., 1912.

MILLING

The addition of grain to the diet precipitated a need in primitive kitchens for methods of reducing tough pericarps on wheat, corn, and other plant foods to release the flavorful kernels inside. Mesopotamian housewives used volcanic rock hand mills for the daily tasks of grinding barley, spice, and sesame seeds. At Jericho, which settlers first occupied around 9000 BCE, archeologist Dame Kathleen Mary Kenyon discovered querns composed of paired rotary grindstones, an early milling technology. To operate the two-layered mill,

Cley Wind Mill North, Norfolk, UK.

the grinder sat alongside the stones to feed grains into the hollow and to turn the upper convex stone to generate enough friction against the bottom stone to separate the kernel from its tough husk. As flour emerged from the two abrasive surfaces, it fell to a mat or container below.

Technological advancement in milling paralleled greater sophistication in cereal recipes and bread baking. In the first century BCE, Hero of Alexander claimed to have invented the windmill. To the north, hand grinding gave place to the water-powered mill in 85 BCE, when the Greeks invented stream-driven edge-runner mill wheels, the world's first food industry. The Romans commonly applied the edge-runner to grain and to olive oil production by placing the fruit in the saucer-shaped hollow of the millstone and leading dray animals attached to the end of a wood radius that circled the crushing stone like the second hand on a clock.

The stone mill was a valuable tool to early Romans, as mentioned by the expert Marcius Porcius Cato in *De Agricultura* (On Farming) when he entered the olive business in the mid-second century BCE. Kitchen slaves or peasant farmers crushed olives, pressed out the juice, and allowed heavy oils to settle from watery fluid called *amurca*. To complete extraction, they used a *trapetum* (roller-mill), a *mortarium* or lava trough that supported a pair of orbs or convex stones attached to each end of a *cupa* (axle). The miller rotated the device in the bowl to release juice for pressing. Various grades of olive oil served as a cooking oil, lamp fuel, bath ointment, and skin unguent.

At Pompeii, archeologists uncovered examples of the two-stage volcanic stone mill six feet tall with a

Water mill. Water flows to the water wheel along a wooden aqueduct.

bell-shaped *meta* (bottom) and a complementary *catillus* (top). The hour-glass figure of these mills allowed slaves, free hirelings, or dray animals to rotate top against bottom while hand-feeding whole grain through the space between. Although found in professional bakeries, one residence, the House of the Labyrinth, had its own full-sized mill. Smaller versions served lesser kitchens. The poor had little choice but to rely on hand mills or to buy professionally baked bread. In the first decade of the first century CE, the architect Vitruvius introduced greater convenience with water mills, which engineers fitted with gears to control the grind.

Persian inventors altered Greek milling technology in 650 CE, when they erected their first windmill, a vertical beam rotated by wind-powered sails. English millers added their own touch with the smock mill, a vertical model of which only the dome was mobile, as opposed to the post mill, which rotated from the ground up around a central beam. Spread west over the continent to Portugal, the milling of grain enhanced kitchen convenience by supplying flour year round.

Grinding equipment in Europe and the New World came in various sizes and types. Most were hand-powered with a hopper holding grain above a striated iron grinder plate. By adjusting the pressure plate, the user would vary the pressure against malt, barley, peas, beans, spices, and corn. On Antigua, a hilltop windmill lessened the labor of slaves, who ground sugar cane and reduced the juice to make syrup for rum. The ubiquitous American corn grinder produced flour of varying grades, from fine milled to middlings and shorts, the coarsest grade, the main ingredient in corn-meal mush.

A drawing of a handmill used at Dorset in the eighteenth century shows a four-sided wooden funnel atop an octagonal box housing the double-stone grinding apparatus. Below, a flywheel connected to a spindle turned by a hand crank. The entire structure fit into a frame 4.5 feet high and three feet square at the base. In 1800, Garnet Terry, a London inventor, devised a similar mechanism with meshed gears and a tin funnel at the top for easy feeding of large grains.

Water mills came in varying design. Whereas the bucket wheel turned by the weight of water, the paddle wheel or undershot variety directed a water force that turned the axle with direct pressure. The plain breast wheel depended on force to hit and press paddles downward. The undershot paddle wheel received its push from below. To assure trouble-free turning, mill builders constructed the kingpin from one immense tree trunk. Less common was the danside, a spiral wheel encased in an inverted cone. As the overshot fell on the blades, it rotated a central shaft and discharged the race through the apex below.

In *The Countryman's England* (1935), the food writer Dorothy Hartley characterized the pleasant industry of the English cider mill. As friends gathered for the annual cider making, the creak of the mill kept pace with the clops of the horse's hooves and the arguments of the millers. Hartley, who promoted traditional food preparation over manufactured goods, declared that cider-making should be a "peaceful family job among ourselves." (Hartley 1980, 62–63)

As technology improved and new ideas replaced the old, mills evolved in size, shape, and mechanism. In 1845, F. G. Witte, an immigrant to Goliad County, Texas, erected the state's first windmill. The twenty-foot wood structure ground a weekly load of five hundred pounds of grain. In 1870, two Germans remodeled it into a thirty-five-foot Dutch mill with the original grind stones and twenty-foot sails attached to a rotating turret that turned according to the prevailing wind. The owners resituated the building numerous times and continued to grind corn for local housekeepers. In 1935, the Victoria Morning Study Club brought the historic mill to Victoria, Texas, as a tourist attraction.

Traditional milling by water, wind, and animal power declined rapidly after steam engines altered technology to safer, more profitable operations. England lost ten thousand windmills; in Holland, they declined by 90 percent. In the same era, American milling reached its height with rural wind-driven water pumps and auxiliary electric generators, especially in the rural Midwest. According to the 1923 Sears, Roebuck catalog, even after considerable electrification rendered home milling obsolete, agrarian families still had need of hand-cranked grist mills, which sold at $7.65 for a pulley-driven model and $3.90 for a smaller geared mill. Less industrialized countries continued hand and wind- or animal-powered milling late into the twentieth century. In the 1960s, residents of the mountainous Ladakh district in northern India hand-milled barley for *tsampa*, the parched meal they ate daily. A conical woven funnel directed the grain into a lap-size milling wheel turned by a stream.

Further Reading

Lunde, Paul, "Muslims and Muslim Technology in the New World," *Aramco World*, Vol. 43, No. 3, (exhibition issue), 38–41.
"The Venerable Windmill," *Aramco World*, March 1960, 12–15.

MINING AND LOGGING CAMP KITCHENS

In the Americas, the cookery for which work camps were famous replicated the bland, unappetizing fare of sailors. Provisioneers bought the easiest foods to transport and store: dry beans, salt meat, coffee, and hardtack. Generally in absence were eggs and dairy items, the staples associated with farmsteads and housewives. According to New England logging history, in 1820, management provided double camps of spruce logs roofed with cedar shingles and a hole chopped out for smoke to escape. The cookhouse and bunkhouse were separated by a dingle, a storage area for casks of codfish and salt pork, tins of bully beef, and barrels of flour.

Camp cooks focused on a simple menu of flapjacks, pickled beef, boiled cod, beans, and tea. One compendium, Mrs. B. C. Whiting's *How We Cook In Los Angeles* (1894), reprised some of the makeshift recipes of the lumber camp, including a mock apple pie, made from soda crackers, brown sugar, water, cinnamon, and citrus acid. For sourdough biscuit, kitchen staff kept a crock at the cook shack door to contain leftover batter, crumbs, and scraps of bread, cake, doughnuts, and pancakes. The mass quickly dissolved into a semi-liquid starter for the next batches of baked goods. According to the California food writer Helen Evans Brown, a mid-twentieth century expert on West Coast cookery, the thrifty camp baker made his own yeast, substituted bear lard for processed shortening, and used few kitchen implements, preferring to squeeze out dough orbs to pat into biscuits without recourse to dough roller or biscuit cutter.

For breakfast beans, the cook started a hot fire and dug a hole alongside it. He scalded presoaked beans, then poured them into a pot on top of an onion. Across the top, he layered sliced sowbelly and finished off the seasonings with thick molasses. After sealing the pot, he lowered it into the hole and topped it off with enough hot coals to line empty spaces down the side. He completed the cooking with a fire on top that burned for twenty-four hours.

When the food was ready, the cook loaded bean kettle, tea urn, and stew pot onto a box sled. After driving to a central location, he blew the dinner horn loud enough for woodsmen to hear from five miles away. Without ceremony, workers swarmed onto the site and wolfed down plates of beans and stew and slugs of hot tea. When the weather was at its worst, tea froze their whiskers. By nightfall, which came as early as 4:00 p.m. in winter, they crowded into the cookhouse. Staff loaded trestle tables with platters of fried mush, piles of flapjacks, pitchers of syrup, pots of brown beans, tins of apple pie, and pans of dried peaches, prunes, and rice pudding. There was no conversation and no argument with the cook, a well-paid hand who knew how to feed a hundred loggers on thirty cents each per day.

The California Gold Rush that followed the 1848 strike at Sutter's mill brought adventurers, rowdies, and entrepreneurs, but few cooks, launderers, or housewives. In token of the badly skewed gender ratio, a frontier poet published "We Miss Thee, Ladies," in *The Miners' Lamentations*, an undated lettersheet summarizing prospectors' privations. Under a picture of a man cooking beneath a tarp beside a one-room cabin, the ten-verse poem began with blandishments, but ended with the realities of an artificial and womanless society. The accompanying essay declared that the lack of women to cook, clean, and keep house was a bitter fault in the otherwise free and easy life of the bachelor miner. Under duress, men discovered that they could learn to cook and spread a decent table when hunger demanded it.

Speculators who arrived in California expecting instant wealth found a hard job, long hours, and only a sprinkle of gold dust to show for panning and examining silt from streams. In shanty towns, rains turned dirt streets into a muddy "sloo" that made shopping and provisioning hazardous. Because foodstuffs passed through Stockton and over muddy traces to mining camps, land pirates gouged shoppers, who had to pay exorbitant rates for staples: one dollar for an egg or a loaf of bread, fifty cents for a quart of milk or pint of molasses, and eleven dollars a pound for flour. Scarce items like onions, apples, cabbage, fresh fruit, and root vegetables sold for even more inflated prices.

Desperate men planted kitchen patches of onions, cabbage, potatoes, and turnips. One survivor, E. Hazard Wells, author of *Magnificence and Misery* (1984), asserted that survival took ingenuity: "No man need starve with a shotgun and fishing appliances during the summer at least. There are some delicious wild currants growing upon the mountainsides near by, and tracks of moose, caribou and silver-tip bears are plentiful." (Wells 1984, 57) Although the cookery was crude, the milieu of San Francisco's mining community produced the area's world-famous sourdough, which married an airborne microbe, *Lactobacillus sanfrancisco,* to a yeast, *Saccharomyces exiguus,* to form a tangy bread that French baker Isadore Boudin invented in 1849.

Where foodstuffs were plentiful or at least sufficient, cooks were lacking. Partners allotted chores by rotating "cook weeks." As John Doble explained, "Sometimes one does the cooking and sometimes another and one only cooks at a time and cooks for all who are in the cabin." (Johnson 2000, 110) At a time when monthly wages averaged ten dollars, one boardinghouse manager offered a bonus of one hundred dollars for someone who would cook for lodgers. In a multicultural environment, Mexican cooks thrived in open-air stalls, where they stirred a fragrant chile and meat soup, sold drinks iced with snow from the Sierras, and offered tamales, pies, and cake to men who seldom saw baked goods. One entrepreneur, Señora Benito Pérez, who served up plates of frijoles and tortillas to willing diners, earned over fifty dollars a day in gold.

Hired females faced the implied duty of sexual service to their employers. In 1850, one cagey woman capitalized on camp hunger for home cooking by establishing a safely chaste kitchen business in fried apple turnovers, which she sold for one dollar each. A Swedish Klondiker, Alice McDonald, journeyed from Cleveland, Ohio, to Dawson to open a boardinghouse, but had to hire out as a waitress and scullery maid. A day's chores included cooking, serving, splitting wood, hauling water, and sleeping with the boss. Disgruntled at the arrangement, she searched for a decent job by advertising in the *Klondike Nugget* as a respectable woman seeking only kitchen work.

Not all situations were as degrading as Alice McDonald's. Mary Thorne of Texas, her slave Diana Caruthers, and Diana's daughters Caroline and Georgeanne set up a successful boardinghouse at the Southern Mines in Mariposa County, an establishment famed for buttermilk and eggs. Disheartened by the lack of choice, Charles Davis, who longed for a better diet, groused that Mariposa miners had to tolerate spartan meals and got "no eggs, no Turkey, no Chickens no pies no doughnuts no pastry. . .unless we take a meal at Mrs. Thornes." (Ibid., 115)

One unusual cooking arrangement occurred in 1850, when a Mississippi planter named Gaster brought his sons and thirty slaves to the mining fields. Although slavery was outlawed in California, the male bondsmen followed the master's orders because he still owned their wives and families. One observer, Timothy Osborn of Martha's Vineyard, took the abolitionist stance and denounced slavery. Against a setting of kitchen chaos, he was forced to admit that the blacks were skilled in cooking, cleaning, and domestic order. Such complaints about division of labor among races failed to set aside the pervasive male complaint that what miners really needed were female housekeepers, a sentiment echoed by Enos Christmas, publisher of the *Sonora Herald.* In the estimation of Lucius Fairchild, "You can't imagine how much more comfortable it is to have a good woman around." (Ibid., 116)

One advantage of mining camps was the mixing of races and cultures in an interdependent community. Miwok Indians, who build snug conical bark dwellings, set an example of living off the land by gathering foodstuffs and unearthing roots and wild onions with digging sticks. In the spring under a strict division of labor, the women, bearing homemade cone-shaped baskets attached to tumplines about the forehead, pulled greens from columbine, clover, larkspur, milkweed, and miner's lettuce. Into summer, they gathered insects and beat balsam and primrose with brush flails to winnow out the seeds. They collected pine nuts and acorns, which they pounded on flat rocks and rinsed to remove bitterness from the meal. More onerous were celebrations, when runners carried bundles of reeds or sticks indicating the number of days until an intertribal get-together. Women gathered and cooked communally for days in addition to making costumes and ear and nose ornaments. In the few idle moments, they clustered about white women's doors to observe unfamiliar styles of cooking and housekeeping.

In contrast to woman's mining camp work, Miwok men fished and hunted, using nets, spears, and bows and arrows and waited while their wives gathered firewood, cleaned and spitted their catch, and roasted it over a fire. A German visitor, Friedrich Gerstäcker, observed the inequities of life for Miwok women and proclaimed it unjust, though necessary. In his opinion, men could not burden themselves with bearing heavy loads because they needed their arms unburdened for the job of hunting. Gradually, the Indians joined gold panners and abandoned subsistence living to earn money to buy food. The Miwok bark and canvas shelter added to the mix of cabins and lean-tos that miners called home.

The common log and canvas cabin of north central California south of Sacramento often perched beside streams for washing and alongside stone ovens and homemade fireplaces for roasting and baking. Archeologists discovered that the miners who baked daily and roasted meats were typically Italian imigrants, who imported home cooking styles and methods to their new locale. Annie Green, a housewife in Greeley, Colorado, realized that a simple kitchen operation could net a steady income. At her home oven, she began baking large loaves and pies to order. She expanded her business by making double use of oven heat to warm flatirons for a sideline in ironing shirts.

For miners in the field, food was a life-and-death issue. At Forty Mile, Emilie Fortin Tremblay reported the same fare three meals a day—beans, sardines, dried potatoes, and sourdough bread. For Christmas, she boosted her menu to include stuffed rabbit, caribou, potatoes, brown beans, plum pudding, and blueberry sauce, but still lacked a variety of vitamins and minerals to maintain health. Dr. J. J. Chambers of Dawson's Catholic Hospital confided to the diarist E. Hazard Wells in November 1897 that miners suffered scurvy in epidemic numbers because of poor nutrition. Chambers predicted that the area case load would rise to five hundred. He surmised that consuming salt pork day after day robbed the system of nutrients.

The answer to Klondike's sufferings came from such expert cooks as Ma Pullen, a bereft widow and contemporary of Chambers. In Skagway in 1897, she brought her four children to settle in fall and found a job as a cook. After hours, she made pies for sale to earn fares for her three sons. Rather than set up in a grub tent, she chose the difficult job of packing provisions in lots that the Canadian Mounted Police estimated at a half ton or more per man. Although she suffered a setback after thieves stole her equipment, she persevered to become the region's only female packer. She expanded business with a wagon team carrying goods over the White Pass on the Brackett toll road, purchased rental property, and opened a restaurant and hotel, called Pullen House.

Further Reading

Backhouse, Frances. *Women of the Klondike*. Vancouver: Whitecap Books, 1995.
Costello, Julia G., "Gold Rush Archeology: Excavating the Mother Lode," *Archaeology*, March–April 1981, 18–26.
Johnson, Susan Lee. *Roaring Camp: The Social World of the California Gold Rush*. New York: W. W. Norton & Co., 2000.
Wells, E. Hazard. *Magnificence and Misery*. Garden City, N.Y.: Doubleday & Co., 1984.
Wharton, David. *The Alaska Gold Rush*. Bloomington: Indiana University Press, 1972.

MIXERS AND BLENDERS

From ancient times, blending food was often no more technically advanced than twirling a leafy twig or palm frond between the hands to aerate liquid. Because of demand in Islamic and Christian cultures of the mid-seventeenth century for purées and sauces, mixers evolved from flat wire beaters, woven wire egg whips, looped and half-moon whisks, and other blending and stirring tools. In the American colonies, cooks learned to whip liquids with a twig by imitating the Indian broom, a splintered birch or beech staff used by East Coast Indians. To increase the whipping power, homemakers soaked a sapling, then splintered the end. After removing the core, they tied the splinters into a head. Several inches below it, they segmented the root and turned the ends over the head to add to the original ruff. Braided fiber held all in position. These homemade gadgets earned their keep by creating extra whipping action out of each twirl of the palms or rotary movement of the arm. They were also handy at the sink for scouring kettles and in the oven for removing ash.

The next level of food blending technology, the rotating barrel food chopper, meat crusher, or meat hasher from the 1860s, contained a blade agitator. When cranked by hand, it hacked out a coarse amalgam of vegetables or meats to be macerated for sausage or mince pies. One recipe, carmeline sauce, began with the grinding of raisins, crushing of almonds, and mixing with sour grape juice, bread crumbs, cinnamon, and cloves. Another dish that demanded heavy mixing was quince paste, an accompaniment to fava beans in meat sauce.

One popular adaptation, the eggbeater, consisted of hand-operated rotary whisk attached to meshed gears. Patented in 1870 and produced by the Dover Stamping company, subsequent designs incorporated numerous changes, such as the addition of ball bearings and rotation on the principle of the bowdrill, a common fire-making device among North American Indians. Updated mixer models could beat and whip without splashing and rinsed clean by repeating the mixing action in soapy dishwater. New York inventor Thomas Holt patented the cyclone eggbeater in 1901, a variant with slotted blades that enhanced the mixing and aerating actions without adding to the labor. In 1929, the Culinary Utilities Company marketed the Keystone Beater, an eggbeater and liquid mixer that capped the work of the beaters within a glass cylinder marked with measurements along the side.

In November 1885, Rufus M. Eastman invented the first electric mixer. The cake beater, patented in 1901, returned to earlier hand-powered technology for better control of batter. The hand-cranked device, fitted with gears and a corrugated wire beater arm, fit over a cake bowl for mixing without slopping batter over the sides or raising a cloud of dry flour. Similarly formed, a drink mixer, invented in 1916 by Stephen J. Poplawski, consisted of a glass jar fitted with a central wire shaft that operated a beater on the principle of the Archimedean screw. Designed to chop, purée, and liquefy solids and liquids in soda fountain beverages, the whirring blade impressed Pennsylvania band leader Fred Waring, who worked with Frederick Osius in 1935 to advance the original blender and market it as the Waring Blender, which became a popular gift for newlyweds.

In 1910, Wisconsin inventors Frederick Osius and George Schmidt perfected the electric food mixer, a scaled-down model of the commercial stirrer that beat milk and ice cream into milk shakes. Sold by Hamilton Beach Manufacturing Company, named for Chester Beach and L. H. Hamilton, the Cyclone mixer reached many home kitchens in the 1930s. It revolutionized menus by speeding up preparation of sauces and encouraged the hesitant to attempt the complex baking projects that once required arduous whipping and folding. In 1926, Air-O-Mix blended two functions in one with a counter-top mixer that could be demounted for hand mixing.

The blender got its start in 1922, when inventor Stephen J. Poplawski devised a bladed tool in a jar. Household engineer Christine McGaffey Frederick studied the blender and mixer for *Efficient Housekeeping or Household Engineering—Scientific Management in the Home* (1925). In her estimation, consumers needed to balance their desire for ease of food preparation with the tedium and difficulty of removing the blades for washing. Her astute understanding of kitchen efficiency holds true with current models, which still require complex breakdown and reassembly during washing and drying of dangerous blades.

In 1927, the boom in hand mixers continued with Chicago inventor A. F. Dormeyer's patent on the electric

beater with detachable blades. In KitchenAid's 1928 catalog, ad copy declared its latest mixer a cheer-bringer that brightened the kitchen, drawing Dad, Junior, and Sister into the act of preparing food. The first Sunbeam Mixmaster, which designer Ivar Jepson streamlined, reached the market in 1930 and held top place for three decades. A heavy machine, it consisted of twin stainless steel beaters that popped out of the head for easy cleaning and a rotating ceramic bowl on a sturdy base. The motor suited mashing potatoes and mixing cakes, but overheated when pressed to blend yeast dough. That same year, the Fitzgerald Manufacturing Company of Torrington, Connecticut, advertised its Star-Rite Magic Maid, a stand mixer with multi-speed motor that promised enough power to rid cookery of hand and arm fatigue.

Companies shifted and regrouped as they vied for control of the mixer-blender market. KitchenAid's designer Egmont Arens brought out a competitor for large-volume tasks that ended Sunbeam's virtual monopoly. The appliance was so powerful that the Hobart Corporation, a subsidary of the Troy Metal Products Company in Ohio, produced an eighty-gallon model in 1931 suited to hotel and restaurant kitchens. Subsequent home versions, intended to appeal to female cooks, came in white, yellow, green, and pink, the latter said to have been inspired by the color of first lady Mamie Eisenhower's inaugural gown. General Electric pressed into the competition with the 1935 Hotpoint portable mixer with three-speed motor, a device so blessed with attachments that it could grate, juice, buff, sharpen knives, mix drinks, chop meat, shred, and slice. In 1949, Dormeyer reinvented the mixer as a multi-purpose Meal-Mixer, which offered juicing and mincing attachments, thus ridding the kitchen of additional counter-hogging appliances.

In 1947, as Britain pulled itself out of rationing and bombed-out flats, the electrical whiz Ken Wood abandoned radar and electronics to take up domestic appliance design at his home workbench in Surrey, England. He invented the A100 Turn-over toaster, the first appliance of a respected kitchen design firm. With thirty laborers, he began manufacture, turning himself into a household name and a billionaire by 1949. He is best known for the Kenwood Chef, a mixer invented in 1950. Engineering a suitable mixer required pinpointing the chores that cooks most often performed. After studying the competition, especially American electrical appliances, Wood assembled the best elements, adding a spaghetti maker from Italy, can opener from the United States, and potato peeler from Germany. The completed machine—marketed as "Your Servant Madam!"—sold nine million units, remaining largely unchanged on the market until 1960. One unusual feature, planetary action, turned the bowl in one direction and the beaters counter to it. For its ability to mix, knead, whisk, liquify, blend, purée, extract juice, slice, mince, grind, sieve, peel, and open cans, the Kenwood Chef earned recognition at the London Science Museum. In 2001, De Longhi Pinguino of Italy purchased the company.

Jean Mantelet, the French inventor-industrialist who established the Moulinex company, brought his tin-plate Mouli hand food mill from Leipzig to France in 1932. His innovation required one more advance to complete his fame. In his words, "It occurred to me that some day women would get tired of turning the handle, so I immediately decided to motorize my appliance." (Rowley 1999, 69) In the 1950s, shortly after Ken Wood invented his Chef, Mantelet applied an electric motor, the beginning of a line of electric kitchen appliances known by the trade name Moulinex. It presaged an age of powerful food processors evolved by such electronics giants as Cuisinart, Hamilton Beach, KitchenAid, Krups, Philips, and Sunbeam. Max Braun, an electronics magnate in Frankfurt, Germany, added mixers and shavers to his line of radio components. In 1957, the company marketed its Kitchen Machine, a minimalist food mixer that earned respect for sleek simplicity and easy assembly and cleaning, qualities lacking in most over-engineered designs.

Within a few years, Braun met stiff competition in the Lady Casco Chef Mate blender-mixer, one of a family of products for the kitchen backed by a guarantee from Lloyd's of London. In France in 1963, inventor Pierre Verdun marketed the Robot Coupe, the first official food processor, as an aid to professional cooks. Cuisinart did not make a serious move into the market until a decade later, when it demonstrated its food processor at Chicago's National Household Exposition. Invented in 1971 by New York-born engineer and amateur cook Carl G. Sontheimer, who contributed a microwave direction finder to NASA's moon missions, the processor was a scaled-down model of the industrial blender that chopped, grated, kneaded, sliced, ground, puréed, and blended food.

Unlike blenders and stand mixers, processors had a narrower range of speeds and limited range of uses. In 1984, *Atlantic* published an overview of the food processor fad, an escalation of high-tech equipment by Cuisinart, Robot Coupe, and KitchenAid that claimed to replaced the labor of a large kitchen staff for such complex and messy recipes as pie crust, forcemeat, purée, paté, and soufflé. Along with praise for time- and effort-saving, the article noted that the machines were cumbersome and less effective at uniform cutting and grating. Authors Barbara and James Goldman complained of leaks around the central shaft, messy and dangerous blade removal, high cost, and motor burn-out.

At century's end, KitchenAid had met the challenge of Braun, Cuisinart, and others by re-introducing a tough, powerful chrome-plated machine that shredded, juiced, minced, stuffed casings, and extruded pasta. The updated KitchenAid mixer featured a beater triad—flat for mixing, balloon wire whisk for whipping, and dough hook for kneading. Dubbed the "little pro," the workhorse mixer appealed to serious bakers and also answered the needs of restaurant kitchens for making desserts. In 2000, KitchenAid brought out its Epicurean mixer in black, cream, red, gray, blue, green, navy, and white with a 475-watt motor and the Pro 6, fifty watts stronger and equipped with burnished steel attachments, six-quart bowl, pouring shield and chute for adding ingredients, and a sensor that adjusted torque to suit the load.

Introduced in the 1930s, Electrolux mixers advanced to the Swedish-made Magic Mill, a heavy-duty mixer for serious bakers working up family-sized batches. The largest capacity machine on the market, the Magic Mill consisted of stainless steel two-gallon bowl and alternate plastic whipping bowl, power arm with grooved pestle, timer, and bottom-mounted transmission. It accommodated a full line of add-ons—blender, slicer-shredder, flake and grain-spice mills, citrus-berry and cookie presses, pasta-maker, meat grinder, nut grinder, and sausage stuffer. In 2001 this machine was priced around five hundred dollars.

European cooks popularized a number of innovations in mixing and blending, including the BonJour Caffe Froth Turbo, a stick blender suited to whipping espresso and cappuccino in the cup, and the HalfPint Cream Whipper from iSi, a home-sized whipper that came with a charge for aerating topping, mousse, dip, and salad dressing. American cooks liked the cordless rechargeable Cuisinart hand blender, a light, shapely tool with petite whirling blade at one end for mixing gravies, sauces, and desserts right in the pot. Easily recharged and dishwasher safe, the device ran up to fifteen minutes per charge and came with a two-cup beaker for whipping cream, making smoothies, and mixing salad dressing and emulsions. A British favorite was the 2001 aluminum Kenwood, a squarish design with 650-watt motor, balloon whisk and flat paddle, and seven-quart bowl. The machine earned acclaim from the New England Culinary Academy.

MOCUCKS

In the progression of cooking technology from basket boiling and stone boiling to roasting over a fire, Native American cooks needed a means of cooking ground seeds in water to make porridge. Before designers hit on carved wood and clay containers, they fashioned

MOLDS

the mocuck, a cylindrical skin and bark container or square bark trough. The Huron of Canada expanded the use of mocucks from cookery to the warming of squash seed over a fire before sowing in rotted stump pith. The treatment caused early germination and helped food growers make the most of a short growing season. The Ojibway of Mille Lacs, Minnesota, hand-rubbed boiled maple sap into *ziinzibaakwad* (sugar granules) and retained them in mocucks for use in cooking porridge, fish, fruits and vegetables, and dried berries and for sweetening summer drinks and hot teas.

The early French *coureurs de bois* (woodsmen) visiting Lake Superior found Chippewa cooks pounding roast venison into tenderized jerked steak for packing in mocucks for winter use. When the fur trader Alexander Mackenzie, author of *Voyages from Montreal on the River St. Laurence through the Continent of North America to the Frozen and Pacific Oceans in the Years 1789 and 1793* (1801), visited Pacific Coast tribes, he marveled at the gift of watertight wood boxes that his hosts gave him as creels to contain the salmon he caught on a fishing expedition.

Shaping a basket from felled birches required careful peeling of the bark with chisels or wedges. From the bark, the mocuck-maker folded one bark sheet, fastened it at the sides, and tempered it over a fire or over steam to make it pliant before bending it into a box shape. He sewed the square-bottomed vessel and lid with basswood fiber, braided sweet grass, cedar or spruce root, willow withes, or wood splints. After a curing over a fire, a smear of pitch sealed them to hold liquids or store water. Attached to a willow hoop and handle, the bark box hung over a fire for cooking. Another form of mocuck was not watertight and served as a tray and serving dish.

The Algonquin, early North American forest Indians from the Great Lakes region, the Chilcotin of British Columbia, and the Penobscot of Maine shaped the mocuck from thin, sturdy birch bark for kitchen storage, for adapting into pans to collect maple sap, or for tying to a lodge pole or longhouse beam with cording or thongs as a shield to protect the family cook fire from wet weather. The Carrier of Canada scraped the rough outer layer with a wood scraper or knife before cutting the bark into the shape of a basket.

Bark buckets served as collectors for maple sap or storage for berries, fruit, or wild rice. The Mono amassed acorns in a mocuck for drying to ready the nut meats for grinding on a mano and metate or with mortar and pestle. Others used the mocuck to transport tools and dishes to a fish-drying frame, herb bed, winnowing floor, salt pit, or fish weir. To free hands of the load, the user tied the box to the forehead with a tumpline. The bark storage boxes were also profitable trade items.

In 1946, the Ojibwa artist Patrick Des Jarlait, who grew up on the Red Lake Indian Reservation, painted *Maple Sugar Time*, a dynamic, cubistic view of sugar making. He drew the group activity from a snapshot of the Martin Kegg family sugaring at Mille Lacs, Minnesota, that same year. One female figure stirs syrup in a kettle; behind her, a male reduces the syrup to crystals. At front, a woman readies a mocuck to receive the granular sugar that another cook pounds in preparation for storage. The folk vignette characterizes the Ojibwa respect for traditional sugaring as a vital part of tribal sustenance.

Further Reading

Mandelbaum, David G. *The Plains Cree: An Ethnographic, Historical and Comparative Study*. Regina, Sask.: Canadian Plain Research Center, 1979.
Underhill, Ruth M. *Red Man's America*. Chicago: University of Chicago Press, 1971.

MOLDS

Molds have had numerous home uses from early times, from forging bronze into pots and rice into cakes in China to shaping plinths for food displays in French *haute cuisine*, freezing ice cream in animal shapes for the White House wedding of Grover Cleveland and Frances Folsom, and shaping gelatins and confections in American dessert shops in the 1920s. Digs at the Mari palace on the Middle Euphrates in Syria from the eighteenth century BCE unearthed circular clay molds in the shape of fish and mammals, which suggest the efforts of the Babylonian cook to please royalty. Simple molding of axes and knives in stone served until a more sophisticated system came into use in 3000 BCE, when technicians carved models in wood and fashioned a clay surface. After they removed the wood, the two halves of the mold served for making pots from molten metal. During the Shang period of Chinese history, from 1766 to 1100 BCE, pot makers created bronze cooking vessels with the lost wax technique. The creator made a wax model, then surfaced it in clay. After decanting the melted wax, the caster poured in melted bronze. When it cooled, removal of the clay exterior left a useful vessel, such as the three-legged cook's kettle with extended handles.

A millennium after Chinese confectioners began molding candy, Egyptians sketched candy-making in tomb friezes. Royal confectioners used molds to shape honeyed treats in such iconic forms as geese and sacred bulls. The candies appear to be bribes that enabled the soul to elude underworld terrors, sweet-talk deities, and escape the court of judgment to return to earth, a human ambition portrayed in *The Book of the Dead* (ca. 1554 BCE), a compendium of spells, magic formulas, and incantations that served as a passport for the dead. Harvest scenes from the Tomb of Menena in Egypt show ritual grain harvesting and preparation, which preceded placement of dough in a triangular or lozenge-shaped mold to produce fragrant loaves in a pleasing uniform configuration.

In Mille Lacs, Minnesota, Ojibwa sugar-makers traditionally gathered each winter to drain sap from maple trees and boil the liquid down to syrup or crystalline sugar. For *zhiiwaagamizigan* (hard sugar), cooks scooped the reduced slurry from the bubbling cauldrons and solidified it over ice or snow. To give it shape, they packed the brown granules into shells or birchbark cones for storage and stitched the tops shut with basswood fiber. For sugar cakes, they poured the sweet syrup into wooden molds greased with deer tallow to make it easier for homemakers to remove solid cakes without breaking them.

In England, gingerbread molds earned the name "fairings" for their sale at local fairs. The most famous, Smithfield's St. Bartholomew's Fair, held from 1123 to 1850, sold molded gingerbread at baker's stalls for over seven centuries.

A viable home business, cookies in the shape of Punch and Judy and alphabet letters opened new outlets for the homemaker's skills and, at the same time, encouraged literacy in children. In small or isolated villages, another market, the church, depended on home kitchens for molded or stamped communion bread.

In the 1400s, Swabian chefs invented the Würzburger marzipan or springerle, a Christian holiday biscuit molded on a carved wood board and painted with bright colors. The brittle cookie was a favorite in Nuremberg as *Eierzucker* and in Switzerland as *Anisbröti*. In the early Renaissance, European banquets favored molded blancmange, a rice, chicken, and almond milk purée seasoned with sugar and pork fat. In 1688, ordinary European cookbooks published the first recipes for homemade springerle dough. Pressed onto carved or intaglio plaques for baking, the anise-flavored cookies acquired fine details and perforations that neatly separated each like a block of postage stamps. Elaborate cookie presses, favored by royalty and nobility, displayed seasonal motifs and figures, such as geese, crosses, and tulips for Easter and reindeer, angels, candles, and nutcrackers for Christmas. Two similiar traditions from Italy, the *pandoro* and *panettone* molds, shaped holiday raisin or citron cakes and breads in similarly ornate motifs.

A royal innovation, the *baba au rhum*, a molded raisin sponge cake soaked in rum or kirsch, brought fame to King Stanislaus Leczinski of Poland. In 1736, he started with a *kugelhopf*, a raised pastry which had originated in Lemberg in 1609, then sprinkled it with rum and set it aflame. A masterstroke when it was introduced at the court of Lorraine, the cake bore the name of Ali Baba, picaresque hero of the Arab classic fable collection *A Thousand and One Nights*. After the Polish pastry chef Sthorer presented baba in Paris in the early 1800s, bakers either brushed them with wine or soaked them in rum-flavored syrup. Two variants, the *fribourg* and the *savarin* yeast cake, achieved similar success. A third, molded into a hexagon, bore the name *gorenflot*, a character in Alexandre Dumas *père*'s romantic novel *La Dame de Montsoreau*, coauthored with Auguste Maquet in 1888.

Molding even simple semi-solids gave servings presence and style. A decorative tin blancmange mold held flavored gelatin to be compressed during the chilling process. Shapes ranged from ziggurat style to flowers, birds, and fluted columns or towers. In the early 1700s, a German favorite compendium, *Goethe's Grandmother's Cookbook*, identified with the era's most influential Romantic poet, advocated molding, dyeing, and decorating sweet pastries as a boost to food presentation at table and for entertaining. Recipes for molded sweets from the mid-1800s suggested wetting the interior of the mold with milk or water before pouring in the thickened mixture as a means of loosening the bond during unmolding to preserve the image.

Molds for cheese were essential to the growing dairy trade. On the Åland Islands between Finland and Sweden, woodworkers produced a three-part rectangular mold. The middle section was a four-sided container to hold the mass. The cheese-maker set the frame in a larger rectangular box stamped with a design. A short-handled tamper fitted into the top of the middle section replicated the motif for a two-sided decoration. Homemakers toiled at smoking, washing in juniper water, and prettying their goat cheeses, which were standard traveler's food, festival items, and gifts to the clergy. Families served molded cheese and black bread to field hands during haying and harvesting and for holiday celebrations.

From the Middle Ages into the early 1900s, throughout France and neighboring countries, the osier basket was the most common mold for cheese. Cooks also used tin, wood, and clay molds, which they shielded from insects and dust with molding cloths. Employed in the draining of curds, the last stage before curing, the mold held curds in a tight round while fermentation altered lactose into lactic acid and the culture formed fungi. Turned out on a cheeseboard, molded cheeses maintained their shape during slicing.

For this reason, they were often centerpieces at receptions and banquets.

For daily use, the favorite mold from the era was the butter mold or butter print, which developed from hand-carved artistic patterns or flowers to late nineteenth-century factory-made molds, including the three-tiered curd cheese shaper made of glazed china in Staffordshire in the 1800s. Whether circular or oblong, each supported a shapeless mass for pressing and tamping into a dense solid, then stamping with a decorative end piece, which contained incised initials, crests, or images that identified the dairy from which the product originated. To create the design, a wood shaper either cut wood parts with a lathe and chiseled the outlines into the grain or forced designs in metal into the surface with heavy pressure. A significant design, the Maltese cross butter mold, consisted of a square at center hinged to four flared side pieces, each bearing a carved design. When the user fitted the sides together and slipped on a hoop to hold the box in place, the pressing of butter and removal of the hoop resulted in a neat block.

The colonial American box maker shaped the round box on a block mold, which ranged from a one-and-a-half inch pill container to a two-foot quilt scrap box or cheese mold. After plunging wood or bark into boiling water, the maker settled the piece hoop-style in a vise and used a wood gauge as a compass to describe circles for top and bottom. Ovals demanded a bit more geometric ingenuity of superimposing a small circle over the edge of a larger one and filling in the gaps to make an oval. After nailing the two ends of the strip around the mold, the shaper fitted the tops and bottoms to strips and secured them with wooden shoe pegs. Another home-made mold was the aspic shaper, which a smith soldered from cookie cutters and tin pie pans. As of 1850, purchasers could buy factory-made boxes from Hingham, Massachusetts, where woodworker Edmund Hersey turned out 1,500,000 fig, strawberry, and salt boxes annually shaped on the steam-powered machinery he devised. A comparable system produced flat molds for shaping maple sugar cakes with attractive designs to enhance trade or advertise products from home kitchen businesses.

The Pennsylvania Dutch, a loose designation encompassing Amish, Brethren, Dunkard, and Mennonite settlers who settled in North America in 1682, kept a Christmas tradition dating to 1560 requiring the making of marzipan or marchpane. Before January 6, called Twelfth Night or Little Christmas, cooks ground almonds or pulverized apricot kernels into paste, which they blended with flour or meal, and sweetened with honey, syrup, brandy, or wine. After rolling out the dough, they hand-pressed it into wood molds carved with animals, flowers, or patterns. With a brass pastry jigger, they zipped away excess dough before sliding the molds into the oven.

Many styles and types of molds made from various materials suited particular food-shaping needs:

Baba mold is a stamped copper mold that shaped a traditional German pound cake.

Barquette tin is a fluted boat-shaped tin or tinned steel pan for baking small *hors d'oeuvres* and tarts, such as the Scandinavian *sandbakkelse*. Other tart pans came in round, scalloped, square, lozenge, and diamond shapes or in frames containing multiple shaped indentations.

Biscuit mold is a copper or ceramic mold that shaped frozen meringue desserts called iced biscuits.

Border mold is a ringed tin mold used for forming mashed potatoes or carrots, gelatins, and force meat into decorative motifs for filling with mayonnaise or sauce and embellishing with garnishes.

Breton cake molds are a series of lightly tinned fluted pans ranging in capacity from one to nine cups for stacking into a multi-tiered *gâteau Breton* (wedding cake).

Brioche mold is a fluted or scalloped glass, aluminum, stoneware, ceramic, or tin-lined copper vessel for baking egg dough into bread. The name may derive from brie, a cheese that may have been an ingredient in an original recipe. The elegant pan enhanced the kitchen both as usable bread shaper and visible culinary decor.

Bundt pan is a scalloped teflon-surfaced aluminum tube pan that produced a dense German coffeecake.

Carenflot mold is a hexagonal border mold.

Cassata mold is a container designed for layering ice cream with Chantilly creme and crystallized fruit soaked in brandy.

Charlotte russe mold is a stamped tin or aluminum cup that compressed *Bavarois* (Bavarian cream), fruit charlotte, bombes, jelly, blancmange, fruit-filled moscovites, and other puddings. The dish may have taken the name of Charlotte-Sophia, Duchess of Mecklenburg, the queen of George III.

Chessel mold is a specialty of the treen carver, who incised crests, portraits, and other respected images to identify the diary worker or farm from which the cheese derived

Confusable mold is a cast-iron pan designed to shape cornbread or other breads into sticks. The name refers to the fusing of sticks into a perforated or aligned series of uniform shapes.

Cornucopia form is a horn-shaped tinned steel mold for making cornets, cream horns, ham rolls, or lady locks, a pastry fitted at the tip with a corkscrew strip, which Germans called *schillerlocken* (Schiller's locks).

Corrugated loaf mold is a two-part cylindrical shaper that created a finished surface on a loaf by marking grooves for slicing.

Croquembouche mold is a tinned steel cone flattened at one end. The buttered mold formed a standard around which the pastry cook fashioned mounds of cream puffs cemented with caramel glaze. The architecture held its airy shape after the mold was removed.

Croquette mold is a conical shaper of meat croquettes that produced mounds suitable for dressing with sauce or gravy. One clever variety was the cutlet mold, which took the shape of drumsticks, leg of mutton, ham shanks, and lamb or pork chops compressed out of mixtures of chopped meat and onion, an egg binder, bread crumbs, and spice.

Dariel or dariole mold is a tin custard cup dating to the 1300s and used for shaping *chartreuses* and desserts.

Flan ring is a circular mold or hoop for jellied deserts, flan, and pastries.

Fritter mold is a long-handled metal implement shaped in seasonal or geometric patterns for dipping batter into hot fat to produce pastries.

Galantine mold is a porcelain or tin loaf pan that held a boned and poached bird until it set or baked into a firm shape for unmolding and garnishing.

Glacé mold is a container for shaping ices for *fromage glacé* (iced cheese).

Kugelhopf mold is a glass, stoneware, ceramic, or tinned steel cake pan marked with geometric motifs to shape a traditional Middle European yeast dough filled with raisins, almonds, and lemon peel. Legend states that a baker invented the pan in 1685 as Turkish insurgents battered Vienna. Because the resulting sweet bread or coffeecake bore the shape of the sultan's turban, the victorious Austrians popularized kugelhopf at pastry shops and coffeehouses. An older legend connects the name to yeast bread shaped like a monk's *gugel* (cowl).

Langues de chat pan is an indented "cat's tongue" or ladyfinger pan producing *biscuits a cuiller*, individual hourglass-shaped cake bites dipped in chocolate or iced for teas and banquets.

Losaid or losset is the Irish dough mold or wooden trough in which the cook left bread overnight to rise.

Madeleine mold is an ornate baking sheet indented to make madeleine cakes, also called cat's tongues. After baking, they received a quick dip in dark chocolate at one end. A long-lived cookie, the madeleine may derive from an earlier recipe baked in scallop shells.

Manque mold is a container for baking *savarin* cakes. When soaked in syrup, they were called *marignans*.

Mary Ann spring pan is a baking tin clamped shut until released to display finished cake. The underside shaped by the Mary Ann base contained a shallow depression for holding filling or fruit and whipped cream.

Obsttortenform is a seamless fluted tin or enameled aluminum plate with diamond-patterned bottom for molding a shallow fruit tart. A variant pan with bundt fluting created an elegant one-layer cake with scalloped sides for decorating or drizzling with chocolate or fruit syrup.

Pâté mold is a five-piece hinged framework that latched into place to hold jelly aspic and meat pastes. By releasing the clips that held the sides in place, the cook could safely remove the molded loaf.

Rehrucken mold is a long tin plate marked by regular ribbing for molding breads or a log cake indented for icing, studding with candied fruit and almonds, and cutting into uniform slices.

Savarin mold is a ceramic ring pan for baking a dough similar to a baba for soaking in kirsch, glazing, decorating, or filling with fruit and whipped cream. The cake took its name from Jean Brillat-Savarin, a French food critic and culinary commentator.

Shortbread mold is a Scottish stoneware baking dish that impresses designs and imprints scoring lines for breaking the cookie into wedges.

Springform pan is a tinned steel pan tube pan with grooved edge to hold a removable side for baking cheesecake and heavy torts similar to kugelhopf.

Timbale is a cooking cup shaped like a truncated cone for molding rice to serve with curried meat or fricassee.

Turkish bonnet baking mold is a domed cake pan shaped with regular convolutions. Thomas Jefferson numbered one of these pans in his inventory at Monticello.

Into recent times, molding devices perpetuate the tradition of shaping foods into identifiable objects, such as the nonstick gingerbread house mold that produces individual walls, roof sections, and chimney for separation and reassembly into a three-dimensional holiday decoration suitable for icing. A simple plastic set with interchangeable dies, the sushi kit, compresses sushi rolls into circles, squares, triangles, or hearts. Another gadget that applies pressure to foods is the stack mold, available in triangular, round, and square shafts with plunger for layering biscuits with berries and cream, tomato slices with peppers and mozzarella, and other combinations of baked, chilled, or frozen combinations.

See also **Cheese; Ice Cream; Tinware**

Further Reading

Roosevelt, Priscilla. *Life on the Russian Country Estate.* Hartford, Conn.: Yale University Press, 1995.

MOLOKHOVETS, ELENA

For over five decades, the food writer Elena Burman Molokhovets supervised the reissues of her classic Russian illustrated cookbook, *A Gift to Young Housewives* (1861). When she was born in 1831 in Archangel, Russian culinary writing had come into its own only in the previous decade. At about the time that Molokhovets was studying at the Imperial Educational Society for Noble Girls, Katerina Alekseevna Avdeeva was producing an energetic kitchen manual entitled *Ruchnaja Kniga Russkoj Opytnoj Khozjajki* (Handbook of an Experienced Russian Mistress of the Household, 1842), the first food compendium to influence Molokhovets. A strict Tsarist and adherent of the Russian Orthodox Church, she married an architect and bore nine sons and a daughter. She enjoyed the leisure of keeping house with a full staff of servants, but considered the compilation of menus to be the task of the mistress alone. She ruled her family with benign severity, running the kitchen by a tight schedule that primed her household to expect meals at a set time and tables arrayed with prescribed utensils, china, and glassware for *zakuski* (appetizers) or a full meal.

When Molokhovets's husband secretly published her stockpile of recipes in honor of her thirtieth name day, the book skyrocketed to instant success. In the introduction to a later edition, she stated three goals: introducing housewives to the kitchen and larder, teaching them to reduce expenses and garner stores, and explaining how to generate daily menus. She took a particular interest in the woman who cooked without kitchen staff. After she revealed her identity in the fourth edition, Molokhovets became a household name for authenticity in Russian cuisine. Her fans called her *baba-povarikha* (old woman cook), a fond title akin to the sobriquet of American folk artist Grandma Moses. A traditional measure of worth for a Russian housewife was pleasing the palate of her husband; the editors of *Novoe Vremja* (New Time) praised Molokhovets for ingratiating a quarter million husbands.

A treasured heirloom passed from woman to woman, Molokhovets's text preserved bourgeois kitchen history from the emancipation of serfs in 1861 to the outbreak of the Russian Revolution in 1917. Her advice strayed from elegant banquet tables and painting *grenochko* (croutons) with small feathers to choosing well water or river water for preserving lemons, the use of the traditional stove and smaller ranges, wrapping jam jars in hay to insulate them for boiling, hanging undressed ducks in the icehouse through the winter, preserving butter and eggs in salicylic acid, and preparing cheap dishes to feed servants. She was well versed in European cookery and included in her recipes a Scottish wedding cake derived from a custom of baking a shortbread "bride's bonn[ach]" at weddings in the Shetland Islands. (Molokhovets 1992, 345)

Molokhovets's domestic advice offered pragmatic solutions to kitchen problems, such as how to smoke fish over damp straw, how to cool jam in china basins rather than metal pans to avoid a metallic taste, how to store currant juice in iron boxes, and how to coat peaches in paraffin before storing them in straw-filled chests. She suggested methods of using a summer oven for cheese-making, baking bread and cakes, and dehydrating fruit leather. In lieu of the correct molds, pots, and kitchen implements, her makeshift *batterie de cuisine* included upending a stool to hold a napkin strainer, roasting coffee beans in a brazier, and cooking chocolate in a mortar. She packed a portable samovar on her saddle for outings.

Molokhovets's knowledge of the pitfalls of preserving food suggests a woman not too elevated above peasantry to perform common culinary tasks that were heavy, messy, and time-consuming. She specified the addition of swallows' nests to barrels of vinegar, a practice common among previous generations. On the use of wood, which was a common storage material in Russia, without understanding the scientific principles involved, she cautioned that absorbent cucumber barrels and wheat or rye bread troughs could not be recycled for use with other foods. She proposed sealing sauerkraut kegs with rye dough before pickling shredded cabbage in brine. By the twentieth edition, issued in 1897, the compilation had expanded from 1,500 recipes to 3,218. In Berlin in the 1920s, a final edition added another one thousand dishes, which lacked the authenticity and Russian spirit of her originals.

Reviled by Communists during the Soviet era, Molokhovets's style of cooking symbolized a gentility and dependence on serf labor that Bolsheviks labeled decadent and elitist. Upon the collapse of the Russian Marxist state, her cookbook returned to the streets of

Moscow with its glimpses of an agrarian preindustrial society, a defunct culture recalled by the dishes and menus in her recipe collection. Slavicist and food historian Joyce Toomre translated Molokhovets' work into English in 1992.

Further Reading

Grants, Musya, and Joyce Toomre, eds. *Food in Russian History and Culture*. Bloomington: Indiana University Press, 1997.

MONASTERY KITCHENS

European and Asian monasteries have contributed much to the originality and spirit of kitchen history. The monastery kitchen provided meals for the order, distributed alms and medicine for the poor, and in many cases created unique and highly valued baked, cooked, or fermented provisions.

In *Regula Monachorum* (Rules for Monks, ca. 515), a classic of moderate Western monasticism, St. Benedict the Great of Nursia, advised designers of monasteries like his own Monte Cassino in central Italy to set up their cloisters so that they enclosed water, mill, kitchen garden, and workshop and walled out anything that would distract from their mission. But he also taught hospitality, "Let all guests that come be received like Christ." (Platt 1996, 202) In reponse to Benedict's command, houses opened their portals to the public. The obedient abbot appointed an official *portarius* (house gatekeeper) to distribute alms to wayfarers. He considered each a welcome *hospes* (guest). Brothers offered meals and set aside guest rooms for homeless wanderers.

Unlike medieval homes and villas, monasteries were among the few residences that devoted one room or suite of rooms solely to cookery. For staff, the abbot appointed a head chef, who was exempt from religious obligation, and set up a food service hierarchy:

- The cellarer or treasurer attended to provisioning and oversaw catering.
- The kitchener managed food preparation, which a rotating list of appointees cooked and served and afterward cleaned the kitchen.
- The refectorer superintended dining hall furnishings.
- The gardener oversaw local produce.
- The pittancer provided foodstuffs for extra dishes.
- The infirmarian superintended the infirmary, which had its own kitchen, garden, and dining area.
- The *questarius* (alms seeker) found the cash from donors and patrons to keep the monastery solvent.
- The almoner distributed charity in the form of food, clothing, and blankets.

Monastery Kitchen, Ladakh.

Monasteries like Bourgueil, Pontlevoy, and Vendôme maintained kitchens in windowless annexes, which protected living quarters, chapel, and the valuable scriptoria from flame. Encouraged by Charlemagne in 800 CE, Christian monk-cooks reclaimed techniques of Roman bakers after a three-century lapse. They revived oven technology and unearthed the hydraulic mills that the architect Vitruvius had engineered. In fields surrounding cloisters, they hired workers to grow and harvest wheat. A daily breaking of bread served residents, guests, pilgrims, and the poor, who counted on monastic altruism during times of pestilence, war, and famine.

When monasticism expanded to double housing for monks and nuns, design indicated the importance of internal sequestering by gender. At the Gilbertine double priory, built at Watton, Yorkshire, around 1150, a mirror-image site plan relegated male diners to a north wall refectory in their compound and females to a similar northern dining area in their compound. In both settings, diners ate in silence while listening to a *lector* (reader) intone a homily or read from patristic writings and hagiography as a means of nourishing body and soul simultaneously. A third kitchen and dining facility served the prior separately. Fountains Abbey, founded in 1220, offered the sick twelve individual rooms in their infirmary. An adjacent walled passage led directly to a spacious kitchen and scullery for direct service of dietetic meals to the sick.

As identified by archeologists, abbey food courts in Egypt, Syria, and Palestine contain remnants of querns, silos, oil presses, and wine presses, evidence of the elements of monastic diets in the eastern and southeastern reaches of Christianity. Monks appeared to have oil, wine, and grain as pantry staples. They baked small round loaves in domed ovens, the center of monastic cuisine. At St. Catherine's cloister in Sinai, workers tiled the oven floor and ceiling with ceramic brick. For daily fare, cooks served vegetable dishes of wild thistle, saltbush, capers, reed, legumes and lentils, lupine seed, beans, hearts of palm, carobs, dates, and figs. Some abbey culinary records name fennel, cinnamon, and pepper as additives to *eukration* (spiced wine). On the conservative extreme of monasticism, anchorites spurned so luxurious a diet and fled to huts, caverns, or brick cells, where they lived on wild honey and greens, gifts of passersby, and limited income from basket weaving. A *laura* (hermit group) that sprang up might erect a church and a communal oven, where they baked loaves solely to serve partakers of the Eucharist.

Abbey kitchen staffs distributed alms, curatives, and nourishing foods as well as *panforte* (fruitcake) for travelers and ritual *panes coronati* (bread crowns) shaped for votive offerings. Although Cistercians favored a diet of beans, hearty Benedictine monks stocked ponds with eels and pike, operated weirs to catch salmon, evolved their own dairy styles, and developed distinctive cheese, one of the staples of the brotherhoods of Ireland and Scotland. According to Paul Bouillard, a French essayist of the 1920s, Alsatian Benedictines recognized the advantages in swine breeding to produce a firm, delicately flavored pork. Abbey recipes include St. Bernard's sauce, a twelfth-century condiment made of bread crumbs, almonds, sugar, anchovies, vinegar, and chocolate. For sharing these taste treats with pilgrims and travelers, they expected no fees, but welcomed donations.

Simultaneously, in Japan, Zen Buddhists followed strict asceticism, which limited their meals to a breakfast of plum tea, *kahu* (rice gruel), and pickled daikon radish, which individuals ate from a personal set of five wood bowls. Polite wayfarers left the brothers' monastery a *cha-dai* (tip), which equalled the price of tea. They wrapped the offering in paper to avoid the gaucherie of handing money directly to the receiver's palm. Some monks chose a hermit's life, which allowed no cooking and food offerings only from pilgrims. On *takhuhatsu* (begging rounds), they took lunch at the kitchens of laypersons, but ate no food prepared by their own hands.

During the renaissance of Tibetan Buddhism, at Piyang, a building campaign produced the Old Temple

and a fourteen-acre adobe-block compound that missionaries completed in 997 CE. Nearby, eighty spartan caves sheltered ascetics. Multi-roomed caverns afforded hermits wall niches for icons, hearths for warmth, and cooking areas to supply their minimal needs. Under the edict of Ye-shes-'od, a local ruler and Buddhist patron who abdicated his powers in 985 CE to join the brotherhood, farmers in the valley below set aside land and grain seed for the monks; herders presented gifts of butter for flavoring the brothers' bread and fueling their lamps.

The best of monastic viticulture came from Avignon, Rheims, and Trier. At Châteauneuf following the Babylonian captivity of the Roman Popes in France in 1309, the papal vineyard earned the highest reputation for fine wine. In the New World, Franciscan missionary brothers became California's outstanding vintners. A parallel interest in herding and cheese-making resulted in cheese known by a monastic name, in particular the *Trappiste Port-Salut,* made in Mayenne, France; the Burgundian *trappistes de Cîteaux*; *Trappiste de Bricquebec* in Normandy; *Trappiste de Mont-des-Cats* in Picardy; the Breton *Trappiste de Sainte-Anne-d'Auray*; and Savoy's *Trappiste de Tamie.*

Benedictines developed pharmacology and promoted hygiene, an outgrowth of their interest in botany and herbalism. The sect maintained healing recipes. Essential to curative decoctions, infusions, salves, and nostrums from monastery kitchens were herbal treatments. For spirit-based beverages, herb growers perfected sweetened infusions or herbal distillations and dispensed them as crèmes, elixirs, balms, tonics, digestives, and love potions. One herb, the common thistle, the brothers blessed for its effectiveness in treating pox.

Priories stocked their *officinas* (workshops) with medicinal herbs, in particular, soapwort, the common name for *saponaria officinalis*, a plant that cleansed the hands of wanderers who came for care and feeding. The tradition of monastic cures in Florence began adjacent to a church in 1221 when Dominican friars opened the *Officina Profumo-Farmaceutica di Santa Maria Novella*. Distilling nostrums from their kitchen garden, the monks established sickrooms and grew the plants needed to restore health and personal sanitation. The pharmacy, no longer operated by the church, was still in business in the early twenty-first century and displayed implements and stills that Leonardo da Vinci originated.

The Bavarian monastery of Weltenburg, which Eustasius established in the early 600s, claims to be the world's oldest monastery brewery. It contains documents attesting to a brewing operation as early as the eleventh century. A favorite of pilgrims, Weihenstephan abbey, also in Bavaria, received a brewing license in 1040 for ale production that was already several centuries old. Visitors gave cash and gifts of grain that supported the brewhouse, which bottled *celia* for the privileged, *cervisa* for ordinary arrivals, and *conventus* for the monks. Late in the feudal period, the abbey grew so wealthy that it could afford serfs to do the brewing and free the brothers for less worldly work.

Sale of ales and beer enriched some houses, where monks turned breweries into lucrative businesses founded on mass production in clean surroundings. The brewing business spread, for example to Switzerland at the Monastery of St. Gall, where, since 820 CE, the brewhouse and bakehouse functioned as one and even used the same troughs as dough trays and fermentation vats. Saint Arnold became the patron of Belgian brewers after he offered consecrated beer to Oudenburg followers as a substitute for polluted water. In 1031, near Regensburg, the St. Emmeram abbey planted hop gardens to enhance brewing. Andechs of Bavaria, founded by Duke Albrecht III in the mid-thirteenth century, encouraged the marketing of monastery beverages, which enriched Benedictine monasteries. Into the twenty-first century, Belgian Trappists operated breweries in Chimay, Orval, Rochefort, Westmalle, and Westvleteren.

Brothers bottled the first Benedictine liqueur in 1510; Carthusians at Grenoble, France, distilled the mysterious chartreuse in 1607. Three aromatic types—green, white, and yellow—were not perfected until 1757. In 1901, when persecutors drove the brothers out of France, they set up production at Tarragona, Spain, under the label *Liqueur des Pères Chartreux* (Liqueur of the Chartreux Fathers). The recipes for other liqueurs bore the flavors and bouquet of monastery herb beds—mint in *crème de menthe*, caraway and cumin in Kümmel, anise in Pernod, artemisia or wormwood in vermouth, bitters in Campari. As of 2000, Belgian Trappists and Bavarian Benedictines operated the few medieval monastic breweries that survive.

In the late medieval period, the cook at the abbey of Notre Dame de Fontevrault (or Fontevraud) in Anjou, France, designed a functional, efficient, and unusually elaborate kitchen, the only Romanesque example to survive. The hearth-centered kitchen, called Tour d'Evrault, attached to the refectory. Beginning with an eight-sided structure, the unknown builder added semi-circular bulges to the outside of the kitchen to contain five hearths and three pantries. Above each fireplace, chimneys, camouflaged with conical towers, and additional flues drew smoke from the work space, making it cleaner and protecting natural light. At the core of the cooking center, a central basket funnel ventilated the room and supplied a draft for each fire.

At the height of medieval monasticism, some abbeys held a communal family of nine hundred monks. For the feeding of so many, each setting appended outbuildings and equipment for baking, cooking, brewing, and dairying. At Glastonbury, with its eight-sided, lantern-roofed kitchen, monks are said to have created English cider as a Christian alternative to sour British wine and heady mead. Whereas, a castle required outdoor roasting of an ox, the abbey fireplace accommodated the roasting of a whole beast along with pig boiling and spit-cooking of poultry.

The productivity of monastery kitchen gardens and the quality of their cuisine made them local gathering spots. Peasants, perpetual onlookers who paid each monastic and priest a fee, resented the quality of their lives and their ample table. Yet charity was the focus of monastery labors. By the late thirteenth century, northwestern Italy was producing enough wheat, rye, and millet to launch a steady feeding ministry beyond the Alps. Most religious houses managed a balance of charity and welcome without excess. In the 1400s, the Cistercian brothers of Basingwerk, Flintshire, in Wales encouraged guests with a new guest quarter and meals served with French and Spanish wines. At Durham, the brothers, led by Prior John Wessington from 1416 to 1446, served up a healthy diet of foods from their prior's own stock. (Platt 1996, n. p.)

From the Balkan monasteries came compendia of native tradition, wisdom, lore, and such local recipes as *mamaliga*, the daily corn mush that monks at Sinaia monastery served with onions, cheese, and red wine to the poor on the abbey's saint's day. Balkan brothers mastered wine making, vegetable cookery, and elegant pastry reflecting a holiday spirit—Romanian All Saints' Day crescents, German Advent *stollen*, Polish Christmas Eve wafers, Easter *babka, mazurek* (flat cakes), monastery bread, and *faworki*, fried strips iced with sugar and nicknamed "God's mercy." (Chamberlain 1989, 419)

The donation of honey and beeswax, common offerings to churches and monasteries called wax-scots or wax-shots, symbolized the sweetness and light of Christianity. Traditionally, wax candles lighted the way for church processionals from dormitory to chapel. The brothers at St. Augustine's Abbey, Canterbury, demanded tithes of honey in 598. Similar honey offerings were welcome in Wessex, Saxony, Yorkshire, Schleswig-Holstein, and Hertfordshire. To add to the foods the brethren enjoyed, in 965, Otto I presented Magdeburg's abbey an annual allotment of honey, but more precious to religious work was the bestowal of wax for candles. Additional gifts from the bee acknowledged monastic piety. In 1551, Ivan the Terrible presented honey to Russian monastics for candymaking.

To maximize hygiene at abbeys constantly receiving the poxed and dying, medieval monastery design outperformed residential architecture by tapping running water from an upland spring or stream. Stone conduits of lead or wood channels attached to kitchen and lavatorium. Monks washed regularly at a cloister trough before sitting at communal tables in the refectory, as pictured in Giovanni Antonio Bazzi's sixteenth-century fresco *The Story of Saint Benedict* at Monteoliveto Maggiore, Italy. Kitchen waste exited by way of drains, which collected sewage from the rere-dorter or necessarium and carried it far enough away from the residence to assure good health and no residual sludge or odors.

As European tables grew more ornate after the Renaissance, monks, too, altered their outreach and attitudes. Although Christian cooks like the nuns of the Abbey of Saints Nabbore and Felice in Bologna continued turning out prized recipes such as Spanish sponge cake as fund raisers, the eighteenth-century monastery menu attested to a change in styles of piety. That the clergy had rich larders was evident by their display of wealth. On Maundy Thursday in 1731 at the banquet room of Whitehall, house staff, described by *Gentleman's Magazine*, served ninety-six poor men and women a boiled dinner and ale, followed by a distribution of cod, herring, and loaves on a platter as well as a leather bag of coins plus clothing and shoes. The nurturing ceremony ended with the Lord Archbishop of York washing the feet of guests in the Royal Chapel in the style of former kings of England. In 1796, the Convent of San Domenico in Palermo, Sicily, made known its wealth at a reception for a new provincial, for which kitchen staff cooked and served a dinner featuring eighty-eight main dishes accompanied by appetizers and desserts.

In the Victorian era, one monk applied science to improve plant food for all people. In 1865, the work of Austrian botanist Johann Gregor Mendel, the abbot at Brünn, broadened the understanding of plant genetics, a science that allowed the kitchen gardener control over numerous aspects of plant cultivation, hybridization, and performance such as resistance to wilt and production of root vegetables with a long shelf life. He published his findings the next year in *Transactions*, the journal of the Natural Sciences Society, but the research received little interest until its acceptance by European botanists Hugo De Vries, Carl Correns, and Erich Tschermak in 1900.

In 1904, Giuseppe Pitrè's reflective *La Vita in Palaermo Cento e Più Anni Fà* (Life in Palermo a Hundred or More Years Ago) saluted the Martorana, Origlione, and Stigmata, wealthy convents where nun/cooks turned produce from their own land into pastries and candies. With the help of special collections to underwrite such costly goods as marzipan and babas, they outperformed lesser monasteries, which cooked up such pedestrian fare as roast chickpeas, pumpkin seeds, and stuffed olives.

In the 1970s, anthropologist Sulamith Heins Potter gathered data for *Family Life in a Northern Thai Village* (1977). She visited Chiangmai Village Temple, the community's social center. In the courtyard, monks, novices, children, and local people gathered for communal meals. Potter explained that the temple congregation ended the usual practice of begging when it began to cook and serve food to the residents each morning by depositing it directly into temple bowls. Special treats included flavored and sugared rice rolled into banana leaf packages cut into intricate shapes before they were cooked. The communal kitchen provided generous space for cooking on a grand scale for residents and guests. Women squatted on the floor around large bowls of ingredients and heated great woks three feet in diameter as they shared the work involved in a menu of curried water buffalo and coleslaw with ground peanuts. For steaming rice, they boiled water below hollowed tree trunk vessels. At fairs, villagers set up stalls at the temple to sell sweets and dried cuttlefish. During pilgrimages, they milled rice in sufficient quantity to feed participants proceeding to the nearby mountains.

In the United States, cooking turned into kitchen business for various monasteries. Kentucky's Abbey of Gethsemani is the nation's oldest Trappist monastery. It evolved from agrarian beginnings to a producer of breads, Port du Salut cheese, sausage, country ham, Canadian bacon, cheese, bourbon-soaked fruitcake, and chocolate bourbon and butter walnut fudge. Their carpenter encased their cheeses in hand-crafted poplar boxes. In 2004, sixty-five monks survived on profits from a barn, bakery, and confectionery.

The Trappist Abbey formally known as Our Lady of Guadalupe, in Lafayette, southwest of Portland, Oregon, had moved to the Pacific Northwest in 1955. In 2004, the elderly monks meditated, worshiped, and worked for profit to earn their way by harvesting hardwood, binding and repairing books, labeling bottles of riesling and pinot noir for vintners in Willamette Valley, keeping a garden and apiary, and baking ginger date-nut cake, honey-almond biscotti, and fruitcake. The monastery's distinctive fruitcake is enriched with brandy, glacéed pineapple and cherries, boiled raisins, honey, cinnamon, mace, pecans, and walnuts. The modern bakery produced twenty thousand cakes a year in one-, two-, and three-pound sizes. The kitchen staff shelved them for three months, then sold them for holiday gift-giving. Annual sales reached $100,000.

Other monastery kitchen businesses prepared delicacies for the table including Monk's bread, butterscotch, creamy caramels, fruitcake, cookies, vinegar, wine vinegar, jam, jelly, marmalade, conserves, preserves, cheese, culinary herbs, dips, sauces, salsa, cookbooks, table wine, and dessert wine.

Since late in the twentieth century, Brother Victor-Antoine d'Avila-Latourrette, a Benedictine monk and author of *From a Monastery Kitchen* (1997) and *Simplicity from a Monastery Kitchen: A Complete Menu Cookbook for All Occasions* (2001), cooked for the assembled brothers and their guests at the Our Lady of the Resurrection Priory in Cold Spring, New York. For the homemaker, his compendium sets up a list of advisories to substitute herbs and spices for salt, reduce the fat content of dairy foods, dress with light sauces, sauté in olive or canola oil, cook with whole grains and fresh vegetables, substitute fruit for pastry, and control portion sizes. His skill at turning discarded food from groceries into tasty meals was a tribute to his thrift and knowledge of food. On feast days, he created festival menus as a release for men devoted to self-restraint, silence, and sobriety. In addition to residential cooking, he grew food for a farmers' market to assure the monastery's fiscal self-sufficiency. As an introduction to his book's second edition, Brother Victor-Antoine wrote, "Monastic cookery, as it has been practiced through the centuries, is cherished for its emphasis on simplicity, wholesome frugality, basic good taste, and the seasonal rhythms of the ingredients used." (d'Avila-Latourrette 1997, 3)

See also **Wine**

Further Reading

Aldenderfer, Mark, "Roots of Tibetan Buddhism," *Archaeology*, May/June 2001, 64–66.
Aprile, Dianne. *The Abbey of Gethsemani: Place of Peace and Paradox*. Louisville, Ky.: Trout Lily Press, 1998.
Downey, Michael. *Trappist: Living in the Land of Desire*. New York: Paulist Press, 1997.
Johnston, William M., ed. *Encyclopedia of Monasticism*. Chicago: Fitzroy Dearborn, 2000.
Moses, Mohandas, "The Old Monastery Kitchen of Hemis," *Asian Age*, July 17, 1999.
Platt, Colin. *The Abbeys and Priories of Medieval England*. New York: Barnes & Noble, 1996.

MONEL

Monel metal got its start from the work of two metallurgists. Ambrose Monell, a member of the Inventor's Guild, created an alloy of copper and nickel named for an adaptation of his own name. Much of the credit for the substance belongs to New Jersey-born metallurgist Robert Crooks Stanley, author of *Nickel . . . Past and Present* (1927), who joined the International Nickel Company in 1901. In 1905, in conjunction with Ambrose Monell, he patented monel, an alloy offering a shiny patina, tensile strength, and resistance to corrosion.

In the 1930s, whole-page ads in *Good Housekeeping* exalted monel, made in ten sites in the United States and four in Canada, as the metal of the future. Color pictures featured the Voss Monel Metal Washer as rust-free, impervious to washing compounds, and durable for a lifetime of heavy use. Text described the shiny uncoated tank as solid, glass-smooth, and gleaming like fine sterling silver. Free booklets offered more information about monel sinks, table tops, and household equipment. In the twenty-first century, monel maintained a niche in the world's metals market for domestic goods, including valves, gauges, pumps, hoses, and ball bearings, especially those surfaces regularly bathed in seawater.

MONGOLIAN HOT POT

A thrifty method of heating the home while cooking derives from the Mongolian *huokuo* (hot pot) or Chinese *ta pin lo* (fire pot), a ring-shaped trough that early northern Chinese cooks fitted around a kitchen chimney to heat water and broth for cooking individual servings of meat and vegetables. This one-dish style of cookery originated in the Asian steppes to the north in the early Middle Ages, where keeping warm at a communal fire was a major concern among Mongolian nomads, who lived in tents. The favored implement was a pair of bamboo chopsticks for dipping foods into boiling water for fast cooking of thinly sliced meat.

The communal cookpot reached southern Chinese kitchens early in the seventh century CE during the Tang dynasty, when foursomes sat at *shuan yang rou* (goat, kid, or mutton) dinners cut into bites and cooked on individual skewers. Coastal families applied the hot pot to seafood. After the rise of the Manchu during the Ch'ing dynasty, the hot pot became a national standard for family dining, a time when people enjoyed face-to-face communication during a relaxed meal.

In 1211, when Genghis Khan and his Mongolian invaders overran China, they suppressed the national rice-based diet by introducing their staple, mare's milk. Under the Yuan (Mongolian) dynasty, which ruled China from 1271 to 1387, at great feasts, their cooks centered dining on coarse, bland dairy foods and whole mutton boiled in cauldrons. These mass cookouts, which the Chinese despised for their insensitivity to the palate, were the forerunners of hot pot cookery, which spread south to Guangzhou Canton. The traditional Mongolian pot was a copper kettle with a hollow center to hold charcoal to warm broth in the surrounding moat. A small chimney vented smoke. Unlike the

Mongols, Chinese cooks used the red hot pot as a place to grill sliced lamb.

A communal at-table cooking device similar to a Swiss fondue set, the Cantonese *shacha* or Szechuan *maotu* hot pot, Peking chrysanthemum hot pot, the stocky Korean stone hot pot, Japanese "Genghis Khan cuisine," and the modern electric stainless steel table model mimicked the chimney-and-pot shape with a gas, charcoal, butane, or ethyl alcohol fuel source in a cylinder at center of a circular pot on a pedestal. The meal began with trays or bowls of diced or thinly sliced pieces of beef, shrimp, snow peas, cabbage, or mushrooms arranged around the pot. Accompaniments were usually soy or chile sauce for flavor. Presentation favored the Chinese emphasis on beauty, color, and precise cutting as well as texture, aroma, and flavor.

The Vietnamese version stressed the fragrance of chrysanthemum greens, mint, or cilantro along with lettuce, tomatoes, okra, and bean sprouts. Alternate recipes stressed saffron with seafood stock, thin rice noodles, fennel, basil, turmeric, cream, and coconut milk. In Laos and northeastern Thailand, for *tom saep* (boiled delicious), cooks presented ceramic pots over coals and flavored cooked bites with kaffir lime leaf, lemon grass, young galangal, and shallots.

To cook meat and vegetables, diners skewer pieces on chopsticks or fondue forks or dip them in bamboo tongs or wire ladles into the boiling broth or stock for quick, low-fat poaching. A choice of dips, soy or curry sauce, and condiments, including garlic, green onions, and chili, allows the individual to flavor according to taste. The hot pot creates an informality that encourages conversation, good manners, and involvement in food selection and cooking.

The style of hot pot cookery influenced the *nabemono* (table cookery) of Japan. As summarized in *Japanese Cooking: A Simple Art* (1980), by Shizuo Tsuji, the owner of Ecole Technique Hoteliere Tsuji in Osaka, Japan's largest school training professional chefs in Japan, and the author of twenty-nine books, the cook placed vegetables on a platter alongside fish, meat, and poultry. Guests used chopsticks to lower tidbits into a centralized cast-iron or clay pot filled with seething broth and either chicken or *kombu* (seaweed) heated over a gas or electric heating ring. After removing the cooked portions, diners dipped them into condiments served in individual bowls.

A late twentieth-century tabletop cooking style, *shabu-shabu*, which takes its name from the sound of food swished in hot fat, consists of a large brass urn filled at center with a funnel of charcoal embers. In New York City's Inagiku, a Japanese restaurant at the Waldorf-Astoria hotel, staff served thinly sliced beef, napa cabbage, onions and scallions, shiitake mushrooms, and carrots for immersing in fish broth. The

diner's taste experience concluded with dipping bites into creamy sesame sauce or ponzu sauce flavored with dai dai (citrus fruit) and a side dish of udon noodles.

Mongolion hot pot cookery suits winter appetites for comfort food. Dietitians recommend such quick, light hot pot cuisine because the diner can control cholesterol, fat, and sodium and can retain nutrients by not overcooking morsels. To stimulate appetite, hot pot cooking adds flavor and variety through fresh ingredients and saucing. The slow pace of cooking and eating steadies the intake of food and produces relaxation conducive to digestion.

Further Reading

Lau, Grace, "Mongolian Hot Pot: Where Guests Cook Their Own Meals," *Diabetes Forecast*, January 1998, 32–38.
Perkins, Dorothy. *Encyclopedia of China.* New York: Facts on File, 1999.

MORTAR AND PESTLE

The forerunners of blenders and electric food processors, the mortar and pestle were vital pieces of equipment dating to prehistory. Found worldwide, they served a long list of needs, as depicted in Japanese prints picturing Ainu women in native dress wielding double-ended pestles as they pulverize rice to shape into cakes. Working in tandem, the pair wield the essential

Assorted dry spices in a mortar with pestle.
[© *Foodcollection.com / Alamy.*]

two-part device for pounding or pulverizing hard substances into paste or powder. The book of Proverbs mentions the metaphoric use of the mortar as a refinement for character: "Though thou shouldest bray [pulverize] a fool in a mortar among wheat with a pestle, yet will not his foolishness depart from him." (27:22)

People worldwide applied the hand-powdered pair for crushing rock salt, maple sugar, spices, grain, nut meats, and tobacco for snuff. In southern India, the black trap mortar provided a harder, more durable surface than earlier quartzite vessels. A variant, the foot-powdered drop-hammer crusher found in China and Japan after 900 CE, suggests a ritual demand for hulled rice for temple use rather than the simpler technology of the home mortar and pestle.

Native Americans used a variety of stone on stone and stone pestles on wood mortars. The Chinchorro of the Chile-Peru coast of South America employed mortars, knives, and *chopes* (sharpened rib bones) from as early as 9000 BCE to prepare meals of shellfish, sea mammals, and seaweed. The standard pair of mortar and pestle ranged in size from a small bowl or prehistoric bedrock mortar and palm-size grinding stone to the Caddo version, a hollowed tree trunk fitted with a paddle as tall as the user. When the French *coureurs de bois* (woodsmen) observed Ojibwa food preparation, they found women digging a hole, lining it with skins, and using it as a mortar bowl for the pounding of dried meat with a stone pestle to make pemmican for trail food.

From 2500 BCE, when the diet shifted from venison to salmon and acorns, the unremitting labor of detoxifying acorns and pounding them into pulp may have shortened the lives of women, who appear to have born the brunt of acorn processing and the feeding of weaned toddlers on acorn gruel. The demands of the acorn-based diet appear to have defined the social organization and settlement system of late prehistoric times. The Mono of the California Sierras settled near oak groves, where women could gather, process, and store whole nuts and acorn flour, for which they designed a mortar and pestle in bedrock and nearby storage silos.

Other diets required the culinary use of the mortar and pestle. Southwestern desert Indians used the mortar for pulverizing agave heart to ferment into beer; for nut butter, they mixed the resulting pulp with piñon nuts, walnuts, or sunflower seeds. The juice they saved went into homemade healing salves, shampoo, and soap. Similarly, the early Inuit pounded caribou fat, fish liver, and fish oil and blended the mass with snow and sugar for a cold dessert called a-gu-tuk. For preparation, they whipped the batter, sprinkled it with bilberries gathered from the northern tundra, and served it like ice cream. The Seminole applied pestle to mortar to pound coontie (or *kuntíi*), product of a common palm plant, into arrowroot flour, a staple in the diet of infants, the elderly, and invalids. In Central and South America, the North American southwest, and Hawaii, creaming of the *ahuacatl*, the Nahuatl name for the avocado or alligator pear, survives with modern electric tools in the making of guacamolé, a dip served with tortilla chips and vegetable crudités.

The Pee-Posh of the Colorado River preferred a hollow cottonwood or mesquite trunk for pulvering mesquite beans, their dietary staple; similarly, the Pima of Arizona and Mexico used cottonwood mortars for crushing corn into meal for daily preparation of cakes and porridge. Forest Indians ground corn with wood-on-wood grinding tools and also pulverized dried fish to enhance blending with other foods. The typical shape of their kitchen vessels paired the dumbbell pestle with a two-handled mortar charred or scraped from a log hollowed by fire and refined with a stone or bone adze. Whole log mortars set on end elevated the work waist-high for ease of filling and emptying without stooping. In New York Bay, the natives of Governor's Island puréed whole hickory nuts in a pulverizing bowl to produce a milky drink; other tribes used the implements to pound popcorn into portable meal for travel.

One labor-saving version preferred by forest Indians involved lashing the pestle to a sapling, a system called a sweep and mortar mill. By crushing downward onto food, then releasing the pestle, the user allowed the spring in the sapling to lift the heavy plunger. The system, as described in colonial American records, evolved into a communication system, by which signalers tapped out messages in code. The replication of mortar use in colonial communities allowed isolated parturient women to tap out an SOS to neighboring midwives.

Another version of the pestle, the beetle was a heavy wooden mallet with a flattened end. Because of its value to cooks preparing chewy cuts of meat for the table, it also went by meat-centered names—meat maul, steak maul, meat fret, steak pounder, meat tenderer, or meat tenderizer. The lathe-turned handle supported a firm grasp for crushing potatoes and vegetables for fritters, pounding veal for *wiener schnitzel*, or tenderizing venison or meat for country-style steak, a Southern specialty simmered to fork tenderness in thick brown gravy.

In England during the Middle Ages, the mortar and pestle were essentials of the clever cook, a claim made by *The Forme of Cury* (1390), an anonymous royal recipe book from the court of Richard II. Because of the need to disguise and otherwise reshape foods, preparation required mincing and pounding of spices into meats and fish, which cooks served on different days—fish on holy days and meat at non-festal or ordinary meals. Dairy workers used finely powdered salt blended with sugar and saltpeter (potassium nitrate) to cure and preserve butter, which they proportioned at one ounce of curing powder to a pound of butter. The *Noble Boke of Cookry for a Prynce Houssolde or eny other Estately Houssolde* (ca. 1470), another anonymous compendium, centers the making of wheat starch on careful beating of the grain in a mortar before the boiling, straining, and drying of the mass on a cloth. Essential to the blending of almond paste and milk, the mortar reduced the nuts to a near liquid for separating whey from solids. The resulting almond paste was the basis for much of medieval cookery, especially marzipan confections, cakes, and icing.

In 1651, master chef Pierre François de La Varenne, author of *Le Cuisinier Français* (1651), devised a sauce that presaged the French culinary masterworks of the seventeenth and eighteenth centuries. He explained that *poivrade* (pepper sauce) required a base of vinegar, onion, citrus peel, and salt in addition to pepper. For green sauce, he described a lengthy process of pounding in a mortar green wheat, toast, vinegar, salt, and pepper, then straining the mass through cloth to produce a hearty meat dressing.

European settlers emulated the kitchen tools of forest Indians. To produce samp or nawsamp, they hollowed logs and shaved limbs into pestles. David Lion Gardiner's *Chronicles of East Hampton* (1940) explains how users anchored the mortar into a tree crotch for support. The pestle acquired a natural springiness by attachment to a long, flexible pole planted in the ground. He expanded, "This instrument might be heard in operation every Saturday afternoon, preparing the samp and hominy for the coming week." (Beard 1975, 121)

In the colonial Pennsylvania, the manufacturer Ann Page produced cylindrical mortars and pestles as well as spindles, spinning wheels, and bench screws. A variant of the upright mortar and pestle was a circular rolling grinding wheel with handles at right angles. The cast iron device fit the slot of a footed herb or tray that held herbs and medicial roots for kitchen preparation. Another style of mortar and pestle was the pasteboard-decked *lignum vitae* mortar on which basket makers rounded woven straw and bonnet makers pressed crowns into shape.

When New World foods entered Mediterranean markets, they introduced a variant to traditional pesto. One Americanized recipe from Lipari, an island off the Sicilian coast, derived from the work of mid-sixteenth century cooks. With mortar and pestle, they pounded tomatoes with blanched almonds to create *salmoriglio rosso*, a vinegary sauce served with wide pasta noodles. Still produced in home kitchens, the favorite red sauce is currently made in seconds in food processors.

In Rurutu in the Society Islands, the preparation of taro root perpetuates a technique that dates into Polynesia's past. After the farmer yanks a dozen starchy tubers from the muck, he carefully replants part of the stalks before moving to the kitchen. For a family, the cook boils the root as an accompaniment to fish, or pounds it in the mortar into a viscous native dish called poi, which the eighteenth-century British sea captain and explorer James Cook once proclaimed a wholesome vegetable.

Today, the mortar and pestle survives in laboratory, pharmacy, herbalism, and kitchen ritual. Materials for making mortars and pestles include brass, ironstone, marble, lignum vitae, burl from hardwoods, bronze, bell metal, glass, pottery, and a fine Wedgwood pair featuring a turned walnut handle. The pestle may be the same material as the mortar, as with the wood spice grinder or glass apothecary's mortar and pestle, or may employ paired materials, as with the stoneware kitchen mortar with wooden pestle. The mortar is usually a deep-sided bowl with rounded lip and pouring spout at the top of the mantle or may resemble a tall urn. The pestle varies from an oblong stone or straight tree limb shaped like a club to an L-shaped wooden pulverizer.

The sausage makers of the Dominican Republic maintain a *pilón* and *mazo* (mortar and pestle) for crushing the garlic and herbs that flavor meat for longaniza sausage, a favorite breakfast food. Similarly, Puerto Ricans pound garlic, onion, sweet and hot peppers, cilantro, and annatto into *sofrito*, an oil they strain and reserve for cooking; the *campesinos* of Margarita off the coast of Venezuela often pair two children at the heavy *mazo* and *pace*. They pound to the rhythm of a shared folk song such as "Arroz con Pollo, Me Quiero Cazar" (Rice with Chicken, I Want to Get Married). In Nigeria, the base or mother stone of the home grinding equipment lies embedded in the earthen floor for daily pulverizing of *wake* (black-eyed peas) with the daughter stone. Kurdish cooks manage a wood mallet and stone bowl to reduce parboiled *bulgur* wheat for bread. In southern Sudan, the Nuer create a hole-in-the-ground vessel in which to place sorghum for tamping with a stout log.

Among the Senufo of Burkina Faso, use of mortar and pestle is gender and age specific. On planting day, women take turns pounding bran from corn kernels by working the pestle, beginning with the oldest down to the youngest cook. They follow with a sharing of the winnowing basket and grinding stones. In token of unity, at dinner, they sit down to a communal bowl to dip hand-rolled balls of mush into sauce.

419

In Kashmir, the traditional preparation of *gustava* (meat balls) dates to prehistory. Cooks use a *mundhi*, a rectangular stone grinding bowl, in which they pound goat meat with a wood mallet for two hours. The process crushes sinew and meat fiber, which cooks periodically moisten with water. The silky meat pulp they produce is the soul of the tender meat ball, which diners eat at low tables as finger food with rice and bread.

See also **Colonial Kitchens, American; Dyes and Colorants; Kitchen Cures; Masters, Sybilla Righton; Nuts and Seeds; Taro**

MUSHROOMS

In the quest for berries, fruit, and tubers, prehistoric hunter-gatherers added to their dietary list the world's forty thousand varieties of fungi, a plant wreathed in mystery from the time of stories of elves and fairies in Celtic Britain into the era of Louis XIV, who had his own farm beds in caves. Because mushrooms grow in varied types of humus, they are ubiquitous and fall into classifications of *Agaricus, Amanita, Auricularia, Boletus, Cantharellus, Cortinarius, Lactarius, Marasmius, Psalliota,* and *Russula.* Trial and error sampling allowed cooks to separate good-tasting and fragrant varieties from those that burned the mouth or caused illness and death, especially when eaten raw. The early Mesopotamians were eating mushrooms and truffles by 1800 BCE.

Mushrooms appeared in classic literature, including the Perseus mythos from Mycenae, which connects the hero's name to the Greek for mushroom. Although the Greek acquired from the Egyptians a belief that mushrooms conferred immortality and were therefore a dish for royalty, both Euripides and Hippocrates warned of fungal poisoning. Among Roman authors, Ovid, Horace, Juvenal, and Martial described mushrooms as table fare and Apicius offered recipes for them, but an historical footnote added that Livia, wife of Rome's first emperor Augustus, used poison mushrooms to murder him. So too did Agrippina, who dispatched her husband, the Emperor Claudius, with a dish of braised mushrooms.

The Aztec, Olmec, Mixtec, Mazotec, Zapotec, Maya, and Mexica valued *teonanácatl,* the nahuatl word for "divine food," a beneficial hallucinogen that Mesoamericans treasured as a godly gift from about 2000 BCE. In Guatemala, artisans began carving holy icons of the mushroom as early as 1000 BCE. In 1953, the amateur mycologist Robert Gordon Wasson, author of *Mushroom Ceremony of the Mazatec Indians of Mexico* (1959), deduced the centrality of the mushroom to Central American culture, where believers venerated it as a tonic, aphrodisiac, and panacea. Similarly, the natives of Borneo, New Guinea, and Kamchatka on the Bering Sea reserve one variety for its healing properties.

In the Pacific, the mushroom acquired similar value. Although Japanese cooks regularly gathered shiitake mushrooms from glades, around 1368, the beginning of the Ming dynasty (1368–1644), kitchen gardeners began cultivating the shiitake as a restorative and health food reserved for the emperor and renamed the "emperor's food." In contrast, the Maori had access to local mushrooms, but they cooked them only during famine. On his voyage to Tierra del Fuego aboard the *Beagle,* naturalist Charles Darwin remarked on local dependence on raw mushrooms as the only vegetable in the diet. In the Americas, cooks rested unpeeled mushrooms at the edge of an open-hearth and added them to plates as side dishes.

Mushrooms continue to appear in culinary history of Africa, India, the Pacific isles, and North America, especially among the Yosemite, who relish a salty mushroom soup. The popularity of amateur mycology in western Europe, particularly among Swiss gourmets, the use of recreational hallucinogens, and the natural food craze in the United States since the 1970s boosted the number of accidental poisonings, 90 percent of which resulted from the ingestion of one variety, the *Amanita phalloides.* In Europe and the Americas, gourmet shops exploited the late twentieth-century gourmet cooking and rise in vegetarianism with powdered morels, shiitake, chanterelles, porcini, cepes, oyster mushrooms, reishi (also called ganoderma or *ling zhi*), portabellas, matsutake, and black trumpets as well as mushroom sauces and pâtés. Drawing on traditional Chinese pharmacopoeia, dietitians prescribed mushrooms for their proteins, iron, zinc, chitin, chiton, fibers, vitamins, and low calories.

Further Reading

Haspel, Barbara, "Mushrooms: From Mystery to Mastery," *Vegetarian Times,* September 1996, 48–56.

N

NEEDLES, KITCHEN

Oversized kitchen needles called *aiguilles à piquer* (picks) or *lardoires* (larding needles) assist the cook in such meticulous chores as adding fat to rump cuts for veal fricandeau, flavoring venison and game birds, adding slivers of olive or capers to roasts, and trussing stuffed geese and turkeys before roasting. An essential for the expert veal and venison roaster, the larding needle is a six- to nine-inch steel shaft open at one end to hold strips of plain, spiced, or marinated bacon or ham. The point at the other end penetrates the meat parallel to the grain. Either by forcing the lardoon out with a plunger, by pushing it with a knife point, or by trailing it behind the needle, the cook artificially marbles the meat.

For French cooks intent on larding, traditionally, the choice fat was the *lard gras* (pork fat), the hard fat layer lying closest to the skin, which was firmer and less easily rendered than the fat closer to the flesh. As described by a wealthy French merchant to his young wife in the anonymous *Ménagier de Paris* (The Goodman of Paris, ca. 1394), the larding process allowed the cook to trim all surface fat from a haunch for an attractive surface while studding substitute fat into the muscle for flavor and moisture. One expert, Louis XIII, who came on the French throne in 1611, used a vermeil needle to force lardoons into beef loin, which his staff served with panache. Austrian cooks pierced game birds, rabbits and hares, and saddles of venison with fat as a method of internal basting to enhance flavor and tenderize succulent meat. To educate the ordinary cook, Urbain-Dubois's *L'Ecole des Cuisinières* (The School for Cooks, 1898) pictured poultry and hares marked anatomically to demonstrate how and where to insert skewers and larding needles.

In the early 1800s, a manufacturer in Birmingham, England, made brass and steel larding pins. A sharp-pointed cube from six to ten inches long, the needle held bacon or suet for threading juice and flavor into meat. In Chapter 12 of Fannie Farmer's classic, *The Boston Cooking School Cookbook* (1896), she particularized the use of such needles for daubing, the forcing of large lardoons through meat from surface to surface. She added that draping meat in fat was an easier method of moistening dry meat, but it lacked the full flavor of fat forced into flesh with a larding needle.

Unlike barding, a method of overlaying dry roasts with bacon strips, the French method of larding held *lard à piquer* (lardoons) on ice before piercing the entire body of meat to assure essential oils for baking. Another method of adding fat involved dicing and frying lardoons to garnish beans and season hare and *boeuf à la bourguignonne*. Larding needles from the late nineteenth century came in a tin or japanned case, which contained a small emery bag for sharpening needle tips. Other varieties of culinary needles included the stuffing needle, for stuffing olives and forcing garlic slivers into roasts, and the *aiguille à brider* (trussing needle), a steel sewing punch for cording butcher string through the openings of poultry to hold in stuffing or to make a compact shape for roasting.

In the 1900s, the chef's *batterie de cuisine* required a number of types of skewers and needles. The tinned or stainless steel turkey lacer held stuffing in the bird. Graduated sets of skewers both round and flat offered varied lengths for making shashlik, grilling lamb kidneys, or trussing poultry varying in size from Cornish hens and capons to geese. A German larding needle from Gerhard Recknagel applied a tiny hinge to the hollow end of a steel shaft and narrow teeth on the sides to simplify the job of pushing chilled fat into tough layers of muscle.

An early twenty-first-century version, the hand-pumped plastic baster, consisted of a plunger, tank for sauces and condiments, and pointed tube for injecting flavorings under the skin of fowl or into fish, hams, and roasts. A chrome-plated version, the pressure seasoner, was a two-stage implement suited to grilling or oven roasting. The barrel at the top contained herbs and spices, which fed into the insertion tube for infusing roasts and poultry as heat drew the liquid downward.

Further Reading

The Goodman of Paris. London: Routledge, 1928.

NUTS AND SEEDS

Nuts and seeds are flavorful, nutritious, and, in comparison with meat and fish, more easily collected, processed, and stored. The Cantonese song "Bright, Bright the Moon" speaks of the chopped betel nut, a fragrant treat served on the year's last day. Still the focus of kitchen activity for ceremonial and holiday meals, such as the Serbo-Croatian *sirnica* (cheese strudel) filled with walnuts for a yuletide treat, nuts represent nature's goodness locked away in its own self-preserving casings.

Rich in protein, nuts and seeds have bolstered human diet from the advent of hunter-gatherers. Peanuts or groundnuts, which originated in Brazil, appeared in burial offerings of early Peruvians. Asian hunter-gatherers relied on acorns before they adapted cereal grains to cultivation. Iraqi cave dwellers could diversify their foodstuffs with acorns, chestnuts, pine nuts, and walnuts.

Twice a year, the Greeks boiled seeds for *panspermia,* a ritual porridge that honored Apollo, the healer and bringer of light. Prehistoric nut collectors in the forests of the British Isles garnered acorns as well as hazelnuts. During famine, the Romans baked acorn bread. The Narragansett of eastern North America valued the butternut for its kernels and oil. Aborigines to the west of the continent elevated acorns to the core of life, even though processing the bitter nut meats required repeated soaks and rinses. The Luiseño and other Mission Indians of California were still garnering, soaking, and grinding acorns into meal in the early 1900s for use in traditional hot cereals and breads.

Peanut harvesting in Alabama. Peanuts on vines ready for combing.
[© *Courtesy of Agricultural Research Service, USDA. Photo by Don Schuhart.*]

The early Swiss and Scandinavians preferred beechnuts as a source of food and cooking oil. Germanic tribes roasted acorns, as did peoples farther south and in North Africa. Less ubiquitous were almond trees, which grew on Crete and in Greece. After 618 CE, Chinese pharmacologist Weng Shen began a health-conscious trend toward fruits and nuts for the royal diet and promoted the establishment of an imperial orchard and the growing of hothouse varieties. In Zambia as early as 900 CE, food preservers stored the Bambara groundnut in pits.

The New World produced a variety of native nuts, including the common *Pinus edulis* (also piñon, Indian nut, or pine nut), pecan, beechnut, buckeye, brazil nut, cashew, and acorn, all of which could be pounded into porridge, added to pemmican, shaped into cakes, or carried in pouches and parfleches (storage envelopes) as trail food. Traditionally, the Catawba, a tribe native to the Carolinas, kept pecans in baskets and used flat stones for cracking them at hearthside. Pacific Coast nations, which based their subsistence on acorns, evolved a regimen of cracking, hulling, pulverizing with rocks, and rinsing and sieving the pulp to wash away bitterness before boiling it into a hot cereal.

Near the Grand Canyon, the Havasupai gathered piñon cones, heated them over a fire, and removed nut meats to store as a major food crop. Parching was a tricky business of lining shallow basket trays with a protective gel of peach purée or piñon pulp. The cook dropped hot coals and nut meats onto the tray and swung it about in a circular pattern to heat the food without igniting the basket. Before the nuts were ready to eat or grind into meal, they required further winnowing to remove charcoal from the grains.

The Algonquian *pawcohiccora*, a delicacy made from pulverized nuts, evolved into a designation for the hickory tree. In addition to sweet meats, pressed nuts produced milk and oil for cooking. Of the pulverizing and cooking of nut meats among forest natives, Irish trader and chronicler James Adair wrote in *The History of the American Indian* (1775) about a recipe combining boiled and sliced chestnuts with cut corn, which women pounded in mortars before kneading them into dough. The corn-chestnut dumplings went into corn shucks for stone-boiling into a favorite bread.

Just as the Indian cook labored over nuts with pounding staff and sieve, the medieval cook had to approach nuts with energy. A recipe for crayfish from the anonymous *Le Ménagier de Paris* (The Goodman of Paris, ca. 1394), an unsigned text that may have been written by Guy de Montigny, servant of the Duc de Berry, offered a lengthy series of preparations beginning with shelling the tails and pounding the carcasses. That done, the cook had to do the same with unpeeled almonds before blending the pulp with grilled bread crumbs. Numerous other recipes began with an almond paste, especially marzipan, a confection that spawned an entire cooking industry.

Drawings from the Middle Ages depict the fall collection of nuts after a member of the gathering party struck the branches with a long stick. At Irish hearths, cooks placed chestnuts in a pierced metal holder and suspended it on a chain from the trammel bar for gentle roasting in the warm updraft. In France, pre-revolution peasants complaining of their miserable lot declared that they lived on water and chestnuts.

In upland Italy, where mountain folk had little land to devote to wheat, the chestnut offered a suitable substitute for grain flour. Before sugar was available, cooks relied on the natural sweetness in ground and milled nut meats for bread, cake, fritters, pudding and fillings, soup, stew, and pasta or for dropping hot from the griddle into red wine. In addition to perfecting iron pans to suspend over open flame for browning nuts, they preserved the aromatic chestnut leaves for enfolding flatbread to bake on stone hotplates and for nestling delicate patties on ceramic tile. Farm families of the Po River plains made double use of chestnuts by fattening pigs for *prosciutto*, the region's salty, air-cured ham. Vendors turned hot nuts into street food and doubled their profits by selling fruit juice and wine to wash them down.

In the American colonies, children awaited the shaking of the tree over a ground cloth for easy retrieval. Gleaners returned to the site with baskets to hold the leftovers. By the hearth, they often shelled the nuts immediately with stones or boiled them briefly to soften the shells. Woodwrights and metalworkers created a variety of nutcrackers—a wood vise shaped like a wrench, the typical spring-loaded hinged-tong variety, which tended to crush meats; the screw type, a cast-iron hemisphere with a screw that forced the whole nut against the opposite side of the casing; and the lever style, a creative method of applying pressure.

The coquilla nut *(Atalea funifera)*, also called the tagua nut, from the piassaba (or piassava) palm of Ecuador and Brazil was a favorite of sailors, who enjoyed hobbies that took up little bunk space and required a minimum of materials and equipment. A form of treen, nut carving, like scrimshaw, produced pleasant "pretties" and love tokens, such as salt and pepper shakers, to carry home from a voyage. The hard coquilla shell, which is a beautifully streaked brown color, produced snuff boxes, jewelry, netsukes (toggles), dice, dominoes, chess pieces, cane and umbrella handles, pipes, mah-jongg tiles, buttons, needle cases, thimbles, and nutmeg graters. The piassaba nut was also a source of oil and stiff, wiry, chocolate-hued leaf fiber, material for making brooms, brushes, and rope.

The peanut arrived in North America with African slaves, who had long valued them for snacks and as thickeners for creamed soup. Southern colonial planters of North America coordinated livestock and produce by fattening quality hogs on peanuts. The Tidewater area south of the James River rivaled Westphalia ham production with their own Virginia hams. By 1639, home pork producers began shipping nut-fattened, hickory-smoked bacon and ham to England. Hams carried the Smithfield label, named for Arthur Smith, an owner of hog-raising land since 1752.

During the food daydreams of the Civil War, Confederate soldiers, who often had only peanuts to eat during long marches, boasted of the best pan-fried fish and the best home-cured ham in their memory. One Southerner could not escape reveries of mast-fed hogs, home-fattened on "hickory nuts and big white- and bur-oak acorns." (Mitchell 2000, 7) The quality meat, smoked over hickory wood, produced a sweet, nutty flavor that cooks paired with sweet potatoes, biscuits, and homemade butter.

Roasting nuts brought out the flavor, but placed demands on the cook to stand near the fire and stir and turn to keep delicate meats from scorching. Around 1860, inventor Thomas Burkhard marketed a patented hand-revolving nut roaster. The cumbrous device consisted of a rotating drum attached to gears and a hand crank. Perched on a stand, it fit neatly against a fire box for roasting almonds in confectionery kitchens. In this same period, Elena Molokhovets, author of *A Gift to Young Housewives* (1861), championed the addition of raw poppy seeds to wafers and other baked goods. To boost texture, nutrition, and color, she used blue, brown, gray, and white varieties, which grew in Saratov, Ukraine, and Voronezh.

The 1900s saw the patenting of numerous nutcrackers, including variations on the pliers type and the knee-warmer, a simple arced thigh shield with raised platform on which the seated user placed a nut for pounding with a mallet. Cast-iron and nickel-plated as well as enameled varieties took such zoomorphic shapes as dogs, squirrels, monkeys, and dragons, usually with the animal's mouth opening to receive the whole nut and the tail serving as the lever that crushed it. Nutcrackers were popular gift items for holidays and weddings. More practical for baking and snack making was the bladed Memco nut chopper from Moore Enameling and Manufacturing Company in West Lafayette, Ohio.

In Hawaii, sauce makers initiated an island business selling *see mui* (cracked seeds). The Yee family, who immigrated from Canton, China, in 1898, set up shop dispensing salty dehydrated *li hing mui*, a favorite snack food for soldiers on the move. The seed company began stocking cherry stones and mango pits. Two Yee brothers spread the business with a neighborhood branch and carriage vending. The Yees extended their stock to ginger, apricot, cranberry, olive, plum, kumquat, prune, and lemon seeds plus peels and slices of fruit offered in three flavors—sweet, sour, or salty. The popular snack food, eaten as a confection, accounted for most of the sales. Other Pacific Asian customers bought seeds to make into holiday wine, as the base for a sugary beverage, in homemade cough syrup, and to fill *musubi* (rice balls).

Nut and seed lore describes the choice of foods eaten out of hand for sporting events and parties. In Edward R. Emerson's *Beverages, Past and Present: An Historical Sketch of Their Production, Together with a Study of the Customs Connected with Their Use* (1908), an anecdotal history of nut-eating in Siberia characterizes the separation of the sexes at social gatherings. Men were the active participants, while women sat along the walls as ornaments. To keep young females occupied, their hosts offered kedrouvie nuts, a flavorful treat so filled with small seeds that the women had to work at separating them from the nut meats, leaving little time to flirt or converse.

In the 1920s, women's magazines, which began introducing readers to brand-name foodstuffs, added Sunkist citrus fruits, Chiquita bananas, Baker's coconut, and Diamond walnuts to the kitchen vocabulary. In an April 1925 issue of *Good Housekeeping*, the Diamond company lauded its California-grown product as the perfect addition to salads. Text promoted tender, plump kernels from thin shells that easily yielded whole, uniform nut meats. Claiming to grow fifty million pounds of nuts per year, Diamond guaranteed that the consumer could use vacuum-packed nuts without worry that they contained trash and pieces of shell.

A moving paean to nuts and seeds occurred during the resettlement of Polish deportees from Vilna on the Russian steppes, where the sunflower flourished after its introduction by Peter the Great late in the seventeenth century. Esther Rudomin Hautzig, who was nine years old at the time of the Jewish diaspora, reminisced in her memoir, *The Endless Steppe* (1968), on the joy of shopping with her grandmother among Russian *baracholka* (food stalls) with the family's first rubles. In delight, Esther recalled: "The first purchase was a small glassful of sunflower seeds. I slit the shell between my teeth and extracted the tiny nut. I nursed it as if it were a piece of precious candy and it could not have tasted better. Siberians love sunflower seeds and I think ninety percent of them bore a little notch in a front tooth to prove it." (Hautzig 1968, 70)

In 1972, the political journalist John Gunther published *Inside Australia*, which describes the use of the green betel nut, fruit of the areca palm, as a narcotic and a source of protein in a diet typically bereft of meat. A nut technology developed with perforated containers of brass, copper, and silver for storing betel and crackers that split and shredded the nut meats. For flavor, users chewed the nut with a pod from the betel pepper plant. To stem the laxative effect, they added lime juice. Chewers addicted to the nut developed blackened teeth and darkened gums.

Into recent times, nuts are popular snack foods, additives to stir fry, and toppings for desserts. Western fanciers of chestnuts buy special chestnut pans with perforated bottoms that have changed little since the days of nut roasters advocated in Platina's *De Honesta Voluptate et Valitudine* (On Right Pleasure and Health, 1475). Cooks hold the container over an open fire, a gas flame, or stove to roast fresh nut meats that they have first scored with a knife. In Spain, cooks roast nuts of the ballota oak and grind them as a coffee substitute. Mediterranean cooks depend on almond milk or almond extract for soup bases. In India, a variety of nuts flavor curries, including almonds, a mild nut that blends with garlic and vegetables. Chinese and European cooks prefer bitter almonds.

The Tepehuan of Chihuahua, Mexico, either gather piñon nuts after they fall or extract them from green cones and beat them with rocks to extract the meats for roasting. In the Caribbean, peanut vendors sell bags of roasted nuts on city streets or at the beach. On Grenada, a familiar pushcart owner heats sugar and spices and adds nuts for peanut brittle, which he cools in large slabs and breaks into pieces for sale to shoppers and tourists.

Nuts are staples in African kitchens and home businesses and a source of social activity as workers gather, sort, and shell them. West Africans chew cola nuts for stimulus and stir them into drinks to relieve drunkenness and quell hunger pangs. In South Africa, the stones used for cracking nuts may be generations old and worn from constant hammering. Groundnuts and peanuts roasted in a skillet of river sand serve as snacks; crushed nuts produce chips for a grainy condiment called *dukkah* and oil for cooking and fueling lamps. Zambian cooks soak dry groundnuts for roasting and pulverizing into flour. For weddings, births, baptisms, and special guests, Zairian kitchens resonate with the roasting, hulling, and pulverizing of peanuts into meal and sauce. For much of a day, the females of the !Kung and the Bushmen living near the Nyae Nyae Conservancy of Botswana forage as did neolithic hunter-gatherers for energy-rich *mangetti* or *mongongo* nuts, which ripen on the ground. When they return home with bulging pouches, they have food to expand a diet that includes beetles and game. Providing up to half their vegetable intake, the nuts consist of a sweet kernel and flavorful outer shell.

In the wooded savannas of the African Sahel, known as the shea belt, the Kassena of Ghana gather, shell, and cream shea nuts from the *Butyrospermum paradoxum* tree into karite butter for cooking, skin treatment, and oiling hides and drum heads. They store unused nut meats in calabash bowls and use them as currency. Because shea (or galam) butter enhances cosmetics and the processing of margarine and chocolate, the commodity liberates Kassena women from patriarchy by giving them a viable staple on the world market, a cause embraced by the United Nations Development Fund of Women (UNIFEM).

The extraction of butter and oil from the nut impacts the design of flat village roofs, on which women dry nuts and grain and gather for cooking and socializing. Plastered clay walls of their huts and compound carry bold designs honoring women's work—the Zanlenga motif to represent the fiber nets that hold calabashes, Wanzagese to imitate a smashed gourd and the interlocking relationships of family, and an hourglass pattern that emulates the mortar in which nut harvesters crush the extracted meats. For trade, the women mold the butter into balls or loaves, from which vendors slice pieces to suit customer requests. Current scientific study of shea butter may enable marketers to compete with the margarine and cocoa butter industries.

Further Reading

Godwin, Peter, "Bushmen," *National Geographic*, February 2001, 90–117.
Hautzig, Esther. *The Endless Steppe.* New York: Harper & Row, 1968.
Nemacek, Sasha, "Who Were the First Americans?," *Scientific American*, 2000, 80–87.
The Williamsburg Cookbook. New York: Holt, Rinehart and Winston, 1971.

NYLON

The invention of the superpolymer nylon on May 23, 1934, did not immediately impact the kitchen. The Iowa-born organic chemist and Harvard professor Dr. Wallace Hume Carothers and his team produced a preliminary fiber at Du Pont research laboratories in 1927 and worked out chain condensation compounds with associate Julian W. Hill in 1930. The miracle fiber was pliant and tough, yet as delicate and lightweight as a spider web, but weakened by hot water and dissolved by cleaning fluids. Carothers applied polyamides to the problem of molecular linkage to spin out a stronger filament, which he extruded through a hypodermic needle. On February 28, 1935, he achieved a mix of penta-methylene-amine, sebacic acid, and xylenol. The first successful superpolymer, initially called "polymer 66" and then "nylon," filled market needs. Du Pont launched commercial nylon manufacture in 1938. News reports claimed that the fiber could be drawn to one-tenth the diameter of silk, yet retained tensile strength 150 percent stronger than silk. Lustrous and flowing, the refined fibers were impermeable by moisture and quick to recover from stretching.

Gradually, factories began turning out sewing machine parts, indoor-outdoor carpet, cording and clothesline rope, injection molded kitchen utensils and hand cranks, tough home scrub brushes, and washable scouring pads. Unlike metal scrubbers, nylon pads did not score metal surfaces or rust. Homemakers could easily rinse, air-dry, and reuse them without fear of souring or bacterial contamination. In 1960, Volk Enterprises of Turlok, California, began supplying poultry houses with microwave-compatible nylon trussing and handles to assist purchasers in lifting and positioning frozen turkeys in shopping carts, on freezer shelves, and during thawing and cooking.

Further Reading

Meikle, Jeffrey L. *American Plastic: A Cultural History.* New Brunswick, N.J.: Rutgers University Press, 1995.

O

OBENTOS

A cultural obligation placed on Japanese women is the packing of multiple courses in an obento, a lunchbox with moveable and interchangeable partitioning to serve four-year-olds at *yochien* (nursery school) or for outings. Similar *ekiben* (boxed lunches) for adult workers are available at convenience stores and train stations, where box sellers pass them to commuters through the train window. On a par with rice-cooking as proof of a bride's skill, the cooking of rice, meat, pork, vegetables, and fruit to suit a nursery school child's taste once determined the reputation of a woman for parenting.

The obento equated with security by becoming a child's away-from-home comfort food. The packing of the lunchbox with bite-size servings between neat boundaries became a school-day ritual for housewives, who made home-cooked food a final slender umbilical cord to tie children to mother's care. In turn, their preschoolers learned early that it was a duty to a *kyoiku mama* (committed parent) and to the school as well to eat all their meals so they would perform well at their studies. After the first year, children, ideally prepared for the rigors of public education, ate institutional cafeteria meals.

Criteria for an appealing obento begin with nutritious, palatable food purchased daily for freshness and presented in five or six courses. The ideal obento requires aesthetic arrangement, a natural preference for a nation that bases its stability on cultural order. Each day's assembly of foods may require up to forty-five minutes, including reheating leftovers or freezing portions for use later in the week. For children's meals, mothers begin with *uruchi mai* (non-glutinous rice), the core food, and cut complementary items into miniature portions, shape them according to the dictates of the season, and arrange them precisely in varied containers fitted into the sturdy trays.

To raise interest in the meals, mothers purchase for embellishments plastic skewers and colored toothpicks, flags, paper flowers, fluted cups, tiny baskets, foil tins, and napkins or handkerchiefs. One aspect of packing is facilitation of eating with *o-hashi* (chopsticks), a boon to the well ordered school program. Another is the structuring of a variety of meat, starch, and vegetables in contrasting and complementary shapes, colors, and textures as an enticement to picky eaters. Anne Allison's article "Japanese Mothers and Obentos: The Lunch-Box as Ideological State Apparatus" in *Anthropological Quarterly* (October 1991) lists as models of motherly creativity a wiener sliced like a segmented worm or dressed like a doll, lemons carved into butterflies, carrots trimmed into shoes, boiled eggs decorated with leaf and pickle to resemble a rabbit, fruit smilies, rolled omelette slices, and tulip-shaped vegetables.

The mother's elaborate kitchen creativity results in a stylized meal that equates with love and concern for the child, who receives food as carefully planned and organized as a dinner for guests. Part of the child's receipt of the gift box is a nursery school ritual of singing songs, thanking Buddha and the mother, and honoring the father for earning a living. Structured mealtimes require helpers to pour tea and monitor behavior for a communal eating session that ends when all the boxes are empty. Teachers turn obentos into an instructional opportunity by cajoling, scolding, and encouraging all to finish in the prescribed amount of time, an injunction echoed by the other children.

Japan's domestic culture at large and Mothers' Associations in particular promote the obento as an adjunct to health and obedience training as well as an art form. Preparation by mothers clarifies for children the rigid gender-specific roles that women accept when they marry and assume command of the home. Companies market numerous styles of lunchboxes, drawstring obento bags, and implements as well as cookbooks and obento magazines, including a journal issued by Shufunotomo, a women's publisher. Food stores offer obento sections with racks of utensils, bags, ribbon, and paper dividers. High-tech boxes allow the purchaser to heat the food by pulling a string on the box. Simpler obentos can be heated in a microwave oven or eaten cold with chopsticks.

Further Reading

Allison, Anne, "Japanese Mothers and Obentos: The Lunch-Box as Ideological State Apparatus," *Anthropological Quarterly*, October 1991, 195–208.

Khor, Diane, "Organizing for Change: Women's Grassroots Activism in Japan," *Feminist Studies*, Fall 1999, 25 (3), 633–662.

Nagatanien, "Ready Meals: Pokemon Obento Carry Carton," *New Food Products in Japan*, April 15, 1999.

White, Merry I., "Japan: The Childless Society?," *Journal of Asian Studies*, February 1, 1999, 58(1), 199.

OIL (AS FOOD)

Oil from olives, avocados, nuts, fish, and other natural sources is a marvel of domestic utility: It provides vitamin A, soothes burned skin, rejuvenates freshly washed hair and flagging libido, lights lanterns, binds dry foods into cakes and casseroles, and lubricates comallis, dumas, woks, and skillets for frying. From study of fossilized leaves found on the island of Santorini, scientists surmised that the olive plant, which dates to 37,000 BCE, was the world's first cultivated tree. Mediterranean lore places the olive tree's emergence in the Nile Delta. Myth proposes that the first olive producer was Adam. Archeologists unearthed evidence from Haifa of oil production in an olive mortar from 5000 BCE. Using hand presses, a Philistine kitchen near Tel Aviv generated five hundred gallons of oil annually.

Traditionally, the extraction of oil from the Egyptian butternut, poppy, radish seed, olive, rape, soya, and cod was a seasonal task. The Egyptians took oil from moringa fruit and the seeds of lettuce, radish, and rape;

Nebuchadnezzar's pantry staff preferred sesame, as did Iraqi cooks, who had limited access to the olive oil used in Syrian recipes. Herodotus's histories describe hempseed as a favorite of Scythians. In Scandinavia, the British isles, Holland, Germany, Switzerland, and Spain, oil pressers chose flax for its fiber as well as its nutrients. The Spanish also gathered flowering nabiza, a turnip plant pressed for cooking oil.

Native Americans used natural liquids from the whale, walrus, passenger pigeon, ducks and geese, walnuts, and hickory nuts, the source of cooking oil for the Creek of Alabama and Georgia and the Yuchi and neighboring Powhatan of the Carolinas. Among the Canadian Cree, the extraction of oil from wild geese suspended from the rafters of a meechwap (cooking lodge) preceded basting the birds while they cooked over a fire. The Natchez of Mississippi used bear fat; the Micmac of Nova Scotia pounded moose bones to yield marrow for an animal butter.

On the West Coast, the eulachon (also oolachon or candlefish) was a prized source of oil among the Nootka, Kwakiutl, and Bella Coola of Queen Charlotte Sound and Queen Charlotte Strait, British Columbia, and by the Chinook of the Columbia River Delta. The fish was so rich in oil that it doubled as a small candle. The Tsimshian of Alaska boiled rotted eulachon and skimmed off the fat to store for cooking grease and as a trade item, which they exchanged with interior tribes for skins, quills, and furs. Passage of oil inland over established routes earned them the name "grease trails." (Dickason 1992, 79)

Among the Maya and Aztec of Peru, the avocado provided the oil to balance a diet rich in amaranth, quinoa, peppers, tomatoes, squash, corn, and beans. It also fueled lamps and lubricated dumas, the smooth baking stones on which they cooked unleavened bread. For each type of oil, correct extraction and processing required settling, filtration to remove bitter elements, heating, storage, and air-tight seals.

For the Mediterranean region, the olive was sacred. From the eastern end of the Mediterranean, where cultivation began before 6000 BCE, farmers learned to graft and domesticate the olive tree. In the Homeric Hymns (eighth to sixth centuries BCE) of classical Greece, the "Hymn to Hestia" speaks of Apollo's hearth keeper as dripping olive oil from her hair. The versatile giant of the oil industry, olives were the source of cooking oil, a youth-perpetuating health food rich in vitamin E, skin cleanser and emollient, fuel for illumination, and common currency. Even the pits could be recycled into charcoal for braziers. Olive wood from ancient cultures turns up in jars from Greece, frescoes from Minos, and bas relief from Egypt.

At the 114 olive oil mills at Ekron in Palestine, presses consisted of granite stone cylinders that rolled olives in a crushing vat. Philistine millers wove round grass mats to line the hardwood frame and activated a lever made from stones tied to wood beams. As it ran into clay jars for separation, the millers poured in hot water that forced the oil to the top, which they removed with bronze dippers.

For good reason, the olive branch symbolized peace as well as prosperity to growers. Oil was a home gift to temples and the olive itself a focal food on fast days. For peasants, farm workers, and urbanites, kitchens maintained a stock of both oil and fruit for daily use, for example, as a flavoring for bread that the cook toasted at a brazier. As the Greek presence grew among nations, so did the plantings of olives, which helped stabilize and enrich the economy.

Home use of olive oil by Syrians and Palestinians passed to Crete and Greece five centuries later, when Crete became the Mediterranean's largest oil exporter and home of grafting experts. To prepare batches for the table or export, pressers soaked the fruit in hot water. The two-part liquid required cooling and separation in a clay container similar to the modern gravy separator. The need for containers sparked manufacture of large numbers of pithoi (storage jars).

The olive passed on to the west in the packs of Greek colonists, who civilized Sicily around 700 BCE, by building communes and planting olive groves, a silvery-leafed tree that became a standard motif in mosaic, ceramic art, and wall painting. Traders equipped a fleet with amphorae intended solely for the oil market. From Greek colonies, farmers popularized the plant in Italy, France, Spain, Croatia, and Tunisia, where pickers devised an artificial harvesting claw from the tips of goat horns, which they slipped over their fingers to grapple for ripe olives. When the Peloponnesian Wars raged, Athenians withdrew into walled towns and sat out the siege under their olive trees. Even when Spartan attackers scorched them, the trees continued to bud. Two literary olive oil enthusiasts, the late fourth-century BCE philosophers Theophrastus and Epicurus, admired the island of Lesbos for its oil, which vied with local wine for culinary supremacy.

Italian olive groves met the needs of Rome, where upper and lower classes daily ate the fruit and oil cakes and filled lamps with the oil, which traveled to all parts of the nation and its territories in sealed amphorae. Early in the Empire, encyclopedist Pliny the Elder, author of Natural History (c. 77 CE), accounted for the value of olive oil: "The property of oil is to warm the body and to defend it against the injuries of cold; yet a sovereign thing it is to cool and mitigate the hot distemperature of the head." (Pliny 1962, 151) He set the best time for picking when the berries began to turn dark.

In characteristic style, Pliny mused on the Greek use of oil as a body emollient for wrestlers. Athletes tied wrist flasks of oil to their arms and dabbled on drops to tone skin and moisturize skin. As a food, oil developed a mystique for strengthening the body and warding off ills. The emperor Nero took oil from the sports arena to present to spectators, who carried gift containers of the best quality oil to their own kitchens.

In Roman colonies in Morocco, olive preservers cured the black fruit in salt or brine. They spiced green olives with red chilies or lemon confit, and violet olives with garlic, parsley, oregano, rosemary, thyme, and turmeric. To crack green olives for the press, they layered them on a stone base to strike with a wood paddle. At the table, Afro-Roman cooks offered diners heaps of couscous laced with meat chunks and vegetables and drizzled in oil. Eating required sliding the right hand palm up into the mass, grasping a fistful to squeeze into a ball and pop into the mouth. At Volubilis, Mauretania, Berber olive growers devoted much of the city to merchandising slave-milled olive oil. At the oil dealer's mansion, when diners overindulged, they spewed up oil-rich dinners into a vomitorium, which slaves emptied into buckets to recycle oil and gastric juices for treating leather.

The British Isles stood apart from the predominence of olive oil, which was a costly import so far north of its source. Eastern Europe had its own source of vegetable oil for cooking and flavoring. According to Elena Burman Molokhovets, compiler of the classic Russian cookbook, A Gift to Young Housewives (1861), poppy seed oil was a favorite staple in Russia. She turned poppy seeds or hempseeds into milk by scalding with boiling water and pouring the sweetened liquid onto dry biscuits. Lithuanians preferred hempseed for oil, parched seeds for snacks, and salted seeds for topping rye loaves and making into a dip for potatoes.

Into current times, Italian cooks demand quality olive oil, as do Americans, who have made it the nation's third-best-selling oil. Whether from California, Lebanon, Sardinia, Portugal, Greece, Italy, or Spain, the world's largest producer of olive oil, a fresh harvest demands a regimen of picking, sorting, crushing in a stone or steel mill, and immediate pressing, extrusion and centrifuging, filtering, and siphoning off of water. Labeling established by law in the European Community follows these standards:

> Best oil is the prize oil of the year, which comes from the first cold pressing of hand-gathered fruit. It yields fruity, green, fragrant extra virgin oil, which producers hold to high standards of color, fragrance, stability, and acidity at less than

1 percent. The best must also rank high in comparisons of organoleptic quality of aroma, taste, and consistency as well as long shelf life.

Virgin oil is the second-best grade, which is pressed under heat. It may have an acidity of up to 2 percent and offers a shorter shelf life than the best grade.

Pure olive oil is the third class, also called just olive oil, which derives from windfalls or preserved stock. It passes through steam processing, refining, and addition of carbon sulfate before being mixed with extra virgin stock. It is best used for frying and lubricating or for industrial applications.

Pomace, the lowest and cheapest grade, comes from further extraction of oil from the remaining olive paste. Because of its high acidity, it serves best as lamp oil.

Affecting each year's production are elements of variety, cultivation, pests and disease, climate, rainfall, and soil. Also, the type of equipment used for pressing of green or black olives or some combination of the two affects the color, flavor, aroma, and consistency. Purist cooks match oil with recipe, choosing Ligurian stock for that region's dishes and Puglian and Calabrian for southern Italian fare. Northern Italian foods, which bear French influence, rely on butter and cream bases. The French season their toasted bread with tapenade, a Provençal spread made from pitted olives, anchovies, capers, olive oil, and seasonings. For aïoli, an olive oil mayonnaise, they blend oil with fresh garlic, egg yolk, and salt. Palestinians prefer olive oil for the making of jaz *mussakhkhan*, a chicken dish seasoned with allspice, pine nuts, sumac, cardamom, and onion for spreading on flat bread.

A second source of oil, *'nzugna* or *sugna* (lard), rendered from pork fat in Sicily and southern Italy, derives from the Latin *axungia,* a fat used in cooking and filling lamps. To supply a household with clay jars of congealed fat, cooks have traditionally simmered fat from a recent slaughtering, drained it of water and scurf, removed bits of hardened meat, and blended it with bay leaves and salt. Refrigerated as purified solid shortening, it requires only a parchment covering tied to the neck of the vessel for long shelf stability.

In the United States, cooks began buying commercial oil in the 1930s. An advertisement for Mazola oil, published in a 1932 edition of *American Cookery Magazine* (formerly the *Boston Cooking School Magazine*), illustrated the newness of canned shortening for frying and salad dressing. The accompanying picture depicts home economists in a revolutionary role — spokespersons for new and improved kitchen products and foodstuffs.

Oil figures in the homemaker's demand for clean, wholesome food. In 1981, olive oil importers earned a reputation for bilking Spanish customers expecting a pure product. Unscrupulous Spanish merchants adulterated stocks with industrial rape seed oil from France colored with red aniline dye. The oil, intended as a machine lubricant, caused the deaths of 402 and toxicity in twenty thousand others. The courts imposed a total of 106,000 years in prison on the thirty-eight who duped their Madrid customers. Aftershocks forced conviction of thirteen businessmen. The seven bureaucrats implicated in the scam did not come to trial for fourteen years.

The U.S. Food and Drug Administration formulated standards to halt fraudulant labeling. In the mid-1990s, the North American Olive Oil Association established its own internal controls. In 1996, the *New York Times* exacerbated a climate of distrust by misreporting the results of trials conducted on 73 oils. They first reported 96 percent of erroneous claims of purity. In a few days, they retracted the article and found only one brand out of compliance.

Chinese cooks depend on oil as a lubricant in wok cookery. Used subtly in stir-fry cooking, oil speeds the heating of foods without soaking them in fat. Since the end of the first century BCE, they have flavored oils by pressing rape seed, unrefined or toasted sesame seed, and turnips and by adding onions and scallions, garlic, shallots, coriander, and peppers to oil before cooking meats, seafoods, and vegetables. The arrival of the peanut in Asia produced a dependable oil that absorbs the aroma and savor of vegetables and spice.

Among Karnali peasants in Tarakot, Nepal, journalists Lila M. and Barry C. Bishop from *National Geographic* found cooks making oil from the *Cannabis sativa* (marijuana) plants that grow wild in the area. In addition to sale of harvests as a cash crop, they turn fiber into twine and press the oil from the plant as a hair dressing and a drug to ease sore muscles. For women who can't afford clarified butter made from buffalo milk, pressing leaves into paste involves kneading them in rectangular wood troughs. Users claim that eating foods cooked with the oil makes people dizzy.

Nutritionists and cooks in industrialized countries have puzzled over late twentieth-century findings concerning fats and health. In addition to reducing butter and oil from the diet, health-conscious families differentiate between the saturated oils in coconut, cocoa, and palm kernels used to harden margarine and the unsaturated fats in hazel oil, walnut oil, and grape seed oil, which have rebounded to popularity in British food markets. Another element in the choice of cooking oil is the smoking point, when degradation sets in. The most common vegetable oils break down (in degrees Fahrenheit) in this order: safflower at 510, soybean at

495, corn at 475, olive and canola at 450, and peanut and sunflower at 440. Popular in American markets are peanut, canola, and safflower oil as well as artisanal nut oils from pecans, almonds, hazelnuts, and pistachio nuts, which serve well in the kitchen for salad dressing and stir-frying.

See also **Amphora; Roman Cookery**

Further Reading

Dickason, Olive Patricia. *Canada's First Nations*. Norman: University of Oklahoma Press, 1992.

Jansen, Michael E., "To the Olives!," *Aramco World*, July-August 1972, 2–9.

Rosenblum, Mort. *Olives: The Life and Lore of a Noble Fruit*. New York: North Point Press, 1996.

Speake, Graham, ed. *Encyclopedia of Greece and the Hellenic Tradition*. Chicago: Fitzroy Dearborn, 2000.

OILCLOTH

An offshoot of table runners, tapestries, and wall hangings, oilcloth—also called waxcloth in England—dressed homes for centuries as a waterproof covering for floors and tables. Developed in England in the Middle Ages from the oiled cloth or parchment that filled window frames, oilcloth paralleled the evolution of painted duck or canvas floorcloths, a common upgrading of drab wood in colonial homes. Around 1685, Richard and Edward Greenbury obtained a patent for "painting with oyle cullors upon wollen cloath, kerseys and stuffes, being proper for hanging (and alsoe with the said cullors upon silke for windows)." ("Complete History of Nairn") In the next decade, a London merchant patented a method of printing "upon oyl cloath...gold and silver flowers and other figures in all sorts of colors, which said flowers and so printed will last as long as the stuffe itself." (Ibid.)

Oilcloth covered galley tables in barges and sea-going vessels and accompanied settlers to the outback as waterproof wrappings for flour and meal, wagon beds, firearms, maps and charts, cookbooks and herbals, and precious papers. Its primary purpose was prevention of stains, mold, and additional laundering of domestic items. The original sizing of jute or burlap with glue and oil paint and leveling with pumice produced a durable cloth finished with varnish and rolled flat with a weighted cylinder. A less cumbrous version began with soaking linen or canvas in linseed oil and block printing the surface with novelty print, gingham, floral, fruit, and tattersall designs.

Around 1850, American inventor Otis Ferrin patented a waterproof painting cloth, a heavy material made from low-grade cotton fiber permeated with oil.

It evolved into the current version of oilcloth, a global standard for rainwear, camping ground cloths, shelf liner, and table coverings. A durable, stain-resistant, if homely commodity, oilcloth enriched English factories while supplying working-class families with a touch of decoration for kitchen and dining area. In late Victorian England, the Storey family of Lancaster, England, abandoned linoleum, a commodity dominated by the rival Williamsons, the "lino" kings, and concentrated on manufacturing blinds, tablecloths, and oilcloth.

In Catharine Beecher and Harriet Beecher Stowe's *The American Woman's Home, or Principles of Domestic Science* (1869), a classic text on home economics, the famous sisters introduce the vision of the kitchen as the core of the home. Text describes each aspect, down to shelves, drawers, and room dividers. Of the floor, the duo advise: "To procure a kitchen oilcloth as cheaply as possible, buy cheap tow cloth and fit it to the size and shape of the kitchen. Then have it stretched and nailed to the south side of the barn and, with a brush, cover it with a coat of thin rye plaster. When this is dry, put on a coat of yellow paint and let it dry for a fortnight. Then put on a second coat." (Harrison, 1972, 126) The handbook promises good service over many years if the oilcloth maker lets it dry for two months.

Because the early coatings aged, discolored, and peeled, in the age of plastics, factories replaced outdated oilcloth technology by permeating cotton mesh with vinyl and backing in flannel to keep the underside from scratching finished furniture. By the early 1900s, variety stores and five-and-dimes stocked solids and patterns, available on rolls like yard goods for measuring out and slicing clean with a knife. Families made annual pilgrimages to Woolworth's or studied the Sears, Roebuck catalog to select a new tablecloth. The neatly cut piece, sometimes zigzagged around the edge with pinking shears, was ready for the table or for packing along on picnics as a groundcloth.

Stiff competition from synthetic finishes and fabrics gained strength in the post-World War II years. In the October 1947 issue of *Woman's Home Companion*, Munising of Chicago advertised Marvalon, a plastic-coated and fiber-backed kitchen material sold by the roll in department and variety stores in solid colors, plaids, and patterns. Suited to covering tables, concealing under-sink storage space, or lining cupboards and shelves, it offered strength and soft texture. Unlike oilcloth, it had no odor and did not fade, stain, fray, crack, or peel. Firestone marketed its own domestic fabric called Velón, a plastic film sold in sheer, lacy, flowered, gingham, and dotted swiss versions for draperies, aprons, screening, and food wrapping and storage.

Further Reading

Beecher, Catharine E. *The New Housekeeper's Manual.* New York: J. B. Pond & Co., 1873.

OLLAS

The olla is the traditional wide-mouth earthen water jar, fermentation vat, medicine jar, or stewing pot essential to the cuisine of the Mexica and Pueblo Indians. Looped handles on each side aid the user in pouring hot liquids from the unwieldy vessel. To the ancient Mesoamerican, the olla functioned in life-affirming activities: the olla was analagous to the womb, from which came life.

In 1586, historian Thomas Harriot, author of *A Briefe and True Report of the New Found Land of Virginia,* reported to interested Europeans on New World foodstuffs, healing, hunting, and cookery. Along with native American fish grilling and table etiquette, he described the use of the olla. Like other vessels and kitchen implements in use by Indians, stewing in ollas was a female province: "Their woemen fill the vessel with water, and then putt they in fruite, flesh, and fish, and lett all boyle together like a galliemaufrye, which the Spaniarde call, olla podrida." (p. 60)

Among the Tepehuan of Chihuahua, Mexico, and their neighbors, the Tarahumara, potting ollas begins with grinding clay on a mano and metate, mixing in sand or pulverized potsherds, and kneading the mass to a workable consistency. The container rises from a clay pot bottom, which they fit into a hole in the ground. More dabs and long coils of clay attach to the base for smoothing with a stick. Those pots that will be used for boiling extend into a lip at top for easy removal with two sticks laid parallel to each other at each side. When the vessel reaches a useable height, the potter smooths the interior with a stone or potsherd and attaches handles. After drying in the sun or on stones set over a dung and oak branch fire for an hour, the olla is ready for polishing and coloring with red beans.

The finished olla holds stores of maize grains for toasting before they go to the mano and metate for grinding and into the pot for pinole, a daily staple at breakfast, lunch, and dinner. Other uses include roasting rattlesnake meat; boiling fresh cut corn kernels, green beans, amaranth grains, or squash squares; cooking squash blossoms in suet or fat; and the parching of corn for esquite, which requires a bed of sand in the bottom of the olla to distribute the heat. For fermenting a maize drink, they pound sprouted maize in a hollow log, then strain and store the mash in a double olla, an hour-glass device that the potter forms by setting pot on pot. A similar boiling, mashing, and fermenting turns agave heart into maguey or mescal.

For cooking soft corn into atole (mush) or yoriki, Tepehuan cooks must work a bit harder. They boil water in the olla, then remove it from the flame to add grain for softening before straining it through a basket sieve. The mush goes to a metate for grinding, during which the cook pours more of the soaking water from the olla. Before serving, the reduced mush receives flavoring with salt, chile, chickpeas, or sorghum seed. For yoriki, the cook goes through a similar process as for atole, but boils the meal several hours in the olla.

To make posole or pozole, the Spanish name for hominy, the Tepehuan cooks soak soft maize in oak ash or crushed limestone rock, which they store in an olla. After rinsing maize in fresh water, they drain the jar, hull the softened grain, and boil it briefly before seasoning with oregano and sow thistle. For a one-dish meal, they add meat or menudo (tripe) and beans. In Nicaragua, cooks celebrate Catholic saints' days by making *indio viejo* (Old Indian Stew) in large ollas, which they place over wood fires and stir with wood paddles.

See also **Mano and Metate**

Further Reading

Pennington, Campbell W. *The Tepehuan of Chihuahua: Their Material Culture.* Salt Lake City: University of Utah Press, 1969.

OPEN-HEARTH COOKING

Both a culinary method and a lifestyle, open-hearth cooking defined the communal activities of paleolithic peoples, who stooped, bent, and squatted by the fire during meal preparation. As characterized in "The Culinary Triangle" in *The Origin of Table Manners: Introduction to a Science of Mythology* (1968) by French cultural anthropologist Claude Lévi-Strauss, acceptance of open-fire roasting allied people with nature. When food cooked over flame, two elements of the natural world—fire and food—complemented each other to produce tasty, palatable meals. For good reason, primeval religious ritual exalted both warmth and sustenance as the bedrock of human subsistence on earth.

Into embers, the early Peruvians sank papaya or pawpaws, also called custard apples, much as they baked sweet potatoes. Egyptians made clay and metal stewpots that perched on supports or trivets over an open flame. The *tannur* (charcoal oven) favored by Arabs functions well outside the dwelling. In ancient Rome, open-hearth cooking was an equally primitive affair

Cooking over an open fire.
[© *Dex Image / Alamy.*]

on a raised platform for igniting a wood or charcoal fire. Vessels consisted of a gridiron, iron or bronze pot on a trivet near the flame, or a cauldron slung on a chain directly over the heat or to the side.

Archeological digs offer a full panorama on open-hearth cooking technique. At two hearths in the Tequendama rock shelter of pre-Columbian Sabana de Bogotá, Colombia, fire tenders cooked fish, turtles, and mollusks and the deer, skunk, guinea pig, armadillo, hare, and cotton rat meat they acquired by hunting, netting, and snaring. For cooking implements, they used flaked edges, awls, grinders, hammerstones, knives and scrapers, choppers, and wooden and bone tools. A later civilization, the Cahto of Mendocino County, California, broiled insects, birds, fish, bear, and small game over coals or on spits. At Old Testament Jericho, which London-born archeologist Dame Kathleen Mary Kenyon unearthed in the 1950s, central courtyard kitchens featured multilayered clay hearths. The strata of polished red or white clay over ash suggest that homemakers took pride in their firesides and refurbished soiled surfaces periodically with clay, which they smoothed with large oval stones.

For Roman slaves and kitchen help, working "down hearth" was hot, dirty work. They vented smoke through a wall vent or out the roof. For people living in insulae (tenements), open-hearth cooking in rooms was dangerous to wooden walls. Without appropriate fire-proofing, families had to eat cold meals, buy food from the street-level thermopolia (hot shops), or use communal ovens, which allowed families to share a fire in a tiled courtyard under an open sky, an obvious disadvantage during cold and wet weather.

The open fireplace or down hearth of medieval England, such as that found at Penshurst, Kent, usually filled the middle of a hall and centered activity about the roasting of whole oxen, boiling of pigs, and spit-roasting of poultry and game birds. Near the shores, the menu featured huge ocean fish. To sustain the heat of intense, long-burning fires, builders made floors and walls of stone slabs or brick. When wall-mounted fireplaces replaced central fire pits, masons used fire brick as a wall and covered it in an iron fireback, which protected the wall while radiating heat.

In medieval France and Italy, hearth cookery suited the making of focaccia or fougasse, a primitive unleavened bread seasoned with olive oil and herbes de Provence. Isadore of Seville, the "Schoolmaster of the Middle Ages" and author of *Etymologiarum Sive Originum Libri Viginti* (Twenty Books of Etymologies or Origins, c. 620), describes it as a flat loaf shaped on a cooking stone. Its simplicity parallels the Central American tortilla, Indian chapati, and Middle Eastern pita. In data obtained from medieval monastery records, focaccia was a subcinericius (under the ash) bread, a product of high quality flour passed to attendees at formal church blessings. In 1553, Flemish journeyman Peter Coeck of Alost described a trek into Greece, where local cooks presented him with similar ash-baked loaves.

Among the homes of eleventh- and twelfth-century Scandinavia, Iceland, Greenland, and England, Viking cooks worked at long central hearths, the focus of family activity. Cooking consisted of boiling in pottery or soapstone embedded in hot coals or in iron cauldrons suspended over the fire. They removed roasted meat from the embers with iron hooks and ate it on unleavened bread formed from barley, rye, and pulses. After dinner, extended families and guests rolled themselves in skin robes and slept near the hearth on fixed benches. The position of the sleeping space determined status—the closer to the fire, the higher the rank.

When Christopher Columbus first saw the Arawak on Haiti in 1493, he observed a protein-rich diet of fish, manatee, iguanas, rodents, bats, dogs, birds, worms, snails, and spiders. The largest portions cooks roasted on skewers at a beachfront wood fire, the ancestor of the barbecue. The Carib, who left the Orinoco Basin to settle parts of the West Indies, preferred coal-roasting plantain, which they pounded and creamed, and breadfruit, which they served in slices. The natives of New Caledonia considered themselves civilized after they abandoned such grilling and roasting and took up boiling tubers in a pot, a human creation. Their concept of fire-roasting as aboriginal and unmediated by human food preparers parallels commentary by the Greek philosopher Aristotle, who dismissed roasting as an ancient cooking method.

Preparing food over an open flame was—and still is—a back-breaking labor profiting from a good eye for coals and signs of diminishing heat and a ready hatchet, ax, wedge, or machete for hewing and splitting fuel to increase heat. The open-hearth system devoured fuel at a fast rate and flourished in areas where fuel cost and availability were not a problem. Mesopotamians referred to the ember-roasting of fish as "touching with fire," an indication of controlled cookery. (Nemet-Nejat) For a steady temperature, cooks varied materials, using corn cobs, dried pith, vine trimmings, fruit and nuts, suckers, down timber, and twigs as fire starters and hardwood splits and backlogs for a slow-burning fire. The constant crouching and bending of cooks to clean shellfish and prepare hides for domestic use developed the human ankle bones and predisposed fireside cooks to compression fracture and spinal arthritis.

Ash roasting from early times allowed cooks to bake a quick flat bread, such as the mafruka of the Saharan Bedouin, roast potatoes and other root vegetables, and steam tender new corn in cold ash under hot coals for the Seminole and Iroquois Green Corn Festival. Women cooked eggs and food wrapped in clay and fragrant leaves, a favorite baking method among the Caribbean tribes. Native Americans prized the camassia quamash, a virtually work-free bulb food that baked into a sweet cake. Camassia consumption was so widespread that the Walla Walla, Shoshone, and Nez Percé jealously guarded rich fields. Purveyors established tuber trade routes over Idaho and Washington state to exchange camassia for dried salmon, buffalo hide, corn, shells, tobacco, moccasins, and feathered bonnets.

In the American colonies, cookware makers devised vessels and utensils to suit open-hearth techniques. A standard item for direct-flame cookery was the long-handled iron, graniteware, or clayware braising pan, a flat-bottomed container in which seared meats continued heating beneath a tight lid. A variant was the round braising pot topped with a flat tin lid that doubled as an indirect source of heat for warming biscuits to accompany the one-dish meal inside.

To keep fat out of the ash and avoid a burnt taste, Colonial cooks often sealed meat in a crust for roasting in front of the flame and used a drip pan to retain cracklings and juices for making sauce and gravy. By placing dishes on a hand-held or two-legged iron salamander, they could shove the head into the fire, then retrieve the device by pulling the handle end and laying it directly on the tops of pies and haunches of meat for contact browning in the style of a hair dresser applying a heated curling iron to tresses. Subsidiary fires increased the variety of menu items. Steady heat was also useful for rendering cooking grease from heavy suet. Cooks turned fatty meat trimmings into pocket soup, a forerunner of bouillon cubes that had a long shelf life and provided tasty meat base for outdoor cooking during long travels.

Well into the 1800s, when stoves replaced open-fire cooking, the kitchen fire burned constantly. A lug pole, also called a chimney crook or chimney bar made of seasoned hardwood or iron, traversed the space above the hearth to hold chains and trammels or pot hooks for positioning pots and griddles above the flame. For retrieving baked potatoes, yams, or chestnuts, cooks employed an iron raker, a handle attached to a curved metal spatula for probing ash for remaining foods. Among New World colonists, birch plants served as roasting gear for shad.

Settlers limited primarily to seafood often supped on oysters, terrapin, or fish alone, which they caught in weirs with their hands Indian style, or by pounding them with sticks in shallow water. Lobster reached six feet in length in New York harbor; crabs fed up to four diners each. French Labadist pietists evangelizing in Brooklyn reported in 1697 that cooks roasted oysters in the fire by the pailful, some a foot long, a fact corroborated in chronicler and first secretary of the Virginia colony William Strachey's *Historie of Travaile into Virginia* (1612). The thrifty householder wisely pickled extras in casks to sell in Barbados and burned the shells for lime.

The French invented the couvre-feu or curfew, a half or quarter dome of sheet metal with an attached handle. It served two purposes: holding heat in embers overnight and reducing the danger of fire from sparks or scattering of ash in a downdraft. For a quick hot drink or medicinal concoction, the kitchen staff could heat an iron loggerhead or muller, a knobby rod, in the embers. The user plunged the bulbous end into tankards of ale or rum or mugs of spiced wine for instant contact heating. The method also purified water for cleansing wounds or feeding to infants.

In seventeenth-century English kitchens, some open-fire hearths featured a built-up brick surface beneath which the cook stoked charcoal through archways. To increase the heat, users built small fires on the surface to heat pots on metal rings. A century later, farmhouse kitchens were wide enough to offer seats and small spirit and tobacco cupboards on each side of the hearth for warmth and convenience. Niches and recesses in the facia held tinder box and brimstone matches. A polished meat screen placed before a roasting joint or fowl kept juices from spurting onto the floor or cook's apron at the same time that it reflected heat onto the outer surface of the meat.

In Scandinavia, northern continental Europe, and the Americas, a round-topped iron fireback or back plate attached to the back wall of the chimney. Iron casters created an ornate design, emblem, mythic or religious scene, or the family's heraldic crest by stamping a design in sand before pouring molten iron over it to harden. A smoke chamber in the flue held bacon slices, which the cook loaded and removed from chimney side after they were dry. Unpeeled mushrooms broiled at the edge. A levered crane lifted and lowered the heavy cauldrons. An iron bar suspended down the chimney fastened to a pot with a hook.

A complex spit on a pulley wheel operated by an overhead smokejack. An innovation in andirons equipped the end pieces with a cup-shaped finial to hold containers of spiced ale. On the hearth, a wooden toasting dog was a whimsical implement. Its head held a spiked rack for impaling bread. The dog's tail turned back to the body to form a handle for moving the implement closer to the fire without overheating the user's hand. A clever container was the ale boot, a long-handled lidded metal container with a toe projection at one side that the cook pressed into the hot coals to heat ale.

Europeans and colonial Americans perpetuated the kitchen traditions of Elizabethan and Jacobean cooks into succeeding centuries. Their list of favorite recipes included collared beef, souse, sop, marrow pudding, gooseberry fool, curd pudding, shrewsbury cake, and jumbal, a thin, crisp, delicate, ring-shaped cake or cookie made with sour cream and flavored with coconut, citrus zest, and spice and scented with rose water. Much hearth cooking of side dishes to accompany roasts required the setting of small pots on three-legged trivets perched over hot coals. Children enjoyed the chestnut-roaster, a shallow perforated skillet like a wire corn popper held over flame and shaken to distribute heat.

For baking on all surfaces at once, eighteenth-century open-hearth cooks favored the girdle plate for making oatbread and pancakes and the posnet, an earthenware braising dish covered with a concave lid that held hot coals, for breadmaking. A nested roaster called a diable allowed the cook to double the menu, for example, by pairing potatoes and chestnuts or manioc and shellfish. The iron oven debuted around 1850. As skill at forging and soldering improved, cooks acquired more sophisticated metal devices to make shifting heavy loads easier and more accurate. Of particular use was the ratchet, which eased a suspended cauldron into place in small increments.

A standard item for open-hearth cookery was the long-handled iron, graniteware, or clayware braising pan, a flat-bottomed container that allowed seared meats to continue cooking beneath a tight lid. As described in Alexis Soyer's The Modern Housewife (1850), braising was a French method named for braise, the wood residue in an oven. He explains that topping a pan with coals required a deep, tight-fitting lid to blend aroma with flavor and create an appealing succulence. Such heavy containers at the open fire endangered the family of Captain Denny. When a trammel bar broke in the flue, a kettle fell, spilling boiling liquid on four children asleep on the hearth, scalding one immediately to death.

Fireside holiday celebrations centered food preparation on goods that could be heated, roasted, or boiled at close range. In 1858, Henry Harbaugh described the Yuletide boiling of chestnuts over an open fire in Franklin County, Pennsylvania. According to Samuel M. Sener, a state folklorist writing in the New Year 1892 edition of Christian Culture, another traditional kitchen chore was the gathering of neighbors for slaughtering pigs. Women shared the jobs of making sausage and pudding meat in wooden tubs for metzel soup, a nourishing food for invalids and sickly children. The festive kitchen sported polished andirons and apples in baskets alongside the great crane of a working fireplace. Children took their turn at cracking hickory nuts and butter nuts at hearthside with mallets. Groups ferried the soup and gift baskets to the poor.

In 1830, German prince Maximilian von Wied presented a picture of aboriginal life in his drawing of a Puri family's open-hearth cooking. In a line drawing of a trio residing in a jungle on the Brazilian Amazon's east coast, he depicted two naked children at play, a dog curled up in sleep, domestic utensils neatly stacked to the left of the palm frond shelter, and a woman resting in a hammock while their supper cooks. In the foreground, a monkey impaled on a stick roasts over a fire outside the entrance.

A painting by J.L. Charmet entitled Hafászcsárda depicts a 1930s tavern setting in which women cook outside a tavern while Hungarian fishers eat at trestle tables. A tripod of branches holds a broad kettle of soup over the fire. Alongside, a pair of women gut and clean fish next to a wrack of drying seines and fish baskets. A stooping figure lifts fish into place on a drying rack over embers. The scene conveys the stoop labor involved in tending food over an open fire. When this plain open-hearth kitchen gave place to the iron hob grate and cookstove, it further separated cooks from the danger of fire during laborious tasks of turning, stirring, and removing foods from flame.

Although much of the industrialized world moved away from open-hearth technology, pockets of primitive cookery persisted where fuel was plentiful. In *Four Years in Paradise* (1941), Kansas-born naturalist Osa Helen Leighty Johnson, who photographed Africa, Borneo, and Oceania with her husband, adventurer and film-maker Martin Johnson, described a Kenyan style of cooking of hot coals. To roast fish or birds, the cook left them intact. After receiving a coating of two or more inches of clay, the meat went into hot embers for an hour. When the surface baked hard, the cook cracked it open and removed the meat, leaving skin and feathers or gills and scales intact.

In the mid-twentieth century among the Tepehuan of Chihuahua, Mexico, roasting over an open fire perpetuated traditional cooking methods that date to prehistory. For roasting squash, women set the rind in hot coals. When the meal was ready, they sliced free a bit of the rind to use as a spoon for scooping out the softened interior. Another favorite meal from hot coals was roasted potatoes and fava beans or cowpea pods, which they baked in ash.

According to Eliot Wigginton's *The Foxfire Book* (1968), a compendium of folkways from the southern Appalachians, open-fire cooks were adept at heavy food preservation chores completed at hearthside in mountain cabins. After slaughtering hogs, preparers collected trimmings from hams, shoulders, entrails, and backbone and let them chill in a lard pot. After slicing into egg-size pieces, they covered the mass with hot water and suspended it over a slow fire for all-day simmering. When the fat boiled out and water evaporated, the remainder was lard and cracklings, the hard pieces that fell to the bottom. The preparer scooped the lard into containers to harden and saved the cracklings for snacks and eating with bread.

Today, open-hearth cooking is the standard method in pre-industrial lands such as Niger, where women sit by the hearth frying kosai (bean cake) or beignets (doughnuts), and among the migratory Lapps of Norway, who live in tents and gather at a communal pot for meals of dried reindeer meat, bread and butter, and coffee. South Africans make a campfire bread called ashkoek (ashcake), the Afrikaan name for a buttermilk batter yeast bread rolled into balls and heated in hot coals. Malawians set up a cook pot either on a mudbrick kitchen floor or on stones outdoors. Chadians continue to prepare meals over a three-rock fire pit, as do some residents of the Marshall Islands. The islanders on Kiribati use an open fire for frying and baking. Cameroonians segregate by gender, with men eating at the table and women and small children remanded to the hearth. In Japan, the custom of cooking yaki-mono (grilled fish) over embers remains a popular form of cookery.

See also **Colonial Kitchens, American; Communal Meal; Pennsylvania Dutch Kitchens; Rumford, Count Von**

Further Reading

Batey, Colleen, Helen Clarke, R. J. Page, and Neil S. Price. *Cultural Atlas of the Viking World.* Abingdon, Oxfordshire: Checkmark Books, 1994.

Gardiner, Anne Gibbons. *Mrs. Gardiner's Family Receipts from 1763.* Boston: Rowan Tree Press, 1989.

Kritzman, Lawrence D., ed. *Food: A Culinary History from Antiquity to the Present.* New York: Columbia University Press, 1999.

Shoemaker, Alfred. *Christmas in Pennsylvania.* Mechanicsburg, Penn.: Stackpole Books, 1999.

OVENS

A workable oven was an essential to the first permanent dwellings. In the earliest models from the Harappan era or before, native Indian cooks of the Indus Valley depended on clay vessels sunk in the ground to store water or grain. Indian cooks used the earliest in-ground tandoor pottery oven around 26,000 BCE at Kalibanga. Ovens built in the Ukraine around 20,000 BCE were simple pits filled with coals and covered with ash, on which the cook set food wrapped in leaves, then mounded the whole operation with soil. Paleo-Indians created ovens as a means of making unpalatable foods edible. Central American natives depended on baked agave heart as a source of food during the cold dry season, when there was a scarcity of game, berries, roots, cactus fruit, and bean pods.

Bread ovens date to around 3000 BCE, when the Sumerians of Ur began baking loaves in stone ovens. The principle involved retaining heat after burning fuel warmed the walls. Re-radiated heat held best in tightly sealed cubicles. The first ovens constructed of fired brick were in use around 2500 BCE in Sumer and Egypt. Sumerian bakers advanced their technology by developing oven tops on which they could set pots and fry pans. Discovered by Sir Leonard Woolley, workable

Removing a pie from an oven.
[*NARA/Franklin D. Roosevelt Library.*]

remains of these sophisticated kitchens survive at Ur from 1800 BCE. In addition to hot-ash roasting, broiling, grilling, and spit-cooking, Babylonian cooks applied radiant heat from a domed oven, a closed chamber that indicates a subtle culinary technology.

At Glastonbury and Meare, Somerset, Iron Age cooks must have reworked the beehive or conical clay ovens on a regular basis, as they did the hearths that they replaced with a new baked clay surfacing for heating wheat cakes bound with honey. On the northern plains of Mongolia, China's nomadic Hokka people baked chicken in a shallow hole, which they lined with stones and heated with fire before covering the chicken with lotus leaves and salt for baking. In Old Testament times, Syrian cooks flattened wheat or barley dough to wafer thinness, then plastered each disk on the wall of their oven to make unleavened bread. Egyptian cooks followed the same process still practiced in Salamant, Egypt, where women stack circlets of battaw bread in ovens each day.

The early Persians made ovens of clay similar to Egyptian styles. Persian bakers nestled dough on pebbles for their rough-textured *sangak* (flatbread). At outdoor sites, Greeks hooded their barley and wheat loaves with *klibanoi* (baking cloches). In Greek kitchens of the fifth century BCE, innovators achieved a breakthrough in baking technology—the *avli* (beehive oven), a circular domed oven for home, or the commercial-size fourno of professional bakeries. Bakers, whether slaves or peasants, blended dough with honey, suet, milk, poppy, anise, or cheese flavorings and placed it in lidded earthenware pots for oven baking or topped the pots at fireside with hot coals. Romans were so taken with bread that they celebrated the annual feast of Fornax, the oven deity, each June 9 by decking ovens and mill donkeys with flower garlands. At Pompeii, the Forno di Modesto (Modestus's oven)

Horne ovens used for cooking and baking at Taos Pueblo, New Mexico.
[© *Library of Congress, Prints and Photographs Division (LC-USF34-001771-D)*]

demonstrates the huge capacity and iron door of a professional bake site, where the eruption of Vesuvius halted his staff in the process of baking 81 loaves.

Medieval Arab cooks perfected cooking in buried ovens in the early Middle Ages. By heating dishes in sealed clay jars, Sicilian cooks applied a technology paralleled in Corsica, Sardinia, and Tunisia. From the age of nationalism in the eighteenth century, legends declare that the Greek klephts, bands of Christian raiders, perpetuated the use of subterranean ovens to conceal their hilltop military positions from pursuing Muslim Turks. However, the motivation was more likely a matter of expedience for an army on the move seeking a convenient way to hold heat until their dinner was ready.

The masonry involved in building a permanent oven was a costly job that the poorer classes paid for in trade or with labor. Those who patched together makeshift ovens risked house fires, which started easily when sparks ignited thatched roofs. The wealthy in manor houses made bread in their own bakehouses and sometimes baked the dough of the serfs on their demesne for a set fee. People fortunate enough to have money and live near town could buy professionally baked bread. Those without ovens could access municipal baking chambers built to accommodate large batches. In one example from the 1300s, middle-class Genoese women dispatched their Arab slaves to do their baking in the community oven.

Additional public facilities became necessary after 1343, when the Black Death carried off so many grain growers, millers, and bakers that mills and bakeries shut down from lack of staff. In Rome, where only thirty thousand citizens survived bubonic plague, Pope Clement VI supplied ovens and imported German professionals to staff bakeries. The arrival of new recipes and techniques rejuvenated the market and improved the nation's attitudes toward bread, which Italians tended to discount below pasta in the diet.

Improvement in oven technology revolutionized medieval cuisine, which, before the twelfth century, had been limited primarily to boiling and roasting. The shift away from spit-roasting supported sophisticated cookery and sauce-making, both elements of extensive feasting. One favorite meal, plank steak, called for coating a wood saucer in drippings and topping with garlic, rosemary, bay leaf, and steak for baking in a hot oven, where it acquired a smoky savor. By the end of the fourteenth century in Provence, new homes had ovens built into the wall out of fireproof stone or brick. In Ireland, families enjoyed the smoky flavor of loaves baked in the oven cavity beside the hearth.

Into the fifteenth century in Tunisia and Muslim Spain, baking was a communal task. Because few homes had their own ovens, cooks gathered at the public market to share the neighborhood facility for bread-baking. Likewise, Sardinian bakers assembled at the community oven to make panade, a doughy tort that they stuffed with minced lamb and vegetables. While the chamber was hot, families could slide in pans of delicate cookies and tarts, bottle fruit, pot fish and birds, dry herbs and feathers, preserve meat, and season green firewood.

English manor houses of the late Renaissance replaced the medieval brick-lined kitchen oven with separate bakehouses. Working-class folk depended on an iron baking box set in the fire or constructed a brick side oven adjacent to the chimney. Until the development of the cast iron door in the 1800s, the front cover was made of wood or tin. Two-stage ovens paired a smokehouse with a baking chamber equipped on the floor with an ash chute or trap for catching residue. The addition of an ash oven below the main chamber stored ashes for soap making. As needs changed with the rise of neighborhood bakeries and wood became less plentiful with the advance of towns, the home oven shrank from six-by-four feet to a more manageable oblong four-by-two feet.

For royalty, bakeries often reached huge proportions to supply tables for state visits and court meals. In the culinary history of Basavaraja of Keladi, India, poet-king and compiler of an encyclopedia, *Shivatattvaratnakara* (c. 1714), the text describes the royal kitchen, which extended 8 feet wide and 32 feet long. At the conical iron ovens on the east side, nine cooktop stations accommodated various types and styles of cookware. On the southeast side, bakers placed loaves in the wood-fired ovens.

In the American Southwest, native American women living in pueblos baked in hornos, the knee-high beehive adobe ovens built outdoors or under a ramada for making corn loaves. The Hispanic equivalent, the hornilla, operated similarly. Through a round door, the baker shoveled dough on a peel into the inner chamber, which they fired with quick-burning mesquite branches and swept clean of ash. By sealing the front with a wooden door, the user could count on enough retained heat for an afternoon's baking. In a similar earth oven, the Tepehuan of Chihuahua, Mexico,

baked agave hearts or crowns as their ancestors did before crushing, boiling, and fermenting them into maguey or mescal.

During a stay with New Mexico natives, researcher Barbara Tedlock collected material for *The Beautiful and the Dangerous: Dialogues with the Zuñi Indians* (1993), which included a study of a woman, Tola, stoking an outdoor oven for traditional bread-baking. Tedlock described the meticulous chore of sweeping hot coals into an iron bucket and cooling down the clay floor with the swish of a cedar bough dipped in water. By sprinkling cornmeal, studying the color, and continuing the water treatment, Tola followed the gradual cooling until the oven was ready for baking. After placing twelve loaves in the oven, she plugged the vent at top, sealed the oven door with a stone slab, and topped off the door with sackcloth and wet adobe for the 35-minute baking.

Pioneer cooks made makeshift ovens on the trail. When heavy rains prevented campfire cooking, women sometimes dug a hole, lined the fire pit with rocks, placed their bread on the sagebrush coals, and topped the in-ground structure with dirt. To allow the fire to breathe, they stuck a hollow ramrod through the center as a flue. Whatever the dough, the finished product tasted of its environment, primarily dirt, ash, and sagebrush.

According to colonists of Quebec, "We were brought up in the shadow of the oven." (Boily & Blanchette 1979, 97) Paralleling styles of northwestern Europe, colonial baking of *pain de famille* (family bread) became national symbols of the Canadian way of life and brought honor to such masonry specialists as Onésime "Beau Poil" Laforêt and Léon des Bonnes Âmes. Up both sides and among the river isles of the St. Laurence Seaway and west to Lac Saint-Jean, bake ovens marked the early settlements with cemented and stone shapes that resembled large loaves of bread, symbols of its role in family continuity. Some homemakers began the oven's service with a ritual baptism, toast, and blessing by the village priest.

The province of Quebec produced some outdoor and semi-indoor ovens roofed to protect the baker in foul weather. The earliest were outdoor stone and clay types, later augmented with rejected brick from village brickyards. Horseshoe-shaped and thick-walled for the best baking, they stood on a leveled-earth or fieldstone base extending a foot into the ground and incorporated a sand buffer between stones and frame insulation of stone, straw, jute, or cedar bark to maintain heat. Positioning away from prevailing winds prevented smoke and sparks from engulfing the living quarters.

The hearth was a large flat stone or double thickness of brick, later replaced by cast iron or sheet metal. A single thickness of crumbly blue river clay, trodden in a trough with salt hay or horse or cow hair, improved the oven's durability and efficiency. Shaping the oven began with a framework of alder, hazel, aspen, or birch lattice encompassing a barrel and attached at crossing with cord, twin, or fishing filament, it resembled the Iroquois longhouse. The shape, which needed an elevated back for maximum heat circulation, began with the building up with turf, compacted sand, firewood, or compressed clay. Another variation was discarded sled runners covered in chicken wire. Lumped clay weighing fifteen to twenty-five pounds formed the exterior as the mason slowly covered the frame. The top received a thinner clay except for the front, which rose to a ridge and surrounded the door like a collar. After tapping and sealing, the mason glazed the shell with sealant, mortar, or chalk.

Following one to two weeks of hardening, the oven was ready for the final drying from a series of small cedar-wood fires, each progressively hotter to vitrify the clay. A final sealing of hairline cracks preceded the erection of a pitched roof, slanted sheet metal shelter, or wood-shingled dome and the terracing of the yard with brick or packed earth. The total project cost very little beyond labor and iron doors because local people recycled material or used natural substances.

The ovens that have survived from colonial Canada were the indoor or summer varieties, which encountered no harsh weather. When the builder added a flue, the user had to reach through the fireplace to access the oven interior, an awkward pose that limited the use of the outer hearth. A more convenient model attached to the side of the oven. Stacked nearby was the supply of cedar, pine, spruce, balsam fir, aspen, or driftwood. The baker selected fifteen pieces and crisscrossed, latticed, or tented them for maintaining air currents to feed the flame.

Long, slow baking devoured a stock of hickory ovenwood cut and split for its weekly use, which kept the interior warm for a full day or more. After bakers kindled a hot flame, they swept out ash and embers, shut the draft, and began filling the space with vessels of dough, meat, and vegetables or meal-sprinkled loaves spaced on cabbage or oak leaves, which children going "a-leafing" gathered and strung on limbs. (Earle 1975, 67) Cooks inserted a week's baking along with sweet *gâteau d'habitant* (farmer's bread), pot pie, tourtière (meat and potato pie), cookies, buns, raisin cake, and fruit cobbler. An intermediate steaming was a way of taming the heat to allow the loaves to rise further before the yeast died.

For other tasks, the oven at low temperature dehydrated fruit and winter squash, which cooks cut into chunks and spread on mesh trays. The internal dry heat deodorized and disinfected feathers and down for bed pillows and cushions and sterilized dishes, clothing,

and mattresses used by the sick. For a damp harvest, the oven removed moisture from flax, which perched in bundles above bars to keep it from scorching. Heat also hurried the desiccation of medicinal herbs. During the processing of cloth newly dyed, oven-drying filled and tightened the weave. The clever baker also used the rest of the heat for aging splits and firelogs and for browning flour for thickening stew.

Oven lore influences much of Canadian art. Painters Edmond Massicotte, Horatio Walker, Yves Lemelin, and Blanche Bolduc have traditionally focused on the oven as a center of home activity. Parade floats on Saint-Jean-Baptiste Day emphasize the value of bread-making as a strengthener of native health and well-being. A painting by Canadian artist William Kurelek depicts the domestic task of lifting loaves on a peel or slice at a free-standing masonry oven built alongside a frame farmhouse on the frontier. The curve of the baker's back implies the amount of labor involved in accessing fired bake ovens.

According to Martha Dandridge Washington's *Booke of Cookery: or, Accomplished Gentlewoman's Companion* (1799), colonial American cooks baked in a brick kitchen oven or at a large outdoor oven in an outbuilding. After settling dough into bread pans, the baker swept ash from the oven floor and quickly placed the pans inside and closed a tight-fitting iron door to preserve heat. The gradual decrease of temperature caused evaporation that produced a crunchy bread crust, and chewy, springy crumb. For a wetter heat, the baker could place shallow pans of water to raise humidity for popovers, a quick bread muffin made from flour, water, and eggs. The soapstone floor held heat and increased danger of burning hand and forearm. To counter this danger, cooks kept potholders nearby, used long-handled baking paddles to place pots in the slowest cooking section of the oven floor, and kept on hand burn ointment, pain killers, and scar treatments made from home recipes.

For the plantation or manor kitchen, smoke ovens distributed heat on outer surfaces inward for curing meats. The addition of ovens at a cellar landing, upper floor staircase, or external wall or ham room opening to the yard turned a simple domestic flue into a multi-use bake center. Wall hooks or meat hooks attached to horizontal poles held haunches and hams securely. An alternative was a meat sled, on which the cook placed raw meat and slid it in and out to check the smoking or curing process. To deter pilferers, owners often padlocked the outer door. Variant ovens were available in tin and copper. A nineteenth-century tin hearth oven was a boxy baking surface with grip handles at each side, built-in drip pan, shelves, and a reflecting lid. Alternately known as an apple roaster or poultry roaster, it compared in shape and use to the dutch oven.

In the July 1930 *Good Housekeeping,* the Smooth-top gas range, distributed by standard Gas Equipment Corporation of New York City, featured the insulated oven. The clean white appliance offered cool cookery in the era preceding the air-conditioned home. Simplifying the use of the Smoothtop was an oven heat regulator and time-and-temperature chart. The advertiser stated the concept in appealing terms: "The heat stays where it belongs, in the oven… and out of the kitchen." ("Cook" 1930, 170) An October issue of the magazine featured the Washington Kitchenette, a stand-alone electric oven on legs that prepared whole meals with safe, adjustable heat. Available from the Gray & Dudley Company of Nashville, Tennessee, and easily portable for use in homes and professional kitchens, it came with either plain metal or porcelain enamel surface for easy cleaning.

To the bread-centered Sicilian kitchen, the wood-burning tanura (oven), faced with Majolica tile, was a handsome source of loaves as well as embers to turn into charcoal and ash for shining copper. After World War II, professional bakeries replaced home bread production with standard loaves.

The revival of adobe ovens in the late twentieth-century has reminded bread fanciers of the advantages of slow baking with fragrant wood to produce an even crust and tender interior. One oven, constructed in 1988 outside Greenmount, Quebec, blends the strengths of clay and sand, which Norbert Senf and Heikki Hyytiainen hand-molded in a wood frame and air dried. A layer of vermiculite concrete undercoated the final surfacing with cement plaster, which fired to a light pink.

Many in the world have to engineer masonry stoves and ovens from the materials at hand. As explained in Josie Stow and Jan Baldwin's *The African Kitchen* (2000), in South Africa, a defunct termite mound converted easily into a pizza oven. After checking the inside for insect activity or predators, builder Edouardo Jalapeño mixed a slurry of mound material and water to seal the oven chamber. Because of the hot climate, drying the oven took only minutes. The open-door oven sat below a natural chimney, from which wafted smoke filtered through the termite tunnels below.

In the twenty-first century, ground ovens cook much of the food of the South Seas. Samoans and Niue islanders depend on both the umu (earth oven) and gas or electric ranges for cooking taro and pork for Sunday dinners and family feasts. Fijians maintain the culinary tradition of roasting in a lovo (ground oven); French Polynesian cooks wrap foods in banana leaves and roast them in the umu or ahimaa, both meaning "ground oven." Native Hawaiians refer to their version as an imu, the cook pit in which they bake taro before pounding it into paiai, a purplish pulp that keeps more

easily than the fresh-dug tubers. The Marshallese, Tuvuluans, and Micronesians also prefer the ground oven and supplement with open-fire cookery for roasting and barbecuing meat and fish.

Specialty ovens suit multiple culinary and living styles, as with the open-air beehive ovens built by the farm women of Turkey. Tunisian cooks make *tabuna* (round bread) in a cylindrical clay oven designated by the same word. In Barbuda and Antigua, cooks work outdoors at a coal pot, the local term for clay oven. Portuguese Hawaiians, once distinguished by their six-foot beehive fornos, have given up traditional baking in which they once produced potato bread a dozen loaves at a time. Their descendents, living in a Pacific ethnic mix, retain only holiday, wedding, baptism, and birthday *pao doce* (sweet bread), a creamy dough spiced with lemon peel and nutmeg.

Modern Indian restaurants perpetuate the style of the traditional *tandoor* (or *tandir*) oven, a round, clay-lined pit cooker shaped like a barrel or dome. Oven builders often sink them into the ground for maximum insulation and fire them with wood, brush, or dung. In the wide mid-Asian span encompassing Turkmenistan, Uzbekistan, Tibet, western China, and northern Pakistan, tandoori cooking takes place inside the protective walls of a portable yurt, the low sheepskin tent favored by nomads. Baking begins with the sticking of rounds of dough against the inner side of the oven. When the chewy rounds are done, the baker removes them with a wire tool and serves them to diners, who dunk or break them into bowls of black tea and eat them with yogurt. Variations include the Tunisian *taboona* and the Kurdish *tanoor,* free-standing clay and brick domes, and the Moroccan *kanoon,* a portable ceramic cylinder.

In industrialized countries, cooks have a variety of oven choices, including radiant heat, microwave, or convection styles, which regulate cooking throughout the chamber with a heat-circulating fan. For a large family or a dedicated cook, a pair of ovens offers more options for organizing food preparation at different temperatures. For those living alone, a counter-top toaster oven can heat, bake, toast, or broil a variety of foods.

The promise of speed cooking, a new wave in kitchen convenience derived from a combination of technologies. The one-cubic-foot GE Advantium, which premiered in 1999, harnessed microwaving to halogen radiant heat, a concept that professional cooks have used for nearly a decade. On the exterior, halogen lights browned the surface and heated the exterior of dense foods with conduction; meanwhile, the microwave cooked the inside by heating inner moisture.

At the January 2001 International Housewares Show in Chicago, the Ultravection countertop oven sped cooking and defrosting by sixty percent with conduction, convection, and radiant heat. The Sanyo Hello Kitty oven combined Asian design with convenience in a vertical tri-level heating chamber fronted with an expanse of glass. The appliance belonged to a line of popular Japanese goods that included toaster, waffle maker, and rice cooker. The Samsung microwave oven with Internet connection allowed the user to retrieve recipes from the company web site to a cartridge that programmed settings automatically for each dish.

Just as gas companies wooed housewives away from wood stoves in the 1880s, modern oven sellers have begun their own kitchen campaigns. To ease concerns of homemakers, Nestlé began marketing Stouffer's Oven Sensations, frozen meat kits explaining how to speed-cook pot roast and chicken. Home builders have begun equipping kitchens of new houses with GE's Adventium oven. The endorsement of chef Martin Yan, host of the PBS-TV cooking program *Yan Can Cook,* assured viewers that the speed-cooker equals and even outperforms conventional ovens. Linda Sparrow, winner of the 2000 Pillsbury Bake-Off, added another inducement to change—easy clean-up of an interior that wipes clean without scrubbing.

See also **Microwaving; Pit Ovens**

Further Reading

Boily, Lise, and Jean-François Blanchette. *The Bread Ovens of Quebec.* Quebec: National Museums of Canada, 1979.

Jacob, H. E. *Six Thousand Years of Bread: Its Holy and Unholy History.* Garden City, N. Y.: Lyons Press, 1997.

Rai, Ranjit. *Tandoor.* New Delhi, India: Viking Press, 1995.

Read, Kenneth E. *The High Valley.* New York: Charles Scribner's Sons, 1965.

Tedlock, Barbara. *The Beautiful and the Dangerous: Dialogues with the Zuñi Indians.* New York: Penguin Books, 1993.

P

PAPER

Paper, which the Chinese originated, was the first man-made flexible packaging. It began around the second century BCE with food wrappings made from mulberry bark. Around 105 CE, Tsi Lun, a courtier, invented fiber technology by grinding and soaking woody plant fiber to pound and press into sheets dried on a screen. His product, refined and simplified over the ages, slowly passed west to the Middle East and Europe. It reached Britain in 1310 and the New World in 1690, when the first papermaker set up shop in Germantown, Pennsylvania.

Shortly after 1600, the Chinese also invented cardboard, which was first produced in England in 1817. By 1850, factories were turning out corrugated paper, a lightweight crating material that replaced wood slatting for egg and produce boxes. In 1870, Robert Gair, a Brooklyn bag maker, began cutting and creasing paperboard to create semi-flexible packages. Food distributors were shipping foodstuffs safely in heavily faced paper cartons in 1900, when shippers attempted to reduce freight charges and handling of bulky wood crates.

Paper acquired multiple kitchen uses. In the Renaissance, cooks experimented with beef, which they grilled *en papillote* (in buttered paper) as a flavor-enhancing and tenderizing method. Because women carved at table, they applied paper trim to the feet of roast chickens to improve their grip and ward off slips of the knife. For adorning turkey or lamb legs or the bone protruding from a cutlet or pork chop or a cutlet-shaped croquette, they attached a cut-paper *manchette* (frill) in a circlet before presentation of the dish at table. The domestic writer John Cordy Jeafferson's *A Book about the Table* (1875) explained that such dressing had additional value as a small napkin to keep fingers well anchored and free from grease while the other hand cut into the meat. Fannie Farmer, an educator at the Boston Cooking School, sparked up cheese croquettes with a paper frill for eye appeal. In later years, one special commodity, rice paper, made from the pith of a Chinese shrub, offered an edible wrapping for macaroons and other bite-sized candies.

During the rise of Continental *haute cuisine* after the French Revolution, restaurants enhanced ambience with such niceties as dripless candles, silver-footed wine rests, and the butler or waiter's pocket crumb trays and brushes for a quick cleanup after each course. To keep soufflés neat for table service, kitchen staff wrapped casserole tops in a folded collar of white paper tied in place with string. The addition of a paper doily to the leg of lamb or crown roast of beef cost little, but added to the flair of service and the aura of sanitation. Buttered paper also served as a wrapping for pot roast or fish baked whole in the oven. For desserts, breads, and side dishes, the addition of a lacy paper doily beautified a bon bon, madeleine, or peach Melba. In *Ices Plain and Fancy: The Book of Ices* (1885), the food teacher and author Agnes B. Marshall promoted the use of dish papers to separate a saucer from the ice cream container above it.

Some types of paper had more than one kitchen use, for example, the plain paper bag, which Creole cooks used for wrapping fish for baking, and wallpaper samples, which clever decorators cut with scissors into geometrics and designs for pasting onto cabinets and kitchen wainscoting. During the sugaring of *petit fours* or condiments for table presentation, the pastry cook got extra mileage from the doily by using it as a round or rectangular template. After sprinkling a sugar cloud over the crust, the cook removed the doily to reveal the design. Another popular form of domestic paper recycling was the working-class housewife's soaking of clothes in water containing the blue wrapper traditionally tied around lump sugar, which grocers marketed in fourteen-pound cones about a yard high. As explained in an October 1836 issue of *The Farmer's Cabinet*, the paper, permeated with indigo, was worth saving for laundry, for dyeing cloth, and for shampooing gray hair, which tended to yellow otherwise.

An unassuming kitchen vessel, the flat paper bag, first made in Bristol, England in 1844 by Frances Wolle, held seed heads for drying, roots for healing potions and dyes, and herbs for cooking. Brown butcher paper or parchment kept direct sun from weakening colors, fragrance, and taste. One valuable invention from the paper bag industry was a machine designed by the inventor Margaret Knight of York, Maine, which folded brown paper into the square-bottomed shopping bag. Subsequent machine upgrades added gussets for more stretch to replace cotton flour sacks. In 1905, bag-making machinery added printing for advertisements and demonstrations of cooking with the products inside, such as corn meal, grits, flour, oatmeal, and brown and cane sugar. In 1925, additional technology produced multiwalled paper sacks sewn shut at the ends, a sturdier pantry container that held onions, potatoes, and citrus fruit. Before packaged goods rid the housewife of a need for stores of paper, the saving of wrappers and twine eased common household packaging tasks.

A thrifty domestic adviser, Jonathan Periam, author of *The Home & Farm Manual: A Pictorial Encyclopedia of Farm, Garden, Household, Architectural, Legal, Medical and Social Information* (1884), compiled methods of putting waste paper to household use. He suggested rubbing a newly blackened stove each day with paper. Likewise, he advocated paper polishing for mirrors, lamp chimneys, and windows. He added that "Rubbing with paper is a much nicer way of keeping the outside of a tea-kettle, coffee-pot and tea-pot bright and clean, than the old way of washing them in suds. Rubbing with paper is also the best way of polishing knives and tinware, after scouring." (Periam 1884, 783)

Periam suggested using flour as a polishing medium for tinware and spoons. When the housewife had gleaned all possible use of each piece of polishing paper, she could twist it into a paper spills for kindling stove fires. His long list of uses for paper included tying over preserves and pickle jars, sealing the top of canned fruit to halt mold, and lining a carpet to insulate floors. He summarized a quick floor-painting method that was easier and cheaper than floor cloths: paste on several layers of newsprint, layer with wallpaper, and varnish the top.

On the Australian frontier, where hessian or burlap curtains were the norm, homemakers seeking a bit of refinement at a station kitchen, shanty, or mining camp resorted to crêpe paper trimming. A frill of crimped paper around tinned food elevated simple trade goods to a holiday treat. Christmas called for table crackers, the bright cylinders that pulled apart with a pop to deliver a trinket or burst of confetti. Homely cupboards got a boost from application of fringed or scalloped paper lining that draped the outer edge of shelving to add color and a sense of order and cleanliness, such as that sold in Wanaaring, New South Wales, in 1905. As decor, paper was cheap, easily fashioned to individual tastes, and renewable.

In the United States, Scott Paper Company, founded in 1879 by brothers Irvin and Clarence Scott and later merged with Kimberly-Clark, introduced paper toweling in rolls in 1907 to improve sanitation in Philadelphia schools. In 1921, the company improved the fiber to make it thirstier and scored a hit with housewives with Scott Towels. Throughout the century, more paper kitchen items came from the fiberboard and wood pulp industry, which molded lightweight, disposable pails, scoops, jars, and other containers from chemically treated pulp. The industry failed, but preceded other twentieth-century disposables.

During the increase of socialism in the 1880s and 1890s, the advent of community kitchens, dining clubs, and cooking services alleviated women's kitchen chores. In the June 1919 edition of *Ladies' Home Journal*, Myrtle Perrigo Fox and Ethel Lendrum published "Starting a Community Kitchen" with instructions on running a low-cost co-op. For transporting food during the hardship years of World War I, the co-authors described a method of recycling cereal boxes, oatmeal cartons, and newspaper into cylindrical insulators for fruit jars or basket liners for casseroles. The reuse of paper that would have gone out with the trash enabled deliverers of goods to secure breakables and maintain cold or hot foods at ideal temperature without requiring investment in thermos bottles or other cumbrous containers.

Paper candy cups and confection cases came on the market in 1904 and were featured items in the Duparquet, Huot & Moneuse catalog. Fluted sides, lace edging, and handles enhanced simple serving containers, which machines shaped as baskets, hearts, cups, dishes, bowls, firkins, and pails. The party cups upgraded servings of fudge and candies as table decorations and party favors, which children carried home from birthday and holiday celebrations. By 1932, Sears, Roebuck was selling paper crinkle cups for baking that promised no burned bottoms on cupcakes and impressive display of nuts and candies for parties. One box of one thousand cups sold for 92 cents.

Paper uses and recycling methods became standard topics in women's magazines and newspaper domestic columns. In the June 1922 issue of *House & Garden*, Ethel R. Peyser's essay "Tinware, Rubber and Paper for the Kitchen" listed wise and unwise uses for paper. She advocated wiping a greasy stovetop with crumpled paper, lining shelves with paper and lacy edging, draining french fries on absorbent brown paper, and serving on disposable paper plates for camping, picnics, and retreat cabins. Specific paper goods worked well for lining drawers and placing under finger bowls; waxed paper wrapped sandwiches and pastries for travel. On the down side, she advised against wrapping ice or fresh produce in paper to preserve it in the refrigerator because of the transfer of flavors to foods.

Into the 1930s, paper goods remained regular features in women's magazines. Regal Paper Company of Pulaski, New York, advertised regularly in *Good Housekeeping* the many uses of Pic-Wax, a domestic waxed paper available in sheets or rolls. Photos and line drawings depicted women selecting sheets for wrapping sandwiches for bag lunches and pulling off lengths for encasing slices of pie. The company promised convenience and economy from a product that kept foods from drying out or swapping flavors and odors with other foods in the pantry or refrigerator. Long lists of suggestions advanced from the mundane packaging in the school lunch box, waxing irons, and lining baking tins to wrapping flowers and unmolding homemade candy.

Smaller ads touted the Burgess Kitchen Memoranda, a roll of paper with pencil that fed down a metal strip to provide space for jotting dates and shopping lists, and the William M. Bevan Company's Liberty paper baking cups and table decorations, made from "specially prepared" material that withstood heat and required no oiling. ("Liberty Paper" 1930, 234) For one dollar mailed to the company in Everett, Massachusetts, the homemaker could order 428 assorted pieces—pie collars, tea cake cups, chop frills, croquette skewers, and doilies—and could receive a free recipe book, a standard lure. Milapaco, makers of lace paper doilies, exploited trends toward inexpensive elegance with snowy white imitation-linen liners for china to set the tone for refined home dining and entertaining.

In the 1940s, postwar domesticity increased the demand for domestic paper goods. In the February 1947 issue of *Woman's Home Companion*, an ad from Scott Paper for Cut-Rite offered the obligatory recipe along with suggestions for use of waxed paper to solve kitchen quandaries. A photo tutorial showed a method of melting chocolate in waxed paper in the top of a double boiler to save scouring burned-on crust. A second photo showed how to wrap and twist paper around celery stalks and lemon halves to save space. Additional suggestions included wrapping a knife in waxed paper for slicing butter. During the rise of home food preservation in freezers rather than canning jars, the same magazine advertised freezer cartons from Interstate Folding Box Company in Middletown, Ohio. The product, a collapsible pint or quart carton with liner, came with the Frostofold Kit, which included cellophane, stockinette, bags, string, funnel, and instructions on how to package foods in disposable paper freezer cartons.

Women's and family magazines fed homemakers' demand for more and better products. In 1925, *Good Housekeeping* published an ad for Rapinwax, a food wrapping product from Minnesota Wax Paper Company of Saint Paul that prefaced a deluge of commercial and home products for keeping foods fresh. The January 16, 1930, issue of *Saturday Evening Post* advertised the Seabright waxed paper carton, a spiral-bound canister with matching paper lid for transporting oysters, pickles, sauerkraut, and slaw from the deli or grocery store. In the 1930s, *Woman's Home Companion* featured full-color ads for Trimz, a ready-pasted wallpaper made by United Wallpaper of Chicago. For kitchen redecoration, the product line offered patterns like Palmetto and Berry Patch in washable, fade-proof paper to enhance plain walls. Advertisements paired husbands and wives at work cutting and applying without special tools and boasted that work begun at lunch could be finished by supper, a domestic emphasis on mealtime and reviving the kitchen. For simpler, less expensive updating of the kitchen look, Royledge offered shelf liner and dye-cut edging that quickly altered a plain wood cabinet to a lace-trimmed, scalloped, or fruit motif.

Currently, paper remains a valuable, but underrated, material for its assistance to domestic chores. The paper vacuum cleaner bag and furnace filter make home clean-ups easier and less expensive. Disposable paper bibs simplify the chore of cleaning up food dribbles and milk stains after feeding a toddler. Either on a roll or pre-shaped, silicone-coated, reusable vegetable parchment paper, available from gourmet or baker's shops, lines pans for nonstick baking and covers casseroles during baking. Fluted candy cups and muffin cups still hold confections and batter for the baking and transportation of corn, bran, and breakfast muffins. Decorative paper loaf pans, made of grease-proof material, offer the holiday baker a container for cooking as well as a one-use vessel for gift loaves. In

Europe, meat prepared for holidays is often on skewers or toothpicks topped with crêpe paper flowers, animals, boats, religious symbols, and flags, for example, the French flag for Bastille Day or American flags on the Fourth of July. Favorite table decorations in most industrialized countries include disposable tablecloths, napkins, favors, and centerpieces in seasonal and holiday themes. French parchment shaped and colored like leaves adds a naturalistic touch to banquet and buffet tables and cheese trays.

See also **Garbage**

Further Reading

Hayden, Dolores. *The Grand Domestic Revolution: A History of Feminist Designs for American Homes, Neighborhoods, and Cities.* Cambridge, Mass.: MIT Press, 1985.

PAPIN, DENYS

The cast brass disgester (or digestor) prefigured the pressure cooker and autoclave. Called a *marmite* (boiler), it was the creation of Denys Papin, French Huguenot innovator of the steam engine and member of England's Royal Society. Born in Blois on August 22, 1647, he studied at the University of Angers, where he earned a medical degree. His interests ranged from medicine to physics, applications of vacuum and hydraulics, invention of a grenade launcher, and the preservation of food in cans. He assisted at the lab of a mentor, Christiaan Huygens, at the Royal Library at Paris and directed experiments at Ambrose Sarotti's Accademia Publicca di Scienze in Venice.

While working in the London laboratory of physicist Robert Boyle in 1679, Papin altered a stewpot into an all-in-one pressure steamer by adding a screw-top lid and fuel chamber. He built from iron and bronze a wood-handled iron cylinder, in which the user added fuel through a small door. Above, in a bronze cylinder, the cook heated food in a hermetically sealed chamber capped by the cover and cranked into place at two iron catches. Because the seal remained tight, Papin could heat water above the boiling point.

When clamped into place with weights attached to the pressure lever and heated over a bunsen burner, Papin's apparatus raised pressure within the pot to dissolve bone and gristle and cook meat to a pulp in minutes. The pressure was the source of the speedy heating and the reason that the *marmite* killed microbes. When the basin heated liquid to steam, the temperature rose as high as 266 degrees Fahrenheit. Because of the increase, food absorbed heat rapidly, cooked quicker without losing as many nutrients, and contained fewer bacteria to spoil the contents.

Holding as much as fifty-five gallons, the *marmite* benefited humble kitchens by tenderizing cheap cuts of meat. Papin demonstrated its application in a pamphlet for the Royal Society in hopes of impressing and earning patronage from Louis XIV. Because Papin's first model lacked a safety valve, the digester endangered the user. A more complicated adaptation supplied a safety arm steadied at one end with a set of weights. The improved apparatus fit onto its own charcoal brazier.

For his ingenuity with steam devices, furnaces, and pistons, in 1687, Papin advanced to chairman in mathematics at Marburg, Germany, but died in poverty after a lifetime of seeking patronage. The upgraded straight-sided *marmite*, advertised in *American Home Cook Book* (1854), served hospitals, cafeterias, and ships' galleys. The device enabled the merchandising of gelatin, which French army cooks prized for its light weight and versatility. French nutritionists applied gelatin from Papin's digestor to treating cancer, diabetes, infection, jaundice, tuberculosis, and ulcers and advocated it to nourish starving people.

Further Reading

Fallon, Sally, "Broth Is Beautiful," *The World & I*, July 2000, 132–139.

PARERS

An apple parer is a valuable labor-saving apparatus for peeling, slicing, and storing apple pieces for drying. Some also suit the preparation of hard pears, potatoes, carrots, parsnips, kohlrabis, and other vegetables and fruits with firm meat and smooth exteriors. Whether of wood or iron, the device originated in a complex arrangement of wheels and shafts. Later upgrades to peeling machines added cogwheels, meshed gears, and belts for versions that fit on the lap or at a table. Some models cored as well as peeled. Large parers stood on legs to allow peelings and scraps to fall into a bucket, which the thrifty householder could boil into jelly to make the most of the fruit.

The hand-cranked apple parer with exposed blade or spoke shave is datable to several inventors. In 1778, thirteen-year-old Eli Whitney launched his tinkering career with a parer. Three years later, Vermont inventor Joseph Sterling claimed to have perfected the first gearless model. Dr. Anthony Florian Willich, compiler of *Domestic Encyclopedia* (1804), credits mechanic Moses Coates of Dowingtown, Pennsylvania, who patented his peeling device on February 14, 1803. Its simplicity and speed impressed Willich, who predicted the parer's success.

PASTA

After 1820, cast iron models, some made more efficient with gears, replaced the homemade styles, such as the wooden bench model, which resembled a three-legged knife grinder, and the straddle or saddle parer, a leather and iron model that provided a wood seat for the user. A rarer version was a small unit equipped with a two-prong fork to hold the fruit and a leather strap to attach the device to the leg, thus leaving the hands free for positioning apples and cranking the handle. The addition of a spring to the blade enabled the parer to save more pulp because the movable blade glided more evenly around the surface. According to Edward Knight's *A Practical Dictionary of Mechanics* (1874), the patent office had already processed over eighty innovations in paring. Subsequent alterations include devices to spiral slice, segment, and core.

In 1974, master chef James Beard and others compiled *The Cook's Catalogue*, which offered suggestions from experts on outfitting the home kitchen. The book recommends the White Mountain apple parer and corer, a painted cast-iron frame that screwed to the table or counter top. Formed of stainless-steel shaft with tinned iron prong and wood knob handle, it bore kinship with the familiar cast-iron meat grinder. Made by the Goodell Company, it retained early American styling, but streamlined the chore of impaling the apple and steadying it against a blade. A sharp hook removed the core at the same time it cut the fruit into uniform slices.

PASTA

The provenance of *pasta secca* (dried pasta) is unclear, particularly among paleoagronomists who reconstruct the agriculture and diet of ancient times. Pasta appears as a first in the anecdotal culinary history of ancient Rome as well as of Arabia, China, Etruria, and Greece. In Book I, Stanza 6 of his *Satires* (35 CE), the odist Horace looked forward to leaving the Circus Maximus and Forum to return home to a simple menu: *ad porri et ciceris refero laganique catinum* (to a bowl of leeks, chickpeas, and fried strips), an indefinite food item that may have been a dumpling, the offshoot of the Greek *laganon*, a pancake. (Chase 1905, 153)

One version of pasta's creation declares it the product of Tartar and Chinese kitchens, which Marco Polo introduced to Venice in the early 1300s. However, evidence from trade and cuisine in China points to strips of dried paste compounded from breadfruit or the sago palm, which would produce the grainy flavor that he recognized as barley. More likely is the speculation that the Arab military invented *itriya* (pasta) to replace *sawiq* (dried barley) as a portable, shelf-stable foodstuff. However, research on this supposition is sketchy.

One clue is the mention of *aletria* or macaroni in the writings of alchemist Arnaud of Villaneuve, an early fourteenth-century translator of the medical texts of Kazakastanian physician Avicenna, author of *Qanun fi at-tibb* (The Canon of Medicine, c. 1050).

Evaluation of pasta-making flour turns to literary, graphic, and forensic evidence of the appearance of durum wheat, a warm-weather, high-protein grain that flourishes in Australia, Ethiopia, North Africa, North and South America, and Russia. In the first century BCE, in the last days of the Roman Republic, the orator Cicero referred to pasta as *laganum*, but he speaks of its source as a product that paleobotanists identify as *Triticum aestivum* (soft bread wheat), a mutation of Egyptian emmer wheat and wild grass that occurred as early as 6000 BCE. Shoring up arguments against the early appearance of durum wheat is the absence of sufficient grinding apparatus to turn hard kernels into refined flour suited to making bread and cake. With primitive mills, the type of grain grown in Republican Rome could have produced only coarse flour, suited to couscous, porridge, and *pasta secca*. However, no surviving evidence points to a cuisine based on pasta.

Durum wheat surprised journeyman Chau Ju-kua, a Chinese tourist in Muslim Spain in the 1100s. He remarked on the ten-year storage of wheat in granaries, a hedge against hunger not possible with China's softer, less hardy wheat. As of 1150, said geographer and encyclopedist Al-Sharif al-Idrisi (or Dreses) in *The Book of Roger,* the port of Trabia, Sicily, supplied Italy and Arab lands with pasta. Subsequently, brief mention of pasta crops up here and there:

- In a Tuscan menu surviving from 1188, the staff of the bishop of Luni served a dish similar to macaroni.
- Another reference to strings of dried pasta survived from a document notarized in 1244 in Genoa.
- In a second notarized paper, Ponzio Bastono mentions a listing from 1279 that includes a box filled with macaroni.
- In 1284, a Pisan baker employed staff to make and sell vermicelli.

Without doubt, by the late 1200s, a century before Marco Polo's return from the Far East, Italians were making ravioli and lasagna, which they called pasta *tagliatelle,* out of *Triticum turgidum* (hard durum wheat or semolina), the only high-gluten grain that accommodates stretching during the drying stage. Obviously, he had observed pasta-making of *vermicelli, lasagne*, and *lagana* (a thin crêpe) in Italy from boyhood. In this same period, Sicilian kitchens were also producing a version of *maccheroni,* which the *Declarus* (c. 1380) of Palermo philologist Angelo Senisio described as dough boiled in water, a suggestion of the cooking method for *gnocchi* (dumplings) rather than thin-walled pasta.

In general, Europeans attributed pasta to the south, as characterized in Sicilian soup, a time-consuming macaroni recipe found in Platina's *De Honesta Voluptate et Valitudine* (On Right Pleasure and Health, 1475), and in macaroni preparation in *Il Libro de Arte Coquinaria* (The Book of Culinary Art, 1548) of Christoforo (also Cristoforo or Christofaro) di Messisbugo (or Messisburgo), steward of Hippolyte d'Este, cardinal of Ferrara. In the former, the daunting task of inserting a wire into the core of a length of dough would hardly encourage the average cook, but would increase the savory blend of sauce tunneling through the bland, wheaty exterior. Platina also explained how to beat flour, dye it with saffron, and form vermicelli for sun-drying. His recipe for sauce called for almond juice, goat's milk, and sugar.

However and wherever it evolved, pasta was a momentous addition to world civilization for several reasons. It stored well, thus allowing the warehousing of foodstuffs against famine and fueling monetary speculation during peacetime and war based on predictions of price and demand. More important to the global economy, the formation of hardtack and pasta from durum wheat permitted galley kitchens to feed ships' crews over long ocean journeys of the type that introduced Europe to the Western Hemisphere.

By the 1500s, macaroni had become an Italian and Provençal staple, produced in Naples, Genoa, and Marseilles. In 1586, a Bolognese inventor applied for a patent on a pasta maker as though he expected to profit from selling the gadget to home cooks. The *chitarra*, a stringed device, allowed the cook to press slabs of dough into thin strips for cooking with sauce. Recipes for pasta with spice or topped with cheese appeared in southern European cookbooks. As stated in the anonymous *Thrésor de Santé* (Compendium of Health, 1607), southern France produced spaghetti and vermicelli, which cooks flavored Arab style with cheese, goat's milk, nutmeg and cinnamon, rose water, and almond milk.

At this point in pasta history, the tomato was the Western Hemisphere's contribution to its development. It was hardly new to native Americans—Peruvian containers from 500 BCE carry the remains of a tree variety. The arrival of the tomato in Naples in 1522 did not immediately transform pasta sauce into the familiar marinara. Described by historian Paul Lunde, yellow varieties called *pomodori* (gold apples) thrived in Spain and Italy, but carried an ill savor as a poisonous fruit. To rid them of toxins, cooks boiled them thoroughly into sauce, a natural accompaniment to bland pastas.

As factories opened, like Bologna's first pasta mill, founded by Giovanini dall'Aglio in 1586, home cooks had less work to do to make Italy's national dish. At a faster pace, recipes for vermicelli, lasagne, macaroni, and filled and ribbon pastas dotted Mediterranean texts, including the *ragù de maccheroni* (macaroni stew) made by chef Alberto Alvisi, cook for Gregorio Chiaramonti, the Cardinal of Imola and later Pope Pius VII. In the kitchen of Marie Louise, Duchess of Parma and wife of Napoleon, chef Vincenzo Agnolloti filled tortellini, nicknamed the "sacred navels of Venus," and baked macaroni in molds to assuage some of the unhappiness of his mistress's marriage to an exiled king.

The use of macaroni in cookery was so established in the 1700s that it became a slang term for foppery. Scoffers connected the powdered ringlets on the wigs of dandies with the curvy pasta. The term formed a curious conclusion to the colonial tune "Yankee Doodle," which describes a self-absorbed swain who "stuck a feather in his cap and called it macaroni."

Vegetable enthusiast F. Vincenzo Corrado, Neapolitan author of *Il Cuoco Galante* (The Gallant Cook, 1778), one of Italy's first well-rounded cookbooks, grew lyric on the possibilities of marrying pasta to the tomato. Among his recommendations was the inclusion of the tomato in sauce to top macaroni as well as eggs, fish, meat, and vegetables. He proposed a universal base to be garnished and flavored in a variety of ways. In his estimation, the tomato was flavorful and beneficial to digestion because of its high acid content. His text explained how to hold a tomato over hot embers, then submerge it in boiling water to loosen the skin, a process that became the kitchen standard. He suggested removing seeds through a hole in the stem end.

The hard work of macaroni making altered in the Renaissance to wrapping dough around iron rods, smoothing out the tubes, then cutting the whole into appropriate lengths. More creative cooks spiraled strands into *fusilli* (coils), dimpled small lumps into *orecchiette* (little ears), and twisted strips into *cappelletti* (little hats), supposedly inspired by Napoleon's tricorns. German poet Johann von Goethe's *Italian Journey* (1788) summarized the Girgenti family's process of making dough from *grano forte* (durum wheat) and molding it around a finger. He commented that the work required manual dexterity. The method shifted from the use of fingers to *busi* (straws), around which the pasta-maker rolled macaroni makings. After sliding the straw from the pasta, the cook formed *maccarruna di zitu,* one of many common Sicilian pastas made and dried in the sun for the food fair that concluded the annual Lenten carnival.

By the time of Thomas Jefferson, in 1802, the chef was stocking pasta in the presidential kitchen, according to an account of a diner, the Reverend Manassah Cutler, a Federalist senator, who discussed pasta ingredients with explorer Merriwether Lewis. The conversation, recorded in Cutler's *Life Journals and Correspondence* (1888), described "a rich crust filled with the strillions of onions, or shallots, which I took it to be, tasted very strong, and not agreeable. Mr. Lewis told me there were none in it; it was an Italian dish, and what appeared like onions was made of flour and butter, with a particularly strong liquor mixed with them." ("Jefferson's Table") Cutler's unfamiliarity with macaroni suggests that it was just making its debut in the United States.

Into the nineteenth century, because of the high cost of flour, pasta had not yet found a place in the pantries of the working class. It acquired versatility when paired with a tomato sauce mentioned in *La Cucina Teorico-Pratica* (The Theoretical and Practical Kitchen, 1837), written by Italy's premier food author, Ippolito Cavalcanti, Duke of Buonvicino, who also offered recipes for fish and clam dressings and carbonara, an egg and cheese sauce. Late in the 1800s, new milling methods made white flour more available to all classes of pasta makers. As a result of the leveling effect of the Industrial Revolution, peasant cooks and chefs to the wealthy began the transformation of pasta to an egalitarian staple. The poor were able to buy small amounts of meat, stretch the pot with sauce, and serve it over tagliatelle, a popular form of fettucine.

In 1920, Roman restaurateur Alfredo di Lellio added to the popularity of pasta dishes by inventing fettuccine Alfredo. Unlike the current cream-heavy version, he made a light, flavorful *parmigiano reggiano* cheese sauce, as described in Gil Meynier's *Conducted Tour* (1931): "A spoon in one hand, a fork in the other, he made a few graceful passes over the dishes on which butter, cheese and *fettucini* were waiting to be mixed by the master. The spoon delved into the heap of flat, golden, ribbon-like spaghetti and lifted it toward the caress of the fork which in its rapid movements carried a piece of fast-melting butter. The grated cheese penetrated into the lower layers of the deftly malaxated mass." (Levy 1997, 225) Legend claims that honeymooners Mary Pickford and Douglas Fairbanks, Jr., named the dish to honor the inventor. In 1928, George Rector, world-class food critic and owner of New York City's Rector Restaurant, reprised the recipe in *The Rector Cook Book*.

In the United States, the Golden Grain Macaroni Company introduced North American diners to Italian-style pasta. Founded in New York in 1890 by immigrant Domenico DeDomenico, renamed Charlie at Ellis Island, five years later, the business reopened in California as a fresh produce store, the first of a chain. After marriage into the Ferrignos, owner of a Salerno pasta factory, in 1912, DeDomenico and his sons began wholesaling pasta. In 1958, the company established itself as an American original with the television marketing of an Armenian rice pilaf recipe as Rice-A-Roni and, in 1964, with Noodle Roni Parmesano.

In the 1930s, women's magazines promoted the use of dry packaged pasta as a time saver. Images of a clock showing the lapse of five minutes accompanied text that promised no pot watching for the cook choosing Quaker Quick Macaroni, a "strength-building product of the Quaker Oats Company." ("Don't Buy Macaroni" 1930, 221) In addition to free sample packages, the company offered a Tudor Plate spoon in the Mary Stuart pattern for two labels from pasta boxes.

The time-minded post-World War II generation popularized a pasta innovation—all-in-one meals from a box, a saver of work and pantry space. In the March 1947 issue of *Woman's Home Companion*, Kraft presented a vividly colored meal made in seven minutes from boxed macaroni-and-cheese. Ad copy stressed the elegance possible from manipulations and enhancements of ready-to-cook meals. A competitor, Chef Boy-ar-dee, lauded its spaghetti and meatballs in a can and a three-part spaghetti dinner in a box, which contained sauce, grated cheese, and dry spaghetti.

In parts of the world where boiling pasta was not a standard culinary technique, cooks have tried imaginative methods of making it palatable. When Salvadoran refugees filled Honduran settlement camps during the 1980s, they faced an unusual quandary. In the absence of tomatoes and margarine, gifts of macaroni from the Italian government were going to waste. Camp cooks improvised a dish of deep-fried macaroni, a nut-flavored snack, and ground macaroni into flour for bread. For a drink, they crushed toasted macaroni and blended with water, sugar, and cinnamon.

In the twenty-first century, Mediterranean cooks create over seven hundred shapes of *pasta secca*. Favorites are pappardelle noodles, fettuccine strips, fusilli spirals, and tortellini pockets or cannelloni tubes suited to stuffing with cheese or meat. On Sardinia, cooks shape semolina flour into *filindeu* (strings), which they cook in fresh pecorino cheese and lamb broth. Another specialty, *makkarrones de busa* (knitting needle maccaroni), is typical of hand-rolled pasta that begins as a ball of dough and spreads out thinner than a pencil in the hands of the experienced cooks of Orosei.

Italian cooks include pasta with almost every meal, serving the first dish after soup. The style varies—in the north, it comes with a white cream sauce; to the south, a red tomato-based sauce. Pasta soup, penne, ziti, rigatoni, vermicelli, and spaghetti fit an everyday menu. For holidays and Sundays, cooks tend toward entrees of meatballs, sausage, grilled meats, or a lamb or veal roast. Calabrians create home-style pasta shapes to suit church feasts. In addition to fusilli, they die cut a *paternostri* (our father) as well as the *ricci di donna* (ladies' curls) and *cappieddo 'i prievido* (priest's hat). Apulian pasta-makers make *orecchiete* (little ears); Sicilians created *cavatelli*, a shape made from ropes of dough formed of durum and softer flours. Japanese cooks value Italian-style pasta, which they emulate with *udon* (noodles), *somen* (corn vermicelli), and *soba* (buckwheat vermicelli).

Pasta-making devices range from the expensive appendage added to food processors, the chrome crank-out variety found in specialty shops, and the plastic extruder, which squeezes out spaghetti, angel hair, linguini, noodles, gnocchi, and spaetzle, a German noodle, in the same style as pastries from a cookie press.

See also **Renaissance Kitchens**

Further Reading

Andrews, Colman. *Everything on the Table*. New York: Bantam, 1992.
Costantino, Mario, and Lawrence Gambella. *The Italian Way*. Lincolnwood, Ill.: Passport Books, 1996.
"Don't Buy Macaroni," *Good Housekeeping*, September 1930, 221.
Kasper, Lynne Rossetto. *The Splendid Table*. New York: William Morrow & Co., 1992.
Lunde, Paul, "New World Foods, Old World Diet," *Aramco World*, Vol. 43, No. 3, (exhibition issue), 47–55.

PATTEN, MARGUERITE

Marguerite Brown Patten, Britain's wartime food commentator, continued her role as food maven by hosting one of the first televised cooking programs. She was born on November 4, 1915, to teacher Elsie Anne and Wallace Henry Brown. After her father died, she wanted to study acting and spent seven months with the repertory company at Oldham. When actors discouraged her ambitions because she was only five feet one inch tall, she found work as the senior home economist for Frigidaire to explain to homemakers the importance of refrigeration to food hygiene. During World War II, she was a consultant for the Ministry of Food's advisory bureau at Harrods department store. In 1943, she began broadcasting five-minute radio segments called *The Kitchen Front*.

While her husband, squadron leader Charles Alfred Patten, served in West Africa as a relief commanding office at war's end, Patten made friends with refugees, who attended her demonstrations and shared their recipes from home. She went on BBC-radio's series *Woman's Hour* in 1946 as a practical cook dealing with the privations of postwar rationing and shortages. The next year, she hosted one of the nation's first televised cooking programs, sharing with Philip Harben the weekly *Designed for Women*. Against gray curtains on a stripped-down set, she trusted her normal persona and expertise before an audience of war brides. Her job lasted into the early 1960s, but the influence of such books as *Marguerite Patten's Post-War Kitchen: Nostalgic Food and Facts from 1945–1954* (1998), *We'll Eat Again: A Collection of Recipes from the War Years* (1985), and *The Victory Cookbook* (1995) remained strong as records of the years of rationing and shortages. Additional cookery programs for television included *On This Day, Cookery Club, Food and Drink,* and *Marguerite Makes a Meal*.

After years of teaching England to cook with a minimum of equipment, Patten promoted frozen foods and took up late twentieth-century kitchen electronics by championing the food processor. Her accomplishments include publication of some 165 titles selling over seventeen million titles plus cooking cards and articles composed with the ordinary cook in mind. In addition to serving on the Forum on Food for the Royal Society of Medicine, she presided over the Guild of Food Writers' Microwave Association. She delivered eleven cookery shows at the Palladium and many lectures, speeches, and demonstrations. In 1991, she earned an Order of the British Empire for contributions to the culinary arts. In 1995, she received the Guild of Food Writers's lifetime achievement award, followed by the Andre Simon Award and the BBC Good Food Awards.

In 1999, Patten published two hundred classic recipes from the 1900s in *Marguerite Patten's Century of British Cooking*, which BBC-Radio presented in ten half-hour segments. For research on World War I, she collaborated with her grandson. Her selection of dishes from each era began with historical background, as with Victorian and Edwardian taste for pulled rabbit, shoulder of mutton, brown Windsor soup, and deviled kidneys, all delivered on ornate salvers by armies of servants. She depicted the 1950s as the era of the hostess cook and characterized 1960s modernism with such European and Mediterranean fare as prawn cocktail, Sole Veronique, Pavlova, and Black Forest Gateau. For the 1970s, she wrote about the emergence of the banana in recipes and depicted postmodern multiculturalism with Thai green curry, polenta *au gratin*, and sticky toffee pudding. She referred to classic recipes as esteemed old friends.

Still working from her Brighton home in her nineties, Patten published a culinary nostalgia book, *Spam: The Cookbook* (2000), drawing on history and memorabilia from the 1930s. The book emphasized that, by the last years of World War II, 90 percent of

Hormel's canned meats were bound for military field kitchens. Among the twenty recipes she included were Thai Spam Cakes and Spam steaks in Port Wine.

Patten hosted the SPAMmie Awards 2000, an annual event acknowledging the favorite working-class convenience food. For her publication of a Spam cookbook and such recipes as Spam and mushroom ramekins and Spam slippers, she received a lifetime achievement award for sixty years of service to the chopped meat product. In December 2000, she was cameoed on BBC-TV's *This Is Your Life* as England's prime culinary historian. In interviews summarizing her career, she admitted to a fondness for *Cookery in Colour* (1993), her first book to employ color photos, and for *Everyday Cookbook* (1968), which gave more of her personal views than previous works. She also enjoyed covering the history of tea in *Complete Book of Teas* (1989).

Further Reading

Milton, Jane, "Out to Lunch with Marguerite Patten," *Candis Magazine*, January 2000.
Pattinson, Georgina, "Ability to Touch on Powers of the Mind," *Irish News*, September 7, 1999.
"SPAM: The Cookbook," *Publishers Weekly*, June 4, 2001, 76.

PEMMICAN

Pemmican was North America's first camping food. Because of their itinerant life, Eastern Cree, Ojibwa, Kiowa, and Naskapi cooks had need of packable, manageable food that required little preparation and cooking on the trail. The answer to their quest was pemmican, a high-energy trail mix formed of minced fish, jerky, venison, or other meat pounded with a maul and congealed with kidney fat, marrow, ground nuts, honey or molasses, marrow, and wild greens. The French *coureurs de bois* (woodsmen) described how Ojibwa women dug a hole, lined it with skins, and used it as a mortar for pounding dried meat with a stone pestle. The blend, seasoned with pulverized cherries and sealed with melted fat for packing in hide containers, could remain up to three years in the ground. Cooks in the Pacific Northwest varied the recipe with seal or sturgeon oil. The Chipewyan, itinerant caribou hunters of the Hudson Bay, dried meat for stuffing into caribou intestines. The nutrient value of pemmican was roughly four times that of fresh meat, a boon to tribes during long sieges, epidemics, and famines.

A task relegated to women, the job of making pemmican called for stocking snack carriers and travel containers of animal intestines with protein-rich foods. By slicing pemmican into quarter-inch strips, drying it on willow lattice into *viande seche* (dried meat), and

stuffing it into the casings, they provided trail provisions that stored well up to five years in the open air. According to minerologist and frontier journalist William Hypolitus Keating's *Narrative of an Expedition to the Source of St. Peter's River, Lake Winnepeek, Lake of the Woods* (1824), the main meat for Indians was buffalo minced thin, jerked or smoked, dried crisp before a fire, then pounded. A variation involved stuffing casings with chopped meat to form treepies, an Indian sausage. Some recipes also called for grasshoppers, a common substitution when game was scarce. An Inuit variation called *giviak* involved stuffing baby birds into sealskin, which the cook buried in a cache to ripen for several months.

Flavored with unseeded pounded buffalo berries, wild grapes, cherries, chokeberries, juniper berries, elderberries, wild plums, gooseberries, currants, serviceberries, or soapberries and molded into cakes or pressed into casings, the Dakota Sioux *wasna* (pemmican) was a nutritious meal requiring no preparation. It provided snack food and the makings of soup, which needed only a quick rehydration in boiling water. Pemmican figures in the American history of the French-Canadian woodsmen, fur trappers and traders, and expeditions into the wild. In the Great Lakes region, pemmican was a trade item among the Métis trappers, who regularly shipped pemmican, furs, dried buffalo haunches, and moccasins and skin shirts in exchange for manufactured goods, cook pots, and tools from the East. One explorer, fur trader Alexander Mackenzie, author of *Voyages from Montreal on the River St. Laurence through the Continent of North America to the Frozen and Pacific Oceans in the Years 1789 and 1793* (1801), traversed the continent from east to west in 1793 with the aid of pemmican.

In the 1850s, the Red River Métis, who dominated the pemmican market, specialized in dried meat. Over their long canoe and ox-cart journeys to the Hudson's Bay trading headquarters, they relied on pemmican as a tasty, low-bulk traveler's food that would not spoil and needed no additional ingredients and no stopping to build cook fires. To save space for other goods, they cached it along regular routes to St. Paul, Minnesota, and across the Dakota border along the Red River Valley to Fort Edmonton in Canada. The company provisioned northern outposts and the *voyageurs* of the boat brigades with pemmican, which they stored on rocks like fire logs to reserve for hard times.

Colonial American cooks emulated native American recipes for pemmican by adding local wild cherries, dried fruit, and maple sugar to rendered fat. Hunters and trappers stocked strings of pemmican in frontier cabins, where they stayed fresh suspended from beams. At a meal with natives in 1804, explorer George Rogers Clark of the Lewis and Clark expedition commented that hosts honoring them with a meal "put before us the dog which they had been cooking, and Pemitigan (pemmican) and ground potatoe and several platters." (McCutcheon 1993, 183)

Pioneers also relied on stored meat for trail food, which they learned to preserve by emulating native American cooks. The best storage containers were buffalo hide sacks, which they sewed during the winter to ready them as carryalls for the spring herd migration. In 1820, seven years after New York inventor Thomas Kensitt developed the tin can, Sir John Richardson, surgeon and naturalist in Sir John Franklin's exploration of the Canadian Arctic coast, advanced the primitive style of making pemmican by drying it in a malting kiln and preserving it in tins for use by campers and explorers. According to *Life with the Esquimaux* (1862), when Captain Charles Francis Hall made his way around the Greenland shore, mariners aboard his ship, the *Polaris*, relied on meat biscuit and pemmican.

In the settlement of the North American west, professional guides and amateur travelers came to depend on pemmican. In the bestselling *The Prairie Traveler: A Hand-Book for Overland Expeditions* (1859), containing advice, maps, and intineraries over the principal routes between the Mississippi River and the Pacific Ocean, army captain Randolph Barnes Marcy gave a recipe for buffalo pemmican preferred by trappers of the Northwest. The preparation called for drying flakes of meat in the sun or over a fire, pounding the flakes between stones into powder, and packing it into animal hide bags. After soaking the grainy meat in melted grease, the pemmican maker sewed the bag shut to keep the mix fresh.

The choice of pemmican was fully acceptable in expedition preparation in 1886, when Arctic explorer Robert E. Peary carried pemmican as instant food on his trek from Greenland to the North Pole. Likewise agreeable to pemmican as trail food in the wild, Dr. Frederick Cook, one-time associate of Peary, traveled Greenland and the Baffin Bay islands from 1907 to 1909. On a small foray with Eskimo companions Ahwelah and Etukishook and twenty-six dogs to pull two sleds, Cook set out with a minimum of food preparation equipment—a lamp, three aluminum pails, six pocket knives, a tablespoon, two butcher knives, saw knife, long knife, and carry bags, plates, teaspoons, and cups for three. Of his food supply of milk, tea, coffee, sugar, soup, and meat, over 75 percent of the total 1289 pounds was pemmican, primarily beef with added walrus pemmican, and musk-ox meat. To cook the food, he carried a pound of matches, two pounds of wood alcohol, and forty pounds of petroleum. Of the trio's pared-down diet, he explained, "We planned our future food supply with pemmican as practically

the sole food; the other things were to be mere palate satisfiers." (Mowat 1989, 390) Because the pemmican contained no water, it was unfrozen. Dried granite-hard, it needed prodigious chewing followed by washing down with hot tea, the one luxury of the day.

The pemmican method of cutting, seasoning, and storing food flourished in other locales. Into the early 1900s in southern Bulgaria, cooks salted pork haunches, wrapped them in hemp or linen, and laid them in high traffic areas for pulverizing under foot. Another Bulgarian method of curing meat involved pounding salt pork, seasoning with wild oregano, peppermint, savory, and thyme, and stuffing the mix into a clean animal intestine, bladder, or stomach to make *baba, starec,* or *tarbuf.* The finished product required no heating and was easily transported to laborers in the fields or at a wine harvest.

See also **Caches; Military Kitchens**

Further Reading

"Dakota Indians," *Fork, Fingers, & Chopsticks*, Spring, 2001, 3–6.
Hollander, John, "Writing of Food," *Social Research*, Spring 1999, 197–211.
Mandelbaum, David G. *The Plains Cree: An Ethnographic, Historical and Comparative Study.* Regina, Sask.: Canadian Plain Research Center, 1979.

PENNSYLVANIA DUTCH KITCHENS

From Germanic or *Deutsch* settlers—Amish, Brethren, Dunkards, and Mennonites—who began arriving in the North American mid-Atlantic states in 1682, the plain people of Pennsylvania earned the name *Deutsch* (German), which evolved into Pennsylvania Dutch. Their kitchen innovations simplified the chores of hearth cooking and food preservation. To relieve the tedium of domestic work, they made such niceties as carved and painted wood boxes for storing candles, painted tin cream cheese molds, tulip incised butter molds, and painted pottery jars. Treen carvers made elaborate spoon racks, plate racks, and dresser boards. Scallops and painted hearts, tulips, scrollery, and stars adorned lidded dough trays and troughs; bands in bright colors encircled sugar barrels. Stress on tidiness inspired them to allow adequate time for sweeping, mopping, and dusting knickknacks.

The practical Pennsylvania Dutch housewife suspended a patterned and decorated covered salt box on the wall to contain enough crystals for preserving meat or as a granular extinguisher for dousing a kitchen fire. They faced pie safes and cupboards with punched tin or zinc paneling to air baked goods and casseroles without admitting flies. Some tacked on supports at the

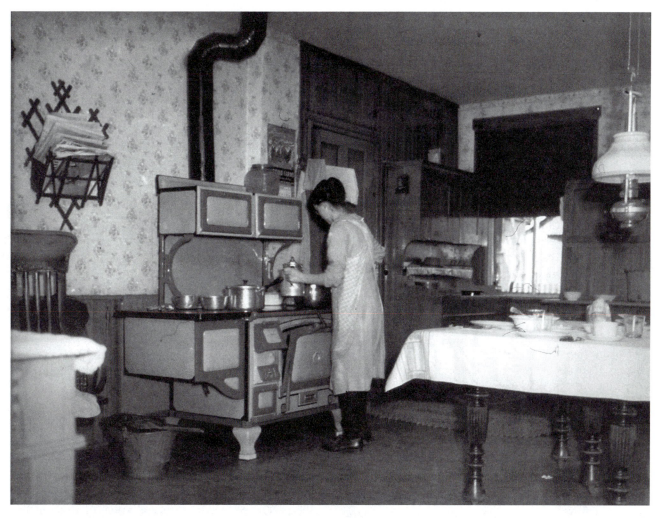

Amish Kitchen in a Mennonite home (Lancaster County, Pennsylvania, 1941).
[© *Courtesy of National Archives and Records Administration.*]

corners for suspending the entire cabinet from ceiling beams away from damp floors. For work space, they made sawbuck tables by setting sturdy narrow bread-boards on X-crossed legs with one stretcher between them. By removing a peg or bolt, the user could separate board from supports and fold all out of the way against a wall. When needed for holding serving dishes or such team activities as making apple butter, rolling out dough for turkey pot pie and homemade noodles, or canning soup mix, the tables quickly came together with a turn of a screw.

One idea to simplify drudgery was the combination measuring cup and dipper, a funnel-bottomed device that allowed the user to attach strainers of various gauges or to pour rich batter into hot oil for *Drechterkuche* (funnel cakes), which they drained on brown paper and powdered with sugar while the pastries were still steaming. Other ideas were the wall-mounted plate rack and the hanging cupboard with indented spoon rack and mug hooks for maximum tidiness of

loose objects. Cooks, who took original recipes from the German *Die Geschickte Hausfrau* (The Clever Housewife, 1848), America's first ethnic cookbook, stirred up scrapple for slicing and frying, combined sausage and apple dumplings for a typical German one-pot dish, parboiled rabbit in vinegar for *hasenpfeffer,* and built broad window shelf-sills for cooling rye loaves, apple cake, and shoofly pie.

The Easter season bore numerous superstitions. Shrove Tuesday, the day before Lent, inspired a flurry of yeast-raised mashed potato doughnuts called *Fastnachts*. If cooling pies and cookies disappeared, the fairies ate them. Such a loss to the spirit world meant that the baker would have a year's good luck.

For a meatless Lenten dish, German immigrants excelled at *Schnitz-un-Gnepp*, a layering of dried apples with dumplings in an earthenware pot like the Roman stewpot and the French *cassoulet*, both containers with a lengthy peasant history. The beauty of one-pot meals was the ease with which Pennsylvania

Dutch cooks could assemble ingredients from whatever they had on hand and cook them evenly in the tall spouted pot to pair with pickled tomatoes, ketchup, or other acidic home-made condiments. The close-fitting lid solved the usual open-hearth problems with smoke and ash tainting food. To maneuver these heavy pots about the hearth, cooks relied on iron pot pushers and hooks on a wood handle, a rough-handed treatment for clayware. After the 1700s, the three-footed redware *gumbis* pot such as those made by Willoughby Smith of Womelsdorf, Pennsylvania, gave way to cast-iron.

On Good Friday, the anniversary of Christ's crucifixion, cooks avoided all baking and burned the eggs they collected from their poultry. In place of their usual kitchen work, they applied their energies to cleaning cupboards, sweeping, and leaving home solutions of peppermint oil, sugar, and borax to kill ants and moths. The day was auspicious for making folk medicine to cure thrush and goiter or remove birthmarks and for concocting nostrums to ward off lightning from the house.

On the Saturday before Easter, thrifty cooks used catkins and onion skin to die Easter eggs. For stronger color, they steeped boiled eggs in solutions of madder for red, hickory bark for yellow, walnut shell and coffee grounds for brown, or a calico wrap in boiling water to transfer patterns from fabric to shell. At kitchen tables surrounded by children, the most creative egg decorators used pith coiled from binsa straw or rushes and glued them to the shells.

In a Christmas tradition dating to 1560, the Pennsylvania Dutch outdid themselves making marzipan or marchpane. Before Twelfth Night or Little Christmas on January 6, bakers mixed ground almonds or pulverized apricot kernels into paste, added flour or meal, and sweetened with honey, syrup, brandy, or wine. After flattening the mass, they pressed it into patterned wood molds carved with animals or flowers. A brass pastry jigger clipped off excess dough before the molds went into the oven. Finished marzipan received an icing tinted with vegetable juice. For gingerbread, a similar process involved readying spicy brown dough into pans and pressing the top with a repeating pattern. Before the baked confection cooled, the baker sliced between patterns to make individual cookies.

In 2001, Verna Dietrich, a traditional artisanal butcher from farmland outside Krumsville, Pennsylvania, perpetuated the recipes and meat products she derived from her grandmother. At her shop, by mail, and at a weekend stall at Renninger's farmers' market in Kutztown, she sold the goods derived from weekly slaughter of four lambs, five cattle, and twenty pigs plus varying amounts of capons, ducks, geese, partridges, pheasants, quail, rabbits, and turkeys, all raised on her property. Buyers felt safe cooking her meats,

because none of her stock ate the animal-contaminated feed that has caused outbreaks of mad cow disease in Europe. Certain of meat origins, Dietrich's company made traditional Pennsylvania Dutch salami and smoked and cured ham, bacon, wieners, and jerky. At a huge kettle, daughter Debbie Deitrich fried *Fastnachts* by the old method, boiled in freshly rendered lard. Of her company's meat kitchen, Verna Dietrich declared, "You won't find many places that slaughter their own pork, beef, and lambs and do their own processing....We make everything here." (Kummer 2001, 144)

See also **Amish Kitchens; Cookie**

Further Reading

Igou, Brad. *The Amish in Their Own Words.* Scottsdale, Pa.: Herald Press, 1999.
Kummer, Corby, "Sausages, Souse, and Shandybookers," *Atlantic Monthly,* July/August 2001, 143–147.
Shoemaker, Alfred. *Eastertide in Pennsylvania.* Mechanicsburg, Penn.: Stackpole Books, 2000.

PEWTER

A blend of tin with a small quantity of lead, pewter is a patinaed metal treasured as the working man's silver. The earliest extant piece, a flask made of a comparable alloy, survives from a grave of 1580–1350 BCE at Abydos in Upper Egypt. However, in comparison with antique treen, silver, wrought iron, and crockery from the past, early pewter, especially that of Roman Britain, did not survive well enough to last into current times.

Once known as "garnish," the term "pewter" also names a set of tableware, which owners have traditionally given as wedding gifts and displayed with pride on sideboards and in china cupboards. (Jekyll & Jones, 1939, 100) Pieces made by the pewterer include condiment saucers, bowls and basins, flagons, jugs, tankards, cups, and chargers for warming plates. In addition, families prized pewter salt cellars, pepper mills and pepper pots, candlesticks and snuffers, bedpans, and inkstands. Pewter ware supplied late medieval Europe with fireplace tools, eating utensils, and fenders and footmen, two necessities for the hearth that protected the floor from scorching and popped clinkers. Sets of spoons and porringers, also called tasters or posnets, flanked the table on cup hooks for a show of attractive and serviceable domesticity.

In England, pewtering dated to the Middle Ages. In 1348, the Pewterers' Company of London established ordinances standardizing alloys used to fashion chargers, salt cellars, and saucers. Pewter came into general use no later than 1533, when the Pewterers' Company

Pewter dishes at the dinner table.

listed plain-rimmed trenchers that evolved into broader, flatter edgings by 1675. Wait staff tended to blend table settings of trenchers with silver implements and vessels. Chaplain William Harrison, author of *Description of Elizabethan England* (1577), summarized the growth of the pewter industry. Of unadorned household pewter, he noted that crafters were beginning to alter flat design to deeper shapes, which held broth and sauce in wells to keep them warm. He explained that people bought these useful dishes by the garnish (set), containing a dozen each of dishes, platters, and saucers.

In 1579, an English commentator described convivial drinks poured into "pots of earth, of sundry colors and moulds, whereof many were garnished with silver, or leastwise with pewter." (Earle 1975, 98) Perhaps because of pewter's durability and ease of care, taverns sported pewter funnels, dram cups, and monogrammed drinking mugs for regular patrons. Pewter plates dominated the market until pottery took its place, introducing the headaches of careless kitchen staff explaining broken crockery. For refined tables, pewter sugar nippers accompanied the tin tea caddy to the table for afternoon refreshment.

Culinary historians summarize the amount of pewter in the New World colonies by reading wills, in which pewter and silver items received special mention as prized heirlooms. When Bethia Cartwright died in Salem, Massachusetts, in 1640, she left her sister three pewter platters, a salt cellar, six spoons, and a porringer. Upon Robert Massey's death at Ipswich in 1643, he bequeathed his two sons and daughter about the same amount that Cartwright left. At Newbury, the Reverend James Noyes died in 1656 leaving fourteen

pewter platters, four drinking pots, a basin and salt cellar, and a charger. Another proof of pewtering is a collection of molds and metalsmithy tools owned by Benjamin Day, one of the earliest pewterers working in Newport, Rhode Island, who flourished in the first half of the eighteenth century.

Ownership of these items brought the obligation to polish, repair, and resurface dull, broken, and thinning dishes. In ordinary homes in the colonial Americas, the child delegated to scrub the family pewter collected horse-tail or scouring rushes from boggy land, but the job of soldering and straightening dented items was more complex. Because of the high cost of equipment and low demand among colonists, few professional pewterers operated smithies in New England. Housewives depended on the itinerant tinker to remold spoons and solder handles.

In the winter of 1642–1643, one pewterer, Richard Graves, of Salem, Massachusetts, acquired a sullied name for multiple incidents of wickedness—firewood theft, assault, gaming, and womanizing—for which a judge sent him to the stocks and had him whipped. According to George Francis Dow's *Every Day Life in the Massachusetts Colony* (1935), Graves "was mulct by the Quarterly court" for public drunkenness at Charlestown. (Dow 1988, 88) From such lowlife came the execration "not worth a tinker's damn." In 1714, David Lyell of New York, who obviously wanted to avoid the prevailing estimation of pewterers, posted an ad in the August 23 *Boston News-Letter* that he was willing to pay good wages to any journeyman pewterer with a worthy reputation.

At the home of progressive John Endicott, governor of the Massachusetts Bay Colony, pewter was the table

PICKLES

standard. Massachusetts-born patriot John Hancock preferred pewter to porcelain, which he disliked for the sound it made when stacked. Worn pieces could be remolded and new metal applied. By 1737, families sending sons to be educated at Westminster School, according to a notice in the October 24, 1737, *Boston Gazette*, had to prove them literate and had to provide bedding and table goods consisting of six napkins, a silver spoon, a knife and fork, and a pewter porringer. These items were non-refundable.

A variant of pewter, alchymy—also alcamy, arkamy, or occamy—blended pan brass and arsenicum for a common spoon material. From the mid-eighteenth century, a favorite was britannia or white metal, compounded of antimony, copper, and tin without lead to create a glossy sheen resembling that of silver. Through brisk trans-Altantic trade in precious metals and luxury items not available in North America, colonists stimulated the prosperity of James Vickers of Sheffield, England, who went into the pewter business in 1769. His white metal tea and coffee services emulated the friezes and decorations of quality neoclassic silverplate while applying the latest technology to mass production, notably, cold rolling britannia metal into sheets and shaping it over dies, and the masking of seams beneath a raised fillet at the upper and lower sides of the spout. Owners of teapots and coffee urns made of britannia had to tolerate the metallic smell and taste that an abundance of copper caused.

The appeal of pewter held true into the twentieth century. In the 1930s, women's magazines touted pewter with connotative words like lustrous, craftsmanship, antique, and heirloom. An ad in the September 1930 *Good Housekeeping* for Pewter by Poole from the Poole Silver Company of Taunton, Massachusetts, pictured coffee service with a satin finish and assured housewives that it harmonized with its surroundings and offered no problems with cleaning and polishing.

Further Reading

Davis, John D., "Metals for the Fashion-Conscious Consumer," *Antiques*, January 2001, 220.

Mayor, Alfred, "Pewter at the Victoria and Albert Museum," *Antiques*, September 1999, 246.

Moulson, David, "The Museum of British Pewter," *History Today*, June, 2001, 3.

PICKLES

In areas where gardening is seasonal, preservation in brine or acidic liquid is one method of storing perishables. The pickling cucumber, which Persians called *soukasa*, may have been grown around 1200 BCE in the Fertile Crescent, from 2000 BCE in India, and in Egyptian soil when Moses led the Hebrews out of bondage. Writing around 77 CE, the Roman encyclopedist Pliny the Elder outlined the erection of cucumber frames for succulent pickling goods to satisfy royal taste buds at Tiberius's court. Acknowledging the need for preservation methods, the Roman Apicius, author of *De Re Coquinaria* (On Cooking, late 300s CE), the world's oldest cookbook, described a fresh sweet-and-sour dressing for cucumber salad, but indicated that the vegetable was delicate and had to be eaten fresh.

From Roman times, the cucumber as well as the calabash was preserved in brine for a long shelf life. After diners ate the solids, they drank the pickling liquid as a watered-down vinegar beverage. Roman legionaries carried the sharp brine in their ration gear because it took up little space, yet could expand with water for numerous servings.

Since 200 BCE, when the cucumber appeared in Chinese kitchen gardens, it received extensive study for its crisp texture and moist, pungent flavor. According to the *Rites of Chou* (c. third century BCE), to extend the cucumber's best qualities, the emperor's staff required sixty-one meat picklers plus sixty-two experts who pickled *zu* (vegetables), including bamboo shoots, leeks, mallow, rape turnips, and water dropwort. From contact with the Chinese pickling crew, Tartar visitors carried pickling techniques west. A Chinese pickler's guide, *Qimin Yaoshu* (Essential Ways for Living of the Common People, sixth century CE), summarized written recipes and preservation methods, 40 percent of which covered sauerkraut.

Around the eastern Mediterranean, preservation of vegetables provided the cook with numerous condiments to relieve the tedium of bread and meat. The caper, a tight bud of the *Capparis spinosa*, produced a savory flavor replicated in the Caucasus by the pickled *Capparis herbacea*, a perennial grass. The pickling of olives inspired individual creative styles among different cultures. For some, the perfect olive needed an overnight soak in water. One recipe called for slitting fruits and dropping them into a brine blended with lemon juice, lemon zest, and chili peppers. An alternate recipe recommended marination in bitter orange leaves. Variations added wild thyme, bay leaf, lemon leaf, and garlic to the mix to produce a pickled olive indigenous to the area.

The wide range of pickled goods explains the popularity of pickling as a means of preservation. The early Navaho stabilized harvests of prickly pear, a versatile cactus fruit found in the deserts of the southwestern United States. According to traveler John Locke, in Cyprus in 1553, fanciers of the *beccafico* (figpecker), a small, chubby songbird, packed them in salt and vinegar. The popular pickled bird, which cost one cent per dozen, became an eastern Mediterranean gift item dispatched to an embassy in Venice. Food writer Amaranth Sitas, author of *Kopiaste: The Cookbook of Traditional Cypriot Food* (1968), reported that Cyprus food shops still stocked the tasty bird pickles in the mid-twentieth century.

Around 1690, Indian exporters were shipping piccalilli, a popular piquant condiment made from carrots, cauliflower, cucumbers, and onions flavored with sugar, garlic, mustard, and vinegar. The original Indian pickle, piccalilli, became an English favorite for spicing up cold meat after the East India Company imported it to sell along with standard curry and chutney. Piccalilli was of value for providing hot and exotic flavor during the cold months when the table lacked flavorful vegetables.

Piccalilli appeared as end-of-the-garden relish in the Americas, where colonial housewives spread the bounty of garden, shore, and forest by preserving, candying, spicing, and marinating. For pickles, recipes applied to oysters, asparagus, elder buds, fennel, green walnuts, lemons, mushrooms, nasturtium buds, parsley, purple cabbage, and samphire, a fleshy vegetable in the carrot family. Amelia Simmons's *American Cookery* (1796), the nation's first cookbook, honored the West Indian gherkin as the best vegetable for pickling in comparison with the humble radish pod, barberry, and purslane. *Hoofland's Almanac and Family Receipt Book for 1875*, published in Philadelphia by the Johnston, Holloway Company, instructed the home pickler on use of the stoneware firkin and the creation of an acidic pickle from cider vinegar and spices. To assure good coverage, the cook sterilized a china plate to place face-down over vegetables to force them below the surface of the brine. Smaller containers required a parchment top tied into place with string or leather cording.

Late in the 1700s, Jewish traders from Baghdad infiltrated Bombay and Calcutta, bringing to India their cuisine. In 1874, the Nahoum family set up shop at New Market, a prosperous kosher food mart and bakery, where they sold fabric, produce, fish, meat, and condiments. A trademark of the Nahoum kitchen was homemade chutney and pickles, for which the cook rinsed chopped ingredients in vinegar and bottled them in small quantities for aging on the shelf. The death of scion Norman Nahoum in 1999 provoked much nostalgia over such delicacies as pickled lady's fingers [okra], preserved lemons, and bamboo shoot pickle, available only at New Market for over a century.

In late Victorian England, cooks depended on relishes and chutneys as accompaniments to meat and dry beans, which seemed bland and unappetizing without a bit of savory side dressing. From close association with the Indian subcontinent, cooks imported flavorings to produce an Anglo-Indian culinary cross-fertilization. For

the Indian *chatni*, English chutney-makers concocted a piquant side dish of fruit and vegetable bits or walnuts added to a mix of ground herbs and spices blended to a paste with coconut, garlic, lime, or tamarind. The emergence of manufactured sauces in the 1800s prefaced a flurry of grocery items in the twentieth century, including the ubiquitous brown sauce, Major Grey's chutney, and bottled ketchup.

In this same period, the question of pickling equipment caused concern. Charles Ranhofer, chief cook at Delmonico's, New York, honorary president of the Societe Culinaire Philanthropique, and author of *The Epicurean: A Complete Treatise of Analytical and Practical Studies on the Culinary Art* (1893), delivered mixed advice on the perennial question about the safety of food cooked in copper pans. He recommended tinned copper over solid copper for cookery to prevent toxins from poisoning the liver. However, in his cornichon recipe, he described boiling in spiced vinegar solution in a copper basin before pouring the pickled in a jar or barrel to marinate. The text implied that copper was safe if acid foods remained only a short period to soak up metallic toxins.

Into the 1900s, pickling was so valuable to Lithuanians and Poles that they honored a pickle folk god. Their pantries bulged with jars and crocks of prepared beet, cabbage, carrot, cucumber, rape, and turnips as well as mushrooms, apples, and pears. For *bigos*, the national Polish dish, food preparers boiled cabbages whole or heated them in an oven or outdoor bonfire. In ditches and barrels, neighbors worked together to tread the heads underfoot or beat them with clubs to extract gases and liquids. After covering the pulp with linen cloths, they pressed it—either alone or along with sour apples—into vats with heavily weighted wood lids and set them in a warm stable or kitchen for several weeks before skimming the top and storing the vessels in a root cellar or pantry over the winter.

In the late 1980s, Moroccan housewives kept lemons for cooking and for adorning tea trays by pickling them in salt. The method resembled the jarring of sauerkraut. After scoring the fruit longitudinally, the pickler stuffed the slits with rock salt and covered them with water in a jar. Several removals of mold and rejarring in a scalded container kept the lemons soft and tart for a month. In the *suq* (marketplace) of Tetouan, picklers covered tables with clay bowls of olives and pickled beets, peppers, carrots, eggplant, and onions. At Tunis, a specialist marketed miniature lemon pickles and arranged vegetable mosaics in a glass jar. Shoppers bought his goods to accompany kebabs of meat and fish.

In 1894, Karl Baedeker's travel guide to Syria and Palestine captured the contrasting cries of street hawkers in the *suq*. He reported on vendors packing their pickled *shawender* (beets), *lift* (turnips), and *khiyar* (cucumbers) in brine or vinegar and loading wooden tubs on donkeys. With plaintive cry, the seller implored, "O father of a family, buy a load; for thirty *paras* a *rotl* of cucumbers!" (Taylor 1971, 14) The Muslim homemaker immured above the street behind lattice discreetly lowered a *sallah* (basket) to make a purchase.

In the early twentieth century, Sophie Trupin's parents pickled produce to supply the family during a long prairie winter. In *Dakota Diaspora: Memoirs of a Jewish Homesteader* (1984), she explains the seasonal preservation of eggs in salt, sauerkraut in wood barrels, vats of dill pickles, and a root cellar for carrots, onions, and potatoes. The unusual pickling was watermelon, "the last things to ripen in the garden." (Trupin 1984, 60) She remembers them as "round, the size of honeydew melons, and had diagonal stripes of dark and light green. When they were ripe and very pink inside, my mother would put them in large barrels and pickle them whole." (Ibid.) To Trupin, nothing was more delicious.

Pickling has not gone out of use, even though refrigeration has lessened the need for it as a food preservative. Mauritians pickle vegetables to eat with fowl and squid; South Africans pickle fish. In Antigua, St. Kitts, Nevis, and Barbuda, *souse* is a popular pickled pigs' feet, which cooks marinate with vinegar to lessen the fatty taste. Cooks in the southern United States also make souse, but mainly in poor households. For Dingus Day, a Midwestern U.S. frolic held on Easter Monday, Polish-American cooks make *bigos* from sausage, mushrooms, and pickled cabbage to serve with corn and beer.

See also **Condiments and Seasonings; Kimch'i**

PINEAPPLE

Over the last millennium, kitchens around the globe have welcomed pineapple. A favorite of Peruvians before 1000 CE, the pineapple moved across northern South America during the campaigns of the nomadic Tupi-Guarani, who occupied vast stretches of southern Brazil, Uruguay, Argentina, and Paraguay. The fruit passed to the home gardens of the Carib of Hispaniola and from there to Europe on the second voyage of Christopher Columbus in 1493. The spiny-shelled fruit suited his galley cooks because it remained fresh for long periods. In Abu al-Fazel's description composed in 1590, the fruit earned the name *kathal-i safari* (traveling jackfruit) "because young plants, put into a vessel, may be taken on travels and will yield fruits. In color and shape they resemble an oblong orange." (Lunde n. d., 48) He continued his characterization by

describing hand-shaped leaves ending in saw-toothed edges.

Because the pineapple was difficult to acclimate to nontropical locales, its fragrant pulp and juice were affordable only to the privileged. During the rococo period, from the late 1700s to the early 1800s, placement of the long-lived pineapple as the centerpiece in massive fruit bowls preceded its symbolism as a gesture of welcome. Architects incorporated the prickly body and jutting green top in mantle carvings and over dining room doors. Designers of finials for pewter and silver coffee pots and kettles employed the pineapple and flame, replaced in the classical period by the pine cone and Grecian urn.

According to the Arabist Paul Lunde, the Ottoman Empire, a self-absorbed civilization seemingly unchanged by European discovery of the Americas, admitted curiosity about new lands and new cultures in the late 1500s. Among the first flavors and aromas to transform the closed society was the pineapple, followed by the custard apple, potatoes, peanuts, manioc, corn, and the turkey. The unusual shape of the pineapple soon appeared in woodcuts featuring plants of the Western Hemisphere. At the same time that importation of these foods introduced Eastern foods to the West, they shifted the economy and opened trade routes and exchanges with the non-Arab world. By 1657, a gift of pineapples to Oliver Cromwell had his cooks wondering how to prepare and serve them.

In 1813, the Hawaiian horticulturist Don Francisco de Paula Marin introduced the fruit to his home garden from contacts with mainlanders, who regularly shipped plants, bulbs, and slips for him to plant in his kitchen garden. Many alien plants failed to take hold, but the *holakahiki* (pineapple) was his success story. To his collection, Captain John Kidwell added the smooth cayenne pineapple in the 1880s, which he brought from English hothouses and planted near Pearl Harbor in 1890. Local cooks began pickling and preserving pineapple and adding it to cool fruit drinks, ices, and sherbets. The pineapple shape became a popular form for treen carvers, who made salt containers by chip-carving wood with a knobby exterior and a stem left hollow for filling and emptying.

After Massachusetts-born entrepreneur James Drummond Dole and William Eames established the Dole and Del Monte fruit plantations at the beginning of the twentieth century, Dole established his first 75,000 pineapple plants in 1901. Quickly dominating nearly 75 percent of the trade, the islands marketed an appealing fruit that became a symbol of privilege and hospitality. The secret to Dole's fortune in fruit was the sale of canned fruit rather than the uncertain fresh marketing strategies that had failed in the past. In 1911, he paid engineer Henry Ginaca to design a peeler-corer that could process one hundred and five pineapples a minute. To build demand, advertisers depicted the fruit as exotic and lush and available already trimmed and cored for table use. American buyers welcomed canned pineapple as a new commodity that could turn everyday meals into an island-spiced treat.

In the 1930s, women's magazines extolled pineapple in sunny yellow advertisements pairing succulent halved fruit alongside tin cans, an easy source for busy cooks. Dole's full-page advertisements in *Good Housekeeping* simplified for the shopper the meaning of first, second, and third grades, which indicated the quality and uniformity of slices, tidbits, and chunks. To introduce the prickly fruit to the uninitiated, Hawaiian Pineapple Company of Honolulu offered a free booklet, "The Kingdom That Grew Out of a Little Boy's Garden," which contained history along with thirty-nine recipes.

The magazine's forum corroborated the data on graded pineapple by explaining that No. 2 followed less standardization of color, shape, and texture and had a lower sugar content in the syrup than prime quality. The third grade contained broken slices, but was no less nutritious or sanitary. The author concluded that economy and presentation should guide the cook in choosing the best grade for canapés, mid-grade for fruit salad, and third grade for cooking. In the February 1947 *Woman's Home Companion*, Hawaiian Pineapple Products displayed recipes tested by Patricia Collier, Dole home economist.

In 1968, Tongan farmers raised coconuts for copra and oil and bananas for export to Japan and New Zealand. For their own use, they harvested breadfruit, taro, and pineapples as kitchen staples. In this same era, Okinawan pineapple farmers applied botanic technology to increase harvests and boost income from Japanese markets. Near the village of Izumi, growers sprayed growth hormones to stagger blooming over a longer period and to lengthen the harvest season. To curtail incursions of wild pigs, they resorted to an old trick—fermented mash, which left drunk pigs as easy pickings for butchering and cooking into a popular blend of pineapple with ham.

Current use of pineapples extends from pure fruit pulp and juice to ingredients for shish kabab, baked ham, and ice cream. Honduran cooks extract every drop of flavor from fresh pineapple by scraping and simmering peelings with rice and cinnamon for a nourishing beverage. Antiguan and Barbudan cooks take pride in dishes exhibiting their indigenous sweet pineapple, called the Antigua black. In South Africa, brewers blend pineapple and raisins into *imfulafula,* a popular beer. For ease of use, grocery stores sell ready-to-eat fruit peeled, cored, and sliced or chunked for addition to salads, garnishing meats, or serving on cocktail picks as an *hors d'oeuvre*. A home plunger-slicer performs the same services with a single spring action while keeping the shell intact for service as dessert dish or drink holder.

Further Reading

Billard, Jules B., "Okinawa, the Island Without a Country," *National Geographic*, September 1969, 422–448.
Lunde, Paul, "New World Foods, Old World Diet," *Aramco World*, Vol. 43, No. 3, (exhibition issue), 47–55.
_____ "Voyages of the Mind," *Aramco World*, Vol. 43, No. 3, (exhibition issue), 2–5.
Marden, Luis, "The Friendly Isles of Tonga," *National Geographic*, March 1968, 345–367.

PIT OVENS

Baking over rocks in pit or rock ovens dates to prehistory, for example, in Tahiti, New Zealand, and Samoa, cooks heated sugary ti roots in communal depressions over a 48-hour period for village feasts. To the early Celts, the breaking of an egg in hot coals was a suitable way to cook, but it required some brushing away ash before the delicacy was edible. Like the pit oven, the rock pit is a subterranean cooking chamber made by lining a hole with rocks. To slow-cook food, the user extinguishes a hot fire, then secures foods in a sealed clay pot covered in hot coals. Common around the globe, this style of cookery, a forerunner of dutch oven cookery, required cooks to crouch near the ground and maneuver from a squatting position that is still evident in pre-industrial societies.

The Maya of southern Mexico and Central America, who established a corn-based culture from 250 to 900 CE, developed an intense cookery that kept women constantly employed in preparing food. At the simple thatched pole cottages they built at the end of their fields, they divided space evenly between sleeping and eating. In the kitchen pavilion, cooks made tamales, fermented a corn drink, and spiced porridge over a pit fire. A clear division of labor kept women at domestic chores while the men cultivated the fields.

Indians of the North American plains cleaned and softened kouse or squamash roots and roasted them on hot rocks. On the long trek from North Dakota to the Pacific Ocean and back, Sacagawea demonstrated the harvesting and baking of kouse and squamash under hot coals to members of the Lewis and Clark expedition, for whom she guided, translated, and assisted in trading for mounts. Early Southwestern Indians used a stone pit oven for baking and selected juniper limbs for adding fragrance and flavor to food. They regularly baked crowns of the agave plant, which they seasoned with cattail pollen and ate leaf by leaf like artichoke heart. The Pueblo used the sugary pods of the *misquitl* or mesquite, a common desert shrub from Sonora to Texas, for mesquitamal, a cereal dish made of bean flour moistened with water, which they cooked at a pit oven. Early Navaho cooks roasted prickly pear fruits or pads into a sweet, syrupy cake; to the east, cooks baked the papaya or pawpaw whole or added its sweet pulp to nutbread. The Aztec roasted squash blossoms stuffed with minced meat and spices and tied with string.

Central and South American cooks baked manioc flour into loaves and stirred some of the starch into boiling water for a hot cereal. The fire of the pit oven, fed with buffalo chips or small limbs, served multiple purposes, for example, as heat and light for making craft materials. At pit fires of the Otomi of Mexico, they boiled amate bark and stretched it near the heat in layered strips, which they pounded with a stone mallet into coarsely textured brown paper. The Cherokee dried wapatoo roots and rounds of pumpkin at the fire, then stored them for winter stew or as handy trail food.

Another native fire pit specialty, ash cake, took shape either as an oval patty or a pone formed from a stiff corn batter and blended with the pulp of cooked beans. For wrappings, cooks used a layer of oak leaves and positioned the loaf on a heated stone, heaped on more leaves and coals and left the cake in the fire pit to cook thoroughly. When individuals were on the move, they kept nokehick or nocake, a fine meal of parched corn, in a leather sack. They added water and formed the small cakes on makeshift fire pits in the wild. They also roasted camas root in earth depressions filled with coals and covered with grass, on which the vegetables cooked under a soil lid. The finished product was shriveled and ashen, but served Northwestern tribes in winter with a sweet, succulent vegetable that could be made into bread.

Among the Havasupai living near the Grand Canyon, the preparation of a roasting pit was man's work. After gathering firewood for the sandy hollow, they received mescal heads collected by women wielding buckthorn sticks to protect their hands from sharp spines. The fire, which burned brush and wood beneath a thick layer of stones, required tamping down with poles and filling with gravel and a layer of grass on which the mescal cooked. Sealing the cook pit was more grass and a layer of dirt for a heating period that varied from twelve hours to four days. The cook's work extended to drying thin slices of mescal and flattening whole heads for drying on racks made from reeds, agave, or bear grass stalks tied with yucca leaves or rawhide.

The pit oven accommodated the foods native to other locales. The Alaskan Eskimo cooked siwash fruit cake, a specialty loaf made from the gel from the inner tissue of the hemlock that is mixed with berries and baked in cakes. Munsi cooks dug pit ovens for roasting quahogs, a heart-shaped clam. The Creek made large pit ovens for accomodating tender new corn, an annual feast that celebrated the harvest and welcomed a new agricultural year. The ritual concluded with rekindling of the hearth fire and a Green Corn Dance, a seven-day ceremony observed in midsummer.

European settlers of the Old West and cavalrymen and fur traders on the move emulated the Algonquin pit-style cooking and called their baked loaves hoecake or johnnycake, which reflects the use of the loaves as journey cake to be packed in a saddle bag for travel. On the trail, cooks dug pit ovens and sheltered them with branches to nurture hot coals in wet weather. By digging fire pits and placing pots over the flames on rocks, they set up a workable solution to soggy campfires. They improved the setup by holding umbrellas overhead and inserting hollow reeds to supply ventilation to the fire.

Into the mid-twentieth century, primitive societies continued the wearying job of supplying home cooking stations with fuel for baking. Among the Stone Age Txukahamei of Brazil, cooks heated stones to roast armadillos and turtles in the shell. From hot rocks, they layered turtles onto long slabs and tied them to poles. For baking, they maneuvered the slabs over the heat. At the end of the cooking process, hosts served the meat on neat layers of leaves for a communal village meal.

A trek for *National Geographic* by Robyn Davidson rewarded her with insights into aboriginal behaviors in outback Australia. In *Tracks* (1980), a travelogue of an overland journey by camel, she describes Eddie, a polite native dinner guest who tolerates her camp food, but would prefer coal-roasted kangaroo. Davidson describes it as "delicious meat…cooked by first singeing the hair and rubbing it off, then burying it in a mixture of sand and coals and leaving it for an hour. The insides are still bloody and red, but the meat and the offal sweet and juicy." (p. 180)

Today, the pit oven continues to serve the cook who lives far from stoves and modern fuel technology. The Tepehuan of Chihuahua, Mexico, prepare limestone for use in soaking maize by roasting stone chunks in a pit oven lined with manure or green oak and covering them with embers for a day of slow heating. They also roast liliacea bulbs or agave crowns on hot stones in deep fire pits and cover them with soil. Further heat from fires on top slowly heats the fibrous foods for an immediate feast. Cooks shape leftover agave into cakes and slice and dry lily bulbs before storage.

For the natives of Papua, New Guinea, a celebratory *mumu* (feast) begins with the digging of a pit steamer-oven to be lined with rocks and filled with firewood. Over the hot pavers, cooks place bamboo tubes and banana leaves to hold corn, yams, sweet potatoes, taro, and tapioca topped with pork. Covered with more leaves and dirt, the oven gets a sluicing of water down the bamboo tubes to create steam and a careful plugging to retain heat. Within three hours, the meat and vegetables are tender and ready for dishing up on banana leaves for eating with the fingers.

Natives of Tonga in the South Pacific celebrate with feasts prepared in an *umu* (earth oven) much as they greeted and feasted English sea captain James Cook, who explored the area in the 1760s. Using standard banana leaf packaging, cooks wrap hunks of *kape*, an indigenous vegetable, for roasting. Alongside, they cook *lu ika*, fish pieces soaked in coconut milk and baked in taro leaf. Accompaniments include spit-cooked chicken or suckling pork, *melong*, and *lu pulu*, a dish of taro greens boiled alongside the pit oven.

See also **Fireplace; Ovens**

Further Reading

Davidson, Robyn. *Tracks*. New York: Pantheon Books, 1980.
Gray, William R. *Voyages to Paradise: Exploring in the Wake of Captain Cook*. Washington, D.C.: National Geographic Society, 1981.
Rogers, Ken E. *The Magnificent Mesquite*. Austin: University of Texas Press, 2000.
Weber, Steven A., and P. David Seaman, eds. *Havasupai Habitat*. Tucson: University of Arizona Press, 1985.

PLASTICS

The invention of plastics changed forever the basic materials that had dominated cookware and kitchen goods for centuries. In the 1950s, advertisers made promises about the usefulness of plastic. New materials freed the homemaker from heavy utensils and rigorous cleaning tasks. Magazines featured families enjoying handsome, inexpensive chairs, tables, and vessels that need no extra care or protection from damage. The slogan of the era, "Better Living Through Chemistry," seemed to promise a complete break from past drudgery.

Although plastic seems new, early forms of pliant materials preceded the miracle fibers of the mid-twentieth century. In the pre-plastic era, the creation of pliant, lightweight goods advanced from ancient technology that called for the shaping of wax, gum, pitch, tar, amber, or resin for home use as sealants, lacquers, and varnishes. In 1000 BCE, Chinese resin workers collected sap from the *Rhus vernicflua* tree to coat and waterproof textiles. In 1731, explorers of the Amazon basin discovered that South American aborigines had been exploiting latex for several millennia. The Romans, according to the encyclopedist Pliny the

Elder's *Natural History* (c. 77 CE), had their own source of thermoplastic resin in amber imported from the Baltic.

Gutta percha, a natural polymer and forerunner of rubber manufacture, had a long history of use. Around 800 CE, Malayans fashioned items from the sticky substance, a gum gathered from girdled sapodilla trees, evergreens that produce a stiff, water-resistant sap similar to latex that could be molded and extruded. In 1650, Suffolk-born gardener and naturalist John Tradescant, whom Charles I named Keeper of His Majesty's Gardens, Vines and Silkworms, introduced gutta percha in England. It suited the manufacture of where it served in the making of furnishings, match safes, and garden hose. Thomas Hancock, an English manufacturer from Marlborough, worked in gutta percha before dabbling in rubber, which made items more elastic. Other work with malleable materials in the nineteenth century began the rush of experimentation and manufacture of synthetics that continues into the twenty-first century.

1838—French chemist Henri Victor Regnault of Aix-le-Chapelle experimented with vinyl chloride a year before Parisian agricultural chemist Anselme Payen isolated cellulose from wood, a marketable plastic resembling horn and ivory that shapes easily into casings, boxes, and frames.

1843—English inventor Dr. William Montgomerie began molding cutlery handles from gutta percha, which he sent to the English Royal Society for analysis. During the Civil War, gutta-percha served domestic needs in the flasks and containers that accompanied soldiers into field kitchens and tents.

1851—Nelson Goodyear commercialized ebonite, a form of rubber vulcanized with excess sulfur. The first thermosetting material, ebonite was valuable in the manufacture of pot handles.

1866—Engineer John Wesley Hyatt of Albany, New York, working with his brother, Isaiah Smith Hyatt, created nitrocellulose, a tough, flexible commercial thermoplastic that manufacturers could carve and shape into the first successful commercial plastic. At the close of the Civil War, the product replaced ivory. The substance had a profound effect on kitchen items. An associate, Charles F. Burroughs, helped engineer blow molding and extrusion technology for cutlery handles, among many other uses.

1900—Swiss inventor Dr. Henri Dreyfus created cellulose acetate, a less flammable thermoplastic than Hyatt's celluloid, and launched a business with his brother, chemist and industrialist

Camille Dreyfus. Used in injection molding, the material they made took shape as food packaging, refrigerator dishes and trays, egg cups, and place mats. That same year, Swiss engineer Dr. Jacques Edwin Brandenberger made cellophane, a clear packaging material that wiped clean. In 1913, he began working out the production of the first pliant, waterproof wrap, which served bakeries and candy-makers as the ideal protective window for their goods. By 1940, when cellophane tape was sealing plasma and pill containers bound for combat zones, wrapping ration packets to feed U.S. soldiers fighting in North Africa, and stabilizing window glass from concussion and flying shrapnel, the A&P was marketing meat in cellophane wrappers to extend shelf life and seal out contaminants and moisture. In the home, tape sealed picnic supplies, held recipes at eye level, marked canisters, and repaired frayed cookbooks and torn curtains.

1909—The introduction of Bakelite began a vast twentieth-century success story in domestic wares. Within eleven years, the United States was turning out five million pounds of plastic annually for use in kettle and iron handles and stove knobs.

1912—Russian scholar Ivan Ostromislensky perfected vinyl chloride as synthetic rubber. In the home, it provided aprons, curtains, films, dish covers, tablecloths, and flexible implements. In 1947, the introduction of molded squeezeable bottles greatly altered kitchen packaging and camping supplies. Vinyl chloride evolved into containers for water and cooking oil, wipe-clean decorative panels for appliances, and squirt bottles for cleaning windows, grills, and countertops.

1923—Austrian chemist Fritz Pollack commercialized urea plastic for light fittings, molded tableware, and household goods.

1924—English chemist Edmund Rossiter of British Cyanides Company formulated a ureaformaldehyde that accepted powder dye for shaping into appliance parts and picnic supplies marketed under the trade names Bandalasta and Beetle, a thermosetting molding powder. English Beetleware, a popular picnic set, intrigued the American Cyanamid Corporation, which copied the dishes for giveaway in packages of Bisquick, Ovaltine, and Wheaties. By the 1930s, children were clamoring for Little Orphan Annie shake-up mugs. From 1930 to 1941, General Mills distributed thirty million plastic premiums as incentives to buyers of their foods. Ads for

Beetleware skippy bowls lauded dishes "light as a feather—amazingly strong—guaranteed sanitary and tasteless." (Wahlberg 1999, 14) These brittle items, available free with the purchase of two boxes of Wheaties and later merchandised in five-and-dimes, did little to dispel the reputation for plastic as cheap, fading goods that offered little esthetic or utilitarian advancement to the kitchen.

1925—Women's magazines began running the ads of companies producing name brand plastic products, including Du Pont's Tontine washable window shades and Duco waterproof tabletops, both featured in the March 1925 issue of *Good Housekeeping*.

1926—Polyvinyl chloride (PVC), the invention of organic chemist Waldo Semon for B. F. Goodrich in Akron, Ohio, was a durable, flame-resistant, moldable plastic commonly found in sheet and block flooring, which quickly replaced linoleum in the mid-1900s.

1929—I. G. Farbenindustrie marketed polystyrene, a product first distilled from balsam trees in 1831. Seized by Dow Chemical and put into production in 1933, the substance transformed homes with inexpensive injection molding of wall paneling, disposable plastic forks and spoons, and wall tiles. It evolved as high impact, low waste commercial plastic in 1950; two years later, Federal Tool Corporation in Chicago could stamp out 56,000 picnic plates per shift. A major feature of molded goods was the absence of screws and nuts. Because uniform fittings took shape with the body of each part, plastic lamps and canisters snapped together without tools.

1930—Harvard instructor Dr. Wallace Hume Carothers and his associate Dr. Julian W. Hill produced elastic super-polymer fibers, forerunners of nylon and neoprene, used in netting, bristle brushes, and invisible sewing thread for upholstery and curtains.

1931—Union Carbide began marketing vinyl, developed in 1925, in upholstery, no-iron mildew-free curtains, and flooring for housing built atop concrete slabs. Consumers quickly rejected vinyl because of fading and darkening, flaking, scratching, and ripping free from adhesives. They particularly disliked shrinkage, which left crevices full of dirt and insects. Vinyl did not recover from its bad reputation until 1954, when better pigmentation and adhesives reduced complaints about upkeep and quality of flooring. Furniture manufacturers replaced wood table and chair legs with wood-grain plastic, which reduced prices for dinette sets and made them lighter to warehouse and easier to maintain. As U.S. entertaining became less formal, stackable and nestable plastic tables for entertaining suited suppers, buffets, snacks, brunches and coffees, and barbecues.

The addition of microscopic holes in the 1950s enhanced breathability and restored vinyl's competitive edge against woven goods. In textured tweed, tortoiseshell, damask, bamboo, bark, wicker, and rope patterns, vinyl seemed less synthetic. Combined with wrought iron in dinette sets, Naugahyde created an airier kitchen ambience than the bulky chromium-rimmed tables and chairs popularized in 1950 by such designers as Raymond Loewy, creator of the Premium saltine box and Coca-Cola bottle.

1933 — Dow chemical lab researcher Ralph Wiley discovered polyvinylidene chloride, marketed as Saran. It got its first use as a protective covering of military equipment, then entered the kitchen market as a stretchy, clingy covering for dishes and pans to halt the spread of odors and flavors in the refrigerator and to protect foods from drying out.

1937 — Devine Foods of Chicago, which had been merchandising hot lunches in metal vessels since 1928, replaced metal with Melamine. A trade name for Melmac, made by American Cyanamid, the new material was rigid and did not dent, rust, melt, or sour food. It entered domestic markets in dishes, heat insulation, handles, trays, and lamp shades. The vessels influenced the military during World War II, when the navy began dispensing food in unbreakable packages that withstood gunfire and rough weather. In the same year, I. G. Farben/Monsanto turned vinyl acetate into glue, paint, and safety glass, an essential in see-through oven doors, which allowed bakers to check the progress of baking without opening the door.

1938 — Nylon made from coal became the world's first synthetic fiber, an asset to the Allies during World War II for its light weight, elasticity, quick drying, and strength. Nylon and other synthetic fibers freed homemakers from ironing garments, drapes, and table linens.

1939 — Swiss chemist Pierre Castan invented epoxy resin, which functioned well as adhesive, surface coating, and laminant.

1940 — I. G. Farben produced polyurethane, a slick finish for fabric in forcing bags, interior moldings, and exterior walls; it earned regard for ease of spray application, use, and washability.

1943 — Dow-Corning brought out silicone plastic, a more malleable material than earlier plastics.

1946 — For Watertown Manufacturing Company in Watertown, Connecticut, Jon Hedu designed Lifetime Ware, a tableware that featured the rimless coupe plate, currently a collector's item. His pieces, guaranteed for life, earned the Good Housekeeping seal of approval. Advertised in the July 1947 issue of *Crockery and Glass Journal* and in the March 1949 *Better Homes and Gardens*, the line expanded in the 1950s with more colors and patterns and reduced weight. Hedu's most successful designs included Monterey, Woodbine, and Balmoral dinnerware.

1949 — Designer Charles Eames of the Herman Miller Company made a splash in home decor with the fiberglas-reinforced polyester (FRP) shell chair, manufactured by the Zenith Plastics Company of Gardena, California. Formed by a hydraulic press in three minutes, these versatile shapes, as well as his Eiffel Tower side chair on a wire cat's cradle base, combined the sturdiness of steel rod legs with aircraft-quality plastics. Against three thousand entrants from thirty-one countries, the shell chair won the Museum of Modern Art's International Competition for Low Cost Furniture award and remained popular into the early 1970s.

CIBA/Cyanamid pioneered melamine formaldehyde, a commercial success as glue, fabric finish, veneer, kitchen utensils, buttons, lamp shades, and unbreakable tableware sold under the trade name Fiesta. Simultaneously with the invention of melamine formaldehyde, the plastics industry entered a dynamic phase. At Imperial Chemical Industries (ICI), chemists R. Hill and J. W. C. Crawford developed polymethyl methacrylate or acrylic, marketed under the trade names Lucite, Perspex, and Plexiglas, an extruded thermoplastic used in refrigerator dishes, bowls, place mats, graters, juicers, clothespins, stirrers, spoons, and pastry knives. At the same time ICI chemist R. O. Gibson and researcher E. W. Fawcett's creation of polyethylene from ethylene gas extended plastic flexibility beyond the brittle Bakelite to a durable, flexible, waxy-surfaced substance.

In Japan, dependence on bamboo, vine, and wood baskets and trays shifted after World War II as plastic and vinyl replaced natural materials. By the mid-1950s, farm wives could buy rice and mushroom sieves, fish creels, crab traps, sake barrels, bait canteens, pickle tubs, and buckets made from plastic instead of wood or bamboo. Kitchens displayed bright-hued plastic cups, bowls, and chopsticks rather than the natural tones of bamboo vessels and implements.

Drawbacks to the use of cheap plastic goods were their brittleness in winter and their tendency to warp and melt near charcoal burners. They also violated a strong tradition of bamboo implements and vessels as a natural alliance of human need with renewable substances from nature.

The only plastic light enough to float, polyethylene could substitute for acrylic in items for the home. It suited the manufacture of shopping bags, recloseable lids, squeeze tubes, swivel closures, bread bags, six-pack connectors, blister packs, garbage bags, dish pans and laundry baskets, garbage cans, brushes, lamps, coasters, and milk carton coatings and bottles. It adapted to injection molding, extrusion, casting, and powder coating. Because of its range of colors, non-abrasive surface, and noise reduction, it fueled the Tupperware industry after Earl Silas Tupper found ways to turn polyethylene slag from Du Pont oil refineries into extrudable plastic.

Early plastic was not without hazards. When manufacturers produced low-standard goods, postwar housewives soon discovered that irons scorched buttons, container lids rolled under radiators and melted into puddles, dishwashers reduced thin-walled measuring cups to amorphous blobs, and pot handles burst into flame on the stove.

To entice the homemaker and gift buyer, department stores showcased tables set with popular Boontonware, manufactured by Boonton Molding Company in Boonton, New Jersey. Boonton achieved a classic Melamine line with industrial designer Belle Kogan's Boonton Belle, featuring a blocky shape renowned as the squared circle. Kogan, who designed kitchenware for Red Wing Pottery, Libbey Glass Co, and Dow Chemical, was one of the first New York artists to abandon pewter and silver for plastic.

Despite advances and touches of artistry, by 1948, the reputation of plastic items plummeted. Housewives returned to natural fiber, china, wood, and metal kitchen goods. Bolstering a flagging industry, giants like American Cyanamid, Bakelite, Catalin, DuPont, and Monsanto began policing fabricators and empaneling advisers to provide technical support to replace shoddy goods with quality products. Brand names and labeling offered shoppers more detailed information about the application and upkeep of a wide array of plastics.

Gradually, homemakers rebuilt trust in such identifiable plastics as American Cyanamid's Melmac, U.S. Rubber's Naugahyde, Westinghouse Electric's Micarta, Dow Chemical's Styron, and Union Carbide's Vinylite. By 1951, azlon, nylon, fiberglass, orlon, and vinyon outstripped every natural fiber except cotton and jute and dominated textiles sold to homemakers and the military. Shoppers chose bright-colored, unbreakable goods such as Micarta table tops for the child-centered home of the 1950s. Budget-minded housewives depended on plastic for its toughness, portability, and informality during their children's growing-up years and valued lightweight goods for casual dining and a kitchen that invited guests to pull up a chair and chat while the cook finished the *hors d'oeuvres* tray. *House Beautiful* supported the consumer who chose to reduce the number of breakables in the kitchen and dining room. Plastics replaced metal on lunch boxes, picnic sets, coolers, and thermos bottles. *Better Homes and Gardens* advocated such durable goods as an enticement to teens to entertain at home rather than seek street hangouts. The success of Naugahyde as a puncture-resistant stool and dining chair covering forced the leather industry to fight for its turf by promoting traditional upholstery as luxurious and high quality.

1953—The Formica Company tripled its output of cabinet laminates, which originated in 1913 as electrical insulation. Chemist John D. Cochrane, Jr., invented Formica, an easily cleaned, fireproof laminated surface available in a glossy or matte finish in many colors and grains for topping cabinets. The do-it-yourself market lauded Formica for use in furnishings and appliance casings. New pressure-sensitive adhesives allowed families more home-decorating options in countertops, backsplashes, and paneling. Corrugated window panels admitted light, but assured privacy in housing projects; polystyrene tiles replaced ceramic for quick domestic makeovers. Its bright colors and patterns made kitchens so visible and decorative that brand names like Formica became a major selling point in middle-class homes.

1954—Italian scholar Guilio Natta invented polypropylene, a durable substance that won him the 1963 Nobel Prize for chemistry, shared with his collaborator, German chemist Karl Ziegler. The substance made tough milk crates, appliance casings, chairs, tables, and placemats.

1955—Ekco, a thriving manufacturer in London's Southend, produced a range of goods in plastic, including bakeware, kitchenware, cleaning products, and pantryware.

1956—Melamine, developed in 1949, won the Museum of Modern Art's design award in 1953–1954. Its growing popularity provoked the Vitreous China Association to issue warnings that Melamine released formaldehyde into hot foods and that dents and slices in the surface harbored microbes. Nonetheless, by 1956, a quarter of American kitchens contained Melamine dinnerware.

When the name Saarinen combined with domestic goods, plastic entered the realm of art. Yale-trained achitect Eero Saarinen of Finland apprenticed in furniture design before partnering with Charles Eames. *Life* magazine featured Saarinen's functional, inexpensive one-piece pedestal chair for Knoll, Incorporated. Called a tulip chair, the plastic shell on plastic-coated aluminum base reduced the clutter of legs because his dinette chairs fit under a table.

1957—At a time when Plastics Manufacturing Company of Dallas, Texas, was popularizing Texasware, designer Russel Wright abandoned the substance and produced a stabler, less rigid polyethylene line called Idealware from Fortiflex, a product of the Celanese Corporation. Unlike its predecessor, it stored food for extended periods without staining. With the equipment of Ideal Toy Company, he produced his Idealware line of pitchers, storage containers, soup plates, salad sets, and utensils. A forerunner of microwaveable dishes, his idea had potential, but failed in the marketplace.

1958—Research by Bayer in Germany and General Electric in the United States resulted in the commercialization of polycarbonate resin. A clear, lightweight glass substitute, polycarbonate approached the look and weight of crystal, but needed no special handling. Beverage, wine and bar sets, and salad bowls could go from microwave to table and dishwasher without clouding. The cost paralleled that of glass. A popular item in polyethylene, Gino Colombine's lemon squeezer, patented in 1958, allowed the cook to position a lemon half on a corrugated post and activate a level that forced juice down the center to a catch basin.

The late 1960s saw a wave of nostalgia for natural materials in the kitchen—metal canisters, wood bowls, and glass tumblers. To compete, plastics took on subtler tones and textures. Floor tiles mimicked marble, slate, brick, and tongue-and-groove planking. Melamine dishes appeared in a broader range of colors and competed directly with the patterns, shapes, and feel of traditional china.

1968—Corian, a pure, marblescent acrylic resin, is another addition to kitchen technology that holds promise for future products. DuPont introduced the polymer in 1968 and presented it in 1971 at the National Association of Home Builders (NAHB) Show in Houston, Texas. Naturally nonporous and hygienic, it was cast in sheets and cut to specific lengths. It blended delicately veined color in sixty-five shades into natural

minerals to produce a stonelike translucence enhanced by matching adhesives. DuPont put it to use on counter tops, molding, wainscoting and wall cladding, switch plate covers, soap dishes, knife blocks, cabinet knobs, and cutting boards as a deterrent to microbial contamination.

1973—Hoover Rainbow Autoboil made an electric kettle out of acetal, a thermoplastic resin sharing the characteristics of brass, aluminum, zinc, and stainless steel and used in food processing.

1979—A polypropylene kettle created for Redring Autoboil offered a water level gauge. Still popular for kitchen goods, polypropylene egg cups poached eggs in the microwave and went directly to the table for serving.

1999—Copco, a division of Wilton Industries, introduced a line of nylon kitchen tools with ergonomic santoprene grips, including fork, pasta spoon, utility spoon, slotted turner, fork, and ladle. According to an ad in the July-August 1999 issue of *Kitchenware News*, the synthetic material survived temperatures up to four hundred degrees Fahrenheit. In the same issue, Browne & Company launched a non-slip silicone base for anchoring its mixing bowls. The starburst inset held bowls straight or tilted for whisking egg whites or vinaigrette. That same year, the Robinson Knife Company updated traditional cutlery with bright colors and comfortable, sure-grip handles made from Santoprene, a fluid thermoplastic elastomer (TPE) injection-molded over polypropylene to form a watertight seal. Marketed as Oneida and Colourgrip, the items adorned the kitchen while assuring the consumer of durable, ergonomically sound, and dishwasher-safe materials.

Currently, plastic gadgetry offers the food preparer a variety of answers to kitchen problems, from egg timers, expandable bread keepers, implement drawer separators, scrub brushes with nonstick bristles, lattice pie crust cutters, and postage and food portion scales. A simple tool, the bowl scraper extracts the last of batter from a vessel. For quick draining of salad greens, the double-walled salad spinner removes water through slots in the inner bowl and retains it in the base. Plastic pepper or salt grinders allow the user to see supplies without guessing when they need refilling.

For cutting, plastic shapes easily into citrus peelers, lettuce slicers, bread slicing guides, steel-blade equipped herb and vegetable choppers and mandoline slicers, measured dough-rising buckets and lids, and odorless and taste-free cutting boards that are easy to disinfect. The Joyce Chen Spiral Slicer, a hand-cranked see-through vegetable cutter, uses stainless steel blades to produce uniform slices, cubes, spaghetti strands, or julienne strips, which collect in the attached plastic cup. Silicone renders spatulas heat-resistant, nonscratching, and flexible.

The ubiquitous plastic bag has altered the way families shop for groceries, transport them home, and recycle. In the town of Ubeda, Spain, west of the Sierra de Segura, freelance olive pickers spread a *manta* (tarp) of black plastic mesh for catching fruit that they whack from each tree. After they drag the mesh to the next tree, a few workers remain behind to glean any olives that fall through the holes or outside the plastic ground cover. Another popular addition to cook sets are plastic lids, both snap-on and screw-on. See-through plastic allows quick examination of leftovers in the refrigerator and reduces the trading of odors and flavors. The firm top also protects meals from splashing or spilling for transportation without adding appreciable weight.

See also **Bakelite; Garbage; Nylon; Plunkett, Roy; Rubber; Teflon**

Further Reading

"Corian: 30 Years Later," *DuPont Magazine*, Vol. 94, No. 4.
Gentry, Patricia. *Kitchen Tools*. San Francisco: 101 Productions, 1985.
Love, Steve, and David Giffels, "The Father of Vinyl," *Beacon Journal*, April 6, 1997.
McNulty, Lyndi Stewart. *Price Guide to Plastic Collectibles*. Radnor, Penn.: Wallace- Homestead Book Co., 1992.
Meikle, Jeffrey L. *American Plastic: A Cultural History*. New Brunswick, N.J.: Rutgers University Press, 1995.
Taylor, Graham D., and Patricia E. Sudnik. *Du Pont and the International Chemical Industry*. Boston: Twayne Publishers, 1984.
Wolf, Nancy, and Ellen Feldman. *Plastics: America's Packaging Dilemma*. Washington, D.C.: Island Press, 1995.

PLATINA

The star cook and most stylish culinary writer of the early Italian Renaissance, Bartolomeo Platina set the tone for period dining. Named Bartolomeo de' Sacchi in infancy, he was born in poverty in 1421 outside Mantua, Italy. A cultured humanist, he assumed his nickname, Il Platina, as a pun on *piadina*, flatbread indigenous to Emilia-Romagna, or Piàdena, his home town. In the house of Duke Ludovico Gonzaga, Marquis of Mantua, Platina tutored the sons, Federigo and Francesco Gonzaga, and remained in the family's good graces after leaving their employ. In 1457, Platina studied philosophy in Florence, then settled in Rome under the patronage of his former pupil, now Cardinal Francesco Gonzaga, where he assumed the post of writer of papal briefs, conferred in 1464 by Pope Pius II.

Platina's contribution to food history came at a low point in his life, a four-month confinement in 1464 to Castel Sant'Angelo, Rome's grim prison, for disagreeing with Pope Paul II, a stickler for orthodoxy. The intervention of Gonzaga set him free. A charge of conspiracy to assassinate the pope returned Platina once more to prison at age forty-seven, but he gained acquittal sixteen months later for lack of evidence.

After his second imprisonment, he continued to collect recipes for the first dated cookbook, *De Honesta Voluptate et Valitudine* (On Right Pleasure and Health, 1475). Begun around 1463, before his first incarceration, the text was a toast to the good life. In ten chapters imitating Apicius's cooking classic, Platina sang the praises of fresh sea bass with green sauce, fried chicken, elderberry pie, chestnut tort, pasta, and egg dishes of all types and wrote essays on nutrition and culinary poisons. He recommended eating mustard for a healthy stomach and lungs, as an expectorant to ease a cough, and as a stimulant to the menses and urination. Ironically, he was working on the text when his enemy, Paul II, died of stroke in the Vatican gardens.

Platina, who was the first competitor for medieval cooks Leone and Taillevant, was an admirer of Roman essayist Pliny the Elder's encyclopedia of around 77 CE; of Apicius, the famed Roman gastronome and author of *De Re Coquinaria* (On Cooking, late 300s CE); of Arabic medical writer Ibn Butlan, author of *Calendar of Health* (c. 1050)*;* and of *Libro de Arte Coquinaria* (Book of Culinary Art), written by contemporary caterer Martino de'Rossi of Como. Platina revered Martino as "another Carneades" and "the prince of cooks of our age." (Platina 1999, 119, 14) From Martino's beginnings, the text of *De Honesta Voluptate et Valitudine* rose to a classic amalgam of Mediterranean kitchen art. Book I commented on kitchen hygiene, clean table linens, sharp knives, and clean white salt. At table, Platina insisted on pleasant, fragrant surroundings and seasonal flowers as well as polite conversation and post-prandial entertainment.

With no kitchen experience, Platina refined the cookery of more extravagant professionals, but avoided strong personal opinions. For the sake of both pleasure and health, he advocated restraint and the selection of digestible foods, for example, tender kid over goat and partridge over quail. In reference to bread, he advocated balance: "Let the baker be careful not to put in too much or too little leaven, for, from the former bread can acquire a sour taste, and, from the latter, it can become too heavy to digest and too unhealthy, since it binds the bowels." (Ibid., 16)

The heavy moralizing that opens Book VIII reflects Platina's correlation of cooking with all phases of life and emotion. He describes condiments as the "best spurs to arouse deadened appetites." (Ibid., 151) However, he admits that they are powerful enough to arouse "luxury, lust, and intemperance." (Ibid.) With an insider's self-assurance, he singles out Rome as one of certain Italian cities devoted to wealth, greed, and gluttony and assures the reader that his recipes are for honest workers who gain strength from stimulus to their taste buds.

On Platina's second release from prison, he researched *Liber de Vita Christi ac Omnium Pontificum* (Book on the Life of Christ and All the Popes, 1474), which he dedicated to the new pope, Sixtus IV. Platina's recognition as an historian and his amicable relationship with the new administration brought rewards. Fully pensioned as the first director of the new Vatican library, he gained status for organizing documents into a functioning reference library. Platina settled at a comfortable home on the Quirinal in Rome, where he died of plague in August 1481 at age sixty.

Further Reading

Platina. *On Right Pleasure and Good Health.* Asheville, N.C.: Pegasus Press, 1999.

PLUNKETT, ROY

Roy J. Plunkett, a polymer chemist for Du Pont, introduced the first nonstick surfacing in kitchen history. A native of New Carlisle, Ohio, he was born on June 26, 1910 at the height of experimentation with new domestic synthetics. He completed degees at Manchester College and Ohio State University before accepting a post in research and development at Du Pont's Jackson Laboratory in Deepwater, New Jersey, at age twenty-six. Among his achievements were breakthroughs in refrigeration, aerosol containers, and plastics.

In researching nontoxic refrigerants for Kinetic Chemicals, a joint effort of Du Pont and General Motors to commercialize chlorofluorocarbons, Plunkett unintentionally created the polytetrafluoroethylene (PTFE) resin while studying gases similar to freon. It appeared as a white powder caked around the nozzle of a steel cylinder of freon. He feared a leak, but deduced by weighing the tank that it still contained the original substance. Working with Jack Rebok, he sawed open the valve assembly of the malfunctioning tank and discovered that the compressed gas, left in cold storage overnight, had shifted to a polymerized solid white powder.

A remarkably heat-tolerant, inert, acid-impervious, and non-adherent surface, PTFE has a molecular weight exceeding thirty million, making it one of the largest known. Kinetic Chemicals patented it in 1941, but developers doubted that they could work with the difficult material for commercial benefit. In 1939, Du Pont promoted Plunkett to chemical supervisor for the manufacture of tetraethyl lead at the Chambers Works, the company's largest factory, a position he held until 1952, when he began managing Du Pont's freon products division. At the height of his career, he patented Teflon, the trade version of his discovery, in 1945, thus creating a new and lucrative product division for Du Pont.

After the military applied it to separate uranium isotopes in atomic bombs during World War II, the waxy, nonwetting, noncorroding product also aided the production of gaskets, vessel linings, and tubes. It reached the civilian public in 1946 as a versatile, noncracking coating for surgical implants and tubing, satellite elements, electric wires and tape, pharmaceuticals, fabrics, air conditioning, and metal cookware. Almost immediately, the application of nonstick surfacing altered the way people cooked, ate, and cleaned.

For his innovative work, Plunkett earned honorary degrees from Manchester College, Washington College, and Ohio State and entry into the Plastics Hall of Fame in 1973, two years before his retirement to Corpus Christi, Texas. In 1985, he was named to the National Inventors' Hall of Fame; three years later, the Society of Plastics Engineers awarded him the John W. Hyatt Award for creating a product in the spirit of Hyatt, father of plastics. Teflon earned Du Pont the National Medal of Technology, presented by President George Bush in 1990, four years before Plunkett's death on May 12, 1994. In his honor, Du Pont offers the Plunkett Awards for Innovation with Teflon.

See also **Teflon**

POMIANE, ÉDOUARD DE

A food scholar and practical cook, Édouard de Pomiane pioneered a simple approach to cuisine that survives into the twenty-first century. He was born in 1875 in Cracow, Poland, but fled to France with his mother during the struggle for Polish independence. After training as a physician, Pomiane lectured on nutrition at the Institut Pasteur, but he made his reputation as a cookbook writer and as the first radio broadcaster on food topics. In *La Cuisine en Dix Minutes ou l'Adaptation au Rhythme Modern* (Cooking in Ten Minutes or Adapting to Modern Rhythm, 1930), he focused on simple food preparation. Readers enjoyed his wit and appreciated the applicability to daily menus of such dishes as breaded veal on green peas, onion soup, and french fries. To introduce English cooks to French techniques, he wrote *Cooking with Pomiane* (c. 1930s), which demystified classic recipes.

De Pomiane traveled to Poland to collect recipes for *Cuisine Juive: Ghettos Moderns* (Jewish Cookery: Modern Ghettos, 1929), an ethnography based on a Polish-Jewish community later obliterated by the Holocaust. His food philosophy respected kosher ingredients, which he researched with the help of the rabbi of Dobczyce.

An unusual viewpoint for the period was Pomiane's *La Cuisine pour la Femme du Monde* (Cuisine for a Woman of the World, c. 1930), in which he made clear his sympathy for working women who, in addition to their jobs, still had to cook and clean at home. He amassed a wealth of tips and techniques for his radio programs, through which he disseminated simple balanced menus lower in protein and fat than the diet of the day. He advocated packaged and canned foods and fresh fruit and he also recorded aspects of the efficient kitchen in *Radio-Cuisine* (1949), one of a long list of works he compiled over his half-century career. His heart-healthy dishes revolutionized meals a half century before their time and influenced the cookery of Jéhane Benoît, M. F. K. Fisher, and Elizabeth David, who penned an introduction to a 1976 reissue of his collections.

Further Reading

Pomiane, Édouard de. *Cooking with Pomiane.* New York: Modern Library, 2001.

_____. *French Cooking in Ten Minutes: Or Adapting to the Rhythm of Modern Life.* New York: North Point Books, 1994.

This, Hervé, "La Gastronomie Moléculaire et Physique," *Science Tribune*, 1997.

POST, CHARLES WILLIAM

The imitator of the Kellogg family of cereal makers, advertiser Charles William "C. W." Post survived competition to found the Post empire, maker of Postum,

Portrait of Charles William Post, 1914.
[© *Library of Congress, Prints and Photographs Division (LC-USZ62-121002)*]

Grape Nuts, and Post Toasties, rival of Kellogg's Corn Flakes. Born on October 26, 1854, in Springfield, Illinois, he attended the Illinois Industrial University and settled in Battle Creek, Michigan, home of the corn flake. He traveled the West selling farm implements before moving back to Springfield to superintend a plow factory.

Poor digestion and nervous collapse sent Post to Texas to work as a cowboy, realtor, and maker of woolens. He returned to Michigan to seek treatment at the Sanitarium, run by vegetarian reformer Dr. John Harvey Kellogg. The regimen of water therapy, massage, and strict diet of health food failed to restore him to health. Kellogg warned Ella Post that her husband was incurable. In 1891, Kellogg sought a religious cure from Elizabeth Gregory, exponent of Mary Baker Eddy and Christian Science.

Post pursued projects intended to better domestic life. At age thirty-seven, he opened La Vita Inn in Battle Creek as a haven for the sick. In addition to his interest in subconscious suggestion, he denounced coffee as a poison and concocted Postum, a coffee imitator touted to build blood and to encourage children to drink their milk. He held stock in the Buck's Stove and Range Company, studied methods on rain-making employing gunpowder and balloons, and experimented with foods. In competition with 107 other brands of corn flakes manufactured in Battle Creek, his health food business made him a multimillionaire. Famous for sanitation and anti-unionism, he founded the National Trades' and Workers' Association, a substitute for unions, which opened a retirement home for destitute workers.

Post was beloved in Post City, Texas, a planned municipality built from profits from Postum and Elijah's Manna, which he renamed Post Toasties. From the efforts of pioneers, ranchers, and cowboys, in 1906, he founded his city on a 333-acre parcel and increased his land holdings to a quarter million acres. The intent was to improve his health from rest and relaxation, but he soon involved himself in building affordable housing for members of his experimental colony.

Post's firm, the Double U Company—shortened from "Double Utopia"—lured settlers to Texas on reduced-fare railroad tickets. He offered prospective colonists a four-room rock-and-stucco cottage and a larger home featuring a porch. Post ruled out alcohol and rowdies and set up a planing mill, lumber yard, mail and water-hauling services, pharmacy, laundry, hotel, and grocery stores to aid families in settling in and acquired a spur line of the Santa Fe Railway to link families with the outside world. On an experimental farm, he planted fruit trees, cotton, corn, kaffir cotton, oats, milo, Sudan grass, cowpeas, wax beans, broom corn, and peanuts.

By 1908, the growing town had schools, churches, a fire department, sewing circle, literary society, and baseball and basketball teams. When his health deteriorated after an appendectomy, he shot himself on May 9, 1914, at his residence in Santa Barbara, California. His only child, Marjorie Merriweather Post, inherited his empire and built Post cereals into one of the nation's most prolific convenience food processors. By the end of the twentieth century, Americans were purchasing Post cereals at the rate of 2.7 billion boxes a year.

See also **Birdseye, Clarence**

Further Reading

Carson, Gerald. *Cornflake Crusade.* New York: Rinehart & Co., 1957.

POTATOES, SWEET POTATOES, AND YAMS

Root crops appear to have redirected the human diet soon after cooler, drier climates limited the abundance of fruit. As shown in the research of Bernard Wood and Alison Brooks, anthropologists at George Washington University, prehistoric gatherers found the subterranean foods most abundant on savannahs. The most valuable tuber, the white potato, first achieved status as an edible in the New World. Among South American mountain folk, the potato was a pre-Columbian staple. Andean farmers began cultivating it for food in South America around 3000 BCE. An enduring form of potato starch is the Peruvian *chuño*, a dried form made by pressing frost-bitten tubers and air-drying them in the sun into potato flour. After Spaniard Pedro de Cieza de León traversed Colombia's Cauca Valley in 1538 and discovered the white potato, it developed into one of the world's first miracle crops.

Long before reaching Europe, the sweet potato became a kitchen staple in the Americas, Caribbean, and Pacific rim. In Oceania, voyagers packed bags of pre-cooked yams to sustain them at sea. Peruvian gardeners cultivated it under the name *kumara*. From early times, the Arawak made meals of fresh and dried tubers, which their cooks prepared along with cassava for Columbus and his crew when they landed in the Caribbean islands. The Spaniards transported sweet potato slips from Haiti to Spain in 1493.

According to Dr. Mistugu Sakihara of the University of Hawaii, Okinawans owe their sweet potato crop to a sailor. When ship's purser Noguni Sokan introduced the tuber to Okinawa in 1605, he knew it by the Chinese term *fan-shu* (barbarian potato). Under pressure from the agricultural magistrate, island farmers introduced it to their fields under the name *han-shu*. Because cultivation of the sweet potato saved Japan from the 1733 famine, Sokan earned hero status, a stone statue, and elevation of his descendants to samurai.

The arrival of potatoes—sweet and white—in Europe made a dramatic change in menus and nutrition. Expeditioner John Hawkins, who began the slave trade between Guinea and the West Indies, returned from his second voyage to the New World in 1565 with England's first tobacco and sweet potatoes. When Francisco Hernandes collected data on the New World for Philip II, he compiled *Treasures of Medical Matters of New Spain* (1570), a compendium of pharmacological application of cinchona, curare, and ipecac from South America and of the Mayan reliance on capsicum, chenopodium, guaiacium, and vanilla. In addition, he learned about growing the white potato, which reached European gardens from Peru via Cartagena, Colombia, in 1573.

Although the French disdained the white potato, by 1581, chef and food writer Marx Rumpolt added potato dishes to the first printed cookbook in Germany, *Ein Neue Kochbuch* (A New Cookbook), which named the starchy tuber a boon to the robust menus of sauerkraut, goose, dumplings, and strudel common in winter. In the estimation of a more recent food commentator, Clifford A. Wright, author of *A Mediterranean Feast* (1999), the common potato eased bouts of famine in Europe by providing an easily grown, digestible tuber adapted to many styles of cooking, menu pairings, and condiments.

When growers transported the white potato to northwestern Europe, most cooks hesitated to accept it as a vegetable. Although it diminished the number and virulence of famines and doubled the continent's population, food lore of the 1600s typified it among foods that "nourish the whole Body, restore in Consumptions, and provoke Lust," a rumor that also plagued the tomato. (Pfeiffer 1975, 36) After an Irishman introduced the potato to Cantyre peninsula, Scottish gardeners grew them as a curiosity alongside turnips, which were new root crops imported from Holland. The first recorded potato purchase in Scotland occurred in 1701, when the Duchess of Buccleugh entered into a household account her purchase of a peck of tubers from Edinburgh.

Leery Scottish peasants suspected that they were being maneuvered into accepting a replacement for oats, their staple carbohydrate. Gradually, people began boiling and stewing white potatoes at mealtime for serving with butter and cream, using them as a grain in gruel, or baking them with apples. Irish mothers left tubers overnight in fireplace ash to serve double duty next day—on the walk to school, their children carried potatoes in their pockets as hand warmers and ate them at lunch.

In 1733, when Augustus III became king of Poland, the white potato received royal affirmation. He had German growers settle on royal lands to popularize the potato among the peasantry. Over denunciation of priests who feared that potato flour would sully communion wafers, royal cooks continued serving potatoes until they won a place in Lithuanian, Polish, Czech, and Ukrainian kitchens. When General Kazimierz Pulaski received his first sack of potatoes, he sent them to a puzzled cook who improvised a dish of scrambled eggs and boiled, heavily seasoned potatoes, which pleased the officers at Pulaski's mess.

In 1761, potato promoter Antoine-Auguste Parmentier survived a year in a German prison on mostly potato dishes. A decade later, he published a monograph attesting that the potato was nourishing enough to end famine. Because Louis XVI agreed to wear one of Parmentier's potato flowers in his lapel, the humble tuber became the rage. By the late 1700s, the white potato was one of Europe's star crops except in Russia, where Orthodox church-goers rejected it in favor of traditional rye. Only after the 1840 potato riots, when the government decreed the planting of potatoes on common land, did peasants increase consumption.

Ironically, potato-loving European immigrants brought its cultivation to their New World homes, thus reintroducing them from a European perspective. In this same period, colonial Quebec bakers depended on the white potato for a makeshift yeast. In the absence of sourdough starter, they mashed solid meat into pulp and left it to mold or blended potato, hops, flour, and water to ferment overnight in a stock jug to make leavening for the next day's baking.

Like other cuisines, potato cookery suited the kitchens and condiments of the place and time. In 1802, Swedish author Carolina Weltzin devoted an entire cookbook to her own experimentations with the potato. Her *Anwisning Till Potäters Mångfaldiga Begagnande* (Directions for Diverse Uses of Potatoes), the first published in Sweden, went through reprints in 1806 and 1819, no doubt because the scope and applications suited the needs of Scandinavian tastes. The peasant focus of her writing is obvious in a subsequent book, *Daglig Helpreda i Köket: Eller Anwisning Till en Tarflig Matredning för Hvarje Dag i Aret* (Daily Helper in the Kitchen: Or Direction for Frugal Cookery for Each Day of the Year, 1808).

Similarly, Englishwomen generally relegated potato cookery to the lower classes. In a rare bit of culinary filler, Charlotte Elizabeth, editor of *Christian Ladies' Magazine* in London, completed a column with a comment on boiling potatoes for "the delicate stomachs of children and invalids." ("Boiling" 1834, 501) Her explanation of how to sort large from small to boil uniform sizes together precedes a description of heating them in their jackets in water about two inches from their tops. After explaining how to temper the hot water occasionally with cold to keep the outsides from bursting before the centers were done, the instructions conclude with friendly advice about quality: "Late in the season, when potatoes become specky, it is better to pare them before boiling." (Ibid.)

Unlike the high-minded ladies' magazines of England and their disdain of domestic work, American lore championed commentary and recipes involving white and sweet potatoes. In the turpentine distilling camps of the piedmont Carolinas, make-do camp cooks dug baking holes, dropped wet moss over white potatoes, and topped them with kindling, pineheart, and a dollop of gum. A quick light set off the pit cooker. When it burned itself out, the resin-coated potatoes were ready to peel and eat.

Potatoes established a social pecking order in the mid-Atlantic and Southern states. The upper Appalachian Scotch-Irish settlers, called Cohees, ate white potatoes and looked down on Virginian whites, who ate sweet potatoes and tuckahoes, the equivalent of arrowroot, which they obtained from local Indians. Despite the stigma, Virginia bakers made puddings and blancmange from tuckahoe, a natural thickener.

During the mid-nineteenth century westering that began settlement of the American frontier, families valued potatoes for preventing and fighting scurvy. Trail blazer John M. Bozeman earned the adoration of women at Fort Phil Kearney after he dispatched to them a supply of potatoes grown on his ranch. In the words of Dee Brown's *The Gentle Tamers: Women of the Old Wild West* (1958), potatoes meted out to the wives of officers and infirmary staff were "as precious as grain in the sacks of Israel's sons in Egypt." (Brown 1958, 195)

In 1853, Native American chef George Crum made the first potato chip at Cary Moon's Lake House in Lake Saratoga, New York. When a VIP, railroad baron Commodore Cornelius Vanderbilt, complained that the french fries were too thick, Crum prepared slices paper thin, soaked them in ice water to keep them from wilting, them fried them crisp and golden brown. After heavily salting the batch, he presented them to the complainer, who lauded their crunch and flavor. From a localized demand for Saratoga chips, manufacturers began production and marketing. As snack food, the chips reached the public in grocery stores after a Mrs. Scudder devised wax paper chip bags in 1926.

In 1908, the Sears, Roebuck catalog simplified the tedious job of potato peeling with a Vermont parer and eye cleaner selling for 51 cents. By mounting the potato, quince, or pear to the far end, the user of a table-mounted shaft turned a hand crank to begin paring. The copywriter boasted that the simple framework skinned away thinner strips that saved "at least fifty percent of the outside of the potato that is ordinarily wasted." (Schroeder 1971, 469) For four cents, the homemaker could purchase a wood-handled potato masher with box-shaped wire head that "is well made and is the best masher on the market." (Ibid., 464) A two-handled combined potato masher and vegetable press that also removed boiled potato skins cost fourteen cents.

In summer 1917, the potato took on a touch of elan with the creation of *crème de la vichyssoise*. A creamy, cold leek and potato soup, it was the creation of Frenchman Louis Felix Diat, who worked at the Paris Ritz and in New York at the Ritz-Carlton, served *Gourmet* as a consultant, and authored *Cooking à la Ritz* (1941), *French Cooking for Americans* (1946), *Sauces, French and Famous* (1951), *French Cooking for the Home* (1956), and *Gourmet's Basic French Cookbook* (1961). The recipe of Diat's mother, which she based on a peasant soup by naturalist André Parmentier, received mention in a 1923 issue of *La Revue Culinaire* (Culinary Review). At the height of protest against the Vichy government in 1941, French chefs revolted against the name vichysoisse, which commemorated Diat's home town, and tried to substitute *crème gauloise,* but failed to dislodge from American parlance the original name of a favorite hot weather soup.

The study of potatoes worldwide helped to explain how foodstuffs passed from culture to culture. The unexplained appearance of the bottle gourd and *Ipomoea batatas* (sweet potato) in the South Seas influenced the theories of Swedish ethnologist Erland Nordenskiöld and Norwegian expeditioner Thor Heyerdahl, author of *Fatu-Hiva: Back to Nature* (1974). Because the crops originated in the Americas and required human cultivation to thrive, the two deduced that immigrants sailed on rafts from South America to Polynesia, bringing with them indigenous foodstuffs. One unmistakable proof of linkage was the shared term *kumara*, the word for "sweet potato" in Peru, Ecuador, and the South Seas.

In 1998, the Hayman sweet potato from Chesapeake Bay and the eastern shore of Virginia gained popularity for its unique green color. A palm-sized tuber that flourished in warm temperatures and cushy loam, the potato had a creamy white interior until cooked, when it developed a nutty flavor and greenish tinge. The Hayman arrived on the Atlantic seaboard in the 1800s when a sea captain named Hayman brought them from the Caribbean. Although it accounted for under one percent of the 25 million bushels of sweet potatoes harvested annually in the United States, it became a holiday treasure for Chesapeake Thanksgiving and Christmas feasts.

The potato remained a pantry staple at the beginning of the twenty-first century. It was number one in Ireland, followed by Germany, where farmers still baked tubers over an open fire and shared them for an outdoor meal. In contrast, sweet potatoes and yams were a staple of African cookery. For daily service to family, Ivory Coast cooks favored *foutou*, a boiled yam or plantain pounded into a sweet mass. In South Africa, yams and sweet potatoes were central elements of feasts celebrating births and marriages and honoring survivors after funerals. Yam slices were available from street vendors for a quick snack or for a worker's lunch. Cooks grated sweet potatoes and blended with egg, milk, flour, and flavorings to make pancakes, which they fried in a skillet coated with olive oil.

Yams also enhanced a tribal ceremony among the Krobo of east Ghana, where women traditionally welcome purified maidens into womanhood with ritual bathing and a meal of yam porridge and palm oil cooked by their mothers. Among the Ewe of Togo and Ghana, homemakers withheld cooking a yam until they had thanked the gods at the village shrine for first fruits. Priests touched slices of the new yam to the tongues of harvesters; the chief shared the first yams and ritual palm wine with the community. Afterward, women fed their families on boiled, roasted, or pounded yam, which they used like flour. According to a popular adage, it was only right that all should profit from the yam harvest: "If you labor for something, you must enjoy its sweetness." (Beckwith & Fisher 1999, Vol. 2, 80)

See also **Root Cellars**

Further Reading

Beckwith, Carol, and Angela Fisher. *African Ceremonies*. 2 vols. New York: Harry N. Abrams, Inc., 1999.
Morris, Helen. *Portrait of a Chef: The Life of Alexis Soyer*. Cambridge: University Press, 1938.

POTTERY

Pottery, in domestic use since prehistory, continues to serve the humblest cooking, baking, boiling, and storage needs as well as providing backsplash tiles, oil lamps, vases, ewers and basins, candlesticks, drug jars and crucibles, and refined table service for food and beverage. In Asia, the Americas, Europe, and parts of Africa, the evolution of handmade pots followed the settling of families, sowing of crops and regularizing of harvests, storage of foods and planning of meals, and herding of animals. For archeologists, whole pieces and shards help to date and particularize the

Pottery kiln.

crafts, symbolism, language, cooking and eating, and trade of cultures. Artisans form ceramic items from clay, which they prepare into a paste, coil or shape into greenware, decorate, and temper or fire to strengthen the body integrity and brighten a finish. Experts identify materials by the grade of grain, pigment, and such organic material as crushed shell or bone fragments as well as punctation with a drilling tool, shrinkage, conical or rounded shape, flattening, castellation into points around the rim, frilled or beaded collaring about the neck, constricted or wide neck, lobed or flat profile, and round or crenellated lip.

Clayworking developed first among agrarian cultures in river valleys as a means of storing harvests and quickly became the domain of female artisans. After preserving foodstuffs in whatever lay at hand—wood, bark, fiber, skin, shell, and bone—the woman learned how to harden clay in fire. The earliest, clay animals molded by Moravian hunters around 30,000 BCE, received a firing at the hearthside.

The first formal shapers and firers of ceramic kitchen vessels began their production around 12,000 BCE. The earliest known pot, dating to this period, was a domestic container at Shimomouchi, Japan. Such prehistoric fired vessels appear to have held seeds or acorns for cooking. The next oldest find, sun-dried pottery, places Near Eastern clay goods from Iran as early as 9000 BCE.; northern Thai pottery appeared around 7000 BCE.

Because of the variance in food staples, pottery did not spread globally at an even rate. Grain producers depended on clay canisters to keep stores free of vermin. For those relying on pit cookery, an advantage to clay cookware was an improvement to flavor and the absence of ash, smoke, and soil contaminants, but a deterrent was the growth of bacteria not killed by direct contact with flame. The last to need storage containers were fishers of the southern Pacific rim, herders and nomads, and subsaharan African tribes, whose supply of fish, yams, and fruit required less cooking and storing than grain. Thus, their sophistication with clay cookware never reached that of Europe, Asia, and the Americas.

A plastic art, potting allowed clayworkers to create by hand or turned wheel a usable commodity that satisfied a kitchen need while reflecting the personal involvement of the ceramicist. The resulting utilitarian and art items range from the simplest pinchpot to altar vessels and figurines and a complex clay oil separator, created by a Cretan potter with a low spout to access usable oil that sank to the bottom. These imaginative containers replaced such primitive vessels as the drinking horn, a piece of bullock's horn fitted at the bottom with a disk for serving ale, mead, and cider held the reed rushlight.

Pottery is identifiable by type and style characterized by known materials and method of firing.

Earthenware—Potters fired the original clay vessel at 1,470 to 1,830 degrees Fahrenheit to produce variant colors from ecru and red to charcoal and black. More advanced surfacing with tin resulted in Majolica, faience, and Delft, a distinctive style originated in seventeenth-century Holland. Familiar Delft blue-and-white tiling, a popular covering for fireplace slips between fire surround and hearth, replicated Chinese porcelain with ornate oriental settings, windmills, European landscapes, ships, or religious motifs.

Stoneware—A more durable material that took the color of stone, stoneware was formed of a high silicate fireclay and fired at 2,280 to 2,370 degrees Fahrenheit for a harder body. This style, dried in a downdraft kiln, originated in China's Shang dynasty in 1400 BCE and passed to Korean potters around 57 BCE and Japanese in the 1200s CE. Three centuries later, German, Dutch, and English artisans took up the craft, which they emulated from Chinese teapots packed in shipments of tea. Variant glazes included a heavy crystalline surface, a thinner slip glaze, rock salt or sodium silicate glaze, lead or alkaline frit glaze, organic ash glaze, and raku, a lustrous lead or alkaline surfacing heavily mixed with grog or fired clay particulate.

Porcelain—A hard, glossy pottery made of pure white kaolin clay and powdered petuntse, a decomposed granite vitrifier, porcelain was the standard domestic material used in sinks and cookware. The Chinese were the first to make hard-paste porcelain, also called natural or true porcelain. From the early 600s CE, workers hand-molded translucent vessels for specific needs and fired them at heights reaching from 2,280 to 2,640 degrees Fahrenheit, which melted the petuntse and fused it to the kaolin to create a nonporous glass. By 960 CE, factories were making palace porcelain goods for Chinese royalty. Court control lasted until 1100, when Korean artisans opened their own porcelain works. In the late 1200s, potters molded worthier shapes on a rotating wheel. Because of China's dominance in early porcelain manufacture, sellers dubbed its tableware "chinaware" or simply "china." By the 1500s, Japan made its own porcelain, specializing in Kakiemon and Imari, also called Arita. In the 1700s in the New World, a land little accustomed to china tableware, Dutch colonists prized their "purslin cupps" and earthenware, probably imported from India until the Revolutionary War spawned global trade. (Earle 1975, 100)

Bone china—English industrialist Josiah Spode's addition of bone to porcelain in 1797 produced a translucent variant called English bone china, a British specialty that became one of the nation's most profitable trade items.

Because of the potter's reliance on local clay and pigments and the development of characteristic designs and motifs, archeologists can locate and date the beginnings and evolution of pottery worldwide:

Near East and Orient

Artisans in Susa applied dark frieze art on a buff ground as early as 3200 BCE; Ur potters turned a wheel about 3000 BCE to shape their pieces. They connected the flywheel at bottom to the upper wheel by means of a sturdy shaft. By controlling speed with the feet, the potter could leave hands free to shape, striate, and smoothe clay. A benefit to clay work was a handy jar of water for lubricating the fingers. By holding one hand inside the pot shape and the other on the outer surface, the artisan could control the thickness of the base, wall, shoulder, and lip to suit utilitarian needs.

Around 3000 BCE, potters of the Fertile Crescent and Manchuria painted designs on pottery. Simultaneously, potters in India turned out earthenware altar bowls and painted figures. Around 1100 BCE, Assyrian and Mesopotamian potters used a tin slip to smooth brickwork in Susa and Babylon. An Islamic and Chinese variant, sgraffito, began with slip application, then the scratching or carving of a design through the surface into the contrasting color layer of the core. Around 1000 CE, Mediterranean potters began varying their designs by adding ornamental knobs, rolling carved cylinders over the surface, piercing, and creating relief and repoussé, a method of shaping by pressing on the inner wall to create a bulge or rim.

To the east, Chinese potters initiated coiled earthenware, stylized key motifs, and funerary stoneware. They created porcelain from plentiful kaolin, a white clay named for China's Kaoling hill country. To produce a polychromatic effect, experimenters mingled slips of several colors and inserted them with a toothed implement. Another decorative finish required the shrinking of the surface glaze for an intentional netting of hair-line cracks.

The prosperity of the Han dynasty, beginning in 206 BCE, produced five centuries of innovation in ceramic ware and hard-paste porcelain as well as ribbed, crenellated stoneware. With the advent of the T'ang dynasty in the 600s CE, pottery advanced from utilitarian to artistic quality with terra cotta funerary figures painted in bright colors. Mid-tenth century Chinese stoneware stood out from earlier techniques with a vitrifying glaze of feldspar. Mishima, a Korean innovation, called for carving a design into the core, then filling in with white or black slip.

China's Ming ware, initiated under the Emperor's patronage in the late 1300s, reached its height in 1465 and set a standard emulated throughout the Middle East, Japan, and Europe, when a stable native rule extended to Korea, Mongolia, Turkistan, Vietnam, and Burma. Powered by Portuguese, Dutch, English, and American trading vessels, world markets featured incised celadon ware, porcelain from Ching-te-chen, Yüan blue and white ceramics, and the familiar court scenes of bright birds and flowers in stylized settings. British imitators produced Minton china with a blue willow pattern valued in middle-class homes and displayed with pride in cupboards and on sideboards. Into the twentieth century, Asian pottery perpetuated the classic delicacy and subtle coloration.

Isolated from the east Asian mainland, Japan evolved its own unique style. Beginning with Jomon clayware in the ninth century BCE, local potters perfected a thin-walled decorative tableware and ceremonial urns for drinking sacred liquids and interring corpses. Closer ties with China produced an imitative carved stoneware and luxurious celadon ware in the twelfth century CE. In the 1500s, the discovery of kaolin in Kyushu empowered the Kakiemon family to found a porcelain industry. A parallel artistry known as Imari exported ornate polychromatic tableware to eager purchasers in Europe, where anything Japanese brought a high price. Simultaneously, the influence of Zen returned tastes from rich dishes to the folk terra cotta, turned out by Bizen, Echizen, Seto, Shigaraki,

Takonabe, and Tamba, Japan's famous six clayworking centers.

Okinawans selected a crock for processing salt pig each winter. Chinese cooks relied on a *sah wor*, a rough-textured sand clay pot, a nonstock vessel used in soaking and preparing dried abalone and a regional *sah wor yung yuk* (lamb stew in a clay pot). Unlike metal vessels, the *sah wor* was valuable for retaining flavor and aroma. Glazed inside with a brown finish, the two-handled pot with fitted lid, which has been in use since open-fire cooking, suited modern stove-top cooking and doubled as a rice steamer, soup and stew maker, and braising pan.

Greece and Rome

About 3000 BCE, Thessalian pottery influenced the artistry of Boeotia and the Peloponnese. Farther east and south, the Greek isles produced refined ornamentation by carving abstract ripples and spirals and the outlines of sea-going vessels. As the artist's skills matched the cook's needs, items took on shape, weight, and qualities food preparers valued. With porous glazing, the Greek *chytra* (stew pot) and *kakkabi* (three-legged cauldron) slow-cooked fowl and casseroles over a steady, controlled fire without scorching or sticking. For delicate dishes, the cook often used a virgin pot rather than pots retaining flavors of past cookery.

A major influence on food storage and trade, the *pithoi* (storage jar), like those surviving at Knossos, Crete, held grain and oil for shipping as early as 2000 BCE. Minoan potters sketched light imagery on a dark background until the 1700s BCE, when they reversed images to dark on light for carafes, spouted jugs, votive pieces, and drinking bowls. By 1400 BCE, the Mycenaeans on mainland Greece, Cyprus, and Rhodes were trading their fine round-shouldered vases, stemmed goblets, cups, and storage jars to Asia Minor, Egypt, and west to Italy and Sicily. With the Doric overthrow of Mycene in the thirteenth century BCE, Greek pottery surged to the height of Mediterrannean artistry.

A shift in the power base put the Athenian potters of 800 BCE in dominance with distinct geometric designs on amphorae, funeral urns, and the figured *calyx krater,* a graceful two-handled drinking bowl shaped like an open flower and used for thinning wine with water. In 750 BCE, Corinthians crafters introduced petite decorative vases and *aryballos*, or perfume and bath-oil vials, to pan-Mediterranean trade, which influenced imitators in Italy and Sicily.

About this time in Italy, Etruscan potters were carving funerary urns and producing their trademark shiny, black *bucchero* ware. Etruria continued to generate new styles with intaglio designs rolled onto wet clay with a carved cylinder. Late in their civilization, trade brought a strong Greek influence far to the south in Italy. Sixth-century Attic artistry returned to prominence with *amphorae* (tall storage jars), *hydria* (water urns), and *oenochoe* (wine pitchers). They added red ochre and a black surface sheen, mastered around 550 BCE by Exekias, who excelled at mythological scenarios on vases, funerary plaques, and amphorae. During the Hellenistic era, Athenians increased their polychromatic repertoire with yellows, orange, white, and blue and dominated the market until the decline of their trade around 320 BCE.

Like their Greek and Etrurian predecessors, Roman ceramicists made clay pieces for specific purposes—jars for cultivating snails, *boletaria* for heating mushrooms, and an earthenware bucket for fattening dormice, a table delicacy served with pepper, pine nuts, asafoetida, and garum. For baking rice dishes, the rice nappy was a multi-use deep-sided baking dish of yellow ware, often made with fluted lip or corrugated bottom. Pieces developing cracks or breaks at the handle or base could be mended with tin, usually applied by the tinsmith or tinker.

Roman cooks preferred coarse red ceramic dishes that potters mass-produced. Erroneously called Samian or Arretine ware, it had no tie with the island of Samos. More properly known as *terra sigillata* (figured earth) or red-gloss ware, from the first century BCE until the third century CE, Samian bowls, platters, beakers, and cups took shape in a bisque mold into a smooth-surfaced kitchen containers of a vividly oxidized brick-red. The most ornate displayed motifs of palm fronds, wreaths, and stars as well as identifiable human and animal figures in the glossy surface, created by stamping, sometimes accompanied by an identifying mark of the artisan. At the height of Samian production in 40 BCE at the beginning of the Augustan empire, the town of Arretium in northern Tuscany, Italy, began producing quality goods, which followed the military and traders to the far reaches of the empire. Colchester, Essex, and Aldgate-Pulborough, Sussex, Britain; Montans and Graufesenque in Gaul, the Argonne Forest; and parts of the Rhone Valley west of Helvetia took precedence in the first century CE, providing provincials with a viable trade in kitchen ware. The pieces, shaped in a mold impressed with designs at Arezzo, Italy, stayed in fashion for sixty years. Popular designs for lamps include scenes from the Circus Maximus and copies of Greek mythological friezes. A handy dairy item, the *latka*, held fresh milkings for separating milk from cream through a small hole at the bottom.

As with other elements of engineering and creativity, Rome followed the styles and tastes of Etruria and Greece. Columella, author of the twelve-book *De Re Rustica* (60 CE), explains the preservation of purslane in an earthenware crock by layering leaves with salt and drenching the whole in vinegar. He particularizes one pot style, a pitch-lined jar in which cooks preserved marinated salsify in a syrup of *defrutum* (fruit purée) or *passum.* The ancient Roman storage and transport amphorae and Samian ware survive as whole cook pots, *pingui* (jars for fat), lidded platters, jars, *urcei* (one-handled jugs), bowls, beakers, flagons, and cups and in abundant shards over western Europe, around the Mediterranean rim and Black Sea, and into Africa and Asia Minor—wherever Roman civilization spread.

Middle East and Africa

The eastern Mediterranean produced indigenous styles of pot-making. Anatolian potters in Catal Hüyük were at work in 7000 BCE, followed by Mesopotamian, Syrian, Afghan, and Persian crafters. Mesopotamian potters developed the slow wheel around 4500 BCE and advanced to a fast wheel in 2000 BCE for thinning walls on vessels they fitted with handles, spouts, and lids and etched with reliefs. Mass production, which melded iron pigment and clay, turned out kiln-fired brick and pottery for urban domestic wine and oil storage, grain caching, and ritual offering containers as large as 250 liters. Top-grade Assyrian pottery shone from glazing and enameling.

Egyptians owned a quantity of kitchen basins, jugs, cups, and bowls, many carved from wood and alabaster as well as some of gold and silver. The al-Fayyum and Tasian cultures began producing clay goods in 4500 BCE and reached a height of scene-painting in 3300 BCE. For the wealthy, clay wine jars kept honeyed grape juice clean and unspoiled during fermentation in systematic cellaring. Peasants relied on wheat and barley beers fermented in vats. Because of limited communication with China, local potters did not fall under Asian influence. They developed no porcelain because of the absence of kaolin and, like India and Rome, concentrated skills on utilitarian tableware, alabaster and stone sculpting, and metalcraft.

Like China, the Islamic civilization mastered ceramics. Around 660 CE, Damascus potters thrived on the flow of styles from east and west. By 800, Baghdad's pottery began to mimic the panache of China's T'ang dynasty. Influenced by delicate dappling, *zillij* (geometric designs), flower painting, and glazing techniques from China, from the 800s to the 1200s, Middle Eastern courts nourished artisans. Shaking off dependence on the Orient, Middle Easterners perfected lustrous glazes and evolved indigenous characteristics.

Samanid style from beyond the Oxus River emphasized Arabic interlaced calligraphy, floral arabesques, and stylized figures. Few household items remain, in part because Muslims did not follow the widespread custom of securing pottery and clay items in tombs with their dead.

From the 900s to the 1400s, Palestinian tile-makers cast brightly colored ceramic tile in molds, a method still used by the Wazwaz family business in Al-Ram outside Ramallah. Artisans chose both indigenous patterns and European motifs to enhance sale of goods along the Mediterranean rim. French, Spanish, Portuguese, and Italian homeowners valued Islamic ceramics as luxury tiling and kitchen and tableware, which they obtained from Muslim traders. Of medieval Islamic and Mudejar ceramics, specialist Judith Molera notes detailing that migrated from the eastern Mediterranean world and traveled north and west into Europe during the Christian conquest of James I of Aragon during the Seventh Crusade.

Gabri ware, a lustrous crockery, was the creation of Islamic clayworkers. From the Middle East, the painting technique spread to Muslim Iberia, where potters covered dishes with a shiny silver and copper surfacing to simulate metal vessels that Islamic law forbade. When they fired their wares, the pieces took on hues varying from red and brownish-gilt to yellow, green, and olive. Eleventh-century gabri pieces began as reddish clay washed with white slip. Potters scratched on motifs by a sgraffito method, incising a flower, animal, or arabesque design into the base material to rise with brown or green glaze. The style remained in vogue in the Eastern Mediterranean and north Africa into the 1200s.

Twelfth-century Persian potters double-fired pieces to produce minai ware, a banded and gilded enameling against a white ground on beakers, cups, bowls, and tankards. Except for the Kashan tile works, the Mongol invasions ended local pottery production in the 1200s. Under Mongol control, the influence of Chinese Ming pottery increased, flooding trade routes with blue and white ware. In the 1400s, Nicaean clayworks created ewers, tiles, painted lamps, and sizeable serving pieces and footed bowls. The Kerman clayworks of eastern Iran perfected an imitation celadon ware in the 1500s and polychromatic surfacing in the next century.

Subsequent decline in techniques left Turkistan folk pottery and Syrian tile and furmah (tesserae) as the major sources of competition with the global pottery market. The placing of individually cut tile pieces into infinite patterns and calligraphic borders produced walls and flooring for public fountains, flower planters, and counter tops for cafes. The art, which spread to Muslim Spain and reached its zenith in the 1600s came back into style in Fez after 1961 under King Hassan II. In the 1970s, Bahraini potters perpetuated their trade in traditional amphorae. Near Aali, they baked goods in a volcano-shaped kiln heated above a hillside cavern fired with palm branches.

In twenty-first-century Malawi, women shaped wide-mouth earthenware pots in traditional sizes to conform to daily cooking chores. For nshima (corn mush), they make a cylindrical nkhali; for carrying water and cooking vegetable and meat sauce, they fashion the mtsuko, a curved pot of medium height. The tallest vessel, the mbiya, stores water and holds home-brewed beer. In a gender differentiated culture, the men's contribution to housewares were gourd canisters and wood spoons and stirrers, which they adorned by burning in motifs.

Europe

From the 700s to the 1500s, Islam influenced Iberian claywork. Medieval Spain maintained techniques derived from tile and amphora manufacture during the Roman Empire. Under Moorish influence, potters turned out distinctive blue-on-white slim-waisted alborelli (apothecary jars), and pieces adorned with Arabic calligraphy. Beginning in the 1200s, Muric and Málaga excelled at luster ware, which thrived in Manises in the 1400s. Madrid porcelain, named for a cowrie shell, was a focus of the mid-eighteenth century, when cooks considered the slick surface appropriate for acid fruit or sticky confections.

By comparison, Italy outproduced Spain with multiple skills and styling gained from Byzantine and Islamic culture. One innovative piece, the grolla, applied convenience to group needs by adding spouts around a multi-handled loving cup for passing at table to share wine or coffee. In the 1200s, specialists refined Majolica, a highly decorated polychromatic family of stove and hearth tiles, tableware, and large serving pieces coated with coperta, a lustrous lead glaze, and with madre perle, a silvered surfacing. Italian tin-glazing found favor in France in the 1200s, initiating quality faience at Saint-Porchaire, Rouen, Lyon, and Nevers. Baroque scrollery reached a height in the mid-seventeenth century with the production of lambrequin ware.

Into the Renaissance, Majolica carried symbols of prestigious genealogy, such as the cruet set decorated with the arms of the Gonzaga, Mantuan rulers. Orvieto became a center for distinctive native style, as did Florence under the patronage of the Médicis. By the early 1500s, Faenza took precedence for stylized painted china.

In 1575, employees of Duke Francesco de Médicis were the first European porcelain specialists to copy Asian methods. In the 1690s at Saint-Cloud and Chantilly, factories mass-produced soft-paste porcelain serving pieces. A shift in European formulation occurred in 1707, when German chemist Johann Friedrich Böttger and Ehrenfried Walter von Tschirnhaus experimented with pulverized feldspar as a softening agent. With the resulting mellower, sleeker substance, called soft-paste porcelain, factories at Meissen, Germany, popularized beverage sets and vases, which imitators in Copenhagen, Furstenburg, Nymphenburg, Strasbourg, and Vienna soon marketed. Factories at Vincennes, Sèvres, Mennecy, Marseilles, Capodimonte, Doccia, and Belgium set new standards for luxury with hard porcelain dinnerware painted with delicate landscapes and birds and edged in gold.

Although France dominated manufacturing of *grès cérames* (stoneware), centers in the Basses-Alpes increased the French reputation for highly ornate pieces that were prized more for art than for utilitarian purposes. By 1800, France was best known for a creamware called *faience fine*. Among serving pieces for the refined home was a silvered flatware basin. When filled with water, it remained on the sideboard for diners to rinse the serving spoons that became soiled during a meal.

Italy's craft energized Germany, Holland, England, and Scandinavia during the early Renaissance. The German Rhineland, rich in clay, supported production of a durable, utilitarian stoneware, which flourished at Cologne, Frechen, Grenzau, Grenzhausen, Höhn, Raeren, and Seigburg. By 1350, local potters excelled at hafner ware, a glazed earthenware tile for stoves and egg-shaped drinking jugs known as Hafnergeschirr. The skill evolved into surfacing carved in high relief and polished to a remarkable sheen. The industry spread from Silesia and Nuremberg to Austria and Switzerland.

After German potters made technological innovations in the 1400s, they transformed stoneware with a subtler glaze achieved in an upgraded kiln that fired pieces at 1,250 degrees Celsius. Hot-firing thoroughly waterproofed the clay by reducing porosity and vitrified it by vaporizing salt and fusing to the core a shiny, hard, transparent glaze. Their diligence in perfecting durable clay goods allowed Rhenish and Flemish potters to dominate the stoneware market with a dependable product line known as Grès-de-Flanders.

Centers sprang up in the fifteenth century in Cologne and Aachen and spread over Belgium, Holland, and northern France. The humbler jugs came from Frechen; embellished versions were products of Raeren and Siegburg, which turned out the characteristice brick-red metallic hue of brown stoneware and a line of white ware. Siegburg's designers led the market in jugs bearing a funnel neck and piecrust base, which resembled the crimping around the edge of a pie. Westerwald was the primary maker of gray ware

decorated in blue, which thrived locally and as trade goods. Cologne's contribution was a sixteenth-century spherical Bellarmine jug called Cologne ware. As headquarters for Rhenish clay goods, the city became the major wholesaler in stoneware commerce, which still produced domestic wares at the beginning of the twenty-first century.

The world pottery trade flourished in the 1600s. In the 1700s, Parisian factories rivaled established porcelain works, as did manufacturers in Lille, Chantilly, and Vincennes, an operation backed by Louis XV and Madame de Pompadour as the royal potter. By 1756, manufacture of the king's tableware passed to Sèvres. Meanwhile, Germany became a major producer of Meissen ware, lead-glazed earthenware, porcelain, and detailed faience.

Low country kitchens profited from cheap Asian goods imported by the Dutch East India Company; English housewives could purchase Germany's *Bartmannkrug* (bearded-man jugs) and Dutch Delft china as well as an indigenous salt-glazed stoneware and the popular Staffordshire goods that supplanted Cistercian ware and imitation Ming porcelain. The first renowned producer of British goods, Joseph Wedgwood of Staffordshire, England, made a creamy earthware called creamware or Queen's ware, then diversified with a distinctive black and white stoneware that rivalled Germany's Messenware and Sèvres china and made "Wedgwood" a household name. Fine English china of the 1700s featured gilded and silvered edging and transfers that printed a scene on the surface. Ironstone, which appeared in the 1800s, became a standard material for the next two centuries for tableware, serving pieces, and an infant's pap boat, a spouted dish for the dispensing of thin gruel.

In the early 1800s, outside Strasbourg, where potters had shaped clay since prehistory, nine workshops at Soufflenheim employed guild members to manufacture roof tiles, ceramic tiled heating stoves, and characteristic Alsatian pieces handpainted folk-style with open-eyed daisies. At these family-owned enclaves, the staff prepared their own clay and glazing, split logs for the kiln, and passed to their womenfolk the finished pieces, ready for designs, animal shapes, sayings, or family names. To inscribe each, the workers used a *barolet*, a quill-ended paintpot. For a *Backeoffe* (baker's oven), the cook hermetically sealed the popular lidded casserole with a dough strip to lock in juices and flavor as the contents baked.

By 1837, Soufflenheim flourished, supporting fifty-five kilns and employing thousands of villagers. The decline during wars, the Great Depression, and mounting competition reduced traffic in pottery until 1960, when cooks once more demanded the folksy, decorative pots, jars, roasters, gratin dishes, soup terrines, mugs, pots, pitchers, jars, crocks, platters, and baking dishes. One popular shape, the fluted Kugelhopf mold, returned to kitchens to shape yeast-raised cakes for betrothals, christenings, Easter, and other family occasions. The familiar tawny yellow glazing expanded to include darker browns, blues, and greens for new shapes in egg cups, candlesticks, wine coolers, snail platters, garlic pots, and lamp bases.

In this same period, Vince Stingl of Hungary followed the lead of northwestern European artistic porcelain manufacture for princely and royal courts and founded the small factory of Herend in 1826. The company's stoneware and porcelain, superintended by Mór Fischer, entered the high-end porcelain market in 1839, when eastern Europeans had difficulty replacing old classical pieces or buying new dinnerware sets from Asia and Europe. For pattern names, designers chose Esterházy, Batthyány, Rothschild, and Apponyi, all surnames of aristocratic customers. The china pantries of Francis Joseph I, Maximillian of Mexico, and Queen Victoria featured company designs that later found their way into private and museum collections.

In Germany, ceramicists manufactured Bunzlau ware, brown glazed goods for cooking, baking, and frying as well as dairying. These functional pieces—hot water bottles, washbowls, candlesticks, smoke pots for beekeeping, and water troughs for poultry—took their hue from a trace of titanium dioxide in the soil. In 1830, Johann Gottlieb Altmann elevated quality by replacing lead oxide with feldspar for coating the inner clay surfaces. Ranging in hue from bluish-black to moss green and honey, the glaze varied from alterations to the mixture, temperature, and baking process. The center of productivity in Silesia, Lusatia, Bohemia, and Moravia extended to factories in Brandenburg, Bavaria, and the Upper Palatinate, which rivaled traditional potteries from the rest of Germany and Czechoslovakia. Marketed by itinerant vendors, the popular tableware sold briskly in central Europe.

The production center, which Poland annexed in 1945 as Boleslawiec, departed from the typical German salt-glazed and sgraffito-decorated tableware. Bunzlau marketed upscale, high-fired earthen coffee pots, pitchers, goose roasters, pancake plates, pickled gherkin and sauerkraut containers, and tankards easily recognized for their rich, chocolaty slip edged in white relief angels, blossoms, crests, Prussian eagles, and stags similar to the artistry of Josiah Wedgwood. With government aid, these table goods stayed in demand in Europe until the mid-nineteenth century, when some fifty kilns flourished.

As mass production began subsuming the market for folk aesthetics, in 1898, German authorities founded *Keramische Fachschule Bunzlau* (Bunzlau Ceramic Technical School). Director Wilhelm Pukall introduced new production and marketing measures and encouraged urbane decor that appealed to a new generation of homemakers. In 1910, local potters began turning out small plates and bowls, dinner services, milk and coffee pots, bread baskets, and vases in blue, green, and orange. Lusatian artisan Paul Schreier of Bischofswerda helped to popularize a new oriental motif, the *Pfauenauge* (peacock eye), which workers hand brushed or sponged onto the surface.

Into the twenty-first century, a standard item in German kitchens was the lidded ceramic *römertopf* jar, the tureen-shaped vessel filled with rum or brandy and fruit. After marinating for several months, the cook stirred the fruit from the bottom upward before it was ready for eating. Cooks could add to the pot when a fruit came into season. Modern ceramic slow cookers carried the *römertopf* name, as did other pieces of earthenware bakeware.

The Americas

Clay implements and dishes evidence the Western Hemisphere's ancient civilization. Archeologists have carbon-dated native American pottery to as early as 30,000 BCE, thus proving it as an essential to daily life. One theory proposes that pottery evolved from the lining of baskets with mud and clay to make them waterproof. As a result of the division of labor into hunting and gathering, it appears that women were the chief basket- and potmakers.

Because native Americans lacked the potter's wheel, the pre-Columbian clay and volcanic ash vessels of the Anasazi, Hohokam, Aztec, Toltec, and Maya were hand-shaped, producing styles both unique and universal. They enabled users to gather and store fresh water, cook over an open fire, protect grains and liquids from contamination or infestation by insects or rodents, and preserve seeds for the next planting.

The Yavapai of Arizona centered their cookery on food boiled in clay pots, as did the Luiseño, one of California's Mission Indian nations. Cherokee and Soco potters shared their craft with white settlers, who advanced their unglazed utilitarian style with gray and green glazes made by pulverizing bottles and broken dishes or window panes between millstones. Throughout the Americas, potters displayed the ritual and tribal symbolism stamped, raked with a coggling tool, painted in vegetal or pigment wash, or hand-drawn on the surface. Such items were valuable enough to rest on a sacred altar or accompany corpses to the grave.

Potters also shaped votive vessels to hold ceremonial drinks. Peruvian, Ecuadorian, and Chilean aborigines produced a stirrup-spouted jug bearing a hollow handle and the face of a deity. The Nazca preferred animal and geometric shapes. Around 100 CE, the Teotihuacán shaped brown-surfaced ritual pots on three legs, a style that also occurred among the Maya of Guatemala and Yucatán and the Mixtec of southern Mexico, who carved sides and handles with temple motifs and hieroglyphs. Details identify particular periods of history, for example, the dual-spouted tankards of the Tiahuanaco of Peru. Early Alabama Indians formed drinking cups with round bottoms so the users could not set them down until they had consumed all of the black drink, a bitter ritual concoction of dahoon holly, ilex, or yaupon to purify the body of evil spirits.

Western natives excelled at pottery, beginning with the Casas Grandes of northern Mexico and spreading north. The Aztec used a covered pot to soak white corn in wood ash to make their staple bread called *tlaxcalli*, a thin pancake or tortilla. Navaho clay workers evolved a more efficient kitchen pot—a bullet-shaped vessel that perched easily in sand and increased the surface conductivity of heat.

Native artisans of the southwestern United States treasured their clay sources so highly that they kept them secret from all but practitioners and apprentices. Pueblo potters tempered their work in open-air bonfires at a height of 1,300 degrees Fahrenheit. The arrival of the railroad brought a tourist demand for native work. By the 1920s, potters like Maria Martinez and Nampeyo of Hano offered signed clay ware that has since appreciated in value from humble kitchen vessels to works of folk art.

In central New York, the Owasco, an Algonquian culture, coiled clay tempered with crushed granite or shell. They paddled the rounded exterior to raise an elongated pot that curved graceful from rounded bottom to a decorated neck. With a cord-wrapped paddle they textured the outside and finished in an incised, stamped, or punched geometric motif. These pots performed daily duty over ash or a hearthstone. A later version of the Owasco pot flared into a collar or rim for piercing with thongs and suspending over flame from crotched sticks.

South of New York, Iroquois created cook pots from early historic times and into the colonial period, when they used them as trade items. Globular with tight necks and tall collars, the pots began as gray clay coils smoothed with a flat lath before sun-drying and firing in hot ash. They displayed geometric designs incised, scalloped, indented, or appliquéd with bone. The pots served as kettles for cooking corn dishes or boiling maple sap into sugar.

Into the twenty-first century, the clay workers of Mexico and Guatemala continued in traditional styles of production. Whereas, gender roles used to assign men the digging of clay and women the grinding and sifting, more recent manufacture placed more women in charge of ceramics. In Actlán, Mexico, whole families participated at all stages of pot making. Cooperative efforts prepared and shaped greenware, dried it in open-air areas, exposed it to sunlight, and completed glazing and ornamentation. As the surface hardened to a leathery exterior, workers applied handles, redried, then fired the items.

In the colonial period, on the Atlantic coast, Afro-colonial potters produced the mundane eating bowls and vessels that anthropologists find at most digs. Marked on the bottom with an inexplicable X, these pieces appear to have been an outlet for pent-up West African religious mysticism that Christian slave masters had suppressed. Emancipation ended the slave ceramic industry, which collectors currently value as Southern folk art that bore daily meals before the invention of Mason jars.

In 1586, watercolorist John White sketched an Algonquian meal cooking in a clay pot over a fire of kindling. He titled his work *The Seething of Theire Meate in Potts of Earth*. Models from this period display an idiosyncratic checked surface in the potting of the Cherokee, who smoothed the interior with a stone and applied a stamped design to the exterior with a wood paddle. Unlike the labor-intensive work of stone boiling, the use of ceramic vessels strong enough to withstand direct underheating at high temperatures over long periods relieved the tedium of heating stones to drop into skins. This shift in cookery broadened the range of foods in the native American diet at the same time that it increased the number of trade items for intertribal commerce.

Like other skilled crafters, European potters came to New England in the early years of settlement to earn a living from the growing demand for cookware. In the Massachusetts Bay Colony, in 1641, John Pride opened a business in Salem; in 1681, a competitor, William Vincent, set up shop. The town of Peabody, Massachusetts, became a potting center. At Charlestown, John Webber and Thomas Symmes were established potters in 1745.

Domestic stoneware filled the gap in productivity. One artisan, Dr. Abner Landrum, owner of Landrum Brick and Pottery Company in Edgefield County, South Carolina, established a potting operation in 1810 to supply kitchen and smokehouse. Traveling by wagon throughout South Carolina and Georgia, he sold his alkaline-glazed containers for storing vinegar, lard, salt meat, and liquor. The pots found favor with the public, who soon supported Pottersville, an industrial village of workers in his employ. Because competitors enticed laborers to other locales, Landrum began apprenticing some fifty slaves to learn the trade. One prolific practitioner, a slave named Dave or Dave Pottery trained as a typesetter for Landrum's pro-Union paper

The Edgefield Hive. He passed from Abner Landrum to his brother-in-law Miles Davis in 1831 to stoke a kiln outside Aiken, South Carolina. Over a period of forty-three years, Dave personalized his pots and huge wide-shouldered jars with rhymed couplets, his name, and the date. The spirit of uplift and immediacy in Dave's work marked other potters' efforts, especially in face jugs, anecdotal containers bearing brash, impudent expressions in eyes, nose, mouth, teeth, and jaws.

Mexican, Pennsylvania Dutch, and English colonial potters brought European techniques and devised their own innovations in Vermont earthenware, Boston yellowware, and Rockingham creamware. Absolom Day's brownware, made in Norwalk, Connecticut, earned a paragraph in the *Christian Advocate and Journal* dated June 21, 1839, urging cooks to temper these vessels in cold water raised to boiling with a handful of bran added to the water to preserve the finish. The salt-glazed redware of southeastern Pennsylvania fueled a river trade that sent pie plates and batter pots south into Tennessee and Virginia. Carolina potters, some newcomers from Connecticut, devised their own salt-glazing technique for wood-lidded stoneware pickling crocks to protect the clay from acid baths, stoneware clabber jars that sterilized easily to rid them of bacteria, and straight-sided cake crocks that kept out moisture. The humbler meat pot, shaped smaller at the bottom than the top, allowed the cook to slide sausage, breakfast mincemeat, and gelled meats out by upending them. The unglazed exterior was easy to grip with greasy fingers.

In an exchange from South to North and across the Atlantic Ocean, the noteworthy work of Andrew Duché at his porcelain and clay works in Savannah, Georgia, influenced English porcelain formulae. The success of the Philadelphian William Ellis Tucker at porcelain ware and Bennington or Rockingham stoneware from Vermont and New Jersey preceded mechanization of American china during the Industrial Revolution. Style-conscious Americans continued to patronize Spode, Wedgwood, and Staffordshire craft into the early twentieth century.

American clay cookware remained a staple of the culinary arts throughout the early twentieth century. The civil engineer Olive W. Dennis, employee of the B & O Railroad, set out to improve sleeper service, lavatories, and the ambience of the dining car. She patented the company's Blue China, a series that featured scenic views along the company's routes and innovative machinery that carried passengers and goods. She researched historic details, such as the posting of guard units during the Civil War. In 1928, the company marketed nineteen hundred souvenir plates and skipped $4,000 worth of orders for other pieces. For its contribution to American culinary history, Den-

nis's china series earned a place of honor in Baltimore's Railroad Museum.

In the southern Appalachians, according to Eliot Wigginton's *The Foxfire Book* (1968), preservers of fruit have traditionally used crocks for storing muscadines (also called fox grapes) through the winter. The picker dried and culled the grapes to remove any split or soft fruit from the batch. After layering them gently in a crockery jar or churn, the preparer poured boiling syrup or molasses over them to begin a mild fermentation. Sealing required dipping one cloth in melted beeswax and one in hot tallow and tying them individually over the container top.

Into the twenty-first century, earthenware pots range from artisanal pieces to collectables manufactured by Schlemmertopf, T. G. Green, Limoges, Dansk, and Stangl, the clayworks that got its start in Pennsylvania in 1805 as a craft shop and developed into a supplier to Tiffany & Company. The finer examples survive competition from Pyrex, Corning ware, and teflon-coated bakeware sold at cut-rate prices at malls and outlet stores. Their familiar, homey shapes appear on the market as Boston bean pots and electric crockpots, some with removable interiors for easy cleanup. One kitchen artist, Dina Angel-Wing of California, referenced the Japanese tea ceremony in the stoic rectangular shape of her raku-fired teapot and two cube-shaped cups on delicate legs. An East Coast potter, Peter Saenger, focused on the organic tea service. In smooth, matte-finished pieces that interlock like a three-dimensional puzzle, his teapots accommodate mugs, creamer, and sugar bowl. A unitized set called "Service for One" pictures a cast porcelain teapot atop a round tray, which holds single mug, creamer, and sugar bowl in a satisfying sculpted stack.

As of this writing, Southern ceramicists perpetuate the clay-working traditions of their ancestors. The Browns, family folk potters in Georgia, continue the methods of clay clans dating back over ten generations. Others—Lanier Meaders in Georgia, Kim Ellington in North Carolina, Norman Smith in Alabama, and Gerald Stewart in Mississippi—research and follow methods of digging clay, shaping pots, and firing them in wood-stoked kilns much as pioneer potters did in the seventeenth and eighteenth centuries.

See also **Bellarmine; Ollas**

Further Reading

"Bouches-du-Rhône Istres," *Athena Review*, Vol. 1, No. 4, 41–42.

Childe, V. Gordon. *What Happened in History.* Harmondsworth, Middlesex: Penguin, 1960.

Hawkes, Jacquetta. *The Atlas of Early Man.* New York: St. Martin's Press, 1976.

Mack, Charles R., and Ilona S. Mack, "The Bunzlau Pottery of Germany and Silesia," *The Magazine Antiques*, July 1997, 88–95.

Mason, Otis Tufton. *Women's Share in Primitive Culture.* New York: Appleton, 1911.

McKittrick, Rosemary, "Stoneware Jugs and Crocks," *Colonial Homes*, August/September 1999, 42–43.

Reed, Evelyn. *Woman's Evolution from Matriarchal Clan to Patriarchal Family.* New York: Pathfinder Press, 1975.

Tyers, Paul. *Roman Pottery in Britain.* London: Routledge, 1999.

Underhill, Ruth M. *Red Man's America.* Chicago: University of Chicago Press, 1971.

POULTRY

Poultry has been a part of home food production since 7000 BCE. Paleolithic hunter-gatherers appear to have snared and trapped birds rather than aim at them in flight and then presented wild birds to tribal cooks for preparation. When first domesticated in southeast Asia, birds expanded to the barnyard and diet appeared successively in each culinary history. In the Middle East, Mesopotamians began raising geese for meat and eggs in the third millennium BCE, followed at thousand year intervals by ducks and chickens. The Maori concentrated on the giant moa until the extermination of the species, when fish replaced fowl in the diet. As depicted on tomb art from 1350 BCE, Tutankhamun may have favored the cock as an entrée.

In China, poultry was a common food among the P'ei-li-kaang around 7000 BCE. Chicken came to symbolize the phoenix, emblem of regeneration and of the empress. Because of the bird's majesty, individuals served poultry on the second day of the lunar New Year to enhance rejuvenation in the coming months and carried squab, pigeons, ducks, geese, partridge, quail, pheasant, sparrows, and chickens to ancestral altars and temples as divine offerings. By the 1400s, among the nine thousand imperial cooks, specific staff members sacrificed animals to the gods in the ratio of 18,000 pigs to 138,000 chickens.

Domestication of chickens began around 1000 BCE, when Chinese cooks added fowl to the diet in steamed, braised, smoked, fried, roasted, boiled, and stir-fried form or chopped as an additive to dim sum, soup, stuffing, and noodles. The traditional *hot yee gai* (beggar's chicken) appears in lore as a mud-coated dish cooked in a lowly fire pit. The peasant cook then peeled the covering and ate the rich meat. For more privileged tables, a boneless stuffed chicken required deft cutting

The Beltsville Small White turkey was bred to have lots of breast meet.
[© *Courtesy of Agricultural Research Service, USDA.*]

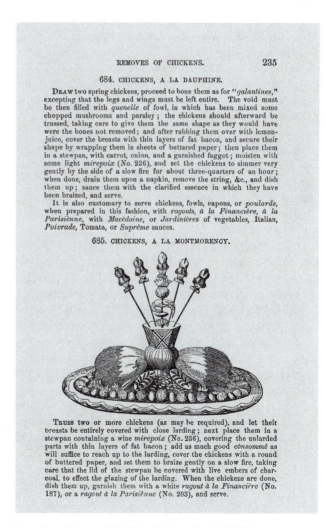

Page from Francatelli's *The Modern Cook* (1860).

with a sharp boning knife and kitchen shears to remove the skeleton without penetrating the skin.

The modern henyard got its start in the Indus Valley and advanced worldwide in sophistication as poultry raisers marketed a ready supply of chicken for the table or trade. Geese appear to have thrived on similar domestication. On its arrival in Europe from north Africa, the guinea fowl became a delicacy in Greece in the 600s BCE and remained in steady demand for discerning Roman diners. By 520 BCE, Greek livestock included "the Persian bird" (peahen), which was already common on Persian farms. (Walker 1996, 81) Cock lore permeated literature as the *alektryon* (awakener) crowing to households each morning. At table, breaking the wishbone produced one small section and one large one, which became the "lucky break."

The Romans revered geese as sacred guardians of the Capitolium and valued goose liver and meat. Like the food history from Asia and the Mediterranean that list home-style methods of fattening the duck and peafowl, Roman poulterers also force-fed to plump up birds, which were trade items in the first century BCE. To swell the organs for cooking, gastronome Quintus Metellus Scipio, who was elected consul in 52 BCE, sweetened freshly removed livers in milk and honey.

In the Middle Ages, poultry organ meats, especially *foie gras* (goose liver), were also specialty items in the kitchens of Austria, Czechoslovakia, France, and Luxembourg. For impounding a broody fowl, the poultry keeper could upend a one-handled piggin or wash tub over the nester. The diameter of the wood pen enabled the hen to warm eggs. The slight rise at one side of the rim allowed her a bit of fresh air and a glimpse of freedom. Similar incarceration assured the cook that the bird did not run off fat while chasing insects in a common henyard.

After slaughter, poultry pluckings produced feathers for household bedding and pillow stuffing. To ready fresh stock for use, the householder gathered them into a net and steeped them in running water to remove blood, grease, and muck. A salt steeping and second rinse preceded a *ley* soak and final rinse. After the feathers dried in a net or sheet, they required a stout shake to jostle clumps. Because they could rot and spread contagion, laws governed the sale of feathers and down for upholstery and mattress stuffing.

In the late Middle Ages, John of Garland's *Dictionary* (1220) particularized the types of birds suitable for eating. He reported on the fowler's job to secure the phoenix, eagle, gerfalcon, sparrow hawk, blackbird, starling, parrot, and nightingale for the table, but not the kite, crow, raven, owl, heron, or pelican. Sellers carried birds door to door on a shoulder pole with trussed birds dangling from each end. Cooks developed hinged pâté molds in tin and copper in which to shape succulent potted liver. To remove the shape whole, they spread the mold with a clear jelly so the mass would remain solid. For a terrine, they pressed ground liver into a loaf pan, topped it with pastry, and steamed it gently in a *bain-marie*. Wait staff learned to flay a chicken leg to make the meat stand out in a whirl around the top gristle.

After the opening of the Ottoman Empire to New World trade, cooks throughout Asia added table exotica—pineapples, sweet potatoes, corn, and turkeys, which had flourished in the wild from Canada to Belize from ancient times. In 1612, Jehangir reported that his retainer, Muqarrab Khan, had traveled to the Moghul court in Goa, India, where he saw a strange animal "larger than a peahen and smaller than a peacock. When it is in heat and displays itself, it spreads out its feathers like the peacock and dances about." (Lunde n. d., 49) The colorful turkey strut appeared in Islamic art by court painter Mansur with wattles and head ablaze in carmine in contrast to dull feathers and claws.

The Spanish wrote extensively on the wild turkey in the 1500s. Late in the 1600s, Jesuits imported turkeys from the Americas to Europe and raised flocks at a poultry farm in Bourges for table use. For the connection with holy men, people often referred to the turkey as a "Jesuit." The French named the female of the species *dinde*, derived from *d'Inde* (from India), a reference to Columbus's incorrect identification of the Caribbean isles as the West Indies. For its variance of the standard poultry menu, food critic Jean Anthelme Brillat-Savarin considered the turkey one of the New World's finest contributions to Old World cooking.

On the American frontier, homesteaders relied on chickens and turkeys for eggs and meat. As settlements grew, chickens and eggs were prime trade items for women who had little access to cash. One settler, Anna Lehfeldt, explained that she liked raising chickens because she could trade eggs for food or staples. To build up a flock, farm women recycled vegetable peels and dishwater, from which hens plucked bits of food. Any water that dampened their backs helped reduce poultry mites, which lessened their productivity and threatened necessary weight gain. One compendium, Mrs. Stephen J. Field's *Statesmen's Dishes and How to Cook Them* (1890) offered an antidote to the scrawny turkey—coop up a Yule bird for three days before slaughtering and force-feed it walnuts and sherry three times a day to encourage succulent, tender meat.

In the Amana colonies, commune-raised poultry had to serve fifteen hundred residents. Each kitchen house supervised a flock of three hundred to four hundred chickens to produce meat and eggs for cooking and trade at the village store. They processed pullets each spring for baking and roasting as a relief from a winter of beef and pork. Late in summer and into autumn, cooks preserved eggs in crocks in a gelatinous solution for winter, when layers lessened production. Amanites did not add geese, turkeys, and ducks until after the dissolution of the commune in 1932.

In a summary of English henyards, food writer Dorothy Hartley denounced scientific poultry farming. With keen-edged wit, she reminisced about the time when every kitchen had a few hens scratching about the door. In *The Countryman's England* (1935), she particularized, "A lot of lazy nondescript hens, snooping round, are no credit to anyone, but some diligent domesticated 'fair layers' are all to the good. Sometimes their pedigree is known but mixed, at other times this sort of hen is called 'barn-door' to prevent further enquiry." (Hartley 1980, 55) The main hindrance to the housewife was the bother of locating eggs scattered about by a single-minded hen. Hartley's memories of British country folk reprised some of their dearest poultry-raising customs. Good husbandry called for watching broody hens and checking on their offspring, because "all eggs in a sitting don't chip out at the same time." (Ibid., 56) She described the placement of a blanket in a round basket at the kitchen fender for gently heating unhatched young in spring. The peaceful farmhouse kitchen, its dinner dishes washed and the floor swept, came alive with cheeps "like a smothered cricket, coming out of the basket in the corner." (Ibid., 57) Widely traveled, Hartley recalled a similar experience in Rondavel, Rhodesia, where the housewife nurtured chicks in a tin oven.

Late in the twentieth century, poultry breeding enabled farmers to produce broader-breasted birds with firm, moist meat. In the early 1980s, an innovation in cooking, the pop-up timer, consisted of an automatic plastic device inserted in the thick of a meaty turkey breast to register doneness. When the timer heated to 178 degrees Fahrenheit, the appropriate temperature for thorough cooking, the lower layer melted, releasing a spring that expanded and pushed a plastic button above the surface. Volk Enterprises of Turlok, California, a family-operated firm founded by Tony J. Volk in 1960 to make and distribute sanitation systems and food service supplies, was the inventor and prominent supplier of the pop-up timer, a microwave-compatible device that also sensed temperatures in ham, lamb, beef, fish or pork. Volk's product line began with the invention of the Hok Lok, a turkey truss that prevented damage to wings and legs during storage and transport, and expanded with Cook'd Right Sensors, thermochromic devices that changed color when meats, poultry, or fish cooked to food safety standards; the Handi-Clamp, a flexible nylon turkey-trussing device; the Clucker-Truss, elastic strings that secured legs and wings to poultry bodies; Vue-Temp cooking timers that announced rare, medium, or well-done internal temperatures; and the Hand-Ler, a carrying handle attached to bulky frozen poultry to make them easier to carry from grocery store to car and home.

Further Reading

Rubin, Barbara Blatt, trans. *The Dictionarius of John de Garlande.* Lawrence, Kans.: Coronado Press, 1981.

PRECIOUS METALS

The molding of precious metals for decorative items dates to the early discovery of tin, gold, and silver as malleable metals. When excavators discovered Mohenjo-Daro in the upper Sind of the Indus Valley in 1921, they unearthed silver and lead cooking utensils from as early as 3000 BCE. Written descriptions of professional silversmithy in Egypt date to 2500 BCE. The earliest domestic items made from precious metals attached a cachet of wealth and ostentation to

A goldsmith's shop, depicting the accountant on the left, the smith bargaining with a customer, and his servant carrying other purchases, or bringing in wares to repair.

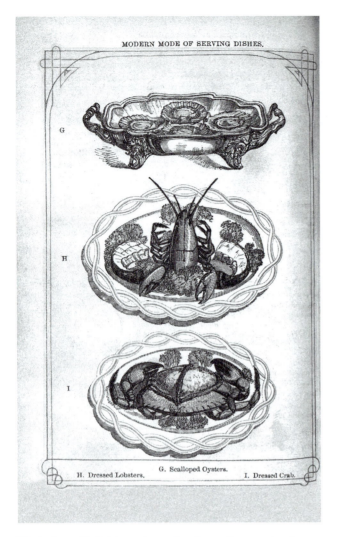

MODERN MODE OF SERVING DISHES.

H. Dressed Lobsters.   G. Scalloped Oysters.   I. Dressed Crab.

Illustration of lobster, oyster, and crab on silver serving trays from *Book of Household Management* (1861) by Isabella Beeton.

their ownership. From the thirteenth and twelfth centuries BCE, remains of Thracian treasure attest to meticulously modeled gold and silver jugs, *phiale* (bowls), lamps, and exquisite *rhyta* (drinking horns) shaped like does, rams, boars, and horses. For the best kitchen ware of the Homeric age, eighth-century BCE householders prized silver and gold as well as more serviceable tin and bronze. In 300 BCE, a Greek goldsmith fashioned a gold wheat stalk ostensibly as a permanent source of food in the tomb. In Rome, a Syrian emperor, Elagabalus, whose palace guard executed him in 222 CE for his extravagance, had his water heated in silver vats. Even more decorous and extravagant, Persian wealth of the seventh and eighth centuries, now part of the Khalili Collection of Islamic art, featured ornate table spoons and ewers of bronze inlaid with silver and finely carved with eagles and griffons, no doubt for the sole use of royalty.

Early in the Middle Ages, European royalty and church hierarchy found gold and silver tableware useful as a status-laden portable wealth. The placement of dishes and implements belonging to a deceased seventh-century chieftain buried at Sutton Hoo at Woodbridge, Suffolk, included silver items wrapped to keep them from tarnishing, thus preserving the prestige of the honoree. During good times, items crafted of precious metals impressed visitors and enhanced the honor and prestige of the householder. Three examples are the *tâte-vin* (wine-taster), a shallow bowl in which the sommelier presented wine for the host's inspection; drum-shaped *timbales*, bowls or vessels used as drinking cups or vegetable dishes; and the silver *sauciére* (gravy boat) with false bottom to hold hot water to keep the gravy from cooling and fats from congealing. Esthetically, silver pieces coordinated with white damask cloths and reflected the soft light of overhead chandeliers. Practically, silver held heat longer than other metals and, fortuitously, turned black in the presence of some poisons, a hazard of dynasties and contested successions. When the economy turned sour or war required liquidation of assets, implements of precious metals could be quickly melted down into ingots for trading, hiding, or transferring to a safer locale.

On a mission to Central Asia, Friar William of Rubruck observed the drinking parties that the Mangu Chan held at his Caracorum palace. In a report to Louis IX of France in 1255, Rubruck described the service of *koumiss*, fermented mare's milk. In place of the usual rawhide vats, the Chan hired goldsmith William of Paris to craft a huge tree-shaped silver fountain twined with fanciful serpent shapes. Wait staff filled the container with the milk beverage and opened jets to four conduits: "One of the pipes discharges wine, a second *caracosmos* (refined mare's milk), a third *boal* (a drink made from honey), and a fourth rice ale, known as *terracina*. Each beverage has its own silver vessel at the foot of the tree, ready to receive it." (Lysaght 1994, 134) Servants heeded the butler's call for service and blew on the pipe to force the liquid out into carafes for pouring into cups.

From donations, monasteries, although dedicated to poverty and charity, acquired a stock of gold and silver. According to an audit of the priory at Steventon conducted on October 18, 1324, the prioress owned two coverlets, six sheets, three chests, forty-three shillings in cash, two trestle tables, nine cushions, a bench and three chairs, lavabo, and copper pots and pans in the manor kitchen. Most unusual was a larder stocked with silver plate, two silver cups, twelve spoons, and a silver-edged serving vessel. In contrast to such sumptuous tableware, Wilsford had two mazers and six silver spoons while Ogbourne had only one silver cup and four spoons.

During the Renaissance, prestige and wealth received attention from banqueters, who observed the fineness of blown glass, faience, and silver and gold serving dishes and pieces both in use and displayed on elegant credenzas. One humanist, Giovanni Pontano, wrote of the luxury at the court of Naples in *De Splendore* (On Splendor, 1498). He affirmed the value of eating from expensive and ornate plates and flatware as appropriate to those of high station. A ritual that carried more ceremonial pomp than sanitation was the presentation of grand ewers and basins for hand washing. Meanwhile, as emissaries of courts and diocese, the *conquistadores* kept watch for any indication of gold plate in the New World and earned rewards for their vigilance when they examined the ornate chocolate-mixing implements of the Mesoamerican Aztec.

At the height of Polish ostentation, making a show at banquets was more important than serving fine foods. Liveried wait staff carried elegant gold and silver dishes, pitchers, and goblets to the table, making a display as they crossed exotic carpets and passed elegant tapestries and coats of arms. At table, they poured drinks into costly glass and served from gold salvers onto rich porcelain. In palaces, royalty collected artful serving pieces more for display than for kitchen use. When King Sigismund III entertained Gaetano, the papal legate, in 1596, he instructed kitchen staff and stewards to serve food on gold plates and bread baskets. In 1646, when Ladislas IV received his fiancée, Marie Louise de Gonzague-Nevers, at the palace in Warsaw, he had the wait staff spread reception tables in satin and silk embroidered with gold and silver threads and deck them with rich plate.

Fine silver pieces ranged from the ordinary to the exotic—the ubiquitous salt cellar, loving cups, caudle or posset cups, punch bowls and dram bottles, flagons, wine coolers, and pap boats, a spouted dish resembling a gravy boat or invalid's cup for delivering thin gruel to an infant's lips. In the American colonies, Thomas Howard of Jamestown began molding silver table objects in 1620; John Mansfield set up a similar operation in Charlestown, Massachusetts, in 1634. Around 1640, the Marques de Mancera, Viceroy of Peru, ordered a Lima silversmith to make collared saucers to hold chocolate cups to keep the brown contents from soiling female drinkers' dresses. In contrast to such prosperity, Lionel Chute, a settler of Essex County, Massachusetts, died in 1645 and bequeathed his treasure—one silver spoon—to his son James. In the next century, the French designed even more ostentatious serving sets than de Mancera's with the first silver *chocolatières*, refined, three-legged vessels into which the server plunged a wood *molinet* (swizzle) for beating the liquid to a froth.

Among royalty, precious metals remained the choice for creating cookware that rid foods of poisons and causes of indigestion. The Indian poet-king, Basavaraja of Keladi, compiler of an encyclopedia, *Shivatattvaratnakara* (c. 1714), listed copper as a destroyer of gas and spleen problems from rice. He recommended bronze for general purpose, gold to halt jaundice and consumption, and silver rice pots to remove liver complaints and phlegm. Clay pots had their own value, as improvements to skin, blood, and the immune system. Seated on a gilded wood dais, the king dined solely from gold vessels, on which servers arranged his food with the chewier items to the left of rice, which occupied supreme importance at center.

In 1759, Matthew Boulton of Birmingham, England, inherited his family's toy and buckle factory and set out to fight snobbery from Londoners who demeaned West country goods as shoddy. Using the latest technology, he impressed china expert Josiah Wedgwood as being "the most complete manufacturer in England in metals." (Davis 2001, 220) To flourish in the high-end market, he employed precision machines to mass produce goods cheaper than his competitors. Among his luxury items were gilt brass and gilt bronze called ormolu, a favorite material for candlesticks, some of which he sold to Catherine the Great of Russia. Among his silverplate goods was the Argand lamp featuring an oil reservoir feeding a hollow circular wick for a cleaner burn and brighter light.

Unusual uses of precious metals permeate nineteenth-century memoirs. Royal heads of Europe prized the coco-de-mer nut, the world's largest seed, which bears the curvacious shape of a woman's thighs and pudendum. Rudolph II, a Hapsburg emperor, was one of many who bought the erotic shape for rimming in gold and silver and use as a drinking vessel. For ordinary gentry, Elena Burman Molokhovets's classic Russian illustrated cookbook, *A Gift to Young Housewives* (1861) passes on an old folk tradition. For leavening a boiled fermented milk, she advised leaving a silver coin or teaspoon in the liquid for four days to produce silver leaven. More from superstition than science, peasants employing this method of clotting cream appear to have passed on good fortune in their desserts rather than flavor, for silver is a relatively inert metal that reacts slowly in the presence of lactic acid.

In the American colonies, punch, named for the Hindi for "five," combined five ingredients—water, rum, lemons, sugar, and green tea—to make a gentleman's drink served at taverns and receptions. The cost of silver or porcelain serving bowls and ladles as well as of Spanish and Portuguese lemons contributed to the mystique of the drink as a beverage preferred by the elite.

Just as in Europe, well-to-do colonials displayed food and salvers and conducted formal teas with the best of implements. Scrolled and adorned like most tea sets of the eighteenth century, such equipage attested to the taste and refinement of the lady serving her guests. Demand for such luxuries, contributed to expanded trans-Atlantic trade in precious metals for table and buffet service.

In 1743, while repairing a decorative copper and silver table knife handle, Thomas Boulsover (or Bolsover), a metalcrafter for the Cutlers Company in Yorkshire, England, discovered that plating copper with silver produced a bond that expanded evenly. His economical process of fusing the two metals resulted in Sheffield silver, England's first silver plate. One of the nation's valued industries, centered in Birmingham, the Sheffield plating process served the manufacturers of snuffboxes, buckles, spurs, pillboxes, and buttons. In France, silver was the metal of choice for making a *galerie de plat*, a central coaster set in the well of a serving vessel to hold garnishes in place.

The staff of Louis XV displayed a magnificent rococo soup service crafted in 1733 by goldsmith François-Thomas Germain, whose works are on display at the Louvre Museum. To honor a royal table, he heaped the lid with a bird, shellfish, and vegetables, shaped feet and handles like a boar, and nestled the finished piece on a stand resembling a reed pool of swans. The piece survived a general melting of precious metals in 1759 during the raising of funds to finance the Seven Years' War and the widespread destruction of beautiful tableware during the French Revolution. On November 13, 1996, the piece doubled the previous record sale for silver when Simon de Puy auctioned it among items belonging to George Ortiz for $10,287,500.

In 1770, the double sandwich method of fusing sterling silver to copper ingots produced a new range of domestic items — punch cups and bowls, mugs, candlesticks and snuffers, ink stands, trays, meat covers, and repoussé tea urns and coffee pots. A particularly showy utensil, the *manche à gigot* (leg of lamb sleeve), clamped to the end of the joint to assure the carver extra grip. Screwed into place, it became a graceful extension of the meat for use in the home and in restaurants and hotel dining rooms. In the *empire* style established during Napoleon's reign, metalsmith Pierre-Philippe Thomire began crafting gilt bronze *surtouts* (centerpieces) in 1810, the same year that Prince Boravitch Kourakine introduced French diners to improved Russian-style service. The purpose of Thomire's mirrored trays, neoclassic epergnes, and patinaed candelabra with filigree baskets was to fill the center of a table denuded of serving dishes after serving staff began slicing and plating food and ladling on sauce in the kitchen for presentation at table.

For ordinary householders, a few touches of silver went a long way toward enhancing the flavor and formality of a meal. In 1801, Newport, Rhode Island, the domestic writer Ruth Gibbs Whitehorne compiled information on bottling tomato ketchup in *Sugar House Book*. To preserve flavor of one hundred puréed tomatoes, she advised pulping, boiling, and pressing the hot mass through a fine sieve with a silver spoon to guard against metallic off-flavors. As described in Mrs. A. P. Hill's *Mrs. Hill's New Family Receipt Book* (1870), ice cream makers chose silver spoons and *coupe* cups for maintaining the temperature of sundaes. Victorians prized silver needle cases, tape measures, picture frames, vanity boxes and trays as well as kitchen and table items. For fine dining, they displayed vinaigrette casters for jams and condiments, footed dishes with filigree handles, dumbbell-shaped knife rests, silver spooners to hold sugar and beverages utensils, serving spoons engraved on both sides of the bowl, filigree pastry spatulas and napkin ring sets for weddings and parties, silver ice buckets and matching tongs, and a fluted tea strainer for high-toned entertaining. For infant presents, they chose sterling napkin rings, rattles, pablum spoons, and child-sized place settings of knife, spoon, and fork.

More impressive was the silver or pewter wine fountain, a centerpiece from which the staff pumped wine through spouts into the basin below. In addition, butlers made a show of positioning the silver salt boat and the silver charger, a commanding display piece that superceded wood and pewter varieties used by humbler folk. These silver disks lined sideboards, particularly among house-proud Marylanders and Virginians, and came to table beneath large servings of meat or vegetables to keep them hot. For utilitarian purposes, cookbooks in seventeenth-century England recommended a silver knife for slicing clean, dry herbs and greens for salad. Such pieces were so treasured that owners listed them individually or by sets in their wills.

In the mid-1800s, metalsmiths created gold, silver, and ivory steelyard and balance beam scales for merchants and outré designs for table use. Chef and inventor Alexis Benoît Soyer created a serving dish insulated with silver sand. An exotic entrée bowl capped with an umbrella top, it stood at the center of four side dishes to hold sauces. A piece from 1870 manufactured by the H. & H. Manufacturing Company of New York City topped a glass salt shaker with a silver embossed lid fitted with a plunger. By pulling up on the knob, the user elevated a series of pins that unclogged holes in the lid.

Care of these Victorian silver treasures required polishing with abrasive silver polish, soaking in warm soapsuds, drying with a soft cloth, and storage in cloth wrappings. Revered items developed a "proud" edge as the wear on silver allowed a patina of copper to shine through. In Victorian England, kitchen servants cleaned holloware with hartshorn or pulverized antlers, which they dampened with spirits of wine. Using bits of rag boiled in milk and hartshorn, they rubbed at chasing and forced tight rolls of cotton waste between tines.

In Washington, D.C., the White House had served food with gold spoons from the time of James Monroe and first lady Elizabeth Monroe. True opulence came in the 1920s with the election of Warren Harding and his wife, Elizabeth Kling Harding, who had the state flatware triple-plated in gold. She instructed wait staff and chef Lee Ping-quan, who was also steward aboard the presidential yacht *Mayflower*, to cease mentioning silverware and to refer to table settings as goldware. Offset by gilt-edged china and fifteen-branch gold candelabra placed on mirrors, the introduction of yellow tones dramatized state dinners in an era of austerity caused by Prohibition.

In 1912, environmental chemist Ellen Henrietta Richards and Sophronia Maria Elliott wrote at length about the value and care of silver in *The Chemistry of Cooking and Cleaning*. The text notes the perpetual burden of polishing: "The matron of fifty years ago took care of her silver herself or closely superintended its cleaning, for the articles were either precious heirlooms or the valued gifts of friends." (Richards & Elliott 1912, 112) After characterizing the thin surfacing of plated silver, they warned of scratches and tarnish and the carelessness of "the table-girl," whom they assumed would use the quickest, easiest method of polishing. (Ibid., 113)

After summarizing the makeup of thirty-eight silver powders, the two authors concluded that three were soaps, ten were part liquid, and twenty-five were dry powder, either all diatomaceous earth or sand. Other brands contained alcohol, ammonia, sassafras, and chalk plus jeweler's rouge. Their preference was for household whiting blended to a paste. They instructed the user to apply it with a cloth, remove with tissue paper or soft unbleached muslin, and polish with chamois. For large quantities of silver, they suggested boiling them for an hour in a laundry boiler or kettle in a strong solution of soda ash, potash, or borax. They confided that the addition of a piece of zinc to the solution cleaned away sulfides, which silver acquired from contact with eggs.

Women's magazines of the 1920s featured modest ads for high-end goods made from precious metals, for example, collectable silver flatware and pitchers

from the Stieff Company in Baltimore. In the 1930s, to spark flagging sales of luxury items, department stores introduced the bridal registry. The sales promotion centered on silverware and featured ad copy and pictures of the starry-eyed couple choosing a pattern that suited their lifestyle. The concept of gift registration extended to china, small appliances, and children's clothing and toys.

Late in 1998, Wallace Silversmiths, a division of Syratech Corporation in East Boston, Massachusetts, brought out flatware reminiscent of Europe's opulent past. Crafted from eighteen-karat gold for the high-end market, the 192-piece service for twelve cost $1.2 million. Called Gold Grand Baroque, the name of the best-selling silverware in the country, the set's oversized pieces came in a mahogany storage chest. The lowest priced piece was a $2,000 demitasse spoon; the highest, an asparagus server for $33,000. The set weighed a total of 500 ounces.

Further Reading

Davidson, Marshall B. *The American Heritage History of Colonial Antiques.* New York: Simon & Schuster, 1967.
Davis, John D., "Metals for the Fashion-Conscious Consumer," *Antiques*, January 2001, 220.
Paunov, Evgeni, "Thracian Treasures from Bulgaria," *Athena Review*, Vol. 1, No. 4, 76–82.
Shah, Tahir, "The Khalili Collection of Islamic Art," *Aramco World*, November–December 1994, 38–47.
Solis-Cohen, Lita, "Record Silver," *Maine Antique Digest*, 1996.
"Wallace Creates Solid Gold Flatware," *Kitchenware News*, December 1998, 19–20.

PRESSES

The press employs force to extract food, either raw or cooked, from containers. Madagascar natives applied a primitive honey press to extract sweetness from the comb. In North America, forest Indians extracted milk from hickory nuts for moistening maize and baked sweet potatoes. Throughout Europe, the French *passe-presser* was a general utensil for puréeing fruit, vegetables, fish, or meat. A specialty item, the tongue press, was a popular gadget from the 1800s for preparing a favorite dish served cold for informal family dinners. Another kitchen tool, the *presse à canard* (duck press), extracted oily juice from fowl.

A variety of presses survived attrition that destroyed other evidence of ancient cuisine. Around 500 BCE, Dravidian treacle makers invented a device to force juice from cane to make *guda* and crystalline sweetener, which they added to curds for a dessert called *payasya*. In the thirteenth century, Norman cider makers, whom Charlemagne's chronicles mentioned in the

Pilchard fish in a barrel after pressing to remove oil.
[© *Nigel Reed / Alamy.*]

early 800s CE, perpetuated a national cider-making style that called for the pressing of one part sweet to two parts sour fruit. After the first extraction of juice, the remaining *marc* (pulp) underwent a second pressing before cider was fermented in casks.

Throughout the Middle Ages, the press or brake, which forced juice from fruit and vegetables, enabled the cook to separate useful liquid and retain pulp for drying, salting, or pickling. The sauerkraut press, which fit into a barrel, consisted of a flat tray that sat atop the lid. After stabilizing it by three prongs to the barrel walls, the user twisted a central screw to force the lid against the chopped vegetables, thus mashing out the brine. Kraut was ready for the table after a quick rinse and heating. In China and Tibet, tea harvesters pressed tea leaves into bricks with ox-drawn equipment. The compression of leaves into solid blocks made it easier to weigh, sell, dispense, and store.

In the home dairy, the levered butter press enhanced the strength of the arm against mass by applying lever action against butter held in a rectangular shaft. The operator could sit in a chair and apply pressure or place one foot on the edge of the press bench for additional force. The user then released the catch that allowed the presser foot to force the finished block from the press bottom. Applying similar principles of physics, the cheese press framed with a yoke and weights suspended from chains forced cheese rounds into thinner circles as whey exuded from the mass.

Unlike early cylindrical stone presses, which operated with a counterweight and central screw, the iron-screw cheese press employed an upright wood frame to hold a cheese board. Placement of one or more hooped cheeses wrapped in muslin cheesecloth within a circular depression allowed fluids to run around the rim and out a small spout into a basin to save for feeding pigs. To force out the small amount of liquid remaining after processing, the cheese-maker topped the cheese board with the *folla* or *foller*, a pressure plate forced against the top by a screw to condense and harden the cheese. Overnight pressure readied the cheese round for a surface dressing and storage.

Shaker communities became America's pioneers of marketing by going into the wholesale seed business, an outgrowth of kitchen gardening. From their success came the impetus to propagate and market herbs. In 1826, they began harvesting rose hips, sweet marjoram, cicuta extract, saffron, and lobelia. Daily at the New Lebanon, Pennsylvania, commune, a press applied three hundred tons of force to turn out 250 pounds of herbs. Turned by a wheel, the press at Niskeyuna commune activated a lever that pushed a pair of blocks into a two-chambered bucket. The whole apparatus fit into a square frame made of four wood beams bolted together and attached to an exterior barn wall. By 1849, workers marketed 16,500 pounds of dried herbs, roots, bark, and extracts.

For the pioneer to the American West, *The Prairie Traveler: A Hand-Book for Overland Expeditions* (1859), a compendium of advice, maps, and intineraries over the principal routes between the Mississippi River and the Pacific Ocean, army captain Randolph B. Marcy explained the importance of packing well. He listed the staples and quantities required per family. In addition to canvas sacks of bacon and flour, canisters of clarified butter, and rubber containers of sugar, he instructed neophyte travelers to slice vegetables thin for desiccation. Drawing on army campaign experience in making foods portable, his method "[subjected] them to a very powerful press, which removes the juice and leaves a solid cake, which, after having been thoroughly dried in an oven, becomes almost as hard as a rock." (Marcy 1978, 31) Rations of vegetables for one person reduced to portions weighing an ounce; a cubic yard produced sixteen thousand servings. From a small cut half the size of an adult hand, cooks could rehydrate enough vegetables to fill a dish to serve four men.

PRESSES

Marcy added that desiccated vegetables retained the antiscorbutic properties that prevented scurvy, a hazard of the long trek West.

In the United States in 1868, the invention of a tinned iron press suited the needs of a single household. For forcing food through a fine, medium fine, or coarse screen, which fit in the bottom of the cylinder, the user activated a curved iron handle. Four extensions of the bottom frame held the container over a larger vessel to catch the runoff. According to the drawing accompanying an advertisement, the iron device, which paired the top lever with a handle for two-handed operation, mashed potatoes, vegetables, grapes, and oatmeal. A variant of the kitchen press was the boxed cutter or corer. Shaped like a thermos bottle, the device, advertised in an F. A. Walker catalog from the 1870s, bore down on vegetables and fruits with a hinged conical lid. The self-contained cylinder prevented juices from splashing work space or cook.

In 1908, the Sears, Roebuck catalog offered several domestic presses in its kitchenware pages. The $1.37 wine and jelly press with two-quart capacity applied a top plunger against a vertical tin cylinder for making jelly, lard, or wine. A fancy japanned screw movement press and sausage stuffer simplified food preparation chores with a four-quart tank and side-mounted hand crank. A $2.77 model wine and jelly press, shaped like a sausage grinder, exuded pure fruit purée in one operation of the crank for condiments and fruit butters and leathers.

Advances in press molding and multi-cavity tooling allowed manufacturers to shape inexpensive dinnerware in elegant designs. In 1916, Madeline Turner patented a fruit press that pulverized pieces of fruit for jams, jellies, and fruit leathers. Similar to sausage mills, patented versions ranged from a gear-driven hand-cranked model for table use to a sturdier press that clamped to a table top. The julienne soup cutter combined ornate geometric cutting disks with a press handle and stabilizing frame. The user forced vegetables through slots in the disk to create fanciful shapes for cooking and table decoration.

Well into the 1900s, Lebanese oil presses followed the same technology and methods of their Mediterranean forebears. Stone wheels weighing over a ton rotated over fresh olives, pulverizing meat and pit. Workers added cold water to cause the reddish-brown oil to flow down a gutter at the edge of the crushing bed and into marble basins. In the final collection, golden oil rose naturally to the top for skimming into a centrifugal clarifier and from there to containers. Workers traditionally claimed the cakes of desiccated waste from the press, which they saved for fueling their ovens.

Presses were among the gadgetry that women's magazines debuted for readers. In the May 1947 issue of *Woman's Home Companion*, a doughnut dispenser from Hom-Ade, Inc., simplified the measurement of uniform servings by pressing out a standardized dollop of batter from the cylindrical well. Held in one hand over a pot of hot oil, the device allowed the homemaker to adjust heat and turn, lift, and drain hot doughnuts with the other hand. Another useful press, the margarine mixer from Plastic Molded Products, Inc., offered a chamber for blending coloring with white solids for extrusion out the far end in stick form.

The press is very much at home in the twenty-first-century kitchen, including the push-up measuring cup for scooping, leveling, and forcing out such semisolids as peanut butter, lard, and sour cream. Standard items range from the waffle iron, screw-topped meat press, and cheese press to the stainless steel potato ricer and garlic or lemon press, a double-handled, hinged device that squeezes out garlic juice or a single serving of lemon juice while freeing hands from garlic odor and citrus pulp and oil. In Mexican cookery, the tortilla press, made of wood and iron or aluminum, is a household necessity, as are the wood or metal bean masher for refried beans and the lime press, which forces juice from an uncompromisingly firm citrus fruit. Familiar to children is the cookie press, a tin syringe with geometric and decorator discs on the end for extruding cookies or shaping pats of butter. A more complicated decorator gun with multiple tips allows the garnisher to fill deviled eggs and baked potatoes, spread soft cheese or dip, and top cupcakes and cookies.

For the everyday hamburger patty, the plastic press shapes meat uniformly for immediate use or freezing. A round or square type with handled tamper or indented tray shapes six ounces of meat to standard size. One variety offers ridges for texture; another by Kuhn Rikon of Switzerland also extrudes dough for cookies and pastries through one of twenty decorative disks. The see-through plastic barrel and steel trigger simplify messy jobs by leaving one hand free for other utensils. An ideal meat press, made by Fox Run Craftsmen, contains a handle that dents patties at center to halt shrinkage and releases the meat onto the cooking surface.

See also **Milling; Oil (as Food)**

Further Reading

Andrews, Edward Deming, and Faith Andrews. *Work and Worship: The Economic Order of the Shakers.* Greenwich Conn.: New York Graphic Society, 1974.
Jansen, Michael E., "To the Olives!," *Aramco World,* July–August 1972, 2–9.
Yzábal, María Dolores, and Shelton Wiseman. *The Mexican Gourmet.* McMahons Point, Australia: Thunder Bay, 1995.

PRISON KITCHENS

PRISON KITCHENS

Conditions in prisons have traditionally deprived inmates of creature comforts. During hard times for a population, jails are the first to suffer rationing and nutritionally unbalanced meals. In Paruta and Palmerino's *Diario della Città di Palermo, 1500–1613* (Diary of the City of Palermo, 1500–1613), 1592 was a catastrophic year of hunger and pestilence. The authors describe the fate of a stray cur wandering into the city prison, which inmates grabbed, slew, and ate half-cooked.

One of the most famous prison cooks, Chandelier, followed Napoleon Buonaparte to exile on the island of St. Helena on October 15, 1815, along with chamberlain Emmanuel Las Casas, several servants, an aide-de-camp, and two generals. At Longwood, Chandelier piqued the fallen emperor's appetite with interesting dishes. The task foundered after Napoleon began sequestering himself indoors to write and converse with Las Casas. Napoleon dined at 7:00 each evening on a generous, well-cooked menu, but sickened late in 1817 from stomach ulcers or cancer that rumors claimed was food poisoning.

For ordinary prisoners exported from England to Australia, food in transports was spartan and bland. To satisfy sailors, guards, and officers, the fleet galleys cooked up simple fare. The weekly ration per man according to navy standard called for four pounds of beef and two of pork, two pints of dried peas, three pints of oatmeal, seven pounds of hardtack, twelve ounces of cheese, six ounces of butter, and a half pint of vinegar. Each convict received enough to stay alive: male inmates survived on two-thirds the sailors' ration; female prisoners got less than half. The insubstantial mess condemned most to scurvy and led them to gnaw gristle and bone for the maximum nourishment they could manage.

When the fleet called in at Table Bay port in South Africa, officers loaded livestock for the last leg of the journey. From a well guarded stock of two bulls, five cows, twenty-nine sheep, nineteen goats, seventy-four pigs, eighteen turkeys, thirty-five ducks, thirty-five geese, two hundred nine chickens, and five rabbits, galley cooks were able to improve menus. In August 1788, after the disappearance of a sheep fattened for a dinner honoring the birthday of the Prince of Wales, the captain offered to liberate any convict who would name the thief.

For the remainder of the voyage, galley kitchens continued to give prisoners bland, unpalatable menus based on salt meat and johnnycake cooked at fireside on a shovel. On the fleet's landing at New South Wales, prison farm self-sufficiency failed to materialize. Fish added substantially to the diet, with ten pounds replacing the regular ration of two and a half pounds of salt beef. Of 966 men, fifty were invalids or aged and others incapable of agriculture; only 320 could work the farm. The men had no plow or draft animals. The first crop failed; the second was so meager that all forty bushels had to serve as seed for the next season. The prison beds, planted on Garden Island in the harbor to prevent pilfering, produced a scraggly harvest that barely fed the patients in sick bay tents. Officers who set inmates to work in private kitchen gardens confessed that the men were so desperate that they ate the crops before they matured. There was little game and not enough gunpowder for bird hunting. Beyond the kitchen gardens, some men ate wild spinach and smilax, which they named "sweet tea." (Hughes 1987, 96-97)

During the American Civil War, at Camp Douglas, Illinois, a prisoner of the Union army, John M. Copley, author of *A Sketch of the Battle of Franklin, Tenn.; with Reminiscences of Camp Douglas* (1893), explained the arrangement of men into fifteen barracks, each equipped with a kitchen on the north end and a "crumb hole" through which cooks distributed food. He described equipment as forty to sixty-gallon kettles and kitchen fueled by coal hauled in by a military detail assisted by inmates. Water service consisted of free-standing sinks conveying water from a lake to a reservoir and from there to the prison. Hydrants supplied washhouses, which contained tubs, buckets, and soap, but no towels. The storehouse, called the "Sutler's store," sold provisions plus cheap merchandise and "bust-head" whiskey, which cost a dollar for two teaspoonfuls. (Copley 1893, 89, 90)

During the immuring of Everett Alvarez, Jr., in Ha Lo Prison, a North Vietnamese lockup, the American flier knew the misery of injuries, vermin, torture, and unpalatable food, which he described in an autobiography, *Chained Eagle* (1989). Captured on August 4, 1964, he lost faith in medical workers who brought him remedies and survived on cold water from a tap and rancid rations from the prison kitchen. The combined sufferings cost him fifty-five or a third of his usual 165 pounds. His spirits rose from the intervention of a compassionate jailer, who brought from his own table chicken and eggs, fruit and vegetables, and bread.

One biomedical concept, the Mediterranean diet, became a late twentieth-century nutritional template that Western peoples accepted as ideal for both taste and nutrition. Greece, Italy, Spain, Portugal, and Southern France emerged as privileged areas in terms of health and long life. Their regimen reflected the dietary rule of Dr. Peter Cunningham, a British Naval surgeon who, in 1821, escorted convicts from England to Australia. To acclimate his charges to a hot, arid southern climate, he fed them less meat and more

490

cereals, fruits, and vegetables than common to the British diet, but made no comment on fats. From the low mortality of felons along the way, he deduced that his regimen was beneficial. The diet resurfaced in the 1970s as a potential deterrent to cardiovascular disease.

Further Reading

Alvarez, Everett, Jr. *Chained Eagle*. New York: Donald I. Fine, 1989.

Copley, John M. *A Sketch of the Battle of Franklin, Tenn.; with Reminiscences of Camp Douglas*. Austin, Tex.: Eugene von Boeckmann, Printer, 1893.

Hughes, Robert. *The Fatal Shore*. New York: Alfred A. Knopf, 1987.

Pitch, Anthony S., "A Prisoner's Tale," *Reader's Digest*, August 1990, 39–42.

PYREX

Pyrex, a common glass invented for railroad signal lanterns, but found in most homes, has been cooking, storing, and serving foods safely since 1915. Before its invention, several European glassworks projects presaged the addition of a tough glass to cooking containers. Optician Carl Zeiss of Weimar, Germany, tinkered with heat-resistant glass in the mid-1800s. He first strengthened silicon with boric acid for use in microscopes for the University of Jena and went into partnership with Ernst Karl Abbe, a German mathematician and physicist, who directed research at the Zeiss workshop, maker of optical equipment, cameras, binoculars, and microscopes. The French invention of Duralex, an unbreakable glass, increased the product line of Bormoioli Rocco et Figlio, a company established in Parma, Italy, in 1854.

Based on the advances of Dr. Otto Schott of Jena Glass Works in Leipzig, Germany, and of Dr. Eugene G. Sullivan, inventor of Corning's Nonex borosilicate glass, in 1915, the American Corning Glass Works of Corning, New York, created the Pyrex brand, a dependable line of casseroles, beverages sets, bakeware, and serving items. The company supplied American homes for over eighty-five years. The offshoot of laboratory work by a physicist, Dr. Jesse T. Littleton, Pyrex derived from a casserole he improvised for his wife, Bessie Littleton, in 1913 by cutting down a Nonex battery jar. For a month, she field-tested various glass containers for heating uniformity and ease of use, food removal, and cleaning. Pyrex earned the praise of master chef James A. Beard, who said of the baking dishes, "They are practical, easy to clean, inexpensive and, being transparent, they allow you to oversee the contents closely." (Beard 1975, 280) He especially admired the dimensions and capacity information stamped into the glass for easy reference.

After Corning removed lead from the formula, the company engaged Sarah Tyson Rorer, food editor for *Ladies' Home Journal* and director of the Philadelphia Cooking School, and consultant and food writer Mildred Maddocks Bentley, co-author of the *Rumford Receipt Book* (1911) and compiler of *The Business of Housekeeping* (1924), to corroborate Bessie Littleton's tests on heat-resistant glass cookware. They concurred that glass produced more efficient cooking and baking. The dishes absorbed heat and were attractive, unbreakable, and sturdier than tin, earthenware, porcelain, or enamelware. Pyrex produced no residual flavors or odors and served the kitchen without corroding or exuding toxins.

According to varying industrial histories, the company named the product for the Greek word for fire or for "pie rex," a hybridized English-Latin name implying "pie king." In addition to the kitchen wares section of Jordan Marsh department store in 1915, Pyrex found appreciative markets in Belgium, France, Germany, Italy, Japan, the Netherlands, and Spain for pie plates, cake and bread pans, custard cups, and later products. According to the March 1925 issue of *Good Housekeeping*, its goods received the endorsement of Alice Bradley, principal of the Fannie Farmer's School of Cookery in Boston. The line expanded with the addition of Range Top Ware (1930), Flameware stovetop skillets and saucepans and mixing bowls for the DeLuxe Hotpoint Mixer (1934), double boilers, percolators, and tea kettles with a detachable handle to fit all parts of the set (1938), and the Chemex coffeemaker (1941), a popular advancement created by Dr. Peter Schlumbohm in the shape of an Erlenmeyer flask and funnel, which other companies copied.

Throughout the 1930s, ad copy in women's magazines recommended Pyrex for boilable bell-top invalid dishes, divided dishes, lidded refrigerator sets, and nursing bottles. Sold in pharmacies and allegedly doctor-recommended, tempered glass baby bottles resisted breakage from sudden temperature change. Available either wide-mouth or narrow-necked in six-sided shape for easier grasp by parent or infant, the bottles were flat-bottomed to sit in pot or electric bottle warmer and displayed ounce and half-ounce markings for easy monitoring of intake.

After the redesign of earlier products in 1948, the company began manufacturing Pyroceram, a crystallized ceramic glass invented by Dr. S. Donald Stookey to remain stable under a wide range of temperatures. During this period, Ann Mikell, consultant to the U.S. Department of Agriculture and former domestic consultant for Frigidaire, traveled the Midwest and Southwest to determine needs and trends through department store lectures, public utility seminars, sampling to retailers, and radio and television programs. In the late

PYREX

1950s, the company produced its popular white Corn-
ingware, an oven-to-table service marked by the company's signature cornflower.

Corning continued producing innovations in glass
and ceramics. Pyroflam fireproof ovenware entered the
market in 1964; the next year, William M. Curtis won
an IDI design award for Terra, a bake-serve ware. The
Pyrex Store 'N' See ware, designed by R. Greer, A.
Samuels and S. Balbach, appeared in 1968, the same
year the company pioneered Jerry E. Wright's
Counter-that-Cooks electric range. Enhancing the use
of the Pyroceram four-unit cooktop was a set of Cook-
mate pots ground and polished to sit securely on the
heat elements.

As plastic dinnerware declined in popularity,
Corelle LivingWare filled a niche. Marketed in 1970,
it extended a two-year guarantee for its break-resistant
tri-layered glass fabrication. During the spectacular
rise of microwave cookery in the next two years, Corning sold sixty million pieces; by 1996, some two billion were in use. The company's intent to challenge
the market into the twenty-first century was obvious
at the January 2001 International Housewares Show in
Chicago, where Corning introduced a potluck dish that
came with vented plastic lid and insulated thermal
carrier.

See also **Maltby, Lucy**

Further Reading

Mauzy, Barbara. *Pyrex: The Unauthorized Collector's Guide.*
Atglen, Penn.: Schiffer Publications, 2000.
"Where Mrs. Homemaker Is Never Forgotten: Consumer Prod-
ucts Divison's Proving Ground for Corning Glassware,"
Corning Glass Works Gaffer, October 1946, 3.

Q

QUERNS

During the Neolithic age, from 10,000 BCE to 2500 BCE, the quern—a primitive handmill for grinding grain—applied stones to remove inedible husks and grind to grit or powder indigenous plants and seeds, the foods that enabled wanderers to enjoy a settled lifestyle. This technology of the Mesopotamians was adapted centuries later by the ancient Chinese, Egyptians, Greeks, Indians, Koreans, and Romans. Querns, which date before 8000 BCE in Mesopotamia, introduced wild grass grains and nuts to the human diet by grinding to make them edible. The technology passed about the Mediterranean to Italy, Spain, and northwestern Africa, where cultivation of grain demanded some means of crushing heads to make flour for bread.

Images of women squatting by wide, shallow stone querns to knead doughy masses appeared in cave paintings in Bhimbetka, India. The precise course of development is difficult to date, depending on the type of grain. For rice- or millet-centered cuisines, a mortar and pestle or an edge-runner mill would have sufficed to grind supplies to powder. For wheat-centered societies, the rubbing action of the muller or grinding stone against a saddle quern would have cracked the hard hull more efficiently than hand pounding with a pestle. The householder depended on a small mortar or saddle quern, such as an artifact unearthed at a dig at Whitby Abbey in northern Britain and the numerous cereal grinders found in Jordan dating to 2500 BCE. The discovery of such domestic tools offers to archeologists proof of a site's occupation as a residence.

For hand milling grain, pigment, or spice, a hard, gritty material like beachrock, porous basalt, tuff, or sandstone worked best. The operator gripped the smaller stone with both hands and rubbed it back and forth over grains scattered over the larger one in the style of the Mesoamerican mano and metate. The work was so laborious that all members of a family might participate, especially if the grinders needed a large quantity of flour for brewing beer or preparing a tribal feast.

For the Hualapai (or Walapai) of Arizona, flat pounding stones and rotary grinders were key technology for a diet heavy in mesquite beans, piñon nuts, and corn. Fine particles from milling in stone querns appear at fault for the wear on teeth that have survived with body remains from early times. Eventually, the larger hour-glass mill turned by slave or dray animal for commercial bakeries made the quern obsolete.

Rotary querns were Roman domestic tools dating before 100 BCE and may have been a British invention shortly before that time. After 2 BCE, about the time that water mills came into use in the Roman empire, essayist Cato the Elder described the rotary quern, an advanced grinder comprised of two nested stones, the top convex fitted to a spindle or axle that matched a slot in the concave bottom. Hand rotation of a wood handle back and forth in an arc or a full 360 degrees provided the friction for grinding meal from grain. The upper layer or bedstone had a hole or funnel for feeding grain into the space next to the bottom stone. Pulverized grain held in the bosom of the lower stone spun out the seam as finished flour. Adjustment of the grind took place at the rynd, an iron or wood block that bridged the underside of the funnel. The technology simplified the job of the saddle quern and offered convenience for cooks who wanted a small quantity of freshly ground grain flour or meal. During the Roman occupation of the British Isles, technology revamped the rotary quern into a pot quern, a similar device pierced at the top by a funnel to simplify the act of filling with grain.

For hand rotary mills, ship's crews probably paid a substantial price for a means of grinding grain during voyages. The cook's task took more than an hour per day to supply flour for the bread of a crew of five or six sailors. The use of space for a quern appears to have been a compromise over carrying flour in the hold, which did not travel as well as whole grain. In addition, heavy querns provided ballast along the keel. Roman legionaries preferred fine Rhenish lava stone from Mayen, Germany, the chief European exporter. Users recycled worn-out or broken quern stones in walls, roads, and building projects. The location of identical grinding technology in Japan suggests a link between Rome and the Far East. As recorded in the *Nihon-shoki* (720 CE), Japan's earliest chronicle, the technology did not permeate the island nation until the establishment of Buddhism, when querns became essentials to the making of tofu.

According to the domestic expert Dorothy Hartley's *The Land of England* (1979), querns were outlawed under early feudal laws, which intended to force smallholders to grind their harvest at the master's mill. People generally ignored the stricture and made stone grinders with one or two off-center grips. In the American colonies, querns or quarnes, called samp mills, were the sole method of grinding grain until newcomers built European windmills, a technology that terrorized forest Indians. By the time that settlers had mastered corn cultivation, they set up English water mills, beginning in 1633 at Dorchester, Massachusetts, and two years later at Ipswich.

In Scotland, cooks of the highlands and islands favored the quern called a "knocking stone." For the simplest kitchen, the quern also served as a toasting stone for finishing oatcakes. In Ireland, because of the dominance of grain meals, the kitchen quern occupied a central location near the hearth. For *práipin* (porridge), the cook griddle-roasted wheat, then ground the grains in a quern. The thin meal, topped with cream and sugar, was a favorite breakfast.

Still in use in the late twentieth century, the quern suited the preparation of durum wheat in the Maghrib, the western half of the Arab world covering roughly central Libya to the Straits of Gibraltar. To ready the hardy wheat for use in couscous, Moroccan women dropped grains into the center of the top stones and rotated tops above bottom stones with wood handles hammered into the cover. The lap-size implement was easily transported and stored. Sturdier models stood on three wooden legs.

See also **Mano and Metate; Mortar and Pestle**

Further Reading

Dickason, Olive Patricia. *Canada's First Nations.* Norman: University of Oklahoma Press, 1992.

Hawkes, Jacquetta. *The Atlas of Early Man.* New York: St. Martin's Press, 1976.

Noakes, Greg, and Laidia Chouat Noakes, "Couscous: The Measure of the Maghrib," *Aramco World*, November–December 1998, 16–23.

R

RAFFALD, ELIZABETH

Elizabeth Whitaker Raffald, a native of Doncaster, Yorkshire, spoke authoritatively on the English kitchen of the late eighteenth century. She was born in 1733 and received the standard education for young women. Raffald chose on-the-job training, beginning in 1748. Under Sir Peter and Lady Elizabeth Warburton, Raffald, at age twenty-seven, became housekeeper at Arley Hall, Cheshire, where she refined her knowledge of food preparation. Three years later, she married the gardener, botanist John Raffald, who originally recommended her for her job. After six years, she moved on to better herself, but remained a close associate of the Warburtons.

Revered as a confectioner, caterer, food writer, hotelier, and purveyor of goods and services, Raffald thrived in Manchester. When her husband established himself at his brother's Market Place nursery stall, she opened the city's first confectionery while mothering her sixteen daughters. In addition to supplying upscale larders with quality provisions, she rented out storage space and maintained a servant referral agency. She compiled directories of local traders and merchants and advertised imported goods and a cooking school in the *Manchester Mercury* and *Prescott's Journal*.

Raffald's *The Experienced English Housekeeper* (1769), which covered kitchen matters from banquets of fifty dishes to fireside family meals, remained a home cooking staple for two centuries. Dedicated to Lady Warburton, the book boasted eight hundred original recipes, which Raffald guaranteed were plain, tested dishes rather than fancy cookery stolen from

ELIZABETH RAFFALD.

Published as the Act directs, by R. Baldwin, 31 July, 1782.

Illustration from *The Experienced English Housekeeper* (1786).

less practical texts. Her forte, the elaborate dessert, filled a chapter with table decoration, a fantasia of jellies, gilded fish, sweets, silvery webs, edible nests, and other goods like those she marketed from her Manchester establishment.

Raffald's book, which went through seven editions, succeeded at the same time that the author was battling loss of business and an alcoholic, spendthrift husband. She opened a refreshment stand at the race track on Kersal Moor and catered meals for the Exchange Coffee House, which her husband supervised. After a lifetime of hard work, she died on April 19, 1781. Her book survived well into the Victorian era in totality and also served John Farley, the London Tavern's head cook, pirater of recipes for *London Art of Cookery, and Housekeeper's Complete Assistant, on a New Plan* (1783), ghost-written by Richard Johnson. Despite its replication of Raffald's recipes, Farley's book remained in print through thirteen editions.

RAMADA

The ramada, a pavilion cook site, grew out of the need to circumvent natural elements. The Potawatomi of Michigan built their cook sheds of limbs roofed with bark to shelter women while they boiled maple sap for sugar, smoked cranberries, made mocucks from birch bark, or pounded beechnuts into flour. In a desert climate, the early Pima constructed the ramada as an outdoor sunshade, arbor, portable work station, and covered veranda. Under a wheat straw roof or cattail and arrowwood stem thatch on mesquite posts, families could enjoy relief from the sun. Maricopo children napped or did chores while weavers made mats and cooks shelled beans, winnowed grain, and ground meal.

Like the chickee of southeastern Indians, the ramada offered a loft of cottonwood or willow beams for storage. In summer, women of the Taos pueblo established food preparation cooking operations outside their homes under shady arbors and built clay hornos for baking trade items. When missionaries first contacted pueblo dwellers, they set up church services in ramadas and dined in the open air with converts. Sodbusters arriving to nearby lands emulated the native ramada by setting up sheltered cook sites in lieu of cabin fireplaces and replicated the pavilion method of shading work stations in distant fields, which required weeks of rock removal and tillage before they were arable. During this period of separation from home conveniences, farm families sometimes cooked and slept under a brush ramada.

During the California gold rush of 1849, miners observed hard-working Miwok women, who made baskets for gathering fresh spring greens, berries, pine nuts, and acorns to process for winter. Shaded from the sun by brush ramadas, they worked at hulling and pulverizing nuts into meal, which they rinsed at streamside to leach out bitter tannic acids. However, their makeshift protection from the sun failed to cool them because their work required stone boiling—heating tightly woven baskets of water and nut meals with stones laid in a fire for dropping into the broth.

In the Montagnard villages of Vietnam, American soldiers found families living in open-air co-ops in the late 1960s. At Buon Rocai, householders rebounded from burned-out villages by quickly reconstructing thatched pavilions. Along the sides, they strung rolled bamboo shades, which protected residents from seasonal wind and monsoons and offered a measure of privacy. Between pavilions, women carried bamboo baskets for winnowing rice and set up hand looms for weaving fabric and knee-high log mortars for pounding grain into meal with a pestle.

In 1974, the Tuareg living in the Nigerian Sahara Desert conducted limited family activity and food preparation under a short version of the ramada. A leather canopy held aloft by sharpened poles, it supported goatskin water bags and sheltered the acacia limbs needed for firewood. While camel herds foraged farther from home, drought forced women to cook millet porridge without milk. Similar to the Bedouin goat-hair tent of Algeria, the desert shelter suited family living, cooking, and dining because it screened out hot sun while welcoming breezes.

In the early twenty-first century, the traditional semi-permanent porch remained in service for displaying wares to tourists and sheltering attendees at rodeos and dance festivals.

See also **Chickee**

Further Reading

Johnson, Susan Lee. *Roaring Camp: The Social World of the California Gold Rush.* New York: W. W. Norton & Co., 2000.

Linthicum, Leslie, "More Than Beauty," *Albuquerque Journal,* September 6, 1998.

Sochurek, Howard, "Viet Nam's Montagnards," *National Geographic,* April 1968, 443–487.

RANDOLPH, MARY

The respected Southern cook Mary Randolph compiled a cookbook that preserves the culinary heritage of Virginia plantations. Born on August 9, 1762, to Anne Cary and Thomas Mann Randolph, a member of the state house of burgesses, she was the first of thirteen children. After marrying a cousin, David Meade Randolph, she settled at Presque Isle in Chesterfield County and had eight children. Her husband, a veteran army officer during the American Revolution, served General George Washington as a federal marshal.

A cousin of Mary Custis whose husband was General Robert E. Lee, and sister-in-law to Thomas Jefferson's daughter, Mary Randolph's lineage included the FFV, First Families of Virginia. She took pride in her reputation as Richmond's best cook. In a familiar colonial upheaval, her family lost social standing during a political shift. She turned to kitchen business to sustain them. From grand style, they settled into an upscale boardinghouse, where her table impressed discerning patrons.

From this experience at professional cookery, Randolph collected English and colonial recipes for *The Virginia House-wife: or Methodical Cook* (1824), an historical landmark in American home economics. The practical and incisive style moved directly to the point: "Nothing is more simple than [making butter sauce], and nothing so generally done badly." (*The Williamsburg Cookbook* 1971, 90) The text contained such classics from local produce as apricots in brandy, walnut catsup, tansy pudding, gooseberry fool, Henrietta pudding, pickled nasturtiums, vinegar of the four thieves, and her rich fruit cake, a pound cake base studded with nine pounds of assorted raisins, currants, almonds, and citron. She also preserved the traditional Atlantic coast communal pot of fish chowder, thickened with the starch of fresh corn, and explained how to corn beef to preserve it through summer weather and how to make french fries in a skillet. Her text included Southern household recipes for soap, starch, cologne, and silver polish.

To save on groceries, Randolph stressed such native produce as stewed sweet potatoes, okra soup, curried catfish, barbecued shoat, field peas, beaten biscuits, homemade berry cordials, and tomato and pumpkin dishes along with Continental specialties from England, France, Spain, and Italy and a Jewish delicacy, pickled fish. Her instructions for a pig roast are typical of her book's straightforward presentation of recipes. She selected a clean, fat pig that would fit in her dish. For stuffing, she minced the liver and mixed it with bread crumbs, onion, parsley, pepper, and salt and blended it with butter and egg to make a paste. After stuffing the cavity, she sewed it shut, speared the pig with a spit, and basted with saltwater while it roasted. For a crisp skin, she rubbed the outside with lard wrapped in linen. Serving called for presenting carcass, head, ears, and feet along with a gravy boat of drippings.

While nursing an invalid son, on January 23, 1828, Randolph died in Washington, D.C., and became the first person buried in Arlington Cemetery, the former home of Mary Custis Lee. Randolph's book maintained its appeal on both sides of the Atlantic and went through new editions in 1825, 1831, 1838, 1850, and 1860. Her tomato ketchup recipe was the first ever published. To her credit, the Randolph cooking style, known as Virginia's best, influenced Civil War cookery above and below the Mason-Dixon Line.

Further Reading

Gardiner, Anne Gibbons. *Mrs. Gardiner's Family Receipts from 1763*. Boston: Rowan Tree Press, 1989.
Hess, Karen, intro. *Martha Washington's Booke of Cookery*. New York: Columbia University Press, 1981.
James, Edward T., ed. *Notable American Women, 1607–1950*. Cambridge, Mass.: Belknap Press, 1971.
The Williamsburg Cookbook. New York: Holt, Rinehart and Winston, 1971.

REFRIGERATION

From ancient times, home-chilling has enabled householders to keep fish, meat, dairy items, and other perishables over a longer period than fresh goods generally allow. Naturalist Zubeir Ibn al-Awwam of Basra described a clever method of cooling beverages for banquets held in the sumptuous Zisa palace in Palermo, Sicily. Norman overlords left to Arab wine stewards the job of chilling and serving a fresh fruit drink. As described in al-Awwam's *Book of Agriculture* (1180), staff smeared the interior of earthenware jars with honey mustard mixed with sweet grape juice. After a day for the blend to permeate the jar, they poured in clarified grape juice and set the jars in the flowing waters of a fountain to chill. The refreshing drinks floated on the current to the banquet tables.

Kitchen workers in India supposedly learned the use of saltpeter as a coolant from Akbar, the great moghul who came to power in 1556. When philosopher-scientist François Bernier, author of *Travels in the Mogul Empire AD 1656–1668*, passed by the Ganges River in 1665, he found people pouring water into tiny flasks and lowering them into a saltpeter solution. By the 1700s, British colonists hired *abdars* (water coolers) to agitate clay jugs of drinking water in a similar solution during the night to chill liquids for breakfast.

In the British Isles, the placement of a shed over a spring provided a farmstead with a keep for milk and a source of water for sluicing salting troughs fashioned from slate. A natural refrigerator, the constant flow of water melting from snow-capped peaks to the north served the family through continual recycling as it passed through the stone sink of the laundry hut, henyard and apiary, and the family privy. The wooden hoggin extended the period of coolness in water supplies by dampening the outside and allowing natural evaporation to chill the interior. For this reason, the trekker frequently attached water bottles, jack pots, and gourds from a long pole swung over the shoulder to encourage free circulation of air and a natural chill for a beverage.

On the Australian outback, bush cooks made their own ovens and cooling devices and preserved food by Fowler's Vacola canning system. For storing recently slain meat, they created a homemade cooler in a shed with a tank on top. By dripping water through the building's charcoal walls, they caused enough evaporation to chill, but not freeze the contents.

In more refined homes, a short period of chilling foods on a stone or marble pantry floor sufficed temporarily to preserve perishable goods, which butchers, fishmongers, and milkmen delivered daily. As described in Randle Holme's *The Academy of Armoury* (1688), the 1677 inventory of Ham House at Chester, the invention of the cistern or cellaret in the late Renaissance offered a more decorative way to chill bottles at table. Holme describes the container as "brass, pewter or lead to set flagons of beer and bottles of wine in." (Wilson 1991, 45)

Although Dr. William Cullen, a Scottish physician and renowned authority on evaporation and neuroses, began making artificial ice in 1755, English families relied primarily on imported ice blocks. Sarah Josepha Hale's *The Good Housekeeper* (1839) instructed the thrifty housewife to wrap ice in flannel and store it in the cellar. To maintain the lowest temperatures, the ice chest served households into the late nineteenth century. London housewives could shop Harrods department store for attractive ash models insulated with charcoal and lined in zinc. Unlike earlier styles that blanketed the ice in a box with lift-out compartments, a cumbrous system patented in 1856, the upgraded Alaska Ice Chest consisted of two square lids fitted into the top.

Mrs. Cornelius's *The Young Housekeeper's Friend* (1859) featured a full-page ad for Nathaniel Waterman's ventilated refrigerator, patented in 1825 in Boston. A horizontal chest with thick walls and handles at each end, the box perched on four legs and offered a metal shelf for holding stores. A competitor, Jewett & Day, listed a larger chest with horizontal lid on top and a small door at the bottom. Cornelius's alternative to these time- and labor-saving appliances was a nesting of pails to form a freezing compartment similar to an ice cream churn. By placing the cream pail inside a larger container of ice and coarse salt, the homemaker could freeze a dairy dessert by agitating the pail within its freezing bath and applying the heat transfer principle as ice changed from a solid to a liquid.

Mechanical refrigeration evolved after the transportation industry worked out solutions to long distance hauling of perishables. With the invention of the refrigerated rail car, designed in 1867 by George Henry Hammond and William Davis, shippers could pack meat and fish directly on a bed of ice for transportation from butcher's bench to seller. A compartmented version, invented by George K. Wood, intended to circulate air through hollow tubes, but the design failed. Joel Tiffany attempted to improve on the car in 1868 by installing ice tanks and bunkers and heat-deflecting doors. A new concept launched in 1872 placed ice in V-shaped vessels at front and rear of the car. Within five years, Tiffany patented a more efficient double-decker Summer-Winter Car, which railmen called "reefers." In 1882, shippers refreshed ice up to four times on the Chicago-to-New York route. The laborious, time-consuming job boosted prices of transported goods.

For the home, numerous types of ice boxes and ice caves chilled by holding chunk ice in a tin container at the top and allowing it to melt and flow down the interior to a catch basin at bottom. Such trickle-down refrigeration encouraged the fad of the late Victorian era—ice cream, sorbets, and flavored ices made from fruit, vegetables, wine, and liqueurs. In 1871, A. M. Lasley of New York advertised in the *American Artisan* a cooler built on the prevailing technology. He declared, "The design will afford a hint for the construction of an ice safe which may be ornamental as well as useful, and if the space between the outer and inner vessels is filled with non-conducting material, one charge of ice would last for a considerable time." (Hartley 1964, 202)

A quaint, but appealing moss water cooler, pictured in Jonathan Periam's *The Home & Farm Manual: A Pictorial Encyclopedia of Farm, Garden, Household, Architectural, Legal, Medical and Social Information* (1884), suggested covering a porous water vase with ordinary brook moss, held in place with silver wire. He explained, "The water, percolating through the pores, helped to keep the moss damp, cooled the water, and, when much evaporation and consequent coolness were wanted, the vase was set in a draft of air. The family have ice now, and the old water-cooler is now a living vase." (Periam 1984, 744) To extend the beauty of the home water cooler, he suggested sowing the moss with fine seeds to grow garden cress and ornamental grasses on the exterior.

The key to refrigerating without ice blocks was latent or absorbed heat, a phenomenon that occurred when heat transformed a liquid to vapor. The process displaced heat when the gas returned to a liquid state. From 1830 to 1880, the demand for refrigeration prompted the invention and patenting of more coolant methods to assure the quality of food that produces shipped over longer distances as people moved from farms to urban centers. In 1874, Swiss inventor Raoul Pictet designed a theoretical compressor system based on sulfur dioxide; German scholar Karl von Linde simplified logistics in 1876 by inventing a commercial system chilled with methyl ether. In 1879, he applied the new technology to the home refrigerator, to which he attached a steam-driven pump. The machine, which he manufactured in Munich, sold poorly in Europe and the United States because of its cumbersome size and noisy operation.

In the 1870s and 1880s, Philip Danforth Armour and G. F. Swift set out to dominate the Chicago meat-packing industry. To undercut New York prices, they built their own fleet of cars. Engines maneuvered the pre-chilled cars to Chicago slaughterhouses, where loaders hung whole sides of beef and pork on meat hooks. On the way east, cooled air circulated among the loosely packed carcasses. In contrast to cattle cars, the refrigerated car carried 50 percent more beef.

When a commercial steam-driven refrigerating system became available in 1880, it arrived in England aboard the SS *Strathleven*, which carried a load of meat from Australia. The standard ammonia refrigerant worked by vaporizing, then dissolving and condensing. The quiet, motorless process began when a timer or thermostat turned on a gas jet. The flame heated the liquid to a gas, which dissolved into water or other liquid. Its dissolution lowered temperatures in the icebox. Reduced pressure allowed the ammonia to flow, carrying heat from the inside and releasing it on the outside.

In the next decade, shippers experimented with cooled gas and brine and replaced ammonia refrigerants with carbon dioxide. The installation of a compressor maintained a regular flow, thus removing heat from the cooling chamber and expelling warm exhaust. In 1890, most brewers applied the principles of thermodynamic transfer to the warm fermentaion of beer and to the cooling of bottled goods. By the beginning of the twentieth century, frozen meat from Argentina, New Zealand, and the United States was no longer a rarity. Ocean liners boasted of their stocks of quality meat cuts and ice creams, which they kept in cold storage during lengthy sea voyages. Into the 1920s, commercial refrigeration progressed, but home refrigeration lagged behind. A major reason was the danger of leaking refrigerants which were both poisonous and flammable.

Ice distributors flourished in towns and cities to stock the safe, but inefficient, home icebox, a technological dinosaur that still directed chilled air from the ice downward into the food. Drippy and malodorous, the first home refrigerators were a mixed blessing. Home and industrial ice boxes began as ash, elm, or oak cabinets lined with tin and topped by a 25-, 50-, 75-, or 100-pound ice block, which melted into a drip

pan below. To change that image, builders of a 1894 home model attached an attractive sideboard with beveled mirror.

In 1895, at the height of the Gilded Age, completion of Biltmore Estate, the George Vanderbilt mansion in Asheville, North Carolina, included installation of a power grid to serve telephones, heating, elevators, and refrigerators. Its builder Richard Morris Hunt supplied a walk-in general storage cooler and separate units for kitchen, pastry room, pantry, and servants room. Power came from two horsepower of steam up to six hours per day. Chilling resulted from a brine solution operated by distilled ammonia and passing through a loop of pipes in the refrigerator cases. The system made three hundred pounds of ice per day and cooled fifty gallons of liquid and a quarter ton of vegetables and meat.

In 1900, the Sears, Roebuck catalog showcased seven styles of ice boxes on wheels priced from $4.00 to $26.50 for an ash model with double doors enhanced by bronze trimmings. None of the entries depicted a cabinet in use. A single cutaway drawing characterized the movement of air from the upper ice chamber through two wire shelves to the bottom and back up the sides of the interior. The 1908 catalog featured six models of ice boxes, ranging in price from $4.45 to $17.95. The cheapest, an Economy brand ice chest, sported a quality exterior of elm and wheels for easy maneuvering. At the other end of the scale, the spacious double-door model, also on wheels, contained insulated walls lined in galvanized steel and a system of circulating air to chill three shelves of food below the ice chamber. The Puritan refrigerator, in the medium price range, drained waste water through a pipe into an unobtrusive drip cup. Enhancing the aura of sanitation was a white enamel lining. The Guardian, first marketed in 1915, offered the first refrigerator fitted with an oak freezer unit insulated with seaweed.

Fifteen years later, stock from Sears had shrunk to five models offering the same features. Prices had risen from $9.95 for the ice chest to $44.00 for a forty-seven-inch dark oak ice box with enameled lining. A curious in-ground iceless ice box selling for $16.95 provided farm families a practical adjunct to the drilled or dug well. Built on the principle of the dumbwaiter, the framed apparatus could be installed directly in a well shaft under the kitchen for hand-cranking to the surface for loading and unloading three shelves of food. A picture of a woman operating the device with one hand suggested easy raising and lowering of the cylinder. The copywriter promised, "It protects your foodstuffs from insects and prowling animals as well as keeping them cool and preventing their spoiling even in hottest summer weather." (Schroeder 1973, 710)

Dr. Mary Engle Pennington, a bacteriologist and chemist, streamlined the process of transporting frozen foods into cities. From her office at the Philadelphia Clinical Laboratory, she analyzed microbes and aided the local health department in reducing impurities in milk. As head of the Household Refrigeration Bureau in 1923, initiated by the National Association of Ice Industries, she affirmed the cold chain from farmer to consumer through education. Her concepts fit the domestic science paradigm of economy, efficiency, nutrition, and hygiene, in particular, the purchase of fresh meat for family use and of sanitary milk for infant feeding.

Pennington's task of educating consumers called for the addition of a lecturer, publication of illustrated brochures for women's clubs and high school home economics classes, and an exhibit on refrigeration for the 1928 convention of the Federated Women's Clubs of America. At the request of Dr. Harvey W. Wiley, head chemist for the U.S. Department of Agriculture, Pennington served the government as first supervisor of the U.S. Food Research Laboratory and devised a method of controlling humidity, which caused frozen foods to mold. Her innovations improved food packaging, storage, and shipping for home and military, winning her a Notable Service Medal from President Herbert Hoover.

In 1914, Nathaniel B. Wales marked a breakthrough in electric compression refrigeration based on a sulfur dioxide refrigerant. Marketed two years later by the Electro-Automatic Refrigerator Company, the name changed to the familiar Kelvinator, a three-door wood refrigerator the size of an armoire. In 1917, E. J. Copeland of General Motors reduced the danger of toxicity by developing an automatic refrigerant control. Heinrich Zoelly's Autofrigor, patented in Switzerland 1918, was the star appliance of Aktiengesellschaft der Maschinenfabriken Escher Wyss & Cie. Cooled by methyl chloride, it was prone to overheating and provoked little interest in American manufacturers.

Of fifty-six firms jostling to manufacture a popular home refrigerator, Frigidaire muscled into second place in 1919, ending the hopes of appliance builders such as Holmes and Allison, which quickly went bankrupt. The neophyte Frigidaire electric refrigerating system, which functioned separate from the icebox itself, was expensive, dirty, noisy, and unreliable. Homeowners who had $450 to invest in one suffered through motor and thermostat breakdowns, leaking tubes, freeze-ups, re-gasketing of pistons, and compressor failure. In 1920, C. A. Carey of Jackson, Michigan, produced a four-legged cylindrical ice box. Called the White Frost Sanitary, the cork-lined steel model with glass water cooler attached to the side carried a doctor's guarantee of cleanliness. The 1920s, which were

active years for domestic application of thermodynamics, saw the emergence of electric power over gas. In Paris, the Polaire refrigerating chest made its debut at the 1924 Ideal Home Show. The built-in California refrigerator fit into the floor and functioned like a dumbwaiter. One newcomer to such modern technology, Lord Braye of Stanford Hall, Rugby, home of the Cave family since 1430, took pride in electrifying his home. He was especially pleased with his icemaker. When he gave guests a tour of the basement kitchen, however, he found that his cook was not so pleased with the new gadget, which she used as a storage chest for cheese. The following years, the Grand Rapids Refrigerator Company presented the Leonard Cleanable Refrigerator in ads in *Good Housekeeping*. Aimed at the ordinary homemaker, the copy carried testimonials from peers who tested the appliance by hanging a full stem of bananas to prove how well the chamber held cold.

Swedes Carl G. Munthers and Baltzar von Platen, engineering students at the Stockholm University of Technology, produced the Electrolux-Servel absorption system, a mechanism without moving parts that ran constantly without thermostatic controls. Built for homes in 1926, it preceded General Electric's popular new model—the steel-chest, air-cooled refrigerator with built-in motor called the Monitor Top for its top-heavy design, which resembled the Civil War gunship of the same name. Designed by Danish immigrant Christian Steenstrup, GE's chief engineer, and marketed at $525, in 1911, it replaced GE's wood Audiffren refrigerator, invented by Abbé Marcel Audiffren, a Cistercian monk and physics teacher, and sold for $1000, twice the cost of an automobile.

Steenstrup's Monitor Top, manufactured in Fort Wayne, Indiana, led GE's product line and established the company as chief producer of kitchen appliances in the United States. By 1927, GE was offering a fourteen-cubic foot home refrigerator, which impacted the way people shopped and stored food. To promote variations in food preparation based on refrigeration, the company hired food writer Alice Bradley, the principal of Miss Farmer's School of Cookery and cooking editor of *Woman's Home Companion*, to compile *Electric Refrigerator Recipes and Menus* (1927). Within two years, refrigerator sales reached 800,000.

Full-page ads in *Good Housekeeping* pictured home scenes in which families carried on their kitchen duties with a distinct fondness for their bubble-headed GE refrigerator. The copy stated explicitly that the appliance chalked up the best record for quiet, efficiency, economy, and trouble-free service in the history of refrigeration. A later ad in the October 1930 issue depicted models surviving laboratory fire, burial in ice and sand, and a dunking in the Erie Canal. Carrying the message by radio was the *General Electric Hour*, a radio broadcast each Saturday night via NBC.

Not to be outdone were competitors Kelvinator and Majestic. Kelvinator presented its own full-page ads picturing mother and child enjoying iced drinks from four-way cold, which produced the "World's Fastest Freezing Ice in 80 minutes." ("World's" 1930, 147) A schematic drawing illustrated how a stack of freezer bins offered steady cold at top, extremely fast ice and dessert freezing at level two, cold storage for meats and ice cream in the third freezer drawer, and uniform cold below 50 degrees Fahrenheit in the refrigerator bottom. Majestic offered a bold eight-page spread embellished with a glimpse of the Northern lights to announce testing of its refrigerators in ten thousand households. Pages of pictures featured the brand's broom-high legs, flat top, easy-opening latch, and Bakelite facing. Models demonstrated the temperature regulator, double-depth freezing tray, and economical motor, which had no belts, gears, or pistons to fail. Thorough laboratory testing in the Good Housekeeping kitchen resulted in a refrigerator capable of maintaining temperatures throughout the interior and of operating quietly while offering customers good service for their investment.

As proof of the efficacy of domestic advertising, psychologist Carl Albert Naether, the author of *Advertising to Women* (1928), offered a refrigerator ad as an example of methods of appealing to female shoppers. The Success Manufacturing Company of Gloucester, Massachusetts, featured a four-door icebox as an example of a cleanable appliance. Copy noted that the user could remove, wash, and scald the ice chamber, food racks, and drain pipe. According to the copywriter, the technological secret was sheet steel coated with enamel: "Can't absorb moisture, can't crack or chip. Its surfaces are all smooth and flat, no panels to collect dirt and germs. The all-steel lining is positively water-tight. The all-steel doors never warp, swell or stick." (Naether 1928, 172) The strong points of the model suggested the weaknesses of previous iceboxes. Similar ads in French magazines depicted the Frigidaire line, launched in 1926 by Delco-Light & Company, as necessities for the modern woman's kitchen.

The 1929 Kelvinator swept into homes with a new design—a white, floor-level appliance that lacked the furniture legs of earlier models. A year later, Frigidaire marketed the first home freezer, some two decades before the idea generated public demand. The shape and styling revolutionized the appearance of the American kitchen. In the July 1930 issue of *Good Housekeeping*, the company followed with dramatic photographic proof that their refrigerator's hydrator with temperature control maintained freshness in such delicate produce as celery, lettuce, and tomatoes. Text boasted that the appliance body was porcelain-on-steel, which the company claimed was clean and rust-free inside and out. In Sweden that same year, Electrolux crafted the first built-in refrigerator, a compact model suited to the kitchenettes of galley-sized apartment kitchens. The next year, the company marketed the first air-cooled refrigerator.

By 1933, GE and Hotpoint debuted a sleek motor-on-bottom design that displaced the Monitor Top. In 1935, engineer Raymond Loewy designed the Coldspot Super Six for Sears, Roebuck, a top seller in gleaming white and chrome. A 1936 Consumers Union remained dubious of refrigerators, with their made-up marketing names of "Conservador, Shelvador, Eject-O-Cube, Adjusto-Shelf, Foodex, Handi-Bin, Touch-A-Bar." (Landau 1986, 152) Another melodic name, the Crosley Shelvador, advertised in the June 1938 issue of *McCall's*, combined the standard ice unit and door shelving with a new gimmick, a radio in the upper door.

The refinement of air cooling to save the householder work and fuel occupied industrial engineers in the 1930s. Newer refrigerator models sustained ice on extended metal fins for up to seven days at a constant temperature. Odors and gas flowed downward into melted ice to rid the food chamber of unpleasant smells. Chambers moved closer to the floor as legs gave place to disks and gliders. In 1938, Finland's Oy Elektrolux Ab advertised the world's first automatic refrigerator. Equipped with a simple oil lamp and copper pipes, it ran on a combination of gas and kerosene or electricity and kerosene. The workings proved unreliable and prefaced the end of foul-smelling kerosene as a practical refrigeration fuel. According to a 1938 issue of *Consumer Reports*, the generation of cold air by ice, gas, and electricity formed a clear pattern of fuel usage: contrasting three dollars' worth of ice and two dollars in gas, the electric refrigerator cost only one dollar to operate. By 1936, the white-and-chrome exterior distanced the refrigerator from its outmoded parent appliance, the icebox.

Late in the 1930s, creativity dominated the shape and appeal of refrigerators. In 1939, Raymond Loewy built a sleek, shiny Electrolux icebox; the designer Walter Dorwin Teague altered appliance concepts by pioneering door shelves for the Crosley Shelvador. The Delco chemist Thomas Midgely's development of Freon, a non-toxic artificial coolant to replace dangerous refrigerants, and additional innovations in air-cooling, set the style and operating method of refrigeration into the twenty-first century. An unusual answer to home freezing was the 1940 cylindrical food chest, which packed items willy-nilly. A double Deepfreeze, manufactured by Motor Products of Chicago, paired twin cylinders separated by a compressor. General Electric brought out the refrigerator with freezing compartment in 1939.

In 1941, Frigidaire offered a small upper ice chest that held trays of ice and a few other items; eight years later, the freezer compartment filled the upper one-quarter of the refrigerator from side to side, with access through a spring-loaded pull-down inner door. Throughout the 1940s, the home freezer improved in shape and convenience, for example, the sleek, rounded 1946 Deepfreeze from Motor Products in Chicago; the quiet 1947 Servel gas refrigerator from Servel of Evansville, Indiana, the rare model that ran on bottled or piped gas or kerosene for use in areas lacking electricity; and the 1948 Maytag, which featured an enamel fold-down leaf, balanced stay-open lid, wire racks, and quick defroster that ran off motor heat. The April 1952 issue of *Consumer Reports* lauded the home freezer for saving shopping time and bother, keeping food on hand, storing leftovers, and enabling consumers to buy in quantity to take advantage of low prices.

In May 1947, Elizabeth Beveridge, the home equipment editor for *Woman's Home Companion* and author of *The Pocket Book of Home Canning* (1943) and *Pots and Pans for Your Kitchen* (1950), summarized advances in home refrigeration since World War II. After sampling eight American models, she noted the addition of quick-freeze units, freezers that held more than a week's supply of frozen foods, adjustable shelves, door shelves, and a drain system that channeled moisture from defrosting into an easily accessible pan. She advised brides to seek appliances that were made from rustless aluminum, glass, stainless steel, or plastic-coated metal.

In 1956, Electrolux introduced the chest freezer in England. Within the decade, most manufacturers were marketing refrigerators with small freezer units. The chemist Mary Engle Pennington, director of Philadelphia's municipal bacterial lab, further improved food preservation by inventing frozen food containers, setting standards for distribution of ice cream, controlling humidity in refrigerators and freezers, and creating insulated refrigerator rail cars to carry milk. Another adaptation in food preservation, the home vacuum freezer packager, replaced glass jars and rings and lids with an airtight plastic bag that preserved quality and taste while preventing freezer burn. Custom models allow the user to slice off units from a continuous roll of bag material to suit the size of the contents.

Home refrigeration and freezing quickly dominated food storage and preparation in North America, but advanced slowly throughout the British Isles. By 1971, 69 percent of British households had refrigerators, but only 4 percent had freezers, most of whom kept them in the garage or and outbuilding because of lack of space in flats. By 1985, the numbers rose to 95 percent owning refrigerators and 66 percent having freezers.

A major contributor to home models was George C. Foerstner, founder of Amana Refrigeration after the Great Change of 1932 ended the faith's communes. After the Amana colonists disbanded, he managed a home appliance industry and marketed home upright freezers, refrigerator-freezers, and frost-free models. In 1965, the company merged with Raytheon and moved into microwave oven production in 1967. Amana Refrigeration passed to Goodman Company of Houston, Texas, in 1997, and continues making home heating and cooling appliances.

Advancements in ice-making and refrigeration have simplifed an awkward chore. In the mid-twentieth century, a plug-in defroster made by Howell & Company and Shane Manufacturing, allowed homemakers to melt ice from the sides of ice compartments during cleaning. In 1952, Westinghouse marketed an unusual three-part upright freezer that froze foods in the top third and stored them in the two sections below. The first self-defrosting refrigerators, which appeared in the 1960s, ended chipping and scraping accumulated ice by hand. The side-by-side models manufactured in 1972 promised economy as well as convenience.

A welter of concern over the danger of freon to the atmosphere forced engineers to weigh home convenience against depletion of the ozone layer, which protects earth from ultraviolet radiation that causes skin cancer, cataracts, and suppressed immunity. In 1985, in Vienna, the United National Environmental Programme met to assess the danger. In two years, members had outlined the Montreal Protocol, an agreement among European and North American nations to phase out freon and create safe methods of extracting the gas from abandoned models. Meanwhile, the creation of hydrofluorocarbons offered a replacement gas for newer models. In 1991, the introduction of the Electrolux Low-Energy Refrigerator further improved the value of the appliance for home use.

In 1998, *La Cucina Italiana* spotlighted the best in the era's refrigerators. Their first choice, the Jenn-Air WaterColors Collection, featured vivid metallic shades of blue, copper, gold, jade, and red. Inside the seamless frame, cantilevered shelving, humidity control, concealed hinges, and a door dispenser for ice water and crushed or cubed ice composed a total package of kitchen convenience. The attractive Sub Zero model, winner of the Industrial Designers' Society of America Design of Excellence Award, introduced halogen-lighted modules separated to suit cabinetry. Householders could place at will refrigerator and freezer units, fruit and vegetable storage, and dairy goods. The Amana PosiTemp, a built-in refrigerator, tailored units to suit kitchen decor. It filtered water through a carbon-activated system to remove off-flavors and odors from ice.

As industrialized nations skyrocketed to more and better appliances, the contrast with have-not nations grew more stark. In October 2000, the Rolex Award for Enterprise went to Mohammed Bah Abba, a teacher in northern Nigeria, who created a clay device that lowered food temperatures in third world homes that lacked electric power. In an impoverished agrarian area, he applied refrigeration principles to indigenous African technology and invented the Pot-in-Pot, a clay cooling chamber that ended food spoilage that causes disease and loss of income. Late that same year, the Electrolux Group, which pioneered low-energy, CFC-free, and recyclable refrigerators, created a pedestal model called the Lighthouse. The waist-high cube, walled with translucent panels, chilled foods while serving as a work station or kitchen island. At the January 2001 International Housewares Show in Chicago, LG Electronics USA debuted a $10,000 multifunctional refrigerator that employs a digital camera, video message board, and email and Internet connection to combine the appliance with up-to-date media.

See also **Ice; Marshall, Agnes**

Further Reading

Beveridge, Elizabeth, "The Inside Story on Refrigerators," *Woman's Home Companion*, May 1947, 100–101.
Hoppe, Emilie. *Seasons of Plenty: Amana Communal Cooking.* Ames: Iowa State University Press, 1998.
Naether, Carl A. *Advertising to Women.* New York: Prentice-Hall, Inc., 1928.
Nagengast, Bernard, "The History of Sealed Refrigeration Systems," *ASHRAE Journal*, 1996.
Sears, Roebuck and Co. *Consumers Guide, Fall 1900.* Northfield, Ill: DBI Books, Inc., 1970.
"World's Fastest Freezing Ice in 80 minutes," *Good Housekeeping*, July 1930, 147.

RENAISSANCE KITCHENS

"Large tabling and belly cheer" characterized Renaissance dining according to Chaplain William Harrison, author of *Description of Elizabethan England* (1577). For housewives, pamphlets such as *The Book of Cookery* (1500), *The Good House-Wives Treasurie* (1588), *The Good Huswives Handmaid* (1597), Henry Buttes's *Dyets Dry Dinner* (1599), and other guidebooks to domestic supervision spelled out the woman's obligations to the home. Above all, she set an example for her cook and scullions by supervising the cleaning and provisioning of the kitchen, dressing meats, and heaping the buffet with suitable meals for family and guests. The kitchen also turned out tonics, teas, and

cures as well as cloth dye and primitive cosmetics for home use. While her husband was absent from the estate or engaged in war, she controlled accounts of the dairy, croplands, and livestock.

As of the late fifteenth and early sixteenth centuries, European diet improved, at least for the upper portion of society, over the limited offerings of the early and middle medieval period. One of the influences on a healthier diet was a flurry of treatises on nutrition and dietetics, which directed cooks toward a more balanced menu. Prominent in Renaissance cookbooks was a dawning emphasis on vegetable dishes, which proliferated dramatically. Of particular merit was the "love apple," an early name for the tomato, which chefs at the Spanish court were cooking with oil, salt, and pepper in the late 1500s. One Englishman dining on them for the first time, declared them insubstantial nourishment. As for meats, cookbooks increased the number of beef recipes and accorded less space to poultry. Harrison noted that the rich ate well of domestic and imported beef, fish, and fowl. However, the underclass had to make do on lesser foods, notably milk, butter, cheese, and "white meats."

Cookery altered from an emerging interest in beef roast, stew, braised oxtail, tongue *paupiettes*, and grilled ribs and steaks, which sometimes went to the oven *en papilllote* (in buttered paper). An alternative was sliced roast larded with suet and soaked in white wine for baking in a terrine. Central to the new cuisine was the preservation of natural flavors, careful addition of *court bouillon,* and the reduction of additional water or marinade to dilute juices. Butter sauce replaced medieval dependence on almond milk, and bread crumbs gave place to a more flavorful thickening of *rous* (fried flour). Spicing was restrained or abandoned and there was diminished dependence on anise, cardamom, cinnamon, cumin, galingale, ginger, mace, mastic, saffron, and spikenard. Instead, clove, nutmeg, and pepper were favored along with the piquance of citric juice, white wine, and vinegar. Sugar, still in demand in Renaissance kitchens, made its strongest appearance at the end of the meal in cake, custard, pastries, and fruit ades.

In Italy, as cooking turned from subsistence to a high art, Christoforo di Messisbugo (also Cristoforo or Christofaro di Messisburgo), steward of Hippolyte d'Este, cardinal of Ferrara, and author of *Il Libro de Arte Coquinaria* (The Book of Culinary Art, 1548) and *Banquetti Compositioni di Vivande, et Apparecchio Generale* (Foods and General Necessities for Banquets, 1549), spoke of the preparation and service of hearty stews for banquets. In place of vegetables, which he considered too watery for the stomach, he advocated a large number of pies and cold dishes presented on an elaborate *credenza* (buffet). One reason for so much chopped meat was the poor state of European teeth, which were not up to chewing larger cuts.

The Venetian doges and their courts ate well from larders stocked with viands and spices from the cosmopolitan Rialto market. Their preference for savory sauces passed to the French, whose chefs, feasting, and cookbooks reached a culinary height in the 1600s. Regency cuisine under Phillipe d'Orléans produced a true French cookery, enlivened by the work of royal *cordons bleus* (master chefs) at the Palais Royal and Trianon. However, in 1630, Jean-Jacques Bouchard complained about the over-spiced and over-sugared foods in Provence, which leaned toward Italian cookery rather than the evolving Parisian style.

Additions to the world canon of cookbooks were numerous throughout the Renaissance. The royal chef of Fernando of Naples, Master Ruperto de Nola, the author of the Catalan classic *Libre del Coch* (Book of the Cook, ca. 1450), first published in 1520, presented the first work on regional cuisine. His blend of Aragonese, Catalan, French, Moorish, and Italian recipes expressed the spirit of Renaissance adventure and inclusion. In Spain, Diego Granado Maldonado compiled several hundred recipes in *Libro del Arte de Cozina* (Book of Kitchen Art, 1599), which drew from de Nola's compilation and from New World, German, and Spanish sources. To his discredit, he translated freely the writings of Italian chef Bartolomeo Scappi, the chef to Pope Pius V and compiler of *Opera dell'Arte dell Cucinare* (Compendium on the Art of Cookery, 1570) and *Libro Nuovo nel Qual S'insegna a Far Ogni Sorte de Vivande* (New Recipe Book for All Sorts of Foods, 1549). Another text, by royal chef Francisco Martínez Montiño, the cook for Philip III, influenced kitchen arts from 1611 into the 1800s. He instructed the maker of *chorizo* (sausage) to marinate lean pork in wine, spices, salt, and vinegar, stuff intestines, and boil the links to keep them for up to a year.

In Sicily under Spanish influence, the *cucina baronale* (baronial kitchen) produced elaborate meals that contrasted the humble fare of peasant tables. A heavy burden of *gabelle* (domestic taxes) hampered owners of ovens, mill, abattoirs, and wine and oil presses as well as the homemaker endowed with windows and hearth, both of which the authorities categorized as luxuries. As a result of additional heavy duties on home foodstuffs, home cooking centered on grain and vegetables because meat was both scarce and costly.

The French *bouche de roi* (king's service, literally "King's mouth") required a staff of up to five hundred royal caterers. About the kitchen, differentiated tasks placed in position a keeper of table service, a *sommelier*, four aides, a dishwasher, boy apprentices, and

thirteen heads of service. The butler oversaw beverages, bread, water, and ice and distributed clean napkins several times during a meal for tying around the neck of diners to protect fine muslin collars. Ornate napkin-folding in the 1500s produced bird and fruit shapes. At refined gatherings, staff sprinkled napkins, tablecloths, and some foods with rosewater or perfume to sweeten air made heavy by the aroma of cooked meats.

In the kitchen, master cooks, roasting cooks, soup cooks, pastry cooks, and *galopins* (errand boys) joined equerries in producing dishes suitable for a royal table. Platina's *De Honesta Voluptate et Valitudine* (On Right Pleasure and Health, 1475) advocated clean, self-controlled staff who kept a hygienic kitchen and pleasant dining atmosphere for the service of such specialties as caviar and peacock. Supplying the kitchen were carriers of water, fuel, and armchairs. Beyond the king's staff were separate kitchen servers for the queen, dauphins, and dauphines.

In a private royal kitchen, royal personages superintended staff and sometimes cooked their own specialties with a collection of silver implements. One menu glimpses the adventuresome, multi-ethnic tastes of the era:

First course—salt beef with carrots and potatoes
Soups—pike cullis [broth] and duck with turnips
Fish—carp *à l'anglaise*, perch, and pike
Entrées—mutton fillets with gherkins, parsleyed chickens and *espagnole sauce*, pike *à la polonaise*, perch *à la genevoise*, pike with sauerkraut, oysters in cream; *noix de veau à la napolitaine*, partridges *en levrault*, eels *à la Bavaroise*, crayfish, marinated roebuck kidney
Pâtisseries—apricot marmalade cake, iced peach tart
Roasts—smelt, *poulardes*, fried sole, wild duck, followed by four salads
Entremets—veal sweetbread, pig's trotters *Sainte-Menehould*, peas *à la crème*, dessert apples *à la chinoise* (Montagné 1977, 269–270)

A privileged Englishman might dine heartily on beef, veal, chicken, sauces, and oranges or dried fruit at noon, followed at evening with mutton, hare, pig's feet, cold beef, sauces, a boiled vegetable, and cheese. A more elaborate menu could combine beef, mutton, veal, hare, peas, strawberries in cream, cherries, confections, oranges and lemons, white manchet bread, and beer. For variety, Tudor cooks added to daily fare pheasant, swans, peacocks, and chickens and small birds. In 1524, the choice included the first turkey, imported to the English court from South America. Poultry pluckers had the difficult task of cleaning and spitting whole larks, quail, pigeons, starlings, thrushes, and sparrows. Dessert called for fruit, custard, waffles and wafers, and marchpane. For the peasantry, however, a class-based theory of food consumption relegated laborers to the everyday sameness of humble food-stuffs—pottage, sorghum bread, porridge, turnip greens, leeks and onions, scallions, and cheat bread, the coarsest kind.

At the Christmas feast of Philip III of Spain, chef Francisco Martínez Motiño served a splendid table:

First course—ham, stew, roast chicken and turkey, veal pasties, pigeon, bird tarts, partridge, pork loin, sausage, and suckling pig

Second course—capons, cake with quince dressing, escarole-stuffed chicken, arugula-dressed veal, liver, sweetbread seedcake, roast thrush, rabbit empanadas, and fried trout

Third course—stuffed chicken and goat, veal udder, minced fowl, turkey and pigs' feet empanadas, bream stew, dove, citron tart, rice fritters, pigeons, and a *blancmange* mixed with chicken

The emphasis on meats attests to their importance to a royal table and an economy enriched by goods and stores from the New World. Staff displayed luxury at an Italian banquet in the 1400s in the pouring of water for finger bowls in three fragrances—lemon, myrtle, and muscat.

Books of etiquette, such as John Lydgate's *Stans Puer ad Mensam* (The Young Waiter at Table, ca. 1430), *The Babees Book, or A Lytyl Reporte of How Young People Should Behave* (ca. 1475), *The Lytylle Childrenes Lytil Boke* (ca. 1480), and *The Young Children's Book* (ca. 1500), became popular at the end of the Middle Ages as people refined their tastes and behaviors. Whether for children or adults, these reached a needy audience as the merchant class accrued wealth and position. In *The Schoole of Vertue and Booke of Good Nourture for Children* (1557), the author prepared the young for polite society, beginning with rising in the morning, dressing for the day, and sitting at table with adults. To the immature, the text warned about overfilling dishes and spilling food on clothing. He suggested having spare trenchers for unexpected guests. For the helpful youth, he explained how to remove bones to voiders (waste bowls), clear the table, and return dishes to the kitchen on a tray. In terms of priorities, he considered covering the salt first in importance, followed by attending to dishes, sweeping crumbs, and serving after-dinner drinks. The entire table service required an appropriate finale—a "lowe cursie" (a low curtsey). (Furnivall 1868, 231)

Women juggled multiple tasks that entailed awareness of servants' faults and the status of household stocks. When time and circumstance allowed, literate women taught their staff how to read and do fancy needlework. Children needed the housewife's attention, such as lining wood tubs with sponges for bathing and straining herbs over rainwater for rinsing their hair, limbs, and delicate garments. John Fitzherbert's *A Boke of Husbandry* (1525) outlined a daunting list of housewifely chores, beginning with a sweep of the house, ordering of dishes and implements, milking cows, feeding stock, and straining the milk before awakening children to be dressed and fed breakfast with their father. He urged organizing grain loads for the brewery and bakery, cheese and butter making, slopping the hogs, and feeding the chickens before gathering eggs and protecting broody hens from predators. The symbol of wifely command of the household lay in the chatelaine's wristlet of keys, which secured cellar, cupboard, smokehouse, garderobe, and escritoire, in which she kept her personal papers, correspondence, shopping lists, and household accounts.

Before the evolution of cities as trading centers, the Tudor housewife oversaw her family's health and safety. In addition to textile work, dairying, and baking, several times per week, she sold produce at the market. Her wares ranged from milk, butter and cheese, eggs, capons and hens, geese, pigs, and grain to stitched goods, feather pillows, herbal elixirs, and other by-products of her kitchen labors. While attending to household provisioning, she purchased necessities—sewing goods, tapers and candles, simples, spices, and salt. As the patriarchal arrangement demanded, on return, she gave her husband an account of her sales and stores.

The number of people seated at the housewife's table varied with circumstance. As described in the weekly account books of Ingatestone Hall, Essex, home of William Petre, the secretary to Henry VI in 1552, the daily feeding of family plus laborers brought to table a tiler, smith, wheelwright, mason, carpenter, glazier, and sawyer plus their helpers. Over early fall, Petre's cook fed a tailor, maltman, carters, and peddlers. At Christmas, the number increased to include the region's poor, whose presence drained a large quantity of kitchen goods.

The staffing of the household of Elizabeth I devoured a sizeable outlay for domestic service, including livery, food, and lodging. The queen's kitchen staff, one of the largest in her *domus providenciae* (provisioning department), ordered under three master cooks an additional chief clerk, two under-clerks, six yeomen, six grooms, eight pages, and scullery workers called gallapines, who mopped and washed up. These well-paid workers, all swore to a loyalty oath, saw to high standards of cookery from quality foodstuffs, which a clerk recorded on the kitchen account book. The clerks superintended the acatry (catery), bakehouse, boilinghouse, butler, buttery, cellar, chaundry, confectionery, ewery, larder, laundry, pantry, pastry, pitcherhouse, poultry, spicery, wafry, and woodyard. In addition to these, the queen hired ushers for seating guests, pages to deliver messages from the queen to the kitchen staff, embroiderers for her table linens, uniform makers, boatmen and body guard for her progresses through the country side, and mole- and ratcatchers.

Servants' chores at the Tudor hall involved the decanting of wine from casks into bottles for transfer into pewter tankards, leather jacks, or stoneware jugs. For domestic use, cellarers made perry, a kind of pear vinegar, and verjuice, an acidic liquor pressed from sour grapes or crabapples for cooking and medicines. In humbler environs, cooks made their own wine from fruit and blossoms and combined it with custards, jam, and sponge cake for trifle, a popular desert first mentioned in Thomas Dawson's *The Good Huswife's Jewel* (1596). Table service on wood plates set on pewter chargers kept foods hot. Decorative roundels were more delicate wooden circles painted with poetic phrases, which invited comment from diners or recitations called roundelays.

Late in the Renaissance, menus added the sunchoke and the tomato, which the expeditioner Hernán Cortés had brought from New Spain in 1523. Venturesome, creative cookery presaged the coming greatness of European cuisine. The menus that influenced Shakespeare's day and afterward varied foods, seasonings, and herbs. The countryside provided seasonal fruit, greens, roots, and nuts from kitchen garden, hedgerow, and woods. Trappers caught birds to feed up on fragrant herbs. A food board controlled the size, weight, and identification of bread loaves by baker's stamp as well as their ingredients, whether simnel, white, wheat, brown, horsebread, or spice breads for funerals and holidays. By the end of the 1600s, English pantries contained imported goods that broadened tastes. Cookbook shelves stocked instruction on diet, health, alcoholic beverages, tea and coffee, and herbal medicine, including Thomas Moffett's *Healths Improvement; or, Rules Comprizing and Discovering the Nature, Method, and Manner of Preparing All Sorts of Food Used in This Nation* (1655); Francesco Liberati's *Il Perfetto Maestro di Casa...Distinto in Trè Libri* (The Perfect Master of the House . . . in Three Volumes, 1658) a guide to Roman household procedures, equipment, kitchen hygiene, seasonal produce, wine selection, and economics; and Nicholas de Bonnefons's *Les Delices de la Campagne* (The Delights of the Countryside, 1661), a composition by the king's *valet de chambre*.

Wars and invasions brought food ideas and cooking techniques as well as destruction and shortages. Italian bakers adopted the Austrian kaiser bun as the *michetta*, a five-lobed loaf popular in Milan. To the northeast, Venetians embraced the *kipfel*, an Austrian breakfast croissant. Potatoes and corn from the New World supplied new starches for breads and fritters. Across Europe, the innovative dishes of such renowned cooks as Marx Rumpolt, the author of *Ein Neue Kochbuch* (A New Cookbook, 1581) and chef to Denmark's Queen Sophia, and Bartolomeo Scappi, the private cook of Pope Pius V, prefigured the great chefs of the late seventeenth and eighteenth centuries, some of the finest in world culinary history. Scappi's text featured detailed engravings of processional display of ornate entrées. He also categorized culinary tools to illustrate the techniques necessary for the latest food manipulations and presentations.

In honor of its culinary history, in 1988, Ferrara's cooks and culinary historians worked at a recreation of a golden era featuring the glamor of such court food as Certosino cake adorned at Christmas with candied fruit, an unsubtle display of wealth. Chef Sergio Ferrarini arrayed dishes in Renaissance style at the elegant Villa d'Este. Drawing on the descriptions of chef Christoforo di Messisbugo, he reprised the kitchen details, plating, service, decorations, and table settings for which the Renaissance was known.

See also **Banquets; Cookbook; Design; Digby, Kenelm; Markham, Gervase; Médicis, Catherine de; Platina**

Further Reading

Furnivall, Frederick J., ed. *Early English Meals and Manners: John Russell's Boke of Nurture.* London: Kegan Paul, Trench, Trübner & Co., Ltd., 1868.

Hufton, Olwen. *The Prospect before Her: A History of Women in Western Europe, 1500–1800.* New York: Vintage Books, 1998.

The Tudor Kitchens: Hampton Court Palace (brochure). West Drayton, Middlesex: E. J. Associates, 1991.

RESTAURANT KITCHENS

Restaurants, professional cookery, innkeeping, and catering flourished in ancient Greece and Rome, throughout the Middle Ages, in the Renaissance and seventeenth century, into the twenty-first century. Street kitchens are ubiquitous in culinary history. The poorest diner, who had no hearth or oven, frequently bought, begged, or worked for meals at wayside taverns. In Anatolia, a comment by Theodore of Sykeon in his biography, composed in the sixth century CE, was the first known recommendation of an inn based solely on the quality of its kitchen. In Japan, street cooks were the forerunners of modern wheeled *yatai* (cafés), egalitarian outdoor kitchens that dispense soups and noodles in broth to students, white-collar workers, and businessmen.

China

From 60 to 1279 CE, Chinese diners patronized popular spots in Kaifeng and Hangchow, catering primarily to travelers. A painting by Chang Tse-tuan from 1126 pictures a roofed pavilion sheltering diners at tables and benches. One long-lived establishment, Ma Yu Ching's restaurant from the Sung dynasty, opened in 1153 and is still in business. Giant menus offered as many as 234 dishes. Waiters impressed patrons by memorizing orders and carrying twenty bowls up one arm and three more in one hand. Buyers also patronized caterers and take-out establishments, where managers boasted that their staffs were as good as the chefs of the rich. Chinese specialists hung spareribs on racks in outdoor ovens to cook slowly in dry heat, emitting fragrances that lured diners to their door. The Chinese also invented ices, ice cream, and sherbet, which they passed on to Persian, Hindu, and Arab cooks.

The Sung dynasty's restaurant culture produced an outstanding restaurant critic, Meng Yuan-lao, who scoured China's burgeoning restaurants. His writings tell of new places to eat, the beginning of service at chairs and tables rather than on the floor, seasonings and preparations, and menus and markets. According to *The Travels of Marco Polo* (ca. 1299), when the Venetian arrived in China in 1275, he found Hangchow's restaurants specializing in iced dishes, vegetarian meals, dog, and fish and shellfish. Still important to the Chinese in later years, good meals typified the flowering of the Ming dynasty, from 1368 to 1644.

Europe

In Europe, the tavern culture thrived in the English pub, Spanish *bodega*, Greek *taverna*, Italian *trattoria*, and French *guinguette*. In France, the *rôtissieur* specialized so exclusively in roast goose that he earned the title of *oyer* (goose cook). In 1385, poet Geoffrey Chaucer set his story series, *The Canterbury Tales* (1385), at the Tabard, a typical English inn, where Harry Bailly welcomed guests and proposed a storytelling competition to be rewarded with a free meal on the group's return from their pilgrimage to the shrine of St. Thomas à Becket at Canterbury Cathedral. After a Sicilian carried instructions on making ice cream to France in 1660, Paris soon supported 250 ice cream shops and restaurants.

The European convention of an ordered presentation of beverages and professionally cooked dishes owes much to the Florentines, one of whom recorded menus from a nobleman's kitchen for the entire year of 1546. Reflecting the tastes of Renaissance figures from the 1300s, this charting of gastronomy established patterns of foods and the importance of such innovations as caviar appetizers, separation of fish and meat, and oil and vinegar dressing for salad greens. These period regimens prefaced formal *table d'hote* (host's table) dining, which got its start at inns where customers came at an appointed hour to eat from a set menu. Professional cookery, brought to its height by Catherine and Marie de Médicis and Louis XIV, influenced chef Pierre François de La Varenne and food critic Jean Anthelme Brillat-Savarin, author of *Physiologie du Goût, ou Méditation de Gastronomie Transcendante, Ouvrage Théorique, Historique et à l'Ordre du Jour* (The Physiology of Taste, or A Meditation on the Best of Dining, a Theoretical and Historic Work on the Order of the Day, 1825). Since 1825, when Brillat-Savarin promoted restaurant dining as a suitable convenience for the era, diners came to demand a varied menu and quality table service.

The stability of restaurant business did not maintain an even growth. As described in journalist Daniel Defoe's *A Journal of the Plague Year* (1720), the disorder created by spread of bubonic plague interrupted patterns of food purchase and consumption throughout Europe. On July 1, 1665, the Lord Mayor and aldermen of London issued orders to justices of the peace, bailiffs, and local officers concerning methods of containing and reducing contagion from the plague. Observers in each parish looked specifically for "stinking fish, or unwholesome flesh, or musty corn, or other corrupt fruits of what sort soever, be suffered to be sold about the city." (pp. 51–52) Likewise forbidden were polluted casks in breweries and bars.

The injunction against public feasting at taverns, alehouses, coffeehouses, and cellars devastated the careers of professional provisioners, bartenders, cooks, and wait staff. For the remainder of the quarantine, people had to lay in provisions when they could and brew and bake at home rather than risk so much as crossing the street to buy the dairier's butter and cheese or the butcher's meats. When epidemics ended, one of the first signs of rejoicing was a grand feast of thanksgiving.

According to British journalist Quentin Crewe's *The Great Chefs of France* (1978), the *traiteurs* (caterers), tavern hosts, café barkeeps, and innkeepers of Paris were the forerunners of the modern restaurateur. A lawsuit in 1796 that French *traiteurs* lodged against a soup seller named A. Boulanger raised the issue of territory for his broadening of the menu to include all types of food and beverage. The pro-entrepreneur, antiguild judgment prefaced an full egalitarianism yet to come in the French Revolution. After a judge guaranteed Boulanger the right to offer sheep's hooves in white sauce, he characterized his consommés and bouillons as *restaurants*, meaning "restoratives."

Boulanger gloried in the judgment. He decked his establishment with an elemental Latin motto that rephrased a line from the Sermon on the Mount: *Venite ad me, vos qui stomacho laboratis et ego restaurabo vos* (Come to me, you who labor at the stomach and I will restore you.) Parisians flocked to his table to taste his sheep's feet, which even Louis XV had cooked in his Versailles kitchen. The term "restaurant" survives in various spellings in English, French, Dutch, Spanish, Portuguese, Italian, Danish, Swedish, Norwegian, Romanian, Russian, and Polish. Cooks like Boulanger adapted the term into *restaurateurs*, a vocation of satisfying appetites by offering a list of foods purchased *à la carte* (from a menu) at the diner's convenience.

Antoine Beauvilliers, chef to Louis XVIII and author of *L'Art du Cuisinier* (The Chef's Art, 1814), opened the Grande Taverne de Londres, the first official French restaurant in the Palais Royale, in 1783. Located on the Rue Richelieu, it was a luxurious eating establishment praised for mirrors, splendid furnishing, portable room heaters, and banquet lighting to accommodate up to three hundred patrons. His innovations included well dressed wait staff, a prized wine cellar, the addition of the soufflé to dessert choices, choices from the best of English cuisine, and catering to the whims of guests. His high-priced menu offered thirteen soups, twenty-two appetizers, eleven pastries, sixty-five meats and game, twenty-three fish, forty-one side dishes, thirty-nine desserts, twelve liqueurs, and fifty-two wines. Staffing displayed French perfectionism. Beauvilliers acted the role of host and *maître d'hôte* by supervising punctilious service and chatting with foreign guests in their own languages. His hiring of female dining supervisors amazed the prudishly patriarchal English, who banned women from working in public dining establishments.

Within three years, Barthélèmy, Maneille, and Simon launched a competitive restaurant called *Aux Trois Frères Provencaux* (Three Provençal Brothers). When these pioneer chefs fled their homeland during the revolution of 1789, they carried the concept of restaurant dining to England. By 1813, Louis Eustache Ude, court cook for Louis XVI and author of *The French Cook* (1828), introduced English chefs to such French techniques as meringues and velouté, a rich creamy white sauce flavored with meat, fish, or cheese.

In this same period, the first chef to outshine his own restaurant was Marie-Antoine Carême, a cook for King George IV, Périgord Talleyrand, and Czar Alexander. A poor man who made his way cooking for nobles and royalty, Carême became a food designer, master confectioner, and gastronomic critic credited with founding French *haute cuisine*. After he began serving the Prince of Wales, he established a style of dining that influenced the restaurant industry up to the present.

French Cuisine

French cuisine, which some honor as the height of serious Western food preparation, encompassed Provençal olives and seafood, the hearty bistro meals of Quebec and Normandy, and the elegant repasts of the Tour d'Argent. Insistent on complicated technique for sauces and pastries, French chefs insisted that their apprentices master basic steps that brooked no deviations or short-cuts. An epitome of the French chef recognized the highest quality in seasonal foods and the regions that produced the best, as with red wine from Bordeaux, dairy goods from Normandy, beef from Charolais, artichokes from Macau, peas from Saint-Germaine, and strawberries from Pessac. Service style ordered presentation from hot or cold *hors d'oeuvres* and soup to entrées, salads, cheese tray, and desserts, each with appropriate aperitif, wine, or digestif. Such preparation and service of French cuisine dominated much of the Western world, including the White House, where Thomas Jefferson, Martin Van Buren, and James Buchanan installed French chefs, and Abraham Lincoln hired a part-time French caterer.

The French Revolution opened the world of fine dining to all society. Those professional cooks who remained in the newly democratized France perpetuated the illusion of aristocratic service for a rising bourgeoisie uplifted by the prevailing attitude toward *liberté, egalité, fraternité*. By the 1800s, Paris alone boasted nearly six hundred restaurants, which hired the skilled servants who once worked for the privileged class. In such good hands, restaurants met the demands of diners by cooking individual servings in a fry pan over a *piano* (flat), a solid cooking surface that was hottest at the center ranging outward to lower temperatures. To record their comments, restaurateurs invented the convention of the *livre d'or* (visitor's book), on which guests logged in their visits and recorded their likes and dislikes about food and service. In the twentieth century, artist Pablo Picasso limited his remarks to sketches on the linen, which playwright Jean Cocteau and poet Georges Hugnet published as *Nappe du Catalan* (Catalonian Tablecloth, 1952).

Restaurant Staff

As protocol advanced in the restaurant and hotel kitchen, staff began to fit a precise hierarchy of professionals:

Chef de cuisine—The visionary who designed dishes and established the ambience for which an establishment was known.

Executive chef—Kitchen manager of a large restaurant or luxury liner or hotel dining room who interviewed and employed staff, oversaw expenditures, updated menus, coordinated service with the *maitre d'*, and superintended general matters concerning cooking and serving. Early in restaurant history, the *maître d'* was a *grand seigneur* (great man), an aristocrat or royalty who often served in title alone. The post evolved into a more functional adviser on cooking, dining, and wine selection.

Sous-chef (under chef)—A cook who worked more closely with food inventories, daily specials, staffing, and the rhythms of preparation and cooking.

Expediter—The link between cooked dishes and diners, who assured prompt service by directing kitchen traffic.

Pastry chef—A separate food master who guarded fragile spun sugar, chocolates, and soufflés until they were plated and served.

Line cooks—Specialists of the skillet and grill who prepared foods at the command of the expediter.

Chef de garde manger—Manager of the cold station who dished up terrines, salads, desserts, and other foods requiring no heat.

Stagiaires or apprentices—Cooking assistants who located the exact vegetables, plucked and disjointed poultry, rinsed mushrooms, and produced the best loaves.

The ladder of responsibility produced world-famous chefs, who began in their teens doing the work that prepared them for greatness.

The better restaurants based table service on unobtrusive presentation of food and a survey of utensils and beverages to see that diners had what they needed and wanted. The hostess received guests, who left their coats with the checker and followed her to a table. After they perused the menu, the manager determined by their postures and eye movements when they had made a selection. He dispatched a team led by a captain, who coordinated seamless presentation of utensils and dishes and clearing of unneeded items. The service waiter took a drink order; the captain announced specials, answered questions about entrées, recorded food preferences, and suggested appropriate wines.

The service waiter organized glasses and soup spoons, fish knives, oyster forks, lobster crackers, finger bowls, and other special utensils needed for the meal.

Another change in service at the beginning of the nineteenth century were later hours for formal dining, introduced after the French Revolution. At the establishment of Chef Méot, the former cook for the Duc d'Orléans, the framers of the 1793 Constitution labored at his table and ate like nobles. From a standard dinner period from 1:00 to 3:00 p.m. daily, schedules altered to allow deputies of the National Assembly to work until 5:00 p.m. and dine later. French cooks began serving *petit-déjeuner* (breakfast), a pre-noon *déjeuner à la fourchette* (breakfast with a fork), and a formal evening meal. Because restaurateurs maintained flexible hours, clean and attractive surroundings, and a wide choice of dishes, their clientele increased. On the outskirts of genteel dining, the clever dishwasher gathered table scraps and plate scrapings into an *arlequin*, a mish-mash of leftovers to be marketed to the poor at three francs per bucket as *bijoux* (jewels) of the refined table.

In the Napoleonic era, the food journalist Alexandre Grimod de la Reynière, contributing editor of *Almanach des Gourmands* (Almanac of the Greedy Diners, 1812), set the tone for post-French Revolution food writers and elitists. He popularized the term "restaurant," which previously applied only to soups. A regular at the Véry Restaurant, Grimod and a select company of gourmets established the Jury Degustateur to set the parameters for French cuisine. He characterized and critiqued styles of table service and the integration into French cookery such New World foodstuffs as turkey, tomatoes, and potatoes. His favorite creations began with veal. As the era produced sauces with titles attached to aristocrats from the families of Béchamel, Condé, d'Uxelles, Orléans, and Richelieu, he proclaimed that, without these new and innovative accompaniments, dinners were as barren as a house repossessed by the sheriff.

When novelist Victor Hugo looked behind the kitchen doors at the Hôtel de Metz, the sight amazed him with its arrangement of copperware and crockery and central hearth. Amid a cadre of maids, waiters, cooks, and carters, he acknowledged the hard work that went into stoking the cave-like fireplace and managing baskets, lamps, and meat safe. His eye returned again and again to the fireside, with spits, chimney hooks, and cauldron and a dozen fire tools for keeping the blaze going. He described the milieu as a microcosm with the fireplace as the sun.

Late in the 1800s, Georges-Auguste Escoffier, manager of César Ritz's hotel chain and London's Carlton Hotel, further particularized the *brigade de cuisine* (kitchen team), a trained professional staff performing exact duties:

- The leader, a chef, called the *gros bonnet* (big hat)
- Deputy cook or *chef saucier*
- An *entremettier* (side dish specialist)
- His aide, a *potager* or *potagiste* (soup chef)
- The *rôtisseur* (roasting cook)
- An aide, a *grillardin* (grill cook)
- A second aide, a *friturier* (fry cook)
- The *poisonnier* (fish cook)
- The *chef pâtissier* (dessert chef)
- An aide called the *chef glacier* (chef of iced treats)
- A *chef confiseur* (preparer of sweets)
- The *garde manger* (supplier), the supervisor of table accoutrements and cold foods

Attached to each stage of food preparation were the *commis* (assistants), the doers of the hardest lifting and maneuvering of sides of meat and heavy pots.

One of the touchstone French gastronomes, Escoffier was the great restaurant kitchen reformer and pacesetter of his day. Decades before Prosper Montagné compiled *Larousse Gastronomique* (1938), a classic historical encyclopedia of French cookery that discarded the fussy, pretentious techniques and garnitures of past decades, Escoffier and associate Philéas Gilbert supported the move to modernized kitchen procedure. Escoffier modified and reformulated standards by simplifying decoration, removing unnecessary steps from menu-writing, speeding up table service, and following the style of the English chef Alexis Soyer in organizing the kitchen staff into teams to master only one aspect of cookery, such as pastry, salads, or sauces.

To remove obstructions from table service, Escoffier supported the Russian method. By replacing multiple service stages with three divisions—appetizer and/or soup, entrée and accompanying vegetables, and dessert—he reduced trips to and from the kitchen, maintained a stable temperature of servings, and set most of the garnished plates on the table at one time. He invented numerous dishes named for famous places, events, and notables, including poularde Derby, tournedos Rossini, chicken Jeannette, and two tributes to Australian singer Nellie Melba—Melba toast and peach Melba. He opened a series of fine restaurants in Paris, Rome, Madrid, New York, Budapest, Montreal, Philadelphia, and Pittsburgh and published *Le Guide Culinaire* (Culinary Guide, 1921), which clarified changes to French cuisine; *Le Livre des Menus* (The Book of Menus, 1924); and *Ma Cuisine* (My Kitchen, 1934).

England

In the same time period, restaurant dining in England was a province of men. Female gourmands limited themselves to nibbling at street stalls or arranging elaborate dinner parties, for which they hired extra servants and rented crystal, china, linens, and silver to make a gaudy show of their refinement, attention to detail, and tastes. For male clientele or men and women traveling together, families ran taverns and inns. Immigrant cooks opened eateries in cellar dives, where communal tables appealed to working-class and aristocratic gentlemen with a taste for chops, sausages, steaks, and a plowman's lunch, consisting of bread, cheese, pickle, boiled egg, and ale. For the discerning, hotel dining rooms, Thomas's Restaurant, or Simpsons's or the St. James appealed to stylish gentlemen, who paid for a private dining room and a pre-ordered meal, often of lavish proportions.

Nineteenth-century refinement of male tastes and expectations influenced the home kitchen. To assist the domestic cook with details, Christine Terhune Herrick and Marion Harland published the five-volume *Consolidated Library of Modern Cooking and Household Recipes* (1905). Culling advice on etiquette and hospitality, marketing, housekeeping, cooking, and baking from the best of upscale settings, the editors drew on Oscar of the Waldorf for guidance to a formal hotel dinner. The last volume devoted its focus to the gentleman and listed chafing-dish recipes and complementary wines and liqueurs. For women, Nancy Lake's *Menus Made Easy; or How to Order Dinner and Give the Dishes Their French Names* (1900) aided home cooks who replicated restaurant refinements in private entertaining. The popular handbook went through twenty-three printings.

Around the World

Outside Europe and the Americas, formal dining began out of another kind of need. In the 1850s, colonial Australia ended an era of convict markets by establishing inns and fine restaurants. David T. Way founded a chain of fourpenny and sixpenny diners in Melbourne. For a shilling, the upscale Langlois Luncheon Rooms and Scots Pie Shop seated diners in the Royal Arcade, where wait staff served local wines for three cents a glass. In Sydney and Paddington, despite shortages of glassware, tableware, and cutlery, dining opportunities expanded. The oyster bar thrived alongside proper dining rooms serving Continental cuisine and imported wines.

In the 1800s, ethnic laborers in the Hawaiian islands remained loyal to their traditional foods and cooking styles. In addition to growing staples in kitchen gardens and peddling familiar foods door to door from shoulder yokes and pushcarts, newcomers opened cook shacks and restaurants. Chinese, Okinawan, Filipino, Japanese, Puerto Rican, and Portuguese immigrants ate out more frequently than Hawaiian and *haole* (white) islanders and created a demand for ethnic cookery as well as table settings featuring bowls, handleless cups, and chopsticks.

The Americas

In the American colonies, at the same time that Englishmen were patronizing the coffeehouse and establishments selling tea and chocolate, their New World counterparts gathered at watering spots for beer and tavern meals, a *table d'hote* arrangement that characterized Atlantic Coast hospitality. The opening of the Tavern Kitchen in Manhattan in 1762 set caterer/restaurateur Samuel Fraunces on a career path that put him in charge of George Washington's kitchens at Mount Vernon and the White House.

For numerous reasons, American restaurants did not follow the French elevation of style and service. In the United States, travelers from colonial days had touted the fair treatment and worthy table of the Wayside Inn, a roadside respite in Sudbury, Massachusetts. Built on the Boston Post road by David How in 1702, it bears a placard proclaiming it as America's oldest operating inn. Henry Wadsworth Longfellow ennobled the site in "Tales of the Wayside Inn" (1873). The kitchen specialized in Yankee fare; bar staff invented the first American cocktail, called the "coow woow." A full-service hotel and National Historic Site, it still offers rooms and family table service in seven huge dining rooms, each heated by fireplaces, as well as entry to the grist and cider mills, gate house, and barn, where staff once stabled the guests' horses.

In Washington, D.C., professional cooking was limited to inns and stagecoach way stations until 1802. The opening of the Oyster House introduced quality food at reasonable prices, but got off to a bad start in its first three months by attracting mostly men and Baltimore prostitutes. To promote public dining, First Lady Dolley Madison requested that her husband, President James Madison, take her out for seafood. After giving advanced warning to the staff, they arrived to find a spotless dining room and polite diners rather than the usual rowdies. She was so charmed by the good food and quality service that she spread the word. So many Washingtonians patronized the restaurant that two more opened to profit from the boom in dining out.

American-style catering and professional cuisine moved in different directions from formal European table service. Elias Durant, a pharmacist, opened the first soda fountain in Philadelphia in 1825, beginning with stomach-soothing seltzer water served on the spot. Into the 1950s, soda fountains served teens eating confections and ice cream and drinking fizzy dairy drinks. Sweets and sundaes overtook the original quick cures, the forerunners of self-medication with a glass of bromo, ammonia Coke, and Alka-Seltzer.

New York City led the elite restaurant circuit in 1827 with Delmonico's, the patisserie-wine shop of the Swiss emigrés Giovanni and Pietro Delmonico. When the shop burned in 1835, the brothers erected a three-story café and ballroom that evolved into the nation's most prestigious and influential food emporium until its demise in 1923. It developed into a polite dinner house accommodating 125, offering sixty-two imported wines, and a menu in French and English. Delmonico's catered to the likes of Charles Dickens, Walter Scott, Charles Louis Napoleon, Grover Cleveland, Oscar Wilde and Queen Victoria and her heir, Edward, the Prince of Wales. Diamond Jim Brady dined there with Lillian Russell; singer Jenny Lind relaxed with fine food after her performances. The Civil War era brought momentous guests to Delmonico's. Abraham Lincoln entertained his secretary of state, William Henry Seward, who brokered the purchase of Alaska in 1876. The staff honored Seward with a meringue-topped ice cream dessert named baked Alaska in honor of his successful venture.

From one location, Delmonico's became a chain noted for fresh produce grown in the family's twenty-acre Brooklyn farm and such classic American dishes as Lobster Newburg. Staff featured a string of professional chefs beginning with the originators' nephew, Lorenzo Delmonico, who selected goods personally from the Washington Street Market and introduced Americans to European cuisine. The tradition of prize chefs continued through the reigns of Oscar Tschirky, creator of Waldorf Salad; Alessandre Filippini, author of *The Table* (1891); and Charles Ranhofer, who compiled 3,500 recipes in *The Epicurean* (1893).

In the South, Marseilles-born Antoine Alciatore launched a tradition of kitchen élan at his Restaurant Antoine, opened in New Orleans 1840. An immaculate, sand-floored diner, it grew to rival the reputation of Delmonico's and the Café Anglais in Paris from the skill of the master chef, who returned to France in 1885 and left son Jules Alciatore in charge. For forty-five years, the business expanded to international renown before passing to Antoine's grandson, Roy Alciatore, who ran the restaurant for forty-two years. Lining the dining room early in the twenty-first century were mirrors from the grand ballroom of the St. Louis

Hotel. Adorning the gallery were old menus, theater programs, ads, photos, and autographs of two thousand notables who have enjoyed the food, either at the main dining room or one of the fifteen auxiliary banquet halls.

Staff typically remained employed their entire careers at Antoine's. Bus boys began a ten-year apprenticeship to wait tables. The head waiter worked his way up over half a century, serving the same French menu used year-round at lunch and dinner and memorizing orders without writing them down. He typically dimmed the lights for service of Café Brulôt Diabolique and brandy-flamed crêpes Suzette. The most famous dishes of the house were oysters à la Rockefeller and pompano en Papillotte (Pompano in a paper bag), originated to mimic a hot-air balloon. Wines dated to 1884, brandy to 1811.

Antoine's maintained a quiet, unadorned atmosphere devoid of cocktail bar, music, or dancing. Staff continued to cook nineteenth-century style over a coal-fired French range and to grind spices at the original marble mortar with a *lignum vitae* pestle. The private dining room called the Dungeon was once a Spanish prison. The restaurant library housed 400 cookbooks, one of which dated to 1659. Still pleasing aficionados of French fare, the restaurant became an American gustatory legend.

American eateries expanded service to meet the dining needs of a surging economy. As railroads criss-crossed the continent, George Pullman introduced the dining car in 1868. His staffing of professional cooks and waiters rewarded a moneyed traveling public with plush, comfortable service of fresh foods purchased along the rail lines. In Providence, Rhode Island, in 1872, viander Walter Scott's horse-drawn wagon of dishes preceded the diner, an American classic. Four years later, Fred Harvey created his own brand of traveler's food service at a depot dinery in Topeka, Kansas, feeding inbound and outbound guests on the Atchison, Topeka & Santa Fe rail line.

In downtown New York City, the confectioner Louis Sherry founded a hotel-restaurant, which he moved in 1898 to Fifth Avenue and 44th Street. In opulent ambience, he served extravagant dinners. In 1903, the city's Horseback Riding Club honored Sherry's Restaurant by selecting it for the group's founding dinner, which ran up a tab of $50,000.

Twentieth-Century Restaurants

Chain restaurants emerged with the creation of the Howard Johnson restaurant franchise. Begun in Wollaston, Massachusetts, in 1925, the owner parlayed a newsstand/soda shop into a second location on Cape Cod. Lacking the cash to underwrite the second business, he received the backing of a friend, who agreed to invest in a parallel operation serving the same menu and following the same setup. The HoJo chain spread rapidly down the eastern seaboard to Florida by 1941 with the construction of 150 restaurants.

The American diner got its start in 1926 with the hat-shaped Brown Derby, a Hollywood landmark and the home of the Cobb salad. The supper club, an outgrowth of the oft-raided speakeasy, began in 1929 with New York City's 21, a night spot that bore some of the aura of earlier illicit booze distributors. A step up from Charlie Berns and Jack Kriendler's Greenwich Village tea rooms, the club appealed to the glitterati. When wrecking crew readied to raze the building before the erection of Rockefeller Center, 21 staff invited guests to a New Year's Eve bash and passed around sledge hammers and crowbars. At the winding down of the Great Depression, the RCA Building on Rockefeller Plaza hosted the Rainbow Room, a re-emergence of Continental opulence coupled with bright lights, a house organ and orchestra, and a popular dance floor.

Ernest Lessing Byfield built on the concept of elegant ambience with Chicago's Pump Room at the Ambassador Hotel. Emulating the seventeenth-century crush at spas built in Bath, England, he tempered egalitarianism with a rigid pecking order—the Hollywood elite at Table One and nobodies to the rear. Dramatic food service produced the appropriate frisson of anticipation. With the opening of the 1939 World's Fair in Flushing Meadows, Queens, cooks from sixty countries displayed their wares at pavilion restaurants. For Americans, who bore an inferiority complex from colonial days, French cuisine received the strongest following. They gawked at the French chef system displayed by Pierre Franey and Henri Soulé, at Le Pavillion.

On the West Coast in the 1930s, Victor Bergeron, beer seller at the Hinky Dinks, pursued Los Angeles theme restaurants with Trader Vic's, a South Seas supper club. Tiki decor spread to a chain famed for serving the Mai Tai. Multicultural dining surged from the example of the Moosewood Restaurant, which nineteen members composed of restaurateurs, writers, and food consultants opened at Dewitt Mall near Cayuga Lake in Ithaca, New York, in 1972 as a vegetarian collective. From the community project developed more dining experiences based on a diverse menu of whole grains, beans, coffee, beers, spirits, herbs, and spices from regional America and around the world. In addition to a website, the collective spread its innovative recipes through a series of cookbooks: *The Moosewood Restaurant Kitchen Garden* (1992), *The Moosewood Restaurant Cooks At Home* (1994), and *The Moosewood Restaurant Low-Fat Favorites: Flavorful Recipes for Healthful Meals* (1996).

The French introduced *nouvelle cuisine* (new cuisine) in the 1960s, when families began to reconsider heavy styles of cookery in light of emerging data on cholesterol and heart disease. The French flair survived while cooks made lighter sauces and served smaller portions, but charged large prices for their ingenuity. In Indonesia, Padang restaurants followed a more structured approach to dining. In the 1990s, waiters approached the table with small dishes of fish, meat, eggs, and vegetables balanced on the left arm and arranged them buffet-style. The bill for dinner covered only those that the diners ate.

Challenges

In November 2000, France, Europe's main beef-eating nation, teetered on the brink of reducing its annual consumption of 198 pounds per year. The hysteria created by lawsuits and rumors of links to Creutzfeldt-Jakob disease caused Italy, Germany, and Spain to curtail beef imports. Restaurant staffs wrestled with fears of disease, deaths, and lawsuits from a re-emergence of bovine spongiform encephalopathy, commonly called mad cow disease because of its erosion of brain tissue.

In Paris, Michel Del Burgo, chef at Taillevent, a three-star establishment, modified the recipe for *filet pique a la moelle* (filet injected with marrow) and removed *tourte de riz de veau* (veal sweetbread pie) from the menu. Owner Jean-Claude Vrinat noted that fears for health caused businessmen to order more fish than beef. Michel Bocuse, a chef in Collonges-au-Mont d'Or near Lyons, continued to serve beef to a declining demand. At the Moulin de Mougins near Nice, chef Roger Verge considered dropping beef tournedos in brandy and filet mignon with truffles because of patrons' fears.

Chefs in Competition

The most famous chefs gain their reputations from dedication to quality ingredients, meticulous preparation, attractive combinations of color and texture, and service that coordinates the senses—sight, smell, touch, sound, and taste. On January 23–24, 2001, contestants entering the Bocuse d'Or Concours Mondiale de la Cuisine (World Contest of Cuisine) in Lyon, France, brought into the exhibit hall of the Eurexpo Center much of the fresh restaurant talent of the twenty-first century. Chef Paul Bocuse, a Lyon restaurateur and president of the organization, suggested the cook-off to promote the annual International Food Trade Exhibition. The first contest took place in 1987. Past awards by nation attest to stiff competition from France, Belgium, and Scandinavia.

Under flags of their nations and the names of the restaurant's they served, entrants went to work. From Argentina, Australia, Austria, Belgium, Brazil, Britain, Canada, Denmark, Finland, France, Germany, Iceland, Ireland, Italy, Japan, Mexico, South Africa, Spain, Sweden, Switzerland, and the U.S., cooks with their young *commis* (helpers) labored for two days to craft the required plattered centerpieces plus three garnishes each for meat and fish. The competition required contestants to complete dinner for twelve in five hours and to use as ingredients a lamb and two sea bass. Cooking stations offered them miniature work stations fitted with sink, counter, refrigerator, oven and four-burner stove, and implements. Assisting them were Paul Bocuse and former contest winners, who roamed the hall to monitor progress.

In the 2001 competition, the twenty-two jurors—eleven for lamb and eleven for fish—sampled, sniffed, prodded, and decimated artful presentations to evaluate each dish on a scale of six hundred points. At 6:00 p.m., officials began the prize ceremony. The winner was a home-court favorite—François Adamski of Maison Prunier in Paris, France, with 580 points, who won 15,000 euros. Henrik Norström of Bon Lloc in Sweden with 532 points took second place and 10,000 euros; Hákon Mar Örvarsson of Hôtel Holt in Iceland, also earning 532 points, won third and 5,000 euros. In 2005, contestants will include newcomers from China and Lebanon.

See also **Automat; Escoffier, Georges-Auguste; Sailland, Maurice Edmond**

Further Reading

Blake, Anthony, and Quentin Crewe. *The Great Chefs of France.* London: Marshall Editions, Ltd., 1978.

Chelminski, Rudolph, "Le Bocuse d'Or," *Smithsonian*, May 2001, 72–80.

The Williamsburg Cookbook. New York: Holt, Rinehart and Winston, 1971.

RICE

A willowy annual grass plant grown in ponds, paddies, shallow lakes, and river banks, rice is a cereal grain rich in protein and carbohydrates. Its cultivation covers 10 percent of earth's arable land, either in rain-fed lowlands, flood plains, uplands, or labor-intensive paddies artificially dammed and irrigated. Globally, the grain comes in numerous varieties:

- Balilla—a short grained Italian rice favored for sweets
- Calasparra—a medium-grain Spanish rice favored for stove-top cooking or baking in an *olla* (clay casserole) or paella pan

U.S. long grain rice.
[© *Courtesy of Agricultural Research Service, USDA. Photo by Keith Weller.*]

- Calrose—a high-quality favorite of Japanese and Hawaiian cooks, which California agricultural experts developed in the late 1940s. The favorite base for shaping nigiri, maki, temaki, and pan sushi, calrose is distributed under the brand names of Diamond, Fukusuke, and Hinode.
- Cargo—an unhusked rise cultivated in Camargue, France, during World War II
- Carolina or basmati—long-grained, angular white tinged with blue, the dominant variety in the United States
- Italian or Roman—a grayish-white grain lacking luster
- Jasmine—a Thai long-grain variety preferred by Southeast Asians
- Java—a flat long grain that tends to be transparent
- Madagascar—a shiny long grain
- Malagkit rice—a Philippine and southeast Asian variety easily identified by its long purple grains
- Mochi rice—a chalky, short-grain Japanese variety known as sticky rice or sweet rice for its glutinous appearance after steaming for use in confections. When milled as flour, it is called mochiko, sold under the Blue Star logo.
- Oryza sativa japonica—the plump, short grains that come from Italy's Po Valley and Valencia, Spain. It

fuels a profitable riziculture that, during the Renaissance, forced adult and child workers into servitude
- Patna—a soft, milky grain
- Piedmont—a rounded grain darker at the center
- Thai sticky rice—a glutinous long-grain variety prized for its aroma and for clinging to chopsticks. It is the basis for Thai meat, fish, and curry recipes.
- Vialone nano—a Venetian risotto used in Venetian *minestra* (rice soups).

Origins of Rice

Global riziculture forms a lesson in world geography beginning in India, Southeast Asia, and China and moving steadily westward. Neolithic Asians cultivated rice where water was abundant. As indicated by ancient paddies and clay imbedded with grain shapes, Chinese farmers in Yaurhermuduh began cultivating rice around 3000 BCE, simultaneously with the riziculture developed in Non Nok Tha, Thailand, and in Ardicchanallur, India. The first rice growers may have built the granaries in India and coastal China, where rice advanced to an annual crop. Rice growing reached Lothal, Pakistan, in 2000 BCE and spread to Hasthinapur and the Philippines around 1000 BCE, to Turkestan after 500 BCE, and to Japan about 100 BCE. Australomelanesian seafarers brought rice and its culinary heritage to Indonesia, where it shared a place in the regional diet with sago, sweet potatoes, and corn.

For Asian cooking, rice, one of the five revered grains, forms the center of Chinese dishes with *t'sai* (accompaniments) arranged about the exterior. The Chinese refer to dining as *sik fan* (eat rice), an equivalent of the English "break bread." To their children, they relate the ancient myth of hunter Houh Jir, who begged the gods for food to replace game, which was hard to find. The gods gave him five sacks for his son to carry on a hunt for edible grains. They returned with beans, hemp, millet, rice, and wheat. The boy Pahdi gave his name to the damp depressions where rice grows, which still bear the name "paddies." Cultivation required intense stoop labor, involving whole families in planting grains for seedlings, then pulling, rinsing, and bundling sprouts for transplanting. After six weeks' growth, neighbors joined in a cooperative effort of harvesting while women cooked huge meals for participants.

India

Indian creativity produced numerous variations on boiled grains. Cooks added fried aromatics and dressed rice with tamarind, sesame, and sugar. They prepared pulse and rice together and cooked rice with meat and ghee (clarified butter). For the pantry, they ground, dried, husked, and polished grain with an iron-covered pounder, then winnowed and washed grains that they stored up to three years. To make *aval* rice, they soaked grain and roasted it in sand to the puff stage, then pounded it flat. For *pori*, they tossed it on hot sand to expand grains. For hardening, they aged and parboiled rice, a method that improved the yield of whole grain.

In addition to mortars, pestles, boiling pots, pounders, and winnowing baskets, the cooks of India needed concave clay grills for toasting *appam* (pancakes). In pots of water they processed rice for mashing into a dough to extrude for *idi-appam*. In shallow pans, they fried *dosai*, a snack made from fermented dhal and rice. A variant, *adai*, was a similar mix of ground rice and four pulses.

Greece

Greek experience with rice during Alexander the Great's conquests to the East in the fourth century BCE had spread the word about a tasty staple grain, but cultivation moved slowly. Greek texts by third-century philosopher Theophrastus give eyewitness accounts of rice crops in India in 320 BCE. In his *History of Plants*, he characterized *óryzon* (rice) as the source of a digestible boiled cereal. He mused, "When growing, it looks like darnel [grass], though standing for most of its life in water, but it fruits not into an ear but into a sort of plume, like millet." (Walker 1996, 82) Additional commentary on rice in Bactria, Babylonia, and Syria emerged four decades later. In time, rice developed a reputation as a restorative for the sick, which earned recommendations from the Greek physician Galen and from late eleventh-century physician Simeon Seth of Constantinople.

Mideast

After the explosive power of the Islamic revolution in the mid-600s CE, rice reached Palestine around 950, where cooks simmered it in fig pulp. From Iran, it moved on to Egypt, which led Mediterranean production in the eleventh and twelfth centuries, and into Sicily, Italy, Spain, and the Western Hemisphere. Along the way, its delicacy and aroma inspired poets and food historians such as the Indian medical text, *Susrutha Samhita* (1000 BCE), which classified types and nutrient value of rice. In the early ninth-century Iraqi philologist and critic ibn Qurayb al-Asma'i, proclaimed rice with butter and sugar a heavenly taste sensation.

China

By the Sung dynasty, which began in 960 CE, rice was the dietary *fan* (staple) of one hundred million Chinese, who also revered tea, oil, salt, soy, and vinegar, which they could make from delicate brown rice. Cooking among court food preparers developed varied ornate ways to dress and serve rice. During the Ming dynasty, from 1368 to 1644, which rid the kitchen of coarse Mongol influence, the Chinese diet of two thousand calories a day allowed each person over 1.8 pounds of rice daily, totalling 660 pounds a year. Still producing a third of the world's crop, the southern area, particularly Guangdong, supports two annual plantings. At weekly markets among the lake-based Intha of Inle, Burma, woven baskets of rice cakes are a staple kitchen dish for cooks seeking to trade their bounty for cash. Over time, the value of rice to the diet has impressed many of the world's cooks.

Wild Rice

When Native Americans developed riziculture, the fall harvest took on social, political, and religious significance. The Winnebago and Anishinabe of the Great Lakes region made rice gathering woman's work, which accomplished from canoes with sticks. The nearby Menominee of Lake Michigan, who took a name adapted from "wild rice," combed the wild for rice, beat it with a flail and bat to husk it, sun-dried and smoked it for storage in baskets, and cooked grains into a stew sweetened with maple sugar. The Ojibwa used canoe and paddles for navigating rice stands and for beating ripe heads from stalks on the scene, as depicted in a drawing by Seth Eastman. Harvesters developed a ritual involving offering *manomin* (rice) grains along with water and tobacco to nature gods and giving thanks for a healing food and dietary staple, which they cooked with wild blueberries. Surviving from their sacral reverence for wild rice is a recipe for *manomin baquajeegan* (wild rice bread), made from grains roasted in the traditional style before husking. [It should be noted that wild rice is the seed of an aquatic perennial grass, unlike the cereal-grain rice discussed elsewhere in this article.]

Concerning New World wild rice, the Anishinaabeg Ojibwa repeat the legend of Nanaboozhoo, a hunter who returned to camp empty-handed and who depended on the Creator, Gitchi Manidoo, to feed him. A duck perched on his kettle, then flew off, leaving behind *manoomin* (wild rice) in the broth. As Nanaboozhoo ate from the kettle, he enjoyed the first Ojibwa rice gruel. Later, he followed in the direction the duck had taken and found wild rice growing at a lake shore among mud hens, geese, and teal, all pecking at the grains.

The story of the Ojibwa discovery of wild rice accounts for the centrality of the grain to the native diet. Holy figures maintain that wandering Indians anticipated a sign from the Creator, of the location of their new home in the West. Because of its vital role in native sustenance, rice became a focus of home cooking, ritual, and thanksgiving. At Manoominigiizis, the wild rice moon, when the grain reaches its peak, ricing parties in the Tamarac National Wildlife Refuge perpetuate the annual harvest, poling their craft through the shallows of Blackbird Lake and knocking free around five hundred pounds of rice each day for local cooks to winnow and rinse.

In 1946, Ojibwa painter Patrick DesJarlait, who grew up at the Red Lake Indian Reservation, created *Making Wild Rice*, a dramatic cubist watercolor demonstrating the mystic quality of traditional wild rice processing. One figure shod in deerskin boots jogs or dances on the harvest in a barrel sunk in the earth and jostles the handle to separate hulls from grains. Another man parches in a kettle the newly-gathered grains. A native woman lifts a birchbark winnowing tray to toss and waft away the hulls. The fabled grain became a grocery specialty item in the 1960s, when Minnesota paddies first supplied 20 percent of North America's wild rice. In 1977, wild rice became Minnesota's official state grain, but California challenged local production with their irrigated paddies.

Carolina Rice

The arrival of one rice to North America made colonial history. In 1685, when a ship from Madagascar brought a unique rice to the Carolina port of Charles Towne, the recipient, Dr. Henry Woodward, kept and propagated the Carolina Golde Seed species. In the 1700s, the rice went into commercial production on tide-washed lands in hundreds of plantations from Wilmington on the Cape Fear River to northern Florida for shipment to the British Isles. By 1726, the South Carolina port shipped 4,500 tons of rice. Low country cooks also valued the tall, golden grain for the buttery savor it added to seafood dishes, soup, pudding, and rice bread.

The historian Karen Hess stressed that planters owed the success of Carolina Gold rice to slaves who learned riziculture in Africa and performed arduous stoop labor in mosquito- and gator-infested swamps and hand threshed the grain to produce a good crop. After Lincoln freed the slaves, plantations shrank as riziculture became less profitable and Carolina Gold grew scarce in grocery barrels and on pantry shelves.

Soldiers departing Civil War battlefields took riziculture west and south to Gulf Coast plantations, the emerging core of the nation's rice industry. Production returned less profit until mechanization replaced hand sowing, reaping, and threshing. Spurring the rise in rice cookery were the forty thousand Chinese who immigrated to the West Coast during the Gold Rush and demanded a rice-based diet. By 1920, the Sacramento Valley of California produced the next rice boom.

The contribution of riziculture to kitchen history includes recipes for gumbo as well as rice cereal for infants and adult breakfasts. In 1901, Louisa Cheves Smythe Stoney published *The Carolina Rice Cookbook*, a compendium of over 230 recipes that she sold for 25 cents at the South Carolina Interstate and West Indian Exposition. Cooks began adding rice to bread, fritters, pudding, and pancakes and waffles. In 1904, puffed rice, invented by Alexander P. Anders at Columbia University, debuted as snack food at the St. Louis Exposition. Rice took on new significance as a filler during both the Depression and rationing of World War II, when it enabled the cook to stretch meat servings.

Japan

In Japanese farmhouses, rice growing initiated the weaving of bamboo seedling baskets suspended from shoulder yokes, scoops, winnowing fans, and storage canisters. Each January, farm wives used starter and broken grains to make rice yeast, an essential to soybean paste and soy sauce. For rice paste, they cooked glutinous grains in sugar and water, then pounded it with a mallet in a mortar to pat into cakes. When sliced and dried, the cakes supplied the family as snack food and as deep-fried pones for meals. In 1908, entrepreneur Tajiro Sumida, an emigrant from Hiroshima to the Hawaiian Islands, became the West's first *sake* brewer. For the island's Japanese contract laborers, he bottled an affordable rice wine made in his own factory.

Overall, rice constituted sixty percent of the Japanese daily diet up to 1940; during World War II, the percentage rose to 66.6 percent. It was so essential to the Malaysian diet that people greeted each other with the questions *Suda makan nasi?* (Have you eaten rice?) (Rajah 1996, 31) Young housewives learned to pick up every spilled grain rather than to insult it by walking on it or sweeping it out the door. When families moved to a new house, they carried a symbolic store of rice and salt to the new kitchen to assure plenty.

Customarily, rice *mochi* (girdle cakes) accompanied holiday meals in Japan. At fortuitous events, families traditionally cooked *azuki* (red beans) with *sekihan* (red rice), which was also the customary dish prepared on the first and fifteenth of the month. In the late 1930s, Emperor Hirohito cultivated a rice paddy on the palace grounds, thereby setting an example of essential human labor to provide food for the family. Gifts of rice, as described in John F. Embree's *Suye Mura: A Japanese Village* (1939), characterized numerous social gatherings, including condolence calls and for community gatherings, naming ceremonies, memorial services, and parties. Weddings required gifts of fish, rice cakes, or *saki* or *sake* (rice wine) in a red lacquerware bucket. Returned containers always carried a kitchen gift, either vegetables, eggs, or rice cakes. In folk tradition, the superstition of tossing rice into a baby's room eased the unknown disturbance that caused the child to cry in the night.

According to Doré Ogrizek's *Japan* (1957), the nation was the "land of the lush plains of ears of rice," where cooks have been making rice-based meals since the Stone Age." (p. 293) Served with slivers of turnip, cucumber, or pickled plums, rice permeated the meal to the end, when diners poured hot tea into the bowl to make *cha-zuke*. For a hot weather dish, individuals embellished rice with fish flakes, grated bonito, or roasted seaweed. A practical serving of *sushi*, rice dressed with vinegar and salt, or *nigiri-zushi* (pressed rice) began with slicing garnishes of raw fish, boiled cuttlefish, lobsters, or octopus. The Inari style of *sushi* called for riceballs topped with sesame seed and diced *renkon* (lotus bulb) and iced with bean paste. A molded dessert featured a salted plum at the core of a riceball.

The Japanese value rice as a national commodity and reject imported goods as proof of their self-sufficiency. At table, rice complements servings of meat, seafood, vegetables, and fruit or is served as a part of sushi, a delicacy combining fish with rice and vinegar. At home, cooks may place a pot or electric rice steamer at the center of the table for spooning into individual bowls. Rather than heap grains for a mass presentation, they return to the kitchen to refill the container. In a nursery-school child's *obento* (lunchbox), rice occupies central importance in a five- to six-course meal, but, like citizens in an orderly society, the focal starch is unobtrusive among bright colored meats, fruit, and vegetables.

Hawaii

Hawaiians eat sixty pounds of rice annually, contrasting the mainland diet of nine pounds. In 1949, when Hawaiian Orientals wearied of American burgers and Asian stir-fry, Richard Inouye, owner of the Lincoln Grill in Hilo, Hawaii, created a compromise dish that accommodated native tastes. By scooping rice into two mounds, capping it with a fried egg and hamburger patty topped with gravy, he produced the *loco moco*, an island original intended as "people food." Named by teenagers, the lunchtime staple rose to a favorite at mom and pop cafés and on meal wagons selling plate lunches to students, fishers, dock workers, and field laborers. The lunch wagon became an essential mobile kitchen treated to its own parking space in downtown Honolulu.

A Taste of Home

Separation from rice has produced severe longing for the taste of home. In winter 1890, Parma ambassadors working in Rome requested that their favorite cook send a *Bomba di Riso*. A volunteer replied by telegram that he was loading onto the train the familiar domed rice dish encasing braised pigeons. Before the savory *bomba* reached Rome, the telegrapher alerted police, who intercepted the train, roped off the tracks, and searched for an explosive. It took a reply from Parma's police to clarify that a *bomba* was a globe-shaped casserole, not a bomb.

In 1944, a dearth of rice caused mass starvation in English-controlled Bengal, one of the world's most populous and poorest areas, where farmers devoted 80 percent of arable land to riziculture. Like the Irish Potato Famine, the dependence of Bengali families on a single crop proved tragic after a rice crop failure. Among the Montagnards of Vietnam, scarcity of food before the annual rice harvest reduces meals to one a day.

Asian-American soldiers realized their isolation as an ethnic minority during World War II, when military kitchens offered little rice and no soy sauce. Immediately after the war, the introduction of the low-cost electric rice saucepan, pioneered by Konoskuke Matsushita in 1946, revolutionized Japanese cookery. The popularity of his rice cooker boosted Panasonic to a world-class industry of kitchen appliances and electronics.

Rice in Modern Times

Further pre-preparation methods made rice available to the kitchen in multiple time-saving forms, including breakfast cereals and candy bars. After inventor Ataullah K. Ozai Durrani pioneered pre-cooked rice in 1950, he demonstrated that the process produced quick-dried grain that required only ten minutes to cook. The military bought the product for packing in K rations. It became the first rice product ever advertised, boosting the national U.S. consumption from nine to ten pounds annually in 1970 as compared to three hundred pounds per person in Asian countries. Within two decades, as rice gained respect because of its nutrients, the figure for Americans jumped to twenty-six pounds per person, in part because of consumer interest in basmati, risotto, sushi, and koshihikari, a short-grain Japanese rice imported under the General Agreement on Tariffs and Trade (GATT) treaty.

During the 1970s, the anthropologist Sulamith Heins Potter, author of *Family Life in a Northern Thai Village* (1977), studied women's work in a rice-centered culture where the seasons revolved around the annual crop. At a small hearth in the home's central hall, Potter observed the daily jobs of heating blackened braziers, lowering a shelf suspended from the ceiling on ropes, and selecting containers to begin the day's cookery. Rice soaked in a green celadon jar overnight. The next morning, the cook and her daughters steamed it in a straight-sided wood pot for breakfast. Women in the village congregated for special gifts of steamed rice and coconut in banana leaves for presentation at temple.

Rice dominates menu planning in Cuba, the Dominican Republic, Puerto Rico, the Mississippi Delta, and much of Africa, where beans and rice are the staffs of life. The combination of rice and peas is so common in Jamaican kitchens that it is called the Jamaican coat of arms. For Namibians, rice imported from South Africa is popular, but too expensive for the poor. Gambians eat rice for lunch as a basis for a spiced vegetable stew. Guineans spice their rice with a peanut butter sauce made with palm oil, ground leaves, and tomato paste. Mauritanians balance daily meals of rice and couscous, made from sorghum flour and served with *idhin* (liquified butter). In the Congo, where 10 percent of children suffer malnutrition and starvation, rice is a staple starch along with cassava, potatoes, yams, beans, and corn. In Sierra Leone, lean times skew menus toward rice and leaf sauce for adults, who save eggs and meat to nourish their children.

Asia is famous for standardizing the cooking and serving of rice-based meals, such as the Balinese *rijsttafel* (rice table), for which cooks make up to two dozen variations on the theme of rice and its many complements. In India, Hindu families celebrate Annaprashanna, a ritual marking a six-month-old child's first taste of rice. For the event, cooks sweeten and spice *payesh* (rice pudding) with brown sugar, cardamom, clove, cinnamon, and bay leaf. Chinese homemakers stock multiple types of rice—extra long grain for daily cooking, glutinous rice for sweet or sticky grain for molding or using in stuffing and cake, black sweet rice for pastry, red rice for holidays, and white rice powder, which mothers mix with sugar and water for feeding infants. A favorite breakfast staple is *jook* (rice gruel), a congee that has fed families since 1000 BCE. It suits the dietary needs of invalids, toddlers, and the elderly and varies meals with the addition of spice, meat, vegetables, herbs, relishes, stock, and other grains.

In Bangladesh, learning to cook rice is the reponsibility of every young woman, who studies the skill of steaming from her mother or grandmother. The Terai of Nepal focus on rice, and the rest of the nation prefers corn, wheat, and millet. The Hmong of Laos eat steamed rice when it is available and corn as a backup. Pakistani diet calls for *pillau*, a lightly fried vegetable-and-rice dish and a rice pudding called *kheer*. Lao and Thai cooks offer glutinous rice as finger food along with bite-size pieces of meat. The people of Hong Kong cook rice into porridge. In Iran, rice and wheat bread are standard menu items. Comoros imports much rice, which local cooks spice with *putu*, a hot pepper sauce. Rice remains the staple in Cambodia, which is called the "cradle of rice." (Skabelund 1997, Vol. II, 39)

Fortified Rice

A futuristic proposal to end world hunger is the creation of fortified rice. Coming of age at the same time with edible vaccines, the production of "golden rice," a vitamin A-enriched grain developed by Ingo Potrykus of Zurich's Swiss Federal Institute of Technology, might end a form of malnutrition that results in blindness in Asia, Africa, and Latin America. (Rusting 2000, 70) Because one third or more of all people depend on rice as a daily staple, a strain fortified with beta-carotene would supply the building material for vitamin A. In May 2000, Zeneca, an agribusiness, bought the rights to a fortification system created by Peter Beyer of the University of Freiburg, Germany, and Potrykus. Zeneca intends to sell the rice to industrialized nations, but to distribute it free in impoverished areas.

For much of the world, such as Hawaii, Taiwan, Guinea-Bissau, Jordan, Malaysia, Kyrgyzstan, Mauritius, the Philippines, Guyana, Panama, the United Arab Emirates, Vietnam, Thailand, Singapore, and Indonesia, dining without rice is not a real meal. Current innovations in rice cookery includes electronic advances in steaming and holding rice at a stable temperature, a valuable technology for home or restaurant. An expensive model, the Zojirushi Deluxe Rice cooker, steams rice and keeps it warm with automatic, thermostatically controlled heaters. The lid locks into place to hold supplies in a five- or ten-cup nonstick pan for up to twelve hours.

See also **Obentos**

Further Reading

Dickason, Olive Patricia. *Canada's First Nations*. Norman: University of Oklahoma Press, 1992.

Embree, John F. *Suye Mura: A Japanese Village*. Chicago: University of Chicago Press, 1939.

Forristal, Linda Joyce, "A Rainbow of Rices," *The World & I*, August 1999, 150.

Garrett, W. E., "The Hmong of Laos: No Place to Run," *National Geographic*, 78–111.

Maraini, Fosco. *Meeting with Japan*. New York: Viking Press, 1959.

Potter, Sulamith Heins. *Family Life in a Northern Thai Village*. Berkeley: University of California Press, 1977.

Rajah, Carol Selva. *Makan-Lah!: The True Taste of Malaysia*. Sydney, Australia: HarperCollins, 1996.

Sochurek, Howard, "Viet Nam's Montagnards," *National Geographic*, April 1968, 443–487.

RITTENHOUSE, DAVID

The astronomer and mathematician David Rittenhouse gets little credit for his redesign of the Franklin stove. Rittenhouse redesigned Benjamin Franklin's stove by angling the sides and the back plate to direct more heat into the room. The Rittenhouse stove outperformed the Franklin fireplace insert throughout the 1790s. It also impressed the Count von Rumford, who borrowed freely from Rittenhouse and Franklin, but credited neither for his own stove design.

A manufacturer of telescopes and scientific instruments, Rittenhouse was born to Welsh Quakers outside Germantown, Pennsylvania, on April 8, 1732. He taught himself optics from books and tools bequeathed by his uncle before opening an instrument business for regulating clocks. Much admired by Thomas Jefferson and the American Philosophical Society for his experiments, Rittenhouse studied thermometers, planets and comets, magnetism, electricity, clocks, and water compression. Resettled in Philadelphia in 1770, he built an observatory and compiled data on Venus, Mercury, and Uranus. He designed a wood hygrometer, surveyed rivers and canals, and settled boundary disputes in Delaware, Maryland, Massachusetts, New Jersey, New York, Pennsylvania, and Virginia. The Royal Society of London tapped him as a foreign member in 1795 to honor Rittenhouse's many achievements.

See also **Rumford, Count von**

Further Reading

Adams, Robert, "Editorial," *Smithsonian*, December 1986, 10.
Almanac of Famous People. Detroit: Gale Research, 1999.

ROASTING

The combination of embers and roots probably introduced early gatherers to roasting as an easy method of preparing raw foods for consumption. A traditional feast of Yue-Ping, the Chinese thanksgiving, occurred on the eighth month of the year, when cooks celebrated by roasting a pig seasoned with herbs. Along with servings of pork, diners looked forward to moon cakes stuffed with pork bits, watermelon seeds, nuts, and ginger, and raised toasts to the full moon.

As a culinary technology, roasting influenced all cultures. In India, numerous references to spit-roasting kebabs in the *Mahabharata* (ca. 1302 BCE), the Sanskrit epic, and other ancient texts establishes the importance of skewered meats to native culture. The Egyptians roasted white lotus; other Mediterranean cooks roasted iris bulbs, called barbary nuts. Arabs held *méchoui*, a meat cooking event that required turning suckling lamb over charcoal embers. Cooked to perfection, the skin crackled and the kidneys reached a golden brown. Diners traditionally abandoned utensils and sat around the spitted meat, pulling pieces from the bone with their fingers. The dinner ended with the passing of a basin of rose-scented water for rinsing hands.

Ingredients and materials varied widely worldwide. Classical Greece and Rome added numerous roots to traditional Mediterranean roasting stock, especially flavorful elecampane, madder, pursetassel, rampion, and salsify. Native Americans applied the method to the sweet aloe, Jerusalem artichoke, and the tubers of cat tail, canna lily, sedge, and tule. African-American slaves, who had few kitchen utensils, roasted potatoes, yams, and sweet potatoes at their cabin fireside.

European tinsmiths produced elaborate roasters, called roasting kitchens, composed of a hemisphere of metal with a bar and adjustable skewers across the center ending in a crank. A versatile device, the roaster featured a lift-up hatch for basting, a pouring spout at bottom for retrieval of juices, and hooks at top for suspension in the chimney from chains. For small game birds, a wrought iron roasting stand with vertical column and prongs below allowed the cook to impale a fish or bird neck to crop and set the stand on a drip pan near the flame. With an iron tool, the roaster could rotate the bird to assure even cooking. A horizontal roast-dripper on legs held long joints of meat above a drip pan.

In England, the traditional Anglo-Saxon wassail bowl welcomed friends for drinking and toasting Christmas, New Year's Day, and Twelfth Night or Epiphany. For a massive punch bowl, named for the Middle English term *waes hael* (be healthy), cooks roasted apples or crabapples to add to ale, which they sweetened with sugar and nutmeg. Wassailers shared a communal loving cup, both in private homes and abbeys. Scottish revellers carried steaming punch bowl, cheese, and fresh-baked buns, short cake, or bread to neighbors' homes. On Christmas morning in Wales and Devon, celebrants bore roasted apples and cider about the orchard and sang to productive apple trees, which they sprinkled with punch and decked with cider-soaked cakes.

Another occasion for roasting, during the Little Ice Age from 1550 to 1850, when the Thames River froze each winter, locals thronged the first Frost Fair, erected on the ice in 1607. A settlement of blanket tents sheltered booths. As depicted in a print sketched of the fair held from December to February 4, 1683, festivities involved a community in entertainments, toy and jewelry booths, bear-baiting, gaming, ice bowling, barrel rolls, and ice sailing. A circle of pickets separated the cooks who roasted an ox at a great makeshift hearth.

In the sixteenth century, Transylvanians roasted whole oxen for wedding feasts. The master roaster stuffed the stomach with a sheep stuffed with a capon. He spitted the skinned ox on a rod with spikes. Suspended between forked poles, the huge carcass displayed hooves and horns as a young helper turned the broach. The master began a lengthy basting with one ceramic kettle of saltwater and the other with a sop of peppered wine blended with onion, apple, tarragon, marjoram, sage, and thyme. The master made a grand display of carving slices to serve on planks to the one hundred guests.

European-style roasting was a standard cooking method in colonial America. In the May 2, 1737, issue of the *Boston Gazette*, John Jackson, jack-maker, offered made-to-order roasting implements at his shop at the town drawbridge. In addition to cookery supplies, he stocked ironing boxes and locks and keys and also cleaned and mended old jacks, which often bent from heavy loads or rusted from salty marinades. In 1784, clockmaker Simon Willard received his first patent from Massachusetts for making and selling his clock jack, a wind-up device that attached to a mantel and suspended haunches of meat or fowl from a hook to turn in a precise rhythm before the fire.

When settlers moved west, they took their culinary technology on the trail. In the cooking advice offered in *The Prairie Traveler: A Hand-Book for Overland Expeditions* (1859), containing advice, maps, and intineraries over the principal routes between the Mississippi River and the Pacific Ocean, army captain Randolph Barnes Marcy singled out the buffalo as a source of meat for roasting. He suggested skinning and stripping tongue, hump, and bones. In addition to flame-cooking thick cuts over a campfire, he advised roasting bones and cracking them for their marrow, a good source of protein for trans-Mississippi pioneers.

During her residency among aboriginal tribes, Daisy O'Dwyer Bates, author of *The Passing of the Aborigines: A Lifetime Spent among the Natives of Australia* (1938), analyzed native cooking styles and diet and battled infanticide and the roasting of young children. She found reason to enjoy aboriginal roasting methods when it applied to kangaroo, emu, wombat, and wallaby. She said, "They cooked me a delicious meal, a wallaby tail, with the skin left on, thrown into the ashes, and a long fat carpet snake called *goonia* rolled into lengths and roasted." (Bates 1967, 135) Wombat required four hours in hot ash, but she extolled its flavor and tenderness, which equalled roast pork.

At the fireside, Bates rescued botanical and reptilian specimens for the Australian and British Museums that the aborigines would have eaten. When kangaroo and emu were scarce, she observed native cooks eating mallee hens and squeezing water from frogs before roasting them in embers. She explained, "Everything is eaten half raw, save the rabbit, which is well cooked, and every bird and beast and creeping thing provided a meal, including the banded ant-eater and the barking lizard." (Ibid., 209) Gradually, she introduced baked potatoes, onions, and apples hot from the ashes, which kept diners' teeth strong and shiny.

On the Pacific island of Tonga in 1967, the coronation of King Taufa'ahau Tupou IV included a traditional pig roast superintended by royal cooks. At a luncheon for 2,500, staff served whole suckling pigs on top of pandanus matting decorated with melon quarters. Without implements, servers split the skin with a chop of the hand and removed roasted meat from the spine with their fingers. On the king's departure by launch, Nuapapuan villagers floated along with his entourage another roasted pig on a coconut palm stretcher as a parting gift.

Roasted foods remain favorites worldwide. In Greece and the Mediterranean isles, cooks marinate pork and lamb for *souvlaki* (kebabs). Georgian cooks prepare hearty fare, including skewered meats and *satsivi* (fried chicken), which they spice with walnut sauce. Kuwaiti hosts honor guests with *quzi*, a national dish of spring lamb stuffed with rice, chopped liver and kidney, and saffron. In the United Arab Emirates, roasted sheep with rice or bread is a common menu item. When there are guests, hosts offer them organ meats as a delicacy. Cooks on the U.S. Virgin Islands and in Yugoslavia use special occasions as an opportunity to roast a pig, lamb, or goat and display a full range of culinary art. Niue islanders roast pig for weddings and other social events. Cooks heap tables with traditional dishes for buffet-style eating and pack left-overs for guests to take home.

Early twenty-first-century technology simplifies the job of roasting meat, fowl, and fish. The nonstick vertical roasting rack reduces cooking time for turkey, chicken, duck, and Cornish game hen while draining grease into a tray. For the single apartment-dweller of small family, the counter-top roaster oven equipped with a rotisserie encourages varied styles of roasting meats and kabobs.

See also **Spit Cooking**

Further Reading

Frazer, John E., "Kuwait, Aladdin's Lamp of the Middle East," *National Geographic*, May 1969, 633–667.

ROMAN COOKERY

Life in the Roman Empire split into unequal portions, with the privileged few enjoying most of the spoils. Lucky servants in sumptuous homes received scraps from the finest kitchens, which the *analecte* (crumb gatherer) collected from the table and either distributed among the staff or repackaged to sell in the public market. Country folk ate and drank three daily meals of humble gruel from simple wood bowls, also the food of prisoners, soldiers, and slaves. For fragrance as well as convenience, plebeian cooks strung dried herbs and onions on filament about their hearths. Outside the kitchen, they cultivated wild fennel and mint and took pleasure in their fig bushes, which supplied fruit for winter consumption.

An outdoor summer dining room in Pompeii. The built-in couches are of concrete, to be covered with cushions. In the center is a stand for a moveable table; in the rear, a shrine for the household gods.

An ancient kitchen stove with kitchen utensils on top. Staff stoked fires in the lower part.

Roman pot, strainer, and meat hooks.

At street level, outlanders who immigrated to the great metropolis occupied a few rooms in cramped tenement houses called *insulae*. Over a wood *craticula* (grate), the lowly braiser of meat and fish grilled directly on embers. In the style of the Etruscans, who lived in Italia before the Romans, the poor added to the evening *cena* (dinner) of grilled vegetables some chickpeas boiled in a bronze cauldron and a wheat gruel or mealy porridge of fava beans flavored with honey, figs, olive oil, sage, or onions. They simmered one-pot style over charcoal braziers, which also roasted asphodel, squill, and *colocasia* (taro) tubers. Expeditioners to Sicily introduced the island peasantry to *maccu*, a fava purée that remained a dinner-hour favorite. After Roman overlords demanded the defor-estation of Sicily, farmers produced so much wheat on the cleared land that they had to preserve pasta dough by sun-drying it, thus creating an industry in *pasta secca* (dried pasta), which was originally peasant food.

A common Roman bowl was the *mortarium* (pl. *mortaria*) or *pelvis*, a heavy conical or hemispherical kitchen vessel shaped with a flanged pouring spout on the lip and surfaced inside with coarse grit. It served the *pistor* (miller or baker) as a durable bowl for grind-ing grain and gave cooks such as Apicius, author of *De Re Coquinaria* (On Cooking, late 300s CE), the world's oldest cookbook, a vessel for pounding and crushing spice, blending foods, and soaking grain for cereal. Found throughout the empire, *mortaria* were products of professional potters who waterproofed them with bitumen, pitch, resin, or wood tar. Their

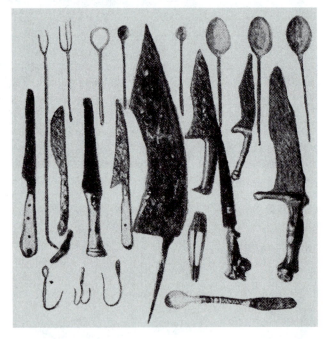

Roman knives, spoons, forks, and other implements.

main faults were attrition from daily grinding with a pestle, which wore down the sides, and subsequent adulteration of food with grit. A sturdier vessel was the *operculum* (work bowl), shaped out of clay and fired in a kiln.

For those who could afford it, inns like the seaside resort at Agro Murecine south of Pompeii, which Vesu-vius covered in volcanic ash in 79 CE, extended hospi-tality to the merchant class, whose business transactions survive on 127 wax tablets known as the Sulpicii Archive. Unearthed during a highway project in mid-2000, the lavish building decorated with brightly frescoed walls featuring images from classical mythology contained a foyer, portico, extensive baths, second-floor sleeping chambers, but only one kitchen to serve five *triclinia* (three-couch dining rooms). The architect limited the food preparation area to a twelve-foot counter, excavated by archeologists Antonio De Simone and Salvatore Ciro Nappo. The innkeeper's slaves served meals at round marble-topped tables convenient to trios of benches on which diners reclined. From the center of each tabletop, a spout dispensed water for hand-washing. The fourth side of the U-shaped arrangement allowed free movement of servers for pouring wine and returning dishes to the kitchen.

For ordinary Romans, street kitchens, *tabernae* (taverns), and cook stalls and barrows offered hot stews and meats as well as bread and beakers of cheap domestic or Corsican wine. Attached to the front of houses, shops featured counters across the front imbedded with storage jars. Their tops stood up even with the surface for the ladling of olives, oil, *garum* (fish sauce), or wine. A hand scale allowed the vendor to weigh goods in sight of the buyer as proof of honesty and good will. For the wayfarer, the *caupona* (inn) extended a form of hospitality that developed into the Italian *osteria*, a rest stop which serves tourists a broad menu of regional foods into the twenty-first century.

Within a cook shop, deep frying in lard produced *globi encytum* (doughnuts), which diners iced with honey and washed down with *thermopolia*, a hot spiced wine heated in a brass *thermopolium* (urn) and dispensed from a spigot. At the end of the serving counter, bread baked in a *clibanus*, a broad-bottomed earthen furnace perforated with small holes. It held a fire or hot coals like a miniature bake oven. The baker spread dough on the surface in the style of Indian tandoori.

Between announcements of the house menu by the *accensus*, who drummed up trade, vendors made their symbolic cries and brandished food symbols: the wine merchant proffered ivy; the butcher, myrtle. Molded terra cotta street signs for the illiterate used coiled snakes to denote an apothecary, an ox for the butcher shop, a goat for a dairy, an ass harnessed to a mill for flour-sellers, a priest leading a bull for the incense-seller, and an *amphora* (storage jar) suspended from a pole or hoisted on two poles for the wine-seller. In Rome's business center, in addition to the *forum boarium*, a cattle market between the shopping district and the Tiber River, merchandisers operated a *forum piscarium* (fish market), *forum pistorium* (bread market), and *forum cupendinis* (luxury items), such as the pungent

vegetable called *silphium*, found only in Egypt, the cosmopolitan fare expected of a world trade center.

The household shopper or slave could find olives at the oil merchant's shop, where he pressed cooking oil from fresh stock into bronze or terra cotta *dolia* (storage vats) buried neck-deep in the cellar. The *holitorium* offered baskets of produce hauled in from the fertile gardens of the countryside. At the *pistrinum* (mill-bakery), families could watch slaves perform the entire bread-making process: carry bags of grain from the loading dock, pour them into the hopper, turn the *catillus* (upper level) of the hour-glass mill, and derive a coarse meal that bore little resemblance to modern flour. From bag to mixing bowl, workers shaped dough into scored, pull-apart ring-loaves and shoveled them into the oven with a wooden peel. For the poorest, the imperial class provided "bread and circuses," the late first-century CE satirst Juvenal's cynical summary of political influence peddling, which office seekers earned by distribution of sops to plebeians.

Roman cooks developed kitchen gardening into an art. As explained in Jonathan Periam's *The Home & Farm Manual: A Pictorial Encyclopedia of Farm, Garden, Household, Architectural, Legal, Medical and Social Information* (1884), they reserved three great Roman names for vegetables: "Fabius, the great general, we should call General Bean [faba]; the great orator, Cicero, was Vice-Chancellor Pea [cicer], and the house of Lentulus got the name from the lentil [lenticulum]." (Periam 1984, 752) Roman horticulturists espaliered apple and pear trees to direct strong limbs toward the sun and grafted fruit and nut stock to shade trees to make the most of growing space. Growers catalogued the tastiest and most prolific apple varieties and used vinegar and *sapa* to preserve apple slices and *defrutum* (fruit purée) in *amphorae* for their own use and as trade commodities. The sour *damascena* (damson plum) they made into table sauce. They classified the pomegranate as *malum punicum* (Punic apple), a name that explains its route from Persia west through their long-time enemies, the Carthaginians. The sophisticated cook puréed peaches with cumin and used apricots in a sweet-and-sour fruit dish flavored with *passum*, mint and pepper, honey, vinegar, and wine.

In 1819, the historian Charles Francois Mazois published *Le Palais de Scaurus; ou, Description d'Une Maison Romaine* (Scaurus's Palace; or, a Description of a Roman House), which contained a detailed examination of the home of Marcus Aemilius Scaurus, who was elected consul in 115 BCE. Mazois was impressed by the enormous arched kitchen, which was 148 feet in length. Scaurus needed a vast cooking space to feed his horde of banquet guests, clients, freedmen, and slaves. The fireplace, at elbow height, drew smoke away from the house. Wall art pictured ritual sacrifice to Fortuna, goddess of luck, and images of spitted venison, fish, ham, birds, and rabbits being readied for cooking. Adjacent storage rooms ordered Scaurus's household supplies. A staffing system allotted jobs to particular slaves for receiving, shelving, and dispersing foodstuffs and utensils.

Mornings began in the black-paved kitchen with preparation of *jentaculum* (breakfast), a brief pause for bread and fruit before the workday commenced. Workers could function barefoot because the floors were heated from below by a hypocaust, a hot-air system maintained by an underfloor furnace. To begin the day's more demanding cookery, staff reached into *dolia* for oil and meal and collected stores of fruit, honey, and meat from the *promuscondus* (pantler), who guarded the *horreum* (pantry). At *prandium* (lunch), they cooked fish, sliced meat, vegetables and fruit, and more bread for their masters, who halted for a leisurely meal. For eggs, they cracked shells directly over the indentations in an *apala* (egg cooker). For the 4:00 p.m. *cena* or *tempestiva convivia* (dinner), the demands of social gatherings required sophisticated cooking for the typical Roman evening dishes, such as basting grilled meat or fish over a *craticula* (gridiron).

The supervision of the kitchen fell to the *coqus* (cook), who served the standard meal in three parts. *Gustatio* (appetizers) comprised a sampling of light wine and *hors d'oeuvres*, such as the poet Martial's service of lettuce and leeks and tunny with sliced egg to his guest Toranius or the wealthy Scissa's wake for a dead slave, whom she honored with seafood and pheasant *isicia omentata* (forcemeat sausages), peacock eggs, and olives and lettuce. An elaborate overstatement of Roman tastes, "Trimalchio's Feast," a chapter of Petronius's *Satyricon* (first century CE), lists honeyed dormice with poppy seed, pomegranate seeds and damsons, wild sow belly stuffed with live thrushes, a rabbit fitted with wings, pork roast carved like fish, and *beccafici* (figpeckers) in spiced egg yolk. *Mensae primae* (entrée or main course) or *cena* (dinner) was the formal presentation of *fercula* (kitchen burdens), a series of three to seven entrées featuring vegetables, sausage, bacon, haunches of meat, game, domestic poultry, fish and shellfish, and stuffed whole carcasses, including pastry-covered roast suckling pig. Petronius's bloated menu flaunted sow belly, whole boar roasted with dates, live thrushes in pastry, and foods representing the twelve signs of the zodiac. *Mensae secundae* (dessert or the last course) was a presentation of fresh pears and apples, grape clusters, *dulciae* (sweets), cheese in grape must, snails, pickled olives, oysters and scallops, goose eggs, and nuts, which varied from roasted local chestnuts to salted almonds and walnuts, an expensive treat. The table beverage to

accompany these courses was usually *mulsum*, a low-alcohol wine drink mixed with honey.

Among discerning cooks, no dish or salad went undressed or came to the table ungarnished. Table serving pieces included: *askos*, a petite pitcher or lipped vessel designed to pour sauces or serve oil or vinegar at table; *boletarion* or *boletar*, the Greek and Latin names for a mushroom server, which often sat on a matching stand; and *oxobaphon* or *acetabulum*, the Greek and Latin names for the vinegar bowl, a container for *garum* or *liquamen*, ancient Rome's universal fish-based condiment. Most kitchen suppliers chose tableware made of bronze, glass, or clay; only the wealthy could afford silver.

Cooks for the rich, who often trained under Greek chefs, turned simple fare into feasts by refeathering roasted peacocks, baking thrushes in boars, and sprinkling finger bowls with rose petals, benzoin, and lemon peel to rinse and sweeten hands stickied with finger food. In *De Agri Cultura* (On Agriculture, ca. 150 BCE), the orator and agronomist Marcus Porcius Cato described the making of one unusual porridge, *alica*, composed of spelt and *creta* (clay) from Leucogee. Also named in *Natural History,* Pliny the Elder's encyclopedia of around 77 CE, and in Martial's second book of epigrams (102 CE), the cereal and a drink made from *alica* so delighted the emperor Augustus that he paid twenty thousand sesterces in rent to control the clay.

Roman kitchens profited from raw materials from the ends of the empire—pork from Gallia Narbonensis (Provence), elephant and roebuck meat from Africa, and exotic spices and additives from Asia and the Middle East. Delicacies such as braised swan brushed with olive oil, marinated artichokes and thistles, and salt fish cooked in brains required skill with egg and cheese sauces as well as vinegars, rue berries, lovage, marjoram, and pepper. The nimble-fingered head chef might superintend the stuffing of dormice with pine nuts or sow's udder with sea urchins while sautéing tree fungi in fish fat, boiling an ostrich, or fricasseeing roses for pastry. Kitchen chores ranged from cooling carafes of Falernian wine in snow hauled from the mountains and folding napkins into dainty shapes.

In the late first century CE, one dissenter, the prim, proper Lucius Annaeus Seneca, condemned the sumptuaries who wasted their lives on gluttony. His contemporary, the satirist Juvenal, ridiculed sybarites who lived for the brief sensual pleasure of rare foods. For himself, Juvenal preferred country-fresh eggs and asparagus, kids fattened on grass, and local apples and bergamot pears. More demanding was the eccentric Syrian-born Emperor Elagabalus, who, around 220 CE, offered a challenge to his sauce cooks: Those who invented tasty accompaniments received sizeable rewards; those who failed stayed locked in the kitchen until they succeeded.

Household accounts for the first six weeks of 1 CE list the foods to be processed: turnips for preservation, wheat for grinding, salt for pickling, and rushes for heating the oven to dry flour and bake cake and loaves of bread made from *siglio* (wheat) or *cicere* (chickpea). Meals called for leeks, asparagus, cabbage, savory barley gruel, sauce, pomegranates, and the much despised beer, a concession that Romans made to living in the uncivilized hinterlands. When used in Britain, other foodstuffs and healing herbs and teas native to Italy required that slaves explain their uses and properties. At an excavated villa near Gloucester, one householder left *marc*, the remains of grape seeds and skins, from an effort to duplicate the vintages of home.

Under the direction of the *archimagirus* (chef in charge), underling cooks began work before daylight to prepare a breakfast of fruit and bread, lay out fish, eggs, and vegetables for lunch, and begin the serious job of planning and preparing dinner, the main meal of the day. For banquets, the work day called for grinding wheat, barley, rye, and oats for bread, which they flavored with honey and cheese. The shaping of foods in molds produced surprising combinations, such as game or goose paté made to look like a dolphin. Magnificent centerpieces included suckling pig stuffed with live doves, which flew upward when the staff sliced open the belly.

Bearing their own napkins and discreetly concealed toothpicks, guests arrived at the *triclinium*, which stood to the right of the peristyle or inner courtyard of Pompeii's House of the Vettii, an elegant home of a class-conscious merchant. The placement of three couches into a U shape allowed servers to move freely about the front to replenish dishes and refresh goblets. For the rich, a personal servant called a "scissor" cut food for the individual plate. Diners changed in their best *caenatoria vestis* (dinner clothes), either white or bright-colored robes, slipped out of their street shoes and into sandals, and stepped forward on the right foot for good luck.

The walls of the dining area gleamed white with *albarium* (stucco) or *opus marmoratum* (fake marble), made from calcinated gypsum stamped with molds into borders, cornices, and wainscoting. Under gold lamps or candelabra, guests reclined or sat on couches raised on pedestals and inlaid with bronze, ivory, and mother of pearl. On the floor, mosaics sometimes created in *trompe l'oeil* fashion the table scraps that typically littered the floor after a banquet. The chief servant placed plates of pottery, glass, silver, and gold before each diner. While listening to the *anagnostes*, the slave who read aloud at meals, guests ate with fingers, spoons, and knives. No one hesitated to overindulge in food or drink, for drunkenness brought no shame to the Roman party-goer.

Early in the second century CE, Rome's notoriety for gluttony found a detractor in the biography of Gaius Suetonius Tranquillus, author of *Lives of the Caesars*. During an era of extravagant consumption, diners took a sensible, enjoyable Mediterranean diet and bloated it into a monstrous display of public gourmandizing. Suetonius chronicled the demands of the emperor Vitellius, who, in 69 CE, banqueted up to four times a day. At one meal, his staff ran through two thousand fish and seven thousand birds, which could include domestic ortolan or bunting, thrush, or *beccaficus* (figpecker) from local aviaries. He was so greedy that he stole sacrificial meats and cakes from sacred altars.

Cooks and wait staff working for the aristocratic and moneyed classes prepared and served strings of gaudy, over-dressed dishes for banquets lasting into the wee hours and costing as much as one hundred million sesterces, an outlay that could feed much of the city for a year. An obsession with dismemberment—calf udders, lamprey milk, pike liver, flamingo tongues, elephant ears, peacock brains—forced diners to try more taste sensations. Those who overindulged fled couches and sought the *vomitorium*, a room designed for disgorging.

During the nearly four centuries that Roman legions occupied Britain, engineers altered an environment decked with crude huts to a sophisticated style of town planning that called for straight streets at right angles. Within residences, central heating systems called *hypocausts* warmed the stone or mosaic floors of rooms and baths through a network of channels that infiltrated the walls as well. Of the five hundred villas that archeologists have excavated, most were built of stone with at least ten rooms and some with upper floors. *Triclinia* emulated the plaster wall designs found in Rome and offered comfortable wooden furnishings for formal dining.

For the adjacent Romano-British kitchens, house slaves stoked the under-floor furnace with coal through a hole in the external wall. At a raised stone hearth, *coqui* (cooks) supervised food preparation in *clibani* (clay pots) and *fretales* or *sartagines* (fry pans) over charcoal fires or on *thermospodia* (stoves), portable bronze hot plates with drawers for hot coals used at tableside for cooking or warming a *lanx* (platter). Into hot coals, cooks could shove the *sartago* (baking dish) or heat *caccabi* or *patinae* (casseroles) for ragouts and stews. The collection of choppers, hooks, kitchens shears, skewers, tripods, mortars, ladles, knives, shellfish spoons, and sieves prefigured open-hearth utensils that remained in use into the nineteenth century. Molds shaped mixtures into a hare, suckling pig, or chicken with wings spread to fly. In the annexed *horreum*, the *atriensis* (housekeeper) stored winter provisions, oil in the *olearium*, and unaged wine in the *cellae vinariae*.

Among Romans living in Antioch, extravagance set the conquerors apart from the conquered. The wealthy flaunted expensive tableware. For banquets, kitchen staff set each place with thirty or more table utensils. A semicircular *stibadium* replaced the standard U-shaped table arrangement after 200 CE. For outdoor dining, servants placed furniture under a canopy. They placed ornately dressed foods on display alongside silver serving pieces. Space for diners allotted a third to serving tables, a third for entertainments, and a third for guest assistance.

Servants lighted overhead chandeliers and washed guests hands in herbed water. After anointing guests' heads with fragrant oil, they distributed flower wreaths and herbs. They filled crystal and fluorspar cups with drink and offered trays of food cut into bite-sized pieces. The *ministerium* (silver service) fell into three categories: *argentum escarium* for eating, *argentum potorium* for drinking, and *argentum escarium* for table setting. They offered eggs in egg cups and foods preserved in brine, honey, and snow, the ultimate extravagance that sent servants into the mountains before daylight for supplies to assure that the cultured Roman ate and drank foods at the optimum temperature.

See also **Amphora; Apicius, Caelius; Cookbook; Garum; Ice Cream; Slavery**

Further Reading

Baker, Rosalie F., and Charles F. Baker. *Ancient Romans*. Oxford: Oxford University Press, 1998.

Bunson, Matthew. *A Dictionary of the Roman Empire*. New York: Oxford University Press, 1991.

Carpiceci, Alberto C. *Pompeii: Nowadays and 2000 Years Ago*. Florence: Bonechi Edizioni, 1977.

Casson, Lionel. *The Ancient Mariners*. Princeton, N.J.: Princeton University Press, 1991.

Edwards, John. *The Roman Cookery of Apicius*. Point Roberts, Wash.: Hartley & Marks, 1984.

Guadagno, Giuseppe, and Rosa Carafa. *Pompeii, Herculaneum, and Stabiae: The Buried Cities*. Venice: Edizioni Storti, 1973.

Harris, Judith, "Five-Star Inn with Great Art," *Archaeology*, July/August 2000, 14–15.

Pliny. *The Natural History of C. Plinius Secundus*. New York: McGraw-Hill, 1962.

Tyers, Paul. *Roman Pottery in Britain*. London: Routledge, 1999.

ROOT CELLARS

Among the root vegetables to survive from prehistory are carrots, parsnips, radishes, swedes, horseradish, and turnips, all of which store well for winter use. In East Asia, farmers grew radishes into massive globes and prized their leaves also as additives to soups and stir-frying. Turnips may have originated in the Caucasus, where families depended on them for cold-weather meals. Roman food commentary relegated turnips to peasants, along with onions and pulses or pap, a porridge of pulverized fava beans. A resurgence of interest in root vegetables after the Black Death of 1348 continued into the American colonial era, when German kitchen gardeners advocated the planting of turnips and kale crops as nutritious food easily grown and cooked. Moravian and Mennonite communities established these vegetables in communal plots heavily laced with fireplace ash to increase longevity.

The root cellar is on the left, away from the heat of the main house.

A popular farm storage area from colonial times, the root cellar was a safe closet for wintering beets, cabbages, carrots, onions, parsnips, salsify, and turnips for daily use when tender vegetables could not survive the cold. Before refrigeration, housekeepers used boxes of sand as methods of absorbing liquids and of anchoring cauliflower, cabbage, and broccoli to keep mold and rot from forming and spreading. Nearby barrels kept apples and hard pears whole and firm. Handfuls of straw or wrappings in tissue or newspaper separated pome fruit to ward off rot.

After Irish and Scotch growers popularized the white potato in the British Isles and transmitted its culture to the eastern seaboard of North America, slatted potato bins became a standard part of home and cellar design. At Hope Lodge in Fort Washington, Pennsylvania, begun by Samuel Morris in 1743, a model of the clay-floored basement alcove survives as an historical monument of colonial food preservation. Built of stone in a dark area against a chimney stack, it appears to have had shelves for banking potatoes, carrots, turnips, beets, and onions as well as apples. The grilled, shuttered windows pierced the walls to ventilate heaped vegetables and equalize temperatures.

In the late 1700s, General G. I. Bibikov's family at Grebnevo, a Russian country estate east of Moscow, anticipated the annual harvest, which enlivened the shift of seasons. In a heavily stratified society, the Bibikovs themselves did little of the work. Grandchildren observed haying, mushroom gathering, and collection of root vegetables for a long and arduous winter. Serfs carried potatoes and cabbages into a huge subterranean root cellar, where they stacked goods to the ceiling.

In St. Jean de Crèvecoeur's *Sketches of 18th-Century America*, published in 1925, the French observer remarked on an innovation—the Dutch cellar, a free-standing storage shed such as the clay-walled model built by the Myburgh family in 1776 at Meerlust Estate near the Helderburg mountains of eastern New York. Preserved in the air flow of a slatted frame out of danger of freezing, white potatoes survived well alongside apples, pumpkins, and cabbages and produced enough sprouted tubers for the spring planting. The sweet potato, a more tender tuber unable to survive in a damp atmosphere, required separate storage in dry sand above the basement level.

For homes farther south, where freezing didn't endanger root crops, householders built the Dutch or Irish clamp, a potato mound formed of tubers layered with straw and roofed with thatching, sod, and soil. A moat around the perimeter drained rain to prevent mold and spoilage from fungi living in the soil clinging to the roots. A compromise between cellar and clamp was the cache, a lined pit where root crops were safe at 63

degrees Fahrenheit if left uncovered. The educator Booker T. Washington, recalling life in Franklin County Virginia around 1860, remarked, "My first memory of life is that of a one-room log cabin with a dirt floor that had a hole in the center which served as a winter home for sweet potatoes." (Thrasher 1969, 5) Supports for the hole began with planking or a wood pallet at the bottom, a framework or stakes up the sides, and a wood door lying across the upper ground surface to keep out predators and deflect rain and snow.

According to Dee Brown in *The Gentle Tamers: Women of the Old Wild West* (1958), on the American frontier, families built root cellars shortly after they laid hearths and dug wells. For good reason, cooks prized fresh fruit, vegetables, herbs, and potatoes as antiscorbutics. Those families anticipating isolation over a long period hoarded potatoes in the root cellar along with barrels of buttermilk to provide milk for children and for moistening flour for biscuits and flapjacks. In addition, underground storage preserved wine, malt and alcohol, pickles and sauerkraut, jerky, buffalo tongue, and bear bacon.

In the Amana colonies, preserving root crops and jars of canned goods was a necessity for the feeding of 1,500 residents. In the fall, when harvesters were filling barns and granaries, kitchen staffs began the chore of cutting squares of newspaper for wrapping apples and pears, preparing barrels of sauerkraut and dilly beans, and storing cheese and calcified eggs in crocks. Into slotted bins went dried onions and carefully culled potatoes to separate whole tubers from those dented or halved with the hoe. From the rafters of the root cellar hung braided ropes of onions and garlic and linen sacks of dried beans and apples, which workers kiln-dried on wood racks in the dry house. In sand, staff buried bushels of root crops, including salsify and celeriac, creamy tubers they introduced from Germany. After sun-hardening, pumpkins and winter squash were ready for storage along with cabbages, pulled up by the root and buried in the cellar's dirt floor.

Eliot Wigginton's *The Foxfire Book* (1968), a compendium of subsistence skills still in use in the southern Appalachians, describes the preservation of vegetables that can't be dried or canned. For cabbage, gardeners traditionally dug a shallow trench with a runnel directing moisture away from the mound. Dirt formed a hillock at center, where cabbages, harvested root and all, spent the winter under a layer of straw. Potatoes remained in a potato bin or, where winters were severe, covered in straw and soil in a hole dug one to two feet below the frost line. Preparation of apple quarters required placing them in a tub, burning sulfur in a saucer, and covering the fumes with a clean cloth to direct the chemical toward hidden pockets of mold. After three days of sulfur bleaching, the apples were ready to be packed into jars or crocks tied at the top with clean cloths.

A modern root cellar or cold cellar functions by keeping bulk supplies of food chilled at high humidity, but not wet or frozen. By positioning an overhead pantry as a shield, the builder centralizes food stores in one area and enables the householder to keep close watch on the cellar's atmospheric conditions. The best way to assure quality is by harvesting produce at the peak of taste and nutrition and hardening cucurbits, potatoes, yams, and sweet potatoes in the sun. Root crops store best untrimmed and unwashed. In addition to root crops and fruit, the cellar preserves endive, savoy and Chinese cabbage, kale, Brussels sprouts, garlic, sunchokes, kohlrabi, radishes, rutabagas, parsnips, celeriac, leeks, soybeans, and collards. Reducing contact between vegetables with mulches of straw, grass, sawdust, and dried leaves and fern fronds or wrapping in tissue or newspaper further protects the stack from harboring yeast and mold.

See also **Potatoes, Sweet Potatoes, and Yams**

Further Reading

Hoppe, Emilie. *Seasons of Plenty: Amana Communal Cooking.* Ames: Iowa State University Press, 1998.

Roosevelt, Priscilla. *Life on the Russian Country Estate.* Hartford, Conn.: Yale University Press, 1995.

Thrasher, Max Bennett. *Tuskegee: Its Story and Its Work.* New York: Negro Universities Presss, 1969.

Tucker, David M. *Kitchen Gardening in America: A History.* Ames: Iowa State University Press, 1993.

RORER, SARAH TYSON

A pioneer of dietetics and home economics, Sarah Tyson Heston Rorer, nicknamed the "Queen of American Cookery," thrived in the lecture hall, in popular print and textbook, and in the classroom and laboratory. At age twenty-one, she married William Albert Rorer, an accountant at his family's surgical instrument factory, and bore two sons and a daughter. Rorer profited from the post-Civil War era, when battlefield nursing and rehabilitation of veterans liberated women from some of the more stifling patriarchal notions of the early nineteenth century. Intellectual curiosity served her during her transition from bored housewife to dynamic spokesperson for domestic science.

After attending lectures on hygiene at the Woman's Medical College and completing three months of kitchen training at the New Century Club in Philadelphia, she took a post as substitute for her former cooking instructor. She studied nutrition, food chemistry, and cookery principles from Isabella Beeton's *Book of Household Management* (1860); Juliet Corson's *Fifteen Cent Dinners for Families of Six* (1878) and "Hints on Domestic Economy" (1880); *Food and Feeding* (ca. 1880) by Sir Henry Thompson, surgeon to Queen Victoria; and J. Milner Fothergill's *Food for the Invalid* (1880). Her teaching expanded to night classes for working women and private tutoring in the homes of wealthy matriarchs.

As founder of the Philadelphia Cooking School in 1883, Rorer influenced the domestic sciences in their infancy. In an era that redirected cuisine from an art to a science, she promoted sensible diet by denouncing indigestible multi-course dinners produced for show. In the one-year normal curriculum, Rorer taught the nation's pioneer dietitians and home economists how to eliminate waste and recycle leftovers into wholesome dishes. Her classes were prepared enough to start their own careers in teaching and lecturing.

Rorer lauded labor-saving devices, particularly dishwashers and gas stoves, an improvement over wood and coal, and advocated agate, granite, and aluminum utensils and vessels as preferable to tin and iron. She promoted the most precise measuring cups and spoons and cooking thermometers and organized work habits that rid the kitchen of drudgery. To the consternation of wealthy women, she supported unions for hired kitchen help. Her lecture-demonstrations were in demand by the Franklin Institute, Jefferson Hospital, and University of Pennsylvania Hospital and earned her a consultancy with Washington Butcher's Sons, makers of olive butter, a lard substitute. She also taught food chemistry at Miss Rebecca Judkins's School.

Because Rorer recommended that Americans eat less and concentrate more on nutrition, especially for invalids and children, she is sometimes called America's first dietitian. Her meal plans characterized a palatable, attractive menu, whether for family or guests. In an era that saw more working women and fewer servants, her cooking classes appealed to women of all types—farm wives, medical students, missionaries, nurses, professional cooks, society girls at a finishing school, a sprinkling of male cooks, and the multi-ethnic fallen women of Philadelphia's Midnight Mission. To the latter, she offered cooking as a better career option than prostitution, ragpicking, or sewing in sweatshops.

When she appeared on the public platform, the halls filled with people who studied her skilled demonstrations and chortled at her wry rejoinders. Unflappable and dramatic, she displayed stage presence and command of her subject by dressing in silk to prove that the cook could be neat as well as capable. For the Retail Grocers', Manufacturers', and Pure Food Exposition of 1889, Rorer debuted on stage in a model kitchen to such throngs that the organizers of the show decided to repeat the exposition the next year with Rorer as star. At Dr. Ellen Richards's Rumford Kitchen, an exhibit at the 1893 Chicago World's Fair, Rorer supervised the corn kitchen, a promotion of corn in flapjacks, mush, hominy, blancmange, pudding, croquettes, pilau, bread, dodgers, and scrapple. The show caused a spurt in the corn market and gained favorable press as far away as Denmark and Japan.

In a thirty-four-year career, Rorer compiled fifty-four domestic pamphlets, articles for the *Medical and Surgical Reporter,* and handbooks, among them *Mrs. Rorer's Philadelphia Cook Book* (1886), *Canning and Preserving* (1887), and the classic *Mrs. Rorer's New Cook Book; a Manual of Housekeeping* (1898), which introduced devil's food cake. Her advice made sense—housewives needed to learn the tasks that they assigned to servants and to master cooking on the kitchen range. Concerning work strain, she blamed improper table height for backache and faulted the walk from work station to stove for fatigue.

For good nutrition, Rorer denounced fried foods, pork, vinegar and mustard, brandy, and sweets. She advocated rice for its digestibility and suggested salads every day of the year. Rorer was known for creditable opinions. In "The Dietary," a regular column for *The Dietetic Gazette,* she expressed her belief that poorly fed people turned to crime. For *Table Talk* magazine, she wrote the articles "How to Live on a Thousand a Year" and "A Christmas Dinner" and the columns "New Things for Table and Kitchen," "Housekeepers' Inquiries," and "Dietetics." In one sharp-edged article for the December 1888 issue of *Table Talk,* she scolded wasters of coal for failing to learn how to regulate a stove damper.

Her personal endorsement of products extended to a column called "Keystone Dishes," recipes based on the use of the Keystone eggbeater, and publication of *Dainty Dishes for All the Year Round* (1890), a cookbook of recipes suited to one company's ice cream freezer and meat grinder. Other cookery pamphlets and advertising campaigns showcased shredded wheat, McIlhenny's tabasco sauce, Wesson oil, Cleveland's baking powder, and the Mudge Patent Processor as her personal choices of the best brands on the market. Throughout her career, Rorer gave testimonials for such new products as Niagara Corn Starch, the Eldridge Cooker, Fleischmann's yeast cakes, Automatic Steam Coffee Cooker, Florence Oil Stoves, and her own blend of coffee. On behalf of bakers, she consulted with food processors and stove manufacturers, to whom she advised placing a thermometer in oven doors. In 1893, she advised owners of the Knox Gelatin Company that they powder gelatin, which had previously come to kitchens in sticky, unmanageable sheets.

After severing her connection with *Table Talk* in annoyance at such frivolous topics as fashionable luncheons and Washington gossip, she launched her own magazine, *Household News,* in July 1893 to pursue dietetics, infant feeding, invalid food, water purity and food adulteration, and home hygiene. The debut garnered praise from *Popular Science Monthly* and *New England Kitchen Magazine* and prefaced a rise in subscriptions to eight thousand by 1896. Among her standard items were printed menus for two weeks' use and commentary connecting social upheaval, labor strikes, and poverty to improper nourishment among the poor. In the February 1894 issue, she listed kitchen essentials, which now included spoons and cups with graduated amounts clearly marked.

Edward Bok, publisher of *Ladies' Home Journal,* persuaded Rorer to abandon *Household News* and join his staff as domestic science editor. Energetic and methodical, she formulated scientific precepts to cookery and taught readers standard principles of stove management and cookery. In "How I Cured My Own Ill-Health," published on June 1905, she explained how she came to Philadelphia's Woman's Medical College and began studying nutrition and cookery. It was her intent to "make cooking a profession, perhaps not second to medicine." (p. 38) By revealing improvement of her own digestion, she displayed a human side to her expertise, one that readers could embrace for its honesty and sincerity.

Among the suggestions in Rorer's columns was an endorsement of tile and linoleum for kitchen floors and of food fanatic Horace Fletcher's concept of chewing each bite thirty times, which he outlined in *Nature's Food Filter: Or When and What to Swallow* (1899). She denounced telephone ordering and home delivery of groceries rather than on-the-scene sniffing, weighing, and selecting fresh produce in person. Her popular articles and question and answer feature helped boost *Ladies' Home Journal* from a circulation of 700,000 to one million, the first American magazine to reach that wide a readership.

When the Exchange for Woman's Work organized in Philadelphia in 1887, Rorer accepted a vice presidency and hoped to raise household work to "a dignified and respected field of labor." (Weigley 1977, 45) With Helen Armstrong, Marion Harland, Mary Johnson Bailey Lincoln, and Lida Willis, Rorer compiled a home economics text, *Home Helps: A Pure Food Cook Book—A Useful Collection of Up-to-Date, Practical Recipes by Five of the Leading Culinary Experts in the United States* (1910). Her example so touched women that they came to her rescue in 1933 when her finances failed. Contributions kept her solvent until her death from bronchial pneumonia on December 27, 1937.

See also **Home Economics**

Further Reading

Hoy, Suellen. *Chasing Dirt: The American Pursuit of Cleanliness.* New York: Oxford University Press, 1995.

Lovegren, Sylvia. *Fashionable Food: Seven Decades of Food Fads.* New York: Macmillan, 1995.

Peiss, Kathy L., "American Women and the Making of Modern Consumer Culture," *Journal for MultiMediaHistory*, Fall 1998.

Rorer, Mrs. S. T., "How I Cured My Own Ill-Health," *Ladies' Home Journal*, June 1905, 38.

Stage, Sarah, and Virginia B. Vincenti, eds. *Rethinking Home Economics: Women and the History of a Profession.* Ithaca, N.Y.: Cornell University Press, 1997.

Weigley, Emma Seifrit. *Sarah Tyson Rorer.* Philadelphia: The American Philosophical Society, 1977.

RUBBER

In the mid-nineteenth century, rubber increased the waterproofing and cushioning of domestic goods. The idea was not new: Mayan and Aztec latex workers had been extracting the sap from rubber trees since 500 BCE and used it for waterproofing and toys. Thomas Hancock, an inventor and manufacturer from Marlborough, England, abandoned gutta percha in favor of latex-based coating for textiles. He patented a masticator, a machine that readied rubber for use in industry, and established a vulcanization process in 1843 that made gutta percha obsolete. His partner, Charles Macintosh, a Scottish industrial chemist from Glasgow, patented a textile surfacing method used on rubberized boots, tarps, and a line of rainwear named macintoshes in his honor.

Another process of vulcanizing rubber, invented by the Connecticut native Charles Goodyear in 1837, brought latex goods into common use. Trained in his father's hardware business, he tinkered with ways to apply the elasticity and water impermeability of India rubber to practical needs. After buying the rights to Nathaniel Hayward's sulfur-blending process, Goodyear unintentionally dropped some of the mass on a hot stove. When it cooled, he realized the value of heat treatment, a process he named "vulcanization" after Vulcan, the Roman god of fire.

Goodyear envisioned rubber goods for industry, farm, dairy, and home—wet suits, waders, rain capes and hats, life belts and buoys, bellows, hose pipe, and buckets. For domestic use, he intended to shape rubber into bath tubs and basins, cushions, sponge and soap bags, nipples, jar covers, and bottle stoppers. He foresaw a baby jumper, a child care device that would keep an infant safely entertained in a springy seat while the mother worked.

Patented in 1844, vulcanized rubber brought Goodyear no profits in the factories he launched in England and France. He held American rights to the process, but lost income from blatant industrial piracy. Although he showed the idea at the Vulcanite Court at London's Great Exhibition held at the Crystal Palace in 1851, he fell into debt and died penniless in New York City on July 1, 1860.

Goodyear's India Rubber Glove Manufacturing Company in New York City was advertising rubber gloves in the *American Agriculturist* in 1870. By century's end, rubber gloves were common in kitchen and institutional use. Rubber domestic items were soon the norm for most homemakers. Frontier guide Randolph Barnes Marcy's *The Prairie Traveler: A Hand-Book for Overland Expeditions* (1859), specified to would-be pioneers that they pack rubber buckets for the trip West rather than less stable wood vessels. A rubber bulb replaced the forcing bag for cake decorating and piping vegetable edging on platters. By 1908, Goodyear's useful products appeared in the Sears, Roebuck catalog as weather stripping, sold at fifty feet for 74 cents. Homemakers could add a storm-proof rubber and hardwood threshold for 64 cents for weatherproofing a door.

A more common application of rubber, tile floors increased the choices of stainproof kitchen floor covering and lessened the work of cleaning spills and scrubbing scuff marks from high traffic areas. Such niceties as the covering on cords of the Spic-Span Premier Electric vacuum cleaner, the bowls of drain plungers, and the rubber holder for Brillo pads, all advertised in *Good Housekeeping* in 1930, promoted the notion that rubber was a time and labor saver and a guarantee of top performance. Copy supplied by Boston Woven Hose & Rubber company, Cambridge Massachusetts, claimed that cheap rings made from poor quality rubber imperiled the foods in a season's canning. Another ad several pages beyond for Good Housekeeping Fruit Jar Rings from Hamilton Rubber Manufacturing Company, Trenton, New Jersey, declared that rubber rings survived long, hard boiling without losing their stretch or becoming spongy, hard, cracked, or curly.

Advertising in *Woman's Home Companion* featured numerous rubber products for the kitchen and pantry. Split-Tab from the Boston Woven Hose & Rubber Company in Cambridge, Massachusetts, simplified the job of opening home canning by creating a jar rubber that separated and pulled free, breaking the seal. A competitor, Kerr Glass Manufacturing Corporation, extolled the self-sealing rubber-cushioned jar lid that ended the need for rubber rings. By 1937, manufacturers were offering isocyanate-based foam rubber, replaced after World War II by styrene-butadiene foam rubber, a handy padding for bar stool seats and benches. In the 1990s, polyurethane accounted for most foam rubber, used in kitchen furnishings and carpet pads.

Early twenty-first-century applications of rubber to domestic needs included spatulas, shovel-shaped dough scrapers, hard-bladed plate scrapers, rubber-bulbed basters, jar openers, and rubber bushings and gaskets for countertop appliances as well as non-slip grips for nutcrackers, pliers, and screwdrivers. Rubber was a major addition to ergonomically designed kitchen tools. Canister lids edged with rubber gaskets tended to keep staples moisture- and vermin-free. Rubbermaid ended separation problems with rubber spatulas by fusing heads to wood handles. A kitchen door mat made of rubber composite had a corrugated surface for cleaning feet of snow or dirt. A lightweight rubber broom facilitated the sweeping of threads, pet hair, and other flyaway debris dispersed by straw brooms. A common safety precaution, the rubber-top step stool, elevated the homemaker for reaching tops of cupboards and cabinets without worrying about slips or falls. Tall folding ladders with rubber steps and feet provided nonslip height for home painting jobs and cleaning ceilings and paddle fans.

See also **Ergonomics**

Further Reading

Gentry, Patricia. *Kitchen Tools*. San Francisco: 101 Productions, 1985.
Haedrich, Ken, "Kitchen Companion: Tools of the Trade," *Kitchen Garden*, December 1998/January 1999, 76–77.
Richards, Ellen H., and S. Maria Elliott. *The Chemistry of Cooking and Cleaning*. Boston: Whitcomb & Barrows, 1912.

RUMFORD, COUNT VON

In addition to being a soldier of fortune and expatriate, Sir Benjamin Thompson, Count von Rumford, was a heating engineer who increased the efficiency of European and American kitchens. In 1775, he criticized the fireplace for fuel use and heat loss up the chimney. To correct the design, he "Rumfordized" the masonry fireplace, reducing the size and efficiency of its fire chamber and angling the sides to radiate more energy into the room. He created the internal ledge or smoke shelf, which kept downdrafts from showering the hearth and floor with cinders and live coals and chilling the room. Developers designed cast-iron stove inserts that emulated his design. Rumford described his fireplace refinement in *Essays: Political, Economical and Philosophical* (1795).

Although not widely recognized by cooks and home economists, Rumford was a domestic engineer native

The comforts of a Rumford stove (June 12th, 1800).
[© *Library of Congress, Prints and Photographs Division (LC-USZ62-58485)*]

to Woburn, Massachusetts. Born to a poor rural family on March 26, 1753, he received a skimpy grade school education and apprenticed as a Salem store clerk while teaching himself French and reading philosophy. At age nineteen, he joined the supporters of New Hampshire's Governor John Wentworth, an outspoken loyalist to George III. When local patriots discovered Rumford's spying efforts for the British, in December 1774, he fled with his family to England and entered service to the British Army as a lieutenant colonel.

In exile, Rumford accepted the posts of Minister of War, Minister of the Interior, undersecretary of colonial affairs, and Royal Scientist to the British crown. For improving ordnance and inventing a mortar to gauge explosive power of gunpowder, at age twenty-seven, he accepted membership in the Royal Society. After serving two years in the colonies as a military officer, his reputation suffered from charges that he sold the French secret information on the British navy, yet he weathered the uproar, received a knighthood, and settled among pro-French Bavarians to spy for the crown.

In Munich, Germany, Rumford shifted allegiance to Karl Theodor, Elector of Bavaria. As minister of police and grand chamberlain, Rumford reorganized the army and designed uniforms and insulated winter coats. In 1784, when Munich's streets harbored two thousand homeless, he established a public works program and organized workhouses to rid the area of beggars while forcing them to cut and sew uniforms.

To lessen the cost of feeding an army, Rumsford promoted the white potato in Europe and concocted Rumfordsuppe, a palatable, satisfying *volkssuppe* (peasant soup) made from white potatoes, pearl barley, peas, crumbs from donated *semmel* bread, vinegar, water, and salt. He invented a double boiler with tin-plate steamer, a two-stage filtered coffee percolator, a thermos bottle, and a kitchen range that he installed in workhouses, orphanages, and hospitals in Europe and the British Isles. In addition, he supplied details of an experimental baking of rye bread at the military bakehouse. In an addendum dated May 1796, he reported on an experimental dinner cooked on a four hundred-gallon iron boiler for 927 inmates of Calecannon, a Dublin workhouse. The menu consisted of boiled or mashed potatoes mixed with greens "cut fine with sharp shovels, and seasoned with butter, onions, salt, pepper, and ginger."

With the intent to feed people with less effort and waste, Rumford set out to revolutionize domestic chores. To improve preparation and storage of foodstuffs, he upgraded the pressure cooker, created a portable field kitchen, invented an oil lamp and a kitchen plaque for hanging pots, and devised the Rumford roaster for cooking meat, a forerunner of the hot-air convection oven. His kettles, submerged in a tight-fitting brick flue, bore conical lids that completed the seal, containing heat below.

In addition to kitchen items, Rumford advanced kitchen science and architecture. After remodeling two hospital kitchens in Verona, he published a treatise, "On the Management of Fire and the Economy of Fuel" (1797), which redesigned the standard chimney into a boxy, insulated stove, which George Bodley patented in England in 1802. Rumford's main contribution to physics was a new theory of calorics, an explanation of heat flow based on his observations of a copper-bulbed thermometer and the overheated workings of a cannon during combat. He devised a calorimeter to measure the release of heat. For his work, he earned the title of Count of the Holy Roman Empire.

At age forty-six, Rumford accepted an appointment as minister plenipotentiary to England and returned to London, where George III rejected his services on the grounds that he was a British citizen serving a foreign government. During his tenure, Rumford worked at refining English fireplaces to improve coal-burning efficiency and created a hot plate heated on a firebox attached to a flue. He and Sir Joseph Banks, the botanist for Captain James Cook's expeditions, organized a technical college, the Royal Institution, to train scientists. To that end, he set up on Albemarle Street and enhanced lecture halls with a laboratory, library, and exhibits.

After retiring to Paris, Rumford received honor from the National Institute of France. His will supported a Rumford professorship at Harvard and the Rumford medals, given by the Royal Society and Boston's Academy of Arts and Science. He died suddenly of fever on August 21, 1814, in Auteuil, France. His extant writings include treatises on lamps, room heating, warm baths, experiments with gunpowder, color harmonics, fuel economy, illumination, double-glazed windows, flues and chimney fireplaces, silk, frigate building, soup kitchens, and reform measures to relieve society of the burden of the poor. A bronze statue on Maximilian Strasse in Munich and a copy in Woburn, Massachusetts, casts him in field marshall's uniform and staff under the inscription "Erected 1867 by Maximilian II, King of Bavaria."

See also **Fireplace**

Further Reading

Delbanco, Nicholas, "Rumford: The Strange Forgotten Life of America's Other Ben Franklin," *American Heritage*, September 1993, 68–77.

Dornberg, John, "Count Rumford: The Most Successful Yank Abroad, Ever," *Smithsonian*, December 1994, 102–11.

S

SAILLAND, MAURICE EDMOND

A famed food critic, Maurice Edmond Sailland wrote under the fanciful pseudonym of Curnonsky. He got his nickname from a pooling of minds after his friend Alphonse Allais suggested he needed a catchy name. Some asked, "Why not 'sky'?" He replied in French, "Cur non 'sky'?" The three words formed Curnonsky, a familiar name to cooks and restaurant owners of the mid-twentieth century.

Sailland was born in Angers, France, on October 12, 1872. After preparing for a journalistic career with a literature major from the Sorbonne, he began writing at age twenty, at the height of the *belle epoque*. His wit earned him a place among the jaunty *boulevardiers* and writers of his day. In addition to mastering the genres of essay, travelogue, and biography, he evolved high standards of restaurant performance; each dish should cause diners to marvel at its inventiveness. Wine selection should coordinate perfectly with the menu. The totality of the meal should not overwhelm the diner.

At the peak of fame, Sailland, called "the Prince," could demand a crackly-skinned leg of lamb with pale pink interior and strike fear into the cook's heart. A negative report on the restaurant could spell financial doom. At Laperousse in Paris, he applauded the first six courses, then lapsed into silence with the seventh. He sniffed, dashed it to the floor, then stalked out. He explained his distaste as a matter of coordination. The rosemary seasoning on the lamb ruined the palate for the partridge that came next. After a meal cooked by Fernand Point, the teacher to chefs Paul Bocuse, Jean

Troisgros, and Alain Chapel, Sailland awarded Point six kisses and analyzed for four and a half hours the virtuosity of his performance.

According to one of many anecdotes, Sailland maintained his integrity by refusing to say in print that margarine was as good as butter. He concluded his public refusal of a bribe from the margarine maker by tearing up a check. His exaltation of Tarte Tatin, created in 1898 by hotel owners Stephanie and Caroline Tatin of Lamotte-Beuvron, France, a French version of apple pie, got the dish a place on the menu of Maxim's in Paris. In 1928, Sailland established the Academy of Gastronomes, a forty-member coterie who occupied seats named for Epicure, Talleyrand, and Brillat-Savarin. After his accidental death in 1956, his many food books and a multi-volume *La France Gastronomique*, co-written by epicure Marcel Rouff, remained classics of world cookery.

Further Reading

"France's Answer to Apple Pie Celebrates Centenary," *Korea Times*, June 2, 1998.

SALT

Common salt is a crystalline compound, sodium chloride (NaCl), that is abundant in nature, essential for health, and necessary to season and preserve food. Globally, salt bears many meanings and purposes, from the English custom of casting spilled salt over the shoulder to avoid misfortune to the Appalachian cleansing of cook pots and teeth with salt after a meal. The Japanese homeowner sprinkles salt on the doorsill after an intruder or rude dinner guest departs and purifies the mourner with salt on return from viewing a corpse or witnessing a burial. For table use, humankind has salted food from Neolithic times, both as a preservative and as a seasoning prefatory to smoking. For example, Sicilian cooks gathered capers from a wild bush growing on the island of Pantelleria and preserved the tasty buds in salt to add pungence to native dishes.

Salt permeates lore and literature. It first appeared in print in the *Peng Tzao Kan Mu* (2700 BCE), a Chinese pharmacopoeia that differentiated forty types of salt. In Assyria, friends denoted welcome and kinship with fellow diners as "a man of my salt," a person trusted to share a valuable flavor enhancer. (Flandrin & Montanari 2000, 33) In societies where commensality equated with peace, those who rejected the sharing of salt at meals displayed a disrespect bordering on open hostility and challenge to combat.

In home kitchens, lump salt was ground between rocks or pounded to a fine grain in a mortar and pestle. Salt-curing took two forms—brining meat, herring, or cod in a salt solution or burying haunches of meat or whole fish in a trough or barrel filled with salt. Both procedures needed careful handling of foods to keep them wholesome in appearance, flavor, and aroma. For a maximum uptake of salt, hams and tongue first steeped in honey water; hares and game soaked best in beer or cider water, which tamed the wild flavor. Tough meat cuts softened when steeped in water and sorrel leaves; bacon profited from soaking in watered cider pomace. Iron hooks served to lift larger carcasses; wood paddles caused the least damage to tender meat fiber. When the cook was ready to prepare ham for the table, the salted meat received a one-day steeping in several changes of fresh water to remove excess salinity.

Herodotus, the author of *The Histories* (ca. 450 BCE), detailed a brining method that remained viable in the ancient Mediterranean for centuries. He explained how village fishermen stored catches of smelt and thunderfish in casks by smashing them with salt into a mealy consistency for forming doughy cakes for baking. In Roman Britain, salt preserved meat, one part of a dietary triad based on bread, meat, and dairy foods. Cato the Censor recorded a method of salt-curing ham that dates to 200 BCE.

As a commodity, nations have rationed, taxed, used as currency, and guarded salt like gold, especially in the outback. Abundant supplies of salt spawned trade routes, for example, those originating at the Indus River and a long trek connecting South America with Mesoamerica. Chinese cooks used salt as a coating for *jiu yim* (pepper salt) shrimp and lotus-wrapped

chicken, around which the grains held in heat like an oven. The concept of salary derived from the Latin *sal* (salt), the Roman legionary's change for shopping for their own foodstuffs in regions where coins were rare.

Salt processing influenced North America's food history before contact with Europeans. For over two thousand years, the Maya carried on a salt trade that linked lower Central America with Mexico. In the Caribbean, the Arawak were so blessed with salt pans that they named the island of St. Martin "Sualouiga" (Land of Salt). The harvest at Bonaire began in the 1600s, where slaves air-dried salt ponds beneath warm trade winds. The Caddo of the Red River Valley made salt in earthen kettles for trade with the Quapaw and Chichimec.

In Central America, the Tepehuan of Chihuahua, Mexico, treasured salt to eat with their three servings per day of pinole, a thin corn gruel. To replenish stores, they brought in lumps from mestizo traders from the west or from Hidalgo del Parral in Chihuahua. Before the salt was table ready, it underwent several grindings at the mano and metate, a traditional stone roller and grinding tray.

Among Native Americans, salt served ceremonial purpose. To the desert Indians, the Green Corn Dance and the busk ritual featured salt as a love amulet. Among Pueblo and Cherokee, it was a burial spice; for the Laguna and Isleta pueblos, salt enhanced cures. The shamans of the Hopi, Navaho, Rio Grande, Tohono O'odham, and Zuñi cleansed themselves before setting out on sacred expeditions to gather salt crystals. At the site, salt pilgrims prayed and worked together while intoning chants, formulas, and hymns to nature and abstaining from food, water, idle conversation, sexual intercourse, and rest. The devout welcomed holy visions and left gifts of corn meal and *bahos* or *pahos* (prayer sticks). Such journeys paralleled the arrival of life on earth from sacred sources.

European fish-salting was a common food processing method in the mid-medieval period, as shown by the *Capitulare de Villis* (The Accounting of Villas, ca. 812 CE), compiled at the decree of Charlemagne. Along the Baltic Sea, fisherfolk preserved large catches of herring in barrels of salt for shipping to southern Poland. As a commodity, salt fish came to prominence in the eleventh century as Christianity influenced cookery in homes, convents, and monasteries. Because strict Catholicism required fasting for nearly a third of the year, cooks chose fish as fast-day food. By the 1400s, the Dutch were enriching their coffers by smoking herring for use in kitchens far to the south.

In Europe, where salt was more precious than gold, purchases from evaporation sites and mines such as the saltworks at Kracow arrived to market in bushels to supply the demands of the fall slaughtering and preserving of meat. In the 1000s, the Irish made the first reference to corned beef, joints of meat preserved with lumps of salt. Also vital to the Arabs, salt was the source of the statement, "There is salt between us," an affirmation of friendship bonded over food. (Pinto 1949, 8) Ibn Battuta, author of the travel memoir *Tuhfat al-Nuzzar fi Ghara'ib al-Amsar wa'Ajaib al'Asfar* (On Curiosities of Cities and Wonders of Travel, 1354), packed the valuable commodity during his travel through West Africa. On an eight hundred-mile journey to Timbuktu, he paid for his nightly purchase of butter and food with aromatics, glass trinkets, and salt, the international coin.

The chronicler Ulrich von Richental (or Richendal) reported about 1423 on an unusual salting of game by the kitchen staff of King Ladislaus Jagiellon of Poland. To honor attendees at the Konstanz synod of Catholic bishops, he dispatched two slaughtered aurochs. One he salted in herring casks by the usual method. The other, left whole and unskinned, his servants gutted and seasoned the cavity with salt and gunpowder.

In medieval Europe, the householder placed such salt-cured meats in the *spic-hus* (bacon-house). Venetian, Sicilian, and Provençal salt makers home-brined *bottarga* (pickled fish roe), artichoke hearts, and morels. They also profited from exporting sea salt north to the Swiss, who lacked the salt necessary for curing meat, fish, and rounds of cheese. In 1439, the Venetian bureaucracy proclaimed salt-making the sole province of the state.

The text of *A Compendyous Regyment or a Dyetary of Helth* (1530) by Andrew Boorde (or Borde), a Carthusian monk and physician from Cuckfield, England, advised storing table salt in a bowl and crushing and serving it with a bone spatula. The cook kept stone jars of salt at the hearth, where the contents flavored foods and served as a handy and effective fire extinguisher. To revive rigid clumps, a brief drying in a bread oven usually restored the mass to free-running crystals. On salting troughs and bacon larders, the recurrence of "salt damp" indicates that dry crystals in the wood have rehydrated and revealed a blood stain. (Hartley 1964, 363)

For its primacy in the household, the salt box was the first container placed on the clean tablecloth at the head table. Platina's Latin masterwork *De Honesta Voluptate* (On Right Pleasure, 1475) declared it necessary to enliven flavors and indicated that salt from Volterra in Tuscany was the clean, white grade preferred at table. It might be placed in the hollow in a cube of stale bread or in metal stemware designed as a salt cellar. Daily, cook staff cleaned silver salt cellars to prevent corrosion.

The host's *nef* (salt boat), a huge, ostentatious table vessel crusted with precious stones and enamel, displayed his wealth. The use of a boat shape connected the white grains with their source in the sea; later symbolism developed from great powerful beasts and dragons to hourglasses, cylinders, and bells. The positioning of salt was a symbol of nobility, with those seated below earning little prestige in comparison with the honored guests above it. As a preservative, salting in closed containers kept fresh herbs flavorful, but drained the color. The salt cellar itself remained covered with a lid or napkin to keep it clean and free of moisture and to discourage would-be assassins from poisoning the contents.

Pickling in brine preserved meat and fish when it flooded the market, enabling the purchaser to buy at a low price and preserve stores for later use. According to Platina, pickling pork meat started the day before butchering, when the livestock manager deprived animals of water to dry the meat. To prevent withering, rot, worms, and grubs, preservers layered chunks of meat skin down on salt in a clay pot or jar and leaving it until it soaked up the brine. The process concluded with hanging haunches on meat hooks over smoke before removing ham, tenderloin, shoulders, bacon, or lard. In addition, Platina's *De Sale*, an essay on salt, summarizes its ability to burn, combat, diminish, and dissolve, but warns that it needs temperate use because its endangers stomach, liver, blood, and eyes.

From the 1400s to the French Revolution in 1789, salt was of primary interest to householders. The *gabelle*, a complicated tax schedule on consumer items levied in 1360, applied specifically to salt used by peasants, but exempted nobles, the clergy, and the elite. After his accession in 1515, Francis I controlled distribution and marketing of salt in the north and central provinces. Because the onus fell on the underclass, families supported a salt underground, which smuggled commodities for illicit sale, and even slew the *gabelleurs* (tax collectors). The government countered by dictating purchase of a standard amount for each household and sent royal forces to plunder the murderers' villages. When peasants rioted and drew up their complaints against the government to present to the Estates-General of 1789, the high tax stood out among other grievances. As a result of a clash between the peasants and crown, in March 1790, the Constitutive Assembly of France abolished its *gabelle*.

Scandinavian salt merchants attempted numerous means of improving their supply. Bishop Olaus Magnus of Sweden, author of *History of the Northern People* (1555), reported on a method of hollowing tree trunks to insert into ocean waves to bring up saltier water from the sea floor. Another method, burning seaweed, produced a black salt adulterated with ash.

SALT

A saltier substance, north European peat, rendered another black salt, which laborers at Vadehavet, Denmark, and Friesland, Holland, burned and boiled to make grains. To season salmon dishes, the Finns simmered Arctic Sea waters and caravaned their granular salt over Scandinavia and Russia. The tedious task of feeding firewood under a salt pan gained ridicule as an elder's job.

To the Native American and colonial European householder, salting was an essential method of preserving food, thus assuring the life and well being of the family and tribe. In colonial homes, free-flowing grains began with placing the salt box near the fire for drying out lumps or removing a brick to make a salt niche. After a pounding in a mortar, loose grains remained at hand for cooking as well as a crude, but effective fire extinguisher. To protect dairy items from spoilage, cheese and butter makers relied on salt to extend shelf life by removing the excess moisture that caused corruption. As described in the anonymous *Le Ménagier de Paris* (The Goodman of Paris, ca. 1394), an unsigned text that may have been written by Guy de Montigny, a servant of the Duc de Berry, setting butter before fire to melt desalinated it. The process divided the mass into a sweet upper portion and a salty precipitate suitable for seasoning pottage.

Colonists imported Liverpool salt for everyday use and saved bay salt from the Bay of Biscay for preserving cod, shad, mackerel, and meat in powdering tubs. When salt boxes ran low, cooks slow-dried thin strips of meat or fish fillets over a fire Indian style. The demand for salt offered business opportunities from as early as the Jamestown, Virginia, saltworks in the 1620s, from which Southern settlers shipped to Puritans in the Massachusetts Bay Colony. In the Dutch colony of New York, Cornelia Lubbetse DePeyster became the first colonist to import salt for domestic use. Her contemporaries applied salt to season and preserve food, especially beef, pork, cod, halibut, and shad. After the meats cured, they maintained a long shelf life and were handy for travel by land or sea. Cooks sliced them thinly for frying or removed some of the salt by simmering with vegetables or in meat stews.

Positioning of salt at table in the American colonies perpetuated the status symbolism of the Middle Ages. At Harvard University in 1644, placement of the footed silver salt cellar, donated by Richard Harris and appraised at £5 1s. 3d., was the dividing line between faculty and graduates from undergraduates. A large family salt bowl preceded the more sanitary and polite use of individual bowls and ladles. In the South, daily servings of fried pork rind nourished slaves and the poor, who ate slices wedged inside cornpone, johnnycake, and biscuits. In the Northeast, salt pork was a major ingredient in baked beans and produced a salty-sweet juice when blended with molasses.

Seasoning became a steady business at the salt ponds of Kauai, Hawaii. From early times, members of the Salt Association of Hanapepe began the salt season each May by clearing debris, smoothing clay from the surface, and hauling buckets of brackish water to a curing pond for evaporation. Salt makers raked in crystals and heaped them into bamboo baskets for winnowing and bagging. From the North American seashore came bay salt or sea salt, as well as from brine springs and salt pans or salt gardens, such as the dried sea beds producing rock salt in West Virginia and Louisiana. By boring into these deposits, miners extracted salt crystals dissolved in hot water, which they pumped out to evaporate in copper or iron kettles or vats.

By the early 1800s, home kitchens sported salt boxes and earthenware salt kits, storage jars with wide sleeves to one side that admitted the hand or scoop for enough crystals to preserve meats. In 1836, before the spread of ice delivery and ice boxes in rural areas, domestic adviser Lydia Maria Child published advice on salting meats in *The American Frugal Housewife*. Concerning corned meats, she described rubbing in a plentiful amount of salt and hanging the meat in a cellar for several days. Because corned haunches did not keep well in summer, she suggested rubbing in additional salt for long periods of storage and covering with cloth to ward off cellar flies. The cooling of curing cellars also allowed the salt-curing of meat year round. The control of temperature at 38 to 50 degrees Fahrenheit produced a revolution in the timing of slaughtering and preserving meats, which had formerly taken place only during the cold months.

Salting proved valuable at Gardiner's Island off Long Island, New York, where local fishermen boosted the worth of sturgeon catch by manufacturing caviar. A fish marketer taught them to separate the egg sac membrane, rinse the roe, and drain it in a sieve. Rock salt preserved it in barrels for shipping to New York City. Repackaging in small tins, labeling in Russian, and reshipping via Russia allowed crafty marketers to sell the roe as true Russian caviar.

In the West, Sophie Trupin's mother, the focus of *Dakota Diaspora: Memoirs of a Jewish Homesteader* (1984), used coarse, hygroscopic grains to cushion a crate of eggs to preserve them through the winter. Trupin recalled: "There must be a fair-sized layer of salt separating each egg from another. The box would be placed in the cellar, and because the salt hardened, keeping out the air, the eggs remained unspoiled." (p. 59) Retrieval was tedious, beginning with a careful spooning away of the crust to free an egg trapped

536

below. From these treasures, her mother made coffee-cake.

Into the twentieth century, salt and storage units remained vital to an efficient kitchen. In 1915, Humboldt Manufacturing Company of Brooklyn, New York, marketed the Kant-Klog, a crystal shaker fitted with a double spiral of non-corrosive metal and knob to break up clumps.

Beginning in the 1930s in the mountain village of Hinokage, Kyushu, folk basketmaker Hiroshima Kazuo crafted filtration cylinders, tea sieves, and grain colanders to meet the needs of farm wives. For sea salt, which the uplanders bought from the buckets of coastal salt peddlers, each household required a conical salt drainer. The handled basket held the impure crystals and directed internal moisture into drops that wept from the tip. The process kept the salt free-running. Thrifty cooks preserved the droplets as *nigari* (bittern), a flavoring for a kitchen staple, homemade *tofu* (soy bean curd).

In 1970, the Guajiro of Manaure, Colombia, were operating the last unmechanized salt industry by scraping crystalline residue from one hundred-acre pans. Tools were limited to hoes, shovels, barrows, and burden bags, the same harvesting devices used in prehistory. Similarly unmechanized, the individual salt miners of seemingly limitless supplies of crystals in Lake Karum, Ethiopia, used poles as primitive levers to maneuver salt slabs from drying ponds to slicers for readying bricks for sale to traders leading mule and camel caravans. For grueling work in hot, corrosive saline chaff, workers lived in salt-block hovels and daily earned around sixty cents, a loaf of bread, and a goatskin of water.

Of the ethnic varieties of salt, cooks hold varied opinions. Some prefer pure iodized table salt, others opt for kosher or sea salt. In "The Goodness of Salt" from *The Artful Eater* (1992), the essayist Edward Behr relates his loyalty to salt and explains that the suffix *-wich* in such place names as Droitwich, Greenwich, Middlewich, and Norwich indicates the original site of a brine spring or saltworks. He finds most interesting gray Armorican grains from the Loire delta. "Close behind are two kinds of coarse white crystals from Mediterranean France, as well as Maldon sea salt from Essex, England, from the Maldon Crystal Salt Company, the only remaining maker of sea salt in England." He extols the crystals for heightening food flavors, fixing the green in vegetables as they boil, lowering the freezing point in ice for hand-cranked ice cream, and preserving anchovies, bacon, cheese, corned beef, ham, olives, pickles, salt cod, sauerkraut, sausage, and smoked beef. Best of all, he claims, salt restores equilibrium between flavors and reduces fat's oily taste.

See also **Smoked Food**

Further Reading

Andrews, Anthony P., "The Salt Trade of the Ancient Maya," *Archaelogy*, July–August 1980, 24–33.

Englebert, Victor, "The Danakil: Nomads of Ethiopia's Wasteland," *National Geographic*, February 1970, 186–211.

Erlandson, Keith. *Home Smoking and Curing*. London: Barrie & Jenkins, 1977.

Stutz, Bruce, "The Rhythm of Bonaire," *Islands*, January–February 2001, 70–83.

Trankina, Michele L. "Living Without Salt?" *The World & I*, April 2001, 142–149.

SANITATION

Sanitation is an ongoing concern of cooks and diners who can't follow their dinners from the original source to food sellers and handlers. Food-borne illness jeopardizes infants and toddlers, pregnant women, the elderly, and people with suppressed immune systems or such chronic life-threatening illnesses as severe allergies, cancer, diabetes, or AIDS. Newly identified pathogens add to the growing list that centers on *E. coli*, vibrio, campylobacter, listeria, and shigella, which can contaminate at any stage of food usage, from purchase and storage to preparation, cooking, serving, and clean-up.

Cleanliness has been a culinary concern since ancient times. In India, the Hindu hearth was a holy shrine that shared space with the domestic worship center. Rules for sanitation regulated placement of the food preparation sits diametrically opposite and out of sight of waste collection and disposal. The devout homeowner bathed and put on freshly washed unstitched clothing before approaching the cook place. A complex series of proprieties set up cooking practice for milk, *ghee* (clarified butter), pulses, rice, dhal, vegetables, and fruit.

Instructions found on three Babylonian tablets from around 1700 BCE instructed the cook to wipe and rinse additives to broth at each step of thirty-five recipes. Such attempts at cleanliness were often a reaction against questionable water sources. The Egyptians valued the annual Nile flood as a natural cleansing, even if it dissolved the mud bricks of their walls and houses. A similar natural process sluiced Venice each day with the influx of tidewaters from the Mediterranean. At meals, it was customary in Egypt, Greece, and Rome to perform table ablutions. As described in the domestic writer Louis-Nicolas Ménard's *Vie Privée des Anciens* (The Private Life of the Ancients, ca. 1875), servants either poured water for washing or diners passed a water basin before and after meals or following presentation of a messy finger food, such as bread dipped in honey.

Republican Rome offered householders more sanitation than earlier peoples by attaching leaded drain pipe to subterranean *cloacae* (sewers). In Londinium in Roman Britain, each householder was obliged to dig a garbage pit per household. When a family filled the pit, they topped it with dirt or plastered it over. These middens have preserved for archeologists the animal bones, smashed wine flagons, bent utensils and tableware, Samianware dishes and vessels, and glass shards that detail the daily kitchen stores of the period.

An unusual device was the coin-operated handwasher, invented around 100 CE by the Alexandrian Heron. An inveterate tinkerer, he had already earned a reputation for clever designs with his solar-powered fountain, water organ, automatic doors, and self-trimming lamp. The slot machine applied a new technology to public ablution. Users dropped a five-drachma piece into the slot of the urn. The bronze coin was heavy enough to trip a lever that dispensed water from a tap for ritual washing of face and hands. When the stream ended, the lever return to its original position and shut the valve.

During the Middle Ages, standards of sanitation improved. Dating to the early thirteenth-century lyrics of Surdas and Namdev and their followers, the *Adi Granth*, Punjabi for "first book," anthologized nearly six thousand Sikh scriptures of instructive sayings, bardic verse, and hymns. In the commentary on food, scripture warns of dangerous foods, particularly alcohol and beef. Of kitchen service, the text asks "Which place can be considered pure, where I can sit and take my food?" (Achaya 1998, 73)

In the British Isles, building design redirected nearby streams as a means of ridding the kitchen and dining areas of waste and muck. The medieval castle contained a privy attached to the outer wall and positioned over a shaft that directed kitchen waste to the moat or river below. The Clunaic priory at Castle Acre, Norfolk, bisected the priory kitchen with a drain leading away from the monks' dormitory. Roche Abbey, a Cistercian cloister begun late in the 1100s, followed a similar sanitation procedure with a drain that flowed south of the kitchen, under the warming house, and beyond the infirmary, a source of serious, sometimes life-threatening contamination. The abbot's residence and kitchen had their own drain, which connected to the abbey west of the infirmary. Alnwick Abbey in Northumberland, built in the late 1300s, carried the plan of natural sanitation to greater efficiency by positioning kitchen and infirmary on the River Alne at the extreme end of the compound's gatehouse, central cloister, and church.

When Marco Polo published *The Travels of Marco Polo* (ca. 1299), his comments on the city-bred habit of bathing suggest that his native city of Venice was not so clean as the urban centers of China. He commented, "It is [the Chinese] custom to wash every day, and they will not sit down to a meal without first washing." (Polo 1958, 215) He also remarked on the people of India, who refrained from touching food with the left hand, "believing that the function of the left hand is confined to such needful tasks as are unclean and foul, such as wiping the nose or the breach and suchlike. Likewise they drink only out of flasks, each one from his own." (Ibid.)

Before Europeans had an understanding of bacterial and viral infections, the washing and polishing of tableware reflected on the host's manners and attendance to the comfort of diners. For individuals, the French and English produced behavior guides that substantiated both the esthetic and hygienic purposes of good manners. Texts reminded diners to come to the table with clean, trimmed nails, to use the finger bowl frequently, and to wipe the mouth on a napkin before drinking, a good suggestion for diners sharing tankards. The handbooks forbade scratching, nose-picking, spitting, belching, and picking the teeth with the tip of the knife.

In medieval England, the punctilious cook required a garderobe pit for sluicing kitchen waste, which bore animal entrails, fish scales, and other offal along with graywater. The kitchen superintendent distributed table linens, napped towels, and a hand towel, which attached to a pole to keep it free of vermin and rodents. For end-of-the-day cleaning, scullery staff assembled pails of boiling water, coarse salt, and bristle brushes for the removal of all evidence of the day's chores. Heather mops or willow or birch brooms were handy for spot cleaning.

Whatever was left over or rejected from the table, diners tossed to the floor for the dogs. Householders layered over spoiled table scraps with rushes and fresh herbs. For flea control, household staff spread alder leaves. More refuse piled up at street level and created a stench under windows. City regulations forced individuals to keep the thoroughfare free from garbage and manure or suffer a penalty.

Upon arrival at the east African harbor of Zeila, now called Djibouti, geographer Ibn Battuta, author of the travel memoir *Tuhfat al-Nuzzar fi Ghara'ib al-Amsar wa'Ajaib al'Asfar* (On Curiosities of Cities and Wonders of Travel, 1354), turned in dismay from a terrible odor. Having crossed the Red Sea from the fragrant coast of Yemen, he concluded that Zeilans deserved a bad reputation for their habit of locating fish markets in the sun and from butchering camels at the dockside. His published opinions influenced much of the civilized world, as did those of Platina, author of *De Honesta Voluptate et Valitudine* (On Right Pleasure and Health, 1475), who stressed a hygienic kitchen and spotless table linens. Concepts of cleanliness necessitated training the wait staff in supplying clean linens, fragrant atmosphere, and sharp knives. Platina added that "the rest of the dishes should be scrubbed clean, whether they are earthen or silver, for this meticulous care arouses even a sluggish appetite." (Scully 1995, 173-174)

Home cleaners were common recipes included in recipe books. Hannah Wooley's *The Queen-like Closet; or Rich Cabinet* (1670) proposes a deodorant for gloves, which the cook concocted from musk, rosewater, civet, gum dragon, and oil of cloves. By mixing in jasmine and cinnamon, the sweetener of gloves created a pungent cleanser for sponging and massaging into leather surfaces permeated with skin oils and table grease. After two days of curing, the gloves needed some limbering to ready them for wear. In the eighteenth century, the revered English cook and food writer Hannah Glasse warned of the danger of verdigris, a poisonous green accretion on brass. In *The Art of Cookery Made Plain and Easy: Excelling Any Thing of the Kind Ever Yet Published* (1747), re-released in America in 1805, Glasse urged the cautious cook to scrub pots and pans, using sand as an abrasive.

Glasse's suggestion fails to mention the major source of nineteenth-century impurities—unscrubbable stone sinks propped up on brick, stone, or concrete columns. Carved natural stone basins, paired with iron pumps, the forerunners of more expensive lead or copper lined wood or sheet metal models, were welcome to cooks accustomed to fetching water in buckets from a well or communal street tap. However, rough soapstone's pitted finish trapped food particles and grease until the user applied a brass-bristled brush and boiling water. Also suspect, the under-sink grease trap and drain offered bacteria a dark, dank environment for proliferation. A shift to the earthenware gamekeeper's sink merely perpetuated septic conditions. Alternate models, including the stand-alone Belfast sink and monstrous ceramic pot sink, were roomy enough to hold large cook pots as well as tableware, but not much easier to sanitize.

A topic examined by Dr. Robert Johnson, Inspector General of Hospitals in the English army in 1845, the placement of military campsites required attention to noxious air and putrefaction near muddy river banks, ponds and fens, and grounds denuded of woods. Johnson drew on his experience with the Hindustani prison at Barrackpore, where damp quarters killed from one-tenth to one-fourth of the forty thousand prisoners annually from cholera and fever. He suggested choosing high ground ventilated by moving air currents than building among thickets and advocated

stretching painted canvas over the tent floor as a barrier against contaminants.

In the United States, one of the least hygienic domestic areas was the farmhouse kitchen, which was often situation on a dirt access road where pigs rooted and poultry roosted at will. Because farmstead chores forced women in and out of the back door to yard and barn, kitchens were rarely free of dust, manure, tobacco spit, and muck tracked or blown in. One solution to sanitizing floors was the clog, a simple food covering that could be scraped clean or left to soak in a pan of water. The worst examples of domestic sanitation were homes regularly invaded by farm animals and yard dogs and cats. Because windows had no screens, and doors did not close tightly, cooks often made drawstring covers or screens for pitchers and bowls to keep out insects and air-borne debris. For meal service, women tended to place a tall object at the center of the table and drape it with a cloth like an umbrella, beneath which they placed prepared dishes. In Charleston, South Carolina, the cook retained young slaves to wave turkey wings or hoist peacock feathers to fan the area in a steady rhythm discouraging houseflies.

In the pioneer's guide *The Prairie Traveler: A Hand-Book for Overland Expeditions* (1859), containing advice, maps, and intineraries over the principal routes between the Mississippi River and the Pacific Ocean, army captain Randolph Barnes Marcy addressed the issue of camp sanitation. He warned of malaria in swampy land near streams, lakes, and rivers surrounded by timber and vegetation. Homes built along the way, such as those of German immigrants in Texas, often stationed wall-mounted wood washstands on the porch with pitcher, bowl, and towel for handwashing before householders entered the kitchen from dairy, henyard, or barn chores. Shuck mats and boot scrapers rid the feet of muck, a major encouragement of flies and gnats.

Acceptable and unacceptable levels of sanitation often divide cultures. When Captain Charles Francis Hall, the author of *Life with the Esquimaux* (1862), accepted the hospitality of an Inuit family in Greenland, he observed Petato, the Inuit cook, handing out pieces of seal meat from a cook pot and ladling broth into bowls. Before filling another bowl with soup, she placed it on the floor for her sled dog to lick clean. The natives accepted her method of cleansing dishes and passed the communal bowl until they had eaten all the seal soup. Hall mused that an outsider attending the meal would have seen "a dirty set of human beings, mixed up among masses of nasty, uneatable flesh, skins, blood, and bones, scattered all about the igloo" and would have been repulsed "when he should see dogs wash [vessels] with their long pliant tongues." (Hall 1972, 476-477)

Munich became one of Germany's first municipalities to regulate dairy products. By an 1862 decree, out of benevolent concern for families with infants and small children, city fathers set up storehouse regulations and hygienic standards for dairy shops, equipment, and storerooms. Inspections ranged upward from ten to twenty-five visits annually. To reduce opportunities for microbial growth, officials tried to re-link buyers directly with dairies and to establish a lapsed interest in vendors to sell milk door to door rather than through a middleman. The campaign was too little too late. From 1870 to 1913, the number of milkmen decreased from 72 percent of the trade to barely 5 percent as commercial dairies drove them out of business. Until World War I, when sealed bottles made inroads into the market, most housewives bought milk at shops, where clerks measured the purchase and poured it into the customer's bottle or stone jar.

In 1912, the environmental chemist Ellen Henrietta Richards and Sophronia Maria Elliott published a household guide to sanitation in *The Chemistry of Cooking and Cleaning*. They discussed in simple terms the value of soap and laundry boosters for antisepsis. As an antidote to pathogens, they described sunlight as "nature's best and cheapest disinfectant." (Richards & Elliott 1912, 166) They urged the housewife to use dry oven heat for cleansing blankets and flannels; boiling water for linens, tableware, floors, and small objects; formalin (formaldehyde and methanol) solutions to kill spores; slaked lime to sanitize human waste; and steam for sturdy substances, such as metals and glass. For a home-rigged sanitizing chamber, they described heating water to boiling in a wash pot over a kitchen fire, topping the vessel with broom handles, and suspending articles and fabrics from them. They concluded, "The whole should be covered with a sheet or cloth to retain the heat, and steamed for an hour or longer, depending upon the degree of penetration required." (Ibid., 169)

Strong in the sanitation market of the 1930s was Clorox, a bleach, stain remover, and bacteria and odor killer carrying the Good Housekeeping guarantee. Ad copy pictured housewives as officers policing danger spots—iceboxes and refrigerators, cabinet shelves, porcelain sinks and table tops, drains, garbage cans, laundry, and sickroom supplies. Clorox distributors promised billions of oxygen molecules in each drop to clean, disinfect, and deodorize. The familiar brown bottles were common sights in grocery buggies and on kitchen and bathroom shelves. Because of the popularity of Clorox with housewives, packaging altered over time to disposable plastic jugs, but marketing claims remained virtually unchanged.

Another popular disinfectant during that era, Lysol, distributed by Lehn & Fink of Bloomfield, New Jersey, promised sterile bottles and nipples, feeding chairs, and floors where baby crawled. An ad in the August 1930 issue of *Good Housekeeping* matched the innocent round eyes of a child suckling from its bottle with a line drawing of a clean electric bottle warmer, obviously rid of microbes with a wipe of cleaning water to which the mother/housewife added Lysol. Extolled as non-toxic to humans, the disinfectant carried strong promises of shielding children during a critical phase of their growth, a topic covered in a free brochure, "Protecting the Home Against Disease."

In the July 1947 issue of *Woman's Home Companion*, Howard Whitman summarized issues discussed at the national Sanitation Foundation at the University of Michigan at Ann Arbor. Headed by Dr. Henry F. Vaughan, the dean of the university's School of Public Health, the consortium pondered the inconsistent tangle of laws and regulations enacted in different states, such as rules regarding the elimination of backwash in sinks and basins, improper handwashing by food handlers, refuse piled in town dumps, ratproof kitchen construction, and pet dogs and cats in commercial food preparation areas. During regular outbreaks of polio, homemakers summoned fears of improper dishwasher design, disparaties in the type of chemical sterilization suited to dishes and sinks, and the temperature of water for sanitizing, which varied state to state from 150 degrees Fahrenheit to 212 or boiling.

In the early twenty-first century, modern sanitation was sometimes a matter of ritual purity. For the Hindu of Nepal, *jutho* (ritual purity) began with full knowledge of the cook's caste and the use of separate plates and utensils. For a feast, the cook had to be a Brahmin, the highest caste, to serve people of lower castes. For the Bangladeshi, Kyrgyz, Somali, Tanzanians, and Cameroonians, washing hands before meals was a necessity because they ate with the right hand rather than with forks. Because they performed bodily hygiene with the left hand, they traditionally refrained from using it to touch dishes or food items. Diners in Burkina Faso offered two options—dining only with the right hand or with aluminum utensils. The people of the Central African Republic, Comoros, Ghana, Eritrea, Fiji, Malawi, Guinea, Kenya, Morocco, Tunisia, Tubuluans, United Arab Emirates, and Zambia showed concern for sanitation by passing soap and water before and after dining.

Variances typify cooking, serving, and dining styles of many nations. A time-honored American method of testing the doneness of cake or pudding is insertion of a broom straw. However harmless seems the contact between food and fibers that have swept the floor, the metal cake tester, wood skewer, or chopstick seems more sanitary. The Beninese eat with either implements or the right hand, particularly for yam *foo-foo*, okra, and *eba*, a thin cassava gruel like grits. Mauritanians wash, lick their fingers after eating, then wash a second time. In India, a wash basin is available in the dining room. Samoans wash their hands after dining, as do the people of Sierra Leone, who also cleanse the face. Sri Lankans wash their hands after meals and drink water to cleanse the mouth.

See also **Canning; Kosher Kitchens**

Further Reading

Hoy, Suellen. *Chasing Dirt: The American Pursuit of Cleanliness.* New York: Oxford University Press, 1995.

MacFadyen, Byron, "Leftovers Shouldn't Be Left Over," *Good Housekeeping*, September 1930, 97, 188.

Richards, Ellen H., and S. Maria Elliott. *The Chemistry of Cooking and Cleaning.* Boston: Whitcomb & Barrows, 1912.

Sauber, Colleen, "When Microbes Are on the Menu," *Harvard Health Letter*, December 1994, 4–5.

Whitman, Howard, "Let's All Be Healthy!," *Woman's Home Companion*, July 1947, 36–37, 48.

SAUSAGE

Sausage has a long and respected history in world cookery, particularly in peasant communities, including kielbasa- and *circinelae*-loving Poles, andouille-cooking Creoles, and chorizo-eating Spaniards. As is evident from regional differences, to oversimply the sausage-making process as mincing meat and adding spices before forcing it into casings or drying in patties robs it of its ethnic characteristics. For example, *Osbane*, an Arabic specialty, begins with chopped

sheep meat and entrails. The cook seasons the forcemeat with pepper, blends in rice, and eases the mix into a sheep's intestines. In the German-French tradition of Alsace, the skilled pork butchers of Strasbourg have traditionally produced a broad range of charcuterie from a variety of sausage meats—knackwurst, saveloys, Thann sausage, Metwurst, black pudding, Schinkenwurst, Schwartenmagen, Bierwurst, veal roll, Schwartwurst, Mulhouse sausage, Lyon sausage, Leberwurst, tongue roll with truffles, and veal roll with *foie gras*.

The first Italian cookbook, *Liber de Coquina* (Kitchen Handbook, ca. 1300s), outlines a fresh fish sausage made from wrapping boiled fish and chopped herbs in cheesecloth before frying it in oil to hold its shape as it heats. The making of mortadella, Italy's pistachio-flavored sausage, is a traditional fried treat derived from an ancient Roman recipe that blended *mortarium* (salt pork) with myrtle berries. The process involved pounding the meat to a slurry and whisking in fat, cinnamon, nutmeg, salt, and pepper before filling casings. Sausage-makers then placed the links in a cool, dry cabinet or shelf to age before cooking. The fragrance alone set mortadella apart from other Mediterranean varieties, which cooks seasoned with the natural flavorings at hand in their region.

Sanitation and quality foodstuffs are the perennial complaint of those suspicious of the varied character of sausage. According to John of Garland's *Dictionary* (1220), medieval intellectuals who sent their servants to buy meat got even with butchers who sold them diseased stock: "In return for the dirty entrails and sausages, the haggis and the tripes which they put together for people in academic robes, these butchers

Mexican butcher in Oaxaca, Mexico preparing sausages.
[© *Brian Atkinson / Alamy.*]

are butchered by wrathful scholars." (Rubin 1981, 37) By the Italian Renaissance, Platina, the author of *De Honesta Voluptate et Valitudine* (On Right Pleasure and Health, 1475), was more sanguine about the goodness of sausage, although he carefully delineated between standard cooking and eating and the less refined style of peasants.

In eastern Prussia in 1601, the Königsberg butcher's guild set out to extrude the longest possible sausage. Cranked out like a long thin hot dog, it incorporated excessive amounts of pepper and stretched to around seven hundred yards. The community spirit generated by the effort attests to the peasant love of spicy chopped meat encased in wiener form. In *The Diary of Thomas Turner, 1754–1765*, the writer, from East Hoathby, Sussex, recorded the baking of sausages in batter in a style that preceded the traditional British toad in the hole. The name didn't take hold until 1787, when Madame d'Arblay wrote of the homely crusted dish to actress Sarah Siddons.

A necessity to American colonists, sausage making was a means of preserving meat for traveling or desperate times, such as epidemics and sieges, when hunters and fishers had no access to the wild. In addition to salting haunches, cooks imitated native American pemmican by devising sausage, a method of recycling animal intestines as casings for chopped, spiced meat. To Massachusetts colonists, links were a delicacy.

Pennsylvania Dutch families exchanged *metzel-suppe*, dishes of sausage meat, as a token of friendship. Into the large intestine, the thinnest of hog innards, they forced chopped meat mixtures with a piston-operated sausage gun or funnels powered by a meat plunger resembling a thin pestle, then tied off the end with string. A less tedious method, the boxed sausage gun held the casing in place while the operator turned a wheel that forced meat out a tube and into the liner. After dividing tubes into links bound with additional cord, sausage makers hung uncut links near a flue to dry.

In the Amana colonies, which supplied food for 1,500 residents, slaughterers retained beef and pork scraps for *Blutwurst* (blood sausage), *Bratwurst* (pork sausage), *Bockwurst* (chive-flavored sausage), *Knackwurst* (spiced sausage), *Leberwurst* (liver sausage), and *Swartenmagen* (headcheese). According to meat worker Carl Schuerer, recipes called for salt, chopped garlic, and hand-ground pepper, allspice, and nutmeg for a quarter-ton batch of processed meat. The value of home-made sausage was its individualized flavor, low cost, and assurance of purity and sanitation, an element lacking in factory-made goods.

In 1908, most of one page of the Sears, Roebuck catalog devoted copy to implements essential to sausage production. A 69-cent Puritan steel chopper with screw-on base for tabletop use pressed food through coarse, medium, and fine plates or one covering designed for extruding nut butter. Ranged below the ad were choppers priced from 96 cents to $7.93 for a butcher-size model with fly wheel and variable size mechanism. In addition to steel knives and plates for choppers, Sears sold stuffing attachments in twelve sizes, a railroad sausage stuffer for 96 cents, and hand-cranked japanned device for farm kitchens and butcher shops for $3.04.

On the Australian frontier, outbackers got by on native foods and such imports or locally made goods as saveloys, a favorite of military cooks during World War I. Saveloy sellers strolled the harbor market and called out the qualities of their wares. The late twentieth-century saveloy, still an Aussie favorite, contained questionable stuffing and an uncommonly bright red color. When parents' and citizens' organizations inveighed against junk food sold in school canteens in 1990, the saveloy was among the foods dietitians labeled as high-fat and low-nutrition for growing children.

In the 1930s, Adolph Levis and his brother developed a cigar, condiment, relish, and pickle business in a Philadelphia cellar into a line of bar sausages. Levis focused on pickled sausage, pepperoni, and pigs' feet. To satisfy customers who wanted bite-size pepperoni snacks, he dried sausages for a longer shelf life. In the 1940s, the meat snacks were a hit in Philadelphia bars. In 1953, he perfected a three-month curing process that boosted flavor and shelf stability. He named the slender sticks, stored in vinegar, Slim Jims and peddled them under the slogan "Less than a meal and more than a snack." (Griffin, 2001, 1D) When he sold out to General Mills in 1967, the company distributed his smoked jerky treat in cellophane wrappers as camping food and as snacks at sporting events. By 2001, the company sold over $150 million of the unique jerked sausages.

Eliot Wigginton, editor of *The Foxfire Book* (1968), describes the sausage making that followed traditional hog slaughtering in the southern Appalachians. Mountaineers prized sausage made from lean meat from hams, shoulders, head, tenderloin, and jowls. Recipes blending salt, brown sugar, sage, black pepper, and red pepper varied from family to family. Sausage makers forced meat through a grinder, sautéed it in a frying pan, then packed it into crocks, which they topped with hot grease before sealing and upending them. For preserving small portions, preservers rolled the meat into balls and packed them in stone crocks to store in the water trough of a spring house. For links, preparers packed the meat into clean small intestines and tied them at each end and at intervals along the length before hanging them from the rafters of a smokehouse.

Preparers substituted corn shucks when casings ran out, then tied or wired the shucks and packed each in a cloth bag for smoking.

Some regions still define their cuisine by their sausages, which are served separately or in soups or pasta sauce. Currently, to the Bedouin of North Africa, *mirqaz* (lamb and mutton sausage), a popular meal dating to the Middle Ages, stores well under olive oil in clay jars. Mixing and sun-drying follow multiple tasks of chopping flank, sweetbreads, and offal and blending with pounded garlic, preserved lemon, spices, and ground pepper before forcing it into links. The savory smell of frying *mirqaz* characterizes the shared meals in a sand-locked terrain where food treats are limited to stock that travels well aboard dromedaries bound for a lengthy trek.

Yugoslavian cooks offer an antipasto of sausage and cheese before dinner. In Germany, cooks in each geographic locale specialize in a *wurst* (sausage). *Boerewoers* (sausage) is a popular treat at South African barbecues. In Rio de Janeiro, cooks make *feijoada* from sausage and black beans. Moldovans make sausage for serving as breakfast *hors d'oeuvres*; Swedes fry sausage with mustard for *stekt falukorv*. The Dutch make a lunch off *kroket,* a deep-fried sausage. Swiss cooks adapt both the German *bratwurst* and French *saucisse* for daily meals. Japanese cooks, who rely heavily on fish, seaweed, and seafood in meal planning, form *kamaboko* (sausages) from fish paste, which they slice into rounds for plating.

A specialty of Botswana and Zimbabwe is the puff adder, a fresh sausage roasted on a *braai* (grill) over a slow fire. To make the snaky length, the cook soaks the intestine of a sheep or wild game in water. Filling begins with diced kidney and liver, onion and garlic, coriander, and pepper. To stuff the casing, the cook ties off the end with cording, and uses a funnel or bottle neck to force the mix into the tube.

In the Pyrénées Mountains that separate France and Spain, hog slaughtering by Aragonese butchers is man's work. However, salting hams and stuffing sausage casings is done by women. They use disparate temperatures for the two. Slow-cured, salted hams store well in a cool basement. Over an open hearth, cooks place blood sausages in a cauldron for boiling, then force minced meat into gut with a *poussoir* (filling machine).

Eastern Europeans use sausage recipes passed from mother to daughter in unchanging kitchen ritual. Bulgarians get their salami and sausage recipes from German pork specialists, whose cooks perfected *leberwürste, schwarzwürste, frankfurter würstchen,* and *schwäbische würste.* Yugoslavian cooks specialize in flavoring salami with chili pepper, olives, and pickled mushrooms and frying or grilling sausages with onion, radish, and horseradish. Poles are famous for their pork and veal *kielbasa,* served with red cabbage. Polish girls working in *wedlina* (sausage shops) dress in white coats and hold out wooden forks bearing steaming *parky, vursty,* and *klobasy,* which they serve with potato salad and sauerkraut.

Early twenty-first-century devices aiding the sausage maker include a device similar to those featured in the Sears, Roebuck catalog for a century—a hand-cranked cast-iron grinder fitted with heavy-gauge steel blades and varied cutting disks. For ease of filling, plastic funnels slip into casings. KitchenAid food processors are available with a sausage stuffer, among other accessories.

Further Reading

Hoppe, Emilie. *Seasons of Plenty: Amana Communal Cooking.* Ames: Iowa State University Press, 1998.

Kummer, Corby, "Sausages, Souse, and Shandybookers," *Atlantic Monthly,* July/August 2001, 143–147.

SERVANTS

The mark of a refined home, whether king's castle or sheik's tent, has been the well trained servant, who mastered the laying of a cloth, carving of bread and meat, and pouring of beverages. In China's classical era, which began in 1122 BCE and lasted over nine centuries, noblewomen devoted themselves to child care and home management. Serving primarily as hostesses, they trained kitchen staff to buy and prepare food and set tables. The aristocratic wife attended personally to training the best head cook in harmonizing flavors and textures, the basic principle of Asian cuisine.

In the late Middle Ages servants worked in hot, sooty, and dangerous environs. Quarreling and cursing warranted discipline from the lady of the house, as did a breaches of curfew, tidiness, and attendance. For those accused of damaging or stealing the master's goods, the punishment was severe. In balance to these liabilities, a manor's retinue dressed in crested livery and never wanted for room, board, bedside candle, or warmth. An English law passed in 1363 promised grooms and servants, in order of their rank, one meal of meat or fish per day at the lord's expense plus the pick of butter, cheese, milk, and leftovers from the table.

Robert Grossteste, the early thirteenth-century bishop of the see of Lincoln, commented that training and supervising kitchen and wait staff required constant vigilance. He asserted that "No one should be kept in your household if you have not reasonable belief that he is faithful, discreet, painstaking, and honest, and of good manners." (Gies & Gies 1974, 108) However, winnowing out the weak employee was not always feasible. The number of kitchen and wait staff per household established status. Gentlefolk housed seven or eight; barons and knights, up to thirty; and aristocrats as many as 150. Royal households functioned on about four hundred. According to the chronicler John Hardyng, Richard II, who ruled England from 1367 to 1400, traveled from court to court with a retinue of family, retainers, and guests numbering ten thousand. To feed so many under these circumstances, he carried with him three hundred kitchen workers. For his attention to victualing, he earned a reputation as an expert viander.

In the late Middle Ages, most households employed servants or apprentices, who learned their art from observing more experienced staff members. Half of the kitchen staff worked as scullions, the lowest ranking of the lot. In the absence of piped-in water and sewage systems, most of these hirelings fetched water and emptied slops. Female kitchen help ranked slightly above dray animals in respect. The ambitious jostled to gain serving posts on large estates. In the estimation of social observer Christine de Pisan, a professional essayist who wrote in the early 1400s, such women were in some ways better off than the freewoman, unskilled laborer, or farm worker because serving women were assured fish, pottage, lard, bread, and milk as well as more choice in placement.

Going into service had its liabilities. In Denchendorff, Germany, female serfs earned eight loaves and two measures of wine to mark the birth of each child, who added to the lord's holdings as though they were livestock. In 1411, the bailiff of Liestal Manor near Basle lined up servants' children of marriageable age and allotted husbands and wives as though he were mating oxen.

Contrasting allotments of food in 1493 attest to inequalities too great for generalization. At priory farm in Indersdorf, Bavaria, over a five-month period from St. George's Day to Michaelmas, serving folk received a fatty soup called *rabl* plus barley bread, cabbage, and milk. Those who, according to the steward, worked well without complaint received what supplies of millet, peas, and fruit were available. In the same year, the staff of Erasmus at Erbach, Odenwald, got two daily servings of meat, side dishes, and a half-jug of wine. On holidays, they received a large portion of fish or roast with a loaf of bread and meat on Sundays. The latter diet surpasses the peasant fare served at the homes of French shepherds, who ate vegetable and meat stew, meat pies, and dairy items.

Bourgeois and upper-class women of Europe supervised servants at carrying packages from the market, seasoning dishes, the poaching of fish in ale, disjointing game for the spit, salting haunches of meat and cod, and the coloring of confections with saffron. For staff, lords and ladies tended to rely on local cooks and kitchen help, some of whom may have been born at the manor and apprenticed in childhood at baking or roasting, brewing or dairying, the skills their parents had mastered. Others brought from distant cultures the cuisine and cooking styles that augmented and enlivened standard fare, as with the Irish oat cakes, Scotch haggis, and Caribbean and Carolina low country hoppin' john simmered in an iron hominy pot. Wherever servants traveled, they carried their kitchen history with them. In the words of the food writer William Woys Weaver in *America Eats: Forms of Edible Folk Art* (1989), "Servants were often the culinary links between two social worlds because they were 'bilingual' in palate." (p. 7)

The superintendent, called the clerk of the kitchen, governed an interdependent team made up of cooks, scullery maids, turnspit boys, pantry keeper, brewer, baker, gardener, buttery maid, and ewer and cellarer. Management required constant monitoring of servant behavior and dress as well as heat and smoke, dirt, and fumes, the products of open hearths. To individual staff, John Russell's *Boke of Nurture* (ca. 1450) explained the mysteries of carving roast and poultry and presenting fish and eels.

In the 1400s, table behavior improved in English manors. Meals for the entire household offered underlings the example of a noble family. To this end, Robert Grosseteste, an advocate of sensible proportions of rest, food, and cheer, advised the Countess of Lincoln: "Make your own household to sit in the hall, as much as you may. . .and sit you ever in the middle of the high board, that your visage and cheer be showed to all men. . . .So much as you may without peril of sickness and weariness eat you in the hall afore your many, for that shall be to your profit and worship." (Girouard 1978, 30) Far from democratic, service delineated high from low by placement of chairs and pouring of beverages—wine for the elite, beer for the lowly. This camaraderie of household continued until around 1450, when the cook and wait staff ate apart in a steward's room, pantry, or below-stairs dining area.

For royalty, servants had to master many ceremonies. A German observer, Lupold von Wedel, attended a state dinner on December 27, 1584, where wait staff hovered about the English Queen Elizabeth I. Before she returned from church, they erected a gold canopy over her table and set out silver meat dishes. When she returned, she stood for a table blessing and rinsed her hands in a covered basin while a servant poured water from an ewer. She dried on a towel, then replaced her rings, which the Lord Chamberlain held during the complex procedure. Court ladies tasted the queen's dish for poison, after which a stout guard bore in dinner to the sound of kettle drums and twelve trumpets. Seated alone, she received meat carved by a young man dressed in black. Another in green poured her drink and remained on his knees until she returned the goblet to him. Supervising these demonstrations of fealty were men clasping the white staffs denoting household officers.

Part of the kitchen staff's daily routine involved carrying heavy loads down long passageways that connected victualing rooms to the main kitchen. Subterranean warrens generally gave no glimpse of the garden or of the private lives of the gentry above stairs. Balancing the hardships of so constrained a life, the best of the kitchen and wait staff could look forward to warmth, plain food, medical care, uniforms, days off, travel, and possible retirement to an estate cottage. Perquisites of the job allotted bones and fat to the cook, soap bits and candle ends to the maid, and cask dregs to the footman. Servants' agencies quickly spread the word about which employers were difficult and likely to cuff the help.

In the sixteenth century, the English term "servants" applied to any who served, be it chaplain or the noble's child employed as a court page. Accommodations were often poor, offering only canvas-covered straw pallets with a log for a pillow. Upon rising, each removed personal bedding and that of knights and their squires before distributing new rushes, smoothing tapestries, and blowing up the fire at the hearth. In small homes, kitchen chores might range from feeding the pigs to shining pewter, rinsing and stretching linens, baking, brewing and stilling, herb gathering, and dairying.

Youngsters remained in service while getting an education. From waiting at table, they learned the order of plates and tableware, kept voiders handy for removing unwanted bits, and a knife for scraping the table. A personal manorial servant, the page, owed a duty to the lord's salt cellar, trencher, knife, napkin, and folded towel used to swaddle bread and keep it at hand. After cleaning the crumbs, the wait staff set out cheese, fruit, and nuts for post-prandial snacking and offered clean towels and hot water for cleansing hands. In their midteens, pages returned to their families better prepared to function in Tudor society. Those that served well often earned the affection of their masters and a mention in their wills.

People seeking employment posted notices at area fairs, such as the Martinmas fair and market each held November 11. Those looking for cooking posts wore colored aprons and carried spoons; dairiers bore stools. The best place to solicit for domestic work was the post-Michaelmas mop fair, a friendly gathering where workers held the symbols of their trades—the mop, shepherd's crook, plowman's cowhide, and wagoneer's whip. In northwestern Europe—western France, Flanders, Holland, and England—women had an equal chance of finding work because of the demand for milkmaids. Farther south, men took precedence at hiring time, even though it was cheaper to hire females. During hard times, it was women who trudged from place to place in search of hearth-tending or scullery, buttery, or laundry work and who risked lives and reputations tramping about unknown roads and farmsteads. In exchange for labor, hirelings expected earnest money, called "God's penny," and guarantee of room, board, and uniforms, which were sewn at the manor. (Hufton 1998, 77) Maid's wear had to be simply cut, unadorned garments and caps from plain fabrics. Skirts hung straight, without ruffles or the lift of a farthingale, a bird-cage underskirt intended for well-born ladies.

For those Europeans operating manors with a full staff, Sieur Audiger, steward for the Countess of Soissons and later to Jean-Baptiste Colbert, France's minister of finance, published a knowledgeable study of household staffing entitled *Le Maison Reglée* (The Well-Ordered Residence, 1692), subtitled, "The Art of Governing a Nobleman's House and Other Gentlemen's Town and Country residences, and the Duties of Senior Staff and Domestics in General." Another handbook on the duties of house staff, *The Compleat Serving Maid*, appeared in 1677 with additions to former positions. The period had added nursery staff, under cooks, and chamber and laundry maids, all sources of employment for the underclass. Wages were usually distributed annually or sometimes twice or four times a year. For the poorest, whom employers rescued from begging on the street, receipt of livery, bed, and board were enough remuneration.

In British colonies in the Virgin Islands, servants were a necessity to the decorous West Indian kitchen and table. Planters entertained with rum swizzle, which the butler soured. Additional help fried fritters and fish, sliced salad greens and fruit, and spit-roasted meats while yams, eddoes, and sweet potatoes roasted over hot coals. After the staff served tea, coffee, and brandy to the gentlemen, they felt entitled to pies, coocoo, whole chickens, and anything else left in the kitchen, which the butler dispensed evenly to all.

By the 1700s, better employment situations existed for many kitchen workers who served the elite. In 1758, the Scottish architect Robert Adams designed much of Kedleston Hall, Derbyshire, a handsome Georgian residence featuring a spacious, well-lighted kitchen with ample storage and roasting screen. At the far end of the room, a dining nook offered private space for servants to eat together in comfort. The high-backed settles on opposite sides of the table protected them from drafts. One item, the silver or glass butler ball, provided the butler with a view of the family at meals without interrupting them. The discreet observer could look from the door to the gazing ball on mantle or sideboard. Like a fish-eye lens, the surface mirrored the entire room. In general, male servants prospered over females, who remained suspect and bound by prudish rules concerning comportment, dress, companions, and amusements during free time. According to Anthony Rowley, author of *The Book of Kitchens* (1999), masters feared that women padded accounts to add to their income. Gender discrimination forced female cooks to assume less demanding work at the grill or stew pot rather than the glory jobs of roasting, pastry-making, and carving at table.

For the ornate banquet, the wealthy treated their servants as part of the display. Just as Roman magnates bought slaves from the market in matched pairs, Europeans dressed up the most attractive wait staff and stewards in garments that complemented the room decor, epergnes of flowers, and table settings. In less sumptuous surroundings, the servants of smallholders were frequently lonely and isolated. Daily pressures and unusual periods of stress often caused sniping among staff or caused the young and inexperienced to flee in vain hope of coming upon a better position. Those who returned in shame to plead for their old jobs received punishments varying from a brief cuffing to a thorough caning.

To smooth the way with employers, books were available for the literate servant. In 1743, *A Present for a Serving-Maid* discussed not only recipes, but the problem of behavior in desperate circumstances, especially the chaste pot girl seduced by the master or his sons or guests. Menon's *La Nouvelle Cuisinière Bourgeoise* (The New Middle-Class Cook, 1746) suggests ways of recycling food, using time- and effort-saving implements, and varying table arrangements to display creativity and dedication. To establish authenticity, Elizabeth Raffald, author of *The Experienced English Housekeeper, for the Use and Ease of Ladies, Housekeepers, Cooks, &c.* (1769), subtitled her work "written purely from practice; dedicated to the Honourable Lady Elizabeth Warburton, whom the author lately served as housekeeper: Consisting of near nine hundred original receipts, most of which never appeared in print." As a tutorial and desk reference for the uncertain domestic worker, compendia such as William Augustus Henderson's *The Housekeeper's Instructor; or, Universal Family Cook* (1794) filled in details on cookery, confectionary, pickling, preserving, making and keeping wines, brewing malt liquor, table setting, and carving, the most public test of the professional food worker.

Women acquired a majority of kitchen positions in the 1800s, thus compensating for the gender inequities of the past. However, class distinctions perpetuated separation between gentry and servants into the 1900s. A tax on liveried male servants went into effect in 1853 at the rate of twenty-one shillings yearly for men and ten shillings and sixpence for youths. To escape high taxation, householders began employing more female domestics, who made up 12.8 percent of England's women workers by 1871. Within a decade, 1.25 million women found employment in other people's homes. Despite the liabilities of their trade, poor female kitchen workers were glad to secure bed and board among the wealthy.

The day's chores for a maid-of-all-work involved emptying slops, scrubbing lamps and chimneys, removing wax from candlesticks, changing linen and making beds, blacking firedogs and collecting ashes, laying fires on hearths, polishing brass and silver, shaking rugs, cooking, serving meals, washing dishes, and answering the bell summons. Her day stretched from 6:00 a.m. to 11 p.m. or later, depending on the extent of home entertaining. Payment of five to ten pounds annually with Sundays and one evening free and two weeks of vacation was typical compensation for a young woman who single-handedly ran an entire household. Even if she worked for a kind family, she endangered herself from falls, burns, exhaustion, and physical strain exacerbated by homes that relegated the kitchen to the basement.

For the servant attending a family of aristocrats, life among a staff of hundreds mimicked a small village like Erddig (or Erthig) Hall, estate of the Yorke family built in northern Wales by Joshua Edisbury, sheriff of Denbighshire, in the 1680s. It maintained a below-stairs housekeeper's room, agent's office, servants' hall, and butler's pantry plus walled garden, laundry, bakehouse, stables, tackroom, sawmills, smithy, and carpentry shop. At Alnwick Castle, the 1867 festivities marking Lord Warkworth's coming of age welcomed all 1,650 tenants and marshalled a staff of 160 waiters to plate salmon, turbot, sole, beef, venison, mutton, chicken, ham, lamb, veal, jelly, pie, tart, pastry, creams, cake, nougat, meringue, baba, and pudding. The main menu had 435 meat and 260 fish dishes, 226 fowl, and 712 desserts. Manorial specialization assigned individual staff members to manage only one aspect of kitchen work, whether the wine cellar, kitchen garden, or silver. Over all, the housekeeper or butler set the tone of attention to duty, propriety, and virtual invisibility to their masters.

In the American South, slave kitchen help and wait staff maintained standards reflecting the lifestyles of European residences. For the table staff, daily use of earthenware or brass lamp bases and glass chimneys and chandeliers kept them busy cleaning, filling, and wick trimming. The messy job took time and care to keep oil from spilling and creating a fire hazard, one of the main causes of destruction in antebellum plantation houses. Constant surveillance by the *major domo* or mistress halted pilfering of foodstuffs, clothing, silver, and spirits, all of which were saleable items for cash.

Whether paid, apprenticed, or indentured, kitchen workers toiled at heavy, sometimes debilitating tasks before technology made domestic work less demanding. For around seventeen pounds, a householder could indenture an immigrant worker by placing him or her under contract for a set time limit. Bound by law to work out the investor's outlay for passage, board, clothing, and training, the indentured servant was not bred like livestock and had the hope of freedom at the end of the term. However, like slaves, survival was limited to those who avoided accidents, strain, disease, despair, and crippling or capital punishment for disobedience or running away.

In Russia, the elegant manor and country house operated on a complement of serfs. Living like grandees at Titovo, the elite Miliutin family had so many specialists—carpenters, bakers, orchardists, woodcutters, smiths, linen weavers, pastry chef, and chandlers—that they claimed they couldn't count them all. Such staffing was necessary to accommodate huge house parties, such as men and their wives and children who assembled for hunting to hounds. Prince Peter Kropotkin described the population of his Moscow home as fifty servants for up to twelve family members. The number of staff rose by 50 percent at their country house, where the masters had three cooks and the servants two. He added, "There were an abundance of servants in the room, so that a man with a platter stood behind every chair when dinner was served." (Roosevelt 1995, 179)

Elena Burman Molokhovets, who published her classic Russian cookbook, *A Gift to Young Housewives* (1861), in the year that serfs gained their freedom, addressed the problem of depending on uneducated kitchen servants to measure precisely and plan menus. To protect silver and china from pilferage, she suggested that the mistress store valuables in a locked buffet and carry the key on her person at all times. For the security of the cold cellar, she advocated constant monitoring of bottled and cached foodstuffs. To nourish most of kitchen staff, she advised young housekeepers to feed them leftovers, middle grade flour, and poultry fat poured over their *kasha* (hot cereal). Molokhovets invited workers for daily prayer, but seemed not to worry about spreading typhoid or tuberculosis in a damp room, for she bedded them in the kitchen in niches on the Russian version of murphy beds. The only other amenities were a peg for a towel and a rack for dress and apron. For houses or apartments too small for such cook's quarters, Molokhovets designed a tabletop to fit over a servant's bed.

Nineteenth-century New Englanders brought a return of culinary control to female heads of household rather than to hired cooks. In the Massachusetts author Mary Tyler Peabody Mann's *Christianity in the Kitchen: A Physiological Cook Book* (1857), she establishes in the preface that ladies of the house should supervise the baking of bread, the heart of home cookery. In addition to rejecting substandard goods, they should also knead their own dough and bake it without leaving it in the hands of unscientific domestics.

Catharine E. Beecher and Harriet Beecher Stowe's *The American Woman's Home, or Principles of Domestic Science* (1869) undermines the belief of the rich that they have a right to be served. The duo charge that privileged children "grow up with the feeling that servants are to work for them, and they themselves are not to work." (Beecher and Stowe 1994, 22) Insidious to moneyed women is the equating of ladyhood with idleness. The Beecher sisters conclude that their book must reveal the falsehood of a pervasive expectation that the servant class should perform all labor, leaving the privileged to amuse themselves at the expense of a downtrodden underclass.

The situation in the United States contrasted that of most of Europe and inhibited formation of a servant class. As plumbing and improved sources of kitchen fuel removed men from domestic chores, women found themselves increasingly alone and unaided. A Norwegian immigrant remarked that reports of a life of ease in America failed to describe the overworked housewife, who did all the chores that a European staff of maid, housekeeper, and cook would perform. In the breach created by a lack of servants, farm girls, who wearied of limited opportunity and boredom, often sought positions in comfortable homes. They immediately felt as overworked and haggard as they had at home under the supervision of demanding parents. The concept of democracy countered loyalty to employers' families, causing girls to reject wearing maid's uniforms and to refuse to obey a call bell or answer to their first names. Many looked elsewhere for more dignified, egalitarian positions as unskilled laborers. Some moved from domestic work onto factory lines to gain control of their evenings, weekends, and holidays and to restore their self-esteem.

During settlement of the American West, military outposts hired company wives as cooks and laundresses. In a letter written in spring 1867 and collected in Alice Kirk Grierson's *The Colonel's Lady on the Western Frontier* (1989), she notes the salaries of washwomen, who could earn thirty to forty dollars a month while their low-ranking husbands received only sixteen dollars. The accommodations for their families were hovels, dugouts, sod houses, lean-tos, or tents. More deleterious to their contentment was the snobbery of the caste-conscious military society. On departure of a cavalry company, Captain Byrne "told the men to put their trunks in one of the wagons and told the [laundresses] to walk on until they were out of sight of the Fort, and then they might ride." (Grierson 1989, 17)

Throughout Europe and the Americas, the Gilded Age continued the time-honored system of rich seeking service from the illiterate or semi-literate poor. In Greece, fine ladies avoided kitchen work as demeaning. For staff, they hired the home cooks eager to escape poverty in Egypt or on the islands of Andros, Naxos, and Skyros. Most of them apprenticed in childhood under female relatives who guarded kitchen secrets as though they constituted a dowry.

Kitchen staff in urban North America were standard additions to middle-class and aristocratic households. From the early nineteenth century, 20 percent of New York householders employed servants. As a result of the Irish Potato Famine, so many Irish arrived in Boston and New York and spread to Philadelphia and around the Great Lakes that maids, kitchen girls, and nannies earned the generic names Bridget, Bridey, or Biddy. Their introduction to polite kitchens was sometimes rough because of their agrarian backgrounds in stacked peat cottages where pigs rooted about dirt floors and chickens roosted in the rafters overhead.

For the average family, after World War I, European servant systems declined with the rise in kitchen technology and water, lighting, and heating systems, which made ewer hauling, lantern washing, and ash removal obsolete. Working-class people who had previously supplied domestic and kitchen staff found jobs in manufacturing and business. Remaining staff were subject less to the former chilly relationship between servant and employer because of the danger of offending staff and causing them to quit.

Before the Civil Rights movement freed blacks from domestic enslavement, black cooks elevated African-American cuisine to the patrician tables of the East Coast. White homeowners took credit for elaborate buffets of cheese grits, black-eyed pea salad, spoonbread, and angel biscuits, all of which came from the plantation background of their kitchen staff. Outside the protections of the unionized Northeast, the maids-of-all-work in the American South accepted regular employment as cooks and baby-sitters during periods of hardship when black men found no jobs. During the Great Depression, black domestic workers clustered on street corners hoping for employment as cooks and washerwomen and willing to work without job security

for small daily wages plus a free meal. The three dollars-a-week and car fare of the mid-1930s were less help than the weekly dole of leftovers, on which black children fed during hard times

Late in the twentieth century, when life for South African domestic workers held unfair burdens for 1.3 million poorly paid black servants in white households, Florence De Villiers set out to improve their lot. Having quit school at age fifteen to hire out as cook and maid, she came of age during the anti-Apartheid crusade. She mobilized a 28,000 member women's labor force called the South African Domestic Workers' Union (SADWU), a union that settled grievances, held counsels, and promoted social services and literacy. Still fighting for housing and minimum wage in 1996, she continued to work toward freeing kitchen workers from long hours and low pay.

See also **Banquets; Etiquette; Slavery**

Further Reading

Degler, Carl. *At Odds: Women and the Family in America from the Revolution to the Present.* New York: Oxford University Press, 1980.

Furnivall, Frederick J., ed. *Early English Meals and Manners: John Russell's Boke of Nurture.* London: Kegan Paul, Trench, Trübner & Co., Ltd., 1868.

Girouard, Mark. *Life in the English Country House: A Social and Architectural History.* New Haven, Conn.: Yale University Press, 1978.

Roosevelt, Priscilla. *Life on the Russian Country Estate.* Hartford, Conn.: Yale University Press, 1995.

Sambrook, Pamela A., and Peter Brears. *The Country House Kitchen, 1650–1900.* London: Sutton Publishing, 1996.

Waterson, Merlin. *The Servants' Hall.* New York: Pantheon Books, 1980.

SERVICE À LA FRANCAISE VS. SERVICE À LA RUSSE

Before the Napoleonic era (1799–1815), European cooks and servers had followed a medieval system of self-service from a selection of dishes displayed in a style known as *service à la francaise* (French-style dining). In the kitchen, cooks assisted the wait staff in ordering dishes by laying out empty vessels and platters in the pattern they would arrive at the table. Roasts came from the kitchen largely ungarnished or encircled with kidneys and sweetbreads, artichokes, hard-boiled eggs, grapes, barberries, or dried fruit, as described in Thomas Dawson's *Good Huswife's Jewell* (1596). Stews arrived on a layer of bread cubes called sippets or sops to enable servers to scoop up pieces engorged with juices. (Wilson 1991, 91) Leading the way in the seventeenth century was the grand salad, a processional showpiece comprised of lemons impaled on rosemary stems topped with cherries atop a bed of shredded greens bordered with egg quarters, capers, and lemon slices. The showy plate evolved into an artful arrangement of shellfish, eggs, pickles, and anchovies called *salmigondis*, a food miscellany that the English rendered as salmagundi or Solomon Gundy. (Ibid., 92)

Randle Holme's *Academy of Armoury* (1688), an inventory for Ham House in Chester, described the addition of the dish ring, an ornate footed stand that elevated platters and bowls to add nobility to their placement. Pictured in *Royal Cookery; or The Complete Court-Cook* (1710) by Patrick Lamb—long-lived head chef to Charles II, James II, William and Mary, and Queen Anne—tables for weddings, royal feasts, state dinners, and coronations ranged upward to 114 dishes and 83 *hors d'oeuvres* set precisely according to protocol. An array of dishes for thirty-eight diners required twenty-four *hors d'oeuvres* and forty-three main dishes. The wait staff spread the table with a *surtout* (centerpiece or epergne), a central station of salt and pepper, vinegar and oil, and lemons.

An alternate, a *dormant,* crafted in faience, porcelain, or silver, was a sizeable dish or socle that supported a focal platter, which typically held a whole fish, bird, or haunch of meat and a moat of gravy or sauce. In *Das Menü* (The Menu, 1888), the table scientist Ernst von Malortie, chamberlain to the royal court of Hanover, explained that around these hubs, cooks supplied dishes in exact multiples of twelve. Symmetrically arranged, these consisted of a visual display of one hundred or more dishes, tureens, and eye-catching containers designed to display ingredients and serving implements for particular entrées, soup, rôtis, and relevés, for example, asparagus trays, mustard pots, and shellfish platters.

According to individual rank or prestige, diners at Baroque and rococo feasts helped themselves to servings or asked assistance from waiters, who presented sips of wine in glasses held on trays and removed for refilling. If the waiter removed one dish, an *assiette volante* (flying dish) took its place to preserve a visual and culinary balance. For tidbits that other diners lacked, guests sometimes passed morsels to share the bounty. When the guest of honor or royal host had finished, staff removed the food, regardless of the progress of other diners through their servings.

The faults of *service à la francaise* were primarily logistical. Contributing to cold food were the long distances that separated cook and plating staff from table. These drafty promenades required an army of waiters, who handled each container once it was potted, pitchered, or arranged on a dish. Because of the vastness of the menu, ample leftovers went back to the kitchen for redistribution via a precise pecking order—lesser officials, house staff, servants, and beggars.

Service à la russe, the Russian-style system sometimes called *service à l'allemand* (the German table service), debuted in France in June 1810 at Clichy. The innovation of Russian ambassador Prince Borisovitch Kourakine (or Kourakin), it quickly shifted thinking about the best way to move cooked food to plates. As described by the food historian Joyce Toomre in the introduction to *Classic Russian Cooking* (1992), "Instead of placing whole roasts on the table as formerly, meats were now carved at a sideboard and divided into individual portions before being served to the guests; also the dishes and cutlery were cleared by servants after each course and replaced with clean ones." (Molokhovets 1992, 29) Popularized by Félix Urbain Dubois, the head cook of the Russian Prince Orloff, in 1860, the Russian method rapidly reduced the separation between cook and diner.

Under this simplified table service, guests took their seats at a table decorated with candles, vases of silk flowers, mirrored trays of fruit and attractive sweetmeats, and crystal ornaments, but no substantial food. After the presentation of trays of *hors d'oeuvres* (appetizers or starters), main courses of food arrived sequentially in a set order already sliced, plated, sauced, and garnished. Staff sometimes paraded a particularly picturesque fish or joint of meat before guests before carting it back to the kitchen for carving and plating. The absence of the geometric arrangement of dishes gave place to an artistic *surtout* introduced in 1810 by the metalsmith Pierre-Philippe Thomire, the creator of neoclassic extravaganzas that could be broken down, rearranged, and augmented for large banquets.

In restaurants serving *à la russe,* the end of dramatic presentation allowed cooks to prepare smaller cuts of meat at high heat *à la minute* (in a shorter period of time). This shift in cooking style lessened waste of food prepared to be admired rather than eaten. Each meal began with a printed or calligraphied menu that described in words what guests would receive. The service of an identical plate to each diner was an outgrowth of the French Revolution. It was the service waiter's responsibility to alert the kitchen staff to prepare the next course. The busboy patroled the dining room, refilling water glasses and bread baskets and removing soiled dishes. Some of the flamboyant cooks of this *belle epoch* lent their names to famous *à la russe* dishes, for example, Adolphe Dugléré, the chef of Café Anglais in Paris in the 1850s, the creator of sole Dugléré.

By the end of World War I, *service à la francaise* had virtually disappeared. Charles Ranhofer, the former head cook of Delmonico's, a revered New York restaurant, explained that restaurants and households employed far fewer staff than in previous times. Young homemakers disdained the pretense of showy table service and preferred intimate dining among friends. A handbook, John Henry Walsh's *A Manual of Domestic Economy* (1879), explained with numbered diagrams the setup for a dinner table for eighteen. Amid an array of place settings, a vase of flowers flanked by four china shells marked the center of service. To left and right, paired candelabra and troughs of cut flowers extended decoration. Around the troughs, glass dishes containing fruits, water carafes on velvet stands, and cruets completed the display at the beginning of a *dîner à la russe*. Such a reduction in finery and food for show enabled Victorian families to entertain on a limited budget.

See also **Glass; Precious Metals; Restaurant Kitchens**

Further Reading

Blake, Anthony, and Quentin Crewe. *The Great Chefs of France*. London: Marshall Editions, Ltd., 1978.

SHAKER KITCHENS

A conservative religious sect as well as economic pioneers, the Shakers of United Society of Believers in Christ's Second Appearing, who set up their Mount Lebanon, New York, commune in 1787, lived by benign socialistic principles of thrift, industry, temperance, and liberality. They spread from Maine to New Hampshire, Massachusetts, Connecticut, and New York to Ohio, Indiana, Kentucky, Georgia, and Florida, and resided in spare barracks or rooming houses separated by gender. From biblical example and authority, they assigned to women cooking, cleaning, laundry, and fiberwork.

Communal kitchens serving eighty to one hundred members were models of efficiency and order serving a breakfast of apple and mince pies, bacon and eggs, and home fries. Workers rotated duties to relieve tedium and unfair allotment of hard jobs, which Shakers avoided with clever home and farm design. Aqueducts piped water to sinks. Two- and three-step stools, like the one in the waiting or gathering room at Hancock Shaker Village, founded in 1790, enabled residents to keep belongings in order and to reach foods stored in communal pantries. Seamstresses turned out tow and linen bags for kitchen use as well as unadorned work dresses, caps, and aprons. Kitchen workers superintended dairying, herb drying, and cheese making and filled barrels with pickles, ketchup, berry and apple wines, maple syrup, vinegar, cider, apple butter, and applesauce.

At the Niskeyuna commune, wood strips around the walls held pegs for suspending enormous pots and pans, strainers, and implements. Two of the innovations of the bakery were a hinged loaf slicer and a revolving oven invented by Emeline Hart. An institutional-size cookstove sat on a fireproof pad at the center of the room. Under the stove pipe that attached to one wall, a slender metal bar held dish towels for drying.

The work table occupied a wall beneath a window that admitted natural light for pressing maple sugar cakes, slicing fruit for preserve or jelly, shelling nuts, chopping vegetables for pickles, and blending sauces. One recipe suggested cutting a sheaf of peach twigs at high sap and splaying the ends for beating cake batter. The use of fruit twig whisks in February imparted fruit flavor to the cake. A three-shelved pie safe with ventilated tin front held pastries and breads turned out weekly. Its doors kept out mice; holes allowed circulation of air to prevent mold. For meals, the kitchen staff produced huge platters of food for their refectory and served the men and women at separate trestle or harvest tables. Their work day ended at 8:00 p.m., an hour before mandatory bedtime.

The ingenious Shakers were inventors and manufacturers of useful, labor-saving kitchen and farm implements. The list of their inventions paralleled the growth of the sect and included, among many others: thresher, steel candlestick, broom corn sorter, seed stripper, vacuum pan for drying herbs, corn preserver and drier, sarsaparilla lozenges, corn cutter, revolving oven and apple parer, corer, and quarterer. Other inventions included butter workers, whip handles, stove wood splitter, pea sheller, dumb waiters, cream separator, dough kneader, powder churn, and dairy tram. Of the quality of their practical devices, one commentator noted, "The forged iron of their metal parts is shaped like fine wood, and the rock maple or oak of their frames is put together like furniture. In true Shaker fashion, there is no ornamentation, but no edge is left unfinished and even minor parts are turned and polished." (Andrews & Andrews 1974, 159)

Another lucrative product distributed in 1810 from the New Lebanon colony was the hair sieve, which Shaker weavers turned into an attractive kitchen appointment by forming a plaid of interwoven wires or white and black hair from cows' tails and horses's manes. They molded the mat at a shaping stool and clamped it with an iron rim. After stitching the edge of the mat into place, the maker attached it permanently with nested hoops and finishing nails. Shakers also marketed the brass wire riddle or crible, a utilitarian barn sieve with large holes for separating wheat and seeds from chaff. A double covered model held seeds or herbs in a frame while the user shook it. An example of practical design was the splint winnower, a half circle of hickory the width of an adult's arm span and fitted with handles along the circular edge of the frame. After users shucked peas or kernels, they held the winnower by its handles and thumped the bottom with their knees to lift pods and chaff from the heavy grains. Shaker basket makers also made rush and reed trays, and containers of various size.

Shakers were the first to raise broom corn for manufacturing brooms and invented a brush vise for making scrub brushes, the chief industry of the Canaan commune. Historians credit Theodore Bates of the Watervliet commune with inventing the flat broom in 1798. Sect manufacturers shaped the brooms on a wheel operated by a treadle. Tidy Shakers covered their brooms with cotton hoods and hung them on the wall from garden rake-head peg strips when not in use or used the covered end for dry polishing a floor to revive a wax sheen. In addition, they manufactured tow, cotton, and wool floor mops in the 1840s. Homemakers came to trust the Shaker name on products for quality and value. By 1820, the Pleasant Hill Shaker community in Kentucky was self-sufficient, producing more than enough food for its five hundred residents.

Shakers pioneered a number of kitchen, laundry, and gardening ideas. The most notable is the sale of paper envelopes of onion, radish, beet, carrot, parsnip, cabbage, lettuce, herbs, corn, tomato, cucumber, and squash seeds, which they first marketed in New Lebanon, Ohio, in 1795. In a decade, the commune was the sect's chief income producer. Within a quarter century of seed sales, they marketed over 37,000 pounds worth $33,901. Until the 1830s, they marketed medicinal herbs and most of America's opium, which they extracted from poppies grown in home gardens. Shakers created or refined numerous kitchen tools, including the apple peeler and corer, which they wielded at fall paring bees. For the annual store of dried apples for making sauce, apple butter, and pie, the commune built a two-story drying shed. Heat from the ground-floor stove rose to fruit bins on the upper level. Nearby barrels held dried fruit, which could be scooped into mixing bowls for further preparation.

When cooking down slurry for apple butter, the cautious Shaker cook stayed clear of the hot, sticky liquid by using a wooden scoop with a slotted handle. The pierced end kept the thick sauce from scorching and sticking to copper vats during slow cooking. The scoop transferred it to bowls for tasting. A paddle-headed stirrer between five and nine feet long and pierced with slots distributed cinnamon and sugar and

kept puddles from forming. For their ample iron-banded apple butter buckets, carpenters shaped the inner lid to fit the rim. A flanged edge kept out air and contaminants.

For cider, the Shaker cider maker layered pulp, called pomace, onto straw atop a slotted rack, releasing a tart, fruity aroma. Force from a hand press separated the pulp into two products: thick pomace oozed from the side of the stack as the juice dripped into a catch basin below. By cutting down the ooze from the side, the worker could return the pomace to the stack, add more straw and fresh apples, and begin the process anew. Multiple squeezings made the most of the fruit, which was funneled into a barrel for fermentation. Low quality juice supplied vinegar for pickling and marinade. A more sophisticated press doubled the product per bushel by altering the method. A power press held racks layered with muslin bags of fruit stacked up to twelve high. Application of pressure ended the ooze of pomace and assured the most juice per bushel. The cider maker readied the juice by sealing barrel heads and stopping bungholes with a twist of straw, which swelled with seepage to a tight fit.

The Shaker blacksmith turned out useful kitchen implements. Tinsmiths manufactured measuring cups, watering cans, funnels, scoops and cups, match safes, needle cases, boxes, pans and baking tins, oil cans, and dust pans. The creation of the cup swab exemplifies the Shaker ingenuity at reusing and recycling. A twist of wire around cotton fibers, leftover fringe, or wool yarn thrum (loom waste) produced the fiber column, a cunning dishwashing implement for getting into tight corners and cylinders. Colony innovators made wood bowls to which they tacked copper handles. Their most useful invention was the icehouse, an insulated box padded with straw and sawdust for preserving great blocks of ice. The idea evolved into a miniature icebox for kitchen use.

Further Reading

Abram, Norm, and David Sloan. *Mostly Shaker*. Boston: Little, Brown & Co., 1992.

Andrews, Edward Deming. *The People Called Shakers: A Search for the Perfect Society*. New York: Oxford University Press, 1953.

_____, and Faith Andrews. *Work and Worship: The Economic Order of the Shakers*. Greenwich, Conn.: New York Graphic Society, 1974.

Reeman, Timothy D., and Jean M. Burks. *The Complete Book of Shaker Furniture*. New York: Harry N. Abrams Inc., 1993.

Wolkomir, Joyce, and Richard Wolkomir, "Living a Tradition," *Smithsonian*, April 2001, 98–108.

SIEVES AND STRAINERS

Earthenware strainer.

Straining lobster stock.

Sieving and straining require containers perforated with holes or woven or meshed to allow liquids to escape. In a tomb of the Harappans of the Indus Valley civilization, which flourished from 2600 to 1900 BCE, a tall cylindrical clay strainer featuring holes nearly to the top may have been a tool for beer brewers. Some Egyptian containers of the later dynasties featured sieves, for example, teapots with internal strainers. Homer explains the Cyclopes' preparation of sheep milk in *The Odyssey* (ca. 850 BCE) as a thickening into curds and whey and a straining through withy baskets, dividing curds for making cheese from watery residue, which the one-eyed giant Polyphemus drinks for supper.

In Roman households, the cook teamed horsehair sieves with the quern, the grinding stones used in homes for milling small batches of flour. For producing *vino cotto* (condensed wine), a favorite of Apicius, author of *De Re Coquinaria* (On Cooking, late 300s CE), the world's oldest cookbook, cooks passed grape must through a sieve, then reduced the liquid to the consistency of molasses for use as a sweetener. The Chinese invented a conical tapered mesh strainer that drained broth from soup solids. An adjunct to the wok, the long-handled meshed ladle removed foods from hot oil and submerged stuffed chicken for deep frying.

For native Americans, an acorn-centered diet required lengthy rinsing to remove bitter tannins from the nut. To improve taste, the Pomo and Hupa poured nut meats into leaching pits, which functioned like natural sieves in the sand. The Salinan of south-central California required basket sieves for leaching acorns before pounding them into meal for cakes. Katherine Vigil, a Tesuque artisan from New Mexico, replicated these traditional sifter baskets in the 1940s.

In the Middle Ages, Europeans created simple bolters or sieves from woven splints or goat or calf skin pierced with holes. The bolter, pulled taut through auger holes or slits in the frame, separated rice kernels after the harvester beat them from the stalk with a hinged wood flail. The latter sieves were crude and short-lived because the leather did not hold up under constant wetting and drying. Another style, the *rastel* or *rastelrier*, had a handle to protect the user from hot liquids pouring from the bottom. According to the wordsmith John of Garland's *Dictionary* (1220), sieving was a servant's work. Country women wove their own sieves from clean grass or chaff, which clarified pan drippings for gravy. Recycled, the fibrous strainer went into the henyard to shine up feathers from oily residue.

In Ireland, as described in the domestic historian Olive Sharkey's *Old Days, Old Ways* (1985), agrarian families relied on boiled potatoes as a menu staple. Cooks strained off the water through wickerwork sieves called skibs and carried the potatoes to the table in the basket for diners to select and peel their own. One accounting of this cyclical draining and serving concluded that a family of six could eat 252 pounds of potatoes a week. For sowans, an oat drink favored by haymakers, cooks soaked husks and whole grain in clay pots for a week, then strained the beverage through a rush mat to remove chaff.

A development of the medieval period was a hair sieve that the Gauls called a tammie (also *tamis* or tammy), a soup or stock strainer woven from the mane and tail hair from horses and cows. Before the hair was usable, the sieve maker straightened it in a hatchel, a device formed of parallel platforms connected by screws that cranked the hair into a tight fit. The tamed hair fit into a pair of wooden hoops or into a small loom for weaving into a mat. The finished sieve was useful for draining wet foods, rubbing sauces and purées through the weave, and sifting or winnowing flour. Later models of the tammy featured a linen, cotton, or crash cloth fitted to two handles with metal rings.

The fine-gauge silk, black gauze, or wire sieve improved on the hair mat. The silk sieve aided the doctor or home healer as a sifter of herbal powder. A variant flour sifter was the boultel, bolter, or boulter, a fabric bag filled with flour or powdered sugar and tied at the neck for shaking over flour boards or distributing sugar evenly over cake. In the time of Henry VIII, John Partridge's *The Treasurie of Commodious Conceits and Hidden Secrets* (1584) described the sieving of ingredients for hippocras, a spiced red wine, through a bolter cloth when the beverage was bottled. Such straining cloths were versatile. For crisping salad greens, the humanist John Evelyn's *Acetaria: A Discourse of Sallets* (1699) advised draining wet leaves in a "cullender," then tying in a clean napkin and swinging the lot over the head to remove moisture. (*The Williamsburg Cookbook* 1971, 86)

For general kitchen use, the footed colander, made of aluminum, clay, graniteware, steel mesh, or tin, traditionally served utilitarian needs to separate liquid from solids. The cribble, derived from the Latin *cribum* (sieve), was a variation for sifting flour, sugar, or corn meal. The coarse residue left behind, called cribble meal or shorts, suited the makers of bran muffins and whole wheat bread. An uncomplicated jelly strainer involved the creation of a four-sided wood frame to hold a cloth in place over a container to catch drippings. Among Greek fishermen, the preparation of *kakavia* (fish stew) began with selection of the smallest

fry in a coarse seine. Recipes varied as to the types of fish to pulp through a strainer, along with lobsters, shrimps, and slices of bigger fish.

Colonial American housekeepers used a wooden tallow strainer with a tin head for readying melted tallow for candle making. For sugaring, workers poured maple sap through wool cloth strainers for successive removal of scum and wood fibers. Bakers settled a sieve onto a stick, called a temse or templet, which fitted into the top of a four-sided bread trough or bread tray for screening out coarse bits of grain or bran. Other wooden implements completed the job—a flour shell or scoop for parceling out flour into the sieve and a bread paddle for stirring in liquid. The job of readying dough for the oven concluded with chopping dough into loaves with a wooden blade.

In 1801, the domestic writer Ruth Gibbs Whitehorne's *Sugar House Book*, compiled in Newport, Rhode Island, advised the home cook on how to reduce one hundred tomatoes into bottled ketchup. The wife of Samuel Whitehorne, one of the Atlantic seaboard's merchant princes, she was remarkably conversant with the messy job of squeezing tomatoes to a pulp, salting and boiling them, then pressing the hot mass through a fine sieve with a silver spoon to guard against metallic off-flavors. The lengthy job of removing skins, adding spices and pepper, and boiling the mix down to a suitable table condiment produced only four or five bottles, which kept for up to three years.

During the flurry of theorizing and improvising methods of reducing food to their nutritional elements, manufacturers of beef tea and writers of home recipes required sieves for extracting protein from meat. After the biochemist Justus von Liebig began experimenting with the manufacture of essence of beef, he published instructions on sieving stew for invalid soup in *Familiar Letters on Chemistry* (1843). The concept influenced the cookery of the London chef Alexis Soyer, author of *Soyer's Charitable Cookery, or The Poor Man's Regenerator* (1838) and *Soyer's Culinary Campaign, with the Plain Art of Cookery for Military and Civil Institutions* (1857), who applied the method to feeding the starving of the Irish Potato Famine and soldiers during the Crimean War. He advised readers on dicing beef for stewing, then defatting and straining the solids through a sieve rather than a cloth, which ruined the flavor.

A surprisingly practical cook for her elevated social level, Elena Burman Molokhovets, the author of the classic Russian cookbook, *A Gift to Young Housewives* (1861), suggested upending a kitchen stool and tying a towel or napkin to the legs to create an impromptu device to strain large quantities into a vessel below. For clear *bouillon*, she advised straining once, then lining the cloth with blotting paper for a second pouring. The same method aided the pouring of boiling water through rose petals to make rose syrup, an aromatic flavoring for baking. She also approved the standard flat drum sieve of horsehair or wire, which she lined with blotting paper for draining such specialties as deep-fried pastry straws. For baking an English wedding cake, she suggested cutting the mesh from the sieve and using the rim as a cake mold.

Sieving was a standard stage of culinary procedures for making smooth sauces or liquids. The English food retailer Agnes B. Marshall, author of *Ices Plain and Fancy: The Book of Ices* (1885), was happy to relieve the cook of dependence on horsehair sieves and tammies for reducing the bases of ice cream and sorbet to a pulp. She described the tedious job of puréeing in a food mill, but also advertised for sale her own tammy cloth, superfine felt jelly bags, and horsehair sieves. She recommended the finest strainer for cooling thickened custard and for removing lumps.

The use of sieves and strainers accompanied a number of meticulous recipes, such as the French *soufflé de chou-fleur* (cauliflower soufflé), for which the cook passed boiled cauliflower through a sieve, and *purée d'endive*, an identical process of reducing a solid mass of endive to a pulp. Around 1860, the French chef Fèlix Urbain-Dubois's *La Pâtisserie d'Aujourd'hui* (The Pastry Shop Today) featured the colander-strainer in a new role, upside down to hold skewered glazed oranges as they dried. In Italy, the sieving of chestnut flour preceded the making of a boiled polenta, which cooks either served in slices, grilled, or fried. The *blanchet*, a white wool cloth filter, strained thick, viscous syrups to remove scum and undissolved particles. In Australian kitchens, home brewers traditionally used fine cloth for straining honeyed ginger water, the basis of ginger beer. In the Middle East, homemakers strained yogurt through cloth to make *labnah* (cream cheese), which they served with olive oil and fresh flat bread.

For easy home use, the Tyler manufacturing Company of Muncie, Indiana, produced a super sieve, a cone-shaped colander on legs. It was fitted with a hardwood roller for rotating around the inner surface to force particles through the holes. As advertised in the August 1930 issue of *Good Housekeeping*, it appeared to exude soft substances through the bottom for jelly, fruit leather, apple butter, riced potatoes, and cooked vegetables for infant and invalid feedings. A forerunner of the electric food processor, it made short work of soft foods with a strong circular motion.

Bequians, a polyglot people derived from African, Arawak, English, French, Irish, Portuguese, and Scottish colonists in the Caribbean, developed fruit cheese, a sweet dessert made from guava or mango. After rubbing pulp through a sieve, they boiled down the

mix with lime juice, cut it into squares, and topped with granulated sugar. The sieve was also a needed tool for making guava jelly. Similarly, Arubans depended on strainers for filtering liquid from aloe pulp for beverages; Trinidadian cooks evolved a method of making black pudding that required straining pig's blood for boiling with hops bread and seasonings for filling casings.

The advent of hermetic canning in Finland in 1910 offered Scandinavian housewives a simplified method of preserving fruits and vegetables. To separate liquids from solids, the preparer spread cloth over a sterile canning jar and placed a sieve in the hollow. By filling the strainer with berries or sliced fruit and filling the canning pot with boiling water, the preparer generated steam that caused the juice to drip into the jar. After twenty-five minutes, the cook sealed the jars of juice and reserved the solids in the sieve for marmalade.

In 1975, chef James A. Beard and his colleagues coauthored *The Cook's Catalogue*, a compendium of recommendations on what to buy to make the most of food preparation. A host of offerings in the era bolstered the *batterie de cuisine*. The book preferred a teardrop-shaped coronet sieve with wire screen for easy handling at the kneading board, a heavy-gauge aluminum strainer seated on a metal collar rather than on feet, as well as the Farberware stainless steel model with plastic handles. Other versions included an enameled steel colander from Japan, a porcelain strainer suited to foods that should not touch metal, and a flat-bottomed aluminum spaghetti colander with long handle. Notably absent were the cheap screen-wire models that flooded the market in the late twentieth century.

At the turn of the twenty-first century, couscous makers of the Maghrib, the western half of the Islamic world, purchased both quern and *ghorbal*, a drum-shaped sieve used for straining steamed grain. The labor-intensive job began with soaking dried semolina in salt water and rolling the lumps into pellets, a method of preservation that inverted the grain, enveloping the germ in starch. By continuing the rolling in the *ghorbal*, the preparer standardizes pellets, which reduced to the desired size and dropped through the screen. Continued sifting and rolling resulted in a fine grain that passed to a *tbak* (grain basket). After two steamings over water, the grains were ready for spreading in the sun to dry.

Additional colanders and sieves suit particular household needs. Strainers shaped from wire block the sink or garbage disposer drain for vegetable washing and rinsing greens and steamed shellfish. One model has a folding handle to turn the strainer into a kettle liner to separate cooked food from residue that collects at the bottom of the pot. An unusual style, a ringed cheese strainer, is a bottomless bowl to which the user fastens muslin on pegs. Another variety of strainer, the berry bowl, is a two-part bowl matched with saucer that holds berries while rinse water flows through holes wide enough to allow passage of stems, leaves, and trash. A common item in kitchen catalogs is the colander basket, a stainless steel mesh sieve with eared handles that contains vegetables for spray-washing and rinsing, removing packing liquid from canned foods, or for draining rice or pasta.

Further Reading

Bates, Joanne, "Breakfast in the Middle East," *Aramco World*, November–December 1975, 15.

Marshall, Agnes B. *Mrs. A. B. Marshall's Cookery Book*. London: Simpton, Marshall, Hamilton, Kent, & Co., 1894.

Noakes, Greg and Laidia Chouat Noakes, "Couscous: The Measure of the Maghrib," *Aramco World*, November–December 1998, 16–23.

Tselementes, Nicholas. *Greek Cookery*. New York: D. C. Divry, Inc., 1985.

SLAUGHTERING

From the beginnings of the home and animal husbandry, slaughtering and the accompanying kitchen work has traditionally involved both agrarian and migrant families. One modern example, the semi-nomadic Khanty, herd reindeer on the Russian tundra. After the sacrificial prayer and killing of an animal with one quick blow of an ax to the cranium, they tie off arteries to stop the bleeding. The owner slices pieces from the carcass to eat raw, dipped in either blood or salt. They waste nothing, preserving bone for knife handles, curing hide in fish guts for sleigh bedding, grinding antlers for healing powder, and drying sinew for sewing thread and boot laces. From the blood, collected in buckets, they make pancakes and blood bread. Similarly thrifty, Colombian cooks save the cow's tail as the main ingredient for *sopa de cebada* (barley soup); African householders prize blood of slaughtered animals as a kitchen floor surfacing.

In ancient Greece, slaughter of cattle, oxen, sheep, and goats ended religious festivals. Red meat, which was a rarity in the home kitchen, was a ritual necessity sacrificed to please deities. After presenting thigh meat at altars, temple staff cooked the remaining parts for worshippers, with the best pieces reserved for priests. The pig, which carried a mixed reputation among Mediterranean people, did not receive the same veneration. Herodotus, the Greek traveler and historian and author of *The Persian Wars* (c. 450 BCE), recorded as an oddity the Egyptian attitude toward swine. Because Egyptians regarded pigs as unclean, even to touch, no swineherd could enter a temple or take a wife from outside the society of herders. Greek priests slaugh-

tered pigs only for worship of Dionysus and the moon deity. The temple workers then cooked the meat for immediate eating by priests so that slaughter and pork-eating took place exactly on the day of the full moon. The poor, who couldn't afford to slaughter their pigs for this ritual, shaped offerings out of dough to present to the gods.

The Ainu, Japan's aborigines, centered animistic worship on the bear and took strength and courage from its blood and meat. Similar to the philosophy of cannibals who absorbed the power of their enemies by consuming their flesh, the Ainu reared the sacramental bear from infancy. A female villager became surrogate mother and breastfed it. When it grew to full size, the devout slaughtered it and welcomed all to a banquet, at which they praised its strength as they devoured boiled meat. The celebration concluded with cups of the victim's blood and toasts to the bear's spirit.

A Roman chef, Caelius Apicius, author of *De Re Coquinaria* (On Cooking, late 300s CE), the world's oldest cookbook, improvised on the civic slaughter of sows by first fattening them for the table on dried figs and honeyed wine. He practiced a humane method of killing, by falling suddenly on the sow before it could tense its muscles in fear. Current styles of slaughtering follow this same principle to produce tender cuts of meat, especially for a Christmas meal.

Both Jews and Arabs concerned themselves with the style and method of slaughter and the purity of animals killed for food. The Talmud, a volume of discussion of Torah law derived from oral tradition, described in the section called *Tamid* (continuous offering) the appropriate method of slaughtering lambs. Similarly, Arab-style slaughtering traditionally began with a one-stroke severance of throat and jugular veins, an act requiring a sturdy hand and large knife or cleaver. Devout Muslims applied this technique to poultry, water animals, camels, sheep, oxen, and all birds except predators. The animals forbidden by the Koran, the pig and wild boar, scripture considered unfit for human consumption, as was the blood of any animal. For preparation of *Bouzellouf*, the slaughterer singed the hair from a sheep's head before boiling it and seasoned meat with garlic, vinegar, oil, pepper, and salt.

In medieval England, slaughtering not performed by a professional *margwyne* (butcher) was the job of an entire family or clan. (Hartley 1979, 293) Itinerant pigstickers often assisted cottagers by grasping and subduing live animals with spiked snout holders. The thrifty housewife had hot boiled grain ready to catch the spurting blood, which clotted nicely into a black pudding. She also took charge of sweetbreads, liver, kidneys, and soft meat for immediate use.

Workers sliced pork fat in leaves for wrapping venison roasts, collected trotters for gelatin, split umbilical cords from unborn calves for muggety pie, and soaked intestines for sausage casings and bladders as lard bags to hold fat and flead (inner pork membranes) for late season lardy cakes. A tepee of straw burned over a carcass made quick work of dehairing. For smallholders, a long pig required hanging on a church porch and scraping with a blunt objects, such as a brass candlestick, to remove bristles. The thrifty cook saved sliced skin as coverings to stretch over bottles and jars. In monasteries, where the diet was predominantly vegetables and grain varied with fish, monks escaped rules requiring abstinence from meat on a technicality. By slaughtering pregnant rabbits, they claimed to remove the tender young still *in vitro* before it had become meat.

Platina, the author of *De Honesta Voluptate et Valitudine* (On Right Pleasure and Health, 1475), made specific comment on hog slaughter. He recommended butchery of year-old pigs and explained how to deprive it of water for a day to dry the meat. For brining, he instructed the slaughterer to "put salt in the bottom of a pot or jar, then lay the pieces in with the skin down." (Platina 1999, 42) After absorbing the salt, haunches hung on a rack for smoking. The user could then cut lard at will from the belly, ham, shoulder, and loin.

One Modenese recipe for *zampone*, a stuffed pig's foot, resulted from necessity. When Pope Julius II besieged the town of Mirandola, Italy, in 1510, local people stretched their food to great lengths to forestall hunger. By slaughtering their hogs and saving every tidbit by stuffing them into the intestines, they managed to feed themselves. When they ran short of casings, they stuffed the last scraps into the front feet to make a meat dish they called *manicotti* (sleeves).

In Ireland, the local *búistéir* (slaughterer) went from farm to farm killing the barrow pig, the fattened animal that fed the family through winter. His method was to plunge a blade straight down the throat into the heart for an instant kill. The family then spread the carcass over a pig gib, a bench on which they anchored the body for scraping off hair. After the animal hung for several days, the *búistéir* returned to debone the carcass and remove the head before the owner salted the pieces in a barrel. Prosperous families sliced salt meat from flitches to share with the poor and hung the rest on rafters over the hearth for incidental smoking.

Animal slaughter went to extremes for European royalty. After Queen Jadwiga ascended the Polish throne in 1384, she and her Lithuanian husband Jagiello demanded fresh tripe, a favorite meal that the royal cook prepared with ginger, nutmeg, pepper, allspice, paprika, bay leaf, and marjoram. In 1530, at the coronation of Emperor Charles V, all Bologna enjoyed a triumphal march and a feast arranged by the city authorities. Workers killed and gutted an ox to stuff with suckling pigs, lambs, rabbits, and poultry and roast over a huge open fire. In early eighteenth-century Bologna at the annual celebration of *La Festa della Porchetta* (Feast of the Roast Pig), participants stalked wild boars, bulls, and swine through a holiday pavilion. Unlike polite banquet-goers, diners chased the animals to be captured and slain for the table. In 1716, artist Giusseppe Mazza sketched the greased-pole climb, an event that rewarded the winners with poultry and game birds.

In the New World, after settlers reached the Atlantic shores to make their homes, European-style professional meat cutting was available in Ipswich, Massachusetts, as early as 1641. According to court records in Essex County, Humphrey Griffin supplied settlers with slaughtered meat. In the South, such tasks on plantations fell to slaves trained in the task of killing animals, cutting meat for fresh cooking or preserving, and tanning the hides for home and farm use.

During the era of slavery in Brazil between the sixteenth and nineteenth centuries, when some four million West Africans and Angolans served as domestics and laborers in gold and diamond mines and sugarcane fields, landowners butchered livestock to celebrate festivals. They reserved offal—pig's innards, feet, ears, tails, and snouts—for their African slaves to add to their bean pots and to simmer savory *feijoada* from the leftover meats. Long after emancipation of Brazil's 750,000 slaves in 1888, the dish remained a national favorite. Cooked in restaurants and served over rice with red or black beans, sausage, tongue, ribs, and dried beef, sprinkled with manioc meal, and adorned with sliced oranges, *feijoada* has traveled a long way from its slaughterhouse beginnings.

Europeans were surprised at innovative native methods of slaughtering game. On February 3, 1701, when the speculator John Lawson traveled inland from the Charleston low country with five Englishmen and three native guides, he covered 550 miles in fifty-nine days over an Indian trading path which he described in a journal, *A New Voyage to Carolina* (1701). On a visit to the Enoe, his Indian hosts offered wild turkey, beaver tail, goose, and shad. Lawson commented that the Indians dressed meats "Wood-cock Fashion," that is, without gutting them.

In eighteenth-century England, the butcher set up shop daily outdoors. A heavy beam at the front of the lean-to held whole and half carcasses of beef, venison, birds, and rabbits as well as legs of mutton and gammon. Meat sellers laid each haunch on round butcher blocks on legs and chopped with large cleavers the amount the purchaser specified. Offal, tallow, and unusable scraps fell to the ground to be devoured by stray dogs. Butchers recycled sacs into useful containers for packaging liquids and meal. French butchers prized the *lard maigre* (pork lean), the streaked pig's belly eaten fresh or used to line the *potée*, a clay pot for cooking vegetables and potatoes. Fresh-slain meat seethed in the skin tenderized naturally in pelt fat, which cooked up into thick broth. The English and American cook customarily salted or smoked sow belly for bacon or fat back.

Among North American aborigines, slaughtering was traditionally gender-specific work. Among the Navaho of the Southwest, women did the slaughtering, tanned hides, and parceled out mutton among households. In the Southeast, game hunters made a male-bonding tradition of stringing up deer and other heavy game and completing the gutting and sectioning of haunches and shoulders as a means of sharing a successful kill. At hunting cabins, the elder hunters were often in charge of cooking fresh elk steak, roasting wild turkeys, and cooking Brunswick stew, made from several wild meats plus onions and potatoes.

In 1822, when the expeditioner Sir William Edward Parry led the *Hecla* and *Griper* to the Canadian Arctic on a second voyage in search of a northwest passage, he spent much of his time observing Eskimos at work or hunting food. When one party returned with seals, he described the care with which the hunter manipulated "a little instrument of ivory called *toopoota*, in form and size exactly resembling a twenty-penny nail, with which they stop up the orifice made by the spear, by thrusting it through the skin by the sides of the wound, and securing it with a twist." (Parry 1842, II, 192) The purpose of the skewer was to halt the flow of blood, which cooks valued for gravy. An Eskimo woman anointed the carcass with water on mouth, flippers, and belly and touched it with lamp black and oil. Two elderly women sectioned meat for immediate use. A sense of community pervaded seal slaughter as the women and youngsters snatched up loose scraps to eat raw, "just as an English child of the same age might do for a piece of sugar-candy." (Ibid.)

The dissection of meat proceeded with the allotment of blubber. While driving away foraging dogs, the butchers continued cutting shares for neighbor women, who arrived with their cook pots. When the butchery ended, the workers rolled up the hide and stored the remaining meat and blubber. Late in the evening, they positioned blubber in their lamps and lit them. At the end of a day of hunting, Parry reported, "Every lamp was now blazing, and every *ootkoseek* smoking with a hot mess, which, together with the friendly reception we experienced, and a little warmth and fatigue from travelling, combined in conveying to our minds an idea of comfort which we could scarcely believe an Esquimeaux hut capable of exciting." (Ibid., 294)

Throughout the Americas, fall slaughtering often brought families together to share the stoking of fires under great cauldrons of water and erecting scaffolds on which to hang meat. A woman alone was able to kill chickens and to hold a suckling pig between her knees and secure the snout for a quick swipe of the knife over the throat or a stab to the heart. The more the pig struggled, the quicker it bled to death. From there, it went into the cauldron to soften the hide before the butcher rubbed on rosin, scrubbed off hair, and gutted it.

Homemakers recycled as much of the offal as possible, for example, retaining ox gall to set colors in cotton, silk, and wool, a recommendation published in Lydia Maria Child's *The American Frugal Housewife* (1836). For a calf, she described a careful cleaning of head, heart, and lungs and suggested leaving the windpipe intact and dangling over the side as a funnel to drain foam from the pot. Brains received separate cooking in a bag before being chopped, seasoned, and buttered.

During the Civil War, women left to fend for themselves plowed, planted, harvested, and slaughtered as life-sustaining chores. While David Harris fought for the Confederacy, his wife Emily maintained their farm outside Spartanburg, South Carolina. Her diary contained a record of the farm work vital to keep the family from starvation. On November 25, 1862, she slaughtered eight animals and noted that they weighed a total of 1,148 pounds. She summarized the onerous job in five words: "The day's work was troublesome." (Lee and Chepesiuk 2000, 31) Four days later, she killed six more, but had to stop slaughtering because she ran out of storage space for lard, hams, shoulders, and sausages.

For military kitchens, regiments drove cattle along with them as beef on the hoof. Camp cooks were so eager to acquire fresh rations that they joined in the free-for-all field slaughter of abandoned or stray cattle. When men received fresh portions, they immediately roasted them on sticks over campfires.

In the Romanian teacher Ion Creanga's memoir, *Memories of My Boyhood* (1879), he describes a Yule custom of hog killing. After his father singed and scalded the pig, he wrapped the meat in straw "to make it sweat, in order that the hair would scrape off easier." (Chamberlain 1989, 130) Creanga straddled the carcass and raised an uproar in anticipation of frying the pigtail and filling the bladder with grains to dry and blow up for a drum. His mother waited for flesh from which to make soup, lard, bacon, and sausage.

The Nobelist Wladislaw Stanislaw Reymont presented a pre-Lenten slaughtering ritual in *The Peasants* (1909), in which Polish women joined the children to catch spurts of blood in a bowl for soup making. The cook stood at a four-legged outdoor cooker, complete with fire box and chimney, which boys too young to join male tipplers stoked with kindling. The Moravian food writer Joseph Wechsberg added his own memories of slaughtering in eastern Europe with a description of his second breakfast, a bowl of calf lung soup.

Food writer Alfred Suzanne, author of *La Cuisine et Pâtisserie Anglaise et Americaine* (French and American Cooking and Desserts, 1904), marveled at seasonal religious customs specifying "a great slaughter of turkeys, geese and all kinds of game, a wholesale massacre of fat oxen, pigs and sheep. They envisage garlands of black puddings, sausages and saveloys . . . mountains of plum-puddings and ovens-full of mince-pies." (Montagné 1977, 243). He enlarged on the carnage by remarking that no English citizen would go hungry when so many animals died to produce traditional holiday ham, sausage, and game.

Eliot Wigginton's *The Foxfire Book* (1968) explains the mechanics of slaughtering in the Appalachian Mountains of the southern United States. Hogs fattened on forest mast—acorns, chestnuts, hickory nuts, and pecans—or stall-fed on peanuts or corn were ready for slaughtering, disjointing, curing, or smoking. The best time for home slaughtering was after heavy frost, when cold nights reduced temperatures to keep meat from spoiling. An outdoor furnace fitted with a cast iron basin or oil drum heated water for scalding and scraping. Farm families shared the work of sharpening butcher knives and cleavers for loosening hair and scraping away scurf, the surface scale that covered the hide.

For hog killing, after the slaughterer shot the animal or slit its throat, workers suspended the carcass on a gambrel stick or singletree passed through the leg tendons. Processing involved hard, smelly work. Hoisting the pig on a pole facilitated the heavy knife work of separating carcass from hide. Next, the preparer slit the gut from chin to crotch with a hawkbill or sharp butcher knife, being careful to leave the intestinal membrane intact. A second cut loosened intestines, which fell into a tub below for use in chitterlings, called "chitlins," and as sausage casings. (Wilson & Ferris 1989, 679) After emptying and turning inside out the intestines were ready for soaking in vinegar water.

Before the meat was clean enough for preserving, workers heated water in a half-buried hogshead or cauldron, scalded the hog, and scraped away its hide with a hog scraper. A second dousing of hot water preceeded the major cutting, which chopped head from backbone, liver and gall bladder from side, and lungs, heart, and kidneys from the central portion. The butcher split the head for removal of the tender brains. After the slaughterer made a single cut up the mainline, workers removed liver, kidneys, heart, and maw.

The job continued at an outdoor table or in the kitchen with mincing of pieces for sausage and removal of trimmings and leaf fat for a lard pot and fatback, the Southern cook's all-purpose seasoning. For the remainder of the cutting operation, the cook wielded an ax or saw to separate backbone, tenderloin, chops, fatback, knuckles (ankles), brains, shoulders, hams, and ribs. For souse, the cook permeated pork with wine, ginger, mace, and nutmeg, then encased it in cloth to pickle. Soul food aficionados cleaned, soaked, boiled, and fried small intestines into chitlins. Cooks in Salley, South Carolina, saved enough viscera to hold the annual food orgy known as the Chitlin' Strut festival.

In the early 1900s, a brass mesh meat cutter's glove with wrist strip guarded the hand opposite the blade. The 1923 Sears, Roebuck catalog offered a twenty-gauge steel hog-scalding basin set on steel frame to localize the work and retain mess that could soak the killing floor and track into the kitchen. On a handbarrow, the workers rubbed meat in red pepper to keep out skipper flies and transported the carcass to vats of salt water or a dry salt trough hewn from a huge tree trunk for preserving large haunches of meat. After several months of sugar or salt curing, the meat passed to the smoke house, where it hung on hooks or wood hangers while a light smoking of smoldering hickory, apple, or sassafras wood dried the tissues while imparting flavor and protecting the meat from insect infestation. Children watching the fire made a trip to the smokehouse every two hours for feeding the flame or banking embers. After processing for a week up to four months, the meat was ready for wrapping for storage or soaking for the kitchen. In the meantime, families ate any parts that might go bad if not consumed immediately.

For country ham, a Southern tradition, curers in the kitchens of Maryland, Virginia, and the Carolinas applied ancient British methods of salting meat. To produce the pungent aroma and flavor, smokers selected carcasses of shoats weighing over three hundred pounds, rubbed them with salt, sugar, and saltpeter, then bedded them in rock salt for up to six weeks. Curers rinsed and trimmed haunches, suspended them over smoke in a dark area, and awaited the roan-brown color, which appeared after an all-summer sweating. By early fall, country hams were ripe for boiling in a cauldron, baking, or slicing and frying. To make the popular red-eye gravy, the cook tipped the coffee pot over the pan drippings. The mix of coffee and grease formed red eyes for spooning onto biscuits.

One of the most detailed descriptions of Native American animal slaughter and prioritized distribution of meat came from the anthropologist Vilhjalmur Stefansson, a Manitoba native who lived among the Mackenzie River Dene in 1906 and later with the Herschel

Island Inuit. Of the latter, he explained how the slaying of migratory caribou followed a prescribed dispersal: kidney, shoulder bone, and lower leg marrow to the children and lungs, liver, stomach, and entrails to the dogs. Adults relished the tongue, brisket, ribs, and pelvis. All, including guests, shared the boiled head.

Into the 1900s, Hungarians counted their culinary blessings by accumulating pig fat, a high-energy food that they added to soup, gruel, vegetables, lean meat, pulses, salads, and *roux* (fried flour). From the Middle Ages, they stored up uncut slabs for salting, drying, smoking, or rendering into lard for both civilian and military use. They traditionally greeted their neighbors with the toast "May his pig fat be thick!" (Riddervold & Ropeid, 1988, 27) Pork fat was the basis of Hungarian cookery, as shown by figures from 1884, when rural people ate over 26.5 kilograms of meat fat a year and city folk, who had a higher standard of living, ate over 36.7 kilograms. The migrant workers who helped with slaughtering each summer received and ate up to five kilograms of fat per month as a major perquisite of their employment.

As described by the traveler Daniel Spoerri, author of *The Mythological Travels* (1970), female slaughterers at Agua Amarga, Spain, improvised a method of cutting and weighing meat pieces to sell to shoppers. After hacking into their goats with an ax, they indiscriminately chopped out meat chunks from one end to the other. To assure a standard portion to each customer, they selected a stone as the absolute measure.

A somber ritual accompanied doe slaughter among Native Americans in New Mexico in the researcher Barbara Tedlock's *The Beautiful and the Dangerous: Dialogues with the Zuñi Indians* (1993). To bring fresh kill to the kitchen, the woman led the way to the house, sprinkling cornmeal along the path in blessing. When the hunter and his helpers had laid out the doe on the floor facing east, the family began a ritual honoring her path to the Zuñi. The woman pressed the feminine white corn ear against the doe's chest; the others dusted her with cornmeal while "singing her home." The hunter recreated the scene of her sacrifice while he whetted his knife for the gutting and peeling of skin. He suspended the carcass from a steel hook and drained the blood onto a pail on the kitchen floor. After the initial dismemberment of the meat, he saved small bones to plant in the cornfield as talismans to improve the harvest. A lengthy preparation concluded with fresh venison barbecued on piñon coals alongside scorched chiles.

Among the aborigines in central Australia, according to Margaret-Mary Turner-Neale's *Bush Foods* (1996), hunters killed, gutted, and skewered kangaroos before singeing the split carcass over a fire. The job ended with scraping, putting the carcass in a hole, and covering the meat with hot coals to bake. Serving followed the dissection of the meat into feet, tail, thighs, hips, ribs, stomach, head, and upper and lower back.

Fresh meat was the basis of much social activity among Africans. Among the Somali of northeast Kenya, women hacked newly slaughtered goat or camel meat into small cubes for browning into *nyeri-nyeri*. They stored covered vessels of meat cubes at room temperature in cupboards and under beds for serving to unexpected guests. In Rhamu, a village in northern Kenya, the slaughter of a goat honored guests, especially those who came to help with planting or the building of a mud oven in the family compound. After frying the meat to serve with curry, the host took pride in reimbursing helpers with fresh meat. As with the banquets at northern European castles during the Middle Ages, the Kenyan communal meal ended with the traditional distribution of leftovers to the needy.

Into the twenty-first century, Hungarian peasants continued the communal pig-slaughtering feast *disznotar*, a day-long task for kin and invited guests. After the solemn plunge of the knife into the animal's throat, the hostess served *palinka* (plum brandy) to the blade-wielders. The burning of hair and scraping of hide preceded nibbling at toasted pig skin, ears, and tail. After the dismembering of the carcass and the cleansing of stomach and intestines for sausage casings, the hostess prepared a huge banquet, which began with the elder male's delivery of a thanksgiving blessing. The day was not complete until the hostess had distributed stuffed cabbage, homemade wine, and sausage from her larder to all participants.

In 2000, *Scientific American* reported on the work of beef slaughterers from figures collected by the U.S. Department of Agriculture, National Cattlemen's Beef Association, Soyfoods Association of North America, and American Heart Association. For the nation's kitchens, slaughterhouses dispensed 64.7 pounds of beef per capita, in contrast with 48.8 of pork and 49.2 of chicken.

See also **Kosher Kitchens; Smoked Food**

Further Reading

Coppens, Linda Miles. *What American Women Did, 1789–1920*. Jefferson, N.C.: McFarland, 2001.

Godwin, Peter, "Bushmen," *National Geographic*, February 2001, 90–117.

Kummer, Corby, "Sausages, Souse, and Shandybookers," *Atlantic Monthly,* July/August 2001, 143–147.

Ross, John F., "People of the Reindeer," *Smithsonian*, December 2000, 54–65.

SLAVERY

SLAVERY

In kitchens over much of the world, slaves performed the hard, menial labor that daily meals demanded. In the Greece of Homer's day, around the eighth century BCE, female slaves milled corn into flour and prepared dough for cooking. The *mageiros* (baker), forerunner of the professional chef, accrued so much prestige that he could buy his own slave crews. Serving under an *eleatros* (steward), menials specialized in marketing, tending fires, prepping meat and vegetables for cooking, plating and garnishing, and serving food and drink at table. A separate job of washing dishes and resetting them on the table fell to the *trapezopoios*. The *oinophoros* (wine steward) poured beakers of wine or refreshed cups.

Slaves mastered the rudiments of Greek cookery. They commanded an array of *chytra* (clay pots), *kakkabe* (metal pots) placed near the fire on *eugytheke* (metal supports), *lebes* (metal basins), and *ollas*, the large jar shapes still in use in modern times. For drinks, they heated wine in a double-bottomed amphora or kettle for pouring into a *patarion* (drinking cup). By law, any kitchen slave who invented a dish could make and sell it for profit. In honoring the cook's ingenuity and position close to the heart of home activity, Greek comedy depicted the kitchen slave as important enough to be intrusive, inquisitive, tale-bearing, and manipulative.

By the sixth century BCE, Roman banquets called for a variety of skilled cooks, whom Romans purchased as slaves. In the kitchen, workers assumed specific jobs: the *focarius* tended the hearth, the *coctor* superintended food preparation, the *pistor* ground grain and puréed vegetables and herbs, the *coquus* boiled and grilled, the *structor* plated and garnished dishes, the *captor* carved, the *proegustator* tasted dishes, the *cellarius* managed selection of vintages, and the *aquarius* supplied the house with potable water for cooking and drinking.

A professional Greek baker elevated and refined the Roman loaf and taught matrons about making sourdough from wheat porridge, soaking millet in grape juice, and steeping wheat bran in wine. These skilled slaves earned high salaries and such perquisites as private homes, an award that Mark Antony gave to Cleopatra's cook. Under Hadrian at the beginning of the second century of the Empire, Rome's food workers unionized into a *collegium coquorum* (cook's guild). As of 14 CE, the Roman Empire supported nearly three million slaves for every five million free citizens.

In Roman Britain, when Anglo-Saxon insurgents replaced Roman conquerors in 449 CE, they brought their own system of enslavement. House staff appeared on the auction block like cattle and suffered fettering, whipping, and torture at the whim of masters and mistresses. One of the accomplishments of Christian missionaries was an end to the buying, selling, and tormenting of human beings. In 845 CE, St. Anskar, the "Apostle of the North," converted King Erik of Jutland and influenced him to halt the Danish slave trade.

In Turkey as early as the fourteenth century, Ottoman rulers bought slaves to do their cooking. For slaves' children, the sultan established a cooking school to teach *saray* (palace) cuisine. Only the best rose to the rank of cook, a respected courtier who devoted his life to serving the tables of nobility. Organized into herb collectors, soup cooks, butchers, grocers, bakers, and confectioners, the slave corps worked together, lived in separate quarters, even worshiped in individual mosques. The first native-born cooks were Turks recruited from camps in Bolu, Anatolia, to serve in the Topkapi Palace at Istanbul. They spread vast tables with a sophisticated amalgam of Turkish dishes accompanied by Chinese, Mongolian, Arab, and Byzantine fare. When the army marched, the sultan's cooks journeyed along, bearing with them the taste of home.

Slavery in Iberia was limited after 1492, when indigenous Hispanics drove black-skinned Moorish insurgents south across the Gibraltar Straits into Africa. Grandees kept a contingent enslaved as farm workers. In 1610, an official dispatch to the Valencian monarch claimed that those who stayed on the land survived on "barley bread, honey, raisins, and prickly pears," which they ate without pausing from their labors. (Crane 1999, 505)

In the American colonies and throughout the Caribbean, from the early days of European settlement, slavery was a given for wealthy planters and exporters, who could invest thirty florins in a slave in Africa in 1675 and, under ideal conditions, recoup up to fifteen times the investment in North America. Domestics knew an unending list of home chores that ranged from cooking breakfast while wetnursing the master's children to preserving garden produce, polishing silver and pewter, and washing and shrouding the family's death. When the master whipped runaways and recalcitrant slaves, it was the kitchen worker who made up a brine for pouring into the lash marks to prevent infection.

Paralleling the life of the privileged, in the slave quarters, according to Millie Evans in B. A. Botkin's *Lay My Burden Down: A Folk History of Slavery* (1958), families lived in one or two rooms on dirt floors they swept with brooms made of sage (sedge) tied with string. Alabama Cato added details of a hewn-oak log cabin in a long row of slave housing, where women cooked at a firehalf, the circular hearth of a stick chimney. The main sources

560

of slave meals were the meager provisions allotted by overseers plus what vegetables families could grow in small kitchen plots that they tended after finishing their work for the master. Standard distribution from the main house included chicken necks, gizzards, pig's feet and intestines and kush, a mix of bacon fat and cornmeal. In *Narrative of the Life of Frederick Douglass* (1892), Douglass described working in his master's kitchen along with his sister and aunt. The trio begged and stole for food "when food in abundance lay mouldering in the safe and smoke-house, and our pious mistress was aware of the fact." (Douglass 1968, 66)

Until the outlaw of the slave trade in England in 1807 and in the United States in 1808, slaving continued to supply homes and plantations with cheap labor, which encouraged slave smuggling. Black captives who survived arrived at coastal markets, where sugar planters traded sugar and molasses for human cargo. Under guard, slaves assembled on auction blocks, where sellers demonstrated their strengths and skills and sold them to the highest bidders. A likely household staffer cost upwards of six pounds, but could be resold for five times that amount, in part because of the mastery of such useful domestic and yard skills as brewing, baking, slaughtering, preserving, pickling, weaving, cobbling, and smithing. Slave populations in the Caribbean isles and the Americas rose from 370,000 in the early seventeenth century to around eight million before the Civil War. Overall, kitchen slaves suffered less privation than the short-lived press gangs on indigo and rice plantations, who died quickly and ignominiously in the field at an early age. Often both breeder and cook, the female cook or baker could depend on a warm home and sufficient food and medicines. The division of labor paralleled the lifestyle of lower class white women, who lived a hearth-centered existence devoted to cooking, cleaning, and child care.

Elizabeth Lyle Saxon corroborates the gulf separating white from black in *A Southern Woman's War Time Reminiscences* (1905). While black women labored at the hearth, the white mistress checked on the progress of foods by a go-between—"a little shining-faced negro girl [carrying] a saucer with a small quantity of the cooking fruit for 'misstis' to see how it was progressing." (Saxon 1905, 21) In *The Narrative of Bethany Veney, a Slave Woman* (1889), the author contrasted the crude southern kitchen she had known in childhood with the streamlined homes of the northern families for whom she worked in adulthood. She made no accusation, but implied that, because plantation masters depended on slave labor, they had no motivation to lighten the load of kitchen work with labor-saving devices.

In contrast to the plantation kitchen, Charles Ball, a cook aboard a frigate and author of *Fifty Years in Chains; or The Life of An American Slave* (1859), testified to the same scene from the black point of view: field hands coming in at sundown to cook for masters and wait at their tables. After the gentry were satisfied, black families, who received no scraps from the food they had cooked, ground their pint of rice or corn per person. For the latter, they shaped pones, and baked them in the embers, which they ate as late as 11:00 p.m. Ball added that, on his arrival into service, the plantation's iron kettle served as cookpot for rice, laundry boiler, and bathing and delousing area. For soap, slaves resorted to yellow fuller's earth from the swamp. The liabilities of plantation cookery included burns and scalds, strained muscles, and severe penalties for breakage and loss of equipment. Slaves shared toil with turnspit dogs, bow-legged canine slaves bred for service and forced to trot in a revolving drum attached by pulleys to a rotating meat spit at fireside.

When missionaries began ministering to Hawaiian islanders in 1826, they pressed locals into bondage as kitchen workers. The newcomers' need for assistance in acclimating to local foods and fishing involved trading clothing, scissors, needles, fishhooks, yard goods, and food in exchange for labor. Pressure from antislavery forces coerced missionaries into releasing Hawaiians from servitude and establishing a work-for-pay system.

In 1843, Norbert Rillieux, a New Orleans-born quadroon, liberated slaves from one of the hazardous cooking chores that cost lives in the Caribbean sugar trade. After mastering steam engineering, he designed a sugar evaporating pan, which transformed the processing of cane juice. At the same time that he reduced production cost and turned out cleaner sugar with less effort, he spared workers from the labor-intensive job of stirring cauldrons of juice over a fire.

Some slaves dot the pages of history by name because of their ownership by such powerful or famous people as Thomas Jefferson. Jefferson encouraged kitchen gardening and poultry yards for profit. In a rare master-slave cooperative, some of his slaves sold their own chickens, herbs, and vegetables in Monticello and to other plantations as a source of private income. Jefferson manumitted five slaves in his lifetime and five more at his death. Among them was James Hemings, an underchef he had trained in cookery in France and freed on February 5, 1796.

Throughout slavery, the typical work for the oppressed was either agrarian or domestic. Only the favored few learned trades related to manufacture. When Negroes fled slavery and could select for themselves jobs that used their skills and preferences, many sought employment in food work. According to the

561

1855 New York state census, free blacks overwhelmingly labored as domestics (15.3 percent). Out of a total of 3,501, 499 (14 percent) became waiters, 366 (11 percent) chose laundry work, 151 (4.3 percent) cooked, and 19, less than one percent, became butchers.

For many slaves, kitchen gardening and cooking was the entrepreneurial ticket out of bondage. As early as colonial days, slave women marketed produce and baked goods, gradually dominating a sector of the Southern economy. According to an eyewitness account of slave vendors in Louisiana and South Carolina: "The market places are filled with Negro women selling fruits and vegetables. . . .They have control of the markets in New Orleans [and] bring their products to the market very neatly." (Hine et al. 1993, 395) Some brokered eggs and poultry as well as produce by selling door to door, establishing regular wagon routes, and transporting fresh commodities to farmers' markets. From these beginnings came truck farms, professional butteries, bakeries, cheese-making, canneries, breweries, apiaries, catering services, restaurants, taverns, and inns, like that of Nancy Remond of Salem, Massachusetts. Some former slavewomen immediately exchanged their earnings for the liberation of others.

For those slaves who bridged the era of emancipation, cooking was the skill that liberated them from servitude to private business. An illiterate kitchen worker, Abby Fisher, formerly enslaved in Mobile, Alabama, cooked in the kitchens of San Francisco's elite and won a diploma at the 1879 Sacramento State Fair. The next year, entries in the sauce/pickle and jelly/preserve categories earned her two medals at the San Francisco Mechanics Institute Fair. By dictating laborious recipes for such specialties as watermelon rind pickle and jumble cake to the Women's Cooperative Printing Office, which published *What Mrs. Fisher Knows about Old Southern Cooking: Soups, Pickles, Preserves, Etc.* (1881), she verbalized the hardships of kitchen work on plantations, where owners gave little thought to saving time and labor.

See also **Mining and Logging Camp Kitchens; Roman Cookery**

Further Reading

Ball, Charles. *Fifty Years in Chains; or The Life of An American Slave.* Indianapolis, Ind.: Asher & Co., 1859.

Bankoff, H. Arthur, Christopher Ricciardi, & Alyssa Loorya, "Remembering Africa Under the Eaves," *Archaeology,* May/June 2001, 36–40.

Brown, William Wells. *Narrative of William W. Brown, an American Slave.* London: C. Gilpin, 1849.

de Saussure, Nancy Bostick. *Old Plantation Days: Being Recollections of Southern Days before the Civil War.* New York: Duffield & Co., 1909.

McCunn, Ruthanne Lum. *Thousand Pieces of Gold.* San Francisco: Design Enterprises of San Francisco, 1981.

Saxon, Elizabeth Lyle. *A Southern Woman's War Time Reminiscences.* Memphis, Tenn.: Pilcher Printing Co., 1905.

Steward, Austin. *Twenty-Two Years a Slave, and Forty Years a Freeman.* Rochester, N.Y.: William Alling, 1857.

Veney, Bethany. *The Narrative of Bethany Veney, a Slave Woman.* Worcester, Mass.: n.p., 1889.

SMOKED FOOD

Smoking food as a purifier and preservative dates to early human experience with fire and foodstuffs. Examples range from the communal smokehouses where Romans cured their cheeses, the chimney hoods where Bulgarians hung ox-meat salamis, and the caves in Conway, England, where salmon was smoked, to the disinfectant smoke that purifies the wood containers in which dairywomen of Rhamu, Kenya, carry sweet and sour milk products to market. The concept of smoking as a way to save perishables may have evolved accidentally during the Stone Age from the coincidental hanging of deer carcasses or fish fillets over a shelter fire. The diners may have liked the smoky taste and welcomed a method of extending the use of freshly caught fish and slaughtered game. The new technology could have inspired a mass food-stocking trend toward harvesting salmon on their seasonal spawning run, trapping animals in game pits, or organizing a game surround, a method of corraling a large number of different species or a single herd for mass slaughter, dressing, and curing. Not only did the method preserve and enhance flavor, it also evaporated moisture and shrank pieces, making them lighter in weight and easier to transport and store.

In December 2000, Jan F. Simek, an archeologist from the University of Tennessee, supervised excavators at a Neanderthal cave site in Dordogne, France, where humans first resided before 280,000 BCE. Analysis proved that hunters used the caves as temporary shelters during cyclical hunts. More sophisticated than history had credited, the hunters appear to have smoked fresh game by igniting slow-burning lichen and grasses.

Greek and Roman cuisine showcased imported processed meats, especially the smoked meats from Alexandria, Egypt, and pork flitches from Westphalia in Gaul. Around 190 BCE, the agronomist Cato composed *De Re Rustica* (On Farming) with descriptions of pickling, salting, and smoking. He explained the salt- and smoke-curing of *carnes fumigatae* (smoked ham), a combined method that began with *ofeliae* (pork chunks) salted in a vat and the addition of whole hams with skin down and layered with salt to separate each haunch. After preliminary curing for twelve days, the pieces were ready for air-drying and sponging clean of salt. A smear of olive oil readied them for hanging in the smokehouse.

At a dig in Bishkupin, Poland, in the 1960s, Professor Z. Rajewski studied the remains of thirty-four caches and nearby hearths. A discovery of fish scales and bones of bass, bream, catfish, pike, and roach showed the site to be an eighth- or tenth-century fish smoking plant, which prepared large catches from Biskupin Lake for a large population. At each side of the hearths, holes apparently supported uprights on which the smoker placed a rod strung with brine-cured fish to hang over the fire below. The method was still in use in the early 1400s, according to the chronicler Joannis Dlugossi's *Opera Omnia* (All Works), when his contemporary, King Ladislaus Jagiellon's military kitchens salted and smoked big game as a hedge against his soldiers' needs during wartime.

Native Americans of the East Coast and Caribbean preserved fish and haunches of venison by stretching them over cane or wooden racks above a slow, fragrant fire of grass, herbs, and mesquite or hardwood. When the Spanish expeditioner Hernando De Soto reached Tampa Bay, Florida, he studied the Timucua method of building strong wood scaffolds over a fire for the roasting of deer, dog, alligators, fish, and snake. According to Jesuit observations in 1660, the Eastern Cree of Canada built a rectangular platform grill for smoking, somewhat in the style of the Chippewa. The Northern Saulteaux and Plains Cree preferred a tripod scaffold. Although Southwestern tribes exploited the desert heat, the Catawba, Cherokee, and Creek erected sapling frames and platforms over a fire pit and smoked freshwater fish.

The Skagit and other northwest tribes also relied on smoked goods. A method of smoking small pieces such as abalone or candlefish began with suspending them on forked sticks or stringing them on bear grass over a fire. The Ingalik of the lower Yukon River crafted a gabled smokehouse fitted with racks for drying fish. Smoke not only dried meat into jerky, but also killed flying insects and parasites in the meat. Smoking became a social occasion, when meaty fumes intrigued neighbors to join in and sample savory food.

After the development of the flue chimney in the Middle Ages, families lacking a smokehouse could smoke meats in small quantities at their own hearth. A useful tool was a wrought iron ham hook or meat hook for hoisting ham into the path of smoke for preservation. One area, Algarve in southern Portugal, developed a unique local custom of pride in chimneys. Masons supplying the ornate, idiosyncratic toppers for kitchen flues patterned them after carillons, lanterns, classical buildings, crests, faces, even a slender minaret. The caps rounded out the wide *lareira*, vertical fireplaces that rose straight up from the hearth, allowing homeowners to brush the inner walls clean of soot. Within these tidy chambers, families dried and smoked meats and sausage.

These flue-smoking methods also influenced the bacon of Transylvania and North America. According to D. J. Hall's *Romanian Furrow* (1933), innovative eastern European peasants hung bacon from the rafters of forts. "Every piece had a label indicating the villager to whom it belonged. The tower was kept locked, and anyone wishing to cut a piece off his bacon went to the custodian, who came along to see that he did not take a piece from someone else's store." (Chamberlain 1989, 59) In Quebec, families smoked meat in the outdoor oven by burning sawdust on the inner surface and leaving the doors open to cure molasses-coated haunches of pork and venison. On the American frontier, the second-floor smoke room, a garret space next to a chimney, served as a smoking chamber, where families kindled fires of hickory shavings.

In the Amana colonies, smoking was a convenient and trustworthy method of securing meat for 1,500 residents. According to Carl Schuerer of East Amana, butchers worked at the rate of two beefs per month in cold weather and thirty-five to forty pigs throughout the slaughtering season. The carcasses of steers remained in process from November to March. The family art of smoking passed to sons, grandsons, and nephews, who later managed the society's meat shop and smokehouse. Hams, shoulders, and bacon reposed curing in vats of brine before suspension in the smokehouse. In summer, the smoker lit a sulfur fire to control flies.

In 1923, the Sears, Roebuck catalog offered the home smoker an enclosed meat smokehouse to accommodate three hogs for $21.00. The two-stage portable system promised safety from fire with sturdy casing, firebox, and pipe formed out of heavy-gauge galvanized iron. The smoking cylinder held meat on hooks on four hardwood posts attached to strap iron hoops. Smoke from the adjacent fire box entered the chamber at bottom and circulated upward. Ad copy touted the apparatus as an ideal storage house with screened ventilators to keep out vermin and predators.

In the 1960s, when cultural historian Krzysztof Moszynski studied the foodways of Slavic peasantry, he found that smoking was a coincidental food-curing method. In *The Folkloric Slav Culture* (1967), he reports that hanging dried meat high in the rafters near the smoke hole for a kitchen exposed the meat to drying fumes. In Podlesia, Poland, home slaughterers cut pork and mutton into chunks, soaked them in brine, then sewed them into bags for suspending in a smoky atmosphere under the eaves. The method parallels the Native American drying of deer, fish, moose, and reindeer into pemmican in leather bags and the White Russian curing of elk meat in ovens before hanging it in the loft in sacks.

According to Prosper Montagné's classic *New Larousse Gastronomique* (1977), the French, unlike the neighboring Alsatians, traditionally preferred cold smoking, especially in Boulogne. After stringing salted fish on rods through the gills, the cook left them on racks to drain. For kippers, they slit fish from top to vent and flattened them so smoke penetrated inner flesh. To create the right atmosphere for preserving herring, they hung them away from flame at a temperature of 77 degrees Fahrenheit. For fuel, they chose beech or sawdust rather than resinous wood, which soaked flesh with an undesired flavor.

In industrialized countries in the twenty-first century, smoking is a standard method of flavoring meats, roe, nuts, berries, sausage, eggs, and cheese. Foods profit from exposure to a non-resinous wood that burns at a slow, steady rate. Woods recommended for their burn and fragrance include oak, mesquite, beech, ash, elm, sycamore, hickory, and birch. In the American South, some smokers choose corn cobs, more for their availability than for aroma or flavor. On the island of Bornholm, Denmark, smokers of herring follow a traditional recipe, which places gutted and salted fish on long poles for smoking over alder shavings.

To prevent scorching from flameup, most fire builders select stout logs. The cold smoker takes the shape of a metal, brick, or wood cabinet that supports flame at the bottom and a perforated or slatted shelf to spread the fumes. Adjustable support rods or grates at the top allow the user to vary flavor intensity by moving meat nearer or closer to the heat source. Drip trays catch effluents for basting or fat removal.

Smoking is a welcome home method of preserving food because of antiseptic qualities that kill bacteria and vermin. Two methods work best: cold smoking at an ambient temperature of 85 degrees Fahrenheit, which leaves tissues uncooked, and hot smoking, a conclusion to cold smoking that raises temperature above 180 degrees Fahrenheit for the more delicate flesh of fish and shellfish and as high as 240 degrees Fahrenheit for meat. Equipment needed for home smoking includes a meat thermometer, deep freeze storage space to keep fresh stock from spoiling until it is smoked, and a brining pump, a syringe that forces saline or pickling solution deep into thick tissue. Stovetop smokers constructed of heavy-gauge stainless steel and fired with alder, cherry, hickory, or oak chips allow the cook to ready fish, poultry, and meat indoors or outside on a grill or open fire as a means of preserving moisture while producing low-fat, low-cholesterol meals.

Hot smoking, which results from an intense flame, begins with dry wood and sturdier equipment. For pressure smoking, a Swedish kiln applies the technology of the closed-box stove. A methylated spirit burner generates enough heat to spread smoke to the top and out the sides. The pressure rapidly forces flavor into the meat as it cooks. Home models made from galvanized trash cans fitted with grilles are less efficient and require more fuel. Suspending pieces above on a hook, string, rawhide thongs, or hazel sticks rather than containing meat in a pan evens the smoking process. Another model, the backyard grill/smoker, varies the flavoring and humidity by positioning a pan of water between charcoal at the bottom and meat at the top, a method that moistens turkey, chicken, pheasant, and other dry-meated fowl. Cooks preferring an herbal savor add fresh sage, thyme, tarragon, or lemongrass leaves and stalks to the water and adjust baffles to slow or expedite the cooking time. For a larger operation, the shed smoker accommodates meats in bulk, such as pork ham, shoulders, sausage links, and bacon.

Smoking styles vary according to ethnic and local tastes, cuisine, and supplies. In the Grenadines, smokers of fresh fish fillet them at the pier, season with spices and peppers, and spread them on racks. The essential ingredient is guava wood, which imparts a distinctive flavor. In Lepsa in the Vrancei Mountains of Romania, chimneyless kitchens separated from living quarters have served double duty since the mid-twentieth century. The absence of flues attests to a time when governments taxed chimneys as luxuries. As the householder readies bubbling masses of *mamaliga* (corn mush) with a wood stirring paddle, smoke rises to the ceiling to cure meat suspended from rafters. Among the nomadic Qermezi of southwestern Iran, smoking preserves kidskin for storage bags, in which families secure curds, clarified butter, yogurt, and sour milk. To rid the skin of a smoky taste, the housewife applies grape syrup.

In Gabon and much of the rural South in the United States, families dry or smoke meat as a preservative and choose smoked spareribs, cured beef, steaks, and hamburgers for outdoor cooking and camping supplies. Ghanian smoked meat includes bat or monkey, available at the Kumasi market. James Peterson, the author of *Splendid Soups* (1993), recommends smoked ham, pancetta, or bacon as a complement to soup or as garnish. As described by mountaineers of the southern Appalachians in Eliot Wigginton's *The Foxfire Book* (1968), apples and other fruit keep tasty and insect-free during winter if the cook first smokes them. After placing hickory coals in the bottom of a barrel, sprinkling sulfur on the embers, and suspending a split oak basket at the barrel lip, the food preserver covers the barrel with cloth or paper seal and allows fumes to bleach the fruit. Slices stay fresh all winter in wood barrels or crocks.

At Jokkmok, Sweden, Lapp herders smoke reindeer flank; in Stockholm, game stalls sell unplucked ptarmigan, wood pigeon, capercaillie, badger ham, crayfish, and roe and eels smoked in the traditional *Rökhus* (kiln). Poles are famous for their smoked eel and ham, served with rye bread and mustard. In Iceland, *hangikjöt* is a popular smoked mutton; the Irish smoke salmon as a local delicacy and trade item. Cooks in Luxembourg smoke a pork collar with fava or broad beans for *judd mat gaardebounen*. Scots from Arbroath set barrels over flame to smoke their traditional Arbroath smokies, small haddock or whiting paired and layered over rods until they turn a dark, tarry brown. In South Africa, hunters strip, salt, and sun-dry fresh springbok and ostrich to make biltong, a defatted meat jerky that requires no refrigeration. The Ewe of Togo and Ghana begin fermenting palm sap for wine by first smoking it. The finished wine serves community custodians as a libation assuring a strong yam harvest and tribal prosperity.

Asian smoking grows out of a different tradition from northern European and American oak smoking. The Japanese raise coturnix quail in small cages for smoking, stuffing, and roasting. The Chinese, who developed the selection of fragrant barks and herbs for smoking, have traditionally preferred freshly picked tea to cure poultry and other meats. For tea-smoked duck, they heat *long jing*, an unfermented green tea from Shanghai, in a dry wok at high temperature and stretch a whole duck on a rack above the smoke. In Sichuan, an unusual reversal of methods for *mai fun gai* (chicken smoked with rice and tea) starts with deep-frying and steaming before smoking over dry-fried rice and black tea.

In 2001, many U.S. merchandise catalogs featured home smokers. To appeal to the hunter or gourmet, the Orvis catalog offered a small free-standing smoker/dehydrator for $450. It consisted of a cabinet housing five shelves and a glass door for checking the progress of meats permeated by the fumes of alder, apple, cherry, hickory, maple, or mesquite briquettes fed automatically into an electric side burner. A separate heating system warmed the chamber to an even temperature. A domed gas outdoor cooker had a porcelain base, front-loading door, and high-BTU burner adapted to deep-frying and grilling.

Further Reading

Dimancescu, Dan, Dick Durrence, and Christopher G. Knight, "Americans Afoot in Rumania," *National Geographic*, June 1969, 810–845.
Erlandson, Keith. *Home Smoking and Curing*. London: Barrie & Jenkins, 1977.
Hoppe, Emilie. *Seasons of Plenty: Amana Communal Cooking*. Ames: Iowa State University Press, 1998.
Mandelbaum, David G. *The Plains Cree: An Ethnographic, Historical and Comparative Study*. Regina, Sask.: Canadian Plain Research Center, 1979.
Wong, Kate, "Paleolithic Pit Stop," *Scientific American*, December 2000, 18–20.

SOFT DRINKS

Worldwide, the use of non-alcoholic drinks has a long history. Soft drinks, such as the *ci-da* (ginger ale) that Koreans pour over watermelon dessert, serve as restoratives, table beverages, and refreshments. On a visit to Egypt in the eleventh century, the poet Nasir-i-Khusraw, author of *Safarname* (Diary of a Journey Through Syria and Palestine, 1045), reported the popularity of lemonade made from the *daq* (thin-skinned) lemon. It was still being peddled in the twelfth century. Into the 1200s, exporters traded in bottles of *qatarmizat*, a sweetened lemon juice. A similar kitchen trade in fruit ades made from oranges and lemons, strawberries, tamarinds, bananas, hibiscus blossoms, pomegranates, and sugarcane survives at Egyptian kiosks, where blenders whir sugar and ice with whole fruit for a modern slushie. Less popular were World War II-era vegetables ades blended of carrot, cucumber, or tomato, such as Carrolade, a vitamin-rich drink made from carrots and dispensed to English children during food rationing.

Carbonation brought soft drinks into a new era in 1741, when Dr. William Brownrigg first made soda water in England. His method of infusing plain water with carbon dioxide required immediate bottling to retain the fizz. The English chemist Joseph Priestley used another method around 1771, when he extracted gas from a brewing cask to dissolve in water.

During a period of high alcoholic consumption in the 1800s, individuals also had a wide choice of soft drinks and mineral waters, which were popular with abstainers. In Russia, according to Dr. Rhind, author of *History of the Vegetable Kingdom* (1868), shoppers could buy a honey-ginger drink flavored with orris root, an aromatic ingredient used in brandy and wine. The French immigrant Elias Magloire Durand, former pharmacist to Napoleon's army, sold refreshments at his shop, the forerunner of the drugstore, near Independence Hall in Philadelphia. His drawing card was sparkling water, which appealed to intellectuals and professionals. New Yorkers of the Lower East Side recall that Louis Auster, owner of Auster's Candy Store, invented the egg cream in the early years of the nineteenth century. The regional treat, made with U-bet chocolate syrup, contained milk and seltzer, but no egg and no cream. It was soon available at other lunch counters and candy stores. In the 1930s, another French emigré to Philadelphia, Eugene Roussel, offered flavored soda water, which became a fad drink.

Bottlers in Arkansas marketed mineral water from the local hot springs. Home cookbooks such as *Mrs. Hill's New Family Receipt Book* (1870), by Mrs. A. P. Hill, named the ingredients for ginger beer, a blend of Jamaican ginger, cream of tartar, and water mixed with yeast and bottled for home use. In stalls at city markets, vendors dispensed peppermint water, fruit syrup, lemonade, and cordials as well as coffee, tea, and cocoa. In the mid-Atlantic states, Shaker herb growers produced sarsaparilla in their kitchen gardens for marketing as a nostrum. Dr. Dixie Crowby, a professor of surgery at Dartmouth, used the medicinal herb to formulate Corbett's Compound Concentrated Syrup of Sarsaparilla, a medal winner at the 1876 Philadelphia Centennial. The drink was the forerunner of the American soft drink industry.

In rapid order, additional soft drinks offered homemakers multiple choices of commercially prepared beverages:

- Charles Alderton of Waco, Texas, formulated Dr. Pepper in 1884.
- In 1886, Atlanta pharmacist John S. Pemberton concocted the world's most famous soft drink, Coca-Cola. Marketed as a tonic for the brain, the drink eventually spanned the globe. Cooks in the American South lauded its use as a marinade to flavor and tenderize pork and ham.
- In 1896, Caleb D. Bradham produced Pepsi-Cola at his pharmacy shop in New Bern, North Carolina.
- Two years later, Edward A. Barq concocted Barq's root beer in Biloxi, Mississippi.
- In 1901, Sidney Lee developed Buffalo Rock ginger ale in Birmingham, Alabama.
- Three years after the debut of Buffalo Rock, Dr. John May named his own ginger ale for Blenheim, South Carolina, the city of its origination.
- In 1907, Valentine Merz brewed Dixie beer in New Orleans.
- In 1916, Coca-Cola appeared in stores in its familiar contoured bottle.

The 1920s and early 1930s were a prolific era of soft drink manufacture, including the marketing of Kool-Aid mixes in 1927, a multi-use powdered drink that offered homemakers a handy base in six flavors for frozen dessert, gelatins, punch, cake icing, and frozen ices on a stick. Weeks before the stock market crash, Charles Grigg began marketing Bib-Label Lithiated Lemon-Lime Soda, which he renamed 7-Up, a ginger ale. His choice of the name 7-Up may derive from a cattle brand. Two other explanations of the name choice are a lucky roll in a dice throw or a contention that the drink cured seven types of hangovers. In 1930, marketers lauded the benefits of lithum in 7-Up. An influx of bottled sodas on the Hawaiian Islands in the 1920s influenced Japanese families to serve them for New Year and Obon holidays. R. C. Cola, a popular Southern drink, got its start in Columbus, Georgia, in 1933, when the pharmacist Claud A. Hatcher adapted a former ginger ale recipe he called Royal Crown.

In this same era, drummers in jalopies and caravans traveled New South Wales selling sweets, crisps, ice cream, and Duncan's ginger beer, an easy draw for young customers. The cordial factory at Quirindi, Australia, made ginger beer and raspberry soda, which distributors transported in their familiar wagons. Home brews consisted of hops or ginger beer and honeymead, which mellowed in kegs and bottles until Christmas celebrations. Concoctions of soft drinks continued into the late twentieth century with Dr. Robert Cade's creation of Gatorade in Gainesville, Florida. One gesture to the growing problem with cast-off soft drink containers came from Coca-Cola Company and Hoechst-Celanese, which introduced the first recycled plastic soft drink bottle in 1990. The next year, some 1,875 recycling programs began collecting plastic containers at curbside.

SOUP

Soup appears on tables worldwide, as it has from the evolution of stone boiling and cooking in earthenware pots. The Umpqua of coastal Oregon have traditionally made soup each winter from bones, salmon roe, and dried and rotted fish heads. The eastern Mediterranean generated a body of soup recipes, notably three Babylonian tablets from around 1700 BCE recording thirty-five broths made from vegetables, pigeons, partridges, venison, gazelle, goat, kid, lamb, and ram. One beer-based soup blended bird meat with aromatic wood steeped in vinegar, mint, garlic, and salt. The author carefully noted ethnic origin, for example, from Elam or Assyria.

The Greeks honored Apollo with a bean festival, during which soup sellers offered pea stock to passersby. Greek *makaria* (bread soup), mentioned by the eighth-century BCE wordsmith Hesychius, appears to be the root of macaroni, but is more likely a barley product than wheat based. The Roman gourmet Apicius, author of *De Re Coquinaria* (On Cooking, late

300s CE), the world's oldest cookbook, recommended parlaying barley broth into vegetable soup by adding beet tops and other *viridia* (greens). Tradition preserves other indigenous soup recipes—the Yosemite nation's salty mushroom soup, Tunisian *tharid* (bread soup), Albanian *buke mevaj me kripe* (bread soup), and Andalusian gazpacho, a soup-salad named for the Mozarabic term *caspa* (fragments) and blended of fresh summer peppers, tomato, cucumber, and a spot of olive oil.

Soups fit into three categories: *consommé,* a clear soup or broth made from well seasoned stock; *potage* and *crème,* a thick, crème soup made with heavy cream; and *velouté,* a meat-, fish-, or cheese-flavored soup built on a *roux* or white sauce. Vegetable soups begin with a *mirepoix* of celery, carrots, and onions and the addition a *bouquet garni* (flavor bundle) of bay leaf, parsley, and thyme. For stock, cooks simmer the skeleton and vegetables on a slow fire for hours to enhance rich flavor and body. A light, nonfat vegetarian broth begins with sautéed onions or leeks, celery, and cabbage cooked until soft, then blended with water, spinach, garlic, tomato, and salt before simmering. For the feeding of invalids, broth contains the essentials of mineral nourishment—calcium, magnesium, phosphorus, silicion, sulfur, and traces of zinc. In honor to rich stock, South American cooks made a rallying cry of a common proverb: "Good broth will resurrect the dead." (Fallon 2000, 132)

For peasants, soups or sops, the medieval term for soup, based on such mundane ingredients as garlic, fish, onions, herbs, potatoes, and chickpeas, fed the masses throughout the Middle Ages in Europe. Monks fasted and abstained as elements of piety and observed vows of poverty by preparing the same simple soups, usually from vegetables grown on monastery grounds. According to the encyclopedist and cartographer al-Maqdisi (or al-Muqaddasi) of Jerusalem, author of *Ahson at-taqasim fi ma'rifat al-aqalim* (The Best of Classification for the Knowledge of Regions, 985 CE), in Tunisia and Muslim Spain, traditional soups suited particular groups: Sufis ate *harisa,* a spiced porridge made from pounded wheat; ascetics preferred *tharida,* a simple dish made from crumbling bread into broth; north African sailors chose *asida,* a Moroccan semolina gruel flavored with honey and enjoyed at Muslim holy feasts. Rural Italian cooks favored a simple *minestra* (vegetable soup), parent of *minestrone* that blends grains and vegetables in a rich broth.

Well into the Middle Ages, soups were the daily fare of the poorest Europeans. In a thirteenth-century description of humble diet by Lombard poet Matazone da Calignano, author of *Nativitas Rusticorum et Qualiter Debent Tractari* (The Birth of Country Folk and How They Should Be Managed, ca. 1360), the meal of a *villano* (peasant) on millet "sop" paired the main course with mixed cereal, onions and garlic, beans, and turnip greens. The advantage of soup was its ease of preparation and flexibility of ingredients. At table, homemakers served broths and consommés in cups for sipping and supplied bowl and spoon for heavier soups.

For invalids, toddlers, and the elderly, panada or toast water, a thin gruel thickened with wheat bread, strengthened those on a liquid diet. For treatment of colds, addition of butter, sugar, and rum to hot broth relieved chest congestion. Cooks varied the menu for the sick with tapioca water served with honey and lemon, an oatmeal or barley spoon food laced with brandy, and barley water, a delicately flavored strained broth. Unlike boiled broths, meat drinks called beef water or chicken water derived from pouring boiling water over pounded slices of meat. A souchet (or souchy) of fish consisted of clear broth flavored with green herbs. Platina's *De Honesta Voluptate et Valitudine* (On Right Pleasure and Health, 1475) recommended a hearty bread soup made from bread crumbs rolled in flour and egg and dried for storage. Cooks rejuvenated the mix by heating in broth and coloring with saffron, Platina's favorite food dye. The anonymous *Le Ménagier de Paris* (The Goodman of Paris, ca. 1394) offered a hint to the hurried cook to remove scorching soup from the stove and transfer the surface liquid to another vessel without stirring up the bitter flavors below.

Egg yolk *moyeux,* grated bread crumbs, and Roman wheat starch thickeners stayed in use until about 1500, when cooks replaced them with a finer flour for bulking up soup into vegetable *potage,* stew, gruel, almond milk, and rice or bean pottage. During this era of soup making, the goodwife could dabble in creative urges, blending meal, peas, and beans with roots and greens and sprinkling on top leaves of alexander, borage, chives, fennel, leeks, mallow, marigold, mint, nasturtium, pennyroyal, rosemary, sage, sorrel, succory, tarragon, thistle, or violet. The finished product became "souper," the original of "supper," the final meal of the day, which families sipped with bread and cheese. (Tucker 1993, 21)

In the sixteenth century, Scottish cooks celebrated harvest with a hotchpotch (also *hochepot* or *hoggepot*), a soup that varied with the goods available in the pantry. The food expert Margaret "Meg" Dod, author of *The Cook and Housewife's Manual* (1826), recommended a base of juicy white turnips. A century later, F. Marion McNeill's *The Scots Kitchen: Its Traditions and Lore With Old-Time Recipes* (1929) characterized the *Hairst Bree* (harvest broth) as an aromatic dish filled with tender vegetables growing in the garden.

In 1650, the French created *roux* (butter-fried flour), a subtler, more flavorful additive to soup bases. Another innovation, the graceful lidded tureen or *soupière*, invented in the 1700s, replaced service in the *marmite* or soup kettle, which cooks carried directly to the table or emptied into covered bowls for ladling to individual guests. At the more elegant extreme of soup cookery, the staff of Louis XV treasured a magnificent rococo soup service crafted in 1733 by goldsmith François-Thomas Germain, whose works are on display at the Louvre Museum. The importance of soup to the menu influenced much of Europe, including Russia. Russian kitchen workers applied French technique and refinements to their own cabbage-based *shchi*, but rarely added to indigenous menus the prized light French broths and puréed vegetables, which required a host of kitchen workers for chopping and creaming. As their saying proclaimed, *Shchi da kasha—pischa nasha* (Cabbage soup and kasha, those are our foods). (Molokhovets 1992, 79)

New World colonists from England brought along the old English recipe for "veal glew," a boiled-down stock of fatty meat trimmings reduced to a paste that cooks patted into cakes and sun-dried. (Beard et al. 1975, 234) In New England, the extract earned the name "soup in the pocket," a reference to its portability. (Ibid.) It was shelf-stable and provided a tasty meat base for outdoor cooking during long travels. Like the French *glace de viande* (meat glaze), pocket soup was a traveler's condensed nourishment and forerunner of *bouillon* cubes, campers condensed vegetables, and the tear-open freeze-dried foods packed for the first space travelers.

Soup has long borne the hopes and expectations of cooks who had to stretch scanty supplies. In 1769, the Pacific expeditioner Captain James Cook sailed the *Endeavour* to Anaura Bay, New Zealand, and had his men collect wild celery for the galley cook to add to soup and breakfast oatmeal. According to Nelson Algren's essay "Festival in the Fields" from *America Eats* (1992), among French settlers of North America, bouillon parties were popular. In place of coffee, hosts at card parties offered bouillon along with crackers and bread.

In 1790, Jourdain Le Cointe's *La Cuisine de Santé* (Healthy Cookery) recorded the first recipe for bouillabaisse, a thick fish soup originated by fishing families as a one-pot meal cooked over a beach campfire from such fresh white-fish catch as Mediterranean rascasse. Bouillabaisse derived its named from *bouillir* (boil) and *abaisser* (reduce), a description of the way that cooks emulsified oil into broth to thicken it. Before fish soup became a common addition to restaurant menus, home cooks served it with baguette slices brushed with garlic and olive oil plus *rouille* (red pepper

aioli) before toasting. Enhancers of the folk recipe added such flavorings as fennel, saffron, citrus zest, and Pernod along with sea bass and mussels.

In 1819, the Arctic navigator Sir William Edward Parry of Bath, England, who sailed the *Hecla* and *Griper* across the Canadian arctic from Baffin Bay to Beaufort Sea, had to recalculate the amount of food each sailor could eat without endangering the expedition's provisions. His method was to replace the allotment of salt beef with a concentrated soup, which economized on the dwindling meat supplies. In the June 1874 issue of *The Household*, published in Brattleboro, Vermont, an article on soup differentiated between peasant soup and cookbook soup. The latter, a strained broth, lacked the meat and fat of the former, a hearty family dinner filled with vegetables, meat tidbits, and whatever "commodiments" the cook found to add. (Weaver 1989, 39)

Soup developed a mixed response in nineteenth-century Europe. The food journalist Alexandre Grimod de la Reynière, contributing editor of *Almanach des Gourmands* (Almanac of the Greedy Diners, 1812), coined the term "restaurant" from "restorative," another name for soup. Soup as a main course lost favor in Victorian England among the elite because of its connection with sustenance for the poor and with *bouillon* bars, sold as invalid food in pharmacies. The moralist and social critic Charles William Day further denigrated soup in *Hints on Etiquette and the Usages of Society: With a Glance at Bad Habits* (1844), when he blamed hot liquids for holding up diners or placing them in an awkward position of taking scalding liquid into the mouth.

Lauded as restoratives by Jean Anthelme Brillat-Savarin, author of *Physiologie du Goût, ou Méditation de Gastronomie Transcendante, Ouvrage Théorique, Historique et à l'Ordre du Jour* (The Physiology of Taste, or A Meditation on the Best of Dining, a Theoretical and Historic Work on the Order of the Day, 1825), soups, which he called *magisteres* (grand masters), gave strength to the invalid and renewed "robust and dynamic characters and . . . people who generally wear themselves out by burning up their energies." (Montagné 1977, 571) He acclaimed savory liquid meals for pleasing the stomach, stimulating appetite, and priming the digestive tract. To the east of France, Catholics cooks prepared *zur* soup throughout Lent as a means of avoiding meat. Bohemian cooks saved a pork head at Carnival time to boil with vinegar and vegetables for a main course and soup to follow. Czechs emigrating to America carried their pork-centered cuisine to the New World, offering pork broth and head cheese to the melting pot's culinary mix.

Among the Magyar peasants of Poland, breakfast soup was the norm, including *krupnik* (sour barley soup) and *gramatka* (beer soup), a Paschal specialty claimed by Czechs, Germans, Hungarians, and Romanians as well. By using beer to moisten cooked porridge or bread, cooks tapped cheap, available liquids. However, the addition of intoxicants often sent children on the way to school in an unstable condition. To the west, Austrian soup makers preferred dairy products as a soup base or flavored grain gruel with pork fat.

In Ireland, cooks made use of the kitchen range to heat the house and keep a stock pot boiling. As explained in the *Irish Press* in November 1934, the pot was a good place for tossing cracked marrow bones, rasher rinds, and vegetable scraps. The blended flavors needed only a straining and pouring into a bowl. An alternative, packet soup squares, worked better in stock than in hot water. The food writer warned, "Do not transfer the old stock into the new stock for more than two days in succession, because old stock is most dangerous." ("Make That Kitchen Range," 1934)

In the 1930s, American women's magazines lauded soup concentrates as the quick way to spice up meals without all the labor of ricing vegetables and boiling stock. Steero Cubes, a beef extract distributed by American Kitchen Products in New York City, appeared in the October 1930 issue of *Good Housekeeping* alongside relaxed hands unwrapping cubes to drop into the soup pot. Text suggested dissolving a cube in canned soups and vegetables to add zest and flavor without the hassle and expense of other condiments. The company offered sample cubes along with a recipe booklet, "101 New Dishes," from the expert Bertha M. Becker, the usual enticement to women needing instructions on how to upgrade their cooking.

Perhaps because it encourages culinary creativity, soup fills bowls worldwide, for example, in Libya, Croatia, Liechtenstein, Norway, Peru, Spain, Wales, Yugoslavia, and Latvia, where cooks make soup for lunch, and Ecuador, Slovenia, and Slovakia, where diners expect soup for lunch and dinner. Soup starter or thickener—known to Italians as *battuto* or *soffrito*, to the French as *matignon* or *mirepoix*, and the Spanish as *sofregit*—combines the flavors of onions and garlic, carrots and parsnips, celery, mushrooms, peas, and fennel with parsley, thyme, lemongrass, and marjoram, the typical soup herbs. In Asia, the common taste enhancers range from fish sauce and chilies to peanut or palm oil, shallots, ginger, and garlic. Unique to the soup of Provence is dried citrus peel; in Morocco, cooks season with cinnamon and turmeric.

Distinct from European technique, Asian cooks speed the cooking soup. Chinese chefs hurry the simmering process by adding powdered base to *kung pau* chicken and hot and sour soup. Japanese cooks begin with *dashi*, a broth of dried flaked bonito and seaweed.

Indonesians blend *bumbu* starter from clove, shrimp paste, macadamia nuts, and galangal root. Indian soups vary from the rest of Asia in the versatility and subtlety of their spicing. From a starter of garlic and onion, ginger, and hot pepper sauteed in oil or *ghee* (clarified butter), they add curry powder or *tadka* and top off soups with yogurt. For vegetarian soups, they prefer coconut milk as a flavor enhancer. In Malaysia, a doctor created *bak ku teh* (spicy breakfast soup) as a tonic to boost his children's appetites. In addition to mushroom, pork and chicken, spices, rice wine, and soy sauce or *tamari*, a fermented flavoring made from wheat and roasted soybeans, he added gankuo and dang xin, two Chinese herbs known for fighting hangovers and promoting a feeling of well being.

The uniqueness of ethnic soups sets each apart from the rest, for example, the chopped nuts and dried fruits in savory Moroccan meat soup and the cilantro and tomatillos of Mexican soup. In Moldavia, the Ukraine, and Russia, cooks pride themselves on *borscht* or *borsch*, a thick beet soup flavored with potatoes and carrots and topped with sour cream. In Iberia, a pleasant cool cup of gazpacho has influenced the making and serving of light summer soups in much of Europe and the Americas. The thrifty Chinese cook saves water from steaming vegetables and rice as a base for soup. Bolivians make soup from *chuños*, a freeze-dried potato. In Albania, cooks use a cow head and seasonings to make a traditional cream soup called *paçe*. Bulgarians blend cucumber with yogurt, walnuts, oil, and seasonings to make *tarator*, a cold soup.

Another variant is the choice of finishes or garnishes for ethnic soups. In Ireland, especially on the Aran Islands, soup is incomplete without a dollop of naturally sweet whipped cream. In France and Iberia, cooks rely on saffron, red pepper, shallots, and garlic. Greeks top their savory lemon chicken soup with shredded lemongrass. Southeast Asian cooks rely on coconut milk for flavor and smooth texture.

According to James Peterson, the recipient of the 1992 James Beard Cookbook of the Year award and author of *Splendid Soups* (1993), the simplicity of soup cooking comes down to three utensils—a chopping knife, cook pot, and soup bowl or mug. For cooks specializing in soups, his book recommends some additions to the usual lineup of kitchen ware:

- A food processor for slicing and chopping vegetables and puréeing shrimp or crayfish shells
- A semiprofessional blender for creaming thin mixtures and attachments that grind small quantities of food or spices
- A hand-held blender for immersing into liquids for pulverizing soft solids

- A food mill, a hand-cranked grinder in a metal frame that presses solids through heavy mesh for straining and pulping seedy or fibrous vegetables
- A miniature food processor for mincing small quantities of herbs, shallots, or garlics
- A marble, porcelain, or Mexican black stone mortar and pestle for grinding spice, garlic heads, or aromatic paste
- A Japanese mortar and pestle, called a *suribachi* or *surikogi*, for pulverizing sesame seeds
- A coffee grinder for spice grinding
- A mandoline or Japanese *benriner* cutter with an adjustable blade for julienning vegetables into slices and from slices into matchstick strips
- Pots ranging from a four-quart cook pot to a ten-quart thick-bottomed broth pot, in either copper or aluminum, that cooks down solids without scalding
- A long-handled strainer with fine or medium mesh screens, a shallow device that allows a circular rubbing of the ladle to force liquid through the holes for a smooth purée. Lined with cheesecloth, it traps hard bits and produces an extra smooth base.
- A fine mesh *chinois* or china cap, such as the cone-shaped strainer protected with a steel band, for making clear or creamed soup. It concentrates the stream of liquid into a receptacle and produces a fine purée.
- A fine or coarse china cap, which tolerates hard shell fragments during the process of straining crab or lobsters pieces. Unlike the screen chinois, it is solid metal with perforations for straining liquids through bones and vegetables.
- A collection of single-piece stainless steel ladles featuring bowls from one to twelve ounces in size for pressing mixtures through a narrow-gauge mesh screen and transferring soup from pots to storage containers or bowls
- A wood or stainless steel drum sieve with a circular screen two feet in diameter for placing over a sheet pan or bowl for working solids over the screen with a plastic scraper or rubber spatula

The soup cook also needs wood spoons, rubber spatulas, and clay, porcelain, or enameled iron baking or gratin dishes for altering soup into a *panade* or casserole or for baking eggs on top of the soup before serving. Host serve soup in cups, mugs, and bowls of various sizes and shapes to set off different types of soup and crocks and ramekins for baked soups. Oval soup spoons and round *bouillon* and *consommé* spoons are also useful implements.

See also **Liebig, Justus von; Potatoes, Sweet Potatoes, and Yams; Rumford, Count von**

Further Reading

Clear, Caitriona. *Women of the House*. Dublin: Irish Academic Press, 2000.

Perkins, Dorothy. *Encyclopedia of China*. New York: Facts on File, 1999.

Peterson, James. *Splendid Soups*. New York: Bantam Books, 1993.

Rajah, Carol Selva. *Makan-Lah!: The True Taste of Malaysia*. Sydney, Austr.: HarperCollins, 1996.

SOYBEANS

The annual legume also known as the Manchurian, soja, or soya bean is the world's most cultivated bean. It is a standard foodstuff of the cook's pantry for its nutrients and worth as a high-energy food. In ancient China, families grew soybeans before 2000 BCE and valued it along with barley, millet, rice, and wheat as one of the five sacred grains. Soybeans formed the basis of soy sauce or *tamari*, a fermented flavoring made from wheat and roasted soybeans, the standard condiment and salt substitute of Asia. It developed after 1134 BCE in liquid and solid form and made its way to Europe in the 1600s aboard Dutch trading

Mature soybeans.
[© *Courtesy of Agricultural Research Service, USDA. Photo by Scott Bauer.*]

vessels, where it fetched a high price for use on Renaissance tables.

Soybeans figure heavily in the development of vegetarianism. Although Buddhists did not ban animals from the diet, a tradition that Buddha died from eating spoiled pork cast doubt on red meat. As a substitute, cooks developed tofu, a glutenous soybean curd, as a diet staple containing more protein than any other food. They made it by crushing cooked beans and coagulating them with gypsum. Tofu is a nutritious, quick-cooking vegetable cheese and meat substitute that Japanese, Chinese, and Indonesian cooks consider a staple.

Although sources date tofu to as early as 2000 BCE, according to legend, after 200 BCE, the underpaid Chinese bureaucrats of the Han dynasty invented the curd as a meat substitute. For this contribution to Asian cookery, these impoverished men were known as "tofu officials." (Rajah 1996, 126) The cheese-textured substance appeared in a north Chinese recipe in 220 CE and reached Japanese kitchens around 760 CE under the name *okabe.* In 1183, Hiroshige Nakomi, a Shinto priest at Nara, chose tofu as an altar offering.

The curd didn't acquire the name *tofu* until 1489 and attained popularity among home cooks after 1600, when Jesuit linguists in Nagasaki first recorded the food in an English text. A Dominican missionary to China, Domingo Fernandez de Navarrete, described the ubiquity of tofu in *A Collection of Voyages and Travels* (1665). Ka Hitsujun of Osaka, who wrote *Tofu Hyakuchin Zokuhen* (100 Favorite Tofu Recipes, 1783), introduced a Chinese variety of fermented tofu. From the surface of soy milk, cooks lifted the skin, called *yuba,* dried it, and used it as wrappers and in rolls. They also molded and steamed the skins to resemble meat, fish, or poultry for vegetarian dishes.

When soybeans reached Europe in the 1700s, they grew in French botanic gardens and in England's Royal Botanic Gardens at Kew. In 1770, Benjamin Franklin wrote to the naturalist John Bartram in Philadelphia and enfolded soybeans in his letter. In 1804, Dr. James Mease mentioned their cultivation in the United States, where agronomists experimented with them as alternatives to native grains. After Asian immigrants settled on the American West Coast late in the 1800s, Wo Sing & Company of San Francisco and Hirata & Company of Sacramento produced the first tofu manufactured in the New World. The first caucasian tofu maker, Seventh-Day Adventist T. A. Van Gundy, jelled curds in 1929 in Arlington, California, for La Sierra Industries.

U.S. Department of Agriculture biologists and Canadian researchers began studying improved varieties during the Depression, when manufacturers crushed soybeans as a source of oil. Within six decades, American farmers led the world in growing soybeans as livestock forage or feed and as a cover crop. Related to alfalfa, clover, and peas and grown throughout eastern Asia, soybeans supplied kitchens with fresh, dried, and fermented foodstuffs as major sources of inexpensive protein. In addition to industrial uses, soybeans benefited the homemaker in soap, disinfectant, caulk, resin, fire extinguishers, wallpaper, solvent, varnish and paint, oilcloth, linoleum, wax, and plastics. As a food, soy benefits the cook in many ways. The Japanese *miso* paste, a fermented mass called *jiang* in China and *twoenjang* in Korea, sometimes blended soybeans with barley or rice to contribute a salty or spicy taste to broth, soup, or stir fry.

In 1953, the Milnot Company, an Illinois canned food manufacturer founded by Charles Hauser in 1915, altered its nondairy cream substitute from a cottonseed oil base to soybean oil. The product, which grew from the military's post-World War I demand for dairy products, replaced sweetened condensed and evaporated milk. By 1975, the company was marketing seventy-five private label brands of evaporated milk, which home and galley cooks and campers approved for their long shelf life and smooth, milk-like taste.

In the twenty-first century, American cooks rely on soy in similar coffee creamers, vegetable oil and margarine, mayonnaise, soy cheese and butter, whipped toppings, and meatless main dishes. Soy milk, the liquid drained from puréed beans, supplies lactose-intolerant stomachs with a beverage or topping for cereal; it is also a protein-rich additive to cooking and baking. As a condiment, soy sauce developed into a regular ingredient in soup, gravy, and Chinese foods.

A suitable meat analogue, soybeans fill canisters around the globe, as with the South African larder, which stocks beans for *bobotie* (meat loaf), a common dish served with curry. Vegetarians worldwide rely on soy for hamburger and bacon look-alikes, no-meat hot dogs and sausage patties, bean sprouts, custards, and nutritious beverages. In Japan, tofu is silky and spongy. The Chinese variety, typically firm or extra firm, is available from pushcarts, where vendors sell it in scoops sauced with a warm brown sugar and peanut syrup. After pressing, tofu supplies cooks with a breakfast protein and a soft enhancer of vegetable soup, broth, sauce, pudding, dip, dressing, and one-dish meals.

See also **Baby Food; Carver, George Washington**

Further Reading

Rajah, Carol Selva. *Makan-Lah!: The True Taste of Malaysia.* Sydney, Australia: HarperCollins, 1996.
Reynolds, Biz Fairchild, "The Most Important Food in the World," *Mother Earth News,* June 2000, 62–66.

SOYER, ALEXIS

One of England's nineteenth-century masters of French cuisine, Alexis Benoît Soyer turned his talents to publishing, invention, philanthropy, and the organization of the *brigade de cuisine* (kitchen team). The youngest son of shopkeepers, Soyers was born in October 1809 in Meaux-en-Brie, France. After his brother Philippe encouraged him to become a cook, Soyer apprenticed at Grignon near Versailles and gained experience from three years' service under Chef Douix on the Boulevard des Italiens. In 1830, Soyer was under-chef at the foreign office for Prince Polignac and passed to the kitchen of the Duke of Cambridge at age twenty-one. He later cooked for a series of nobles.

As cook for 1,500 aristocrats at London's upscale Reform Club in Pall Mall, Soyer rose to the enviable position of first chef. One of the original proponents of gas energy for home cookery, in 1841, he further modernized the huge club kitchen with gas cookers, which improved efficiency and flexibility for group dinners, private meals, and banquets. After the death of his wife, artist Emma Jones Soyer, he began a long career in cookbook publishing and bottled Soyer's Sauce for sale. To express his image of the professional, Chef Soyer wore tailor-made jackets and a red velvet beret. He achieved fame for designing work spaces and inventing kitchen tools.

In February 1847, during the Irish Potato Famine, Soyer sketched plans for a soup boiler. Two months later, he volunteered to set up feeding stations at the Royal Barracks in Dublin and in London, to solicit donations, and to supply recipes to nourish the hungry. Measuring forty feet by forty-eight inches, a station consisted of a board and canvas frame around a coal oven and a three hundred-gallon steam boiler on wheels. Around the outside of Soyer's boiler he set eight *bain-maries* to hold one thousand gallons of water. Alongside he assembled cutting tables, tubs on wheels, chopping blocks, storage boxes, and water butts. At the far end, he devised a row of tables holding enamelled food basins and metal spoons on chains. A parallel row of tables held wash basins and sponges for dishwashing. At the opposite end, a portrait of Queen Victoria looked down on cooks and diners. He zigzagged the line of the hungry to keep them from crowding together and spreading disease. Each entered at the sound of a bell, paused for grace, and ate a quart of soup before exiting. The whole meal required six minutes for a total of one thousand meals served per hour.

Suffering appalled Soyer. One of his innovations to end famine was meatless soup, an inexpensive, nutritious broth that stimulated appetites and improved digestion. Comments by the media about watery soup so demoralized the Irish that they turned on Soyer and

Frontispiece from Pantropheon (1853).

forced him to flee. Undaunted, he continued to inveigh against waste while any person starved.

Working at society's extremes, Soyer served both poor and rich. In 1838, he published a pamphlet, *Soyer's Charitable Cookery, or The Poor Man's Regenerator*, a handbook for altruists that earned more money for charity. That same year, he received a commission from a Mr. Harbottle to design a galley for the *Guadalquiver*, a steamboat carrying passengers around Cuba. Built at Liverpool, it bore Soyer's design, carried out by outfitters Bramah and Tristige of Piccadilly. Typical of Soyer's genius, the eight-by-seventeen-foot kitchen was compact and convenient.

In addition to his pragmatic drawings of restaurant kitchens in *Gastronomic Regenerator, a Simplified and New System of Cookery* (1846), Soyer published advice to the middle class in *The Modern Housewife or Ménagère* (1849), prettily dedicated "to the Fair Daughters of Albion." The text, like that of Eliza Acton's *Modern Cookery for Private Families* (1845), spoke directly to the bride learning to cook well on a budget.

...on to cooking and writing, Soyer tinkered ... low-cost innovations for the kitchen. He ... all spirit stove, called Soyer's Magic ... for cramped spaces or ... the stove along on a ... by cooking in the wild. ...ring Cross company sold ... returned no profit to the ... or a gas cooker, cottager's ... coffee pot, egg cooker, and ... enrich him because his true ...

...ciples of quality food service we... of advice. He thought that guests should know the menu before dinner. To the server, he advised limiting the number of wine glasses to one, cutting meat cross-grain on a slant, and serving vegetables well done. He instructed guests not to move dishes, but to leave table arrangement to the staff. His advice concerning digestion was to avoid unsavory food and not to take more food or wine out of deference to the host.

Against the English tide of hearty meats, Soyer proposed a vegetarian diet, especially for those who could ill afford meat. Among his chosen vegetables, he lauded potatoes, broccoli, cauliflower, artichokes, parsnips, mushrooms, beans, onions, and turnip tops. His dicta called for plain salad leaves rather than chopped assortments of numerous greens and herbs. For tenderizing meats, he promoted the leaves of the papaw tree, which loosened the fiber of old pigs and poultry and newly-slaughtered meats. He spurned leftovers on subsequent days unless the food took on a new texture, flavor, and appearance.

During the Crimean War, he revolutionized field kitchens at Scutari, Turkey, for the English military by instituting order and pragmatic use of supplies, equipment, and fuel. On his own funds, he visited the battle zone to lift morale by serving more edible meals at the barracks hospital. He rigged up a bakery and replaced rotted vegetables with dried stock. His field stoves, comprising a copper boiler and chimney common to the Victorian laundry, required no tinning nor replacement parts and remained a military standard through two world wars. Near the barracks hospital, he set up a kiosk, called Soyer House, to which he invited medical officers and army personnel from England, France, and Turkey. Guests ate servings from numbered bowls and indicated their surprise at the quality and flavor of Soyer's battlefield meals. Lord William Paulet wrote, "Had I not seen and tasted [the new diet] I could not have believed that such an amelioration could have been produced from the same materials as allowed by Government." (Morris 1938, 145) Soyer credited improvement to organization, skill, and control of proportions.

As a savings to the military, he managed with two civilian cooks and six soldiers what thirty-four untrained men had previously bungled. On passing through the halls, he heard cheers from patients who had the strength to applaud.

On return home, Soyer worked at completing *Soyer's Culinary Campaign, with the Plain Art of Cookery for Military and Civil Institutions* (1857) and a monograph, *Instructions to Military Hospital Cooks, in the Preparation of Diets for Sick Soldiers* (1857). A bout of fever and a fall from his horse in June 1857 compromised his health. His constitution declined over two years of speaking engagements until his death on August 5, 1858.

See also **Cookbook; Military Kitchens; Potatoes, Sweet Potatoes, and Yams**

Further Reading

Morris, Helen. *Portrait of a Chef: The Life of Alexis Soyer.* Cambridge: Cambridge University Press, 1938.

Ray, Elizabeth. *Alexis Soyer, Cook Extraordinary.* Lewes, Eng.: Southover Press, 1991.

Volant, F., and J. R. Warren, eds. *Memoirs of Alexis Soyer.* Rottingdean, Sussex: Cooks Books, 1985.

SPACE KITCHENS

Since the first manned space flights in 1961, National Aeronautics and Space Administration (NASA) kitchens provisioning U.S. space missions have prepared foods on earth that supply adequate nutrients for maximum performance under physically and mentally stressful conditions. Dietitians, engineers, and food scientists follow guidelines evolved at NASA by the Foods Systems Engineering Facility at Johnson Space Center in Houston, Texas, which protects space crew from bacteria and viruses and from mishaps that cause liquids or crumbs to contaminate sensitive equipment. In the 1950s, civilian professionals at the Pillsbury Company evolved the Hazard Analysis and Critical Control Point (HACCP) concept, which predicts the kinds of food safety risks and problems that may jeopardize a crew in space. Staff examined every aspect of ingredient selection, kitchen conditions, temperature monitoring, handling and storage, packaging and distribution, and directions for consumption.

At space laboratories, engineers test the stability of individual items on the zero-gravity KC-135 airplane, a space simulator. Cooks determine the value of foods after freeze-drying and packaging; astronauts evaluate the color, consistency, odor, and taste of dishes about five months before preparers make menus for each flight. The eight categories of food prepared for space meals include these:

Cosmonaut Valery V. Ryumin organizes a meal on the mid deck of the Earth-orbiting space shuttle *Discovery*.
[© *Courtesy of the National Aeronautics and Space Administration.*]

Rehydratable stores—for example, citrus juice concentrate and oatmeal with water removed for easy storage

Thermostabilized food—including fruit, pudding, beef tips with mushrooms, tomatoes and eggplant, chicken à la king, ham, and tuna, which are processed with heat to destroy bacteria and enzymes and stored at room temperature in pull-tab cans, lidded cups, or retort pouches, which combine the conveniences of metal cans and boil-in bags

Intermediate moisture [IM] food—including apricots, beef jerky and dried peaches and pears, which are partially dehydrated to retain a soft texture but remove water in which bacteria can thrive

Natural form [NF] food—such ready-to-eat snacks as chocolate candy, cookies, granola bars, dried apricots, pudding cups, brownies, peanut butter, and almonds, which are placed in flexible pouches

Irradiated goods—meaty entrées, including beef steak, tuna salad, and chicken stew, which are cooked and packaged in flexible laminated foil pouches and sterilized with ionizing radiation to preserve servings at room temperature.

Quick frozen food—such freeze-at-the-source dishes as casseroles, chicken pot pie, and quiche, which retain taste and texture

Fresh food—eat-out-of-hand produce, particularly apples, oranges, and bananas, which require no preparation or preservation

Refrigerated dairy foods—such perishables as cream cheese and sour cream, which require cold storage

In addition, packers supply condiments, for example, individual pouches of ketchup, tabasco sauce, mayonnaise, mustard, and taco sauce plus polyethylene dropper bottles of liquid pepper and salt, which can't be shaken onto foods. The concept proved so flexible that campers, rescue teams, and spelunkers have purchased the same stay-fresh meals for a variety of situations.

About two months before a space launch, NASA staff loads food packages in the order in which they will be consumed. For Space Shuttle flights, they pack the completed food kit in the Shuttle locker and ship it to the Kennedy Space Center in Florida three weeks in advance of departure. A day before launch, food crews enhance the supply of processed foods with stocks of fresh bread and rolls, carrot and celery sticks, pome and citrus fruit, and bananas. The crew stores foods on board in secure containers that will not float away in conditions of microgravity during orbits of Earth, when food, utensils, and scissors enter freefall. To thwart the danger of free-floating liquids or crumbs being inhaled or contaminating equipment requires planning and engineering. Special packages and sipping straws with clamps deliver servings directly to the mouth, but keep contents from escaping into the atmosphere.

The history of space travel has seen the evolution of food preparation from a primitive to a sophisticated state. The first astronauts—Alan B. Shepard, Jr., in *Freedom 7* on May 7, 1961, and Virgil I. "Gus" Grissom in *Liberty Bell 7* on July 2, 1961—traveled only fifteen minutes in space. In preparation, they ate full meals at the commissary before departing Earth. In test situations, crew examined the physiological demands of biting, chewing, and swallowing liquids and solids in a microgravity atmosphere.

On longer voyages in space, crewmen John Glenn, M. Scott Carpenter, Walter M. "Wally" Schirra, and L. Gordon Cooper, Jr., pilots of the next four Mercury missions, relied on unappetizing freeze-dried powder, bite-size cubes, and semi-liquids squeezed from aluminum tubes without the aid of utensils, all developed at the Army's Natick Laboratory. Dehydration gave them problems with rehydrating foods, as did drinking from straws or squeezing solids into the mouth. To ease passage of pulpy foods, preparers developed a coating for the tubes to halt formation of hydrogen gas when applesauce and other acidic meals came in contact with metal. To lighten foods in storage, NASA developed plastic containers.

For more involved test flights, food preparers offered newly created bite-size cubes by compressing and dehydrating purées that rehydrated automatically when it met saliva in the mouth. To prevent crumbs, cooks coated individual pieces with edible gelatin and vacuum-packed servings in individual containers formed from laminated plastic film. These clear food boxes stored easily and protected contents from flavor loss, sogginess, and spoilage, a potential hazard to crew health and agility and to the overall success of the flight.

During the Gemini stage of space exploration, begun with the five-hour mission of Virgil Grissom and John W. Young in Gemini 3 on March 23, 1965, staff broadened the choice of foods, retained more flavor and normal consistency, upgraded packages, and increased nutrient intake. Astronauts enjoyed three meals of .58 kilograms of food per day for maximum performance. Freeze-drying benefited the space program by making their food light, easy to store at room temperature, and safe to eat after long storage. Four-day menus enticed the crew with tasty cinnamon toast, turkey chunks, cream of chicken soup, shrimp cocktail, beef stew, chicken with rice, chicken and vegetables, turkey with gravy, fruit cocktail, butterscotch pudding, applesauce, chocolate, and grape and orange beverages.

To freeze-dry foods, preparers diced, liquefied, or sliced each edible before pressure cooking or processing and wrapping in cellophane. After quick freezing, they dried foods on trays by reducing air pressure in a vacuum chamber. The essence of freeze-drying was a rapid rise in temperature to drive off moisture that might form ice crystals while preserving natural flavors and oils. The diner had only to inject water back into the food with a water gun, then squeeze the contents directly into the mouth. To prevent the growth of bacteria, the user of the package put germicidal tablets in the empty container to decontaminate leftovers.

Begun in 1968, the Apollo program launched Walter Cunningham, Don Eisele, and Walter Schirra, Jr., on October 11, for a 260-hour flight. The mission, which was the first to provide in-flight hot water, built on past success by increasing menu variety. Engineers pioneered the "spoon bowl," a zippered plastic package rehydrated with a water gun and opened for eating with a spoon. Because moisture caused contents to adhere to the spoon, users dined more normally. The menu expanded from similar unappetizing purées to the familiar taste, aroma, and textures of bacon and scrambled eggs, cornflakes, cheese crackers, peanut butter, spaghetti, hot dogs, beef pot roast and sandwiches, tuna salad, chocolate pudding, and coffee. For Christmas 1968, Frank Borman, James A. "Jim" Lovell, Jr., and William "Bill" Anders, the pilots of Apollo 8 who looped the moon on a 150-hour flight, munched turkey chunks and spooned up gravy while envious Mission Control technicians staffed monitors and contented themselves with coffee and sandwiches.

Continuing the search for a genuine dining experience, space food kitchen staff and dietary engineers devised a thermostabilized container called a wetpack, which contained naturally moist food that diners could see and smell while eating. One type of wetpack was a flexible plastic of aluminum foil pouch; another was a can with pull-off lid. With this method, staff could pack a week's worth of rations per astronaut in a container no larger than three shoe boxes. For backup, the astronauts carried the same squeeze tubes that Mercury crewmen had used.

In 1972, before the French geologist Michael Siffre entered Midnight Cave near Del Rio, Texas, for a six-month study of solitude away from natural light, he contacted NASA to aid him in stocking frozen meals. The Marriott In-Flite Service packed the same foods that astronauts John M. Young, T. K. "Tom" Mattingly, III, and Charles M. Duke had eaten on the Apollo 16 lunar mission the previous April 16, including appetizing casseroles, filet mignon, potatoes, and spinach. Siffre grew so lonely and disoriented that he welcomed a mouse and lured it closer with the offering of a pea and jam. NASA studied the effects of Siffre's subterranean mission on physiological rhythms and nutrient use for future application to space missions of similar duration.

When the one hundred-ton Skylab 2 flew from John F. Kennedy Space Center on May 25, 1973, it was the site of a twenty-two-week assignment for pilots Charles Conrad, Jr., Joseph P. Kerwin, and Paul J. Weltz that was more demanding than any previous space flight. Meals came in rehydratable beverage dispensers and packages or aluminum cans. In the ship's circular workshop, ten water tanks held seventy-two gallons each. Storage lockers stowed clothing and meals. In the wardroom below, food heating and service for the nine-man crew made use of a freezer and refrigerator, dining space, and table containing electronic heaters to warm meals. By anchoring their feet to footholds, the men were able to sit for meals and gaze out a circular window to Earth below. To assure their contentment and nutrition, space cooks had expanded the menu to include filet mignon, prime rib, lobster Newburg, chili, ham, mashed potatoes, steak, asparagus, and a dripless ice cream in the form of blue wafers that melt in the mouth.

In microgravity, diners of all three 1973 manned Skylab missions consumed 2,800 calories per day to meet normal physiological needs for their age, weight, and exertions, particularly life science experiments. To ready food for the table, each of three three-man crews warmed packages by conduction on the heated tray, which engineers divided into recessed compartments. As a joke, during the second manned mission aboard Skylab 3 launched on July 28, 1973, electrical engineer Owen K. Garriott smuggled in a tape of his wife's voice saying, "This is Helen in Skylab. The boys hadn't had a home-cooked meal in so long, I thought I'd just bring one up." (Canby 1974, 462)

On the 1975 Apollo-Soyuz Test Project, the first international link-up in space launched on July 15, kitchen staff provided U.S. astronauts Thomas P. "Tom" Stafford, Vance D. Brand, and Donald K. "Deke" Slayton with meals similar to those served on Apollo and Skylab missions. Russian fliers Alexei A. Leonov and Valeri N. Kubasov ate from aluminum tubes and metal cans containing a delicacy, pickled perch. On small heating units, cosmonauts warmed meals of meat, meat paste, cheese, soup, bread, dried fruit, nuts, cake, and coffee. Cooking required only an oven and special containers; no pots were necessary.

For John Young and Robert Crippen, who manned the Space Shuttle *Columbia*, launched from Florida on April 12, 1981, food preparers upgraded packaging and utensils to create a normal dining atmosphere. For a two-day, six-hour mission, they allotted 3.8 pounds of food per person; one pound of the weight consisted of packaging. The orbiter fuel cell produced an adequate supply of potable water for kitchen use. Menu choices coordinated seventy-four foods and twenty beverages in five categories: thermostabilized irradiated, intermediate moisture, rehydratable, natural fruits and vegetables, and beverages. Within dietary restrictions, individual fliers could choose foods that suited their tastes from scrambled eggs, cereal with nondairy milk, chicken consommé, cream of mushroom soup, shrimp cocktail, macaroni and cheese, chicken and rice, and tortillas, which removed the problem of bread crumbs. Crew color-coded choices before storing foods on board.

Remodeled in 1994, the Shuttle galley featured updated electronics and reduction of bulk by one-third the weight and one-half the volume. The Shuttle contained its own modular galley in the orbiter middeck, complete with food locker secured by a net, forced-air convection oven capable of holding fourteen food packages, and a water reservoir, which dispensed fluids in half-ounce increments at three temperatures: warmed to 155–165 degrees, room temperature, or chilled. Within thirty-five minutes, the four-person crew could assemble foods, reconstitute, and heat a full meal to 160–170 degrees on a tray, which velcroed to the middeck stowage locker or lap. Diners opened foil packs with scissors and ate with normal utensils. Because of the length of a mission, designers made rigid box-shaped containers from lighter materials, such as a septum to divide elements within packages and flexible plastic sides with valves for hydrating. A trash compactor reduced the bulk of waste.

The exception to general space food preparation was the sixty billion dollar International Space Station (ISS), which departed for four months of habitation from the launch site in Baikonur, Kazakhstan, on October 31, 2000. The project was a cooperative effort of Belgium, Britain, Canada, Denmark, France, Germany, Holland, Italy, Japan, Norway, Russia, Spain, Sweden, Switzerland, and the United States. For a crew of two Russian cosmonauts, Yuri Gidzenko and Sergei Krikalyov, plus William Shepherd, a former U.S. Navy SEAL, and the mission's commander, who lived in the Habitation Module, preparers delivered food in ninety-day increments via a Multi-Purpose Logistics Module, a pressurized container exchanged regularly at the Space Shuttle payload bay. On arrival, the crew had no way to cook food and only enough oxygen for forty-eight hours, during which they activated life-support systems. Each flight also carried a two-day supplementary provision in case bad weather inhibited the return docking. Unlike the Space Shuttle food system, the ISS had multi-use tables to which trays attached. Utensils fastened to trays with magnets. A joint Russian-U.S. system provided fuel cells that recycled and sanitized wastewater and condensation from oxygen generators as a by-product for drinking and cooking. Crew could access additional cabin moisture for washing, but not consumption.

The food for ISS was frozen, refrigerated, or thermostabilized for storage in the module's refrigerator-freezer. The menu, compiled by both Russian and American provisioners, included Russian-style kielbasa as well as standard American fare—grits and oatmeal, fettucine alfredo, lobster tail, beef goulash, meatballs, chicken salad, stir-fried chicken, and au gratin potatoes as well as fresh and fresh-treated fruits and vegetables, brownies, shortbread, instant breakfast, nuts, trail mix, gum, and

Life Savers and allowed for substitutions chosen three months before launch. Microwaveable foil and plastic packages retarded spoilage over a long shelf life. Within pullout drawers with viewing windows, preparers positioned frozen food in single-serving containers. Cosmonauts selected beverages from a long list that included cocoa, cherry and grape drink, lemonade, peach nectar, cider, punch, tea, and coffee in three varieties—regular, decaffeinated, and kona.

The crew followed a pre-meal protocol involving selection of foods on a computer, locating food, and preparing and heating. To reconstitute beverages, diners added concentrated fruit juice from the refrigerator and rehydrated meals through an adapter on each package. To access a pouch, the user pierced the septum with a needle, selected on a dial the amount of water needed for rehydration, then pressed a light blue button for cold or a yellow button for hot. The pump shut off automatically to prevent pouches from bursting. Low-power microwave or convection ovens heated at bottom and blew warm air onto wrapped dishes. After raising food temperatures to 165 to 180 degrees Fahrenheit—too low to burn foods or melt plastic—diners velcroed containers onto matching oven and tray slots to keep them from floating in space. Utensils stayed in place with magnets. Cosmonauts opened packages with scissors and ate with knife, fork, and spoon, which they washed with packaged towelettes at a hygiene station. Trash disposal in a compactor and stowing of trays and utensils ended the meal.

In case of a delayed docking or on-board system failure, the ISS offered a Safe Haven food system, a backup nutrition pack that could feed crew for twenty-two days. This alternate emergency ration, comprising thermostabilized, dehydrated, or intermediate moisture foods stored at room temperature, provided two thousand calories per member each day. Foods remained edible for two years or longer. To aid clean-up and combat bacteria and mildew, which had hampered the Russian Mir space station, Duane Pierson, the head of microbiology at the Johnson Space Center, insisted on a reduction of condensation. Because elevated radiation could speed mutation of resistant bacterial strains, he supplied the crew with ordinary soap.

Space food and dining protocol was not limited to the sky. Pillsbury's HACCP system that regulated food aboard Apollo spacecraft reached commercial food producers in 1971. The company trained Food and Drug Administration employees in compiling low acid canned food regulations to ensure the sanitation and safety of all U.S. canned foods. Plans to extend HACCP controls to meat and fish vendors projected relief of the public's concern about heavy metal contamination as well as salmonella, insect infestation, and *E coli* bacteria.

From 1975 to 1977, a demonstration project managed by the Johnson Space Center produced Meal System for the Elderly. A multi-agency cooperative sponsored delivery of space meals to home-bound seniors and handicapped people who could not access other federal, state, and charity meal programs. Commercial kitchens such as Sky-Lab Foods, Inc. in Elmsford, New York, marketed NASA's food packages of freeze dried and "retort pouch" meals as a convenience that combined shelf stability and transportability. Food preparation suited the needs of the aged, immobilized, and disadvantaged for easy delivery to home-bound and institutionalized diners.

In 1995, NASA's Hazard Analysis and Critical Control Point system came under renewed consideration of the Food and Drug Administration for application to civilian food service. Unlike standard health department certification, space kitchen scrutiny shifted from clean facilities to hygienic food-handling procedures. By studying provisions from purchase to service, agents reduced the food-borne illness by charting temperatures and cleanliness during storage, thawing, recipes and preparation, holding, cooking, reheating, and plating. The major drawback of instituting HACCP procedures in schools, restaurants, and hotels was the increase in human labor and the training of agents to a new way of thinking about food safety.

Further Reading

Canby, Thomas Y., "Skylab, Outpost on the Frontier of Space," *National Geographic*, October 1974, 441–492.

Collins, Jim, "From Grime to Sublime," *Attaché*, June 2001, 26–30.

Hall, Alice J., "The Climb Up Cone Crater," *National Geographic*, July 1971, 136–148.

Lorenzini, Beth, "Here Comes HACCP," *Restaurants & Institutions*, January 1, 1995, 119.

Philips, Sam C., "A Most Fantastic Voyage," *National Geographic*, May 1969, 593–635.

Siffre, Michel, "Six Months Alone in a Cave," *National Geographic*, March 1975, 426–435.

Weaver, Kenneth F., "Voyage to the Planets," *National Geographic*, August 1970, 147–193.

SPICES

Spice identifies ethnic cooking styles and trading patterns that links far flung peoples in a culinary exchange unprecedented in human history. To the Gabonese, *piment* (hot pepper) is the common flavoring. The Azeris of Azerbaijan specialize in spicy dishes, which they call the "French cuisine of the East." (Skabelund 1997, Vol. II, 15) Over traditional kebabs, pilau, and piti, they add cilantro, cinnamon, dill, garlic, ginger, mint, pepper, or saffron. A soothing after-entrée, *dovga*, a blend of yogurt, rice, and herbs, improves

Spices for sale at an outdoor market in Thailand.

digestion. Korean cooks, who lace hot dishes with chili peppers, obtained their trademark spice from the Portuguese. Similarly, Hawaiians owe their *lomilomi* salmon to Iberian newcomers.

Spice appeared in a wide range of settings in world history. Egyptian morticians used peppercorns to fill the mummy of Ramses III, who died in 1156 BCE. Remains of a patrician woman buried in China around 165 BCE survived in remarkable condition alongside sacks, jars, and bamboo canisters of meat, grain, fish, fruit, cinnamon, and ginger. Ginger so dominated Chinese cookery that on his journey to India, Buddhist monk Fa-Hsien, author of *Fo Kuo Chi* (Record of Buddhist Kingdoms, 406 CE), reported that sailors grew it in containers on board ship.

Piquant seasonings from Asia and the Near East, especially pepper, revolutionized the European diet. Hippocrates, the father of Greek medicine, had recognized the medicinal qualities about 400 BCE, but placed no value on it as a condiment. Caelius Apicius, the Roman gourmet, recorded in *De Re Coquinaria* (On Cooking, late 300s CE) the use of cardamon, cinnamon, clove, costum, ginger, nutmeg, and pepper, all derived from a thriving trade with the eastern Mediterranean shore and beyond. From the Moluccas came nutmeg and clove; from Vietnam, cinnamon and cassia; and white and black pepper from India. The outlay for spice was so unsettling that Roman encyclopedist Pliny the Elder warned in Volume XII of his *Natural History* (ca. 77 CE) that the government was pouring one hundred million sesterces each year into the pockets of Arab, Chinese, and Indian traders. The question of the spice fad concerned the Roman Senate, which held special sessions to discuss the empire's reliance on Asian imports.

The relatively mundane spicing of foods in the Roman Empire pale by comparison with the medieval orgy that erupted during and after the Crusades. The English pepperers' guild existed from the 1150s to 1345, when they merged with the Guild of Grossers (wholesale grocers). In 1328, St. Birgitta of Uppland, Sweden, purchased forty kilograms of almonds, five kilograms of caraway, three kilograms of pepper, one kilogram of ginger, seven hundred grams of saffron, and five hundred grams of cinnamon to host a funeral dinner honoring her father, Birger Persson. In the aftermath of the Black Death in 1348, the medieval beginnings of world trade stirred in the Mediterranean trade centers. Historians question motivation, but reject the long-held fallacy that people spiced questionable meats to hide advancing putrefaction. It is more likely that the wealth of the silk routes and harbor-to-harbor routes of Levantine merchant vessels derived from Europe's boredom with a bread- and gruel-based diet, the aspirations of the rising middle class, and curiosity about the fabled foods and preservatives of distant lands made accessible by improvements in trade and transportation. The 1400s saw the introduction of cloves, dried dates, raisins, and pepper, all derived from western Europe's contact with the Levant during the Crusades.

The advance of pharmacology also stimulated the spice trade. At European *apothecarii* (pharmacies), compounders, drawing on newly translated medical texts from the Arab world, classified pepper, cinnamon, and other stimulants as curatives, digestives, aphrodisiacs, soporifics, and tonics. One example from 1317 was the *pain d'epices* (spice bread), an appetite stimulant fragrant with almonds and rose water, that the physician Gaufridus Isnardi made for Pope John XXII. The papal apothecary, Jaquet Melior, sent spice-rich recipes for

Philip VI of France, featuring coriander, licorice, and mint.

The demand for fresher, more exotic stores of ginger, cardamom, allspice, coriander, cubeba, galingale, and saffron brought ships from Sumatra, India, and, after the discovery of the New World, the West Indies, where the Arawaks preserved meat in the fruit of the wild allspice plant. Brisk turnover in stores transformed Crete into an island warehouse and built Aleppo, Tripoli, Beirut, Acre, Hormuz, Istanbul, Montpellier, Valencia, Ragusa, and Naples into trading meccas. Saffron alone was a caliph's treasure, for it derived from the threads of pistils and stamens at the rate of two hundred pounds of crocus to yield three ounces of dried spice. In 1560, Alexandria handled five million pounds of flavor enhancers on their way to the kitchens of the Mediterranean shores and as far inland as traders ventured.

In the mid-seventeenth century, Pierre de Lune, chef of the Duc d'Orléans and friend of the food writer François-Pierre de la Varenne, invented a culinary masterpiece, the *bouquet garni* (flavor bundle). An aromatic vegetable and herb cluster that the cook wrapped in a cheesecloth square and tied securely with kitchen string or immured in a porous container similar to a tea ball, it typically consisted of bay leaf, parsley, and thyme, depending on the dish it enhanced. Additional herbs bagged for stewing included basil, burnet, celery, chervil, rosemary, savory, and tarragon. The cook used a skewer to fish the bundle out of the dish before plating.

The supreme importer, Venice's Rialto market, became a cosmopolitan gateway, dispatching ships to all quarters, banking coins of global provenance, and setting lavish tables second to none. At *aromatarii* and *speciarii*, storekeepers wafted *sacchetti veneti* (Venice bags) under the noses of shoppers, who could identify alley storefronts by the scent of sandalwood from India and mace from Barbados. Housekeepers pierced oranges and citrons with clove and rolled them in orris root to suspend on ribbons as pantry-freshening pomanders. Cooks traded coins for the pinches of aromatic grains for pickling eel and turning meats into *luganeghe* (sausage). Serafino Amabile Guastella, the author of *L'Antica Carnevale nella Contea di Modica* (The Old Carnival in Modica County, 1887), expressed the attitude of the poor to these additives. For the household lacking much more than bread for sustenance, the wife added an onion and a few olives to augment and vary her husband's meager workday lunch. In lieu of these humble condiments, he had to rely on ginger, which he packed in a holder carved from a cane.

The consensus on spices pointed to their value as flavorings, seasonings, and curatives:

Spice	Culinary Use	Curative Use
Allspice	Rice, curry, pudding, pickles, wine	Colic, flatulence, neuralgia, rheumatism
Anise	Flavoring, beverages	Cough, flatulence, indigestion, poor appetite, rheumatism
Bay leaf	Meat stew, fricassee, fish, soup, sauce, bouillon	Acne, stomach, kidney
Cardamom	Marinade, liqueur, beverages, wine, pickles, fruit salad, curry, cake, bread, biscuits, coffee	Flatulence, halitosis, headache, indigestion
Cinnamon	Tea, fruit, pickles, flavoring	Diarrhea, flatulence, infection, nausea
Clove	Curry, fruit, marinade, pickles, wine, bread, biscuits, cake, pie	Halitosis, nausea, neuralgia, rheumatism, toothache
Cumin	Curry, yogurt, lamb, pickles, liqueur	Colic, diarrhea, flatulence, indigestion
Ginger	Wine, liqueur, cake, biscuits, stew, sauce, stir-fry, cordials, candy	Chills, nausea, sore throat, poor circulation
Nutmeg	Roast meat, milk, cheese, liqueur, cordial	Indigestion, poor appetite
Pepper, black	Flavoring, condiment	Arthritis, edema, flatulence, indigestion, infection, nausea, rhinitis, vertigo
Pepper, cayenne	Seasoning, stew, soup	Colic, indigestion, poor circulation, rhinitis, sore throat
Peppers, chili and sweet	Salads, casseroles, stew, soup, sauces	Indigestion, poor appetite, rhinitis
Saffron	Bread cake, biscuits, fish, meat, food coloring, flavoring	Fever, indigestion, muscle cramp, sexual dysfunction
Turmeric	Food coloring, pickles	Bruises, congestion
Vanilla	Flavoring, food coloring	Malaise

Spice mill with engraved decoration, circa 1540.

Travelers have disseminated spice and recipes from all parts of the globe. Muslim pilgrims visiting Mecca returned with spring water from Zamzam and metalware, Chinese porcelain, and spices from India and the Moluccas. Portuguese sea captains, who navigated the world and established themselves in China, Japan, the Philippines, Hawaii, and Macao, earned their livelihood as spice traders and wine merchants. Along the way, they survived ennui and isolation by adapting native dishes with the spices at hand—Indian cumin, coriander, ginger, and chili peppers; Malaccan five-spice powder; Hawaiian vinegar and chilies; and Caribbean citrus juices and allspice.

According to colonial legend, spice raised spirits during the American Revolution. In the winter of 1777–1778, when General George Washington's forces had little food at Valley Forge, he proposed a cheery dinner. With only tripe, peppercorns, and scraps available, the cook proposed Philadelphia Pepper Pot, a dish whose flavor overcame what it lacked in ingredients. Perhaps a West Indian recipe brought by African slaves, the spicy combination of pepper, salt, soup herbs, clove, onion, and dumplings reputedly retrieved from despair the Continental Army.

Current contributors to the world's spice trade include nations small and large. One of the smallest, Grenada, produces nutmeg and cinnamon. St. George, the island capital, offers cooks visiting the island market a choice of vanilla, mace, cocoa, and nutmeg to carry home for kitchen use. Restaurant and home kitchen produce callalloo soup, lobster creole, and "oildown," a meat and vegetable stew cooked in coconut milk. Other open-air market pavilions in the British Virgin Islands; Pointe-à-Pitre, Guadeloupe; and Bridgetown, Barbados, stock similar fresh food enhancements and their own combinations at bargain prices. Caribbean blends are the heart of the meat-jerking process. Similarly, Ethiopians rely on *berbere*, a red pepper spice paste added to *kifto* (stew); Moroccan cooks depend on *ras el hanout* (head of the shop), the all-round spice blend of twenty or more ingredients reputed to be an aphrodisiac. For *bobotie*, a ground beef or venison curry originating in Cape Malay, cooks enliven the meat with turmeric, paprika, curry powder, ginger, cayenne, and Worcestershire sauce and top the casserole with a baked custard and bay or lemon leaves.

Modern conveniences make storing and dispensing spices easier and more exact. A one- or two-level under-counter carousel organizes labeled spice cells and dispenses exacting measurement in one-quarter teaspoon increments. Over the stove or at table, users of a hand-held plastic pepper or salt ball squeeze the handles to grind condiments to uniform size, from coarse to fine. At the January 2001 International Housewares Show in Chicago, OXO displayed an adjustable spice grinder attached to the spice container for instant grinding of herbs and condiments directly into a dish.

See also **Apicius, Caelius; Condiments and Seasonings; Kitchen Cures; Mortar and Pestle**

Further Reading

Swahn, J. O. *The Lore of Spices: Their History, Nature and Uses Around the World*. Gothenburg, Sweden: AB Nordbok, 1991.

SPIT COOKING

The roasting spit, the first kitchen appliance, earned its place in culinary history by applying physics to browning over an open flame. By turning a wood or

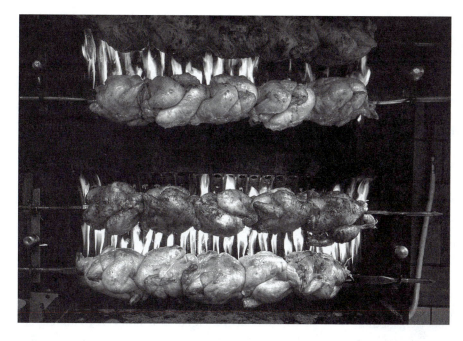

Whole chickens on a spit.
[© *Topix / Alamy.*]

metal skewer, cooks ensured that joints, fish, or poultry impaled on metal rods were thoroughly cooked. Roasters could retain juices longer in the cooking process or halt rotation for frequent daubs of prepared marinade or natural juices accumulating in the *léchefrite* (drip pan). A basting of fat tenderized a roast while it browned. The remaining pan drippings served as a base for gravy and sauces. Another advantage of the spit was the cook's control of hot foods by lifting the metal skewer, placing it away from flame, or serving it at table.

In ancient Egypt, meat roasting was a primitive affair involving spitting of fish, fowl, or goat flanks over an open hearth on wood splints. Early spit-roasting in the British Isles applied the technology to skewers of meat as well as vegetables, and small birds. Anything smaller had to be grilled, fried, or baked. By the Iron Age, spit-making advanced from expendable metal rods to heavy forged metal rods, which had the advantage of conducting heat down the length and through the inner fibers of roasting meat. The thickness of the meat determined the stoutness of the rod chosen for the job.

Early European varieties of oven spits included the dangle spit or poor man's jack, a vertical hook attached by rope or chain to the fireplace crane to hold large joints of meat. To cook all sides evenly, the cook twisted the cord, causing the heavy load to unwind slowly, exposing the entire surface to flame. In Provence, spit roasting of *petits oiseaux* (little birds) made use of the sparrows and larks that farmers and viticulturists downed with lead shot to stop their pilfering of grain and grapes. John of Garland's *Dictionary* (1220) reports that in medieval Europe, rural

Cooking with turnspits. Engraving from Il Trinciante (The Carver), by Vincenzo Cervio, 1604.

cooks roasted geese, pigeons, and fattened poultry on hazelwood spits. He added that they fooled the unwary by covering undercooked meat with garlic and sauce.

With the coming of Buddhism to Japan late in the twelfth century, diners fought new strictures against meat-eating. In the face of pressure to embrace vegetarianism, peasants spit-roasted pork and mutton in the field by skewering it and balancing the rod over a fire between two stones. From their clandestine dining came the term *sukiyaki* (roasted on a spit). The personalized cooking style developed into table service such as the Mongolian hot pot, at which each diner prepared meat, vegetables slices, mushrooms, and bamboo shoots to taste.

In the seventeenth-century English manor house, roasting on spits required the trussing of poultry and joints of meat to secure it to the rod. More delicate skewers suited *foies d'oie* (goose liver) and sweetbreads. Cooks and servants collected drippings in a shallow tray, in which they dipped bread and toast. They also basted dry meats with fats or turned them into sauces or gravies to serve with sliced portions.

A dog or sheep harnessed to a treadmill—and encouraged to run by hot embers tossed at its feet—could operate one variety of spit. One round version of the dog-powered turnspit connected the rotating wheel by pulleys to its source of energy, a round wall niche fitted with a drum in which a small dog ran. English breeders called the long-bodied, short-legged dog a turnspit.

A clockwork or turnspit devised in 1684 was attached to the chimney facing with the spindle piercing the wall. One model, built in the Hospice in Beaune, France, in 1698, consisted of an open framework of geared pulleys. By winding the turnspit, the kitchen staff could end the wearing task of hand turning by allowing the cogwheel to engage the mechanism and slowly rotate the meat. A musical turnspit cranked out up to two dozen different tunes while meats roasted over the flame. The cook could time the progress from across the room by noting when the tune reached its end.

In this same period, Austrian and German cooks developed the *Baumkuchen* (tree torte), a whimsical batter cake formed over a rotating stake or spit. For birthdays, Christmas, and weddings, the torte-maker turned the spit while pouring rounds of batter that formed a row of increasingly smaller circlets. The finished spit cake resembled a tree turned sideways. For a dramatic surprise presentation, German confectioners often placed a sparrow in the vacant center of the cake and penned it inside with a nosegay of flowers. When the presenter removed the bouquet, the bird flew away.

Colonial American cooks secured meat to the spit by pressing it onto a sharp point and forcing it back against a metal basket or prongs, which kept the roasting haunch from slipping into the fire. A variant skewer was the cradle spit, which supported a wrought iron cage at center shaped from iron strips. The hinged top opened to admit birds, pieces of game, or sections of domestic meats. When loaded for cooking, the metal rod rested on firedogs or andirons at the front of the hearth opening, where the cook could collect dripping in a pan and thin with water and herbs for basting. For

families that maintained a strict division of labor, turning the spit was the job of servants or slaves, children, or dogs in harness. Only the elite could afford a clock jack, a wind-up device that contained gears to regulate the rotation of the spit to assure even cooking all around.

An adjunct to the metal rod was a dangle spit, a vertical instrument suspended by a rope that unwound, thus rotating meat impaled on a cluster of hooks at the end. A bottle jack consisted of a metal sleeve containing a clockwork and topped with a rack ring for suspending from a hook clamped to the fireplace fascia. By inserting a key into the spring-wound mechanism, the user could regulate even movement of roasting meats before a flame. The eighteenth-century clock jack or watchwork engine, a gear-driven mechanism operated with weights and flywheels, similarly regulated rotation of the spit. A set of metal vanes or wings at the top of the device governed one model.

Throughout the eighteen century, cooking experts issued recipes on spit-roasting that secured tender meat by wrapping it in buttered paper, the forerunner of the French *en papillote* (in a paper bag). Hannah Glasse's classic *The Art of Cookery Made Plain and Easy: Excelling Any Thing of the Kind Ever Yet Published* (1747) initiated the technique, which John Farley replicated in his *The London Art of Cookery* (1783) and Isabella Beeton in her household guide, *Book of Household Management* (1860). Buttered paper also cropped up in the nineteenth century in American colonial cook Mary Randolph's *The Virginia House-wife: or Methodical Cook* (1824), Louis Eustache Ude's *The French Cook* (1828), and Russian food writer Elena Burman Molokhovets's popular cookbook, *A Gift to Young Housewives* (1861), in which she seasoned poultry and paper with meat juice and bread crumbs to form a savory crust.

Late in the nineteenth century, French chef Georges-Auguste Escoffier, who opened the Savoy Hotel, established rules for spit-roasting, which he considered the superior method of meat cookery. He explained that, whereas oven roasting trapped vapor in an enclosed space and ruined the meat juices, spit-roasting took place in open air. In the dry atmosphere, he explained, nothing contaminated the natural juices. By the time that food writer Mary Ronald published *The Century Cook Book* (1895), oven bake-roasting had gained ground over spit-roasting, even though she acknowledged the superiority of the latter.

Currently in industrialized countries, spit-roasting is largely a nostalgia period piece resurrected for demonstrations of historic kitchens or Southwestern trail cookery. Among the Tepehuan of Chihuahua, Mexico, spit roasting remains the traditional finale of a successful deer hunt. They slice, salt, and hang venison from the rafters and save the blood for boiling. A pecking order determines who receives what portion. The shooter receives the spine; any male over forty years old can demand a shin. Females over forty years may ask for any portion, but younger women may not eat bone marrow, which is a delicacy reserved for men.

See also **Roasting**

Further Reading

Rubin, Barbara Blatt, trans. *The Dictionarius of John de Garlande.* Lawrence, Kans.: Coronado Press, 1981.

SPOONS

Spoons, among the earliest and still the favored eating implements, appear to be contemporary with soup. Scoops and ladles, like the ivory and bitumen models found in Mesopotamian digs, paired with knives to dip liquids and lift cooked vegetables as the knife cut meat. The burial chamber of an aristocratic woman at Alaca Höyük, Turkey, around 2500 BCE revealed alongside her bones a spindle and a large silver spoon.

Varieties of spoons over time include the flat-ended seal spoon of Henry VI, who could use the handle to stamp documents and letters. The maiden spoon featuring the bust of a sedate young woman on the handle became a favorite dowry item. The fastidious snuff takers of the seventeenth and eighteenth centuries could sniff powdered tobacco through a perforated utensil, which fit into the end of the snuff bottle as both stopper and spoon.

The earliest Egyptian tombs contained many spoons, both serving pieces and personal eating utensils. The most primitive spoons survive from a clay culture that formed bowls in a rounded handle or stem. In the kitchen, cooks preferred porcelain ladles for tasting spoons because porcelain did not change the flavor as sometimes happened with metal. The porcelain also cooled hot liquids to protect the taster from burns. Other versions include the ritual incense dipper and tiny cosmetic spoon, each created to perform only one task. Egyptian spoon-makers shaped a double-use implement with bowl at one end and snail-extractor hook or spike at the other.

Classical Greek and Roman spoon-makers preferred silver, gold, and bronze as well as the more common bone spoon, which sometimes tapered to a knob or hole to admit a thong for attaching the implement to a belt or sash. A shellfish spoon ended in a spike for prying open oysters and mussels; another specialty was the egg spoon, which rounded into an egg cup. A Roman *trua* (cooking spoon) found at the house of Pansa at Pompeii was pierced, presumably for stirring

vegetables and straining away excess juice. Persian carvers nested wood sherbet spoons carved to translucent thinness. The more ornate featured boat-shaped bowls inlaid with silver, amber, coral, and mother of pearl. For libations to the gods, priests dipped into jugs of consecrated wine with *simpula*, long straight-edged spoons that resembled spatulas.

From the Saxons at Sutton Hoo, a chieftain's grave near Woodbridge, Suffolk, remains of seventh-century English life survives in remarkable condition. In addition to a ship buried to honor the deceased, coins, Byzantine silver, a Near Eastern bronze cauldron, wooden water buckets, cups, bowls, drinking horns, and tableware characterize a lavish tomb mound. The numbers of spoons and drinking vessels imply that a nobleman offered plenty of utensils to guests.

In the 1300s, each place setting consisted of a spoon, a trencher of bread, and a charger underneath. Forks appeared only with the exceptional dish, for example, oysters, snails, and winkles. Each diner carried a personal knife, but may have received another one from a set owned by a wealthy host. Among the peasantry, into the Renaissance, metalsmiths shaped spoons from treen, copper, pewter, or latten, a yellow alloy. The juniper spoon was a favorite of diners preferring flavored wood for eating salad. Piers Gaveston, a contemporary of Edward II, owned three forks and sixty-nine spoons; in 1328, at the death of Queen Clemence of Hungary, wife of Louis X of France, her will bequeathed to heirs one fork and thirty spoons. In the Khalili Collection of Islamic art, thin-handled bronze and silver spoons from this same era display bowls covered with intertwined dragons and arabesques, a complex and exacting artistry for which Iran and Turkey were famous.

In the 1400s, spoons took on special meaning and particular tasks. The Sicilian cook making cannoli for the Lenten carnival filled the fluted tubes with a coffee spoon to insert a mix of ricotta cream, food coloring, and flavorings. Silver apostle spoons were popular gift items, despite complaints from Puritans that they were sacrilegious. Godparents often presented a newborn with a spoon with one of Christ's twelve followers carved in the handle. By age eleven, the child had collected the remaining spoons. The twelfth birthday and confirmation in the church brought the savior spoon, named for its depiction of Christ on the handle. Puritans were known to decapitate the portrait and produce a spoon with a stump handle.

Aristocratic European homes kept varied sizes of *potlouches* (stirring spoons) and *poches* (soup ladles) for serving and, in the Renaissance, adopted the silver spoon for table use. In Tzarist Russia, aristocrats celebrated Easter at country estates by sharing a feast with peasants and laying each place with a wood spoon, a symbol of fellowship with the poor. The wealthy Este family of Ferrara, Italy, dipped into rice and pasta dishes with lapis lazuli and mother of pearl spoons. A century later, the thin marrow spoon came into use to extract flavorful marrow from such meat dishes as *osso buco*. Meanwhile, the table spoon took a distinctive shape—a seal on the head, baluster handle, and assay mark stamped inside the bowl. The distinctive "knop" at the end of the Elizabethan spoon typically took the shape of a ball or acorn. (Wilson 1991, 67)

By 1660, the fig-shaped bowl gave place to an oval supported by a rib extending from the base along the handle to the tip. Under the Hanoverians, the style altered to the hind's-foot handle—flat, broad-ended stem dentate into three lobes and turned up slightly. For its flanged end split into tripartite shape it earned the name of "trifid" spoon. (Ibid.) Such spaces suited stamping or engraving with initials, crests, or ornamentation. For stability and strength, the smith attached the oval bowl with a narrow ear called a rat-tail.

Native Americans used bone, ivory tusks, nutshells, seashells, and freshwater shells to fashion spoons, scrapers, blades, and dippers for domestic use and as trade goods. The Yaqui of the Sonoran Desert made spoons, mats, shelving, and cutting implements from cane; the Salish of western Montana twined spoons from grass. The Karuk of Siskyou County, California, differentiated by gender, with women cooking and feeding themselves and their children with mussel-shell spoons and men eating with carved wood implements; for the Umpqua of coastal Oregon, under a gender-specific protocol, men used bone spoons, but women had to scoop food with shells or eat with their fingers. When the French *coureurs de bois* (woodsmen) encountered the Chippewa, their women were cooking with clamshell spoons. From 1819 to 1822, when Sir William Edward Parry encountered the Canadian Eskimo on his three voyages to the Arctic in search of a northwest passage, he took note of cups and bowls made from musk ox horn and of the *pat-tekniuk* (marrow spoon), a long, narrow implement carved from hollowed bone that women gathered and tied as a set in a needle case to keep safe. (Parry 1842, II, 184)

After the spoon evolved into the old English version, featuring a rounded handle ridged at the center, it came to the Americas with settlers, who used it to steady food for cutting. Around 1650, the bowl was typically perforated into a strainer for lifting stray leaves from the teacup. A tea service spoon featured a pointed handle intended for ramrodding a spout clogged with residue. Another specialty found in colonial New England was the salt shaker spoon, which combined the bowl with a corked salt cellar at the other end. By the 1770s, the spoon broadened in the bowl, shortened to a rat-tail, and ended with a downward curve of the handle. Specialty spoons accompanied absinthe, hot cereal, jam, coffee and tea, liqueur, mocha, eggs, melon, and syrup. In the British Virgin Islands, locals set an evening meal on ceramic plates and offered only spoons as utensils.

Within a century, middle-class diners emulated the Caribbean table setting. The creation of an *en suite* service of matching spoons grew to ornate tea and coffee service in the 1700s, which featured teaspoons, sugar tongs, strainers, skimmers, and measuring spoons inside caddies for scooping tea leaves into the pot. The privileged household kept condiment and serving spoons shaped especially to accompany salt cellars, mustard pots, sauce bowls, and boiled egg cups and for serving fish slices and extracting marrow from bones. Under the administration of James Monroe, the fifth U.S. president, and First Lady Elizabeth Monroe, the sumptuous White House displayed unusually lavish epergnes, gilded porcelain tableware, and a dessert service paired with gold-plated spoons.

In Wales, a favorite keepsake was the love spoon or a host's gift spoon, an ornately handled treen piece carved with whimsical shapes, letters, stars, and hearts or branded with dates and names. As wooden valentines, they marked betrothals, weddings, anniversaries, and birthdays and hung in a place of honor in a new kitchen as evidence of rural courtship and pledges of faith. Carving spoons, sugar tongs, wall mounts, wood chains, and clips was a specialty of sailors, who pursued a simple hobby on shipboard during idle moments. From the giving of spoons as a prelude to romance came the term "spooning" for "courting" or "wooing." Nested spoons symbolized the closeness of a relationship.

Elaborate boxwood spoons were the treen carvers' gifts for christenings. The church also displayed ornate altar spoons for use at coronations of kings and emperors and for serving chrism, the holy oil used for anointment. A long-handled ritual spoon carved with profiles of the apostles or Holy Family and mounted in silver or gold was common in Russian and German churches. With these, the priest who celebrated eucharist ladled wafers from the ciborus, mixed watered wine in a chalice, and retrieved incense from the navette for placement in a censer.

In the twentieth century, cooks frequently insisted on a wood spoon because it does not bruise delicate vegetables and fruits. The slotted or perforated treen or tin spoon served a dual purpose—draining juice from chunks of vegetables or fruit and agitating batters, which squeezed through the slots. Another standard implement, the measuring scoop, an alloyed spoon sized with quarter-cup and half-cup bowls, was incised with inner bowl markings to measure teaspoons and tablespoons. More familiar were graduated tin or plastic spoons or scoops nested on a ring. In middle-class homes, the copper spoon dripper, like the one manufactured in 1914 by Henry Rogers, Sons & Company of Wolverhampton, England, consisted of a wall rack and drip trough to hold used ladles, basters, and tasting spoons.

In the 1920s, advertising featured innovations in serving and stirring spoons. The January 1925 issue of *Good Housekeeping* presented the multipurpose nickel silver Servespoon from Ace Hardware Manufacturing Corporation of Philadelphia. The slotted spoon, shaped like a rectangular turner, featured open spaces resembling a cream whipper for maximum stirring power and square corners for digging unblended ingredients out of crannies.

The spoon is still essential around the world. Armenian cooks, who squat alongside a *tonir* (pit oven), distribute flat unleavened *lavash* (bread) and spoons as the main mealtime implements for use by diners seated at ground level. The simplicity of dining procedures parallels the concept of humility and reverence for God, the source of all nourishment. In India, the *baghar* method of cookery involves heating spices a spoonful at a time in oil of *ghee* (clarified butter). A quick means of fusing the flavors of ghee with spice is to sizzle the two in a metal spoon held over a flame and pour the mix over kidgeree, an inventive dish of spiced chickpeas.

In the twenty-first century, spoons in wood and stainless steel dominate kitchen chores involving wet food pieces, sauces, gravies, and batters. Some special varieties of spoons include the following:

Bonbon spoon—a serving piece for candies and salted nuts

Jelly server—a serving piece that lifts firm jelly, cottage cheese, and cream cheese

Grapefruit spoon—the serrated spoon with narrow tip for removing sections of citrus fruit from membranes

Gravy ladle—a serving dipper that dispenses gravy and sauces and also soup

Mayonnaise ladle—a small ladle that dispenses mayonnaise, dressings, thin sauce, gravy, or whipped cream

Punch ladle—a deep-bowled dipper sometimes equipped with pouring spouts on each side of the handle for serving individual cups of punch

Salad set—a paired spoon and fork or both united like scissors for grasping and serving salads

Soup ladle—a deep-bowled serving piece with curved handle for dispensing soup

Sugar spoon—also called a sugar shell, a serving piece for granulated or powdered sugar

Tablespoon—a serving piece for berries, casseroles, salads, and vegetables

The oversized stainless steel spoon rest is useful as both receiver for sticky spoons or use as scoop or ladle. Flatware spoons continue to adapt to various uses, for example, a special infant spoon features a large bowl on one end for the feeder to taste the food before spooning in a bite with the smaller end.

Further Reading

Barber, Elizabeth Wayland. *Women's Work: The First 20,000 Years*. New York: W. W. Norton & Co., 1994.
Glants, Musya, and Joyce Toomre, eds. *Food in Russian History and Culture*. Bloomington: Indiana University Press, 1997.
"Knives, Forks, and Spoons," *Aramco World*, March 1960, 16–19.

STEAMING

In such diverse tasks as congealing soap, powering a pressure cooker, releasing oil from olives, readying eel for a Japanese hibachi, and relaxing tough fibers for the weaving of mocucks, steam has traditionally been the ally of the home cook. Properly controlled, it gentles preparation of delicacies like oysters and mussels without harming either flavor or aroma. For the Umpqua of southwestern Oregon and the Blackfeet of the Great Plains, the open-pit steaming of camas root and wild carrot each summer prepared the vegetables for storage. In China, the steaming of *baozi* (buns) lightens yeast dough, which the cook may fill with red bean paste, sugary nuts, or mashed jujubes.

The earliest Indian steamer was a perforated clay cylinder used in the Indus Valley from Neolithic times. Although the seventh-century BCE traveller Xuan Zang, who visited 110 of India's 138 kingdoms, ridiculed the Indian steaming method, cooks in India were adept at heating foods over gentle steam. Another primitive steamer consisted of a wicker basket placed over a wide-mouth boiling pot. To assure the food kept its shape, the cook tied portions in cloth. A more sophisticated steamer was a two-stage vessel consisting of a large cookpot fitted internally with trays or leaves resting on supports. In Kerala, artisans fashioned a cookpot with a fitted bamboo tube and a pierced baffle at the lower end to admit steam. A more sophisticated use of steam was the bathing of cooked food with aromas of spice or *ghee* (clarified butter) generated from a hot tile dropped into a cookpot.

In Algeria, cooks rub a lamb shoulder in cumin and saffron, encase it in cheesecloth, and steam it all day in the *kiskis* or *couscousiere*. The device also cooks pasta and bathes grains in broth for *masfuf*. A detailed description of the steaming and hand-rolling of *kuskus* (couscous) appears in *Fadalat al-Khiwan fi Tayyibat al-Ta'am wa 'l-Alwan* (The Overflowing Table of Delicious Food and Dishes, ca. 1200s), written by Murcian jurist Ibn Razin al-Tujibi. The design of the Algerian steamer appears to have begun as a woven basket set atop a clay water pot; however, no model has survived. Only part of a medieval clay bottom remains from a discovery at Chellala.

According to Lucie Bolens's *La Cuisine Andalouse, un Art de Vivre, du Xi au XIII Siècle* (Andalusian Cuisine from the eleventh to the thirteenth century: A Way of Life, 1991), archeologists unearthed the first whole implement in the tomb of Massinissa, a Berber monarch buried in Numidia around 238 BCE. However, the Arabist Charles Perry, food writer for the Los Angeles *Times,* surmised that couscous did not appear in Arabic kitchens until 632 to 732 BCE, during the Arab conquest of North Africa, when farmers first planted *Triticum turgidum* (durum wheat). The technology appeared in Provence in a travelogue, *Les Confessions de Jean-Jacques Bouchard Suivies de Son Voyage de Paris a Rome en 1630* (Confessions of Jean-Jacques Bouchard Following his Journey to Paris and Rome in 1630), and moved north to Brittany before 1699, when a naval officer, Charles de Clairambault, wrote of a date and couscous dish prepared by 'Abd Allah bin 'Aisha for a Ramadan celebration.

When Europeans first arrived on the shores of North America, they learned about steaming from Indians. Pilgrims observed the Wampanoag clambake, at which cooks dug holes at the shore and cooked freshly gathered mussels and clams in the sand by dropping hot stones onto wet seaweed to generate steam. Joseph C. Hart described the European adaptation of steaming in his Nantucket-based novel, *Miriam Coffin: or, The Whale-Fisherman* (1834). After cooks deposited quohogs in the ground, they topped them with burning embers: "The steam of the savoury liquor, which escaped in part without putting out the fire, preserved the meat in a par-boiled state, and prevented it from scorching, or drying to a cinder, and the whole virtue of the fish from being lost." (Neustadt 1992, 44) The text concluded with an explanation about correct placement of shellfish to prevent them absorbing ash and the value of steaming to melt the hinges of the shells.

Steaming was valuable to Americans at the beginning of the twentieth century. In 1909, Grimwade patented a quick-cooking steaming bowl fitted with a lid forming a tight vacuum, which ended the need of a pudding cloth. The steamer, a forerunner of the pressure cooker, heated from the center to the outside and kept food hot until served. Eunice White Bullard

Beecher, wife of the Reverend Henry Ward Beecher, touted the Hill Champion Odorless Steam Cooker, a two-tiered chamber fitted with an adjustable baffle that shortened cooking times for most foods. The locking cover held in steam and allowed the pot to depressurize through a tube for the range-top cooking of casseroles, vegetables, and puddings.

In 1908, the Sears, Roebuck catalog listed a small two-door steam cooker for $4.87. Praised for economy, the tin chest with copper tank had a domed top that channeled condensation down the sides to the water tank to keep moisture from causing soggy food. The merchandiser declared the cooker safe on coil, gas, gasoline, oil, or wood stove and recommended it for fruit canning up to a dozen quart-size Mason jars. The purchaser received two heavy seamless pans to use in the steamer's four compartments.

The Pueblo peoples of Taos, New Mexico, used the horno as both baking oven and vegetable steamer, a method that parallels Tahitian pit-cooking of breadfruit and manioc wrapped in banana leaves. Early in the twentieth century, Atlantic Coast cooks, following the system invented by Amanda Jones, applied steam to canning jars and chose a lidded tin bread pan to steam Boston brown bread, a dough that requires moisture to preserve texture.

The Maori of New Zealand traditionally steamed *karengo* (seaweed) as a special condiment for feasts. During World War II, Maori soldiers serving with the Allied forces suffered from long marches across the Sahara. Remembering a home remedy, they requested packets of *karengo* from home. On the move over the dusty terrain, they carried strands with them to chew as an antidote to thirst and dry mouth.

In Oceania, Europe, Asia, and the Americas, steaming has maintained its importance in the kitchen. Italians value espresso urns that steam rather than boil delicate ground coffee beans; English cooks place bundles of asparagus in a perforated tray and lower it into a steambath to release subtle flavor while protecting the fragile blossom end. Likewise intent on gentle cooking, Mexican tamale makers steam their meals in a tin pot fitted with a three-section disk that holds the tamales upright. Japanese confectioners prefer steaming to make a sweet mochi rice dumpling called a *dango;* Hawaiian chefs create entire meals on a single leaf by layering fish, vegetables, and spices and placing the serving in a bamboo steamer for rapid cooking that melds the flavors.

The Chinese prefer steaming over a wok in a round woven bamboo or metal basket as a natural, fat-free method of heating without desiccating foods. When cooks first began making bread, they preferred unfilled loaves and rolls steamed or steamed and fried long before they attempted baking dough. Only a quick dash of oil on the steamer bottom is necessary to keep foods from sticking. For individual dishes, cooks can stack steamer baskets for maximum use of steam or can substitute slotted cake racks as a platform on which to set tempered glass, porcelain, metal, or Pyrex dishes. Other substitutions include steamers designed for asparagus, clams, corn on the cob, or pasta. The steamer's penetrating heat softens breads and expands dried vegetables and mushrooms.

Chinese cooks prize the bamboo steaming basket as an essential for cooking rice, the base for stir-fried meats, sauces, and vegetables. The basket fits over pot or wok of boiling water and absorbs moisture, enabling the cook to tenderize vegetables below while using the steam above to plump rice. When foods reach the optimum state for eating, cooks can plate them directly at the table from the steamer basket. A similar set-up in Laos and Thailand calls for nesting the steaming basket in a metal pot of water for the rice served at every meal. The serving is so expected that they invite guests with a standard phrase, *"Thaan khao may?"* (Would you like to eat rice?).

In 1974, the chef James Beard and other food specialists compiled *The Cook's Catalogue*, which surveyed the best in culinary equipment. For steaming, he stressed the importance of selecting equipment that saved vitamins and enhanced the use of energy. He pictured the folding SteaMarvel, an inexpensive sheaf of pierced metal leaves that opened to form a steamer basket. He explained, "For a minimal investment this stainless-steel wonder will transform any pot. . .into a satisfactory steamer." (Beard et al. 1974, 450) For sturdier models, he recommended the three-stage Cuisinart steamer or a competitive model with Bakelite handles from Wearever. A useful German device for serious cooks, the aluminum tubed rice steamer and mold took the shape of a tube pan for holding rice grains in place while steam expanded the mass into a circle suited for molded presentations to be filled with accompaniments.

In the 1990s, steamers offered a method of achieving a healthful, low-fat diet by cooking independent of added fat. The manufacture of electric steamers and rice cookers created an easy, almost foolproof way to cook vegetables tender-crisp, to fluff individual rice grains, and to preserve flavor and juice in poultry and seafood. Steaming preserved not only texture, but also nutrients. To ancient methods, inexpensive electric steaming devices such as those from Farberware, West Bend, Sanyo, Hamilton Beach, Hitachi, Black & Decker, and Oster added control and programming to assure the right span of cooking and hold dishes at optimum temperature until they were ready for plating and serving.

Additional twenty-first-century steaming devices increase the choices of cooks who want gentler cooking than boiling or roasting. Stainless steel cookware sets come with additional steaming baskets and pasta inserts; a loaf steamer produces bread with a distinctive crust. A cylindrical asparagus steamer fitted with a chrome wire rack eases insertion and removal from hot water or broth. Another advancement, the Turbo Convection Steamer, works faster and more evenly by applying moist convection heat to a two-chambered see-through compartment. Additional applications of steam include portable steamers for touching up wrinkled clothing and steam cleaners to reduce bacteria in drains, on counters, and around toilet facilities. DeLonghi's Steam-It-Clean produces a multi-application of high-pressure, high-temperature steam to clean ovens, grills, tile, windows, upholstery, carpeting, wallpaper, and artificial plants. In addition to degreasing and sterilizing, the machine eliminates pollutants from counters and crevices.

See also **Bamboo; Basketry; Rice; Tagines**

Further Reading

Fein, Ronnie, "Food Steamers: One of Today's Hottest New Kitchen Appliances," *Consumers Digest*, September–October 1994, 71–73.

Morse, Kitty, "Couscous Past and Present," *Aramco World*, November–December 1998.

Neustadt, Kathy. *Clambake: A History and Celebration of an American Tradition.* Amherst: University of Massachusetts Press, 1992.

Noakes, Greg, and Laidia Chouat Noakes, "Couscous: The Measure of the Maghrib," *Aramco World*, November–December 1988, 16–23.

Stone, Caroline, "Morocco by Mouthfuls," *Aramco World*, November–December 1988, 18–31.

Yzábal, María Dolores, and Shelton Wiseman. *The Mexican Gourmet.* McMahons Point, Australia: Thunder Bay, 1995.

STEEL

Steel replaced flint, chert, and iron as the metal of choice for shaping table cutlery. It was superior in strength, lightweight, and odor- and taste-free. Two varieties of steel have impacted the manufacture of kitchen implements. Carbon steel, the common material found in table knives, is a resilient metal also favored for blades of butcher knives, Chinese cleavers, and paring knives; it can be sharpened for decades without losing its edge.

Stainless steel is used for shaping cookware and the steamer baskets and strainers for Chinese cooking. In the March 1921 issue of *House & Garden*, an announcement of the arrival of stainless steel on the market elicited joy among professional and home cooks. Professional and amateur cooks praised the metal's high polish, which enhanced switchplates, fittings, hinges, locksets, knife blades, kettles, and pots and pans. Another plus for the new metal was its long wear and the absence of scaling, a problem with iron cutlery.

Steel accommodates a variety of shapes and densities. Common articles formed from steel include:

Blades—cutting edges in implements, for example, the Joyce Chen Saladacco spiral slicer, and hand-cranked tool that churns out paper-thin slices for Asian-style salads and garnishes.

Fruit corer—a sharp-edged cylinder with a side slot and knob or handle for plunging into spherical fruits and extracting inedible and fibrous portions. A smaller dual-purpose corer and parer with serrated edge resembles a paring knife.

Ice chipper or ice chisel—a sturdy rectangular or wedge-shaped blade on a handle, some with hand guards. The pronged end plunged into ice to a standard depth to even uniformity of shards or chips.

Lard pail—a heavy-lidded container for clarifying port and beef fat to be reused as lubricant for griddles or oil for cooking.

Oil can—a vessel with dripless spout, cool handle, and built-in mesh strainer for filtering residue from reusable oil.

Oyster shucker—a levered device that removes meat without endangering or tiring the hand.

Pasta maker—a machine that shapes dough into pasta strips and also slices dough into strips for bread sticks.

Steak knives—table cutlery, featuring high carbon stainless steel blades and heat-resistant plastic or resin handles.

Steamers—either perforated baskets for kettles, or three-stage pot, steamer shelf, and lid for retaining steam during the tenderizing of vegetables or cooking of rice.

Trash can—sanitary receptacle that features a treadle for no-hands opening and a rust-proof liner that lifts out for cleaning and relining with plastic bags.

Trivet—a stand with short feet to protect stoves and counters from hot pans or anchor casseroles on a buffet.

Early in the twenty-first century, the use of stainless steel in trendy, upscale appliances enhanced the postmodern kitchen with a bright, shiny gleam. Breadmakers and deep fryers applied brushed stainless steel to exterior units that required no special cleaners or polishes. High-end stand mixers with ergonomic handles featured polished stainless steel bowls fitted with burnished steel beaters, dough hooks, and wire whips and capped with pouring shields with removable chutes. Smaller pieces include microplane graters, olive oil misters, jar lifters and cap piercers, canister sets, vented compost containers, box-blade and wedge cake cutters, pot racks and brackets, and dish drainers. Merging art with utility, the Bodum tea bowl, Asam tea pot, and Osiris water kettle, designed by Carsten Jørgensen and displayed at New York City's Museum of Modern Art, show master crafting of vessels shaped to suit hand and task.

Stainless steel utensils cover the range of kitchen needs—mixing bowls, measuring cups, ladles and spoons, turners, forks, a six-sided column grater, universal double boiler, flat and balloon whisks, buffet servers, skimmers, tongs, nonstick coated meat racks, and wall racks for hanging pans and skillets. A set of steel spatulas and spreaders with pliable silicone blades comes in varied sizes and shapes. The Mouli food mill, a kitchen classic, harnesses hand-turned pressure to shred vegetabless and force pulp from seeds and skins through discs gauged for purée, sauce, ricing, and baby food. A small steel oval used like handsoap removes cooking and food preparation odors from the hands with a non-allergenic and environmentally safe metal disc.

Stainless steel cookware comes in standard collections of fry pan, covered saucepan, covered sauté pan, and lidded stockpot. A basic nine-piece collection adds a larger fry pan and a steamer insert for the saucepan. The set from All-Clad offers a choice of four metals, including stainless steel with non-stick interiors, brushed aluminum, charcoal anodized exterior, and copper exterior, its high-end product. Demeyere of Belgium markets a full line of five-ply stainless steel saucepans, skillets, and casseroles with a high-gloss finish. Fitted with cool stainless steel handles, the pieces are durable, heat evenly, and survive heavy use in oven and dishwasher.

STONE BOILING

One of the innovations of open-fire cookery was the augmentation of spit roasting with watertight baskets, soapstone bowls, or pits lined with hides. The Assiniboine of the Great Lakes, Montana, and Saskatchewan acquired their name meaning "those who cook with stones," a method of boiling ground seeds and water by heating stones in a fire and plunging them into a woven or skin container of water to boil the mix into hot cereal. Near the Great Lakes, the Iroquois and Shawnee stone-boiled fresh dock, milkweed, wild asparagus, and tender spring poke to round out a diet based on corn, beans, and squash.

Stone boiling.

[*Original illustration by Dan Timmons.*]

Around 2500 BCE, Celtic cooks in the Orkneys, Isle of Man, and English Midlands varied the spit-roasting over embers and baking of meat on hot flagstones by digging a *fulacht fiadh* (outdoor pit cooker) near a water course and lining the trough with timbers or stones. Similar to the Indian method, *fulacht* cookery began with filling a hole with water, adding fresh kill wrapped in hay ropes or fabric, and dropping in hot stones to bring the temperature to a boil. For their one formal meal per day, the Celtic *fianna* (hunters) cooked mutton, venison, wild pork chunks, and birds to doneness and ate them with dried or boiled dulse, carrageen, tangle, bladderwrack, and laver, all seaweeds gathered at the shore. As described in Geoffrey Keating's *The History of Ireland* (ca. 1630, published in 1908), at an adjacent pit, the woodsmen relaxed in a bathing pit/sauna before pitching tents for the night. In 1973, remains of a *fulacht fiadh*, built into a crescent-shaped mound of scattered boiling stones, turned up in Causeway, Ireland.

According to the anthropologist Patrick Vinton Kirch of the University of California at Berkeley, author of *The Lapita Peoples: Ancestors of the Oceanic World* (1997), the Lapita, Pacific seaborne colonists of Fiji, Tonga, and Samoa from as early as 1600 BCE,

heated coral stones at coconut shell fires in their stilt huts for simmering fish in clay pots.

Early Native Americans cooked by this labor-intensive method by adding heated stones to an animal stomach, skin bag, basket, or birch-bark mocuck, the favored stone-boiling container of the Beaver and Cree of Alberta and the Carrier of north-central British Columbia. The method served paleo-Indians of Dust Cave in Florence, Alabama, as a method of cooking hickory nut meats and Minnesota natives as a way to process wild rice. The Pomo boiled with stones for making chemuck, a hot acorn porridge flavored with honey and berries; enabled Atlantic coast tribes stewed *m'sickquatash*, which settlers called "succotash," from mixed vegetables and bits of meat or boiled fiddlehead ferns or pokeweed shoots and onions as spring vegetables. To spare the hands, the cook lifted the stones with long-handled tongs.

The Apache and Gros Ventres of the Great Plains did their stone boiling in a water-filled hole in the ground. The Lakota of the the Great Plains reserved a buffalo stomach for roasting meat with tubers and berries. Similarly, the Dogrib of the Northwest Territories lined holes with caribou stomach for stone boiling; the Kaska of British Columbia and the Yukon Territory dried a moose stomach to preserve it for stone boiling. Massachusetts aborigines used the same method as a means of refining maple sap into syrup for kitchen use. The Bannock and Shoshone of the Great Basin stone-boiled in woven baskets; the Serrano of San Bernardino County, California, stone-boiled meat in watertight baskets and heated blood into a thickened soup. The Nootka of Vancouver Island, British Columbia, added an unusual twist to stone cookery by stone-boiling food in wood boxes. Another variant, internal stone roasting was a favorite of the Inca of Peru. As described in Spanish missionary and historian Bernabé Cobo's *Historia del Nuevo Mundo* (History of the New World, 1893), cooks lined the carcasses of domesticated guinea pigs with hot *calapurca* (pebbles) before baking them in clay dishes.

An original use of local plants enabled the Havasupai, who lived near the Grand Canyon, to stone-boil in cactus pots. They chose a large barrel cactus, burned off its spines, and sliced away the top. For boiling liquid, they bashed in the inner pulp to form a slurry from the soft tissue. Into this liquid they dropped hot stones, thereby boiling and flavoring their meals with the taste of cactus. The method served for cooking small animals, quail, and hen eggs and for mixing dye and paint, cooking arrow poison, boiling corn and small corn or mutton grass dumplings, parboiling tender greens, and steeping medicine tea.

Because skin, grass, and fiber containers burned easily, most native cooks kept liquids hot by dropping hot stones into the mix, removing them, and replacing them with more hot stones. This method of cookery predominated until the invention of pottery, which was durable enough to endure direct contact with flame. Stone boiling precipitated the maple sugar industry in New England and Canada, where colonists imitated the centuries-old process evolved by natives.

The use of stones for cookery in the absence of metal pots struck the imagination of Europeans newly arrived in North America. As described in Kathy Neustadt's *Clambake: A History and Celebration of an American Tradition* (1992), the Wampanoag and Algonquian adapted the concept of dropping stones into skins of water to the sand-baking of shellfish on the Atlantic seaboard. By dropping stones onto wet seaweed, they generated steam to cook delicate clams and mussels. The remains of these clambakes littered sites at New Bedford and Westport, Massachusetts. When the pilgrims arrived in 1620, they learned this seashore tradition, one of North America's contributions to culinary technique.

When Captain James Cook sailed the *Resolution* to Nootka Sound, British Columbia, in 1778, his men observed natives stone boiling. One crewman, the artist John Webber, sketched huge communal dwellings, where native women dried fish and hung them from the rafters. At fire pits, they squatted close to the flame to heat rocks and plunge them into water. Rather than boil food with the stones, they used the resulting steam to cook spitted fish that they held above it.

During the California gold rush, miners observed the labors of Miwok women at close range. According to *Hutching's California Scenes*, a lettersheet dated 1854, Anglo men studied the hardships of women's work. Most fascinating was the task of gathering grasshoppers, seeds, and acorns for grinding and pounding into paste. They formed the mass into loaves to be boiled alone or with rats, rabbits, or squirrels in a tightly woven mocuck, which held two to four pecks. After dropping in stones to heat the mixture, they dipped out servings with their fingers, using the basket as a communal pot.

For most Native American cooks, stone boiling ended after Europeans introduced metal pots and pans as trade items. One man named Ishi, the reputed last Yana-Yahi, who lived at the anthropology museum of the University of California in San Francisco until his death in 1916, recognized stone boiling as superior to the white world's overcooking of meat and vegetables on a modern stove. He explained, "The right way is to cook like acorn mush. Put cold water in basket. Place hot rocks in water till it bubbles. Add acorn meal. It cooks *pukka-pukka*. Then is it done. Same way, make deer stew. Or rabbit stew. Cook *pukka-pukka*. Not too long." (Kroeber 1961, 164) He concluded that stone boiling produced properly cooked food—a clear broth and firm meat and vegetables, "not soft and coming apart." (Ibid.)

See also **Maple Sugar**

Further Reading

Kirch, Patrick Vinton. *The Lapita Peoples: Ancestors of the Oceanic World*. London: Blackwell, 1997.

Kroeber, Theodora. *Ishi in Two Worlds*. Berkeley: University of California Press, 1961.

Mandelbaum, David G. *The Plains Cree: An Ethnographic, Historical and Comparative Study*. Regina, Sask.: Canadian Plain Research Center, 1979.

Mourning Dove: A Salishan Autobiography. Lincoln: University of Nebraska Press, 1990.

Neustadt, Kathy. *Clambake: A History and Celebration of an American Tradition*. Amherst: University of Massachusetts Press, 1992.

Weber, Steven A., and P. David Seaman, eds. *Havasupai Habitat*. Tucson: University of Arizona Press, 1985.

STOVES

After humankind abandoned open fire cookery, the stove became the center of kitchen activity. The essayist Rhys Davies in *These Simple Things* (1965) compared the stove to the bed for its ability to comfort the homeowner. The concept of flat burners atop a fuel source began in antiquity, but did not achieve high technological status until the manufacture of the closed-fire range in the eighteenth century. The Roman version preserved at the house of Pansa in Pompeii featured a counter honeycombed with chambers to hold charcoal and partitions on which the cook could set pots, grills, or an iron egg fryer, which the smithy indented to cook four eggs at a time. The Inca cooked at a knee-high pottery stove, a multi-lobed earthen heater similar to the modern *chiminea*. At two of its branches, jugs and pots sat atop the vent. The third remained open to allow smoke to escape.

In Jacques Le Hay's painting *Ast-chi, Cuisinier du grand Seigneur* (1714), a frontal view of an Asian cook depicts his use of a counter-top stove built out of stone blocks. An arched opening at the base sheds light from a well-stoked fire. Above, a lidded pot steams as the cook prepares to pour oil into a spoon, perhaps for adding to the boiling mixture. With only a few alterations in design and materials, the imaginative eye could picture the same man cooking at an iron cookstove that had yet to be designed. Similarly, in Mexico, a low mud parapet raised on a platform into a U shape held iron bars laid across the open top to create a crude brazier stove. Into the opening at the bottom, the cook

A circular heating stove from Pompeii.

built a wood, brush, and dung fire to heat pots of food placed on top.

A forerunner of the Franklin stove was Benjamin Franklin's New Pennsylvania fireplace, a box-shaped space heater and cookstove engineered in 1742 to burn wood or coal. The Franklin stove, described in *Observations on the Cause and Cures of Smoking Chimneys*, was a compromise between his fireplace and an innovative enclosed cookstove. It increased the amount of heat radiated from the front by inserting a U-shaped flue to make full use of energy before the air current carried the remaining heat up the chimney. The Franklin system, which reduced the firebox and inner passage, succeeded at making the most of heated air currents and at preventing downdrafts of cold air from smoking up rooms. Its faults were many, the most debilitating being the covering of bright flame with an unsightly metal box. In addition, it was typically dirty and rusty.

Around 1750, the advent of iron technology, which alleviated some of the inefficiencies of coal-, peat-, and wood-burning fireplaces, presaged total replacement of open-hearth cookery with the first cast-metal stoves. A heavy material for kitchen furnishings, half-ton iron

stoves required heavy labor during installation and jeopardized insubstantial flooring. In France, the charcoal brazier shared space with the *potager*, a stove equipped with twelve to twenty *foyers* (grates). On these small workhorses, cooks could control heat to blend the delicate sauces that delighted the French court and sparked a true national cuisine. The introduction of the coal-fired stove further improved controlled cooking and encouraged subtle techniques of blending flavors over heat.

In older English homes, the range perched on a brick plinth below a tiled false back to make the new device fit into the fireplace. A plate rack above the cooking surface used rising heat to warm dishes. A saddle boiler captured heat behind the fire for warming water, accessed from either side. In front of the firebox, a bracket out front suspended a bottle jack to roast meat. A small door under the firebox allowed the cook to empty the accumulated ash.

In 1785, a Hungarian ironworks at Kislöd began distributing iron cooking plates for placing on brick hearths for the radiation of heat to the bottom of pots. Those who did the least amount of kitchen work were the first to complain about the absence of romance in these fuel-saving devices. In Poland, a nobleman noted, "The stove gave only heat and was deaf and dumb; a fireplace gave both heat and light and talked with a person." (Lemnis & Vitry 1996, 110-111) Nonetheless, advanced stoves met the demand of a public eager to leave the open hearth behind in a search for more efficient kitchens. An Englishman, Thomas Robinson, created a coal-burning kitchen range in 1780, a compact cast-iron heater containing water closet and oven. He increased oven heat by lining it with masonry and spiking the sides to hold shelving. The inventor David R. Rittenhouse redesigned the Franklin stove, which marketers exploited in the 1790s as the Rittenhouse stove. It was the choice of Thomas Jefferson for Monticello for using half the wood to produce double the heat in the tearoom and dome room.

A patent for a new stove, issued to Exeter foundryman George Bodley in 1802, introduced the first closed-top cooking surface. As depicted in Thomas Webster's *Encyclopedia of Domestic Economy* (1844), the oblong appliance contained a large boiler with tap, roasting range, and oven with separate fireplace. It earned a general nickname—the Leamington—after a factory at Leamington Spa. The name surfaced in the far corners of the British Empire, including the Australian Hotel in Townsville. Temperamental and grimy, the iron box attached to the chimney with an iron flue and suited varied culinary needs. For subsequent coal-burning models, called kitcheners or portable ranges in the United States, engineers mounted them on legs and added a water heater as a convenience.

The technology was a mixed blessing. Housewives who suspected kitchen grime of causing disease also concluded that the acrid, hazy atmosphere contributed to inattention and dawdling in kitchen staff. Furthermore, ovens still lacked temperature gauges and required a bare-handed estimate of readiness. To keep these appliances grime- and soot-free, cooks ended a hard day's kitchen duty with a new task—brushing the metal surface free of crust and blacking the raw metal to prevent rust.

Central European stoves profited from the perfection of cast iron, but introduced the new technology to the home primarily for heating. Scottish open-range styles often placed an iron oven on one side of a fireplace grate. In larger homes, the oven on one side balanced a water boiler and tap on the opposite side. In Ireland, housewives stored black lead in a tall keeper and applied it daily with a polishing rag to the range bodywork to display to best advantage the family cooking place.

In 1815, iron cookstoves served in multiple capacities. They heated foods as well as home and institutional kitchen spaces and ships' galleys, thus ending the dangerous practice of open-hearth cookery at sea. One successful stove inventor, Philo Penfield Stewart, created the popular Oberlin stove from a remodeled style in 1834 in the home of a friend, Mrs. John J. Shipherd of Elyria, Ohio. An ad for the Patent Oeconomical kitchen ranges made by Green and Pickslay ironworks of Sheffield captured the wonder of the enclosed range: "With one small open Fire will Roast, Steam or Bake for a family of from five to fifty Individuals, and afford a constant supply of hot Water." (Schärer & Fenton 1998, 43)

The Harel range, a brick or stone firebox set in a wood frame, began upgrading kitchens in the 1820s. It presented a refined kitchen image by the application of attractive ceramic tile to the outer surface. At the base, one or more terra cotta fireplaces varied depths and heights of cook space. Above, niches and an encompassing rim offered places for warming foods and encouraging dough to rise and milk to clabber.

The traditional *Russkaja pech'* (Russian stove) took up a quarter of a peasant residence as oven, cooktop, drier of fruit, fermenter of *kvass* (fermented mare's milk), laundry dryer, and home heater. A massive facade built of clay, brick, or stone and imbued with female symbolism and fecundity, it filled a space from floor to ceiling and overheated one area of the house usually saved for the elderly, invalid, or very young. In chimneyless houses, a ceiling hole or wall chink vented smoke. The traveler Johann George Kohl, secretary of the Austrian legation at the court of Peter the Great and author of *Russia* (1842), remarked on the placement of benches near the stove and the variety of niches in the structure for drying wet clothes and towels and the snoozing of individuals wrapped sauna-style in sheepskins.

Necessary tools for stoking fires and positioning coals included pokers, shovels or peels, and long-handled forks for moving clay *gorshki* (casseroles), which contained the meals cooked long and slow over constant wood heat. Such shuffling of containers allowed cooks to take advantage of cooler spots on the cooktop, their only means of controlling temperature for such specialties as silver leaven, resulting from dropping a silver coin or spoon into milk to produce a clotted cream. In 1861, Elena Burman Molokhovets's classic Russian cookbook, *A Gift to Young Housewives,* described cast iron plates, which she stacked to one side and lifted by inserting a removable handle just as users of iron stoves lifted lids covering the firebox. She also specified that the stove should possess an iron or wood hood. She declared it "essential for the family's health; without it, the only way to rid the kitchen of fumes is to open doors onto a cold stairwell." (Molokhovets 1992, 116)

Stove cookery found a champion in master chef, inventor, and food writer Alexis Soyer. In *The Modern Housewife or Ménagère* (1848), he recommended the iron stove for hotels and taverns and suggested that housewives could dry laundry nearby without worrying about fire. A later model, manufactured by Home Comfort, graced the grim iron surface with blue graniteware enameling, which matched a popular series of pots and kettles. Scandinavian firms set the pace in stove design with the 1869 Norwegian Aga, a heat-storing model.

John Spence of Boston patented an oven called "The Republican" in 1852 that applied convection to the external heating of the oven. As advertised in Mrs. Cornelius's *The Young Housekeeper's Friend* (1859), the unique shape of his stove drew air around five sides of the oven, an economical method of recycling heat and reducing the amount of fuel necessary for baking, cooking, and heating water.

In this same period, refinements improved the stove's serviceability. In 1850, Mary Evard, a milliner, earned brief success with her Reliance Cook Stove, which she and her husband demonstrated at the St. Louis Fair. In 1867, a New Yorker, Elizabeth Hawks, devised a baking attachment for stoves intended to spread heat thoroughly through loaves while leaving the top crust light and tender. She continued modifying the original design and marketed two thousand units within months of their shipment from the Empire Foundry of Troy.

Technology improved in 1865 after the Edinburgh inventor James Young began extracting paraffin oil from shale for burning as fuel in cookers and stoves.

Design peaked in the Edwardian era, when ironmongers touted the top of the line, some in *art nouveau* style surrounded with tile. Cleveland Metal Products applied oil and kerosene technology in 1925 to the oil space heater, kerosene water heater, and Perfection oil cook stove and oven. Their ad cajoled, "They let Mother come out of the kitchen earlier and less tired." (Celeher 1985, 51) In 1932, Sears marketed the wickless, smokeless, and odorless oil range from E-Z-est-Way, which promised the home cook unencumbered lighting, never-fail baking, recycling of heat from front burners to back, and removable plates for easy clean-ups.

The domestic adviser Jonathan Periam's handbook *The Home & Farm Manual: A Pictorial Encyclopedia of Farm, Garden, Household, Architectural, Legal, Medical and Social Information* (1884) simplified for the uninitiated the use of these new stoves. He explained that the damper was a source of home comfort and economy. He offered a method of measuring economy: if the housekeeper found more ash after adjustment of the damper, the gain proved that she did not lose heat up the chimney.

A Boston financier and philanthropist, Edward Atkinson, vice president of the Anti-Imperialist League from 1898 to 1905 and author of *The Science of Nutrition* (1896), extended stove improvements to cookery for factory workers and common laborers. He invented the Aladdin Oven, an insulated lunch pail cooker that fit atop a kerosene lamp. Using slow-cooking methods, the user could simmer tasty, sanitary soup, stew, oatmeal, vegetables, and puddings for a satisfying workday meal. The low-cost device used a limited amount of fuel and required no pot watching or stirring. His effort to upgrade the diet of the worker earned praise from sanitation expert Dr. Ellen H. Richards and Frances Willard, secretary of the Woman's Christian Temperance Union, who championed improved nutrition to keep men out of saloons. The failure of the Aladdin Oven to sell provoked Atkinson to write an article for the January 1897 issue of *New England Kitchen Magazine*, in which he chided men for not supplying their wives with the latest cooking convenience.

However, the historian Albert Bolles, author of *Industrial History of the United States* (1897), predicted that a mechanized firebox would never replace the cheery, inviting open hearth. He commented that all classes felt repugnance at stoves, which were better received in schools, courtrooms, bars, shops, "and other public and rough places." (Cowan 1983, 56) He concluded that it seemed untenable that the householder would try to bring up a family around an iron stove. More to the point were women's responses to change. Optimism radiated from the diary of the housewife Ann Still of Smoogrow, Orkneys, who bought her grated stove in 1878 and had it in place and working in January 1879, with minor adjustments to the chimney to halt smoking. With terse delight in new technology, she summarized, "Got it put up & room much warmer." (Schärer & Fenton 1998, 42) The domestic author Erzsébet Komáry, a teacher in Budapest, wrote a lengthy overview of improvements in *A Polgári Háztartás Szakácskönyve* (Cookery Book for the Middle-Class Household, 1914). In her opinion, the younger generation had already embraced modernization by choosing iron ranges and cooking plates as time- and work-savers.

A useful piece of stove equipment was the square or round asbestos pad. Formed of a fireproof fibrous mineral, asbestos sheets bound in iron separated pottery and metal pots from flame. Spills readily burned off the mat. Another implement, the carbonizer, was a nested pair of cylinders that fit in a range flue. The inner piece, a perforated or slotted pipe incinerator, held waste material that carbonized as heat and fumes changed its composition. For managing the flue, the householder could clip a flue stopper in the sooty opening left by removal of stovepipes. The round plate, sometimes painted, lithographed, or stamped in a geometric motif, decorated the wall like a mounted plaque.

In 1889, Carpenter Electric Company in St. Paul, Minnesota, sold the electric stove to restaurants, but housewives continued to struggle with the old black wood- or coal-burner. By 1891, the few homemakers who had access to electricity could purchase home units, boxy black stoves that resembled wood burners. They contained a bake oven and warming oven topped with an iron hot plate attached by wires to a switchboard and controlled by switches. The 1900 Sears, Roebuck catalog showcased the Acme Royal Range, a rococo nickel-plated model that sported ornamentation rivaling a parlor organ. Early in the twentieth century, stove linings were often shaped from monel, a shiny alloy of iron, manganese, copper, and nickel. Named for an American metallurgist, Ambrose Monell, the alloy limited heat conduction.

For more conventional cooks in the American Midwest, models pictured in the 1908 Sears, Roebuck catalog extolled the ornate blue polished steel Wehrle range at $29.75 along with a standard cookstove at $15.95. A labeled drawing of the cheapest model pointed out roomy warming closet, damper controls mounted at eye level, elevated tea pot stands, handy coal-feeder door, removable porcelain-lined water reservoir, spring-loaded oven door, and a hearth and removable ash pan. In 1909, the catalog featured ornate nickel scrollery and bossed feet on blue polished steel coal-, coke-, or wood-burners. The stoves sold for $19.88 to $28.33, depending on the height of the closet and such features as a porcelain-lined water reservoir, asbestos insulation, warming closet, six eyes or rondels, and sensitive oven thermometer marked in increments from one to twelve. To encourage the timid customer, the company added in capital letters a promise to furnish repairs.

In 1906, Albert L. Marsh further enhanced electric cookery with the patenting of Nichrome wire. The addition of stovetop hot plates and radiant coils accommodated the various pans and kettles found in most kitchens. Electric boiling rings and oven regulators improved control of temperature. A breakthrough in heating speed derived from General Electric's Calrod unit, an element housed in magnesium oxide and chromium iron that successfully competed with instant-light gas burners. In industrialized nations, women shifted their loyalty rapidly to electricity. In *Der Neue Haushalt* (The New Housekeeping, 1926), the German ergonomics leader Dr. Erna Meyer stated, "We are grateful to gas, but our longing belongs to electricity." (Schärer & Fenton 1998, 68)

The nickel-plated Mayflower range, advertised in the 1923 Sears, Roebuck catalog, displayed the era's sleek design, which contrasted the squat, utilitarian laundry and cook stoves of earlier times. Guaranteed for up to thirty years, the wood-burning model presented a polished cooktop that ended scrubbing, blacking, or shining, three of the dirtiest and most despised home chores. Sold for as low as $69.05 for the eight-burner model, it accommodated a thirty-gallon water boiler for an extra $3.75. The advertiser guaranteed that the popular Mayflower operated at low cost and eliminated waste and heat loss. Cheaper, sleeker, and less obtrusive, the porcelain enameled gas ranges on subsequent pages sold to the city homemaker. Unlike the heavy iron monsters with eight to ten eyes, enameled models perched on long graceful legs supplied the basic four burners and bake and warming ovens. Featuring zinc plating in the oven and polished metal, the newer models suggested both ease and convenience. Prominent in the ad copy was the promise that the stoves lit "instantly without matches and without reaching over the top or moving utensils." (Schroeder 1973, 690)

In the February 1925 issue of *Good Housekeeping*, the Florence Stove Company advertised the Florence Oil Range as channeling flame directly up into the cooking rather than out into the room. The American Stove Company touted the Lorain oven heat regulator, which served gas and oil stoves to assure temperature control. A lengthy article by Arthur J. Donniez of the Good Housekeeping Institute appeared in the May 1925 issue to illustrate advances, including easy-lighting gas ports, oils that prevented rust, and a closed top that allowed the cook to group several pots over a single hot surface to maximize fuel use. By 1930, *House and Garden* was advertising the Caloric gas range, an attractive green porcelainized appliance with stacked ovens and streamlined burners and warming closet.

After World War II, manufacturers turned from military hardware to domestic goods and the stove metamorphosed into a kitchen work station. The deep-well cooker, marketed in the 1940s, replaced the William Campbell Company's cooker range of 1928, which positioned an electric kettle in the space below the oven. The handier stove-top cooker economized on fuel by withdrawing the heat source to the interior for baking, boiling, slow-cooking, and steaming. A later dual-position model, the thrift-cooker, worked in the stove and on top. An upgrade added a third use, pressure cooking. Burners offered faster heating, seven gradations of heat, plate warming, and implement drawers. Designers of gas ranges, such as the Estate range made in Hamilton, Ohio, added fluorescent surface lights, oven lights, child-proof locks on controls, and crisping chests for removing moisture from breads, cereals, chips, crackers, and condiments. Norge, a division of Borg-Warner in Detroit and Toronto, brought out the spirolator burner for different types of gas that spread flame over the whole pan bottom for maximum contact.

Woman's Home Companion offered readers a variety of informational ads, columns, and illustrated features demonstrating changes in kitchen ranges. The February 1947 issue depicted the Grand gas range as the best choice for the busy cook who baked and roasted meat simultaneously in its twin chambers and broiled in the Charcolator. The April issue featured an overview of models compiled by the home equipment editor Elizabeth Beveridge, author of *The Pocket Book of Home Canning* (1943) and *Pots and Pans for Your Kitchen* (1950). Of the ten featured American makes, she praised the General Electric built-in pressure cooker; Norge's deep-well cooker with two-deck rack; Frigidaire's smooth, one-piece top, which made clean-up easier; and the multi-use control clocks and lighted dials of several name brands.

In the 1960s, German cooks made their greatest shift toward convenience and modernity in their kitchens. As listed in the *Jahrbuch für die Bundesrepublik Deutschland* (Yearbook for the German Republic, 1969), by the end of the decade half as many homes were using coal stoves as at the beginning; electric ranges accounted for a threefold increase in use and gas range use increased by 60 percent. Shifts from regional fuels further homogenized recipes and cooking styles. The leveling effect of fuel economy produced a uniformity of experience and expectations in cooks from one end of the country to the other. Modern cookbooks compiled and distributed by agents of utility companies, such as Elizabeth Meyer-Haagen's *Das Elektrische Kochen* (Electric Cookery, 1956), mirrored the technology of gas and electric stoves.

The creation of ceramic stovetops in the 1960s ended the kitchen task of retrieving food dropped into heating coils and cleaning spills, which quickly charred into a serious cleaning chore. A strong competitor to gas ranges, ceramic stoves such as those manufactured by Miele in Austria and Germany, Gaggenau in Germany, and SMEG (Smalteria Metallurgica Emiliana Guistalla) in Reggia Emilia, Italy, beautified the kitchen with glossy surfaces. Although temperature settings were less precise than gas, the units promised instantaneous heating and cooler peripheries, a savings in wasted heat, melted implements, and burned fingers. On the down side, they demanded flat-bottomed cook pots and required careful scrubbing to remove burned sugar and calcium accumulation without marring the surface.

Ceramics faced stiff competition from induction units, a coil-under-glass system that heated only when a ferrous metal pan touched the burner. Touchpad control, quick rise to exact temperature, and spread of heat up the sides of the vessel enhanced such daily techniques as slow simmering. The induction stove, including the drop-in countertop unit manufactured in Austria and Germany by Bulthaup, further coordinated the stove with the surrounding work space. Its sealed heating unit also enhanced the sense of cleanliness and ease in food preparation never before available with earlier methods of cooking.

Stove makers began outfitting their appliances with appealing features in the 1990s, such as the Grande Châtelaine cast-iron model from Godin, a French company that loaded the oversized designer stove with brass fittings, eight gas rings, and two ovens. In 1992, Lacanche, named for a city in the Burgundy region, began producing professional kitchens distinctive in their variety of styles and gleaming enamel surfacing. A year later, Dacor coordinated a commercial-grade gas cooktop with electronic touch pads, sealed burners, and self-cleaning convection oven plus quiet raised ventilation system in a porcelainized case. A variety of interchangeable electric modules coordinated the flexibility of heat elements, woks, barbecue/griddle, grills with lava stones, and rotisserie.

In 1994, General Electric added induction cooking technology to its Profile appliances. The concept was safe, responsive, and energy efficient, but was not an immediate success with builders and homeowners. Cooktops offered glass-ceramic panels and electronic touchpads with ten power settings. Drawbacks for consumers were price as well as the need to convert from ordinary to ferromagnetic cookware and to learn a new

way of controlling heat. To entice the tenuous shopper, some dealers offered a free set of steelcore Nordic cookware.

The editors of *La Cucina Italiana* heralded more versatile kitchen ranges in 1997. They admired the Maytag radiant heat range with self-cleaning convection oven and Insta-Heat surface, a smooth glass top over which cooks could slide pots and pans. Their second choice, the Wolf gas range, advertised automatically re-ignitable flame, precision brass valves, porcelain convection oven, and a broiler that cooked up to 1500 degrees Fahrenheit. The forty-eight-inch Thermador Professional cooking island with hood featured a variety of sealed burners, grill, and griddle arrangements plus convention and auxiliary ovens. The Jenn-Air, a third smaller than the Thermador, packed into its sleek stainless steel frame and backsplash a modular gas cooktop, electric convection oven, nonstick grills, and broiler with variable temperature control.

Reduction of internal grime boosted the cost of domestic ranges, but won over industrious cooks who disliked oven-cleaning. The devices worked by several methods: pyrolysis eliminated crust in a sealed oven generating extra-high temperatures, catalysis absorbed carbonized drips and vapors by oxidating while food cooked, and hydrolysis applied water to the problem. As a boon to the career woman, the self-cleaning oven became a standard option, which Kenmore's gas and electric models modified with vapor-monitoring.

Innovations in stoves keep online and catalogue sources stocked with appealing ideas and safety devices, such as the rail on the SMEG oven that keeps hot vessels from falling. The single-eye professional burner accommodates table-side cooking for catering, buffets, barbecues, and patio gatherings. The Glowmaster Induction Cooker is a simple counter device shaped like a hot plate for warming, sautéing, frying, and boiling. Smaller add-ons include iron burner plates that distribute heat more evenly from electric eyes and decorative covers that conceal eyes when they are idle. A massive Viking professional grill equipped with cast-iron burners, rotisserie, rangetop burners, smoker, barbecue tools, grilling basket, halogen grill light, and other amenities promises top-of-the-line butane or natural gas efficiency for cookouts. The Maytag speed-cook range applies radiant heat and low-level microwaves to complete defrosting and cooking in less than half the time of conventional ranges.

In March 2001, *Consumer Reports* evaluated popular professional-style ranges, which cost eighteen hundred dollars and above for such amenities as heavy grates in a thirty-six-inch stainless steel case, powerful burners to suit stir-frying, continuous grates, automatic oven shut-off, more oven rack positions, a choice of six to eight burners, and dual fuel—gas burners and electric oven. New ranges like the Maytag Accellis and the Maytag Gemini lure consumers with multiple advantages—double ovens, warming drawers, and convection fans, a speedier technology for baking and roasting. The quick cooktops from Hotpoint and Kenmore promise easy clean-up, touchpad controls, larger oven windows, gentler simmering, and fewer repairs.

Frontgate catalog lists a line of gourmet grills, outdoor cooking surfaces in a variety of shapes and sizes for grilling, griddling, smoking, or rotisserie cooking. The Frontgate Ultimate 2001 Edition Grill combines features in demand in the twenty-first century. The stainless steel unit comes with oversized wheels, casters, and pull-out storage drawer. Removable shelves surfaced in Corian withstand sharp knife cuts; a halogen light illuminates the surface for evening use. Ergonomic knobs allow the user to grip controls without slipping. In addition to the propane-powered heating elements and spit-roaster, the stove features a set of forks, knives, and brush for professional grilling and an electronic thermometer-fork. This unit is the top of a full line of outdoor kitchens and cooking centers for patio and pool-side use.

See also **Amish Kitchens; Fireplace; Rittenhouse, David; Victorian Kitchens**

Further Reading

Babyak, Richard J., "Cooler Cooking: Induction Stages Comeback," *Appliance Manufacturer,* January 1994, 97–98.
Beveridge, Elizabeth, "Our 1947 Electric Range-Finder," *Woman's Home Companion*, April 1947, 110–112.

STREET FOOD

Portable snacks, cooked expertly and quickly at streetside stalls or dispensed from pushcarts, are a time-honored culinary tradition around the world. The British archeologist Sir Charles Leonard Woolley, who led a University of Pennsylvania expedition to Ur, discovered the ancient equivalent of a snack bar in the ancient Sumerian center. Dated to 1700 BCE, the brick counter offered bread from an oven or spitted meats grilled on charcoal braziers much like those still in use in the Middle East. The German archeologist Heinrich Schliemann's excavations at Hissarlik in Turkey disclosed the ruins of ancient Troy, the setting of Homer's *Iliad* (850 BCE). Unearthed at the fortified gate to the city was a small food shop, equipped with ovens, storage bins, hearth, and sink, which appears to have dispensed quick snacks or baked goods to passersby.

Street cooking for travelers at train depot.
[© *Shoosh/Up the Res/Alamy.*]

Of Brazier and Bazaar

In late medieval Cairo, strolling street cooks balanced small stoves on their heads. Lines of *tabbakhun* (cookshop owners) in the shaded bazaar sold deep-fried fritters, grilled kabobs and sausages, pickled vegetables, wheat porridge, and date-sweetened confections—a tradition that has changed little over time. Likewise, during China's Sung Dynasty, snacks of noodles and soup were an established street business. Originally dismissed as peasant food, according to historian Shu Hsi, these quick meals of noodles and cakes eventually found favor at the imperial court.

To satisfy the hunger of shoppers and travelers on the thoroughfares of first-century Rome and Pompeii, hawkers sold cool wines, and brazier cooks distributed tasty snacks at some 200 *cauponae* (taverns). Local patrons, businessmen, and visitors clustered around the vendors to select from bread, cheese, and cakes. In the Street of Dried Fruits, described in William Clarke's *Pompeii: Its Past and Present State* (1847), hungry pedestrians had their choice of chestnuts, figs, hemp seed, plums, or raisins. The beverage list included fruit juice, both fermented and fresh, and wine, either straight from the jar or mixed with water or seawater. On cold days, chilly strollers partook of hot spiced and honeyed wine dipped from jars sunk up to the neck in heated marble counters. At high summer, when the

A Street vendor offers fresh fried dough with a sprinkling of powdered sugar as a tasty breakfast treat (Viñales, Cuba. 2002).
[© *Courtesy of Agricultural Research Service, USDA. Photo by Peter Manzelli.*]

Engraving of street bakers during the Renaissance.

Italian sun pushed temperatures over 100 degrees Fahrenheit, sellers depended on regular shipments of snow from the Appenines to line the bottom of stone wine sleeves.

In the late Middle Ages and early Renaissance, Turkish kitchens created street foods sold by vendors in the Istanbul market. One shop specialized in *iskembe corbasi* (tripe soup), a popular dish for late-night suppers following heavy drinking. Cooks marinated morsels of lamb and chicken and spit-roasted them outdoors on a grill, just as soldiers once roasted meat on the tips of their swords. Fragrant bites of hot meat became traditional street fare in cities and at the confluence of major roads.

In the Eastern Mediterranean throughout Egypt and Lebanon, fish kebabs were more popular than those made with meat. As described in *Viaggia* (Journeys, 1384), a travelogue of Leonardo di Niccolò Frescobaldi, a wealthy Florentine, Cairo residents carried a rawhide picnic cloth, spread it on the thoroughfare, and ate *al fresco* from a street menu of kebabs, rice, and fritters. He described the cries of vendors offering

597

spitted lamb to travelers, who had no choice but street food in a city that lacked inns or other travel accommodation. As a precaution against disease, a local food officer supervised the cleanliness and suitability of urban food stalls.

A Surviving Tradition

The tradition of street food persisted into the twenty-first century in the *souvlaki* and baklava stands in the Athenian Plaka and the kebab makers throughout the Arab world. In North Africa, *kushari* peddlers aboard donkey carts in Cairo satisfied the laborer's need for a quick lunch, spiced with a tomato-based chili sauce. In Turkey, the vendors displayed their oval pizzas, or *pide, shushbarak* (crescent pastries), and *lahmacun* (meat pasties), fragrant with onion and spices. For quick snacks or informal lunch breaks, street cooks assembled gyros—rotisserie-cooked lamb, dressed with sour cream, tomato chunks, and onion slices and enveloped in pita bread.

In South Africa, slices of yam sprinkled with sugar became noontime meals for day laborers. Buttery deep-fried *brik* pockets, phylo pastry filled with potatoes and preserved lemons, were the most popular lunch in Tunisia. In Spain, the hot *churro* (fritter) had a long history of street sale. Italian sellers of *panini* (sandwiches) in Paris made inroads into French cuisine, filling sandwiches with mozzarella, prosciutto, tomato, and olive oil and cooking them between grilling plates that marked the bread with a distinctive scored pattern.

Legend has it that the sandwich originated in London in 1762. After a day-long round of dice and cards, the Earl of Sandwich, desiring a simple meal, requested that his cook layer slices of cheese and cold meat between pieces of bread. With a whole meal in a single hand, he could continue rolling the dice with his free hand. From this efficient invention came nearly two and a half centuries of fast food, which freed drivers to continue a journey during mealtime and offered cooks great scope for inventiveness in combining foods and bread for picnic meals, travel food, impromptu dinners, and school lunches.

Another food tradition with roots in England, fish and chips purportedly got its start in 1863 at John Lees's wooden hut in Mossley, Manchester, where he specialized in pigs' feet and pea soup. Another version of the fish-and-chips story claims that the first paired fry-ups began in 1868 at Main's, a food seller in London's East End. Wherever its beginnings, the frying of hake, cod, and haddock chunks along with potatoes in beef fat or oil attracted an immediate following. Not all London residents were equally enthusiastic—in 1876, a health inspector complained about the neighborhood nuisance of fish friers with their smelly oil and late-night hours. In 1912, a fish-and-chips purveyor, Harry Ramsden, began selling his wares in Bradford from 9:00 a.m. to midnight every day except Christmas. He opened his first official location in 1928 at Guiseley, Leeds; from two pan friers, he fed the walkers and cyclists who patronized his hatch window. Prefiguring the fast-food chains that arose later in the century, by the 1930s a chain of Harry Ramsden's Huts was catering to the take-out trade in battered fish; in 1952, the company broke a record, selling 10,000 servings of fish and chips in one day. Branches and kiosks of Ramsden's fish and chips appeared in Glasgow and Dublin and then spread around the globe to Singapore, Hong Kong, Toronto, Melbourne, the Middle East, and opened in many airports and most British military installations. Copies cropped up along the Mediterranean, where cooks substituted squid for finned fish, and in Belgium, where the main dish was mussels and chips.

Streets of San Antonio and Chicago

Chili, a southwestern American street food, originated at stands on the streets of the Military Plaza in San Antonio, Texas, in the 1830s. Sadie Thornhill and Juanita and Esperanza Garcia, who earned the title "chili queens," set up cauldrons of beans and *chili con carne* to serve with tortillas, tamales, eggs, coffee, and chocolate. (Castro 2000, 57) The press of people about the women's oilcloth-covered tables attracted troubadours, musicians, and food lovers of all social levels and races and inspired the O. Henry short story "The Enchanted Kiss." After the town mayor decided to build city hall on the spot, the women moved their enterprise to Alamo Plaza, where they became a tourist attraction. A chili stand sent by the city of San Antonio to the 1893 Chicago Columbian Exposition allowed people from all over the country to sample this unique street cuisine.

The frankfurter, another popular U.S. street food, developed in Frankfurt, Germany, some time before 1500. The Viennese claimed to have invented the wiener, which got its name from the German word for *Viennese*. In 1880, Antoine Feuchtwanger, a Frankfurt native, imported frankfurters to St. Louis. A Bulgarian cook, Tom Kiradjieff, set up a street kitchen selling "coney islands" (chili dogs) in Cincinnati in the 1920s, which launched his innovative Cincinnati chili business. (Flandrin & Montanari 2000, 544).

Rise of Fast Food

In the 1940s, two brothers, Maurice and Richard McDonald, owners of a Pasadena, California, drive-in restaurant, decided to satisfy Americans' demand for speed by providing meals that could be prepared in a matter of minutes. Their menu consisted of only three items—hamburgers, fries, and milkshakes. They eventually sold their business to Ray Kroc, who launched the McDonald's chain. The popularity of McDonald's led inevitably to imitators, resulting in the development of a giant fast-food industry that spread from the United States around the globe. One of the most successful was the Brazilian entrepreneur Alberto Saraíva's Habib's restaurant chain, which catered to the large Middle Eastern population in Latin America.

Despite the widespread presence of fast-food chains, the tradition of street foods remained strong into the twenty-first century, especially in developing countries and in the urban centers of industrial nations. In New York City, office workers gathered around umbrella-covered carts to consume hot dogs and mustard-slathered pretzels; street stalls and pushcarts in Mexico City, Saigon, and Nairobi dispensed local specialties to passersby. Existing alongside these flourishing businesses, fast-food establishments—most catering to drivers rather than pedestrians—provided hundreds of millions of meals per year.

See also **Automat; Convenience Foods; Kitchen Business**

Further Reading

Castro, Rafaela G. *Dictionary of Chicano Folklore*. Santa Barbara, Calif.: ABC-Clio, 2000.
Leibowitz, Ed, "Out from Under the Wrecking Ball," *Smithsonian,* December 2000, 112–122.
Luxner, Larry, "Esfihas To Go," *Aramco World,* November/December 2000, 34–37.
Ritzer, George, "Slow Food Versus McDonald's," *Slow,* July–September 1998.
Schlosser, Eric. *Fast Food Nation: The Dark Side of the All-American Meal*. Boston: Houghton Mifflin, 2001.
_____, "Why McDonald's Fries Taste So Good," *Atlantic Monthly,* January 2001, 50–56.

SWEETENERS

Sweets are integral to the human diet, as evidenced by pictures of jars of honey in ancient Thebes, God's promise to Moses in Exodus of a "land of milk and honey," Assyrian preference for fig syrup, Lydian commerce in a sugary tamarisk syrup, Syrian extraction of sweet *elaiomeli* oil from palms, and Mesopotamian table service of date purée. Egyptian refinement of wild carob, papyrus juice, and grapes yields natural confections, as do the *mnasion* and *sari* plants. The

Berber of southern Morocco expect lavish gifts from a groom to his in-laws, including tea, dates, henna, and sugar. Among tamarisk limbs, Arab nomads gather a sweet insect secretion called "bread of heaven," the original heavenly manna described in Exodus, which they store in earthenware for use as an energy-rich food. Farther east, the Iraqi still collect this sweet for flavoring honey cakes.

Sugar cane emerged in New Guinea around 5000 BCE before passing to India. The Ainu, Japanese aborigines of Hokkaido and Sakhalin Island, made sweetener from sap they collected from sugar maples when it rose in their trunks in early spring. In more recent times, they simmered a rice syrup with malted grain to produce a sweetener as thick as honey and easily metabolized by the body. Early Greek sweetening derived from two main sources—honey and dates. The Roman encyclopedist Pliny the Elder's *Natural History* (ca. 77 CE) described sugar as a white substance collecting in a reed, but he dismissed it as primarily a medicine imported from India and Arabia. The Roman chef Caelius Apicius, author of *De Re Coquinaria* (On Cooking, late 300s CE), the world's first cookbook, stuffed dates as appetizers or puréed the prize Jericho date and added it to meat and fish sauce.

Finnish cooks traditionally relied on the wild blueberry, cloudberry, raspberry, and strawberry for sweetening desserts and liqueurs. Also prominent as sweetmeats were pressed figs and dates. Among natives of the Americas, cooks boiled maple and birch sap into sugar, a process they taught European colonists. Similarly, Chilean syrup makers based their sweetener on coconut sap. The canyon Indians outside Santa Rosa, Mexico, fermented sprouted sugar cane seeds in a pine needle bed as the basis for a popular drink. An unusually powerful sweetener, the West African *katemfe* berry, used in livestock food and chewing gum, is two thousand times as sweet as sugar.

Other sources provided other degrees of sweetening and flavoring. The Hidatsa and Ojibwa of the Great Plains collected box elder sap for a minty-tasting sugar; Native Americans from Idaho and Washington turned the sap of baked camassia squamash into molasses. Southwestern tribes collected agave (or maguey) sap for *agua miel* (honey water) and reduced it to syrup or sugar for sweetening porridge. Fermented sap produced vinegar or pulque, a high-powdered alcoholic beverage.

Sucrose or sugar crystallized from refined cane sap originated in India and was the basis for a Dravidian treacle. From there, it passed to China and Cyprus. Known from 300 BCE, it served the Romans as a restorative or medicine rather than a condiment. After the Arabs conquered Persia in 640 CE, they introduced cane sugar to Syria, North Africa, and Spain. By the 700s CE, Sicilian cooks were using sugar in huge quantities; in 760 CE, Arab cane growers in Motril and Málaga, Spain, were irrigating land for the cultivation of a sugar crop. In the reckoning of Sicilian gastronome Pino Correnti, the author of *il Libro d'Oro della Cucina e dei Vini di Sicilia* (The Golden Book of Sicilian Cooking and Wine, 1976), the Italian cassata, a confection built around a filling of sweet ricotta cream, got its start in Palermo in 998 CE, when Arabs reached Sicily from North Africa, bringing citrus fruit and cane sugar. Sicilian pastry cooks refined traditional confections and invented a cheese-filled dessert built on a base of sponge cake called *pan di Spagna* (bread of Spain). Topped with marzipan and sweetmeats, it became a seasonal treat at Easter and Christmas. In 1150, Granada boasted fourteen sugar mills; tall, willowy cane flourished on farms in the Madeiras in 1240.

Sugar refining began with Arab technology and passed to Europe during the Crusades. It advanced in the 1400s in Venice, a shipping center that exported sweetener to distant lands before Lisbon dominated refining. In "De Saccharo" (On Sugar), Book II of the food author Platina's Latin masterwork, *De Honesta Voluptate et Valitudine* (On Right Pleasure and Health, 1475), text described the sources of his table sugar as Arabia, India, Crete, and Sicily. He preferred it white and finely ground and recommended it for nourishment and digestion.

In 1577, Chaplain William Harrison, author of *Description of Elizabethan England*, commented on the predominance of meat and sweets on the tables of the privileged. Imported into the British Isles from Egypt, Cyprus, Rhodes, Sicily, and Syria, sugar, like quicksilver and frankincense, had to travel by land and water from the East before reaching the kitchen larder. Because of dangerous passage and the threat of loss from piracy, theft, and spoilage, it cost too much for anyone but royalty and the aristocracy, who hired sugar masters to ready it for the kitchen. As pictured in art, the steward suspended a conical funnel above a lidded ewer and placed sugar loaves of the same shape inside. By pouring water through the apparatus, the sugar-maker derived a syrup that was more easily measured and added to recipes than chunks or powder. Perhaps to reduce the cost, vendors sold powdered mace sugar or powdered rose sugar, a sweet-smelling dressing for desserts and some meats.

Sugar was a money-making product of the West Indies and impetus to slavers, who operated tortuous *ingenios* (refineries) to the detriment of their crews' health and safety. After compressing stalks, the cane worker retrieved dark opaque juice through a strainer to filter out impurities and sold the crushed stalks as bagasse, a residue valuable to the paper industry. Cane juice went through a defoaming and heating process to convert to syrup and into vacuum pans for crystallization. Barbados sugar millers first sold crystal sugar in 1642, enriching themselves above the other Caribbean isles. To assure harmonious milling and a steady profit, slave buyers deliberately chose African slaves from different areas and language groups to isolate workers.

Throughout Europe, demand for sugar accompanied home and café consumption of cocoa, coffee, and tea. By 1573, the first German refinery at Augsburg was producing cane sugar for local shops. Cane sweetener altered English cookery in the seventeenth century by replacing honey. It reached the kitchen in cones, hats, or loaves varying in weight from five to fifty pounds. To keep lump sugar safe and clean, the householder placed it in a string cradle suspended from hooks in the ceiling or overhead beams. The user had to chop small hunks and grind them in a mortar and pestle for table use. Fine cakes, cookies, and confections needed sieving and further grinding of lumps to assure uniform melting for icing and fudge.

For banquet tables, confectioners for royalty turned white sugar into architectural sculpture made from a paste of sugar and tragacanth gum. Workers shaped it with sculpting instruments or molded it in wood or plaster frames. In 1738, a Dresden wedding celebration honoring Maria Amalia and Charlies III of Spain and Sicily featured a model of Mount Vesuvius formed from confectioner's paste. In 1780, the encyclopedia of Denis Diderot and Jean D'Alembert pictured the elements of the confectioner's work station, equipped with cutting and shaping tools and wheels, spatulas, and tin molds as well as almond paste and dough.

In the second half of the eighteenth century, beet sugar competed with cane sugar. Long prized in ancient Egypt, India, China, Greece, and Rome, it did not reach the kitchen in crystalline form until 1747, when German apothecary Andreas Marggraf first refined it from liquid of the sugar beet (*Beta vulgaris*). The son of the court pharmacist at Berlin and lab director at the German Academy of Sciences of Berlin, he identified it under a microscope as the same crystal as cane sugar. Because the sweetening industry was slow to act on his discovery, beet sugar did not become a factory-refined product until 1801. Near century's end, his pupil, Franz Karl Achard, improved the Silesian mangel-wurzel as a source of table sweetener and, in 1802, built a sugar factory at Cunern, Poland. Six years later, Benjamin Delessert clarified beet sugar through charcoal, a system that improved flavor for home use. The improvement caught the attention of Napoleon, who financed beet fields, training of scientists, and refineries in France, Belgium, Germany, and Austria.

At the same time that beet sugar manufacture reached Poland, it got its start in Russia, replacing the cane sugar manufacturing established in 1723. Private estates maintained their own production centers. Within ninety-five years, the number of Russian beet sugar processing plants rose to 236. In the next century, beet sugar, although whiter and cheaper, failed to hold its dominance over cane because beets left an unpleasant odor and aftertaste that marred candy, cookies, and beverages. Elena Burman Molokhovets, author of the classic Russian cookbook, *A Gift to Young Housewives* (1861), persisted in buying cones of white cane sugar, which she pounded with citrus zest to add extra flavor to recipes. For treacle, she preferred a sweet potato syrup similar to American molasses.

Colonial American farmers made their own molasses from sorghum, a field crop that also drew game birds, which augmented domestic meats, fish, and venison in the diet. By 1730, sugar was the basis of jam, another valuable food item in a colonial diet limited by place and opportunity. Maple sugar came in syrup and cake form. For pioneers setting out over the Rockies for Western lands, the type of sweeteners they chose—loaf sugar, maple sugar, molasses, honey—was crucial to its preservation during a tough haul in foul weather.

A lighter sugar from cane imported from the Caribbean or grown in Louisiana came to market in large hollow cones or loaves that blended brown stack with white. Refiners broke it into smaller loaves and wrapped it in blue paper for marketing in grocery stores, where clerks unwrapped each lump, threaded it on cord, and hung it for display. Some stores supplied shoppers with a sugar mill for grinding in the store. In lieu of a mill, users cut loaves with sugar nippers, then ground pieces for use and sifted out impurities and lumps. By 1850, Shakers had entered the competitive maple syrup trade and developed sweeteners and fruit preserves, which they shipped by train worldwide. Brown sugar was the most dependable and cheapest. By the 1870s, merchandisers could separate molasses and brown sugar from a premium grade white. Havana sugar, the finest grade, was the choice of bakers and pastry makers, who still subjected stock to crushing in a mortar or with a rolling pin and sifting to assure fine particles.

As the American Civil War deprived Southern planters of slave labor, sugar growers began emigrating to British Honduras, now called Belize. In contrast to farming in the United States, the American colony in British Honduras extended the best opportunity for farming duty free. Lodging at the American Hotel, owned by Mrs. A. Foote, offered cheap rooms, servants, and fresh-cooked meals at a third less than they had cost in the South.

Venturesome frontierswomen learned trail substitutions, the tradeoffs that evened out supplies of staples long after wagons had rolled past the last trading centers and dry goods stores. The absence of sugar was hardest to bear, especially for children and for men who demanded sweetening in coffee. The replacement of granular sugar with wild honey and molasses was the first substitution to come to mind. Less common was a snip of fruit leather, puréed and dried in the sun, or the center of a melon, which clever cooks pulverized, sieved, and mixed with starchy water boiled from corn cobs.

In the Hawaiian Islands, owners of plantations abandoned sandalwood, sea salt, and whale oil as lucrative commodities and looked to sugar production for wealth. Because leprosy and epidemics of measles and other European diseases had decimated natives already weakened by press-gang work, entrepreneurs hired middlemen—Alexander and Baldwin, Castle and Cooke, C. Brewer and Company, H. Hackfeld and Company, and Theo. H. Davies and Company. These competitive jobbers imported Japanese, Filipino, Chinese, Korean, Okinawan, Puerto Rican, and Portuguese laborers for the hot, exhausting work of tending and harvesting cane. The fall of Hawaii's last monarch, Queen Lydia Kamekeha Liliuokalani, to a group of American sugar planters on January 17, 1893, preceded the annexation of the island chain in 1898 and the Americanization of the sugar industry.

Although island sugar manufacture carried dangers of fever and machete injuries, the overwhelming outcry of disillusioned field hands was the absence of home foodstuffs—Japanese *tofu* and *sake* (rice wine), Korean *kimch'i* and soy sauce, and Chinese tea, *gau* (sesame cakes), and *jook* (rice gruel). Smuggled seeds for kitchen gardens satisfied individual families, many of whom developed after-hours pushcart peddling of ethnic vegetables—daikon for *tsukemono* (pickle), ginger, lotus root, and watercress—and homemade confections based on cheap island sugar. The Filipina cook Doreen Fernandez, who surveyed the Filipino Women's League's *Hawaii Filipino's Favorite Recipes* (1975), found little connection between authentic recipes and acculturated island cooking. A Japanese woman reared in Japan and immigrated to Hawaii complained that island sweets had ruined traditional Japanese food.

In Australia, the production of sugar began in 1865. "Blackbirding" enslaved Kanaka workers from the Pacific Islands until 1905. From July to October, workers cut and transported cane to sugar mills for shredding, crushing, extracting juice, and boiling it down into molasses. After selling off refined table sugar, owners recycled the by-products—basse fiber for kitchen fuel, impurities for fertilizer, and molasses to make into ethanol or feed to livestock.

The predominance of sweet over salt, sour, or bitter colored much of human outlook and the way homemakers stocked pantries, cooked, and decorated their kitchens and dining areas. During the 1870 Siege of Paris, Continental cooks and bakers suffered from rationing of cane sugar. As a substitute, they preferred grape sugar to saccharin for taste and texture. Shifts in recipes demonstrate how they accommodated the quirks of both sweeteners, which did not cook with the same flavor or produce the same brown crust in pies, cakes, and cookies.

For display of sugar, late nineteenth- and early twentieth-century sugar and syrup containers underwent a refinement from simple canisters into ornate table vessels. The treen, turned wood, enamelware, or japanned tin sugar bowl often contained holder and small matching spoon exposed through a hole in the lid for ladling out individual servings. A sanitary glass table model, manufactured in 1915 by the Ideal Sanitary Sugar Bowl Company of New York City, dispensed through the bottom when the user pressed a nickel-plated lever. Similar devices dispensed syrup and honey with a one-handed operation.

When the exigencies of World War II forced sugar rationing in the United States on May 5, 1942. American kitchens either managed on stock-piled stores or black market supplies or shifted sweeteners from granulated sugar to honey, maple syrup, and sorghum molasses. The redoubtable maple sweetener industry proved a godsend to the nation's sweet tooth. Sugaring families ferried sugar buckets on sap sleds to maple groves. At the sugarhouses, a plank fire heated evaporating pans, which sent vapors aloft through a roof vent. Boiled down at the rate of thirty to forty barrels of tree ooze per gallon of syrup, the finished product varied according to amount of sweetness borne by that year's sap.

After sugar returned to the market, Grandma's Old Fashioned Molasses and Karo, Sweetose, and other brands of corn syrup competed heavily with crystal sugar for use on breakfast foods, in baked beans, and in the canning and freezing of fresh fruit. To introduce cooks to substitutions for dry sugar, the American Molasses Company offered two booklets, "101 Molasses Recipes" and "Make Your Precious Sugar Go Further." Into the 1960s, shifts in sweeteners were common in the marketplace. In 1969, artificial sweeteners suffered a blow when the U.S. Department of Health, Education, and Welfare banned cyclamates.

In the late twentieth century, sugaring consumed much of the manual labor of the Caribbean. Sidney Mintz studied the folk traditions of field work at Jauca, a rural cane-growing district of Puerto Rico inhabited by the offspring of slaves and by Chinese, Indian, Javanese, and Portuguese contract laborers. He lived in a worker's shack and joined in the seed cutting, seeding and planting, cultivation, fertilizing, ditching, irrigation, cane cutting, and truck loading. In Jamaica, he found the poor still purchasing loaves or heads of hardened brown sugar laced with molasses. He discovered a similar loaf sugar used by homemakers in Haiti, the Creole *rapadou*, a small brown log wrapped in banana leaf. Ironically, for these peasants who powered the sugar industry, their own kitchen and table supply was never the pure white crystals so highly valued by the world's wealthy.

Today, sugar from numerous sources remains the world's prime quick-energy food. In Indonesia, gatherers tap the sweet palm trunk for *gulah merah* (palm sugar). Malawian and Barbadian mothers offer children sugarcane to gnaw for snacks. While sojourning on Fatu-Hiva in the Marquesas Islands, the expeditioner Thor Heyerdahl photographed his wife Liv chewing sugar cane. He declared it sweet, juicy, and good for the teeth, unlike refined sugar, which bears the brunt for the modern era's surge in dental caries. In industrialized countries, weight-conscious cooks try to reduce sucrose by replacing it with calorie-reduced or non-caloric sweeteners, but the aftertaste impedes the complete removal of refined sugars from cooking, carbonated drinks, medicines, and processed foods.

On September 18, 1995, the U.S. Food and Drug Administration cleared for sale a sweetener known as stevia, derived from *Stevia rebaudiana*, a perennial shrub of the aster family grown in Brazil, China, Paraguay, Israel, and Thailand. A favorite of the Guarani Indians for treating obesity and high blood pressure and for sweetening medicine and *yerba maté*, stevia was in use in the 1500s when Spanish adventurers encountered it. A natural sugar requiring no refining, it remained a local sweetener until the early 1900s, when the botanist Moises S. Bertoni studied its unique glycosides. Characterized as non-caloric and three hundred times sweeter than cane sugar, it found appreciative users in Brazil, China, and Japan, where cooks choose it to flavor soft drinks, pickles, and soy sauce.

Limited to sale as a food or food supplement, but not as an additive in the United States, stevia appeared to relieve users of fears of dental caries and weight gain while aiding digestion, regulating heart rate, and lowering blood pressure without endangering diabetics. The food authors Donna Gates and Ray Sahelian, coauthors of *The Stevia Cookbook: Cooking with Nature's Calorie-Free Sweetener* (1999), indicated a rise in public demand for the sugar replacement, which was available in plant form from nurseries and garden centers. Ground into a brownish-green powder, stevia enhanced food with a flavor that left no aftertaste, the main fault of artificial sweeteners.

New sweeteners continued to enter the market in the twenty-first century. Early in October 2000, French genetic engineers announced a fructose-rich potato that could end the world's search for a safe, inexpensive, and tasty sugar substitute. A sweet bonanza, the product of enzyme coding, could ease the dietary hardships of diabetics and allow cooks to dream up sweet, non-fattening desserts. According to a report in *Biotechnology and Bioengineering*, Rajbir Sangwan and the staff of the Université de Picardie Jules Verne in Amiens, France, anticipate that manipulating potato starch into a sugar twenty times sweeter than fructose will aid the food industry, but anger critics of genetically altered foods. In mid-2001, Jim Kastner and Mark Eiteman, chemical engineers at the University of Georgia, were considering the possibilities of extracting xylitol from the wood fibers left over from paper production. Already a commercial success in Finland, where producers make low-calorie sugar from the xylose in birch wood, xylitol is a common additive in Scandinavian candy, chewing gum, pharmaceuticals, and toothpaste.

The arrival of Splenda sugar substitute on the market provoked criticism in the March 2001 issue of *Consumer Reports*. With only two calories per teaspoon compared with fifteen for sugar, the new flavoring seemed ideal. One of its selling points is the appearance and volume of granular sugar. At five to seven times the cost of Equal and Sweet 'N Low, the market leaders, Splenda performed well in iced tea, but produced a salty flavor and aftertaste in cookies and bitterness in the chocolate cake recipe recommended on the box.

Welcome technological advancements currently broaden a number of additional choices in methods of sweetening. The professional chef's torch applies butane to melt sugar for crème brûlée. Baker's catalogs and online gourmet shops list refined caramel-flavored corn syrup, sticky bun sugar, glazing sugar, fine sparkling sugar, snow white glitter, pearl sugar, sanding sugar, and coarse and crunchy sugars for topping cookies and pastry. Another favorite, nonpareils, are tiny sugar spheres in metallic and primary colors for decorating holiday and birthday treats.

See also **Candy; Honey; Maple Sugar; Molds**

Further Reading

Barthes, Roland, "Toward a Psychosociology of Contemporary Food Consumption," *Annales: Economies, Societes, Civilisations*, September–October 1961, 977–986.

Beckwith, Carol, and Angela Fisher. *African Ceremonies*. 2 vols. New York: Harry N. Abrams, Inc., 1999.

Fitzhugh, William W., and Chisato O. Dubreuil, eds. *The Ainu: Spirit of a Northern People*. Washington, D.C.: Arctic Studies Center, National Museum of Natural History, the Smithsonian, 1999.

Levy, Paul. *The Penguin Book of Food and Drink*. London: Penguin Books, 1997.

Platina. *On Right Pleasure and Good Health*. Asheville, N.C.: Pegasus Press, 1999.

Reilly, Lee, "A Spoonful of Stevia," *Vegetarian Times*, September 1997, 96.

T

TABLES

Kitchen tables, which derive from the Latin *tabula*, are the heart of action and the location of the *batterie de cuisine*, from which comes family and institutional meals. Although many cooks, such as traditional Armenians and Amazonian natives, squat alongside a central fire or ceramic pit oven to prepare food and bake bread, the table is the current standard work station. The choice bears out historic kitchen decor.

Ancient Times

From the third millennium BCE, Mesopotamian food service radiated out to diners from stands, trays, and tables, whether plain or carved wood or inlaid with metal or ivory. For royal meals, Babylonian kitchen staff spread tables with linen cloths; servants supplied napkins at the end of the meal for an obligatory hand washing.

Arab customs also depended on formal table service. According to the Koran, the holy scripture of Islam, Muslim diners must eat at a table. As a guard against gluttony, Islamic law forbids crouching, which reputedly causes people to overeat. Instead, each participant at a meal should sit at the table in a pose that allows an immediate rise to the feet.

In past times, worktops accommodated dairying in awkward creamery basins and table churns and held kneading trays, dough boxes, stone troughs, and salting implements. Before the invention of the ironing board, the table was the flat surface on which launderers cleaned stains from garments and pressed coal-bearing irons on wrinkled table linens, collars, and cuffs. For the candy-maker, a cool quarry tile, marble, or alabaster work station helped to solidify mints and toffee. Maple or beech butcher block tops, often scored and worn from heavy cleaving, took on a patina from constant whacks of knives and cleavers.

The placement of dining tables and those who sat at them records the human hierarchy that prevailed at a particular period. In classical times, dining was a tangible link between the affluent patron and the client or hanger-on. Greek hosts set well-scrubbed individual tables in front of each guest or before a couch seating two people and served a three-stage meal: *paropsides* (appetizers), grilled or spit-roasted meat, and *deuterai trapezai* (second tables), the dessert course. The style changed in the time of Alexander the Great, who apparently had little regard for the drunken vulgarities and coarse amusements of his father, Philip of Macedon. After Alexander's campaign through the Middle East, North Africa, and India, egalitarian dining encouraged shared food and drink and reciprocation of invitations. Those who merely gobbled without returning the gesture to their hosts earned the name *parásitoi* (parasites) for their disinclination to open their own homes to dinner guests.

The Roman *triclinium* (three-table dining room) became the focus of banquets. According to the architect William Clarke's *Pompeii: Its Past and Present State* (1847), the palace of Scaurus contained four triclinia that treated guests to the height of luxury: "The table, made of citron wood from the extremity of Mauritania, more precious than gold, rested upon ivory feet, and was covered by a plateau of massive silver, chased and carved, weighing five hundred pounds. The couches, which would contain thirty persons, were made of bronze, overlaid with ornaments in silver, gold, and tortoise-shell." (Vol. ii, p. 15)

Slaves set up tables and couches in a U shape and, at each place, stretched a wool mattress dyed purple and stuffed with feathers. According to the Greek stoic philosopher Chrysippus, who wrote late in the third century BCE, the cushions came from Babylon. The mosaic floor bore a motif of food fragments to give the appearance of an unswept salon. Over the surface, slaves strewed eye-pleasing sawdust dyed with vermilion and saffron blended with lapis.

Medieval to Modern Times

The Roman dining area remained the standard for much of continental Europe and the British Isles into the Middle Ages. A schematic drawing of the table at Tara Hall depicting the seating arrangement used in the second century CE affirms the importance of social levels and the cut of meat that each deserved. The drawing depicts a tun of mead, roasting spit, and steward lighting the way for guests. In Japan, seating arrangements traditionally followed a rigid alternation from first spot to the left, first to the right, second to the left, and on to the end, where the host sat. The safest seat was the *tokonoma*, a ritual wall niche displaying a lettered scroll, at which no attacker could enter the room.

In Europe during the Anglo-Saxon period, the lord of the hall occupied the only chair. His banquet table was a demountable *bord*, from which came the term "bed and board" meaning "dwelling and food." Positioned on trestles, it presented the best of hospitality at the same time that it elevated his stature among those standing in attendance and the family and guests who sat alongside on cushions atop folding chairs. The group, shielded by a *baldachino* (canopy), posed before a grand arras, often embroidered with some family member's contribution to history. All parts were easily removed, stacked, and even transported for outdoor dining or travel.

Upon the board cloth or tablecloth, servants "laid the board," a term meaning "spread a meal." The importance of the Anglo-Saxon *bord* survives in such terms as boardinghouse, boardroom, and chairman/chairwoman of the board. If the guest list was larger than usual, the staff set extensions to the head table in a U pattern and seated honorees on the outside. The inner portion of the U, like the Roman banquet table, remained open for presentation of *divertissements* (entertainments) and for rapid and efficient service by steward and staff. Another purpose of the setup,

the preservation of the host's sightlines allowed him full awareness of other diners, security guards, and visitors entering from the opposite side of the hall.

One model of Anglo-Saxon dining table in the Hadden Hall collection characterizes the front table used by nobles, their family, and honored guests. It was a multipurpose device comprising a smooth, flat surface mounted on three massive carved oak pedestals, which stabilized flagons and trenchers. The placement of the head table with projecting *tester* or rich canopy, called a cloth of estate, was farthest from the door to avoid drafts and enemy attack and to elevate the host as the most important person in the gathering. (Wilson 1991, 31)

John Russell's *Boke of Nurture* (ca. 1450) advised the *sewer* (server) on the exact method of laying a cloth, evening the folds, and stretching out an additional cloth to be positioned over all laps as a communal napkin. He gave explicit instructions as to the placement of loaves, salt cellar, and spoons and knives. He indicated that the salt went to the lord's right and trenchers and knife to the left. After steady service from kitchen hearth to great hall, it was the staff's job to return the room to order. For local sessions of court, staff "turned the tables" by overturning the upper slab to place a clean, unstained tabletop at the disposal of the justice.

In the medieval kitchen, the table was a serviceable furnishing when placed under a window or opposite the hearth after fireplaces moved to the outside wall. In the château of Champ de Bataille, the work table stood beneath a candle-lit lantern to maximize light for rolling dough, cleaning fish, and preparing meat. Racks held implements and braided onions, peppers, and garlic at arm's reach. One drawer at center attached to the underside to hold knives and stirring spoons. Splay-legged benches offered spare seating.

As of the 1100s, the nobleman's kitchen needed more surfaces than the simple trestle table. For mincing cabbage, shelling beans and lentils, and chopping onions, carrots, parsnips, and beetroot, a small table sufficed. For cleaning ducks and domestic poultry, a separate flat surface accommodated the removals of entrails and feathers and scraping and singeing of the skin. At a boiling water bath, the cook added fowl to the pot and skimmed foam from the surface. When the meat was parboiled, a return to the table for stuffing, sewing the cavity, and basting the skin preceded the final roasting at fireside. By the 1500s, the *table dormant*, a permanent four-legged furnishing, replaced the demountable trestle arrangement. (Singman) Wait staff frequently placed it near the fireplace to assure hot food and the warm backs of diners.

For the fifteenth-century diner, Platina's Latin masterwork, *De Honesta Voluptate et Valitudine* (On Right

Pleasure and Health, 1475) established the prototype for seasonal dining. The worthy Italian table should bear perfume and stand in a warm, enclosed dining area in winter and occupy a breezy, open spot for summer. Spring necessitated a floral centerpiece; summer called for fresh evergreen limbs and vines underneath. Fall was the best time to suspend apples, pears, and clusters of grapes from above. By the 1500s, wait staff often covered the tabletop with carpet made by professional *carpyte-makers*. (Hartley 1979, 293)

The Renaissance brought a shift from the crude trestle table with host seated on a dais to a more egalitarian draw-leaf and gate-legged tables. Staff could group these furnishings as individual dining assemblies or one long table for state dinners at which guests sat on upholstered armchairs or armless dining stools, called farthingale chairs for their use by women in panniered dress. (Wilson 1991, 46) Tablemates could converse across the expanse without the rigorous formality of medieval dining on one side of the table only. The replacement of embroidered cloth with gilded leather upholstery produced grandeur while not holding odors of past meals, as did plush and damask cushioning. By the eighteenth century, these tables had evolved into mahogany flap tables, a versatile dining area that staff could extend by raising the flap and by joining two such tables for a banquet.

Colonial woodwrights departed from the standard trestle or sawbuck table, set atop crossed wood beams, and the plain, but serviceable plank table, some fitted with underside boxes or balconies to hold extra rushes for lighting. As depicted in George Francis Dow's *Every Day Life in the Massachusetts Colony* (1988), the home of the colonist John Ward of Salem, Massachusetts, featured two tables. Against the wall under the only window, a small, crude table made the most of natural light over work space. To the sides, shelves and a large, showy dresser presented a picture of prosperity in the amount of pewter plate it bore. Across from the kitchen proper, a stationery oval table seating six held the day's meal.

One popular innovation was the hutch table, which took its name from a Middle English word for "compartment." Unlike the primitive table-board or plank and trestle arrangement, which was the seventeenth-century norm, the chambered piece, often called a chair-table, combined a table with a chest and settle and sometimes an added drawer or trunk. The seat served as storage box for linens and safe for treasured items. As described in the November 1874 issue of *American Agriculturist*, the chair-table user could fold down the hinged seat back over the arms to make a dining table, ironing board, or work space. Backless benches called forms accommodated diners at each side of the table.

Frontierswomen made do with whatever tables they could form from materials at hand. The rear flap of a Conestoga wagon could be pulled down and propped on a single leg to double as food preparation space or chairless serving bar. Drovers engineered the same arrangement for their cooks, who worked out of the back of a chuckwagon. This catch-as-catch-can demountable surface mirrored a similar lack of table and chairs for Europe's working poor. Among laboring-class families, broods of children had to share the stools and chairs that remained after adults seated themselves. Those who lost out had to stand at table.

Russian compiler Elena Burman Molokhovets's *A Gift to Young Housewives* (1861), which set forth sensible instruction to beginners, aimed for a clean, orderly, spacious kitchen. To reduce clutter, she suggested that "a kitchen table with drawers and two or three stools are necessary, as well as a box for firewood." (Molokhovets 1992, 116) To the box, she described the attachment of drop leaves supported by collapsible legs to "turn the box into a table seventy inches long or, with both leaves up, 98 inches long."

The food historian Nelson Algren described in *America Eats* (1992) the elongated Swedish *smörgåsbord* (sandwich table), a nineteenth-century tradition of bounty hosting attendees at weddings, christenings, and funerals. In token of hospitality, women contributed enough food for a lavish display. Among Scandinavian settlers in Nebraska, the typical *smörgåsbord* table had to hold cold plates of sausage and tongue, eggs, meatballs, meat loaf, gravlax (salt-and-pepper cured salmon), beets, carrots and celery, radishes roses, preserves, apple salad, cheese, Swedish crisp breads, butter, and coffee. Added to these were hot scalloped potatoes, brown beans, peas, and an onslaught of desserts, including ginger and butter cookies, fruit compote, and lingonberries with whipped cream. The Russian version of the sandwich table, called a *zakuska*, invited guests to stand around a spread of appetizers, toast with glasses of vodka, and eat canapés before going in to a formal dinner. Reflecting on the hearty custom, novelist Anton Chekhov considered pickled herring the best of the *zakuska*.

In 1803, Dorothy Wordsworth visited humble Highland cottages that she described in *Recollections of a Tour Made in Scotland*. In one kitchen, she found a sanded floor and tiny dresser with benches along the wall, where the cook stored peat. Beside a bag of oatmeal at the hearth, the flour barrel doubled as a table with the addition of a baking board as tabletop. In upscale English homes, the Bushway table offered a high degree of flexibility. For guests, it could extend to six times its original size.

The change from work tables to continuous counters and cabinetry began in the twentieth century.

After her family's arrival from Norway to Montana in 1899, Kaia Lien recalled the log cabin her father built on the Yellowstone River. Makeshift and crude, it rose above a clay floor and sported a dirt roof that grew weeds. For a cupboard and table, her mother made do with apple boxes. A decade later, the simple four-legged work table underwent a transformation that prefigured the Hoosier cabinet, a favorite with farm wives. To accommodate supplies nearer the work station, the possum-belly cabinet table added a tin-lined potato bin and sliding flour bin. A fancier English model topped the curved-belly cabinet table with an open-shelf hutch.

In the 1950s, when plastic experienced its boom, the laminated table top introduced a new luxury and glamor to the kitchen. The combination of a wipe-clean plastic top and tubular chrome legs dominated the market with dinette sets intended for the young family. Available in the same bright hues as canisters, tableware, and kitchen implements, plastic enabled designers to inject a casual elegance to informal home dining and entertaining. By 1951, 85 percent of dinette suits featured protective plastic veneer and vinyl upholstery on the matching chairs. The fashion shifted to wrought iron legs late in the decade, then gave place to the return of wood in the 1960s, when earth tones resumed their dominance.

Table Customs Around the World

Serving meals at a central table to diners seated on chairs is not the pattern for every country. Currently, people in parts of Africa stand for meals or sit on floor mats, the place where diners in Laos and Guinea-Bissau eat from large bowls. The Laotian server duck-walks to the table when company is present to remain lower than the guest's head. Perhaps no table style has so influenced the rest of the world than the Swedish *smörgåsbord*, the pattern for long buffet table offering warm and cold specialities and desserts. Globally, cooks set up these food displays for weddings, community feasts, holiday festivals, and communal meals on cruise ships and at inns, taverns, country clubs, and hotels. The challenge of preparing, cutting, and arranging food in identifiable patterns, such as seasonal themes, animals, fish, and national flags often results in platters edged in blossoms, epergnes of fruit, and ice sculpture at the center.

Asian table arrangement developed apart from the four-legged table. In the Italian traveler Fosco Maraini's *Meeting with Japan* (1959), the first-person text describes the casual charm of a country kitchen at the mountaintop inn at Hanase. From the beaten earth floor, the kitchen worker stepped out of *geta* (wooden sandals) to enter a raised serving area. On *tatami* (mats), politely unshod feet approached shiny wood tables. Diners squatted around the open fire to warm their hands and sip tea.

Gender plays a major role in how diners interact at the table. Mauritanians, Mayas, *mestizos*, and Togolese segregate by gender, with men and women eating in different rooms. Swazis also separate, with women eating in the kitchen and men at the gate to the *kraal* (corral), where they reserve the choice pieces of meat for themselves. Men in Moldavia never admit to knowing how to cook or help in the kitchen. In the Czech Republic, women prepare plates of hearty foods in the kitchen and carry them to male diners. Georgian cooks typically serve and abstain from joining male diners unless there are other women present. In Panama, the female cook is the last person served at the table. In Paraguay, women attending rural festivals eat at a separate table.

Furnishings vary worldwide. I-Kiribati, Togolese, Tuvaluans, Yemenis, and Tanzanian Muslim cooks serve guests sitting cross-legged on floor mats; Mongolians and Tajiks hosts likewise seat guests on the floor or on low stools at a small table. Samoans, Tongans, Tunisians, and Senegalese also vary as to sitting on the ground or at a table. Uzbeks prefer sitting on floor mats and leaning against pillows. Singaporeans vary by ethnic background: Indians and Malays choose floor mats with men dining before women and children; others eat at a table. In the United Arab Emirates, families may sit in a circle on the floor or seat themselves at tables when they entertain guests. Claudia Roden describes Arab tables in *A New Book of Middle Eastern Food* (1985) as metal trays placed on a stool or framework of wood legs. Inlaid with tortoise shell or mother of pearl, these brass, copper, or silver dining tops feature Middle Eastern motifs, charms, blessings, and paeans to Allah from the Koran. To accommodate guests, the host provides cushions before bearing in food and drink from the kitchen.

The evolution of Japanese dining exemplifies the importance of seating and service to food quality. Presentation of a *hakozan* (tray table) begins with plating the food, arranging it in dishes on the surface, and transporting the entire table to the diner. A shift to the *chabudai* (group table) alters service to a more rapid, efficient dispersal of dishes to individuals dining together. The shift reduces fuss and lessens the chance of someone's dinner getting cold.

In some parts of the world, particularly much of Africa, Argentina, Bolivia, Chile, Québec, Mexico, Spain, Uruguay, and the Pacific islands, eating while walking, riding public transportation, or standing on sidewalks is considered rude or in poor taste. For busy Lesothans, the cook pot simmers on the stove for family members to serve themselves, either standing or sitting in groups or alone. The ground suits rural islanders in Papua New Guinea. Sierra Leone's villagers squat on the ground to receive portions. Malaysians eat at a table except for Muslims, who prefer floor mats. Rural Pakistanis eat with their hands from their seats on the ground or floor, which they segregate by gender much like families in Somalia.

See also **Chuckwagons**

Further Reading

Furnivall, Frederick J., ed. *Early English Meals and Manners: John Russell's Boke of Nurture.* London: Kegan Paul, Trench, Trübner & Co., Ltd., 1868.

Glants, Musya, and Joyce Toomre, eds. *Food in Russian History and Culture.* Bloomington: Indiana University Press, 1997.

Maraini, Fosco. *Meeting with Japan.* New York: Viking Press, 1959.

Roden, Claudia. *A New Book of Middle Eastern Food.* New York: Viking, 1985.

TAGINES

A traditional Moroccan, Armenian, and Berber one-dish serving vessel, the *tajin* (tagine or tajine), from the Greek *teganon* (fry pan), consists of a shallow footed terra cotta bowl covered by a perforated lid, which remains in place over hours of slow dry heating. The concept appears to date to the time of Harun al-Rashid, late eighth-century ruler of the Islamic empire and fifth caliph of the Abbasid dynasty. Foods cooked tagine-style appear in *Alf Laylah Wa Laylah* (The Thousand and One Nights), an Arabic story collection begun in the ninth century CE.

The standard covered dish mounts into a tall, open-topped chimney to vent steam. Working over a charcoal brazier, the original tagine users layered vegetables to smother meat on an oiled surface before beginning the process of slow cooking. The *qidra* style of tagine cookery lubricated the surface with *samna* (clarified butter) and added a purée of chopped onion for flavor and aroma. For *muqawlli*, cooks placed ingredients in olive oil to produce a richly spiced food placed on banquet tables to be dipped with shreds of bread.

The early tagine combined the dry stewing action below with the escaping vapors to make omelettes and to complete the steaming of couscous, the national small-grain staple. Late in the twentieth century, Middle Eastern cooks claimed that the tagines from Fez, Morocco, were the best, as were restaurant servings of tagine and couscous. The purpose of the conical top and slow heating over hardwood coals was the enhancement of taste and aroma. Fragrant, slow-cooked dishes featuring meat and fish sautéed in argan oil, olives, and dried fruit and sauced with sweet and sour condiments were also called tagine, which Moroccans traditionally served with wedges of preserved lemons and washed down with mint tea.

Neighboring Mediterranean peoples, including cooks in Provence, adapted the technology of the Moroccan tagine. A recipe recorded for the kitchen of Richard I suggests use of a similar dish. In Tunisia, the finished stew looked like quiche. Algerian cooking focused on tagines, but Islamic taboos limited stewing ingredients by forbidding pork. Current models, which are sturdier and adaptable to modern needs, can be used in the microwave and washed in a dishwasher. Moroccan cooks still prefer the antique glazed earthenware tagines of their ancestors.

Further Reading

Noakes, Greg, and Laidia Chouat Noakes, "Couscous: The Measure of the Maghrib," *Aramco World*, November–December 1998, 16–23.

Stone, Caroline, "Morocco by Mouthfuls," *Aramco World,* November–December 1988, 18–31.

TARO

A staple in Oceania, taro is a large variety of noxious plants of the arum family, all related to anthuria, calla lilies, dieffenbachia, and philodendron. It produces calcium oxalate crystals as well as a fragrant, delicious corm, or small tuber, with a creamy interior tinged with purple threads. Harvesters wear rubber gloves to prevent burning, stinging, and inflammation of the skin.

Although taro has fed peasantry and nobility of the South Pacific for centuries, it is not indigenous to the islands. Rather, it appears to have originated in India or Southeast Asia and spread to Africa, the Caribbean, Latin America, China, Japan, and the South Pacific by traders and explorers. When Polynesians from the Marquesas Islands arrived at the Hawaiian chain in 300 CE, they found native birds and fern, but no carbohydrates. Their introduction of taro and sweet potatoes began a culinary cycle that influenced much of Hawaii's kitchen history. In island kitchen gardens, cultivators shaped paddies and ditches for taro and dry patches for sweet potatoes.

Cooks pounded taro with a mortar to make *poi*, a starch base for other dishes, including breadfruit, yams, coconut, and cane sugar. Peasants ate taro leaves and stems as well as mountain apples and bananas. In addition to fish and seafood, they varied their diet with sea salt, *limu* (seaweed), and ground *kukui* (candlenuts). Royalty invited guests to extravagant *poi* suppers, lavish banquets featuring extended tables dressed

Harvesting Taro in Hawaii.
[© *Photo courtesy of USDA Natural Resources Conservation Service.*]

in fern fronds, flower leis, maile vines, and ti leaves and decked with fruit bowls and coconut halves heaped with *poi* to complement *limu*, shrimp and fish, kalua pig, chicken, and squid.

Roast pig and dogs were the privilege of aristocrats until the 1780s, when the English explorer Captain James Cook reported that the island was a true paradise. His descriptions of sybaritic bliss prefaced the arrival of Congregational missionaries with their preconceived notions of fit diet. European and American traders and travelers also weakened the hold of standard cookery on the populace. The importation of sheep, cows, goats, and salt meats and salmon skewed the native diet away from dependence on taro. In private, Hawaiians perpetuated Tahitian traditions and set up extended tables for *poi* suppers, for which they pulled fresh ti leaves for steaming coconut into *kulolo*, wrapped mullet for baking, steamed pork and salt fish into *laulau,* cooked taro leaves into *luau,* and tenderized taro root into a fibrous dish similar to the Caribbean callaloo.

As the late 1800s saw the decline of native Hawaiians and immigration of Asian, Puerto Rican, and Portuguese laborers, the native kitchen began to lose contact with early food traditions. The Japanese rice-based diet further eroded the value of taro as it vitiated native cultures with a multi-nation blend of customs and menus. Chinese immigrants seized neglected taro patches as suitable rice paddies, but riziculture died out in the 1960s, when Hawaiian farmers found it more profitable and less chancy to grow taro.

The exchange of foodstuffs passed Hawaiian dishes to other Pacific rim cuisine. In the Philippines, the Mansaka readied taro plots with machetes for slash-and-burn cultivation and planted tubers along with rice

and sweet potatoes for a balanced diet. In the mountain kitchens of Hinokage, Kyushu, Japanese kitchen staff depended on a variety of bamboo trays, sieves, and baskets. The taro-washing colander, a shallow rounded tray, received roots that had first been soaked in wood buckets of water and stirred with a pole. Once poured onto the colander, the taro received numerous rinses with fresh water and an extended draining before cooking.

In 1992, to replace menus based on imported foodstuffs, a consortium of twelve Hawaiian chefs compiled a cookbook of island cuisine. In place of international recipes, they began resurrecting old dishes and formulating new ways to cook native-grown seafood, wild boar, and venison. Their campaign for an indigenous food renaissance began with research and extended to shared meals, food fairs at hotels, television appearances, and interviews and articles in the popular press.

Today, for the Marshallese, Niueans, and Micronesians, taro remains a staple agricultural starch along with pumpkin, pandanus, breadfruit, sweet potatoes, and papaya. In Fiji, menus pair fresh-plucked taro greens with boiled manioc. At family socials, the Tanna in the New Hebrides present dinner guests liana-bound leaves encasing *laplap*, a paste of yam or taro. Tongans, who raise coconuts for copra and oil and bananas for commercial export to Japan and New Zealand, keep for their own use breadfruit, taro, and pineapples. They cook taro leaves with *lu pulu* (corned beef) and coconut cream. Papua New Guineans stock pantries with more *kaukau* (sweet potato) and *saksak* (sago palm) than taro. The destruction of Samoan taro in 1993–1994 altered their staple to *ta'amu* (roots), bananas, and yams as well as rice and breadfruit.

See also **Leaves; Mortar and Pestle**

Further Reading

Billard, Jules B., "Okinawa, the Island Without a Country," *National Geographic*, September 1969, 422–448.
Rajah, Carol Selva. *Makan-Lah!: The True Taste of Malaysia.* Sydney, Australia: HarperCollins, 1996.

TEA

Whether cool, sun-dried *tsing tcha* (green tea), fragrant jasmine, or full-bodied, artificially dried red, tea sipping is a universal pleasure. Tea originated in China as a liquid offering to family elders and ancestral gods. Legend says that drinking tea as a beverage began around 2700 BCE when camellia leaves accidentally showered onto the water pot of Shen-Nung, the first tea afficionado and father of Chinese herbalism. As the leaves sank to the bottom and steeped, the fragrance enticed him to take a sip.

From that first taste came a vast world beverage trade that spawned books of commentary on tea as a stimulant and treatment for indigestion. An essay in the Buddhist priest-poet Lu Yu's three-volume *Ch'a Ching* (Classic of Tea, ca. 760 CE) noted the worth of tea for cooling, satisfying thirst, lifting spirits, and relieving headache and joint pain. Tea sales precipitated the standardization of a weight known as the catty, from the Malay *kati*, equal to 1.3 pounds or .6 kilograms. Because of a reliable traffic in tea from Shanghai and area estates, officials taxed the commodity in 793 CE. Over time, hosts served tea as the nation's betrothal and wedding beverage for its representation of longevity, fidelity, and domesticity.

In a myth from the Indus region, Dharma sampled tea leaves as an antidote to sleep; the Japanese claim that the same deity shaped tea from his own eyelids, which refused to stay open during lengthy meditation. Thus, Taoists revered the drink for its value to monks. By 600 CE, the Chinese were a nation of tea devotees. Early in the eighth century, Japan's emperor Saga became the island's first patron of tea, which was distributed in *dancha*, a hard ball of fermented leaves imported from China. At the height of commerce with China, Japan received tea seeds from the mainland after the 700s CE and began growing its own crop. The nation developed an indigenous tea culture around *cha* or *o-cha*, a green camellia leaf introduced with the importation of Buddhism. As a luxury, growers planted tea on temple grounds to serve to priests and the elite. The first formal tea ceremony took place under the Emperor Shomu in the mid-700s.

Bishnoi woman of India making tea.
[© *Nikreates Peops / Alamy.*]

Tea Ceremony

The age-old Japanese *chado* or *sado* (way of tea), or *cha-no-yu* (hot water tea), is a ritual that had its beginnings in Zen Buddhism as a religious or medicinal consumption of *matcha*, a bitter green tea. The elements mimicked the bases of the universe: wood into charcoal, charcoal set afire, fire heating metal, and metal causing water to boil. The esthetic of a formal ritual evolved from yin and yang—self-discipline and an appreciation of beauty and order in the mundane, cyclical events of the day. As a result of practitioners' enthusiasm for formal tea drinking, the ceremony influenced the Japanese *ethos*—its religion, clothing, etiquette, architecture, art, gardening, calligraphy, and philosophy. As a unifier of society, the ceremony perpetuated behaviors conducive to citizenship and ideal rule.

In an ambience sweetened with incense, the host sounded the gong and carried from a shelf in the service room or kitchen pantry the prescribed utensils—a water jar, bamboo ladle and stand, lid rest, bowl washer, bamboo whisk, spatula, and tea caddy. The order of events began with the passing of sweets, then the crushing of tea leaves for stirring into water heated in a *furo* (charcoal brazier) or a sunken *ro* (hearth). The tea, served in a communal bowl, was one of two

TEA

types—a thick *koicha* (heavy tea) or *usucha*, a thin, foamy beverage with an astringent taste. The bowl passed from guest to guest, with the last participant drinking the remainder of the tea. After polite exchanges, the host removed the implements and cups and the guests retired from the room.

The tea cult got its start late in the 1190s in the Kamakura era, when *bonzes* (Zen monks) seeking enlightenment made tea their customary drink. They pulverized expensive green leaves, poured on boiling water, and whisked the powder with a bamboo beater. Daily, they sipped tea to keep them from nodding off during meditation. The use of tea became part of the ceremony ennobling Daruma or Bodhidharma, patriarch of Buddhism.

The prototypical tea house, Kyoto's bare-floored, silver-leafed garden house called the *Ginkakuji* (Silver Pavilion), has remained in service since the Shogun Ashikaga Yoshimasa built it in 1482. An outgrowth of feudalism, the act of participating in a ceremonial tea, like European banquets, regulated and limited negative urges. It promoted consensus and peace among belligerent lords, who approached the table unarmed and composed for a polite exchange. By association, the Japanese equated formalized tea drinking with refinement, courtesy, and artistic taste.

In the 1580s, Japan produced its first tea master, Sen Rikyu or Sen-no-Rikyu, a cultured intellectual, who stressed four principles: *wa,* harmony and balance among guests and utensils and with nature, an esthetic appreciation of the tea garden and tea house that blends with its surroundings; *kei,* respect for people and tea implements, demonstrated through acts of courtesy and consideration for others; *sei,* purity displayed through a symbolic cleansing of hands and rinsing of the mouth before the ceremony; and *jaku,* tranquility demonstrated by the unhurried contemplation of the purpose and act of serving tea.

The concept of a tea ceremony, which was foreign to European and American homemakers, took on an allure of the exotic East and encouraged importers to merchandise tea services comprising matching pieces, complementary implements, and trays. In 1894, the World Food Fair in Boston featured Sarah Tyson Rorer's Japanese luncheon and foreign table settings, notably a "Japanese Ceremonial Tea" by Carrie Dearborn, a faculty member of the Boston Cooking School. Today, the Japanese tea ceremony still follows the principles of Sen Rikyu.

Popularization of Tea

At the end of the twelfth century, tea drinking reached the masses. Historians credit Myoan Eisei (or Yosai),

the founder of Japan's Rinzei Zen Buddhism, who arrived in Kyoto from China in 1191 bearing tea seeds to plant for general consumption. He published a treatise, *Kissa Yojoki* (Tea-Drinking for Health, 1211), a tribute to tea drinking to cure paralysis, beriberi, and boils and to stimulate appetite. Eisei passed tea seed to Myoe, a priest at the Kozan-ji temple in Kyoto as a stimulus to meditation. Myoe planted a productive tea garden on the grounds at Togano-o and lauded the beverage as an antidote to aging.

As the elite samurai demanded tea, cultivation spread to other provinces. After the collapse of the shogunate in 1333, a rising merchant class adapted their leisure time to brewing whole leaf tea and sipping it while enjoying high-stake games of *tocha*, a test of the ability to recognize the area in which tea was grown. Cooks began associating specific teas with certain foods: seafood with green tea, vegetables with white tea, oolong with game, floral-scented tea with chicken, and spareribs, roast pork, and preserved vegetables with black tea.

Chou Kao-ch'i, author of *Yang-Hsien Ming Hu Hsi* (early 1500s), gave an overview of Ishing (Yixing) teapots, made on the Yangtze River near Shanghai. According to his description, Europeans identified the distinctive pots as *boccarro* (large mouths), a name assigned to them by Portuguese traders. From these pots, which contained one-person servings, European potters evolved the familiar home, restaurant, and hotel tea service, reputedly first owned by the Earl of Cadogan at Staffordshire. Other accounts of the characteristic English teapot claim that Europeans emulated Chinese wine urns or Muslim coffeepots of the 1650s. Whatever the source, Chinese tea service perpetuated brewing directly in the cup, a style still in use in Asian restaurants.

In the early 1700s, the East India Company supplied English tea drinkers with pots imported from Asian pottery studios. Potters designed spherical shapes with short spouts, then branched out to scrolls, crests, and Blue Willow designs intended to suit British tastes, as well as the more whimsical melons, pears, bamboo, dragons, monkeys, and elephants. In the 1730s, teapot makers produced the first silver tea services, a specialty mastered forty years later by the American silversmith and Revolutionary War hero Paul Revere, famed for *repoussée* motifs and monograms.

China's domination of the tea trade shaped its national economy. Tea dealers in China and Tibet hitched oxen to presses to concentrate individual leaves into bricks, which offered standard measure for trading purposes. The drink grew so popular with the masses in Japan that, in the early 1400s, vendors steeped it in the streets of Kyoto for sale to passersby.

By 1610, tea sellers brought the cakes to northwestern Europe and exchanged them like money.

Against objections by a Russian ambassador, the Mongol Khan shipped tea to Tsar Michael III, who was not sure what to do with a gift of dried grass. He grew so fond of the beverage that he had his personal cook brew pots of tea to keep him awake during sessions of the Duma. Ordinary Russian households rejected the new drink as another western European frivolity until 1725, when the creation of a Sino-Russian trade increased importation of the costly leaf. Prices did not fall until the 1860s, when bourgeois homes began regular tea service. In 1861, Elena Burman Molokhovets's classic Russian illustrated cookbook *A Gift to Young Housewives* (1861) listed as an ingredient for ladies' punch a teaspoon of yellow tea, a precious commodity from China that was rarely exported. Chinese officials usually hoarded the rare leaves from young shoots for use by court officials and for ritual beverages.

After Catherine of Braganza introduced *camellia thea* (tea) at the court of her husband, Charles II of England, following the restoration of the monarchy in 1660, the Portuguese custom of tea drinking became a staple of the British Isles and colonies and increased consumption of sugar as well. Merchants sold tea by the pound, which produced three hundred cups. Traders warehoused leaves in blocks and transported them much like hunks of sugar. A tea-maker grated the solid mass, then stored loose flakes in caddies or catties, the wood, japanned, or tin boxes often constructed with lockable lids and drawers. The caddy took its name from the Malay or Javanese *kati*, an Asian measure equal to about twenty-two ounces. Colonial Americans from Labrador south to the Caribbean drank tea as a medicinal and a refreshment. On the frontier, tea served as a makeshift currency.

The shift in beverages fueled heavy importation of pots and dishes, lacquerware trays, small table heaters, and elegant tables and screens. From China and Java came tables edged in fretwork for seating guests at tea. The English added chairs and back stools, on which ladies in panniered dress could seat themselves in comfort and propriety. After 1700, local carpenters created a columnar tea table elevated on three small feet to accommodate wide skirts more easily. For the poor, who couldn't afford tea, wait staff distributed spent tea leaves at the kitchen door.

Tea took the place of ale and beer in England and its colonies, where apothecaries sold prime leaf for its medicinal powers. By 1770, England drank tea at the rate of two pounds per person for a total consumption of eighteen million pounds annually. Families regularly bought from smugglers, who helped reduce the price of a heavily taxed commodity. In place of cumbrous brewing of ale and beer, householders used teabags or tea columns, swizzle sticks filled with tea leaves, to brew cups or pots of pekoe and oolong. Pioneers in Australia, who regularly brewed billy tea, replaced it with red sage tea to purify the blood, goldenrod for aching back, red clover for cancer, and foxglove and broom for dropsy.

Tea made political history after England imposed the Boston Port Act, which exacted a tea tax from the American colonies in 1773 to shore up the financially troubled East India Company. Some outraged Middle Atlantic tea-drinkers opted for ribwort, sage, thoroughwort, hyperion or raspberry, strawberry, teaberry, and currant leaf tea or an infusion of loosestrife, called liberty tea. On December 16, 1773, householders encouraged a riot, the Boston Tea Party, culminating in the jettisoning of tea bales from the *Beaver Dartmouth,* and *Eleanor* into the Boston Harbor.

In Poland, tea drinking got off to a slow start because the drink was more valuable as a palliative for stomach ailments. After the privileged began brewing it in fashionable salons, peasants took up drinking tea also. Homemakers served cups with lemon and cream, also with cherry or raspberry juice or red wine.

The end of China's tea trade monopoly came in 1822 when residents of northern India discovered tea growing in the wild. The price of tea fell during the 1800s as colonial tea estates in the Indian subcontinent began competing with China. Distributed by the East India Company, new varieties whetted English shoppers' appetites for hot, sweet beverages. The lower classes had to content themselves with substandard leaves adulterated with fake teas and additives. Tempting home cooks to give up making scones and cakes for tea, the muffin man, a street vendor with bell, tramped residential areas at teatime. By the 1840s, there was enough opposition to his noisy intrusion that parliament enacted a law prohibiting his trade.

For the middle and upper classes, higher quality goods and tin or japanned canisters for storage were the rage of the era. Families displayed their gentility and wealth with ornate silver tea service, including tea strainer, tongs for selecting cubes from a sugar boat, and a spooner, a sugar pot that held spoons on hooks about the lid. As a meal, the afternoon or "high" tea may have begun in the early nineteenth-century salons of Anna, Duchess of Bedford. In the Victorian era, the custom developed into a full meal taken either indoors or outdoors. Timed to the arrival of children home from school, the spread comprised pork pie, sliced ham, sardines and tomatoes, currant and raisin breads, dainty cucumber sandwiches, pickles, scones with jam and butter, cakes or biscuits, and tea. A truncated version, the Devon cream tea, introduced in the 1880s, reduced the menu to scones with jam and clotted cream. When the French imported afternoon tea, they adapted a gallicized term *fivoclocquer* (to take tea at five).

During a sojourn at Cumberland Inlet with Greenland natives, the English expeditioner Captain Charles Francis Hall, author of *Life with the Esquimaux* (1862), met Tookoolito, a traveled woman who had taken up tea drinking during her visit to England. She surprised him by offering tea. After hanging her kettle over a fire lamp, she withdrew a handful of black tea from a tin box and asked whether he liked his cup weak or strong. Because she had only one cup to offer, Tookoolito and Hall shared it along with his proffered sea biscuit. To his question about her twice daily tea-drinking, she explained that she bought an annual supply from English and American whalers.

Tea in the Twentieth Century

By 1902, Frank Clarke, an English inventor, had mechanized tea-making with a spring-loaded automatic pot. Goblin came out with the Teasmade model in 1933, the first electric pot. To counter the sharp-edged industrial style that dominated the market, the Hungarian-American ceramicist Ilonka Karasz, an illustrator for *New Yorker*, returned tea drinking to its warm beginnings with a rounded glazed set of pot, sugar bowl, and creamer in a warm cerulean color lined in gleaming white and topped with white knobs. The set is still marketed through the Metropolitan Museum of Art.

To suit tea-making for individual drinkers, the Tao Tea Company of New York City advertised tins of tea balls in the March 1925 issue of *Good Housekeeping*. Formed from tiny bud leaves harvested in Ceylon, India, and Java, a single ball dropped into a teapot containing four cups of water would instantly brew tea for a luncheon or family use. Joseph Kreiger pioneered individual servings in mesh bags, which Americans popularized in the 1930s. The convenience and savings of brewing tea one cup at a time reduced market emphasis on teamakers and concentrated instead on handy electric water heating coils that perched on the side of a tea mug. Cheap and handy for travel, they were popular in dorm rooms, offices, and efficiency apartments.

Tea became a mealtime standard globally, as discovered by Grey Owl, the pen name of Archie Belaney, author of *Tales of an Empty Cabin* (1936). On a visit to the tepees of east central Canadian Indians in the 1930s, he observed women serving tea in porcelain cups. Likewise, Cree hosts welcomed him to their lodge and set the tea-pail a-boil as a gesture of welcome.

In the twenty-first century, in Kazakstan, Tajikistan, Uzbekistan, Turkmenistan, and Kyrgyzstan, *chai* (black tea), boiled daily in a samovar, uplifts spirits at tea breaks and rounds out the evening meal, which may consist of no more than flatbread and yogurt. In the southern United States, hosts serve tea iced, sweetened, and sometimes garnished with lemon slices and/or mint sprigs. The Austrian custom of *jause* (afternoon tea) calls for plates of sandwiches and pastries; Chileans take *onces* (afternoon tea) with similar foods. Poles prefer tea as an evening beverage. In Bhutan, tea-makers buy supplies of *jari* in triangular cones. Throughout the day, they pinch off enough for a cup or pot and boil the tea in water to extract all the essence, which they blend with baking soda and butter, shake, strain, and pour. Like tea makers in southeast Asia, the Sarhadi of Baluchistan in southeastern Iran brew tea in milk with sugar and spice.

Australians enjoy three daily meals plus tea in the morning and afternoon. Tajiks drink *choi* (tea) at breakfast, as do Zambians. In Iran, Somalia, Taiwan, and Russia, tea is a courtesy offered to guests; Pakistani and Zimbabwean cooks make tea for casual, business, and formal occasions. Saudi Arabians typically end meals with tea or coffee and conversation; in Cape Verde and Sudan, a tea or coffee break with cakes and cookies is the province of the rich.

Tea service varies according to taste and available additives. Fijians serve morning tea in tin bowls; in Eritrea, cooks pour tea at breakfast with honey, yogurt, and *k'itcha* (bread). Mauritians also prefer additives to tea, especially milk and sugar. In Azerbaijan, hosts offer tea to diners at the end of the meal. The Botswana brew tea or *Mageu* (sorghum beverage) for breakfast; Comorians also like morning tea with sweetener. The Muslims of Cameroon drink tea, but water is more common for family meals.

In other parts of the world, tea is a standard beverage, including Malawi, where those who can afford to drink tea consume it every day. In Pacific rim countries, the preparation of tea is a daily task. In Japan, tea, like rice, is a feature at each meal. Homemade stock requires hand gathering, grading and winnowing, kneading into rolls on a tray, and careful storage in airy baskets. The I-Kiribati blend tea with grated coconut, an island staple. South Africans grow their own tea, a caffeine-free bush tea called *rooibos*, a leaf harvested from a plant indigenous to the western Cape.

The highly caffeinated smoky *yerba maté*, an indigenous tea called Brazilian tea, Paraguay tea, Jesuit tea, missionary tea and South American holly brewed by the Argentine gaucho is a natural accompaniment and palate cleanser for a diet dominated by beef. Picked from the *Ilex paraguariensis*, an evergreen in the holly family named in 1822 by French naturalist and botanist

Auguste de Saint Hilaire, it grows wild in Argentina, Brazil, Chile, Peru, Uruguay, and Paraguay, the most prolific source. A hot restorative and anti-depressant, the tea was a favorite in ancient times, when the Guaraní sipped it through a filtered *bombilla* (straw) from a calabash. On the plains, the gaucho depended on *yerba maté* for energy and nutrients. In the Arab world, a number of tea drinkers who have lived in Argentina still drink the bitter *yerba maté*.

Marketed by Jesuit missionaries, *yerba maté* survives in annual exports as both aged leaf and a stimulating carbonated beverage sold under the trade name Matérva. It can be steeped traditional style in a gourd and sipped through a metal straw or brewed in a French press, drip coffeemaker, or tea ball. Most drinkers prefer it plain; some add sugar or honey, milk, lemon juice, mint, or cinnamon.

In China, where tea drinking began, workers still scoop and sort tea leaves by hand for pan firing. On metal pans above wood-fired braziers, workers dry, roll, and hand-shape royal tea from Tai Ping. To present the leaves at their flavorful best, they curl, ball, spiral, or twist the fragrant mass in bamboo baskets by a method as old as tea history. To blot up excess moisture, the preparer spreads the firing basket with rice paper and begins the slow process over a bed of embers at a low temperature. The meticulous work concludes with lifting, fluffing, reshaping, and flat-pressing leaves with a cloth pad.

When these plants reach perfection, fresh supplies greet the home shopper in many varieties at open air markets. To tempt the customer who leans toward something new and different, Shanghai merchants measure out stock into glasses and pour on hot water from metal thermoses to show how the leaves unfurl and slowly suffuse the water with a golden green as they rehydrate. The consumer sips, breathes in the aroma, and decides whether or not to buy.

Further Reading

Brackenbury, Wade. *Yak Butter & Black Tea: A Journey into Tibet.* Chapel Hill, N.C.: Algonquin Books, 1998.

Luxner, Larry, "The South American Leaf," *Aramco World,* November–December 1995, 28–29.

Ogrizek, Doré, ed. *Japan.* London: McGraw-Hill Book Co., Inc., 1957.

Salzman, Philip Carl. *Black Tents of Baluchistan.* Washington, D.C.: Smithsonian, 2000

Tanaka, Sen'o, and Sendo Tanaka. *The Tea Ceremony.* Tokyo: Kodansha International, 1998.

TEFLON

Telfon is the discovery of Du Pont research chemist Roy J. Plunkett, who created the fluoroplastic by accident in a tank of freon in April 1938 while seeking a safer, non-polluting method to lower temperatures in refrigerators. Because the small molecule of two carbon and four fluorine atoms was unusually slippery and resisted aging, degradation, high temperatures, light, mechanical stress, bacteria, growth, discoloration, and brittleness, he carried the concept a step further with Teflon, the trademark name for a solid with the lowest dynamic friction and coefficient of static. Chemically described as polytetrafluoroethylene (PTFE), it could be molded and so benefited the Allies during the Manhattan Project as a packaging for uranium hexafluoride and as a nose cone paint that was invisible to radar.

Postwar applications, pioneered in France, prefaced a shift in kitchenware from crusted pans to smooth nonstick surfaces that wiped clean without scrubbing. In 1956, factories began making Tefal. Although expensive to produce, the substance worked well in the manufacture of the Freeline kettle. By 1960, Teflon-coated kitchenware was selling rapidly in the United States. Late in the 1990s, Tefal introduced the Thermospot, a built-in heat indicator that turned red when the pan was sufficiently preheated.

Donald L. Schmidt developed the hard nonstick polymer coating as a biologically inert material to repel water and most solvents. The secret of nonstick coatings was a dual fluorine polymer like that found in nylon and Plexiglas. The manufacturer, Minnesota Mining & Manufacturing Company (3M), which acquired the patent, synthesized the coating by dissolving it in water, spraying or brushing it on sandblasted surfaces, then heating them to 140 to 248 degrees Fahrenheit. As the water evaporated, the double polymers bonded. Because dirt, tar, paint, and adhesives didn't adhere, the synthetic coating aided homemakers by supplying cookware and utensils that wiped clean without scrubbing. Teflon, the trade name for the most common nonstick coating, exposed fluorine polymers at the surface to lower tackiness, a boon to the manufacture of uniforms, wall coverings, seals and barriers, circuit boards, valves, greenhouse coverings, and stain-resistant carpeting.

Applications of Teflon technology slowed late in the twentieth century. A small disk called a Glisdome, which appeared on the market in 1993, applies Teflon surfacing to the corners of major appliances to ease them over vinyl, hardwood, and kitchen carpet. In 1999, National Steel Corporation of Mishawaka, Indiana, began marketing Teflon coated shingles. In 2000, Lumenyte International Corporation in Irvine, California, coated optical fibers with Teflon to replace neon lamps. Simultaneously, non-conductive electrical tapes came on the market with Teflon coating. Currently, Teflon impacts kitchen work by protecting kitchen carpets and upholstery, waterproofing fabrics and wall coverings, and repelling mildew, stains, odors, and flavors in kitchen wares and on electric waffle irons.

See also **Plunkett, Roy**

Further Reading

"Don't Throw Away Your Pots and Pans Just Yet," *Medical Update,* December 1990, 5–6.
Roberts, Royston M. *Serendipity: Accidental Discoveries in Science.* New York: John Wiley and Sons, 1989.

TELEVISION KITCHENS

Television has made an impact on the home cook. Through the immediacy of hands-on food preparation, programs tutor the unskilled in handling a chef's knife, blending a roux with a wire whisk, and piping decorative edging around entrées. In 1947, the radio and television singer Alma Kitchell hosted the *Kelvinator Kitchen,* the first commercial network series and first televised cooking show on the air. Viewers could watch the TV cook demonstrate a wealth of techniques, convenience foods, specialty items, implements, and major appliances. The following year, the gourmet and food author James Beard debuted on *Elsie Presents,* a popular presentation of food techniques and ideas for varying standard American menus with items from world cuisine. In the 1950s, Bess Myerson, a former Miss America, began a long career as consultant and spokeswoman for the housewife. She appeared on television programs as mistress of ceremonies, appliance demonstrator, panelist, and commentator on beauty pageants.

Among the faces people remember from the 1960s, Julia Child's is one of the most familiar. Paralleling Myerson's instructions to homemakers, French-trained Child launched *The French Chef,* a half-hour television series begun on February 11, 1963. The program, which reduced to the basics the washing of salad greens and uncorking of wine, survived in various formats for thirty-seven years in more than eight hundred episodes filmed with two cameras. Her forthright style and expertise influenced cooks Thomas Keller, Emeril Lagasse, Alice Waters, and Jacques Pepin, the author of *Jacques Pepin: A French Chef Cooks at Home* (1975). TV cook and entrepreneur Martha Stewart remarked, "She's a great teacher. She doesn't leave out anything, and her instructions are clear." (Shriver 2000, 11D) Child's amazing longevity also advanced more types of televised cooking programs.

Jeff Smith, PBS's *The Frugal Gourmet,* came to TV food shows via the ministry. His experience cooking feasts for student demonstrators during Vietnam War protests prefaced a shift from pulpit to stove. From the series *Food as Sacrament and Celebration,* Smith advanced to restaurant ownership of the Chaplain's Pantry. Late in the 1970s, he debuted on public television. The folksy, appealing format aired in Washington and Chicago before becoming a regular series in 1987. To food as art and entertainment, he contributed his own brand of spontaneity, proletarian ingredients, and multicultural theme shows shot in Hong Kong and New Orleans. Like a storefront ministry, his advocacy of humanistic goals rescued cooking from snobbery and turned it toward hospitality and personal satisfaction.

Another folksy favorite on PBS in the 1990s, Justin Wilson, the author of *Justin Wilson Number Two Cookbook: Cookin' Cajun by Justin Wilson* (1980), *Justin Wilson's Homegrown Louisiana Cookin'* (1990), and *Justin Wilson Looking Back: A Cajun Cookbook by Justin Wilson* (1997), departs from the strict formula of television cook and food critic to storyteller and dialect entertainer. Mixed into preparation and description of hoppin' John, dirty rice, and Cajun spiced chicken were his reminiscences and humorous commentary, which always concluded with a recommendation of wine with food. His confident execution of recipes introduced outsiders to such Southern ingredients as ham hocks, andouille (sausage), and okra.

In the mid-1990s, the Food Network offered a slate of TV cooks to appeal to varying skills and interests. For the lover of Asian cuisine, *The Iron Chef* turned cookery into on-air drama. Gordon Elliott produced situational comedy with *Door Knock Dinners* with visits to real kitchens and on-the-spot recipes concocted from whatever the cooking crew found in the fridge. Sara Moulton originated *Cooking Live,* a series of theme meals punctuated by live call-in questions and a partner cooking along at home and reporting by telephone on the progress of the meal.

The most flamboyant Food Network star, Emeril Lagasse, amassed a following for his on-camera cooking, beginning with *How to Boil Water* in 1994 and followed by *Emeril and Friends, The Essence of Emeril,* appearances on *Good Morning America,* and the Food Network's prime-time *Emeril Live,* which taped its one thousandth show in February 2001. Energetic and theatrical, he infused his performances with kinetic grace and cries of "Bam" and "Wow," originally intended to keep the stage crew alert. For the average cook, his transformation of *haute cuisine* into fun in the kitchen and tasty dishes stripped away fears of difficult procedures and innovations in food and technique.

Following the success of Wally Nash's *Cuisine Wok Show* in 1993, appliance makers Braun, T-Fal, DeLonghi, and Meyer advertised on-screen with chefs at work. A method enhancing credibility on TV shopping channels and half-hour infomercials, these live advertisements increased the success of such kitchen products as titanium utensils and silicone bakeware.

In January 2001, PBS aired *America's Test Kitchen,* a thirteen-part series derived from *Cook's Illustrated,* a no-nonsense bimonthly magazine that the *New York Times* called the *Consumer Report* of cooking. Hosted by editor and publisher Christopher Kimball, who founded the magazine in 1979 in Brookline, Massachusetts, each program in the series focused on a single theme, for example, cooking science, cookware testing, and food sampling. The cast included writers, editors, and staff chefs who demonstrated technique, equipment, and cooking wisdom at the company kitchen at Boston Common Press.

See also **Beard, James; Child, Julia; Cookbook; Patten, Marguerite**

Further Reading

Dworkin, Susan. *Miss America, 1945: Bess Myerson and the Year That Changed Our Lives.* New York: Newmarket Press, 2000.

Shriver, Jerry, "Host of 'America's Test Kitchen' Can Take the Heat," *USA Today,* January 5, 2001, 5D.

_____, "Julia Child, Ever the Cutup," *USA Today,* December 1, 2000, 11D.

THERMOMETERS

From the oven's invention, cooks have used the sense of touch as a thermometer. Recipes from early books offered a dare-devil approach to gauging heat. According to the encyclopedic *L'Ecole Parfaite des Officiers de Bouche* (Perfect Instruction for Table Staff, 1682), cooks dipping fruit into sauce for *oranges entières* (whole oranges) should test the boiling liquid with a finger, the only true test of temperature. As described in Molly Harrison's *The Kitchen in History* (1972), bakers held their hands and arms inside the heated chamber for a count of forty, proof of the right temperature for light bread, cake, and pie. Half that count was hot enough for beans, brown bread, Indian pudding, and meat. Della T. Lutes, the author of *The Country Kitchen* (1936), named one chamber a "brown paper oven," which would turn white stationery brown. (Beard et al. 1975, 20)

Graduated thermometers were first sealed for laboratory and domestic use in 1641, when Grand Duke Ferdinand of Tuscany made a glass model. In 1654, Leopoldo, Cardinal de Médicis of the Accademia del Cimento engineered the first enclosed glass liquid gauges, called Florentine thermometers. Preferred in France and England, they measured changes in heat intensity on scales of fifty, one hundred, or three hundred degrees. In 1709, Gabriel Daniel Fahrenheit, a physicist and maker of meteorological devices from Danzig, Poland, drew on the work of Danish astronomer Ole Rímer to invent the alcohol thermometer, upgraded five years later by the mercury thermometer. Fahrenheit calibrated his scale on the freezing of ice and salt at zero and fixed the freezing and boiling points of water at 32 and 212 degrees. The temperature scale that bears Fahrenheit's name flourished in England and Holland and is still commonly used in the United States. The French adhered to Ren, de Raumur's scale, based on alcohol; the Russians used the calibrated scale of Joseph Nicolas Delisle, which he invented in 1732.

The awkward measuring of temperatures on a 180-degree scale changed in 1742, when Anders Celsius, a Swedish professor teacher at the University of Uppsala, presented to the Swedish Academy of Sciences his concept of a thermometer based on one hundred degrees. The standard measure, called the centigrade or Celsius scale, chose zero as a boiling point for water and one hundred as the freezing point. It was botanist Carl Linnaeus who inverted the measures in 1745. It was not until the 1970s that nations began formally replacing all applications of the Fahrenheit temperature scale with the Celsius or centigrade standard. For home use, application of a conversion formula involved multiplying the Fahrenheit temperature by 5/9 and subtracting 32 to reach the Celsius figure.

During this same era, measurement and control of home heating entered a new phase with the invention of the thermostat, an essential control for furnaces, water heaters, ovens, irons, stoves, toasters, coffee pots, and other appliances needing strict regulation of temperature. The first bi-metal measure was the English "grid-iron" pendulum, perfected in 1726 to stabilizing clocks. In 1830, the Glasgow-based chemist Andrew Ure patented a steel-zinc bar element to register changes in temperature. By measuring the variance in metal expansion rate, the riveted strips arc toward dampers or valves to activate or suppress heating systems. The concept of measuring responses in two metals remains in use for regulating heat and maintaining home and appliance climates.

In the first years of the twentieth century, when home economics began evolving from untrained domestic labor to a scientific discipline, the demand for a temperature gauge lay at the heart of the precise control of cookery, a major concern of Sarah Tyson Rorer, the head of the Philadelphia Cooking School. The educational pioneer Dr. Elizabeth Sprague, who had studied domestic science at MIT and the University of Illinois, experimented with kitchen thermometers. Working with an agricultural chemist, she studied the precise cooking of beef roast. By inserting a thermometer into the roast, she particularized gradations of doneness. She taught her methods at the University of Kansas, where she served as home economics department head and supported land grant colleges. Her course "The Application of Heat to Food Materials" influenced the career of her protégée, the domestic consultant Ava Milam Clark.

Quick to capitalize on the drift to scientific cookery, stove manufacturers began touting accurate heat measurement. In 1908, the White House range, an ornate iron stove forged by Cussins & Fearn of Columbus, Ohio, arrived on the market with "up to the minute" features. (Ibid., 19) At the center of a heavily scrolled and ornamented oven door was an oven thermometer with glass face and pointer to register temperatures inside.

Appealing to a growing interest in scientific home management, in the February 1925 issue of *Good Housekeeping,* the Taylor Instrument Companies of Rochester, New York, presented numerous models of domestic thermometers to simplify housework. The candy-making thermometer, housed in a silver-plated copper case, attached to cookpots with an adjustable clip and supplied a wood handle to save fingers from burns. The baking thermometer, mounted on a disk, magnified the readings on the mercury-filled tube for easy reading. For home and outdoors, other models mounted or hung provided clear markings and numerals and red liquid indicating from twenty to 150 degrees Fahrenheit.

By the 1930s, according to James A. Beard and colleagues' *The Cook's Catalogue* (1975), cooking thermometers were common kitchen items. An advertisement in a 1936 issue of the *Washington Post* offered the Bake-O-Meter, a right-angled metal gauge with needle that swung in an arc and an interpretive scale of degrees to guide the cook. The text declared, "Don't stick your hand in the oven to see how hot it is. Vital statistics prove it dangerous." (Ibid., 15) Beard's recommendations of the best on the market included a mercury oven thermometer in a folding stainless steel case; an English color-coded cold thermometer with glass face; dough, deep-frying, candy, and meat thermometers from the H-B Instrument Company; Bi-Therm Centigrade testing gauge; chrome thermometer-spoon; the cork and wood Thermovins from Germany and Swiss aluminum Vinometer for gauging wine temperatures; and a wood-handled candy thermometer and several other models marketed by Taylor, a respected English manufacturer of gauges since 1851.

In mid-2001, high-tech thermometers were a standard offering of the catalog Wind & Weather. Among their products was a wireless thermometer from Oregon Scientific that registered and graphed maximum and minimum temperatures over a twelve-hour period and transmitted long-range up to three hundred feet. Another of their home thermo-hygrometer sensors displayed in jumbo digits on an LCD screen both temperature and humidity, a necessity for proper baking. The device sounded an alarm if either figure exceeded the parameters that the user set. A fancier model included the time calibrated by the U.S. Atomic Clock in Boulder, Colorado.

Further Reading

Ganeri, Anita. *The Story of Weights and Measures.* New York: Oxford University Press, 1996.

66 Centuries of Measurement. Dayton, Ohio: Sheffield Measurement Division, 1984.

TINWARE

Tin has been a major material for shaping cooking and dairy containers and implements since its discovery by St. Piran of Cornwall in the late 500s CE. The original tinware, made of sheet metal, shaped and soldered easily and came in varied sizes, whether as sifters, cake and lady finger pans, molds, jelly and cream strainers, muffin pans, pancake turners, or pot lids. A line of seamless tinware that originated in France and reached the market in the United States earned the name French ware.

From early times, solid and plated tinware has been valuable in humble homes. Farm wives hung tin dippers by outdoor buckets and basins of water and used a small tin horn to summon field workers to wash for meals. They sometimes chose blackened tin for bread pans and shiny tin for cake pans with removable sides. Dough rose in a ventilated bread raiser, a domed tin vessel that protected the warm mass from insects and dust. For hot drinks, a long-handled tin toddy cup allowed the man of the house an evening beverage or warmed healing herbal mixtures or cough syrup. In Ireland, green goose soup came to the Christmas table in tin panniers as the appetizer preceding sliced goose. In French kitchens, tin cutters sliced puff pastry for layered *hors d'oeuvres.* Flan, a one-crust pie popular throughout the Continent and British Isles, baked in a pie tin.

Before tin became common kitchen ware, houseware makers worked in sheets of latten, a thin brass alloy. When tinware arrived on the Atlantic shore, such valuable pieces as a bailed plate warmer or pie dish came brightly lacquered and securely packed in crates. Although slow to reach all the American colonies, tinware earned respect for its serviceability and light weight. As described in Philip William Flower's *History of the Trade in Tin* (1880), for repair, tinsmiths could buy thick, heavy-gauge sheets for roofing or they could work from taggers, a paper-thin sheet used for making or repairing domestic items.

Useful in farm and dairy kitchens were small tin pails, buckets, and containers, known to the Dutch as blickies, which may derive from the German *blick* (tin or shining). Mothers packed their children's lunches in these pails. Restaurateurs and innkeepers used a tin lattice slicer, an undulant serrated blade imbedded in wood, for fluting or lattice potatoes, cucumbers, carrots, and fruit. A hand version, the fruit scalloper, created the same effect with a press of the wire-handled corrugated blade into fruits and vegetables. Another tin device, the twine holder, was a metal sphere suspended on a wire. Through a hole in the bottom, the user could pull off a length of string for meat trussing or tying packages. To keep warm, the needleworker stocked a tin footwarmer or foot stove with embers. The rectangular box, pierced with holes in the tin inserts to let heat escape, served as a footstool that the user could carry from room to room with a wire handle.

Itinerant metal repairmen called tinkers or gypsies traveled from kitchen to kitchen. In Ireland, they traced their beginnings to the Irish Potato Famine of 1845–1848, when enterprising tinsmiths took to the road, some in horse-drawn caravans and more on foot in a round of fair and horse markets. They bore the familiar cylindrical pig on their backs, in which they kept tools—coils of solder, rivets, tongs, tinsnips, hammers, vises, and snarling and soldering irons. When the housewife needed repairs, they plugged holes in basins, fashioned new handles for dippers, tacked metal facings on tools, and recast spoons. A romanticized figure often stereotyped as a scamp or worse, the tinker appeared in numerous memoirs and folk histories, such as *Pinnock's Guide to Knowledge* (1832), which claimed "The tinker, and the other men of the travelling workshop, learned to make the people themselves much more handy than they are now." (Franklin 1997, 195)

The tinker was adept at recycling tin wire into pie holders and coolers, rigging up braces and handles for handle-less pitchers, and soldering together metal scraps to shape into kraut cutters or stampers, strawberry hullers or pincers, napkin rings, and collared milk pans to prevent boil-overs. A specialty was a selection of cookie cutters in animal and seasonal shapes with holes cut in the surface for ease of placement and release onto cookie sheets. The tinsmith's line of goods included kitchen racks to organize implements and cutlery, a rotating towel bar for drying towels, oil cans and lamp fillers fitted with serpentine braces, and a kitchen trousseau, a canvas suitcase holding a sixty-eight-piece collection of gadgets, implements, and kettles for setting up house. The whitesmith, an iron and tin worker, made such items as lanterns and betty lamps with hinged covers, tinderboxes, tea caddies, and roasting ovens.

The author Pinnock Flower esteemed the role of tin in pioneering. When Dutch and Irish newcomers set up tents on the prairies, panned for gold in Nevada, mined silver in the Rockies, or barged down the Mississippi, they carried a standard kit of tinware—a teapot, kettle, pannikin, and wash basin. These inexpensive domestic items awaited the pioneer at trading posts and in country stores.

On the goldfields of Australia, miners made the most of a lidded tin billy. For cooking bread when embers ran low in a camp oven fire, Joe Watson of Caringbah proposed pressing a tin kerosene can into service as a kettle for heating water. After filling the billy two-thirds full with dough, the baker topped it with a clean rag, clapped on the lid, and plunged the pan into the boiling water. As with standard instructions for English boiled puddings, the method heated the bread, but kept it dry.

In the commercial kitchen, tin was a necessity to bakers. They drew flour from a tin flour box and sprinkled flour through the snowflake-patterned holes of a tin flour dredger. One of the ubiquitous baking items in kitchens past and present is the biscuit cutter, a round or fluted body with metal or wooden handle that allowed the baker to cut uniform shapes for biscuits, scones, crackers, or cookies. Some contained metal needles that pricked the surface to keep the dough from puffing; one from the early 1900s was both doughnut cutter and corer. A removeable central dome allowed the user to press out doughnuts or to add a pointed shaft for piercing and coring fruit. An early twentieth-century cutter revolved in a bracket to roll over dough and produce a line of uniform circles.

Tin was a standard item of the Chinese tea trade. Delicate leaves traveled best in tight-lidded tin containers. Tea drinkers stored tea either in the original tin or a similar tin or japanware vessel, but never in glass, which allowed light to fade flavor, aroma, and color. A heating device for metal carafes and samovars was the tin *aetna,* a cone-shaped vessel that the user placed in a saucer of flaming spirits to heat beverages or mull wine.

For open-hearth cooking, the wooden-handled apple or bird roaster, a shovel-shaped innovation, positioned the apple or bird on hooks, racks, or shelves in front of a half dome or box shaped from tin, which reflected heat to the back while the front cooked. The mechanism was adaptable to roasting potatoes, small fowl, or hunks of cheese. Another fruit preparer was the tin apple quarterer, a wooden-handled device that required placement on top of each sphere and a quick downward thrust, which forced crossed blades through the core. The tin Dutch oven cheese toaster offered a variation on the reflector oven. A cruller or potato fryer, advertised in the 1895 Montgomery Ward catalog, attached a graceful brace to the side of a fry pan from which the cook could suspend the pierced tin basket for draining oil back into the pan for the next batch.

Larger tin pieces included a portable tin reflecting oven with tiers of shelves inside, a tin pineapple stand, clam baker, a fish kettle or fish boiler with removable strainer, and an asparagus boiler, an oblong box with lid and handles. For steaming spears upright, the cook tied them in bundles with kitchen string and set them on a perforated tray. Handles enabled the user to extract the fragile steamed asparagus bundle and drain it back into the box before lifting the vegetables with broad-armed tongs and placing them in a serving dish. Also stamped from tin were cake boxes, a round tin cabinet or carrier with top handle, hasp, and lock. The French invented a sink-side tin utensil rack. Stamped with decorative leaf pattern, it held freshly washed implements upright while they dripped into the tray below.

In the United States, tin dominated the nineteenth-century kitchen, In a column for *Table Talk* dated May 1887, Sarah Tyson Rorer, the founder of the Philadelphia Cooking School, advised her readers, "In purchasing kitchen utensils, it is economical to buy the very best. Double plated tin ware will last a lifetime, while the cheap kind scarcely lasts the carrying home." (Weigley 1904, 113) In 1908, the Sears, Roebuck catalog featured a Queen forty-four-piece stove furnishing set, a starter assortment of implements and vessels for cooking, baking, and beverage service. Primarily tin, the set contained a more durable copper-bottomed wash boiler and tea kettle and cast iron spider. The predominence of tin allowed the manufacturer to hold the price at $3.84 because of low-cost materials and light shipping weight. Tin was the essential rust-proofing agent in a cherry stoner, a handy device that forced cherries into one dish and pits into another.

In November 2000, the South Carolina novelist Pat Conroy reported in *Gourmet* magazine on the use of tin at a traditional Southern oyster roast. For a typical cold weather roast, he described placing tin on cinder blocks over an oak fire, shoveling the meaty shellfish on top, and covering them with wet burlap sacks. He declared that diners must eat while the oysters are hot, for "a lukewarm oyster is a disappointment to the spirit." (p. 204)

Further Reading

Conroy, Pat, "An Oyster Roaster . . . Like Tasting Heaven," *Gourmet,* November 2000, 204–206, 209–211.

Weigley, Emma Seifrit. *Sarah Tyson Rorer.* Philadelphia: The American Philosophical Society, 1977.

TREEN

Called treen or treenware, wooden domestic implements took their name from an Old English term referring to a carver's use of wood from green trees. To ready raw material, the hewer split, carved, dried, sanded, and oiled each new piece. The sturdiest of these got its strength from hardwoods—wild cherry, black walnut, bird's-eye maple, sassafras, butternut, birch, poplar, and Italian boxwood as well as less available and less dependable stocks of hornbeam, apple, pear, yew, mahogany, ebony, persimmon, and teak. Handy touches in these items include carved hand-holds, knobs, and piercing to allow the user to insert a thong or attach to a hanging hook. Treen lemon squeezers were ideal for the extraction of an acidic liquid that mottled metal juicers. Colonial American carvers often chose distressed wood or ash burl veneer for an artistic touch derived from forest Indian crafters. Such pieces, shaped from naturally imperfect growth cells, they labeled burl treen or burlware.

Treen extended in application from trays and bowls to heavy agricultural scoops, crooks, hayforks, flails, ship parts, joinery, furnishings, and road vehicles to the dainties of the home: condiment sets, imaginative nutcrackers, shuttles and bobbins, pipe implements, knitting needles and crochet hooks, butter fleeters (ladles) and matching bowls, decorative laundry bats and other love tokens, escritoires, swipples or hand-staffs, spice towers, and holiday wassail bowls. Turned wood became handles for bread rasps, ulus, and dough scrapes. The most common turned drinking cups, called beechen, displayed the least decoration, which the maker burned in with a branding iron. In the humble Welsh kitchen, an oak spoon rack featured holes for each wooden spoon and a cutlery box or drawer below. Upscale versions of treen, some inlaid with Delft tile, replicated angle, banding, and incising for en suite kitchen sets, for example, matched mixing bowl, rolling pin, potato masher, skimmer, and storage jars.

At the beginning of the English Renaissance, treenware begin to lose favor as silver, tin, and other metal competed. In addition to changing the feel and look of wood tableware and kitchen items, the influx of glass and metal changed the sound of condiments passing from hand to hand and the splash of cider into the mug.

In 1840, the traveler Johann George Kohl, secretary of the Austrian legation at the court of Peter the Great, commented on the utensils common in Russian kitchens. In addition to barrels, kegs, vats, tubs, and carboys (demijohns), he noted a "peculiar dexterity in wood-carving." (Molokhovets 1992, 44) Among the treen items he found in place of earthenware or iron were carved jugs, pots, and water pitchers. In Elena Burman Molokhovets's classic Russian cookbook *A Gift to Young Housewives* (1861), she expressed a preference for dry alder, maple, or oak rather than resinous pine or spruce, which flavored butter and other foods stored in wood.

Before automatic lathes, wood turners had to be skilled at operating machinery, judging friction, and selecting grains suited to each piece, whether a simple umbrella rib or walking stick or the more complicated clothes pin, steak mauls, balusters, egg cups, washing dollies, hand-cranked bread breaks, clockworks, mechanical toy, or Norwegian *tine* (lidded lunch box). To true a piece of work required good eyesight and a steady hand on calipers and chisels, especially for incising mottoes such as "Staff of Life," "Waste Not, Want Not," and "Give Us This Day Our Daily Bread." In reference to the tools of Welsh crafters, Dr. Iorweth C. Peate's *Guide to the Collection Illustrating Welsh Folk Crafts and Industries* (1935) praised the pole lathe, which worked pieces with the grain and prevents scrapes to the surface. He acknowledged that the turning device took more effort at the treadle than an ordinary machine.

Late in the nineteenth century in Lancaster County, Pennsylvania, the Mennonite woodcrafter Joseph Lehn added to American folk art with cabinetry and the carving of Lehnware. Shaped like goblets with finialed lids, his utilitarian pantry boxes, seed chests, egg cups, salt cellars, and saffron cups held food items with style. He cranked them out on a treadle lathe and painted them with strawberries, pomegranates, and willow edging. From humble table goods they developed into prized antiques.

Early in the twentieth century, according to Olive Sharkey's *Old Days, Old Ways* (1985), the Irish poor acquired from the Welsh a variety of kitchen treenware. Most common in peat and stone cottages were egg racks and spoon racks to hold the love spoons of courtship. Called "tidies," these framed shelves also held stove polish, cutlery, and dishes. (Sharkey 1985, 48) From the English Midlands north into Scotland, the baker suspended a doughboard from a thong through the handle. To dress up bannocks and oat-cakes, the treen-maker sliced cross-hatching through the surface of haverboards, also called bakbredes or riddleboards.

Currently, individuals prize treen holloware for home use because it adapts to microwave and dishwasher. Crafters sell wood spoons, forks, toaster tongs, and other domestic pieces and such specialty items as snuff boxes and thimbles at crafts fairs and tourist shops. Beginning woodcrafters often choose to make rolling pins, which require turning a foot-long cylinder to create a rounded shoulder and tapered knob. More difficult is the nut pulverizer, an eight-inch piece that uses the same techniques for the short handle. The dowel end fits into a headpiece grooved to give a clean edge on pounded meat. Another useful treen item is the bean spoon, a foot-long implement joining shaped bowl and curved handle. The scoop, a cylindrical shovel-shaped spoon in various sizes to accommodate the grains or solids to be removed, begins with a spindle handle and requires thinning the inner walls.

TSELEMENTES, NIKOLAS

The fount of modern Greek cookery, Nikolas Tselementes won the esteem of a native son and master chef. An Athenian born in 1878, he came from the island heritage of Sifnos in the western Cyclades. He completed high school, served in the army, and clerked for a notary while pondering a career in law. In idle moments, he haunted the kitchen of Aktaion, a fashionable retreat in Neo Faliro owned by his uncle. After studying the culinary arts in Vienna and learning French techniques at the Sacher Hotel, he worked for various embassies and among the rich of Cairo and Istanbul, from whom he began learning recipes. He later studied nutrition at Columbia University and cooked in New York City at the St. Moritz Hotel.

In 1910, Tselementes published a world classic, *Odigos Mageirikes* (A Cooking Guide), the first cookbook in modern Greek. He gave some of the credit for its popularity to the cooking of his wife Ersilia. Of his nation's cuisine, he did not hesitate to criticize tendencies toward fats and over-spicing, a trend copied from Turkish cookery. His refinement of the Greek palate extended to restaurants and cafes, yacht galleys, hotels and inns, and home kitchens.

More than a cook, Tselementes introduced European etiquette, style, and customs to the untutored, untraveled Greek. In native tradition, he urged women to remain ladylike and to fawn over their husbands with compliments and sweetmeats. In an era of parvenus, he instructed the neophyte housewife on hiring and dressing servants. Above all, he believed that skilled cookery was the supreme female adornment, valued far above beauty or high fashion.

In urban pastry shops, Tselementes gave cooking lessons in Athens and Piraeus for beginners. Before live audiences, he demonstrated organization, neatness, and technique. He experimented with foods for invalids. For the military, he trained galley chefs and infantry cooks and contrived moussaka and pastitio from canned corned beef. For Aeg, a German firm, he introduced the electric range to women who were more at home with wood and charcoal stoves.

Throughout his rise in expertise and popularity, Tselementes amassed no fortune and flaunted no pretensions. He was curiously antipathetic to Mediterranean traditions and hated pickles, sour foods, olive oil, spices and herbs, and the smell of cucumber and garlic. To traditional Greek menus, he added creamy dishes topped with bechamel and restored to glory stuffed grape leaves, chickpeas, *melopita* (honey pie), handmade pasta, pilaf, and Lenten dishes. Although he published widely in the media, at his death, his family destroyed his papers and memorabilia when his home was razed. His recipes and cooking style live on at the tavernas of Sifnos and in online collections.

Further Reading

Tselementes, Nicholas. *Greek Cookery.* New York: D. C. Divry, Inc., 1985.
_____. *One Hundred Unusual Dinners and How to Prepare Them.* Boston: Thomas Todd, 1938.

TUDOR, FREDERIC

Frederic Tudor, born to a prominent Boston family in 1784, created a system of shipping ice to tropical climes worldwide. His contribution to culinary history expanded the temperature scale of dishes and the methods by which cooks could devise new taste sensations. At age twenty-one, he borrowed a suggestion from his brother William that New Englanders share their bounty in ice with parts of the world where there was no ice in the kitchen and cooks keyed food selection to seasonal produce. In 1806, he started a global ice business by chopping the surface from Walden Pond and Wenham Lake, Massachusetts. He investigated methods of guaranteeing his product by purchasing sleighs with saw-bladed runners for improved cutting and by promoting the fledgeling ice cream and chilled beverage business and applications of ice in hospitals.

After investing ten thousand dollars, Tudor made his first sale of 130 tons of axe-cut ice to Martinique in 1806. He personally assisted the manager of the Tivoli garden in making ice cream, which brought in three hundred dollars the first night, but meltage over six weeks resulted in a financial loss of four thousand dollars. While trying to get ice to Havana during a yellow fever epidemic, he studied preservation methods with straw and wood insulation and cut the loss to melting from 60 percent to 8 percent. A friend, Nathaniel Jarvis Wyeth, helped him engineer an ice saw that chopped uniform blocks from Fresh Pond near Cambridge. By 1810, he was demonstrating home-style ice cream making in the West Indies, an idea he carried to Iran and South America.

Although Tudor lost agents, experienced an unseasonably warm New England winter, and suffered numerous failures in shipping to the port of Havana, he continued to pack ice in felt, pine chips, and sawdust to ship to the West Indies, South America, and Asia, a major purchaser. In 1833, Tudor succeeded in shipping 180 tons of blocks aboard the Tuscany on a four-month journey to Calcutta. To introduce chilled foods to the Anglo-Indian diet, he distributed apples, butter, and cheese. The novelty of Massachusetts ice chilling Indian foods caused essayist Henry David Thoreau to note that Walden Pond water was mingling with the sacred Ganges.

By 1856, Tudor had become the world's ice king and transformed the menus of the Philippines with 146,000 tons of Massachusetts ice. One essential to his success was the construction of ice depots at the receiving end of his business. To hold his goods in insulation, in 1842, he built the Vivekanandar Illam in Chennai, India, a two-acre ice house replicated in Bombay, Mumbai, and Calcutta. The locker remained in business for nearly forty years, when steam-process ice-making from pure water replaced shipped pond and lake ice.

Further Reading

Boorstin, Daniel J. *The Americans: The National Experience.* New York: Vintage Books, 1965.
Crowe, Mike, "Kennebec Ice," *Fisherman's Voice,* May 2000, 1–2.
Hamilton, Neil A., "The Ice King," *American History,* October 2000, 30–34.

U

ULU

For Eskimo cooks, the ulu (or ulo), a half-moon-shaped cleaver or utility knife, has been a valuable hand tool from prehistory. A lightweight multipurpose bone, ivory, or metal knife and scraper, it suits the hand for skinning and filleting fish and boning animals, chipping ice, cutting moss to make wicks for cooking lamps, piercing duck eggs, and slicing baleen, the tender mouth tissue from the gray whale. To entertain young children, women use their ulus to carve toys from discarded bones and tusk.

Anthropologists have located ulus among the effects of the Dorset, an extinct tribe of nomadic Eskimos native to coastal territory extending from Greenland to Baffin Island from 800 BCE to 1200 CE. In the summer of 1842, when the Arctic navigator Sir William Edward Parry of Bath, England, sailed the *Hecla* and *Griper* in search of a northwest passage, he observed the soapstone cooking vessel, walrus tusk knife, and crude ulu of the Canadian Eskimo. He described the latter as "an instrument for chopping, very much resembling a cooper's adze, which had evidently been secured to a handle of bone for some time past, and of which the iron was part of an old file." (Parry 1842, I, 186) On a second voyage, he observed more closely the Greenland native's knife, "resembling, in its semi-circular shape, that used by shoemakers in England." (Ibid., 225)

Two decades later, Captain Charles Francis Hall, the author of *Life with the Esquimaux* (1862), made a subsequent expedition to the Arctic. During an attempt to rescue an Inuit woman immured in an ice tomb, Hall discovered her frozen body next to an iron pan from which she had tried to chip ice to quench her thirst. Alongside her was a four-gallon tin can containing her treasured personal belongings—whale skin, beads, needles, sewing cord made of reindeer sinew, and an ulu. In reference to the heavy domestic labor performed by Inuit females, he declared, "In the hands of an Esquimaux woman, this simple instrument, made of bone and iron, is equivalent to the knife, hatchet, scraper, and shear of civilization."

The ulu or mezzaluna found favor with American consumers. In 1908, Sears, Roebuck featured a japanned ulu in its catalog for 7 cents. Among other types of forcing tools and can openers, the iron-handled mincer offered a ground steel blade and sturdy handle. In 1975, the chef James Beard joined other food experts in compiling *The Cook's Catalogue*. In featured commentary on curved chopping blades, he characterized the ulu as an essential cutting tool in Chinese cuisine. His text featured an antique French mincing knife, the *hache-viand* (hash knife), a variant of the ulu with paired blades "like a child's double-runner skate" and handles extending beyond them for rocking back and forth over foods. (Beard 1975, 97) He featured an arced blade with vertical wood handle and matching bowl along with a German stainless-steel crescent blade with knobs at each end for chopping apples and fresh horseradish root and for making a sailor's hash of potatoes, corned beef, salt herring, and beets.

Late in the twentieth century, natives of Greenland maintained the all-purpose ulu as a food chopper.

Housewives skillfully slid pointed ends and sharp blade under the skins of seals to separate fat and meat from organs and skeleton. Because of their thrift and talent at dismembering, cooks left little of the seal to toss into the kitchen midden. They immediately served the eyes and livers as delicacies and boiled or dried flanks, hearts, and intestines for subsequent meals. The dried skins fetched up to ninety kroner at markets in Copenhagen, Denmark.

In the twenty-first century, the ulu remains in favor for its ease of use and the safety of its manipulation.

Culinary shops offer a wood-handled variety, called in Italian *mezzaluna* (half-moon), that fits a wooden chopping bowl. A stainless steel version formed of a single metal sheet and grooved to fit the fingers, the twin-bladed ulu is ideal for mincing chives, garlic, herbs, nuts, seeds, and ingredients for salsa.

Further Reading

Parry, W. E. *Three Voyages for the Discovery of a Northwest Passage*. New York: Harper & Brothers, 1842.

V

VACUUM CLEANERS

After years of hauling carpets and rugs to the clothesline for beating, the homeowner prized the carpet sweeper, which revolutionized fiber cleaning by applying the rotating brush technology of street sweepers to napped floor coverings. The English inventor Jane Hume patented a forerunner of the vacuum system in 1811. A wheeled box maneuvered by a handle, it contained a pulley-operated brush that swept crumbs into the container. Advanced in the mid-nineteenth century, the bellows system of drawing air through a closed container produced a balky, cumbrous machine requiring two people—a bellows operator and a floor cleaner. Ives M. McGaffey, a Chicago inventor, created the first suction, fan-driven floor cleaner, a hand-cranked model he called the Whirlwind.

For most home owners, the first name in fiber care was Bissell, an eponymous brand of sweeper invented in Grand Rapids, Michigan, in 1876 by Melville Reuben Bissell. His concept of self-contouring brushes preceded similar designs in vacuum cleaners. In 1908, the Sears, Roebuck catalog offered the improved Bissell Champion Carpet Sweeper for $1.97. Ad copy lauded "improved spring dumping device, pure bristle sweeping brush," and a handsome japanned case. (Schroeder 1971, 468) A middle-grade device, it was 23 cents more than the Leader Carpet Sweeper, which lacked spring action, but 29 cents less than the Seroco model, built of three-ply hardwood and sealed with three coats of varnish. The advertisement extolled the Bissell's copper-plated and triple nickel-plated and

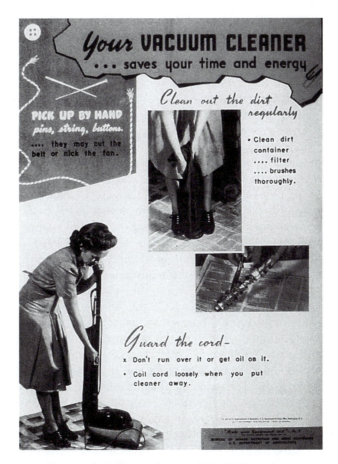

Advertisement for vacuum cleaners, 1941-1945.
[© *Courtesy of National Archives and Records Administration.*]

625

polished metal workings and brushes "made of the finest imported Chinese bristles." (Ibid.)

In 1901, the English inventor Hubert Cecil Booth recognized misapplied technology when he saw a wheeled floor care system that blew an air stream against fabrics and carpeting to dislodge dirt. That same year, he patented a reverse operation, a gas- or electric-powered vacuum cleaner head mounted on a cart. To trap particles, he sewed a cloth filter bag and named his device Puffing Billy. By equipping his device with see-through hoses, he demonstrated to would-be customers the machine's ability to extract dirt. The cumbrous machinery, which a cleaning service drove to homes by horse and van, began work after staff shoved hoses through windows to reach floors. The apparatus remained too bulky, heavy, and impractical for the average homeowner to purchase until 1905, when a San Francisco firm mounted a ninety-two-pound cleaner on a trolley.

It was a tanner and harness-maker, William "Boss" Hoover, of Berlin, Ohio, who pioneered the maneuverable upright model in 1908, invented by a relative, James Murray Spangler. With a broomstick, pillow slip, brushes, fan motor, and soapbox, he jury-rigged an upright device that would assist him in cleaning a department store, where heavy dust worsened his asthma. Hoover capitalized on the successful machine by shutting down his tannery and launching the Electric Suction Sweeper Company. In 1924, Booth resurged and renamed his company Goblin Limited. The successful manufacturer is now located in Tralee, Ireland, as a division of Glen Dimplex, makers of mini vacs, steam cleaners, and wet-dry shop vacuum systems.

Electrolux, one of the enduring names in floor care products, got its start in Sweden in 1919 when Lux merged with Elektromekaniska. Already the marketer of the Lux kerosene lamp, the Lux factory began selling a portable cylindrical vacuum cleaner in 1912. The popular horizontal tank mounted on parallel runners like a sled came on the market in 1921. In 1924, a flexible hose for reaching walls and inside cabinets increased the usability of the machine. A decade later, the firm opened a U.S. factory in New England.

The 1923 Sears, Roebuck catalog highlighted ad copy for the upright Energez Vacuum Cleaner, a pricey cast aluminum model for the mail-order business clientele at $29.85 to $31.50. A schematic drawing of top-mounted attachment point and line drawing of a smiling mother vacuuming while her children play suggested how an electric sweeper promoted harmony and ease in the home. In addition to rotating brush heads, the company listed separately a set of five attachments and hose for $8.70. Guarantees of a heavy, dust-retaining bayonet ring bag and on-off switch at the end of the handle promoted the ideal of cleaning from a standing position without dirtying the home-maker or the atmosphere. On a back page, the catalog also offered a non-electric vacuum cleaner for $18.75. Operated on rotating brushes and suction, the aluminum upright model weighed only eleven pounds and ejected dust into a fabric bag for easy emptying. In 1928, Carl Albert Naether, the author of *Advertising to Women*, chose an ad from the Vital Automatic Vacuum Cleaner Company of Cleveland, Ohio, as a model of direct mail copywriting that appealed to female shoppers. Alongside a letterhead picturing a child vacuuming with her mother, the text notes that a powerful suction fan got all the dirt.

In the late 1940s, the post-World War II generation of homemakers looked for easier, quicker, and more economical ways to performing cyclical chores. One vacuum, the Air-Way Sanitizor, touted an extended wand and a cheap, sanitary throw-away bag made of patented filter paper. The clean-hands method of jettisoning dirt became one of the most appealing features. A full-page ad in the April 1947 issue of *Woman's Home Companion* presented a beautifully dressed and coifed woman in medium heels and suit lifting her Electrikbroom with one finger. Made by the Regina Corporation of Rahway, New Jersey, the multiple-use stick vacuum cleaner swept and dry-mopped and stored in limited space on a closet hook.

After joining the staff of Sears, Roebuck, in 1979 as an industrial designer, Nancy Perkins redesigned the dishwasher, Incredicell car battery, and canister vacuum cleaner. Perkins's vacuum cleaner supplied housewives with a lightweight, easy-to-operate machine featuring improved wheels, bumpers, and handle. With renewed confidence in the field of industrial design, she opened Perkins Design Ltd., which she moved from Chicago to Keichline's building in Bellefonte, Pennsylvania.

A British vacuum cleaner inventor, James Dyson, launched a bagless Dual Cyclone model with a centrifugal system that cleaned the air of heavy particulate. His full-suction model came on the home market in 1984 as the G-Force. He failed to clinch a manufacturing deal with Amway, a U.S. firm launched in 1959 by Rich DeVos and Jay Van Andel, and instead signed with a Japanese firm. When Amway began selling its own cyclone cleaner, he successfully sued the company for stealing his idea and began making the cleaners in upright and canister models at a site in Wiltshire, England.

Subsequent models offer a variety of sizes and motor power for small and large jobs. A hand-held wet-dry super-power model, invented by Dan Brazier in 1977, allowed the homeowner to suction up dry and wet spills. In 1979, Black & Decker drew on technology used for the Apollo moon landing to produce a cordless vacuum, a natural for cleaning kitchen nooks and crannies on shelves and between appliances. Canisters offered reusable cloth bags and disposable paper bags and attachments for kitchen carpet or hard flooring. In the spirit of save-the-planet ecology, Dyson devised the Recyclone vacuum cleaner from recycled plastic and marketed spare parts and accessories over the Internet. The company began the twenty-first century with plans for quieter machines and for a vacuuming robot programmed to follow a planned cleaning grid without a human operator guiding it. Oreck combined technologies to make the XL Radio Vac, an upright cleaner equipped with a headset attached to an FM radio in the handle.

Further Reading

Naether, Carl A. *Advertising to Women*. New York: Prentice-Hall, Inc., 1928.

VERMIN

Control of mice and insects has typically required ingenuity. The Mesopotamian housekeeper used rope handles to hang pots on the wall away from rats. The early English hung elecampane root at window casements and doorsills to trap gnats on the sticky surface, grew mint along an outside wall to stop ant infestation, and strewed such aromatics as shoofly and hemp agrimony under tables and rugs and in closets to mask odor and repel crawling pests and moths. They grew aconite, a poisonous garden flower also called monkshood or wolfsbane, baked it into cakes, and left them in infested areas for vermin to eat.

Traditionally, vermin control fell to women. According to the anonymous *Le Ménagier de Paris* (The Goodman of Paris, ca. 1394), an unsigned text that may have been written by Guy de Montigny, servant of the Duc de Berry, it was the wife's job to create a comfortable home for her mate. For summer influx of fleas in a bedroom, the medieval text offered six antidotes: spreading alder leaves, smearing trenchers of bread with glue or turpentine and luring the insects with candlelight, capturing fleas on cloth spread over the room, trapping them in sheepskin, placing blanchets of white wool on straw to contrast black fleas, or keeping bedding tightly corded in a chest to suffocate insects. To rid the room of mosquitoes, he advised smoking them out with lighted twists of hay or swathing the bed in netting. For flies, he suggested tying up flitches of fern, trapping bugs on glued surfaces, or swatting them with a fly whisk.

Cooks wrapped meat in tansy to ward off flies and dropped pennyroyal in water kegs to keep water sweet. Simpler applications of domestic vermin control brought sprinklings of quassia chip, juniper berry, and other aromatics in cupboards to halt ants and mint and tansy to ward off mice. To repel mosquitoes, outdoor cooks burned citronella candles, artemisia, and myrtle and rubbed skin with an aromatic oil blended from clove, eucalyptus, geranium, and peppermint. A spray made from chives killed aphids and controlled mildew.

Mousetraps, the world's most patented device, have enjoyed a long and colorful history. For halting theft of grain, the home woodcarver devised a drop-weight mouse trap. In late medieval England, drop-lever mousetraps were more complex death-dealers requiring the collaboration of carpenters and smithies. In 1876, Daniel Conner created "The Claws," a box with levered garroting wire. By enticing mice to leap toward bait, the trap killed them and dropped them down a chute into a pail. That same year, L. B. Brown and J. H. Norrow shaped a wire cage that admitted rodents and trapped them there to be killed or released far from the kitchen.

In 1899, John Mast of Lititz, Pennsylvania, began making the Victor, the most popular mouse-killer for the next century. The user activated the flat piece of wood equipped with spring and wire bail by latching the wire into place. When mice sniffed at the baited end, they tripped the latch, causing the spring to slam down the bail. Mast's invention outlasted A. A. Low's electrocuting trap from the 1980s and subsequent glue traps, baffled chambers baited with anti-freeze, and humane catch-and-release models marketed by animal rights agencies.

Flies, the insidious species that breeds in garbage and rotting matter, challenged fastidious housekeepers with a weekly production of five hundred eggs per week. Because houseflies, fleas, and lice made homelife miserable, medieval housewives burned fleabane in a chafing dish as a fumigant. They made kitchen flea lamps, which involved spreading sticky birdlime or turpentine on trenchers of bread and leaving the pieces at floor level near lighted candles. The light drew fleas, which stuck to the mixture. *The School of Arts*, a handbook published in 1754 by the Royal Society of Arts, offered an updated cure for fleas—fumigation with burning sulfur or the strewing of pennyroyal on linens.

In the mid-nineteenth century, Australian pioneers worked at foiling the flies that spoiled their meat. They used kerosene or paraffin oil for cleaning windows and sills. Within the window frame, they hung rags soaked in pungent oil of lavender. Within the room, cloves and fennel pots drove off insects. Brown paper coated with boiled linseed oil, resin, and honey formed makeshift flypaper to protect precious pantry stores.

Catharine E. Beecher and Harriet Beecher Stowe, the authors of the classic handbook *The American*

627

Woman's Home, or Principles of Domestic Science (1869), outlined methods of defeating vermin with home remedies, such as keeping a cat to ward off rats and mice or poisoning the pests with hemlock and old cheese. For bedbugs, homemakers puttied chinks in bedsteads and painted over them. To kill an infestation, the text warns that the housewife needed a strong poison made of corrosive sublimate and alcohol. For cockroaches, readers learned how to pour boiling water into their nests or how to mix arsenic, corn meal, and molasses as a poison or combine sweetened water with lime chloride. Crickets and red and black ants also fled from scalding or from a sprinkle of Scotch snuff.

For flying insects, the Beecher sisters suggested another regimen. Flies died from sipping a poisonous mix of cobalt in sweetened water. Mosquitoes, which were more insidious, failed to suck the blood of victims who slept under tight netting around beds. The authors offered no poison for mosquitoes, but suggested salt water or spirits of hartshorn to ease the bites. Fleas, they advised, decreased from a three-part regimen of sudsing the dog, collecting fleas from the bathwater, and burning them. For moths, they suggested airing winter clothes in hot sun and sewing them in linen bags sprinkled with tobacco powder before storing them in spring.

Proponents of self-reliance rather than faith in patent goods, the Beechers recommended that home kitchen gardeners apply numerous non-pesticide methods of controlling vermin. They listed carefully selected varieties of garlic and herbs for specific jobs. Cautious fig preservation began with a layering of mullein. For storing apples, pears, and root crops, some cooks wrapped fruit in nettle leaves before transporting them to root cellars. A similar casing in nettle deterred insects that attacked moist cheese.

To prohibit insect infestation, snails, and mice from food preparation centers, nineteenth-century housewives planted artemisia by the kitchen door to banish slugs. They resorted to bay leaves in heavy-lidded canisters for air-tight storage of staples, placement of cotton balls dipped in mint to repel ants, boron trails along cracks in the floor, roach bellows, and a kitchen tabby to patrol by night. Terra cotta traps smeared with molasses or molasses and pokeberry juice lured cockroaches into the basin, from which they were unable to escape. A glass bell jar with a single entrance hole baited with sweetened fruit trapped flying insects on the kitchen table or outdoor picnic area. A multipurpose insecticide, pyrethrum, became the favorite nontoxic spray for bedbugs, cockroaches, flies, aphids, mites, ants, and mosquitoes.

Those homemakers following the domestic advice of Jonathan Periam, the author of *The Home & Farm Manual: A Pictorial Encyclopedia of Farm, Garden,* *Household, Architectural, Legal, Medical and Social Information* (1884), could halt cockroaches with a sprinkle of paris green from a flour dredging box and stop ants at the kitchen door by planting wormwood. He recommended flypaper from the month of May into the fall and a wash of laurel leaves and quicklime on walls to stop flies from settling. He suggested planting wild chamomile, which emitted "an empyreumatic odor" that drove away crawling insects. (Periam 1984, 785) For campers, he suggested burning brown sugar on hot coals to rid the cooking area of gnats and mosquitoes.

The 1908 Sears, Roebuck catalog listed its vermicides in lethal terms, beginning with Quick Death Bug Killer and Fertilizer, guaranteed against potato, squash, pumpkin, watermelon, and rose bugs as well as cabbage and currant worms. Introduced in 1902, the preparation sold for 22 cents for five pounds. The advertiser also showcased sulfur fumigation candles to kill insects and rid the home and clothing of infectious diseases and, for specific vermin, a bedbug exterminator at 17 cents per half pint, tins of fly killer at 13 cents, paris green at 28 cents per pound, poison fly paper at 9 cents for four, (unmailable) roach powder at 18 cents a tin, and flake tar moth destroyer at 9 cents per pound.

In 1912, the environmental chemist Ellen Henrietta Richards and Sophronia Maria Elliott summarized correct home methods of sanitizing most surfaces and fibers in *The Chemistry of Cooking and Cleaning.* Their suggestions of useful home insecticides called for kerosene, sticky flypaper, and powdered chrysanthemums, which suffocated water bugs and fleas. Of poisonous flypapers, they noted that the dying insects bore arsenic compounds on their remains as they fell about the house, thus endangering children and pets.

In the 1920s and 1930s, women's magazines carried advertisements for ant and fly poisons. In *Good Housekeeping,* the April 1925 issue decribed Rat Bis-Kit as a tidy way to poison rats and mice. In 1930, Antrol Laboratories of Los Angeles promoted the removal of filthy, destructive pests by placing glass jars of an unspecified syrup that ants eagerly sought out. Carrying the unidentified poison back to their nests, they allegedly exterminated whole colonies without spreading toxins to harm humans. A later issue included in the September Forum of reader's questions the dictum that insecticides are better than homes beset with bedbugs, flies, and moths. For kitchen, pantry, and cellar, editors cited the New Jersey Agricultural Experiment Station, which exonerated spraying with pyrethrum, a non-poisonous method of stunning or paralyzing insects. Instructions for closing rooms to allow the spray to penetrate mentioned no precautions to cover food and dishes or protect cabinet and food preparation surfaces.

As an alternate to home poisons and traps, the entomologist Edith Marion Patch, author of *Science at Home* (1935), advanced additional non-toxic, non-invasive methods of safeguarding the home from vermin. Before becoming a teacher, she worked without salary for Charles D. Woods at the University of Maine. Her research into the aphid's life cycle and publication of *Aphid Pests of Maine, Food Plants of the Aphids, Psyllid Notes* (1912) assisted kitchen gardeners in limiting damage to food plants. For her expertise, in 1930, the Entomological Society of America elected her president.

Another contributor to vermin control, the entomologist and nematologist Marjorie A. Hoy promoted the use of natural predators, parasitoids, and recombinant DNA methods to limit infestation of mites, mealybugs, and citrus leaf miners in Florida and California. In 1996, federal environmental control agencies permitted her to release the first transgenic beneficial predator. In February 2000, she was appointed to the Advisory Committee on Biotechnology, a federal watchdog. For her work and respect for ecology, she earned the Bussart Memorial Award and the Founders Memorial Award from the Entomological Society of America. She continued her work at the University of Florida, Gainesville.

In the same field of interest as Hoy, Amegda J. Overman, a professor of food and agronomy at the University of Florida, began advising the Gulf Coast Research and Education Center in Bradenton, Florida, in 1945. A specialist in nematology, she researched infestations of vegetables, ornamentals, and farm crops. She co-developed a system of plastic mulch and fumigation for kitchen gardens and promoted trickle irrigation and multicrop silage for sustaining bedding plants and herbs in Florida and the tropics. In 1997, she was named an honorary life member of the Soil and Crop Science Society of Florida.

In the twenty-first century, a safe, quiet home device, the Mosquito Magnet, rids homes, yards, and barns of flying insects without emitting poison. The idea began in 1990 with a fishing trip by Bruce Wigton, employee of Southern California Edison, who wanted a better method of killing mosquitoes and gnats than pesticides and bug zappers. The trap is the outcome of his studies on bloodseeking insects begun in 1991 by the American Biophysics Corporation in cooperation with the State Departments of Environmental Management, the U.S. Department of Agriculture, and the U.S. Centers for Disease Control.

Powered by a propane tank, the Mosquito Magnet lures mosquitoes, gnats, sand flies, and black flies by exuding a moist carbon dioxide vapor and an octenal attractant. Flying insects, seeking a warm-blooded prey, mistake the gas for a person. The machine vacuums them into a net and dehydrates them. The expensive gear needs no electricity and extends its effectiveness over an acre. Tested in the Florida Everglades and distributed in Florida and the Caribbean, the machine is capable of a daily kill of 100,000 mosquitoes.

See also **Insects, Reptiles, and Worms**

Further Reading

The Goodman of Paris. London: Routledge, 1928.
Richards, Ellen H., and S. Maria Elliott. *The Chemistry of Cooking and Cleaning*. Boston: Whitcomb & Barrows, 1912.

VICTORIAN KITCHENS

During Victoria's long reign (1837–1901), Europe's population increased greatly, placing more demands on food preparation and distribution. The poorest people, drawn from rural areas to factories in large cities, often subsisted in multi-family dwellings and modest cottages whose cramped quarters consisted of a sitting room and sleeping area. Even in more ornamented versions of the Victorian cottage, floor plans designated no area as a kitchen. The three-room laborer's cottage was the first to contain a true kitchen, a room added to the back of the two-room house and augmented with a wood lean-to to hold cooking and heating fuel. Another version of the laborer's cottage added a washroom and pantry addition to the square floor plan, but relegated cookery to the living room fireplace.

In tenements, poor families ate and cooked in the sitting room and slept in the second room. Humanitarians instructed working-class women in hygienic kitchen cleaning and the wholesome storage and preservation of foods. The first public health nurses visited tenement families to illustrate methods of cleaning and cooking for invalids and small children and of bathing the family in shallow tin bath tubs heated with water from the kettle.

For the lower middle class, the American landscaper and agronomist Andrew Jackson Downing published a farm cottage plan in *Horticulturist* magazine during the 1840s. It proposed a roomy four-room house with enclosed porch, veranda, and two upstairs bedrooms. The modest home with two chimneys contained a real kitchen larger than the parlor. Another home design in Henry W. Cleaveland, William Backus, and Samuel D. Backus's *Village and Farm Cottages* (1856), pictured a mid-Victorian cottage with central hall separating living room and kitchen to the right from a bedroom on the left. A slightly larger cottage separated rooms symmetrically with parlor and living room in the front, two bedrooms behind, and wash room, pantry, and kitchen occupying a smaller area attached at the rear. For the needs of the farm family, Lewis Falley Allen published *Rural Architecture* (1851) featuring a two-story house with downstairs kitchen, containing a back oven and full fireplace. The design preceded the Queen Anne cottage, a suburban dwelling that offered more space upstairs and a kitchen-pantry-dining room complex on the first floor.

In standard multi-story Victorian homes for the gentry, the basement was the nerve-center of the house and the domain of servants. Below stairs, a typical food-preparation center consisted of storage rooms and larders, pantries, and sculleries for dishwashing. To aid the rolling of pastry and making of candies, the typical work table often featured a marble inset on the top level. For the average family, marble was a costly addition that was easily chipped or broken if mishandled.

Regular briefings from the lady of the house on careful use of equipment, fuel economy, menus, and provisioning brought master and worker face to face. Cut off from most of the upstairs activities, food workers remained in the dim, windowless kitchen and communicated with the upper floors by dumbwaiters and stairs. For resident staff, floor-level rooms for butler, housekeeper, and launderer shared hallways with the still room, butler's pantry, wine cellar, toilets, garbage and coal vaults, and entrance to the subterranean ice-house.

At Como House in Melbourne, Australia, a built-in range from the 1860s demonstrates the cooking technology of the era. Within a niche that originally held a hearth, the iron-fronted cooking shelf extended a surface suited to large cook pots and steamers. Below, iron doors to left and right offered shelves for baking. At center, the cook could poke up the embers through a grid. A broad-mouthed hopper protruded at bottom for easy removal of ash and clinkers. Although the fireplace was gone, the hearth remained in position to prevent popping coals from scorching an oiled hard-wood floor or linoleum or from igniting linens. Above the range, a narrow ledge held clock, gas lantern, lamps, hand mill, and canisters. To one side, a wire stand supported a set of seven pots, one above the other.

In the basement warren, function surpassed fashion in cold water taps, sturdy hutches, soapstone game-keeper sinks, scrubbable tin surfaces, wood drain board, plate racks and overhead racks for hanging pots and implements, and brick flooring swept clean and resanded daily. A plate rail offered additional storage space for platters and trays. Corners and available wall space housed small cabinets and shelving for utensils and treasured items, such as lidded tins of coffee, tea, and spices. The dresser, a massive wood cabinet and work station, organized bins, storage jars, linens, and

utensils as well as cup hooks for jugs and tankards. Lighting in the lower level derived primarily from the fireplace, leaving odd corners gloomy and dank. A central table held fresh meats and vegetables for dressing beneath an iron gas chandelier or hanging lamp, fueled with gas or oil. Between meals, house staff accessed the same surface for polishing silver and brass and sharpening cutlery.

Cooks, either plain or "professed" (trained specialists), were typically females who had apprenticed at a manor or inn, then moved on to private service, often to end the misery of maid's work. The economical cook, who fed a large family and house staff, drew on numerous cookbooks and home economics handbooks for advice. For example, they learned to recycle stale bread as college pudding, trifle, treacle tart, apple charlotte, bread pudding, or queen of pudding, heavy sweets that entered English cuisine with the Hanoverian kings, who brought boiled puddings from Germany. Additional help for the budget came from windfall fruit, which they turned into fool, purée, fruit leather, mousse, apple snow, apple amber, pie, or tart.

For the average British cook, kitchen work improved as more homes employed waxcloth or oilcloth table coverings, clocks, accurate scales, coal-fired ranges, and cookbooks, but cleaning remained a chore. For the run-of-the-mill plastered flooring or exposed deal or fir, the rule was daily scrubbing on hands and knees with bristle brush, block soap, and pail. Tongue-and-groove oak-plank flooring, which mass production had regularized into standard widths, sported scatter rugs, stiffened canvas, or oilcloth to protect fine graining, but coverings increased laundry with an unwieldy rectangle that had to be washed and stretched over a sturdy fence or on tenterhooks for annual airing and sun-drying. The invention of linoleum in 1860 lightened the job by covering floors in a durable jute or canvas heat-bonded to an oxidized linseed oil surface fluxed with resin and filled with cork and gum. The new flooring resisted fire, scratches, and dents and did not absorb kitchen fat, oil, or grease.

Unlike the heavy pieces of previous centuries, wood cabinets took on a sleeker look. The Victorian work station combined drawers and bins for storage of flour, sugar, and beans. Pull-out cutting boards enabled the cook to rearrange work space for rolling pie crusts or dressing meat and fish. Small shelves aligned spices in small bottles within easy reach. On the walls, flatware racks held tableware and serving pieces in neat order to display ivory or pearl handles and engraved bowls.

Cooking techniques experienced a vast alteration during Victoria's reign. One of the hardest, messiest jobs was broiling, which involved lifting fish, game, or meat above hot coals on an iron grate set on legs. Home broilers came in various designs:

- A two-part ridged pan made of cast iron with tin lid
- A hinged heavy wire rack resembling a fireside popcorn popper
- A reversible Morgan broiler, patented in 1890, which allowed pan juices to run back to the meat
- A charcoal broiler, a lidded, multilevel cooker from the late 1800s that held a bed of embers in the bottom level to grill meat on the upper shelf
- The brandiron, a griddle for fast cooking meats at the heat
- An American flat iron pot fitted with an internal wire rack and a tin lid
- A cast iron broiler for gas stoves, a flat disk topped with a grid that fits over the gas under a domed ventilated lid

In whatever form, these heavy, awkward devices demanded careful observation during use and long sessions of scrubbing with abrasive cleaners and wire-bristled brushes after a long soak in a tub of hot water.

For the homemaker, the journalist and poet Eliza Acton published *Modern Cookery for Private Families* (1845), a compendium for middle-class cooks that went through a number of editions, including the 1855 issue, which added foreign and Jewish cookery. The first popular author to write for her peers, she simplified the complexities of adding thickeners to soup and gravy, leavening and icing cake and pastry, and boning, trussing, and carving roasts and fowl. She became the first food authority to list ingredients as an introduction to instructions and to specify a cooking time. To her readers, she pledged only kitchen-tested results.

In 1852, Acton wrote *The English Bread Book*, a call to home bakers to avoid unhygienic professional bakeries, which were notorious for adulterating their goods with chalk, alum, and pulverized wood and bone to produce a cheap white loaf. Her advocacy of proper selection of fresh fish, a return to home preservation of fruit, and the baking of nutritious brown bread to restore purity and nutrition to families agreed with sentiments expressed by the English journalist and publicist William Cobbett in *Cottage Economy* (1823). Another strong voice for home cooking was the novelist and social critic Charles Dickens, author of *Household Words*, a weekly journal published in the *Examiner* from 1850 and added to his popular compendium *All the Year Round* (1858).

For the military wife trying to maintain British kitchen standards in the Anglo-Indian colonies, Colonel A. R. Kenney-Herbert compiled several compendia of advice, including *Wyvern's Sweet Dishes* (1881), issued under the pseudonym Wyvern, in which he described trifle as a womanly delight. His *Culinary Jottings* (1885), based on English and Continental cookery, reformed cuisine for Anglo-Indian exiles by compiling thirty detailed menus. Unlike chefs of his era who added crystallized violets to desserts and maiden hair fern to baked items, he stressed the flavor and nutrients of fish, salads, and vegetables over such ornate frippery.

Edward Abbott's *The English and Australian Cook Book: Cookery for the Many as Well as for the Upper Ten Thousand* (1864), the island nation's first cookbook, compiled the recipes of a wealthy cosmopolitan colonist. Drawing on Victorian forerunners Eliza Acton and London chef Alexis Benoît Soyer, Abbott produced 103 chapters on housewifery, drinks, soirées, and defense of meat eaters. For a kangaroo steamer, he advised braising bite-size pieces of meat in milk, shredded onion, and seasoning. After a late addition of salt bacon and ketchup, the meat was ready for eating with jelly.

Victorian homes displayed accumulated wealth in decorated fireplaces decked in white marble and classical detailing or painted white to suggested an airy grace rather than subsistence cookery. Marquetry, carving, and crests on the overmantel made a statement about the family's wealth, family connections, and prestige. Tables, made of dark woods, tended to be large and heavy. Kitchen staff covered them with soft flannel *sous-nappe* (undercloth) or felt molleton beneath the top cloth to pad expensive wood and silence the clink of utensils. They stretched across table cloths the narrow table runners that performed the same silencing for salt and pepper and water carafe. On ornate sideboards, housekeepers arranged serving pieces, Japanware, and showy epergnes and vases filled with fresh flowers and greenery stripped, nipped, and arranged at the kitchen sink. Staff glossed the horsehair upholstery of dining room chairs with furniture polish or a dab of oil.

Conformity burdened households during the first half-century of Victoria's reign, ostensibly in imitation of the staid, proper royal family. One rebel, Charles Lock Eastlake, the secretary of the National Gallery and author of *Hints on Household Taste in Furniture, Upholstery and Other Details* (1868) and *Lectures on Decorative Art and Art Workmanship* (1876), disdained mass produced furnishings for imposing a set standard on personal tastes. Near the end of the Victorian age, he lauded individuality and lighter pieces. As trading with Asian markets prospered, his contemporary, the merchant Arthur Lasenby Liberty, promoted the popularity of Japanese goods at his emporium, Liberty of Regent Street.

Home upkeep required the constant mixing of cleaners and polishes. To protect Turkey or Axminster carpets, staff placed a drugget or temporary floor covering under dining tables to protect from spills. Home life improved considerably after safer stoves curtailed fears of fire. In the 1870s, introduction of tiled and marbled walls, gas, refrigerators, and plumbing eased the daily tasks of scrubbing soot, collecting lamps for cleaning, arranging logs and removing ash and clinkers, hauling ice, and filling and carrying water upstairs and slops downstairs. Linoleum reduced the need for polishing hardwood. Gradually, designers placed these updated and more attractive kitchens at the rear of the house in closer proximity to the dining room.

From advances in chemical fertilizers and railroads, and distribution of canned foods and factory-made jelly and preserves in the 1880s, the variety and quality of foodstuffs burgeoned, teasing the palate and increasing demand for more interesting dishes. Door-to-door vendors found a ready market for country-fresh produce, dairy products, and meats. The kitchens of grand hotels, resorts, trains, and ocean liners and glittering, extravagantly complex table service and carvery satisfied the dreams of the gourmet and social climber, for whom dining was evidence of refinement and culture. Yet, for the poor, survival in an age of excess produced more wrenching ironies, more opportunities to serve the rich.

Demand for servants grew even as the employee pool shrank. More potential servants chose factory work and clerking over bulky laundry, polishing silver, and grilling a heavy English breakfast, which had grown larger and earlier as menus moved away from Continental style pastries and coffee to fried eggs,

bacon and sausage, grilled mushrooms and tomatoes, and toast. For homeowners, the number of domestic staff they employed determined the design and size of the kitchen and adjacent servants' quarters. The organization and convenience of a well planned work space increased the likelihood that kitchen staff would be happy at their posts and remain longer.

The Fabian Society advocated social change in the home through planning and technology rather than revolution. Among their suggestions to end "repetitive and soul-killing drudgery," were proposed alternative housekeeping measures—architectural plans for communal dining and housecleaning in low-maintenance apartments, which would feature toilet and bath facilities and coin-operated gas meters. Leaders like Maud Adeline Brereton proposed that the gas industry make appliances affordable and supply technology to equip homes with hot water as a means of upgrading convenience and sanitation.

See also **Acton, Elizabeth; Brereton, Maud Adeline; Francatelli, Charles Elmé; Gas; Linoleum; Marshall, Agnes; Oilcloth; Stoves; Young, Hannah**

Further Reading

Clendinning, Anne, "Gas and Water Feminism: Maud Adeline Brereton and Edwardian Domestic Technology," *Canadian Journal of History*, April 1, 1998, 2–24.

Grow, Lawrence, comp. *The Old House Book of Cottages and Bungalows.* New York: Sterling/Main Street Books, 1987.

Osband, Linda. *Victorian House Style.* London: David & Charles, 1991.

W

WATER

The availability of water is a crucial element in the choice of campsite or permanent dwelling. Well-digging technology and brick-lined shafts were first found in Harappa, an ancient Indus Valley civilization. An archeological dig at Dholavira in Gujarat, India, disclosed a huge reservoir supplying a city dating to 3000 BCE. The complex water management system held 325,000 cubic yards of rainwater to fill Harappan home cisterns for bathing, cooking, and drinking. A series of brick culverts and drainage lines channeled waste water from the city. The success of hydraulic engineers contributed to the vigor of the community, a mercantile center that traded with Mesopotamia, Persia, and southern Arabia.

The transportation of water from source to kitchen was a major drain on energy, equipment, dray animals, and time. An agrarian family's use of around two hundred gallons per day added up to three hundred tons of water per year lifted bucket by bucket, usually by women or slaves. Thus, the rise of cities produced a need for pipes and plumbing. The Indus civilization south of the Himalayas between Afghanistan and India created a draining system around 2700 BCE to dispose of rainwater and home wastes. Ceramic artisans shaped pipes to standard so each would fit, straight end to flanged end, and would accommodate a tight asphalt cementum. Each householder accessed a sanitation system that drained bathwater, kitchen refuse, and sewage from baked brick privies into gutters and street drains that flowed into under-street mains. At

Water well.

WATER

intervals, civic planners added sedimentation tanks to end problems with clogging.

The technology of city water service reached Europe and the Middle East by 2500 BCE. Within the next half century, planners of the burial monument of Sahurê, an Egyptian pharaoh, installed a quarter mile of copper pipe at Abusir. Scientists consider the shaping of sheet metal into pipe a breakthrough in water technology. At Pergamum in Turkey, the production of a metal conduit allowed city planners to direct a water course two miles to a citadel through a lead pipe positioned on stone stanchions. The only power source was water pressure.

When Sir Arthur Evans unearthed the ancient Cretan palace of King Minos at Knossos north of Egypt in 1900, he revealed a surprisingly well ordered water system from before 2000 BCE that linked cisterns to a source seven miles away. To assure free flow, clay workers had tapered pipes to boost water pressure, thus flushing each segment of sediment. Kitchen drainage passed through interlocking terra cotta pipes. A sanitary water system beneath the Queen's Hall consisted of an earthenware bathtub and flush toilet. To drain sewage from the palace, the user poured water into a stone slab, beneath which waste entered an underground stream.

Water systems became a criterion for judging the complexity and sophistication of rulers and their realms. Persian *qanats*, tunnels directing groundwater to homes, date to 700 BCE and continued to serve the city of Tehran into the 1930s. The Persian king was so taken with the purity of spring water that he demanded it at his table in an early example of bottled drinking water. In 690 BCE, Assyrian water agents, copying an older Armenian network, equipped Nineveh with water piped in from a canal and aqueduct system. In addition to supplying kitchens and baths, the flow moistened King Sennacherib's garden.

Wells for home use replicated in miniature the water systems of cities. Chinese well diggers thrived from prehistory. Around 600 BCE, Austrian woodworkers were shaping winches and windlasses to ease the job of lifting. The technology powered the first water wells. Ancient Greek householders relied on wells cut into bedrock in a courtyard outside the kitchen. For purity, they lined the sides with terra cotta drums. In the fourth century BCE, the Athenian added a bell-shaped cistern at the corner of the roof to make up for a falling water table with collected rainwater. Slaves could also fetch kitchen supplies from public fountains, a common gathering spot for domestics and the poor.

In the home, a regular supply of clean water was a necessary element of table courtesy, as displayed in ancient Egypt, where finger food required ewers and basins of water for frequent hand rinsing. Archimedes, an engineer and mathematician living in Alexandria, invented the hand-turned water screw in 236 BCE, making the householder's transportation of water from its source easier. The later addition of a wing to the shaft applied water force to turning the screw and automatically pumping water for home use. From the fifth century BCE, the Greek Olynthus townhouse situated the kitchen downstairs with access to a fountain house or communal water cistern. The same shared arrangement afforded the women of first-century CE Nazareth only one source, Mary's Well. In Fez, a tiled courtyard at the center of the old city focused on the fountain at center, where kitchen staff filled ewers and guests rinsed mouths and hands before entering the dining area. In contrast, advanced technology offered clay drains and sewers, which turned Athens into a model city.

Descriptions of ancient technology often centered on water and drainage systems. Herodotus, the Greek traveler and historian and author of *The Persian Wars* (ca. 450 BCE) marveled at the ingenuity of Arabs at the Corys River, which flowed into the Red Sea. In Book III, he commented that an Arab king "made a pipe of the skins of oxen and other beasts, reaching from this river all the way to the desert, and so brought the water to certain cisterns which he had dug in the desert to receive it." (Herodotus 1942, 214) The historian added that the three-stage pipeline traversed an expanse the equivalent of a twelve-day ride from river to destination.

Roman water suppliers, masters of engineering, built aqueducts from 312 BCE to 455 CE throughout the empire. Around 97 CE, Sextus Julius Frontinus, a surveyor and superintendent of the city waterworks appointed under the emperor Nerva, described the design and erection of eleven aqueducts totaling 260 miles in length to supply the city from distant reservoirs, lakes, and rivers. Through channels built under and above the surface, the largest, the Aqua Marcia, fed city supplies over a fifty-seven-mile span. Pipelines passed over granite piers graced by the Roman arch, one of the major contributions of ancient engineering to domestic and civic health and stability. The city supplied three hundred gallons per person daily. To halt waste and boost the water department's income, Frontinus installed bronze *moduli* (valves) on mains and positioned pipes to deliver water to each home along the line. The bore of the pipe determined how much homeowners paid for the service. A similar system in Constantinople, Rome's eastern capital, limited mansions to two-inch pipes, smaller homes to one and a half-inch pipes, and the poorest residents to half-inch pipes.

A small private house that survives at Pompeii preserves a self-contained water system fed by rainwater. Perhaps the home of a person too poor to afford a connection to city water lines, it contained a lengthy channel to collect rain and conduct it to a concrete house cistern. Through the well-hole, users drew small amounts for washing and cooking and carried their loads across the courtyard to a tiny L-shaped kitchen.

In Badia, the Jordanian desert, in the first century CE, Roman conquerors of the Nabataean Arabs installed an ingenious water system. To reduce the stress on aquifers to supply homes and farms, engineers installed catchments in native rock and dammed natural depressions. Connected by canals, the system watered shade trees that slowed evaporation. Terracing reduced waste. The system supplied soldiers at the Roman fort and Nabataean homes into the Byzantine and early Islamic eras.

In the New World, native peoples chose home sites near the best water supplies. Water figures in the *Popul Vuh* (1558), the nation's mythos and scripture, were crucial to the life and lore of the Quiché or utlateca, Mayan highlanders of Mesoamerica. Originating north of Guatemala around 700 CE, they evolved a cave culture situated in the limestone caverns along the Caves Branch River and into the Sibun Hills valley. In this life-affirming locale, nature offered dry storage for maize, underground aquifers to supply their homes, and pure water dripping from stalactites for drinking and ritual use.

The Anasazi of the southwestern United States built their multi-storied residences based on the availability of spring water. The surviving housing complexes at Hovenweep, Mesa Verde, and Yellow Jacket bear out this dictum for settling. Another aspect of native settlements was the ability to control water through engineered hydrology. At Chaco Canyon, Hovenweep, Lowry Ruins, and Pueblo Blanco, dams, reservoirs, canals, and water baffles enabled residents of a dry landscape to catch and hold water for gardening and domestic use.

Throughout the Middle Ages, waterbearers' collection from numerous sources—streams, fountains, springs, rivers, swamps, wells—forced the cook to consider water's purity and use for drinking, food preparation, dishwashing, floor mopping, or other purposes. The casual pollution of ponds with drainage from an abattoir, dyehouse, or launderer's tubs was standard procedure, as was the emptying of garbage and dead animals and the scouring of chamber pots. Wise individuals remained wary of the provenance of moats and flowing water, particularly their proximity to privies, and shunned suspect wells.

Along at least one wall of the typical estate kitchen stood a heavy stone sink hollowed out to accommodate cook pots and equipped with drains, which led to cesspools. The washing center suited varied tasks—the cleaning of fresh greens and vegetables, cleansing of dishes and cutlery, and laundering of clothes. Medieval water systems depended on gravity to refill central reservoirs on each floor of a castle or estate. Muslim technology increased the convenience of water to homes in 1300 with the inventions of durable masonry dams and the noria, a hydraulic wheel powered by water or animals. With ample water to the kitchen garden, diets improved and grew more varied with the introduction of citrus trees, rice, and sugar cane.

Water supplies concerned local authorities in the sixteenth and seventeenth centuries, when law enforcers fined householders for watering stock, drowning cats, or rinsing fish or animal entrails at public spigots. From the sixteenth to the nineteenth centuries, country homeowners depended on hand pumps, hoists, or donkey wheels for lifting well water in buckets. Even the kitchen equipped with its own well forced cooks into a cyclic lowering and lifting of buckets. In London, drays carried portable wood water containers attached to shoulder yokes for selling pure water house to house. Where piping was feasible, householders laid charred-out tree trunks or earthenware drainpipe, fitting the tapered end of one pipe into the open mouth of the next section. Because there was pitch but no mortar in the fitting, the shifting of earth during winter heaving and spring thaw sometimes allowed silt to cloud supplies. For this reason, cooks left pots of muddy water standing at the hearth to settle solids to the bottom. Water carters filled heavy hogsheads of fresh spring water and portaged it door to door.

Technology improved these haphazard supplies. In 1681, during the reign of England's Charles II, Sir Samuel Morland connected Windsor Castle with water from the Thames River by means of a water wheel. A similar pump station supplied Blenheim Castle around 1706 by lifting water to a hilltop cistern, England's first water tower. The steam-driven pump, a great kitchen labor saver, didn't come into use until the end of the eighteenth century.

Hawaiian islanders valued their fresh water for themselves and for the whaling vessels that brought trade to the harbors in exchange for a refilling of galley supplies. Because rainfall was erratic and uneven in the Society Islands, locals depended on artesian wells in lava rock or redistributed such abundant sources of rainfall as the two hundred inches per year from Manoa Valley to Lanai, Kahoolawe, and Nihoa, all desert spots. Householders traditionally cut, carved, and lined canals with rock and built and reshaped land masses to direct water to their home ditches, flumes, and aqueducts.

To early Native American women, the rawhide water bag was an essential vessel. Made from hide laced with babiche into a reservoir or from an animal stomach tied with a strap, the bag was an easy burden carried to a stream, maneuvered onto a tumpline around the forehead, and suspended down the back. It bore the household supply of fresh water for cooking and cleaning as well as comforting the sick and washing small children. Because individuals considered water dead after it sat unused overnight, morning rinsing and refilling of the water bag was a standard chore. When water supplies dried up, the Pueblo relied on the heart of saguaro cactus, a reliable source of liquid.

In colonial America, water could be lethal. Most people avoided it in favor of chocolate, coffee, and tea. By boiling kitchen supplies to make these beverages, drinkers killed bacteria that caused amoebic dysentery, cholera, and typhoid, the most feared water-borne diseases. Those who had pure wells used buckets staved in oak for drawing water. The suction bucket improved the process by applying an iron trap door to the bottom. As the bucket entered the well, pressure forced the door upward on its leather hinge. When the filler began cranking the bucket upward, water pressure sealed the bottom into place.

An adjunct of the colonial water system was the springhouse, a stone building or log shed built partially underground. It channeled the flow from a spring through a raised trough or floor-level groove at a stable temperature of 58 degrees. Householders entered the building via stepping stones and placed stoneware crocks of milk and butter and pans of vegetables and fruit directly into the flow. Kept immaculately clean and whitewashed and aired through louvered windows, wire mesh, or shutters, the dark, mossy springhouse was an inviting respite from a hot kitchen or wash pot and also a favorite play area for children during summer months. For backup, the householder caught rainwater in tubs, noggins, jars, and pails. They used their supply quickly, before the growth of "wiggle-tails" and algae. (Algren 1992, 14) For piped-in convenience, families connected hollow logs and limbs, clay pipe, or metal tubing to direct flowing water above a dwelling by gravity into the kitchen. As a filter for trash and sediment, they tied linen or cheesecloth over the spout.

After Jacob Schweppe began bottling mineral water in Geneva in 1783, Schweppe of London made soda water available commercially in the 1790s. It enhanced the American drug store, where customers bought the bubbly drink as a digestive aid. In 1807, Dr. Philip Syng Physick, a Philadelphia physician, had the chemist Townsend Speakman flavor soda water with fruit juice, the beginning of the American carbonated drink industry. At the first soda fountain, Elias Magloire Durand, a French-trained chemist, began dispensing fizzy drinks in Philadelphia in 1825.

At table or on the sideboard, hosts provided soda water from a gasogene (or gazogene), a tall glass device that infused water with a refreshing effervescence. The two-stage, wire-covered body, shaped like an hourglass, held packets of bicarbonate of soda and tartaric acid. The user discharged gas from a small bulb into reserves and filled glasses from a tap at the top of the stem.

Shakers who established communes in New England, New York, Kentucky, Ohio, and Pennsylvania devised innovative water controls. The first hydraulic water system introduced water mechanics to Kentucky in 1831. Matthew B. Carter invented a waterwheel; Thomas Wells and George Wickersham followed with a screw propeller and a turbine waterwheel, the first to feature controlling gates at a given horsepower.

Less convenient, the frontier of Currency Creek in Adelaide, South Australia, offered water to those willing to dig for it. An unidentified letter in the July 1868 issue of *English Woman's Journal* summarized the hard dig through rock for an inadequate spurt. To supply the home, the family made "a large tank, fifteen feet long and six deep; if we can get that full this winter, which bids fair to be a wet one, I think we shall find it enough for all domestic purpose." ("On Assisted," 1868, 334)

Along the American frontier, pioneers encountered their own need to control water supplies to expedite the grueling journey across the Continental Divide to the West. The danger to westerers and their livestock of running dry or encountering alkali springs often precipitated disaster. In a dry season, locating water in dry, porous sand began with a stick or ramrod and some excavation. For sinking a well, diggers had to perforate a flour barrel with small holes to use as a curb of cave-ins and force the siding into the well while removing sand with shovels. Other methods of locating water included looking for green swards or tall grass, cottonwood or willows, flags, and rushes, all of which flourished around water. Fresh animal tracks, herds of bison or deer, and flights of birds and water fowl could also lead to water. During rain, the tent dweller could catch drippings in a suspended cloth or blanket weighted at the center or in a bucket below.

Settlers fortunate enough to build near running water still had to carry buckets indoors for cooking, dishwashing, laundry, and bathing. Some had spring rooms adjacent to the kitchen, where cold water flowed constantly; others kept rain barrels at the end of an eave to catch drinking water, often called soft water for the absence of iron found in springs and branches. One South Dakota family hauled fifty-gallon barrels of fresh water on a stoneboat pulled by a team of horses. To keep the supply palatable and clean, they upended washtubs or draped tarps over the tops. In winter, melting snow at the hearth was easier than carrying water overland.

The lucky household had piped-in water from a spring and drainage that took gray water far enough from the house to prevent contagion. To protect the iron pump station, which was usually situated outside the kitchen door, Lydia Maria Child's *The American Frugal Housewife* (1836) suggested setting the handle at its highest point each night to keep it from freezing. (McCutcheon 1993, 96)

Recycling was a necessity. Housewives bathed their children and themselves in the same water and reused dishwater to mop floors, soak work clothes, or water kitchen beds. During a drought or when rising sap dried up wells, families searched out sinkholes and loaded barrels that they had previously burned out with a handful of sulfur or sanitized with a flaming pine knot. They returned home with cloudy, suspect water that had to be filtered, boiled, and stored in jugs. For toilets, families relied on privies, chamber pots, or the outdoors.

After the installation of municipal water systems, beginning with Croton, New York, in 1842, changes in water quality and supply brought luxury and ease to the home. The water heater got its start in 1868, when Benjamin Waddy Maughan invented the gas geyser. The concept of heating water as it advanced up a hollow coil in a brass and copper tank introduced users to instant hot water. The Boiling Steam Therma, an English model positioned above the kitchen sink, dispensed the same rapidly heated water for culinary use. By the 1890s, the marriage of electricity to water heating further alleviated the homemaker of the heavy job of hauling and heating water on the stove and the danger of scalds from distributing it for household use. Advances notwithstanding, families around the world continued to suffer from inadequate and impure water supplies in slums and in rural areas.

After the railroad improved provisioning of the American West by hauling fresh goods from the East, householders could buy fresh water. Peddlers transported it on wagons and sold it in the streets of frontier towns. The purity improved, but at great price. A woman complained, "The alternative was a choice between the strong alkaline water of the Rio Grande or the purchase of melted manufactured ice at its great cost." (Brown 1958, 198)

For the individual home, the 1923 Sears, Roebuck catalog featured three water heating models. For ease of replenishing a family supply, the Eveready, sold for $99.85, promised self-starting and stopping. The advertiser guaranteed, "Night or Day It Never Forgets

to Pump When Water Is Needed." (Schroeder 1973, 695) At half the price, the Water Boy pneumatic water supply system, operated by a hand-turned balance wheel. None of the ad copy commented on linings, water purity, sediment, taste, or odor.

Women's magazines added water concerns to their list of domestic concerns. Advertisements in *Good Housekeeping* featured Anaconda brass pipe as an answer to health concerns and frequent repairs in water lines. In the April 1925 issue of the same magazine, Wayne Tank and Pump Company boldly entered the field with the water softener. A forbidding photo of a length of pipe corroded with lime and magnesia warned that mounting scale spread particles on foods, chapped hands, and destroyed the taste of coffee and tea. The company offered to filter particulate to produce the most health-affirming water for home use.

The miracle of turning seawater into fresh improved island life considerably. In Curaçao off the coast of Venezuela, rainwater and natural supplies of drinking water were so threatened that, in 1928, residents had to erect desalination plants at Riffort and Penstraat. The updated plant built at Mundo Nobo in 1948 used steam to generate electricity and to heat brine and evaporate water for distillation through calcium and carbon filters. The system worked so well that other islands studied the Curaçao method to ease their own shortages.

Twentieth-century water systems improved with the laying of asbestos cement, ductile iron, reinforced concrete, and steel pipelines. In February 2001, the water expert Peter H. Gleick, author of *The World's Water* (2000) and director of the Pacific Institute for Studies in Development, Environment and Security in Oakland, California, published a projection of the world's water needs. By the year 2025, he predicted, water-use efficiency will fall short of supplying the population. Around 40 percent of 7.2 billion people globally will have to alter their daily needs, especially in the stressed North African countries and Saudi Arabia. Scarcity in India, Pakistan, Afghanistan, South Africa, Sudan, and Ecuador will exceed the needs of northern China and the southwestern United States, both of which are prone to severe shortages. One solution to profligate abuse of water is the curtailment of home leaks, for example, in Mexico City, which wastes enough water to supply the city of Rome. Another possible salvation is the creation of dual systems, with potable water for drinking and cooking and gray water for flushing toilets and watering gardens. Numerous home inventions augment, clean, and distribute supplies of potable water, including on-line or tap-mounted filtration systems, sink-mounted heaters dispensing boiling water for rehydrating soups and making instant beverages, and refrigerator doors equipped with filtered water and chipped or block ice.

Further Reading

Cate, Curtis, "Taking the Waters at Vichy," *Horizons*, spring 1976, 18–21.

Edwards, Mike, "Indus Civilization," *National Geographic*, June 2000, 108–131.

Eigeland, Tor, "Understanding the Badia," *Aramco World*, November–December 1997, 10–17.

Evans, Harry B. *Water Distribution in Ancient Rome: The Evidence of Frontinus*. Ann Arbor: University of Michigan Press, 1994.

Gleick, Peter H., "Making Every Drop Count," *Scientific American*, February 2001, 40–45.

Haley, Bruce. *The Healthy Body and Victorian Culture*. Cambridge, Mass.: Harvard University Press, 1978.

Kumar, M., "Aqua Dholavira," *Archaeology*, November/December 2000, 22.

Periam, Jonathan. *The Home & Farm Manual: A Pictorial Encyclopedia of Farm, Garden, Household, Architectural, Legal, Medical and Social Information*. New York: Crown Publishers, 1984.

Richards, Ellen H., and Alpheus G. Woodman. *Air, Water, and Food: From a Sanitary Standpoint*. New York: John Wiley & Sons, 1901.

Vesey, Tom, "Up on the Roof," *Islands*, December 2000, 51–56.

WEIGHTS AND MEASURES

Standardized measuring is an agreement among nations as to the exact volume or weight of a single unit of a commodity. Sumerians, Babylonians, Egyptians, and Harappans of the Indus Valley were the first cultures to standardize metrology, primarily for weighing grain as an aid to farmers and traders. In answer to the demand for units of measure, the first unit created was the cubit, a measure of length from the elbow to the tip of the extended middle finger on the average Egyptian, Greek, Babylonian, and Hebrew. As a market scale, Egyptian inventors built a rudimentary balance beam or equal-arm balance around 5000 BCE. A primitive hand-held version applied the arithmetic principle of equal measure to two pans suspended on cords equidistant from a center post.

Mentioned in the *Arthashastra* and the *Vajanaseyi Samhita*, the dual-pan device was the standard for market business among the Harappans who flourished in the Indus Valley from 2900 to 2600 BCE. They left polished cube weights in multiples of one, two, five, ten, twenty, one hundred, and upward. At Lothal, gold disks followed a decimal progression. The royal weight system was balanced in the king's favor to take a profit during the weighing process.

In 2600 BCE, the Babylonians based measures on the mina, the world's oldest standard weight, which Hammurabi listed in his law code and Jews and Babylonians applied to their monetary system. Around 2400 BCE, Babylonian traders evolved a dependable system of weights and measures based on weights carved in stone to look like sleeping ducks. Through adaptations in the Egyptian and Babylonian system came the measurements used by Hittites, Assyrians, and Phoenicians.

In Thebes around 1650 BCE, Ahmes (or Ahmose), scribe of Amenemhet III, copied the Rhind Papyrus, which was compiled two centuries earlier. It is named for the Scottish Egyptologist Alexander Henry Rhind, who acquired the document in 1858. A remarkable mathematical text, it summarized Egyptian weights and measures for the inventory and sale of beer and bread.

Hazelnuts on scales.
[© *Topic / Alamy.*]

Another method of standardizing measures was to sound vessels made of the same shape and weight. The sound waves produced identical pitch, which was more accurate than a system based on inconsistent shapes of human anatomy.

The Greeks appointed *metronomoi* (weight measurers), a group of authorities who verified weights and measures in the public market to assure consumers that traders were honest. Each unit of weight bore a symbol from nature, such as a turtle or a dolphin, long considered good luck. In the third century BCE, the mathematician and engineer Archimedes discovered the water displacement method, a means of measuring odd-shaped objects such as a fish or a turnip by placing it in a container of known volume, filling the container with water, then removing the water to calculate how much of the total was water and how much equaled the object. A humble stone measuring cup along with cording, plates, porringers, chalices, bowls, and plaited baskets survives from an archeological dig at Qumran, a desert commune settled around 130 BCE by Jewish ascetics in flight from Herodian persecutions.

Rome had its own idiosyncratic control on grocery purchasing. According to the London chef Alexis Soyer's translation Adolphe Duhart-Fauvet's *The Pantropheon: History of Food in All Ages* (1853), the mication system worked like a hand game. Buyer and seller held out fists. At the same instant they opened their hands to reveal any number of extended fingers. If they showed the same number, the seller's price ruled. When the number varied from hand to hand, the buyer named the price. The mication method ended in 360 CE with an edict calling for a system of weights rather than a battle of fingers.

Roman refinement of the method in the first century CE placed a pin through the beam that held the *bilanx* (dual pans), the word from which "balance" derives. The *pondus* or weight that created the balance evolved into "pound" and *unica* into "ounce. The name *libra* for scale attached to a sign of the zodiac and gave the English language the abbreviation lb. The Roman device was in use in Tangier on the Strait of Gibraltar when Muslim geographer Ibn Battuta, author of the travel memoir *Tuhfat al-Nuzzar fi Ghara'ib al-Amsar wa'Ajaib al'Asfar* (On Curiosities of Cities and Wonders of Travel, 1354), visited the area's vibrant food market.

The first major variant was the Danish and Roman unequal-arm bismar or steelyard, a metal arm on which the user attached an object on the hook end and slid weights on the free end to arrive at a balance. The bismar scale reached common market use in 200 BCE and remained in service for centuries to determine the weight of meat, grain sacks, wool, or silk. It earned so foul a reputation for deception that in 1450, the Archbishop of Canterbury excommunicated anyone owning

one. Nonetheless, the device standardized market exchange in China, Japan, and the Orkney and Shetland islands. In 1640, Francesco Curti painted a market-day picture of Bologna, where a dealer in loose domestic staples held at chest level his steelyard to weigh a housewife's small purchase. The placement was the best way for the eye to assure a balance and to display to the buyer the mark on which the weight freely swung.

Early standardization was a forerunner of the Muslim system of weights and measures that undergirded the trans-Saharan caravan trade from Gao, India, and Niger River settlements to North African commercial centers in Morocco, Tunisia, and Egypt. As an intercontinental exchange of goods flourished throughout the Middle Ages, the *Rus* (Norsemen), the Arabic term for Vikings, adopted Middle Eastern weights and measures and carried them north over the Volga River trade route to Scandinavia. For one specialty, the raisin trade, the Spanish invented the frail as a standard unit of measure.

Throughout Europe during the Middle Ages, consumers complained about lack of standardized measures and about the strike, the leveling stick or flat edge used to strike off quantities rising above a level dry measure. Householders had to learn a specific vocabulary of measurement terms for certain goods. Henry III of France ordered bakers to provide scales in shops, workrooms, and carts for customers to check the accuracy of each sale.

A familiar vessel in marketing and storage was the sack, a standard human measure equivalent to the amount a man could carry on his back. A loosely-filled sack with looped top allowed one man to carry it up a gangplank and down a ship's ladder to storage. For handholds, the user folded down the top and created two convenient ears at each end. For those amounts too heavy or awkward for loading on the shoulder, the carrier walked the sack along by shifting it side to side over the ground or dragged it onto a two-party hand barrow, a flat carryall with four handles resembling the wheelbarrow, which substituted a wheel for one of the human carriers. Stacking in a stairstep fashion rather than symmetrically allowed the user to withdraw one diagonal layer from top to bottom without shifting the rest.

Mechanical devices for direct weighing improved in the 1700s with the advent of knife-edge scales, first used by the Scottish apothecary and physicist Joseph Black. The knife-edged pivot, made from boron carbide, steel, or agate, allowed a beam to oscillate horizontally in response to placement of weights in the empty pan until the two pans reached equilibrium. Adjustable legs allowed for alignment of the balance case to compensate for use on unlevel surfaces or in moving farm wagons. An arrow marker or pointer indicated the center of the fulcrum. The French police regulated the use of these scales by requiring sellers to hang them higher than they could reach with their thumbs. Those bakers who persisted in cheating consumers risked fines, confiscation of their wares, destruction of ovens, and an *amende honorable*, a French euphemism for public flogging.

In the American colonies, Caleb Ray called himself the "Chief Skale-maker of New England" in the April 26, 1708, issue of the *Boston News-Letter*. At his Governours Dock shop, he made and sold weights and scales and strung and mended old ones. Professional regulation of scales was available in 1745. An advertisement in the November 12 issue announced the services of Jonathan Dakin, a mathematical balance maker, for the manufacture and mending of scale beams.

In the nineteenth century, European scales led the market in precision with the equal-arm version, which came in six styles: rider, keyboard, and chain, which needed no pan weights; and damped, constant load, and projection scales, which determine mass rather than weight. The equal-arm method of measurement remained in use until the twentieth-century hydraulic and electronic compensation scales further improved calculation of weight. To further standardize weights and measures to assure the shopper a fair trade, in 1824, the British government imposed a system of Imperial Units. Another nineteenth-century device for weighing small amounts of foodstuffs, the spring-loaded or candelabra platform scale, invented in 1840, was available in ivory, bronze, copper, or silver. A heavy-duty version suspended from overhead ended in a hook suited to weighing baled goods, bailed buckets, and bundles tied with twine.

Wood scales for home and farm were one of the specialties of the treen carver, who chose beech for spindle, crossbar, and swinging pans, bowls, or platters suspended from the opposite ends of the beam. The dairy worker selling blocks of butter or cheese carried goods to market in a tub. An adjunct to sales was the wood butter scale, a variation on the Roman balance beam that dangled square wood disks on wire or cord from each end of the horizontal timber. Asian peddlers made similar devices from bamboo. In England, the record of units sold was called a tally and the recorder a tallier, a term that elided into "teller."

In residential kitchens, homely methods remained in use. Elena Burman Molokhovets, author of the classic illustrated Russian cookbook *A Gift to Young Housewives* (1861), directed the reader to have on hand a silver teaspoon, a copper or iron one-*garnet* measure for flour and milk, and a medium-size glass, which held the same quantity as a large champagne bottle.

For measuring soup and preserves, she slipped a notched story stick or spill into the pot to indicate how far she needed to reduce liquids. She was more exacting with the manufacture of vodka. For measuring liquid density, she used a spirit thermometer or hydrometer, which the English physicist Robert Boyle first applied in his laboratory in 1675. She preferred the Réaumur temperature scale, devised in 1730 for Louis XIV by the French naturalist René-Antoine Ferchault de Réaumur with freezing set at zero and boiling at 80 degrees. Later in the Victorian era, the frozen dessert specialist Agnes Marshall, author of the classic *Ices Plain and Fancy: The Book of Ices* (1885), advertised her saccharometer, a device for measuring quantities of sugar in solutions, which she marketed under her logo from her own warehouse.

In 1908, Sears, Roebuck offered a full line of home and counter weighing devices in its annual catalog. Two models of spring-loaded scales with top hopper and front needle pointer and dial at 96 cents and $1.87 and a beam-suspended steelyard scale for 98 cents contrasted the low cost of a loose-weight balance beam weight scale at 74 cents and the more expensive steelyard scale at $3.73. The latter, resembling union scales used in trade, contained oil-tempered steel bearings, brass beams marked on each side in half-ounce increments, and a capacity of 240 pounds. The device was suitable for market weighing of bags of potatoes, sacks of flour and meal, whole sugar cones, and poultry.

The growing interest in home economics and controlled cookery brought more emphasis on precise measurements. To fulfill the demands of recipes naming exact amounts in cup, teaspoons, and tablespoons, companies began to stock more convenient tin and glass vessels marked in whole, half, third, and quarter denominations. In an instructive article for *Good Housekeeping* in 1930, staff member Dorothy B. Marsh gently explained that inexplicable failures at baking cakes and brewing coffee were usually the result of careless measuring. Her text outlined the scientific concept of proportion, especially flour to leavening for light, fluffy, digestible baked goods. She stressed that the Good Housekeeping Institute issued recipes that had been tried, tasted, and approved according to precise standards. She differentiated between wet and dry measure and discussed sifting, leveling, using the water displacement method of measuring solid shortening, and the importance of scraping or tapping the bottom to dislodge the last of each ingredient. A list of terms—creaming, stirring, beating, folding, kneading, cutting, larding, marinating, boiling, simmering, stewing, braising—complete the tutorial.

A month later, Helen Whitson Kendall, also on staff at the Good Housekeeping Institute, revisited the subject of measuring devices by reporting the findings of the United States Bureau of Standards and the Bureau of Home Economics. At the request of the American Home Economics Association, the staff studied specifications for measuring devices and named the best heat-proof glass and aluminum models with the clearest incremental markings for accurate dry or wet measure. She notes, "Controversy has arisen as to the correct measurement of the teaspoon, but since in household measurements the teaspoon has been considered for some time as 1/3 of a tablespooon, we have accepted this as our standard." (Kendall 1930, 94)

Photos in the February 1947 *Woman's Home Companion* presented the correct method of leveling a cup of sifted flour or teaspoon of baking powder or soda with a knife blade or spatula. For brown sugar, another picture showed the use of a spoon to press the grains into a cup. Wet measure of milk in a glass cup displayed the painted markings on the side for easy portioning of water, milk, syrup, or honey. A clear picture of the water displacement method of measuring solid shortening clarified the filling of the cup with water up to the amount that, added to the desired amount of shortening, equaled a full cup. By dropping shortening in small increments, the cook completed filling the measure up to the correct mark.

James A. Beard and collaborators opened their book, *The Cook's Catalogue* (1975), with lengthy commentary on the matter. Text commented, "To the extent that cooking is chemistry, a life-enhancing science, it imposes on us a degree of precision." Recommendations singled out some utensils by name and material—the Foley stainless steel measuring cups and spoons, plastic measurers with a slide to produce rulerlike accuracy, Pyrex measuring cups, a porcelain measuring pitcher, seesaw balance scoop, Danish wall scale, Pelouze portion-control scale, and French plastic scale and balance beam.

Early in 2001, the House of Lords for the first time since 1876 sat in judgment as the Court of Parliament. The case involved a merchant's right to apply imperial measures and weights rather than accede to the Department of Trade and Industry's Units of Measurement Regulations of 1994. Steven Thoburn of Sunderland, England, a second-generation greengrocer in Southwick, earned the nickname "metric martyr" for being the first to test a European Union Directive to sell commodities by metric units. ("'Metric Martyr' Faces," 2001) After he sold 34 pence worth of bananas by the pound to a local councilman, the Sunderland City Council prosecuted him for noncompliance with metric standards and served seizure notice of his imperial scales. After confiscation of equipment on July 4, 2000, he faced a fine of £5,000, costs of £200,000, and six months in prison. A local fishmonger, Neil Herron, also threatened by muncipal authorities for following

pounds and ounces, managed Thoburn's campaign against draconian trade regulations and launched petitions among customers.

In 1989, holdouts like Thoburn initially found a supporter in Prime Minister Margaret Thatcher, who gained a ten-year reprieve for traders selling loose goods in nonmetric units, but her successor, Tony Blair, did not pursue an extension as England began phasing out the imperial weight system. Pleading the previous Weights and Measures Act of 1985, which allowed trade in both imperial and metric units, Thoburn refused to use grams and kilograms and sold fruit and vegetables in the traditional pounds and ounces. After pursuing his case in the lower courts, Thoburn appealed judgment to the high court. Although he carried the backing of citizens who launched a grassroots resistance to compulsory metrification as a violation of British law, in April 2001, he lost the appeal and faced fines, court costs, and six months of probation.

Into the twenty-first century, home and institutional cooks in developed countries have relied on scales to determine exact amounts of foods allowed on controlled diets. In poorer, less industrialized lands, where government-regulated weights and measures are unknown, cooks and shoppers still weigh by guess and measure with a pinch and a handful. In Bolivia, tuna cans have become a standard measuring cup; West Africans rely on cigarette tins. In the street markets of Nicaragua, shoppers purchase goods gauged on homemade hand-held scales tied together with string and weighted with wood disks.

For the cook who wants to invest in better and more convenient weights and measures, the choices are numerous. For measuring the reduction of liquids, the stainless steel ruler has replaced the story stick, a skewer marked with notches or lines. The triple-beam balance scale, balanced on a knife-edge, supplies accurate weighing of foods placed in a pan at one end. By adding or removing small amounts, the user can determine the exact weight when the beam reaches a balance. A more expensive, but vastly more accurate determination derives from digital electronic scales, which are calibrated to weigh minute amounts. Such meticulous gauging is essential for diets that control metabolic imbalance or disease by maintaining a strict accounting of nutrients in food, for example, the Johns Hopkins high-fat diet used to control epilepsy.

See also **Poultry; Thermometers**

Further Reading

Alexander, David, and Pat Alexander, eds. *Eerdmans' Handbook to the Bible*. Icknield Way, Hertsfordshire: Lion Publishing, 1973.

Edwards, Mike, "Indus Civilization," *National Geographic*, June 2000, 108–131.

Ganeri, Anita. *The Story of Weights and Measures*. New York: Oxford University Press, 1996.

"Here's How We Measure in the Home Service Center," *Woman's Home Companion*, February 1947, 84–85.

Insoll, Timothy A., "The Road to Timbuktu: Trade & Empire," *Archaeology*, November/December 2000, 48–52.

Kendall, Helen Whitson, "Approved Measuring Cups," *Good Housekeeping*, September 1930, 94.

Marshall, Agnes B. *Mrs. A. B. Marshall's Cookery Book*. London: Simpton, Marshall, Hamilton, Kent, & Co., 1894.

WINE

Wine making has traditionally accessed much of the world's sweet fruits, grains, and heady herbs. The oldest extant bottled wine, found in China's Hunan Province in 1980, is over 3,300 years old. It turned up during an archeological dig in a Xinyang grave. The cultivation of vine fruits, which began in the Caucasus in 8000 BCE and Mesopotamia in 6000 BCE, eventually encompassed Russia, Turkey, and bible lands. Surviving seed of vineyard stock and storage vessels found in Georgia date to 5000 BCE. Cuttings were so valuable that, in 3000 BCE, families wrapped them in silver to bury with loved ones.

Fermentation of the wine grape, *Vitis vinifera,* probably began accidentally from the action of sugars and yeast in grape skins. The book of Genesis names Noah as the first viticulturist and winemaker after re-establishing his residence following the great flood. Egyptian vintners bought enough storage jars in 3000 BCE to spawn a jar industry. Meticulous warehousers marked corks and stamped sealed containers to identify wine maker and vintage.

As depicted in wall paintings from the tomb of Nakht at Thebes around 1400 BCE, wine-making was slave work. After stripping each trellis of clusters, laborers trod them in a stone pool, which drained into a vat. The finished product went into clay jugs for capping with perforated stoppers and labeling with estate name and vintage for perusal by tax assessors. An alternate method involved placing grapes in a bag on a frame. Slaves extracted juice from hulls by turning the screw end of the frame.

Galilean wine-making in the first century CE supplied the daily table. Servers watered the wine to accompany communal bowls of beans, lentils, cucumbers, onions, leeks, garlic, olive oil dressing, and desserts of dates, figs, and pomegranates. An energetic viticulture resulted in standardization of containers named for Bible characters:

Jeroboam	3.0 liters
Rehoboam	4.5 liters
Methuselah	6.0 liters
Salmanazar or Shalmaneser	9.0 liters
Balthazar	12.0 liters
Nebuchadnezzar	15.0 liters

Wine-making spread from Phoenicia and Egypt in 3000 BCE to Greece a millennium later, and to Italy, North Africa, and Sicily about 1000 BCE. Viticulture permeated the extremes of continental Europe and Russia by 500 BCE. Wine overtook mead as a standard beverage and relegated honey-based drinks to the tables of peasants who couldn't afford wine.

In China around 2000 BCE, the cook at the court of the emperor Yu accidentally fermented rice into wine. The innovation so overjoyed the emperor that he had the cook brew a quantity of rice wine for guests. Overindulgence so sapped his officials that the emperor issued regulations for serving rice wine, which wait staff should ladle into tiny cups and distribute only after imbibers had eaten and exercised. In

Vineyard scene from the Bayeaux Tapestry, 11th Century.

Wine merchants.

500 BCE, the city of Shao-Hsing became a wine capital for its making of a superior rice wine as payment of tribute. Shao-Hsing stock developed into a favorite cooking wine still favored for its use in poultry dishes.

The bases for wine gradually shifted to dates, grapes, and pears, with aromatic additives including chrysanthemum, pomegranate blossoms, ginger, saffron, honey, bamboo leaves, and pepper. Early Swiss winemakers stewed and sweetened sloes for wine, but to the south and east, the grape was the standard. For its delicacy and bouquet, grape wine entered palaces and homes of the wealthy as an aristocratic beverage envied by lower-class beer and mead drinkers. Around the Mediterranean, grapes and dates provided pulp and juice for sugar, table fruit, pressed cakes, and beverages.

In classical Greece, most wine came from pressed grapes, leaving bits of grape and vine for the server to strain from the liquid. The Greeks epitomized their national drink as the ideal of *yávos*, an amalgam of bright, moist succulence. They became the first oenophiles and displayed their personal preferences for imports as well as the Pramnian vintage that Homer lauded. In the mid-ninth century BCE, the poet also supplied a recipe for *kykeon* (punch), composed of wine, barley meal, honey, and goat cheese.

Standard vintages figure in the writings of Theophrastus, a fourth century BCE wine critic who compared the virtues of Chian, Lesbian, and Thasian imports and commented on blended wines. Descriptions note the dark color, which ranged from amber to black, and a strong aroma, perhaps from the goat or sheep skins in which vintners stored it or the pitch that sealed amphoras for storage and shipping. Home brewers at Rhodes concocted unusual wines from the myrtle berry and from myrrh and rushes, a low-alcohol variety highly prized about the Mediterranean.

At the *andron* (men's quarters), the Greek host followed the custom of serving wine from a *oinochoe* (wine jug) into a larger *krater* (mixing bowl) and adding water from a *hydria* (water pitcher) or of pouring wine into a *psykter* (wine cooler) and adding snow. A custom unknown to Scythians and other Mediterranean cultures, who drank their wine neat, the polite blending always began with wine first. The mingling of clear liquid in a dark base characterized the naming of a particular vessel, the *dinos* (whirlpool). Proportion favored two parts wine to five of water. Stronger blends of half and half or the serving of *akratos* (unmixed) was socially unacceptable in polite gatherings. From the bowl, it was a slave's job to dip blended wine into the *oinochoe* (jug) for serving in cups for long evening symposia, punctuated by frequent toasts and the sharing of communal wine bowls or loving cups.

Farther west, viticulture dominated European farmland because immigrant Attic vintners outnumbered farmers. In Italy, the first grapevines sprouted in Etruria and spread to the Vesuvian slopes of Italian Campania. It was Italy that became the first *oenopatria* (land of wine). The Etruscans planted the peninsula's first vineyards in the seventh century BCE. In the Greco-Roman residence, homemakers deposited the domestic supply of wine in a clay *amphora* (jar) or huge *dolia* (vat) buried in the earth up to the neck. From these, the staff served watered must, a wine concentrate, rather than beer, mead, or tea. The poor contented themselves with *acetum*, a thin wine bordering on vinegar. Only children and invalids drank milk, which was considered medicinal. The Aminean, Falernian, Opimian, and Nomentane vintages rivaled the Greeks' high standards.

Late in the Roman empire, Caelius Apicius, the author of *De Re Coquinaria* (On Cooking, late 300s CE.), the world's first cookbook, concentrated on cooking wines to the exclusion of table beverages and supplied advice on clarifying cloudy vintages with bean meal, vine ash, or egg white. He listed spiced and honeyed wines for serving with the *gustatio* appetizers. For making sauces and flavoring meat, fish, and vegetables, he chose Cretan *passum* (raisin wine) for the musk aroma and taste of the vine-dried muscatel or

WINE

psythian grape. The processing of *passum* began with the picking of dried clusters or hurrying the sun-drying process by spreading stems of grapes on trays or boiling them in olive oil. To make premium raisin wine, vintners soaked the dried fruit in a quality wine, then crushed and pressed them. A second press of pulp soaked in water produced an inferior *passum*.

In addition to raisin wine, Apicius mentioned *vinum* (table wine), *merum* (undiluted wine), *vino cotto* (condensed wine), a syrup made from strained must boiled down to a molasses consistency, and other grape additives to his cookery. He used *cerenum*, the must of pressed grapes, which cooks reduced a third by boiling; a more common flavoring, *defrutum* (pulp), underwent further reduction to a half volume. He also recommended the thickest and sweetest grape pulp, *sapa*, which cooks boiled down two-thirds to a syrup and used to preserve blackberries. His meticulous recipe for spiced wine was a tedious brew of three cookings of honey mixed with a small amount of wine. Skimmed and peppered, the mix was blended with gum mastic, saffron, date pits, and spikenard and heated with hot coals. He also mixed absinthe, a wormwood wine flavored with costmary and spikenard to be drunk as an aperitif. He filtered his violet and rose wines, which he made from fresh petals dried of dew. For dessert wine, his wine stewards added *carenum* or *defrutum* to drinkers' cups. Alternatives included the common *mulsum*, a honeyed wine, and *hydromeli*, a mead fermented from honey and rainwater.

The arrival of Julius Caesar's legions to Britain brought the first Mediterranean wine, an exotic beverage that contrasted to the heavier taste of domestic mead and ale. Troopers insisted that conquered peoples accept wine drinking as a cultural refinement. They also spread throughout the empire the Roman concept of the best vine stock, which they grafted to local vines to hybridize a plant that could survive farther north. An innovation to storage, the English oak vat imparted a wood flavor at the same time that it enhanced the maturing process. English wine makers never approached the skill of vintners to the south, but made tasty cherry liqueur and home brew from currant, damson, elderberry, gooseberry, and parsnips.

In the Middle Ages, wine-drinking was customary at mealtime. Abbeys produced some of Europe's most successful vintages, brandies, and liqueurs. Before vintners used a new wine jar, they steeped it in running water, with the mouth pointing upstream to force the current inside and out the bung hole to remove the clay taste. The favorite table wine in England was Bordeaux, which wait staff could serve soon after bottling. Butlers decanted wine from barrels into jugs and ewers for refreshing cups at table. For the last course, they sweetened drinks with sugar or honey and added spices to complement desserts selections of wafers, fruit, nuts, and cheese. After the English turned clerics out of their strongholds in the Tudor era, the skills developed over centuries dispersed with them and the vineyards were reclaimed by nature. Only the aristocratic oenophile had the leisure and money to pursue a private vineyard.

As for who should consume wine and when, Dr. Giacomo Albini, the author of *De Sanitatis Custodia* (On Guarding Health, 1341), ruled that moderate consumption of table wines aided health and digestion in adult. He believed that children aged five and under should have not wine, which might curdle their milk. Table service to preteens, who were still growing, should consist of watered wine poured sparingly during meals. Late in the era, a Latin treatise opined that wine deserved to be the primary beverage because it was a universal drink in France, Italy, and Iberia. Its benefits included strengthening the body, digesting meals, modifying ill-balanced humors, lifting the spirits, and restoring the mood.

As explained in Bartholomaeus de Glanville's *De Proprietatibus Rerum* (On the Suitability of Things, ca. 1450), hypocras or hippocras, the after-dinner spiced wine, piqued the appetite, comforted the stomach, and cleaned the circulatory system. To corroborate his findings, he cited a venerable source, Arab doctor Isaac ben Honain (ca. 900 CE). A precise service of hypocras derived from a table urn topped with a circle of lidded compartments. By opening a valve, the user could dispense spice into the main vat at table or relegate the task to a steward posted at a sideboard. In simpler surroundings, the spicer of wine suspended a cloth sack into a vat or ewer to unleash such ordinary flavors as cinnamon, clove, rosemary, sage, or nutmeg or more exotic hints of myrtle, hyssop, musk, or artemisia, also called wormwood. Another spiced table wine, claret or claré, received flavoring from a powdered mix of herbs added to honeyed brandy.

Consumption was ample, as with the French fishers of Newfoundland's Grand Banks, who received a ration between 2.5 and three liters daily; however, the quality of their allotment did not produce a constant state of inebriation, as would happen with current vintages. Burghers usually consumed white or rosé, a young vintage that the cook watered to make the bottle last. The moneyed merchant class and aristocrats developed more refined tastes for such imports as Cyprian, Tyrrhenean, and Corsican vintages. They trained sommeliers to select wines with distinct qualities of aroma and flavor for pairing with particular foods.

The national production of standard vintages reflected the status of the economy and the people's well being. To maintain a quality yield, the elite employed a wine steward to secure the cellar, which supplied the family until the next wine-making. A body of wine-rectifying lore protected the wholesaler from heavy losses. Cooking anthologies approved roasted grapeseed to discourage mold and boiled wheat and egg white and a sack of laserwort suspended in the bung hole to improve consistency. In the early sixteenth century, table service simplified with the creation of bottling and corking technology, as mentioned in the court educator and scholar John Palsgrave's *Leclaircissement de la Langue Francoyse* (Clarification of the French Language, 1530), a Renaissance English-French dictionary.

As of 1551, the English had to import from Gascony, Madeira, and the Rhineland their stock of sack, wine, and malmsey, which was of special use in easing parturient women. The use of wine in recipes was common, as demonstrated by instructions for making a gooseberry tart as recorded in the anonymous *A Proper New Booke of Cookery* (1575): "Take Goseberies and parboyle them in white wine claret or ale, and boyle withall a little white bread, then take them up and draw them through a strayner as thick as you can, with the yolkes of five Egges, then season it up with sugar, halfe a dishe of butter, to bake it." (Denny, n.d., 23)

Champagne, which had been in existence since the sixth century, so entranced Vencesilaus of Bohemia during his treaty discussions with Charles VI in 1387 that he extended his mission to Rheims several weeks to drink more. Three kings, Charles VI of Spain, Frances I of France, and Henry VIII of England, maintained personal vineyards at Ay to supply their tables with champagne. The creator of bubbly champagne was a Benedictine, the brotherhood best known for hospitality. At the abbey of Hautvillers, Dom Pérignon, cellarmaster to the monks for nearly half a century, managed the winery from 1668 to 1715. His contribution to the fine wines of France was sparkling wine, which he blended from several stocks, bottled, and corked with wood rather than the traditional oiled flax during secondary fermentation to retain effervescence. Perfected in 1670, monastery champagne was a forerunner of today's popular celebratory and holiday drink.

A Frenchwoman and daughter of the mayor of Rheims, Nicole-Barbe Clicquot, invented pink champagne and simplified the winemaking process by inventing a system of clarifying sparkling wines. Her experience with wine storage began after her marriage to a vintner and shipper in the 1790s. Widowhood forced her to assume responsibility for her husband's business. To solve the problem of yeast and sugar sedimentation over long years of storage, which added grit and reduced sparkle, she initiated *sur pointe* (upended) storage. To shore up the foundering champagne industry, she produced a clearer product by regular shaking, repositioning, and a brief uncorking to expel particles. Her clever use of gravity to solve the problem solidifed the fortunes of the Clicquot vineyard and fattened the profits of the Champagne district.

In Hungary, the creation of *tokaji aszú* (tokay or Ausbruch wine) began in the 1600s. By accident, a vintner had to postpone harvest of grapes that subsequently fermented on the vine. As they air-dried, the sugar increased and acidity dropped. Wine from tokay grapes charmed Louis XIV of France, who named the beverage "king of wines—wine of kings." (Römer, Vol. 1, 1995, 227) The popularity of the scarce vintage elevated it as a trade and gift item exchanged between princes and popes and reserved for table service at state occasions. Still produced the traditional way, wine-makers collect burst grapes for pressing in small quantities to create a floral aroma.

Wine steadily increased in popularity as a mealtime drink, in part because it pleased England's Georgian court. Sir Henry Thompson, Queen Victoria's surgeon and author of the popular *Food and Feeding* (1880), questioned the consumption of alcoholic drinks at the table, particularly aperitifs before dinner. He insisted that only top quality wine suited human physiology and recommended Sauterne with soup, Rhine or Moselle with fish, and Bordeaux and Burgundy with mutton and game. He deplored blending white wine with red or serving champagne, which tickled the tongue, but did nothing for the digestive tract. Not wholly pro-temperance in outlook, his book allowed for liqueur or mature champagne with dessert.

Wine developed into one of several dominant drinks in the Americas. Long before European settlement, the early Papago of southern Arizona fermented the juice of the saguaro cactus into strong wine. Immigrants from France, Italy, and Germany established vineyards. The wealthy imported madeira, malmsey, malvasia, port, sack, or sherry, which they valued for drinking, cooking, and medicinal purposes. Some vintages shipped well in wooden tuns and casks or bottles; Rhine wines made from traminer grapes arrived in stoneware jugs. Pottery used to bottle wines produced the greatest number of archeological finds from the colonial era. Southern settlers harvested tough native muscadines, James grapes, and scuppernongs when cuttings of European varieties failed to produce strong stock. Among those failing to turn the colonies into a wine source was Thomas Jefferson, who farmed the land around Monticello, his Virginia manse.

Punch was in vogue in 1888 when Benjamin Harrison was elected president of the United States. First Lady Caroline Scott Harrison, co-compiler of *Statesmen's Dishes and How to Cook Them* (1890), was fond of festive drinks for receptions and lawn parties. A favorite, regent punch, she based on black tea, which her kitchen staff laced with brandy, rum, orange and lemon juice, and champagne. Theodore and Edith Roosevelt enjoyed a spring punch based on a German *Maibowle*, comprised of woodruff stems and leaves, fresh strawberries, white wine, cognac, and Catawba wine or champagne.

In the Amana colonies, wine-making staff harvested grapes from wood trellises each fall. After the kitchen staff chose bunches for making into pies, jam, and juice, the vineyard crew commandeered helpers from schools and craft shops and handed out willow baskets for picking and delivering clusters to the press house. At the heavy wood press, workers extracted a first press for use in the winery, a cool, deep cellar of the *Saal* (meeting house) or village general store. The grape pulp passed to locally coopered vats for several days' fermentation, followed by two more pressings. The third yielded *Tresterwein*, the best vintage. Vintners added sugar and water and pumped the liquid into barrels, some holding one thousand gallons.

Each village filled from four to eight of these huge wood vats with the annual wine. The commune's vintner issued each adult an allotment of the harvest, around fifteen to twenty gallons, which individuals drew from vats into bottles and jugs. Non-drinkers shared allotments with those who liked wine. When laws forbade home wineries, Amanites complied with authorities. According to the historian Henry Schiff, in 1917, the commune pumped nineteen thousand gallons into the Iowa River.

In 1908, the entrepreneur Tajiro Sumida, an emigrant from Hiroshima to the Hawaiian Islands, became the West's first sake brewer. He met the challenge of supplying Japanese contract laborers with a reasonably priced rice wine equivalent to the beverages in Japan. He found backers for a sake factory, but had difficulty emulating the conditions under which traditional wine was made. Over a five-year period, he found an imported lactic acid to stabilize fermentation and mimicked the Japanese winter by refrigerating the brewing process. Other improvements he initiated include use of California rice stock for sake and stainless steel vats and implements. During the thirteen years of Prohibition, he maintained status as the island chain's top Japanese businessman and resumed operation after the law was repealed in 1933.

In 1973, Nonino winery, the leading producer of grappa in the Friuli section of Italy founded in 1897 by Orazio Nonino, pioneered Picolit, a single-grape vintage. The vintner's innovation revisited a popular, but crude peasant wine similar to *aqua vitae* or cognac that originated in Tuscany and Veneto. Original grappa makers, who were too poor to afford their own products,

distilled the fiery, high-powered drink from pressed leftovers—grape pits, skins, pomace, and stalks. In the 1400s, they sold it to seafarers and traders as a safe, unspoilable table wine. Nonino altered the national Italian spirit, boosting the aroma and quality with the addition of fresh grape stock. The new grappa expanded the market beyond the usual laboring class.

Europe's viticulture still thrives as a dominant element of world trade. In Hungary, farm families grow furmint grapes to make *tookai*, a sweet wine that accompanies meals. Slovenian vintners profit from sale of the Laski Riesling, a sweet white wine; Bosnians foster sauvignon and traminer wines, an addition to local slopes since World War II. Poles, who prefer mead and honeyed fruit wine, import their wines from Hungarian, Bulgarian, and Romanian stocks. In Andalusia, the familiar frosty pitcher of sangria, derived from the Urdu *sakkari* (sugared wine), refreshes native and tourist alike with a blend of citrus juices, apple, peach, or apricot and hearty burgundy.

In the twenty-first century, stores and mail-order catalogs tempted the oenophile with an array of implements. Essential to any wine cellar is a storage rack, where bottles are stored in a slightly damp, airy chamber kept between 50 and 54 degrees Fahrenheit. Hosts retrieve bottles hours before serving and leave them in the kitchen to be *chambré*, a technical term referring to readying them for uncorking and pouring. Bordeaux take the longest time because they must rise to around 64 degrees Fahrenheit. Dessert whites, served between 36 and 41 degrees Fahrenheit, take the shortest time,

Wine racks vary. A favorite shape is the X-shaped wood rack that unfolds accordion style, resembling a Roman library shelf. Home bars often display sterling silver or pewter wine collars to inhibit dripping and ornamental bottle stoppers to identify the vintage while sealing the opening and protecting remnants of wine until the next use. The familiar *tire-bouchon* (corkscrew) attaches to a variety of ingenious devices to remove the plug without risk of dropping pieces into the wine. The process precedes decanting to aerate and to separate wine from residue.

See also **Amphora**

Further Reading

Adam, David, "Physics: Lumps Keep Bubbly Bubbly," *Nature*, January 25, 2001.

Fredriksson, Lars, "The Liquor from Luzhou and the Secret of the Earth Cellar," *Oriental Studies*, No. 49–50, 1984.

McGovern, Patrick, "Meal for Mourners," *Archaeology*, July/August 2001, 28–29.

Römer, Joachim, and Michael Ditter, chief eds. *Culinaria: European Specialties*. Cologne, Ger.: Könemann, 1995.

WIRE

Many unassuming culinary implements are outgrowths of twisted wire, for example, the corrugated spoon and ladle, the dipping fork, the wire cage on a roasting spit, wire baskets for deep-fat fryers and asparagus steamers, and the domed mesh dishcover or fly screen. The Roman *cacabus* (boiling kettle) narrowed to a small mouth and wire handle for enclosed cookery and stewing. In the mid-1500s, macaroni makers inserted wire into the core of a length of dough to form a tunnel to admit flavored sauce.

Wire contributed dish warmers and drainers, egg baskets, potato boilers, pastry blenders, dishmops, and corn dryers. The tinker shaped tin wire into pie holders, cheese slicers, and oven peels for retrieving baked goods. Japanese fanciers of sesame have traditionally toasted seed in a long-handled tin holder topped with a wire mesh screen. In frontier dry-goods stores, wire held cones of sugar and suspended twine for easy access for wrapping packages.

Wire mesh was the main element of heavy-duty sieves, mechanical sifters, the aligner of rollers on spool washboards, and the *garde-manger*, a frame storage chest or larder well-aired and cool for hanging meat, poultry, game, and fish until it was tender. A flexible wire grapple adapted as cork puller, olive retriever, and dish cloth holder, which enabled kitchen workers to scrub the sooty insides of lamp chimneys and narrow-necked jugs. In Australia, a bent wire retrieved dampers (biscuits) from the ash of a cook fire. The fruit scalloper consisted of a wire handle holding a corrugated blade for slicing into fruits and vegetables.

An indispensible wire item, the whisk, blended wet and dry ingredients while incorporating air into the mix. According to Elizabeth (or Eliza) Smith's *The Compleat Housewife; or Accomplish'd Gentlewoman's Companion* (1727), the first printed cookbook in America, the whisk came into use in the eighteenth century as a mechanical means of leavening cake with beaten egg. It served the French chef in the making of cherry soufflé Montmorency, a puréed fruit cooked to the cracking stage in boiling water and blended with stiffly beatened egg white or cream. At the Pâtisserie Frascati, established in Paris around 1800, bakers specialized in the *galicien*, a butter cream cake lightened by whisking the sugar with eggs over low heat. Other uses for the wire pastry blender included mashing avocado for guacamole and chopping eggs and canned tomatoes into sauce.

In Europe, wire benefited some of the innovations of the era. In France, a twist of wire held champagne corks in place under strong pressure of internal gases. The use of wax and a wire wrap on champagne bottles also furnished Nicholas Appert with a suitable closure for the original canned goods. As described in the February 1809 issue of *Courier de l'Europe*, he secured food in glass under a vacuum seal with an airtight closure before boiling the containers to kill food-tainting microbes. Home canners applied a wire bail to glass jars of food before the invention of the Mason jar with screw-on lid. In Victorian homes, the call of the brass wire-and-pulley house bell summoned butler, maid, or kitchen staff, who recognized the tone of one particular bell. Wire also bound straw on handles for brooms and bristle to kitchen pastry brushes and, in the early 1900s, the utility brushes invented by the Nova Scotian businessman Alfred Carl Fuller.

A common wire mesh device for open-hearth cooking in rural America was the screen corn popper, a long-handled box or cylinder that held corn kernels in the heat until moisture trapped inside caused them to explode into fluffy white bits. An article in the *New York Times* dated August 3, 1890, describes the work of Francis P. Knowlton, a New Hampshire inventor who shaped the first wire corn popper in 1837. He intended to sell them at a Concord hardware dealership, but met with derision until users tried and accepted them.

Other wire devices include the electric kettle fitted with wire around the inner circumference, a revolutionary cooker that debuted at the Crystal Palace Great Exhibition of 1851; the wire helix corkscrew that the New York inventor George Blanchard attached to a tubular metal nutmeg grater in July 1856; the open-weave canister that C. A. Mills of Hazel Green, Wisconsin, inserted in his coffee roaster, patented in 1863; and the soap dispenser and dish racks that Josephine Garis Cochrane attached to the inside of the first dishwasher, which she invented in 1886. In *Common Sense in the Household: A Manual of Practical Housewifery* (1871), written by Marion Harland, pseudonym of author Mary Hawes Terhune, text promoted the latest in hand blenders—the wire-bladed egg beater for aerating fluffy desserts and the basis of soufflés.

In this same period, wire functioned as the *sine qua non* in various housewares. It was an essential attribute of the mouse traps—a garroting wire on Daniel Conner's "Claws" in 1876, on L. B. Brown and J. H. Norrow's wire cage trap that same year, and John Mast's popular Victor, a popular design patented in 1899 that remained in use for over a century. In 1897, a wire mesh gas toaster, a long-handled device, suspended bread slices over a gas flame; another innovation, the wire-handled griddle greaser with roller or detachable cloth dauber for spreading fat, aided the cook in lubricating metal surfaces. In 1908, the Sears, Roebuck catalog pictured a wood-handled potato masher for 4 cents with box-shaped wire head that "is well made and is the best masher on the market." (Schroeder, 1971, 464) The 1923 catalog listed wire brushes for cleaning grills and aluminum cookware with functional wire handles, a given on other kitchen items, including coal scuttles and utility and dairy buckets. For the circulation of chilled air around perishables, Sears refrigerators contained lightweight wire shelving that homeowners could position to suit the size of containers.

Wire goods contributed to other domestic items. In 1912, the Belling Company of England manufactured the Standard, an electric radiant-heating unit that passed electricity through wire-wrapped fireclay for heating kettles, warming dishes, and toasting bread. In the 1930s, wire frames enabled confectioners to dip candy eggs in sugar or chocolate coating. In Oklahoma City in 1937, Sylvan N. Goldman perfected the shopping cart and wire basket, the beginning of self-service grocery shopping that discounters later adapted for use in such mega-stores as K-Mart and Wal-mart. In the 1970s, Ettore and Alberto Alessi engineered an attractive wire fruit basket in stainless steel that earned renown at a display of artful household goods in Frankfurt's *Museum für Kunst* (Museum of Modern Art).

See also **Tinware; Vermin**

Further Reading

Periam, Jonathan. *The Home & Farm Manual: A Pictorial Encyclopedia of Farm, Garden, Household, Architectural, Legal, Medical and Social Information.* New York: Crown Publishers, 1984.

WITCHES' KITCHENS

The connection between bubbling cauldrons and witches dates far into the past, including Hindu witches who reputedly flew naked by night to commit acts of cannibalism. Hellish cooking lore also attaches to voodoo practitioners among the Fon of Dahomey, Yoruba of Nigeria, Kongo of Zaire and Angola, and Haitians of the Caribbean. In 1660, the Dutch artist Jacques (or Jakob) de Gheyn II painted *The Witches' Kitchen*, a demonic perversion of normal cooking activity. To prepare a heathen salve to enable them to fly, the subjects search cookbooks; cats, frogs, and skeletal remains lie on the floor, suggesting that animal and human tissue will supply ingredients. Above the kitchen fire, which perverts heat for cooking into energy for demonic ritual, a witch flies away on a broom. Ulrich Molitor's illustrations for *De Lanijs et Phitonicis Malieribus* (1489), the middle panel of Vienna's *Last Judgement* (1510), Peter Bruegel the Elder's *St. James and the Magician Hermogenes* (1565), and David Teniers the Younger's oil painting

Preparations for the Sabbath (ca. 1650) carry similar imagery and themes turning the normal into fearful forms of sorcery.

According to Governor John Winthrop's journal *The History of New England, 1630–1640* (1648), Margaret Jones was the first victim of American witch hunts. Coming under suspicion along with Alice Young, Mary Johnson, Joan Carrington, and Mary Parsons, Jones went to the gallows in Boston in 1648 for failing to refute evidence that she had a malignant touch. A practicing healer and midwife working out of her kitchen and garden, she concocted physics, aniseed, and elixirs and warned patients who failed to take medication that they would not recover. Because some of her predictions came true, the court construed her acts as ominous divinations. Stereotypes of the doer of evil depicted miscreants like Margaret Jones as aged, isolated crones and their work spaces as firesides or kitchens where noxious liquids bubbled in pots, enveloping vapors escaped into the air, and flickering candlelight cast shadows suggesting menace in the mundane. Witches were said to grow secret patches of such poisonous herbs as henbane, mandrake, monkshood, cowbane, belladonna, wormwood, thornapple, rye smut, and datura, a powerful hallucinogen also known as moonflower, which connected it with nighttime devilry. Witches reportedly smeared themselves with home-brewed emollients that enabled them to fly. To enhance their charms, they kept frogs and toads, lizards, snakes, owls, mice, hares, and wolves about the house as familiars to do their evil bidding or as additives to foul-smelling brews.

Word of mouth deepened suspicions that the witch's recipes demanded the unholy and inhumane. European witchhunters suspected their quarry of stirring up cauldrons of nightshade, a common pasture plant that killed livestock. The source of the drug atropine, a powerful nerve block, nightshade (also called henbane or belladonna) had an ancient history in Chinese necromancy as a means of summoning spirits and in Greek worship as a stimulant added to wine.

In secular courts, as described in Reginald Scot's *Discoverie of Witchcraft* (1584), officials used skewers to probe under suspects' fingernails to extract samples of ghastly cookery. Scott reported a recipe in which "The fat of yoong children, and seeth it with water in a brasen vessell, reserving the thickest of that which remaineth boiled in the bottome, which they laie up and keepe, untill occaision serveth to use it." (Scot) To round out the mix, they add "Eleoselinum, Aconitum, Frondes populeas, and Soote." (Ibid.) Witches purportedly intended these hearthside philters to impart supernatural powers and protection from enemies, particularly the church, which declared cauldron art a sacrilege and abomination.

In current terms, the witches of past eras were pagans and animists who revered phases of the moon, shifts of the zodiac, and the efficacy of herbs as abortifacients, toxins, talismans, aphrodisiacs, and charms. In the positive element of their work, they honored nine sacred plants: chamomile, chervil, crabapple, fennel, mugwort, nettle, plantain, sainfoin, and watercress, which they used in charms and elixirs to fend off evil. The prime protector was angelica, as well as clover, dill, garlic, and leek staved off spells, charms, and Satan himself. Those practitioners who chose to concoct poison could select from common plants—henbane, thornapple, arsenic, antimony, mercury, hemlock, wolfsbane, artemisia, or aconite, the head-high stalk with innocent blue flowers known as monkshood.

Traditionally, practice of the forbidden craft has been private. Because of centuries of suspicion and persecution, practitioners concealed their use of tools, herbs, and elements of nature for magical application. The basic needs were few. Sketches by Peter Breughel demonstrate multiple poses of witches with ordinary home and kitchen implements—spindle, rake, produce basket, funnel, keg, tongs, fork, grinding wheel, peel, whisk broom, and bellows.

In Latino culture, the *curandera* (nurse-midwife) has traditionally applied innate talents for making *remedios* to heal the sick and welcome newborns. Often labeled white witches, healers like Josephita Ortiz y Davis and Maria Sabina, a Mazatec herbalist from Huautla, Oaxaca, Mexico, set up kitchen centers for drying curative plants. Using ordinary knives, graters, and mortar and pestle sets, they compounded salves and medicines from roots, hallucinogens and mushrooms, and the *yerba buena* (good weed).

In Germany's Harz Mountains, celebrants reenact *Walpurgisnacht*, the Teutonic Halloween, are celebrated on April 30. Since 1908, a pharmacy, *Zum Roten Fingerhut* (The Red Thimble), has returned to the suspect cauldron for a new supply of *Schierke Feuerstein*, an herbal concoction first brewed by apothecary Willi Druber. The name "Walpurga" demonstrates the shift in folk beliefs from superstition to faith. The original Walpurga was a female hearth spirit who could prophesy from shapes mirrored in the Well of Wyrd and could harry housewives who neglected their domestic chores. Late in the eighth century CE, St. Walpurga, St. Boniface's missionary to the Swabians and abbess at Heidenheim convent, merged in German lore with the witchy Walpurga to bless the home and crops and protect the home cauldron from shortages. However, the shift to this benign medieval saint did not stay other communities from burning 1,500 witches between 1623 and 1633 between Bamburg and Würzberg.

See also **Aphrodisiacs; Kitchen Cures**

Further Reading

Aikman, Lonnelle. *Nature's Healing Arts: From Folk Medicine to Modern Drugs*. Washington, D.C.: National Geographic, 1966.

Kieckhefer, Richard. *Magic in the Middle Ages*. Cambridge: University of Cambridge Press, 1989.

Perrone, Bobette, H. Henrietta Stockel, and Victoria Krueger. *Medicine Women, Curanderas, and Women Doctors*. Norman: University of Oklahoma Press, 1989.

Russell, Jeffrey Burton. *Witchcraft in the Middle Ages*. Ithaca, N.Y.: Cornell University Press, 1972.

Vigil, Evangelina. *Woman of Her Word: Hispanic Women Write*. Houston, Tex.: Arte Publico Press, 1987.

WOKS

Unlike world cuisines that employ a selection of pots and knives, Asian cooking limits most tasks to cleaver, chopsticks, and wok. Originally formed from iron in the shape of a soup bowl to fit its curve into the flame, the wok supplied Chinese kitchens at all levels of society with a sturdy, multi-functional cooking surface that readily conducted heat without requiring large amounts of oil. Whether carbon steel, stainless steel, or aluminum, it adapted to baking, boiling, frying, dry roasting, steaming, and baking. Still performed in the early twenty-first century, stir-frying was the choice cooking method at stops and in dining cars along the Trans-Siberian Railway, where Chinese cooks prepared low-cost meals of fried rice. For the tea worker in the Jiuhua Mountains of China, the wok, whether electric or wood-fired, provided the smooth, seamless surface for pan-firing, drying, and hand-shaping tea leaves. The wok was so central to kitchen work that days suitable for a chef's culinary experimentation were traditionally characterized as *hoy wok* (open wok).

The longevity of the wok attests to its usefulness and versatility. In a Hunan tomb, archeologists discovered a wok along with the cook's remains and bamboo slips recording her recipes and culinary techniques. In Malaysia, wok cookery became a restaurant staple because of the influence of the Baba Nonya (Chinese-Malaysians). These traders arrived on the peninsula in the 1400s and specialized in stir-fry cookery featuring tofu and soy sauce. Their cuisine reached its peak in the late 1900s and early twentieth century. In the twenty-first century, each town has a resident *char koeyteow* (dark-fried Chinese noodles) expert. From a tray of fresh pork, sausage, prawns, garlic, bean sprouts, and sambal oelek, a blend of red chilies, salt, and brown sugar, he selects bits for stirring and tossing with noodles in his wok.

An important link between American and Chinese cooking methods derived from the text of *How to Cook and Eat in Chinese* (1945), a culinary classic by Buwei Yang Chao from Anhui, China, translated into English by her daughter Rulan. The foreword, composed by Hu Shih, credits Mrs. Chao with originating the term *ch'ao* or "stir-fry." The preface by the Nobelist Pearl Buck states that Mrs. Chao deserves a Nobel Peace Prize for "contributing to international understanding." Her book, written in collaboration with her husband, Yuen Ren Chao, preserved authentic Cantonese and northern Chinese cookery with red-cooking in soy sauce and clear-simmering in broth and spurred an interest in stir-frying. The newly coined term entered the cook's vocabulary and cooking skills as a standard term. Preserving the concept, Helen Brown's *West Coast Cook Book* (1952) transmitted to the East Coast kitchen principles and traditions that Californians had long before learned from their Asian cooks.

Woks became a given in studies of Asian domestic chores. In 1982, photographers for the National Geographic Society captured the one-handed work of a Kazak homemaker at an outdoor wok in a Tian Shan meadow. At an open pit over a pot of coals, she warmed yurt, heated a kettle of water for milk tea, and cooked bread at a lubricated metal wok. The work developed a rhythm as one hand held a circle of dough while the other slid a scoop under a nicely browned serving. In another view of wok cookery, Bai villagers simmered a pig's head snout upward in a wok to assure a prosperous year.

Into the twenty-first century, Chinese cooks maintained Taoist principles of balance and harmony, which derive from the *Analects* of Confucius, a series of aphorisms on lifestyle composed in the sixth century BCE. These specialists excel at stir-frying meat with *yow choy* (Chinese oil vegetable), water chestnuts, and other native vegetables, which they traditionally serve over rice. To limit the amount of fat needed, they season a new wok with fat and keep it oiled to lubricate the surface for nonstick cooking. The concept of rapid stir-fry is not limited to Asians. Australians frequently use the method, as do urban Lao cooks.

Chefs prefer the wok because its shape allows rapid stirring of foods in hot oil and removal to a cooler part of the surface to halt the absorption of fat. Classic technique varies for each dish whether it is slow simmering, stir-frying, steaming, sauteeing, marinating, boiling, lengthy simmering, marrying flavors, barbecuing, cold mixing, stewing, pounding, frying with sauce, or deep frying. (Lee 1962, 68–70) For steadiness and control, they place the bowl above a wok ring, a hollow steel circlet that fits over a stove burner.

Sometimes a complex or multi-stage dish requires a combination of wok cookery methods:

- Deep-frying of marinated, battered morsels cooks the inside to tender doneness while forming a crust on the exterior. To assess temperature change from placing cold foods into hot oil, cooks rely on frying thermometers. A Chinese steel-mesh strainer separates, turns, and lifts pieces and holds them above the heat for draining.
- Oil-blanching is a method of sealing exterior surfaces of meats and vegetables without overcooking the interiors. The strainer quickly ends heating by draining hot fat back into the wok.
- Water-blanching, which is similar to oil blanching, requires the boiling of several cups of water for quick processing of vegetables. To create an intense green in broccoli and other green vegetables, cooks add baking soda to the water, then strain and rinse in cold water or soak in an ice water bath to halt the cooking. This method is a standard preparation of foods for freezing and canning.
- Stock-blanching, a low-fat method of cooking foods, follows the water blanching procedure. After heating broth, the cook separates foods by density and size, first heating fibrous vegetables like cauliflower, *bok choy*, *wong nga baak* (Peking celery cabbage), onions, and carrots, then adding thin slices of meat or poultry. Cooking to a simultaneous end allows for a one-time removal of all foods for quick service to plates.
- Dry-roasting of nuts or sesame seeds requires a bare wok heated to a high temperature, then a reduction of heat for stirring of a single layer of pieces with a spatula. Rapid turning prevents scorching. Another use of dry roasting is the cooking of crêpe-thin pancakes as an accompaniment to Peking duck
- An innovative use of rack and Pyrex or porcelain dishes supports wok tempering for steaming. After the water heats in the bowl, the cook places a slotted rack over the bowl and sets dishes of food in the steam. Covering with the wok lid directs steam to the food and prepares them for more thorough cooking in a steamer basket.

Tools for wok cookery include a paddle-shaped wok brush with stiff bristles for cleaning, a wood or steel cover for steaming and boiling, a long-handled Chinese ladle formed from one piece of steel, and a steel mesh strainer. The favorite tool is the Chinese spatula, a spade-shaped utensil that slides over the seamless interior with greater ease than in a flat-bottomed pan. For cooking rice and tenderizing vegetables, the use of one or more circular frame bamboo steamers set on the bowl of the wok offers another method of adaptation to suit delicate foodstuffs. The steel skillet wok is a pierced foot basket with handle that allows the cook to keep delicate foods out of the flame.

See also **Frying**

Further Reading

Chao, Buwei Yang. *How to Cook and Eat in Chinese*. London: Faber and Faber, 1945.

Danforth, Kenneth C., ed. *Journey into China*. Washington, D.C.: National Geographic Society, 1982.

Rajah, Carol Selva. *Makan-Lah!: The True Taste of Malaysia*. Sydney, Australia: HarperCollins, 1996.

WOMEN'S MAGAZINES

Women's magazines followed the era of etiquette books and recipe collections as the next stage in womanly self-improvement. In 1852, publisher Samuel Orchart Beeton brought out the monthly *Englishwoman's Domestic Magazine* at 2 cents per copy. His brainchild, the first affordable women's publication and the first to treat issues of home management, offered essay competitions, columns on cooking for invalids and gardening, advice from Cupid's Letter-Bag, and commentary dignifying the tedious work of kitchen and home management.

After Beeton's marriage to Isabella Beeton, she took over the writing of household hints and kitchen advice and added a column on child care. Valued for her clear, concise style and inclusion of homey proverbs, she produced a spin-off, *The Book of Household Management* (1859), a classic in England, Canada, the United States, and Australia. In 1860, when *Englishwoman's Domestic Magazine* was selling sixty thousand copies a year, she enlarged the series, printed it on a higher grade of paper, and introduced color engravings. Her regular columns published such helpful household advice as making homemade paste from flour and beer, using perfumed oil to preserve leather, laundering blond lace in soft soap, and mixing oil of cloves, oil of caraway, gin or whiskey, and camphor to rid closets of moths. Her woman-to-woman essays brought her fame at the same time that they stimulated competition from other women's magazines.

English publishers, realizing the commercial potential of magazines for women, emulated the Beetons. *The Lady*, an imitation published in 1885, was one of forty-eight startups by the end of the century. Most offered economic and culinary advice and introduction to new kitchen gadgets and machines. For the outback females of Australia, one means of escaping their daily routine was through *Women's Weekly, Woman's Day*, and *New Idea*.

In the United States, one of the most popular publications tailored to a female readership was the Boston-based *American Ladies Magazine*. A didactic, moralistic proponent of the cult of womanhood, the magazine went into production in 1828 under the hand of its primary writer and America's first female editor, Sarah Josepha Buell Hale, author of *The Good Housekeeper* (1841).

When Hale sold her journal to Louis Antoine Godey in 1837, he altered the name to *Godey's Ladies Book* and reshaped content to mimic English journals for gentlewomen. The revamped magazine, which he intended to mold tastes and elevate middle-class American women, promoted household efficiency, fashion, and women's education in a format resembling current magazines. By 1898, competition from *Ladies' Home Companion, Good Housekeeping,* and *Vogue* ended Godey's magazine. The focus shifted from gentility to consumer awareness with the appeal of George Newne's *Homes and Gardens* to the middle-class Englishwoman. Odhams Press cultivated the same market in 1920 with *Ideal Home.*

Mass circulation of *Godey's Ladies Book, Good Housekeeping, McCall's, Pictorial Review,* and *Woman's Home Companion* burgeoned during the 1890s. The media introduced farm journals and sources of dress patterns, the focus of Ebenezer Butterick's *The Metropolitan*, renamed *The Delineator* in 1869. These trade papers issued articles on cooking, kitchen design, fashion, and household management in addition to romantic short fiction and blips of news and trends. They dispensed household hints to an audience composed primarily of women who managed servantless homes. More applicable to the kitchen was Agnes B. Marshall's *The Table*, a London weekly filled with recipes, crisp cooking tutelage, and even crisper opinions on events of the day.

The most successful publication, Cyrus H. K. Curtis's *Ladies' Home Journal*, initially edited by his wife, Louisa Knapp Curtis, debuted in 1883. Louisa Curtis personally conceived and tested domestic ideas, which she published in a column for farm women entitled "Woman and the Home." For its quality and content, *Ladies' Home Journal* became America's most popular and remunerative magazine.

Meanwhile, James McCall, founder of *McCall's*, died in 1883, leaving the magazine to the supervision of his wife. Mrs. George Bladsworth, writing under the pseudonym May Manton, began editing the publication. Her broadening of a fashion journal to include household tips and home management commentary boosted circulation to three hundred thousand. The glory years were shortlived, ending in 1890 when George Bladsworth himself took charge.

A Philadelphia grocer, Finley Acker, established *Table Talk* in 1886. One of the original domestic science magazines, it introduced home cooks to packaged biscuits and other new time-saving foodstuffs in a column called "Grocery News." Acker made a direct appeal to women to inform themselves on advancements in cookery by sponsoring the Philadelphia food exposition of 1892, which promoted such time-savers as Pettijohn's Breakfast Food, Pearline soap, Baker's cocoa, and hygienic, table-ready currants from Purity Dried Fruit. He engaged Sarah Tyson Rorer, "Queen of American Cookery" and the principal of the Philadelphia Cooking School, to write food articles. She established "Housekeepers' Inquiries," a question-and-answer column that popularized the magazine. Her input increased to "New Things for Table and Kitchen," a regular feature introducing new utensils, and "Keystone Dishes," recipes that stressed the recently invented Keystone eggbeater. Her product endorsements extended over a range of products, including Niagara corn starch, and preceded her founding of *Household News*, a more professional and less commercial endeavor than *Table Talk*.

From the late 1880s into the first decade of the twentieth century, women's magazines took up the campaign for pure food, drink, and drugs. The U.S. Congress passed the 1909 Pure Food and Drug Act. Among muckraking magazines, the *Christian Advocate, Popular Science,* and *Outlook* issued condemnations of addictive drugs and adulterated food. One of the strongest voices came from Edward Bok, publisher of *Ladies' Home Journal*.

A Dutch immigrant, Edward William Bok, who married Cyrus Curtis's daughter, edited *Ladies' Home Journal* from 1889 to 1919. Bok opened with a weekly column by the notable pulpit minister Henry Ward Beecher and hired the domestic efficiency expert Christine McGaffey Frederick to write a column. To familiarize himself with the feminine perspective, Bok surveyed his audience with general questions directed at readers. To gain reader confidence, he wrote the column "Side Talk to Girls" under the fictitious persona of the Ruth Ashmore and published such new and radical solutions to kitchen drudgery as community co-ops and kitchenless homes. The pervasive urge for self-improvement created a readership eager for print tutorials. In 1904, during the period when Sarah Rorer wrote kitchen articles for *Ladies' Home Journal*, Bok's magazine became America's first to achieve a circulation of one million readers. In 1917, the *Journal* drew a million letters from readers, many of whom posed direct questions to Rorer.

In 1892, Bok rejected patent medicine advertising as a source of revenue, a bold move for a women's magazine. By 1894, full-page food advertising promoted national brands, beginning with Van Camp. To upgrade family meals, readers began to buy brand names rather than unsanitary generic staples like crackers and pickles sold from open barrels. Bok's use of continued articles forced readers to shuffle through the magazine to additional pages at the back, an action exposing them repeatedly to advertisement. He also paired domestic topics with ads for baking soda and corn flakes. He hired doctors and nurses to compose medical columns to answer housewives' questions about home sanitation, nutrition, and personal hygiene.

During the rise of homemakers' zeal for better products, a parallel contingent read magazines that advised them on how to apportion the household budget. The establishment of *House Beautiful* in 1896 in Chicago introduced to the middle-class homemaker a pleasant method of keeping up with innovations in appliance and kitchen design, domestic management, and cooking techniques. Articles featured photos of real interiors and focused on specific problems with lighting, fireproofing, and economy of space.

Additional assistance to housewives came from *Good Housekeeping, Woman's Home Companion,* and *American Kitchen Magazine*, which boasted one of the most professional editorial staffs in domestic science publications. In 1894, Mary Johnson Bailey Lincoln, a teacher at Lasell Seminary in Auburn Dale, Massachusetts, food lecturer, and compiler of *The Boston School Kitchen Textbook* (1887), began authoring "From Day to Day," a culinary column for *American Kitchen Magazine* (1895–1903) that landed her the post of its food editor.

Along with features on personal development and short fiction, editors covered home concerns such as household help and new home architecture. Founded by Clark W. Bryan in 1885 as "A Family Journal Conducted in the Interests of the Higher Life of the Household," *Good Housekeeping* succeeded by maintaining a home-centered focus. (Tebbel & Zuckerman 1991, 102) In 1900, under the ownership of Phelps Publishing Company, the magazine issued findings of an experimental laboratory that evolved into the Good Housekeeping Institute. Its staff awarded editorial endorsement to Laura Hicks, the inventor of a scrubbing mitt with a corrugated surface for washing delicate laundry items. The magazine's approval helped her market the handy device with ad copy composed to appeal to female consumers.

In 1905, the editor of *Woman's Home Companion* engaged six famous cooks to author individual columns featuring twelve favorite recipes. The list included the food writers Marion Harland and Christine Terhune Herrick, the lecturer Mary Johnson Lincoln, the food editor Janet McKenzie Hill, Elizabeth O. Hiller of the Chicago Domestic Science Cooking School, and the domestic educator Fannie Farmer, the most famous cookbook author of the era. Later in the magazine's history, the food editor Dorothy Kirk compiled the *Woman's Home Companion Cook Book* (1942), a popular text still in print many years later.

Homemaker magazines gave homemakers an outlet for their frustration with heavy home and farm chores. Subscribers sent complaints to farm journals about the length of their workdays and the frustration of unending toil. *Cosmopolitan* magazine launched an essay contest based on the farm wife's daily existence and received grim descriptions of daily tasks.

When women earned recognition as a domestic economic voice, by the 1910s, advertisers took them and their issues more seriously. William Randolph Hearst, who acquired *Good Housekeeping* in 1911, pushed the magazine to first place and hired a nutritionist and U.S. Department of Agriculture chemist, Dr. Harvey W. Wiley, to market product endorsement under the Good Housekeeping Seal of Approval. Under his direction, the magazine's Bureau of Foods, Sanitation and Health reviewed food, toiletries, and pharmaceutical ads from 1912 to 1929. By 1922, the magazine was America's foremost domestic journal.

During a period of advancements in home sanitation, especially in urban areas, women's magazines and publications helped introduce higher levels of cleanliness. In foreign language newspapers and Yiddish magazines, Lever Brothers ran advertisements with photos of immigrant women learning American-style cleanliness and using types of soaps that served unique situations. In 1929, expenditure for ad copy in national periodicals rose beyond $300 million as advertisers shifted from print and line drawings to photos of women scrubbing with Old Dutch Cleanser, rinsing garments in Lux, or washing household grime from hands with Lifebuoy.

Central to the cult of middle-class domesticity, the British version of *Good Housekeeping*, established in 1922, contributed to the rise of consumerism among average citizens, most of whom were women. In 1927, two years after *Ideal Home* began promoting electric kitchen appliances, *Good Housekeeping* joined the campaign to jettison wood, coal, and gas in favor of clean, efficient electric power for heating, lighting, and cooking as well as for laundry and vacuuming floors. The company's institute began issuing cookbooks as inducements to renew magazine subscriptions. The text promised continued research and kitchen experimentation to assure readers of the best ideas, home plans, and recipes. Institute staff offered inexpensive English dishes, outdoor food preparation, weight reduction, recipes for leftovers, introduction to kitchen equipment, and nutritional advice. In the 1930s, the Good Housekeeping Studio was posting regular lists of in-house "folios" teaching women how to select window treatments, paint, woodwork, lighting, braided rugs, and period furnishings. Titles varied from an uncomplicated guide to planting herbs in "A Garden Calendar" to the problem-solving "Furnishing a House for a Family of Five" and "Making the Most of Nondescript Rooms."

The efficiency expert Christine Hunter Frederick, a syndicated columnist and product analyst for *Ladies'* *Home Journal* and author of a domestic handbook, *Household Engineering* (1920), characterized the effect of advertising in *Selling Mrs. Consumer* (1929). Her classic description of the tastes and responses of women to advertising presaged post-World War II consumerism. To insure consumer loyalty, manufacturers of appliances and convenience foods targeted the leisured class, who had the time and means to patronize dry-goods stores and boutiques.

German advertising psychologist Carl Albert Naether, author of *Advertising to Women* (1928), directed *Ladies' Home Journal's* copywriting for clothing, makeup, and food ads to femininity, housewifeliness, and motherhood with evocative language and imagery. He noted how women affected the economy: "With women buying 96 per cent of the dry goods, 67 per cent of the food stuffs, and 67 per cent even of the automobiles, the special ways and means of appealing to women are obviously of paramount importance in the general field of advertising and merchandising." (Naether 1928, xiii) He broke down home purchases item by item, noting that women also bought 87 percent of raw and market foods, 50 percent of meats, 50 percent of ranges, and 48 percent of drugs. He recommended selling to fashionable, prestigious women in *Vogue* and the ordinary housewife in *Good Housekeeping* and *Ladies' Home Journal*. Of *Ladies' Home Journal*, Naether declared its editorial policy "as broad as the activities of a woman who is interested in her home and her community." (Ibid., 9)

After homemakers' hard years of making do in the early 1930s, quality became an issue. According to Helen Damon-Moore's book *Magazines for the Millions* (1994), both *Ladies' Home Journal* and *Saturday Evening Post* helped shape American commercialism by building trust in professional domestic writers. In 1936, *Consumer Reports*, the journal of the Consumers Union, built a strong following for unbiased, ad-free information on such issues as purity of foods, quality of paper products and detergents, and appliances that were kind to the environment. By the beginning of the twenty-first century, the journal claimed 4.6 million readers.

In mid-century, women's magazines, despite their ubiquity, had not kept pace with the undercurrent of discontent that preceded the rise in feminism during the 1960s. In 1955, *Housekeeping Monthly* posted a set of guidelines for the stay-at-home wife. In deference to the male, she should have dinner waiting when he returned home. In addition to cooking to please, the article advised dressing to please, gaiety, household neatness, and clean children.

A new approach countering the long supremacy of *Ladies' Home Journal* derived from Donald P. Hanson and Frank Wheeler, officials of the A & P and creators of a free magazine, *Woman's Day*. Competing against *Family Circle*, Hanson and Wheeler's grocery store journal, later elevated to a sale item, focused on middle Americans on a budget. In addition to articles on housekeeping and grocery shopping, editors suggested ways to do more with less expenditure. By 1973, *Woman's Day* was grossing $45 million a year.

Other homemaker magazines such as *Demorest's Illustrated Monthly Magazine, Godey's Lady's Book, Young Housekeeper's Friend*, and *Farm Wife* have recognized and nurtured kitchen and farm labors since their inception. One example, *People's Journal*, reported the annual production of butter, a daily chore performed by farm women. Because of butter's continuing popularity with consumers, sale of home dairy goods bolstered family income in small, steady increments. Another farm journal lauded women for exhibiting their butter at county fairs for the small, but meaningful blue and red ribbons that honored their devotion to dairying and kitchen business.

The rise of feminism failed to end the reign of women's magazines. In the 1970s, kitchen stars Julia Child and James Beard began writing cookery columns. In Ireland, London-born Theodora Rosling Fitzgibbon freelanced food and travel articles for *Homes and Gardens* and *Harper's Bazaar* and compiled such regional fare as Irish stew, finnan haddie, bread pudding, and Hallowe'en Night's boiled bacon and cabbage for *A Taste of Ireland* (1968) and *Irish Traditional Food* (1983). For years she served *Image* magazine and the *Irish Times* as cooking editor. To the Irish, she was the fount of true Irish dishes of the eighteenth and nineteenth century that had fallen into disuse.

The merger of kitchen magazines with television cooking programs and websites brought the publishing industry into partnership with electronic media. Competing with *Food and Wine, Bon Appetit, Cook's Magazine,* and *Cuisine* was *Gourmet: The Magazine of Good Living*, a purist cook-from-scratch monthly that Earle R. MacAusland started during World War II. The attraction to both print and electronic versions of *Gourmet* were product advice on microwave ovens, food processors, and cooking tools. The monthly journal launched a successful drive for less opulent audiences with a televised cooking hour starring its editor Sara Moulton. Removing obstacles between tutor and home cook, the phone-in element made Moulton accessible. As though addressing the problems of home cooks, she prepared and plated attractive theme meals, for example, fruit-based, vegetarian, Italian, Asian, and American. Viewers could relax and focus on food selection and technique without worrying over writing down ingredients, temperatures, and cook times, all of which Moulton posted on the website.

The series was the design of the International Food Network, an independent research laboratory established in 1987 at the Cornell University Research and Technology Park in Ithaca, New York, and run by eighteen degreed food and nutrition technologists. Fuelled by its early success, in the early years of the twenty-first century, the Food Network airs extensive programming on the world's varied cuisine.

See also **Beard, James; Beeton, Isabella; Child, Julia; Frederick, Christine McGaffey; Hale, Sarah Josepha; Marshall, Agnes; Plastics; Rorer, Sarah Tyson**

Further Reading

Fisher, Katharine A., "Laying the Foundation of Good Housekeeping Institute," *Good Housekeeping*, April 1925, 86–87, 140.

Goodwin, Lorine Swainston. *The Pure Food, Drink, and Drug Crusaders, 1879-1914*. Jefferson, N.C.: McFarland, 1999.

Hale, Sarah Josepha. *Early American Cookery: "The Good Housekeeper, 1841,"* Mineola, N.Y.: Dover Publications, 1966.

Harwood, Catherine, "Housewives' Choice—Women as Consumers Between the Wars," *History Today*, March 1997.

Naether, Carl A. *Advertising to Women*. New York: Prentice-Hall, Inc., 1928.

Tebbel, John, and Mary Ellen Zuckerman. *The Magazine in America, 1741–1990*. New York: Oxford University Press, 1991.

White, Cynthia L. *Women's Magazines 1693–1968*. London: Michael Joseph, 1970.

Zuckerman, Mary Ellen. *A History of Popular Women's Magazines in the United States, 1792–1995*. Westport, Conn.: Greenwood Press, 1998.

WOOD

Sturdy and easily carved and planed, wood has served kitchens from ancient times for door and window frames, containers, tables and benches, and shelving. Derived from the same technology that made the first canoes and pirogues, bowl-making was a matter of burning out the cavity of a branch or log and halting the spread of fire with water, mud, or green bark. Some wood kitchen vessels have had numerous applications, for example, the flat, open bowl used as a gathering vessel, serving dish, and infant carrier by the Coolamon, aborigines of Australia. As early as the third millennium BCE, Mesopotamian kitchen staff sat on wood-frame stools topped with woven reeds. Some of the kitchen furnishings folded for portability and easy storage. Like potters, carvers earmarked vessels and implements with their unique shaping and bench markings since 1500 BCE, when Egyptians first whittled spoons as cooking implements. With copper saw, adze, ax, bow drill, chisel, and scraper, their carpenters worked at cedar, cypress, fir, and pine timbers shipped to the treeless desert from Phoenicia. Design of tables, chairs, cabinets, and chests featured skilled joinery and hardwood pegging. Quality handwork resulted in furnishings that survived to the twenty-first century, in part because dry air kept them from rotting.

The Ainu, the Japanese aborigines of the North Pacific living on Sakhalin Island and Hokkaido, carved wood bowls and spoons, a fish roe masher, and pierced or slotted spatulas, their utensils for eating a diet of skunk cabbage, anemone, parsnips, and wild garlic. Greek carvers made the prototype for personal spoons for eating eggs. According to Pliny the Elder, Romans prized similar goods shaped from rare, expensive wood veneers. Thus, it is not surprising that the cooper's job has been in existence in England since the arrival of Roman legions on British soil, when local crafters began producing tableware to their overlords' specifications. Originally, their wood pails had neither rope handle nor wire bail. For carrying, the user thrust a long dowel through small holes bored in the ears.

Coopering advanced under Gallic influence. From northern Europe, Roman traders imported bulbous oak barrels and casks bound with wood laths. Before these vessels were tight or after a long period of standing dry, they needed a steep in water to swell the joints to prevent them from leaking. For submerging wood vessels in water, the cooper filled them with large clean stones to assure complete coverage. Otherwise, the wood walls swelled unevenly and warped. For fish cleaning, oyster rinsing, pickling, salting, and brewing troughs, the user steeped each container to saturation to assure that the wood didn't absorb too much of the curing liquid. Dairy workers kept their cooperware separate from all other uses and soaked cheese molds and tubs in running water to remove salt.

In the farm kitchens of Modena and Reggio, Italy, as early as 1000 CE, the wood barrel was a family jewel. From great homemade tuns, families steeped a household stock of sweetly acidic balsamic vinegar for home use and for wedding and guest gifts, but never for market. The trick to balsamic's unique flavor was the passage of the aged must to a series of wood barrels—for example, from mulberry to ash, cherry, chestnut, then oak—to enhance enzyme action that produced piquant flavor, hue, and bouquet. When barrels deteriorated, coopers erected new frames around the old or saved chunks of the old frame to bind into the new, lest some valued part of the aging process be lost. Families depended on oak-barrel vinegar to pickle chestnuts and flavor roasting game hens. Lucrezia Borgia attested to its value in easing childbirth. Others purified fetid or malignant air with drops of balsamic vinegar during a rise in pestilence.

European carpenters fashioned rushlight holders of wooden spindles pierced with a series of holes to allow the householder to raise and lower the source of illumination. Another style connected a straight column to a notched rushlight arm by a wooden latch. By lifting the latch and repositioning the notched piece, the user could improve lighting to a window seat, settle, work table, or chair.

Joiners, seated by hearthside or out of the wet in a barn door, whittled pieces for family. By employing a locked lap to interweave ends of hoops, the unhurried hand avoided nails, which split slender withes. Hungarian coopers fitted one sizeable piece, a cauliflower barrel, with a leather shoulder harness so the vendor could hoist it on her back for the long walk to market.

For refined home furnishings, woodworkers rotated wood on varieties of the lathe, a turning device for shaping churn plungers, sugar bowls, laundry mangles, and noggins. Invented in 1290, the lathe used simple geometry to put a perfect edge or lip on a post or spindle, the essential shape of the distaff, reel stand, lace bobbin, and winder used in household fiber work. The mandrel lathe, developed from the spring pole lathe, permitted more detailed ornamentation, for example swizzle sticks and toddy sticks, mixing tools that spun in the palms to blend lemon, herbs, and sugar into drinks or to disperse chocolate in cocoa. Another essential piece, the *fond-de-plat* (plate bottom), a round or oval wood disc, anchored cold dishes on a metal or porcelain plate for garnishing.

Like tinkers and candlers, coopers developed into journeymen who traveled from home to home with tools and supplies in hand to repair broken staves or replace missing ones. While making his rounds, the cooper served a community by repairing large vats and constructing new containers to order. For example, a capacious cask, the hogshead, held from 63 to 140 gallons of salted meats, pickled vegetables, or fish. The two-handled water tub required a smooth, spokeshaved cowstal, a solid splint pole that slid through the holes in the handles for a two-person shoulder carry.

The qualities of wood inspired the householder to ingenious solutions for domestic problems. Platina, the author of *De Honesta Voluptate et Valitudine* (On Right Pleasure and Health, 1475), suggested securing fish to a board with twine before dropping it into poaching liquid. One vessel common to pantries was the mazer or mether, a round-bottomed wooden bowl used by Irish and Scottish mead-drinkers in the thirteenth century. The squared body featured a four-sided lip and handles on each side. By 1405, the invention of the wood screw in Germany opened the way to more sophisticated wood technology that allowed the joining of small pieces such as handled kitchen implements and storage boxes, thus ending waste from the carving of objects in one piece from large pieces of wood or the tedium of pegging pieces into place.

Unlike machine-made goods, the earliest wood pieces bear lathe scorings, uneven cuts, and pegs that belong to less complicated time, when hand-turned goods were meant to last a lifetime. Native American woodworkers used an adze, similar to an ax, for shaping and hollowing out logs for canoes or pirogues or for thinning the sides of smaller wood pieces for burl bowls.

Specialties within the coopering profession include the wet cooper and the dry cooper, who made vessels for either wet or dry storage, and the white cooper, who fashioned the smaller items—wood spigots, canteens, piggins, churns, buckets, and tubs, such as the powdering or pickling tub, a lidded trough in which hams and joints of meat cured in salt or sugar. One master cooper, the famous John Alden, whom Henry Wadsworth Longfellow immortalized in *The Courtship of Miles Standish* (1858), earned passage aboard the overcrowded *Mayflower* solely because he was a skilled carpenter and therefore valuable to the ship's crew, who depended on beer barrels to hold barrel-stock on deck and other wood containers for the ship's galley.

When American colonists arrived in the heavily forested new world, they found a host of native woods to choose from and could buy boxwod, cinnamon bark, ebony, lignum vitae, mahogany, and sweet wood bark at the Long Wharf in Boston as early as 1737. Professional coopers, who made the most durable of wood pieces, were on the job as early as 1751.

Artisans used the adze plus the ax, hatchet, saw, knife, spokeshave, plane, auger, and gimlet, the essentials of their craft. For washtubs and barrels, they forced staves into a finished shape by pressing with scorp and croze. They finished barrel heads and bottoms with a divider and beveled the edge with a chamfer. Additional assistance from the drawknife for shaving and whittling, froe for cleaving, and beetle (or bithel) for hammering wood into place completed the jobs of cooping, pegging, and planing serviceable puncheon floors, like that found in the Arwine cabin at the Museum of Appalachia in Norris, Tennessee. Carpenters chose the same tools for paneling or wainscoting stone walls, framing them in timbers, and adding built-in shelving and niches and for pegging kitchen floors in bleached yew cut with the grain to reveal the wood's soft yellow luster.

In colonial Quebec, Virginia, the Carolinas, and New England, homes seemed sturdier and more durable from the replacement of flimsier door coverings with the oak-plank board-and batten door. Carpenters fitted them with pull rings and ornate iron strap-and-pin hinges extending nearly two-thirds the width of the surface and seated them in matching frames and sills. Inner oak-plank doors guarded stores of wine and staples and protected kitchens from draft. Overhead, a jettied upper floor, hoods, drip moldings, apexed roofs, and porches flanked by louvered or solid shuttered windows kept out rain and snow.

Worldwide, housekeepers depended on lathe-turned and carved wooden items—dashers for vertical broomstick or barrel churns, handles for box churns, dough trays and bake boards, doweled dish drainers, apple butter sticks, and butter molds, Scotch hands, and paddles for turning a humble food into a table adornment.

- Bohemian wood turners studded wood rolling pins with spikes for the pricking of matzot, the unleavened bread that celebrates Passover.
- Quebec dough boxes and the baker's chair offered a seat with convertible backrest that lowered into a kneading table. When bread cooled from the week's baking, it often went back into the dough box or churn as the perfect storage place.
- Pennsylvania Dutch wood plate racks, knife racks, and spoon racks kept items in common use out of the way of sink activity and displayed tableware on the wall in lieu of a hutch or china cabinet.
- Intricate pantry and storage boxes, banded with wood hoops, took numerous shapes and capacities for holding cheeses, butter, herbs, soap, pills, spices, sugar or salt, jewelry, and keepsakes. They came in handled and handleless styles, some lapped at the side and some arrow- or tab-ended. A pie box contained a shelf on legs that allowed storage of one pie below and one on the shelf for easy transportation.
- Paddles, spoons, spatulas, wet and dry scoops, and shapers for stirring apple butter, sorghum squeezings, dye, and hasty pudding, or corn pudding and for scooping soft soap, scraping bowls, seeding raisins, or smoothing feather mattresses. An ingenious device, the Shaker two-way scoop applied a stirrer as the handle for the apple butter scoop.
- Trays included the Irish *losset* or *losad*, a wooden dough tray, as well as the voider or butler's tray for taking dirty dishes to the sink and the "dumb betty," a utility tray.
- Winnowing sieves and strainers separated large grains, hulls, insects, and rodent matter from grits and flour or assisted the healer in loosening powder for packing into capsules.
- A separate category of wood tools specifies a family of tenderizers—cutlet bats or gridded meat frets, needle-faced frets, and wooden mallets and beaters for hammering the fiber of tough rump steak, *entrecôtes*, escalopes, cutlets, and *noisettes*.

- The lard squeezer centered force on muslin bags of cooked leaf lard, the fat that accumulated in a leaf-shaped pattern around hog kidneys. Homemakers stored it in the lidded lard bucket, an unappealing hollowed log also dubbed the tar or slush bucket for its humble, malodorous contents. After pressing, the collected liquid cooled and hardened in bowls. Cooks saved leftover bits of meat to season cooked vegetables.
- Liquid and beverage containers ranged from nog-gins, water buckets, cream tubs, and accompanying dippers to the brewer's firkins, lidded tankards, strainers, spigots, mashers, funnels, and skimmers. One unusual item was the whetstone holder, a hollow limb which the user filled with water to soak the stone before using it to sharpen knives.
- For the barnyard, the home whittler made sheep yokes, horse hobbles, wood chains, and sheep tamps.
- Kegs held cider, oysters, and powder for flintlock rifles. The rundlet or rum canteen contained spirits. The colonial version of the wooden keg was a straight-sided cylinder with one thick stave, into which the maker carved a bung hole and fit a plug. Small ones attached to straps for carrying liquids canteen style; petite swiglers held spirits or noon-time beverages transported to workers in the field or woodlot.
- Tubs and keelers, the mundane domestic do-alls, contained fat or ashes for soap, water for dishwashing and foot soaking, and cooling milk.
- Wooden vats and barrels preserved butter, pickles, salted meats, soft and caked sugar, apples, and root crops.

Favorite raw materials ranged from local pine and ironwood to near-black *lignum vitae* (wood of life) from the West Indies and Central America, a dependable material for making sand shakers, ice pails, coasters, and Scottish *quaichs* or English mazers (communal drinking cups). Woodworkers prized coco-bolo or cocoawood, a brownish-purple native American wood marked with lighter streaks, for carving utensil handles and shaping cutting boards, a flat surface grooved at the side to collect juices. Another import, Central American mahogany, was Sir Walter Raleigh's choice of material for repairing his ship. At the end of the seventeenth century, an English cabinetmaker discovered its beauty while fashioning a bureau and initiated the trade in mahogany veneer, a substitute for *lignum vitae*, for food and linen chests and fine home furnishings. An unusual piece to survive from this period was the running footman's staff, a walking stick fitted at the head with a stoppered flask for spirits. Standard American woods, which native Americans introduced to European settlers, came from local forests.

Ash—Durable and sturdy, black or swamp ash was light in color and resilient and non-splintering as hoop poles, withes, barrel staves, handles, chairs, keg hoops, plows, carts and shafts, goose yokes, and splints.

Basswood—Also known as linden or spoonwood, basswood was a favorite light wood for young whittlers to practice on, but lacked the sturdy grain of hardwoods.

Beech—A deep-colored wood often soaked in cold brine, beech offered density and long wear. It suited woodworkers shaping dairy wares, churns, butter tubs, bowls, platters, scoops, boxes, brooms, mortars and pestles, chopping blocks, cutting boards, and rolling pins. Shoemakers carved kitchen clogs and pattens from beech; mattresses makers chose beech leaves for stuffing.

Birch—Curly, river, and paper birch, an abundant tree, especially near water, was essential to native American carpenters, who hacked bark into canoes, mocucks, canoes, pots, maple sugar pans, brooms, and containers. They charred, scraped, or cut cups and bowls out of burls. Scots immigrants brought to the New World a preference for aromatic birch flavoring in distilled whiskey and smoked herring and haddock and used birch sticks in the bottom of stew pots to keep the contents from sticking and burning. Colonial woodworkers selected the satiny wood to make window paper, stationery, handles, clothespins, staves, washboards, and pantry boxes. Birch wood smoldered into quality charcoal; the ash made soap and bleach

Boxwood—A tough, heavy, fine-grained wood, boxwood produced attractive goods in a rare white or yellow hue. Treen makers carved it into newlywed gift items, including spoons, shakers, pastry wheels, knife and corkscrew handles, and butter stamps.

Cedar—Fragrant, rot-proof cedar, whether red or white, became a favorite moth-proof liner for chests and closets and a source for coffins. Second best was cypress, also a fragrant evergreen found in many locales. In colonial times, woodworkers chose it for washtubs, keelers, firkins, churns, barrels, and pails because it withstood moisture. The piggin, a bucket with one long stave pierced with a hole for a thong to fasten it to the belt, hung handily at the side for egg gathering, nutting, and berrying. Larger versions carried slop to the pigsty. Another use, aromatic grilling, began with cedar planks soaked in water and set on the grill to permeate meats with natural savor.

Chestnut—A hard wood for bowls, boxes, and tableware, chestnut was dark in color, but lightweight and fast growing.

Elm—Elm burl, a favorite of native American dish and bowl makers, carved or scraped easily with bone or stone tools. Because it stood up to waterlogging, elm suited colonial cabinet makers for the shaping of table tops, sink stands, and cupboards. Like the Iroquois, they also used elm bark for roofing and mats.

Hazel—Hazel was a carveable wood for pitchforks and rakes.

Hickory—Hickory, which derived its name from the Algonquian *pawcohiccora* (hickory nut pulp), shaped well into splints, withes, and barrel hoops.

Holly—A white, fine-grained, toughwood, holly did not split or break easily. Toolmakers preferred it for wedges, flails, battens, and goads.

Hornbeam—White-wooded hornbeam, a member of the birch family, supplied colonial whittlers with wood for cogged wheels and latches and hinges for closets, food chests, and cupboards.

Laurel—Laurel or spoonwood from New York and Pennsylvania was a favorite material for smooth-grained spoons, which forest Indians made as trade goods or to sell to European colonists.

Maple—Maple was a preferred wood of the Iroquois and Northeastern colonists. Bird's-eye, rock, curly, or sugar maple burned clean and left quality ash for making soap or fertilizing a kitchen garden. It also produced sturdy, attractive chopping bowls, butter paddles, shoemaker's lasts, and common ware. For colonial butter prints, the carver chose the end of a plant and gouged, branded, or chiseled into the grain the pattern that marked the butter, identifying its provenance. The satin finish and close, hard grain suited chests of drawers, tables, chairs, and bedroom suites. For spinning wheels and distaffs, maple shaped into a true circle or spindle. Itinerant wheelwrights went door-to-door selling wool wheels or clock reels for two dollars and spinning wheels for one dollar.

Oak—Pin and white oak, which supplied odorless, pliant splits for baskets, box rims, handles, meal buckets, and cheese presses, also produced sturdy plank tables, mortars, bettles or beatles (mallets), pillars and posts, ladder rungs, cart-wheel spokes, and barrels. Oak was valuable for its flexibility and strength even when trimmed into thin pieces for binding tubs and piggins and whittling into legs for butter-working tables.

Pine—White and pitch pine, a lightweight wood that had no odor or taste, suited makers of butter tubs and corn cribs. English newcomers cut pine trees into sailboat masts, which enriched the colonists as a trade item for purchase of Cuban and Haitian sugar, wine from the Canaries, and slaves from Guinea and Madagascar. In addition to bridges and highways, hewers valued pine for ceiling and floor panels, blinds, shelves, stools and chairs, tables and benches, and cupboards and bed frames. Pitch pine knots smoldered as temporary outdoor lights and became flashlights when secured in an iron frame at the end of a pole for night fishing or jacklighting.

Poplar—Soft, odorless, tasteless poplar, or whitewood, lacked the resilience of hardwoods, but delighted the carver of spoons, scoops, bowls, plates, butter prints and keepers, tub covers, and wooden chargers. The carver shaved one colonial necessity, the spoon holder, from a hollowed poplar column with a bottom piece pegged into place.

Sour gum—Sour gum, or tupelo wood, was a curly grained material that resisted splitting. Its resilience was preferable for barrels, mortars, and pestles.

Walnut—Black walnut, a relative of butternut, made sturdy utensils and supplied nuts and husks that tanned and dyed to a deep blackish brown. For paneling and the best cabinetry, it polished to a deep luster and produced elegant burl for such ornamental pieces as mantels, trays, and cheese boards. Colonial joiners veneered permeable walnut knot as an inlay for chests and furnishings.

Willow—The common *salix alba*, prized for flexibility, made the best baskets and panniers. Willows in general suited producers of wattle and daub, clubs, sticks, laundry paddles, slats, and bowls, which they waterproofed with wax or grease.

Native American carvers chose the diseased knot, also called the burl or knurl, a venous wood tumor from ash or maple for the carving of bowls. They shaped oval and round containers with one or two handles or flat with no handles for sipping hot beverages and cereals such as samp and *atole*. Hardwoods made suitable trenchers, the wood disks that pairs of diners ate from as a communal plate in homes and at the Harvard college mess table. One variant was the trencher-top table, a rare table board hollowed at intervals into a trencher-sized depression for each diner.

One Connecticut deacon miffed his neighbors by milling wood so each of his family members could have a separate trencher. For his largesse, his neighbor accused him of pretense and extravagance.

Wood was also the choice for everyday porringers, mugs, barrels, fruit and bread bowls, and scrub brush handles. Most homes owned prize wooden objects—long-handled stirring spoons and mallets, salt servers and paddles, small mortars and pestles for crushing and grinding spices and medicinal herbs, larger pairs for pulverizing grain, cheese forms and biscuit molds, spurtles or stirring sticks, dry sinks, hatchet and ax handles, measuring spoons, colanders, and rolling pins. More limited pieces included nutcrackers and nut bowls, wire batter beaters, napkin holders, wine caddies, and lemon squeezers as well as spools and spindles, knitting needles, game boards, glass- or clay-lined inkwells, canes, pipes, mirrors, and storage boxes.

An unusual shape for a wood implement was the thick wooden bannock board, an essential for baking Scottish bannock cakes or Irish bannock bread. The colonial American variant involved mixing a thick paste of wheat flour, corn meal, water or buttermilk, salaeratus or salt, soda, molasses, eggs, and butter or bacon fat and rolling it out with a wooden bannock stick. Cooks cut bannocks with a tin cutter or shaped them by hand to spread in a pan or spider, or on a bannock stone or a bannock board in a hot oven. The simple board and handle perched at an angle before a fire like a picture frame leaning against its prop.

In 1908, the Sears, Roebuck catalog featured materials for refinishing wood chairs and kitchen splashbacks. In addition to tough imitation leather fiberboard, brass-head nails, and hanks of caning, the copywriter tempted the remodeler with 7-cent woven wood splint splashback mats for washstands. Sewed into a rectangle and decorated with varied plant images, the mats repelled soiling easier than linen splashers. The home-centered post-World War II era introduced a mania for do-it-yourself projects. For wood repair, ads in *Woman's Home Companion* praised plastic wood as the answer to broken or warped wood utensils. A line drawing pictured a split in a salad bowl with a promise that plastic wood handled as easily as putty and hardened into wood.

In the 1950s, plank dinners came into fashion as a method for the hostess to serve guests without the aid of a cooking staff. As described in Betty Crocker's *Picture Cook Book* (1950), the one-dish meal began with freshly planed hardwood boards, one per diner. Each placed fresh foods on the surface for heating in the oven. When they emerged, the diners added salads to the far end of the boards. The method paralleled the Finnish board-cooking of salmon trout, which cooks pegged to the board to render the fat and tenderize the flesh.

Grilling and barbecuing in the twenty-first century required a variety of wood chips, vine parings, and planks cut from maple, oak, hickory, alder, peach, and apple. Acacia thorns, raisin bush sticks, and vine prunings, which consumers bought at specialty kitchen stores, worked well as skewers for meat, vegetable, fruit, and seafood kabobs. By soaking them in wine, bourbon, sherry, cider, or port, the cook permeated the food with flavor. More exotic taste from lemon grass, rosemary limbs, cinnamon sticks, or licorice root further turned home-cooked foods into mealtime adventures. In Japan, cooks skewered eels for *domburi* (braising).

In November 1998, *Kitchenware News* announced the formation of Alaska Forest Creations Inc. in Ketchikan, an environmentally responsible firm situated in the largest U.S. national forest. The company began manufacturing wood bowls and salad serving sets from woods previously considered unusable. With state and federal grant money, designers studied ways to recycle wood waste from logging operations and to cut and shape utensils and vessels using computer design programs and pneumatic cutting tools.

Wood technology continues to supply the kitchen with small items like wood nut bowls and serving dishes and trays, bread and cheese boards, salad bowls, countertop butcher blocks, and cutting boards edged with a groove for collecting juices. The coiled wood *brotformen* (dough-rising basket) imprints as it cradles loaves while they expand. Popular large items are the kitchen island and a rolling cart featuring cabinets, pull-out shelves, and drawers topped with a wood cutting board.

See also **Barbecue; Treen**

Further Reading

Boily, Lise, and Jean-François Blanchette. *The Bread Ovens of Quebec.* Quebec: National Museums of Canada, 1979.

Mason, Otis Tufton. *Women's Share in Primitive Culture.* New York: Appleton, 1911.

Reader, Ted, and Kathleen Sloan. *Sticks & Stones: The Art of Grilling on Plank, Vine and Stone.* Minocqua, Wisc.: Willow Creek Press, 1999.

Y

YEAST

To cultures that valued bread and beer above other processed foods, yeast carried central importance, both nutritionally and culturally. A common family of single-celled fungi that reproduce by budding, yeasts include the all important *Saccharomyces cerevisiae*, which ferments the sugars derived from flour to produce the ethanol and carbon dioxide gas that raises dough. A variant strain, called barm or brewer's yeast, ferments cereal, hops, and malt to make ale and beer. Another strain, the *ellipsoideus*, transforms grape juice into sparkling wine. Dried yeasts also supplement other foods with B-complex vitamins, vitamin D_2, and protein.

In Egypt, the monopoly of yeast around 2000 BCE established the supremacy of one group, who also controlled baking and brewing. Until the early 1700s, English bakers leavened with barm or residual yeasts from sugar, potato, grain, or malt left to proliferate in water in a yeast tub or sour tub. These residual yeasts permeated the mix with spores from previous batches. For the New World's colonial bakery, yeast was self-regenerative. When the jar neared empty, the baker made a new batch and added it to the remainder of the old yeast to transfer its fermenting power and keep it alive. Sometimes, just stirring the batch in the wood trough picked up enough spores to make leavening. Left overnight by a banked fire, the action of leaven on flour and water formed a sponge. The next morning, the baker punched it down, added more flour, and kneaded it until the gluten reached the proper consistency, a quality altered by heat and humidity that only an experienced baker could judge. Before baking, the cook divided the mass with a dough cutter and shaped it into loaves in a lidded bread trough or bread tray for a second rising.

For risen dough, some American bakers fermented yeast by cooking hops in a maceration of potatoes and the barm that floated on top of beer mash. The preferred components later shifted to other bases, beginning with flour and water boiled with brown sugar and salt. Cooks bottled the mass, which they called "sots" or "emptins," and stored it in clay jars. Amelia Simmons's *American Cookery* (1796), the first kitchen text written by an American-born food professional, characterized pearl ash or potash as a worthy leavener, a practice also common in Russia. As described in *The New Family Receipt Book* (1819), a Long Island fermentation method began with sourdough yeast made from apples or pumpkins for use in Long Island bread.

Making yeast was a messy chore. M. E. Porter's *Mrs. Porter's New Southern Cookery Book* (1871) quotes John Janney's description of his mother's cookery in Loudoun County, Virginia, in the 1820s: "At night the 'batter pot' was set near the fire to keep warm, and sometimes the batter would become too light. It was not an uncommon thing to find a good deal of the batter run over the hearth in the morning and some crickets in the batter." (Weaver 1989, 8) Holding the pot by the prominent handles, bakers poured out enough for each day's needs.

In the Amana colonies, for yeast, bakers cooked hops in a copper kettle with barley and used a dipper of starter from the last week's brew. After overnight

661

fermentation, the supply was ready for storage in the basement in a stone crock. After generations of home bakers fermented their own leavening, in the late 1700s, Dutch yeast makers began selling cakes of baker's yeast, live cells extracted from the distilling process to puff dough with the release of carbon dioxide during the rising stage. Refined in Vienna, processed yeast gained immediate favor with home cooks. Because of one case of sickness from brewers' yeast, under Louis XIV, bakers could no longer recycle the additive. By the 1820s, saleratus, literally *sal aeratus* (aerated salt), was available for leavening.

In the bone-dry atmosphere of the American desert, frontier breadmakers tested yeast strength by sprinkling it with sugar and watching for a chemical reaction that proved it still had life. To freshen bitter stock, they added toasted bread crumbs or sifted it with bran, the makings of middling bread, a common name for whole wheat bread. From experience, they learned to raise sour dough in a clay crock rather than in tin, which turned it green. When starter dough ran out or dried up, they substituted baking powder and soda or saleratus, the least satisfactory of substitutes, or turned to salt-risen loaves.

Commercial baking powder replaced alkaline powder or pearl ash, which Dutch bakers introduced to New Netherlands, the original name for New York. The store-bought leavening replaced foul-tasting ash and reduced the cost of baking by requiring fewer eggs. Two years after the Civil War, Austro-Hungarian distillers Charles Louis and Maximilian Fleischmann and their partner James Gaff built a yeast factory in Cincinnati, Ohio. They began processing their commercial yeast cakes by the Hungarian method, which they patented in 1870.

The product was slow to capture the market. After introducing it at the 1876 Philadelphia Centennial Exposition at a bread-making demonstration called the Vienna Bakery, the Fleischmann brothers established the nation's most revered leavening product. They drove a spiffy team to grocery stores, where they delivered fresh yeast in person. As compared with the information-less ad for competitor Magic Yeast in the May 1925 issue of *Good Housekeeping*, the Fleischmanns' folksy, door-to-door method plus astute investments in vinegar and beer rightfully turned Charles into a millionaire.

Yeast influenced numerous events in world history. In 1849, San Francisco miners originated the area's world-famous sourdough by applying an airborne microbe, *Lactobacillus sanfrancisco*, to a yeast, *Saccharomyces exiguus*, to form a tangy bread credited to French baker Isadore Boudin. In the 1880s, the rising anger of housewives against impure foods brought action from such backers as the Women's Christian Temperance Union and the magazine *Good Health*, co-edited by activist and dietitian Ella Eaton Kellogg. Nutritionists, recognizing the danger of adulterants, advocated more yeast bread, which took hours to rise before baking, and fewer recipes calling for baking powder, which shortened the job of raising bread to only minutes. During World War II, yeast suppliers marketed active dry yeast as a solution to one of the problems of feeding soldiers in the field. In Europe in the 1970s, yeast marketers began packaging instant yeast, a long-lived product that needed no proofing. Fleischmann's added another innovation, bread machine yeast, in 1994.

Further Reading

Jacob, H. E. *Six Thousand Years of Bread: Its Holy and Unholy History*. Garden City, N.Y.: Lyons Press, 1997.
Negrin, Micol, "Bread Through the Ages," *La Cucina Italiana*, October-November 1997, 34–35.
_____, "Bread Through the Ages," *La Cucina Italiana*, December 1997 January 1998, 50–51.
Ola, Per, and Emily d'Aulaire, "Baking Up a Business," *Smithsonian*, November 2000, 108–116.
Rentschler, Kay, and Julia Collin, "Understanding and Using Yeasts," *Cook's Illustrated*, January/February 2001, 25–27.

YOUNG, HANNAH

In an era that saw the manufacture of saccharine, sugar cubes, synthetic vanilla, root beer, Wheatena, Nestle's Infant Milk Food, milk chocolate, the ice cream soda, and margarine, the foods educator Hannah M. Young was one of the first women to exploit her kitchen success as a demonstrator and advertiser of brand-name products. A native of Birmingham, England, she was born on June 24, 1858, to Cornelius Young, owner of Thynne Street Works, a gas cooker factory in Warrington, Lancashire, which also employed her brother Cornelius, Jr. She earned a degree in cooking and an award from the 1886 Berkhamsted Mechanics Industrial and Fine Arts Exhibition. A pioneer of brand-name ingredients, she readily composed recipes for manufactured provisions and patent foods. She became so famous that her husband, Dr. William Riding, dropped his surname and called himself William Young.

From demonstration lectures for her father's stoves, Young compiled and edited *Domestic Cookery, with Special Reference to Cooking by Gas* (1886), an obvious promotion of the new technology. In the 1897 edition, among the book's five hundred recipes, she appended a series of dishes—beef fillet with tomatoes, Polish stew, pork cutlets, Spanish Stew, stuffed onions—touting goods marketed by the Liebig Extract of Meat Company. The back matter advertised Fletcher

Russel & Company's New Kensington cooker, water heaters, broiler grill, iron, and gas-fired stoves.

Young cultivated a broad constituency by expanding her repertoire from the folksy rook pie to chic foreign dishes. Her philosophy simplified for the average cook a plain, satisfying cookery embellished for the average table. Her second book, *Choice Cookery* (1888), allied middle-class economy with more fashionable, genteel menu items, such as julienne consommé, mock ginger, pomegranate and maraschino jellies, and boeuf à la rosine, a skewered meat dish that began with the mounding of potatoes and mushrooms. Noticeably absent were the mutton recipes preferred primarily by poor immigrants and the laboring class.

Beginning in 1892, Young's company, a collaboration with Fanny Beck, advertised a line of foodstuffs—leaf gelatin, Flor-Ador thickener, and baking powder—and equipment, including molds, forcing bags, sifters, and the Hutchings Patent Steamer, a four-tier vessel with shut-off valve. She issued the lavishly illustrated *Leibig and Company's Practical Cookery Book* (1893), a product-driven collection of game, fried meat, fish, soup, and pudding recipes based on the success of the chemist Justus von Liebig, owner of a meat reducing factory in Fray Bentos, Uruguay. Introducing the text, she summarized advancement in home economics since 1873, when England established the National Training School of Cookery. She used von Liebig's extract as the supreme model of convenience provisions that reduce kitchen labor.

Undated is Young's *The Housewife's Manual of Domestic Cookery* (ca. 1880s), subtitled "Dainty and Simple Dishes for the Year Round in Health and Sickness with Illustrations from Photographs." It demonstrated the folding of serviettes, the type of nicety that middle-class women applied to refine their homes. Her last text, *Home Made Cakes and Sweets* (1904), which she wrote after moving to Harston, Cambridge, illustrates confections and pastries as an element of gentility.

Further Reading

Young, H. M. *Choice Cookery.* London: John Heywood, 1890.

COMMON SOURCES

Achaya, K. T. *Indian Food: A Historical Companion*. Delhi and Oxford: Oxford University Press, 1994.

Adkins, Lesley, and Roy A. Adkins. *Handbook to Life in Ancient Rome*. New York: Facts on File, 1994.

Algren, Nelson., *America Eats*. Iowa City: University of Iowa Press, 1992.

American Indian History and Culture (database). New York: Facts on File, 2000.

American Women's History (database). New York: Facts on File, 2000.

Andrews, Tamra. *Nectar and Ambrosia: An Encyclopedia of Food in World Mythology*. Santa Barbara, California: ABC-Clio, 2000.

Aresty, Esther B. *The Delectable Past*. New York: Simon & Schuster, 1964.

Banham, Joanna (editor). *Encyclopedia of Interior Design*. London and Chicago: Fitzroy Dearborn, 1997.

Bates, Daisy. *The Passing of the Aborigines: A Lifetime Spent among the Natives of Australia*, 2nd edition. London: John Murray, 1966; New York: Praeger, 1967; original edition, London: John Murray, 1938; New York: Putnam, 1939.

Beard, James, et al. (editors). *The Cook's Catalogue*. New York: Harper and Row, 1975; London: Harper & Row, 1976.

Beecher, Catharine E., and Harriet Beecher Stowe. *The American Woman's Home*. Hartford, Connecticut: Stowe-Day Foundation, 1975; original edition, New York: J. B. Ford, and Boston: H. A. Brown, 1869.

Berriedale-Johnson, Michelle. *The Victorian Cookbook*. London: Ward Lock, and New York: Interlink Books, 1989.

Birkby, Robert C. *The Boy Scout Handbook*. Irving, Texas: Boy Scouts of America, 1990.

Biography Resource Center (database). Farmington Hills, Michigan: Gale, 2000.

Booth, Letha. *The Williamsburg Cookbook*. New York: Holt, Rinehart, 1971.

Brothwell, Don, and Patricia Brothwell. *Food in Antiquity: A Survey of the Diet of Early Peoples*. New York: Praeger, and London: Thames and Hudson, 1969.

Brown, Dee. *The Gentle Tamers: Women of the Old Wild West*. New York: Putnam, 1958.

Bruhns, Karen Olsen, and Karen E. Stothert. *Women in Ancient America*. Norman: University of Oklahoma Press, 1999.

Bugialli, Giuliano. *The Fine Art of Italian Cooking*. New York: Times Books, 1989.

Cannon, Poppy, and Patricia Brooks. *The Presidents' Cookbook*. New York: Funk and Wagnalls, 1968.

Celeher, Jane H. *Kitchens and Kitchenware*. Lombard, Illinois: Wallace-Homestead Book Co., 1985.

Chamberlain, Lesley. *The Food and Cooking of Eastern Europe*. London: Penguin, 1989.

Cheney, Joyce. *Aprons: Icons of the American Home*. Philadelphia: Running Press, 2000.

Clarke, William. *Pompeii: Its Past and Present State*. London: M. A. Nattali, 1846.

Cosman, Madeleine Pelner. *Fabulous Feasts: Medieval Cookery and Ceremony*. New York: Braziller, 1976.

Counihan, Carole, and Penny Van Esterik (editors). *Food and Culture: A Reader*. New York and London: Routledge, 1997.

Cowan, Ruth Schwartz. *More Work for Mother*. New York: Basic Books, 1983.

Crane, Eva. *The World History of Beekeeping and Honey Hunting*. London: Duckworth, and New York: Routledge, 1999.

Crowther, Geoff, et al. *Africa*, 7th edition. Hawthorn, Victoria, and London: Lonely Planet, 1995.

David M. Kennedy Center for International Studies, Brigham Young University. *Culturgrams: The Nations Around Us*, vols. 1 and 2. Chicago: Ferguson, 1997.

Davidson, Alan. *The Oxford Companion to Food*. Oxford and New York: Oxford University Press, 1999.

Denny, Roz. *The Tudor Kitchens Cookery Book* (brochure). West Drayton, Middlesex: E. J. Associates, n. d.

Diehl, Daniel. *Constructing Medieval Furniture*. Mechanicsburg, Pennsylvania: Stackpole Books, 1997.

DISCovering U. S. History (database). Farmington Hills, Michigan: Gale, 2000.

DISCovering World History (database). Farmington Hills, Michigan: Gale, 2000.

Dow, George Francis. *Every Day Life in the Massachusetts Bay Colony*. New York: Dover, 1988; original edition, Boston: Society for the Preservation of New England Antiquities, 1935.

Earle, Alice Morse. *Home Life in Colonial Days*. Middle Village, New York: Jonathan David, 1975; original edition, New York: Macmillan, 1898.

Emmerling, Mary Ellisor. *American Country: A Style and Source Book*. New York: Clarkson N. Potter, 1980.

Fahey, Warren. *When Mabel Laid the Table: The Folklore of Eating and Drinking in Australia*. Sydney: New South Wales Press, 1992.

Feeney, John. "… The Good Things of Egypt…," *Aramco World* (November–December 1975): 2–7.

Flandrin, Jean-Louis, and Massimo Montanari. *Food: A Culinary History from Antiquity to the Present*. New York: Columbia University Press, 1999.

Franklin, Linda Campbell. *300 Years of Kitchen Collectibles*. Iola, Wisconsin: Krause Publications, 1997.

Franklin, Linda Campbell. *From Hearth to Cookstove: America in the Kitchen*. Florence, Alabama: House of Collectibles, 1976.

Garland, John. "Daily Life of the Ancient Greeks," *Daily Life Through History* (database), http://greenwood.scbbs.com:8080.

Garraty, John A. (editor). *Dictionary of American Biography*, New York: Scribner, 1960.

Gies, Joseph, and Frances Gies. *Life in a Medieval Castle*. New York: Crowell, 1974; London: Abelard-Schuman, 1975.

Gould, Mary Earle. *Early American Wooden Ware and Other Kitchen Utensils*. Rutland, Vermont: Charles E. Tuttle, 1962.

Graham, Robin Lee. *"Dove."* New York: Harper and Row, and London: Angus and Robertson, 1972.

Grimbly, Shona (editor). *Encyclopedia of the Ancient World.* London and Chicago: Fitzroy Dearborn, 2000

Hall, Charles Francis. *Life with the Esquimaux.* London: S. Low, 1864; reprinted Rutland, Vermont: Charles E. Tuttle, 1970.

Harrison, Molly. *The Kitchen in History.* Reading: Osprey, and New York: Scribner, 1972.

Harrison, William. *Description of Elizabethan England.* http://www.fordham.edu/halsall/mod/1577harrison-england.html.

Hartley, Dorothy. *Food in England.* Boston and London: Little, Brown, 1999; original edition, London: Macdonald, 1954.

Hartley, Dorothy. *The Countryman's England*, 3rd edition. London: Jill Norman, 1980.

Hartley, Dorothy. *The Land of England.* London: Macdonald, 1979.

Hartley, Dorothy. *Water in England.* London: Macdonald, 1964.

Herodotus. *The Histories.* Harmondsworth and Baltimore: Penguin, 1954.

Heyerdahl, Thor. *Fatu-Hiva: Back to Nature.* Garden City, New York: Doubleday, and London: Allen and Unwin, 1974.

History Resource Center: U. S. (database). Farmington Hills, Michigan: Gale, 2000.

Hook, Paula, and Joe E. Heimlich. "A History of Packaging" (fact sheet). Columbus: Ohio State University Extension, 2000.

James, Peter, and Nick Thorpe. *Ancient Inventions.* New York: Ballantine, 1994.

Jekyll, Gertrude, and Sydney E. Jones. *Old English Household Life.* London: Batsford, and New York: Scribner, 1939.

Landau, Irwin (editor). *I'll Buy That: 50 Small Wonders and Big Deals,*. Mount Vernon, N. Y.: Consumers Union, 1986.

Laudan, Rachel. *The Food of Paradise: Exploring Hawaii's Culinary Heritage.* Honolulu: University of Hawaii Press, 1996.

Lee, Su Jan, and May Lee. *The Fine Art of Chinese Cooking.* New York: Gramercy, 1962.

Lemnis, Maria, and Henryk Vitry. *Old Polish Traditions in the Kitchen and at the Table.* New York: Hippocrene Books, 1996.

Lo, Eileen Yin-Fei. *The Chinese Kitchen.* New York: Morrow, 1999.

Macdonald, Anne L. *Feminine Ingenuity: Women and Invention in America.* New York: Ballantine, 1992.

Marcy, Randolph B. *The Prairie Traveler: A Hand-Book for Overland Expeditions.* Williamstown, Massachusetts: Corner House, 1978.

Marks, Copeland. *Indian and Chinese Cooking from the Himalayan Rim.* New York: D. I. Fine Books, 1996.

McCutcheon, Marc. *The Writer's Guide to Everyday Life in the 1800s.* Cincinnati, Ohio: Writer's Digest Books, 1993.

McNeill, F. Marian. *The Scots Kitchen.* London: Blackie, 1929.

Miller, Judith, and Martin Miller. *Period Details.* London: Mitchell Beazley, and New York: Crown, 1987.

Mitchell, Patricia B. *Union Army Camp Cooking, 1861–1865* (brochure). Chatham, Va.: Sims-Mitchell House Bed & Breakfast, 2000.

Molokhovets, Elena. *Classic Russian Cooking.* Bloomington: Indiana University Press, 1992.

Montagné, Prosper. *New Larousse Gastronomique.* London: Hamlyn, and New York: Crown, 1977.

Mowat, Farley (editor). *The Polar Passion: The Quest for the North Pole.* Toronto: McClelland and Stewart, 1973.

National Presto Cooker Recipe Book. Eau Claire, Wisc.: National Pressure Cooker Co., 1946.

Norwak, Mary. *Kitchen Antiques.* London: Ward Lock, and New York: Praeger, 1975.

Ó Céirin, Kit, and Cyril Ó Céirin. *Women of Ireland: A Biographic Dictionary.* Kinvara, Co. Galway: Tír Eolas, 1996.

Parkinson, Rosemary. *Culinaria: The Caribbean.* Cologne: Könemann, 1999.

Patterson, Lotsee, and Mary Ellen Snodgrass. *Indian Terms of the Americas.* Englewood, Colo.: Libraries Unlimited, 1994.

Peavy, Linda, and Ursula Smith. *Pioneer Women: The Lives of Women on the Frontier.* New York: Smithmark, 1996.

Petroski, Henry. *The Evolution of Useful Things.* New York: Knopf, 1992; London: Pavilion, 1993.

Pinto, Edward H. *Treen, or Small Woodware Throughout the Ages.* London: Batsford, 1949.

Platt, Richard. *Smithsonian Visual Timeline of Inventions.* London and New York: Dorling Kindersley, 1994.

Powell, Elizabeth S. *Pennsylvania Butter: Tools and Processes.* Doylestown, Penn.: Bucks County Historical Society, 1974.

Pritzker, Barry M. *A Native American Encyclopedia: History, Culture, and Peoples.* Oxford and New York: Oxford University Press, 2000.

Quennell, Marjorie, and C. H. B. Quennell, *A History of Everyday Things in England*, 2 vols. London: Batsford, and New York: Scribner, 1918, 1919.

Reader's Digest. *Magic and Medicine of Plants.* Pleasantville, N. Y.: Reader's Digest, 1986.

Riddervold, Astri, and Andreas Ropeid (editors). *Food Conservation.* London: Prospect Books, 1988.

Rider, B. C. *The Greek House: Its History and Development from the Neolithic Period to the Hellenistic Age.* Chicago: Argonaut, 1964.

Rowley, Anthony. *The Book of Kitchens.* Paris: Flammarion, 1999.

Schärer, Martin, and Alexander Fenton (editors). *Food and Material Culture.* East Linton: Tuckwell Press, 1998.

Schlabach, Joetta Handrich. *Extending the Table: A World Community Cookbook.* Scottdale, Penn.: Herald Press, 1991.

Schroeder, Joseph J. (editor). *1908 Sears, Roebuck Catalogue*, Northfield, Illinois: DBI Books, 1971.

Schroeder, Joseph J. (editor). *1923 Sears, Roebuck Catalogue.* Northfield, Illinois: DBI Books, 1973.

Scully, Terence. *The Art of Cookery in the Middle Ages.* Woodbridge, Suffolk: Boydell, 1995.

Shapiro, Laura. *Perfection Salad: Women and Cooking at the Turn of the Century.* New York: Farrar, Straus, 1986.

Sharkey, Olive. *Old Days, Old Ways.* Dublin: O'Brien, 1985.

Simeti, Mary Taylor. *Pomp and Sustenance: Twenty-Five Centuries of Sicilian Food.* New York: Knopf, 1989.

Singman, Jeffrey L. "Daily Life in Elizabethan England," *Daily Life Through History* (database), http://greenwood.scbbs.com:8080.

Snodgrass, Mary Ellen. *Encyclopedia of World Scriptures.* Jefferson, N.C.: McFarland, 2001.

Snodgrass, Mary Ellen. *Religious Sites in America.* Santa Barbara, Calif.: ABC-Clio, 2000.

Snodgrass, Mary Ellen. *Who's Who in the Middle Ages.* Jefferson, N.C.: McFarland, 2000.

Snodgrass, Mary Ellen. *Historical Encyclopedia of Nursing.* Santa Barbara, Calif.: ABC-Clio, 1999.

Snodgrass, Mary Ellen. *Encyclopedia of Frontier Literature.* Santa Barbara, Calif.: ABC-Clio, 1997.

Snodgrass, Mary Ellen. *Celebrating Women's History.* Detroit: Gale, 1996.

Stephenson, Sue H. *Basketry of the Appalachian Mountains.* New York: Van Nostrand Reinhold, 1977.

Stow, Josie, and Jan Baldwin. *The African Kitchen*. London: Conran Octopus, 1999; New York: Interlink Books, 2000.

Stowe, Harriet Beecher. *The Oldtown Folks*. Boston: Fields, Osgood, 1869; http://www.digital.library.upenn.edu.

Taylor, Dale. *The Writer's Guide to Everyday Life in Colonial America*. Cincinnati, Ohio: Writer's Digest Books, 1997.

Thompson, Eleanor McD. (editor). *The American Home: Material Culture, Domestic Space, and Family Life*. Winterthur, Del.: Henry Francis du Pont Winterthur Museum, 1998.

Tunis, Edwin. *Colonial Craftsmen and the Beginnings of American Industry*. Cleveland: World, 1965.

Ulrich, Laurel Thatcher. *Good Wives: Image and Reality in the Lives of Women in Northern New England, 1650–1750*. New York: Knopf, 1982.

Vaughan, J. G., and C. A. Geissler. *The New Oxford Book of Food Plants*. Oxford and New York: Oxford University Press, 1997.

Visser, Margaret. *The Rituals of Dinner: The Origins, Evolution, Eccentricities, and Meaning of Table Manners*. New York: Grove Weidenfeld, 1991.

Wahlberg, Holly. *1950s Plastics Design*. Atglen, Penn.: Schiffer Publishing, 1999.

Walker, Harlan (editor). *Cooks and Other People: Proceedings of the Oxford Symposium on Food and Cookery 1995*. Totnes, Devon: Prospect Books, 1996.

Walsh, William S. *Curiosities of Popular Customs*. London: Gibbings, and Philadelphia: Lippincott, 1898.

Weaver, William Woys. *America Eats: Forms of Edible Folk Art*. New York: Museum of American Folk Art, Perennial Library, 1989.

Webb, Pauline, and Mark Suggitt. *Gadgets and Necessities*. Santa Barbara, Calif.: ABC-Clio, 2000.

Werner, Michael S. (editor). *Encyclopedia of Mexico*. Chicago and London: Fitzroy Dearborn, 1997.

Whiting, Alfred F. *Havasupai Habitat*, edited by Steven A. Weber and P. David Seaman. Tucson: University of Arizona Press, 1985.

Wigginton, Eliot (editor). *The Foxfire Book*. Garden City, New York: Doubleday, 1972.

Williams-Sonoma Guide to Good Cooking (CD-ROM). Novato, Calif.: Brøderbund Software, 1996.

Wilson, C. Anne (editor). *The Appetite and the Eye*. Edinburgh: Edinburgh University Press, 1991.

Wilson, Charles Reagan, and William Ferris. *Encyclopedia of Southern Culture*. Chapel Hill: University of North Carolina Press, 1989.

Wilson, Mitchell. *American Science and Invention*. New York: Simon & Schuster, 1954.

Wise, W. H. *The Wise Encyclopedia of Cookery*. New York: Grosset and Dunlap, 1971.

World of Invention, 2nd edition. Farmington Hills, Mich.: Gale, 2000.

Wright, Clifford A. *A Mediterranean Feast*. New York: Morrow, 1999.

INDEX

A

Abbott, Edward, 631
Absinthe, 17
Abstinence from the Flesh of Animals, 273
The Academy of Armoury, 498, 549
The Accomplisht Cook or The Art and Mystery of Cookery, 165, 195
*Acer saccharum*sugar maple tree, 377
Acetaria: A Discourse of Sallets, 222, 276, 289, 335, 553
Acton, Eliza, 1–2, 58, 158, 286, 572, 631
Adair, James, 423
Adams, Andy, 134
Adi Granth Punjabi for "first book," 538
Admonitions and Doctrines from a Wise Parent to His Daughters, 220
Adventures in Good Cooking, 290
Adventures in Good Eating, 290
Adventures of a Home Economist, 297
The Adventures of the Ten Princes, 363
Advertising to Women, 501, 653
Advice to His Son Verified, 220–221
Aertsen, Pieter, 229
Aframomum melegueta, 289
Africa, pottery of, 475–476
The African Kitchen, 48, 441
Agaricus, 420
The Agricultural Almanac, 209
Ainsworth, Richard, 80
Air conditioning, 2–3
Akabori, Minekichi, 3
Akabori Ryori Kogiroku (Akabori Cooking Manual), 3
Akabori School of Cookery, 3
Akron Beacon, 111
Albini, Giacomo, Dr., 644
Alcohol, 4–9
    Arab World, traditions in, 5–6
    Caucasus, traditions in, 4–5
    China, traditions in, 5
    Europe, traditions in, 6
    India, traditions in, 4
    local traditions involving, 8–9
    North and South America, traditions in, 7–8
    religious law, influence on attitudes toward, 9
Alcott, Dr. William A., 336
Alderotti, Taddeo, 6
Alf Laylah Wa Laylah (The Thousand and One Nights), 609
Algar, Ayla Esen, 183
Algeria *kiskis or couscousiere,* 585
Algren, Nelson, 111

Allen, Lewis Falley, 630
Alloys, early, 389
All the Year Round, 631
Almanach des Gourmands (Almanac of the Greedy Diners), 509, 568
An Alphabet for Gourmets, 237
Alphonsi, Petrus, 219
Altamiras, Juan, 166
Aluminum, 9–11
Aluminum foil pie crust shield, 35
Amana colonies, 11
Amanita phalloides, 420
Amanite Kitchens, 11–13
Amelia, or a Young Lady's Vicissitudes, 364
America Eats, 111, 253, 568, 607
America Eats: Forms of Edible Folk Art, 544
American Agriculturist, 82, 100, 259, 530, 607
American Artisan, 498
American Cookery Magazine (formerly) *Boston Cooking School Magazine,* 167, 170, 430, 457, 661
American Cooking, 51
American Council on Science and Health (ACSH), 27
American Fabian, 267
American fries, 253
The American Frugal Housewife, 7, 115, 167, 209, 286, 536, 557, 637
American Home Cook Book, 148, 446
American Journal of Sociology, 267
American Kitchen Magazine, 114, 293, 652
American Ladies Magazine, 651
The American Lady's System of Cookery, 278
American Moderns: Bohemian New York and the Creation of a New Century, 173
The American Weekly, 244
American Wine and Food, 123
The American Woman's Home, 53, 70, 90, 115, 173, 192, 231, 291, 353, 431, 547, 628
The American Women's Cook Book, 168
Americas
    alcohol, traditions in, 7–8
    barbecue in, 46–47
    beer brewing in, 56–57
    brooms, innovations in, 75–76
    cheese variations, 119–120
    chocolate popularity, 128–130
    corn use in, 177–178
    dairying in, 184–185
    etiquette, 221–222
    pottery, 478–480
    restaurant kitchens, 511–512
America's Test Kitchen, 617

Amiczo, Chiquart Master, 43
Amish kitchens, 13–15
Amish Society, 13
Amish Women: Lives and Stories, 15
Amphora, 15–16
Anabasis, 16, 40, 301
Analects, 650
The Ancient Physicians Legacy, 331
Andalusian Cuisine from the eleventh to the thirteenth century: A Way of Life, 586
Andrews, Lucy C., 263
Angas, George French, 221
Anglo-Saxon *meodu,* 383
Anna Maria's Housekeeping, 111
Anonymous Thirteenth-Century Manuscript on Spanish-Arabic Cookery, 163
Anthropological Quarterly (October 1991), 427
Aphid Pests of Maine, Food Plants of the Aphids, Psyllid Notes, 629
Aphrodisiacs, 16–17
Apician Morsels; Or, Tales of the Table, Kitchen, and Larder: Containing, a New and Improves Code of Eatics; Select Epicurean Precepts; Nutritive Maxims, Reflections, Anecdotes, & c., 18
Apicius, Caelius, 17–18, 28, 109, 156, 163, 261, 272, 300, 333, 555, 599, 643
Apiculture, 300–301
Apis mellifera, 299
Appert, Nicolas, 18–19
The Appledore Cookbook, 293
Appleton's, 267
Appliances, 211–215
    percentage of homes equipped with, 213
Applied Motion Study, 264
Aprons, 19–22
Arabella, 256
Arabic *qand,* 91
Arab World, traditions with alcohol, 5–6
Archaeological evidence of cannibalism, 97
Archestratus, Athenian-born Epicurean, food writer, 22
Argonautica, 255
Artemis absinthium (wormwood), 17
The Artful Eater, 537
Arthashastra, 638
The Art of Cookery Made Plain and Easy, 167, 270, 271, 310, 362, 539, 582
The Art of Cooking by Gas, 263
The Art of Eating, 237
The Art of Italian Cooking, 168
The Art of Making Ices, 310

INDEX